Yard & Garden Tractor

SERVICE MANUAL ■ 1ST EDITION

P.O. Box 12901 ■ Overland Park, KS 66282-2901
Phone: 800-262-1954 Fax: 800-633-6219
www.clymer.com

Library of Congress Catalog Card Number 2002108183

July, 2002
October, 2004
May, 2008

This book can be recycled. Please remove cover.

Cover photo courtesy of:
MTD Products, Inc.

Yard & Garden Tractor

SERVICE MANUAL ■ 1ST EDITION

Riding Lawn Mower Manufacturers:

- Ariens
- Cub Cadet
- John Deere
- Ford
- Gravely
- Honda
- Ingersoll
- MTD
- Power King
- Snapper
- Toro
- Yardman

Engine Manufacturers:

- Briggs & Stratton
- Honda
- Kawasaki
- Kohler
- Shibaura
- Tecumseh
- Toro
- Yanmar

Publisher Shawn Etheridge

EDITORIAL

Managing Editor
James Grooms

Editor
Steven Thomas

Associate Editors
Rick Arens

Group Production Manager
Dylan Goodwin

Production Manager
Greg Araujo

Senior Production Editor
Darin Watson

Production Editors
Holly McComas
Adriane Roberts
Taylor Wright

Production Designer
Jason Hale

Technical Illustrators
Matt Hall
Bob Meyer

MARKETING/SALES AND ADMINISTRATION

Sales Managers
Justin Henton
Matt Tusken

Marketing and Sales Representative
Erin Gribbin

Director, Operation–Books
Ron Rogers

Customer Service Manager
Terri Cannon

Customer Service Account Specialist
Courtney Hollars

Customer Service Representatives
Dinah Bunnell
April LeBlond

Warehouse & Inventory Manager
Leah Hicks

Penton Media

P.O. Box 12901, Overland Park, KS 66282-2901 • 800-262-1954 • 913-967-1719

More information available at *clymer.com*

CONTENTS

Dual Dimensions

This service manual provides specifications in both the U.S. Customary and Metric (SI) systems of measurement. The first specification is given in the measuring system perceived by us to be the preferred system when servicing a particular component. The second specification (given is parentheses) is the converted measurement. For instance, the specification "0.011 inch (0.28 mm)" indicates that we feel the preferred measurement, in this instance, is the U.S. measurement system and the metric equivalent of 0.011 inch is 0.28 mm.

ARIENS

931 Series (GT Series)

CONDENSED SPECIFICATIONS

MODELS	931033 (GT18)	931034 (GT20)
Engine Make	Kohler	Kohler
Model	M18S	M20S
Number of cylinders	2	2
Bore	3.12 in. (79.2 mm)	3.12 in. (79.2 mm)
Stroke	2.75 in. (69.85 mm)	3.06 in. (78 mm)
Displacement	42.18 cu. in. (691 cc)	46.98 cu. in. (769 cc)
Power Rating	18 hp (13.4 kW)	20 hp (14.9 kW)
Slow Idle	1200 rpm	1200 rpm
High Speed (No-Load)	3250 rpm	3250 rpm
Crankcase Capacity	3 pt.* (1.4 L)	3 pt.* (1.4 L)
Transmission	See text	See text

*With filter—3.5 pt. (1.7 L).

FRONT AXLE ASSEMBLY

MAINTENANCE

Inject good quality grease into grease fittings found on the wheel hubs, axle and steering components at 50-hour intervals. The recommended lubricant is a multipurpose, lithium base grease.

SPINDLES REMOVAL AND INSTALLATION

Raise and support the side to be serviced. Remove the wheel and tire. Disconnect the tie rod end, and if needed, the steering cylinder rod end (12—Fig. AR1-1). If removing the right spindle (11), drive out the roll pin (8), remove the collar (7), and withdraw the spindle from the axle. If removing the left spindle (21), remove the clamp bolt. Remove the steering arm (13), and withdraw the spindle from the axle.

Inspect the spindle and bushing for damage. Spindle bushings (9) are replaceable.

Install the spindle by reversing the removal procedure. Lubricate with multipurpose grease.

TIE ROD AND TOE-IN

A single tie rod (18—Fig. AR1-1) with replaceable ends (16 and 20) is used on all models.

Front wheel toe-in, measured at the horizontal centerline at the front and rear of the wheel rims, should be $\frac{1}{16}$-$\frac{1}{8}$ inch (1.6-3.2 mm). Measurement at the front should be smaller than the rear measurement.

To adjust toe-in, loosen the jam nuts and rotate the tie rod (18—Fig. AR1-1) to lengthen or shorten it as necessary. Note that one end of the tie rod is equipped with a tie rod end and jam nut with left-hand threads.

AXLE MAIN MEMBER REMOVAL AND INSTALLATION

To remove the axle main member (15—Fig. AR1-1), remove any PTO driven accessories from the PTO drive shaft. Disconnect the steering cylinder rod end from the steering arm (13). Support the front of the tractor. Loosen set screw in the rear bearing locking collar (2—Fig. AR1-2). Tap the collar with a pin punch to rotate it free from the lip of the rear bearing (4). Remove the cap screws attaching the front bearing housing (9) to the frame, then withdraw the PTO shaft assembly from the housing and frame. Unbolt and remove the PTO rear bearing housing (5). Reposition the locking stud (14) to the unlocked position, then withdraw the axle pivot tube (7) from the axle main member. Lower the axle from the frame and roll the axle assembly forward from the tractor.

Install by reversing the removal procedure.

POWER STEERING SYSTEM

SYSTEM OPERATION

All models are equipped with hydraulic power steering. Pressurized oil from the hydrostatic drive unit is supplied to a steering control valve and cylinder to provide the power steering. When the steering wheel is turned, elements in the control valve direct pressurized oil to the right or left turn control valve output ports.

Hydraulic hoses connect the control valve ports to the steering cylinder attached to the left spindle steering arm. During right turns, pressurized oil travels to the front steering cylinder hose. During left turns, pressurized oil enters the cylinder through the rear hose. If hydraulic flow to the steering control valve is interrupted, the steering control valve acts as a pump to maintain steering control.

Refer to the HYDROSTATIC TRANSMISSION and HYDRAULIC SYSTEM sections for maintenance and service information for the hydrostatic drive unit and hydraulic system.

POWER STEERING CYLINDER OVERHAUL

Position the front wheels full right. Remove the left running board. Clean the hoses, fittings and adjacent area, then disconnect the hydraulic hoses. Detach the front and rear ends of the steering cylinder and remove the cylinder.

Refer to Fig. AR1-3 for an exploded view of the steering cylinder. To disassemble the cylinder, unscrew the cylinder head (6) and remove the rod and piston assembly. Unscrew the nut (3) and slide components off the rod toward the piston end of the rod.

Clean and inspect parts. Check the piston (4) and cylinder bore (1) for damage and replace when necessary. Replace the O-ring seals (2, 5 and 7).

Reassemble by reversing the disassembly procedure. Extend the cylinder rod (8) fully before attaching the hydraulic hoses. Start the engine and turn the steering wheel from full left to full right several times to purge air from the system.

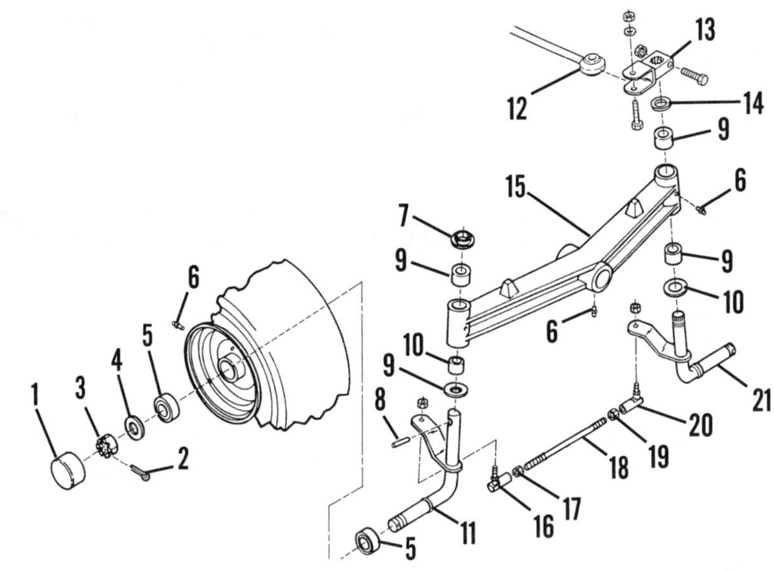

Fig. AR1-1–Exploded view of front axle assembly.

1. Hub cap
2. Cotter pin
3. Castle nut
4. Washer
5. Bearings
6. Grease fitting
7. Collar
8. Roll pin
9. Grease fitting
10. Washer
11. Steering spindle (right)
12. Steering cylinder rod
13. Steering arm
14. Washer
15. Front axle
16. Tie rod end
17. Nut
18. Tie rod
19. Nut (L.H.)
20. Tie rod end (L.H.)
21. Steering spindle (left)

POWER STEERING CONTROL VALVE

Removal and Installation

Detach the battery cables and remove the battery. Unscrew the steering wheel retaining nut and pull the steering wheel off the shaft.

CAUTION: Do not strike the steering wheel when removing it, as the power steering control valve may be damaged.

Remove the floor plate from the tractor. Mark the location of the hydraulic lines on the steering valve and note the steering valve location in reference to the mounting bracket. Clean the hoses, fittings and the area adjacent to the steering valve. Disconnect the hydraulic lines and cap the openings. Remove the nuts from the steering valve mounting bolts, then withdraw the steering valve assembly through the bottom of the frame.

Reinstall by reversing the removal procedure. After installation is completed, start the engine and turn the steering wheel from full left to full right several times to bleed air from the hydraulic system.

Overhaul

Before disassembling the steering control valve, note the alignment grooves (G—Fig. AR1-4) machined in the unit's side. When disassembling, place components in the proper order for reassembly.

NOTE: Do not clamp the steering control valve in a vise for service work. Fabricate a holding fixture as shown in Fig. AR1-5.

Place the steering valve in a holding fixture with the steering shaft down and secure with 5/16-24 NF nuts. Remove the four nuts securing the port cover (44—Fig. AR1-6) and remove the cover. Remove the sealing ring (40) and the five O-rings (41). Remove the plug (43) and ball (42). Remove the port manifold (39) and the three springs (38). Remove the valve ring (35) and discard the sealing rings (34). Remove the valve plate (33) and the three springs (32) from the isolation manifold pockets. Remove the hex drive and pin assembly (31), then remove the isolation manifold (30).

Remove the drive link (29), metering ring (17) and seal rings (16 and 27). Lift

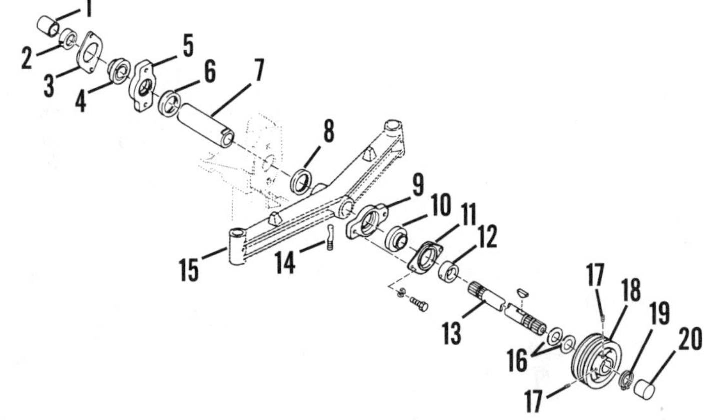

Fig. AR1-2–Front PTO shaft must be removed prior to removing the axle from the tractor. Refer to text.

1. Cover
2. Lock collar
3. Flange
4. Rear bearing
5. Bearing housing
6. Bushing
7. Axle pivot tube
8. Bushing
9. Bearing housing
10. Front bearing
11. Flange
12. Lock collar
13. Front PTO shaft
14. Lock stud
15. Axle
16. Washers
17. Set screw
18. Pulley
19. Snap ring
20. Cover

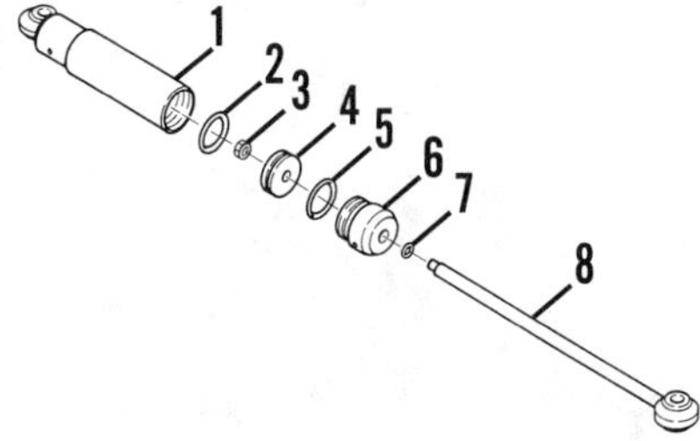

Fig. AR1-3–Exploded view of steering cylinder.

1. Cylinder tube
2. O-ring
3. Nut
4. Piston
5. O-ring
6. Cylinder head
7. O-ring
8. Rod

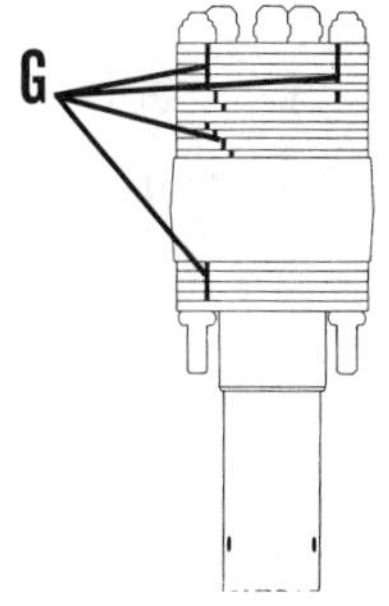

Fig. AR1-4–Components of steering control valve having alignment grooves (G) must be positioned as shown, or unit will not operate properly.

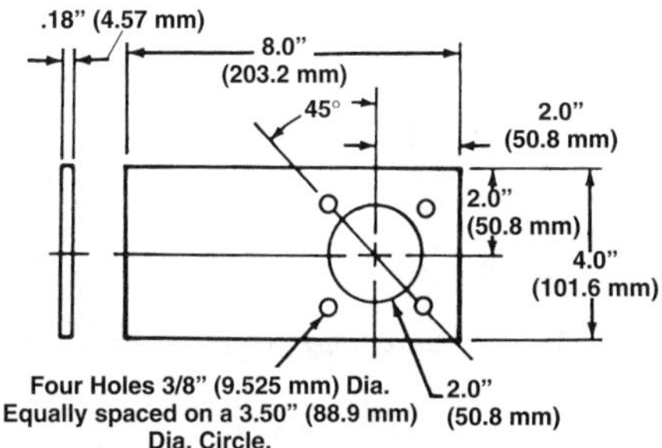

Fig. AR1-5–Fabricate a holding fixture as shown to aid service work on power steering control valve used on models with power steering.

Fig. AR1-6–Exploded view of power steering control valve.

1. Nut
2. Dust cover
3. Steering shaft
4. Bracket
5. Cap
6. Bearing
7. Tube assy.
9. Snap ring
10. Washer
11. Upper cover plate
12. Face seal
13. Seal spacer
14. Thrust bearing
15. Spacer
16. Seal ring
17. Metering ring
18. Drive plate
19. Stator
20. Drive link spacer
21. Rotor
22. Alignment pins (5)
23. Commutator
24. Commutator ring
25. Commutator cover
26. Commutator seal
27. Seal
28. Screws (11)
29. Drive link
30. Isolation manifold
31. Hex drive assy.
32. Springs
33. Valve plate
34. Seal ring
35. Valve ring
36. Seal ring
37. Alignment pins (2)
38. Springs
39. Port manifold
40. Seal ring
41. O-ring
42. Ball
43. Plug
44 Port cover
45. Fitting

off the metering assembly and remove the commutator seal (26). Remove the 11 Allen head screws (28) and lift off the commutator cover (25). Remove the commutator ring (24), then carefully remove the commutator (23) and the five alignment pins (22). Remove the drive link spacer (20) and separate the rotor (21) from the stator (19). Remove the drive plate (18), spacer (15), thrust bearing (14), seal spacer (13) and face seal (12). Remove the upper cover plate (11). Remove the steering shaft (3).

The bushing (6) is retained by crimps in the steering column. Be sure to crimp the metal after installing the bushing. The steering column (7) is welded in the upper cover plate tube. The unit must be replaced if the column is loose in the cover plate tube.

Clean and inspect all parts and replace any showing signs of damage. Springs (38) should have a free length of 0.75 inch (19 mm) and springs (32) should have a free length of 0.50 inch (12.7 mm). Springs must be replaced as sets only. The commutator (23) and commutator ring (24) are a matched set and must be replaced as an assembly.

Check rotor-to-stator clearance using a feeler gauge as shown in Fig. AR1-7. Note the height of rotor and stator. If the rotor and stator height is 0.75 inch (19 mm) or less, replace the rotor and stator assembly when the clearance exceeds 0.003 inch (0.08 mm). If the rotor and stator height is greater than 1.00 in. (25.4 mm), replace the rotor and stator assembly when clearance exceeds 0.005 in. (0.13 mm).

Replace all seals and O-rings and lubricate all parts with hydraulic fluid prior to installation.

Reassemble by reversing the disassembly procedure and referral to the following notes: Be sure the alignment grooves on the upper cover plate (11—Fig. AR1-6), isolation manifold (30) and port manifold (39) are on the same side. Install the rotor (21) so the pin holes face out. Install the commutator so the long grooves (G) are out as shown in Fig. AR1-8. When installed, pins (22) must not protrude above the commutator face (23). Apply low strength thread-locking solution to the threads of the screws (28—Fig. AR1-6) and install the screws finger tight. Insert the metering valve assembly in the metering ring (17) with the commutator cover (25) facing downward.

Place a suitable size wood block under the metering valve assembly so the drive plate (18) is partially out of the metering ring. Make six shims that are

Fig. AR1-7–Use a feeler gauge to check rotor to stator clearance. Refer to text.

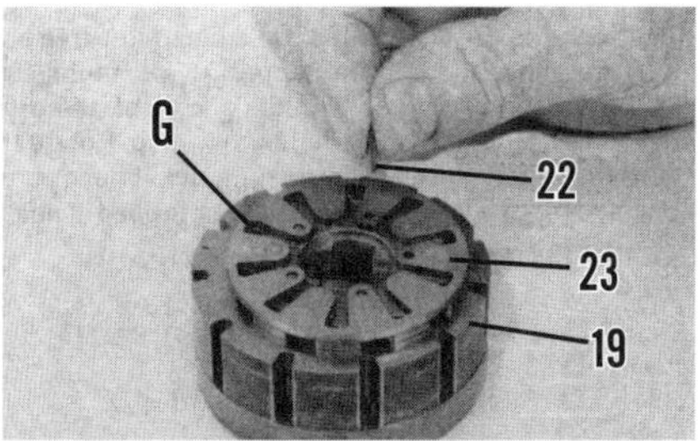

Fig. AR1-8–Install commutator so long grooves (G) are out.

Fig. AR1-10–Install valve plate so "PORT SIDE" on plate is opposite from alignment grooves (A) on isolation manifold.

0.007 inch thick, ½ inch wide and 1½ inches long. Insert shims between the drive plate and metering ring so two shims touch every 120°. Remove the wood block and push the metering valve down until the drive plate is flush with the surface of the metering ring. Tighten the screws (28) in several steps to the final torque of 11-13 in.-lb. (1.24-1.47 N·m) using the sequence shown in Fig. AR1-9. Commutator ring (24—Fig. AR1-6) should now be concentric within 0.005 inch (0.127 mm) of drive plate (18).

Insert the large tang end of the drive link (29—Fig. AR1-6) into the slot in the rotor (21) and rotate the metering assembly to make certain the parts do not bind. Install the commutator seal (26) so the yellow mark on the seal is toward the commutator cover (25). Be sure ½ inch (13 mm) springs (32) are installed in the isolation manifold (30) and ¾ inch (19 mm) springs (38) are installed in the port manifold (39). Install the valve plate (33) so the spring slot with the smallest cavity and the words PORT SIDE are positioned opposite from the alignment grooves (A) on the isolation manifold as shown in Fig. AR1-10. Tighten the valve assembly nuts in a crossing pattern to 20-24 ft.-lb. (27-33 N·m). Tighten plug (43—Fig. AR1-5) to 97-151 in.-lb. (11-17 N·m). Make sure that all parts with alignment grooves are aligned as shown in Fig. AR1-4, otherwise the unit will not operate correctly.

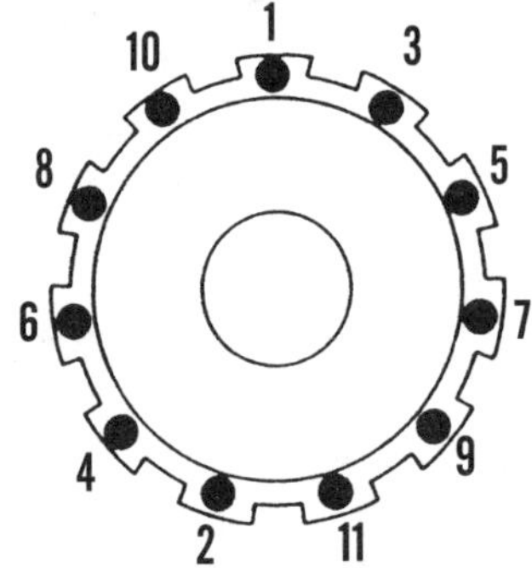

Fig. AR1--9–Tighten the 11 Allen head screws to 11-13 in.-lb. (1.2401.47 N•m) in sequence shown. Refer to text.

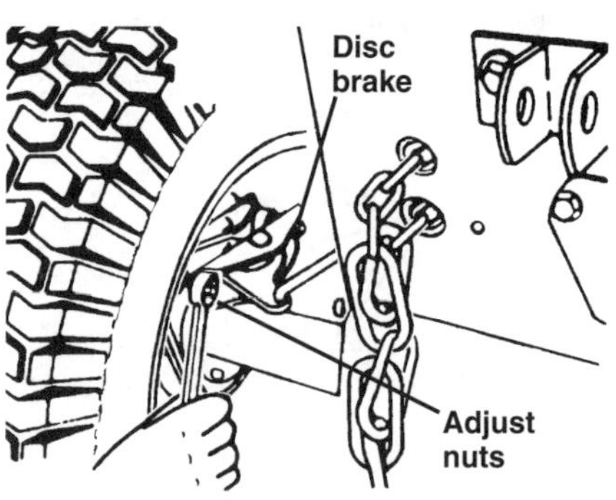

Fig. AR1-11–Drawing showing location of brake adjustment nuts.

ENGINE

REMOVAL AND INSTALLATION

To remove the engine, disconnect the wires to the headlights and remove the hood, grille and side panels. Hood, grille and side panels can be removed as a unit. Remove the PTO belts and disconnect the wire to the PTO clutch at the front of the engine. Disconnect the battery cables and electrical wires to the engine. Disconnect the choke and throttle cables from the engine. Detach the fuel line from the carburetor. Unscrew the cap screws attaching the drive shaft coupling to the flywheel. Remove the four bolts mounting the engine to the frame. Lift the engine toward the front and remove the engine from the tractor.

OVERHAUL

Engine make and model are listed at the beginning of this section. Refer to the appropriate Kohler engine section in this manual for tune-up specifications, engine overhaul procedures and engine maintenance.

BRAKES

ADJUSTMENT

If the brake pedal can be depressed more than two inches (51 mm), adjust the brakes. Raise and support the rear of the tractor so the wheels clear the ground. Open the free-wheeling valve on the hydrostatic transmission so the wheels may be rotated. Tighten the two adjusting nuts (Fig. AR1-11) evenly while rotating the wheel until a slight drag is felt. Back each nut off ⅛ turn. Repeat the procedure for the remaining side.

BRAKE PADS

Raise and support the rear of the tractor. Remove the rear wheel. Remove the axle flange retaining nut and pull the axle flange from the axle shaft. Disconnect the brake rod (1—Fig. AR1-12). Remove the nuts (7) and carriage bolts (15). Withdraw the friction plate (13) and caliper plate (14).

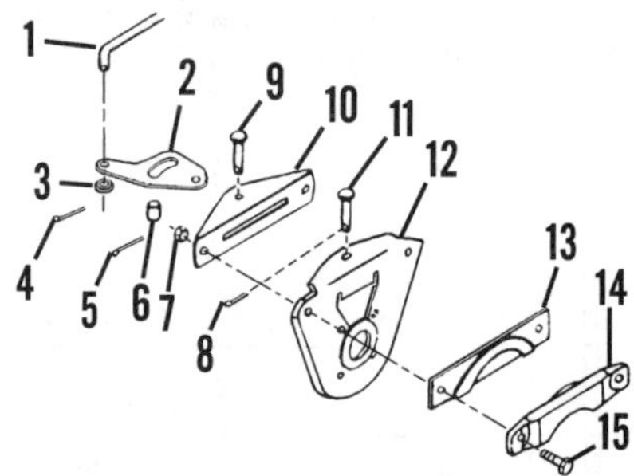

Fig. AR1-12–Exploded view of disc brake system.

1. Brake rod
2. Actuator plate
3. Washer
4. Cotter pin
5. Cotter pin
6. Roller
7. Nut
8. Cotter pin
9. Pin
10. Pressure plate
11. Pin
12. Caliper mounting plate
13. Friction plate & pad
14. Caliper plate & pad
15. Bolt

To disassemble the brake further, remove the pin (9) and roller (6). Remove the pin (11) and plate (2). Separate the brake disc from the carrier plate when the disc is to be replaced. Unbolt and remove the caliper mounting plate (12).

Reinstall by reversing the removal procedure. Adjust the brakes.

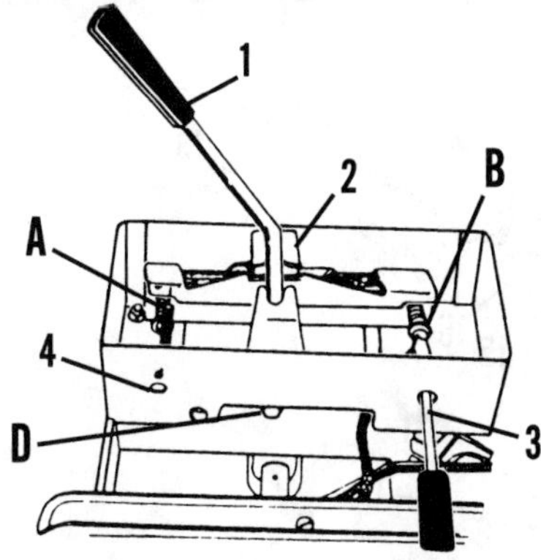

Fig. AR1-13–Drawing of control lever friction adjustment screws (A and B), control lever (1), control fork (2), screwdriver (3) and access holes (4).

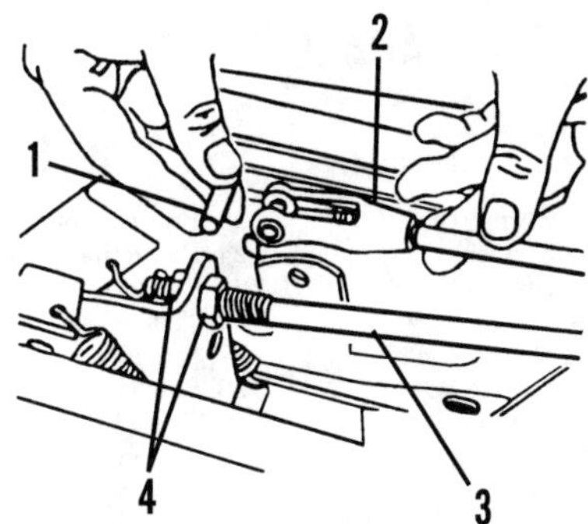

Fig, AR1-14–To adjust hydrostatic shift linkage, shift rod (2) must be disconnected from neutralizer rod (3). Refer to text.

1. Pin
2. Shift rod
3. Neutralizer rod
4. Adjusting nuts

SHIFT CONTROL LINKAGE

FRICTION ADJUSTMENT

If the hydrostatic control lever (1—Fig. AR1-13) will not maintain the set position, adjust the friction plate spring pressure. Raise the rear deck and insert a screwdriver (3) through the access holes (4) and tighten screws (A and B) evenly. If the tractor tends to gain speed, tighten the first screw (A) more than the second (B). If tractor loses speed, tighten the second screw (B) more than the first (A).

NEUTRAL ADJUSTMENT

Raise and support the rear of the tractor so the wheels are free to turn. Remove the floor plate. Disconnect the shift rod yoke (2—Fig. AR1-14) from the neutralizer rod (3). If the shift lever does not return to NEUTRAL when the neutral return pedal is depressed, adjust the neutralizer rod's length using the adjusting nuts (4). Loosen the jam nut (1—Fig. AR1-15) so the eccentric (2) can be turned with a wrench. Start engine and move shift lever to NEUTRAL.

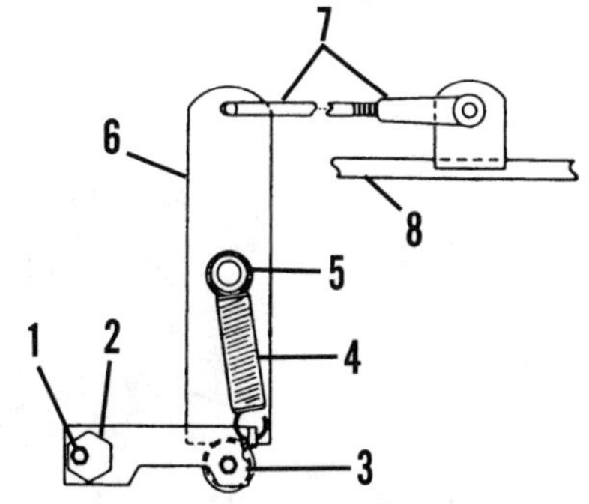

Fig. AR1-15–View of hydrostatic shift linkage. Refer to text for adjustment.

1. Jam nut
2. Eccentric
3. Bearing
4. Spring
5. Pintle arm
6. Transmission lever
7. Shift rod
8. Shift lever

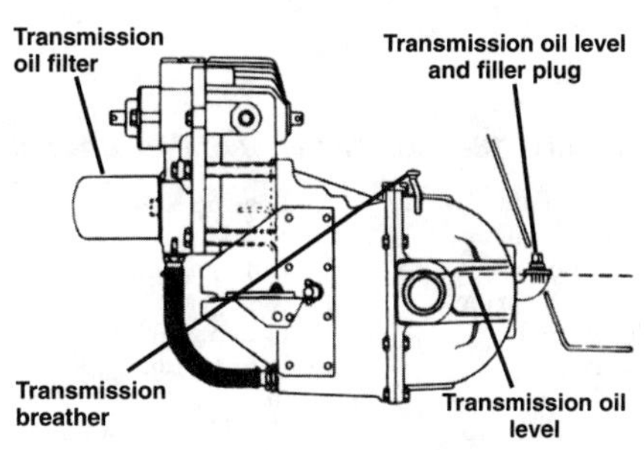

Fig. AR1-16–Hydraulic system, hydrostatic drive unit and final drive share a common oil sump in final drive housing. Oil should be level with filler plug opening.

CAUTION: Use care when working around the rotating drive shaft and tires.

With the engine running at full throttle, adjust the eccentric until the wheels stop turning and tighten the jam nut. Shut off the engine and adjust the shift rod yoke so the shift rod (7—Fig. AR1-15) is centered in the slot in the transmission lever (6).

HYDROSTATIC TRANSMISSION

LUBRICATION

Oil for the transmission is routed from the oil sump in the final drive housing. A spin-on filter (Fig. AR1-16) mounted on the transmission protects the hydrostatic transmission and other hydraulic components.

Refer to the FINAL DRIVE section for the oil change procedure. Change the oil filter after every 500 hours of operation. Fill the new filter with clean oil prior to installing. Oil level should be maintained at the top of the filler elbow.

Periodically inspect the transmission for oil leakage.

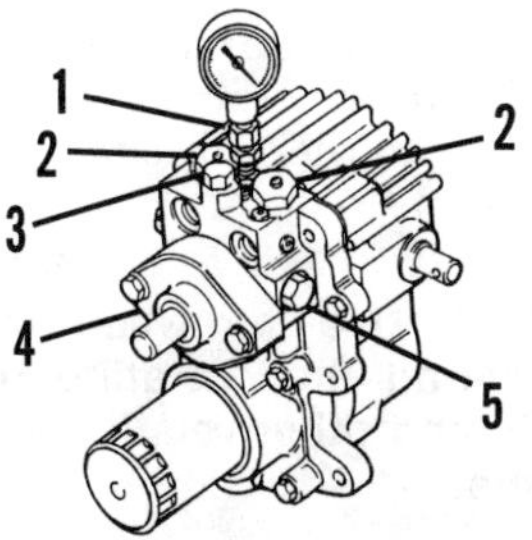

Fig. AR1-17–Install a pressure gauge as shown to check system pressures. Refer to text.

1. Pressure gauge
2. Check valves
3. Implement pressure relief valve
4. Charge pump
5. Charge pressure relief valve

TROUBLESHOOTING

The following problems and possible causes should be used as an aid in locating and correcting transmission problems.

Loss of power or tractor will not operate in either direction.
1. Low oil level.
2. Park lock engaged.
3. Plugged oil filter.
4. Locked hydrostatic unit.
5. Air entering charge pump suction side.
6. Transmission oil temperature too hot.
7. Broken speed control linkage.
8. Free wheeling valves depressed or stuck down.
9. Faulty charge pump or charge pressure relief valve.
10. Damaged transmission pump and/or motor.
11. Internal damage to reduction gear assembly.

Transmission operating too hot.
1. Low transmission oil level.
2. Wrong oil in transmission.
3. Plugged oil filter.
4. Overloaded tractor.
5. Faulty charge pump or charge pressure relief valve.
6. Worn transmission pump and/or motor.

Transmission jerks when starting or operates in one direction only.
1. Faulty speed control linkage.
2. Faulty charge check valve.

Tractor creeps when in NEUTRAL. Could be caused by a worn or incorrectly adjusted control linkage.

PRESSURE CHECK

To check hydrostatic transmission charge pressure, install a 0-1000 psi (0-7000 kPa) test gauge as shown in Fig. AR1-17. Raise and support the rear of the tractor so the tires are off the ground. Start and run the engine at 1/4 throttle. Move the transmission speed control lever to the full forward or reverse position.

CAUTION: Use care when working around the rotating rear wheels and other rotating components.

Note the pressure gauge reading, then increase engine speed to full throttle. Pressure may increase but should not decrease.

Transmission charge pressure should be 70-150 psi (485-1035 kPa). Pressure can be adjusted by the use of shims on top of the charge pump relief valve (5–Fig. AR1-17) spring.

REMOVAL AND INSTALLATION

Disconnect the battery cables. Remove the rear deck and fuel tank. Disconnect the drive shaft rear coupler and remove coupler half from the transmission input shaft. Thoroughly clean the transmission and surrounding area. Place a drain pan under the tractor, then disconnect the hose from the axle housing and drain the lubricant. Disconnect hydraulic hoses and cap all openings to prevent contamination. Disconnect the transmission control linkage. Remove the transmission mounting screws. Tilt the transmission back and remove it from the tractor.

Installation of the transmission is the reverse of removal. Tighten transmission mounting bolts to 25-30 ft.-lbs. (34-40 N·m). Make certain the hoses are reconnected properly.

Note that the transmission must be primed with oil before operating to prevent internal damage. To prime the transmission, remove the implement relief valve plug (3—Fig. AR1-17), spring and poppet. Pour one pint of clean oil in the port. Install the relief valve, then start the engine and check for leaks. Add oil to the reservoir as necessary to bring the oil level to the top of the filler elbow.

OVERHAUL

All models are equipped with a Sundstrand Series 15 U-type hydrostatic transmission. Refer to the HYDROSTATIC TRANSMISSION SERVICE SECTION at the rear of this manual for overhaul information.

FINAL DRIVE

LUBRICATION

The final drive housing is the oil reservoir for the hydrostatic transmission and the hydraulic system. Maintain oil level at the filler plug on the final drive housing (Fig. AR1-16). The recommended fluid is SAE 5W-30 engine oil for normal service. If ambient temperature exceeds 80° F (27° C) or tractor service is severe, recommended oil is SAE 30. Oil in the final drive should be changed after every 500 hours of operation. The approximate capacity is 5.5 quarts (5.2 L).

NOTE: After changing oil, the transmission must be primed before operating to prevent internal damage to the transmission.

To prime the transmission, remove the implement lift relief valve plug (3—Fig. AR1-17), spring and poppet. Pour one pint (0.5 L) of clean oil into the relief valve port. Install the relief valve, start the engine, and check for leaks. Add oil to the reservoir as necessary to bring the oil level to the top of the filler elbow.

OVERHAUL

To remove the final drive, remove the hydrostatic transmission as described in the previous section. Detach the parking pawl assembly from the final drive housing and disconnect the brake control rods. Support the rear of the tractor and unbolt the axle brackets from the frame. Roll the unit forward until the oil filler pipe is clear of the rear hitch plate, raise the tractor and roll the assembly away from the tractor.

To disassemble the unit, drain the oil from the housing. Remove the wheels and hubs (1—Fig. AR1-18) from the axles (6). Unbolt the axle bearing retainer and withdraw the axle and bearing assemblies from the rear housing (7). Unbolt and separate the front and rear housings (23 and 7).

Be sure the differential bearing caps are marked for the correct reassembly as they are matched to the front housing. Unbolt and remove the bearing caps, then pry the differential assembly out of the housing. Drive a pointed punch through the pinion shaft expansion plug and out of the housing. Remove the snap ring (19) and shim (18) from the end of the pinion shaft. Remove the side cover (25) and place a screwdriver blade under the edge of the reduction gear (24) to prevent the gear from binding. Press the pinion gear (13) out of the housing and remove the outer bearing (21), spacer (17) and reduction gear (24). Press the pinion shaft out of the pinion bearing (14). Press the bearing cups (15 and 22) out of the housing.

To disassemble the differential, drive the lock pin (2) out of the pinion shaft (3) as shown in Fig. AR1-19. Drive the

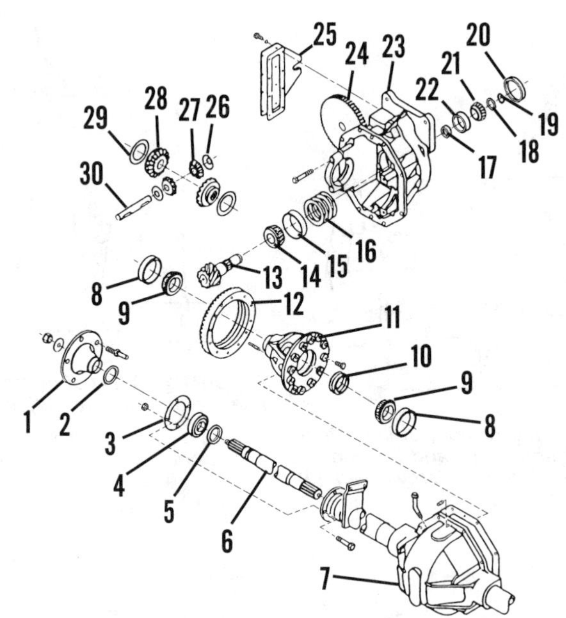

Fig. AR1-18–Exploded view of final drive and rear axle assembly.

1. Hub
2. Felt seal
3. Retainer
4. Axle bearing
5. Oil seal
6. Axle
7. Axle housing
8. Bearing cup
9. Bearing cone
10. Shims
11. Differential case
12. Ring gear
13. Pinion gear
14. Bearing cone (inner)
15. Bearing cup (outer)
16. Shims
17. Spacer
18. Shim
19. Snap ring
20. Expansion ring
21. Bearing cone (inner)
22. Bearing cup (outer)
23. Front housing
24. Reduction gear
25. Cover
26. Thrust washer (2)
27. Pinion gear (2)
28. Side gear (2)
29. Thrust washer (2)
30. Pinion shaft

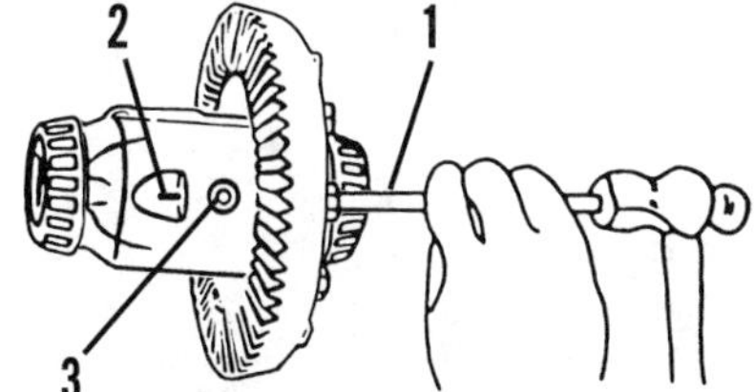

Fig. AR1-19–Use a long, thin punch (1) to drive retaining pin (2) out of pinion shaft (3), then drive pinion out of differential case.

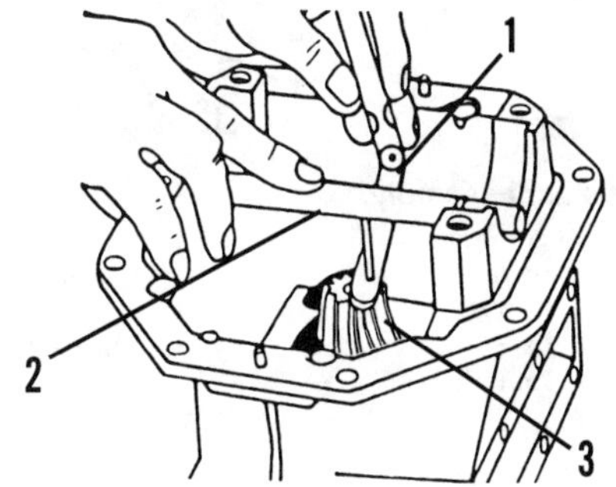

Fig. AR1-20–If front is replaced, measure from bottom of bearing cradles to pinion gear surface as shown to determine pinion shaft shim pack thickness. Refer to text.

pinion shaft (3) from the housing. Rotate the pinion gears (27—Fig. AR1-18) 90° to the differential case openings and remove the pinion gears (27), side gears (28) and thrust washers (26 and 29).

Use a suitable puller inserting the puller jaws into the indentations provided in the differential case, to remove the differential case bearings (9). Remove cap screws securing ring gear (12) to the case, then drive the ring gear off the case using a hammer and wood block.

Clean and inspect all parts and replace any damaged parts.

Reassemble by reversing the disassembly procedure. Reuse the original shim pack (16), when reinstalling the inner bearing cup (15) in the original housing (23). If the housing (23) is being replaced, determine the proper shim pack by installing the bearing cup (15) in the housing without shims. Press the bearing cone (14) on the pinion shaft and position the shaft and bearing in the housing. Using a depth measuring tool similar to the one shown in Fig. AR1-20, measure the distance from the bottom of the bearing cradles to the pinion gear surface. Subtract the measured dimension in inches from 1.2097 and the difference will be the required shim pack thickness in inches. Remove the inner bearing cup, install the required shim pack and reinstall the cup in the housing.

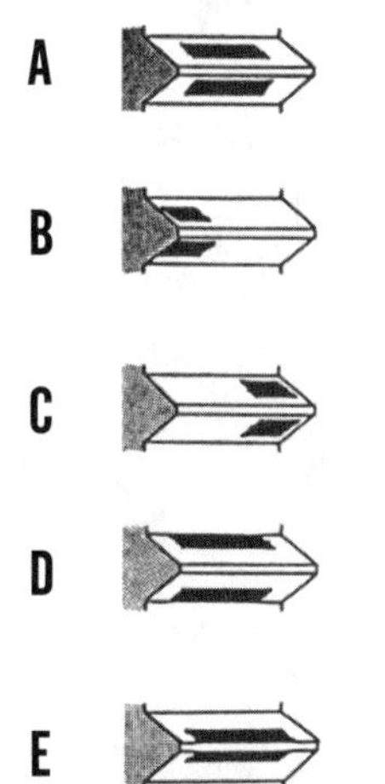

Fig. AR1-21–Drawings showing typical gear teeth contact patterns encountered when checking ring gear and pinion. "A" pattern is desired; "B" too close to toe; "C" to close to heel; "D" contact too low; "E" contact too high. Refer to text and correct as necessary.

Position the pinion gear, reduction gear (chamfered side of splines toward the pinion gear) and spacer in the housing. Press the outer bearing cone onto the pinion shaft until a slight drag is felt when the gear is turned by hand. Then, install the thickest shim (18—Fig. AR1-18) possible which will still allow snap ring (19) installation. Use a sealer when installing the expansion plug (20) and side cover (25).

Position the ring gear (12) on the differential case (11) and pull the gear into place by tightening the retaining cap screws evenly. Tighten cap screws to 50-55 ft.-lb. (68-75 N·m).

Press bearing cones (9) on the original differential case (11) using the original shims (10). If the differential case is replaced, install a 0.020 inch shim pack under each bearing. Position the differential assembly in the front housing with the ring gear facing the same side as the reduction gear cover. Install bearing caps in their original positions and tighten cap screws to 40-45 ft.-lb. (54-61 N·m).

Using a dial indicator, check for the proper ring gear to pinion backlash of 0.003-0.007 inch (0.076-0.178 mm). If necessary, adjust backlash by moving shims (10) from one side to the other until the correct backlash is obtained.

To check the gear teeth contact pattern, paint teeth with a gear pattern compound, then rotate the pinion while applying a light load to the ring gear. Compare contact area on the teeth with the patterns illustrated in Fig. AR1-21. Correct as necessary. The desired tooth contact pattern on ring gear is shown at A. To move toe pattern B toward the heel, shim the ring gear away from the pinion,

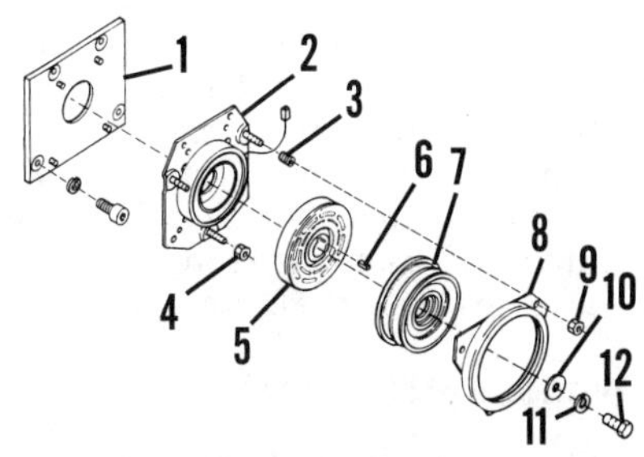

Fig. AR1-22–Exploded view of PTO clutch assembly.

1. Adapter plate
2. Field assy.
3. Springs (3)
4. Nuts
5. Rotor
6. Key
7. Pulley
8. Brake flange
9. Nuts
10. Washer
11. Lockwasher
12. Screw

within 0.003-0.007 inch (0.076-0.178 mm) backlash limits. To move heel pattern C toward the toe, shim the ring gear closer to the pinion, within the backlash limits. If the pattern is low D, remove the shims located under the pinion inner bearing cup. If the pattern is high "E", increase the shim pack under the pinion inner bearing cup.

Assemble the front housing to the rear housing and tighten the retaining screws to 18-23 ft.-lb. (24-32 N·m).

POWER TAKE-OFF (PTO)

FRONT PTO

Testing PTO Clutch

Use the following procedure for locating a PTO malfunction. Turn the ignition switch ON, depress the seat safety switch, and actuate the PTO switch. If the clutch does not engage, disconnect the wiring connector at the clutch and use a 12-volt test lamp to check the wire continuity coming from the PTO switch. If the lamp lights, either the PTO or the wiring connector at the clutch field coil is defective.

To check the field coil, disconnect the wiring connector at the PTO clutch. Using an ohmmeter set on the low scale, check the resistance between the PTO connector and the ground wire. The specified resistance is 0.3-0.5 ohm. A reading other than the specified reading indicates the field coil is faulty and the unit should be replaced.

Adjust PTO Clutch

The PTO clutch must be adjusted if the clutch has been disassembled or when the operation becomes erratic. With the clutch disengaged, insert a feeler gauge through the slots in the brake plate (8—Fig. AR1-22) and measure the clearance between the clutch rotor (5) and field (2). There should be 0.015 inch (0.38 mm) clearance between armature and clutch rotor at each of the clutch plate slots. To adjust, tighten or loosen the clutch adjusting nuts (9) to obtain the correct clearance.

Overhaul PTO Clutch

To remove the PTO clutch, release the idler spring tension and remove the PTO belts. Disconnect the wiring connector at the PTO clutch. Unscrew the retaining nuts (9—Fig. AR1-22) and remove the brake flange (8). Unscrew the cap screw (12) from the center of the clutch. Use a suitable puller to remove the clutch pulley (7) and rotor (5). Unbolt and remove the field assembly (2).

Inspect bearings for damage. Inspect for broken or distorted springs (3). Check contact surfaces of the rotor and armature for damage. Be sure the wires are in good condition.

To reassemble the clutch, reverse the disassembly procedure. Adjust the clutch as previously described.

Overhaul PTO Shaft Assembly

Remove the PTO driven equipment from the tractor. Relieve the idler pulley tension and remove the belts (20—Fig. AR1-23) from the front pulley (15). Loosen the set screws in the rear bearing locking collar (2). Tap the collar with a pin punch to rotate it off the lip of the rear bearing (4). Remove the bolts attaching the front bearing housing (3 and 5) to the frame. Slide the PTO shaft assembly forward out of the axle and frame. Note that the axle pivot tube (7) may remain in place when removing the PTO shaft assembly. The pulley (15) and bearing lock collar (2) are locked in place by set screws. Loosen the set screws, then tap the side of the collar with a punch to rotate the collar off the bearing. Remove the bearing housings (5) and bearings (4).

Inspect all parts for damage and replace when necessary. When installing the PTO assembly, tap the side of the bearing collar (2) with a pin punch to lock the collar to the lip of the bearing. Then, tighten the locking collar set screws to secure the bearings to the PTO shaft.

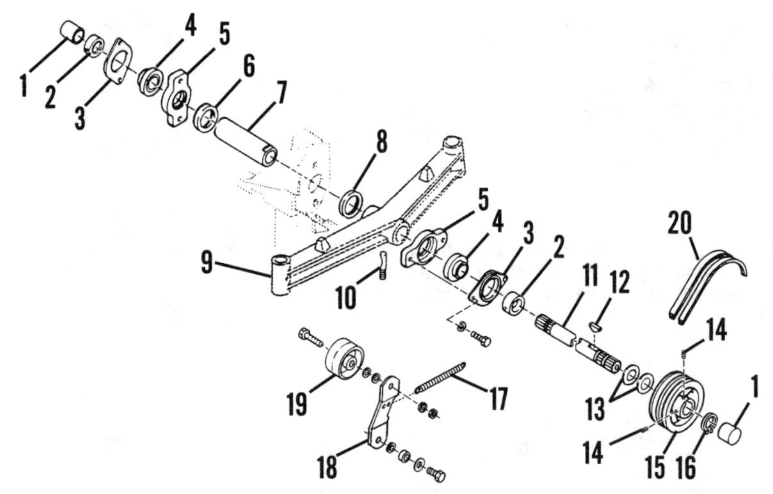

Fig. AR1-23–Exploded view of front PTO output shaft assembly.

1. Cover
2. Locking collar
3. Flange
4. Bearing
5. Flange
6. Bushing
7. Tube
8. Bushing
9. Front axle
10. Locking stud
11. PTO shaft
12. Key
13. Washer
14. Set screws
15. Pulley
16. Snap ring
17. Spring
18. Idler arm
19. Idler pulley

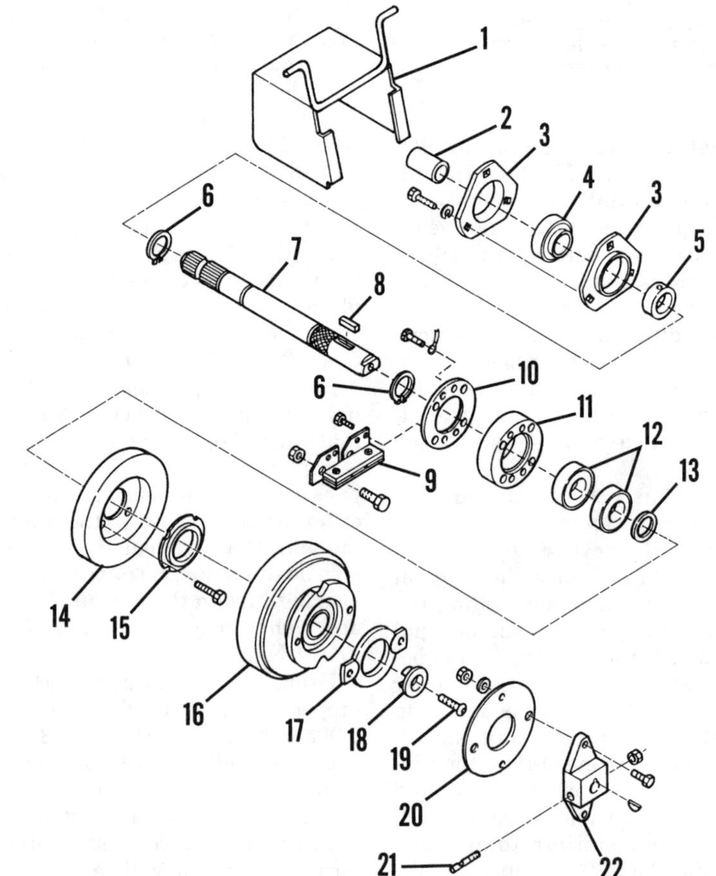

Fig. AR1-24–Exploded view of rear PTO assembly.

1. Shield
2. Cover
3. Flange
4. Bearing
5. Locking collar
6. Snap ring
7. PTO shaft
8. Key
9. Torque bracket
10. Ring
11. Bearing hub
12. Bearings
13. Washer
14. Clutch driven flange
15. Flange
16. Clutch driven flange
17. Flex coupling flange
18. Retainer
19. Cap screw
20. Flex coupling disc
21. Stud
22. Flex coupling flange

REAR PTO

Testing PTO Clutch

Use the following procedure for locating a PTO malfunction. Turn the ignition switch ON, depress the seat safety switch, and actuate the PTO switch. If the clutch does not engage, disconnect the wiring connector at the clutch and

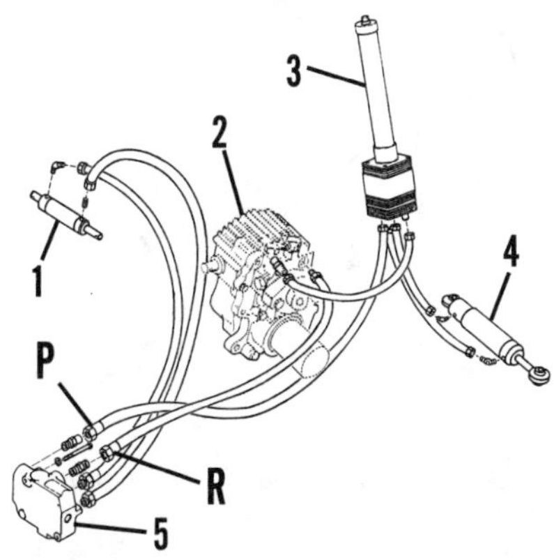

Fig. AR1-25–Drawing of hydraulic system components.

P. Pressure line
R. Return line
1. Lift cylinder
2. Hydrostatic transmission
3. Power steering control valve
4. Power steering cylinder
5. Lift control valve

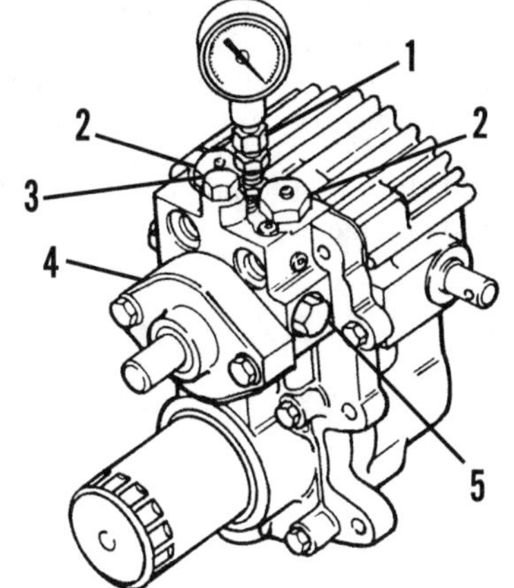

Fig. AR1-26–Install a pressure gauge as shown to check system pressures.

1. Pressure gauge
2. Check valves
3. Implement pressure relief valve
4. Charge pump
5. Charge pressure relief valve

use a 12-volt test lamp to check the wire continuity coming from the PTO switch. If the lamp lights, either the PTO or wiring connector at the clutch field coil is defective.

To check the field coil, disconnect the wiring connector at the PTO clutch. Using an ohmmeter set on the low scale, check the resistance between the PTO connector and ground wire. The specified resistance is 0.3-0.5 ohm. A reading other than the specified reading indicates the field coil is faulty and the unit should be replaced.

Overhaul

Remove the cover plate over the top of the rear PTO clutch. Detach the rear PTO clutch wire lead and ground lead.

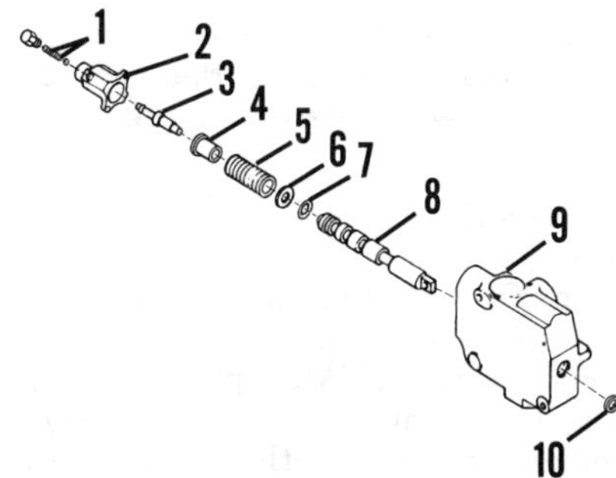

Fig. AR1-27–Exploded view of implement lift valve.

1. Float spring & ball
2. End cover
3. Float valve arm
4. Spring retainer
5. Spring
6. Washer
7. O-ring
8. Valve spool
9. Valve body
10. O-ring

Unbolt torque bracket assembly (9—Fig. AR1-24). Remove the rear PTO shield (1). Loosen the set screw in the rear bearing lock collar (5) and use a punch to rotate and free the collar from the bearing. Disassemble the bearing flange plates (3) and remove the plates, rear bearing (4) and collar. Unscrew the two bolts securing the clutch to the flex coupling (20 and 22). Move the clutch and shaft back to clear the remaining bolts in the coupling, then remove the assembly.

To disassemble clutch, unbolt and remove retainer (18) and clutch assembly (14 and 16) from the PTO shaft.

Reinstall by reversing the disassembly procedure. Note the gap between the outer ring and clutch must not be more than 0.062 in. (1.57 mm).

HYDRAULIC SYSTEM

SYSTEM OPERATION

All models are equipped with the hydraulic system shown in Fig. AR1-25. The charge pump mounted on the front of the hydrostatic transmission provides pressurized oil for the transmission, hydraulic lift and power steering systems. The hydraulic system uses oil contained in the final drive housing. Oil from the housing sump travels to the charge pump. Pressurized oil from the charge pump travels internally to the transmission (2). An implement relief valve on top of the transmission valve block protects the system from excessive pressure. Pressure oil from the charge pump travels to the power steering control valve (3) and hydraulic lift circuit (5).

Also refer to the power steering and transmission sections.

LUBRICATION

The final drive housing is the oil reservoir for the hydrostatic transmission and the hydraulic system. Refer to the FINAL DRIVE section for lubrication requirements.

PRESSURE CHECK

To check the hydrostatic drive transmission charge pressure and the hydraulic system lift operating pressure, install a 0-1000 psi (0-7000 kPa) test gauge as shown in Fig. AR1-26. Raise and support the rear of the tractor so the tires clear the ground. Start and run the engine at $\frac{1}{4}$ throttle. Move the transmission speed control lever to the full FORWARD or REVERSE position.

CAUTION: Use care when working around rotating rear wheels and other rotating components.

Transmission charge pressure should be 70-150 psi (483-1034 kPa). Increase the engine speed to full throttle. Charge pressure may increase but should not decrease. Shims are available for installation on top of the charge pressure relief valve spring to adjust the pressure.

To test lift system pressure, place transmission speed control lever in NEUTRAL. With the engine running at $\frac{3}{4}$ throttle, operate the lift control valve lever so the lift cylinder reaches the end of the stroke. The gauge pressure reading should be 500-1000 psi (3450-6900 kPa).

Shims are available for installation on top of the implement relief valve spring to adjust the pressure. One 0.015 inch shim will change the implement relief valve pressure approximately 100 psi (670 kPa).

If pressures are low and shimming the relief valve does not correct the problem, refer to the HYDROSTATIC TRANSMISSION section for service procedures.

LIFT VALVE

To remove the lift valve, first thoroughly clean the valve and hydraulic hoses. Disconnect hoses from the valve. Remove the pin attaching the control lever to the valve spool. Unbolt and remove the valve from the tractor.

To disassemble, remove two screws retaining the spring end cover (2—Fig. AR1-27) to the valve body (9) and remove the cover. Push the valve spool (8) out of the valve body.

Individual parts for servicing the valve are not available. Replace the valve assembly when the spool or body is damaged.

HYDRAULIC CYLINDER

To disassemble the lift cylinder, first remove the adapter fittings from the cylinder body (8—Fig. AR1-28) and rod cap (2). Unscrew rod cap from the cylinder body, then withdraw the piston rod (4) and piston (5) from the body. Unscrew the retaining screw (7) to remove the piston from the rod.

Inspect the cylinder body, piston and rod for scoring or other damage and replace when needed. Replace O-ring seals (3 and 6) and wiper seal (1). Coat all parts with clean oil when assembling.

ELECTRICAL SYSTEM SAFETY INTERLOCK SYSTEM

A safety interlock system grounds the engine ignition circuit, preventing the engine from starting unless the following conditions are met: The operator must be sitting on the seat, the speed selector lever is in the PARK/START position, the brake/neutralizer pedal is depressed and the implement power (PTO) is disengaged.

NOTE: When checking switches for continuity, disconnect wiring from the switches before testing to prevent possible damage to the meter or interlock module.

The ignition switch (Fig. AR1-29) has three positions: OFF, START and RUN. In the OFF position, there should be no continuity between any switch contacts. In the START position, there should be continuity between the B, I and S terminals and the X and Y terminals. In the RUN position, there should be continuity between the B, I and A terminals and the X and Y terminals.

To test the interlock switches that are normally open, connect an ohmmeter across the switch terminals. The meter should indicate infinite resistance (open circuit). Actuate the switch and the meter should indicate 0.01-0.1 ohm resistance (closed circuit) indicating the switch is functioning normally.

To test the interlock system, connect the voltmeter black lead to ground on the frame. Connect the meter's red lead to the white wire at the ignition switch terminal (B). With the speed selector lever in the park/start and the PTO switches OFF, the battery voltage should be read on the meter. If there is no voltage at the white wire, check for a faulty selector lever switch, PTO switches, blown fuse or diode.

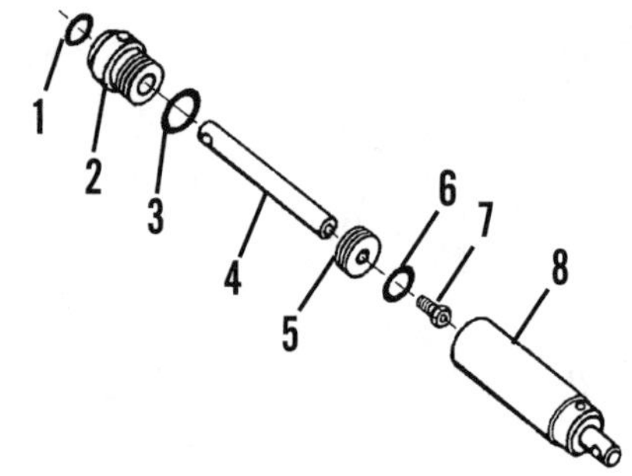

Fig. AR1-28–Exploded view of hydraulic lift cylinder.

1. Wiper seal
2. Rod cap
3. O-ring
4. Piston rod
5. Piston
6. O-ring
7. Cap screw
8. Cylinder body

Connect the voltmeter's red lead to the yellow wire at the module connector. Turn the ignition switch ON and depress the seat switch. The meter should indicate battery voltage. Engage the PTO switch, the implement light should illuminate and the PTO clutch should engage.

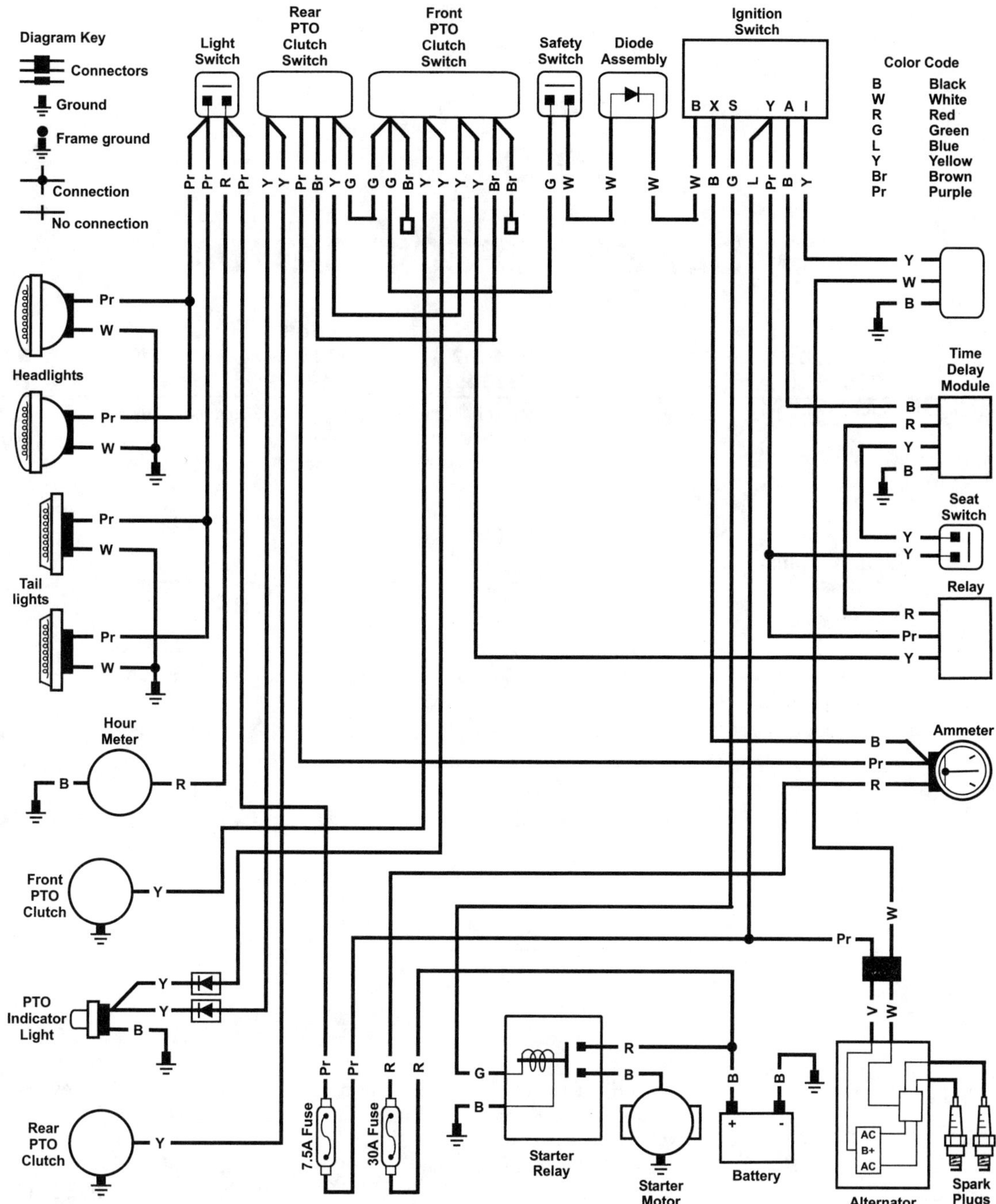

Fig. AR1-29–Typical wiring diagram.

ARIENS

Series 934 (HT Series)

CONDENSED SPECIFICATIONS

MODELS	934005 (HT16)	934006 (HT16)	934007 (HT14s)	934008 (HT14T, HT1442)	934019 (HT16)	934020 (HT18)
Engine Make	Kohler	Kohler	B&S	B&S	Kohler	Kohler
Model	MV16	MV18	261777	294777	MV16	MV18
Number of cylinders	2	2	1	2	2	2
Bore	3.12 in. (79.2 mm)	3.12 in. (79.2 mm)	87 mm (3.43 in.)	68 mm (2.68 in.)	3.12 in. (79.2 mm)	3.12 in. (79.2 mm)
Stroke	2.75 in. (69.85 mm)	2.75 in. (69.85 mm)	73 mm (2.86)	66 mm (2.60)	2.75 in. (69.85 mm)	2.75 in. (69.85 mm)
Displacement	42.18 cu. in. (691 cc)	42.18 cu. in. (691 cc)	435 cc (26.5 cu. in.)	480 cc (29.3 cu. in.)	42.18 cu. in. (691 cc)	42.18 cu. in. (691 cc)
Power Rating	16 hp (11.9 kW)	18 hp (13.4 kW)	14 hp (10.5 kW)	14 hp (10.5 kW)	16 hp (11.9 kW)	18 hp (13.4 kW)
Slow Idle	1750 rpm	1750 rpm	1400 rpm	1400 rpm	1750 rpm	1750 rpm
High Speed (No-Load)	3600 rpm	3600 rpm	3600 rpm	3600 rpm	3600 rpm	3600 rpm
Crankcase Capacity	See text	See text	See text	See text	See text	See text
Transmission Capacity	See text	See text	See text	See text	See text	See text

FRONT AXLE AND STEERING SYSTEM

MAINTENANCE

All models are equipped with grease fittings at the outer axle ends and the steering pivot shaft. Periodically inject a good quality grease into the grease fittings.

TIE RODS AND TOE-IN

Two tie rods, each with replaceable ends, are used on all models. Check tie rod ends for excessive play and replace when needed.

Front wheel toe-in (measured at horizontal centerline of wheel rim flange) should be $\frac{1}{16}$-$\frac{1}{8}$ inch (1.6-3.2 mm). Front measurement should be smaller than rear measurement.

To adjust toe-in, loosen the jam nuts and rotate the tie rod (10—Fig. AR2-1). Note that one end of the tie rod is equipped with a tie rod end and adjacent jam nut with left-hand threads. Turn the tie rod clockwise to decrease toe-in or counterclockwise to increase toe-in. Tie rods must be adjusted equally to provide the correct turning radius in each direction.

STEERING SPINDLES REMOVAL AND INSTALLATION

To remove the steering spindles (20—Fig. AR2-1), raise and support the front of the tractor and remove the front wheels. Disconnect the tie rod end from the spindle. Drive out the roll pin (19) at the upper end of the spindle, then lower the spindle from the axle main member.

Inspect the spindle and bushing for damage and replace when necessary. Install spindle by reversing the removal procedure.

AXLE MAIN MEMBER REMOVAL AND INSTALLATION

Raise and support the front of the tractor. Disconnect the tie rod ends from the spindles. Support the axle main member, remove the pivot bolt and lower the axle from the tractor.

Inspect all parts for damage. Install axle by reversing the removal procedure.

DRAG LINK AND STEERING PIVOT

Adjustment

A steering pivot (9—Fig. AR2-1) transfers steering motion to the tie rods. A drag link (1) transfers the steering motion from the steering gear as-

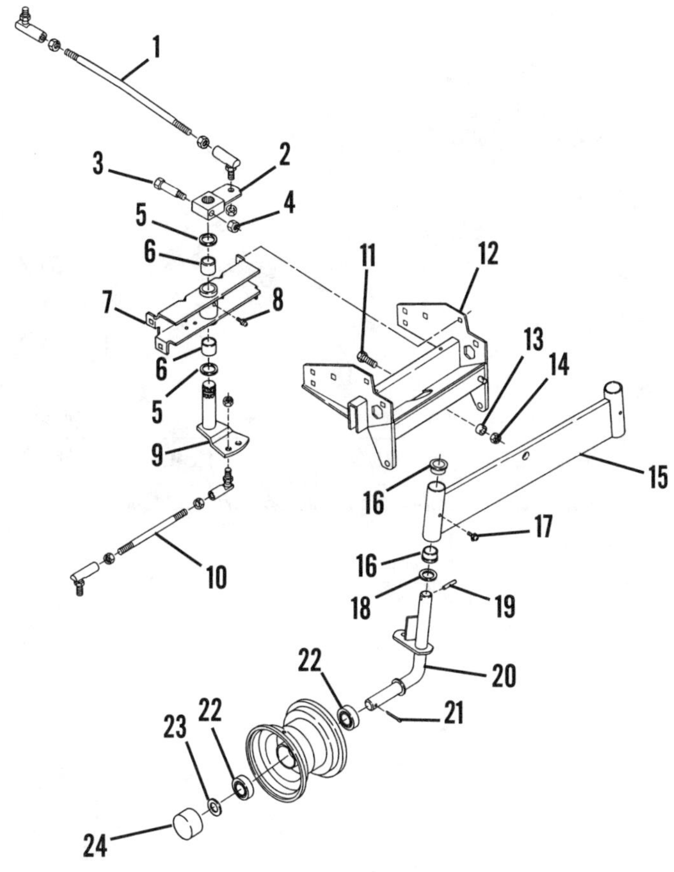

Fig. AR2-1–Exploded view of front axle assembly used on Series 934 models.

1. Drag link
2. Steering arm
3. Shoulder bolt
4. Locknut
5. Plastic washer
6. Bushing
7. Pivot bracket
8. Grease fitting
9. Steering pivot
10. Tie rod
11. Bolt
12. Axle support
13. Spacer
14. Nut
15. Front axle
16. Flange bushing
17. Grease fitting
18. Washer
19. Roll pin
20. Steering spindle
21. Cotter oin
22. Bearing
23. Washer
24. Hub cap

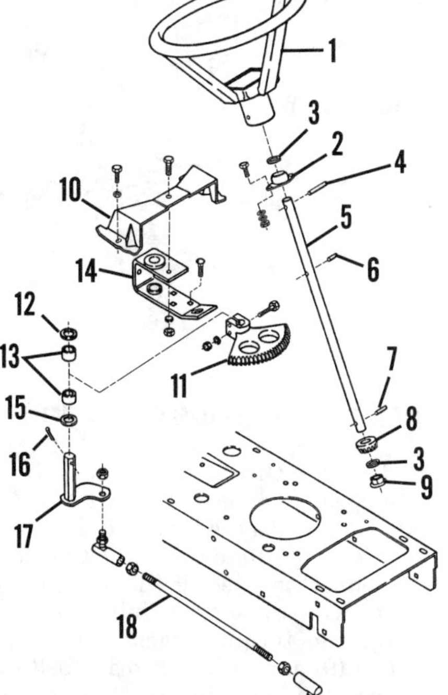

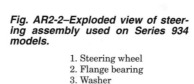

Fig. AR2-2–Exploded view of steering assembly used on Series 934 models.

1. Steering wheel
2. Flange bearing
3. Washer
4. Roll pin
5. Steering shaft
6. Roll pin
7. Roll pin
8. Steering gear
9. Flange bushing
10. Brace
11. Sector gear
12. Washer
13. Bushings
14. Steering bracket
15. Washer
16. Cotter pin
17. Steering arm
18. Drag link

sembly to the steering arm (2) attached to the steering pivot.

Adjust the length of the drag link (1—Fig. AR2-1) so the steering wheel is centered and the full steering range is obtained.

Removal and Installation

To remove the steering pivot (9–Fig. AR2-1), detach tie rod ends from the steering pivot. Detach the drag link from the steering arm (2). Mark the steering arm and pivot shaft end so the steering arm can be reinstalled in its original position. Remove the steering arm retaining bolt (3), then remove the steering arm. Remove the steering pivot.

Inspect for damage. Bushings (6) are replaceable. Reinstall by reversing the disassembly procedure. If the alignment marks are not present on the steering arm and pivot shaft, assemble as follows: Place the front wheels in the straight ahead position and center the steering gear on the sector gear (11—Fig. AR2-2). Assemble the steering arm to the pivot shaft and tighten clamp bolt securely.

STEERING GEAR OVERHAUL

Detach the drag link from the steering lever (17—Fig. AR2-2). Loosen the clamp bolts on the sector gear (11), then remove the steering lever (17) and sector gear (11). Drive out the roll pin (4) beneath the flange bearing (2). Pull up the steering shaft to gain access to the roll pin securing pinion gear (8). Drive out the roll pin and remove the shaft and gear.

Inspect all parts for damage and replace when needed.

Reassemble by reversing the disassembly procedure. Lubricate gears and bushings during assembly with multipurpose grease. During assembly the pinion gear (8) must be centered on the sector gear (11) with the front wheels in the straight ahead position.

To adjust backlash between the pinion gear (8) and sector gear (11), loosen the two clamp bolts securing the sector gear to the steering lever shaft. Raise or lower the sector gear on the steering lever shaft to obtain the desired backlash, then tighten the sector gear clamp bolts.

SAFETY INTERLOCK SYSTEM

The tractor is equipped with a safety interlock system that prevents inadvertent starting of the tractor engine or operation when the operator leaves the tractor seat. The tractor engine should not start if the following occurs:

- Operator in tractor seat, shift lever in NEUTRAL, brake engaged and PTO clutch lever in the ON position.
- Operator in tractor seat, the PTO clutch lever in the OFF position, brake engaged and shift lever in a position other than NEUTRAL.
- Operator in tractor seat, shift lever in NEUTRAL, the PTO clutch lever in the OFF position and brakes released.
- Operator not in seat when starting engine.

The seat switch should kill the engine when the operator is not in the seat or leaves the seat when the PTO clutch is engaged. The seat switch should kill the engine when the operator leaves the seat when the brakes are not locked.

Refer to wiring schematics at the end of this section.

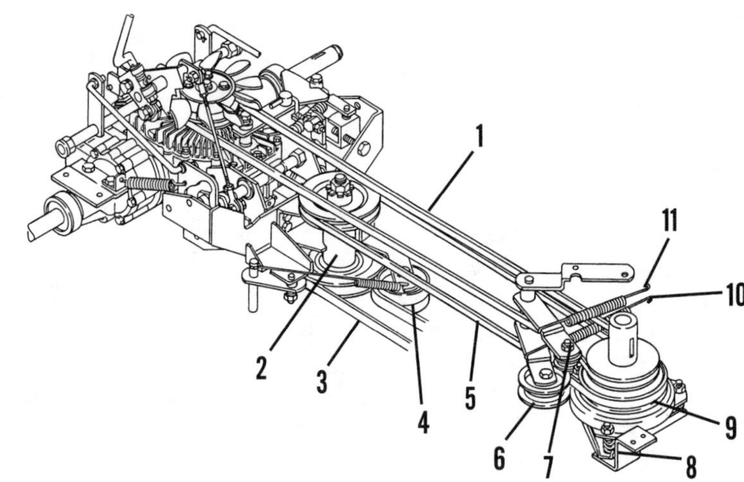

Fig. AR2-3–Drawing of drive components used on Series 934 models.

1. Traction drive belt
2. Jackshaft
3. Lower PTO drive belt
4. Idler
5. Upper pto drive belt
6. Idler
7. Idler
8. Torque bracket
9. PTO clutch
10. Spring
11. Spring

ENGINE

REMOVAL AND INSTALLATION

Disconnect the battery leads. Remove the mower deck, if so equipped. Remove the PTO drive belt (3—Fig. AR2-3) from the jackshaft pulley. Detach the jackshaft idler spring (10) to relieve belt tension. Disconnect the PTO clutch electrical wire connector. Unbolt and remove the torque bracket (8), PTO clutch (9) and jackshaft drive belt (5). Detach the idler spring (11) to relieve the transaxle drive belt tension. Remove the transaxle drive belt (1) from the engine pulley. Remove the engine pulley and extension shaft assembly from the engine crankshaft. Detach the throttle and choke cables from the engine. Disconnect the engine electrical wiring. Remove interfering air shrouds and baffles. Disconnect the fuel line. Remove the hood and grill. Unscrew the engine mounting fasteners. Lift the engine out of the tractor.

Reverse the removal procedure to install the engine.

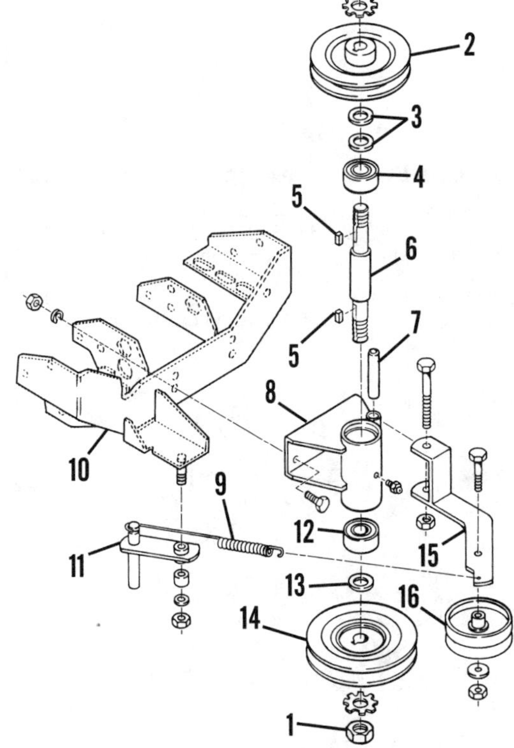

Fig. AR2-4–Exploded view of jackshaft assembly.

1. Nut
2. Pulley
3. Washers
4. Bearing
5. Key
6. Jackshaft
7. Sleeve
8. Housing
9. Spring
10. Bracket
11. PTO actuator
12. Bearing
13. Washer
14. Pulley
15. Idler arm
16. Idler

OVERHAUL

Engine make and model are listed at the beginning of this section. Refer to the appropriate engine section in this manual for tune-up specifications, maintenance and overhaul procedures.

DRIVE BELTS

Series 934 models are equipped with a single primary traction drive belt (1—Fig. AR2-3) transferring engine power to the hydrostatic transaxle. The secondary drive belt (5) transfers engine power to the jackshaft (2). The PTO drive belt (3) transfers power from the jackshaft to the implement. Spring-loaded idlers (4, 6 and 7) apply tension to the drive belts and no adjustment is necessary. If belt slippage occurs, inspect drive belt for damage and replace when necessary.

REMOVAL AND INSTALLATION

Remove the mower deck, if so equipped, and the PTO belt (3—Fig. AR2-3). Detach the jackshaft drive belt idler spring (10) to relieve belt tension. Disconnect the electric PTO clutch electrical wire connector. Unbolt and remove the torque bracket (8), PTO clutch (9) and jackshaft drive belt (5). Detach the idler spring (11) to relieve

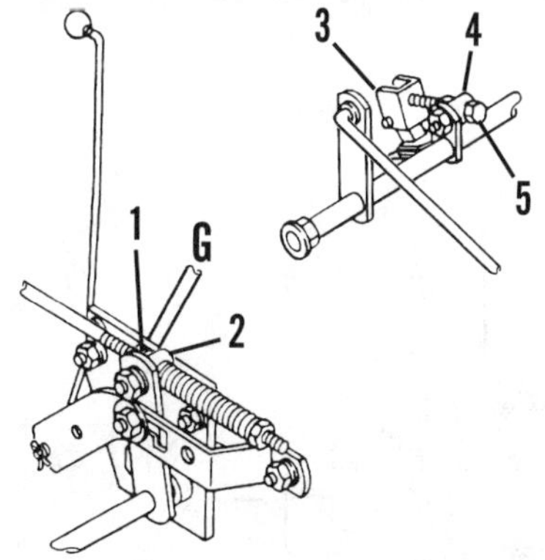

Fig. AR2-5–On Series 934 models, gap between washer (1) and pivot (2) should be approximately 1/8 inch (3.2 mm). Refer to text for adjustment.

1. Washer
2. Pivot
3. Clevis
4. Brake acutating pivot
5. Pivot bolt

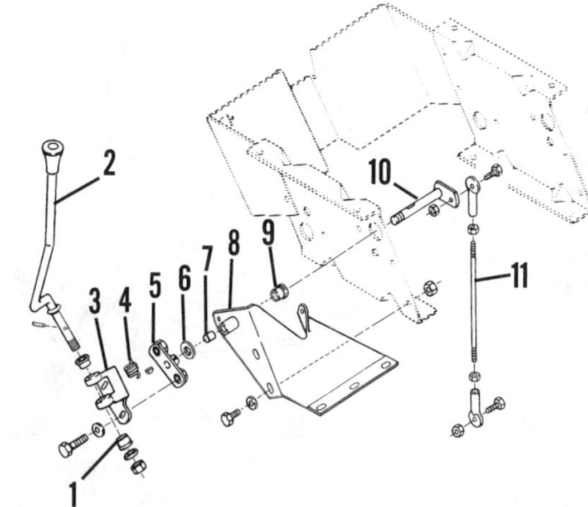

Fig. AR2-6–Exploded view of speed selector linkage.

1. Bushing
2. Selector lever
3. Outer arm
4. Spring
5. Inner arm
6. Thrust washer
7. Bushing
8. Brace
9. Bushing
10. Selector rod
11. Shift rod

transaxle drive belt tension. Remove the transaxle drive belt (1) from the engine pulley and then from the transmission pulley.

Reverse the removal procedure to install the transaxle drive belt.

JACKSHAFT

All models are equipped with a jackshaft (2—Fig. AR2-3) that transfers power via drive belts from the engine pulley to the implement.

LUBRICATION

Periodically inject a multipurpose grease into the grease fitting on the jackshaft housing.

OVERHAUL

To remove the jackshaft assembly, first remove the drive belts as previously outlined. Then unbolt and remove the jackshaft housing (8—Fig. AR2-4) from the transaxle mounting bracket (10).

To disassemble, remove the nut (1) from the top of the jackshaft. Remove the jackshaft pulley (2), key (5) and washers (3). Withdraw the jackshaft (6) with the lower pulley (14) and bearing (12) from the jackshaft housing. Remove the nut, PTO pulley (14), washer (13) and bearing (12) from the jackshaft. Drive the upper bearing (4) from the jackshaft housing.

Inspect parts for damage and replace when needed. After assembly, inject multipurpose grease into the grease fitting (2).

BRAKE/NEUTRALIZER

934 Series tractors are equipped with a disc brake located inside the transmission unit. When the brake pedal is depressed, the hydrostatic transmission control linkage is returned to NEUTRAL and then the brake is applied.

Adjustment

Engage the parking brake. Check the gap between the clutch rod collar washer (1–Fig. AR2-5) and pivot (2). The gap (G) should be approximately $\frac{1}{8}$ in. (3.2 mm). To adjust the gap, loosen the locknut at the rear brake actuating pivot (4) and rotate the pivot bolt (5) to obtain the specified gap. Retighten the locknut. Release the parking brake, then engage the brake and check the gap.

Overhaul

The brake is located in the transaxle. Refer to the HYDROSTATIC TRANSMISSION section for service information.

HYDROSTATIC TRANSAXLE

LUBRICATION

The transaxle housing serves as a common reservoir for the hydrostatic transmission and gear reduction unit. An oil expansion tank is located below the instrument panel, directly below the battery. A dipstick is attached to the tank cap. To check the oil level, raise the hood and clean the area around the expansion tank cap/dipstick, then remove the dipstick. When the transmission is cold, the oil level should be at the mark indicated on the dipstick. Premium quality hydraulic oil or SAE 30 engine oil is the recommended oil.

If oil appears to be milky or black, it is possible that the oil is contaminated or overheated. The problem should be corrected, then the oil should be drained and refilled. Change oil after every 500 hours of operation or more often when operated in severe conditions. To drain the oil, disconnect the hose from the bottom of the transmission and allow the oil to drain into a container.

The transaxle is equipped with a spin-on oil filter. Change the oil filter when changing the oil.

NEUTRAL ADJUSTMENT

When the brake pedal is depressed the speed control lever should return to NEUTRAL position and the transaxle should shift to NEUTRAL. The tractor should not creep in either direction when the brake pedal is released.

If the speed control lever does not return to NEUTRAL when the brake pedal is depressed, loosen the cap screws at the outer arm (3—Fig. AR2-6) of the speed selector lever (2). Reposition the speed selector lever to the neutral detent, and tighten the cap screws..

If the tractor creeps (transaxle does not shift to NEUTRAL) when the brake pedal is depressed, proceed as follows: Remove the rear deck and fuel tank for access to the transaxle control linkage. Raise and support the rear of tractor so the rear wheels do not contact the ground.

CAUTION: Exercise care when working around rotating wheels and transaxle cooling fan.

Check the shift rod length (7—Fig. AR2-7). The distance between ball joint studs must be $10\frac{3}{4}$ inches (273 mm). Loosen the jam nuts and rotate the rod to adjust the length.

Depress the brake pedal and engage the parking brake. Pivot bearing (3—Fig. AR2-7) should be centered in the notch of the control arm (1). To adjust the bearing position, loosen the locknuts (4) on the neutral link. Loosen the pivot bracket (5) retaining screws. Start the engine and run at idle. Position the pivot bracket (5) so the rear wheels do not rotate. Retighten the pivot bracket screws. Adjust the position of the neutral link (2) so the pivot bearing (3) is centered in the notch of the control arm (1). Retighten the locknuts (4). Recheck the speed control lever adjustment as previously described.

FRICTION ADJUSTMENT

Freedom of shift linkage movement may be adjusted by altering the spring pressure against the cross shaft (18—Fig. AR2-8) flange. Turn the bolt (19) or nut (25) to adjust spring pressure.

REMOVAL AND INSTALLATION

Remove the mower deck, if so equipped. Remove the rear deck and seat. Remove the implement drive belts and traction drive belt. Detach the brake rod (14—Fig. AR2-7) and neutral rod (11) from the brake shaft. Disconnect the clevis (12) from the transaxle. Remove the flange bushing from one end of the brake shaft, and slide the brake shaft out of the frame. Disconnect the towing valve linkage. Disconnect the spring (8) from the shift cam. Unbolt and remove the transaxle cooling fan and pulley. Detach the control arm (1) from the transaxle shift shaft and neutral link (2). Disconnect the oil hoses from the transaxle and plug or cap the openings.

Raise and support the rear of the tractor. Remove the rear wheels. Disconnect the neutral switch wiring. Support the transaxle. Remove the screws securing the transaxle to the transaxle mount (6). Remove the screws securing the axle mounting plates (9) to the tractor frame. Lower and remove the transaxle.

Reinstall the transaxle by reversing the removal procedure. Adjust the control linkage as previously outlined.

OVERHAUL

Model 934007 is equipped with an Eaton Model 751 hydrostatic transaxle. All other Series 934 models are equipped with an Eaton Model 850 or 851 hydrostatic transaxle. Refer to the HYDROSTATIC TRANSAXLE section at the rear of this manual for overhaul information.

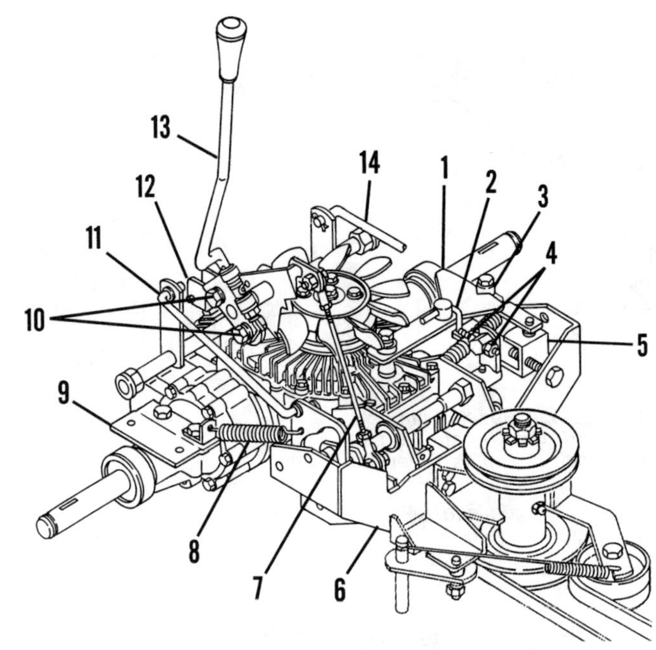

Fig. AR2-7–Drawing of shift mechanism used on Series 934 models.

1. Control arm
2. Neutral link
3. Pivot bearing
4. Nuts
5. Pivot bracket
6. Transaxle mount
7. Shift rod
8. Spring
9. Axle mounting plate
10. Screws
11. Neutral rod
12. Clevis
13. Speed selector lever
14. Brake rod

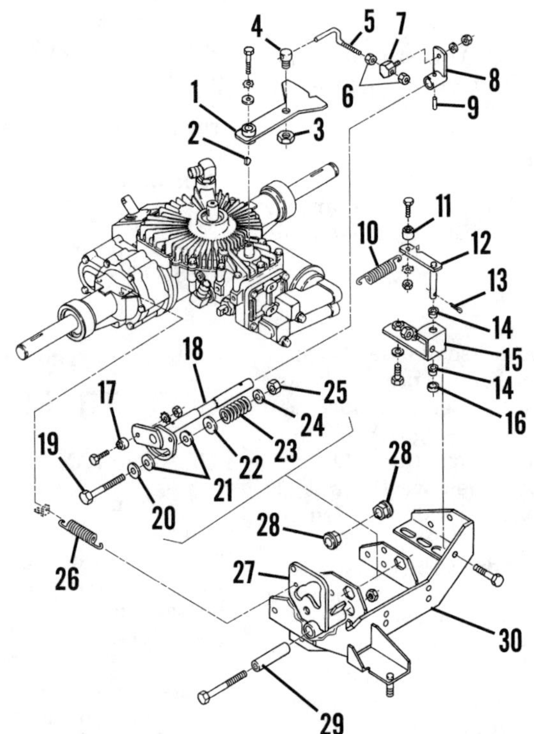

Fig. AR2-8–Exploded view of shift mechanism used on Series 934 models.

1. Control arm
2. Key
3. Nut
4. Adapter
5. Neutral link
6. Nut
7. Rod pivot
8. Neutral arm
9. Roll pin
10. Pivot bearing
11. Pivot bearing
12. Pivot arm
13. Cotter pin
14. Flange bushing
15. Pivot bracket
16. Bushing
17. Pivot bearing
18. Cross shaft
19. Bolt
20. Washer
21. Friction washer
22. Washer
23. Spring
24. Washer
25. Nut
26. Spring
27. Cam
28. Flange bushing
29. Spacer
30. Transaxle mount

ELECTRIC PTO CLUTCH

TESTING

Use the following procedure for locating a PTO malfunction. Turn the ignition switch ON, depress the seat switch,

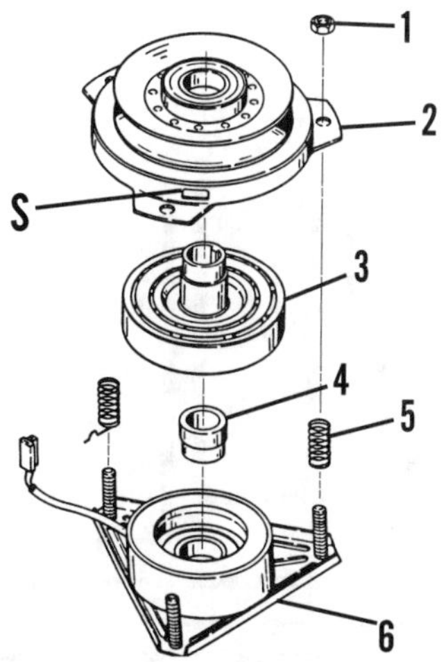

Fig. AR2-9–Exploded view of electric PTO clutch used on Series 934 models

1. Nut (3)
2. Armature assy.
3. Rotor assy.
4. Adapter
5. Spring (3)
6. Field assy.

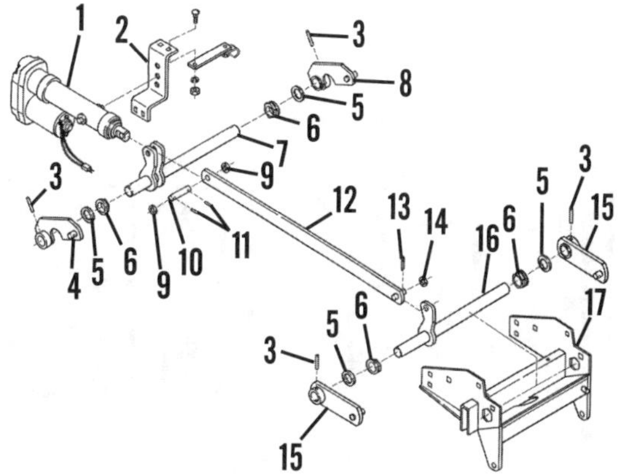

Fig. AR2-10–Exploded view of electric lift assembly used on Series 934 models.

1. Actuator assy.
2. Bracket
3. Roll pin
4. Lift arm
5. Washer
6. Flange bushing
7. Lift pivot
8. Lift arm
9. Washer
10. Pin
11. Roll pin
12. Lift link
13. Cotter pin
14. Washer
15. Lift arm
16. Front lift pivot
17. Axle support

and actuate the PTO switch. If the clutch does not engage, disconnect the wiring connector at the clutch and use a 12-volt test lamp to check the wire continuity coming from the PTO switch. If the lamp lights, either the PTO or the wiring connector at the clutch field coil is defective.

To check the PTO field coil, remove the clutch from the tractor. Ground the field coil frame and energize the coil lead wire with a known 12-volt source. Hold a piece of metal next to the coil and note if the metal is attracted. If the metal is not attracted to the coil, replace the field coil assembly.

ADJUSTMENT

The PTO clutch must be adjusted when the clutch has been disassembled or operation becomes erratic. With the clutch disengaged, insert a feeler gauge through each of the slots (S—Fig. AR2-9) in the clutch plate and measure the clearance between the clutch rotor (3) and armature (2). There should be 0.015 inch (0.38 mm) clearance between the armature and clutch rotor at each of the clutch plate slots. To adjust, tighten or loosen the clutch adjusting nuts (1) to obtain the correct clearance.

OVERHAUL

To remove the PTO clutch, remove the front or center mounted equipment from the tractor. Disconnect idler arm spring to remove tension from the PTO belt. Disconnect the electric clutch wires. Unbolt and remove torque bracket from the clutch. Remove the jackshaft belt. Remove the clutch retaining bolt and withdraw the clutch from the extension shaft. Use a plastic hammer to tap and loosen the clutch from the extension shaft if necessary.

To disassemble the clutch (Fig. AR2-9), remove the adjusting nuts (1) and separate the armature (2) and rotor (3) from the field coil housing (6). Press the bearing from the armature if necessary.

Inspect bearings for damage. Inspect for broken or distorted springs (5). Check contact surfaces of rotor and armature for damage. Replace parts when necessary.

To reassemble the clutch, reverse the disassembly procedure.

Apply antiseize lubricant to the extension shaft before installing the clutch assembly. Tighten the clutch retaining cap screw to 50 ft.-lb. (68 N·m). Adjust the clutch as previously outlined.

ELECTRIC LIFT

Series 934 models are equipped with an electric lift. Refer to Fig. AR2-10 for an exploded view of the lift assembly. Motor and actuator (1) are available only as a unit assembly.

WIRING SCHEMATICS

Fig. AR2-11 illustrates the circuit for the engine when running. Fig. AR2-12 illustrates the circuit for the PTO when engaged.

Figures AR2-11 and AR2-12 are on the following pages.

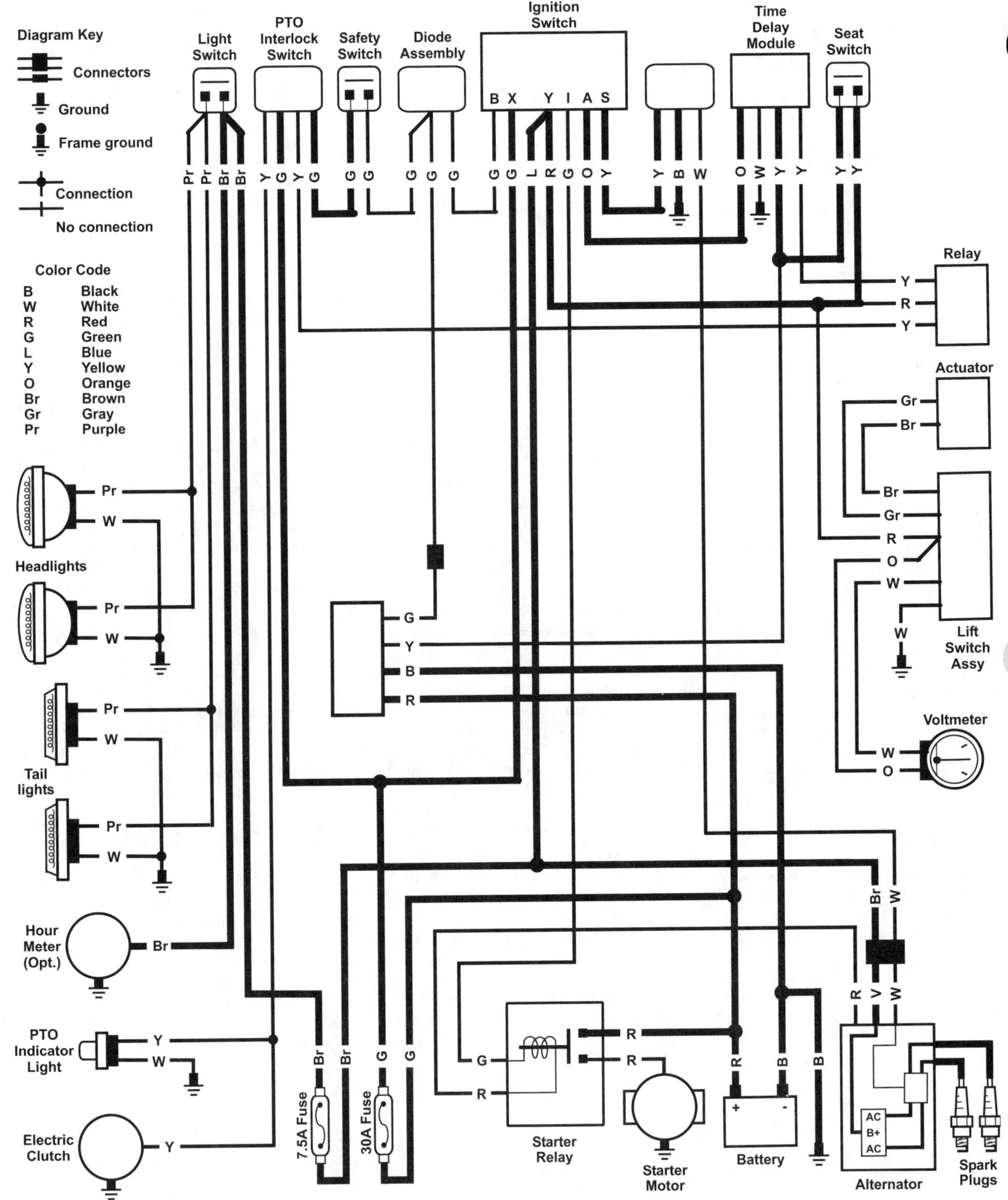

Fig. AR2-11–Wiring schematic for the tractor running circuit.

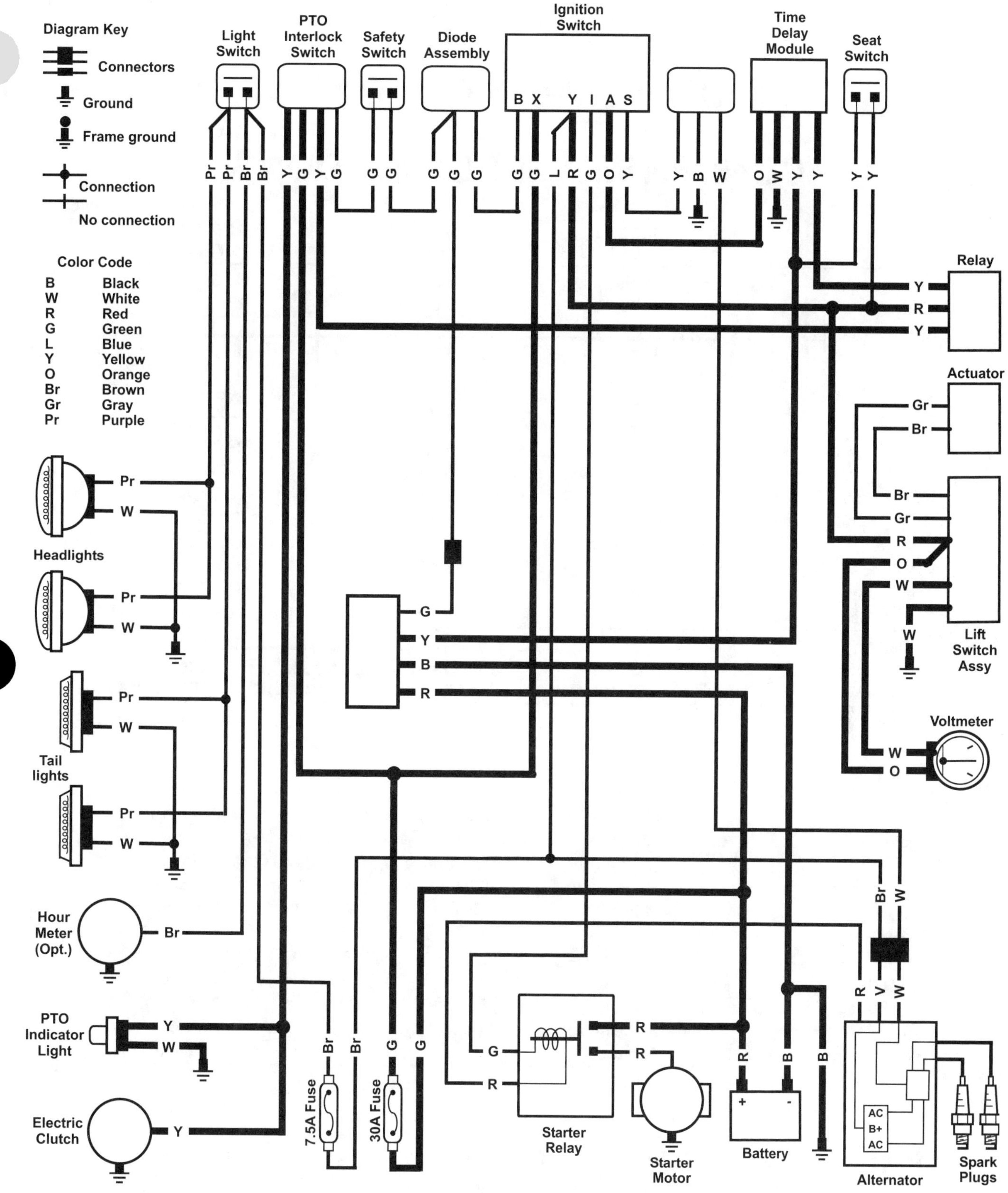

Fig. AR2-12–Wiring diagram for the PTO circuit.

ARIENS

935 Series (YT Series)

CONDENSED SPECIFICATIONS

Models	935025 (YT1232HK)	935026 (YT1238HK)	935027 (YT1232GB)
Engine Make	Kohler	Kohler	B&S
Model	CV12.5	CV12.5	286707
Number of cylinders	1	1	1
Bore	87 mm (3.43 in.)	87 mm (3.43 in.)	3.438 in. (87.3 mm)
Stroke	67 mm (2.64 in.)	67 mm (2.64 in.)	3.06 in. (77.7 mm)
Displacement	398 cc (24.3 cu. in.)	398 cc (24.3 cu. in.)	28.04 cu. In. (465 cc)
Power Rating	9.4 kW (12.5 hp)	9.4 kW (12.5 hp)	12.5 hp (9.4 kW)
Slow Idle	1750 rpm	1750 rpm	1750 rpm
High Speed (No-Load)	3600 rpm	3600 rpm	3600 rpm
Crankcase Capacity	See text	See text	3 pt. (1.4 L)
Transmission Capacity	See text	See text	See text

Models	935028 (YT1238GB)	935029 (YT1232HB)	935030 (YT1238HB)	935031 (YT1438HK)
Engine Make	B&S	B&S	B&S	Kohler
Model	286707	286707	286707	CV14
Number of cylinders	1	1	1	1
Bore	3.438 in. (87.3 mm)	3.438 in. (87.3 mm)	3.438 in. (87.3 mm)	87 mm (3.43 in.)
Stroke	3.06 in. (77.7 mm)	3.06 in. (77.7 mm)	3.06 in. (77.7 mm)	67 mm (2.64 in.)
Displacement	28.04 cu. in. (465 cc)	28.04 cu. in. (465 cc)	28.04 cu. in. (465 cc)	398 cc (24.3 cu. In.)
Power Rating	12.5 hp (9.4 kW)	12.5 hp (9.4 kW)	12.5 hp (9.4 kW)	10.5 kW (14 hp)
Slow Idle	1750 rpm	1750 rpm	1750 rpm	1750 rpm
High Speed (No-Load)	3600 rpm	3600 rpm	3600 rpm	3600 rpm
Crankcase Capacity	3 pt. (1.4 L)	3 pt. (1.4 L)	3 pt. (1.4 L)	See text
Transmission Capacity	See text	See text	See text	See text

FRONT AXLE AND STEERING SYSTEM

MAINTENANCE

All models are equipped with grease fittings at the outer axle ends and at the steering pivot shaft. Periodically inject a multipurpose grease into the grease fittings.

TIE RODS AND TOE-IN

Two tie rods (11—Fig. AR3-1), each with replaceable ends (12), are used on all models. Check tie rod ends for excessive wear and replace when necessary.

Front wheel toe-in should be $\frac{1}{16}$-$\frac{1}{8}$ inch (1.6-3.2 mm). Measure toe-in at wheel hub height at the front and rear of the wheel rims. The front measurement should be smaller than the rear measurement.

To adjust the toe-in, loosen the jam nuts and rotate the tie rod (10—Fig. AR3). Note that one end of the tie rod is equipped with a tie rod end and adjacent jam nut with left-hand threads. Tie rods must be adjusted equally to provide the correct turning radius in each direction.

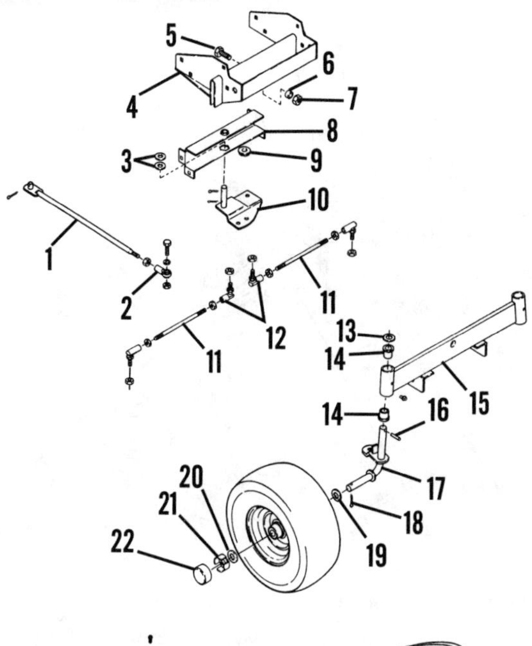

Fig. AR3-1—Exploded view of front axle assembly used on Series 935 models

1. Drag link
2. Rod end
3. Washers
4. Axle support
5. Cap screw
6. Spacer
7. Nut
8. Steering pivot channel
9. Flange bushing
10. Steering pivot
11. Tie rods
12. Rod ends
13. Washer
14. Bushings
15. Axle main member
16. Roll pin
17. Steering spindle
18. Cotter pin
19. Washer
20. Washer
21. Spindle cup
22. Hub cap

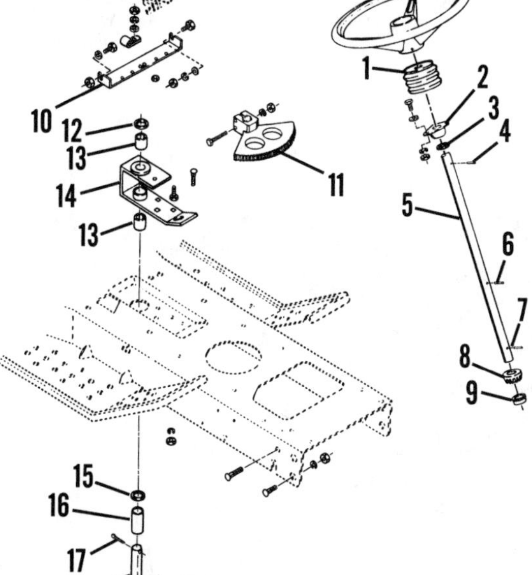

Fig. AR3-2—Exploded view of steering assembly used on Series 935 models.

1. Bellows
2. Flange bearing
3. Washer
4. Roll pin
5. Steering shaft
6. Roll pin
7. Roll pin
8. Steering gear
9. Flange bushing
10. Brace
11. Sector gear
12. Washer
13. Bushings
14. Steering bracket
15. Washer
16. Spacer
17. Cotter pin
18. Steering arm
19. Drag link

STEERING SPINDLES REMOVAL AND INSTALLATION

To remove the steering spindles (17—Fig. AR3-1), raise and support the front of the tractor and remove the front wheels. Disconnect the tie rod end from the spindle. Drive out the roll pin (16) at the upper end of the spindle, then lower the spindle from the axle main member.

Inspect spindle and bushing for damage and replace when necessary. Install spindle by reversing the removal procedure. Lubricate with multipurpose grease at the grease fitting in axle end.

AXLE MAIN MEMBER REMOVAL AND INSTALLATION

Raise and support the front of the tractor. Disconnect the tie rod ends from the spindles. Support the axle main member (15—Fig. AR3-1), remove the pivot bolt (5) and lower the axle from the tractor.

Inspect all parts for damage. Install the axle by reversing the removal procedure.

DRAG LINK AND STEERING PIVOT

Adjustment

Adjust the length of the drag link (1—Fig. AR3-1) so the front wheels and steering wheel are centered and the full steering range is obtained.

Removal and Installation

A steering pivot (10—Fig. AR3-1) transfers steering motion to the tie rods and spindles. A drag link (1) transfers steering motion from the steering gear assembly to the steering pivot.

To remove the steering pivot, detach the tie rod ends from the steering pivot. Detach the drag link from the steering pivot. Remove cotter pins in the steering pivot shaft and withdraw the steering pivot.

Inspect the steering pivot shaft and flange bushing (9) for damage and replace when needed. Install by reversing the disassembly procedure.

STEERING GEAR OVERHAUL

Detach the drag link from the steering lever (18—Fig. AR3-2). Loosen the clamp bolts on the sector gear (11), then remove the steering lever (18) and sector gear (11). Drive out the roll pin (4) beneath the flange bearing (2). Raise the steering shaft to gain access to the roll pin (7) securing the pinion gear (8). Remove the shaft and gear.

Inspect bushings for damage and replace when needed. Reassemble by reversing the disassembly procedure. Lubricate the gears and bushings during assembly. During assembly the pinion gear must be centered on the sector gear with front wheels in the straight-ahead position.

ENGINE

REMOVAL AND INSTALLATION

Disconnect the battery leads. Remove the mower deck, if so equipped. Detach the idler spring (4—Fig. AR3-3) to relieve drive belt tension. Remove the drive belt (2) from the engine pulley (1). Detach the throttle and choke cables from the engine. Disconnect the engine electrical wiring. Remove interfering air shrouds and baffles. Disconnect the fuel line. Unscrew the engine mounting fasteners. Lift the engine out of the tractor.

Reverse the removal procedure to install the engine.

OVERHAUL

Engine make and model are listed at the beginning of this section. Refer to

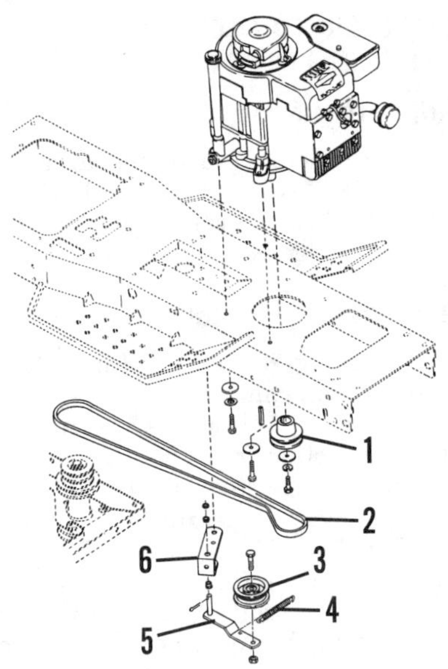

Fig. AR3-3–Drawing of engine and main drive belt typical of all models.

1. Engine pulley
2. Primary drive belt
3. Idler pulley
4. Spring
5. Idler arm
6. Idler pivot

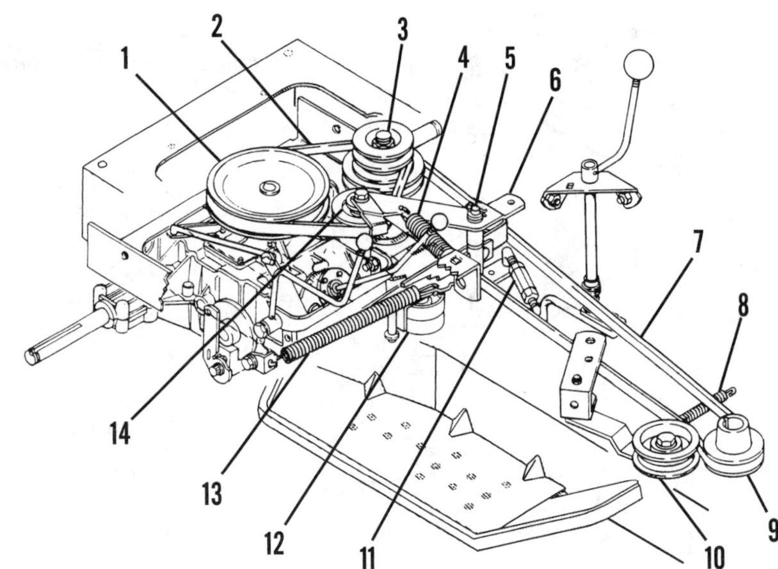

Fig. AR3-4–Illustration of belt drive system typical of gear drive models.

1. Transaxle pulley
2. Traction drive belt
3. Jackshaft pulley
4. Spring
5. Idler pivot shaft
6. Idler arm
7. Primary drive belt
8. Spring
9. Engine pulley
10. Idler pulley
11. Idler adjuster link
12. PTO idler
13. Extension spring
14. Traction clutch idler

the appropriate engine section in this manual for tune-up specifications, maintenance and overhaul procedures.

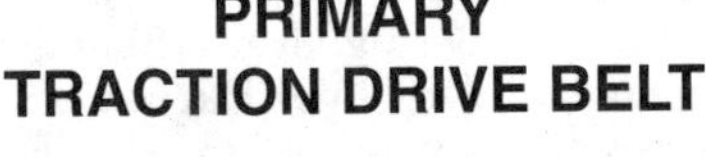

PRIMARY TRACTION DRIVE BELT

Series 935 models are equipped with two traction drive belts. The primary drive belt transfers engine power to the jackshaft. The secondary drive belt transfers power from the jackshaft to the transmission or transaxle pulley.

HYDROSTATIC DRIVE MODELS REMOVAL AND INSTALLATION

Remove the mower deck, if so equipped, and implement drive belt. Detach the transmission disconnect actuating rod from the idler arm. Detach the main idler spring from the frame to relieve drive belt tension. Remove the primary drive belt from engine pulley and jackshaft pulley.

Reverse the removal procedure to install drive belt.

GEAR DRIVE MODELS REMOVAL AND INSTALLATION

Remove the mower deck, if so equipped, and implement drive belt. Remove the secondary drive belt as described in the following section. Detach the spring (4—Fig. AR3-4) from the rear idler arm. Loosen the three screws attaching the jackshaft housing to the transaxle mounting bracket to provide clearance for belt removal from the jackshaft pulleys (3). Detach the spring (8) from the front idler to relieve drive belt tension. Detach the extension spring (13) from the frame. Remove the primary drive belt (7) from the engine pulley (9). Disconnect the actuating rod (11) from the PTO idler arm. Detach the clevis pin at the top of the idler pivot shaft (5), then lower the PTO idler assembly until the traction idler arm (6) is free of the shaft. Slide the primary drive belt between the traction idler arm and the PTO idler assembly, and remove the belt from tractor.

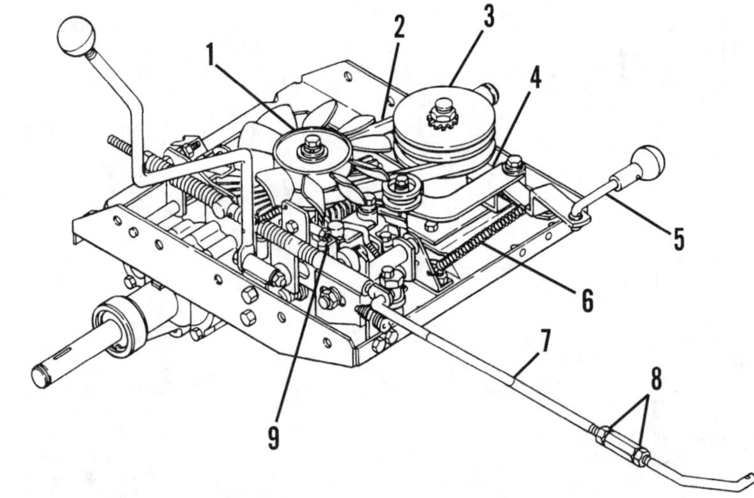

Fig. AR3-5–Illustration of drive belt system typical of hydrostatic drive models.

1. Transmission pulley
2. Traction drive belt
3. Jackshaft pulley
4. Clutch idler
5. Tramission disconnect lever
6. Extension spring
7. Brake rod
8. Jam nuts
9. Brake bracket

Reverse the removal procedure to install drive belt.

SECONDARY TRACTION DRIVE BELT

HYDROSTATIC DRIVE MODELS REMOVAL AND INSTALLATION

Remove the primary traction drive belt as previously described. Move the transaxle disconnect control (5—Fig. AR3-5) to the disengaged position. Re-

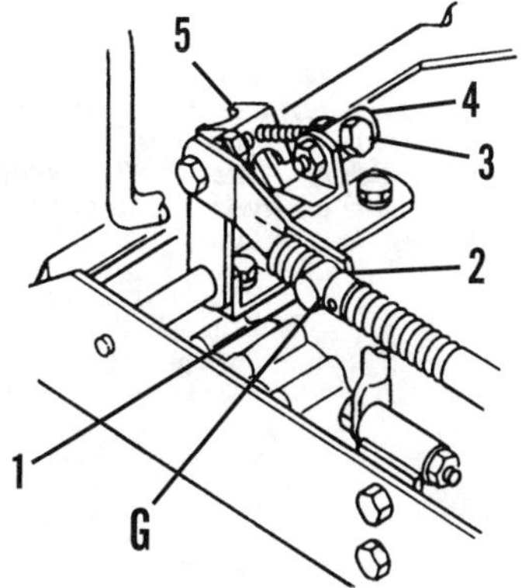

Fig. AR3-6–Drawing showing adjustment point for brake linkage on hydrostatic drive models. Refer to text for procedure.

1. Pivot
2. Collar
3. Brake adjustment bolt
4. Pivot
5. Brake clevis

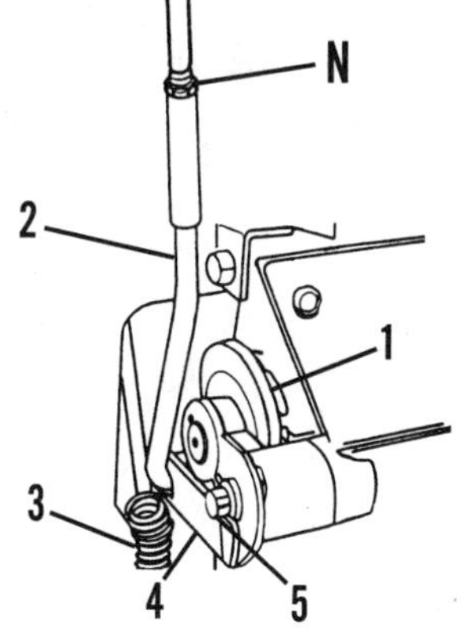

Fig. AR3-7–Drawing showing adjustment point for brake linkage on gear drive models.

1. Brake disc
2. Brake rod
3. Spring
4. Brake lever
5. Shoulder bolt

move the secondary traction drive belt (2—Fig. AR3-5) from the jackshaft pulley (3) and then the transmission pulley (1).

Reverse the removal procedure to install the drive belt.

GEAR DRIVE MODELS REMOVAL AND INSTALLATION

Loosen the screws securing the belt guides at the pulleys (1 and 3—Fig. AR3-4) and idler (14), and move the guides to provide clearance for belt removal. Depress the clutch pedal and remove the secondary traction drive belt (2) from the idler and pulleys.

Reverse the removal procedure to install the drive belt. Position the belt guides $\frac{1}{16}$-$\frac{1}{8}$ inch (1.6-3.2 mm) from the belt.

Fig. AR3-8–Exploded view of brake assembly typical of all gear drive models.

1. Spring
2. Inner brake pad
3. Outer brake pad
4. Spacer
5. Brake holder
6. Brake lever
7. Washer
8. Shoulder bolt
9. Woodruff key
10. Brake disc

CLUTCH

GEAR DRIVE MODELS

Gear drive models are equipped with a spring-loaded idler (14—Fig. AR3-4) that applies tension to the secondary traction drive belt (2). No adjustment is required. If clutch malfunctions, check the drive belt and operating linkage.

BRAKE

HYDROSTATIC DRIVE MODELS

Adjustment

Disengage the parking brake. Move the speed selector to the full forward position. Depress the brake pedal. Brake bracket (9—Fig. AR3-5) should move an additional $\frac{1}{32}$-$\frac{1}{16}$ inch (0.8-1.6 mm) after the speed selector moves to the NEUTRAL position. Adjust the bracket movement by loosening the jam nuts (8) on the brake rod (7) and rotating the coupler. Retighten the nuts and check adjustment.

Engage the parking brake. Check the gap (G—Fig. AR3-6) between the pivot (1) and collar (2). The gap should be approximately $\frac{1}{16}$ in. (1.6 mm). To adjust gap, loosen the jam nut at the brake clevis pivot (4) and turn the pivot bolt (5) until specified gap between the pivot and collar is obtained. Release the parking brake, then depress the brake pedal and check the gap.

Overhaul

Brake components are located in the hydrostatic transaxle. Refer to HYDROSTATIC TRANSMISSION section for service information.

GEAR DRIVE MODELS

Adjustment

Loosen the jam nut (N—Fig. AR3-7) on the brake actuating rod (2). Disconnect the spring (3) and brake actuating rod from the brake lever (4). Pull back the brake pedal to its rearmost position. Push the brake lever (4) as far forward as possible. Rotate the brake rod so it enters the hole in the brake lever. Reattach the brake rod to the brake lever and tighten jam nut.

Overhaul

Disconnect the spring (3—Fig. AR3-7) and brake rod (2) from the brake lever (4). Unscrew the shoulder bolt (5) and remove the brake holder assembly. Remove the brake disc (10—Fig. AR3-8), inner brake pad (2) and spring (1).

Inspect components for damage. Replace the brake disc and/or pads if signs of overheating or burnishing are evident. Check for damaged threads in the transaxle case.

Reverse the removal procedure to install the brake assembly. Apply Loctite to the shoulder bolt threads and tighten the bolt to 200-250 in.-lb. (23-28 N·m). Adjust the brake as previously described.

JACKSHAFT

All models are equipped with a jackshaft. The jackshaft transfers power via drive belts from the engine pulley to the implement. The jackshaft also transfers power from the engine to the transaxle.

LUBRICATION

Periodically inject a multipurpose grease into the grease fitting on jackshaft housing.

OVERHAUL

To remove the jackshaft assembly (3—Fig. AR3-4 or Fig. AR3-5), first remove the drive belts as previously outlined. Unscrew the top nut (14—Fig. AR3-9) and remove the upper pulley (15), washer (16) and Woodruff key (20) from the jackshaft. Remove the cap screws attaching the jackshaft housing (18) to the frame, and lower the jackshaft assembly from the tractor. Remove the lower nut (14), pulley (22), washer (16) and Woodruff key (20) from the jackshaft. Remove the jackshaft and bearings (17) from the housing.

Inspect all parts for damage and replace when needed. Assemble in the reverse order of disassembly. After assembly, inject multipurpose grease into the grease fitting.

MANUAL TRANSAXLE (MODELS 935027, 935028)

REMOVAL AND INSTALLATION

Raise and support the rear of the tractor, then remove the rear wheels. Remove the speed selector knob and boot, if so equipped. Detach the Hi-Lo shift rod. Detach the brake rod. Remove the screws attaching the front of the transaxle to the mounting bracket. Support the transaxle, remove four cap screws attaching rear of transaxle to mounting bracket, and remove the transaxle.

Reverse the removal procedure to install the transaxle.

OVERHAUL

Tractor is equipped with a Foote Series 4000 transaxle. Refer to the rear of this manual for overhaul information.

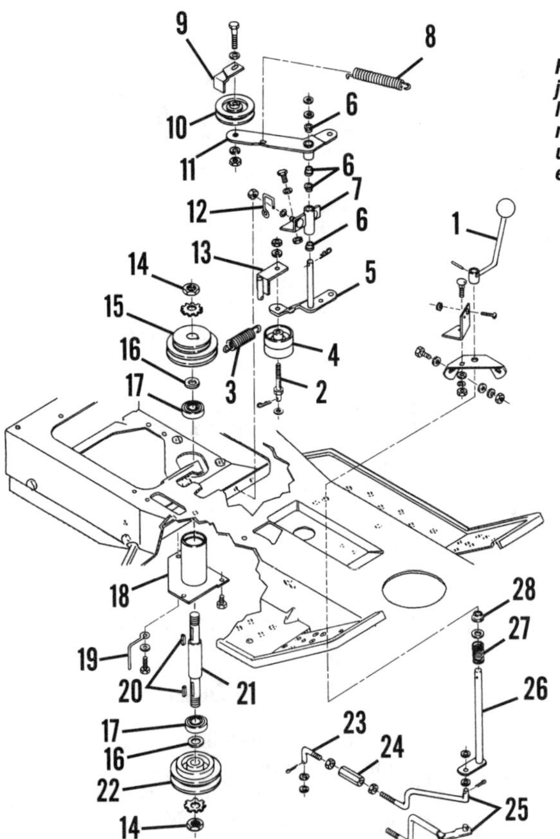

Fig. AR3-9–Exploded view of jackshaft assembly and control linkage typical of gear drive models. Jackshaft assembly used on hydrostatic drive models is similar.

1. PTO control lever
2. Idler spindle
3. Spring
4. PTO idler
5. Idler arm
6. Flange bushing
7. Idler pivot
8. Spring
9. Belt retainer
10. Clutch idler
11. Idler arm
12. Belt guide
13. Bracket
14. Nut
15. Upper pulley
16. Washer
17. Bearing
18. Jackshaft housing
19. Belt retainer
20. Key
21. Jackshaft
22. Lower pulley
23. Idler adjuster link
24. Coupling nut
25. Idler link
26. PTO lever shaft
27. Spring
28. Flange bushing

HYDROSTATIC TRANSAXLE (MODELS 935025, 935026, 935029, 935030, 935031)

LUBRICATION

The recommended oil is SAE 20 or SAE 30 engine oil. The oil reservoir is equipped with a dipstick attached to the cap. Maintain the oil level at the proper level on the dipstick with the transaxle cold.

Change oil after every 500 hours of operation or more when operated in severe conditions. If the color of the oil is milky, it is possible that the oil has become water contaminated. Locate and correct the problem, then refill with new oil.

NEUTRAL ADJUSTMENT

When the brake pedal is depressed, the speed control lever (1—Fig. AR3-10) should return to its neutral position and the transaxle should shift to NEUTRAL. The tractor should not creep in either direction when the brake pedal is released.

If the speed control lever does not return to its neutral position when the brake pedal is depressed, adjust the length of the shift rod (3—Fig. AR3-10) so the lever is centered in the neutral slot. If the tractor will not maintain a set speed (the speed control lever moves without being manually moved), turn the friction adjusting bolt (2) to increase friction pressure on the control lever.

If the tractor creeps (the transaxle does not shift to NEUTRAL) when the brake pedal is depressed, proceed as follows: Raise the rear deck for access to the transaxle control linkage. Raise and

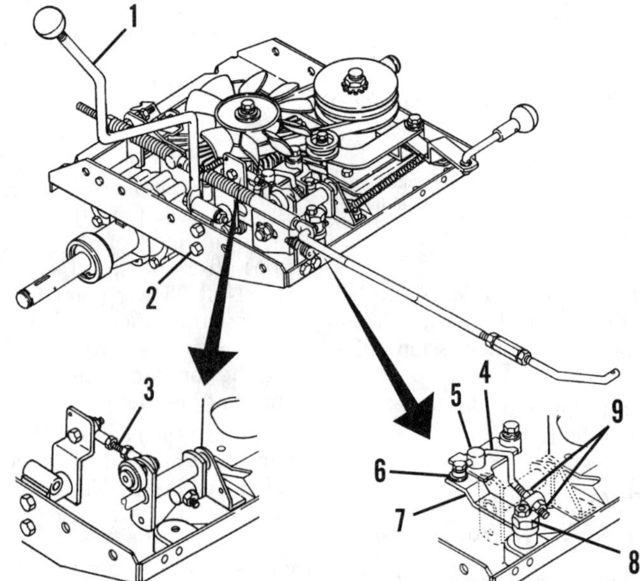

Fig. AR3-10–View showing adjustment for hydrostatic transmission linkage. Refer to text for procedure.

1. Speed selector lever
2. Friction adjusting bolt
3. Shifter rod
4. Shift rod link
5. Pivot
6. Bearing
7. Detent arm
8. Eccentric
9. Jan nuts

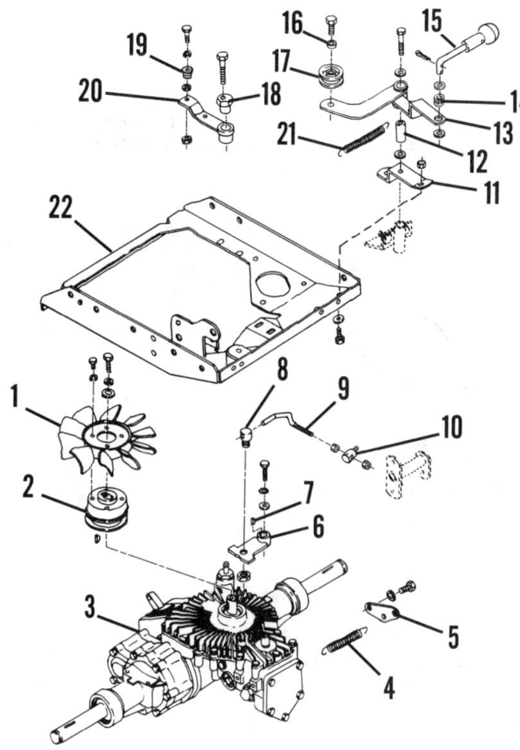

Fig. AR3-11–Exploded view of hydrostatic transmission control linkage.

1. Fan
2. Transmission pulley
3. Hydrostatic transaxle
4. Extension spring
5. Spring anchor
6. Nut
7. Shift arm
8. Pivot
9. Shift link
10. Pivot
11. Idler bracket
12. Spacer
13. Idler arm
14. Grommet
15. Transmission disconnect arm
16. Bushing
17. Idler
18. Eccentric
19. Bearing
20. Detent arm
21. Spring
22. Transaxle mount

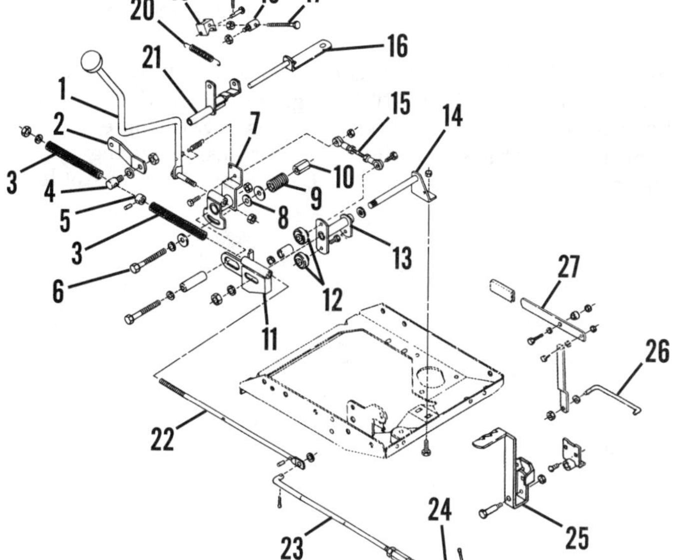

Fig. AR3-12–Exploded view of hydrostatic drive speed selector linkage and brake linkage. See Fig. AR3-11 also.

1. Speed selector lever
2. Brake link
3. Spring
4. Pivot
5. Collar
6. Friction adjusting bolt
7. Shift bracket
8. Friction washer
9. Spring
10. Guide nut
11. Brake bracket
12. Bearings
13. Shift control
14. Brake pivot
15. Shift rod
16. Brake bracket
17. Brake adjuster screw
18. Pivot
19. Brake clevis
20. Spring
21. Brake arm
22. Rear brake rod
23. Center brake rod
24. Front brake rod
25. Brake pedal
26. Brake link
27. Park brake handle

support the rear of the tractor so the rear wheels do not contact the ground.

CAUTION: Exercise care when working around rotating wheels and the transaxle cooling fan.

Check fit of the shift rod link (4—Fig. AR3-10) in the pivot (5). The link should move slightly in the pivot. Adjust the link position in pivot by rotating the jam nuts (9). Loosen the nylon locknut on the bottom end of the cap screw retaining the eccentric (8) just enough so the eccentric can be turned with a wrench. Start the engine and run at idle. Depress then release the brake pedal. Rear wheels should not rotate. If the wheels rotate, turn the eccentric so the wheels do not rotate. Turn the eccentric in both directions and find the midpoint at which the wheels do not rotate. Hold the eccentric and tighten the nylon locknut. Recheck the adjustment.

If turning the eccentric does not stop wheel rotation, remove the battery and tray assembly. Loosen the screw securing the pivot bearing (6) in the detent arm. Rotate the eccentric (8) so the cap screw is on the left side. Run the engine (jump start engine) and move the speed control to the neutral position so the pivot bearing (6) centers on the shift arm. Tighten the pivot bearing retaining screw. Perform the neutral adjustment using the eccentric as described in the previous paragraph.

REMOVAL AND INSTALLATION

The transaxle is located in a subframe that is removed from the tractor with the transaxle. Remove the mower deck, if so equipped. Remove the knob from the speed control lever. Disconnect the neutral switch wiring. Remove the rear deck. Remove the battery and tray assembly. Raise and support the rear of the tractor. Remove the rear wheels.

Remove the primary drive belt and traction drive belt. Disconnect the spring from the idler arm. Remove the speed selector lever (1—Fig. AR3-10). Detach the brake control linkage from the transaxle. Support the transaxle and subframe. Remove the screws attaching the subframe and drawbar plate to the tractor frame. Separate the subframe with the transaxle and drawbar plate from the tractor.

Disconnect the oil hose from the transmission, drain the oil and plug or cap the openings. Remove the transaxle fan (1—Fig. AR3-11) and pulley (2). Disconnect the spring from the detent arm (20). Unbolt and remove the shift arm (6) and key from the transaxle shaft. Disconnect the brake link (2—Fig. AR3-12) from the clevis (19).

Unbolt and remove the brake bracket (16) and arm (21). Disconnect the shifter link (15). Remove the screws securing the transaxle to the subframe and separate the transaxle from the subframe.

To reinstall the transaxle, reverse the removal procedure. Perform the neutral adjustment and brake adjustment as previously described.

OVERHAUL

935 models are equipped with an Eaton Model 750 hydrostatic transaxle. Refer to the HYDROSTATIC TRANSAXLE section at rear of this manual for overhaul information.

ATTACHMENT LIFT

A mechanical attachment lift (Fig. AR3-13) is used on all models. To remove the lift linkage, first remove any mounted attachment. Disconnect the adjustment link (8) from the rear hanger (11) and lift lever (10). Remove the rear hanger from the hanger bracket (9). Disconnect and remove the lift link (6). Drive out the roll pin and withdraw the lift arm (5) and bushings (4). Unbolt and remove lift quadrant (3) and lift handle (2).

Inspect all parts for damage and replace when necessary. Assemble in the reverse order of disassembly.

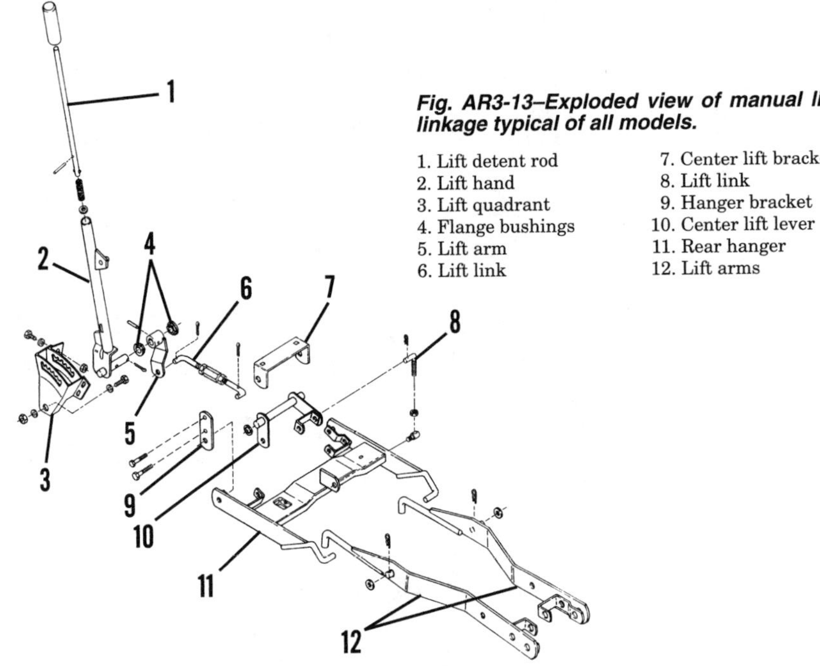

Fig. AR3-13–Exploded view of manual lift linkage typical of all models.

1. Lift detent rod
2. Lift hand
3. Lift quadrant
4. Flange bushings
5. Lift arm
6. Lift link
7. Center lift bracket
8. Lift link
9. Hanger bracket
10. Center lift lever
11. Rear hanger
12. Lift arms

SAFETY INTERLOCK SYSTEM

The tractor is equipped with a safety interlock system that prevents inadvertent starting of the tractor engine or operation when the operator leaves the tractor seat. The tractor engine should not start if the following occurs:

- Operator in the tractor seat, shift lever in NEUTRAL, the brake engaged and the PTO clutch lever in the ON position.
- Operator in the tractor seat, the PTO clutch lever in the OFF position, the brake engaged and the shift lever in a position other than NEUTRAL.
- Operator in the tractor seat, the shift lever in NEUTRAL, the PTO clutch lever in the OFF position and the brakes released.
- Operator not in the seat when starting the engine.

The seat switch should kill the engine when the operator is not in the seat or leaves the seat when the PTO clutch is engaged. The seat switch should kill the engine when the operator leaves the seat when the brakes are not locked.

Refer to the wiring schematics at the end of this section.

WIRING SCHEMATICS

Fig. AR3-14 illustrates the wiring diagram for models equipped with a Briggs & Stratton engine. Fig. AR3-15 illustrates the wiring diagram for models equipped with a Kohler engine.

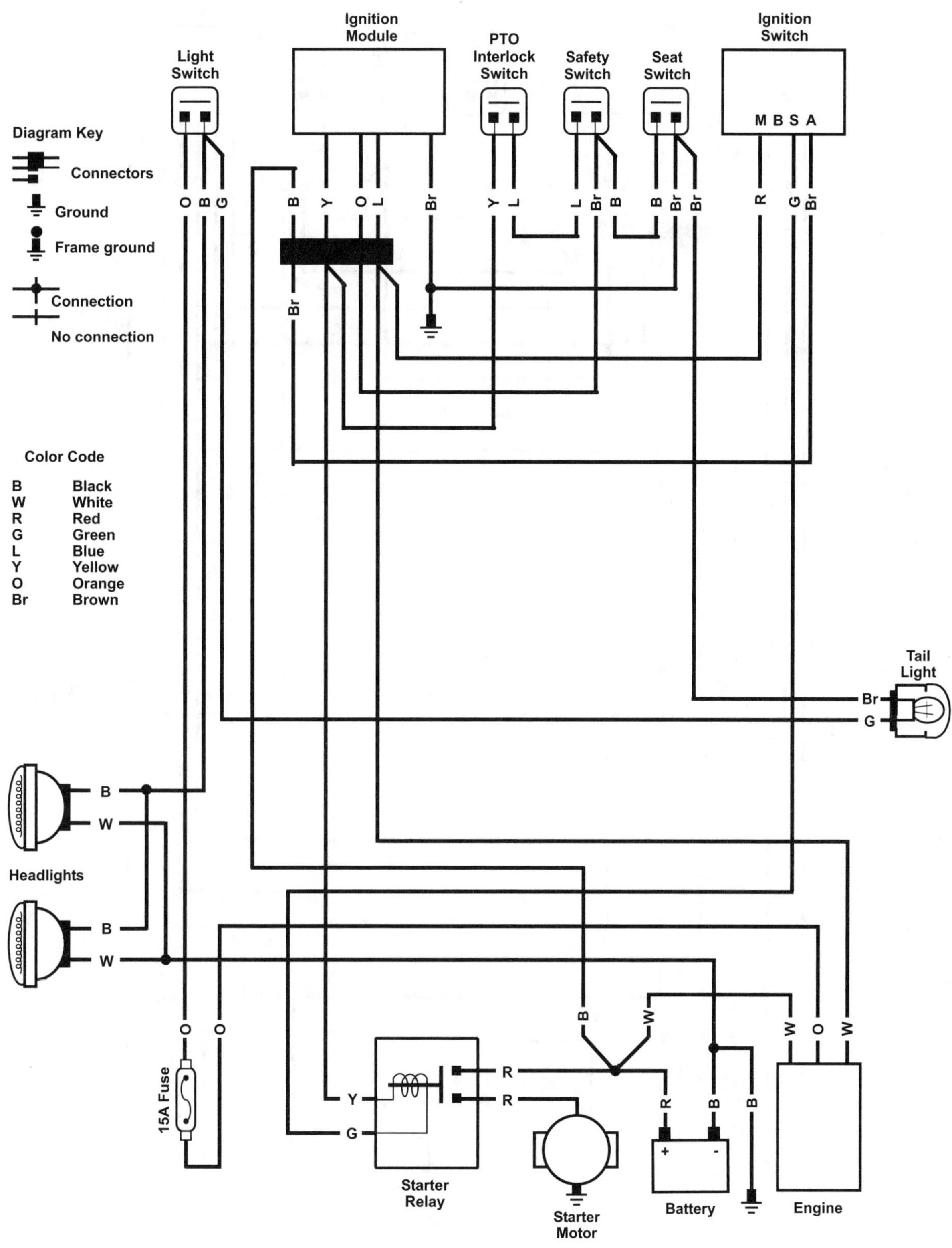

Fig. AR3-14–Typical wiring schematic for models with Briggs & Stratton engine.

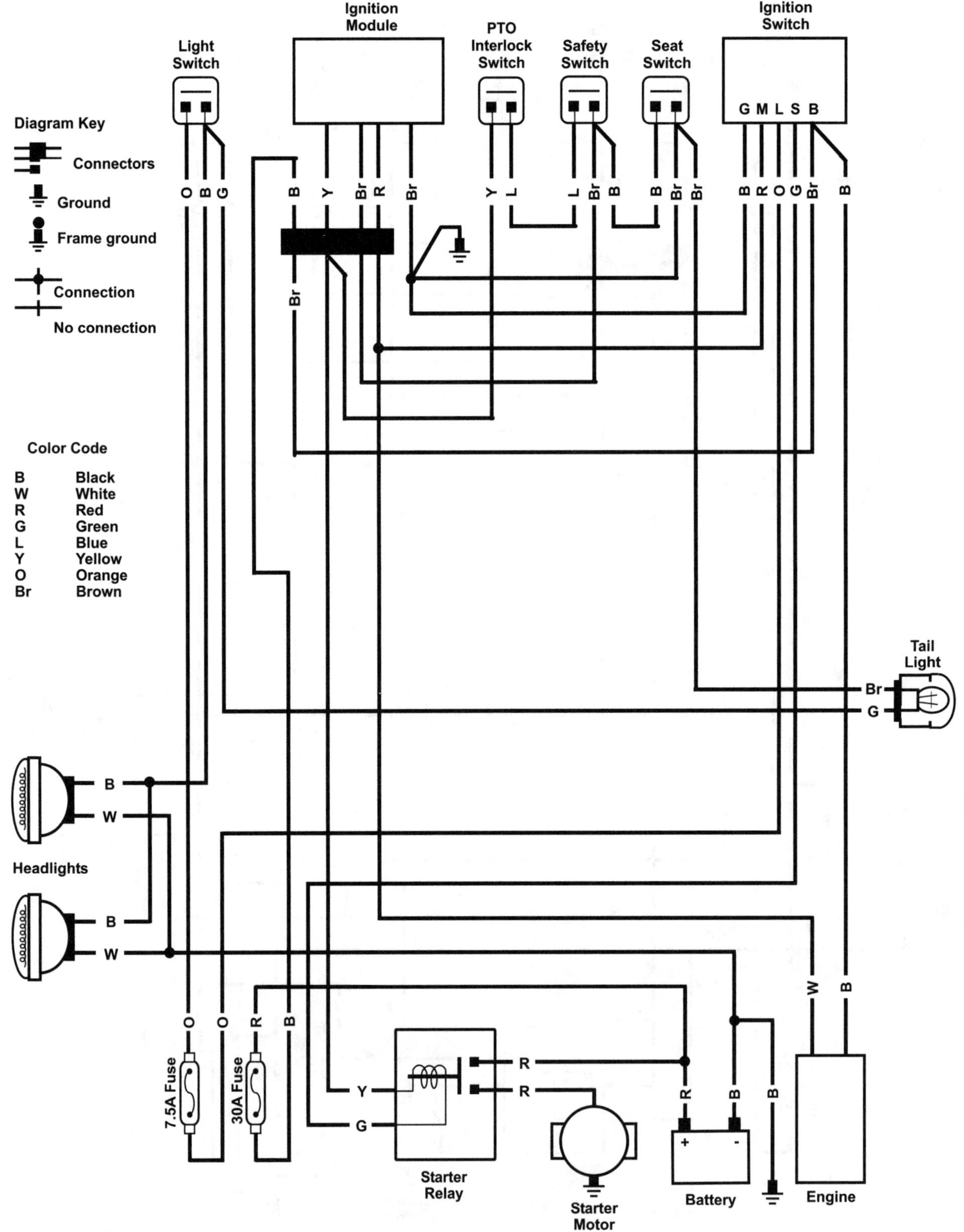

Fig. AR3-15–Typical wiring schematic for models with Kohler engine.

CUB CADET

CONDENSED SPECIFICATIONS

Models	1015	1020	1225
Engine Make	B&S	B&S	B&S
Model	251707	251707	283707
Number of cylinders	1	1	1
Bore	3 7/16 in. (87.3 mm)	3 7/16 in. (87.3 mm)	3 7/16 in. (87.3 mm)
Stroke	2 5/8 in. (66.7 mm)	2 5/8 in. (66.7 mm)	3.06 in. (77.7 mm)
Displacement	24.36 cu. in. (399 cc)	24.36 cu. in. (399 cc)	28.4 cu. in. (465 cc)
Power Rating	10 hp (7.4 kW)	10 hp (7.4 kW)	12 hp (9 kW)
Slow Idle	1750 rpm	1750 rpm	1750 rpm
High Speed (No-Load)	3400 rpm	3400 rpm	3400 rpm
Crankcase Capacity	3 pt. (1.4 L)	3 pt. (1.4 L)	3 pt. (1.4 L)
Transmission Capacity	36 oz. (1065 mL)	*	36 oz. (1065 mL)

*Refer to Hydrostatic Transmission section.

Models	1315, 1325	1320, 1330, 1340	1405, 1415
Engine Make	Kohler	Kohler	Kohler
Model	CV12.5	CV12.5	**
Number of cylinders	1	1	**
Bore	3 7/16 in. (87.3 mm)	3 7/16 in. (87.3 mm)	**
Stroke	2 5/8 in. (67 mm)	2 5/8 in. (67 mm)	**
Displacement	24.29 cu. in. (398 cc)	24.29 cu. in. (398 cc)	**
Power Rating	12.5 hp (9.3 kW)	12.5 hp (9.3 kW)	14 hp (10.5 kW)
Slow Idle	1800 rpm	1800 rpm	**
High Speed (No-Load)	3400 rpm	3400 rpm	**
Crankcase Capacity	4 pt. (1.9 L)	4 pt. (1.9 L)	**
Transmission.	36 oz. (1065 mL)	*	36 oz. (1065 mL)

*Refer to Hydrostatic Transmission section.
**Note engine model number on engine and refer to engine service section in this manual for engine specifications.

Models	1420, 1430	1440	1541, 1641
Engine Make	Kohler	B&S	Kohler
Model	**	**	**
Number of cylinders	**	**	2
Bore	**	**	3.125 in. (79.2 mm)
Stroke	**	**	2.75 in. (69.85 mm)
Displacement	**	**	42.18 cu. In. (691 cc)
Power Rating	14 hp (10.5 kW)	14 hp (10.5 kW)	15 hp (11.2 kW)
Slow Idle	**	**	1200 rpm
High Speed (No-Load)	**	**	3600 rpm
Crankcase Capacity	**	**	3.5 pt (1.7 L)
Transmission Capacity	*	*	*

*Refer to Hydrostatic Transmission section.

**Note engine model number on engine and refer to engine service section in this manual for engine specifications.

MODELS	1715	1720, 1730	1860
Engine Make	Kohler	Kohler	Kohler
Model	MV17	MV17	MV18
Number of cylinders	2	2	2
Bore	3.125 in. (79.2 mm)	3.125 in. (79.2 mm)	3.125 in. (79.2 mm)
Stroke	2.75 in. (69.85 mm)	2.75 in. (69.85 mm)	2.75 in. (69.85 mm)
Displacement	42.18 cu. in. (691 cc)	42.18 cu. in. (691 cc)	42.18 cu. in. (691 cc)
Power Rating	17 hp (12.6 kW)	17 hp (12.6 kW)	18 hp (13.4 kW)
Slow Idle	1200 rpm	1200 rpm	1200 rpm
High Speed (No-Load)	3600 rpm	3600 rpm	3600 rpm
Crankcase Capacity	3.5 pt.*** (1.7 L)	3.5 pt.*** (1.7 L)	3.5 pt.*** (1.7 L)
Transmission Capacity	*	*	*

*Refer to Hydrostatic Transmission section.

**Note engine model number on engine and refer to engine service section in this manual for engine specifications.

***With filter—4.0 pt.(1.9 L).

FRONT WHEELS

Lubricate the front wheel bearings after every 30 hours of operation. Inject No. 2 multipurpose lithium grease into each wheel hub through the grease fitting on the wheel hub. Two or three shots from a hand-held grease gun should be sufficient.

The front wheels are equipped with replaceable bearings (1—Fig. C1). To remove the bearings, raise and support the front of the tractor. Remove the hub cap (7), bolt (6) and washers (4 and 5). Slide the wheel off the axle. Drive the bearings from the wheel using a long punch.

Lubricate the new bearings with grease prior to assembly. Press them into the wheel hub, applying force to the outer race only. Slide the wheel onto the axle and secure with the bolt and washers.

FRONT AXLE SYSTEM

AXLE MAIN MEMBER

The front axle main member is mounted directly on the main frame. On Models 1340, 1440, 1541, 1641 and 1860, the axle main member pivots on the center mounting pivot pin. On all other models the axle main member pivots on a bushing (1—Fig. CC2).

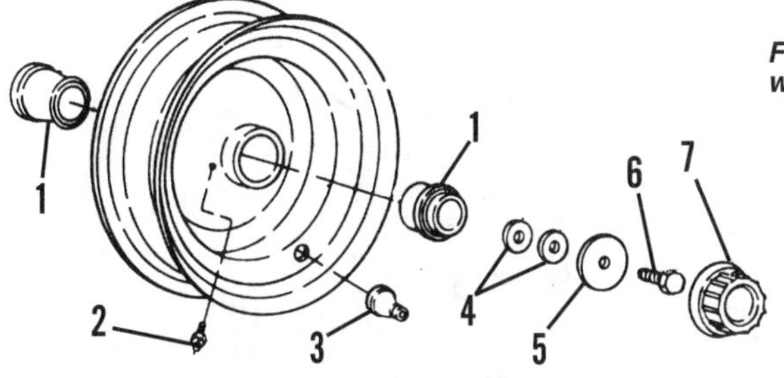

Fig. CC1–Exploded view of wheel assembly.

1. Bearing
2. Grease fitting
3. Air valve
4. Washers
5. Washer
6. Bolt
7. Hub cap

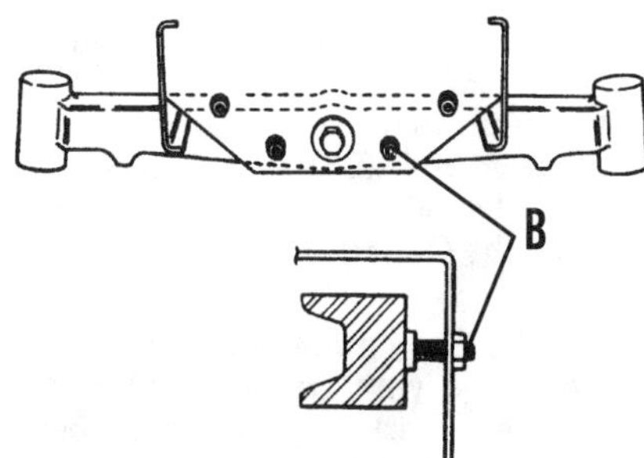

Fig. CC3–On models equipped with axle adjustment bolts, the head of both bolts (B) must contact axle main member.

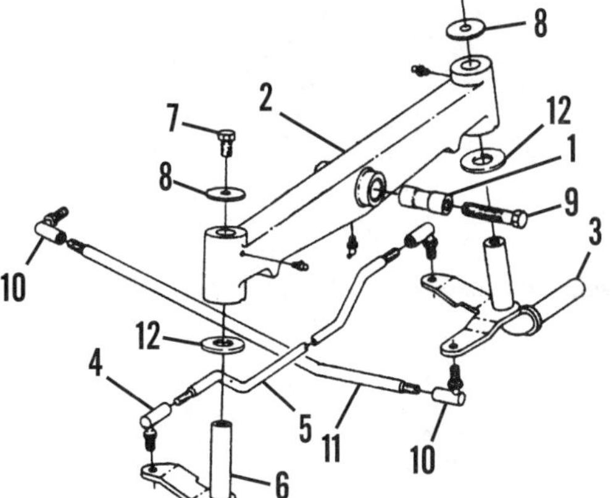

Fig. CC2–Exploded view of front axle assembly used on Models 1015, 1020, 1225, 1315, 1320, 1325, 1330, 1405, 1415, 1420, 1430, 1715, 1720 and 1730.

1. Pivot bushing
2. Axle main member
3. Left spindle
4. Tie rod end
5. Tie rod
6. Right spindle
7. Cap screw
8. Washer
9. Bolt
10. Drag link end
11. Drag link
12. Thrust washer

To remove the front axle main member assembly, raise the front of the tractor and remove the front wheels. Disconnect the steering drag link from the steering arm or steering spindle. Remove the axle pivot pin bolt and lower the front axle assembly from the tractor.

To reinstall the axle main member, reverse the removal procedure. Lubricate the pivot pin and bushing, if so equipped, with multipurpose grease. On models equipped with axle adjustment bolts (B—Fig. CC3), adjust each bolt until the head of the bolt contacts the axle main member, then tighten the jam nut.

TIE ROD

Front wheels should toe-in $\frac{1}{16}$ to $\frac{1}{8}$ in. (1.5-3 mm). To check toe-in, set the front wheels straight ahead. Measure the distance between the front and rear of the front wheels at hub height. Subtract the front measurement from the rear measurement to determine toe-in.

To adjust toe-in, disconnect one tie rod ball joint from a steering spindle. Loosen the ball joint jam nuts, if so equipped, and turn tie rod in or out as necessary. Note that some tie rods (5—Fig. CC2) have a bend in the center for clearance and the bend must face downward when the tie rod is installed.

Replace the tie rod ball joint ends when excessively worn. Refer to Fig. CC2 or CC4.

STEERING SPINDLES

Models 1340, 1440, 1541, 1641 and 1860

Lubricate the front wheel spindles after every 10 hours of operation or monthly, whichever occurs first. Inject No. 2 multipurpose lithium grease into the front axle main member through the grease fitting (16—Fig. CC4) at each end. Two or three shots from a hand-held grease gun should be sufficient. Check for looseness and binding in the front axle components.

To remove the steering spindles (18 and 30—Fig. CC4), first raise and support the front of the tractor. Remove the front wheels. Disconnect the tie rod (23) from the steering spindles. Disconnect the drag link (5) from the steering arm (11). Remove the steering arm clamp bolt (6). Remove the left steering spindle retaining bolt (9) and washer. Detach the steering arm from the steering spindle, then remove the left spindle (18). Remove the bolt from the top of the right steering spindle (30), then remove the spindle.

Inspect the spindles, axle, wheels and bearings for wear or damage and renew as necessary. Install the steering arm on the left spindle so the steering arm is 20° ahead of the axle as shown in Fig. CC5.

All Other Models

Lubricate the front wheel spindles after every 10 hours of operation or monthly, whichever occurs first. Inject No. 2 multipurpose lithium grease into the front axle main member through the grease fitting at each end. Two or three shots from a hand-held grease gun should be sufficient. Check for looseness and binding in the front axle components.

To remove the steering spindles (3 and 6—Fig. CC2), first raise and support the front of the tractor. Remove the front wheels. Disconnect the drag link (11) and tie rod (5) from the steering spindles. Remove the bolts from the top of the steering spindles and lower the spindles from the axle main member.

Inspect the spindles, axle, wheels and bearings for excessive wear and replace when necessary.

TILT STEERING (MODELS 1340, 1440, 1541, 1641 AND 1860)

Models 1340, 1440, 1541, 1641 and 1860 are equipped with a joint allowing relocation of the steering wheel. The joint connects the upper and lower steering shafts.

Overhaul

Remove the front side panels. Remove the battery. Remove the battery tray and adjoining panels. Remove the steering wheel. Remove the washer (6—Fig. CC6) and steering shaft boot (7). Remove the joint retaining bolt (31). Remove the joint housing bolts

(33). Remove the lower joint housing (30). Remove the screw (29), washer (28), lower drive coupling (27), balls (24), drive hub (25), upper drive coupling (23) and boot (22). Remove and discard the O-ring (26).

NOTE: Early models may not be equipped with an O-ring (26). If desired, early models may be upgraded by installing couplings (23 and 27) equipped with an O-ring groove.

CAUTION: The torsion spring (12) is under tension. Wear safety glasses when removing or installing the spring.

Remove the cotter pin (13), clevis pin (14) and torsion spring (12). Remove the tilt control button (16) and tilt control plate (17). Remove the shaft guide bushing (11) and guides (10).

Inspect all components for damage. Assemble the drive hub (25), without the balls, and drive couplings (23 and 27). The drive hub must move freely in the drive couplings without grabbing. Inspect the balls for nicks, galling or other damage.

Reassemble the upper steering shaft and joint by reversing the disassembly procedure. A special tool 759-3596 is available from Cub Cadet to assist in installation of the torsion spring (12). Pack the drive couplings with CV joint grease during assembly.

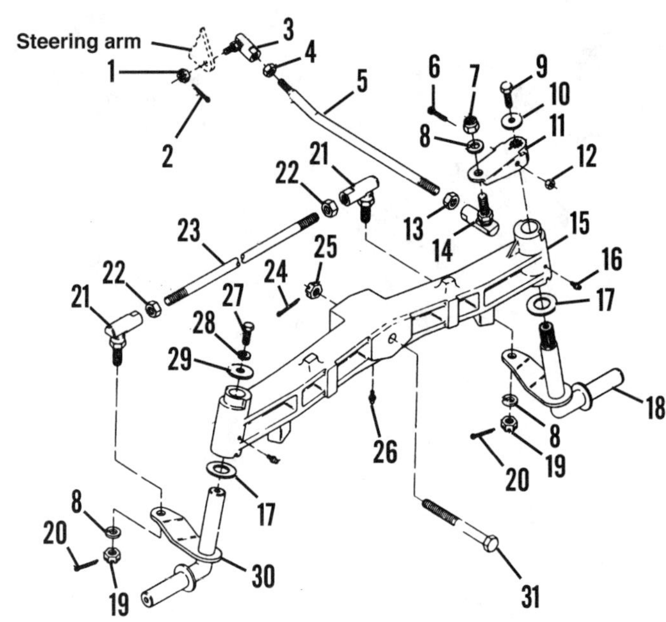

Fig. CC4–Exploded view of front axle assembly used on Models 1340, 1440, 1541, 1641 and 1860.

1. Nut	9. Bolt	16. Grease fitting	24. Cotter pin
2. Cotter pin	10. Washer	17. Washer	25. Nut
3. Rod end	11. Steering arm	18. Spindle (left)	26. Grease fitting
4. Jam nut	12. Nut	19. Nut	27. Bolt
5. Drag link	13. Jam nut	20. Cotter pin	28. Lockwasher
6. Cotter pin	14. Rod end	21. Rod end	29. Washer
7. Nut	15. Axle main member	22. Jam nut	30. Spindle (right)
8. Lockwasher		23. Tie rod	31. Pivot bolt

STEERING GEAR OVERHAUL

MODELS 1340, 1440, 1541, 1641 AND 1860

Remove the front side panels. Remove the battery and battery tray. Remove the joint retaining bolt (31—Fig. CC6). Disconnect the drag link from the steering arm plate (14—Fig. CC7). Remove the mounting bolts retaining the steering gear housing and tube. Lower the steering gear housing out of the tractor.

To disassemble, clamp the steering arm plate (14—Fig. CC7) in a vise and remove the nut (11) and jam nut (12). Separate the housing and tube assembly (4) from the steering arm plate. Remove the cotter pin (21) and adjustment plug (20). Remove the steering shaft and cam assembly (8) and the bearings from the housing and tube assembly.

During reassembly, coat the cam, bearing balls and races with multipurpose grease. Install the steering shaft and cam, balls and races into the housing and tube assembly. Make certain that the races enter the housing squarely and are not cocked. Thread the adjustment plug (20) into the housing until cam end play is removed but the shaft still turns freely. Insert the cotter pin (21) into the nearest hole in the adjustment plug.

Fill the housing with lithium base grease. Loosen the jam nut (12) and back the cam adjustment bolt (13) out two turns. Install the seal (16), retainer (15) and steering arm plate (14). Install the washer and nut (11). Tighten the nut until there is $^{3}/_{32}$ inch (2.4 mm) clearance between the steering arm plate and housing (Fig. CC8). Install a jam nut against the nut (11—Fig. CC7) and tighten the jam nut to 40 ft.-lbs. (54 N·m).

Inject grease into the fitting (17) until grease begins to appear between the steering arm plate (14) and housing. Center the steering cam by rotating the steering shaft halfway between full right and full left turn. Turn the cam adjustment bolt (13) inward to eliminate backlash, then tighten the jam nut (12) to 40 ft.-lbs. (54 N·m). The steering shaft should rotate smoothly with minimum backlash.

ALL OTHER MODELS

To remove the steering gear assembly, first disconnect the battery cables.

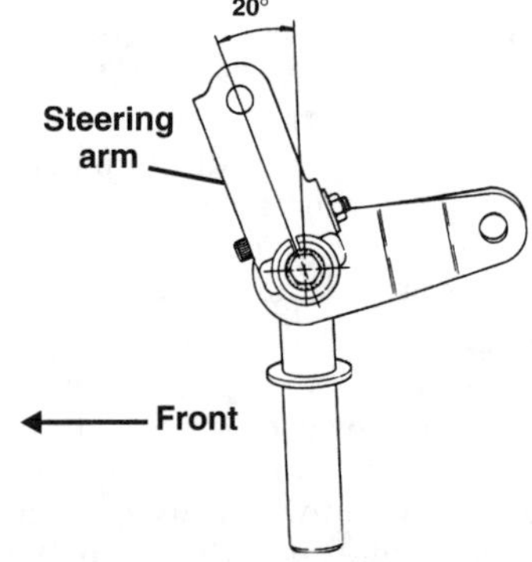

Fig. CC5–On Models 1340, 1440, 1541, 1641 and 1860, install the steering arm on the left spindle so the steering arm is 20° ahead of the axle as shown.

On models with a console-mounted fuel tank, remove the fuel tank. On all models, remove the steering wheel cap and retaining nut and pull the steering wheel off the steering shaft. Disconnect the throttle cable, choke cable, PTO electric clutch wire harness (if equipped), engine ground wire, starter cable and main wire harness

Remove the nuts or screws attaching the steering shaft bearing to the dash. Remove the nuts attaching the dash pedestal to the frame and lift the pedestal up over the steering shaft. Discon-

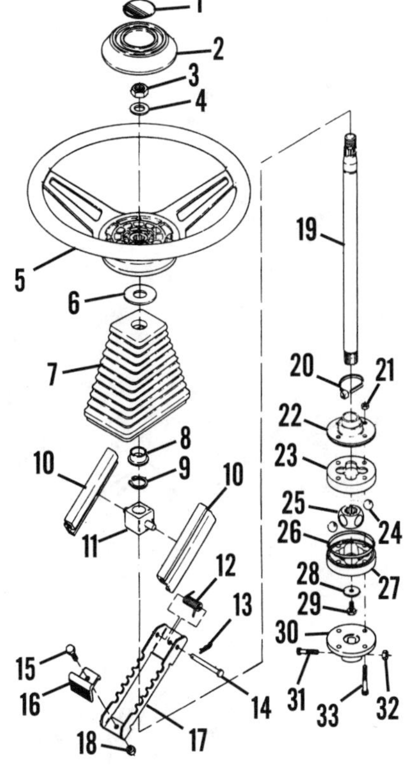

Fig. CC6–Exploded view of tilt steering assembly used on Models 1340, 1440, 1541, 1641 and 1860.

1. Label
2. Cap
3. Nut
4. Washer
5. Steering wheel
6. Washer
7. Boot
8. Flange bushing
9. Snap ring
10. Guides
11. Guide bushing
12. Torsion spring
13. Cotter pin
14. Clevis pin
15. Screw
16. Tilt control button
17. Tilt control plate
18. Locknut
19. Upper steering shaft
20. Tie strap
21. Locknut
22. Boot
23. Upper drive coupling
24. Ball
25. Drive hub
26. O-ring
27. Lower drive couplng
28. Washer
29. Screw
30. Steering adapter
31. Bolt
32. Locknut
33. Bolt

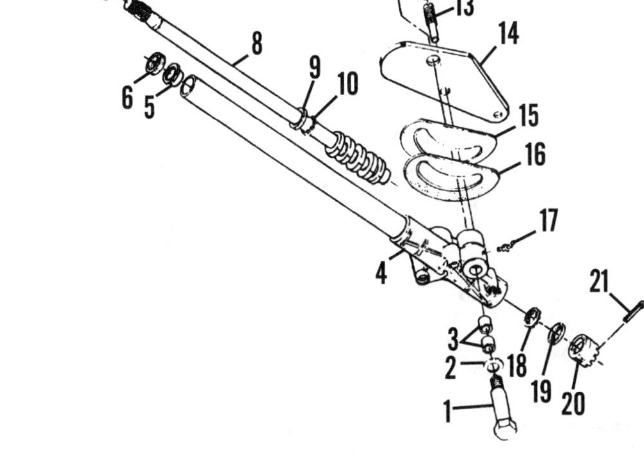

Fig. CC7–Exploded view of steering shaft and gear assembly used on Models 1340, 1440, 1541, 1641 and 1860.

1. Pivot bolt
2. Washer
3. Bushings
4. Housing & tube assy.
5. Bearing
6. Seal
7. Nut
8. Steering shaft & cam
9. Bearing race
10. Nut
11. Nut
12. Jam nut
13. Cam adjustment bolt
14. Steerng arm plate
15. Seal retainer
16. Seal
17. Grease fitting
18. Bearing & retainer
19. Bearing race
20. Adjustment plug
21. Cotter pin

nect the drag link from the steering arm. Remove the bolts attaching the steering box to the frame and remove the steering gear assembly.

To disassemble the steering gear, refer to Fig. CC9 and remove the cap (10), nut (9) and bolt (8). Remove the nut (19) from the end of the steering arm shaft (5), disengage the snap ring (22) from the groove in the shaft and withdraw the shaft and bevel gear (21) from the steering box (11). Remove the nut (18) and pull the steering wheel shaft out of the steering box and pinion gear (16).

Inspect the bushings for damage and replace when necessary. Check for broken gear teeth or bent shafts and replace parts when necessary.

To reassemble, reverse the disassembly procedure. Turn the adjusting bolt (8—Fig. CC9) to obtain the minimum amount of backlash between the bevel gear and pinion gear, while still allowing the steering wheel shaft to turn freely. Install the steering gear assembly. With the front wheels in the straight-ahead position, the pinion gear must be in the center of the bevel gear.

ENGINE

REMOVAL AND INSTALLATION

Models 1340, 1440, 1541, 1641 and 1860

To remove the engine, first disconnect the battery ground cable. Disconnect the headlight wiring and remove the grille housing, hood and side panels. Remove the battery. Remove the battery tray and adjoining panels. Disconnect the starter wires, charging wires, electric clutch wires, ignition wires and ground wires. Disconnect the choke and throttle linkage. Disconnect the fuel line.

Detach the drive shaft from the engine as described in the DRIVESHAFT section. Remove bolts attaching the engine to the frame. Slide the engine forward and use a suitable hoist to lift the engine from the frame.

Install by reversing the removal procedure.

All Other Models

To remove the engine, disconnect and remove the battery. Disconnect the two extension springs from the bottom of the grille. Loosen the grille pivot bracket retaining bolts on each side of grille. Remove the pivot bracket bolts from one side only and pull the grille and hood off the pivot brackets.

Disconnect the choke cable and throttle cable. Disconnect fuel line from fuel pump. Disconnect the ground wire, main wiring harness and starter cable at the engine.

On models equipped with an electric clutch, disconnect the wire to the electric clutch. Raise the front of tractor and unbolt and remove the electric clutch, engine pulley and belt guard, crankshaft spacer and drive belt idler pulley. On all other models, remove the engine pulley and drive belt idler pulley.

On all models, remove the four bolts attaching the engine to the frame and lift the engine from the frame using a suitable hoist.

Install the engine by reversing the removal procedure while noting the following special instructions: Be sure that the four spacers are located be-

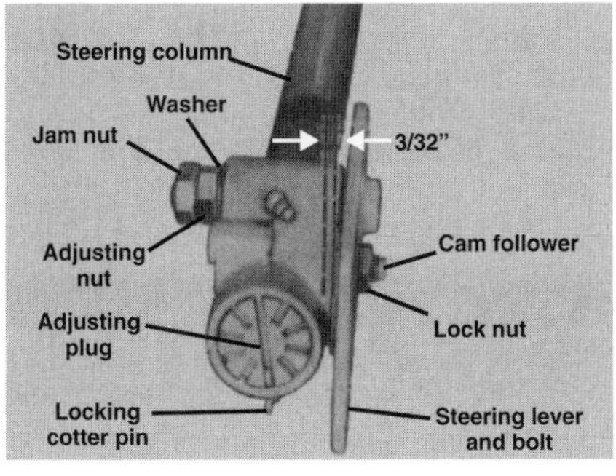

Fig. CC8–view of assembled steering unit. Tighten adjusting nut until steering lever is 3/32 inch (2.4 mm) from housing.

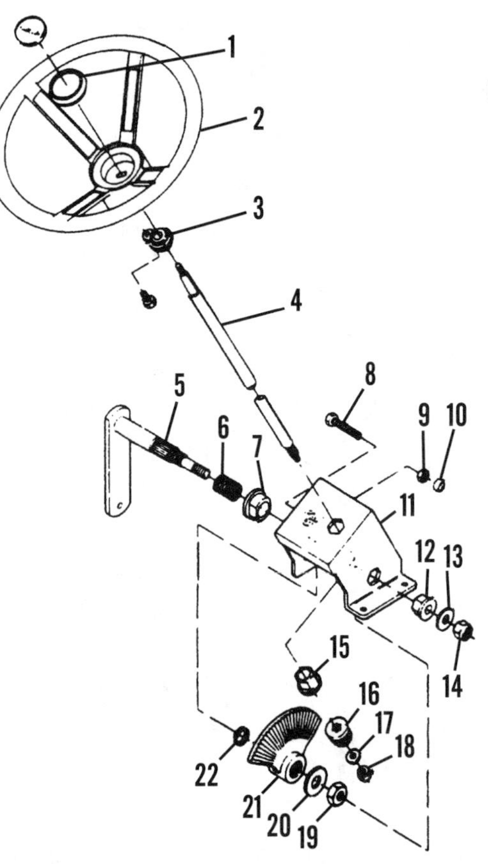

Fig. CC9–Exploded view of steering gear assembly used on all models except 1340, 1440, 1541, 1641 and 1860.

1. Steering wheel cap
2. Steering wheel
3. Column bearing
4. Steering shaft
5. Steering arm shaft
6. Spring
7. Flange bushing
8. Cap screw
9. Jam nut
10. Cap
11. Steering box
12. Flange bushing
13. Thrust washer
14. Locknut
15. Flange bushing
16. Pinion gear
17. Thrust washer
18. Locknut
19. Jam nut
20. Thrust washer
21. Bevel gear
22. Snap ring

tween the engine and frame. When installing the engine belt guard mounting plate, be sure that the welded bolts on the plate face downward (away from the tractor frame). The hub side of the idler pulley must face upward (toward the tractor frame).

OVERHAUL

Engine make and model are listed at the beginning of this section. To overhaul engine components and accessories, refer to the KOHLER or BRIGGS & STRATTON section of this manual.

DRIVESHAFT OVERHAUL (MODELS 1340, 1440, 1541, 1641 AND 1860)

Open the hood and remove the side panels. Remove the frame cover. Remove the engine coupling screws (7—Fig. CC10). Remove the tie strap (2) and slide the drive shaft coupling away from the engine. Remove the coupling components (1, 9, 10, 11, 12, 13 and 14) from the drive shaft. Set aside the coupling components for inspection. Withdraw the drive shaft from the rear coupling.

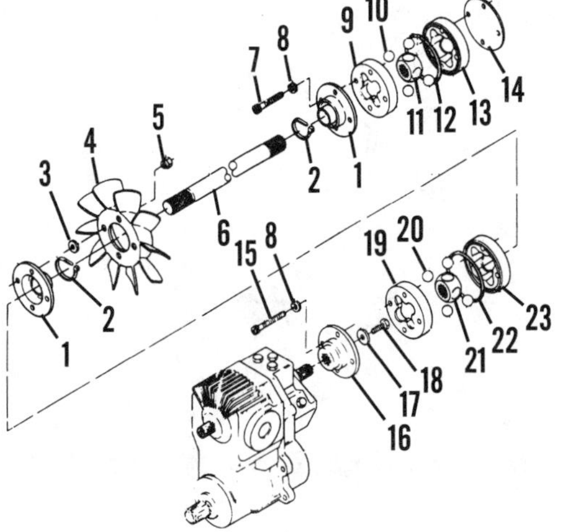

Fig. CC10–Exploded view of drive shaft assembly used on Models 1340, 1440, 1541, 1641 and 1860.

1. Boot
2. Tie strap
3. Washer
4. Fan
5. Nut
6. Drive shaft
7. Bolt
8. Lockwasher
9. Coupling
10. Ball
11. Drive hub
12. O-ring
13. Coupling
14. Adapter
15. Bolt
16. Adapter
17. Washer
18. Screw
19. Coupling
20. Ball
21. Drive hub
22. O-ring
23. Couping

NOTE: Early models may not be equipped with O-rings (12 or 22). If desired, early models may be upgraded by installing new coupling halves equipped with an O-ring groove.

Remove nuts retaining the fan (5) and remove the fan (4). Remove the washers (3) and tie strap (2). Remove the boot (1). Remove the components (23, 22, 21, 20 and 19) from the rear coupling. Set aside the coupling components for inspection. Remove the screw (18) and drive the flange (16) from the hydrostatic pump shaft.

Inspect all components for damage and replace as needed.

Assemble the drive hub (11 or 21), without the balls, and the drive coupling halves. The drive hub must move freely in the drive couplings without grabbing. Inspect the balls for nicks, galling or other damage.

Reassemble the drive shaft and joints by reversing the disassembly procedure. Pack the drive couplings with CV joint grease during assembly.

BRAKES

MODELS 1340, 1440, 1541, 1641 AND 1860

Adjustment

The brakes should engage when the gap from the brake pedal lever to the pedal lock tab is no more than one

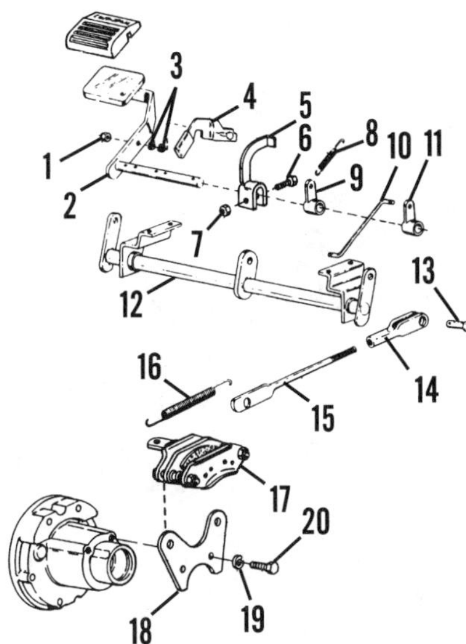

Fig. CC11–Exploded view of brake control linkage used on Models 1340, 1440, 1541, 1641 and 1860.

1. Locknut
2. Brake pedal
3. Wave washers
4. Parking brake bracket
5. Start switch bracket
6. Bolt
7. Locknut
8. Spring
9. Brake lever
10. Rod
11. Brake lever
12. Pivot shaft
13. Clevis pin
14. Rod end
15. Brake rod
16. Spring
17. Caliper assy.
18. Mounting bracket
19. Lockwasher
20. Bolt

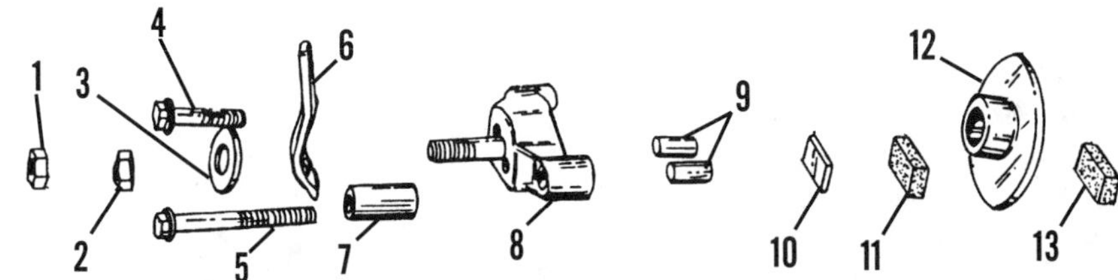

Fig. CC12–Exploded view of disc brake assembly used on all models except 1340, 1440, 1541, 1641 and 1860. On some models, a single nut is used in place of nuts (1 and 2).

1. Nut
2. Nut
3. Washer
4. Bolt
5. Bolt
6. Brake lever
7. Dowel pin
8. Caliper
9. Pins
10. Back-up plate
11. Brake pad
12. Brake disc
13. Brake pad

inch (25 mm). To adjust the brakes, support the rear of the tractor so the rear wheels can rotate freely. Disconnect the brake rod (15—Fig. CC11) on each side. Shorten or lengthen the brake rod as needed by rotating the clevis (14).

The brakes must have equal stopping action at both wheels. With the rear wheels supported off the ground, start the engine and operate in forward gear. Apply the brakes. If one wheel stops sooner than the other wheel, adjust the brake rod on the wheel that does not stop until both wheels stop simultaneously.

Overhaul

The disc brakes on these models are mechanically actuated and located at the end of both rear axles. Braking action is accomplished by brake pads contacting a disc attached to each rear wheel hub and axle.

To disassemble the brakes, remove the wheels and disconnect the brake rod (15—Fig. CC11). Remove the bolts attaching the brake assembly to the mounting bracket (18).

Inspect parts for damage and replace when necessary.

ALL OTHER MODELS

Adjustment

To adjust the brake, the pedal should be in the released position.

Loosen the jam nut and turn the adjusting nut (2—Fig. CC12) in until the brake disc (12) is locked.

NOTE: Some models may not be equipped with a jam nut. The adjusting nut is a locknut or castellated nut.

Back off the adjusting nut $\frac{1}{4}$ turn and tighten the jam nut. Recheck braking action.

Overhaul

The disc brake is located on the right side of the transaxle. To disassemble the brake, remove the rear wheel and disconnect the brake rod spring from the brake lever. Unbolt and remove the brake assembly from the transaxle.

Inspect all parts for damage and replace when needed.

When installing the brake, be sure the hub side of the brake disc (12—Fig. CC12) faces away from the transaxle housing.

DRIVE BELT REMOVAL AND INSTALLATION (MODELS 1015, 1020, 1225, 1315, 1320, 1325, 1330, 1405, 1415, 1420, 1430, 1715, 1720 AND 1730)

A spring-loaded belt idler clutch is used on these tractors. No adjustment is required. If the belt slips due to excessive wear or stretching, replace the belt.

To replace the drive belt, first remove the mower from the tractor. If equipped with an electric PTO clutch, unbolt and remove the clutch assembly. Loosen the cap screws retaining the pulley belt guards and swing the guards out of the way. Remove the idler pulley, and on hydrostatic drive models remove the fan from the transaxle pulley. Slide the belt over the transaxle input pulley and remove the belt. Install the new belt by reversing the removal procedure.

TRANSAXLE

LUBRICATION (ALL MODELS SO EQUIPPED)

Models 1015, 1225, 1315, 1325, 1405, 1415 and 1715 are equipped with a Peerless 920 series transaxle. Transaxle fluid capacity is 30 ounces (887 mL) of Bentonite grease.

REMOVAL AND INSTALLATION (MODELS 1015, 1225, 1315, 1325, 1405, 1415 AND 1715)

Disconnect the battery cables and remove the battery. Disconnect the seat safety switch and remove the seat and seat bracket. Remove the center panel and fenders. Disconnect the fuel line and remove the fuel tank.

Remove the belt keeper from the top of the transaxle housing. Depress the clutch/brake pedal and engage the parking brake lever. Disconnect the shift linkage at the transaxle. Remove the fixed belt idler pulley and work the drive belt off the transaxle pulley. Release the clutch/brake pedal and disconnect the brake rod spring from the brake lever.

Raise and support the rear of the tractor. Place a wooden wedge between the front axle and frame on both sides to prevent the tractor from tipping. Remove the drawbar hitch plate. Remove the U-bolts attaching the transaxle to the frame and roll the transaxle out from under the rear of the tractor.

To install, reverse the removal procedure.

OVERHAUL (MODELS 1015, 1225, 1315, 1325, 1405, 1415 AND 1715)

Refer to the appropriate TRANSAXLE SERVICE section in this manual for overhaul procedure.

HYDROSTATIC TRANSMISSION

LUBRICATION

Models 1020, 1220, 1320, 1330, 1420, 1430, 1720 and1730

These models are equipped with either a Hydro-Gear or Sundstrand hydrostatic transmission. Periodically check the fluid level and maintain the level at the full mark on the reservoir. Recommended transmission fluid is Cub Cadet Transmission Hydraulic Fluid.

Models 1340, 1440, 1541, 1641, 1860

These models are equipped with a Hydro-Gear or Sundstrand hydrostatic transmission. The transmission uses oil contained in the differential housing. Replace the transmission oil filter after every 100 hours of operation or annually, whichever occurs first. Also refer to the DIFFERENTIAL AND REDUCTION GEAR section.

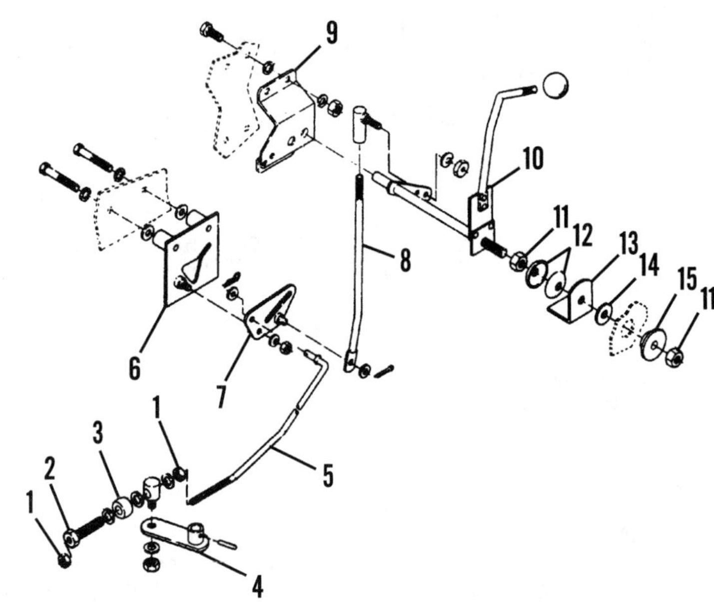

Fig. CC13–Exploded view of hydrostatic transmission control linkage used on Models 1020, 1220, 1320, 1330, 1420, 1430, 1720 and 1730.

1. Nuts
2. Adjustment stud
3. Rubber washer
4. Control arm
5. Hydrostatic control arm
6. Cam plate
7. Cam lever
8. Control rod
9. Support bracket
10. Control lever
11. Jam nuts
12. Belleville washers
13. Friction bracket
14. Friction washer
15. Shoulder spacer

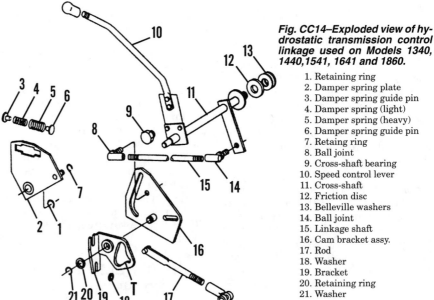

LINKAGE ADJUSTMENT

Models 1020, 1220, 1320, 1330, 1420, 1430, 1720 and 1730

A pull of approximately 10 lbs (5 kg) should be required to move the speed control lever (10—Fig. CC13). If the speed control lever friction setting is too loose or too tight, turn the friction adjusting nuts (11) on the speed control lever shaft as necessary.

Raise the rear wheels off the ground and support the rear frame securely. Start the engine and move the speed control lever to neutral "N" position. If the rear wheels turn with the control lever in neutral, shut off the engine and adjust the linkage as follows: If the tractor creeps forward, loosen the jam nuts (1—Fig. CC13) and turn the adjuster stud (2) counterclockwise until the wheels stop turning. If tractor creeps rearward, turn the adjuster clockwise.

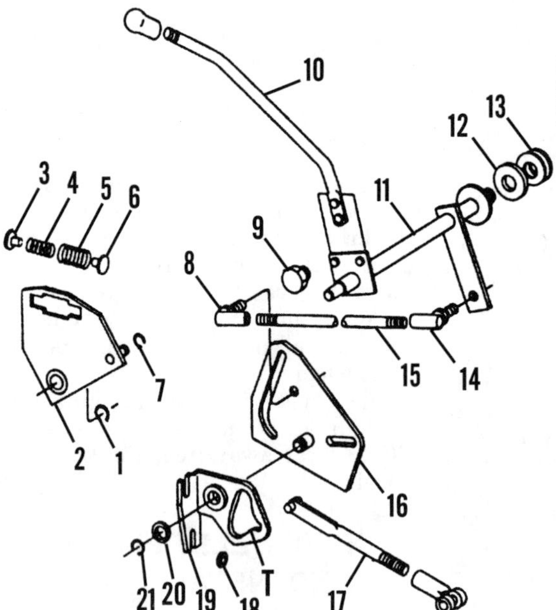

Fig. CC14–Exploded view of hydrostatic transmission control linkage used on Models 1340, 1440,1541, 1641 and 1860.

1. Retaining ring
2. Damper spring plate
3. Damper spring guide pin
4. Damper spring (light)
5. Damper spring (heavy)
6. Damper spring guide pin
7. Retaing ring
8. Ball joint
9. Cross-shaft bearing
10. Speed control lever
11. Cross-shaft
12. Friction disc
13. Belleville washers
14. Ball joint
15. Linkage shaft
16. Cam bracket assy.
17. Rod
18. Washer
19. Bracket
20. Retaining ring
21. Washer

Models 1340, 1440, 1541, 1641 and 1860

Speed Control Lever Adjustment

A pulling force of 7 to 8 lbs (3.2 to 3.6 kg) should be required to move the speed control lever. If the control lever friction setting is too loose or too tight, adjust by removing the left side engine panel and tighten or loosen the friction control nut as necessary.

Cam Bracket Adjustment

If the tractor creeps when the speed control lever is in NEUTRAL or if the linkage has been removed and is being installed, adjust the brake pedal and speed control lever, then raise and support the tractor so the rear tires clear the ground.

CAUTION: Use caution when working near rotating tires or parts.

Remove the frame cover and lubricate the T-slot (T—Fig. CC14). Move the speed control lever to the fast forward position. Loosen the cam bracket mounting bolts and move the cam bracket to its highest position in the slotted holes and tighten the bolts slightly to retain in this position. Start the engine and use a punch and hammer to adjust the cam bracket downward until the wheels stop turning.

Move the speed and directional control lever to the forward position. Depress the brake pedal and lock in this position. If there is excessive transmission noise or vibration with the brake pedal depressed, adjust the cam bracket until the transmission noise or vibration stops. Release the brake and shut off the engine.

Move the speed control lever to the fast forward position and tighten the cam bracket retaining bolts. Start the engine, move the speed control lever to the fast forward position, depress the brake pedal fully and release. The wheels should stop turning and the speed control lever should return to the NEUTRAL position.

If the speed control lever is not in the NEUTRAL position, loosen the jam nut on the neutral return rod and adjust until the lever is in the NEUTRAL position. Tighten the jam nut.

The speed control rod should not touch the end of the slot when the brake pedal is fully depressed. If the rod touches, disconnect the clevis from the brake cross-shaft, loosen the jam nut and lengthen the rod until the clearance is obtained. Tighten the jam nut and connect the clevis to the brake cross-shaft.

REMOVAL AND INSTALLATION

Models 1020, 1220, 1320, 1330, 1420, 1430, 1720 and 1730

To remove the hydrostatic unit, raise and support the rear of the tractor. Disconnect the brake control rod and the transmission speed control rod. Remove the knob from the dump valve rod. Remove the drive belt from the transmission input pulley. Remove the transmission mounting bolts and axle housing U-bolts. Roll the transmission assembly rearward from the tractor.

Unbolt and separate the hydrostatic unit from the differential housing. Note that the couplings on the hydrostatic input and output shafts are held in place with Loctite. It may be necessary to heat the couplings and use a puller to remove the couplings from the shafts.

Install the transmission by reversing the removal procedure. Adjust the brake linkage and speed control linkage when necessary.

Models 1340, 1440, 1541, 1641 and 1860

Disconnect the hydraulic lines from the hydrostatic unit to the hydraulic lift valve if so equipped. Detach the drive shaft from the transmission as described in the DRIVESHAFT section. Disconnect the brake rod from the transaxle. Disconnect the transmission suction line. Remove the cam bracket mounting bolts and move the cam bracket and linkage up out of the way. Unbolt the hydrostatic transmission from the differential housing and remove the unit.

Install the hydrostatic transmission by reversing the removal procedure. Adjust the brakes and control linkage when necessary.

OVERHAUL

Models 1340, 1440, early 1541 and 1860 are equipped with a Sundstrand 15 series U-type hydrostatic transmission. Models 1020, 1220, 1320, 1330, 1420, 1430, later 1541, 1641, 1720 and 1730 are equipped with a Hydro-Gear BDU-10S series hydrostatic transmission. Refer to the appropriate Hydro-Gear or Sundstrand section in the HYDROSTATIC TRANSMISSION SERVICE section for overhaul procedure.

DIFFERENTIAL AND REDUCTION GEAR

LUBRICATION

Models 1020, 1220, 1320, 1330, 1420, 1430, 1720 and 1730

A Hydro-Gear 210-1010S transaxle is used on these models. Refer to the Hydro-Gear section in the REDUCTION GEAR AND DIFFERENTIAL SERVICE section for lubrication information.

Models 1340, 1440, 1541, 1641 and 1860

The differential housing contains oil that is also routed to the hydrostatic transmission. Maintain the oil level in the differential housing at the proper mark on the oil dipstick. The oil should be replaced annually. Refill with 14 pints (6.6 L) of Cub Cadet Transmission Hydraulic Fluid.

OVERHAUL

Models 1020, 1220, 1320, 1330, 1420, 1430, 1720 and 1730

Remove the hydrostatic drive unit and transaxle as previously outlined in the HYDROSTATIC TRANSMISSION section. Separate the hydrostatic unit from the transaxle housing. Remove the wheel and hub assemblies from the axles.

A Hydro-Gear 210-1010S transaxle is used on these models. Refer to the Hydro-Gear section in the REDUCTION GEAR AND DIFFERENTIAL SERVICE section for overhaul procedure.

Assemble the hydrostatic unit on the reduction gear housing and tighten the mounting bolts to 80-120 in.-lbs. (9.0-13.6 N.m).

Models 1340, 1440, 1541, 1641 and 1860

Remove the transmission as outlined in the HYDROSTATIC TRANSMISSION section.

Drain the fluid from the differential and remove the axles and their carriers. Remove the left and right hearing cages (29—Fig. CC15) and note the thickness of each shim pack (31). Turn the differential assembly in the housing until it can be removed.

NOTE: It may be necessary on some models to remove one of the bearing cones (4 or 11) before the differential can be removed.

Remove the differential flange (5), snap rings (7), shaft (9) and spider gears (8). Remove the axle gears (10). The ring gear and case assembly (6) are serviced as an assembly only.

Remove the expansion plug (28) and snap ring (22), spacer (21), gear (20) and snap ring (19). Remove the bevel pinion shaft (12) from the housing (18). Remove the bearing cup (14) and shim pack (15).

To reassemble, install the differential assembly in the housing and adjust the preload on the bearings (4 and 11) by varying the thickness of shim packs (31) until a steady pull of 4 to 14 lbs (1.8 to 6.4 kg) is required to rotate the differential assembly (Fig. CC16). Remove the differential assembly, keeping the shim packs (31–Fig. CC15) with their respective bearing cage.

Install the differential and pinion shaft assemblies in the case. Paint the ring gear teeth with Prussian Blue and rotate the ring gear. Observe the contact pattern on the tooth surfaces. Refer to Fig. CC17. If the pattern is too low (pinion depth too great) as in B, remove shims (15—Fig. CC15) as necessary to correct the pattern. If the pattern is too high (pinion depth too shallow) as in C, add shims (15) to correct the pattern. Make certain the ring gear backlash is correct after each shim change. Adjust as necessary.

If a new bevel pinion shaft, transmission case or rear bearing and cup are installed, the pinion shaft bearing preload must be adjusted. The snap ring (27—Fig. CC15) is available in various thicknesses for adjustment purposes. Install a snap ring (27) that establishes a preload of 0.001-0.006 inch (0.03-0.15 mm).

Check the rolling torque required to turn the pinion. Adjust the thickness of the snap ring (27) as needed to obtain a rolling torque of approximately 2 in.-lb.

Install the pinion shaft and bearing assembly in the housing. Install the snap ring (19), gear (20), spacer (21) and snap ring (22). Install the cover (24), bearing cup (25) and bearing (26).

Install a snap ring that will allow 0.003 in. (0.0762 mm) pinion shaft end play. Snap rings are available in a variety of thicknesses. Install a new expansion plug (28).

Install the differential assembly and install a dial indicator to measure the ring gear backlash. Move the shims (31) from side to side until 0.003-0.008 in. (0.08-0.20 mm) backlash is obtained.

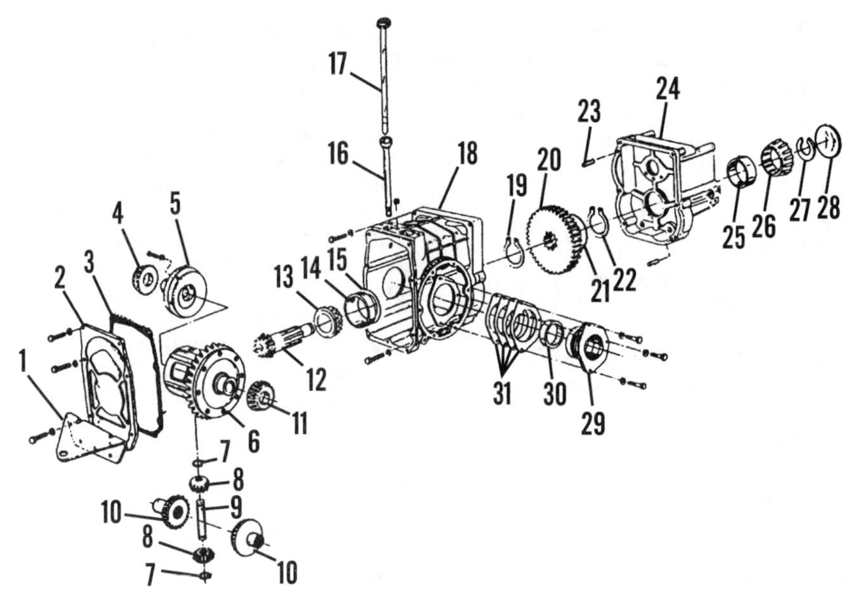

Fig. CC15–Exploded view of reduction gear and differential assembly used on Models 1340, 1440, 1541, 1641 and 1860.

1. Drawbar
2. Cover
3. Gasket
4. Bearing
5. Differential flange
6. Ring gear & carrier
7. Snap rings
8. Spider gears
9. Cross-shaft
10. Axle gears
11. Bearing
12. Pinion shaft
13. Bearing
14. Bearing cup
15. Shims
16. Dipstick tube
17. Dipstick
18. Case
19. Snap ring
20. Reduction gear
21. Spacer
22. Snap ring
23. Dowel pin
24. Cover
25. Bearing cup
26. Bearing
27. Snap ring
28. Expansion ring
29. Cage
30. Bearing cup
31. Shim pack

ELECTRIC PTO CLUTCH OVERHAUL (ALL MODELS SO EQUIPPED)

If the PTO clutch fails to engage, perform the following checks: Verify that voltage is present at the clutch electrical lead with the PTO switch engaged and the engine running. Refer to the wiring diagram and verify that the pto switch and other electrical components are operating properly.

Clutch coil resistance should be 2.4-3.4 ohms. Clutch coil current draw should be 3.5-4.0 amperes.

To remove the PTO clutch, disconnect the wire from the clutch. Remove bolt retaining the clutch and withdraw the clutch from the engine crankshaft. Remove the stud nuts (2—Fig. CC18) and separate the armature (4) and rotor (5) from the field coil (6).

To install the clutch, reverse the removal procedure. Adjust the clutch as follows: With the PTO switch OFF, insert a feeler gauge through each of the three slots (S—Fig. CC19) in the armature housing and measure the air gap between the armature and rotor. The air gap should be 0.010-0.025 inch (0.25-0.63 mm) and is adjusted by tightening or loosening the three stud nuts (2).

When the PTO clutch has been replaced, the clutch and brake friction surfaces should be burnished as follows: Run the engine at ½ throttle and engage and disengage the clutch five times (10 seconds on and 10 seconds off). Increase engine speed to ¾ throttle and engage and disengage the clutch five times.

Fig. CC16–Differential bearing preload is correct when a steady pull of 4 to 14 pounds (1.8 to 6.4 kg) on a spring scale is required to rotate differential assembly as shown.

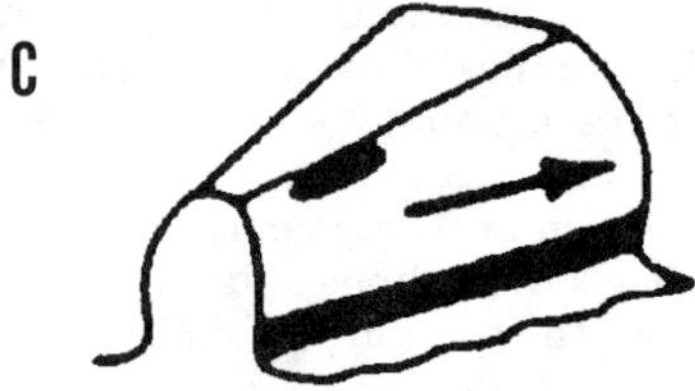

Fig. CC17–Bevel pinion tooth contact pattern is shown at "A", too low at "B" and too high at "C".

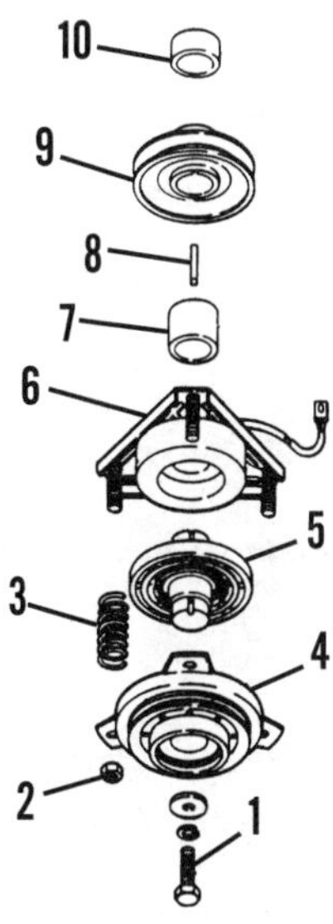

Fig. CC18–Exploded view of electric PTO clutch used on some models.

1. Retaining nut
2. Nut (3)
3. Spring (3)
4. Armature
5. Rotor
6. Coil assy.
7. Bushing
8. Key
9. Engine pulley
10. Spacer

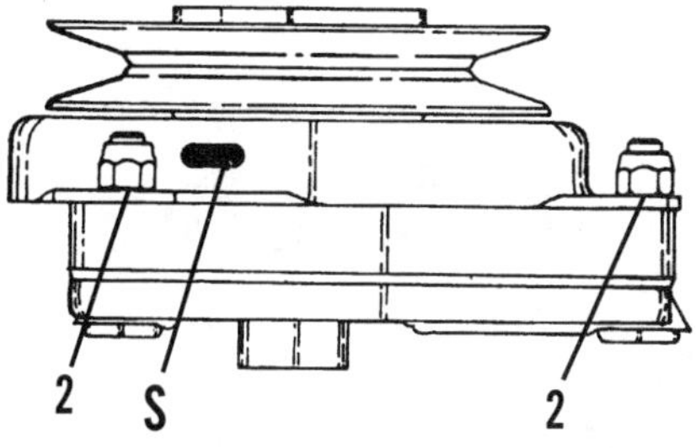

Fig. CC19–Check air gap setting between armature and rotor using a feeler gauge at the three slots (S) in cover. Specified gap is 0.010-0.025 inch (0.25-0.63 mm). Tighten or loosen mounting nuts (2) to obtain desired gap.

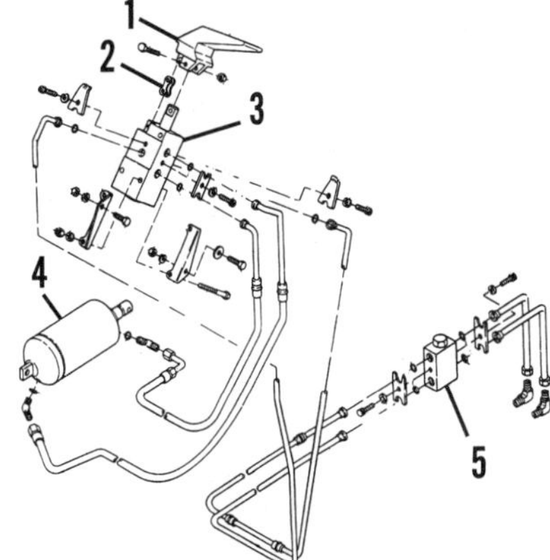

Fig. CC20–Exploded view of hydraulic lift components used on some models.

1. Operating level
2. Link
3. Control valve
4. Hydraulic cylinder
5. Relief valve

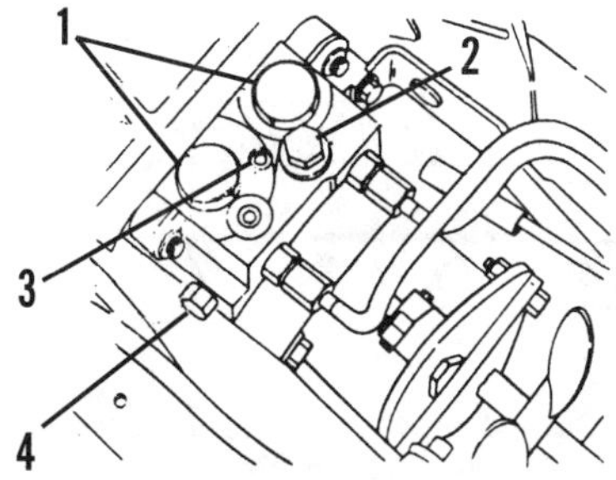

Fig. CC21–On models equipped with hydraulic lift, hydrostatic charge relief valve is located on right side of transmission center housing and lift relief valve is located on top of center housing.

1. Check valves
2. Hydraulic lift relief valve
3. Lift pressure test port
4. Charge relief valve

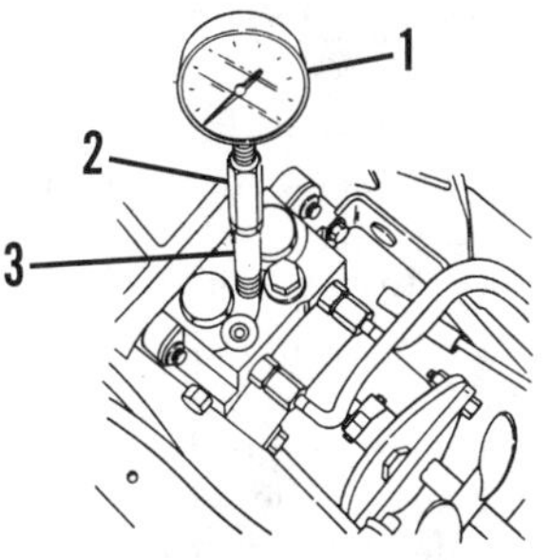

Fig. CC22–Install pressure gauge in center housing test port to check lift pressure.

1. Gauge
2. Adapter
3. Nipple

HYDRAULIC LIFT

OPERATION (ALL MODELS SO EQUIPPED)

The hydrostatic drive charge pump furnishes fluid to the hydraulic lift system. Refer to Fig. CC20 for a drawing of the hydraulic lift system. Refer to the HYDRAULIC TRANSMISSION section for fluid recommendation.

The charge pump relief valve is located on the right side of the transmission center housing under the plug (4—Fig. CC21). The hydraulic lift system relief valve is located on top of the center housing under the plug (2).

The lift relief valve regulates the hydraulic lift pressure at 500-625 psi (3450-4310 kPa). The single spool control valve is used to direct pressurized fluid to the double-acting lift cylinder.

PRESSURE CHECK AND ADJUSTMENT (ALL MODELS SO EQUIPPED)

To check hydraulic lift pressure, install a 1000 psi (7000 kPa) test gauge in the pressure test port as shown in Fig. CC22. Start the engine and operate at approximately ⅔ full engine rpm.

With the lift control valve in NEUTRAL, the test gauge should indicate charge pressure of 90-200 psi (620-1300 kPa). With the control valve in the raise position and the lift cylinder at the end of its stroke, the test gauge should indicate maximum lift pressure of 500-625 psi (3450-4310 kPa).

If the lift pressure is not within the specified range, remove the lift pressure relief valve and add or remove spring shims as required.

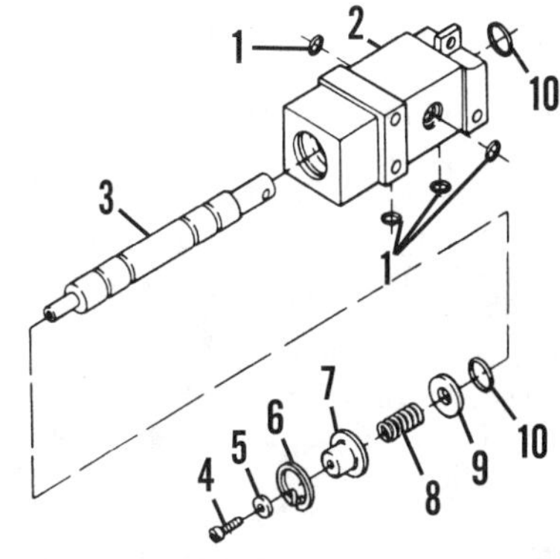

Fig. CC23–Exploded view of control valve.

1. O-rings
2. Body
3. Spool
4. Screw
5. Washer
6. Snap ring
7. Boot
8. Spring
9. Washer
10. O-ring

CONTROL VALVE OVERHAUL (ALL MODELS SO EQUIPPED)

Remove the side panels and battery to access the control valve. Make certain any mounted equipment is in the fully lowered position. Clean the valve and hydraulic lines to prevent dirt or foreign matter from entering the hydraulic system. Identify and disconnect the hydraulic lines from the valve. Unbolt and remove the valve assembly.

To disassemble the control valve, refer to Fig. CC23. Remove screw (4), washer (5) and snap ring (6). Remove the boot (7), spring (8) and washer (9). Withdraw the spool assembly.

Clean and inspect all parts for damage. If the spool (3) or valve body (2) is scored or otherwise damaged, replace the control valve as an assembly as the spool and body are not serviced separately.

When reassembling, use new O-rings and lubricate all parts with clean hydraulic fluid. To prevent internal damage to the O-rings during installation, proceed as follows. Install one O-ring on the rounded end of the spool. Insert the spool into the valve body until the O-ring groove on the flat end of the spool is just exposed (Fig. CC24). Install the remaining O-ring, then push the spool back into the body so it is in operating position.

After installing the control valve, start the engine and operate at approximately ⅔ full engine speed. Cycle the lift cylinder several times to expel air from the system and check for leaks. Check the fluid level in the differential housing and fill to the proper level with hydraulic fluid.

LIFT CYLINDER OVERHAUL (ALL MODELS SO EQUIPPED)

Remove the frame cover and right foot plate to access the hydraulic lift cylinder. Clean the cylinder and hydraulic lines to prevent dirt or foreign matter from entering the hydraulic system. Identify and disconnect the hydraulic lines from the cylinder. Remove the cylinder mounting bolt and pin and remove the cylinder.

Identify and remove the hydraulic fittings from the cylinder. To disassemble the hydraulic cylinder, secure the mounting end of the cylinder in a vise. Using a suitable spanner wrench with $\frac{3}{16}$-in. pins, rotate the cylinder head counterclockwise as shown in Fig. CC25 so the retaining wire is exposed. Pull the retaining wire out of the access slot while rotating the cylinder head. Remove the cylinder head. Note that the internal O-ring (5—Fig. CC26) may become wedged in the wire groove in the cylinder during cylinder head removal.

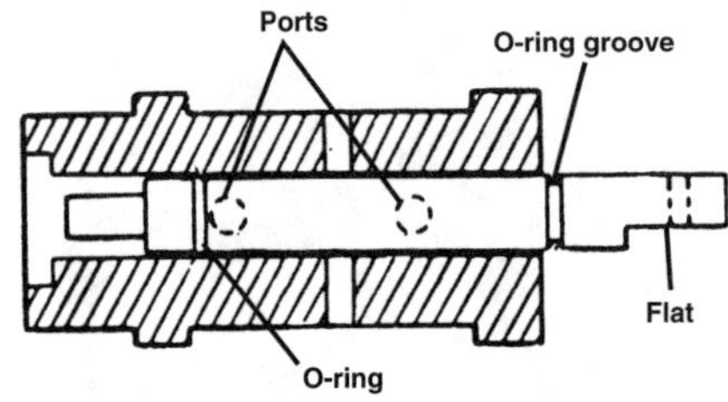

Fig. CC24–Follow procedure in text when installing spool and O-rings.

NOTE: If the O-ring catches in the wire groove in cylinder, insert a tool through the wire access slot and cut the O-ring.

Pull out the piston and rod. Discard the O-rings and seal. Inspect the components. The piston, rod and cylinder are available only as a unit assembly.

Lubricate all components with hydraulic fluid before assembly. To install the cylinder head, align the hole in the cylinder head with the wire access slot in the cylinder. Insert the retaining wire through the access slot and engage the hooked end of the wire in the hole in the cylinder head. Using a spanner wrench, turn the cylinder head clockwise so the wire is pulled completely into cylinder.

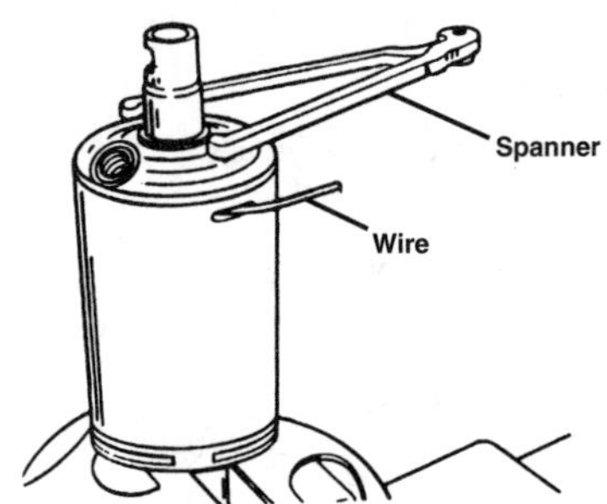

Fig. CC-25–Using a suitable spanner, rotate cylinder head as described in text to removing retaining wire.

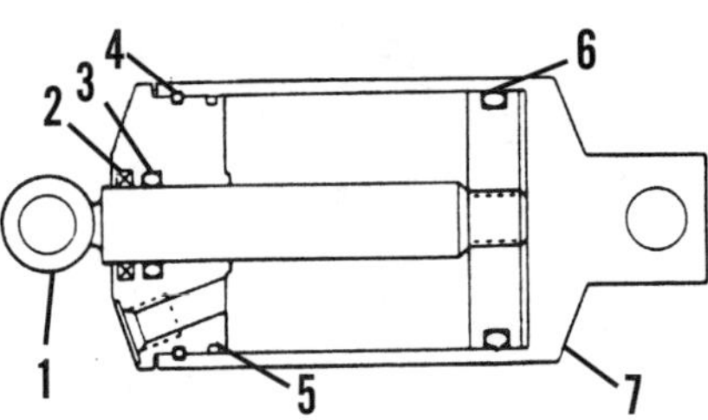

Fig. CC26–Cross sectional view of hydraulic cylinder.

1. Piston & rod
2. Seal
3. O-ring
4. Retaining wire
5. O-ring
6. O-ring
7. Cylinder

ELECTRICAL WIRING DIAGRAMS

Refer to Figs. CC27, CC28 and CC29 for typical wiring diagrams.

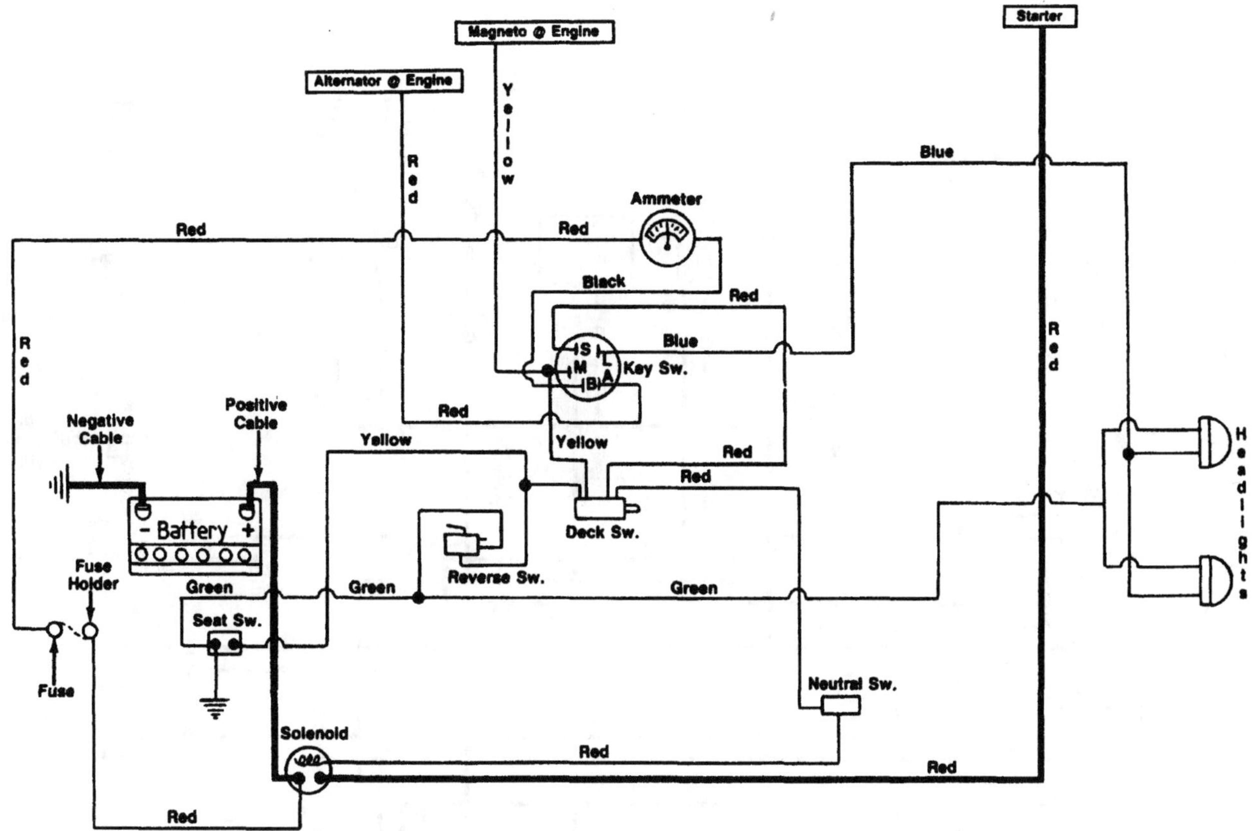

Fig. CC27–Electrical diagram for Models 1015, 1020, 1315 and 1320.

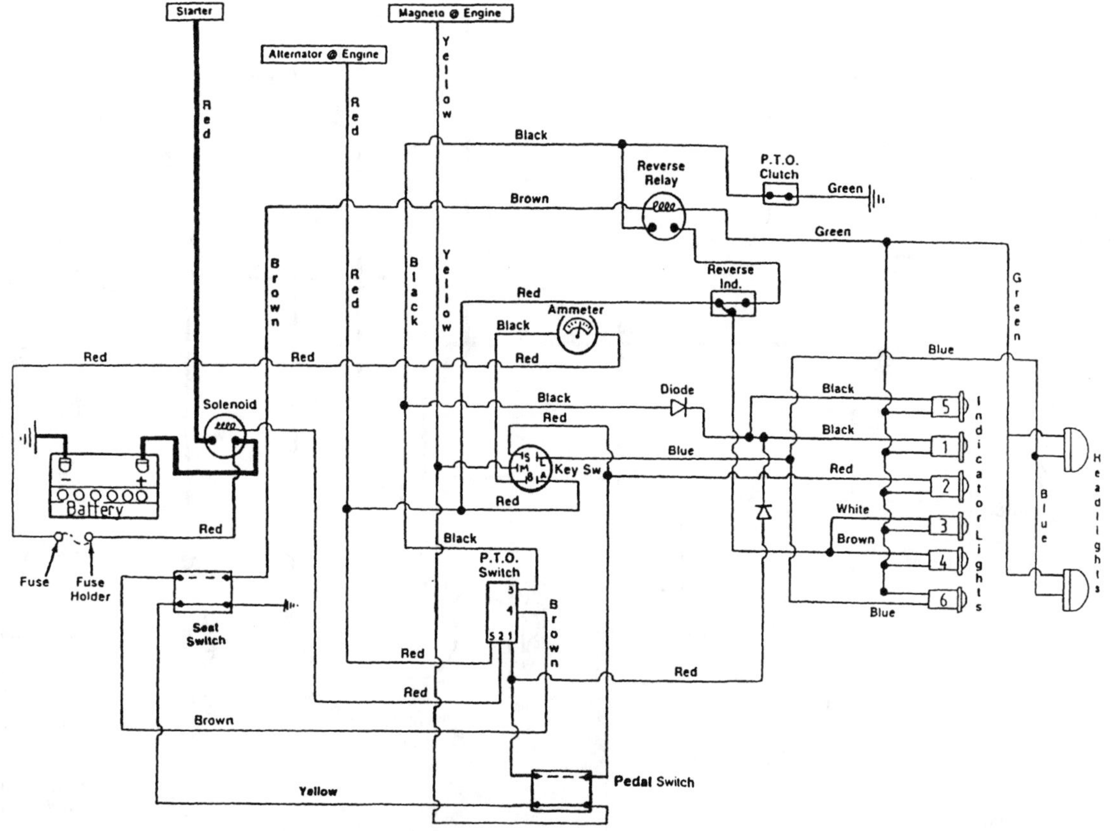

Fig. CC28–Electrical wiring diagram for Models 1405, 1420 and 1720.

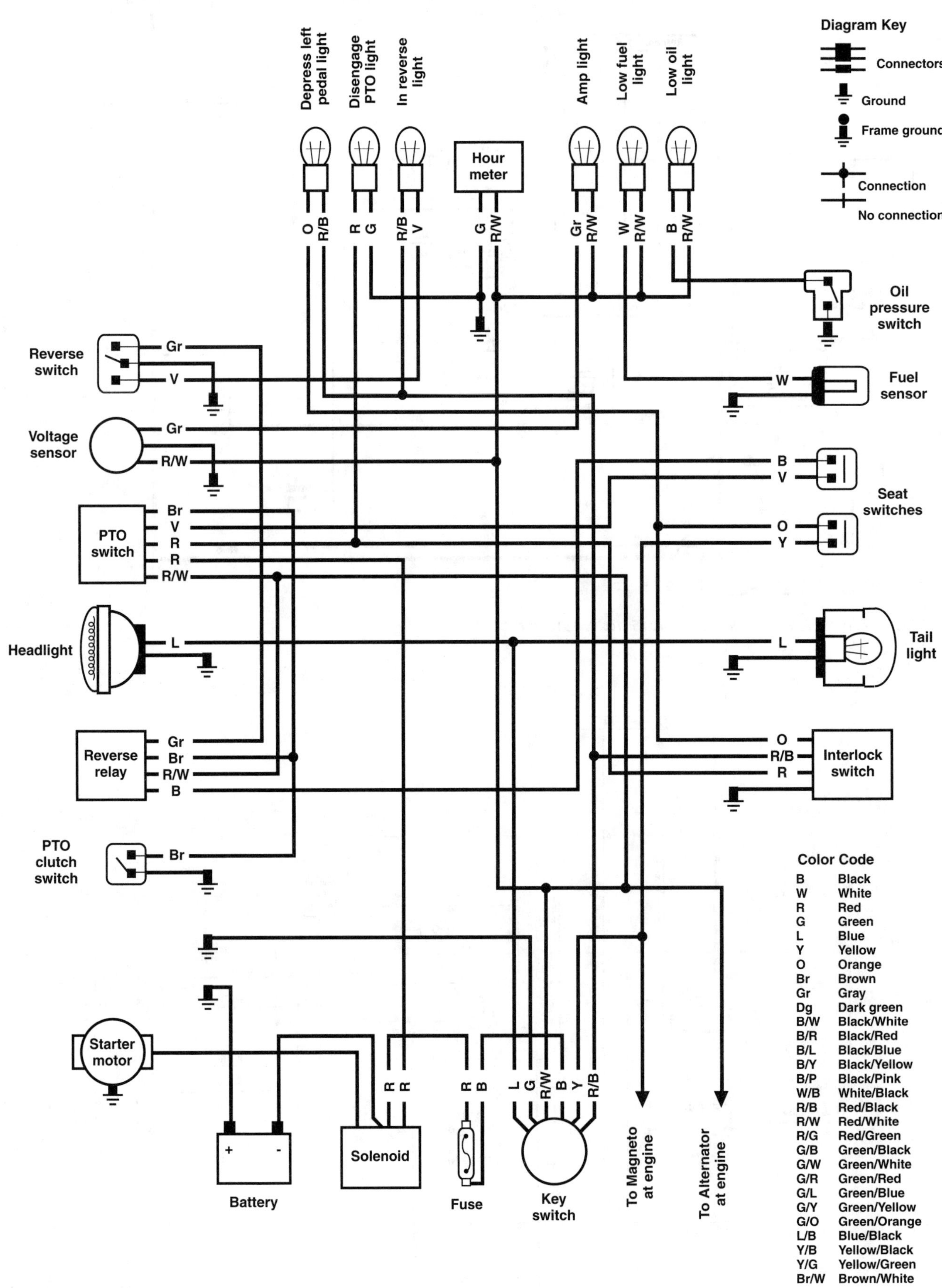

Fig. CC29–Electrical wiring diagram for Models 1340, 1541 and 1860.

CUB CADET

CONDENSED SPECIFICATIONS

Models	1862	1882	2082
Engine Make	Kohler	Kohler	Kohler
Model	M18	M18	M20
Number of cylinders.	2	2	2
Bore	3.12 in. (79.2 mm)	3.12 in. (79.2 mm)	3.12 in. (79.2 mm)
Stroke	2.75 in. (69.85 mm)	2.75 in. (69.85 mm)	3.06 in. (78.0 mm)
Displacement	42.18 cu. in. (691 cc)	42.18 cu. in. (691 cc)	46.98 cu. in. (769.8 cc)
Power Rating	18 hp (13.4 kW)	18 hp (13.4 kW)	20 hp (14.9 kW)
Slow Idle	1200 rpm	1200 rpm	1200 rpm
High Speed (No-Load)	3600 rpm	3600 rpm	3600 rpm
Crankcase Capacity	3 pt.* (1.4 L)	3 pt.* (1.4 L)	3 pt.* (1.4 L)
Transmission Capacity	**	**	**

*With filter—3.5 pt.(1.7 L).
**Refer to Hydrostatic Transmission section.

FRONT WHEELS

Lubricate the front wheel bearings after every 30 hours of operation. Inject No. 2 multipurpose grease into each wheel hub through the grease fitting on the wheel hub. Two or three shots from a hand-held grease gun should be sufficient.

The front wheels are equipped with replaceable bearings (1—Fig. CC101). To remove the bearings, raise and support the front of the tractor. Remove the hub cap (7) and bolt (6). Slide the wheel off the axle. Drive the bearings from the wheel using a long punch.

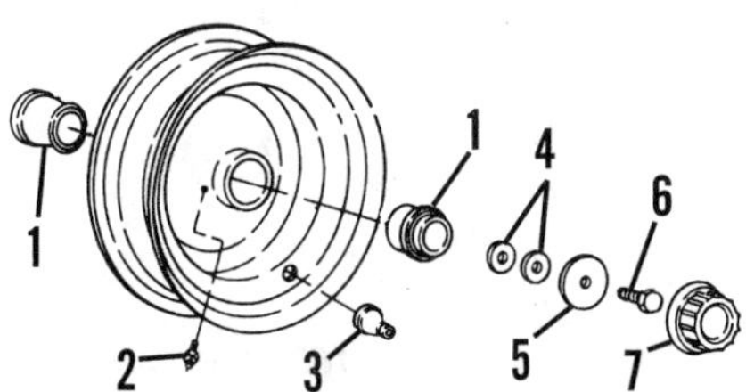

Fig. CC101-Exploded view of wheel assembly.

1. Bearing
2. Grease fitting
3. Air valve
4. Washers
5. Washer
6. Bolt
7. Hub cap

Lubricate the new bearings with grease prior to assembly. Press them into the wheel hub, applying force to the outer race only. Slide the wheel onto the axle and secure with the bolt and washers.

FRONT AXLE SYSTEM

AXLE MAIN MEMBER

The front axle main member is mounted directly on the main frame. The axle main member pivots on the center mounting pivot pin. Refer to Figs. CC102A and CC102B.

Lubricate the pivot pin bolt after every 10 hours of operation. Inject No. 2 multipurpose grease into the grease fitting on the axle main member. Two or three shots from a hand-held grease gun should be sufficient.

To remove the front axle main member assembly, raise and support the front of the tractor. Remove the front wheels. Disconnect the hydraulic steering cylinder from the steering arm. Remove the axle pivot pin bolt and lower the front axle assembly from the tractor.

To reinstall the axle main member, reverse the removal procedure. Lubricate the pivot pin by injecting multipurpose grease into the grease fitting on the axle main member.

TIE ROD AND CENTER STEERING LEVER

Front wheels should toe-in 1/32 to 1/8 inch (0.8-3.0 mm). To check the toe-in, position the wheels straight ahead and place a chalk mark at wheel hub height on each rim at points (A—Fig. C103). Measure the distance between the two points.

Move the tractor forward until the chalk marks are at points (B). Measure the distance between the two points. The distance between points (B) must be 1/32 to 1/8 inch (0.8-3.0 mm) less than the distance between points (A).

To adjust the toe-in on Model 1862, disconnect one tie rod ball joint from a steering spindle. Loosen the ball joint jam nuts, and turn the tie rod (22—Fig. CC102A) to shorten or lengthen it as necessary.

Adjust the toe-in on Models 1882 and 2082 by lengthening or shortening each of the two tie rods (16—Fig. CC102B) as necessary. Tie rods should be as nearly equal in length as possible.

Replace the tie rod ball joint ends if excessively worn. Refer to Fig. CC102A or CC102B.

Models 1882 and 2082 are equipped with a center steering lever (23—Fig. 102B). Lubricate the pivot pin after every 10 hours of operation. Inject No. 2 multipurpose grease into the grease fitting on the center steering lever. Two or three shots from a hand-held grease gun should be sufficient.

To remove the steering lever (23), disconnect the tie rod ends (17) and remove the snap ring (24). Withdraw the pivot pin (22) and lever.

STEERING SPINDLES

Lubricate the front wheel spindles after every 10 hours of operation or monthly, whichever occurs first. Inject No. 2 multipurpose grease into front axle main member through grease fitting at each end. Two or three shots from a hand-held grease gun should be sufficient. Check for looseness and binding in the front axle components.

To remove the steering spindles, refer to Fig. CC102A or CC102B. Raise and support the front of the tractor. Remove the front wheels. Disconnect the tie rod from the steering spindles. Disconnect the hydraulic cylinder rod end from the steering arm.

Remove the steering arm clamp bolt (8). Remove the left steering spindle retaining bolt and washer. Detach the steering arm from the steering spindle and remove the left spindle. Remove the bolt securing the right steering spindle and lower the spindle from the axle.

Inspect the spindles, axle, wheels and bearings for excessive wear and replace when necessary. Install the steering arm on the left spindle so the steering arm is 0-6° ahead of the axle as shown in Fig. CC104.

TILT STEERING

All models are equipped with a joint allowing relocation of the steering wheel. The joint connects the upper and lower steering shafts.

REMOVAL AND INSTALLATION

Remove the front side panels. Remove the battery. Remove the battery tray and adjoining panels.

Remove the steering wheel cover and retaining nut. Pull the steering wheel off the steering shaft. Remove the

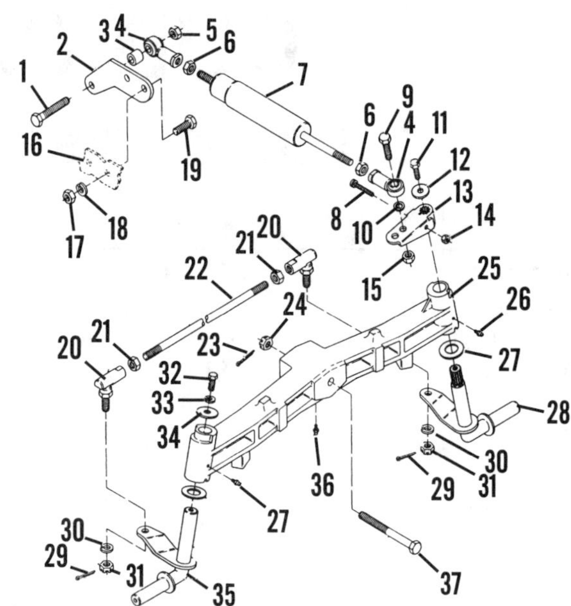

Fig. CC102A–Exploded view of front axle assembly used on Model 1862.

1. Bolt
2. Bracket
3. Spacer
4. Rod end
5. Locknut
6. Jam nut
7. Hydraulic cylinder
8. Bolt
9. Bolt
10. Washer
11. Bolt
12. Washer
13. Steering arm
14. Nut
15. Locknut
16. Frame
17. Nut
18. Lockwasher
19. Bolt
20. Rod end
21. Jam nut
22. Tie rod
23. Cotter pin
24. Nut
25. Axle main member
26. Grease fitting
27. Washer
28. Spindle (left)
29. Cotter pin
30. Lockwasher
31. Nut
32. Bolt
33. Lockwasher
34. Washer
35. Spindle (right)
36. Grease fitting
37. Pivot bolt

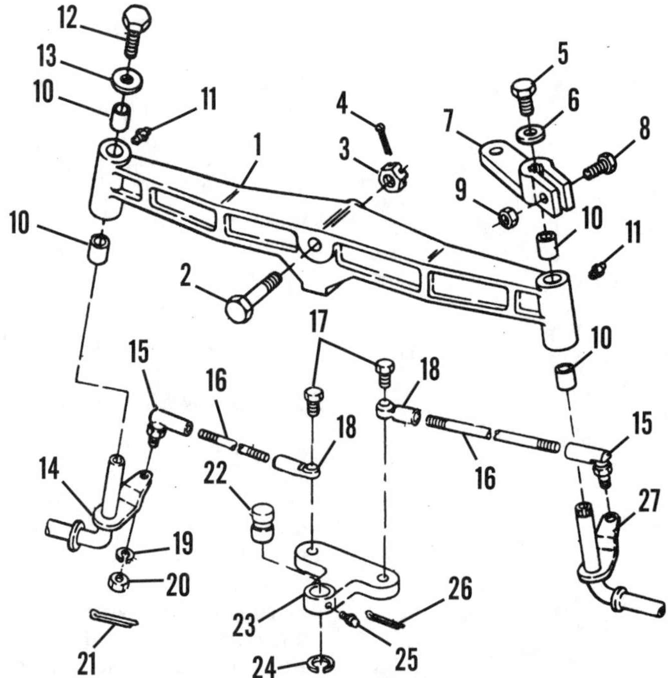

Fig. CC102B–Exploded view of front axle assembly used on Models 1882 and 2082.

1. Axle main member
2. Pivot bolt
3. Nut
4. Cotter pin
5. Bolt
6. Washer
7. Steering arm
8. Bolt
9. Locknut
10. Bushing
11. Grease fitting
12. Bolt
13. Washer
14. Spindle (right)
15. Rod end
16. Tie rod
17. Bolt
18. Rod end
19. Lockwasher
20. Nut
21. Cotter pin
22. Pivot pin
23. Center steering arm
24. Snap ring
25. Grease fitting
26. Cotter pin
27. Spindle (left)

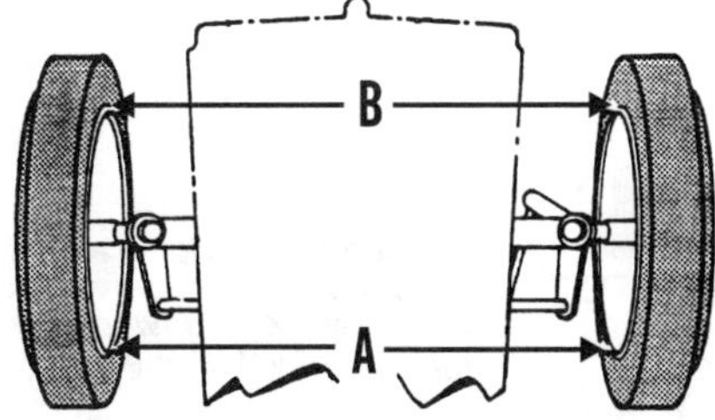

Fig. CC103–To check front wheel toe-in measure distance at points A and B.

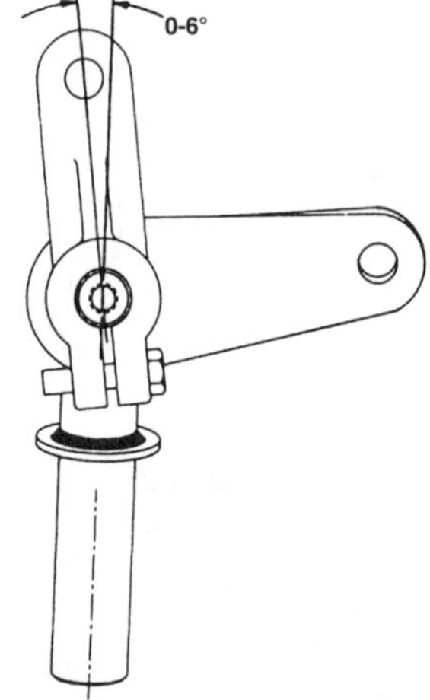

Fig. CC104–Install the steering arm on the left spindle so the steering arm is 0-6° ahead of the axle as shown.

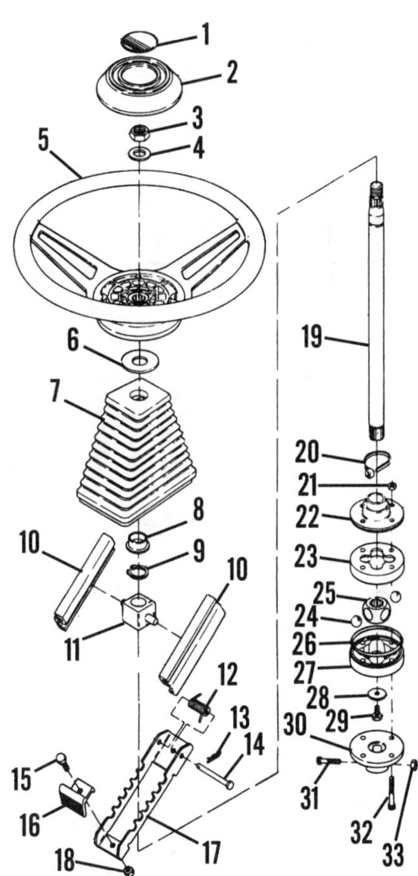

Fig. CC105–Exploded view of tilt steering assembly used on all models.

1. Label
2. Cap
3. Nut
4. Washer
5. Steering wheel
6. Washer
7. `Boot
8. Flange bushing
9. Snap ring
10. Guides
11. Guide bushing
12. Torsion spring
13. Cotter pin
14. Clevis pin
15. Screw
16. Tilt control button
17. Tilt control plate
18. Locknut
19. Upper steering shaft
20. Tie strap
21. Locknut
22. Boot
23. Upper drive coupling
24. Ball
25. Drive hub
26. O-ring
27. Lower drive coupling
28. Washer
29. Screw
30. Steering adapter
31. Bolt
32. Bolt
33. Locknut

washer (6—Fig. CC105) and steering shaft boot (7).

Remove the joint retaining bolt (31). Remove the joint housing bolts (32). Remove the lower joint housing (30). Remove the screw (29), washer (28), lower drive coupling (27), balls (24), drive hub (25), upper drive coupling (23) and boot (22). Remove and discard the O-ring (26).

NOTE: Early models may not be equipped with an O-ring (26). If desired, early models may be upgraded by installing couplings (23 and 27) equipped with an O-ring groove.

CAUTION: Torsion spring (12) is under tension. Wear safety glasses when removing or installing the spring.

Remove the cotter pin (13), clevis pin (14) and torsion spring (12). Remove the tilt control button (16) and tilt control plate (17). Remove the shaft guide bushing (11) and guides (10).

Inspect all components and replace if excessively worn.

Assemble the drive hub (25), without the balls, and the drive couplings (23 and 27). The drive hub must move freely in the drive couplings without grabbing. Inspect the balls for nicks, galling or other damage. Complete the installation by reversing the removal procedure.

POWER STEERING SYSTEM

Pressurized oil from the hydrostatic drive unit is supplied to a steering control valve and cylinder to provide power steering. Refer to section on HYDROSTATIC TRANSMISSION for maintenance and service information on hydrostatic unit.

STEERING CONTROL VALVE OVERHAUL

To remove the control valve, remove the hood and side panels. Remove the battery and battery tray. Remove the connector bolt (31—Fig. CC105) located in the bottom of the steering adapter.

Remove the screen from the tractor frame and place a suitable container under the tractor to catch hydraulic fluid. Identify then disconnect the hydraulic lines from the bottom of the steering control valve. Cap the openings to prevent the entrance of dirt or foreign matter. Remove the control valve support plate (1—Fig. CC106). Remove the side bracket (3). Remove the steering control valve.

NOTE: Do not clamp the steering control valve in a vise for service work. Fabricate a holding fixture as shown in Fig. CC107.

Before disassembling the steering valve, note the alignment grooves machined in the side of the unit. All marked components must be reinstalled in their original positions.

Place the steering valve in the holding fixture with the steering shaft down and secure with 5/16-24 NF nuts. Remove the four nuts securing the port cover (4—Fig. CC108) and remove the cover. Remove the sealing ring (6) and five O-rings (5). Remove the plug (1) and ball (3). Remove the port manifold (7) and the three springs (8). Remove the valve ring (9) and discard the sealing rings (6).

Remove the valve plate (11) and the three springs (10) from the isolation manifold pockets. Remove the hex drive

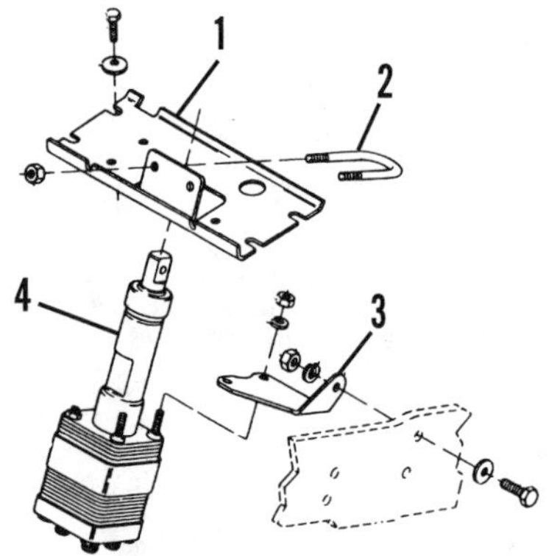

Fig. CC106–Exploded view of power steering mounting brackets.

1. Support plate
2. U-bolt
3. Bracket
4. Power steering control valve

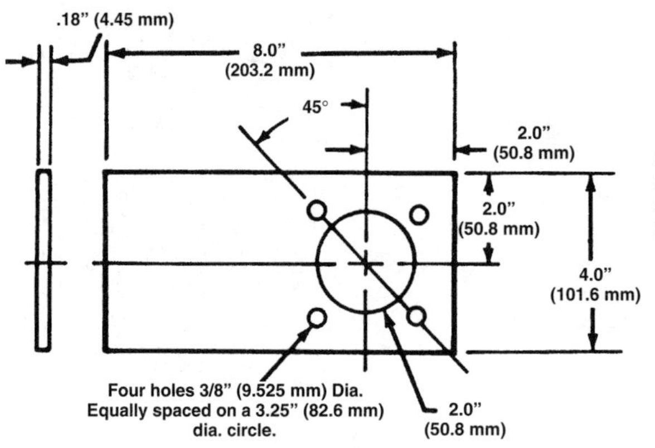

Fig. CC107–Fabricate a holding fixture as shown to aid service work on power steering control valve used.

and pin assembly (12), then remove the isolation manifold (14). Remove the drive link (15), metering ring (16) and seal rings (6).

Lift off the metering assembly and remove the commutator seal (18). Remove the 11 Allen head screws (17) and lift off the commutator cover (19). Remove the commutator ring (20), then carefully remove the commutator (21) and the five alignment pins (22). Remove the drive link spacer (23) and separate the rotor (24) from the stator (25).

Remove the drive plate (26), spacer (27), thrust bearing (28), seal spacer (31), face seal back-up ring (30) and face seal (29). Remove the upper cover plate (32). Remove the steering shaft (36) and service the retainer plate (35), upper bushing (38) and seal (39) as necessary.

Clean and inspect all parts and replace any showing signs of damage. Springs (8) should have a free length of 0.75 inch (19 mm) and springs (10) should have a free length of 0.50 inch (12.7 mm). Springs must be replaced as sets only.

The commutator (21) and commutator ring (20) are a matched set and must be replaced as an assembly. Check the rotor to stator clearance using a feeler gauge as shown in Fig. CC109. If rotor height is 1.0 inch (25.4 mm) or more and clearance exceeds 0.005 inch (0.13 mm), replace the rotor and stator assembly. If rotor height is 0.75 inch (19 mm) or less and clearance exceeds 0.003 inch (0.08 mm), replace the rotor and stator assembly. Replace all seals and O-rings and lubricate all parts with clean hydraulic fluid prior to installation.

Reassemble by reversing the disassembly procedure and referral to the following notes: Be sure the alignment grooves on the upper cover plate (32–Fig. CC108), isolation manifold

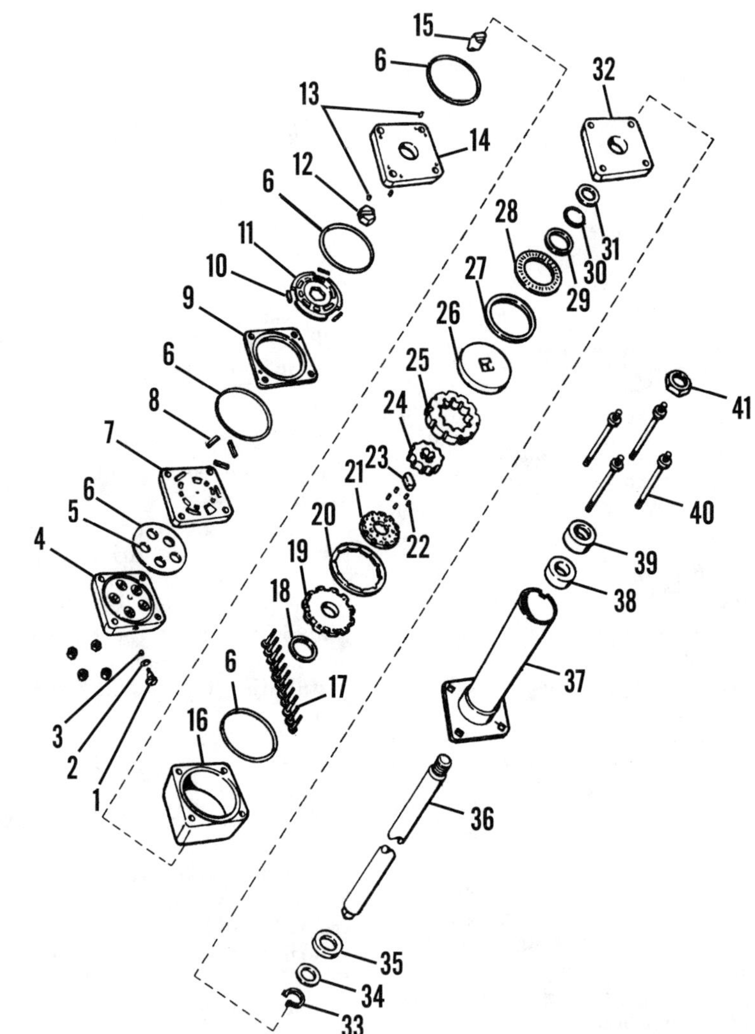

CC108–Exploded view of power steering control valve used on models equipped with power steering.

1. Plug
2. O-ring
3. Ball
4. Port cover
5. O-rings
6. Seal rings
7. Port manifold
8. Springs
9. Valve ring
10. Springs
11. Valve plate
12. Hex drive assy.
13. Alighment pins (2)
14. Isolation manifold
15. Drive link
16. Metering ring
17. Screws
18. Commutator seal
19. Commutator cover
20. Commutator ring
21. Commutator
22. Alignment pins (5)
23. Drive link spacer
24. Rotor
25. Stator
26. Drive plate
27. Spacer
28. Thrust bearing
29. Face seal
30. Back-up ring
31. Seal spacer
32. Upper cover plate
33. Snap ring
34. Washer
35. Retainer
36. Steering shaft
37. Steering tube
38. Bearing
39. Dust seal
40. Special bolts
41. Nut

Fig. CC109–Use a feeler gauge to check rotor to stator clearance. Refer to text.

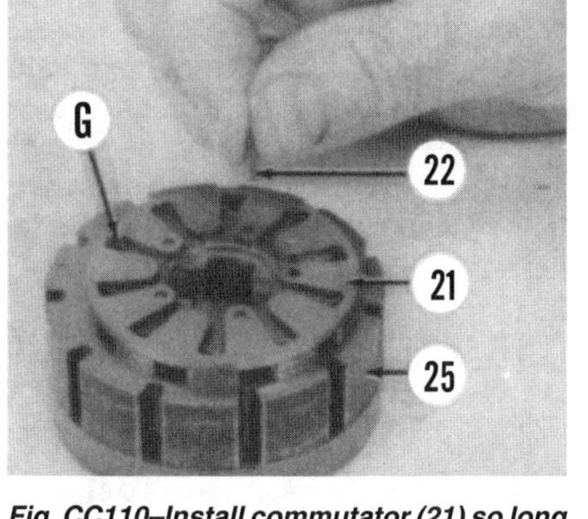

Fig. CC110–Install commutator (21) so long grooves (G) are out.

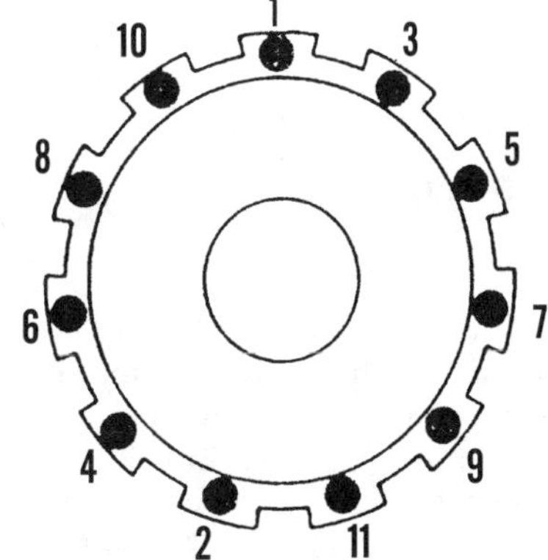

Fig. CC111–Tighten the eleven Allen head screws in metering assembly to 11-13 in.-lb. (1.24-1.47 N•m) in sequence shown. Refert to text.

(14) and port manifold (7) are on the same side. Install the rotor (24) so the pin holes are out. Install the commutator so the long grooves (G) are out as shown in Fig. CC110. When installed, the pins (22) must not protrude above the face of the commutator (21).

Apply low strength thread-locking solution to the screws (17) and install the screws finger tight. Insert the me-

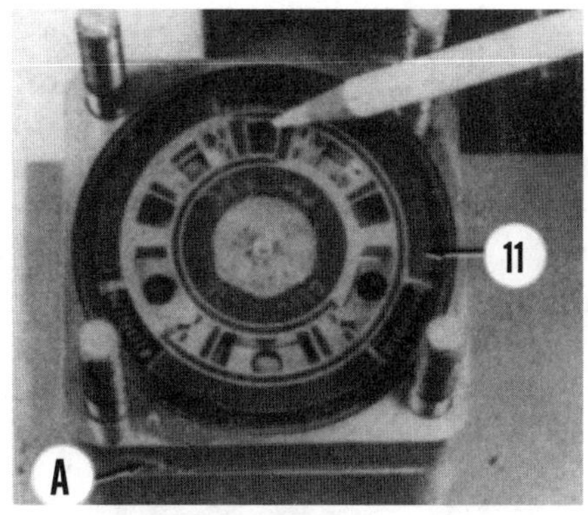

Fig. CC112–Install valve plate (11) so "PORT SIDE" on plate is opposite from alignment grooves (A) on isolation manifold.

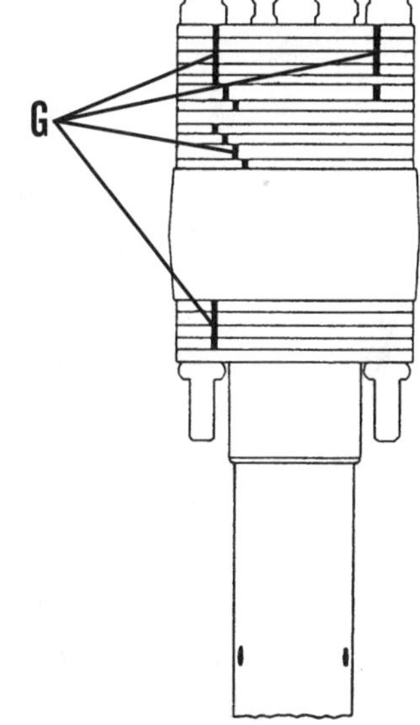

Fig. CC113–Components of steering control valve having alignment grooves (G) must be positioned as shown, or unit will not operate correctly.

tering valve assembly in the metering ring (16—Fig. CC108) with the commutator cover (19) facing downward. Place a suitable size wood block under the metering valve assembly so the drive plate (26) is partially out of the metering ring. Make six shims that are 0.007 inch thick, 1/2-inch wide and 1 1/2 inches long. Insert shims between the drive plate and metering ring so two shims abut every 120°. Remove the wood block and push the metering valve down until the drive plate is flush with the surface of the metering ring. Tighten the screws (17) in several steps to final torque of 11-13 in.-lb. (1.24-1.47 N·m) using the sequence shown in Fig. CC111.

The commutator ring (20—Fig. CC108) should now be concentric

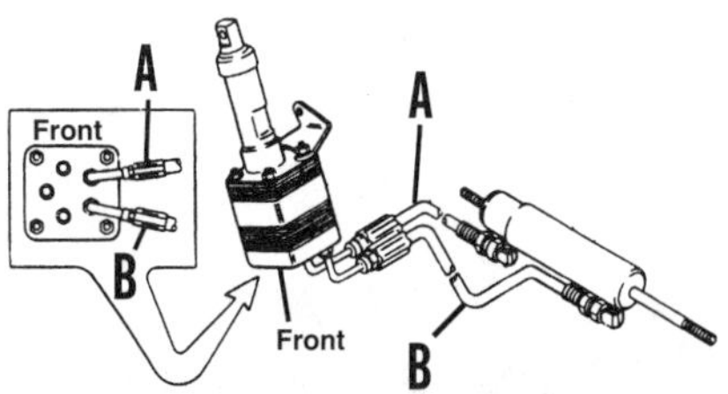

Fig. CC114–Diagram showing routing of hydraulic lines from control valve to hydraulic steering cylinder. If unit is equipped with a hydraulic lift system, refer to CC115 for routing.

within 0.005 inch (0.127 mm) of the drive plate (26). Insert the large tang end of the drive link (15) into the slot in the rotor (24) and rotate the metering assembly to make certain the parts do not bind.

Install the commutator seal (18) so the yellow mark on the seal is towards the commutator cover (19). Be sure the 1/2 inch (13 mm) springs (10) are installed in the isolation manifold (14) and the 3/4 inch (19 mm) springs (8) are installed in the port manifold (7).

Install the valve plate (11) so the spring slot with the smallest cavity and the words "PORT SIDE" are positioned opposite from the alignment grooves (A) on the isolation manifold as shown in Fig. CC112. Tighten the valve assembly nuts in a crossing pattern to 18-22 ft.-lb. (24-30 N·m). Tighten the plug (1—Fig. CC108) to 97-151 in.-lb. (11-17 N·m). Make sure that all parts with alignment grooves are aligned as shown in Fig. CC113, otherwise the unit will not operate correctly.

To reinstall the steering control valve, reverse the removal procedure. Refer to Figs. CC114 and CC115 when connecting the hydraulic lines. Start the engine and turn the steering wheel from full left to full right several times to bleed air from the system.

STEERING CYLINDER REMOVAL AND INSTALLATION

Refer to Fig. CC102A and CC116. Turn the steering wheel fully to the right. Mark the hydraulic hose locations prior to disconnecting the hoses. After disconnecting the hoses, plug the opening to prevent dirt from entering the system.

Disconnect the steering cylinder from the steering arm and the anchor bracket. The steering cylinder used on all models is a welded assembly and must be replaced as a complete unit.

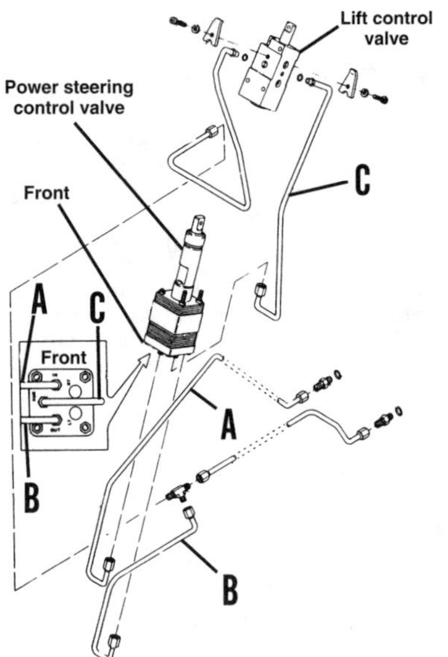

Fig. CC115–Diagram showing routing of hydraulic lines on models equipped with a hydraulic lift system.

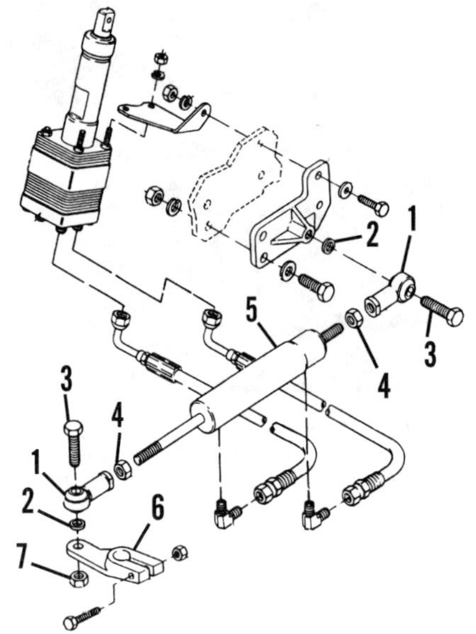

Fig. CC116–Exploded view of typical hydraulic steering cylinder installation.

1. Rod end
2. Washer
3. Bolt
4. Jam nut
5. Hydraulic cylinder
6. Steering arm
7. Locknut

ENGINE

REMOVAL AND INSTALLATION

To remove the engine, first disconnect the battery ground cable. Disconnect the headlight wiring and remove the grille housing, hood and side panels. Remove the battery. Remove battery tray and adjoining panels.

Disconnect the starter wires, charging wires, electric clutch wires, ignition wires and ground wires. Disconnect the choke and throttle linkage. Disconnect the fuel line.

Detach the driveshaft from the engine as described in the DRIVESHAFT section. Remove the engine mounting bolts. Slide the engine forward and use a suitable hoist to lift the engine from the frame.

Install by reversing the removal procedure.

OVERHAUL

The engine make and model are listed at the beginning of this section. To overhaul engine components and accessories, refer to the KOHLER or BRIGGS & STRATTON section of this manual.

DRIVESHAFT REMOVAL AND INSTALLATION

Open the hood and remove the side panels. Remove the frame cover. Remove the engine coupling screws (7—Fig. CC117). Remove the tie strap (2) and slide the driveshaft coupling away from the engine.

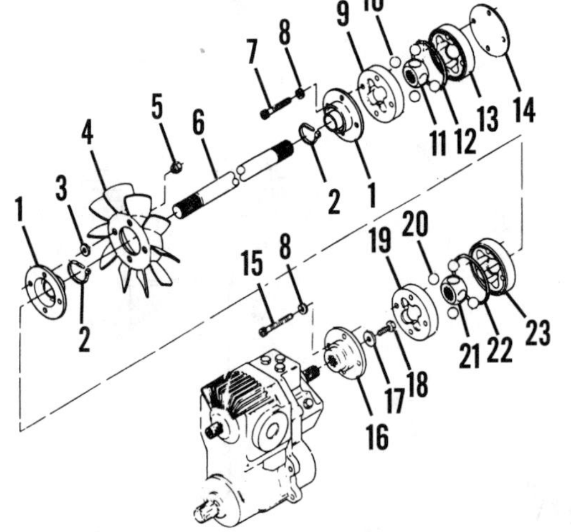

Fig. CC117–Exploded view of driveshaft assembly.

1. Boot
2. Tie strap
3. Washer
4. Fan
5. Nut
6. Driveshaft
7. Bolt
8. Lockwasher
9. Coupling
10. Ball
11. Drive hub
12. O-ring
13. Coupling
14. Adapter
15. Bolt
16. Adapter
17. Washer
18. Screw
19. Coupling
20. Ball
21. Drive hub
22. O-ring
23. Coupling

Remove the coupling components (1, 9, 10, 11, 12, 13 and 14) from the driveshaft. Set aside the coupling components for inspection. Withdraw the driveshaft from the rear coupling.

NOTE: Early models may not be equipped with O-rings (12 or 22). If desired, early models may be upgraded by installing coupling halves equipped with an O-ring groove.

Remove the fan retaining nuts (5) and remove the fan (4). Remove the washers (3) and tie strap (2). Remove the boot (1).

Remove the rear coupling components (23, 22, 21, 20 and 19). Set aside the coupling components for inspection. Remove the screw (18) and drive flange (16) from the hydrostatic pump shaft.

Inspect all components for damage.

Assemble the drive hub (11 or 21), without the balls, and drive coupling halves. The drive hub must move freely in the drive couplings without grabbing. Inspect the balls for damage.

Reassemble the driveshaft and joints by reversing the disassembly procedure. Pack the drive couplings with CV joint grease during assembly.

BRAKES

MODEL 1862

Adjustment

The brakes should engage when the gap from the brake pedal lever to the pedal lock tab is no more than one inch. To adjust the brakes, block the front

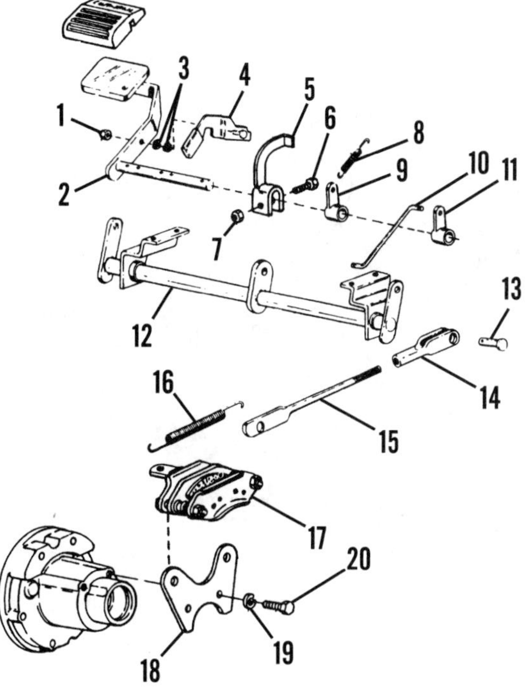

Fig. CC118–Exploded view of brake control linkage used on Model 1862.

1. Locknut
2. Brake pedal
3. Wave washers
4. Parking brake bracket
5. Start switch bracket
6. Bolt
7. Locknut
8. Spring
9. Brake lever
10. Rod
11. Brake lever
12. Pivot shaft
13. Clevis pin
14. Rod end
15. Brake rod
16. Spring
17. Caliper assy.
18. Mounting bracket
19. Lockwasher
20. Bolt

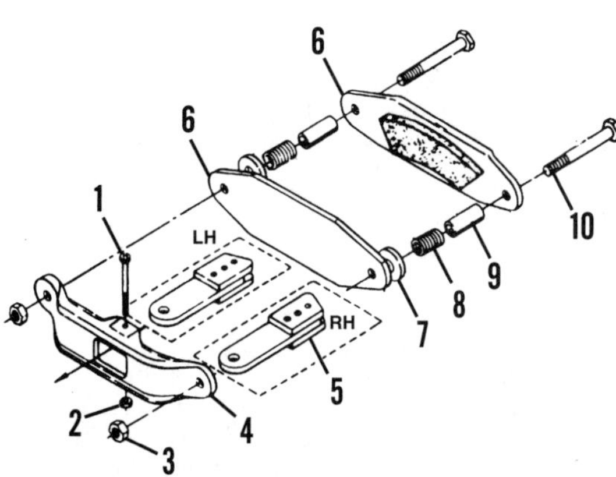

Fig. CC119–Exploded view of brake caliper assembly. Note installation direction of actuating cam (5) used on left side (LH) or right (RH) side brake assembly.

1. Bolt
2. Nut
3. Nut
4. Cam bracket
5. Actuating cam
6. Pad
7. Washer
8. Spring
9. Spacer
10. Bolt

wheels so the tractor cannot move. Raise and support the rear of the tractor so the rear wheels can rotate freely. Disconnect the brake rod (15—Fig. CC118) on each side. Shorten or lengthen the brake rod as required by rotating the clevis (14).

Brakes must have equal stopping action at both wheels. With the rear wheels supported off the ground, start the engine and operate in forward gear. Apply the brakes. If one wheel stops sooner than the other wheel, adjust the brake rod on the wheel that does not stop until both wheels stop simultaneously.

Overhaul

The brakes are mechanically actuated and located at the end of both rear axles. The brakes are disc type with brake pads contacting a disc attached to the wheel hub and axle.

To disassemble, raise and support the rear of the tractor. Remove the rear wheels and disconnect the brake rod (15—Fig. CC118). Remove the bolts attaching the brake assembly to the mounting bracket (18).

Inspect parts (Fig. CC119) for wear and replace when necessary. Reverse the removal procedure to install the brakes. Adjust as previously outlined.

MODELS 1882 AND 2082

These models are equipped with three brake pedals—two pedals provide differential braking while another pedal engages both brakes and acts as the parking brake.

Adjustment

To check brake adjustment, engage the pedal latch on the right side brake pedals. The brakes should engage when the gap from the left-side brake pedal lever to the pedal parking lock tab is no more than one inch.

To adjust the brakes, block the front wheels so the tractor cannot move. Raise and support the rear of the tractor so the rear wheels can rotate freely. Disconnect the brake rod (19—Fig. CC120) on each side. Shorten or lengthen the brake rod as required by rotating the clevis (17).

Brakes must have equal stopping action at both wheels. With the rear wheels supported off the ground, start the engine and operate in forward gear. Apply the brakes. If one wheel stops sooner than the other wheel, adjust the brake rod on the wheel that does not stop until both wheels stop simultaneously.

Overhaul

The mechanically actuated brakes are located at the end of both rear axles. The brakes are disc type with brake pads contacting a disc attached to the wheel hub and axle.

To disassemble, raise and support the rear of the tractor. Remove the rear wheel and disconnect the brake rod (19—Fig. CC120). Remove the bolts attaching the brake assembly (20) to the mounting bracket (21).

Inspect parts (Fig. CC119) for excessive wear and replace when necessary. Reverse the removal procedure to install the brakes. Adjust as previously outlined.

HYDROSTATIC TRANSMISSION

LUBRICATION

These models are equipped with either a Hydro-Gear or Sundstrand hydrostatic transmission. The transmission uses oil contained in the differential housing. The oil filter should be replaced after 50 and 100 hours of initial operation. Thereafter, replace the filter after every 100 hours of operation or annually, whichever occurs first. Also refer to the DIFFERENTIAL AND REDUCTION GEAR section.

LINKAGE ADJUSTMENT

Speed Control Lever Adjustment

Speed control lever should require a pulling force of 3-5 lbs. (1.4 to 2.3 kg) to move the control lever. To adjust, remove the left side engine panel and tighten the friction control nut (7—Fig. CC121) to increase the pulling force or loosen it to decrease the lever friction.

Cam Bracket Adjustment

If the tractor creeps when the speed control lever is in neutral position or if the linkage has been removed and is being reinstalled, adjust the brake pedal and speed control lever, then raise and support the tractor so the rear tires are off the ground. Block the front wheels so the tractor cannot move.

Remove the frame cover and lubricate the T-slot (T—Fig. CC121). Move the speed control lever to fast forward position. Loosen the cam bracket mounting bolts and move the cam bracket (26) to its highest position in the slotted holes and tighten the bolts slightly to retain in this position. Start the engine and use a punch and hammer to adjust the cam bracket downward until the wheels stop turning.

CAUTION: Use caution when working near rotating tires or parts.

Move the speed and directional control lever to the forward position. Depress the brake pedal and lock in this position. If there is excessive transmission noise or vibration with the brake pedal depressed, adjust the cam bracket to a position where the noise or vibration stops. Release the brake and shut off the engine.

Move the speed control lever to the fast forward position and tighten the cam bracket retaining bolts. Start the engine, move the speed control lever to the fast forward position, depress the brake pedal fully and release. The wheels should stop turning and the speed control lever should return to neutral.

If the speed control lever is not in NEUTRAL, loosen the jam nut on the neutral return rod and adjust until the lever is in NEUTRAL. Tighten the jam nut.

The speed control nod should not touch the end of the slot when the brake pedal is fully depressed. If the rod touches, disconnect the clevis from the brake cross shaft, loosen the jam nut and lengthen the rod until clearance is obtained. Tighten the jam nut and connect the clevis to the brake cross shaft.

Removal and Installation

Detach the driveshaft from the transmission as described in the DRIVESHAFT section. Disconnect the hydraulic lines from the hydrostatic unit to the hydraulic lift valve if so equipped. Disconnect the brake rod from the transaxle. Disconnect the transmission suction line. Remove the cam bracket mounting bolts and move the cam bracket and linkage up out of the way. Unbolt the hydrostatic transmission from the differential housing and remove the unit.

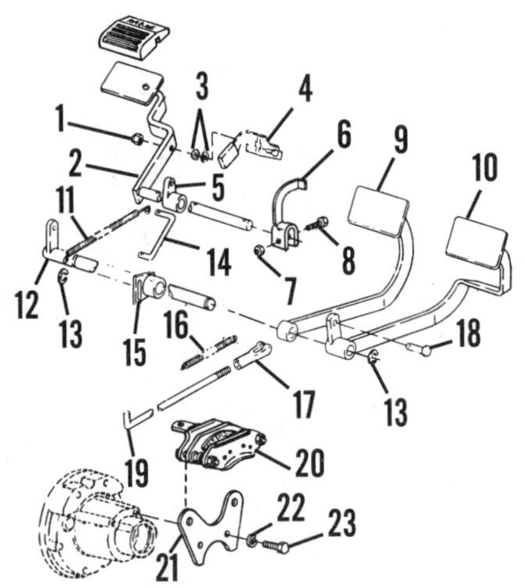

Fig. CC120–Exploded view of brake control linkage used on Models 1882 and 2082.

1. Locknut
2. Brake pedal
3. Wave washer
4. Parking brake latch
5. Brake lever
6. Start switch bracket
7. Locknut
8. Bolt
9. Brake pedal (left)
10. Brake pedal (right)
11. Spring
12. Cross-shaft
13. Snap ring
14. Link
15. Parking brake arm
16. Spring
17. Rod end
18. Clevis pin
19. Brake rod
20. Caliper assy.
21. Mounting bracket
22. Lockwasher
23. Bolt

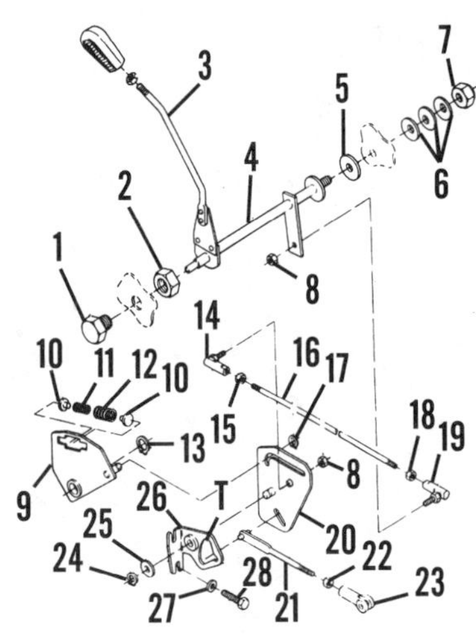

Fig. CC121–Exploded view of hydrostatic transmission control linkage.

1. Cross-shaft bearing
2. Nut
3. Speed control lever
4. Cross-shaft
5. Friciton disc
6. Belleville washers
7. Nut
8. Nut
9. Damper spring plate
10. Damper spring guide pin
11. Damper spring (light)
12. Damper spring (heavy)
13. Snap ring
14. Ball joint
15. Jam nut
16. Linkage shaft
17. Snap ring
18. Jam nut
19. Ball joing
20. Cam bracket assy.
21. Rod
22. Jam nut
23. Ball joint
24. Snap ring
25. Washer
26. Bracket
27. Washer
28. Bolt
T. T-slot

Install the hydrostatic transmission by reversing the removal procedure. Adjust the brakes and control linkage as necessary.

OVERHAUL

The unit may be equipped with either a Hydro-Gear or Sundstrand hydrostatic transmission. Refer to the appropriate Hydro-Gear or Sundstrand section in the HYDROSTATIC TRANSMISSION SERVICE section for overhaul procedure.

DIFFERENTIAL AND REDUCTION GEAR

LUBRICATION

The differential housing contains oil that is also routed to the hydrostatic transmission. Maintain the oil level in the differential housing at the proper mark on the oil dipstick. The oil should be replaced annually. Refill with 14 pints (6.6 L) of Cub Cadet Transmission Hydraulic Fluid.

OVERHAUL

Remove the transmission as outlined in the HYDROSTATIC TRANSMISSION section. Drain the fluid from the differential and remove the axles and their carriers. Remove the left and right bearing cages (29—Fig. CC122) and note the thickness of each shim pack (31). Turn the differential assembly in the housing until it can be removed.

NOTE: It may be necessary on some models to remove one of the bearing cones (4 or 11) before the differential can be removed.

Remove the differential flange (5), snap rings (7), shaft (9) and spider gears (8). Remove the axle gears (10). The ring gear and case assembly (6) are serviced as an assembly only.

Remove the expansion plug (28) and snap ring (22), spacer (21), gear (20) and snap ring (19). Remove the bevel pinion shaft (12) from the housing (18). Remove the bearing cup (14) and shim pack (15).

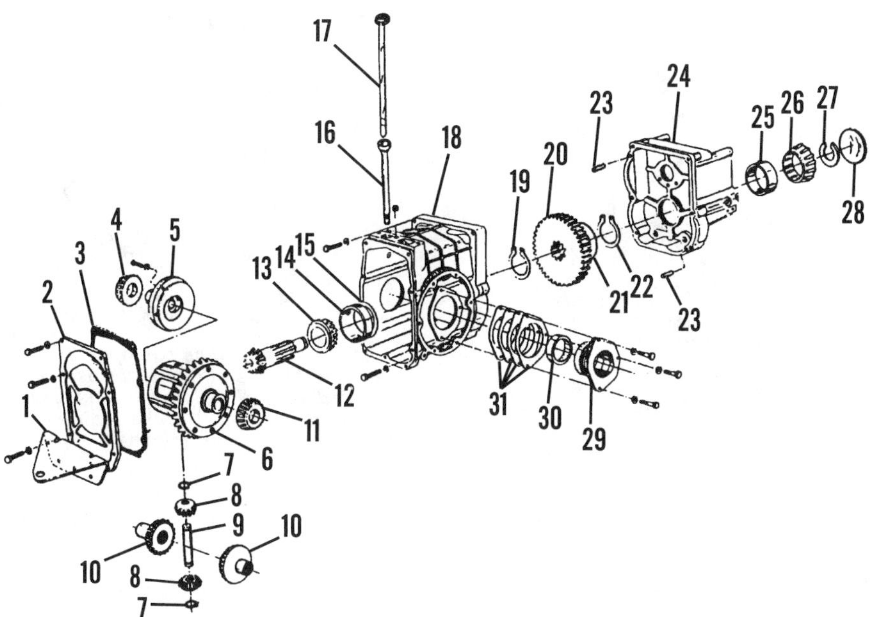

Fig. CC122–Exploded view of reduction gear and differential assembly.

1. Drawbar
2. Cover
3. Gasket
4. Bearing
5. Differntial flange
6. Ring gear & carrier
7. Snap rings
8. Spider gears
9. Cross-shaft
10. Axle gears
11. Bearing
12. Pinion shaft
13. Bearing
14. Bearing cup
15. Shims
16. Dipstick tube
17. Dipstick
18. Case
19. Snap ring
20. Reduction gear
21. Spacer
22. Snap ring
23. Dowel pin
24. Cover
25. Bearing cup
26. Bearing
27. Snap ring
28. Expansion plug
29. Cage
30. Bearing cup
31. Shim pack

Fig. CC123–Differential bearing preload is correct when a steady pull of 4 to 14 pounds (1.8 to 6.4 kg) on a spring scale is required to rotate differential assembly as shown.

To reassemble, install the differential assembly in the housing and adjust the preload on the bearings (4 and 11) by varying the thickness of the shim packs (31) until a steady pull of 4-14 pounds (1.8 to 6.4 kg) is required to rotate the differential assembly (Fig. CC123). Remove the differential assembly keeping each shim pack (31) with its respective bearing cage.

Install the differential and pinion shaft assemblies in the case. Paint the ring gear teeth with Prussian Blue and rotate the ring gear. Observe the contact pattern on the tooth surfaces. Refer to Fig. CC124. If the pattern is too low (pinion depth too great) as B, remove shims (15—Fig. CC122) as necessary to correct the pattern. If the pattern is too high (pinion depth too shallow) as C, add shims (15) to correct the pattern. Make certain the ring gear backlash is correct after each shim change. Adjust as necessary.

If a new bevel pinion shaft, transmission case or rear bearing and cup are installed, the pinion shaft bearing preload must be adjusted as follows: Different thickness snap rings (27—Fig. CC122) are available to adjust the preload. Install a snap ring (27) that establishes a preload of 0.001-0.006 inch (0.03-0.15 mm). Bearing preload is correct when a slight drag can be felt when rotating the pinion shaft (a rolling torque of approximately 2 in.-lb.). If the shaft spins freely, a thicker snap ring is required.

Fig. CC124–Bevel pinion tooth pattern is shown at "A", too low at "B" and too high at "C".

Install the pinion shaft and bearing assembly in the housing. Install snap ring (19), gear (20), spacer (21) and snap ring (22). Install cover (24), bearing cup (25), bearing cone (26) and snap ring (27). Install a new expansion plug (28).

Install the differential assembly and install a dial indicator to measure the ring gear-to-pinion backlash. Move shims (31) from side to side until 0.003-0.008 inch (0.08-0.20 mm) backlash is obtained.

ELECTRIC PTO CLUTCH OVERHAUL (ALL MODELS SO EQUIPPED)

If the PTO clutch fails to engage, perform the following checks: Verify that voltage is present at the clutch electrical lead with the PTO switch engaged and the engine running. If there is no voltage present, check that the PTO switch and other electrical components are operating properly.

If voltage is present, check the PTO clutch coil for proper operation. Clutch coil resistance should be 2.4-3.4 ohms. Clutch coil current draw should be 3.5-4.0A.

To remove the PTO clutch, disconnect the wire to the clutch. Remove the clutch retaining bolt and withdraw the clutch assembly from the engine crankshaft. Remove the stud nuts (2—Fig. CC125) and separate the armature (4) and rotor (5) from the field coil (6).

To reinstall the clutch, reverse the removal procedure. Adjust the clutch as follows: With the PTO switch OFF, insert a feeler gauge through each of the three slots (S—Fig. CC126) in the armature housing and measure the air gap between the armature and rotor. The air gap should be 0.010-0.025 inch (0.25-0.63 mm) and is adjusted by tightening or loosening the three stud nuts (2).

When the PTO clutch has been replaced, the clutch and brake friction surfaces should be burnished as follows: Run the engine at ½ throttle and engage and disengage the clutch five times (10 seconds on and 10 seconds off). Increase the engine speed to ¾ throttle and engage and disengage the clutch five times.

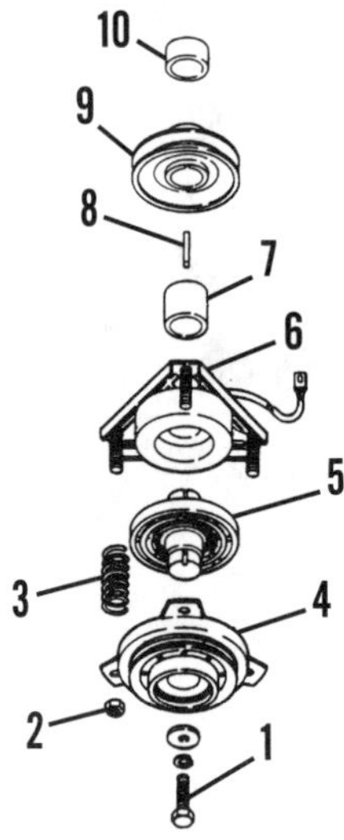

Fig. CC125–Exploded view of electric PTO clutch used on models so equipped.

1. Retaining bolt
2. Nut (3)
3. Spring (3)
4. Armature
5. Rotor
6. Coil assy.
7. Bushing
8. Key
9. Engine pulley
10. Spacer

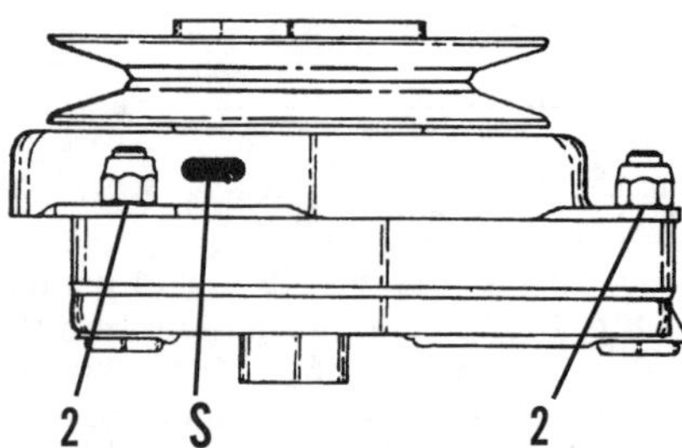

Fig. CC126–Check air gap between armature and rotor using a feeler gauge at the three slots (S) in cover. Specified gap is (0.010-0.025 inch (0.25-0.63 mm). Tighten or loosen mounting nuts (2) to obtain.

HYDRAULIC LIFT (ALL MODELS SO EQUIPPED)

The hydrostatic drive charge pump furnishes fluid to the hydraulic lift system (Fig. CC127). Refer to the HYDRAULIC TRANSMISSION section for lubricant information.

The charge pump relief valve is located on the right side of the transmission center housing under the plug (4—Fig. CC128). The hydraulic lift system relief valve is located on top of the center housing under the plug (2). The lift relief valve limits the pressure in the lift system to 500-625 psi (3450-4310 kPa). The single spool control valve (3—Fig. CC127) directs pressurized fluid to the double-acting lift cylinder (4).

PRESSURE CHECK AND ADJUSTMENT

To check the hydraulic lift pressure, install a 1000 psi (7000 kPa) test gauge in the pressure test port as shown in Fig. CC129. Start the engine and operate at approximately ⅔ full engine rpm.

With the lift control valve in neutral, the test gauge should indicate charge pressure of 90-200 psi (620-1300 kPa).

With the control valve in the raise position and the lift cylinder at the end of its stroke, the test gauge should indicate maximum lift pressure of 500-625 psi (3450-4310 kPa).

If the lift pressure is not within the specified range, remove the lift pressure relief valve and add or remove spring shims as required.

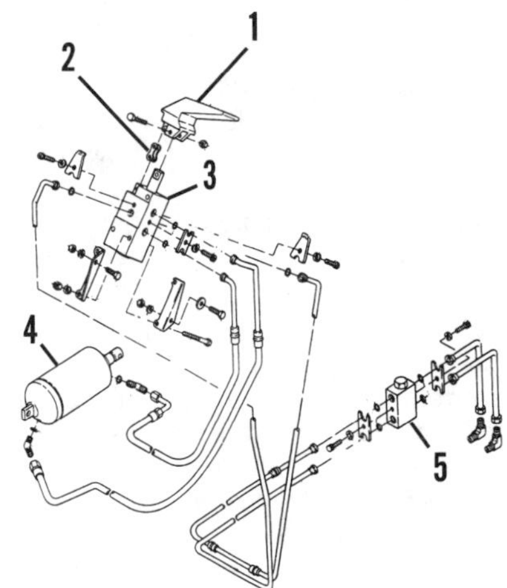

Fig. CC127–Exploded view of hydraulic lift components used on models so equipped.

1. Operating lever
2. Link
3. Control valve
4. Hydraulic cylinder
5. Relief valve

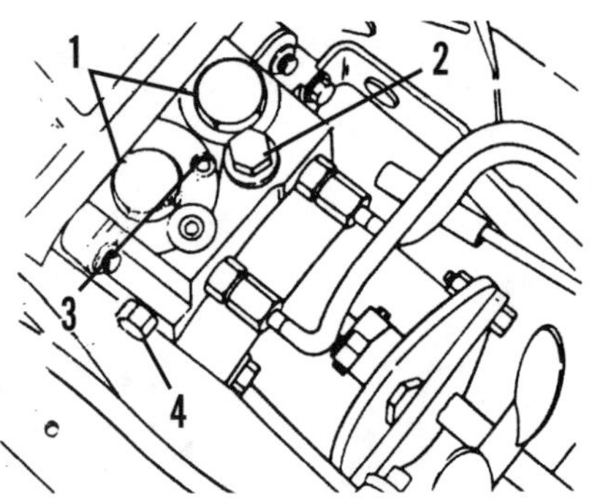

Fig. CC128—On models equipped with hydraulic lift, hydrostatic charge relief valve is located on right side of transmission center housing and lift relief valve is located on top of center housing.

1. Check valves
2. Hydraulic lift relief valve
3 1Lift pressure test port
4. Charge relief valve

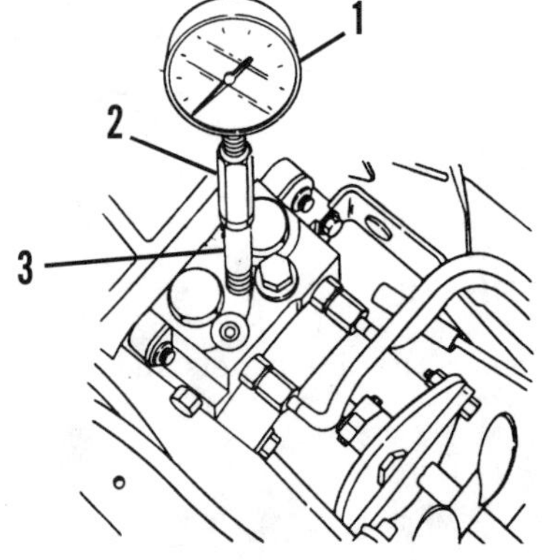

Fig. CC129–Install pressure gauge in center housing test port to check lift pressure.

1. Gauge
2. Adapter
3. Nipple

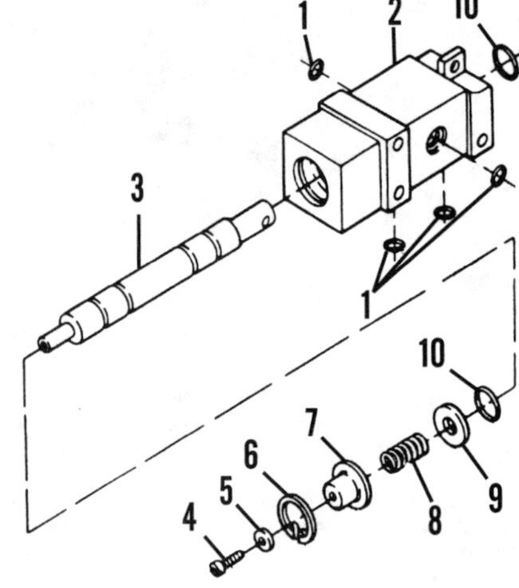

Fig. CC130–Exploded view of control valve.

1. Piston & rod
2. Body
3. Spool
4. Screw
5. Washer
6. Snap ring
7. Boot
8. Spring
9. Washer
10. O-rings

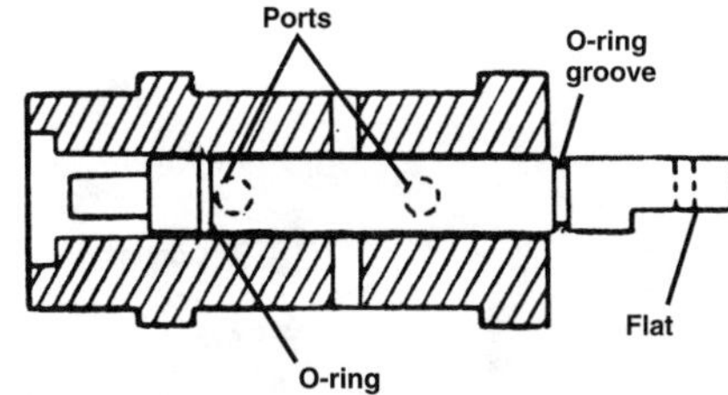

Fig. CC131–Follow procdure in text when installing spool and O-rings.

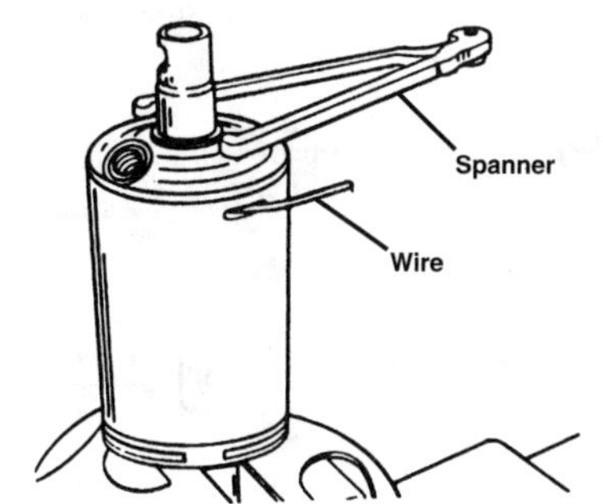

Fig. CC132–Using a suitable spanner, rotate cylinder head as described in text to remove retaining wire.

CONTROL VALVE OVERHAUL

Remove the side panels and battery for access to the control valve. Make certain any mounted equipment is fully lowered to relieve pressure in the hydraulic system. Clean the valve and hydraulic lines to prevent dirt or foreign matter from entering the hydraulic system. Identify and disconnect the hydraulic lines from the control valve. Unbolt and remove the valve assembly.

To disassemble the control valve, refer to Fig. CC130. Remove the screw (4), washer (5) and snap ring (6). Remove the boot (7), spring (8) and washer (9). Withdraw the spool assembly.

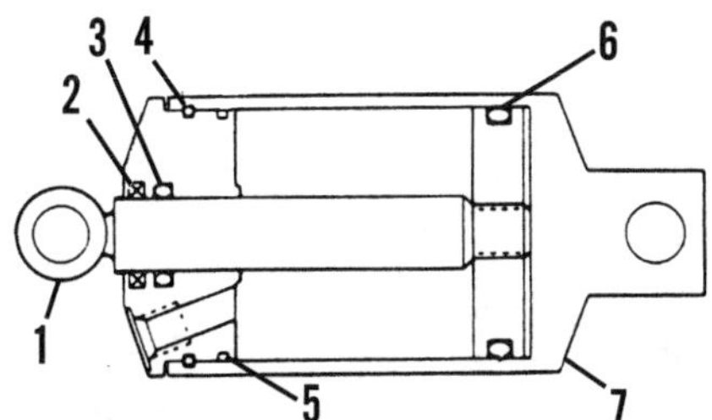

Fig. CC133–Cross-sectional view of hydraulic cylinder.

1. Piston & rod
2. Seal
3. O-ring
4. Retaining valve
5. O-ring
6. O-ring
7. Cylinder

Clean and inspect all parts for wear or other damage. If the spool (3) or valve body (2) is scored or otherwise damaged, replace the control valve assembly as the spool and body are not serviced separately.

When reassembling, use new O-rings and lubricate all parts with clean hydraulic fluid. To prevent damage to the O-rings during installation, proceed as follows. Install one O-ring on the rounded end of the spool. Insert the spool into the valve body until the O-ring groove on the flat end of the spool is just exposed (Fig. CC131). Install the remaining O-ring, then push the spool back into the body so it is in operating position.

After installing the control valve, start the engine and operate at approximately ⅔ throttle. Cycle the lift cylinder several times to expel air from the system and check for leaks. Check the fluid level in the differential housing and fill to the proper level with hydraulic fluid.

LIFT CYLINDER OVERHAUL

Remove the frame cover and right foot plate for access to the hydraulic lift cylinder. Clean the cylinder and hydraulic lines to prevent dirt or foreign matter from entering the hydraulic system. Identify and disconnect the hydraulic lines from the cylinder. Remove the cylinder mounting bolt and pin and remove the cylinder.

Identify and remove the hydraulic fittings from the cylinder. To disassemble the hydraulic cylinder, secure the mounting end of the cylinder in a vise. Using a suitable spanner wrench with ³⁄₁₆-inch pins, rotate the cylinder head counterclockwise as shown in Fig. CC132 so the retaining wire is exposed. Pull the retaining wire out of the access slot while rotating the cylinder head. When removing the cylinder head, the internal O-ring (5—Fig. CC133) may snag the wire groove in the cylinder and bind the cylinder head in the cylinder.

NOTE: If the O-ring catches in the wire groove in the cylinder, insert a tool through the wire access slot and cut the O-ring.

Pull out the piston and rod. Discard the O-ings and seal. Inspect components for wear. The piston, rod and cylinder are available only as a unit assembly.

Lubricate all components with hydraulic fluid before assembly.

To install the cylinder head, align the hole in the cylinder head with the wire access slot in the cylinder. Insert the retaining wire through the access slot and engage the hooked end of the wire in the hole in the cylinder head. Using a spanner wrench, turn the cylinder head clockwise so the wire is pulled completely into the cylinder.

ELECTRICAL WIRING DIAGRAM

Refer to Fig. CC134 for a wiring diagram typical of all models.

Figure CC134 is on the following page.

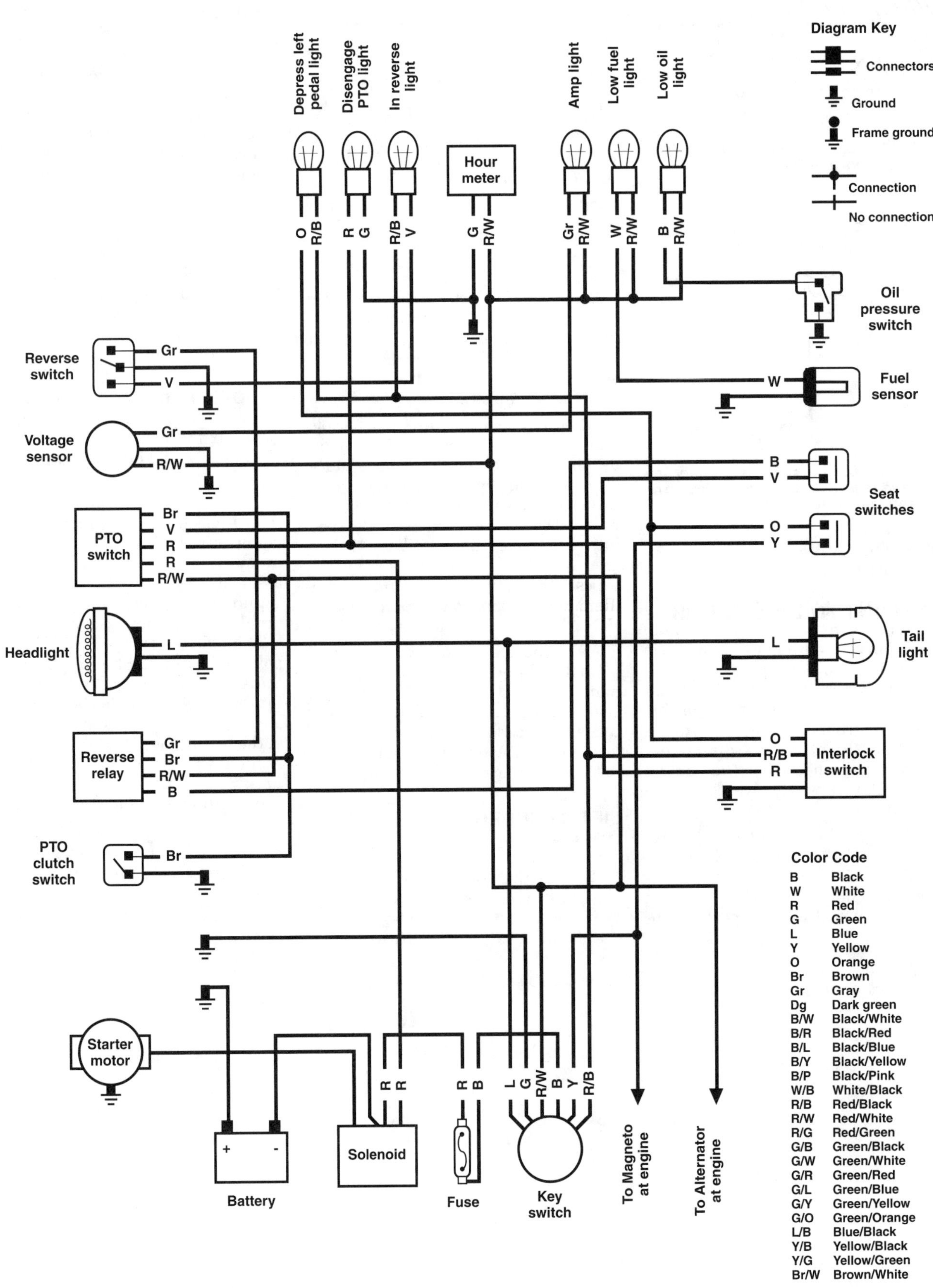

Fig. CC134–Typical electrical wiring diagram.

JOHN DEERE

CONDENSED SPECIFICATIONS

MODELS	STX30	STX38
Engine Make	Kohler	Kohler
Model	CV12.5S	CV12.5S
Bore	87 mm (3.425 in.)	87 mm (3.425 in.)
Stroke	67 mm (2.638 in.)	67 mm (2.638 in.)
Displacement	398 cc (24.3 cu. in.)	398 cc (24.3 cu. in.)
Rated Power	6.7 kW* (9 hp)	9.3 kW (12.5 hp)
Slow Idle Speed—rpm	1350	1350
High Idle Speed (No-Load)—rpm.....	3350	3350
Crankcase w/Filter Capacity	1.9 L (2 qt.)	1.9 L (2 qt.)
Fuel Tank Capacity	4.7 L 1.25 gal.)	4.7 L (1.25 gal.)

*7.5 kW (10 hp) on 1992 models.

FRONT AXLE SYSTEM

AXLE MAIN MEMBER REMOVAL AND INSTALLATION

To remove the front axle assembly, raise and support the front of the tractor. Remove the front wheels. Disconnect stabilizer arms from the axle. Disconnect the tie rods from the spindles. Unbolt and remove the muffler. Remove the axle pivot bolt (10—Fig. JD1-1) and lower the axle assembly (8) from the tractor. Remove the hub cap (1), snap ring (2) and wheel hubs (4) from the axle spindles.

Inspect the axle bushing (9) and pivot bolt (10) for damage and replace when necessary. Steering spindles (11) are not serviced separately. Axle assembly must be replaced if spindles or axle are damaged. Check wheel bearings (3) and wheel hub (4) for damage and replace when required.

To install axle assembly, reverse the removal procedure. Tighten axle pivot bolt to 54 N·m (40 ft.-lb.). Tighten tie rod retaining nuts to 22 N·m (16 ft.-lb.).

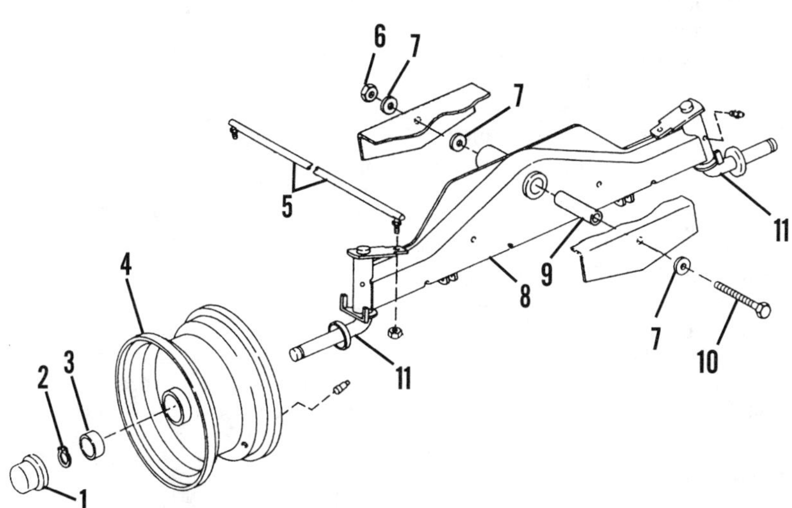

Fig. JD1-1–Exploded view of front axle assembly. Spindles (11) are not replaceable.

1. Cap
2. Snap ring
3. Bearing
4. Wheel hub
5. Tie rods
6. Nut
7. Washers
8. Axle main member
9. Pivot bushing
10. Pivot bolt
11. Spindles

STEERING GEAR

REMOVAL AND INSTALLATION

Remove the bolt (2—Fig. JD1-2) and steering wheel (1) from the steering shaft. Shut off the fuel and disconnect the fuel line at the filter. Disconnect the throttle control cable at the engine. Remove the dash retaining screws and remove the dash and fuel tank. Disconnect the tie rods from the steering sector gear (14). Remove the upper cotter pin (6) and washers (3, 4 and 5) from the steering shaft (7). Push the shaft down until the pinion gear (9) is accessible and remove the cotter pin (8), washers (10) and pinion gear.

NOTE: Washers (10), if used, are not interchangeable with other washers on the steering shaft. Later production tractors do not use washers (10).

Pull the steering shaft (7) up through the console. Remove the snap ring (11) and washers (12), then the withdraw sector gear (14).

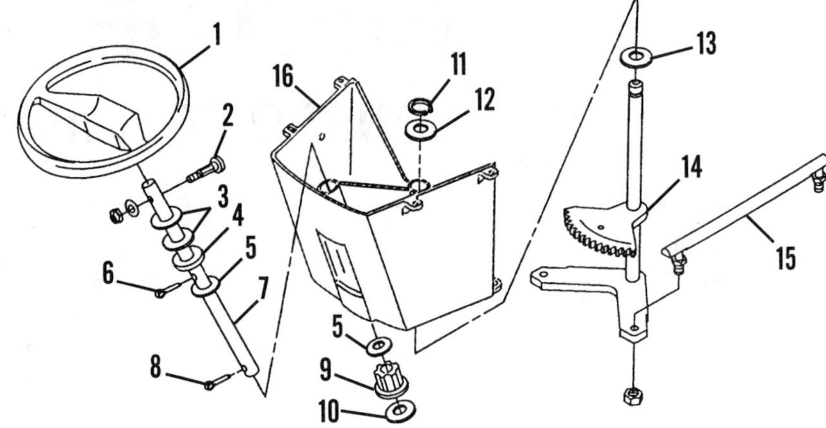

Fig. JD1-2–Exploded view of steering gear assembly. Washers (10) are not used on some tractors.

1. Steering wheel
2. Retaining bolt
3. Washers
4. Washer
5. Washer
6. Cotter pin
7. Steering shaft
8. Axle main member
9. Pinion gear
10. Washer
11. Snap ring
12. Washer
13. Washer
14. Sector gear & shaft
15. Tie rod (2 used)

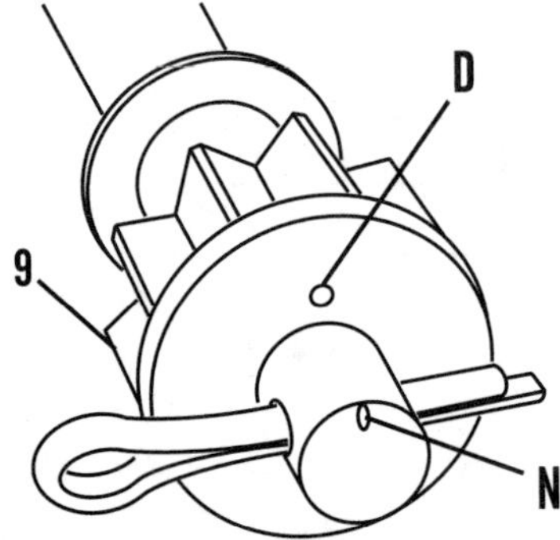

Fig. JD1-3–Dimple (D) on pinion gear (9) should be aligned with notch (N) in end of steering shaft.

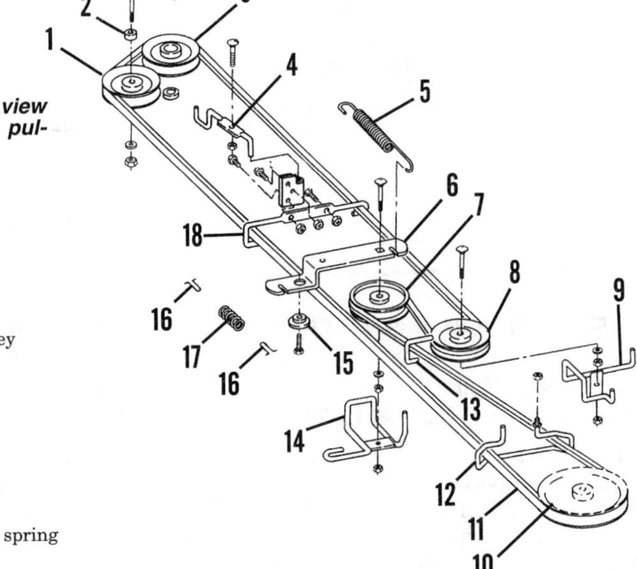

Fig. JD1-4–Exploded view of traction drive belt, pulleys and belt guides.

1. Idler pulley
2. Spacer
3. Engine drive pulley
4. Belt guide
5. Belt tension guide
6. Clutch arm
7. Clutch pulley
8. Adjusting idler pulley
9. Belt guide
10. Transaxle pulley
11. Traction drive belt
12. Belt guide
13. Belt guide
14. Belt guide
15. Bushing
16. Link
17. Clutch compression spring
18. Belt guide

Inspect gears and shafts for damage and replace when required. Inspect the four bushings located in the steering console (16) and replace if excessively worn.

When reinstalling the steering gears, adjust the quantity of washers on the top and bottom of the sector gear shaft and steering shaft to obtain the minimum amount of backlash without binding. When installing the pinion gear (9—Fig. JD1-3), align the dot (D) on the gear with the notch (N) on the steering shaft. Tighten the tie rod retaining nuts to 22 N·m (16 ft.-lb.).

ENGINE

REMOVAL AND INSTALLATION

To remove the engine, first disconnect the battery ground cable. Raise the hood and disconnect the springs from the hood brackets, then lower the hood and move forward to remove the hood from the tractor. Shut off the fuel and disconnect the fuel line from the engine. Disconnect the throttle control cable. Disconnect the starter wires and ignition wires. Remove the heat shield and muffler. Slip the mower drive belt off the PTO clutch. Disconnect the PTO clutch wire harness, remove the clutch retaining bolt and remove the clutch from the crankshaft. Remove the traction drive pulley and key from the crankshaft. Remove the engine mounting cap screws and lift the engine from the tractor.

To reinstall the engine, reverse the removal procedure. Tighten the engine mounting cap screws to 32 N·m (24 ft.-lb.). Apply antiseize compound to the crankshaft, then install the drive pulley and PTO clutch assembly. Tighten the PTO clutch cap screw to 73 N·m (54 ft.-lb.).

OVERHAUL

Engine make and model are listed at the beginning of this section. To overhaul engine components and accessories, refer to the KOHLER engine section of this manual.

CLUTCH AND TRACTION DRIVE BELT

All models are equipped with a spring-loaded belt idler clutch. When the clutch pedal is depressed, the clutch arm (6—Fig. JD1-4) moves the idler pulley (7) to loosen the drive belt from the drive pulleys, stopping forward or reverse movement.

DRIVE BELT

To remove the traction drive belt (11—Fig. JD1-4), first lower or remove the mower deck. Note that the drive belt can be removed without removing the mower deck, but removing the mower deck will provide better access to components on the underside of the tractor. Remove the PTO clutch from the engine crankshaft. Disconnect the tie rods from the steering arm. Remove the belt guides (9 and 14) from the idler

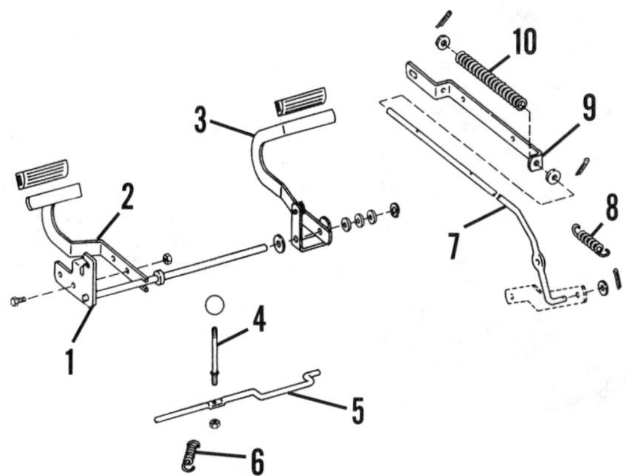

Fig. JD1-5–Exploded view of clutch and brake pedals and associated linkage.

1. Clutch shaft
2. Clutch pedal
3. Brake pedal
4. Park brake rod
5. Park brake shaft
6. Return spring
7. Brake rod
8. Return spring
9. Brake strap
10. Compression spring

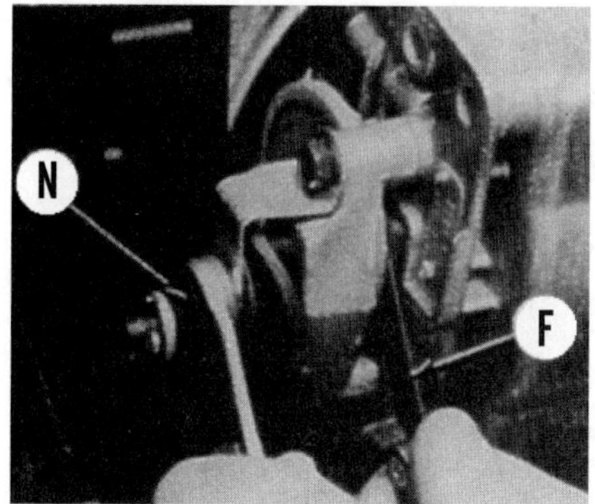

Fig. JD1-6–Clearance between brake disc and brake pad should be 0.5 mm (0.0020 in.) with brake disengaged. Turn nut (N) to adjust.

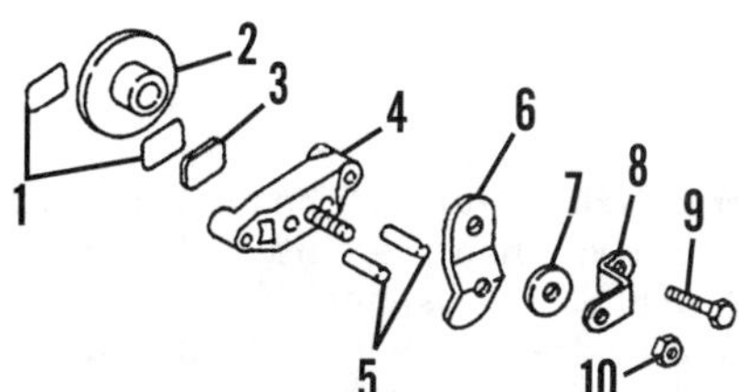

Fig. JD1-7–Exploded view of disc brake assembly.

1. Brake pads
2. Brake disc
3. Back plate
4. Brake holder
5. Actuating pins
6. Brake lever
7. Washer
8. Bracket
9. Cap screw
10. Adjusting nut

pulleys. Disconnect the spring (6—Fig. JD1-5) and remove the park brake rod (4). Remove the drive pulley (3—Fig. JD1-4) from the engine crankshaft, then slip the belt out of the transaxle pulley and remove from the tractor.

To install the belt, reverse the removal procedure. Apply an antiseize compound to the crankshaft before installing the drive pulley and the PTO clutch.

To adjust belt tension, engage the park brake. Move the adjusting pulley (8—Fig. JD1-4) to remove all slack from the belt and tighten the pulley retaining bolt. Release the park brake. The length of clutch release spring (17) should be 47 mm (1.85 in.) if the belt is properly adjusted. Repeat the adjustment procedure if necessary.

CLUTCH ARM

To remove the clutch arm (6—Fig. JD1-4), engage the park brake and remove the belt guide (14) and clutch idler pulley (7). Release the park brake and disconnect the spring (5) from the clutch arm. Remove the mounting cap screw, bushing (15) and arm (6) from the tractor.

To reinstall, reverse the removal procedure. Apply Loctite 242 to threads of the clutch arm mounting cap screw and tighten to 34 N·m (25 ft.-lb.).

BRAKE

ADJUSTMENT

To adjust the brake, first make sure the park brake is disengaged. Use a feeler gauge to measure the clearance between the brake disc and pad as shown in Fig. JD1-6. Clearance should be 0.5 mm (0.020 in.). Turn the nut (N) to obtain the correct clearance.

REMOVAL AND INSTALLATION

To remove the brake assembly, raise and support the rear of the tractor. Remove the right rear wheel. Disconnect the brake rod from the brake lever (6—Fig. JD1-7). Remove the brake mounting cap screws and withdraw the brake holder (4), disc (2) and pads (1).

To reinstall the brake, reverse the removal procedure. Adjust the brake as previously outlined.

TRANSAXLE

LUBRICATION

The transaxle is filled at the factory with SAE 90 GL5 gear lubricant and does not require periodic checking of lubricant level. If an oil leak develops, the leak should be repaired and the unit refilled with gear lubricant. Transaxle capacity is approximately 890 mL (30 oz.).

On models equipped with grease fittings at the outer end of the axle housings, inject with multipurpose grease after every 25 hours of operation.

REMOVAL AND INSTALLATION

To remove the transaxle, raise and support the rear of the tractor. Remove the rear wheels. Remove the belt guide from the adjusting pulley (8—Fig. JD1-4) and move the pulley forward to loosen the traction drive belt. Remove the drive belt from the transaxle pulley. Disconnect the transaxle shift linkage and brake linkage. Disconnect the wiring from the safety start switch located on top of the transaxle. Remove cap screws attaching the transaxle to the frame and lower the transaxle from the tractor.

To install the transaxle, reverse the removal procedure. Adjust the drive belt tension as previously outlined.

OVERHAUL

The tractor may be equipped with a Peerless Model 915, 920 or 930 transaxle. Refer to the Peerless section in the TRANSAXLE SERVICE section for the overhaul procedure.

PTO CLUTCH

ADJUSTMENT

The clutch should be adjusted if the clutch has been disassembled or when operation becomes erratic. With the clutch disengaged, insert a feeler gauge through the slot in the clutch plate (Fig. JD1-8) and measure the clearance between the clutch rotor and armature. Clearance should be 0.41 mm (0.016 in.). To adjust, tighten the adjusting nut (B) next to the slot until the feeler gauge (A) just begins to bind. Do not overtighten. Repeat the adjustment at each of the slots in the clutch plate.

TESTING

Use the following procedure for locating a PTO malfunction. Turn the ignition switch ON and actuate the PTO switch. If the clutch does not engage, disconnect the wiring connector at the field coil and use a 12-volt test lamp to check the wire continuity coming from the PTO switch. If the lamp lights, either the PTO or the wiring connection at the clutch field coil is defective.

To check the field coil, remove the clutch from the tractor. Ground the field coil frame and energize the coil lead wire with a 12-volt battery. Hold a suitable piece of metal adjacent to the coil and note if the metal is attracted. If the metal is not attracted, replace the field coil assembly.

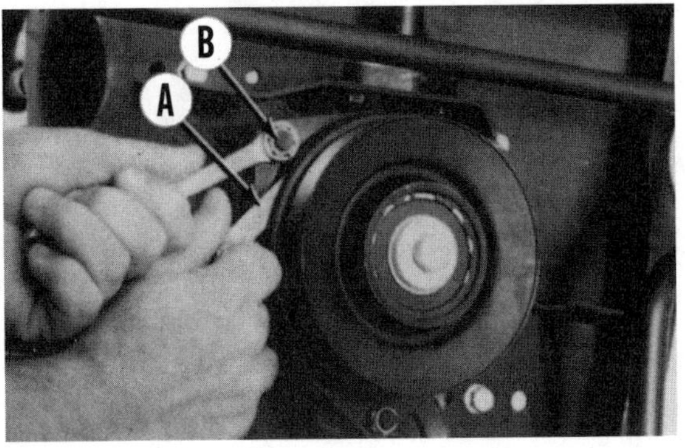

Fig. JD1-8–Use a feeler gauge to measure clearance between PTO clutch rotor and armature. Turn nuts (B) to adjust clearance. Refer to text.

OVERHAUL

To remove the PTO clutch, remove the mower deck or lower the mower deck to the lowest position and move the mower belt tension lever to the release position. Disconnect the clutch wire harness connector. Slip the drive belt out of the clutch pulley. Hold the clutch assembly and remove the retaining cap screw. Remove the clutch assembly from the crankshaft.

To disassemble the clutch, remove the three nuts (7—Fig. JD1-9) and separate the armature assembly (9), rotor (8) and field coil (5).

Inspect the bearings in the field housing and armature for damage and replace the bearings or housing assemblies when necessary. Inspect rotor and armature contact surfaces for damage and replace when needed.

Apply an antiseize compound on the crankshaft before reinstalling the clutch. Install the clutch and tighten the retaining cap screw to 73 N·m (54 ft.-lb.). Adjust the clutch as previously outlined.

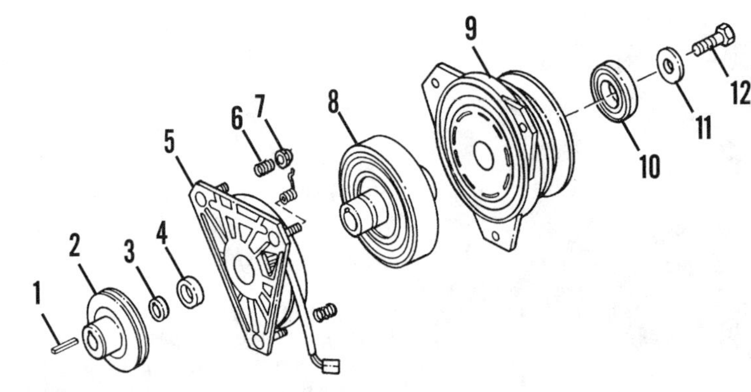

Fig. JD1-9–Exploded view of Warner electric PTO clutch used on early production models. Clutch used on later models is similar except that collar (4) is not used and bearing (10) is not available separately.

1. Key
2. Pulley
3. Hub
4. Spacer
5. Coil assy.
6. Spring
7. Nut
8. Rotor
9. Armature & pulley assy.
10. Bearing
11. Washer
12. Cap screw

ELECTRICAL SYSTEM

SAFETY INTERLOCK SYSTEM

A safety interlock system prevents the engine from starting unless the following conditions are met: The key switch is in the START position, the shift lever is in NEUTRAL and the PTO switch is in the DISENGAGED position.

The interlock starting system operation is as follows: Current flows from the battery positive terminal (Fig. JD1-10) to the starter soleniod terminal, then to the fusible link and key switch battery terminal. With key switch in the START position, current flows to the PTO switch. With the PTO switch in the DISENGAGED position (switch closed), current flows to the neutral start switch. The neutral start switch is located in the top of the transaxle and is actuated by the transaxle shift fork. The neutral switch is closed when the shift fork is in the NEUTRAL position. Current then flows to the key switch S1-S2 terminals and then to the starter solenoid, engaging the solenoid and allowing the starter motor to operate.

NOTE: When checking switches for continuity, disconnect wiring from the switches before testing to prevent possible damage to the meter or interlock module.

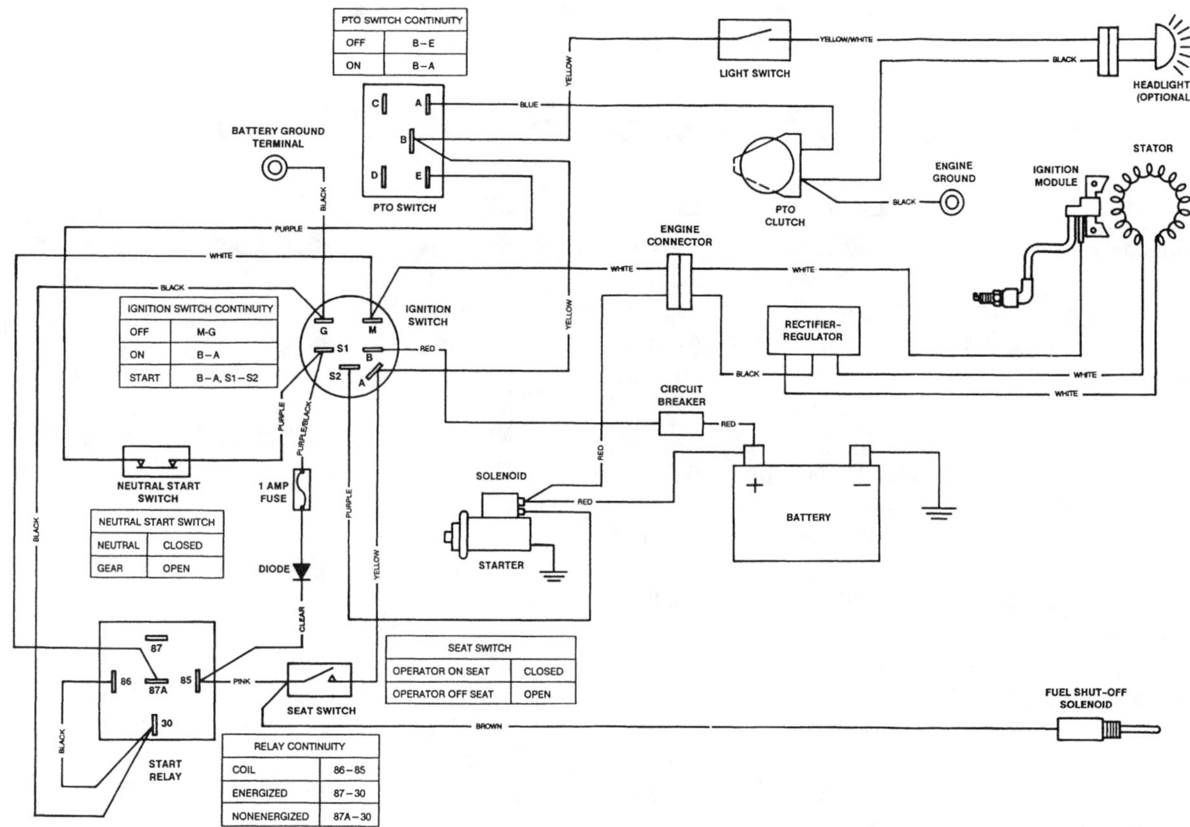

Fig. JD1-10–Wiring schematic typical of all models.

JOHN DEERE

CONDENSED SPECIFICATIONS

MODELS	LX172	LX176	LX178	LX186	LX188
Engine Make	Kawasaki	Kawasaki	Kawasaki	Kawasaki	Kawasaki
Model	FC420V	FC420V	FD440V	FC540V	FD501V
Bore	89 mm (3.5 in.)	89 mm (3.5 in.)	67 mm (2.64 in.)	89 mm (3.5 in.)	67 mm (2.64 in.)
Stroke	68 mm (2.68 in.)	68 mm (2.68 in.)	62 mm (2.44 in.)	86 mm (3.38 in.)	62 mm (2.44 in.)
Displacement	423 cc (25.8 cu. in.)	423 cc (25.8 cu. in.)	437 cc (26.7 cu. in.)	535 cc (32.6 cu. in.)	437 cc (26.7 cu. in.)
No. of Cylinders	1	1	2	1	2
Power Rating	10.4 kW (14 hp)	10.4 kW (14 hp)	11.1 kW (15 hp)	12.6 kW (17 hp)	12.6 kW (17 hp)
Slow Idle Speed—Rpm	1400	1550	1550	1550	1550
High Idle Speed (No-Load)—Rpm.	3350	3350	3350	3350	3550
Crankcase Capacity	1.3 L* (2.8 pt.)	1.3 L* (2.8 pt.)	1.1 L* (2.3 pt.)	1.6 L* (3.4 pt.)	1.1 L (2.3 pt.)
Transmission Capacity	1.0 L (36 oz.)	3.4 L (3.6 qt.)	3.4 L (3.6 qt.)	3.4 L (3.6 qt.)	3.4 L (3.6 qt.)
Fuel Tank Capacity	9.5 L (2.5 gal.)	9.5 L (2.5 gal.)	9.5 L (2.5 gal.)	9.5 L (2.5 gal.)	9.5 L (2.5 gal.)

*Add 0.2 L (0.4 pt.) with filter change.

FRONT AXLE SYSTEM

FRONT WHEELS AND BEARINGS

The front wheels may be removed after removing the hub cap (15—Fig. JD2-1) and detaching the snap ring (14) on the end of the spindle. Install the front wheels so the valve stem (12) is toward the inside of the tractor.

The front wheel bearings (13) are replaceable. Remove the bearings using a suitable puller or press. Prior to installation, pack the bearing with EP grease. After installation, pack the area behind the bearing with grease. Install the bearing so it is flush with the end of the hub.

STEERING SPINDLES

Lubrication

Lubricate steering spindles after every 50 hours of operation. Inject EP grease into the fittings in the outer ends of the axle.

Overhaul

To remove steering spindles (7 and 8—Fig. JD2-1), raise and support the front of the tractor and remove the front wheels. Disconnect the tie rod (6) and drag link (9) from the spindles when necessary. Remove the snap ring (2) retaining the spindle in the axle, then the lower spindle from the axle main member.

Inspect spindle bushings (3) for wear and replace when necessary. The bushings are a press fit in the axle. During assembly, tighten the tie rod retaining nuts to 23 N·m (204 in.-lb.). Tighten the drag link retaining nut to 37 N·m (27 ft.-lb.). Lubricate the steering spindles

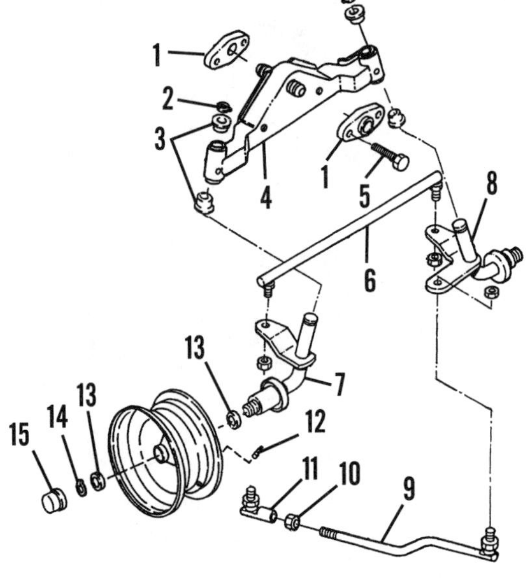

Fig. JD2-1–Exploded view of front axle assembly.

1. Pivot anchor
2. Snap ring
3. Bushing
4. Axle main member
5. Screw
6. Tie rod
7. Spindle (right)
8. Spindle (left)
9. Drag link
10. Jam nut
11. Rod end
12. Valve stem
13. Bearings
14. Snap ring]
15. Hub cap

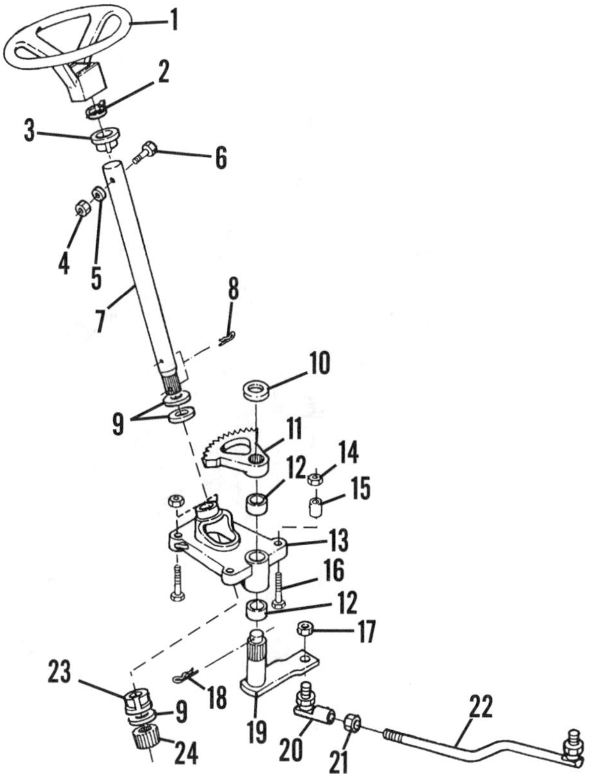

Fig. JD2-2–Exploded view of steering components.

1. Steering wheel
2. Snap ring
3. Bushing
4. Nut
5. Washer
6. Bolt
7. Steering shaft
8. Cotter pin (2)
9. Washers
10. Washer
11. Sector gear
12. Bearing
13. Support
14. Nut
15. Spacer
16. Bolt
17. Locknut
18. Cotter pin
19. Steering arm
20. Rod end
21. Nut
22. Drag link
23. Bearing
24. Pinion gear

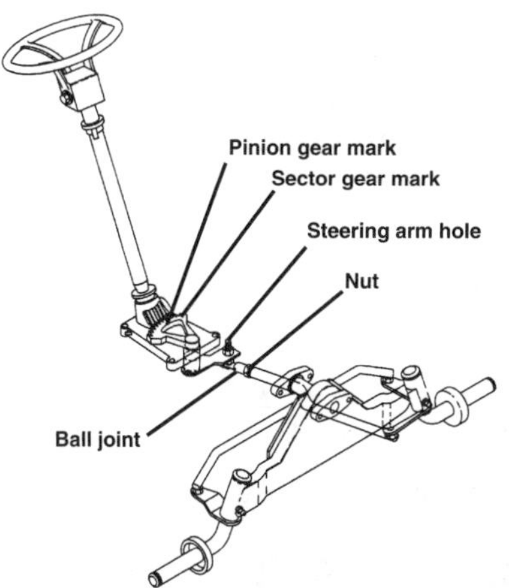

Fig. JD2-3–During assembly align marks on pinion gear and steering sector gear as shown.

by injecting EP grease into the grease fittings.

AXLE MAIN MEMBER OVERHAUL

To remove the front axle assembly (4—Fig. JD2-1), remove the mower deck, muffler and electric PTO clutch. Remove the crankshaft drive pulley. Raise and support the front of the tractor. Remove the front wheels. Disconnect the drag link (9—Fig. JD2-1) from the left steering spindle (8). Remove the cap screws retaining the axle pivot anchors (1). While supporting the axle, turn the pivot anchors onto the axle pivot shaft. Lower the axle and remove from the tractor.

Inspect the axle pivot shaft and anchors for wear and replace when necessary. To reinstall the axle, reverse the removal procedure. Tighten the pivot anchor retaining screws to 25 N·m (221 in.-lb.). Tighten the drag link retaining nut to 37 N·m (27 ft.-lb.).

STEERING SYSTEM

TIE ROD AND TOE-IN

Unscrew the retaining nuts to remove the tie rod (6—Fig. JD2-1). Tighten the tie rod retaining nuts to 23 N·m (204 in.-lb.). Toe-in is not adjustable.

DRAG LINK ADJUSTMENT

Adjust the drag link end (11—Fig. JD2-1) so the steering wheel is centered when the front wheels point straight ahead. If adjustment is not possible, check for damaged components and proper indexing of the steering gears.

STEERING GEAR OVERHAUL

To remove the steering gear assembly, remove the mower deck. Remove the bolt (6—Fig. JD2-2) and lift the steering wheel off the shaft. Raise the hood, disconnect the battery cables and remove the battery. Remove the cotter pins (8). Withdraw the pinion gear (24) and washer (9) from the lower end of shaft. Loosen four screws retaining the dash panel. Pull or push the steering shaft (7) up through the dash panel.

NOTE: It may be necessary to force the snap ring (2) through the dash panel.

To remove the sector gear (11) and steering arm (19), disconnect the drag link from the steering arm. Remove the cotter pin (18), then separate and remove the sector gear and steering arm.

To reinstall the steering gear assembly, reverse the disassembly procedure while noting the following. First, install the steering shaft (7—Fig, JD2-2) and washers (9). When installing the pinion gear (24), make sure the mark on the pinion gear aligns with the mark on the lower end of the steering shaft. When installing the sector gear (11), make sure the front wheels are positioned straight ahead and the mark on the sector gear is aligned with the marks on the pinion gear and steering shaft as shown in Fig. JD2-3. If the front wheels are not in the straight-ahead position with the marks aligned, adjust the drag link length.

ENGINE

LUBRICATION

Check the oil level before operation and after every four hours of operation. Determine oil level by resting the dipstick on top of the dipstick tube; do not screw in.

The recommended oil is a premium grade oil meeting the latest API service classification. Use SAE 15W40 oil for temperatures above 32°F (0°C); use SAE 10W-30 oil for temperatures between -4°F (-20°C) and 86°F (30°C); SAE 5W-30 may be used between 68°F (20°C) and -22°F (-30°C).

Change oil and filter after first five hours of operation and then after every 100 hours of operation, or more frequently when operation is severe.

REMOVAL AND INSTALLATION

To remove the engine, first remove the hood and muffler. Disconnect the battery ground cable. Close the fuel shut-off valve and disconnect the fuel line. Disconnect the throttle control cable. Disconnect the ground wire, starter wires and ignition wires from the engine. Remove the electric PTO clutch. Engage the parking brake to relieve tension on the traction drive belt. Remove the drive pulley and key from the engine crankshaft. Remove the engine mounting cap screws while noting the screw length for proper installation. Lift the engine from the tractor.

To install the engine, reverse the removal procedure. Apply an antiseize lubricant to the crankshaft before installing the drive pulley. Tighten the engine mounting screws to 16 N·m (142 in.-lb.). Tighten the PTO clutch mounting cap screw to 75 N·m (55 ft.-lb.).

OVERHAUL

The engine make and model are listed at the beginning of this section. To overhaul engine components and accessories, refer to the KAWASAKI engine section in this manual.

CLUTCH AND TRACTION DRIVE BELT

MODEL LX172

Adjustment

To adjust the clutch, stop the engine and release the clutch pedal. Measure the distance between flanges on clutch pedal spring retainer caps (6—Fig. JD2-4). The distance should be 31-35 mm (1.22-1.38 in.) for proper belt tension.

To adjust distance on Model LX172 prior to serial number 43870, loosen the nut on the front idler pulley (15—Fig. JD2-5) and move the front idler pulley as needed. Position the belt guide attached to the idler pulley so the guide is parallel to the belt between the engine pulley and idler pulley, then retighten the nut.

On later Model LX172, loosen the nut on the front idler pulley (15—Fig. JD2-4) and move the front idler pulley so it is centered in the slot. Position the belt guide (13) attached to the idler pulley so the guide is parallel to the belt between the engine pulley and idler pulley, then retighten the nut. Loosen the retaining nut on the front bellcrank idler pulley (9) and move the pulley in the slot to obtain the desired belt tension. Note that both the idler pulley and the front bellcrank pulley can be used

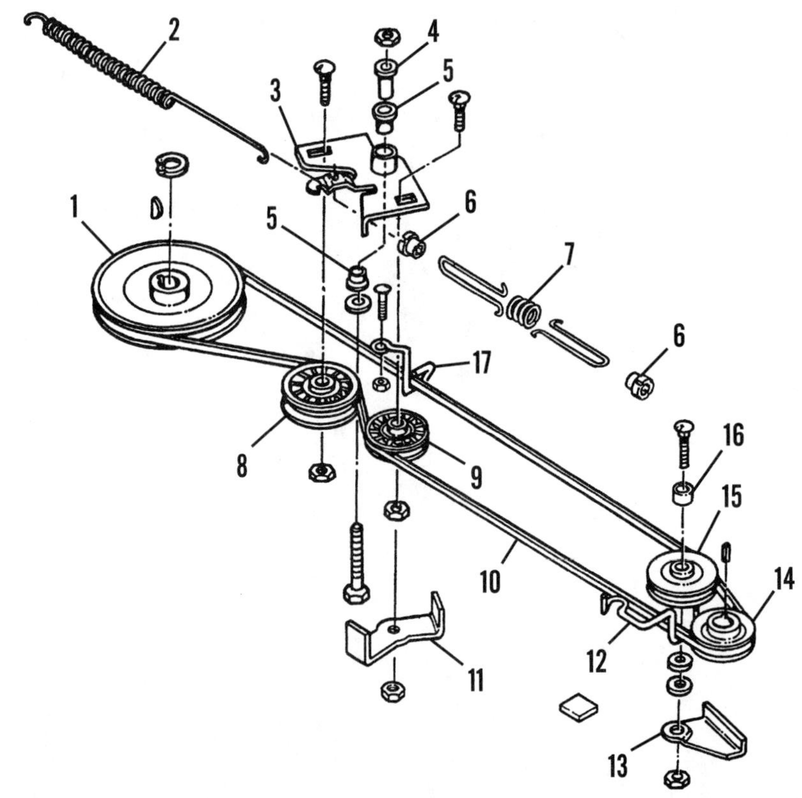

Fig. JD2-4–Exploded view of traction drive belt arrangement on Model LX172.

1. Transaxle pulley
2. Belt tension spring
3. Bellcrank
4. Bushing
5. Bushings
6. End caps
7. Clutch pedal spring
8. Flat idler
9. V-idler
10. Traction belt drive
11. Belt guard
12. Belt guide
13. Belt guard
14. Engine pulley
15. Idler pulley
16. Bushing
17. Belt guide

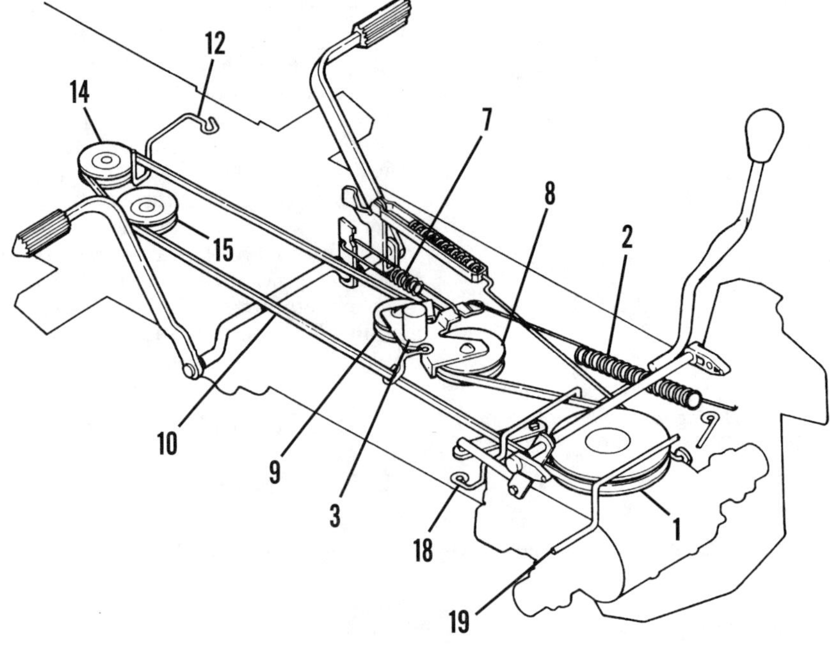

JD2-5–Drawing of traction drive components for Model LX172.

1. Transaxle pulley
2. Belt tension spring
3. Bellcrank
7. Clutch pedal spring
8. Flat idler
9. V-idler
10. Traction drive belt
12. Belt guide
14. Engine pulley
15. Idler pulley
18. Belt guide
19. Belt guide

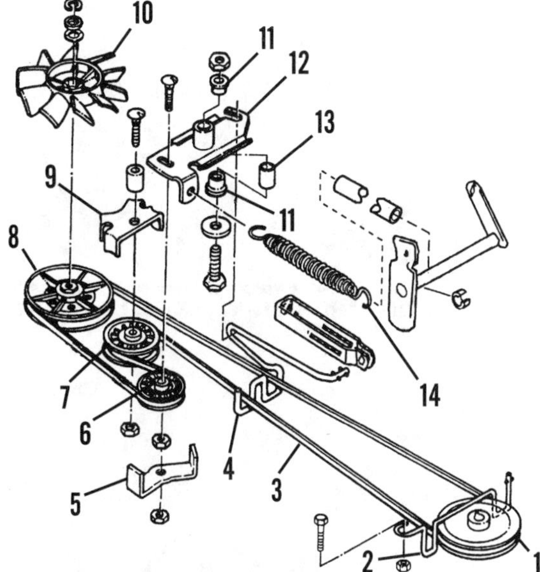

Fig. JD2-6–Fig. JD2-6—Exploded view of traction drive components.

1. Engine pulley
2. Belt guide
3. Traction drive belt
4. Belt guide
5. Belt guard
6. Belt tension pulley
7. Idler pulley
8. Transaxle pulley
9. Belt guide
10. Fan
11. Bushings
12. Idler assy.
13. Bushing
14. Belt tension spring

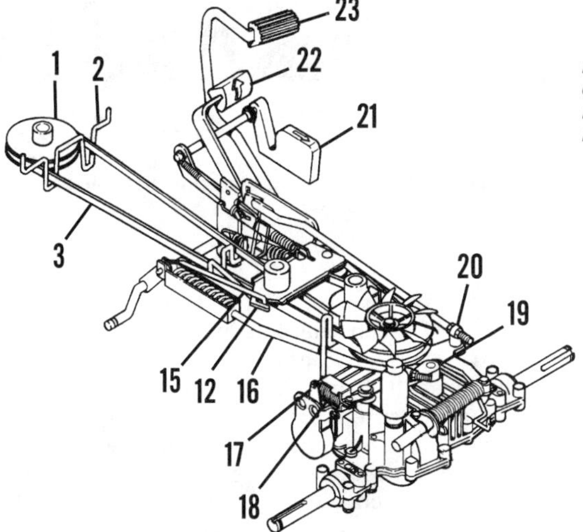

Fig. JD2-7–Drawing of traction drive components on Models LX176, LX178, LX186 and LX188.

1. Engine pulley
2. Belt guide
3. Drive belt
12. Bellcrank
15. Release rod
16. Brake control rod
17. Brake arm
18. Brake actuating rod & spring
19. Brake lever
20. Speed control rod end
21. Reverse pedal
22. Forward pedal
23. Brake pedal

to adjust belt tension if needed. If the belt is tensioned correctly, the distance between the caps (6) on ends of clutch pedal spring should be 31-35 mm (1.2-1.3 in.). Adjust the bellcrank belt guide (11—Fig. JD2-4) so the guide is parallel with the belt as it wraps around the pulley.

Removal and Installation

Remove the mower deck. On early models, raise the seat and disconnect the wire connector. Unscrew the seat adjustment knobs and remove the seat. Remove the mower depth control knob. Unscrew fasteners securing the rear fender and foot panels and remove the rear fender assembly. Disconnect the fuel hose and remove the fuel tank. On all models, push down the clutch pedal and engage the parking brake. Loosen the transaxle belt guide (12—Fig. JD2-5). Separate the drive belt from the transaxle pulley. Detach the belt guide (11). Remove the pulleys (8 and 9) from the bellcrank (3). Remove the nut and belt guide from the front idler pulley (15). Detach the front belt guide (12). Disconnect the wire connector from the PTO clutch. Disconnect the drag link from the steering arm. Remove the drive belt.

Replace the drive belt by reversing the removal procedure. Adjust belt tension as previously described. Adjust the pulley belt guides so they are parallel with the belt.

MODELS LX176, LX178, LX186 AND LX188

Adjustment

To adjust belt tension, stop the engine and move the forward/reverse pedals to NEUTRAL. Remove the mower deck. Loosen the nut attaching the tensioner pulley (6—Fig. JD2-6) to the bellcrank (12). Move the pulley towards the rear to increase belt tension or towards the front to decrease tension. The belt is tensioned correctly when the alignment mark on the bellcrank (12—Fig. JD2-7) is aligned with the mark on the release rod (15). Retighten the idler bolt.

NOTE: If the mark is not visible, make a mark 16 mm (0.63 in.) from the end of the slot.

Removal and Installation

Remove the mower deck. Push down the brake pedal and engage the parking brake. Disconnect the wire connector from the PTO clutch. Detach the front belt guide (2—Fig. JD2-6). Disconnect the drag link from the steering arm. Remove tensioner pulley (6) and idler pulley (7). Remove center belt guard (4). Loosen the belt guide at the transmission pulley. Remove the drive belt (3).

Replace the drive belt by reversing the removal procedure. Adjust the belt tension as previously described.

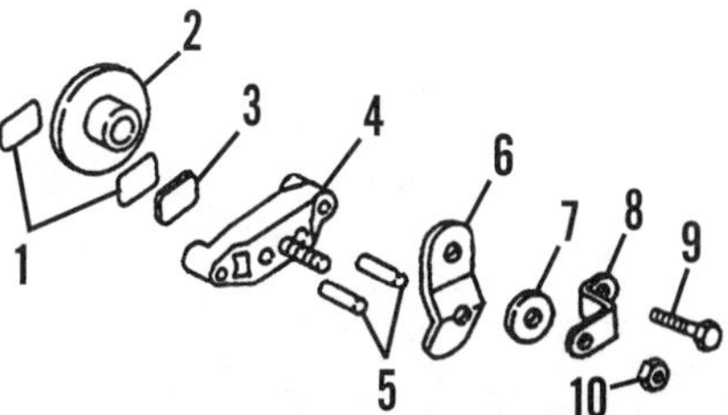

Fig JD2-8–Exploded view of disc brake assembly used on Model LX172.

1. Brake pads
2. Brake disc
3. Back plate
4. Brake holder
5. Actuating pins
6. Brake lever
7. Washer
8. Bracket
9. Cap screw
10. Adjusting nut

BRAKES

MODEL LX172

Adjustment

To adjust the brakes, first make sure the park brake is not engaged. Use a feeler gauge to measure the clearance between the brake pad (1—Fig. JD2-8) and brake disc (2). Clearance should be 0.13 mm (0.005 in.). Turn the adjusting nut (10) on the brake arm (6) to obtain the correct clearance.

Overhaul

Remove the mower deck. Raise and support the rear of the tractor and remove the right rear wheel. Disconnect the brake rod from the brake arm. Remove the brake arm guide plate. Remove the retaining cap screws and withdraw the brake holder (4—Fig JD2-8), plate (3) and outer brake pad. Slide the brake disc (2) outward and remove the inner brake pad.

Inspect the parts and replace when necessary. Replace the brake pads when the thickness is less than 6 mm (0.24 in.). Reassemble in reverse of the disassembly procedure. Adjust the brake as previously outlined.

MODELS LX176, LX178, LX186 AND LX188

Operation

Depressing the brake pedal (23—Fig. JD2-7) forces the brake control rod (16) to rotate the brake lever (19). An internal transaxle rod and shaft rotates an external lever. The lever pulls actuating spring and rod assembly (18), which pulls the brake arm (17) to tighten brake band around the brake drum. When the brake control arm rotates to apply the brake, internal transaxle components shift and lock the transaxle in NEUTRAL. The linkage activates the brake switch so engine starting is possible. Depressing the brake pedal also deactivates the tow (freewheeling) valve, if previously engaged.

Adjustment

Raise the seat and disconnect the wire connector. Unscrew the seat adjustment knobs and remove the seat. Remove the mower depth control knob. Unscrew fasteners securing the rear fender and foot panels and remove the rear fender and deck assembly. Detach the brake control rod (16—Fig. JD2-7) from the brake lever (19) on the transaxle. Detach the actuating rod (18) from the brake arm (17) on the brake assembly. Push the brake lever (19) back as far as possible and hold in this position. Adjust the length of the actuating rod (18) by rotating the rod so it slides easily into the hole in the brake arm (17). Hold the brake lever (19) back and adjust the jam nuts on the control rod end (16) until the control rod end slips easily into the hole in the brake lever (19).

Overhaul

Raise and support the rear of the tractor. Remove the left rear wheel. Disconnect the brake actuating rod, then unbolt and remove the brake cover and band assembly (4—Fig. JD2-9). Detach the snap ring (3) and remove the brake drum (2).

Inspect brake parts for damage. Reinstall by reversing the disassembly procedure. Apply a light coat of Lubriplate to the transaxle shaft (1) splines. Adjust the brake as previously described.

SHIFT LINKAGE

NEUTRAL ADJUSTMENT (MODEL LX172)

If the transaxle gear indicated on the shift indicator quadrant is not properly engaged, perform the following neutral adjustment.

Move the gearshift lever to NEUTRAL. Loosen the shift linkage nuts (1—Fig. JD2-10) located on each side of the rear frame behind the rear wheels. Move the linkage support brackets (2) so the shift lever is centered in NEUTRAL on the shift indicator quadrant. Tighten the nuts. Operate the shift lever to determine if all the gears are properly engaged.

PEDAL HEIGHT ADJUSTMENT (MODELS LX176, LX178, LX186 AND LX188)

The pedal height must be correct to obtain the full speed range and to prevent transaxle internal components from acting as mechanical stops.

Raise the seat and disconnect the wire connector. Unscrew the seat adjustment knobs and remove the seat. Remove the mower depth control knob. Unscrew the fasteners securing the rear fender and foot panels and remove the rear fender assembly. Move the gas tank forward to provide access to the control linkage. With the transmission in NEUTRAL, adjust the speed control rod end (20—Fig. JD2-7) until the distance between the forward pedal shaft to the frame member just below the pedal is 76-80 mm (2.99-3.15 in.).

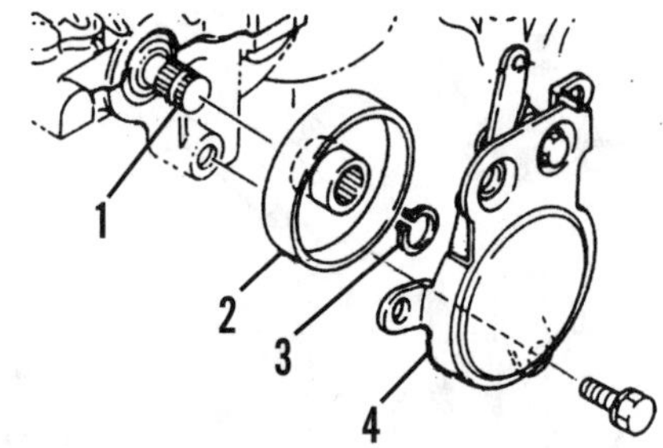

Fig. JD2-9–Exploded view of brake assembly used on Models LX176, LX178, LX186 and LX188.

1. Shaft
2. Brake drum
3. Snap ring
4. Brake cover & band assy.

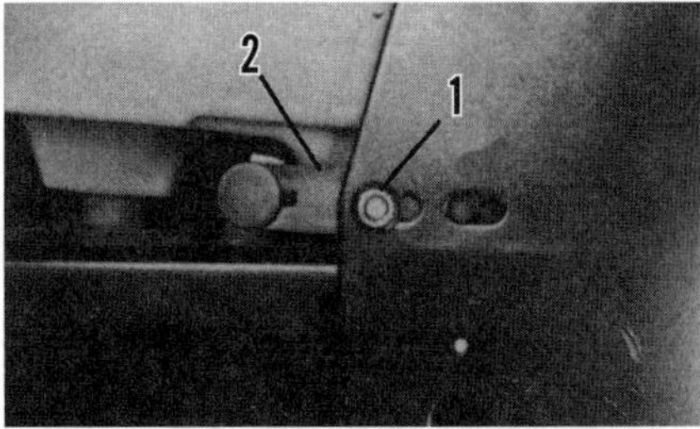

Fig. JD2-10–To adjust shift linkage on Model LX172, loosen nut (1) and move support bracket (2) on both sides of tractor so shift lever is centered in neutral position. Refer to text.

TRANSAXLE

MODEL LX172

Lubrication

The transaxle is filled at the factory with SAE EP90 lithium grease and does not require periodic checking of the lubricant level. If an oil leak develops, the leak should be repaired and the unit refilled with lubricant. Transaxle capacity is approximately 1.0 liter (36 oz.).

Removal and Installation

Remove the mower deck. Push the clutch pedal down and engage the parking brake. Raise and support the rear of the tractor. Remove the rear wheels. Detach the belt guide adjacent to the transaxle pulley and remove the drive belt from the pulley. Disengage the parking brake. Disconnect the shift linkage and brake linkage from the transaxle. Disconnect the neutral switch wire from the transaxle. Support the transaxle, remove the nuts securing the transaxle to the frame, then lower the transaxle from the tractor.

To install, reverse the removal procedure. Tighten the mounting bolts and nuts to 9 N·m (80 in.-lb.).

Overhaul

Model LX172 is equipped with a Peerless Model 801 transaxle. Refer to the PEERLESS section in the TRANSAXLE SERVICE section for the overhaul procedure.

MODELS LX176, LX178, LX186 AND LX188

Lubrication

Maintain the oil level between the marks on the reservoir located adjacent to the rear of the fuel tank. The recommended oil is John Deere Low Viscosity HY-GARD (J20D) Transmission Oil. To add oil, move the seat forward for ac-

Fig. JD2-11–Loosen locknut (A) and rotate eccentric shaft (B) to adjust neutral position on Modles LX176, LX178, LX186 and LX188. Refer to text.

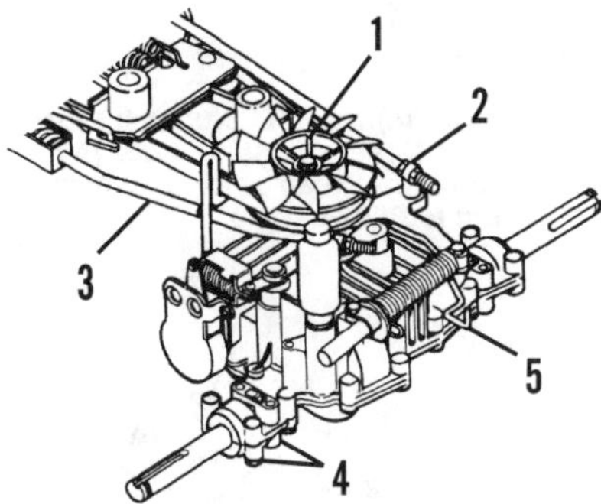

Fig. JD2-12–View of transaxle used on Models LX176, LX178, LX186 and LX188.

1. Fan & drive pulley
2. Shift control rod
3. Brake control rod
4. Transaxle mounting nuts
5. Tow rod

cess to the reservoir cap. Clean the area around the reservoir cap, then remove the cap and foam filter. Fill the reservoir to the desired level on the reservoir. Approximate oil capacity is 3.4 liters (3.6 qt.).

Air must be bled from the system after repairs are made requiring the oil to be drained from the transaxle. Raise and support the rear of the tractor so the rear wheels clear the ground. Start the engine and run at slow speed. Alternately depress the forward and reverse pedal, and engage and disengage the free wheel valve lever. Repeat this procedure until the rear wheels rotate. Stop the engine and lower the rear wheels to the ground. Push the tractor forward and back to rotate the hydrostatic pump. Start the engine and operate at fast idle. Depress and release the forward and reverse pedals until the tractor moves without hesitation.

Neutral Adjustment

Remove the seat and rear fender deck. Move the fuel tank forward to gain access to the transmission linkage. Raise and block up the rear of tractor so the wheels clear the ground. Connect a jumper wire to the seat switch wire so the engine will run. Start the engine and run the engine at idle speed. With

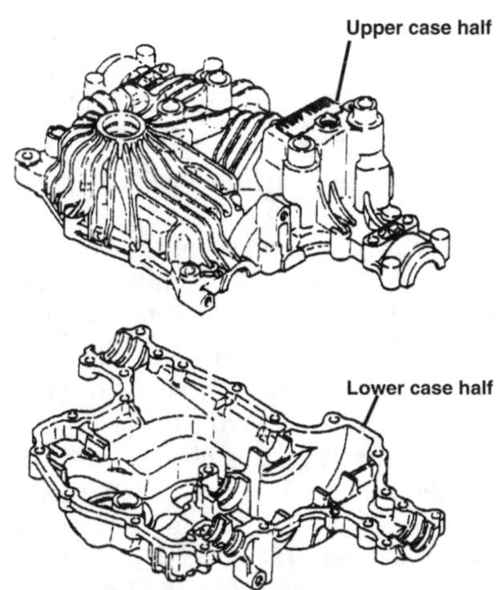

Fig. JD2-13–Model K60 Kanzaki transaxle is used on early Model LX176, LX178, LX186 and LX188.

the transmission in NEUTRAL, the rear wheels should not rotate.

If the wheels rotate, loosen the locknut (A—Fig. JD2-11) and adjust the eccentric shaft (B) as follows: Turn the eccentric clockwise until the wheels just begin to rotate in reverse. Then, turn the eccentric in the opposite direction until the wheels just begin to turn forward. Position the eccentric at the midpoint. Hold the eccentric and tighten the locknut (A).

Troubleshooting

The following list of problems that may occur and possible causes should be used as an aid in locating and correcting transmission problems.

Loss of power or transmission will not operate in either direction.

1. Low transmission oil level or wrong oil.
2. Plugged transmission oil filter.
3. Slipping or broken traction drive belt.
4. Improperly adjusted or damaged forward/reverse control linkage.
5. Binding free wheel linkage.
6. Worn or damaged internal hydrostatic transmission components.
7. Damaged final drive components.

Tractor jerks when starting or operates in one direction only.

1. Faulty speed control linkage.
2. Faulty forward or reverse check valve.
3. Binding or damaged shock absorber.

Tractor creeps when in NEUTRAL.

1. Improperly adjusted or damaged forward/reverse pedal linkage.
2. Improperly adjusted neutral eccentric.
3. Binding shock absorber.

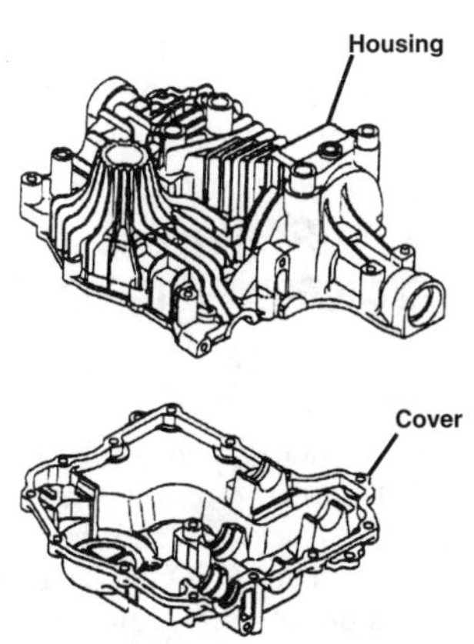

Fig. JD2-14–Model K61 Kanzaki transaxle is used on late Models LX176, LX178, LX186 and LX188.

4. Worn or damaged variable swash plate components.

Noisy operation

1. Low transmission oil level or wrong oil.
2. Contaminated oil contaminated.
3. Air in system.
4. Plugged hydrostatic oil filter.

Removal And Installation

Remove the mower deck. Raise the seat and disconnect the wire connector. Unscrew the seat adjustment knobs and remove the seat. Remove the mower depth control knob. Unscrew the fasteners securing the rear fender and foot panels and remove the rear fender assembly. Disconnect the fuel hose and remove the fuel tank. Raise and support the rear of the tractor. Remove the rear wheels.

Engage the parking brake. Remove the fan and pulley (1—Fig. JD2-12) from the transmission. Disengage the parking brake. Disconnect shift control rod (2) and brake rod (3) from the transaxle. Disconnect the brake switch wire from the transaxle. Support the transaxle and remove the nuts (4) securing the transaxle to the frame. While lowering the transaxle from the tractor, disconnect the tow (freewheel) control rod (5) from the transaxle lever.

To install, reverse the removal procedure.

Overhaul

Models LX176, LX178, LX186 and LX188 are equipped with a TUFF TORQ hydrostatic transaxle manufactured by Kanzaki. Early models use a Model K60 transaxle which can be identified by the transaxle case being split into upper and lower halves (Fig. JD3-13). Later models use a Model K61 transaxle which can be identified by the case being split into an upper housing and lower cover (Fig. JD2-14). Refer to the KANZAKI section in the HYDROSTATIC TRANSAXLE SERVICE section for overhaul procedure.

POWER TAKE-OFF (PTO)

TESTING

Use the following procedure for locating a PTO malfunction. Turn the ignition switch ON, close the seat switch and actuate the PTO switch. If the clutch does not engage, refer to the wiring schematic and check for faulty wiring or electrical component.

To check the PTO field coil, disconnect the wiring connector at the PTO clutch and measure the resistance across the coil terminals. Resistance should measure 2.4-2.7 ohms. Normal current draw with the clutch engaged is about 4 amps.

To check field coil magnetism, remove the clutch from the tractor. Ground the field coil frame and energize the coil lead wire with a known 12-volt source. Hold a piece of metal next to the coil and note if the metal is attracted. If the metal is not attracted to the coil, replace the field coil assembly.

ADJUSTMENT

The PTO clutch must be adjusted when the clutch has been disassembled or operation becomes erratic. With the clutch disengaged, insert a feeler gauge through the clutch plate slots and measure the clearance between the clutch rotor and armature as shown in Fig. JD2-15. There should be a clearance of 0.38-0.64 mm (0.015-0.025 in.) at each of the clutch plate slots. To adjust, tighten or loosen the clutch adjusting nuts (N) to obtain the correct clearance.

OVERHAUL

To remove the PTO clutch, disconnect the electrical wires and remove the clutch retaining screw. Remove the clutch assembly from the crankshaft. Use a plastic hammer to tap and loosen the clutch from the crankshaft if necessary.

To disassemble the clutch (Fig. JD2-16), remove the adjusting nuts (4) and separate the armature and rotor (3) from the field coil housing (1).

Inspect the bearings for damage. Inspect for broken or distorted springs. Check contact surfaces of the rotor and armature for damage. Replace parts or the clutch assembly when necessary.

To reassemble the clutch, reverse the disassembly procedure. Apply an antiseize lubricant to the crankshaft before installing the clutch assembly. The slot in the field coil plate must fit over the pin on the engine platform. Install a washer (5—Fig. JD2-16) with the concave side toward the engine. Tighten the clutch retaining screw to 75 N·m (55 ft.-lb.). Adjust the clutch as previously outlined. If installing a new clutch, break in the clutch by engaging the PTO at least eight times unloaded before attaching a load to the clutch.

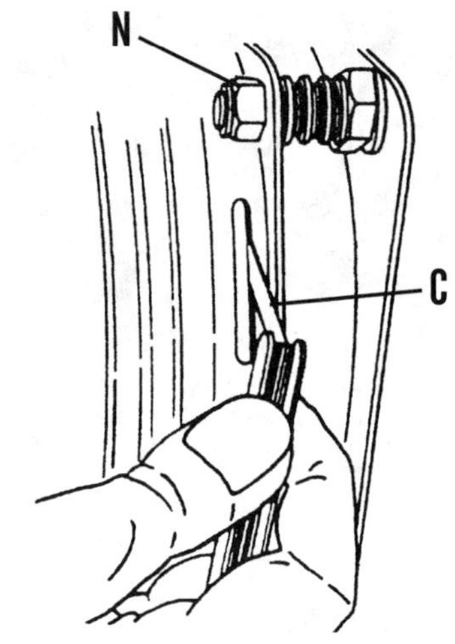

Fig. JD2-15–Adjust PTO clutch by turning each of the three adjusting nuts (N) until clearance (C) between rotor and armature is 0.51 mm (0.020 in.).

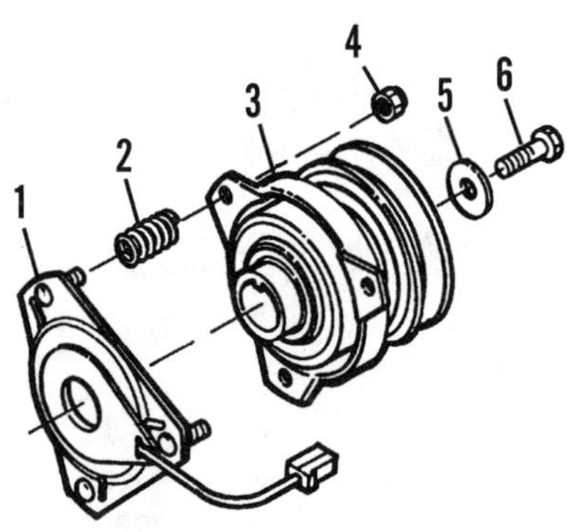

Fig. JD2-16–Exploded view of electric PTO clutch

1. Field coil assy.
2. Spring
3. Armature & rotor assy.
4. Adjusting nut
5. Washer
6. Screw

SAFETY INTERLOCK SYSTEM

The tractor is equipped with a safety interlock system preventing inadvertent starting of the tractor engine or operation if the operator leaves the tractor seat. The tractor engine should not start if the following occurs (engage parking brake):

- Operator in the tractor seat, the shift lever in NEUTRAL, the brake engaged and the PTO clutch lever in the ON position.
- Operator in the tractor seat, the PTO clutch lever in the OFF position, the brake engaged and the shift lever in a position other than NEUTRAL.
- Operator in the tractor seat, the shift lever in NEUTRAL, the PTO clutch lever in the OFF position and the brakes released.
- Operator not in the seat when starting the engine.

The seat switch should kill the engine when the operator is not in the seat or leaves the seat when the PTO clutch is engaged. The seat switch should kill the engine when the operator leaves the seat when the brakes are not locked.

Refer to wiring schematics at end of this section.

WIRING SCHEMATICS

Refer to Fig. JD2-17 or Fig. JD2-18 for identification and location of electrical components. Electrical wiring schematics are illustrated in Fig. JD2-19 and Fig. JD2-20.

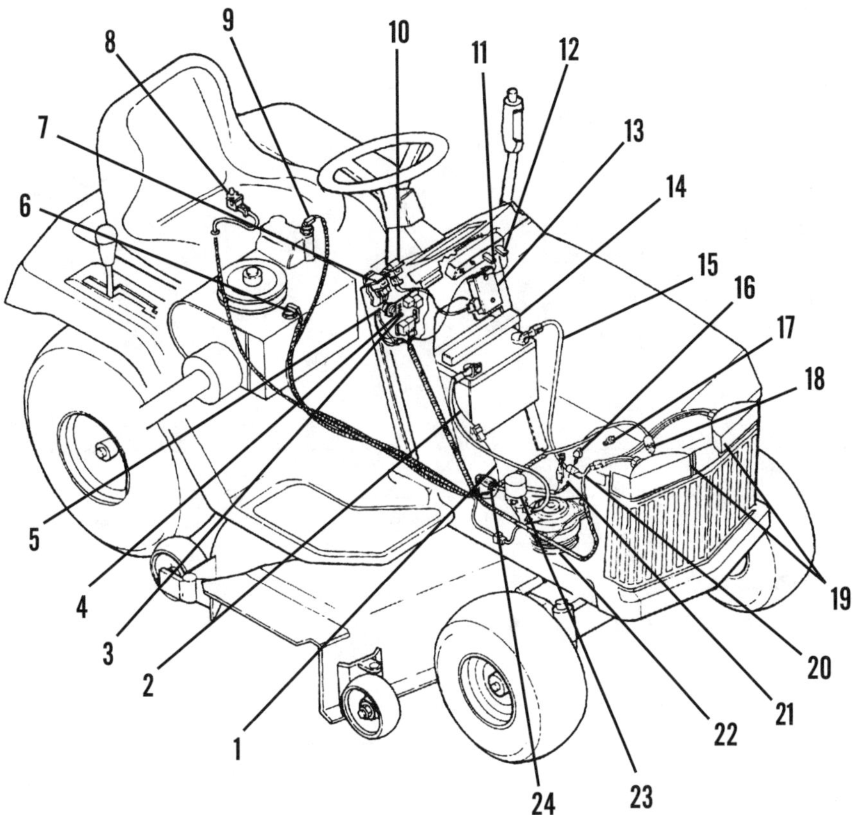

Fig. JD2-17–Drawing illustrating the location of electrical components on Models LX172, LX176 and LX186.

1. Fusible link
2. Battery positive cable
3. 15 amp fuse
4. Interlock module
5. Key switch
6. Neutral start switch
7. PTO switch
8. Seat switch
9. Brake switch (LX176, LX186)
10. Headlight switch
11. Engine oil pressure light
12. Battery discharge light
13. Voltage regulator
14. Battery
15. Battery negative cable
16. Ignition module
17. Engine oil pressure switch
18. Fuel shutoff solenoid
19. Headlights
20. Wiring harness ground
21. Stator connector
22. PTO clutch
23. Starter motor
24. Engine controller

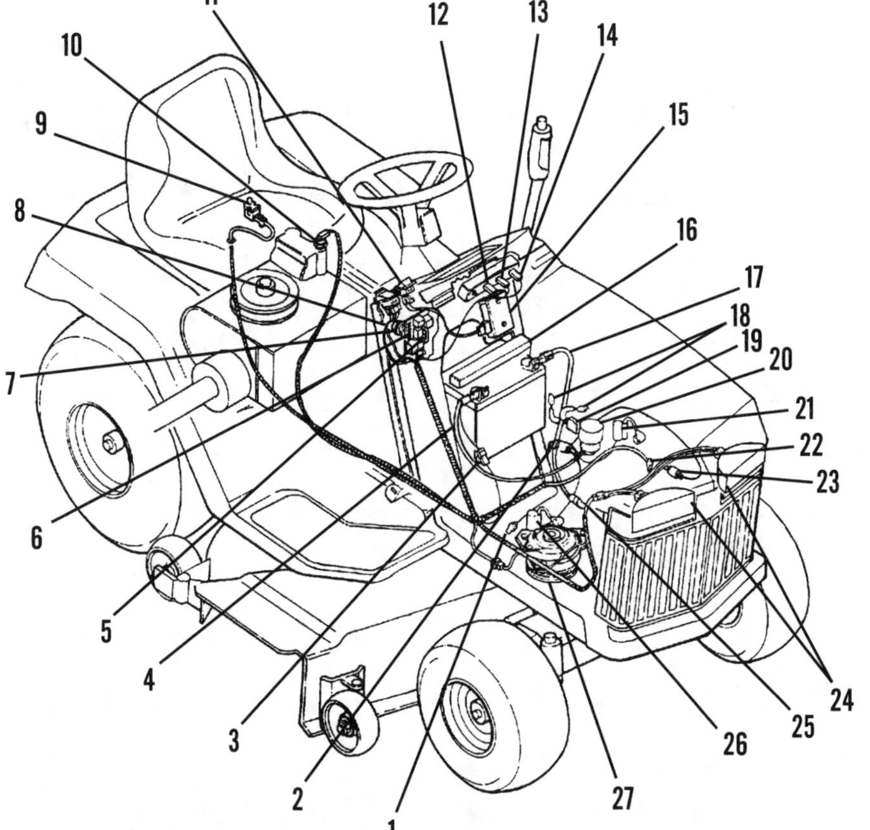

Fig. JD2-18–Drawing illustrating the location of electrical components on Model LX178 and LX188.

1. Engine oil pressure switch
2. Engine connector
3. Fusible link
4. Battery positive cable
5. 15 amp fuses
6. Interlock module
7. Key switch
8. PTO switch
9. Seat switch
10. Brake switch
11. Headlight switch
12. Coolant temperature light
13. Engine oil pressure light
14. Battery discharge light
15. Voltage regulator
16. Battery
17. Battery negative cable
18. Ignition module connector
19. Ignition module
20. Starter motor
21. Ignition coil
22. Coolant temperature switch
23. Fuel shutoff solenoid
24. Headlights
25. Wiring harness ground
26. Ignition coil
27. PTO clutch

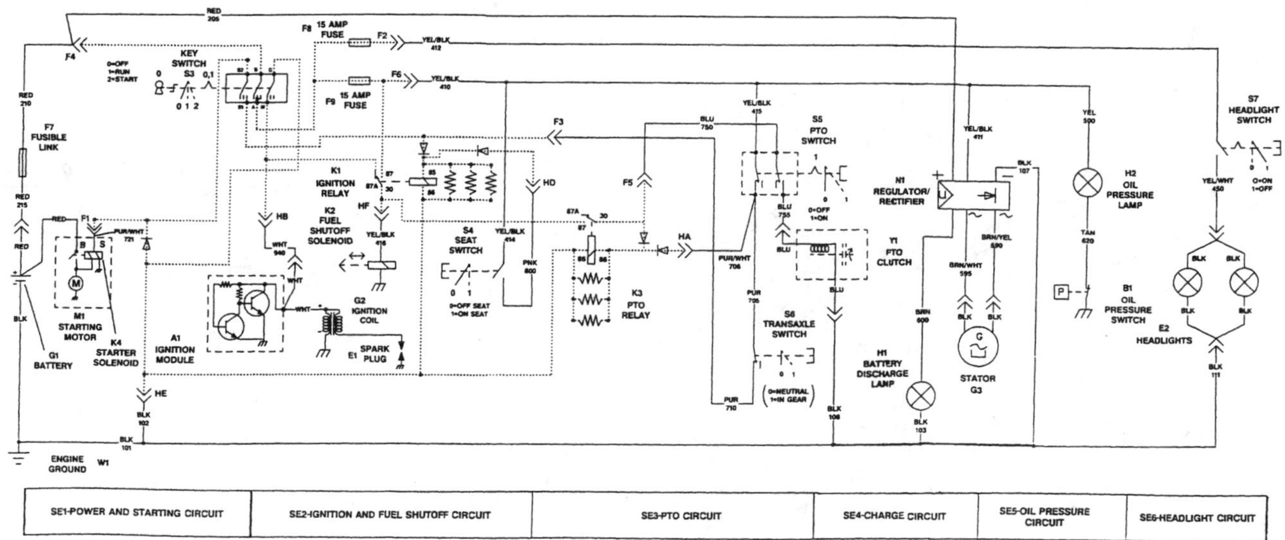

Fig. JD2-19–Wiring schematic for Models LC172, LX176 and LX186.

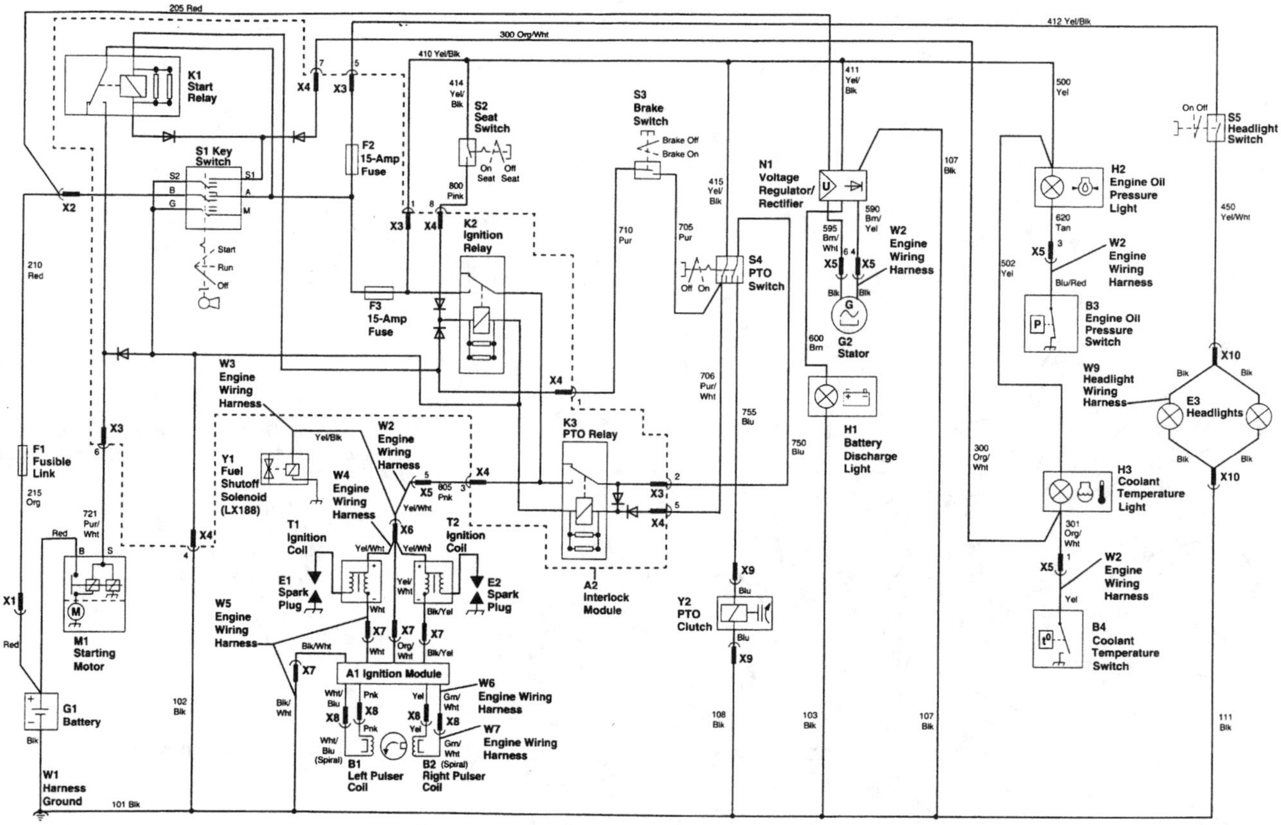

Fig. JD2-20–Wiring schematic for Models LX178 and LX188.

JOHN DEERE

CONDENSED SPECIFICATIONS

MODELS	GT242	GT262	GT275
Engine Make	Kawasaki	Kawasaki	Kawasaki
Model	FC420V	FC540V	FC540V
Bore	89 mm (3.5 in.)	89 mm (3.5 in.)	89 mm (3.5 in.)
Stroke	68 mm (2.68 in.)	86 mm (3.38 in.)	86 mm (3.38 in.)
Displacement	423 cc (25.8 cu. in.)	535 cc (32.6 cu. in.)	535 cc (32.6 cu. in.)
Power Rating	10.4 kW (14 hp)	12.6 kW (17 hp)	12.6 kW (17 hp)
Slow Idle Speed—Rpm	1400	1400	1400
High Idle Speed (No-Load)—Rpm	3350	3350	3350
Crankcase Capacity	1.3 L* (2.8 pt.)	1.6 L* (3.4 pt.)	1.6 L* (3.4 pt.)
Transmission Capacity	3.6 L (3.8 qt.)	3.6 L (3.8 qt.)	4.3 L (4.7 qt.)
Fuel Tank Capacity	9.5 L (2.5 gal.)	9.5 L (2.5 gal.)	10.4 L (2.8 gal.)

*Add 0.2 L (0.4 pt.) with filter change.

FRONT AXLE SYSTEM

FRONT WHEELS AND BEARINGS

The front wheels may be removed after removing the hub cap (15—Fig. JD20-1) and detaching the snap ring (14) on the end of the spindle.

The front wheel bearings (13) are replaceable. Remove bearings using a suitable puller or press. Prior to installation, pack the bearing with EP grease. After installation, pack area behind the bearing with grease. Install bearing so it is flush with the end of the hub.

Install the front wheels on Model GT262 so the valve stem points toward the outside of the spindle. Install the front wheels on all other models so the valve stem (12) is toward the inside of the tractor.

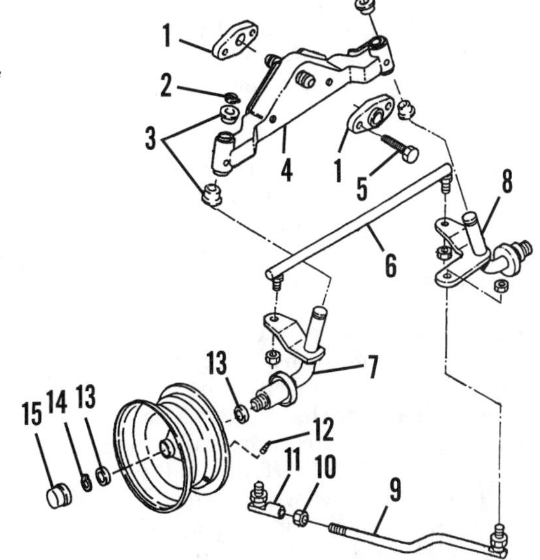

Fig. JD20-1–Exploded view of front axle assembly.

1. Pivot anchor
2. Snap ring
3. Bushing
4. Axle main member
5. Screw
6. Tie rod
7. Spindle (right)
8. Spindle (left)
9. Drag link
10. Jam nut
11. Rod end
12. Valve stem
13. Bearings
14. Snap ring]
15. Hub cap

STEERING SPINDLES

Lubrication

Lubricate steering spindles after every 50 hours of operation. Inject EP grease into the fittings in the outer ends of the axle.

Overhaul

To remove the steering spindles (7 and 8—Fig. JD20-1), raise and support the front of the tractor and remove the front wheels. Disconnect the tie rod (6) and drag link (9) from the spindles when necessary. Remove the snap ring (2) retaining the spindle in the axle, then lower the spindle from the axle main member.

Inspect the spindle bushings (3) for wear and replace when necessary. Bushings are a press fit in the axle. During assembly, tighten the tie rod retaining nuts to 23 N·m (204 in.-lb.). Tighten the drag link retaining nut to 37 N·m (27 ft.-lb.). Lubricate steering spindles by injecting EP grease into the grease fittings.

AXLE MAIN MEMBER OVERHAUL

To remove the front axle assembly (4—Fig. JD20-1), remove the mower deck, muffler and electric PTO clutch. Remove the crankshaft drive pulley. Raise and support the front of the tractor. Remove the front wheels. Disconnect the drag link (9—Fig. JD20-1) from the left steering spindle (8). Remove the cap screws retaining the axle pivot anchors (1). While supporting the axle, turn the pivot anchors onto the axle pivot shaft. Lower the axle and remove from the tractor.

Inspect the axle pivot shaft and anchors for wear and replace when necessary. To reinstall the axle, reverse the removal procedure. Tighten pivot anchor retaining screws to 25 N·m (221 in.-lb.). Tighten drag link retaining nut to 37 N·m (27 ft.-lb.).

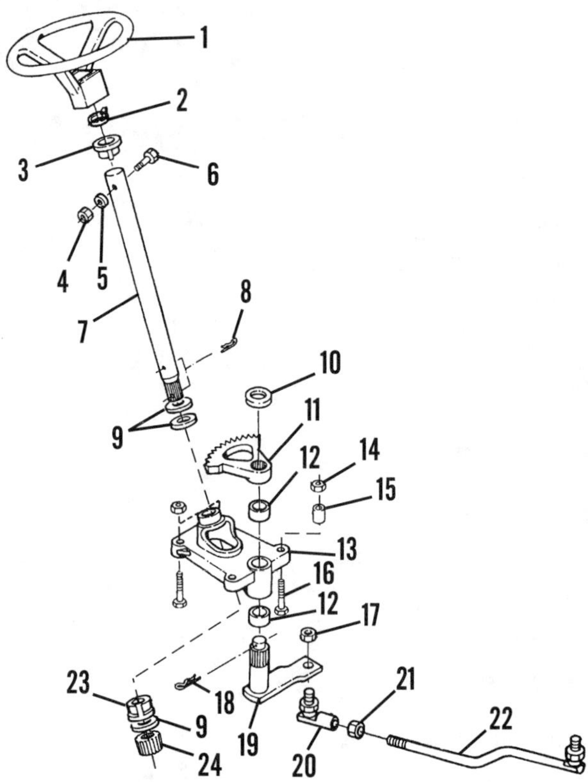

Fig. JD20-2–Exploded view of steering components.

1. Steering wheel
2. Snap ring
3. Bushing
4. Nut
5. Washer
6. Bolt
7. Steering shaft
8. Cotter pin (2)
9. Washers
10. Washer
11. Sector gear
12. Bearing
13. Support
14. Nut
15. Spacer
16. Bolt
17. Locknut
18. Cotter pin
19. Steering arm
20. Rod end
21. Nut
22. Drag link
23. Bearing
24. Pinion gear

STEERING SYSTEM

TIE ROD AND TOE-IN

Unscrew the retaining nuts to remove the tie rod (6—Fig. JD20-1). Tighten the tie rod retaining nuts to 23 N·m (204 in.-lb.). Toe-in is not adjustable.

DRAG LINK ADJUSTMENT

Adjust the drag link end (11—Fig. JD20-1) so the steering wheel is centered when the front wheels point straight ahead. If adjustment is not possible, check for damaged components and proper indexing of the steering gears.

STEERING GEAR OVERHAUL

To remove the steering gear assembly, remove the mower deck. Remove the bolt (6—Fig. JD20-2) and lift the steering wheel off the shaft. Raise the hood, disconnect the battery cables and remove the battery. Remove the cotter pins (8). Withdraw the pinion gear (24) and washer (9) from the lower end of the shaft. Loosen the four screws retaining the dash panel. Pull or push the steering shaft (7) up through the dash panel.

NOTE: It may be necessary to force the snap ring (2) through the dash panel.

To remove the sector gear (11) and steering arm (19), disconnect drag link from the steering arm. Remove the cotter pin (18), then separate and remove the sector gear and steering arm.

To reinstall the steering gear assembly, reverse the disassembly procedure while noting the following. First, install the steering shaft (7—Fig, JD20-2) and washers (9). When installing the pinion gear (24), make sure the mark on the pinion gear aligns with the mark on the lower end of the steering shaft. When installing the sector gear (11), make sure the front wheels are positioned straight ahead and the mark on the sector gear is aligned with the marks on the pinion gear and steering shaft as shown in Fig. JD20-3. If the front wheels are not in the straight-ahead position with the marks aligned, adjust the drag link length.

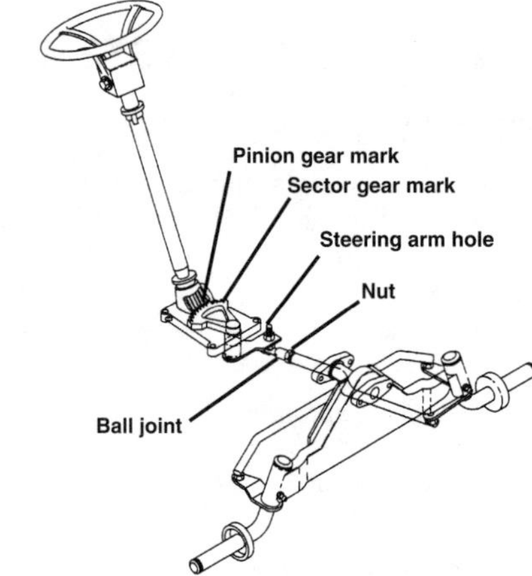

Fig. JD20-3–During assembly align marks on pinion gear and steering sector gear as shown.

ENGINE

LUBRICATION

Check the oil level before operation and after every four hours of operation. Determine oil level by resting the dip-

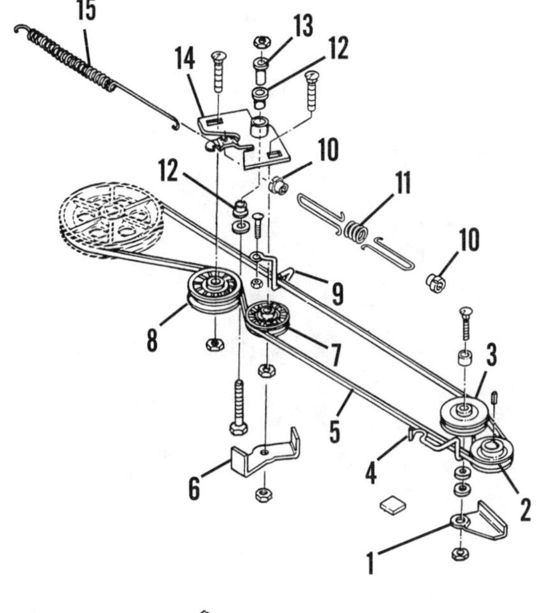

Fig. JD20-4–Exploded view of traction drive belt components for Model GT242 and GT262.

1. Belt guard
2. Engine pulley
3. Idler
4. Belt guide
5. Drive belt
6. Belt guard
7. V-idler
8. Flat idler
9. Belt guide
10. Spring caps
11. Clutch pedal spring
12. Bushings
13. Bushing
14. Bellcrank
15. Spring

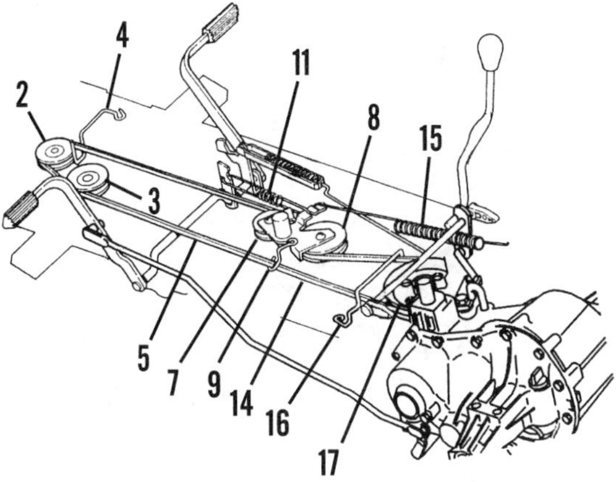

Fig. JD20-5–Drawing of traction drive belt arrangement on Models GT242 and GT262.

2. Engine pulley
3. Idler
4. Belt guide
5. Traction drive belt
7. Idler
8. Idler
9. Belt guide
11. Clutch pedal spring
14. Bellcrank
15. Spring
16. Belt guide
17. Transaxle pulley

stick on top of the dipstick tube; do not screw in.

The recommended oil is a premium grade oil meeting latest API service classification. Use SAE 15W40 oil for temperatures above 32°F (0°C); use SAE 10W-30 oil for temperatures between -4°F (-20°C) and 86°F (30°C); SAE 5W-30 may be used between 68°F (20°C) and -22°F (-30°C).

Change oil and filter after the first five hours of operation and then after every 100 hours of operation, or more frequently when operation is severe.

REMOVAL AND INSTALLATION

To remove the engine, first remove the hood. Remove the heat shield and muffler. Disconnect the battery ground cable. Drain the engine oil. Close fuel shut-off valve and disconnect fuel line. Disconnect the throttle control cable. Disconnect the ground wire, starter wires and ignition wires from the engine. Remove the electric PTO clutch. Engage the parking brake to relieve the tension on the traction drive belt. Remove the drive pulley and key from the engine crankshaft. Remove the engine mounting cap screws while noting the screw length for proper reassembly. Lift the engine from the tractor.

To install the engine, reverse the removal procedure. Apply an antiseize lubricant to the crankshaft before installing the drive pulley. Tighten the engine mounting screws to 16 N·m (142 in.-lb.). Tighten the PTO clutch mounting cap screw to 75 N·m (55 ft.-lb.).

OVERHAUL

Engine make and model are listed at the beginning of this section. To overhaul engine components and accessories, refer to the KAWASAKI engine section in this manual.

CLUTCH AND TRACTION DRIVE BELT

MODELS GT242 AND GT262

Adjustment

To adjust the clutch, stop the engine and release the clutch pedal. Make certain the engine idler (3—Fig. JD20-4) is positioned in the center of its mounting slot. Measure the distance between the flanges on the clutch pedal spring retainer caps (9). The distance should be 31-35 mm (1.22-1.38 in.) for proper belt tension.

To adjust belt tension, loosen the nut on the engine idler pulley (3—Fig. JD20-4), if necessary, and move the idler pulley so it is centered in the slot. Position the belt guide attached to the idler pulley so the guide is parallel to the belt between the engine pulley and idler pulley, then retighten the nut. Loosen the retaining nut on the bellcrank idler pulley (7) and move the pulley in the slot to obtain the desired clutch spring compressed dimension of 31-35 mm (1.22-1.38 in.). Retighten the nut.

If drive belt slips after performing the preceding adjustment procedure, increase the belt spring tension by moving the rear end of tension spring (15—Fig. JD20-5) to the rear spring attachment hole or notch. Recheck the clutch pedal spring adjustment.

If drive belt engagement is abrupt or rough after performing the preceding adjustment procedure, decrease the belt spring tension by moving the rear end of the tension spring (15—Fig. JD20-5) to the forward spring attachment hole or notch. Recheck the clutch pedal spring adjustment.

Removal and Installation

Remove the mower deck. Push down the clutch pedal and engage the parking brake. Separate the drive belt (5—Fig. JD20-5) from the transaxle pulley (17). Detach the belt guide (9). Remove the idler pulleys (7 and 8) from the bellcrank (14). Remove the nut and belt guard (1—Fig. JD20-4) from the engine idler pulley (3). Detach the front belt guide (4). Disconnect the wire connector from the PTO clutch. Disconnect the drag link from the steering arm. Remove the traction drive belt.

Replace the drive belt by reversing the removal procedure. Adjust belt tension as previously described.

MODEL GT275

Adjustment

To adjust belt tension, release the clutch pedal and engage the parking brake. Remove the mower deck, if so equipped. Remove the belt guard (4—Fig. JD20-6) from the idler pulley (5). Loosen the nut attaching the idler pulley (5) to the bellcrank (16), and slide the idler in the bellcrank adjustment slot to obtain the desired belt tension. Retighten the idler retaining nut. Install the belt guard (4).

Removal and Installation

Remove the mower deck. Remove the seat and unscrew the seat adjustment knob. Unscrew the fender deck retaining screws and remove the fender deck. Move the fuel tank forward. Detach the spring (13—Fig. JD20-7) from the bellcrank. Disconnect the electric PTO wiring connector on the underside of the frame. Remove the belt guide (9). Disconnect the steering drag link. Remove the idler (8). Remove the belt guide (4—Fig. JD20-6) from the moveable idler (5). Disconnect the tension release rod (12). Remove the drive belt (2) from the pulleys.

Reverse the removal procedure to install belt. Adjust belt tension as previously described.

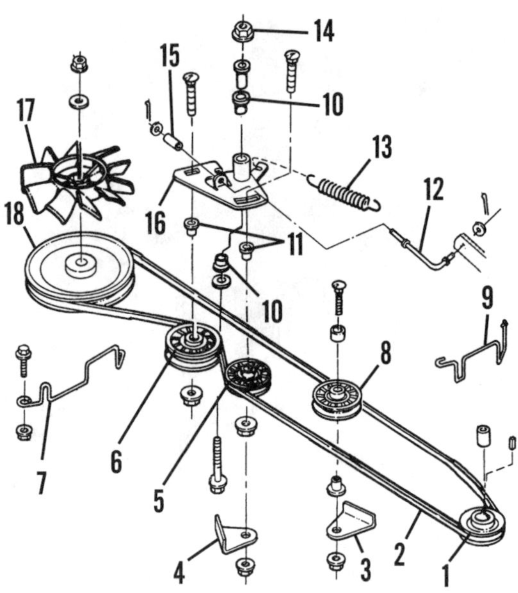

Fig JD20-6–Exploded view of traction drive belt coponents for Model GT275.

1. Engine pulley
2. Traction drive belt
3. Belt guide
4. Belt guard
5. V-idler
6. Flat idler
7. Belt guide
8. Idler
9. Belt guide
10. Bushings
11. Bushings
12. Tension release rod
13. Spring
14. Bushing
15. Sleeve
16. Bellcrank
17. Fan
18. Transmission pulley

BRAKES

MODELS GT242-GT262

Adjustment

Remove the mower deck. Engage the parking brake. Measure the distance (D—Fig. JD20-8) from the rear of the brake rod bracket (11) to the cotter pin (P) in the brake rod (10). Distance should be 18-20 mm (0.71-0.79 in.). Rotate the adjusting nuts (9) at the end of the brake rod to obtain the desired distance.

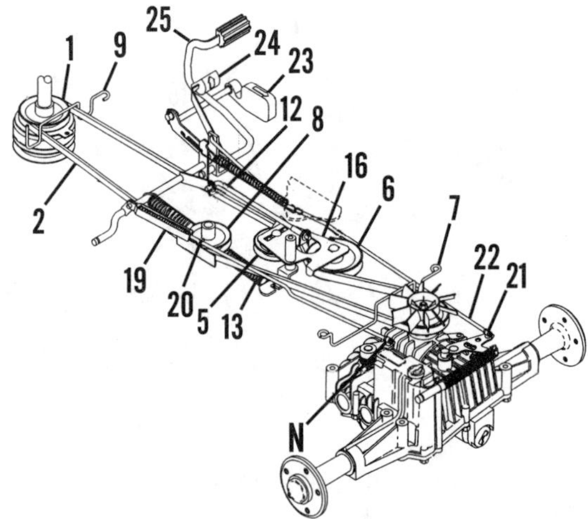

Fig. JD20-7–Drawing of traction drive belt arrangement on Model GT275.

1. Engine pulley
3. Belt guide
5. Idler
6. Idler
7. Belt guide
8. Idler
9. Belt guide
12. Tension release rod
13. Spring
16. Bellcrank
19. Brake rod bracket
20. Brake rod
21. Speed control rod end
22. Speed control rod
23. Reverse pedal
24. Forward pedal
25. Brake pedal

Overhaul

Drain oil from the transaxle. Detach the brake rod from the brake arm (8—Fig. JD20-8).

NOTE: Be prepared to catch loose balls (5) when removing the cover.

Remove the cap screws attaching the brake cover (6) to the transaxle housing. Remove the cover, actuator (3), brake plates (1) and discs (2). Detach the snap ring (4) and remove the brake arm (8) from the cover.

Inspect the brake components for damage. Replace the discs if the radial grooves are worn away. The specified diameter of the brake arm shaft is 19.95-20.00 mm (0.785-0.787 in.). The specified diameter of the cover bore is 20.02-20.05 mm (0.788-0.789 in.).

Reassemble the brake by reversing the disassembly procedure. Install the seal (7) flush with the cover surface. Lubricate the seal before installing the brake arm. Use grease to hold the balls (5) on the actuator (3). Apply gas-

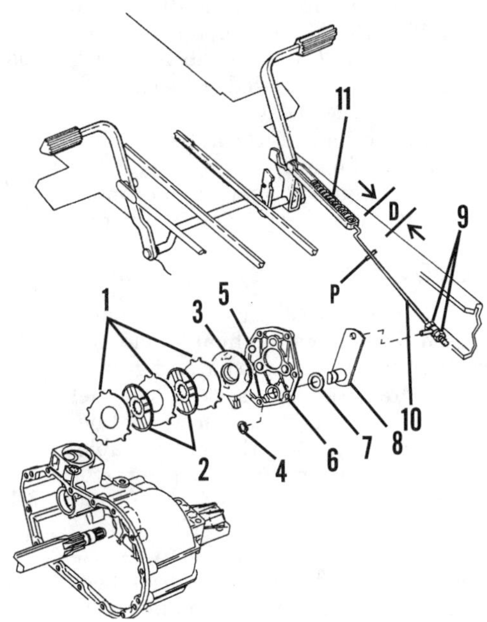

Fig. JD20-8–On Models GT242 and GT262, distance (D) from rear of brake spring bracket (11) to cotter pin (P) in brake rod should be 18-20 mm (0.71-0.79 in.). See text.

1. Brake plate
2. Brake discs
3. Actuator
4. Snap ring
5. Ball (3 used)
6. Cover
7. Seal
8. Brake arm
9. Jam nuts
10. Brake rod
11. Brake bracket & spring

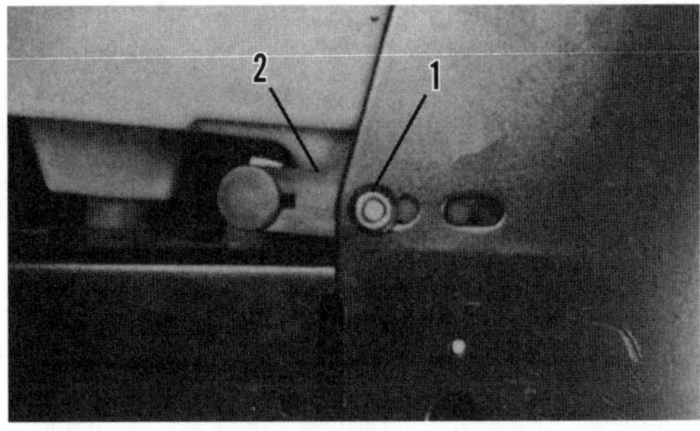

Fig. JD20-9–To adjust shift linkage on Models GT242 and GT262, loosen nut (1) and move bracket (2) on both sides of tractor so shift lever is centered in neutral position. Refer to text.

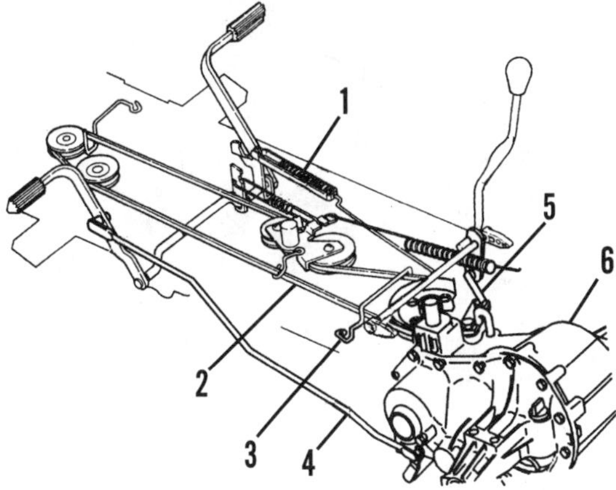

Fig JD20-10–Drawing of tractor drive system for Models GT242 and GT262.

1. Brake rod
2. Traction drive belt
3. Belt guide
4. Clutch interlock rod
5. Shift lever
6. Transaxle

ket-forming sealer to the cover and transaxle mating surfaces. Apply Loctite to the cover screws. Tighten the cover screws to 24 N·m (212 in.-lb.) on a used transaxle case or to 29 N·m (22 ft.-lb.) on a new transaxle case. Adjust the brake as previously described.

MODELS GT275

Adjustment

Remove the mower deck. Remove the seat and fender deck to gain access to the brake linkage. Engage the parking brake. Measure the distance from the rear of the brake rod bracket (19—Fig. JD20-7) to the cotter pin in the brake rod (20). The distance should be 3-5 mm (0.12-0.20 in.). Rotate the adjusting nuts (N) at the end of the brake rod to obtain the desired distance.

After adjusting the brake, check for the following correct functions: With the brake pedal released, the engine should not crank over or start. The forward and reverse pedals must pivot freely and return to NEUTRAL without binding. The tractor should roll freely without brake drag when the free wheeling valve is actuated.

Overhaul

Brake components are contained in the transaxle. Refer to the HYDROSTATIC TRANSMISSION section for brake service.

SHIFT LINKAGE

NEUTRAL ADJUSTMENT (MODELS GT242-GT262)

If the transaxle gear indicated on the shift indicator quadrant is not properly engaged, perform the following neutral adjustment.

Move the gearshift lever to NEUTRAL. Loosen the shift linkage nuts (1—Fig. JD20-9) located on each side of the rear frame behind the rear wheels. Move the linkage support brackets (2) so the shift lever is centered in NEUTRAL on the shift indicator quadrant. Tighten the nuts. Operate the shift lever to determine if all gears are properly engaged.

PEDAL HEIGHT ADJUSTMENT (MODEL GT275)

Pedal height must be correct to obtain the full speed range and to prevent transaxle internal components from acting as mechanical stops.

Remove the mower deck. Remove the seat and unscrew the seat adjustment knob. Unscrew the fender deck retaining screws and remove the fender deck. Move the gas tank forward to provide

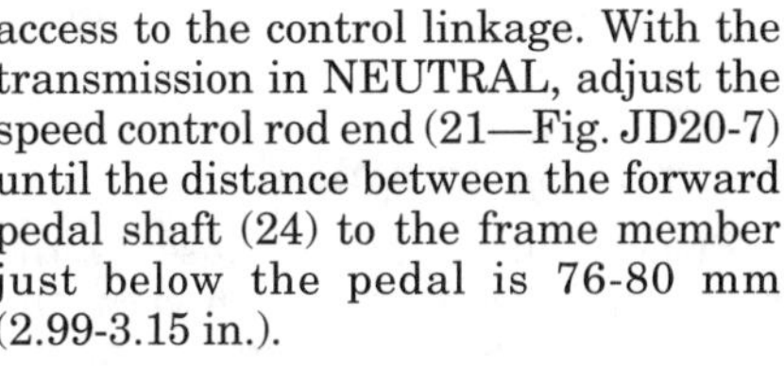

access to the control linkage. With the transmission in NEUTRAL, adjust the speed control rod end (21—Fig. JD20-7) until the distance between the forward pedal shaft (24) to the frame member just below the pedal is 76-80 mm (2.99-3.15 in.).

TRANSAXLE

MODELS GT242-GT262

Lubrication

Check the transaxle oil level after every 25 hours of operation. The oil level should be maintained at the top mark on the dipstick, which is located at the rear of the transaxle. Add oil when necessary. The approximate oil capacity is 3.6 liters (3.8 qt.).

Recommended oil is John Deere Low Viscosity HY-GARD (J20B) Transmission Oil.

Removal and Installation

To remove the transaxle, remove the mower deck. Raise and support the rear of the tractor. Remove the rear wheels. Drain the oil from the transaxle housing. Engage the parking brake. Detach the belt guide (3—Fig. JD20-10) adjacent to the transaxle pulley and remove the drive belt (2) from the pulley. Disengage the parking brake. Disconnect the brake linkage (1), clutch interlock linkage (4) and shift linkage (5) from the transaxle. Disconnect the neutral switch wire from the transaxle. Support the transaxle. Remove the transaxle mounting bolts and nuts, then lower the transaxle from the tractor.

To reinstall, reverse the removal procedure. Tighten the mounting bolts and nuts to 50 N·m (37 ft.-lb.). Fill the transaxle with oil to the full mark on the dipstick.

Overhaul

Models GT242 and GT262 are equipped with a TUFF TORQ transaxle manufactured by Kanzaki. Refer to the KANZAKI section in the TRANSAXLE SERVICE section for the overhaul procedure.

MODEL GT275

Lubrication

Transaxle oil level should be checked prior to use of the machine. The oil fill cap is equipped with a dipstick. The oil level should be maintained between the dipstick marks. The recommended oil is John Deere Low Viscosity HY-GARD (J20B) Transmission Oil. Clean the area around the cap before removal.

The approximate oil capacity is 4.3 liters (4.7 qt.).

Neutral Adjustment

Remove the seat and unscrew the seat adjustment knob. Unscrew the fender deck retaining screws and remove the fender deck. Move the fuel tank forward to gain access to the transmission. Raise and support the rear of the tractor so the wheels clear the ground. Connect a jumper wire to the seat switch wire so the engine will run.

Start the engine and run at fast idle speed. With the transmission in NEUTRAL, the rear wheels should not rotate. If the wheels rotate, loosen the locknut (A—Fig. JD20-11) and adjust the eccentric shaft (B) as follows: Turn the eccentric clockwise until the wheels just begin to rotate in the reverse direction. Then, turn the eccentric in the opposite direction until the wheels just begin to turn forward. Position the eccentric at the midpoint. Hold the eccentric and tighten the locknut (A).

Fig. JD20-11–Loosen locknut (A) and rotate eccentric B) as described in text to adjust neutral position on Model GT275.

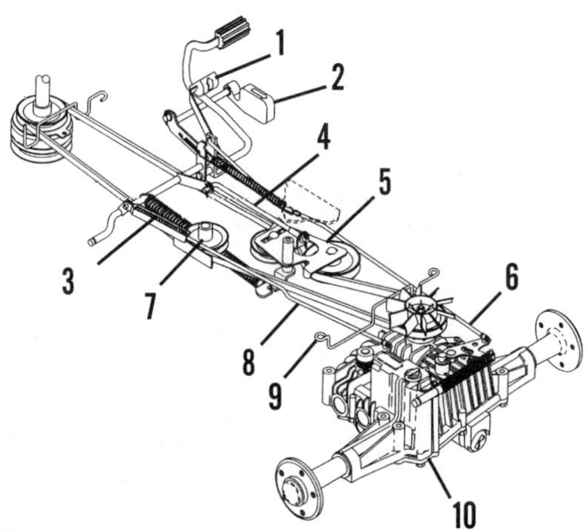

Fig. JD20-12–Drawing of traction drive system for Model GT275.

1. Forward pedal
2. Reverse pedal
3. Spring
4. Tension release rod
5. Bellcrank
6. Speed control rod
7. Idler
8. Brake control rod
9. Belt guide
10. Hydrostatic transaxle

Troubleshooting

The following list of problems that may occur and possible causes should be used as an aid in locating and correcting transmission problems.

Loss of power or transmission will not operate in either direction.
1. Low transmission oil level or wrong oil.
2. Plugged transmission oil filter.
3. Slipping or broken traction drive belt.
4. Improperly adjusted or damaged forward/reverse control linkage.
5. Binding free wheel linkage.
6. Worn or damaged internal hydrostatic transmission components.
7. Damaged final drive components.

Tractor jerks when starting or operates in one direction only.
1. Faulty speed control linkage.
2. Faulty forward or reverse check valve.
3. Binding or damaged shock absorber.

Tractor creeps when in NEUTRAL.
1. Improperly adjusted or damaged forward/reverse pedal linkage.
2. Improperly adjusted neutral eccentric.
3. Binding shock absorber.
4. Worn or damaged variable swash plate components.

Noisy operation
1. Low transmission oil level or wrong oil.
2. Contaminated oil.
3. Air in system.
4. Plugged hydrostatic oil filter.

Removal and Installation

Remove the mower deck. Remove the seat and rear fender deck. Disconnect the fuel line and remove the fuel tank. Remove the battery. Disconnect the belt tension release rod (4—Fig. JD20-12). Remove the traction drive belt from the transaxle pulley. Disconnect the neutral switch wire connector. Disconnect the shift control rod (6) from the transaxle. Disconnect the brake control rod (8) from the brake arm. Disconnect the free wheel release rod from the transaxle. Raise and support the rear of the tractor. Remove the rear wheels. Support the transaxle, and remove the transaxle mounting bolts and transaxle.

To install, reverse the removal procedure. Tighten the transmission front mounting nuts to 27 N·m (20 ft.-lb.) and rear mounting nuts to 54 N·m (40 ft.-lb.). Fill the transmission with Low Viscosity HY-GARD Transmission oil. Adjust the transmission control linkage and brake linkage as previously discussed.

Overhaul

Model GT275 is equipped with a TUFF TORQ Model K70 hydrostatic transaxle manufactured by Kanzaki. Refer to the KANZAKI section in the HYDROSTATIC TRANSAXLE service section for the overhaul procedure.

POWER TAKE-OFF (PTO)

TESTING

Use the following procedure for locating a PTO malfunction. Turn the ignition switch ON, engage the parking brake, close the seat switch and actuate the PTO switch. If the clutch does not engage, refer to the wiring schematic and check for faulty wiring or electrical component.

To check the PTO field coil, disconnect the PTO clutch wire connector and measure the resistance across the clutch connector terminals. The specified resistance is 2.4-2.6 ohms. The normal current draw with the clutch engaged is about 4 amps.

To check clutch coil magnetism, remove the clutch from the tractor. Ground the field coil frame and energize the coil lead wire with a known 12-volt source. Hold a piece of metal next to the coil and note if the metal is attracted. If

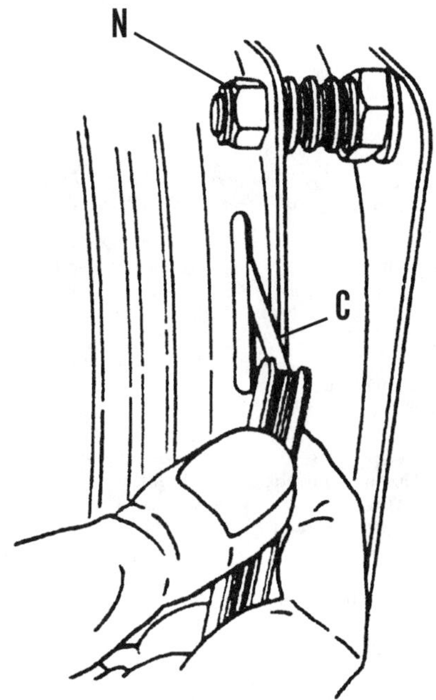

Fig. JD20-13–Adjust PTO clutch by turning each of the three adjusting nuts (N) until clearance (C) between rotor and armature is 0.51 mm (0.020 in.)

the metal is not attracted to the coil, replace the field coil assembly.

ADJUSTMENT

The PTO clutch must be adjusted if the clutch has been disassembled or if the operation becomes erratic. With the clutch disengaged, insert a feeler gauge through the slots in the clutch plate and measure the clearance between the clutch rotor and armature as shown in Fig. JD20-13. There should be a clearance of 0.38-0.64 mm (0.015-0.025 in.) at each of the slots in the clutch plate. To adjust, tighten or loosen the clutch adjusting nuts (N) to obtain the correct clearance.

OVERHAUL

To remove the PTO clutch, disconnect the electrical wires and remove the clutch retaining screw. Remove the clutch assembly from the crankshaft. Use a plastic hammer to tap and loosen the clutch from the crankshaft when necessary.

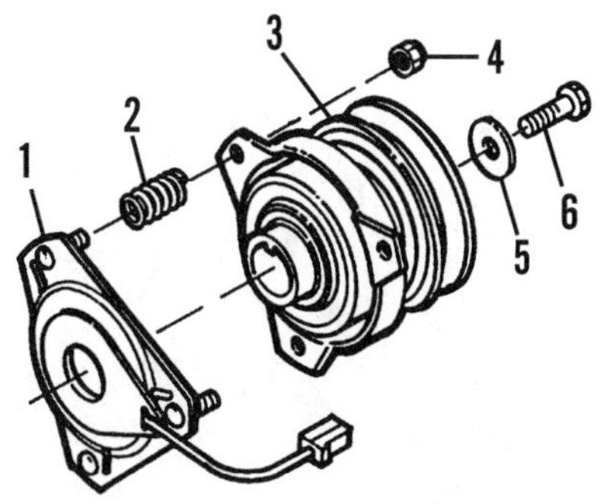

Fig. JD20-14–Exploded view of electric PTO clutch.

1. Field coil assy.
2. Spring
3. Armature & rotor assy.
4. Adjusting nut
5. Washer
6. Screw

To disassemble the clutch (Fig. JD20-14), remove adjusting nuts (4) and separate the armature and rotor (3) from the field coil housing (1).

Inspect the bearings for damage. Inspect for broken or distorted springs. Check the rotor and armature contact surfaces for damage. Replace parts or clutch assembly when necessary.

To reassemble the clutch, reverse the disassembly procedure. Apply an antiseize lubricant to the crankshaft before reinstalling the clutch assembly. The slot in the field coil plate must fit over the pin on the engine platform. Install a washer (5—Fig. JD20-14) with the concave side toward the engine. Tighten the clutch retaining screw to 75 N·m (55 ft.-lb.). Adjust the clutch as previously outlined. If installing a new clutch, break in the clutch by engaging the PTO at least eight times unloaded before attaching a load to the clutch.

SAFETY INTERLOCK SYSTEM

The tractor is equipped with a safety interlock system preventing inadvertent starting of the tractor engine or operation when the operator leaves the tractor seat. The tractor engine should not start if the following occurs (engage parking brake):

- Operator in the tractor seat, the shift lever in NEUTRAL, the brake engaged and the PTO clutch lever in the ON position.
- Operator in the tractor seat, the PTO clutch lever in the OFF position, the brake engaged and the shift lever in a position other than NEUTRAL.
- Operator in the tractor seat, the shift lever in NEUTRAL, the PTO clutch lever in the OFF position and the brakes released.
- Operator not in the seat when starting the engine.

The seat switch should kill the engine when the operator is not in the seat or leaves the seat when the PTO clutch is engaged. The seat switch should kill the engine when the operator leaves the seat when the brakes are not locked.

Refer to the wiring schematics at end of this section.

WIRING SCHEMATICS

Refer to Fig. JD20-15 for identification and location of electrical components for Models GT242 and GT262. Refer to Fig. JD20-16 for identification and location of electrical components for Model GT275. Wiring schematic and harness diagram for Models GT242 and GT262 is illustrated in Fig. JD20-17. Wiring schematic and harness diagram for Model GT275 is illustrated in Fig. JD20-18 for Model GT275.

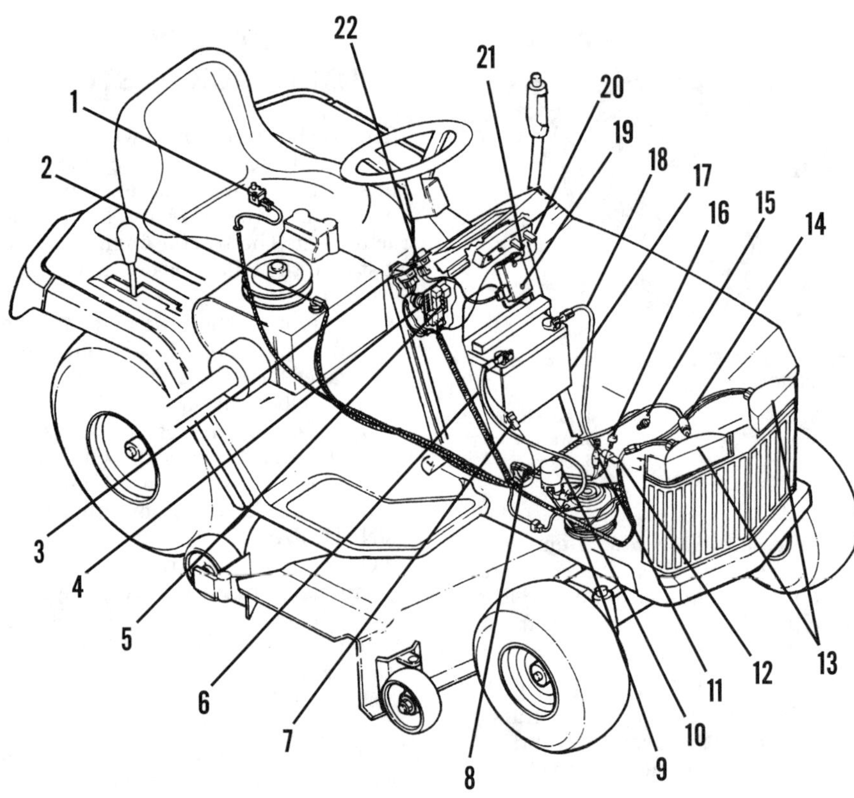

Fig. JD20-15–Drawing showing electrical components for Models GT242 and GT262.

1. Seat switch
2. Neutral start switch
3. PTO switch
4. Key switch module
5. 15 amp fuses
6. Battery positive cable
7. Fusible link
8. Engine connector
9. PTO clutch
10. Starter solenoid
11. Stator connector
12. Wiring harness connector
13. Headlights
14. Fuel shut-off solenoid
15. Oil pressure switch
16. Ignition module
17. Battery
18. Battery negative cable
19. Regulator/rectifier
20. Battery discharge lamp
21. Oil pressure lamp
22. Headlight switch

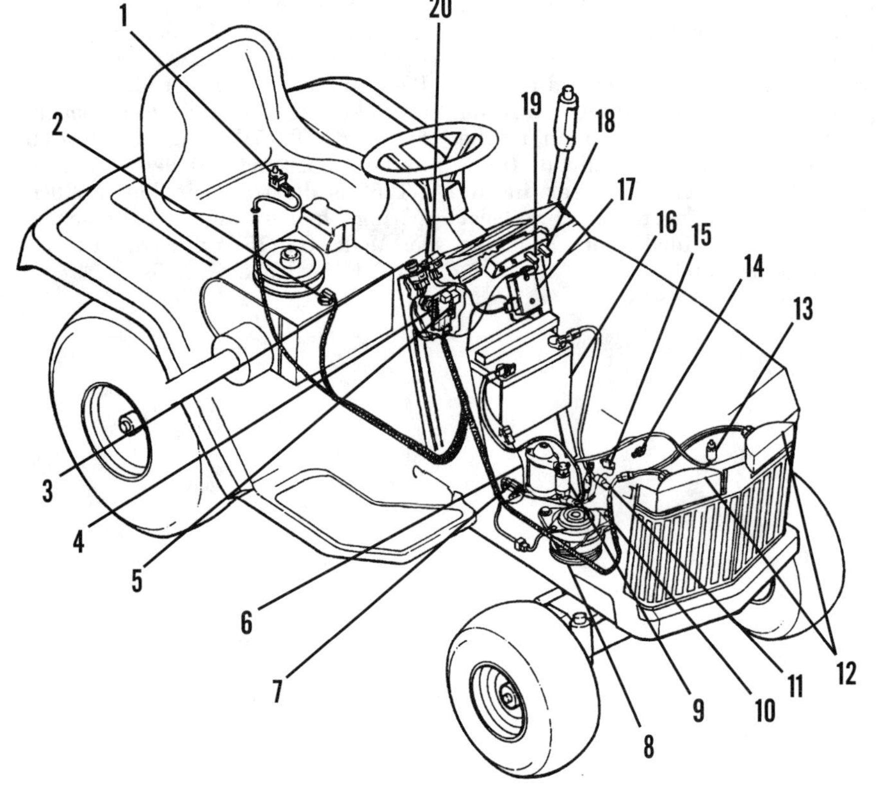

Fig. JD20-16–Drawing of electrical components for Model GT275.

1. Seat switch
2. Neutral start switch
3. PTO switch
4. Key switch & interlock module
5. 15 amp fuse
6. Engine connector
7. Engine connector
8. PTO clutch
9. Starting motor
10. Stator connector
11. Wiring ground
12. Headlights
13. Fuel shut-off solenoid
14. Oil pressure switch
15. Ignition module
16. Battery
17. Regualtor/rectifier
18. Battery discharge light
19. Oil pressure light
20. Headlight switch

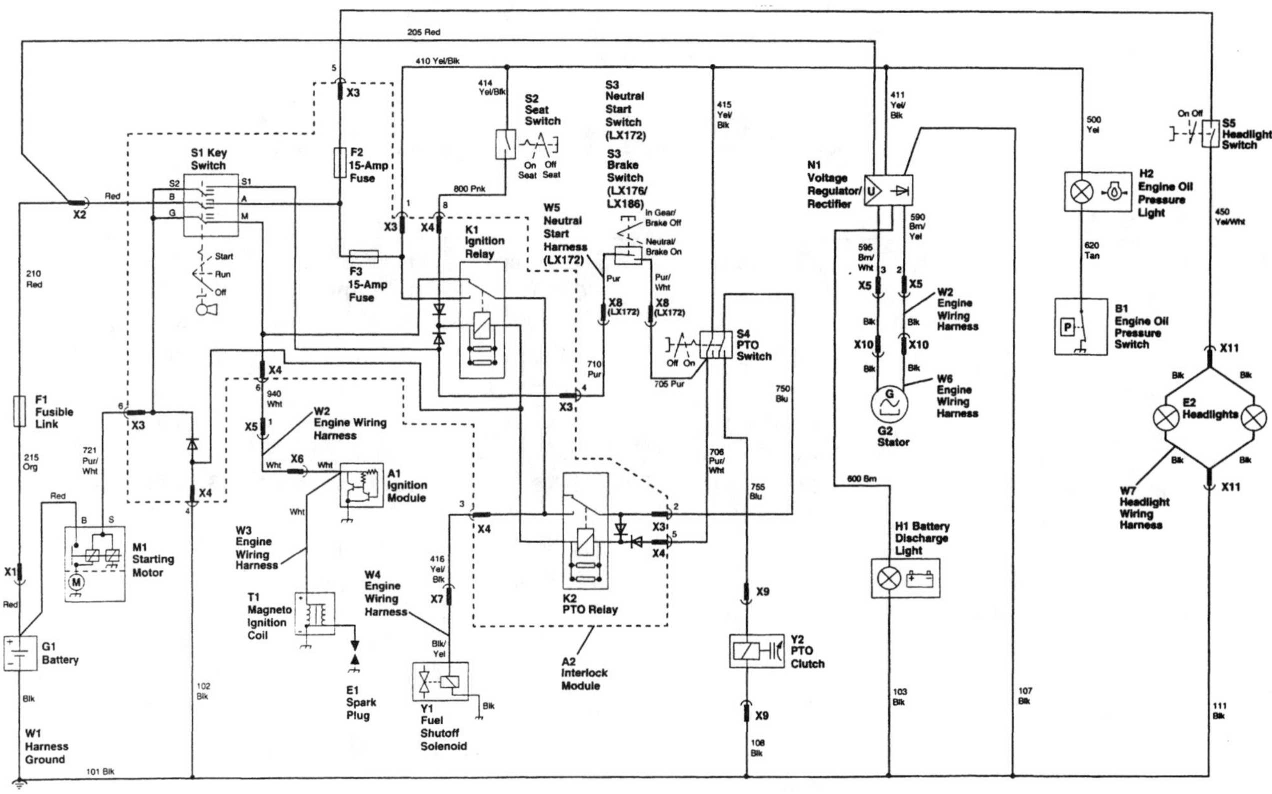

Fig. JD20-17–Wiring schematic and harness diagram for Models GT242 and GT262/

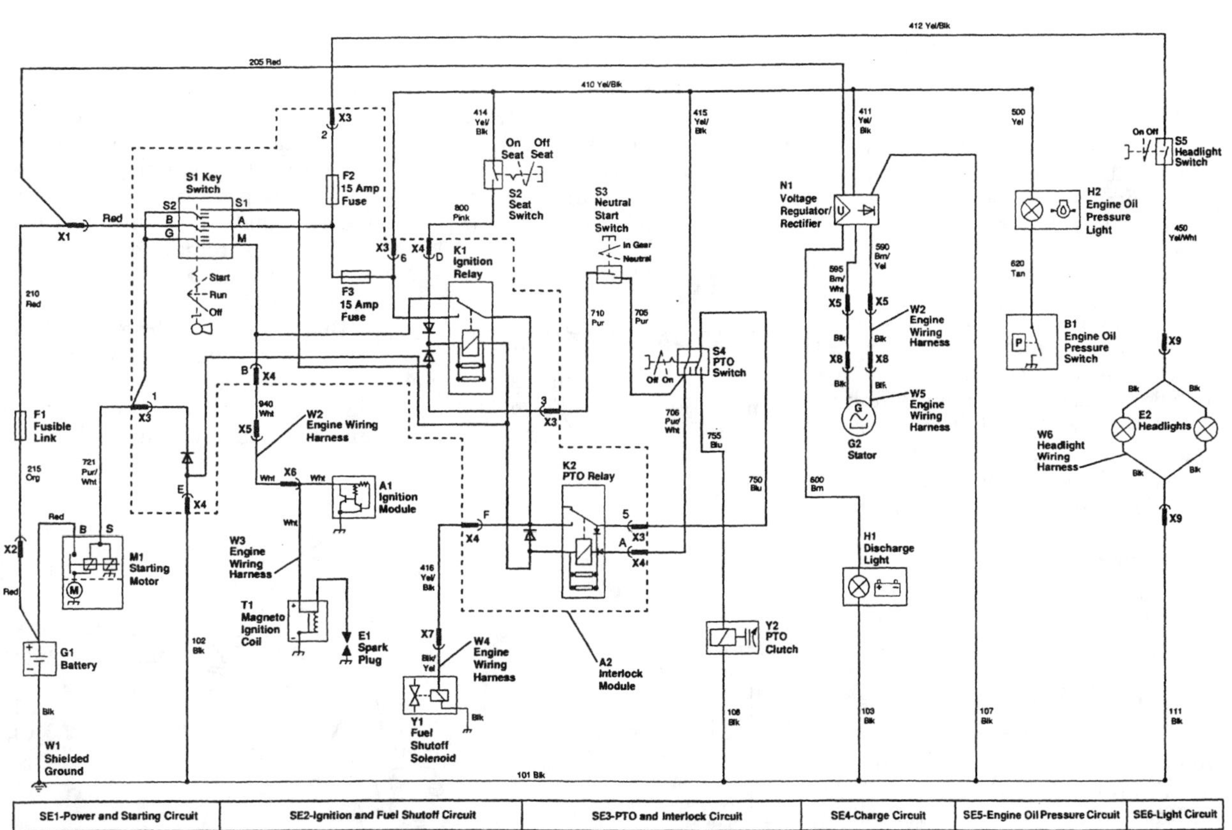

Fig. JD20-18–Wiring schematic and harness diagram for Model GT275.

JOHN DEERE

CONDENSED SPECIFICATIONS

MODELS	170	175	180	185
Engine Make	Kawasaki	Kawasaki	Kawasaki	Kawasaki
Model	FC420V	FC420V	FC540V	FC540V
Bore	89 mm (3.5 in.)	89 mm (3.5 in.)	89 mm (3.5 in.)	89 mm (3.5 in.)
Stroke	68 mm (2.68 in.)	68 mm (2.68 in.)	86 mm (3.38 in.)	86 mm (3.38 in.)
Displacement	423cc (25.8 cu. in.)	423cc (25.8 cu. in.)	535cc (32.6 cu. in.)	535cc (32.6 cu. in.)
Power Rating	10.4 kW (14 hp)	10.4 kW (14 hp)	12.6 kW (17 hp)	12.6 kW (17 hp)
Slow Idle Speed	1400 rpm	1400 rpm	1400 rpm	1400 rpm
High Idle Speed (No-Load)	3350 rpm	3350 rpm	3350 rpm	3350 rpm
Crankcase Capacity	1.3 L* (2.8 pt.)	1.3 L* (2.8 pt.)	1.6 L* (3.4 pt.)	1.6 L* (3.4 pt.)
Transmission Capacity	1.0 L (36 oz.)	See Text	1.0 L (36 oz.)	See Text

*Add 0.4 L (0.8 pt.) with filter change.

FRONT AXLE SYSTEM

TIE ROD AND TOE-IN

Refer to Fig. JD3-1 and note the tie rod (9) and ball joints are integral and must be replaced as an assembly. Toe-in is not adjustable.

STEERING SPINDLES

To remove the steering spindles (1 or 5—Fig. JD3-1), raise and support the front of the tractor. Remove the front wheels. Disconnect the tie rod (9) and drag link (3) from the spindles when necessary. Remove the snap ring (7) retaining the spindle in the axle, then lower the spindle from the axle main member.

Apply multipurpose grease to the spindles before installing in the axle. Install spindles by reversing the removal procedure.

AXLE MAIN MEMBER

To remove the front axle assembly, first remove hood, muffler and muffler guard. Remove the electric PTO clutch. Raise and support the front of the tractor. Disconnect the drag link (3—Fig. JD3-1) from the steering spindle. Remove the cap screws retaining the axle rear pivot anchor (8). Turn the pivot anchors onto the axle pivot shaft and lower the axle from the tractor.

Inspect the axle pivot shaft and anchors for wear and replace when necessary. To reinstall the axle, reverse the removal procedure.

STEERING GEAR

REMOVAL AND INSTALLATION

To remove the steering gear assembly, remove the bolt (3—Fig. JD3-2) and lift the steering wheel off the shaft. Raise the hood, disconnect the battery cables and remove the battery. Disconnect all wires from the dash. Disconnect the throttle control cable. Remove nuts retaining the dash panel and lift the dash off the steering shaft. Remove the cotter pins (5 and 10). Drive the steering shaft (4) up through the pinion gear (11) and remove the gear, bearings (2 and 8), washers (7), spring (6) and steering shaft.

Disconnect the drag link from the sector shaft (20). Remove the shaft support (17) retaining nuts, then unbolt and remove the sector gear support (12) and sector gear (15) assembly.

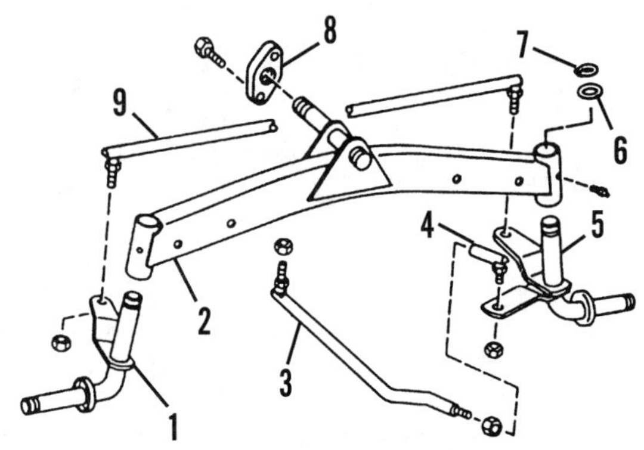

Fig. JD3-1–Exploded view of front axle assembly.

1. Steering spindle (right)
2. Axle main member
3. Drag link
4. Ball joint
5. Steering spindle (left)
6. Washer
7. Snap ring
8. Pivot pin anchor
9. Tie rod

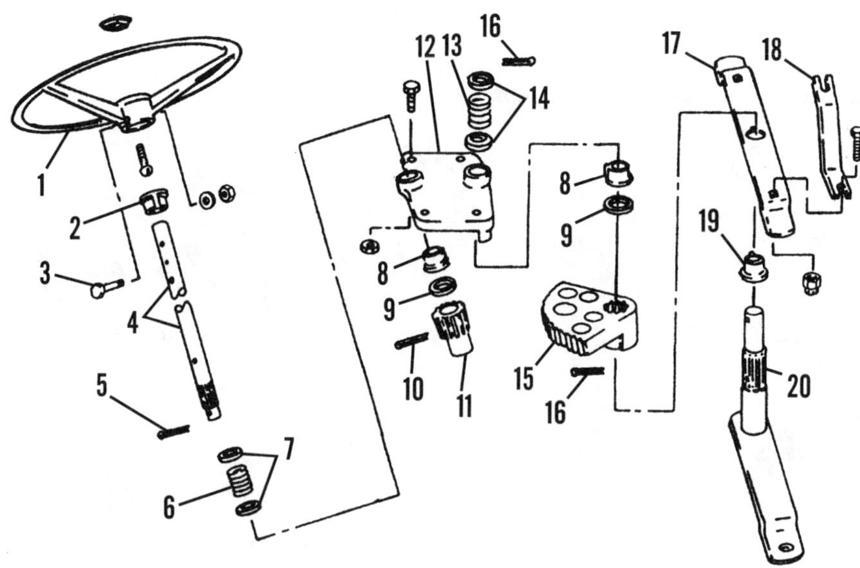

Fig. JD3-2–Exploded view of steering gear.

1. Steering wheel
2. Bushing
3. Bolt
4. Steering shaft
5. Cotter pin
6. Spring
7. Washers
8. Bushing
9. Washer
10. Cotter pin
11. Pinion gear
12. Support
13. Spring
14. Washers
15. Sector gear
16. Cotter pin
17. Sector shaft support
18. Strap
19. Bushing
20. Sector shaft

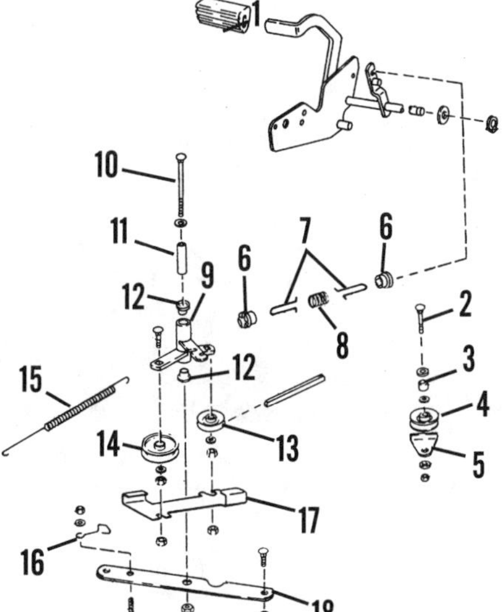

Fig. JD3-4–Exploded view of clutch bellcrank assembly used on Models 170 and 180

1. Pedal assy.
2. Bolt
3. Spacer
4. Idler pulley
5. Belt guard
6. Cap
7. Link
8. Spring
9. Bellcrank assy.
10. Bolt
11. Bushing
12. Bushings.
13. Idler pulley
14. Idler pulley
15. Spring
16. Belt guide
17. Belt guard
18. Support

To install the steering gear assembly, reverse the disassembly procedure while noting the following special instructions. Be sure the mark on the sector gear (15) is aligned with the mark on the sector shaft (20). When installing the pinion gear, make sure the mark (A—Fig. JD3-3) on the pinion gear is aligned with the mark (B) on the sector gear. With the dots aligned, the front wheels should be in a straight-ahead position. If not, disconnect the drag link (3—Fig. JD3-1) from the steering spindle (5) and move the wheels to a straight-ahead position. Adjust the length of the drag link so the ball joint end (4) fits into the steering spindle without moving the front wheels. Reconnect the drag link to the spindle.

OVERHAUL

To disassemble the steering gear, remove the cotter pins (16—Fig. JD3-2), washers (14), spring (13) and support (12) from the sector shaft (20). Mark the sector gear and shaft to ensure correct alignment when reassembling, then remove the bearing (8), washer (9) and gear (15) from the shaft. Remove the support (17) and bearing (19) from the sector shaft.

Inspect bearings, springs, steering shaft, sector shaft and steering gears

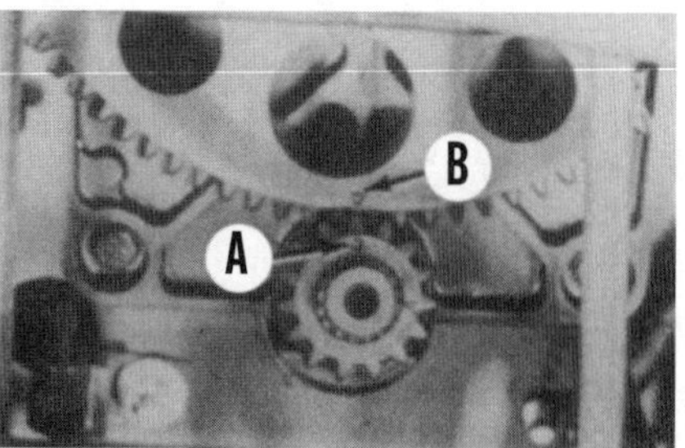

Fig. JD3-3–When assembling steering gears, make sure that dot (A) on pinion gear is aligned with dot (B) on sector gear.

for damage and replace when necessary.

When reassembling, be sure the marks on the sector gear and shaft are aligned.

ENGINE

REMOVAL AND INSTALLATION

To remove the engine, first remove the hood, muffler and pedestal shroud. Disconnect the battery ground cable. Close the fuel shut-off valve and disconnect the fuel line. Disconnect the throttle control cable. Disconnect the ground wire, starter wires and ignition wires from the engine. Remove the electric PTO clutch. Relieve tension on the traction drive belt and remove belt from the drive pulley. Remove the drive pulley and key from the engine crankshaft. Remove the engine mounting cap screws, rotate the engine to clear the oil drain hole in the frame and lift the engine from the tractor.

To install the engine, reverse the removal procedure. Apply an antiseize lubricant to the crankshaft before installing the drive pulley. Tighten the PTO clutch mounting cap screw to 45 ft.-lb. (56 N·m).

OVERHAUL

Engine make and model are listed at the beginning of this section. To overhaul engine components and accessories, refer to the appropriate KAWASAKI section in this manual.

CLUTCH AND BRAKE

MODELS 170 AND 180

Operation

Separate pedals operate the clutch and brake. When the clutch pedal is depressed, the bellcrank assembly (9—Fig. JD3-4) pivots and loosens the drive belt from the drive pulleys stopping forward or reverse movement. The brake pedal actuates a disc brake located on the transaxle.

Adjustment

To adjust the clutch, first remove the mower from the tractor. Put the transmission in gear, but do not engage the parking brake. Loosen the nut on the front idler pulley (4—Fig. JD3-4) and slide the idler in the slot until the distance between the inside of the frame and flat idler (14) is 3.7 in. (94 mm). Adjust the belt guard (5) to be parallel with the drive belt and provide clearance of 0.020 in.(5 mm) between the guard and belt. Tighten the idler pulley nut. Replace the drive belt if belt slippage occurs as a result of belt wear or stretching.

To adjust the brake, first be sure the parking brake is not engaged. Use a feeler gauge to measure the clearance between the brake pad and brake disc. Clearance should be 0.020 in. (0.50 mm). Turn the adjusting nut (10—Fig. JD3-5) on the brake lever (6) to obtain clearance.

Overhaul

Raise and support the rear of the tractor and remove the right rear wheel. Disconnect the brake rod from the brake lever (6—Fig. JD3-5). Unbolt and remove the caliper assembly (4). Remove the brake disc (2) and inner brake pad from the transaxle.

Inspect parts and replace when necessary. Reassemble in the reverse of the disassembly procedure and adjust as outlined in the ADJUSTMENT paragraph.

MODELS 175 AND 185 (PRIOR TO SERIAL NUMBER 475001)

Operation

These tractors are equipped with a hydrostatic drive and do not use an engine disconnect clutch. A disc brake is located on the left side of the rear axle housing. When the brake pedal is depressed, the brake is actuated and the hydrostatic transmission control linkage is returned to the NEUTRAL position.

Adjustment

A spring-loaded idler maintains the proper drive belt tension. No adjustment is required. If belt slippage occurs due to belt stretch or wear, replace the belt.

To adjust the brake, first make sure the park brake is not engaged. Use a feeler gauge to measure the clearance between the brake pad and brake disc. The clearance should be 0.020 in. (0.50 mm). Turn the adjusting nut (10—Fig. JD3-5) on the brake lever (6) to obtain the correct clearance.

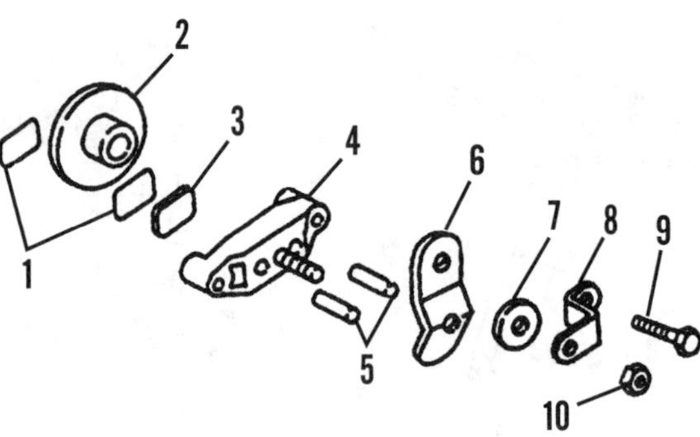

Fig. JD3-5–Exploded view of disc brake assembly typical of all tractors except Model 185 S.N. 465001 and later.

1. Brake pads
2. Brake disc
3. Back plate
4. Brake holder
5. Actuating pins
6. Brake lever
7. Washer
8. Bracket
9. Cap screw
10. Adjusting nut

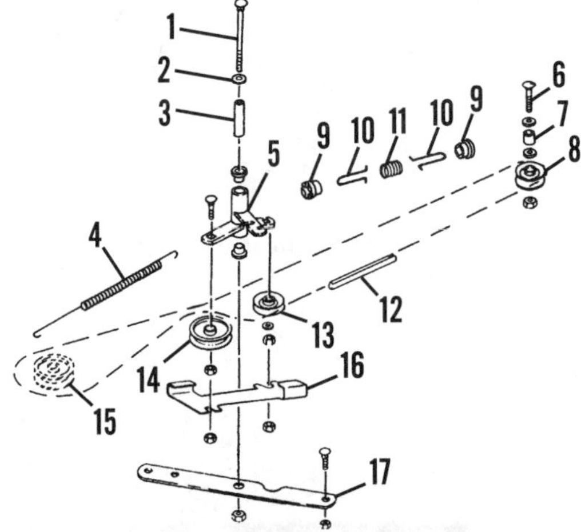

Fig. JD3-6—Exploded view of clutch bellcrank assembly used on Model 185 S. N. 475001 and later.

1. Bolt
2. Bushing
3. Bushing
4. Spring
5. Bellcrank
6. Bolt
7. Spacer
8. Pulley
9. Cap
10. Link
11. Spring
12. Drive belt
13. Idler pulley
14. Idler pulley
15. Pulley
16. Belt guard
17. Support

Overhaul

Raise and support the rear of the tractor and remove the right rear wheel. Disconnect the brake rod from the brake lever (6—Fig. JD3-5). Unbolt and remove the caliper assembly (4). Remove the brake disc (2) and inner brake pad from the transaxle.

Inspect parts and replace when necessary. Reassemble in the reverse of the disassembly procedure and adjust as outlined in the ADJUSTMENT paragraph.

MODEL 185 (SERIAL NUMBER 147001 AND AFTER)

Operation

A spring-loaded belt idler bellcrank assembly (5—Fig. JD3-6) serves as the engine disconnect clutch and maintains the proper drive belt tension.

The brake assembly is mounted internally in the rear axle housing. When the brake pedal is depressed, the brake is applied, the hydrostatic transmission control linkage is returned to NEUTRAL and the bellcrank assembly (5) pivots and loosens the drive belt from the drive pulley.

Adjustment

There is no adjustment required for the spring-loaded clutch bellcrank assembly or for the transmission brake. Replace the drive belt if belt slippage occurs as a result of belt stretch or wear.

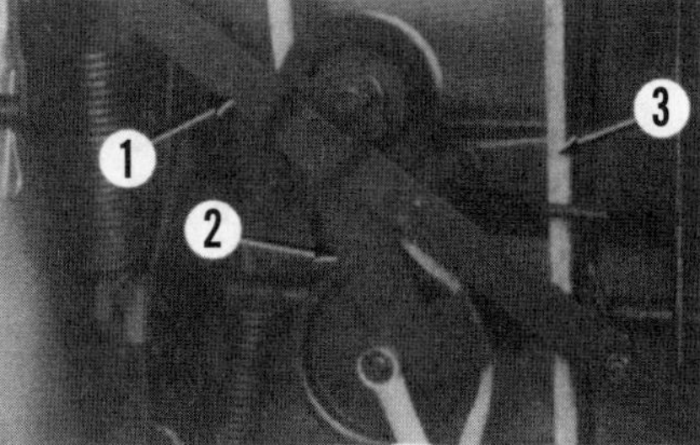

Fig. JD3-7–Underside view of traction belt clutch assembly used on Models 170, 180 and 185 S.N. 475001 and later.

1. Clutch support
2. Belt guide
3. Drive belt

Overhaul

Removal and installation of brake components are covered in the FINAL DRIVE service section.

DRIVE BELTS REMOVAL AND INSTALLATION

MODELS 170, 180 AND 185

To remove the drive belt, first remove the mower from the tractor. Disconnect the wiring harness from the electric

Fig. JD3-8–On Model 170 and 180, distance (A) between inner surface of flat idler pulley and inside of frame should be 3.7 inches (94 mm) with clutch engaged. Refer to text for adjustment procedure.

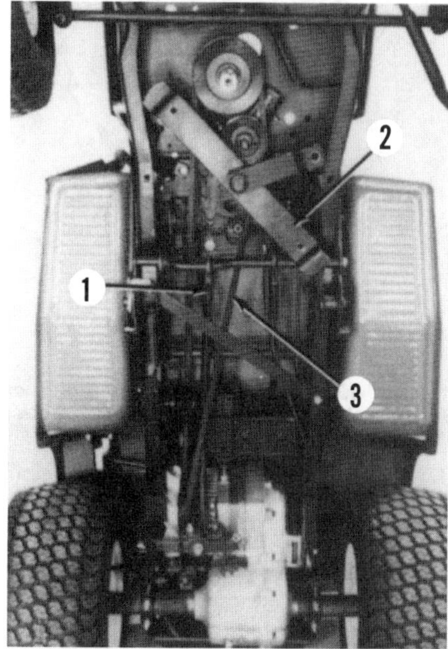

Fig. JD3-9–Underside view of traction drive belt on Models 175 and 185 prior to S.N. 475001.

1. Neutral return rod
2. Steering support
3. Drive belt

PTO clutch, then unbolt and remove the PTO clutch. On all models except Model 185, loosen the adjusting idler retaining nut. Remove the steering support mounting cap screws and turn steering support so it is parallel to the drive belt. Disconnect the steering drag link from the steering shaft arm. Remove the belt guide (2—Fig. JD3-7) from the clutch idler pulleys. Remove bolts attaching the clutch support (1) to the frame and turn the support so it is parallel with the drive belt (3). Depress the clutch pedal and slip the drive belt out of the pulleys.

To install the drive belt, reverse the removal procedure. On all tractors except Model 185, slide the belt adjusting idler in its mounting slot until clearance of 3.7 in. (94 mm) is obtained between the flat idler and inside of the frame as shown in Fig. JD3-8. Tighten

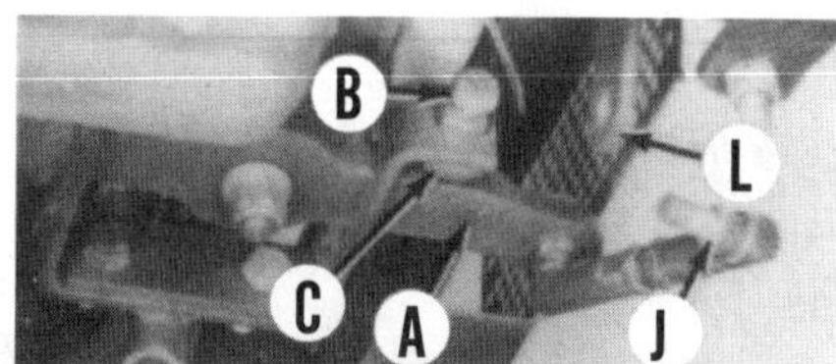

Fig. JD3-10–Underside view of hydrostatic transmission control linkage used on Models 175 and 185 prior to S.N. 475001.

A. Control arm
B. Adjusting screw
J. Control link ball joint
L. Control lever

the nut on the adjusting idler. Tighten the PTO clutch mounting cap screw to 45 ft.-lb. (56 N·m).

MODEL 175 AND 185 (PRIOR TO SERIAL NUMBER 475001)

To remove the drive belt, first remove the mower from the tractor. Disconnect the electrical leads from the PTO clutch, then unbolt and remove the PTO clutch. Remove the steering support mounting bolts and turn the support (2—Fig. JD3-9) so that it is parallel with the drive belt (3). Disconnect the drag link from the steering shaft arm. Disconnect the transmission neutral return rod (1) from the brake cross shaft. Push against the spring-loaded belt idler to relieve the spring tension or disconnect the spring, then remove the drive belt from the pulleys.

To reinstall the drive belt, reverse the removal procedure. No adjustment is required on the spring-loaded idler pulley assembly. Tighten the PTO clutch mounting cap screw to 45 ft.-lb. (56 N·m).

TRANSAXLE (MODELS 170 AND180)

REMOVAL AND INSTALLATION

To remove the transaxle, first remove the mower. Raise and support the rear of the tractor. Depress the clutch pedal and slip the traction drive belt off the transaxle drive pulley. Disconnect the brake control rod from the disc brake lever. Disconnect the neutral start switch wire located on top of the transaxle. Disconnect the transaxle shift arm. Remove the bolts attaching the hitch plate to the frame, then roll the transaxle back from the tractor.

To install, reverse the removal procedure. Adjust the traction drive belt, brakes and shift linkage when necessary.

OVERHAUL

Models 170 and 180 are equipped with a Peerless 800 series transaxle. Refer to the appropriate transaxle section in this manual for overhaul procedure.

HYDROSTATIC TRANSMISSION

MODELS 175 AND 185 (PRIOR TO SERIAL NUMBER 475001)

Lubrication

The transmission oil level should be checked when the oil is cold. Park the tractor on a level surface and raise the seat. Clean the area around the oil fill tube, then remove the filler tube cap. The oil level should be just above the screen in the reservoir, or 5½ in. (140 mm) from the top of the fill tube. If the oil level is low, add oil to bring the level just above the screen. The recommended oil is SAE 30 engine oil. Capacity is approximately 1.5 pints (0.7 L).

NOTE: DO NOT drain or change the transmission oil while the tractor is covered by manufacturer's warranty, otherwise the warranty will be void.

To refill the hydrostatic transmission with oil after the unit has been serviced, remove the oil reservoir cap and vent plug from the top of the transmission housing. Fill the reservoir with SAE 30 engine oil until oil flows from the vent hole. Rotate both the input and output shafts several revolutions to purge air from the system, then add oil to the reservoir until oil again flows from the vent hole. Install and tighten the vent plug. Continue to refill the reservoir until the oil is at the cold level FULL mark on units with a dipstick, or until the oil is 5½ in. (140 mm) below the top of the reservoir on units without a dipstick.

Linkage Adjustment

If the tractor creeps when the brake pedal is fully depressed, the neutral return linkage should be adjusted as follows: Raise and support the rear of the tractor so the rear wheels clear the ground. Move the hydrostatic control lever to NEUTRAL. Disconnect the brake rod from the disc brake lever. Disconnect the transmission control rod ball joint (J—Fig. JD3-10) from the hydrostatic control lever (L). Engage the parking brake and start the engine. Loosen the jam nut and turn the adjusting bolt (B) until the rear wheels stop turning. Tighten jam nut.

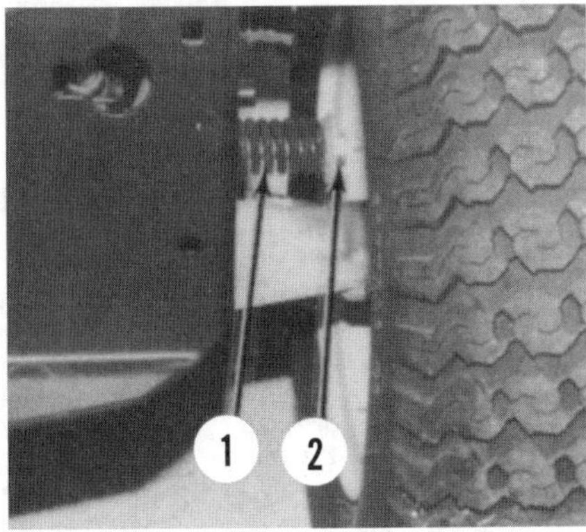

Fig. JD3-11–To adjust hydrostatic control lever friction adjustment, turn nut (2) to compress spring (1) until control lever will hold in position.

Disengage the park brake and move the hydrostatic control arm (A) to the rear as far as it will go. There should be 0.030-0.100 in. (0.7-2.5 mm) clearance (C) between the adjusting bolt and the control arm. If not, disconnect the neutral return rod yoke from the brake cross shaft and turn the yoke as necessary to obtain the correct clearance.

Reconnect the neutral return linkage and brake linkage. Engage the park brake. Loosen the jam nut on the hydrostatic control rod ball joint (J) and turn the joint as required so it slips into the hole in the hydrostatic control lever (L).

If the hydrostatic control lever will not stay in position when released or if the lever is hard to move, tighten or loosen the adjusting nut on the linkage compression spring (Fig. JD3-11).

Removal and Installation

To remove the hydrostatic transmission, first remove the mower. Raise and support the rear of the tractor. Drain lubricant from the final drive housing. Remove the mower height knob, the park brake knob and transmission tow valve knob. Disconnect the seat safety switch. Unbolt and remove the pedestal shroud and platform. Shut off the fuel and remove fuel tank. Remove the transmission cooling fan shield.

Disconnect the transmission control rod ball joint (8—Fig. JD3-12) from the transmission control arm (11). Remove the control arm retaining nut and remove the control arm and key from the transmission. Disconnect the brake control rod from the brake lever. Remove three cap screws and two U-bolts attaching the final drive housing to the frame and lower the final drive and transmission assembly. Remove the traction drive belt from the transmission pulley, then remove the final drive and transmission from the tractor. Remove the transmission mounting cap screws and separate the transmission from the final drive housing.

To install the transmission, reverse the removal procedure. Refill transmission with SAE 30 engine oil and refill final drive housing with SAE 90 gear lubricant. Adjust the transmission linkage as previously outlined.

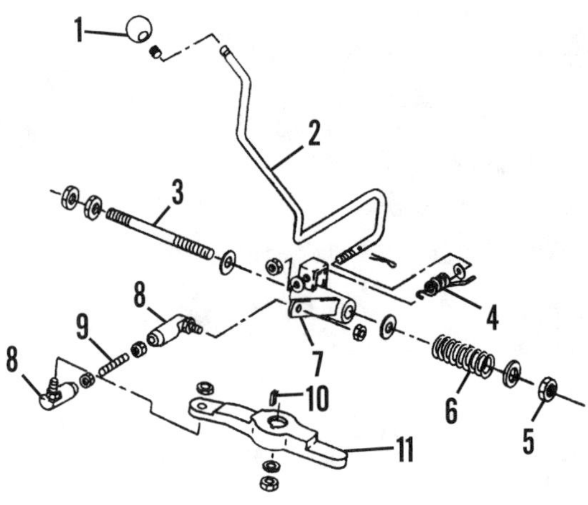

Fig. JD3-12–Exploded view of hydrostatic transmission shift lever and control linkage used on Models 175 and 185 prior to S.N. 475001.

1. Knob
2. Shift lever
3. Stud
4. Torsion spring
5. Nut
6. Friction spring
7. Pivot
8. Ball joint ends
9. Control link
10. Key
11. Control arm

Overhaul

Models 175 and 185 prior to Serial Number 475001 are equipped with an Eaton Model 7 hydrostatic transmission. Refer to the appropriate Eaton section in the HYDROSTATIC TRANSMISSION service section for the overhaul procedure.

MODEL 185 (SERIAL NUMBER 475001 AND AFTER)

Lubrication

The transmission oil level should be checked when the oil is cold. Park the tractor on a level surface and look under the right fender to see the oil reservoir. The oil should be up to the OIL LEVEL line on the reservoir. If not, raise the seat and clean around the oil reservoir cap. Remove the cap and fill to the proper level with SAE 10W-30 engine oil. The capacity is approximately 28.7 fluid ounces (850 cc).

NOTE: DO NOT drain or change transmission oil while the tractor is covered by the manufacturer's warranty, otherwise the warranty will be void.

To refill the hydrostatic transmission with oil and bleed air from the system after the unit has been serviced, proceed as follows: Fill the oil reservoir to the FULL line. Raise and support the rear of the tractor so the rear wheels clear the ground. Start the engine and run at idle speed for about three minutes. Then, move the transmission control lever to full forward for 10 seconds, return the lever to NEUTRAL for five seconds, push the tow (bleed valve) for two seconds, move the lever to full forward for 15 seconds and stop the engine. Fill the reservoir to the FULL line. Start the engine and run at idle speed. Place the transmission control lever in NEUTRAL for 10 seconds, then move the lever to full forward for 10 seconds and return the lever to NEUTRAL. Stop the engine and fill the reservoir to the FULL line.

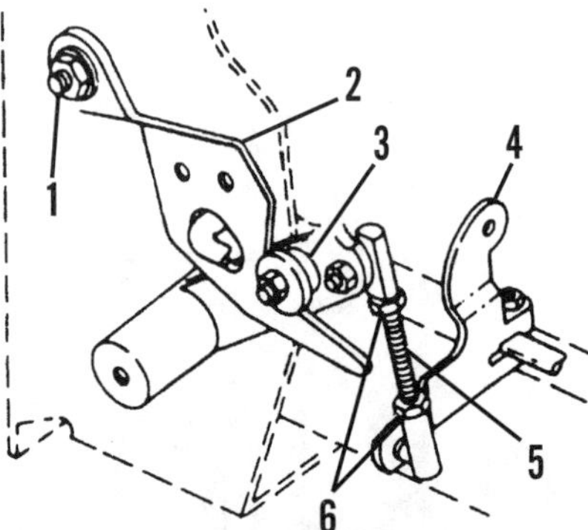

Fig JD3-13–Refer to text for adjustment of hydrostatic contol linkage used on Model 185 S.N. 475001 and later.

1. Nut
2. Cam
3. Roller
4. Control arm
5. Control link
6. Jam nuts

Linkage Adjustment

If the tractor creeps when the brake pedal is fully depressed, the neutral return linkage should be adjusted as follows: Raise and support the rear of the tractor so the rear wheels clear the ground. Move the hydrostatic control lever to NEUTRAL. Loosen the cam pivot nut (1—Fig. JD3-13) and engage the park brake. Move the cam (2) so the roller (3) is centered in the V of the cam. Hold the cam against the roller and tighten the retaining nut. Loosen the jam nuts (6) on the hydrostatic control link (5). Start the engine

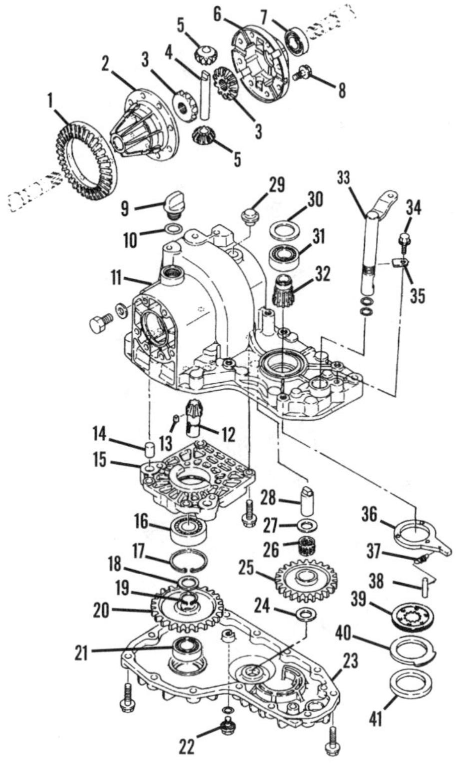

Fig. JD3-14–Exploded view of final drive unit used on Model 185 S.N. 475001 and later.

1. Bevel ring gear
2. Differential case
3. Axle side gears
4. Pinion shaft
5. Pinion
6. Differential case
7. Bearing
8. Cap screw
9. Oil filler cap
10. O-ring
11. Final drive housing
12. Bevel pinion gear
13. Key
14. Dowel
15. Bearing retainer
16. Bearing
17. Snap ring
18. Thrust washer
19. Snap ring
20. Counter ring
21. Bearing
22. Plug
23. Cover
24. Thrust washer
25. Idler gear
26. Needle bearing
27. Thrust washer
28. Idler shaft
29. Bleed valve
30. Spacer
31. Bearing
32. Motor drive gear
33. Brake camshaft
34. Cap screw
35. Plate
36. Brake actuator
37. Spring
38. Pin
39. Brake disc
40. Plate
41. Spacer

and turn the link until the rear wheels stop turning, then tighten the jam nuts.

Operate the transmission in FORWARD and REVERSE and apply the brake and release. The rear wheels must stop turning when the brake is applied and released. If the wheels continue to turn, readjust the linkage as needed.

If the hydrostatic control lever will not stay in position when released or if the lever is hard to move, tighten or loosen the linkage compression spring adjusting nut (Fig. JD3-11) as necessary.

Removal and Installation

To remove the hydrostatic transmission, first remove the mower. Raise and support the rear of the tractor. Disconnect the transmission tow valve linkage. Disconnect the oil reservoir hose. Disconnect the transmission control rod ball joint from the transmission control arm. Disconnect the neutral return control rod. Disconnect the brake control rod from the brake camshaft. Remove the traction drive belt from the transmission pulley. Remove the bolts attaching the hitch plate to the frame, then roll the final drive and transmission assembly back from the tractor.

Drain oil from the final drive housing and hydrostatic transmission. Remove the transmission cooling fan and drive pulley. Remove the transmission mounting cap screws and separate transmission from the final drive housing.

Install the hydrostatic transmission assembly. Install the transaxle assembly in the tractor and refill the final drive housing to level the plug opening with SAE 10W-30 engine oil. Refill the hydrostatic reservoir with SAE 10W-30 engine oil and bleed air from the system as previously outlined in the HYDROSTATIC TRANSMISSION LUBRICATION paragraph.

Overhaul

Model 185 Serial Number 475001 and later is equipped with a Hydro-Gear BDU series hydrostatic transmission. Refer to the HYDRO-GEAR section in the HYDROSTATIC TRANSMISSION service section for the overhaul procedure.

FINAL DRIVE

MODELS 175 AND 185 (PRIOR TO SERIAL NUMBER 475001)

Removal and Installation

To remove the final drive assembly, first remove the mower. Raise and support the rear of the tractor. Drain the lubricant from the final drive housing. Remove the rear wheels. Remove the mower height knob, park the brake knob and the transmission tow valve knob. Unbolt and remove the pedestal shroud and platform. Shut off the fuel and remove the fuel tank. Remove the transmission cooling fan shield.

Disconnect the transmission control rod ball joint from the transmission control arm. Remove the control arm retaining nut and remove the arm and key from the transmission. Disconnect the brake control rod from the brake lever. Remove the three cap screws and two U-bolts attaching the final drive housing to the frame and lower the final drive and transmission assembly. Remove the traction drive belt from the transmission pulley, then remove the final drive and transmission from the tractor. Remove the transmission mounting cap screws and separate the transmission from the final drive housing.

To install the final drive, reverse the removal procedure. Refill the final drive housing with SAE 90 gear lubricant until the lubricant level is just below the oil fill/check plug opening. Adjust the transmission linkage as previously outlined.

Overhaul

Models 175 and 175 (prior to Serial Number 475001) are equipped with a Peerless 1300 series final drive. Refer to the FINAL DRIVE section at the rear of this manual for the overhaul information.

MODEL 185 (SERIAL NUMBER 475001 AND LATER)

Removal and Installation

To remove the final drive assembly, first remove the mower. Raise and support the rear of the tractor. Disconnect the transmission tow valve linkage. Disconnect the oil reservoir hose. Disconnect the transmission control rod ball joint from the transmission control arm. Disconnect the neutral return control rod. Disconnect the brake control rod from the brake cam shaft. Remove the traction drive belt from the transmission pulley. Remove the bolts attaching the hitch plate to the frame and roll the final drive and transmission assembly from the tractor. Drain oil from the final drive housing and hydrostatic transmission. Remove the transmission cooling fan and drive pulley. Remove the transmission mounting cap screws and separate the transmission from the final drive housing.

Install the hydrostatic transmission assembly. Install the transaxle assem-

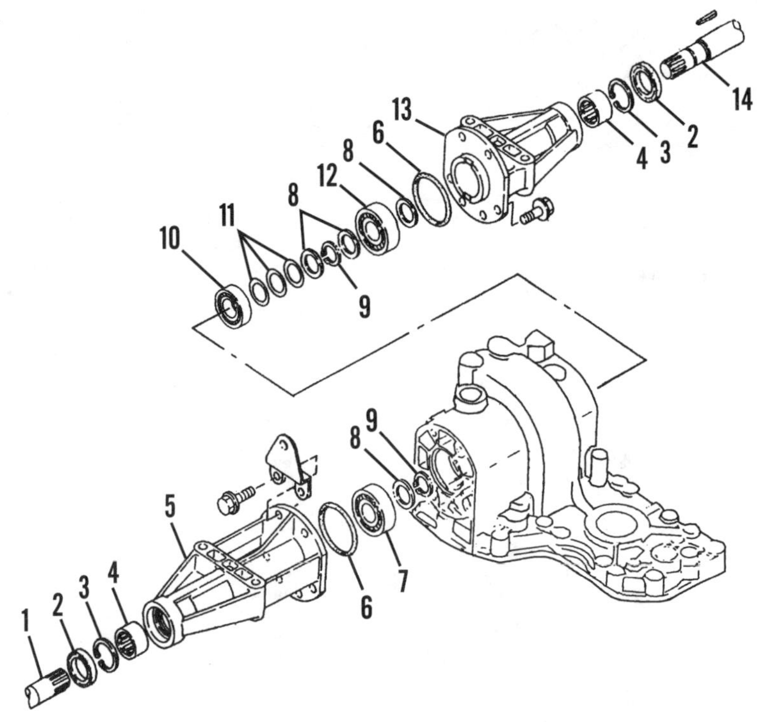

Fig. JD3-15–Exploded view of rear axle assembly used on Model 185 S.N. 475001 and later.

1. Axle (right)
2. Seal
3. Snap ring
4. Bearing
5. Axle housing
6. O-ring
7. Bearing
8. Washer
9. Snap ring
10. Bearing
11. Shims
12. Bearing
13. Axle housing
13. Axle (left)

bly in the tractor and refill the final drive housing to level the plug opening with SAE 10W-30 engine oil. Refill the hydrostatic reservoir with SAE 10W-30 engine oil and bleed air from the system as previously outlined in the hydrostatic transmission LUBRICATION paragraph.

Overhaul

To disassemble the final drive, first unbolt and remove the hydrostatic transmission from the final drive housing. Unbolt and remove the cover (23—Fig. JD3-14) with the idler gear (25) and shaft (28). Remove the drive gear assembly (30, 31 and 32) and brake assembly (33-41). Unbolt and remove the axle housings with axles from the final drive housing. Unbolt and remove the bearing retainer (15) with the counter gear (20) and bevel pinion shaft (12). Remove the final drive assembly from the housing. Remove the differential case cap screws (8) and separate the differential components (1-6).

Inspect all parts for damage. Refer to the following wear tolerance specifications:

Idler gear (25) ID . . . . **0.827-0.828 in. (21.01-21.03 mm)**
Idler shaft (28) OD . . . . **0.668-0.669 in. (16.99-17.00 mm)**
Counter gear (20) ID . . . . **0.788-0.789 in. (20.01-20.03 mm)**
Bevel pinion shaft (12) OD . . . . **0.787-0.788 in. (20.00-20.02 mm)**
Brake lever shaft(33) OD . . . . **0.786-0.789 in. (19.97-20.03 mm)**
Brake lever bore ID in cover (23) . . . . **0.791-0.795 in. (20.10-20.20 mm)**
Brake lever bore ID in housing (11) . . . . **0.789-0.790 in. (20.05-20.08 mm)**
Differential pinion shaft (4) OD . . . . **0.549-0.550 in. (13.97-13.98 mm)**
Differential pinion gear (5) ID . . . . **0.552-0.553 in. (14.03-14.05 mm)**

To reassemble, reverse the disassembly procedure. Apply Loctite 242 to threads of differential case cap screws (8) and tighten to 230 in.-lb. (26 N·m). Position the differential assembly in the housing.

NOTE: Ring gear and bevel pinion gear backlash must be checked after the bevel pinion drive assembly and axles are installed. Install items (13, 20 and 21) after checking the backlash.

Assemble the bevel pinion drive assembly, except the key (13), counter gear (20) and bearing (21), in the bearing retainer (15). Note the new final drive housing (11) has untapped bolt holes. If the final drive housing is replaced, tighten the bearing retainer cap screws to 260 in.-lb. (29 N·m). If the original housing is reused, tighten the cap screws to 220 in.-lb. (25 N·m). Install the left and right axle assemblies. Tighten the axle housing mounting cap screws to 260 in.-lb. (29 N·m) if the final drive housing was replaced, or 220 in.-lb. (25 N·m) if original housing was reused.

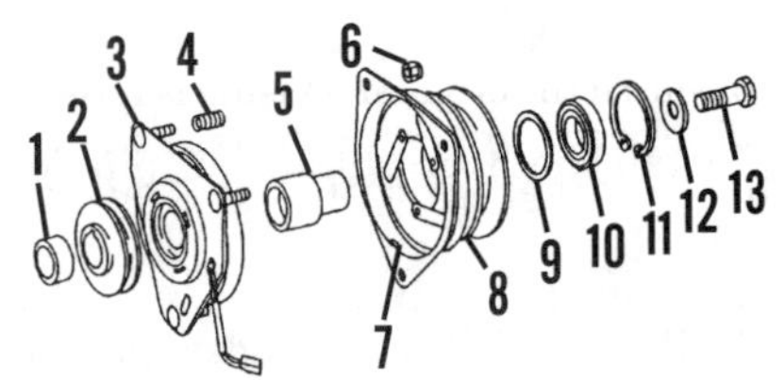

Fig. JD3-16–Exploded view of Ogura electric PTO clutch used on some tractors.

1. Collar
2. Pulley
3. Field coil & rotor assy.
4. Spring (3)
5. Bearing collar
6. Adjust nut (3)
7. Adjustment slot (3)
8. Armature & pulley assy.
9. Spacer
10. Bearing
11. Snap ring
12. Washer
13. Retaining screw

Check and adjust the ring gear to bevel the pinion gear backlash as follows: Position a dial indicator on the housing so the indicator pointer is against the edge of the keyway in the bevel pinion shaft. Hold the axle and differential assembly from moving, then move the bevel pinion shaft back and forth and measure the ring gear to bevel the pinion gear backlash at the pinion shaft keyway. The specified backlash is 0.006-0.012 in. (0.15-0.30 mm). To adjust backlash, add or remove shims (11—Fig. JD3-15) from the left axle shim pack.

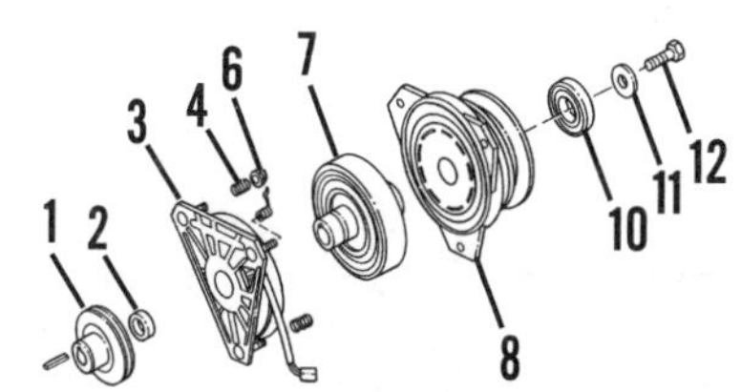

Fig. JD3-17–Exploded view of Warner electric PTO clutch used on some tractors.

1. Collar
2. Pulley
3. Field coil
4. Springs
6. Adjsting nut
7. Rotor
8. Armature & pulley assy.
10. Bearing
12. Spring washer
13. Retaining screw

When the gear backlash is properly adjusted, install the key (13—Fig. JD3-14), counter gear (20) and bearing (21) on the bevel pinion shaft (12). Install the brake assembly and drive gear assembly (30-41). Assemble the idler gear (25) and shaft (28) assembly in the cover (23). Apply liquid gasket maker to the final drive house and cover mating surfaces. Tighten the cover retaining cap screws to 260 in.-lb. (29 N·m) if the final drive housing was replaced, or 220 in.-lb. (25 N·m) if the original housing is reused.

Install the hydrostatic transmission assembly. Reinstall the transaxle assembly in the tractor and refill the housing to level the plug opening with SAE 10W-30 engine oil. Refill the hydrostatic reservoir with SAE 10W-30 engine oil and bleed air from the system as previously outlined in the HYDROSTATIC TRANSMISSION LUBRICATION paragraph.

AXLE SHAFTS

MODELS 175 AND 185 (PRIOR TO SERIAL NUMBER 475001)

Differential housing must be disassembled in order to service the axle shafts and bearings on these tractors. Refer to the REDUCTION GEARS AND DIFFERENTIAL paragraphs for the overhaul procedure.

MODEL 185 (SERIAL NUMBER 475001 AND LATER)

Axles, seal, bearings and hubs can be serviced without removing the final drive housing from the tractor. To remove the axle assemble, block up tractor under the frame and remove the rear wheel. Unbolt and remove the rear axle housing from the final drive housing.

To disassemble, remove the snap ring (9—Fig. JD3-15) and pull the axle shaft (1 or 14) out of the axle housing (5 or 13). Pry the oil seal (2) out of the housing. Remove the snap ring (3) and drive needle bearing (4) from the housing as required.

To reassemble, reverse the disassembly procedure. Tighten axle housing mounting cap screws to 220 in.-lb. (25 N·m).

ELECTRIC PTO CLUTCH

TESTING

Use the following procedure for locating a PTO malfunction. Turn the ignition switch ON and actuate the PTO switch. If the clutch does not engage, disconnect the wiring connector at the clutch and use a 12-volt test lamp to check the wire continuity coming from the PTO switch. If the lamp lights, either the PTO or wiring connector at the clutch field coil is defective. To check the PTO field coil, remove the clutch from the tractor. Ground the field coil frame and energize the coil lead wire with a known 12-volt source. Hold a piece of metal next to the coil and note if tge metal is attracted. If the metal is not attracted to the coil, replace the field coil assembly.

ADJUSTMENT

The PTO clutch must be adjusted if the clutch has been disassembled or if operation becomes erratic. With the clutch disengaged, insert a feeler gauge through the slots in the clutch plate and measure the clearance between the clutch rotor and armature. There should be a 0.015 in. (0.38 mm) clearance between the armature and clutch rotor at each of the slots in the clutch plate. To adjust, tighten or loosen the clutch adjusting nuts (6—Fig. JD3-16 or Fig. JD3-17) to obtain the correct clearance.

OVERHAUL

To remove the PTO clutch, disconnect the electrical wires and remove the clutch retaining bolt. Remove the clutch assembly from the crankshaft. Use a plastic hammer to tap and loosen clutch from the crankshaft if necessary.

To disassemble an Ogura clutch (Fig. JD3-16), remove the adjusting nuts (6). Support the armature housing (8) and press the bearing collar (5) out of the armature assembly. Remove the snap ring (11) and press the bearing (10) and spacer (9) from the armature housing.

To disassemble a Warner clutch (Fig. JD3-17), remove the adjusting nuts (6) and separate the armature (8) and rotor (7) from the field coil housing (3). Press the bearing (10) from the armature if necessary.

Inspect bearings for damage. Inspect for broken or distorted springs (4). Check the contact surfaces of the rotor and armature for damage. Replace the parts when necessary.

To reassemble either type of clutch, reverse the disassembly procedure.

Apply an antiseize lubricant to the crankshaft before reinstalling the clutch assembly. Tighten the clutch retaining cap screw to 45 ft.-lb. (56 N·m). Adjust the clutch as previously outlined.

SAFETY INTERLOCK SWITCHES

All models are equipped with transmission and PTO neutral-start interlock switches. Some models are also equipped with a seat interlock switch.

On models equipped with an electric PTO clutch, the PTO switch must be OFF to activate the PTO neutral-start switch. The safety switch is not adjustable and must be replaced if testing indicates a switch failure.

On models equipped with a manual PTO clutch, the neutral-start switch is closed when the control lever is placed in the ngaged position. If necessary, loosen the switch mounting screws and adjust for proper operation. Be careful not to bottom out the switch plunger to prevent damage to the switch.

All models are equipped with a transmission neutral-start switch. To adjust switch, loosen the mounting screws or nuts and move the switch until it closes when the transmission shift lever is placed in NEUTRAL. On hydrostatic transmission models, the switch should close when the hydrostatic control lever is placed in NEUTRAL or when the brake pedal is fully depressed. To prevent damage to the switch, be sure the switch is not bottomed out after adjustment.

WIRING SCHEMATICS

Refer to Fig. JD3-18 or Fig. JD3-19 for the electrical wiring schematics.

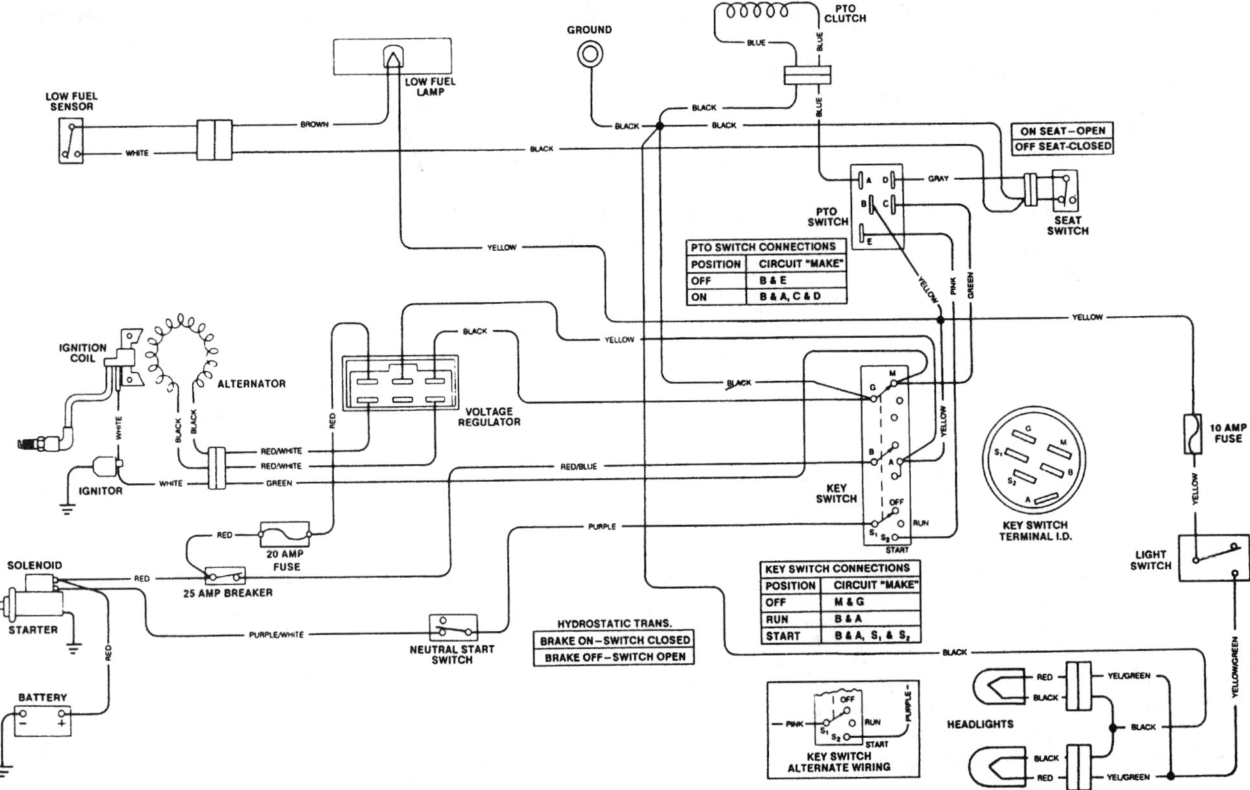

Fig. JD3-18–Electrical wiring diagram typical of Model 175.

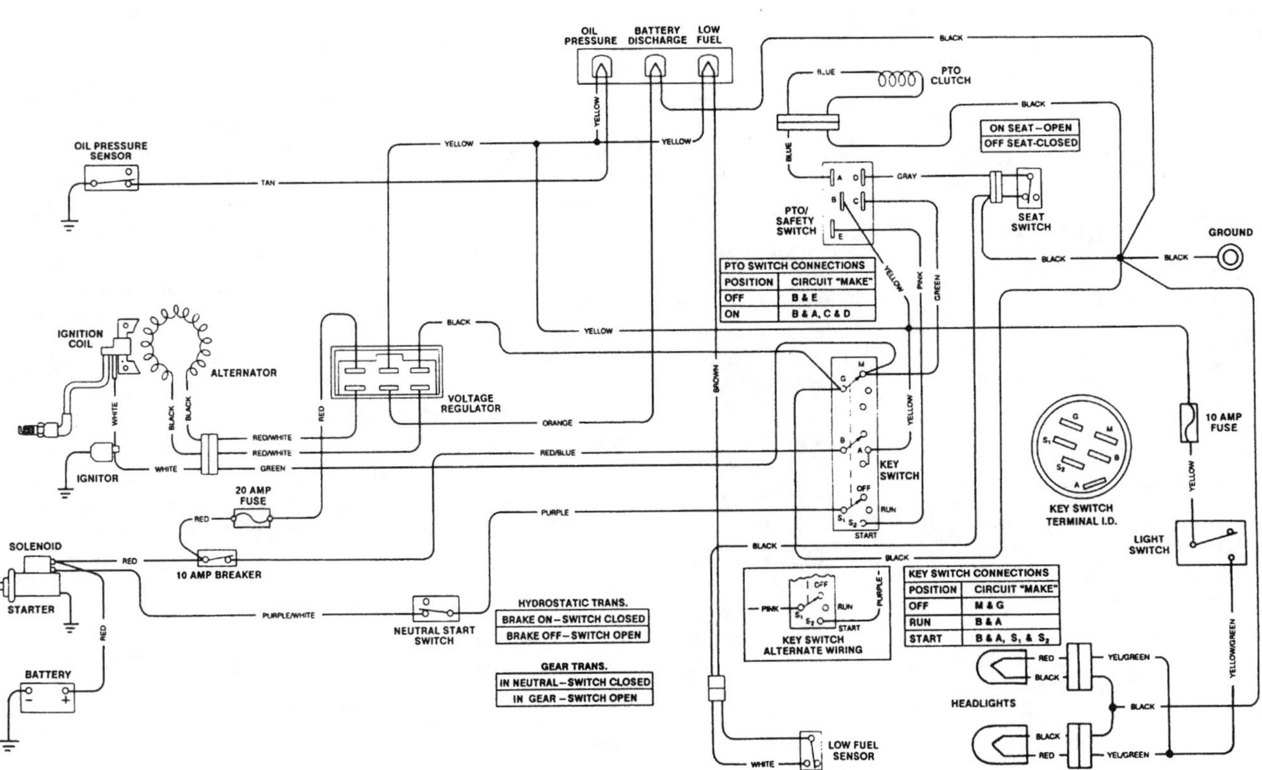

Fig. JD3-19–Electrical wiring diagram typical of all other models.

JOHN DEERE

CONDENSED SPECIFICATIONS

MODELS	240	245	260	265
Engine Make	Kawasaki	Kawasaki	Kawasaki	Kawasaki
Model	FC420V	FC420V	FC540V	FC540V
Bore	89 mm (3.5 in.)	89 mm (3.5 in.)	89 mm (3.5 in.)	89 mm (3.5 in.)
Stroke	68 mm (2.68 in.)	68 mm (2.68 in.)	86 mm (3.38 in.)	86 mm (3.38 in).
Displacement	423cc (25.8 cu. in.)	423cc (25.8 cu. in.)	535cc (32.6 cu. in.)	535cc (32.6 cu. in.)
Power Rating	10.4 kW (14 hp)	10.4 kW (14 hp)	12.6 kW (17 hp)	12.6 kW (17 hp)
Slow Idle Speed	1400 rpm	1400 rpm	1400 rpm	1400 rpm
High Idle Speed (No-Load)	3350 rpm	3350 rpm	3350 rpm	3350 rpm
Crankcase Capacity	1.3 L* (2.8 pt.)	1.3 L* (2.8 pt.)	1.6 L* (3.4 pt.)	1.6 L* (3.4 pt.)
Transmission Capacity	See Text	2.5 L (2.6 qt.)	See Text	2.5 L (2.6 qt.)
Fuel Tank Capacity	11.4 L (3.0 gal.)	11.4 L (3.0 gal.)	11.4 L (3.0 gal.)	11.4 L (3.0 gal.)

*Add 0.4 L (0.8 pt.) with filter change.

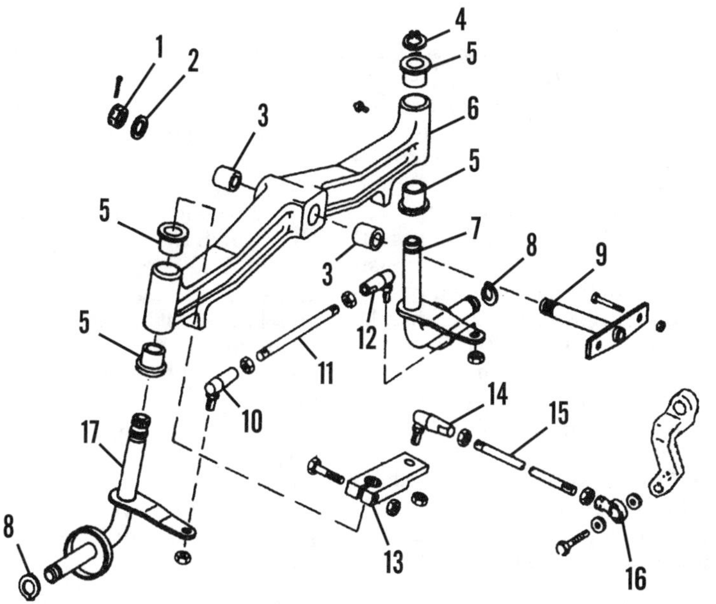

Fig. JD4-1–Exploded view of front axle assembly. Note that rod ends (12 and 14) have left-hand threads.

1. Slotted nut
2. Washer
3. Bushing
4. Snap ring
5. Bushing
6. Axle main member
7. Spindle (right)
8. Snap ring
9. Pivot
10. Tie rod end
11. Tie rod
12. Tie rod end
13. Steering arm
14. Drag link end
15. Drag link
16. Drag link end
17. Spindle (left)

FRONT AXLE AND STEERING SYSTEM

MAINTENANCE

The front wheel spindles should be lubricated after every 50 hours of operation. Jack up the front axle so the wheels are suspended and apply grease to the spindles through the grease fitting at each end of the axle. One or two shots from a hand-held grease gun should be sufficient. Use lithium based grease. Check for looseness and binding in the front axle components.

FRONT WHEEL BEARINGS

Front wheel bearings are sealed and should not require lubrication. Wheel bearings are a press fit in the wheel hub.

TIE ROD AND TOE-IN

The tie rod (11—Fig. JD4-1) is equipped with replaceable ends that are not interchangeable.

Front wheel toe-in should be 3-6 mm (1/8-1/4 in.). Adjust toe-in by altering the tie rod length.

STEERING SPINDLES

Raise and support the front of the tractor. Remove the wheel and tire. Disconnect the tie rod end, and if needed, the drag link end. If removing the right spindle (7—Fig. JD4-1), detach the snap ring securing the top of the spindle and withdraw the spindle from the axle. If removing the left spindle (17), mark the end of the spindle and steering arm (13) so the arm can be returned to its original position. Remove the clamp bolt, remove the steering arm and withdraw the spindle from the axle.

Inspect components for damage. Replaceable bushings (5) are located in the axle.

DRAG LINK

A drag link (15—Fig. JD4-1) with adjustable ends is located between the steering arm and pitman arm. Adjust the length of the drag link so equal turns of the steering wheel are required to reach the full left and right turn from NEUTRAL.

Steering effort and response can be adjusted by changing the connecting point of the drag link in the pitman arm. Connecting the drag link to the lower hole in the pitman arm will provide quick steering response when the tractor is not heavily loaded. Connecting the drag link to the pitman arm's upper hole will provide reduced steering effort when the tractor is equipped with heavy loads on the front axle, but the steering response will be slower because more turns of the steering wheel will be required to turn the front wheels.

AXLE MAIN MEMBER REMOVAL AND INSTALLATION

Raise and support the front of the tractor. Disconnect the drag link end (14—Fig. JD4-1) from the steering arm (13). Using a suitable jack, support the axle assembly. Unscrew the pivot pin nut (1). Unscrew the pivot pin mounting screws and lower the axle assembly out of the tractor.

Inspect components for damage. The axle bushings (3) are replaceable.

When installing the axle, tighten the pivot pin nut (1) until the axle end play is removed but the axle still pivots freely.

STEERING GEAR OVERHAUL

Detach the drag link from the pitman arm. Scribe match marks on the pitman arm and end of the pitman shaft, then remove the pitman arm. Raise the hood and remove lower the pedestal panel. Disconnect the steering column shaft from the gearbox shaft. Unscrew the fasteners securing the gearbox and remove the gearbox.

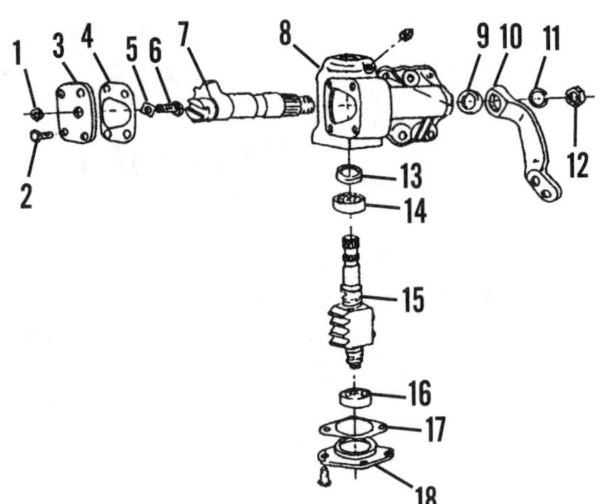

Fig. JD4-2–Exploded view of steering gearbox.

1. Nut
2. Screw
3. Cover
4. Gasket
5. Shim
6. Adjuster
7. Pitman shaft
8. Gearbox
9. Seal
10. Pitman arm
11. Lockwasher
12. Nut
13. Seal
14. Bearing
15. Shaft & nut assy.
16. Bearing
17. Shim
18. Cover

The steering gear is a recirculating ball type. Refer to Fig. JD4-2 for an exploded view of the gearbox. To disassemble, remove the side cover (3) and end cover (18) and withdraw the pitman shaft (7) and wormshaft assembly (15). The wormshaft is available only as an assembly and no attempt should be made to disassemble the unit.

When assembling the gearbox, perform the following adjustments: Back out the adjusting screw (6) until it stops. Turn the wormshaft (15) clockwise until it stops, then turn back one-half turn. Install needed shims (17) so the rolling torque when turning the steering shaft is 0.4 N·m (3.5 in.-lb.). Install the thickest shim (5) allowed when assembling the unit and make sure the pitman shaft (7) is centered on the ball nut when the nut is at the midpoint of travel. Turn the adjusting screw (6) so the steering shaft rolling torque increases to 1.1 N·m (9.5 in.-lb.), then tighten the locknut (1) while holding the adjusting screw in place.

Gearbox oil capacity is 170 mL (6 oz.). The recommended oil is SAE 90 gear oil rated GL-5. After installation, check the oil level by removing the plug (19). The oil level should be 25 mm (1 in.) below the top of the plug hole.

ENGINE

LUBRICATION

Check the oil level before operation and after every four hours of operation. Determine the oil level by resting the dipstick on top of the dipstick tube; do not screw in.

The recommended oil is a premium grade oil meeting the latest API service classification. Use SAE 30 oil for temperatures above 32°F (0°C); use SAE 10W-30 oil for temperatures between -4°F (-20°C) and 86°F (30°C); SAE 5W-30 may be used between 50°F (10°C) and -22°F (-30°C).

Change oil after first five hours of operation and then after every 50 hours of operation, or more frequently when operation is severe. Change the oil filter, on engines so equipped, after first five hours of operation and then after every 100 hours of operation.

REMOVAL AND INSTALLATION

To remove the engine, first remove the hood, muffler and pedestal shroud. Disconnect the battery ground cable. Close the fuel shut-off valve and disconnect the fuel line. Disconnect the throttle control cable. Disconnect the ground wire, starter wires and ignition wires from the engine. Remove the electric PTO clutch. Relieve traction drive belt tension and remove the belt from the drive pulley. Remove the drive pulley and key from the engine crankshaft. Remove the engine mounting cap screws and lift the engine from the tractor.

To install the engine, reverse the removal procedure. Apply an antiseize lubricant to the crankshaft before installing the drive pulley. Tighten the PTO clutch mounting cap screw to 56 N·m (45 ft.-lb.).

OVERHAUL

Engine make and model are listed at the beginning of this section. To overhaul the engine components and accessories, refer to the KAWASAKI engine section in this manual.

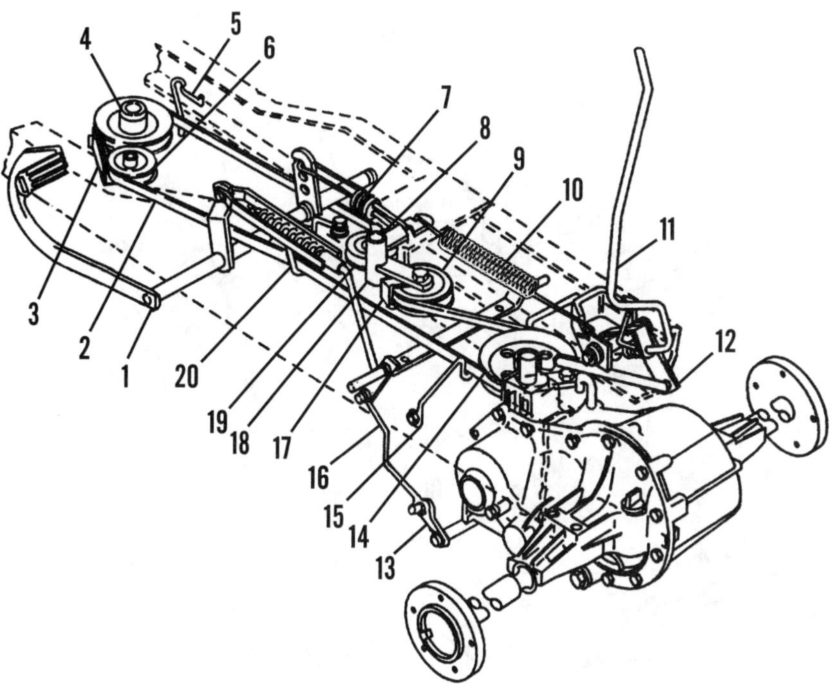

Fig. JD4-3–Drawing showing power train components for gear drive Models 240 and 260.

1. Clutch pedal
2. Traction drive belt
3. Belt guide
4. Engine pulley
5. Belt guide
6. Belt tension idler pulley
7. Clutch tension spring
8. Belt guide
9. Bellcrank idler
10. Belt tension spring
11. Shift lever
12. Shift linkage
13. Shift interlock arm
14. Transaxle pulley
15. Belt guide
16. Interlock linkage
17. Belt guide
18. Clutch bellcrank
19. Bellcrank idler
20. Belt guide

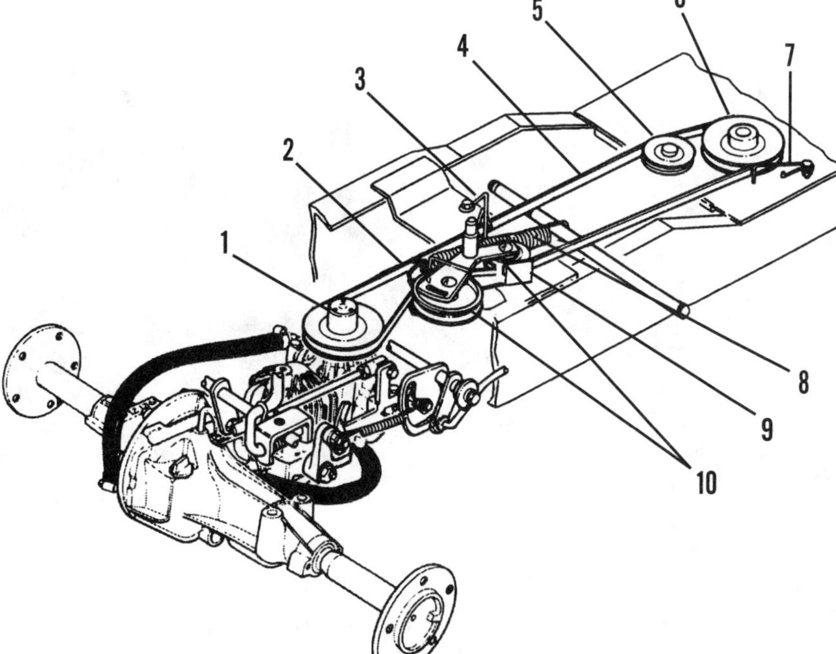

Fig. JD4-4–Drawing showing power train components for hydrostatic drive Model 245 and 265.

1. Transmission pulley
2. Belt guide
3. Belt guide
4. Traction drive belt
5. Belt idler
6. Engine pulley
7. Belt guide
8. Belt tension spring
9. Belt guide
10. Bellcrank idler

CLUTCH AND TRACTION DRIVE BELT

MODELS 240 AND 260

Adjustment

When the clutch pedal (1—Fig. JD4-3) is depressed, the bellcrank assembly (18) pivots and loosens the drive belt (2) from the drive pulleys, stopping the tractor's forward or reverse movement. At the same time the clutch is disengaged, the transmission interlock linkage, which is connected to the clutch pedal shaft, moves the interlock arm (13) to unlock the shifter fork and allow a shift to be made.

To adjust the clutch, stop the engine and release the clutch pedal. Loosen the nut on the front idler pulley (6). Move the front idler pulley until the clutch pedal spring (7) is 54 mm (2 in.) long. On some models, the bellcrank idler pulley (9) can also be adjusted to make up for belt stretch.

Drive Belt

To remove the traction drive belt (2—Fig. JD4-3), first remove the mower deck. Disconnect the wiring harness from the electric PTO clutch, then unbolt and remove the PTO clutch. Remove the adjusting idler pulley (6) and belt guide (3). Remove the remaining belt guides (5, 8, 15, 17 and 20) when necessary. Depress the clutch to relieve spring tension or disconnect the spring (10), then slip the belt out of the pulleys.

To reinstall the belt, reverse the removal procedure. Adjust the belt tension as previously outlined.

MODELS 245 AND 265

The hydrostatic power train used on Models 245 and 265 uses a spring-loaded idler pulley and belt drive system as shown in Fig. JD4-4. The belt tension is held constant by the spring (8) and no adjustment is required. If belt slippage occurs due to wear or belt stretch, replace the drive belt.

Drive Belt

To remove the traction drive belt, first remove the mower deck. Disconnect the electrical wiring from the PTO clutch, then unbolt and remove the PTO clutch. Remove the belt guides when necessary. Disconnect the belt tension spring or move the idler pulley pivot to relieve spring tension on the belt, then slip the belt out of the pulleys.

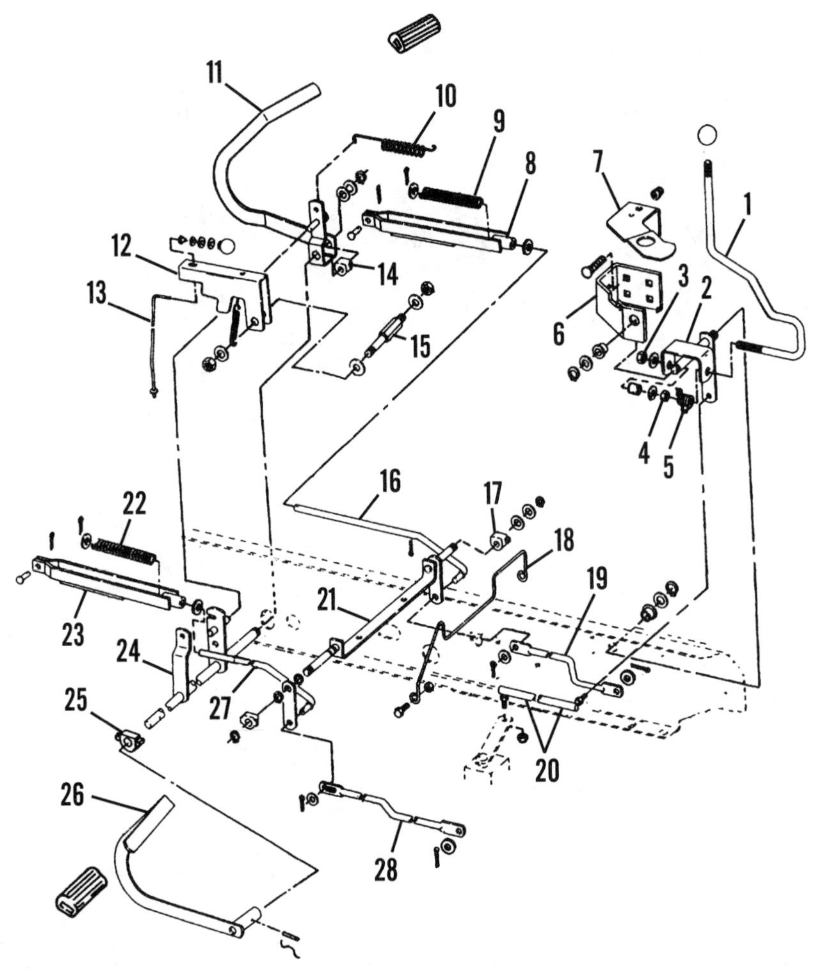

Fig. JD4-5–Exploded view of clutch, brake and shift linkage used on Models 240 and 260.

1. Shift lever
2. Shift bracket
3. Nut
4. Nut
5. Torsion spring
6. Bracket
7. Support
8. Spring retainer
9. Brake compression spring
10. Return spring
11. Brake pedal
12. Park brake latch
13. Brake rod
14. Bearing
15. Stud
16. Brake rod
17. Bearing
18. Belt guide
19. Brake rod
20. Shift rod
21. Brake shaft
22. Clutch compression sprng
23. Spring retainer
24. Clutch shaft
25. Bearing
26. Clutch pedal
27. Interlock rod
28. Interlock rod

To reinstall the belt, reverse the removal procedure.

BRAKES

Models 240 and 260 prior to 1992 are equipped with a shoe and drum brake located on the right side of the transaxle housing. Model 240 after 1991 is equipped with a disc brake located inside the transaxle. Models 245 and 265 are equipped with a shoe and drum brake located on the left side of the final drive housing.

ADJUSTMENT

Refer to Fig. JD4-5 for an exploded view of the clutch and brake linkage used on Model 240 prior to 1992 and Model 260. No brake adjustment is required on these tractors.

To adjust the brake on Model 240 after 1991, engage the parking brake. Measure the distance from the rear of the bracket (B—Fig. JD4-6) to the cotter pin (P) in the brake rod. The distance should be 22-28 mm (0.87-1.10 in.). Rotate the adjusting nuts (N) at the end of the brake rod to obtain the desired distance.

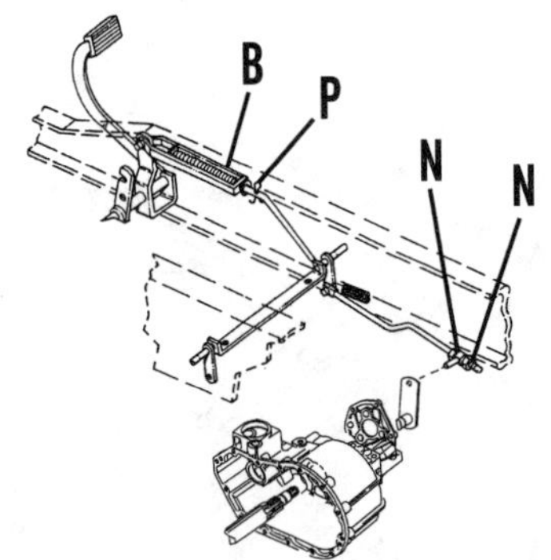

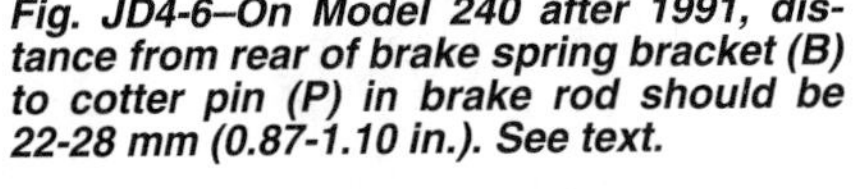
Fig. JD4-6–On Model 240 after 1991, distance from rear of brake spring bracket (B) to cotter pin (P) in brake rod should be 22-28 mm (0.87-1.10 in.). See text.

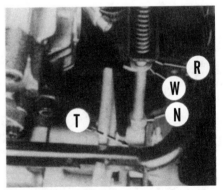

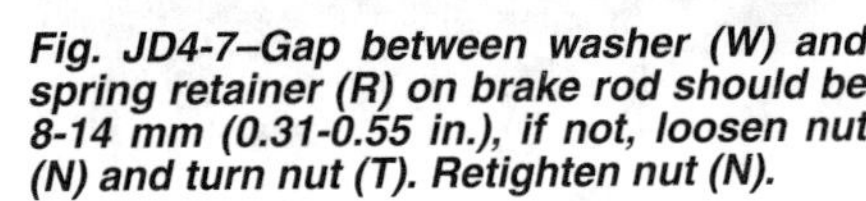
Fig. JD4-7–Gap between washer (W) and spring retainer (R) on brake rod should be 8-14 mm (0.31-0.55 in.), if not, loosen nut (N) and turn nut (T). Retighten nut (N).

To adjust the brake on Models 245 and 265, place the parking brake in the locked position. Measure the gap between the washer (W—Fig. JD4-7) and the spring retainer (R). The gap should be 8-14 mm (0.31-0.55 in.), if not, the loosen jam nut (N) and turn the nut (T) when necessary. Retighten nut (N).

REMOVAL AND INSTALLATION

Model 240 after 1991

Drain oil from the transaxle. Detach the brake rod from the brake arm (8—Fig. JD4-8).

NOTE: Be prepared to catch loose balls (5) when removing the brake cover.

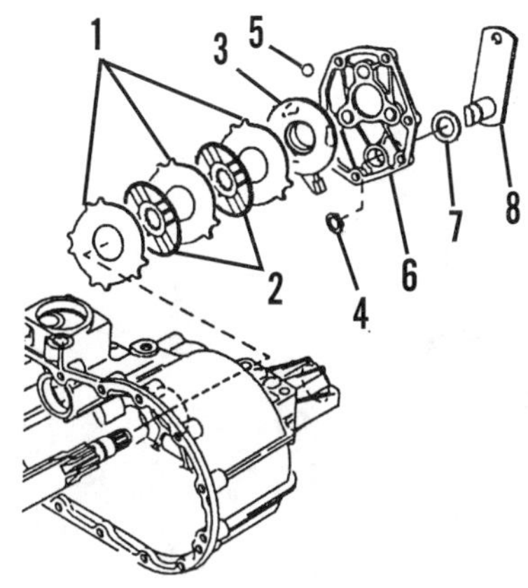

Fig. JD4-8–Exploded view of disc brake assembly used on Model 240 after 1991.

1. Plate (3)
2. Disc (2)
3. Actuator
4. Snap ring
5. Ball (3)
6. Cover
7. Seal
8. Brake arm

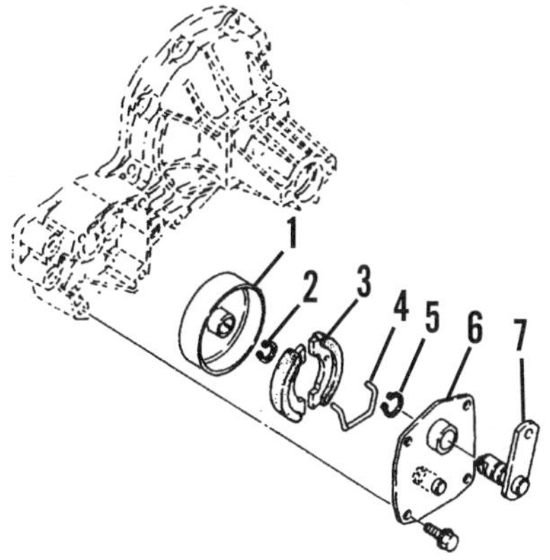

Fig. JD4-9–Exploded view of brake assembly typical of all models except late production 240 models.

1. Drum
2. Snap ring
3. Brake shoes
4. Spring
5. Snap ring
6. Cover
7. Arm

Unscrew and remove cover (6). Remove actuator (3), brake plates (1) and discs (2). Detach the snap ring (4) and remove the brake arm from the cover.

Inspect brake components for damage. Replace the discs if the radial grooves are worn away. The specified brake arm shaft diameter is 19.95-20.00 mm (0.785-0.787 in.). The specified cover bore diameter is 20.02-20.05 mm (0.788-0.789 in.).

Reassemble the brake by reversing the disassembly procedure. Install the seal (7) flush with the cover surface. Lubricate the seal before installing the brake arm. Use grease to hold the balls (5) on the actuator (3). Apply gasket-forming sealer to the cover and transaxle mating surfaces. Apply Loctite to the cover screws. Tighten the cover screws to 24 N·m (212 in.-lb.) on a used transaxle case or to 29 N·m (22 ft.-lb.) on a new transaxle case. Adjust brake linkage as previously described.

All Other Models

Refer to Fig. JD4-9 for an exploded view of the brake assembly used on all models except Model 240 after 1991. To disassemble, detach the rod from the brake arm and remove the screws securing the cover (6). Note the position of the brake spring (4) for reassembly. Remove spring (4) and brake shoes (3). Remove snap ring (2) and withdraw brake drum (1).

Inspect components for damage. On Models 240 and 260, brake lever shaft (7—Fig. JD4-9) diameter should be 19.95-20.00 mm (0.785-0.787 in.). The shaft bore in the cover (6) should be 20.02-20.05 mm (0.788-0.789 in.). The maximum allowable shaft to cover clearance is 0.5 mm (0.020 in.).

On Models 245 and 265, the brake arm shaft (7) diameter should be 17.96-18.00 mm (0.707-0.709 in.). The shaft bore in the cover (6) should be 18.02-18.04 mm (0.709-0.710 in.). The Maximum allowable shaft-to-bore clearance is 0.5 mm (0.020 in.).

To reinstall the brake, reverse the removal procedure. Install the spring (4) so the open portion is toward the brake arm. Apply grease to the brake arm shaft. While tightening the cover screws, push the brake arm forward so the brake shoes will contact the drum thereby centering the cover. Tighten the cover screws to 24 N·m (18 ft.-lb.) if the holes are threaded, or to 29 N·m (22 ft.-lb.) on new cases with untapped holes. Adjust the brake as outlined in the previous section.

TRANSAXLE (MODELS 240 AND 260)

LUBRICATION

Check the transaxle oil level after every 25 hours of operation. The oil level should be maintained at the dipstick's top mark, which is located at the rear of the transaxle. Add oil when necessary.

NOTE: Several different lubricants have been used in production of transaxle. Check the oil color to determine the correct oil to use. Do not mix lubricants.

GL-5 gear lubricant (thick, honey colored oil) was used in early production. This lubricant is no longer recommended. Drain and refill using John Deere Low Viscosity HY-GARD Transmission/Hydraulic oil.

John Deere All-Weather Hydrostatic Fluid or Type F automatic transmission fluid (red in color) was used in later production.

John Deere Low Viscosity HY-GARD (J20B) Transmission/Hydraulic oil (thin, honey colored). Use in transaxle equipped with wet disc brake. John Deere All-Weather Hydrostatic fluid or Type F Automatic Transmission fluid may be used in the transaxle with a dry shoe and drum brake.

NEUTRAL ADJUSTMENT

Move transmission shift lever to NEUTRAL and shut off the engine. If the shift lever is not positioned in the neutral notch in the deck quadrant slot, adjust the shift lever as follows: Loosen nut (3—Fig. JD4-5) and turn the nut (4) forward to move the lever forward in the quadrant slot or turn nut back to move the lever back. Hold the nut (4) and tighten the other nut (3).

REMOVAL AND INSTALLATION

To remove the transaxle, securely block up the rear of the tractor. Place the shift lever in NEUTRAL, then disconnect the shift rod from the transaxle shift arm. Disconnect the brake control rod and transaxle interlock control rod. Depress the clutch pedal and remove the drive belt from the transaxle pulley. Remove the transaxle mounting bolts and lower the transaxle from the tractor.

To install, reverse the removal procedure.

OVERHAUL

Models 240 and 260 are equipped with a TUFF TORQ transaxle manufactured by Kanzaki. Refer to the KANZAKI section in the TRANSAXLE SERVICE section for the overhaul procedure.

HYDROSTATIC TRANSMISSION (MODELS 245-265)

LUBRICATION

Check the transmission fluid level after every 25 hours of operation. The fluid level should be maintained at the top mark on the dipstick attached to the fill plug (P—Fig. JD4-10). The fluid level should be checked when the transmission is warm. Be sure the tractor is on a level surface and the engine is stopped when checking.

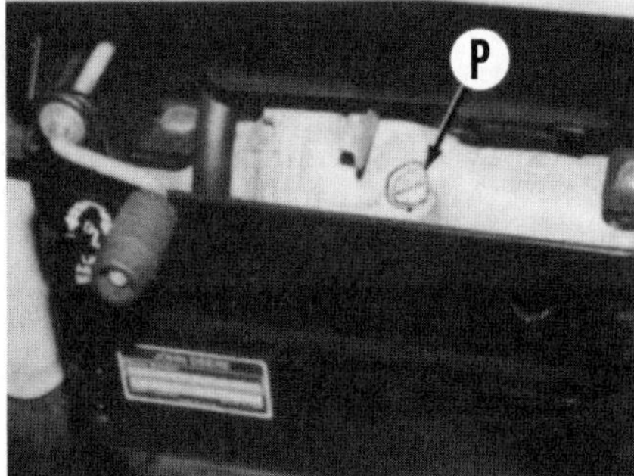

Fig. JD4-10–View showing location of transmission fill plug (P).

Fig. JD4-11–Adjust hydrostatic control lever friction by rotating nut (N) so force required to move control lever is 22-36 N (5-8 lb.).

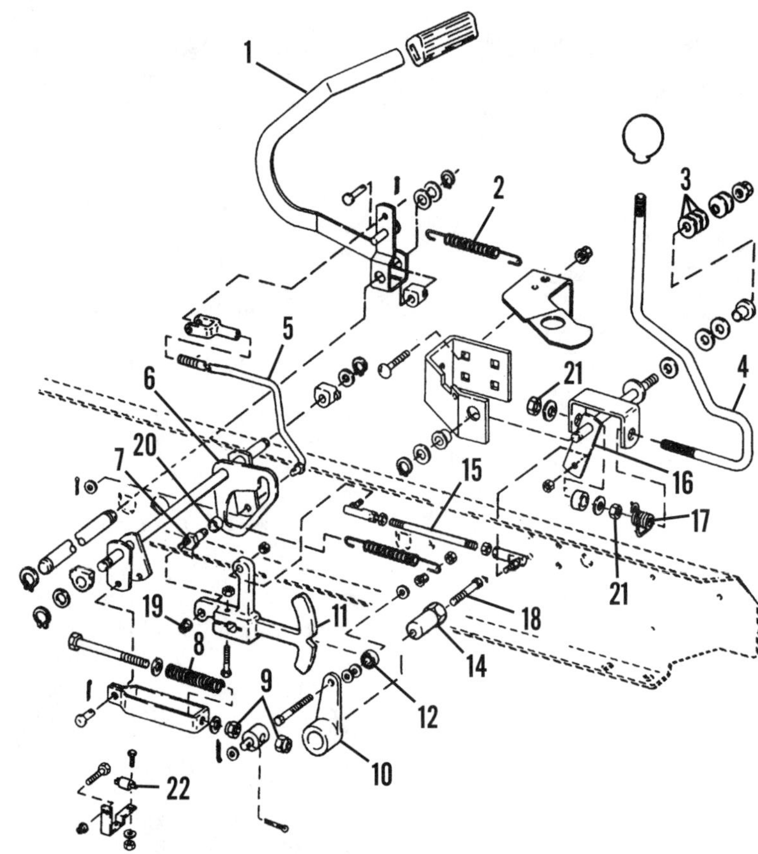

Fig. JD4-12–Exploded view of hydrostatic control linkage.

1. Pedal
2. Spring
3. Spring washers
4. Shift lever
5. Control rod
6. Cam plate
7. Eccentric
8. Spring
9. Nuts
10. Control lever
11. Control arm
12. Roller
14. Eccentric
15. Rod
16. Lever
17. Spring
18. Screw
19. Nut
20. Roller
21. Nut
22. Neutral switch

NOTE: Two different lubricants have been used in production of hydrostatic transaxle. Check the oil color to determine the correct oil to use. If oil is honey colored, use John Deere Low Viscosity HY-GARD Transmission/Hydraulic fluid. If oil is red, use John Deere All-Weather Hydrostatic Fluid or type-F automatic transmission fluid. Do not mix lubricants.

Transmission fluid and filter should be changed after first 50 hours of operation and then every 250 hours of operation thereafter. Partially fill new filter with oil before installing. Oil capacity is approximately 2.5 liters (2.6 qt.).

CONTROL LEVER FRICTION ADJUSTMENT

The force required to move the hydrostatic control lever should be 22-36 N (5-8 lb.). Adjust the control lever friction by rotating the nut (N—Fig. JD4-11).

NEUTRAL ADJUSTMENT

Securely support the rear of the tractor so the rear wheels clear the ground. Run the engine at the fast throttle setting and move the transmission control lever so the wheels stop turning. This may not be the neutral position indicated on the shift panel. Stop the engine.

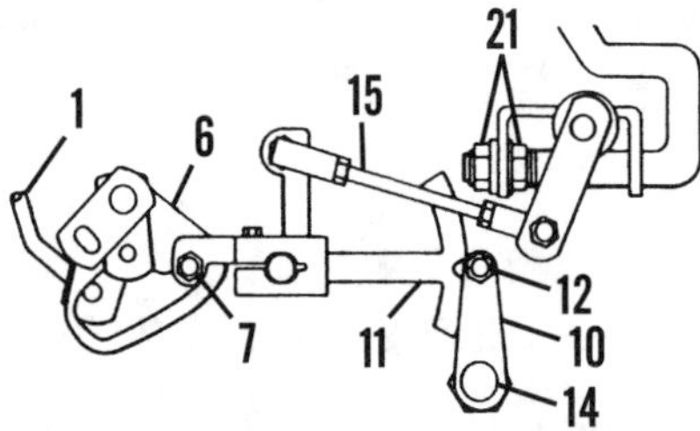

Fig. JD4-13–Drawing of transmission control mechanism. Refer to text for adjustment.

Loosen the eccentric retaining screw (18—Fig. JD4-12) and rotate the eccentric (14—Fig. JD4-12 and Fig. JD4-13) so the roller (12) is centered in the control arm (11) notch. Loosen the nut (19—Fig. JD4-12). Engage the parking brake. Turn the eccentric (7) so the roller (20) is centered in the slot of the cam (6), then retighten the nut (19). Being certain the roller (12) is centered in the control arm (11) notch, turn the nuts (21) so the shift control lever is centered in the neutral notch of the shift panel.

Fig. JD4-14—Connect a suitable pressure gauge to either port (P) to check hydraulic pressure. See text.

Run the engine and check the adjustments. The shift lever should return to NEUTRAL when the brake is depressed and the rear wheels should not turn when the shift lever is in NEUTRAL.

Fig. JD4-15–Adjust PTO clutch by turning each of the three adjusting nuts (N) until clearance between rotor and armature is 0.41 mm(0.016 in.)

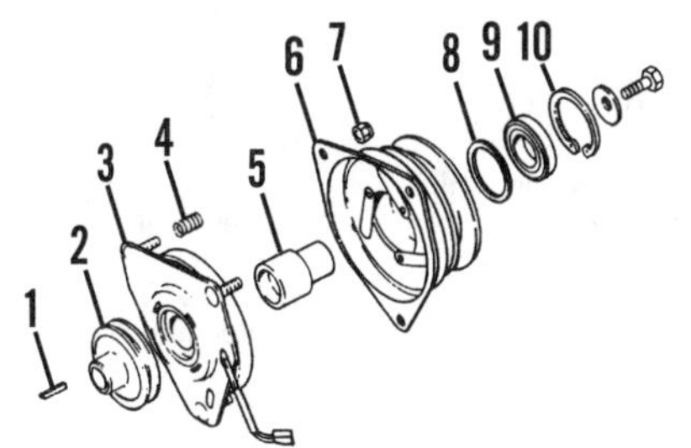

Fig. JD4-16–Exploded view of Ogura electric PTO clutch.

1. Key
2. Traction drive pulley
3. Field coil assy.
4. Spring
5. Collar
6. Armature & pulley assy.
7. Adjusting nut
8. Spacer
9. Bearing
10. Snap ring

CHARGE PUMP PRESSURE TEST

To check the charge pump pressure, first start and run the engine at fast idle until the transmission oil is warm. Stop the engine and install a 0-150 psi (0-1000 kPa) pressure gauge in either port (P—Fig. JD4-14) located in front of the transmission. On early models, only the Allen head port plug must be removed. On later models with a hex head plug, remove the surge relief valve in either port. See the TRANSMISSION repair section).

Move the transmission control lever to NEUTRAL, run the engine at slow idle and check the pressure.

NOTE: Transmission must be in NEUTRAL and the wheels must not rotate. Do not move the transmission control lever out of NEUTRAL as the pressure will increase and may damage the pressure gauge.

Charge pump pressure must be 193-490 kPa (28-71 psi). If low, be sure the transmission filter and charge pump relief valve are in good condition. The relief valve pressure is not adjustable.

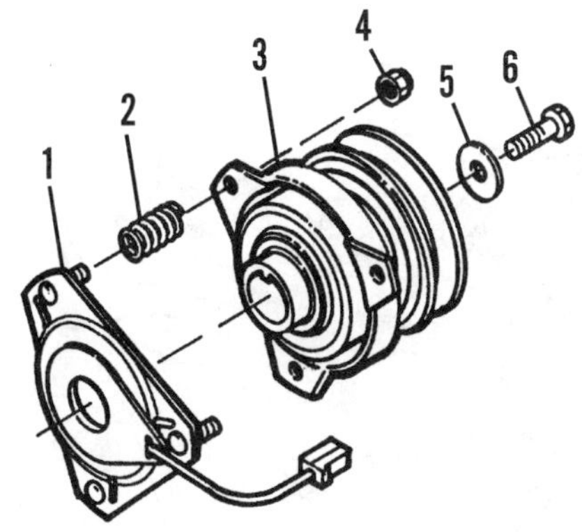

Fig. JD4-17–Exploded view of Warner electric PTO clutch.

1. Field coil assy.
2. Spring
3. Armature & rotor assy.
4. Adjusting nut
5. Washer
6. Cap screw

REMOVAL AND INSTALLATION

To remove the transmission, securely block up the rear of the tractor. Disconnect the hydrostatic transmission control linkage and brake control linkage. Disconnect the traction drive belt tension spring or move the belt idler pulley pivot to relieve belt tension, then slip the belt out of the transmission pulley. Remove the transaxle mounting nuts and bolts and lower the transaxle assembly from the tractor.

Drain the oil from the transaxle housing. Disconnect the hydrostatic transmission suction and return hoses. Unbolt and remove the hydrostatic transmission from the transaxle housing.

To install, reverse the removal procedure.

OVERHAUL

A Hydro-Gear Model BDU-21L hydrostatic transmission is used on Models 245 and 265. Refer to Hydro-Gear section in the HYDROSTATIC TRANSMISSION SERVICE section for the overhaul procedure.

FINAL DRIVE OVERHAUL (MODELS 245-265)

Remove the final drive and transmission assembly from the tractor as outlined in the TRANSMISSION section. Separate the hydrostatic transmission from the final drive. Remove the wheels and brake components. To reinstall the unit, reverse the removal procedure.

Models 245 and 265 are equipped with a Kanzaki final drive. Refer to the KANZAKI section in the FINAL DRIVE section for the overhaul procedure.

POWER TAKE-OFF (PTO)

TESTING

Use the following procedure for locating a PTO malfunction. Turn the ignition switch ON and actuate the PTO switch. If the clutch does not engage, disconnect the wiring connector at the clutch and use a 12-volt test lamp to check the wire continuity coming from the PTO switch. If the lamp lights, either the PTO or the wiring connector at clutch field coil is defective. To check the PTO field coil, remove the clutch from the tractor. Ground the field coil frame and energize the coil lead wire with a known 12-volt source. Hold a piece of metal next to the coil and note if the metal is attracted. If the metal is not attracted to the coil, replace the field coil assembly.

ADJUSTMENT

The PTO clutch must be adjusted if the clutch has been disassembled or if operation becomes erratic. With the clutch disengaged, insert a feeler gauge through the slots in the clutch plate and measure the clearance between the clutch rotor and armature as shown in Fig. JD4-15. There should be a clearance of 0.38-0.64 mm (0.015-0.025 in.) on a Warner clutch, or 0.30-0.51 mm (0.012-0.020 in.) on an Ogura clutch at each of the slots in the clutch plate. To adjust, tighten or loosen the clutch adjusting nuts (N) to obtain the correct clearance.

OVERHAUL

To remove the PTO clutch, disconnect the electrical wires and remove the clutch retaining bolt. Remove the clutch assembly from the crankshaft. Use a plastic hammer to tap and loosen the clutch from the crankshaft when necessary.

To disassemble an Ogura clutch (Fig. JD4-16), remove the adjusting nuts (7). Support the armature housing (6) and press the bearing collar (5) out of the armature assembly. Remove the snap ring (10) and press bearing (9) and spacer (8) from the armature housing.

To disassemble a Warner clutch (Fig. JD4-17), remove the adjusting nuts (4) and separate the armature and rotor from the field coil housing.

Inspect the bearings for damage. Inspect for broken or distorted springs. Check the rotor and armature contact surfaces for damage. Replace the parts or clutch assembly when necessary.

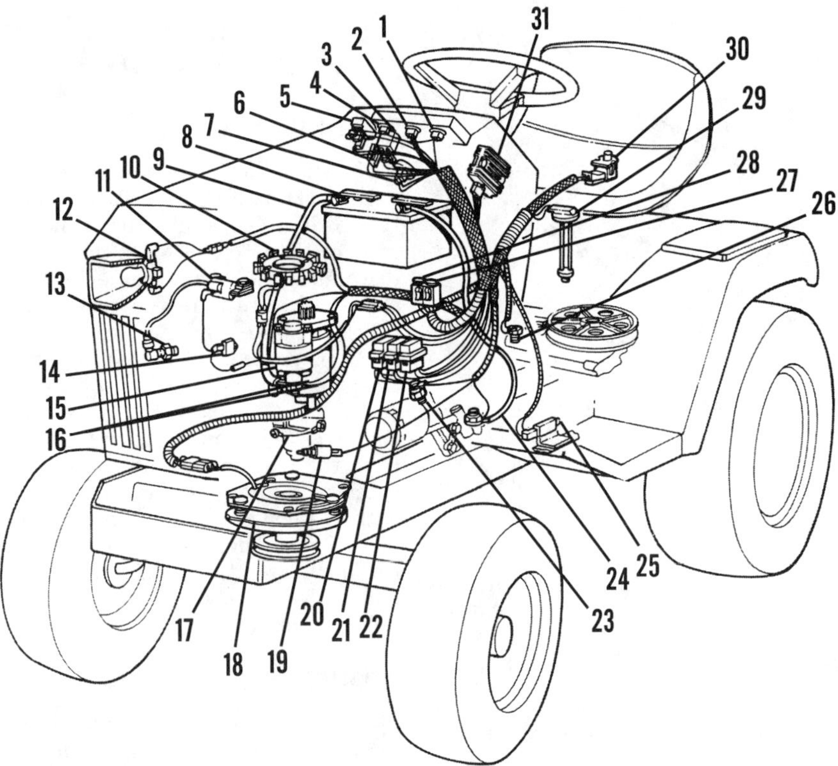

Fig. JD4-18–Drawing showing tractor electrical component location typical for all models.

1. Oil pressure lamp (optional on 240 & 245)
2. Discharge lamp
3. Hour meter (optional on 240 & 245)
4. Low fuel lamp
5. Light switch
6. PTO switch
7. Key switch
8. Battery
9. Battery positive cable
10. Stator
11. Ignition coil
12. Headlight
13. Spark plug
14. Ignition module
15. Starter/solenoid
16. Fusible links
17. Fuel shut-off ground wire
18. PTO clutch
19. Fuel shut-off solenoid
20. Ignition relaty
21. PTO relay
22. Starter relay
23. Oil pressure switch
24. Battery negative cable
25. Transmission neutral start switch (hydro)
26. Transmission neutral start switch (gear)
27. 20 amp fuse
28. 10 amp fuse
29. Low fuel switch
30. Seat switch
31. Rectifier/regulator

To reassemble either type of clutch, reverse the disassembly procedure.

Apply an antiseize lubricant to the crankshaft before reinstalling the clutch assembly. Install a washer under the retaining screw with the concave side toward the engine. Tighten the clutch retaining screw to 56 N·m (45 ft.-lb.). Adjust the clutch as previously outlined. If installing a new clutch, break in the clutch by engaging the PTO at least eight times unloaded before attaching a load to the clutch.

SAFETY INTERLOCK SYSTEM

The tractor is equipped with a safety interlock system preventing inadvertent starting of the tractor engine or operation when the operator leaves the tractor seat. The tractor engine should not start if the following occurs (engage parking brake):

- Operator in the tractor seat, the shift lever in NEUTRAL, the brake engaged and the PTO clutch lever in the ON position.
- Operator in the tractor seat, the PTO clutch lever in the OFF position, the brake engaged and the shift lever in a position other than NEUTRAL.
- Operator in the tractor seat, the shift lever in NEUTRAL, the PTO clutch lever in the OFF position and the brakes released.
- Operator not in the seat when starting the engine.

The seat switch should kill the engine if the operator is not in the seat or leaves the seat when the PTO clutch is engaged. The seat switch should kill the engine if the operator leaves the seat when the brakes are not locked.

Refer to wiring schematics at the end of this section.

WIRING SCHEMATICS

Refer to Fig. JD4-18 for tractor electrical component location for all models. Refer to Fig. JD4-19 for electrical wiring schematic and harness diagram for Models 240 and 245. Refer to Fig. JD4-20 for electrical wiring schematic and harness diagram for Models 260 and 265.

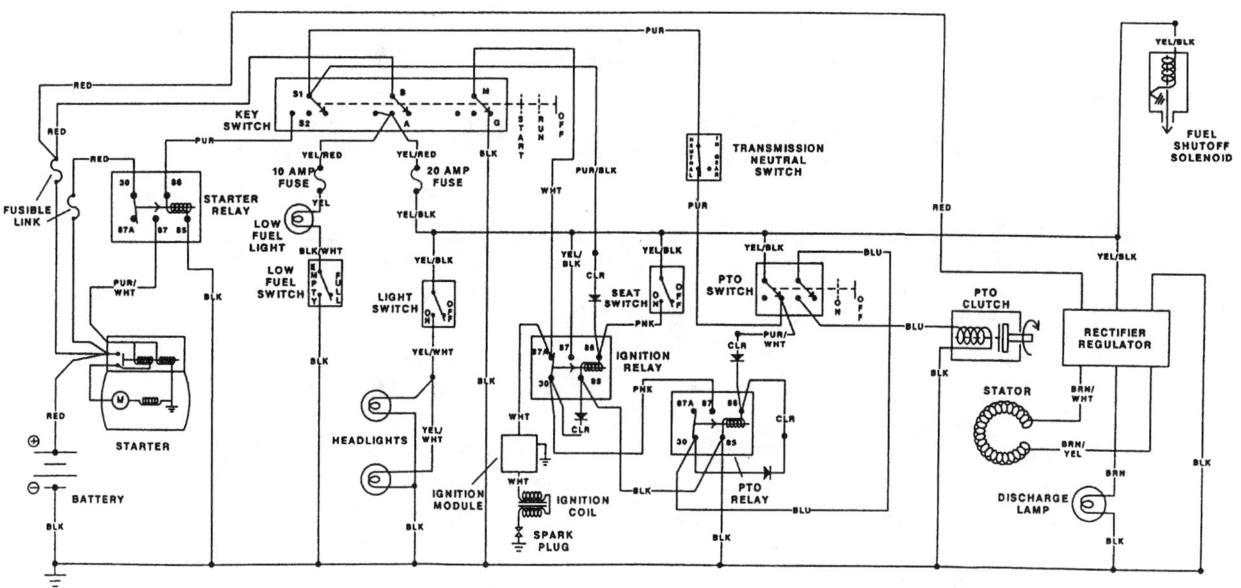

Fig. JD4-19–Electrical system schematic for Models 240 and 245.

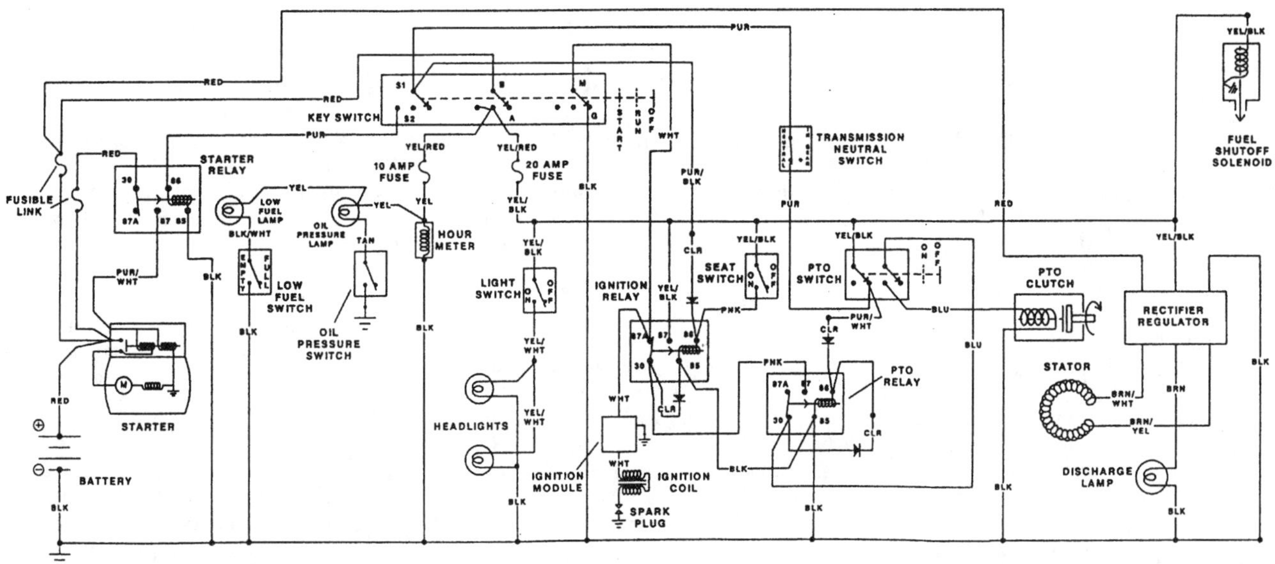

Fig. JD4-20–Electrical system schematic for Models 260 and 265.

JOHN DEERE

CONDENSED SPECIFICATIONS

Models	285, 320
Engine Make	Kawasaki
Model	FD590V
Bore	74 mm (2.91 in.)
Stroke	68 mm (2.68 in.)
Displacement	585 cc (35.68 cu. in.)
Power Rating	13.4 kW (18 hp.)
Slow Idle	1400 rpm
High Speed (No-Load)	3350 rpm
Crankcase Capacity	1.9 L (2 qt.)
Hydrostatic Transmission Capacity	2.5 L (2.6 qt.)
Cooling System Capacity	3.1 L (3.3 qt.)
Fuel Tank	11.4 L (3.0 gal.)

FRONT AXLE AND STEERING SYSTEM

MAINTENANCE

The front wheel spindles should be lubricated after every 50 hours of operation. Jack up the front axle so the wheels are suspended and apply grease to the spindles through the grease fitting at each end of the axle. One or two shots from a hand-held grease gun should be sufficient. Use lithium based grease. Check for looseness and binding in the front axle components.

AXLE MAIN MEMBER REMOVAL AND INSTALLATION

Raise and support the front of the tractor. Disconnect the drag link end (14—Fig. JD5-1) from the steering arm (13). Using a suitable jack, support the axle assembly. Unscrew the pivot pin nut (1). Unscrew the pivot pin mounting screws and lower the axle assembly out of the tractor.

Inspect components for damage. The bushings (3) in the axle are replaceable.

To install the axle, reverse the removal procedure. Tighten the axle pivot nut (1) until the front-to-rear axle free play is eliminated, but the axle still pivots freely.

TIE ROD AND TOE-IN

The tie rod (11—Fig. JD5-1) is equipped with replaceable ends (10 and 12) that are not interchangeable. Install new tie rod ends when excessive wear is evident.

Front wheel toe-in should be 3-6 mm ($^1/_8$-$^1/_4$ in.). To adjust toe-in, loosen the jam nuts on the tie rod ends. Turn the tie rod to change its length when necessary to obtain the desired toe-in.

STEERING SPINDLES

Raise and support the front of the tractor. Remove the wheel and tire. Disconnect the tie rod end, and if needed, the drag link end. If removing the right spindle (7—Fig. JD5-1), detach the snap ring (4) securing the top of the spindle and withdraw the spindle from the axle. If removing the left spindle (17), scribe match marks on the steering arm (13) and spindle so they can be returned to their original position. Remove the clamp bolt from the steering arm, remove the steering arm and withdraw the spindle from the axle.

Inspect components for damage. Replaceable bushings (5) are located in the axle.

Lubricate steering spindles with multipurpose grease prior to installing in the axle. Be sure the steering arm is installed in its original position. Check and adjust the toe-in as previously outlined.

DRAG LINK

A drag link (15—Fig. JD5-1) with adjustable ends is located between the steering arm (13) and pitman arm. Adjust the drag link length so equal turns of the steering wheel are required to

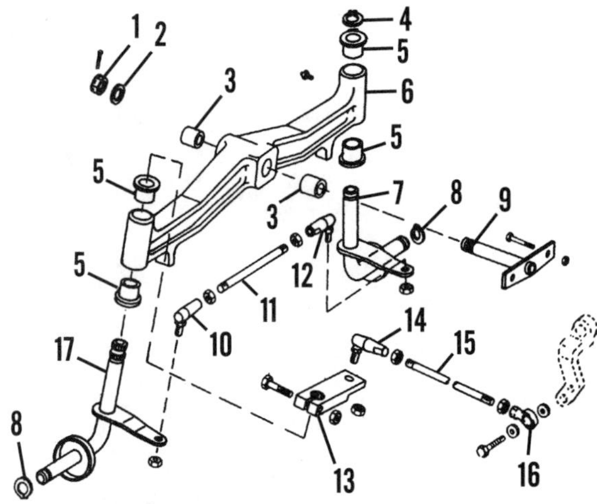

Fig. JD5-1–Exploded view of front axle assembly. Note that rod ends (12 and 14) have left hand threads.

1. Slotted nut
2. Washer
3. Bushing
4. Snap ring
5. Bushng
6. Axle main member
7. Spindle (R.H.)
8. Snap ring
9. Pivot
10. Tie rod end
11. Tie rod
12. Tie rod end
13. Steering arm
14. Drag link end
15. Drag link
16. Drag link end
17. Spindle (L.H.)

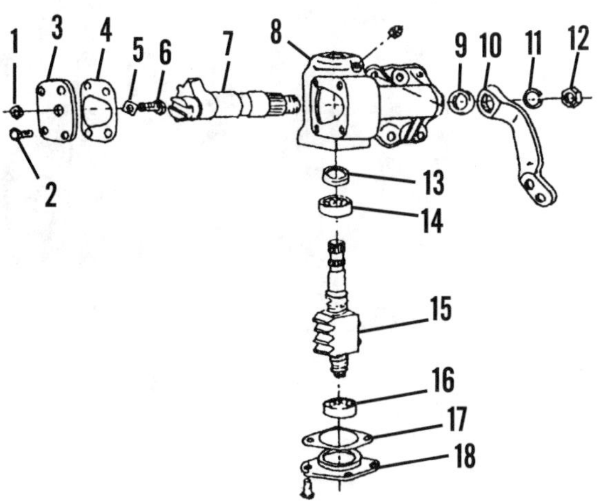

Fig. JD5-2–Exploded view of steering gear box.

1. Nut
2. Screw
3. Cover
4. Gasket
5. Shim
6. Adjuster
7. Pitman shaft
8. Gearbox
9. Seal
10. Pitman arm
11. Lockwasher
12. Nut
13. Seal
14. Bearing
15. Shaft & nut assy.
16. Bearing
17. Shim
18. Cover

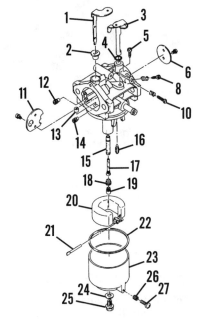

Fig. JD5-3–Exploded view of carburetor.

1. Choke shaft
2. Bushing
3. Throttle shaft
4. Seal
5. Idle jet
6. Throttle plate
7. Spring
8. Idle mixture screw
9. Spring
10. Idle speed screw
11. Choke plate
12. Air jet'
13. Bushing
14. Air jet
15. Nozzle
16. Fuel inlet valve
17. Nozzle
18. Jet holder
19. Main jet
20. Float
21. Pin
22. Gasket
23. Fuel bowl
24. Gasket
25. Screw
26. Spring
27. Drain screw

reach the full left and right turn from NEUTRAL.

FRONT WHEEL BEARINGS

The front wheel bearings are sealed and should not require lubrication. Wheel bearings are a press fit in the wheel hub.

STEERING GEAR OVERHAUL

Detach the drag link and remove the pitman arm. Raise the hood and remove the lower pedestal panel. Disconnect the steering column shaft from the gearbox shaft. Unscrew the fasteners securing the gearbox and remove the gearbox.

The steering gear is a recirculating ball type. Refer to Fig. JD5-2 for an exploded view. To disassemble, unbolt and remove the side cover (3) and end cover (18). Withdraw the pitman shaft (7) and wormshaft assembly (15). The wormshaft is available only as an assembly and no attempt should be made to disassemble the unit.

When assembling the steering unit, perform the following adjustments. Back out the adjusting screw (6) until it stops. Turn the wormshaft (15) clockwise until stopped, then turn back one-half turn. Install needed shims (17) so the rolling torque when turning the wormshaft is 0.4 N·m (3.5 in.-lb.). Install the thickest shim (5) allowed when assembling the unit and make sure the pitman shaft (7) is centered on the ball nut when the nut is at the midpoint of the travel. Turn the adjusting screw (6) so the wormshaft rolling torque increases to 1.1 N·m (9.5 in.-lb.), then tighten the locknut (1).

Gearbox oil capacity is 170 mL (6 oz.). The recommended oil is SAE 90 gear oil rated GL-5. After installation, check the oil level by removing the plug (19). The oil level should be 25 mm (1 in.) below the top of the plug hole.

ENGINE

MAINTENANCE

Lubrication

Check the oil level before operation or after every four hours of operation. Determine oil level by resting the dipstick on top of the dipstick tube; do not screw in.

The recommended oil is a premium grade oil meeting the latest API service classification. Use SAE 30 oil for temperatures above 32°F (0°C); use SAE 10W-30 oil for temperatures between -4°F (-20°C) and 86°F (30°C); SAE 5W30 may be used between 50°F (10°C) and -31°F (-35°C).

Change oil and filter after first five hours of operation and then after every 100 hours of operation, or more frequently when operation is severe. Crankcase capacity is 1.9 liters (2 qt.).

Air Filter

The air filter consists of a foam precleaner element and a dry paper filter element. Both elements should be cleaned after every 25 hours of operation or more frequently when operating conditions are severe.

Clean the dry paper element with low pressure compressed air blown from the inside towards the outside. Clean the foam precleaner element by washing in a solution of mild detergent and water. Allow to dry completely, then apply approximately 30 mL (1 oz.) of clean engine oil. Squeeze out excess oil and install.

Cooling System

Drain, flush and refill cooling system annually. Manufacturer recommends low silicate antifreeze that does not contain stop leak additive. Cooling system capacity is 3.1 liters (3.3 qt.).

A thermostat maintains cooling system temperature. The thermostat should open at 82° C (180° F) and open fully at 95° C (203° F).

Spark Plug

The recommended spark plug is NGK BMR6A. The spark plug gap should be 0.7 mm (0.028 in.). Tighten spark plug to 20 N·m (180 in.-lb.).

Fuel Filter

The fuel filter should be changed periodically based on fuel cleanliness and operating conditions. Pay particular attention to clean fuel on fuel injected models due to problems that may occur if contaminated fuel is used. The fuel filter on carbureted engines is located in the fuel hose adjacent to engine. The fuel filter on fuel injected engines is located at the rear of the tractor on a panel attached to the rear of the tractor frame.

Carburetor

Carbureted engines are equipped with the float carburetor shown in Fig. JD5-3.

Adjust the carburetor control cables as follows: Place the engine throttle lever in the fast position. Align the holes in the throttle lever (6—Fig. JD5-4) and plate (5) and insert a $^{15}/_{64}$-inch drill bit (4). Loosen the throttle cable housing clamp (1), pull the cable housing tight and retighten the cable clamp. Rotate the screw (2) so there is a gap between the screw and choke control lever (3), then turn back in until the screw just touches the choke lever. Remove drill bit. Move the throttle control lever to the choke position. The carburetor choke plate should be closed, if not, repeat the procedure.

The initial setting of the idle mixture screw (8—Fig. JD5-3) is $1\frac{1}{8}$ turns out from the lightly seated position. To adjust the idle mixture screw, turn the idle speed screw (10) so the engine runs at 1400 rpm. Run the engine until it reaches the normal operating temperature. Turn the idle mixture screw (8) in until the engine runs rough, then turn the screw out until the engine runs rough again. Turn the screw to the midpoint position (it should be the highest engine speed) then back out ¼ turn. Adjust the idle stop screw so the engine idles at 1400 rpm.

High speed mixture is controlled by the fixed main jet (19). Standard main jet is 112.5 and should provide satisfactory operation up to 3000 feet. The main jet 110.0 is available for use from 3000 to 7000 feet, while the main jet 107.5 is designed for operation above 7000 feet.

To disassemble the carburetor, refer to Fig. JD5-3 and remove the float bowl (23), float (20), fuel inlet needle (16), main jet (19), idle jet (5) and idle mixture screw (8).

Clean the carburetor fuel passages with a suitable carburetor cleaning solvent. Do not use wires or drill bits to clean the passages as the carburetor's calibration could be upset if the passages are enlarged or damaged. Inspect the fuel inlet needle (16) and seat for wear. The fuel inlet needle is replaceable.

When assembling the carburetor, note the float should be parallel with the carburetor float bowl mating surface when the carburetor is inverted (fuel inlet needle is on its seat). Bend the float tab to adjust the float level, being careful not to push on the fuel inlet needle.

Governor

To adjust the governor linkage, first check the throttle cable adjustment as outlined in the CARBURETOR section. Place the throttle control lever in the fast position. Loosen the governor lever

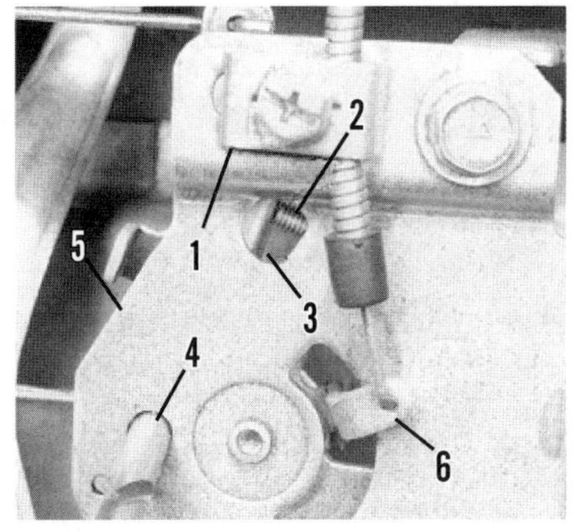

Fig. JD5-4–Refer to text for throttle cable adjustment.

1. Clamp
2. Screw
3. Choke lever
4. Drill bit
5. Throttle plate
6. Throttle control lever

clamp bolt (7—Fig. JD5-5), hold the lever and turn the governor shaft (6) as far as possible counterclockwise. Retighten nut.

The maximum no-load engine speed should be 3250-3450 rpm on carbureted engines and is adjusted as follows: Run the engine until the normal operating temperature is reached. Align the holes (5) in the throttle lever (2) and plate (4) and insert a $^{15}/_{64}$ inch drill bit (3). Run the engine with the transmission in NEUTRAL and determine the engine speed using an accurate tachometer. If the engine speed is not 3250-3450 rpm, loosen the plate retaining screws (1) and reposition the plate to obtain the desired engine speed. Retighten the screws and recheck the engine speed. Check the choke operation as outlined in the CARBURETOR section.

Ignition System

A breakerless, solid-state ignition system is used. Ignition timing is not adjustable. If a malfunction is suspected, refer to the REPAIRS section for the service procedure.

Valve Adjustment

The engine must be cold when checking the valve stem end clearance. Remove the rocker arm cover and unscrew the spark plug for the cylinder being checked. Rotate the crankshaft so the piston is at top dead center on the compression stroke. Both the intake and exhaust valves should be seated and the rocker arms loose. If not, the piston is not on the compression stroke and the crankshaft must be turned one complete revolution.

Measure the clearance between the valve stem and rocker arm with a feeler

Fig. JD5-5–Refer to text for governor control linkage adjustment.

1. Cap screws
2. Throttle control lever
3. Drill bit
4. Throttle plate
5. Hole
6. Governor shaft
7. Clamp bolt

Fig. JD5-6–Loosen locknut (N) and turn screw (W) to adjust valve clearance.

gauge. Clearance should be 0.25 mm (0.010 in.). Loosen jam nut (N—Fig. JD5-6) and turn adjusting screw (W) to obtain the desired clearance. Tighten the jam nut to 9 N·m (79 in.-lb.) and recheck clearance.

REMOVAL AND INSTALLATION

To remove the engine, first remove the hood, muffler and pedestal shroud. Disconnect the battery ground cable. Close the fuel shut-off valve and disconnect the fuel line. Disconnect the throttle control cable. Disconnect the ground wire, starter wires and ignition wires from the engine. Remove the electric PTO clutch. Relieve the tension on the traction drive belt and remove the belt from the drive pulley. Remove the belt pulley and key from the engine crankshaft. Remove the engine mounting cap screws and lift the engine from the tractor.

To reinstall the engine, reverse the removal procedure. Apply an antiseize lubricant to the crankshaft before installing the drive pulley. Tighten PTO clutch mounting cap screw to 61 N·m (45 ft.-lb.).

REPAIRS

Tightening Torques

The recommended tightening torque specifications are as follows:

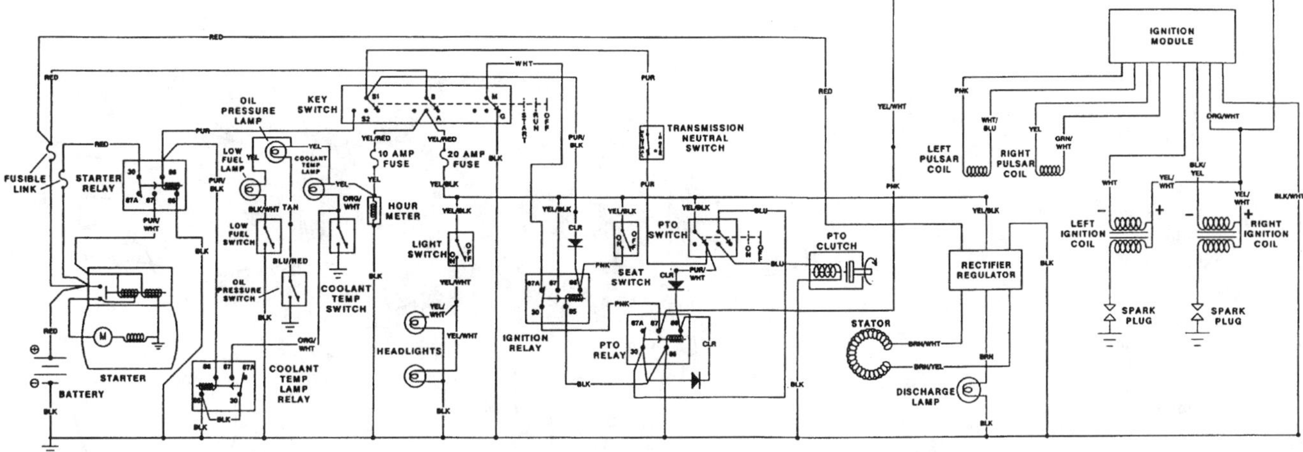

Fig. JD5-7–Wiring diagram for Model 285 with carbureted engine. Refer to Fig. JD5-10 for fuel injection wiring diagram.

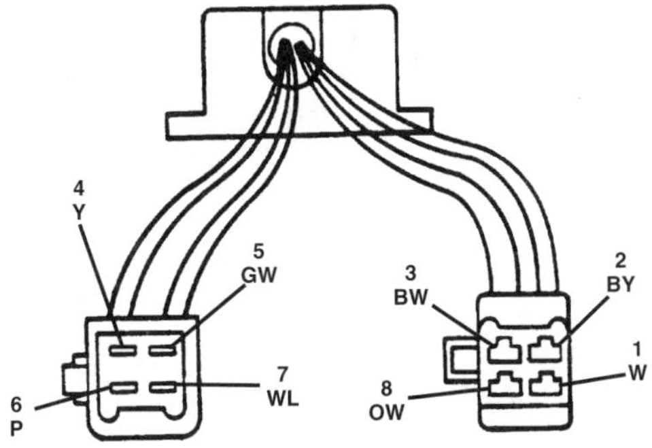

KΩ		TESTER (+) TERMINAL (RED)							
	TERMINAL	1	2	3	4	5	6	7	8
TESTER (-) TERMINAL (BLACK)	1		∞	1~8KΩ	4~16	2~8	4~16	2~8	2~10
	2	∞		1~8	4~16	2~8	4~16	2~8	2~10
	3	∞	∞		1~6	0	1~6	0	0.5~2
	4	∞	∞	1~6		0	3~12	1~6	2~8
	5	∞	∞	0	1~6		1~6	0	0.5~2
	6	∞	∞	1~6	3~15	0.5~2		1~6	1~6
	7	∞	∞	0	1~6	2~8	1~6		0.5~2
	8	∞	∞	0.5~2	2~8	0.5~2	2~8	0.5~2	

Fig. JD5-8–To check ignition module, detach lead connectors and using an ohmmeter set on K ohm scale, then perform resistance checks as indicated in table.

Connecting rod . . . . 21 N·m (186 in.-lb.)
Cylinder head . . . . 21 N·m (186 in.-lb.)
Flywheel . . . . 108 N·m (79 ft.-lb.)
Oil pan . . . . 21 N·m (186 in.-lb.)
Rocker arm . . . . 9 N·m (79 in.-lb.)
Spark plug . . . . 20 N·m (180 in.-lb.)

Ignition System

The ignition system consists of an ignition module, two pulsar coils and two ignition coils. A 12-volt battery supplies current to the ignition system. A safety switch operated by weight on the tractor seat disconnects current to the ignition system if the operator leaves the seat while the engine is running.

Refer Fig. JD5-7 which includes the ignition system components. Before testing the ignition system, be sure the safety circuit components are not faulty and affecting the ignition system's performance. Note the following test specifications when troubleshooting the ignition system:

Pulsar coil resistance . . . . 85-270 ohms
Ignition coil resistance:
Primary . . . . 3.4-4.6 ohms
Secondary . . . . 10.4-15.5k ohms

To check the ignition module, detach the lead connectors and using an ohmmeter set on the K-ohm scale perform resistance checks as indicated in Fig. JD5-8. Note the values in the table are approximate and the actual test values may be different depending on the accuracy and condition of the ohmmeter.

Fuel Pump

The fuel pump on carbureted engines is a mechanical pump driven by a lobe on the camshaft. The pump should maintain a minimum fuel pressure of 19.6 kPa (2.8 psi) at full throttle. Fuel flow at full throttle should be 160 ml (5.4 oz.) in 15 seconds. The fuel pump must be serviced as a unit assembly.

The fuel pump on fuel injected engines is driven electrically. Check fuel pressure at the inlet line to the fuel injector. The pressure should be 274-284 kPa (40-41 psi). Check for restrictions and leaks in the filter and hoses, and pressure regulator if pressure is insufficient. Replace the pump if pressure remains low. Check the return line, pressure regulator vacuum hose and pressure regulator when pressure is high.

Fuel Pressure Regulator (Fuel Injected Engines)

A vacuum-controlled fuel pressure regulator is located on the throttle body of the fuel injected engines. The regulator varies fuel pressure according to the air pressure in the intake manifold through a vacuum hose. When the manifold pressure decreases, the fuel pressure is increased, and the reverse

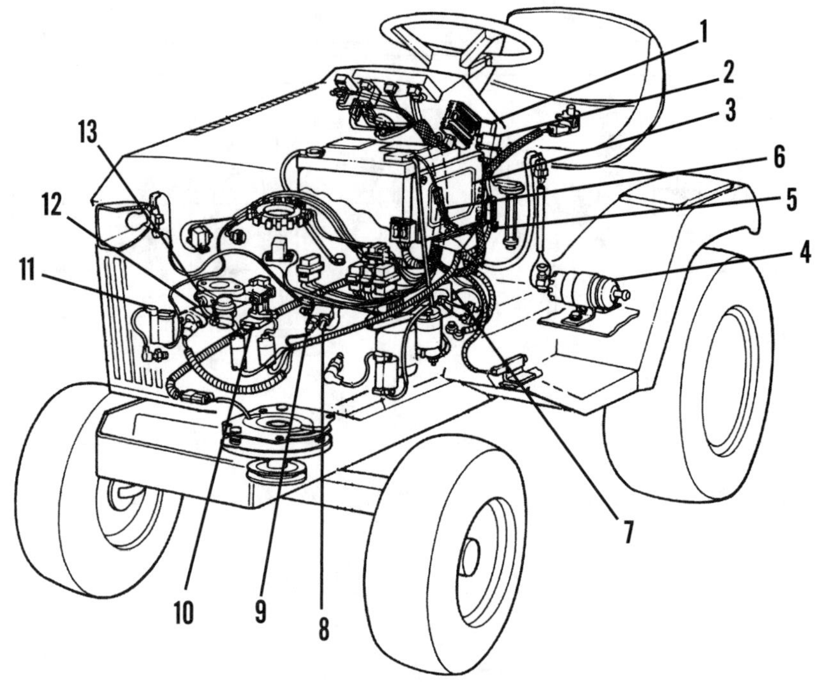

Fig. JD5-9–Drawing showing location of fuel injection system components.

1. Fuel injection module relay (green)
2. Fuel pump relay (blue)
3. Fuel injection module
4. Fuel pump
5. Altitude compression switch
6. Fusible links
7. Ignition module
8. Fuel injection coolant temperature sensor
9. Coolant temperature sensor
10. Throttle sensor
11. Ignition coil
12. Fuel injector
13. Air temperature sensor

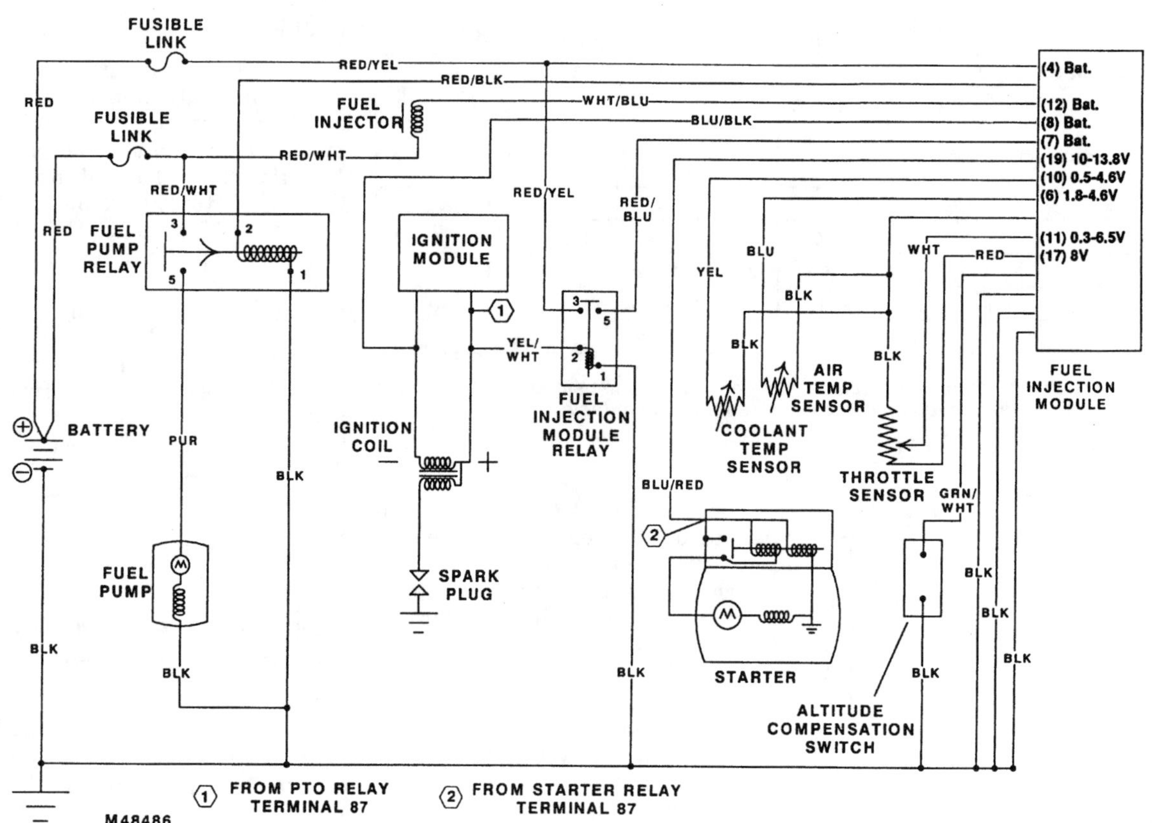

Fig. JD5-10–Wiring diagram for fuel injection system on models so equipped. Note test voltage readings at fuel injection module and connector. Reading is taken at module or connector depending on current direction.

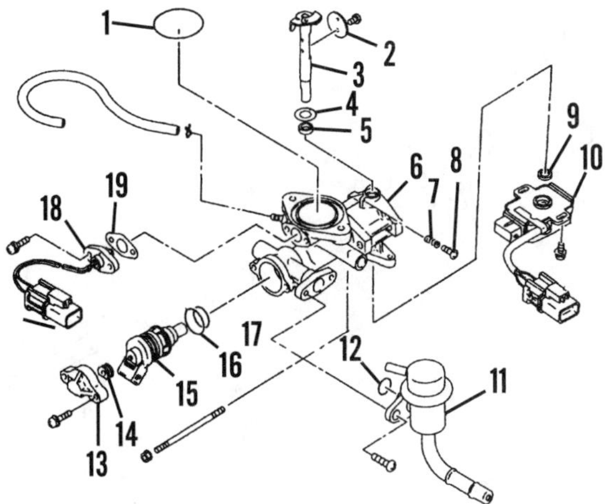

Fig. JD5-11–Exploded view of throttle body injection components.

1. O-ring
2. Throttle plate
3. Throttle shaft
4. Washer
5. Seal
6. Body
7. Spring
8. Idle speed screw
9. Seal
10. Throttle sensor
11. Fuel regulator
12. O-ring
13. Cap
14. Damper
15. Injector
16. O-ring
17. O-ring
18. Air temperature sensor
19. Gasket

when the manifold pressure increases. The fuel pressure regulator must be serviced as a unit assembly.

Fuel Injection System

The engine may be equipped with a fuel injection system. Refer to Fig. JD5-9 for a diagram indicating the location of the fuel injection components. Refer to Fig. JD5-10 for the wiring diagram of the fuel injection electrical circuit.

Operation

The fuel injection system is an electronically controlled, throttle body system. The system is divided into two subsystems, fuel delivery and control.

The fuel delivery system consists of the fuel filter, fuel pump, fuel injector and pressure regulator. Fuel from the fuel tank passes through the filter to the fuel pump. Pressurized fuel from the pump is directed to the fuel injector, which is located in the throttle body attached to the intake manifold (see Fig. JD5-11). Excess fuel is routed from the injector to the pressure regulator, which maintains system pressure (see FUEL PRESSURE REGULATOR). Leak-off fuel from the regulator is directed back to the fuel tank.

The control system consists of the fuel injection control module, module relay, fuel pump relay and several sensors. The sensors provide the control module with voltage readings related to the throttle position, coolant temperature and air temperature. The control module also senses engine speed, starter circuit voltage and battery voltage. The control module relay directs current to the control module when the ignition key switch is in RUN. The control module energizes the fuel pump relay when output from the fuel pump is required. The control module regulates the time and duration of the fuel injector output. Activation of the injector by the control module is determined by input from the sensors and related circuits. Note that the two fusible links are located in the system to protect system components.

Troubleshooting

Refer to Fig. JD5-10 for voltage readings that will help determine a faulty component. Normal troubleshooting techniques will serve to isolate the faulty component. Voltage readings are taken with the connectors connected.

The following fuel system circuits may prevent engine from starting if a malfunction occurs (including starter and ignition circuits):

- Fuel injection module.
- Fuel pump circuit.
- Fuel injector circuit.
- Engine speed circuit.
- Starter sensing circuit.

A rough running engine may be caused by a malfunction in the following:

- Air temperature sensor circuit.
- Coolant temperature sensor circuit.
- Throttle sensor circuit.
- Engine speed circuit.

Note the following when performing voltage checks:

Throttle sensor—voltage reading of 0.3-6.5 V at pin 11 of fuel injection module is obtained when the throttle plate is closed and the throttle lever is moved from slow idle to fast idle.

Starter voltage sensing—voltage reading of 10-13.8 V at the blue/red wire terminal on solenoid and pin 19 of the fuel injection module is obtained with the ignition key switch held in the START position. Ground the spark plug wires to prevent starting.

Fuel pump circuit—when the ignition key switch is turned ON there should be battery voltage for 5 seconds at the fuel injection module pin 21, if not replace the module. Battery voltage should be present at the fuel pump relay terminal 2 for 5 seconds when the key switch is turned to the ON position. With the spark plugs grounded, turn the key switch to ON until the fuel pump stops, then turn to START and measure the voltage at the fuel pump relay terminal 2; there should be 10-13.8 V. If not, check the circuit and replace the fuel injection module if no other cause is found. Turn the key switch to ON until the fuel pump stops, then apply negative battery voltage to the blue/black connector between the ignition coil and ignition module and measure the voltage at the fuel pump relay terminal 2; the reading should indicate battery voltage. If not, check the circuit and replace the fuel injection module if no other cause is found.

Component Testing

The following components may be tested using an ohmmeter. The ignition key switch must be OFF.

THROTTLE SENSOR. Detach the throttle sensor connector. Connect the ohmmeter leads to the black wire pin and red wire pin. Move the throttle lever while noting the meter reading. Resistance should decrease when the throttle lever is moved from slow to fast. Resistance readings should fall in range from 3.3k to 6.8k ohms. Connect the ohmmeter leads to the white wire pin and black wire pin. The resistance should be 0.2-0.5k ohms when the throttle lever is in the idle position.

AIR TEMPERATURE SENSOR. Detach the air temperature sensor connector. Resistance reading between the sensor connector terminals at 68° F (20° C) should be 1.9-3.1k ohms. At a temperature range of 32°-86° F (0°-30° C) resistance readings should be in range of 7.4k-1.3k ohms. Resistance should decrease as temperature increases.

COOLANT TEMPERATURE SENSOR. Specified temperatures and resistance readings are same as for the air temperature sensor.

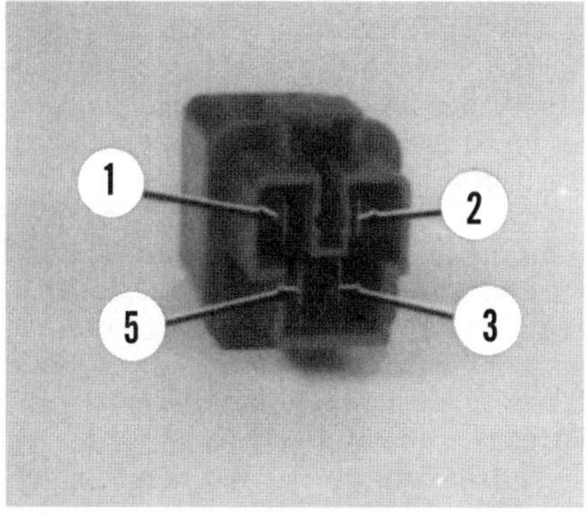

Fig. JD5-12–View of fuel pump relay pins. Refer to text for resistance tests.

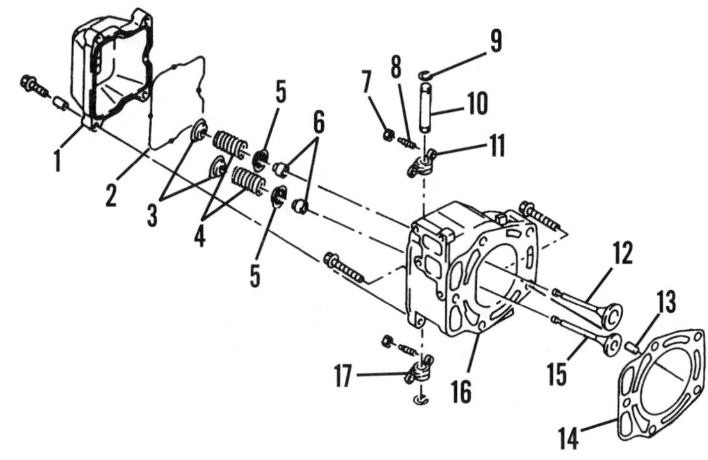

Fig. JD5-13–Exploded view of valve system components.

1. Rocker cover
2. Gasket
3. Spring retainers
4. Valve springs
5. Spring seats
6. Valve stem seals.
7. Jam nut
8. Adjusting screw
9. Snap ring
10. Rocker shaft
11. Rocker arm
12. Intake valve.
13. Alignment dowel
14. Head gasket
15. Exhaust valve
16. Cylinder head
17. Rocker arm

FUEL PUMP RELAY. Refer to Fig. JD5-12 for connector pin identification. Continuity should exist between pins 1 and 2. There should be infinite resistance between pins 3 and 5. Apply positive battery voltage to pin 1 and negative voltage (ground) to pin 2. Continuity should now exist between pins 3 and 5.

FUEL INJECTION MODULE RELAY. Follow the testing instructions for the fuel pump relay.

FUEL INJECTOR. Detach injector wire connector. Resistance between the injector pins should be 11.1-12.9 ohms. Apply negative battery voltage to one injector pin and tap a wire from the positive battery terminal to the other injector pin. The injector should "click" each time a connection is made. If not, replace the injector.

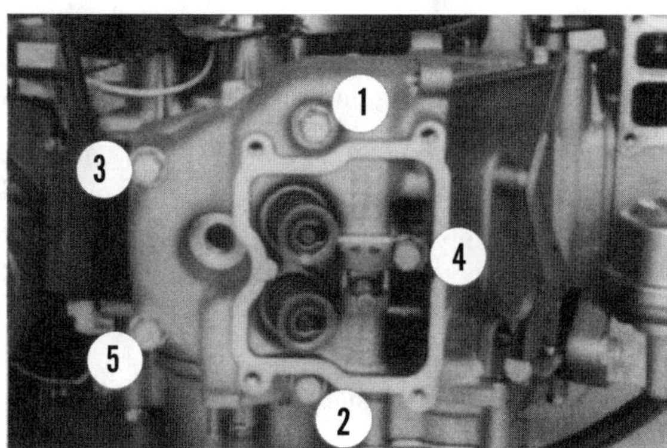

Fig. JD5-14–Tighten cylinder head screws in sequence shown above.

Cylinder Head

To remove the cylinder head (16—Fig. JD5-13), first drain the coolant from the engine. Remove the intake manifold and detach the exhaust pipe. Rotate the crankshaft so the piston is at top dead center on the compression stroke. Remove rocker arm cover (1). Detach the snap rings (9) on the rocker shaft (10), withdraw the rocker shaft and remove the rocker arms (11 and 17). Remove the push rods and mark them so they can be reinstalled in their original position. Unscrew cylinder head screws and remove cylinder head.

Clean cylinder head and inspect for damage. Use a feeler gauge and straightedge or surface plate to check the cylinder head gasket surface for distortion. Replace if a 0.05 mm (0.002 in.) feeler gauge can be inserted under the head and surface.

Install the cylinder head with a new gasket. Lightly oil the threads of the cylinder head screws, then tighten in the sequence shown in Fig. JD5-14. Tighten the screws in steps of 3 N·m (27 in.-lb.) until a final torque of 21 N·m (186 in.-lb.) is attained. Adjust the valve clearance as outlined previously in the ENGINE MAINTENANCE section.

Valve System

The valves are located in the cylinder head (16—Fig. JD5-13). To disassemble, remove the snap rings (9) and withdraw the rocker shaft (10) and rocker arms (11 and 17). Press down on the valve spring retainers (4) to disengage the retainer from the valve stem. Removal of the lower spring seat (5) will result in damage to the valve stem seal (6). If the retainer and seal are removed, install the new stem seal. Keep all parts separated and identified as they are removed so that they can be installed in their original locations.

Valve seats and guides are not replaceable. The valve face and seat angles should be 45°. Valve seat width should be 0.80 mm (0.031 in.). Minimum valve margin is 0.60 mm (0.024 in.). The Maximum allowable valve guide inside diameter is 6.05 mm (0.238 in.). The minimum valve spring length is 29.70 mm (1.170 in.). The maximum valve stem runout measured with the valve supported at ends is 0.03 mm (0.001 in.). The maximum push rod runout measured with the push rod supported at the ends is 0.30 mm (0.012 in.). The minimum rocker shaft diameter is 11.95 mm (0.470 in.). The maximum rocker arm inner diameter is 12.07 mm (0.475 in.).

Piston, Pin, Rings and Rod

Remove cylinder head. Separate the crankcase cover (34—Fig. JD5-15) from the cylinder block for access to the piston and rod assemblies. Unscrew the rod cap screws, detach the rod cap and remove piston and rod assembly through the cylinder bore.

Specified piston clearance in bore is 0.030-0.170 mm (0.0012-0.0067 in.). The specified standard piston diameter

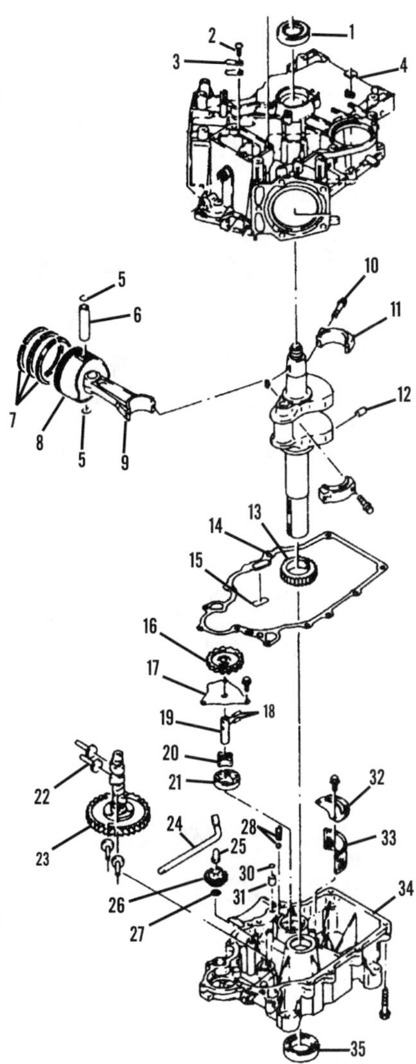

Fig. JD5-15–Exploded view of internal engine components.

1. Seal
2. Plate
3. Breather valve
4. Cylinder block
5. Retaining ring
6. Piston pin
7. Piston rings
8. Piston
9. Connecting rod
10. Rod cap
11. Crankshaft
12. Pin
13. Gear
14. Gasket
15. O-ring
16. Oil pump gear
17. Cover
18. Pins
19. Pins
20. Inner rotor
21. Outer rotor
22. Tappets
23. Camshaft
24. Governor shaft
25. Sleeve
26. Governor
27. Washer
28. Relief valve spring
29. Relief valve
30. O-ring
31. Dowel pin
32. Plate
33. Strainer
34. Oil pan
35. Seal

is 73.935-73.950 mm (2.9108-2.9114 in.). Measure the piston diameter 11 mm (0.43 in.) from the bottom of the piston perpendicular to the piston pin.

Maximum allowable pin bore in the piston is 17.04 mm (0.671 in.). The minimum allowable piston pin diameter is 16.98 mm (0.668 in.). The maximum allowable piston ring end gap is 1.00 mm

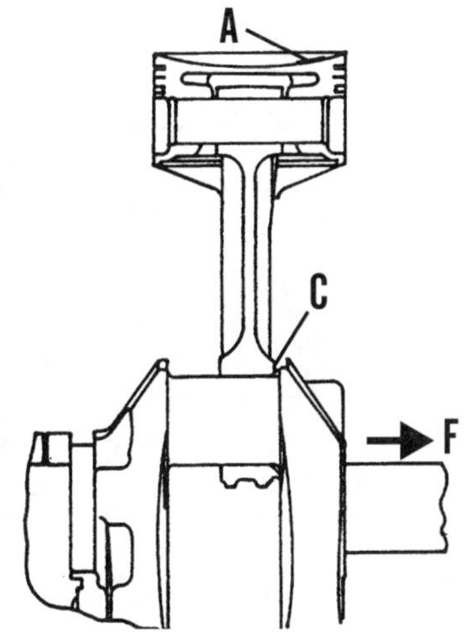

Fig. JD5-16–Assemble piston and rod so arrow (A) on piston crown is toward flywheel (F) and chamfer (C) is toward adjacent crankshaft web (W). Note that when both rods are installed on crankshaft the non-chamfered sides will be together.

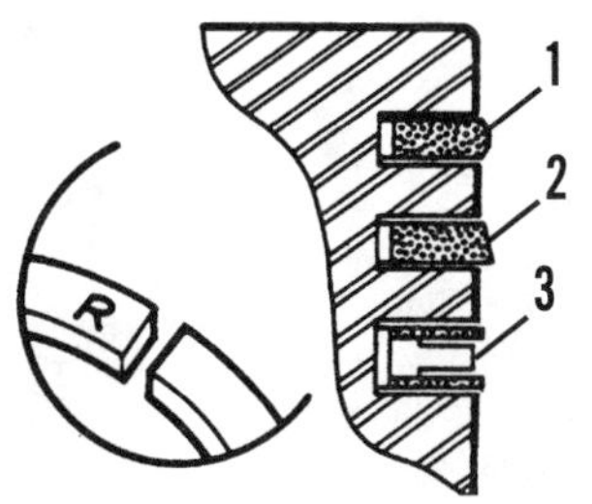

Fig. JD5-17–Cross section of piston and rings showing correct installation. Be sure that "R" and "NPR" mark on end of top ring (1) and second ring (2) faces up. Oil ring (3) can be installed either way.

(0.039 in.). The maximum allowable piston ring side clearance is 0.10 mm (0.004 in.) for compression rings. Pistons and rings are available in standard and 0.50 mm oversize. Refer to the CYLINDER BLOCK section if oversize pistons are required.

The connecting rod rides directly on the crankpin. The maximum allowable inside diameter at the big end of the rod is 34.06 mm (1.341 in.). Minimum allowable crankpin journal diameter is 33.93 mm (1.336 in.). The Maximum allowable inside diameter at pin end of rod is 17.05 mm (0.671 in.). The connecting rod is available with the standard size big end diameter as well as with 0.50 mm undersize big end diameter.

Assemble the piston and rod so the arrow on the piston crown will be towards the flywheel as shown in Fig. JD5-16 and the chamfered side of the rod big end is next to the crankshaft web. Install piston rings with the lettered side towards the piston crown. See Fig. JD5-17. Position the piston rings so the ring gaps are 180° apart. Install the piston and rod assembly so the arrow on

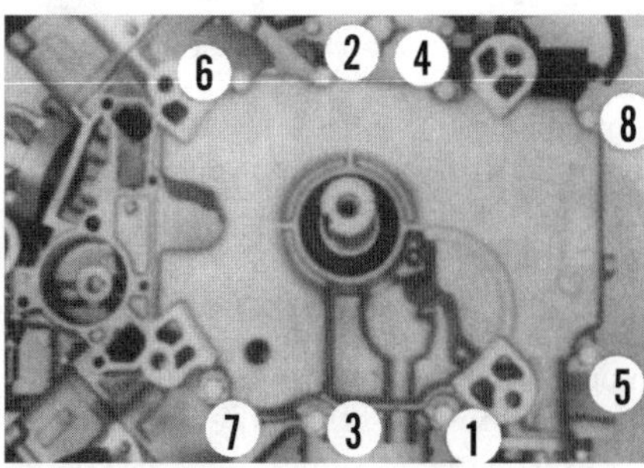

Fig. JD5-18–Tighten oil pan screws in sequence shown above.

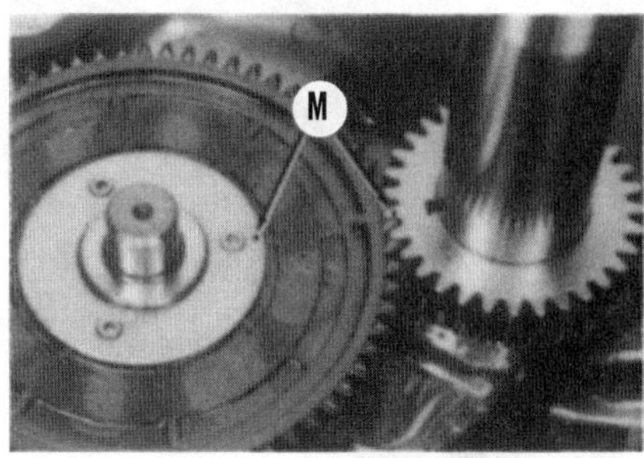

Fig. JD5-19–Align timing marks (M) on crankshaft and camshaft gears when installing camshaft.

the piston crown points towards the flywheel end of the crankshaft. Make sure the rod cap matches the rod and tighten the rod screws to 21 N·m (186 in.-lb.). Tighten the crankcase cover screws to 21 N·m (186 in.-lb.) in the sequence shown in Fig. JD5-18. Install the cylinder head as previously outlined.

Camshaft

The camshaft (23—Fig. JD5-15) is accessible after removing the crankcase cover (34). Rotate the crankshaft to align the timing marks (M—Fig. JD5-19) on the camshaft and crankshaft gears before removing the camshaft.

The camshaft rides in nonreplaceable bushings in the cylinder block and crankcase cover. Replace the cylinder block or crankcase cover if the bushing diameter is greater than 16.07 mm (0.633 in.).

Minimum allowable camshaft bearing journal diameter is 15.91 mm (0.626 in.). Minimum allowable camshaft lobe height is 25.23 mm (0.993 in.). Minimum fuel pump lobe height is 19.50 mm (0.768 in.).

When installing the camshaft, be sure to align the timing marks (M—Fig. JD5-19). Tighten the crankcase cover screws to 21 N·m (186 in.-lb.) in the sequence shown in Fig. JD5-18.

Crankshaft and Main Bearings

To remove the crankshaft (11—Fig. JD5-15), remove the engine flywheel and separate the crankcase cover (34) from the cylinder block. Remove the connecting rod caps (10). Withdraw the crankshaft from the cylinder block.

The crankshaft rides in nonreplaceable bushings in the cylinder block and crankcase cover. Maximum allowable bushing diameter in block and oil pan is 34.07 mm (1.341 in.). Minimum allowable crankshaft main bearing journal diameter is 33.91 mm (1.335 in.). Minimum allowable crankpin diameter is 33.93 mm (1.336 in.). The crankpin may be reground to accept a connecting rod with a 0.50 mm undersize big end. Maximum allowable crankshaft runout is 0.05 mm (0.002 in.) measured at main bearing journals with the crankshaft supported at the ends.

Be sure the timing marks (M—Fig. JD5-19) on the crankshaft and camshaft gears are aligned. Tighten the crankcase cover screws to 21 N·m (186 in.-lb.) in the sequence shown in Fig. JD5-18.

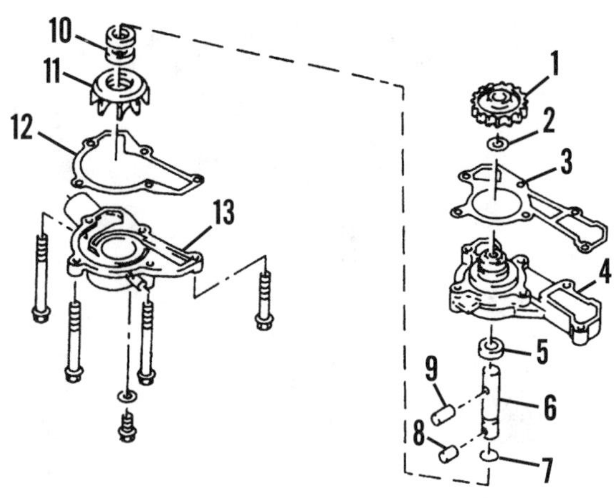

Fig. JD5-20–Exploded view of fuel pump.

1. Gear
2. Washer
3. Gasket
4. Housing
5. Seal
6. Shaft
7. Pin
8. Pin
9. O-ring
10. Seals
11. Impeller
12. Gasket
13. Cover

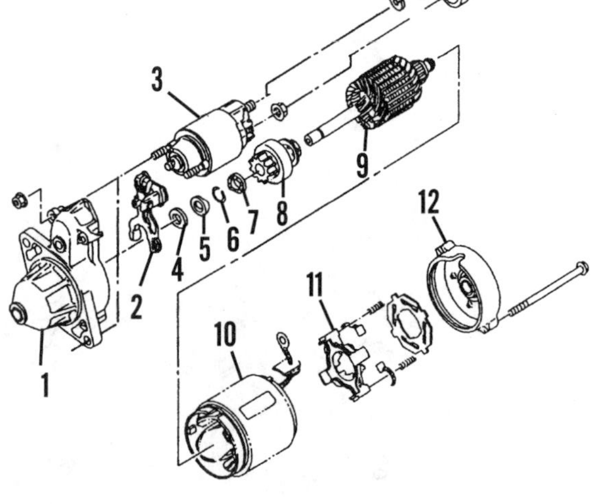

Fig. JD5-21–Exploded view of starter.

1. Drive housing
2. Fork
3. Solenoid
4. Washer
5. Pinion stop
6. Retaining ring
7. Pinion stop
8. Clutch
9. Armature
10. Frame
11. Brush plate
12. End cap

Cylinder Block

The cylinders may be bored to accept oversize pistons. The standard bore diameter is 73.98-74.00 mm (2.9126-2.9134 in.) and the maximum wear limit is 74.07 mm (2.916 in.). Be sure to check the bore diameter when the cylinder is cold.

Governor

A flyweight governor (26—Fig. JD5-15) is located in the crankcase cover (34). The camshaft gear drives the governor gear. Remove crankcase cover for access to the governor assembly. Governor components must move freely without binding.

NOTE: Removing governor assembly from the shaft will damage the governor and require installation of a new governor assembly.

Remove governor assembly by prying or pulling it off the shaft. The shaft must protrude above the boss 32.2-32.8 mm (1.27-1.29 in.). Install the governor by pushing down until it snaps onto the locating groove. Tighten crankcase cover screws to 21 N·m (186 in.-lb.) in the sequence shown in Fig. JD5-18.

Oil Pump

A gerotor oil pump is located in the crankcase cover. The pump provides pressurized oil directed to the crankshaft main bearing journals and crankpin. Drilled passages in the connecting rods squirt oil on the underside of the pistons.

To check oil pressure, remove the oil pressure switch in the cylinder block side adjacent to the oil filter and connect an oil pressure gauge. With the engine at the operating temperature and running at fast throttle setting, oil pressure should be no less than 240 kPa (35 psi).

Remove the crankcase cover for access to the pump. Note the oil pump cover (17—Fig. JD5-15) holds the oil pressure relief valve ball and spring (28) in place. The maximum inner rotor-to-outer rotor clearance is 0.3 mm (0.012 in.). The minimum allowable shaft diameter is 10.92 mm (0.430 in.). Maximum allowable bore diameter in crankcase cover and pump cover is 11.07 mm (0.436 in.). Maximum rotor bore diameter in crankcase cover is 40.80 mm (1.606 in.). Replace the relief valve spring (28—Fig. JD5-15) if the length is less than 19.50 mm (0.768 in.).

Water Pump

Refer to Fig. JD5-20 for an exploded view of the water pump. The impeller (11), shaft (6) and pin (8) are available as a unit assembly only. Minimum allowable diameter of shaft is 9.94 mm (0.391 in.). Maximum allowable diameter of housing bore is 10.09 mm (0.397 in.). Install the seal (10) using the driver provided in the seal kit. Tighten 6 mm mounting screws to 8 N·m (71 in.-lb.) and the 8 mm mounting screw to 21 N·m (186 in.-lb.).

Electric Starter

Refer to Fig. JD5-21 for an exploded view of the electric starter. Place alignment marks on the pinion housing, frame and end cover before disassembly so they can be reinstalled in its original position. Replace the brushes if the length is less than 6 mm (0.24 in.). Starter no-load current draw should be 50 amps at the starter speed of 6000 rpm. The starter current draw under load should be 72 amps at starter speed of 500 rpm.

Alternator

The alternator stator is located under the flywheel. To check the alternator,

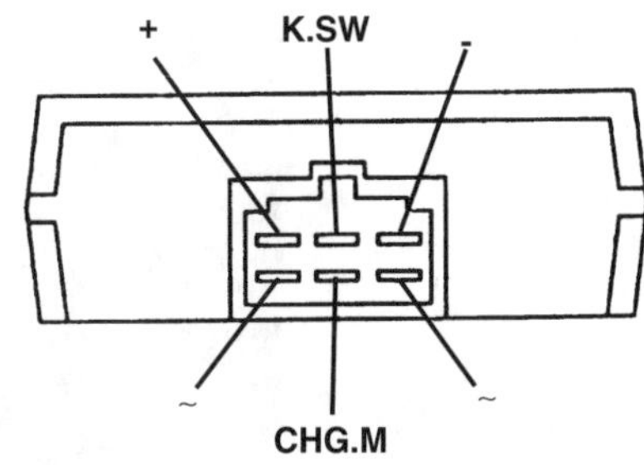

Range: RX1KΩ

Tester (+ / -)	+	K.SW	—	~	~	CHG.M
+		∞	∞	∞	∞	∞
K.SW	4KΩ ~20KΩ		200Ω 1KΩ	1KΩ 5KΩ	1KΩ ~5KΩ	200KΩ ~∞
—	3KΩ ~15KΩ	200Ω ~1KΩ		1KΩ 5KΩ	1KΩ 5KΩ	200KΩ ~∞
~	1KΩ ~5KΩ	∞	∞		∞	∞
~	1KΩ ~5KΩ	∞	∞	∞		∞
CHG.M	10KΩ ~50KΩ	1KΩ ~5KΩ	1.5K ~7.5KΩ	4KΩ ~20KΩ	4KΩ ~20KΩ	

Note: Resistance value may vary with individual meters.

Fig. JD5-22–Refer to table and diagram shown above to perform resistance readings on regulator/rectifier.

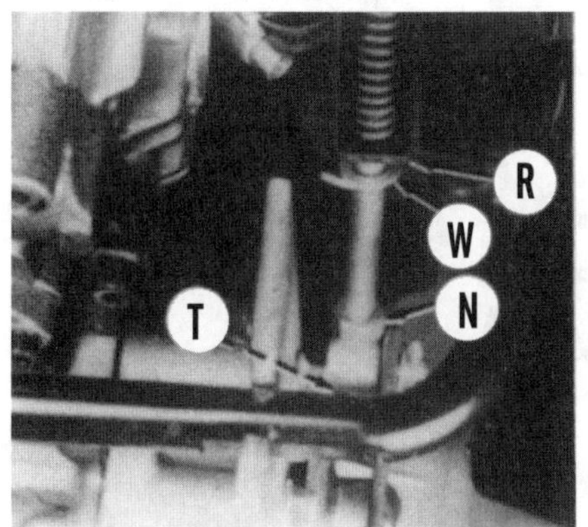

Fig. JD5-23–Gap between washer (W) and spring retainer (R) on brake rod should be 8-14 mm (0.31-0.55 in.), if not, loosen nut (N) and turn nut (T). Retighen nut (N).

disconnect the stator from the regulator/rectifier, refer to the wiring diagram in Fig. JD5-7 and check the voltage reading at the stator leads. With the engine running at fast throttle the minimum voltage reading is 26 volts AC. If the voltage is insufficient, check the resistance of the stator (engine stopped) by attaching ohmmeter leads to the stator wires. Replace the stator if resistance is not within the range of 0.12-0.19 ohms.

Regulator/Rectifier

The regulator/rectifier should provide 15 amps direct current at 12.2-13.8 volts at full engine speed. If regulator/rectifier is suspected faulty, refer to Fig. JD5-22 and perform resistance checks. Replace the regulator/rectifier if desired readings are not obtained.

Battery

The tractor is equipped with a 12 V, group 22F battery. Cold cranking amp rating is 341 amps with a reserve capacity of 68 minutes.

BRAKES

All tractors are equipped with a drum brake located on the differential housing. The brake drum is attached to the differential shaft. Depressing the brake pedal operates the brake and shifts the transmission into NEUTRAL (see the TRANSMISSION section).

ADJUSTMENT

To adjust the brake, place the parking brake in the locked position. Measure the gap between the washer (W—Fig. JD5-23) and spring retainer (R). Gap should be 8-14 mm (0.31-0.55

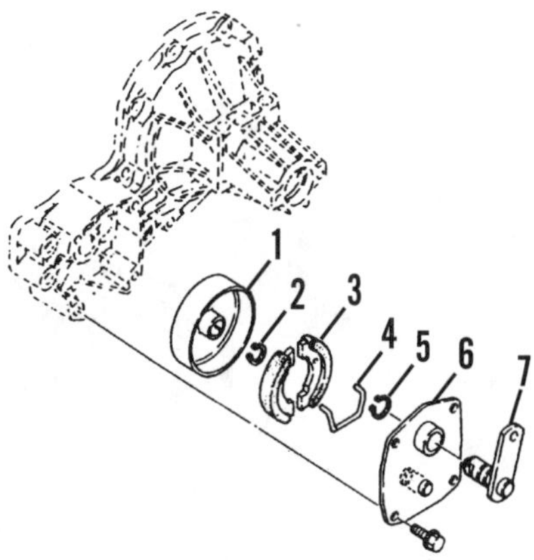

Fig. JD5-24–Exploded view of brake assembly.

1. Drum
2. Snap ring
3. Brake shoes
4. Spring
5. Snap ring
6. Cover
7. Arm

in.), if not, loosen nut (N) and turn nut (T). Retighten nut (N).

REMOVAL AND INSTALLATION

Refer to Fig. JD5-24 for an exploded view of the brake assembly. To disassemble, detach the rod from the brake arm and remove the screws securing the cover (6). Disengage the spring (4) and remove the brake shoes (3). Remove the snap ring (2) and withdraw the brake drum. Remove the snap ring (5) and separate the brake arm (7) from the cover (6).

Inspect components for damage. The brake arm shaft diameter should be 17.96-18.00 mm (0.707-0.709 in.). The shaft bore in the cover should be 18.02-18.04 mm (0.709-0.710 in.). Maximum allowable shaft clearance is 0.5 mm (0.020 in.).

To reassemble, reverse the disassembly procedure. Install the spring (4) so the open portion is towards the brake arm. Apply grease to the brake arm shaft. While tightening the cover screws, push the brake arm forward so the brake shoes will contact the drum thereby centering the cover. Tighten the cover screws to 24 N·m (18 ft.-lb.) if the holes are threaded, or to 29 N·m (22 ft.-lb.) on new cases with untapped holes. Adjust the brake as outlined in the previous section.

TRANSMISSION

MAINTENANCE

Check the transmission fluid level after every 25 hours of operation. Fluid level should be maintained at the top mark on the dipstick attached to the fill plug. Operate the tractor with the en-

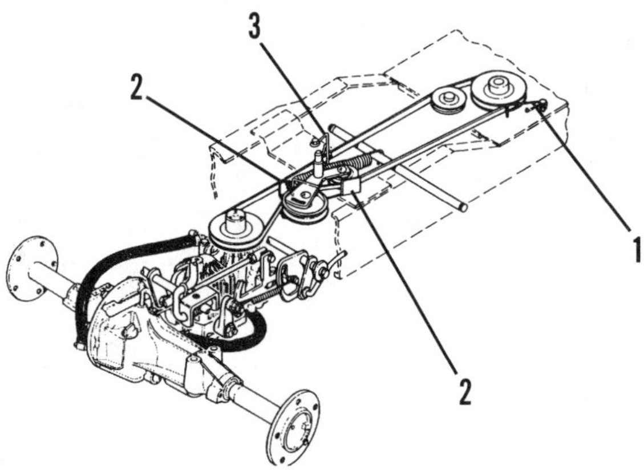

Fig. JD5-25–Drawing of traction drive belt system. Position guides (1,2 and 3) as specified in text.

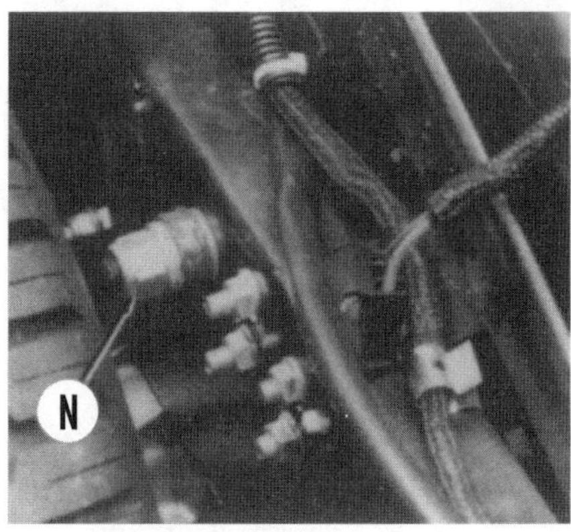

Fig. JD5-26–Adjust control lever friction by rotating nut (N) so force required to move control lever is 22-36 N (5-8 lb.).

gine running and shift several times into FORWARD and REVERSE before checking the level. Be sure the tractor is on a level surface and the engine is stopped when checking.

The transmission fluid and filter should be changed after first 50 hours of operation and then after every 250 hours of operation thereafter. Partially fill filter with oil before installing.

Two different oils have been used in the transmission. Check the oil color in the transmission. If the oil is red, the recommended oil is good quality F-type automatic transmission fluid or John Deere All-Weather Hydrostatic Fluid. If the oil is honey color, the recommended oil is low viscosity John Deere HY-GARD (J20B) Transmission and Hydraulic oil. Do not mix oils.

Oil capacity is 2.5 liters (2.6 qt.).

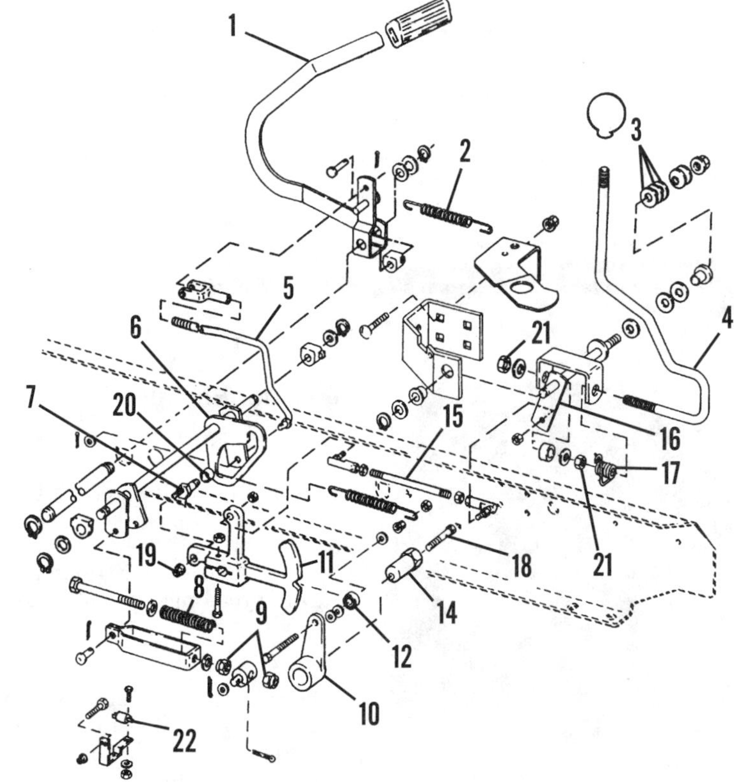

Fig. JD5-27–Exploded view of transmission control linkage.

1. Pedal
2. Spring
3. Spring washer
4. Shift lever
5. Control rod
6. Cam plate
7. Eccentric
8. Spring
9. Nuts
10. Control lever
11. Control arm
12. Roller
13. Spring
14. Eccentric
15. Rod
16. Lever
17. Spring
18. Screw
19. Nut
20. Roller
21. Nut
22. Neutral switch

ADJUSTMENTS

Belt Guides

Adjust the belt guide locations so the guide (1—Fig. JD5-25) is 1-4 mm (0.04-0.16 in.) from the belt, guides (2) are 1-5 mm (0.04-0.20 in.) from belt, and guide (3) is centered over the belt.

Control Lever Friction

The force required to move the control lever should be 22-36 N (5-8 lb.). Adjust the control lever friction by rotating the nut (N—Fig. JD5-26).

Neutral Start Switch

The tractor is equipped with a neutral start switch preventing engine starting unless the brake pedal is depressed and the transmission is in NEUTRAL. The plunger on the switch (22—Fig. JD5-27) should be forced in when the brake pedal is depressed. Adjust the switch's position by loosening the switch mounting bolts and moving the switch.

Neutral Position

Securely support the rear of the tractor so rear wheels clear the ground. Run the engine at fast throttle setting and move the transmission control lever so the wheels stop turning. This may not be the neutral position indicated on the shift panel. Stop engine.

Loosen the eccentric retaining screw (18—Fig. JD5-27) and rotate the eccentric (14—Fig. JD5-27 and Fig. JD5-28) so the roller (12) is centered in the notch of the control arm (11). Loosen

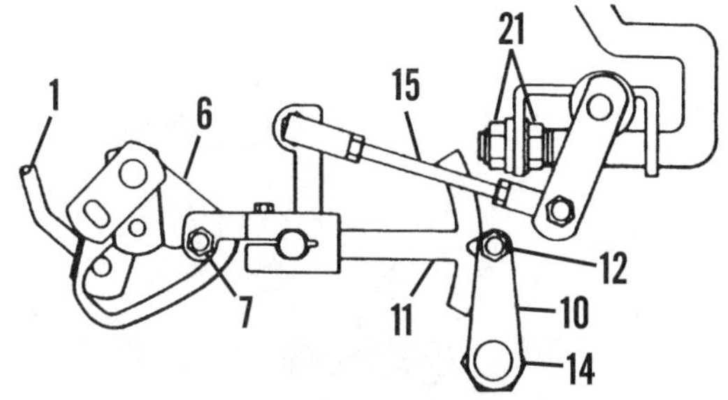

Fig. JD5-28–Drawing of transmission control mechanism. Refer to text for adjustment.

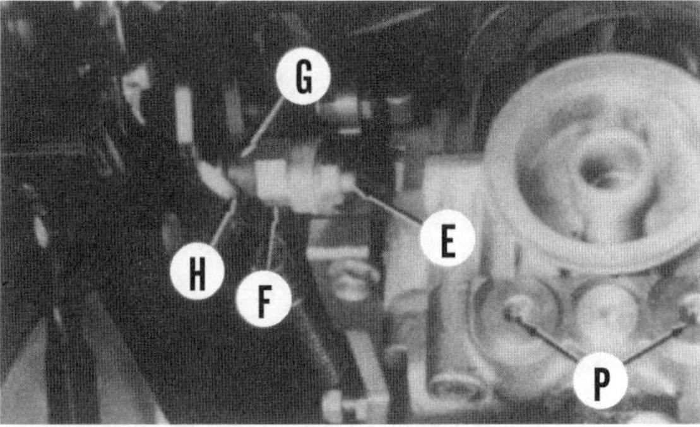

Fig. JD5-29–Connect a suitable pressure gauge to either port (P) to check hydraulic pressure. Later models use a hex plug and surge relief valve instead of Allen head plug shown. See text.

Fig. JD5-30–Adjust PTO clutch by turning each fo the three adjusting nuts (N) until clearance between rotor and armature is 0.38-0.64 mm (0.015-0.025 in.) on Warner clutch or 0.30-0.51 mm (0.012-0.020 in.) on Ogura clutch.

the nut (19—Fig. JD5-27). Engage parking brake. Turn the eccentric (7) so the roller (20) is centered in the slot of the cam (6), then retighten the nut (19). Being certain the roller (12) is centered in the notch of the control arm (11), turn the nuts (21) so the shift control lever is centered in the neutral notch of the shift panel. Run the engine and check adjustments. The shift lever should return to NEUTRAL when the brake is depressed and the rear wheels should not turn when the shift lever is in NEUTRAL.

PRESSURE TEST

Charge Pump Pressure Test

Install a 0-7000 kPa (0-1000 psi) pressure gauge in either port (P—Fig. JD5-29). On early models, only the Allen head port plug must be removed. On later models with a hex head plug, remove surge relief valve in either port. See the TRANSMISSION repair section.

Start and run the engine at the fast idle until the transmission oil is warm. Move the transmission control lever to NEUTRAL, run the engine at slow idle and check pressure.

NOTE: Transmission must be in NEUTRAL and the wheels must not rotate. Do not move the transmission control lever out of NEUTRAL as the pressure will increase and may damage the pressure gauge.

Charge pump pressure on Model 285 must be 193-490 kPa (28-71 psi). Charge pump pressure on Model 320 must be 270-621 kPa (40-90 psi). If low, be sure the transmission filter and charge pump relief valve are in good condition. Relief valve pressure is not adjustable.

OVERHAUL

To remove the transmission, first remove the lower pedestal cover, seat and platform. Close the fuel shut-off valve and disconnect the fuel line. Disconnect the wiring and remove fuel tank. Drain the oil from the transmission. Remove the drive belt. Disconnect the hydraulic hoses and plug all openings. Disconnect the transmission control linkage. Remove the cap screws attaching the transmission to the final drive housing and lift the transmission from the tractor.

Models 285 and 320 are equipped with a Hydro-Gear Model BDU-21L hydrostatic transmission. The charge pump on the Model 320 transmission also provides hydraulic fluid for the hydraulic lift system. Refer to the Hydro-Gear section in the HYDROSTATIC TRANSMISSION SERVICE section for the overhaul procedure.

DIFFERENTIAL OVERHAUL

To remove the transmission and differential assembly, first remove the mower deck. Raise and support the rear of the tractor. Remove the drive belt. Remove the rear wheels. Drain the oil from the transmission and differential assembly. On Model 320, disconnect the hydraulic lines to the hydraulic lift. Disconnect speed selector linkage and brake linkage from the transmission and differential. Support the transmission and differential assembly. Remove the four bolts mounting bolts and remove the transmission and differential assembly from the tractor.

After removing the differential and transmission assembly from the tractor, separate the transmission from the differential as outlined in the TRANSMISSION section. Remove brake components.

Models 285 and 320 are equipped with a Kanzaki final drive unit. Refer to the KANZAKI section in the FINAL DRIVE section for the overhaul procedure.

POWER TAKE-OFF (PTO)

ADJUSTMENT

Adjust the electric PTO clutch by turning each of the three adjusting nuts (N—Fig. JD5-30) until the clearance between the rotor and armature is 0.38-0.64 mm (0.015-0.025 in.) on a Warner clutch or 0.30-0.51 mm (0.012-0.020 in.) on an Ogura clutch. Do not over-tighten nuts. Operate the clutch several times and recheck the clearance.

OVERHAUL

Two types of electric PTO clutches have been used. Refer to Fig. JD5-31 for an exploded view of an Ogura PTO clutch or to Fig. JD5-32 for an exploded view of a Warner PTO clutch. Either

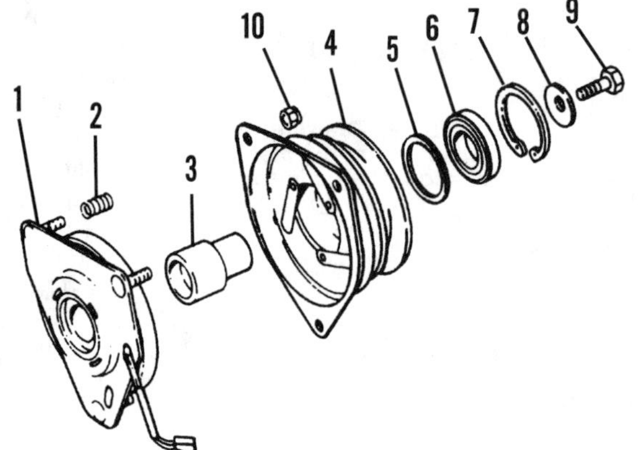

Fig. JD5-31–Exploded view of Ogura electric PTO clutch.

1. Coil
2. Spring
3. Bearing hub
4. Armature & pulley
5. Washer
6. Bearing
7. Snap ring
8. Belleville washer
9. Screw
10. Nut

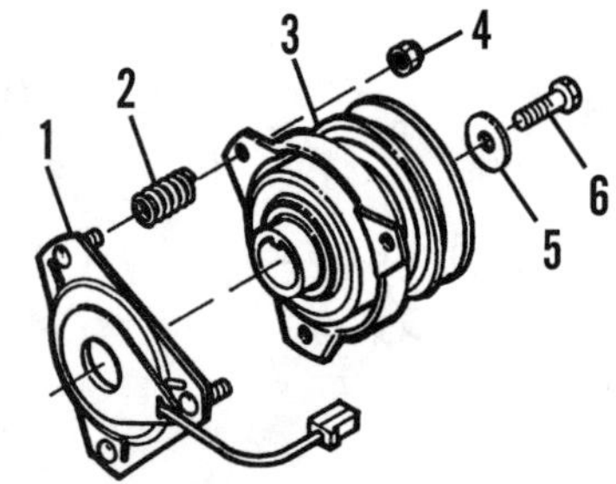

Fig. JD5-32–Exploded view of Warner electric PTO clutch.

1. Coil
2. Spring
3. Armature & pulley
4. Nut
5. Belleville washer
6. Screw

clutch may be removed after unscrewing the center screw. The bearing of the Ogura clutch may be removed by pressing out the bearing after removing the snap ring. The Warner clutch is available only as a unit assembly.

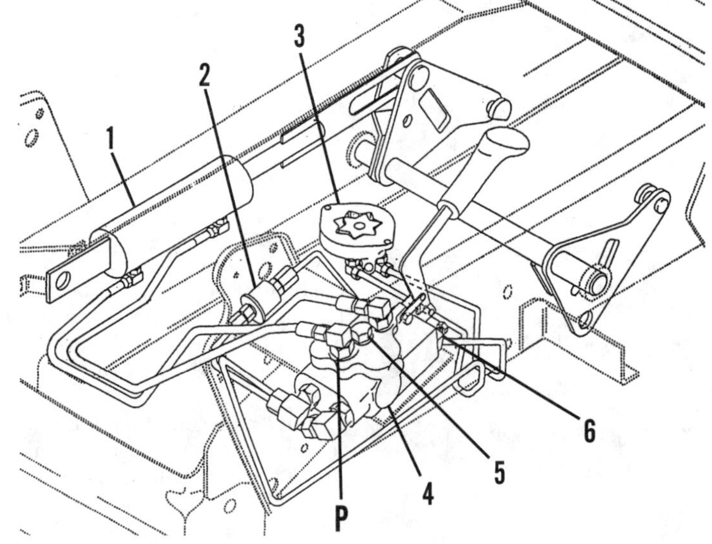

Fig. JD5-33–Drawing showing location of hydraulic lift components.

1. Cylinder
2. Filter
3. Transmission charge pump
4. Control valve
5. Check valve
6. Relief valve

HYDRAULIC LIFT (MODEL 320)

MAINTENANCE

The hydrostatic drive unit supplies pressurized oil for the hydraulic system functions. Refer to the appropriate TRANSMISSION section for maintenance and service information for the hydrostatic drive unit.

No system maintenance is required other than checking for leaks and damage. An inline filter removes foreign matter from the oil in the return circuit. Install the filter so the arrow points toward the transmission.

LIFT SYSTEM PRESSURE TEST

Before performing the lift system pressure check, perform and record the charge pump pressure as previously described.

Disconnect the cylinder hose from the rear port (P—Fig. JD5-33) of the control valve. Install a 0-7000 kPa (0-1000 psi) pressure gauge in the port. Start and run the engine at 3350 rpm. Move the hydraulic lever to raise the position to obtain the pressure reading. Record the reading, then subtract the charge pressure reading. The system pressure should be 550-650 psi (3795-4485 kPa). If low, check the condition of relief valve at the front of the control valve. The relief valve is not adjustable. If the valve is faulty, replace the valve.

CONTROL VALVE

The control valve is available only as a unit assembly. If removed, install the check valve so the groove in the valve body is toward the plug (5—Fig. JD5-33). Replace the valve if internal or external leakage is apparent.

HYDRAULIC CYLINDER

To check cylinder seals for internal leakage, first fully extend the piston rod. Disconnect the hydraulic hose from the rod end of the cylinder. Start the engine and hold the lift control valve in the lower position (extend rod). There may be an initial flow of oil out of the open cylinder port, then the oil flow should stop. If oil continues to flow from the cylinder port, the cylinder piston seal is faulty.

The hydraulic cylinder is a welded assembly and no service parts are available. Replace the cylinder if internal or external leakage is apparent.

WIRING

Electrical component locations for 285 and 320 standard tractors are illustrated in Fig. JD5-34. Electrical component locations for 285 fuel injection tractor are illustrated in Fig. JD5-35. Refer to Fig. JD5-7 and Fig. JD5-10 for electrical wiring schematics.

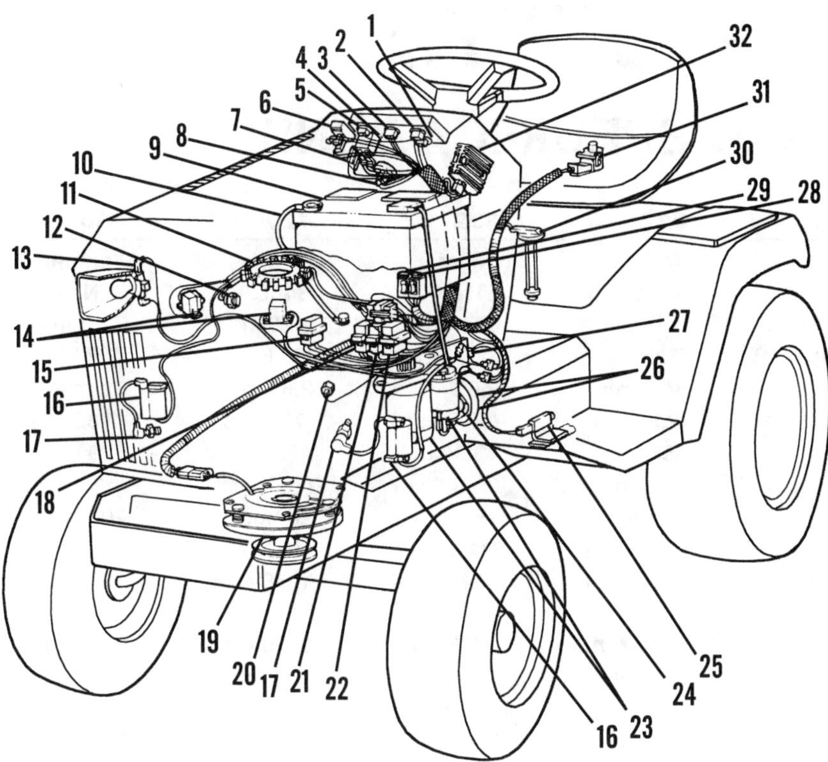

Fig. JD5-34–Drawing showing location of electrical components for 285 and 320 standard tractors.

1. Coolant temp. light
2. Oil pressure lamp
3. Discharge lamp
4. Hour meter
5. Low fuel lamp
6. Light switch
7. PTO switch
8. Key switch
9. Battery
10. Battery negative cable
11. Stator
12. Oil pressure switch
13. Headlight
14. Pulsar coils
15. Starter relay
16. Ignition coil
17. Spark plug
18. Ignition relay
19. PTO clutch
20. Coolant temp. Switch
21. PTO relay
22. Coolant temp. lamp relay
23. Starter/solenoid
24. Battery positve cable
25. Transmission neutral start switch
26. Fusible links
27. Ignition module
28. 20 amp fuse
29. 10 amp fuse
30. Low fuel switch
31. Seat switch
32. Recitifer/regulator

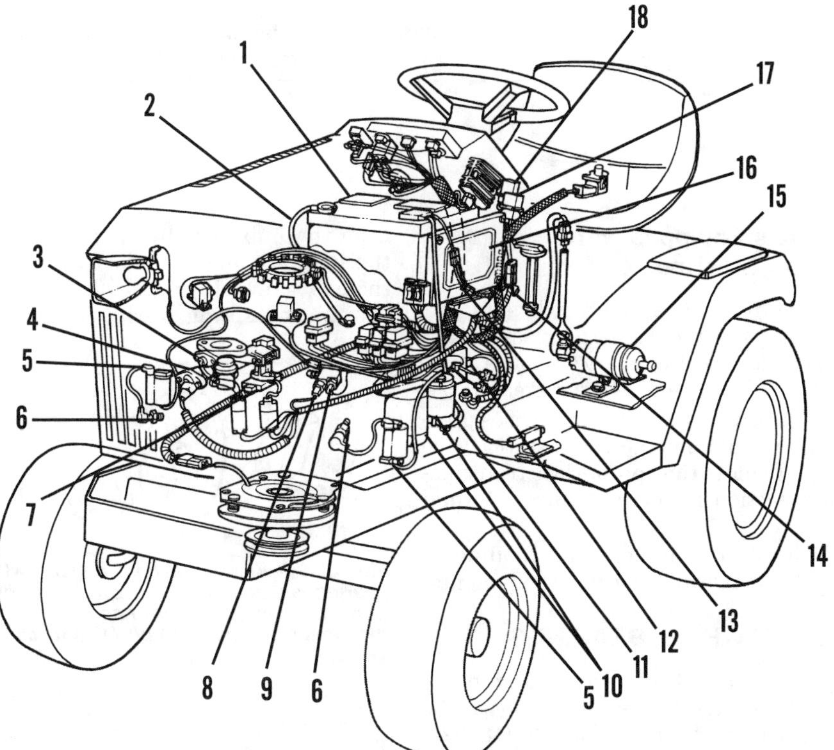

Fig. JD5-35–Drawing showing location of electrical components for 285 tractor with fuel injections.

1. Battery
2. Battery negative cable
3. I.I. air temp. sensor
4. Fuel injector
5. Ignition coil
6. Spark plug
7. F.I. throttle sensor
8. Coolant temp. sensor
9. F.I. coolant temp. sensor
10. Starter/solenoid
11. Battery positve cable
12. Ignition module
13. F.I. fusible links
14. F.I. altitude compensation switch
15. Fuel pump
16. Fuel injection module
17. Fuel pump relay (blue)
18. Fuel injection module relay (green)

JOHN DEERE

CONDENSED SPECIFICATIONS

Models	316	318	322	332	420	430
Engine Make	Onan	Onan	Yanmar	Yanmar	Onan	Yanmar
Model	B43M	B43G	3TG66UJ	3TN66UJ	B48G	3TNA72UJ
Bore	3.25 in. (82.55 mm)	3.25 in. (82.55 mm)	66 mm (2.6 in.)	66 mm (2.6 in.)	3.25 in. (82.6 mm)	72 mm (2.83 in.)
Stroke	2.62 in. (66.6 mm)	2.62 in. (66.6 mm)	64.2 mm (2.53 in.)	2.62 in. (66.6 mm)	2.88 in. (73 mm)	72 mm (2.83 in.)
Displacement	43.3 cu. in. (712.4 cc)	43.3 cu. in. (712.4 cc)	658 cc (40.2 cu. in.)	43.3 cu. in. (712.4 cc)	47.7 cu. in. (781.7 cc)	879 cc (54 cu. in.)
Power Rating	16 hp. (11.9 kW)	18 hp. (13.4 kW)	18 hp. (13.4 kW)	16 hp. (11.9 kW)	20 hp. (15 kW)	20 hp. (15 kW)
Slow Idle	1350 rpm	1250 rpm	1300 rpm	1325 rpm	1250 rpm	1200 rpm
High Speed (No-Load)	3600 rpm	3500 rpm	3425 rpm	3425 rpm	3500 rpm	3350 rpm
Crankcase Capacity	1.5 qts. (1.4 L)	1.5 qts. (1.4 L)	2.6 qts. (2.5 L)	2.6 qts. (2.5 L)	1.5 qts. (1.4 L)	2.6 qts. (2.5 L)
w/filter	2 qts. (1.9 L)	2 qts. (1.4 L)	2.9 qts. (2.8 L)	3.1 qts. (2.9 L)	—	3.1 qts. (2.9 L)
Hydraulic System Capacity	5 qts. (4.7 L)	4.7 qts. (4.5 L)	6.5 qts. (6.2 L)	5 qts. (4.7 L)	4.6 qts. (4.4 L)	7.5 qts. (7.1 L)
Transaxle or Transmission Capacity	See Text	See Text	See Text	See Text	See Text	See Text
Cooling System Capacity	—	—	2.9 qts. (2.8 L)	2.9 qts. (2.8 L)	—	4 qts. (3.8 L)
Fuel Tank Capacity	4.5 gals. (17 L)	4.5 gals. (17 L)	4.5 gals. (17 L)	4.5 gals. (17 L)	6.5 gals. (24.6 L)	6.5 gals. (24.6 L)

FRONT AXLE

MAINTENANCE

Models Equipped with Manual Steering

The front wheel hubs, axle spindles, steering pivot and steering gear should be lubricated after every 25 hours of operation.

NOTE: Do not over-lubricate the steering gear. Two strokes of a hand grease gun are usually sufficient.

Use lithium-based grease. Check for looseness and binding in the front axle and steering components.

Models Equipped with Power Steering

The front wheel hubs, axle spindles, steering pivot and steering gear should be lubricated after every 25 hours of operation. Use lithium-based grease.

The power steering system uses pressurized oil from the hydrostatic drive unit. Refer to the appropriate transmission section for maintenance information.

Check for looseness and binding in the front axle and steering components.

FRONT WHEEL BEARINGS

To remove the front wheel bearings/bushings, raise and support the side to be serviced. On Models 318, 322, 332, 420 and 430, remove the dust cap from the hub and the snap ring from the spindle end. On Model 316, remove the cap screw (1—Fig. JD6-1), spindle cap (2) and spring washer (3). On all

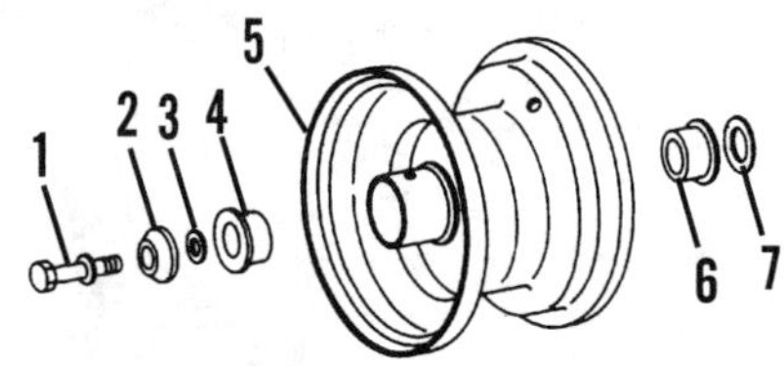

Fig. JD6-1–View showing typical wheel bearing asssembly used on all models. Some models may use a snap ring to retain the wheel in place of bolt (1) and cap (2) shown.

1. Bolt
2. Cap
3. Washer
4. Bearing
5. Wheel & hub
6. Bearing
7. Washer

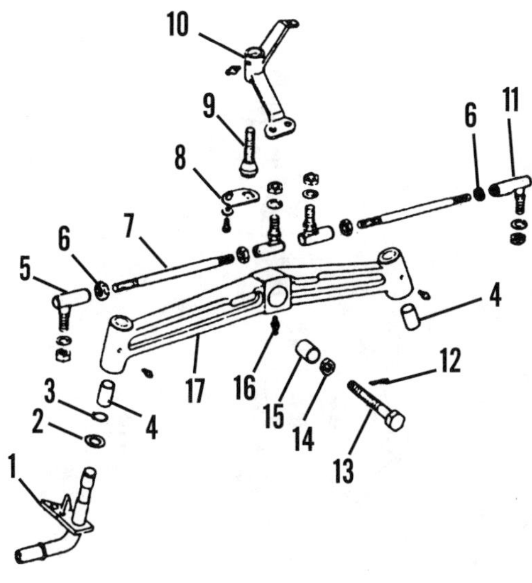

Fig. JD6-2–Exploded view of front axle assembly used on Model 316.

1. Spindle
2. Washer
3. Snap ring
4. Bushing
5. Tie rod end
6. Jam nut
7. Tie rod
8. Lock plate
9. Conical bolt
10. Steering pivot arm
11. Tie rod end
12. Cotter pin
13. Pivot bolt
14. Nut
15. Bushing
16. Grease fitting
17. Axle main member

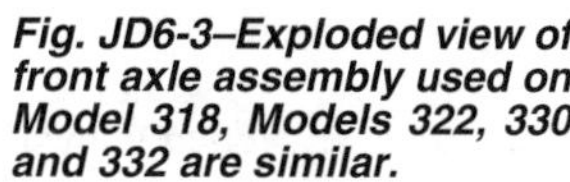

Fig. JD6-3–Exploded view of front axle assembly used on Model 318, Models 322, 330 and 332 are similar.

1. Spindle
2. Bushing
3. Jam nut
4. Snap ring
6. Bolt
7. Tie rod end
8. Jam nut
9. Tie rod
10. Jam nut
11. Tie rod end
12. Steering arm
13. Axle main member
14. Spindle
15. Pivot bolt
16. Bushing
17. Bushing
18. Bushing
19. Bushing

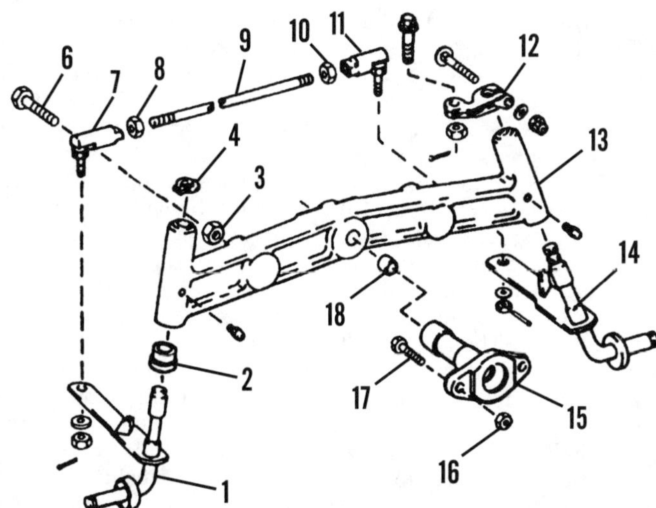

Fig. JD6-4–Exploded view of front axle assembly used on Models 420 and 430.

1. Spindle
2. Bushing
3. Jam nut
4. Snap ring
6. Bolt
7. Tie rod end
8. Jam nut
9. Tie rod
10. Jam nut
11. Tie rod end
12. Steering arm
13. Axle main member
14. Spindle
15. Axle pivot
16. Nut
17. Bolt
18. Bushing

models, slide the wheel and hub assembly off the spindle. Wheel bearings/bushings are a press fit in the wheel hub. If the bearings/bushings are a loose fit in the hub, replace or repair the hub when necessary.

Pack the bearings/bushings and hub with multipurpose, lithium-base grease. Reinstall by reversing the removal procedure. Tighten the cap screw (1) to 35 ft.-lb. (46 N·m).

STEERING SPINDLES

To remove the steering spindles (1—Fig. JD6-2, Fig. JD6-3 or Fig. JD6-4), raise and support the front of the tractor and remove the front wheels. Disconnect the tie rod ends, drag link or steering cylinder from the spindles when necessary. Remove the snap ring retaining the spindle (1) or the clamp bolt securing the steering arm (12—Fig. JD6-3 or Fig. JD6-4), then lower the spindle from the axle main member.

Inspect the spindle and bushing for damage and replace when necessary.

Lubricate the spindle and bushing with multipurpose grease prior to installation. Install the spindle by reversing the removal procedure.

AXLE MAIN MEMBER REMOVAL AND INSTALLATION

Model 316

Raise and support the front of the tractor. Disconnect the tie rod ends (5 and 11—Fig. JD6-2) from the spindles. Support the axle main member (17), then remove the cotter pin (12) and nut (14). Remove the pivot bolt (13) and lower the axle from the tractor.

Inspect all parts for damage. The bushing (15) and pivot bolt (13) are replaceable.

Install the axle by reversing the removal procedure.

Models 318, 322 and 332

Raise and support the front of the tractor. Disconnect the drag link from the steering arm (12—Fig. JD6-3). Disconnect and remove the power steering cylinder, if so equipped. Support the axle main member and loosen the jam nuts (3) at the left and right sides, then turn the axle deflector adjustment bolts (6) in to provide maximum axle movement. Remove the pivot bolt (15). Lower the axle assembly and roll away from the tractor.

Inspect all parts for damage. Replace the bushings (16, 17, 18 and 19) and pivot bolt (15) if necessary.

Install the axle by reversing the removal procedure. Adjust the left and right axle deflector adjustment bolts outward until the axle just pivots freely and tighten the jam nuts (3).

Models 420-430

Raise and support the front of the tractor. Disconnect the drag link from the steering arm (12—Fig. JD6-4). Disconnect and remove the power steering cylinder. Refer to the POWER TAKE-OFF section and remove the front PTO driven pulley and shaft. Support the axle main member, loosen the jam nuts (3) at the left and right sides, then turn the axle deflector adjustment bolts (6) in to provide the maximum axle movement. Remove the axle pivot (15) and lower the axle assembly from the tractor.

Inspect all parts for damage. Install the axle by reversing the removal procedure. Adjust the left and right axle deflector adjustment bolts outward until the axle just pivots freely and tighten the jam nuts (3).

MANUAL STEERING SYSTEM

TIE ROD AND TOE-IN (MODEL 316)

Two tie rods (7—Fig. JD6-2), each with replaceable ends (5 and 11), are used on Model 316.

Front wheel toe-in should be 3/16 inch (5 mm). To adjust toe-in, loosen jam nuts (6) and turn tie rods to lengthen or shorten them when necessary. Tie rods must be adjusted equally to provide the correct turning radius in each direction.

MANUAL STEERING GEAR OVERHAUL (MODEL 316)

To remove the steering gear, proceed as follows: Remove the steering wheel. Do not strike the end of the steering shaft. Remove the battery, side panels and battery base. Disconnect the seat safety switch and push the switch through the hole in the deck. Remove the rear deck/fender assembly and screen under the frame. Detach and plug the interfering hydraulic lines. Detach the brake neutral return linkage. Detach pitman arm. Detach the brake arm from the left side of the frame. Remove the left pedestal panel. Disconnect and remove the drive shaft. Detach the brake arm components on the right side of the frame and withdraw the brake cross-shaft. Detach the interfering rockshaft link, remove the steering gear mounting screws, and remove the steering gear with the shaft. Detach the steering shaft from the steering gear.

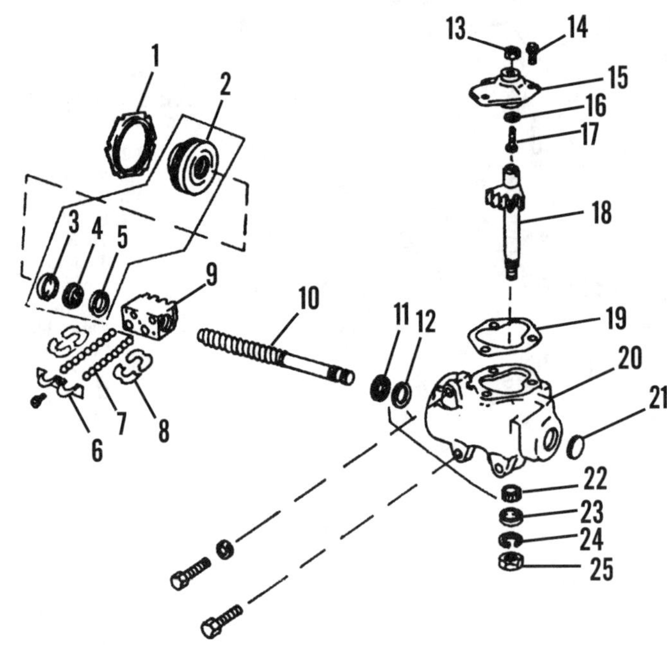

Fig. JD6-5–Exploded view of steering gear used on Model 316.

1. Lock nut
2. Adjuster
3. Thrust bearing
4. Bearing
5. Retainer
6. Clamp
7. Balls (50)
8. Ball guides
9. Ball nut
10. Wormshaft
11. Bearing
12. Thrust bearing
13. Nut
14. Screw
15. Cover
16. Shim
17. Adjuster
18. Pitman shaft
19. Gasket
20. Gearbox
21. Seal
22. Bearing
23. Seal
24. Lockwasher
25. Nut

Position steering gear in a vise and remove the cover (15—Fig. JD6-5) screws. Loosen the nut (13) and remove the pitman shaft (18) and cover assembly. Unscrew the wormshaft nut (1) and adjuster plug (2). Withdraw the wormshaft assembly while being careful not to rotate the shaft to the end of its travel as the ball guides may be damaged.

Inspect the components for damage. Detach the ball guide clamp (6) to remove the balls so the wormshaft (10) and ball nut (9) can be separated. There are 50 balls, which are available only as a set. Balls must be replaced if damaged. The wormshaft and ball nut are available only as a set. The tips of ball guides (8) must not be bent.

Lubricate the wormshaft with multipurpose grease, then assemble the wormshaft and ball nut so the narrow end of the ball nut teeth face upward and the splined end of the wormshaft is located on the left side of ball nut. Install one half of the ball guide (8), install half of the balls (7) and other half of the ball guide. Install the remaining ball guides and balls and secure the ball guides with a clamp (6). When installing the wormshaft and ball nut in the housing, be sure the ball nut is centered in the housing so the middle of the nut is aligned with the pitman shaft bore. Fill the housing with 312 g (11 oz.) of multipurpose grease.

The end play of the adjuster (17) must be less than 0.05 mm (0.002 in.). Install shims (16) as needed to obtain the desired end play. Install the pitman shaft in the cover and turn the adjuster counterclockwise until bottomed, then turn the adjuster ½ turn clockwise. Install the pitman shaft assembly in the housing so the pitman gear teeth are centered on the ball nut teeth. Tighten the side cover screws to 40 N·m (30 ft.-lb.).

To adjust the wormshaft bearing preload, tighten the adjuster plug (2) until bottomed, then back out ¼ turn. Rotate the wormshaft until at the end of travel—do not force—then rotate in the opposite direction ½ turn. Tighten the adjuster plug so a rolling torque of 0.6-1.0 N·m (5-9 in.-lb.) is required to rotate the wormshaft. Do not rotate the wormshaft to the end of travel when reading torque. Install nut (1).

Back out the adjuster (17) and turn back in one turn. Turn the wormshaft so the gear is centered and check the rolling torque required to turn the wormshaft. Rotate the adjuster in so an additional 0.5-1.2 N·m (4-11 in.-lb.)

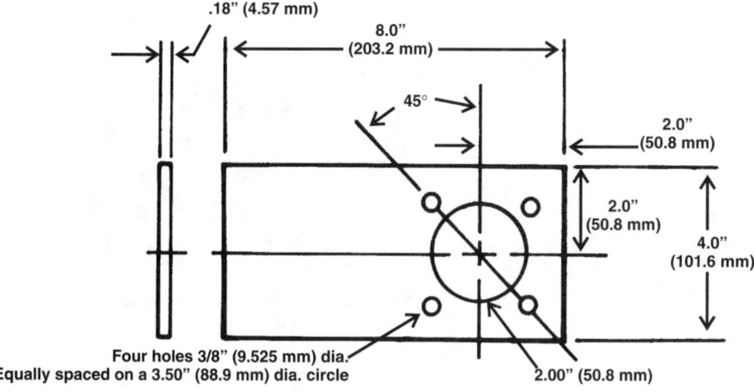

Fig. JD6-6–Fabricate a holding fixture as shown to aid service work on power steering control valve.

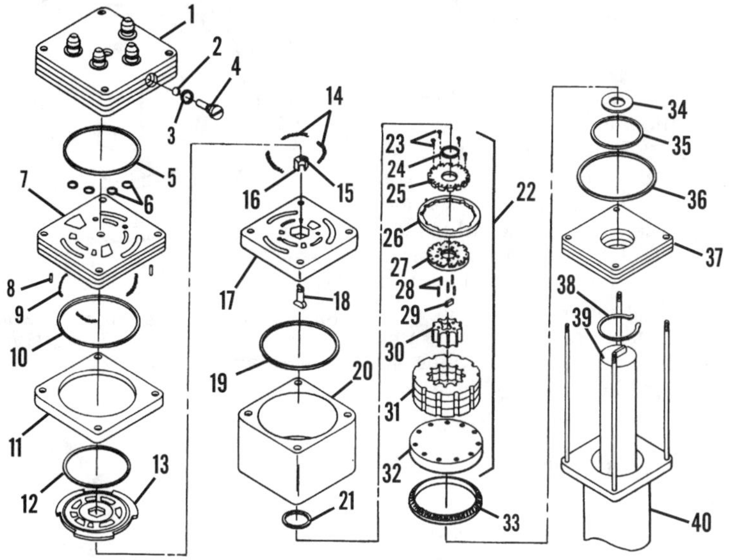

Fig. JD6-7–Exploded view of power steering control valve used on Models 318, 322, 420 and 430.

1. Port cover
2. Ball
3. O-ring
4. Plug
5. Seal ring
6. O-ring
7. Port manifold
8. Alignment pins (2)
9. Springs
10. Seal ring
11. Valve ring
12. Seal ring
13. Valve plate
14. Springs
15. Pin
16. Hex drive assy.
17. Isolation manifold
18. Drive link
19. Seal
20. Metering rng
21. Seal
22. Metering assy.
23. Screws (11)
24. Commutator seal
25. Commutator cover
26. Commutator ring
27. Commutator
28. Alignment pins (5)
29. Drive link spacer
30. Rotor
31. Stator
32. Drive plate
33. Thrust bearing
34. Seal spacer
35. Face seal
36. Face seal back-up ring
37. Upper cover plate
38. Snap ring
39. Steering shaft
40. Tube assy.

torque is required to rotate the wormshaft. Tighten the adjuster locknut (13) to 34 N·m (25 ft.-lb.) while preventing rotation of the adjuster.

Tighten the steering gear retaining screws to 95 N·m (70 ft.-lb.). Tighten pitman arm retaining nut to 224 N·m (165 ft.-lb.).

POWER STEERING SYSTEM

Pressurized oil from the hydrostatic drive unit is supplied to a steering control valve and cylinder to provide power steering on Models 318, 322, 332, 420 and 430. Refer to the appropriate TRANSMISSION section for maintenance and service information for the hydrostatic drive unit.

TIE ROD AND TOE-IN (MODELS 318, 322, 332, 420 AND 430)

All models are equipped with a single tie rod (9—Fig. JD6-3 or Fig. JD6-4) with replaceable ends.

Front wheel toe-in should be $\frac{3}{16}$ inch (5 mm). To adjust toe-in, loosen jam nuts (10) and turn the tie rod to lengthen or shorten it as necessary.

STEERING CONTROL VALVE (MODELS 318, 322, 332, 420 AND 430)

Removal and Installation

Model 430

Remove the grille and side engine covers. Remove the battery and battery base. Disconnect the seat safety switch and taillight wire connectors. Detach the interfering handle knobs and remove the rear fender and deck. Remove the bottom frame guard. Detach the battery cable clamp from the firewall. Disconnect the wire leads from the circuit breaker on the right pedestal panel and detach the fuse block from the panel. Remove the right pedestal panel. Detach the shock absorber attached to the hydrostatic control mechanism. Mark the location of the hydraulic lines on the steering valve and note the steering valve location in relation to the mounting bracket. Disconnect the hydraulic lines and cap openings. Remove the steering wheel; do not strike the end of the steering shaft. Unscrew the mounting nuts and remove the steering valve.

Models 318, 322, 332 and 420

The power steering control valve is attached to the lower end of the steering shaft. To remove, use a suitable puller and remove the steering wheel. Remove the battery and battery tray. Remove the right side panel and remove the protective screen/shield from the lower side of the frame. Disconnect the drive shaft. Mark the location of the hydraulic lines on the steering valve and note the steering valve location in reference to the mounting bracket. Disconnect the hydraulic lines and cap openings. Remove the nuts securing the steering unit and lower the unit through the dash and remove.

OVERHAUL

Observe the following before proceeding with service on the steering control valve.

NOTE: Do not clamp the steering control valve in a vise for service work. Fabricate a holding fixture as shown in Fig. JD6-6.

Before disassembling the steering valve, note the alignment grooves machined in the unit's side. Place the steering valve in a holding fixture with the steering shaft down and secure with 5/16-24 NF nuts. Remove the four nuts securing the port cover (1—Fig. JD6-7) and remove the cover. Remove the sealing ring (5) and four or five O-rings (6). Remove plug (4) and ball (2). Remove the O-ring (3) from the plug. Remove the port manifold (7) and the three springs (9). Remove alignment pins (8). Remove valve ring (11) and discard sealing rings (10 and 12). Remove the valve plate (13) and the three springs (14) from the isolation manifold pockets. Remove the hex drive and pin assembly (16), then remove the isolation manifold (17). Remove drive link (18), seal (19), metering ring (20) and seal (21). Lift off the metering assembly (22) and remove the seal (24). Remove the 11 Allen head screws (23) and lift the commutator cover (25) off. Remove the commutator ring (26), then carefully remove the commutator (27) and the five alignment pins (28). Remove the drive link spacer (29) and separate rotor (30) from the stator (31). Remove the drive plate (32), thrust bearing (33), seal spacer (34), face seal (35) and face seal backup ring (36). Remove the upper cover plate (37). Remove the steering shaft (39) and service the upper bearing seat, washer and retaining ring when necessary.

Clean and inspect all parts and replace any showing signs of damage. Springs (9) should have a free length of 0.75 inch (19 mm) and springs (14) should have a free length of 0.50 inch (12.7 mm). Springs must be replaced as sets only. Check the rotor-to-stator clearance using a feeler gauge. If clearance exceeds 0.003 in. (0.076 mm) replace the rotor and stator assembly. Replace all O-rings and lubricate all parts with clean hydraulic fluid prior to installation.

Reassemble by reversing the disassembly procedure and referral to the following notes: Be sure the alignment grooves on the upper cover plate (37), isolation manifold (17) and port manifold (7) are on the same side. See Fig. JD6-8. Install the rotor (30—Fig. JD6-7) so the pin holes are out. Install the commutator so the long grooves are out as shown in Fig. JD6-9. When installed, the pins (28—Fig. JD6-7) must not protrude above the commutor face. Apply low strength thread-locking solution to the screw threads (23) and install the screws finger tight. Insert the metering valve assembly in the metering ring (20). Make six shims that are 0.007 inch thick, ½-inch wide and 1½ inches long. Insert the shims between drive plate and metering ring so two shims abut every 120°. Turn the assembly over and push the metering valve down until bottomed. Tighten the screws (23) to 11-13 in.-lb. (1.24-1.47 N·m) using the sequence shown in Fig.

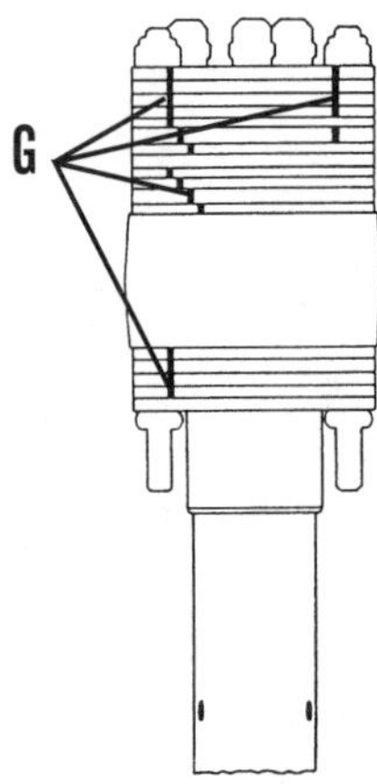

Fig. JD6-8–Components of steering control valve having alignment grooves (G) must be positioned as shown, or unit will not operate properly

JD6-10. The commutator ring (26—Fig. JD6-7) should now be concentric within 0.005 in. (0.127 mm) of the drive plate (32). Install the commutator seal (24) so the yellow mark is towards the commutator cover (25). Install the valve plate (13) so PORT SIDE is opposite from the alignment grooves on the isolation manifold (17) as shown in Fig. JD6-11. Tighten the valve assembly nuts in a crossing pattern to 20-24 ft.-lb. (27-33 N·m). Tighten the plug (4—Fig. JD6-7) to 97-151 in.-lb. (11-17 N·m).

STEERING CYLINDER OVERHAUL (ALL MODELS SO EQUIPPED)

Mark the hydraulic hose locations and disconnect hoses. Disconnect the steering cylinder at each end. Steering cylinder used on all models is a welded assembly and must be replaced as an entire unit.

ENGINE

MODELS 316, 318 AND 420

Maintenance

Regular engine maintenance is required to maintain peak performance and long engine life.

Check the engine oil level and clean the air intake screen at five-hour intervals. Clean the engine air filter precleaner at 25-hour intervals.

Change the engine oil, perform the tune-up, adjust the valves and clean carbon from the cylinder heads as recommended by the engine manufacturer.

Removal and Installation

Remove the grille, side panels, hood, hood support and, if necessary, the air cleaner and muffler. Disconnect all interfering wiring, cables and hoses. Remove the PTO belts and disconnect the drive shaft at the engine. Detach the motor mounts and lift the engine out of the tractor.

After installing the engine on Model 420, tighten the PTO belt tension spring so the spring length is 1.38 in. (35 mm) if the spring is vertical, or so the spring length is 1.6 inches (41 mm) if the spring is horizontal.

Overhaul

Engine make and model are listed at the beginning of this section. To overhaul engine or accessories, refer to the appropriate engine section of this manual.

Fig. JD-9–Install commutator so long grooves (G) are out.

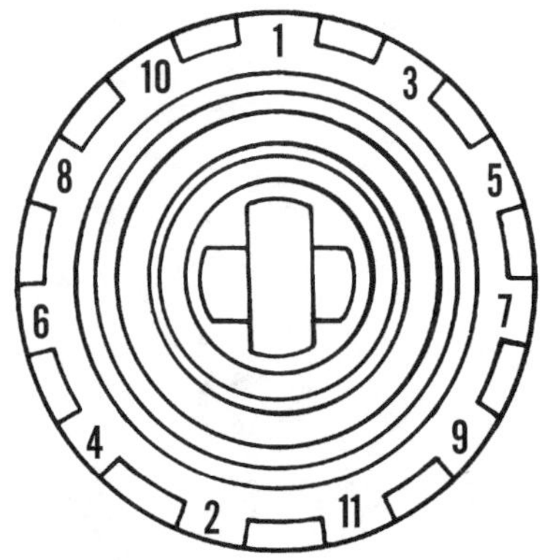

Fig. JD6-10–Tighten the 11 Allen head screws to 11-13 in.-lb. (1.25-1.45 Nm) in sequence shown. Refer to text.

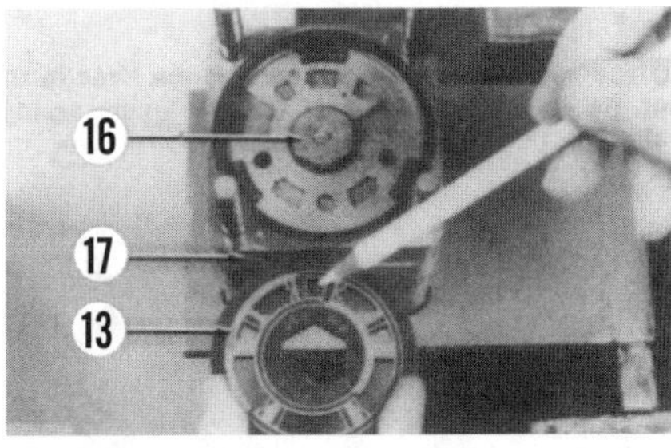

Fig. JD6-11–Install valve plate (13) so "PORT SIDE" is opposite from alignment grooves on isolation manifold (17).

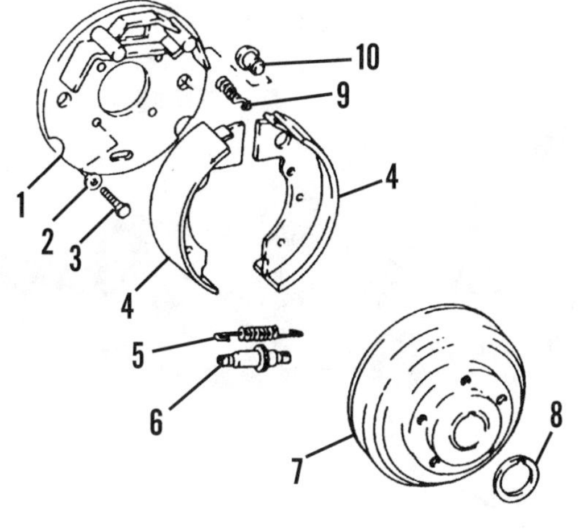

Fig. JD6-12–Exploded view of brake assembly.

1. Backing plate
2. Nut
3. Bolt
4. Brake shoes
5. Return spring
6. Adjuster
7. Brake drum
8. Lock plate

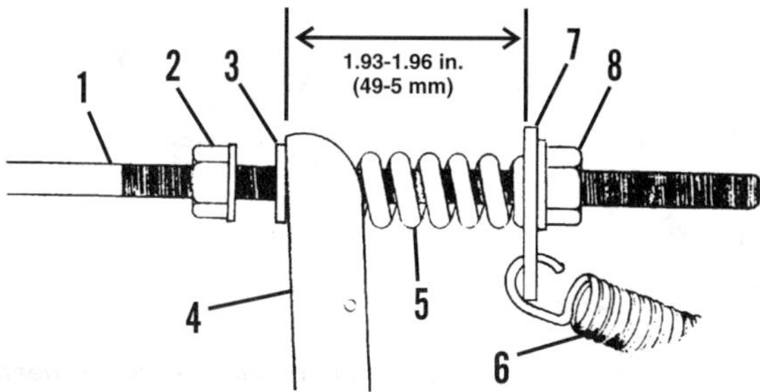

JD6-13–Drawing showing correct adjustment specification for brake adjustment.

MODELS 322 AND 332

Maintenance

Regular engine maintenance is required to maintain peak performance and long engine life.

Check the engine oil level and clean air intake screen at five-hour intervals. Clean the engine air filter precleaner at 25-hour intervals.

Change the engine oil, perform tune-up, adjust valves and clean carbon from the cylinder heads as recommended by the engine manufacturer.

Drain, flush and refill cooling system annually. The manufacturer recommends low silicate antifreeze not containing stop leak additive.

Removal and Installation

Remove the grille, side panels, battery, battery base and panel on the tractor underside. Disconnect the leads for the headlights and hourmeter. Remove the hood, hood support and support for the battery base. Drain the cooling system. Disconnect all interfering wires, cables and hoses. Detach the rubber drive shaft isolator at the engine. Loosen the screws securing the drive shaft universal joint at the transmission and slide the drive shaft towards the transmission. Detach the motor mounts and lift the engine out of the tractor.

When installing the engine, tighten the engine mount nuts to 27 ft.-lb. (36.7 N·m). On Model 332, bleed the fuel injection system as outlined in the Yanmar engine section.

Overhaul

Engine make and model are listed at the beginning of this section. To overhaul the engine or accessories, refer to the appropriate engine section of this manual.

MODEL 430

Maintenance

Regular engine maintenance is required to maintain peak performance and long engine life.

Check engine oil level and clean air intake screen at five-hour intervals. Clean engine air filter precleaner at 25-hour intervals.

Change the engine oil, perform tune-up, adjust valves and clean carbon from cylinder heads as recommended by engine manufacturer.

Drain, flush and refill the cooling system annually. The manufacturer recommends low silicate antifreeze that does not contain stop leak additive.

Removal and Installation

Remove the grill and side panels. Remove the battery and base. Drain the cooling system. Remove the fuel/water separator. Disconnect the fuel injection pump inlet hose and fuel return hose. Cap the fuel lines to prevent contamination. Remove the coolant tank and disconnect the water pump inlet hose. Disconnect the headlight wire. Remove the hood. Disconnect any interfering wiring and cables. Remove the muffler. Detach the belts from the PTO pulley and disconnect the drive shaft. Remove the fan shroud. Attach the lift to the engine, detach the engine from the mounts, and lift the engine from the tractor.

When installing the engine, tighten the engine mount nuts to 33-40 ft.-lb. (44-54 N·m). Tighten the drive shaft screws to 17-21 ft.-lb. (23-29 N·m). Tighten the PTO spring retaining nut so the spring length is 1.38 in. (35 mm). Bleed the fuel injection system as outlined in the Yanmar engine section.

Overhaul

Engine make and model are listed at the beginning of this section. To overhaul the engine or accessories, refer to the appropriate engine section of this manual.

BRAKES

ADJUSTMENT

Raise and support the rear of the tractor. Insert the brake adjusting tool or screwdriver through the brake adjustment slot in the backing plate (1—Fig. JD6-12) and turn the adjustment wheel (6) until a slight drag is felt as the tire and wheel are rotated. Depress the brake pedal firmly to seat the shoes. Back the adjuster wheel off until the slight drag is just removed. Adjust the opposite side in the same manner making certain the left and right pedal height is equal. Apply both brakes and set the parking brake so the tractor will not move. Turn the adjusting nut (8—Fig. JD6-13) until the spring (5) compressed length is 1.93-1.96 in. (49-50 mm) on Models 316 and 420, or 1.65 in. (42 mm) on all other models. Turn the nut (2) until the nut and washer (3) just contact the brake lever (4).

REMOVAL AND INSTALLATION

Raise and support the rear of the tractor. Remove the tires and wheels. Bend the lock plate tabs from the axle nut and remove the nut. Remove the brake drum (7—Fig. JD6-12). Disconnect the hold-down springs (9) and spring (5). Remove the brake shoes (4).

Install by reversing the removal procedure. Tighten axle nut to 50-80 ft.-lb. (68-108 N·m) and secure the nut with lock plate. Adjust the brakes as previously outlined.

HYDROSTATIC TRANSMISSION

LUBRICATION

The hydrostatic transmission uses oil contained in the final drive. A spin-on oil filter is mounted on the transmission.

The oil level should be checked before operating the tractor. The transmission must be cold and the tractor must be on level ground. Maintain the fluid level at the midpoint in the sight tube at the rear of the tractor (Fig. JD6-14). The recommended fluid is John Deere All-Weather Hydrostatic Transmission Fluid.

The transmission oil and filter should be changed after every 200 hours of operation. Refer to the specifications table at the beginning of this section for fluid capacity. Do not overfill.

Fig. JD6-14–View showing location of fill tube (A), sight tube (B) and accumulator-vent (C). Refer to text.

NEUTRAL POSITION ADJUSTMENT

On all models, block up the rear of the tractor so the rear wheels can rotate and remove the bottom frame cover. Three different linkage configurations have been used. Inspect the shift linkage and determine if the tractor has a J-bolt (J—Fig. JD6-15), turnbuckle (T—Fig. JD6-16) or detent spring (D—Fig. JD6-17).

To adjust linkage on models with a J-bolt (J—Fig. JD6-15) and turnbuckle, proceed as follows: Movement of the hydrostatic control lever should require 7-10 lbs (31-44.5 N). If not, remove the side panel and turn the nut (A) to obtain the desired lever friction. Apply both brakes and allow the hydrostatic control lever to return to NEUTRAL. Loosen the jam nut (N) and adjust the eccentric nut (E) so the lever goes squarely into the notch of the slot in the tractor dash. Move the lever forward, apply the brakes and make certain the lever correctly returns to NEUTRAL. Adjust the jam nuts (M) on the J-bolt (J) so the roller (R) just enters the neutral slot in the cam plate (C) when both brakes are applied. See the following section for TRANSMISSION NEUTRAL ADJUSTMENT.

To adjust linkage on models with a turnbuckle (T—Fig. JD6-16) but no J-bolt, proceed as follows: Movement of the hydrostatic control lever should require 7-10 lbs (31-44.5 N). If not, turn the locknut (A) to obtain the desired lever friction. Apply both brakes and allow the hydrostatic control lever to return to NEUTRAL. Loosen the nuts (N) and position cam plate (C) so the neutral roller (R) enters the slot; the roller must not touch the top of the slot. Tighten nuts (N). If the control lever is not in the neutral notch in the tractor dash, loosen the locknut and turn the eccentric nut (E). Retighten locknut. See the following section for TRANSMISSION NEUTRAL ADJUSTMENT.

To adjust the linkage on models with a detent spring (D—Fig. JD6-17), proceed as follows: Remove the right ped-

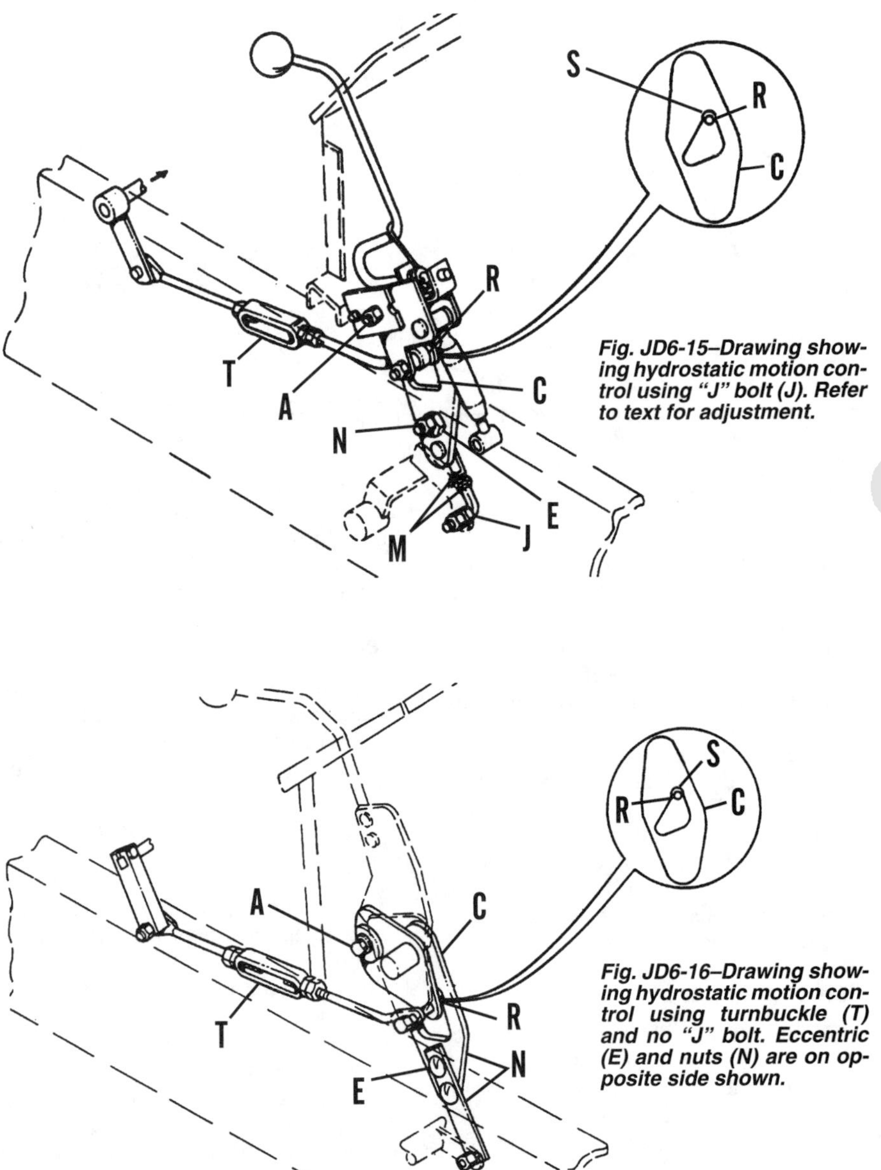

Fig. JD6-15–Drawing showing hydrostatic motion control using "J" bolt (J). Refer to text for adjustment.

Fig. JD6-16–Drawing showing hydrostatic motion control using turnbuckle (T) and no "J" bolt. Eccentric (E) and nuts (N) are on opposite side shown.

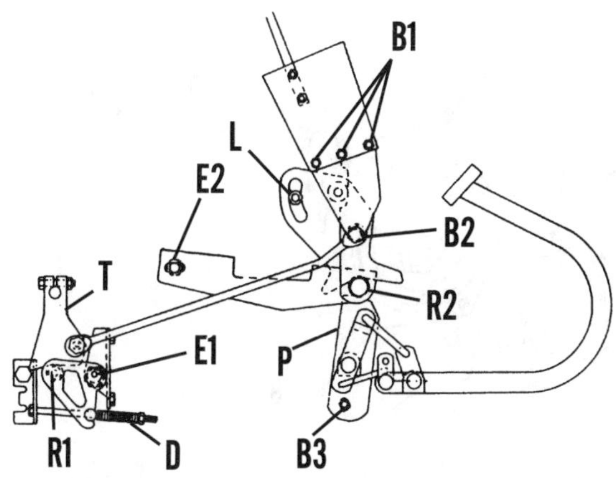

Fig. JD6-17–Drawing showing hydrostatic motion control using detent spring (D).

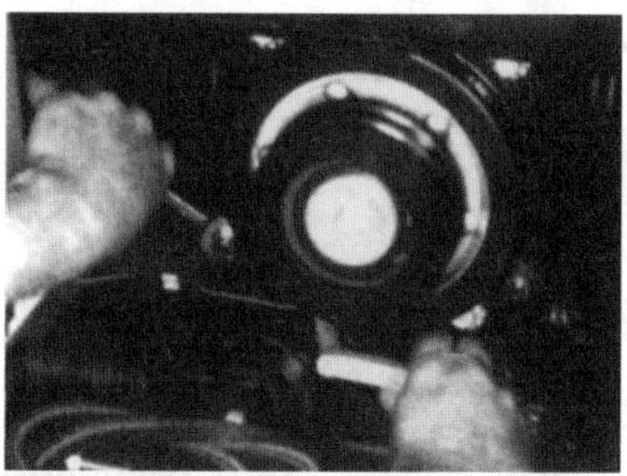

Fig. JD6-18–Use a 0.018 inch (0.46 mm) feeler gauge to check electric PTO clutch adjustment. Refer to text.

estal panel and fender deck. Block up the rear of the tractor so it is securely supported and the rear wheels can rotate. Start and run the engine at fast idle with the hydrostatic control lever in NEUTRAL. The wheels should not rotate. If the wheels rotate, stop the engine and loosen the bolts (B1 and B2). Move the transmission control arm (T) so the roller (R1) is centered in the detent notch. Rotate the nut adjacent to the detent spring (D) so the spring length is 1.97 in. (50 mm).

CAUTION: Exercise extreme caution during the next steps as the rear wheel and drive components will be spinning near the work area.

Start and run the engine at fast idle. Rotate the eccentric (E1—Fig. JD6-17) so the rear wheels do not rotate. Tighten eccentric and stop engine. Turn the eccentric (E2) so the bolt (B2) is centered in the hole; the roller (R2) must be centered in the cam plate notch. Tighten the eccentric (E2) and bolt (B2). Engage the parking brake and loosen the bolt (B3); some models have two bolts. Move the plate (P) up until the plate is against the roller (R2) and tighten the bolt (B3). Position the hydrostatic control lever in NEUTRAL in the dash panel. Tighten the bolts (B1) and disengage the parking brake. Check the force required to move the hydrostatic control lever. If more or less than 7-10 lbs (31-44.5 N), turn the locknut (L) as needed.

TRANSMISSION NEUTRAL ADJUSTMENT

On models with a turnbuckle (T—Fig. JD6-15 or Fig. JD6-16), movement of the shift mechanism and transmission shift arm must be synchronized. Remove the fender deck and block up the rear of the tractor so it is securely supported and the rear wheels can rotate. On Model 420, shift the two-speed axle to the low position. Start and run the engine at fast idle with the hydrostatic control lever in NEUTRAL. The wheels should not rotate. If the wheels rotate, stop the engine and loosen the jam nuts on the turnbuckle.

CAUTION: Exercise extreme caution during the next step as the rear wheels and drive components will be spinning near the work area.

Start and run the engine at fast idle. Rotate the turnbuckle so the rear wheels do not rotate and tighten the jam nuts.

REMOVAL AND INSTALLATION

Disconnect the necessary electrical wiring and two-speed shift knob, if so equipped, then remove the seat and deck assembly. Note the location of the fuel lines, disconnect the fuel lines, then drain and remove the fuel tank. Remove the drain plug at the bottom of the differential housing and drain the fluid. Disconnect all hydraulic lines, filler hose and sight tube. Cap all openings. Disconnect the transmission control linkage and brake rods. Disconnect the transmission shift linkage and differential lock linkage, if so equipped. Raise and support the frame of the tractor. Support the transmission assembly, remove the mounting bolts and lower the assembly. Roll the assembly away from the tractor.

Separate the hydrostatic drive unit from the final drive housing making certain the spacers between the hydrostatic drive unit and final drive housing are marked for correct reassembly.

Install by reversing the removal procedure. Adjust the transmission linkage and brakes.

OVERHAUL

All models are equipped with a Sundstrand U-type hydrostatic transmission. Refer to the HYDROSTATIC TRANSMISSION section at rear of this manual for overhaul information.

FINAL DRIVE

LUBRICATION

The final drive serves as the reservoir for the oil used in hydrostatic transmission. Refer to the HYDROSTATIC TRANSMISSION section for lubrication information.

OVERHAUL

Refer to the HYDROSTATIC TRANSMISSION section for the removal and installation procedure.

All models are equipped with a Peerless 2600 series final drive. Refer to the FINAL DRIVE section at rear of this manual for overhaul information.

POWER TAKE-OFF (PTO)

ADJUSTMENT

Adjust the electric PTO clutch by inserting a 0.018 inch (0.46 mm) feeler gauge between the rotor and armature through the slots in the brake plate (Fig. JD6-18) and turning each adjusting nut, four adjusting nuts on early models and three adjusting nuts on late models, until the feeler gauge can just be removed. Adjust all nuts equally.

REMOVAL AND INSTALLATION

Remove the side panels, grille, cover and hood. Remove the PTO drive belt. Remove the adjustment nuts (4—Fig. JD6-19). remove the cap screw (14) and washer (13). Disconnect the clutch electric lead and remove the pulley assembly (8) from the crankshaft. Remove the springs (3), rotor (6) and key (7). Remove cap screws (1) and coil (5).

Install by reversing the removal procedure.

OVERHAUL

Remove snap ring (11—Fig. JD6-19) and carefully press the bearing (10) out of the bearing bore. Remove shims (9). Press the hub (2) from the bearing (10).

Windings in the coil assembly (5) may be checked by connecting the lead wire to the positive (+) battery post and touching the metal flange of the coil assembly to the negative (-) battery post. A strong electromagnetic field should be present at the face of the coil.

Reassemble by reversing the disassembly procedure.

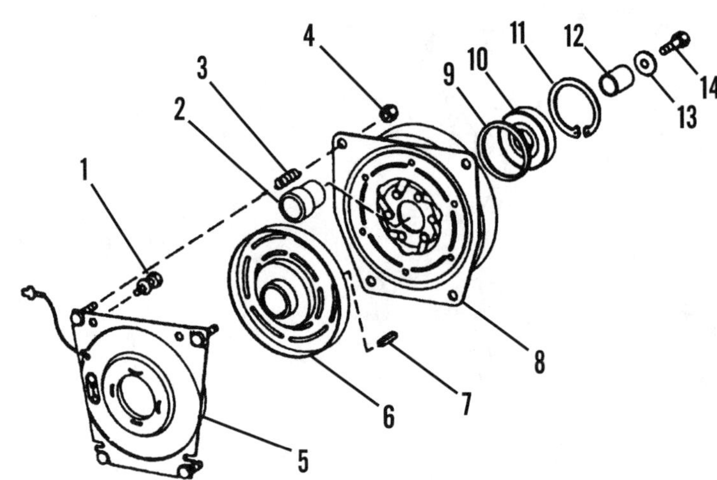

Fig. JD6-19–Exploded view of electric PTO clutch used on some models.

1. Cap screw
2. Bearing hub
3. Spring
4. Adjustment nut
5. Coil
6. Rotor
7. Key
8. Armature & pulley
9. Spacer
10. Bearing
11. Snap ring
12. Bushing
13. Washer
14. Cap screw

HYDRAULIC SYSTEM

MAINTENANCE

The hydrostatic drive unit supplies pressurized oil for the hydraulic system functions. Refer to the appropriate TRANSMISSION section for maintenance and service information for the hydrostatic drive unit.

PRESSURE TESTS

Charge Pump Pressure Test

Install a 0-1000 psi (0-7000 kPa) pressure gauge in the port (P—Fig. JD6-20). Start and run the engine at fast idle. The charge pump pressure must be a minimum of 90 psi (620 kPa). If low, be sure the transmission filter and charge pump relief valve are in good condition. On some models, the relief valve pressure setting is adjustable using shims in the charge relief valve. See the TRANSMISSION section.

Lift System Pressure Test

Install a 0-3000 psi (0-20,000 kPa) pressure gauge in the test port (P—Fig. JD6-20). Start and run the engine at fast idle. Operate the hydraulic lever to obtain the pressure reading. The system pressure should be 850-950 psi (5865-6555 kPa). If low, be sure the transmission filter and implement relief valve are in good condition. On some models, the relief valve pressure setting is adjustable using shims in the implement relief valve. See the TRANSMISSION section.

CONTROL VALVE

A variety of multi-spool control valves from various manufacturers have been used according to model, optional equipment or serial number. Refer to Fig. JD6-21 for an exploded view of a typical three-spool control valve.

Before removing the control valve from the tractor, mark all hydraulic lines to assure the correct installation during reassembly. Cap all openings.

To disassemble control valve, remove button plugs (1—Fig. JD6-21). Remove spool cap (5) and carefully remove detent balls (6) and spring (7). Remove spool (8), spool caps (2) and spools (24). Remove plugs (12), spring (14) and plungers (15). Remove the relief valve plug (20), shims (19), spring (17) and poppet (16). Remove all O-rings from the valve body and plugs. Remove the retaining rings and springs from the spools only if replacement is required.

Inspect all parts for damage. Replace all O-rings.

Reassemble by reversing the disassembly procedure.

HYDRAULIC CYLINDER

Hydraulic cylinder used on all models is a welded assembly and no service parts are available. Replace the cylinder if internal or external leakage is apparent.

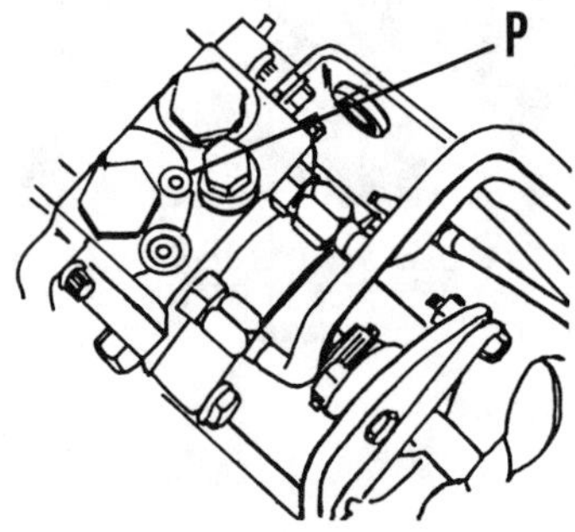

Fig. JD6-20–View showing location of test port (P) on hydrostatic drive unit.

ELECTRICAL SYSTEM MAINTENANCE AND SERVICE

Battery electrolyte level should be checked at 50-hour intervals of normal operation. If necessary, add distilled water until level is just below the vent well base. DO NOT overfill. Keep the battery posts clean and cable ends tight.

For alternator or starter service, refer to the appropriate engine service section in this manual.

Refer to the appropriate wiring diagram for the model being serviced (Fig. JD6-22 - JD6-26).

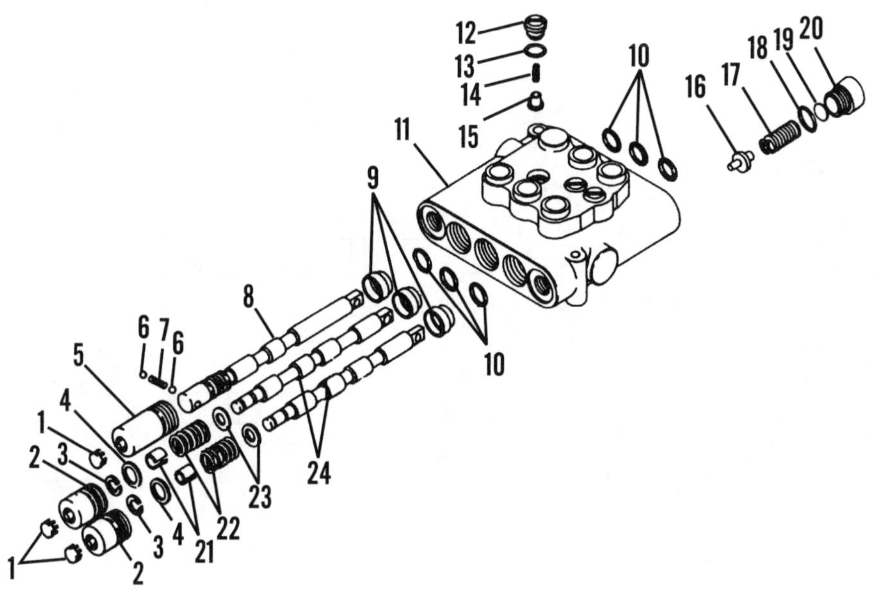

Fig. JD6-21–Exploded view of typical three-spool valve.

1. Button plugs
2. Spool caps
3. Retaining rings
4. Washers
5. Spool cap
6. Detent balls
7. Detent spring
8. Spool
9. Bushings
10. O-rings
11. Valve body
12. Plug
13. O-ring
14. Spring
15. Plunger
16. Poppet
17. Spring
18. O-ring
19. Shim
20. Plug
21. Spacers
22. Springs
23. Washers
24. Spools

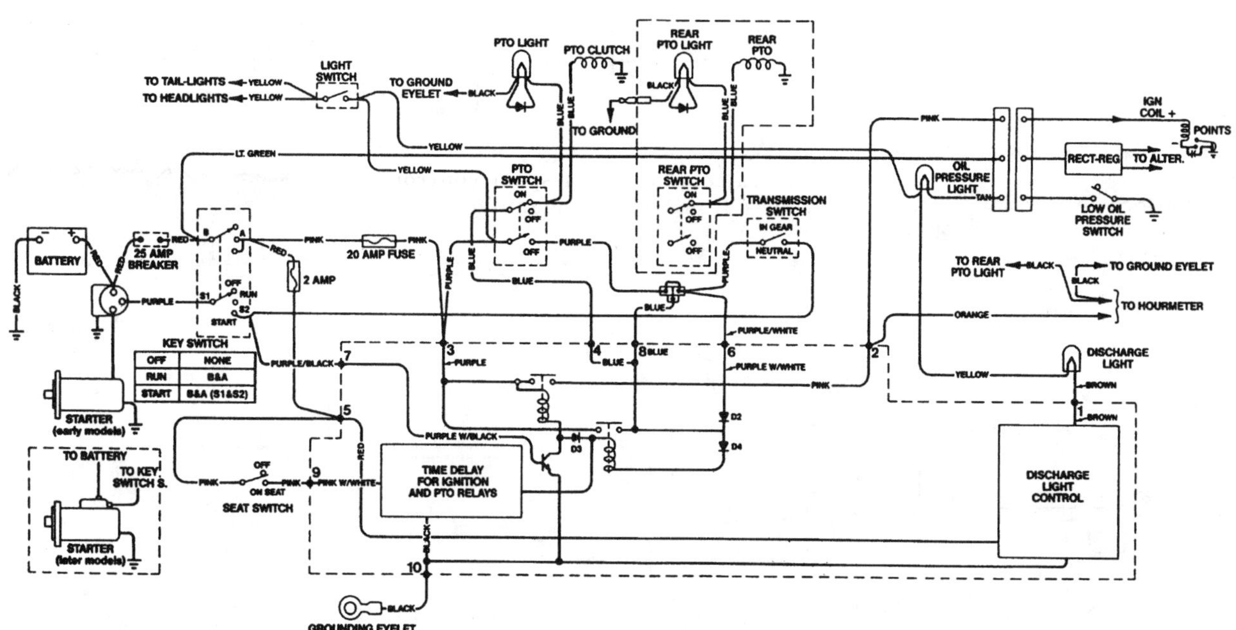

KEY SWITCH	
OFF	NONE
RUN	B&A
START	B&A (S1&S2)

Fig. JD6-22–Wiring diagram for Model 316.

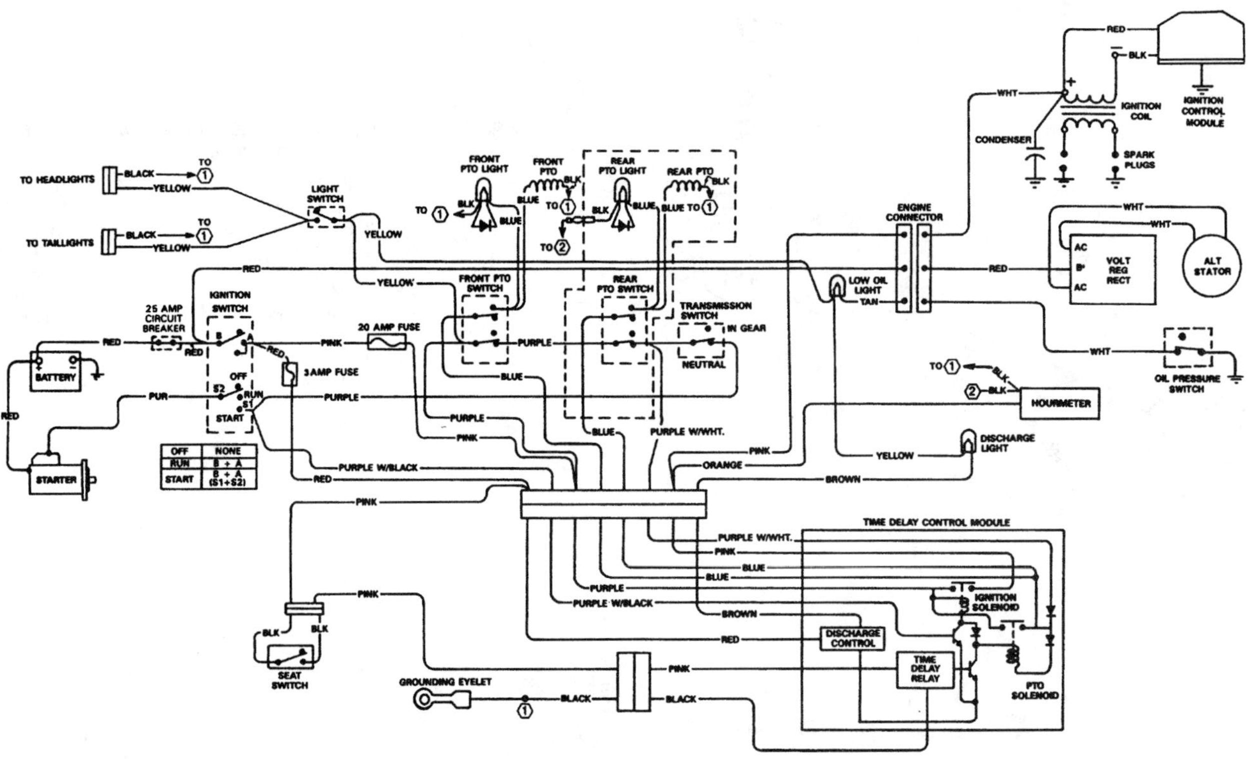

Fig. JD6-23–Wiring diagram for Models 318 and 420.

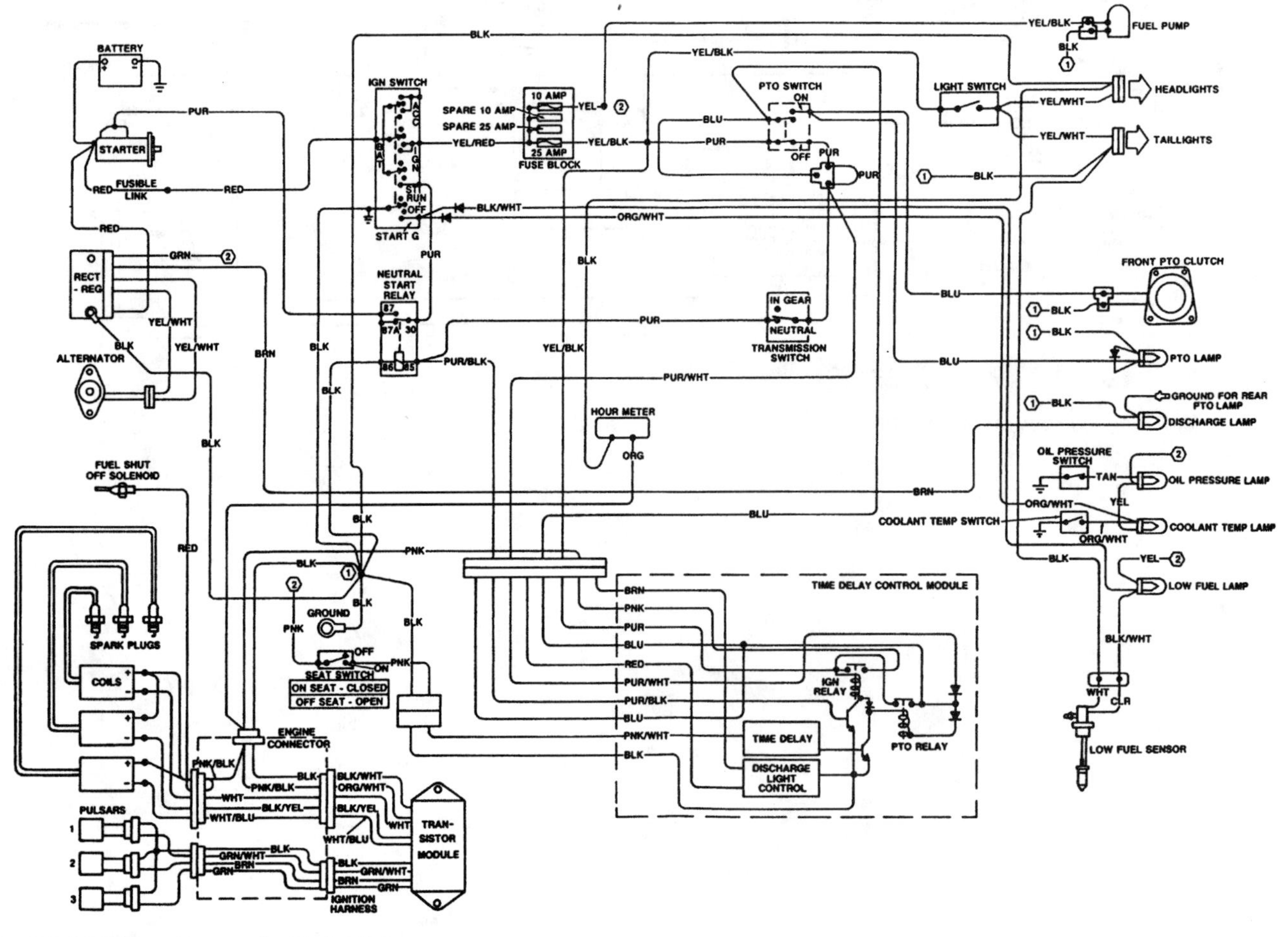

Fig. JD6-24–Wiring diagram for Model 322.

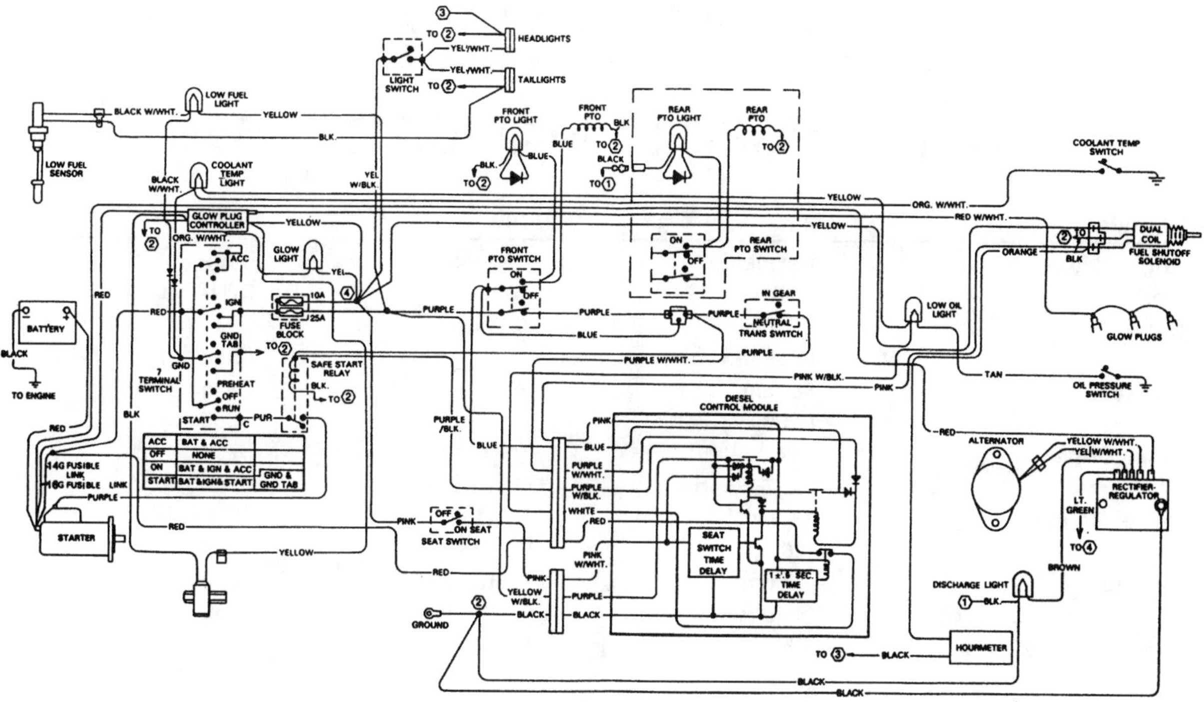

Fig. JD6-25–Wiring diagram for Model 332.

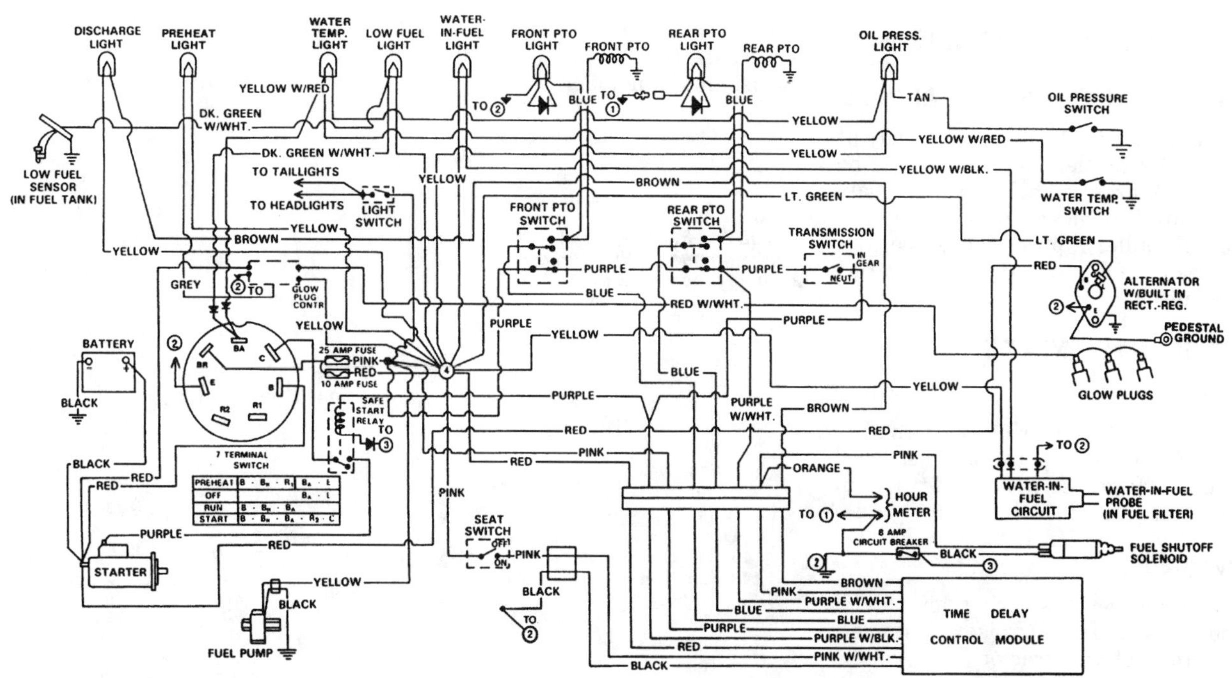

Fig. JD6-26–Wiring diagram for Model 430.

JOHN DEERE

CONDENSED SPECIFICATIONS

Models	425	445	455
Engine Make	Kawasaki	Kawasaki	Yanmar
Model	FD620D	FD620D	3TNA72UJ3
Bore	76 mm (2.99 in.)	76 mm (2.99 in.)	72 mm (2.83 in.)
Stroke	68 mm (2.68 in.)	68 mm (2.68 in.)	72 mm (2.83 in.)
Displacement	617 cc (35.7 cu. in.)	617 cc (35.7 cu. in.)	876 cc (53.44 cu.in.)
Power Rating	14.9 kW (20 hp)	16.4 kW (22 hp)	16.4 kW (22 hp)
Slow Idle	1450 rpm	1450 rpm	1650 rpm
High Speed (No-Load)	3550 rpm	3550 rpm	3350 rpm
Crankcase Capacity	1.5 L* (3.2 pt.)	1.5 L* (3.2 pt.)	2.8L* (3 qt.)
Reduction Gear Capacity:			
2-Wheel steering	5.6 L (6 qt.)	5.6 L (6 qt.)	5.6 L (6 qt.)
4-Wheel steering	6.6 L (7 qt.)	6.6 L (7 qt.)	6.6 L (7 qt.)
Cooling System Capacity	2.8 L (3 qt.)	2.8 L (3 qt.)	2.8 L (3 qt.)
Fuel Tank Capacity	24.6 L (6.5 gal.)	24.6 L (6.5 gal.)	24.6 L (6.5 gal.)

*Includes filter.

FRONT AXLE SYSTEM

FRONT WHEELS AND BEARINGS

Front wheels (2—Fig. JD7-1) may be removed after detaching the retaining screw (4). Front wheel bearings (1) are renewable. Remove bearings using a suitable puller or press. Wheel bearings are sealed and no additional lubrication is required.

STEERING SPINDLES

Lubrication

Lubricate the steering spindles after every 50 hours of operation. Inject good quality EP grease into the fittings in the outer ends of the axle.

Overhaul

To remove the steering spindles (6 and 13—Fig. JD7-1), raise and support the front of the tractor. Remove the front wheels. Disconnect tie rods (18) from the spindles as necessary. Remove the snap ring (8) retaining the spindle in the axle, then lower the spindle from the axle main member.

Inspect the spindle bushings (7) for excessive wear and replace when necessary. Install the spindle bushings so the

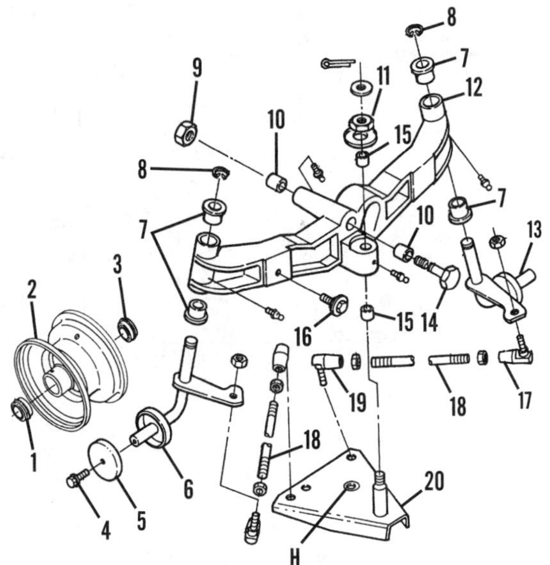

Fig. JD7-1–Exploded view of front axle assembly used on 2-wheel steer models.

1. Bearing
2. Wheel hub
3. Bearing
4. Cap screw
5. Cap
6. Spindle, L.H.
7. Bushings
8. Snap ring
9. Nut
10. Bushings
11. Nut
12. Axle main member
13. Spindle, L.H.
15. Bushing
16. Flange screw
17. Rod end
18. Tie rod
19. Rod end
20. Pivot plate

gap between bushing flange and axle end is no more than 1mm (0.04 in.).

During assembly, tighten the tie rod retaining nut to 61 N·m (45 ft.-lb.). Lubricate the steering spindles by injecting EP grease into the grease fittings.

AXLE MAIN MEMBER OVERHAUL

To remove the front axle assembly, raise and support the front of the tractor. Remove the front wheels. On 4-wheel-steer models, disconnect the rear steering rod from the steering plate (20—Fig. JD7-1). Detach the steering cylinder from the steering plate and axle.

NOTE: Steering cylinder may be removed without disconnecting the hydraulic hoses. The cylinder end studs are tapered and a forked tool or soft-faced hammer may be required to dislodge the end stud.

Support the axle, unscrew the pivot bolt (14—Fig. JD7-1), and remove the axle (12).

Inspect the axle pivot bolt and bushings (10) for wear and replace when necessary. Install the bushings flush with the outer end of the axle bore.

To reinstall the axle, reverse the removal procedure. Be sure the guide plate on the frame fits behind the guide bolt (16) flange on each side. Tighten the pivot bolt to 68 N·m (50 ft.-lb.). When installing the steering cylinder, be sure the guide pin in the cylinder fits in the hole in the axle. On 4-wheel-steer models, tighten the rear steering rod retaining nut to 170 N·m (125 ft.-lb.).

TIE RODS AND TOE-IN

Unscrew retaining nuts to remove the tie rods (18—Fig. JD7-1). The tie rod ball joint ends (17 and 19) are replaceable. Tighten the tie rod retaining nuts to 61 N·m (45 ft.-lb.).

The initial length of the tie rod should be 292 mm (11.5 in.) on 2-wheel-steering models or 313 mm (12.3 in.) on 4-wheel-steering models. Measure the tie rod length between the centers of the rod end studs.

Accurate toe-in measurement is only possible with the front end of tractor unsupported and on level ground. Rotate the steering wheel so an 8 mm screw can be inserted through the steering plate hole (H—Fig. JD7-1) into the hole in the front axle (12). Measure the distance between the front wheels at the front and rear of the wheels at the hub height. The front distance must be 1-6 mm (0.04-0.24 in.) less than the rear distance. To adjust toe-in, loosen the tie rod end jam nuts and turn the tie rods to adjust the tie rod length until the toe-in is 1-6 mm (0.04-0.24 in.). The tie rods must be adjusted equally to provide the correct turning radius in each direction.

For proper steering operation on 4-wheel-steer models, rear wheel toe-in should be checked as described in the REAR-WHEEL STEERING SYSTEM.

FRONT STEERING SYSTEM

All models may be equipped with a 2-wheel-steering system, while Model 425 may be equipped with a 4-wheel-steering system. The front wheel steering mechanism is similar for all models. On the 4-wheel-steer system, a rod attached to the front steering plate (20—Fig. JD7-1) transfers steering motion to the rear wheel steering mechanism. Refer to the REAR STEERING SYSTEM section for related service information.

On all models, the hydrostatic drive unit supplies pressurized oil to a steering control valve and cylinder to provide power steering. Refer to the HYDROSTATIC TRANSMISSION section for maintenance and service information for the hydrostatic drive unit.

STEERING LEAKAGE TEST

The following test procedure will help identify and isolate internal leakage in the steering control valve and cylinder.

Operate the tractor until hydraulic oil temperature is 110° F (43° C). Operate all hydraulic components (transaxle, lift, etc.) so all hydraulic oil reaches the desired temperature. Turn the wheels fully to the right. Stop the engine. Disconnect the outer return hydraulic hose from the steering cylinder and cap the hose end. Start and run the engine at fast idle. Remove the steering wheel cap. Using a torque wrench, rotate the steering wheel retaining nut clockwise at a constant torque of 6.8 N·m (60 in.-lb.). Count the number of turns in one minute while also checking for fluid leaking from the open cylinder port.

In one minute, no more than four turns should be possible at the specified torque. If excessive fluid exits the cylinder port and more than four turns is possible, then the cylinder is leaking internally and should be replaced. If the excessive cylinder leakage is not apparent, but more than four turns of the steering wheel are possible, the control valve is leaking internally and should be repaired or replaced.

STEERING CYLINDER OVERHAUL

Mark the hydraulic hose locations and disconnect the hoses. Disconnect the steering cylinder at each end. The cylinder end studs are tapered and a forked tool or soft-faced hammer may be required to dislodge the end stud.

The steering cylinder is a welded assembly and must be replaced as an entire unit.

When installing the steering cylinder, be sure the guide pin in the cylinder fits in the hole in the axle. If the hoses are unmarked, connect the outer hose to the L-port on the steering control valve and the inner hose to the R-port.

STEERING PLATE

Lubrication

Lubricate the steering plate after every 50 hours of operation. Inject EP grease into grease fitting at the front of the axle.

Overhaul

To remove the steering plate (20—Fig. JD7-1), detach the tie rods (18) from the steering plate. On the 4-wheel-steer models, detach the rear steering rod from the steering plate. On all models, remove the steering cylinder without disconnecting the hydraulic hoses. Detach the cotter pin, remove the washer and unscrew the retaining nut (11). Remove the steering plate.

Inspect the bushings (15) and pivot stud. Install the bushings flush with the outer surface of the axle bore. Reverse disassembly to install the steering plate. Tighten the retaining nut securely, but the plate should not bind when rotated. Install washers as required to fill the gap between the nut (11) and cotter pin. Tighten tie rod retaining nuts to 61 N·m (45 ft.-lb.). On 4-wheel-steer models, tighten rear steering rod retaining nut to 170 N·m (125 ft.-lb.).

STEERING COLUMN OVERHAUL

Remove the steering wheel cap (1—Fig. JD7-2), unscrew the retaining nut (2) and withdraw the steering wheel (3). Raise the hood and remove the side panels. Remove the radiator screen. Remove the dash panel instrument module. Remove the choke control knob, if so equipped, and the throttle control knob, then remove the boot. Disconnect the PTO switch wiring connector.

To gain access to the lower dash panel fasteners, remove the footrest. Remove the knobs on the hydraulic control levers and remove the boot. Detach the parking brake control rod. Disconnect the light switch. On models so equipped, disconnect the cruise control lever. Unscrew the ignition switch retaining nut. Unscrew the dash panel fasteners and remove the dash panel. Unscrew the steering column fasteners and remove the steering column (8) and shaft (12).

Inspect bushings (7) and replace if excessively worn. The steering shaft is available only as a unit assembly.

Reinstall the steering column and shaft by reversing the disassembly procedure. Lightly lubricate the splined end of the steering shaft with multipurpose grease. Make certain the foam washer (13) contacts the steering control valve. Tighten the steering wheel nut to 38 N·m (28 ft.-lb.).

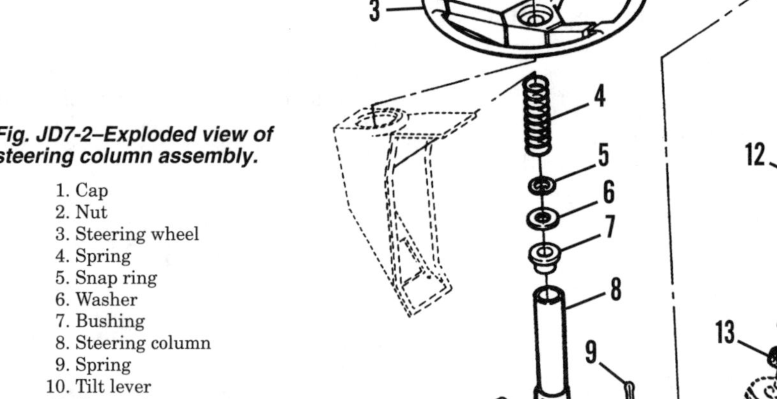

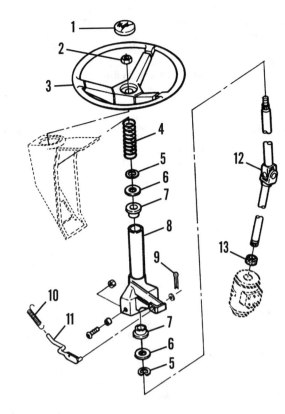

Fig. JD7-2–Exploded view of steering column assembly.

1. Cap
2. Nut
3. Steering wheel
4. Spring
5. Snap ring
6. Washer
7. Bushing
8. Steering column
9. Spring
10. Tilt lever
11. Cotter pin
12. Steering shaft assy.
13. Foam washer

STEERING CONTROL VALVE

Removal and Installation

Raise the hood and remove the side panels. Drain coolant from the radiator. Disconnect the hydraulic lines to the radiator and drain the hydraulic fluid from the radiator. Disconnect the coolant hoses. Remove the radiator screen and coolant reservoir. Unscrew the fan shroud and move out of the way. Disconnect the choke control cable, if so equipped, and throttle control cable.

Remove radiator mounting fasteners and remove the radiator. Mark the hydraulic lines and hoses so they can be reinstalled in the proper position. Unscrew the retaining plate securing the lines and hoses to the control valve. Disconnect the lines and hoses from the control valve. Unscrew the mounting screw and remove the control valve.

Install the steering control valve by reversing the removal procedure.

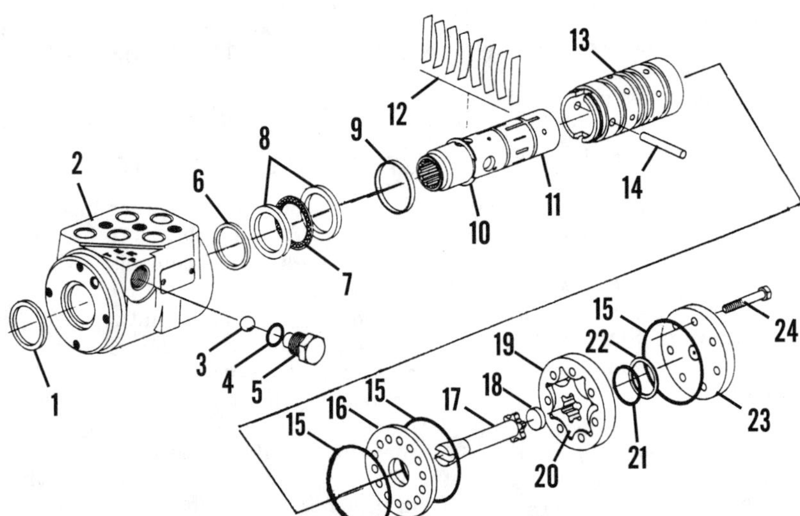

Fig. JD7-3–Exploded view of power steering control valve.

1. Dust seal
2. Housing
3. Check ball
4. O-ring
5. Plug
6. Quad seal
7. Thrust bearing
8. Thrust race
9. Collar
10. Snap ring
11. Spool
12. Leaf springs
13. Sleeve
14. Pin
15. O-ring
16. Wear plate
17. Drive shaft
18. Spacer
19. Outer gear
20. Inner gear
21. O-ring
22. Seal ring
23. End cover
24. Screw

Overhaul

An exploded view of the steering control valve is shown in Fig. JD7-3. Prior to disassembly, thoroughly clean the outside of the valve. Scribe a match mark on the steering valve component parts and valve body so that they can be installed in their original locations.

NOTE: The valve components are machined to extremely close tolerances. Use caution when disassembling and reassembling to avoid scratching or nicking the valve components.

Thoroughly clean all parts prior to assembly.

To disassemble the control valve, remove screws (24—Fig. JD7-3) and remove components (15-23) from the valve housing (2). Withdraw the spool (11) and sleeve (13) assembly from the valve housing. Remove the thrust bearing assembly (7 and 8), and carefully extract the seals (1 and 6) from the valve housing.

NOTE: Springs (12) are under tension.

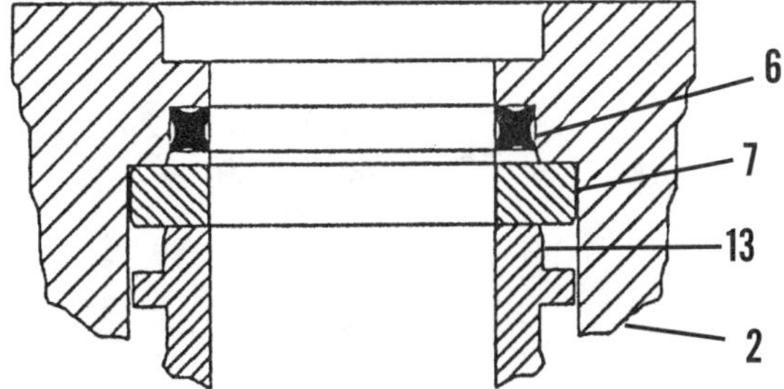

Fig. JD7-4–Cross sectional view showing assembly of sleeve (13), quad seal (6) and bearing race (7). See text.

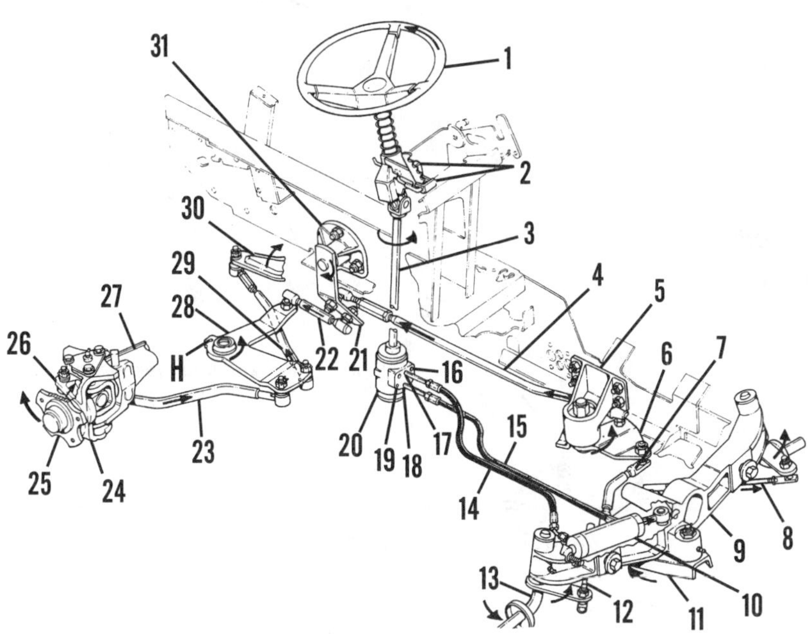

Fig. JD7-5–Drawing of 4-wheel steering components.

1. Steering wheel
2. Tilt steering assy.
3. Steering column
4. Drag link
5. Front pivot housing
6. Front steering arm
7. Front steering link
8. Tie rod
9. Front axle
10. Steering cylinder
11. Front pivot plate
12. Tie rod
13. Front spindle
14. Left turn hose
15. Right turn hose
16. Return port
17. Left turn port
18. Right turn port
19. Inlet port
20. Steering valve
21. Rear pivot arm
22. Rear link
23. Rear tie rod
24. Rear spindle housing
25. Rear hub
26. Rear spindle plate
27. Rear axle
28. Rear pivot plate
29. Rear tie rod
30. Rear spindle plate
31. Rear pivot housing

Remove the pin (14) and separate sleeve (13) and spool (11). Carefully remove the collar (9), which will release the spring leaves (12).

Inspect components for damage, including scratches, burrs and nicks. A seal kit is available, otherwise, the control valve must be serviced as a unit assembly.

Install a quad seal (6) using the following procedure: Place one bearing race (7) in the valve housing, then insert the sleeve (13) into the housing and hold the race tightly in the bore as shown in Fig. JD7-4. Install the quad seal (6) in the groove as shown. Remove the bearing race and sleeve.

Install the snap ring (10—Fig. JD7-3) on the spool (11). Insert two flat spring leaves (12) in the spool slot. Then install the remaining curved leaves, three at a time, between the flat leaves. Position the collar (6) around the springs. Lubricate the spool with clean hydraulic oil and insert the spool in the sleeve (13). Position the springs into the notches in the sleeve. Insert pin (14).

Install the dust seal (1) with the open side out. Lubricate the lips of the dust seal and quad seal with petroleum jelly. Lubricate and install the thrust bearing (7 and 8). Lubricate the spool assembly and carefully insert it into the housing and through the seals.

Position the housing with the open side up in a vise. Only use sufficient clamping force to hold the housing or damage may occur. Install the O-rings (15) and wear plate (16). The holes in the wear plate must match the holes in the housing. Insert the drive shaft (17) so the notch engages the pin (14). Install the gerotor (19 and 20) so the holes match the wear plate holes. Install the remainder of components. Tighten the end cover retaining screws to 17 N·m (150 in.-lb.) in a crossing pattern. Tighten plug (5) to 17 N·m (150 in.-lb.).

REAR-WHEEL STEERING SYSTEM

Models 425 and 455 may be equipped with a 4-wheel steer system (see Fig. JD7-5). The front pivot plate (11) steering motion provides directional force for the rear steering system. Linkage transfers steering motion to the rear pivot plate (8). Tie rods connected between the rear steering plate and steering arms force the steering knuckles to turn in the desired direction.

When the front pivot plate is rotated clockwise, the linkage moves the rear pivot plate counterclockwise. Thus, in a turn, the front and rear wheels pivot in opposite directions. This allows a shorter turning radius than can be accomplished with front wheel steering only.

Refer to the FINAL DRIVE section for service information concerning steering knuckle and bearing assemblies.

TIE RODS AND TOE-IN

Unscrew the retaining nuts to remove the rear tie rods (23—Fig. JD7-5). Tighten the tie rod retaining nuts to 45-57 N·m (33-42 ft.-lb.).

To check and adjust the rear wheel toe-in, first adjust the toe-in of the front wheels as previously outlined and leave the 8 mm screw in the alignment holes (H—Fig. JD7-1) of the front pivot plate and front axle.

Insert a 10-mm screw through the alignment holes (H—Fig. JD7-5) of rear the pivot plate (28) and mounting plate. It may be necessary to adjust the length of the middle link (4) by turning the adjuster at the rear end of the link so the screw can be inserted through the alignment hole (H) and mounting plate hole. The alignment screws installed in the front and rear pivot plates coordinates the front and rear wheel alignment.

NOTE: The alignment screw must be perpendicular to the pivot plate and mounting plate when installed for proper toe-in alignment.

Toe-in of rear wheels should be zero (front distance equal to rear distance). Adjust toe-in by loosening the jam nuts and rotating the adjusting nut on each tie rod (23—Fig. JD7-5). Note the inner jam nut has left-hand threads. Be sure the tie rods are adjusted equally to maintain the proper wheel alignment.

STEERING ARM PIVOTS AND LINKS

Refer to Fig. JD7-5 for the diagram showing the location of front and rear steering arm pivot assemblies (5 and 31) and connecting links (7 and 22).

NOTE: Do not attempt to rotate rod ends on intermediate links (7 and 22). The rod ends are peened to lock them in place. Link length is not adjustable.

Exploded views of pivot assemblies are shown in Figs. JD7-6 and JD7-7. Unscrew retaining nut and detach the snap ring to remove the steering arm from the pivot housing.

Inspect components for wear and replace when necessary. During assembly, tighten the retaining nut to 108 N·m (80 ft.-lb.). Tighten pivot housing mounting bolts to 84 N·m (62 ft.-lb.).

REAR PIVOT ASSEMBLY

Refer to Figs. JD7-8 and JD7-9 for an exploded view and cross-section of the rear pivot assembly. To remove the pivot assembly, disconnect tie rods and steering arm link from the pivot plate (4). Remove the cap screws attaching the pivot bracket (1) to the frame and lower the assembly from the tractor.

Working through the access holes (A—Fig. JD7-9) in pivot plate, pry the cap (12) from the bottom of pivot plate (4). Use a punch through the access holes to drive the spring pin (11) out of the retaining nut (10). Remove the nut and withdraw the pivot plate assembly from the pivot bracket stub shaft. Pry the seal (2) from the pivot plate.

Inspect components for wear and replace when necessary. When assembling the rear pivot assembly, install the seal (2) so the open side is up and the seal is flush with the top of the bore. Pack bearings with EP grease prior to installation. While tightening the nut (10) to 67-83 N·m (49-61 ft.-lb.), align the slot in the nut with the pin hole in the pivot stud. Insert the spring pin (11). Install the cap (12), then fill the cavity with EP grease through the grease fitting.

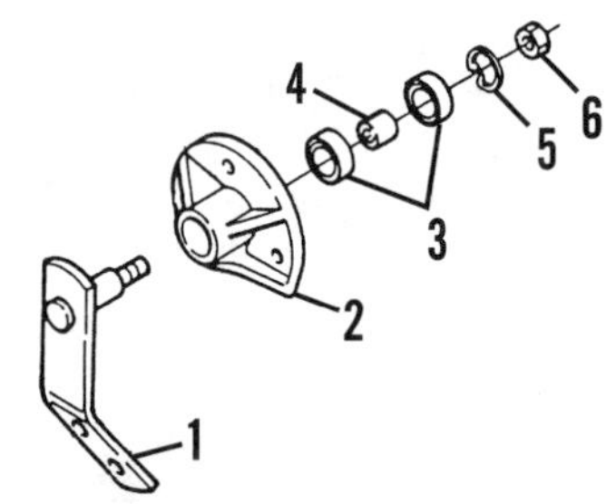

Fig. JD7-6–Exploded view of rear steering pivot.

1. Pivot arm
2. Pivot housing
3. Bearing
4. Spacer
5. Snap ring
6. Nut

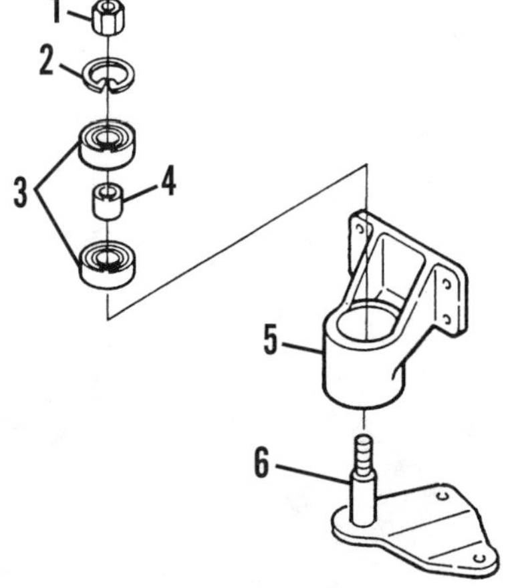

Fig. JD7-7–Exploded view of front steering pivot.

1. Nut
2. Snap ring
3. Bearings
4. Spacer
5. Pivot housing
6. Pivot arm

ENGINE

MAINTENANCE

Lubrication

Models 425 and 445

The engine oil level should be checked prior to operating the engine. Check the oil level with the oil cap not screwed in, but just touching the first threads.

The recommended oil is any premium grade oil meeting the latest API service classification. Use oil viscosity based on the expected ambient temperature range during the period between oil changes as indicated in the chart shown in Fig. JD7-10.

Change the oil after the first five hours of operation and then after every 50 hours of operation, or more frequently when operation is severe. Change the oil filter, on engines so equipped, after the first five hours of operation and then after every 100 hours of operation.

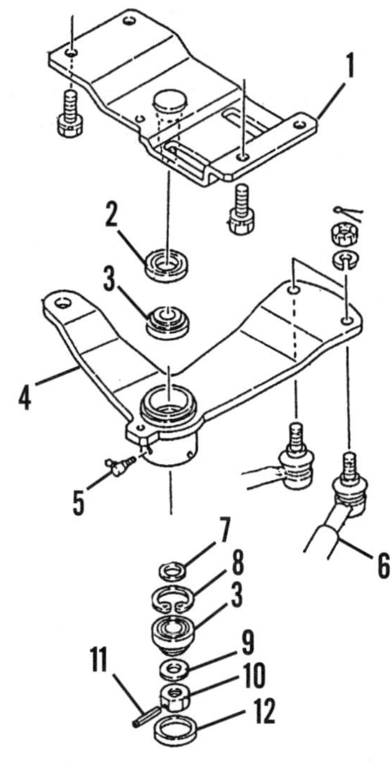

Fig. JD7-8–Exploded view of rear steering pivot plate assembly.

1. Pivot support
2. Seal
3. Bearing
4. Pivot plate
5. Grease fitting
6. Tie rod
7. Washer
8. Snap ring
9. Washer
10. Nut
11. Roll pin
12. Cap

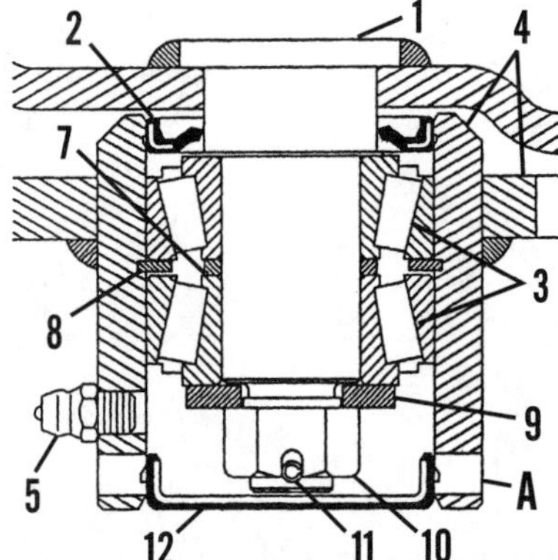

Fig. JD7-9–Cross-sectional drawing of rear pivot plate assembly. Small holes (A) are located in the pivot plate hub to provide access for removal of cap (12) and roll pin (11). Refer to Fig. JD7-8 for parts identification.

An oil pressure switch on the engine activates the dash panel warning light.

Model 455

Engine oil level should be checked prior to operating engine. Maintain the oil level between the F (full) mark and the L (low) mark on the dipstick.

The recommended engine lubricant has the API classification CD. Select oil

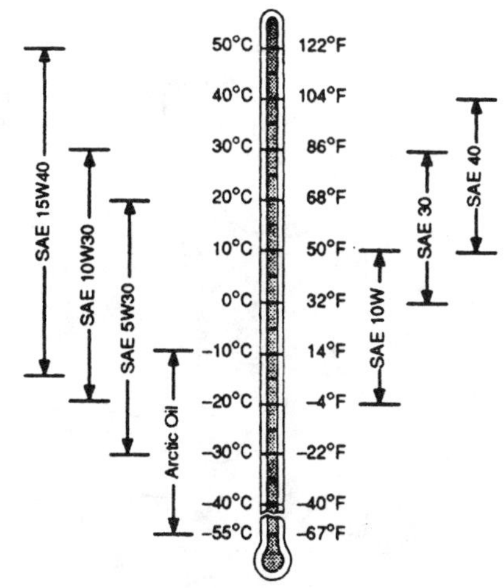

Fig. JD7-10–Chart showing recommended oil viscosity for ambient temperature.

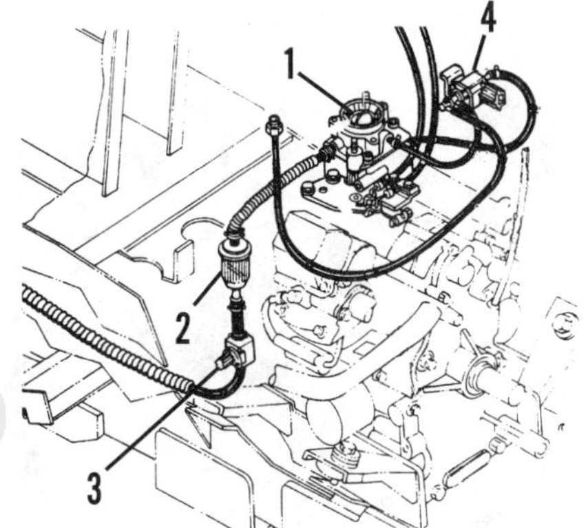

Fig. JD7-11–Drawing of Model 425 fuel system showing carburetor (1), fuel filter (2) and fuel shut-off valve (3). The carburetor vent solenoid (4) stops fuel flow to the engine when de-energized.

viscosity based on the expected ambient temperature range as shown on temperature chart in Fig. JD7-10.

The recommended oil change interval is after every 200 hours of use. The oil filter is a spin-on paper element cartridge. On new and reconditioned engines, lubricating oil and filter should be changed after the first 50 hours of operation.

Air Filter

Models 425 and 445

The engine is equipped with a dry air filter. Clean or change the filter when the air restriction indicator's yellow plunger reaches the red line.

Remove foam and paper air filter elements from the air filter housing. The foam element should be washed in a mild detergent and water solution, rinsed in clean water and allowed to air

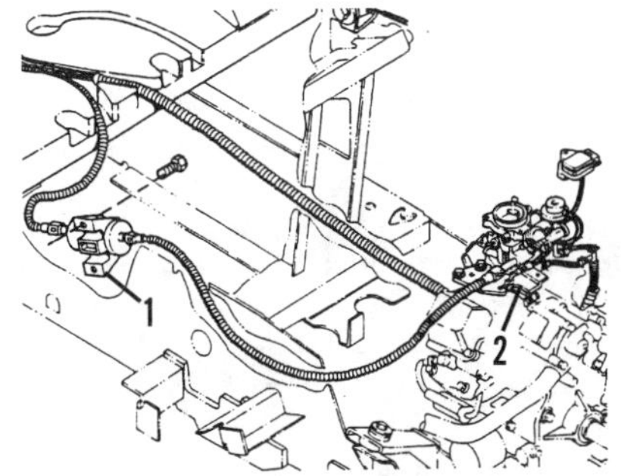

Fig. JD7-12–Drawing of Model 445 fuel system showing location of fuel filter (1) and fuel pressure relief screw (2).

dry. Soak the foam element in clean engine oil. Squeeze out excess oil.

The paper element cannot be cleaned and must be replaced when dirty. Reinstall filter elements.

Model 455

The tractor is equipped with an outer primary filter element and an inner safety element. The primary filter element should be removed and cleaned after every 200 hours of operation or more frequently when operating in extremely dusty conditions. Remove dust from the filter element by tapping lightly with your hand, not on a hard surface. Compressed air at pressure under 30 psi (210 kPa) may also be directed inside the filter element, but be careful not to damage the element. Do not wash the air filter element. Replace the filter once a year or more often if damaged or extremely dirty.

The inner filter element should not be cleaned. If contaminants are evident on the inner filter, the outer filter has failed and both filters should be replaced.

Cooling System

Periodically clean debris from the radiator screen and check the radiator's coolant level.

WARNING: The cooling system is pressurized. Remove the radiator cap only when the engine is cold.

Periodically inspect the coolant hoses. Replace damaged or deteriorated hoses.

Coolant system capacity is approximately 2.8 liters (3.0 qt.). The recommended coolant is a 50/50 mixture of clean water and permanent antifreeze. The antifreeze must be suitable for use in aluminum engines.

Flush the cooling system after every 12 months.

A thermostat maintains cooling system temperature. On Models 425 and 445, the thermostat should begin to open at 63-66°C (145-150°F) and open fully at 80°C (176°F). On Model 455, the thermostat should begin to open at 71°C (160°F) and be fully open at 82°C (180°F). A coolant temperature sensor on the engine controls the dash panel gauge.

Spark Plug (Models 425 and 445)

The recommended spark plug is NGK BMR4A for Model 425 and NGK BMR6A for Model 445. The spark plug gap should be 0.76 mm (0.030 in.). Tighten the spark plug to 20 N·m (177 in.-lb.).

Fuel Filter

Model 425

The fuel filter (2—Fig. JD7-11) should be replaced after every 250 hours or operation or annually, whichever comes first. Stop the engine and let it cool before removing the filter.

Close the fuel shut-off valve (3). Squeeze the hose clamps and disconnect fuel hoses from the filter. Install the new filter with the arrow on the filter housing pointing in the direction of the fuel flow.

Model 445

The fuel filter should be replaced after every 500 hours of operation.

NOTE: Fuel system pressure must be relieved before performing any service to the fuel injection system.

To relieve fuel pressure, first stop the engine and let it cool. Open the fuel tank cap to relieve pressure in the fuel tank. Raise the hood and remove the side panel from right side. Loosen the fuel pressure relief screw (2—Fig. JD7-12) one-half turn counterclockwise to relieve the fuel pressure in system.

The fuel filter (1) is located under the platform on right side of tractor. Squeeze the two clips to disconnect fuel hoses from the filter. Remove the screws attaching the filter to the frame and remove the filter. Install the new filter so the arrow on the filter housing is pointing in the direction of the fuel flow. Tighten the fuel pressure relief screw.

Model 455

A replaceable paper element fuel filter (7—Fig. JD7-13) is located between the fuel feed pump and fuel injection pump. Water and sediment should be drained from the filter bowl (11) after every 50 hours of operation or when necessary. To drain water, unscrew the retaining ring (12) and remove the bowl and filter assembly. If an unusual amount of water or sediment is evident, locate the source of contamination and correct it. Clean the filter bowl and install filter assembly.

The filter element should be replaced annually or sooner if the loss of engine power is evident. Air must be bled from the system after installing the filter.

Bleed Fuel System. Air must be bled from the diesel fuel system anytime the fuel lines are disconnected or a fuel system component is removed. To bleed air from fuel system, first loosen the bleed screw (1—Fig. JD7-13) on the filter housing. Turn the key switch ON to activate the fuel feed pump. When air-free fuel flows from the bleed screw, tighten the screw. Loosen the bleed screw on the fuel injection pump fuel inlet fitting. When air-free fuel flows from the bleed screw, tighten the screw and turn the key switch OFF. If the engine will not start, loosen the fuel injector line fittings at the injectors and crank the engine until the fuel flows from all lines. Tighten the injector line fittings and start the engine.

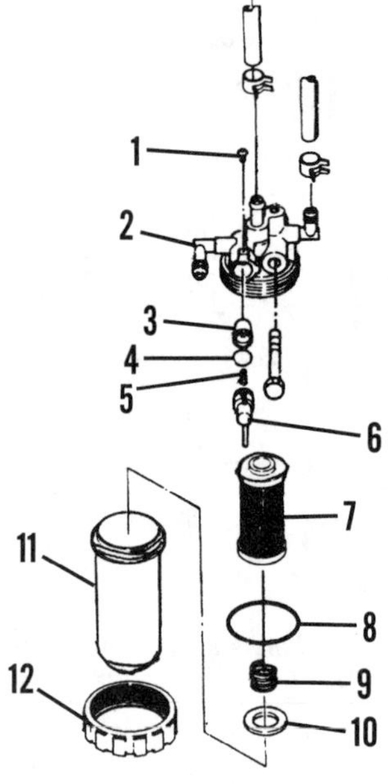

Fig. JD7-13–Exploded view of fuel filter for Model 455.

1. Bleed screw
2. Filter housing
3. Shutoff valve
4. O-ring
5. Spring
6. Knob
7. Filter element
8. O-ring
9. Spring
10. Gasket
11. Fuel bowl
12. Retaining ring

Fig. JD7-14–Adjust throttle and choke control wires as described in text.

1. Throttle cable clamp
2. Choke cable clmap
3. Throttle control lever
4. Slot
5. Cap screws
6. Control plate

Fig. JD7-15–View of fuel shutoff used on Model 455.

A. Locknut
B. Link
C. Cable link
D. Pump shutoff lever
E. Rod end
F. Solenoid plunger

Engine Control Cables (Models 425 and 445)

Adjust the throttle control cable as follows: Loosen the throttle cable clamp (1—Fig. JD7-14) at the engine end. Move the throttle lever on the instrument panel towards the fast idle until the throttle lever arm at the cable end is 2-3 mm (0.08-0.12 in.) from the pedestal opening edge. Pull the throttle cable housing so the control lever (3) at the engine end is against the end of the slot (4) in the plate. Retighten the clamp. Check the throttle for a full range of movement without binding.

On Model 425, loosen the choke cable housing clamp (2—Fig. JD7-14) and adjust the position of the cable housing so the choke carburetor plate operates through the full range.

To adjust the maximum unloaded engine speed (fast idle), run the engine with the throttle control lever in the maximum speed position. Using an accurate tachometer, check the engine rpm. The engine speed should be 3450-3650 rpm. Loosen the control plate retaining screws (5—Fig. JD7-14) and move the control plate (6) to adjust the fast idle speed. Retighten screws.

Throttle Control Cable (Model 455)

The throttle hand lever should move smoothly, but have enough tension to maintain throttle setting. To adjust throttle friction, turn the adjusting nut located on the hand lever quadrant clockwise to increase tension or counterclockwise to decrease the tension setting.

Throttle cable should be adjusted so the governor lever on injection pump moves fully to the slow and fast idle positions. To adjust, loosen the throttle cable clamp (C—Fig. JD7-15) located adjacent to the injection pump. Move the hand lever towards the fast idle position until the cable end of the lever is 2-3 mm (0.080-0.120 in.) away from the end of the slot in the frame. While holding the throttle control lever against

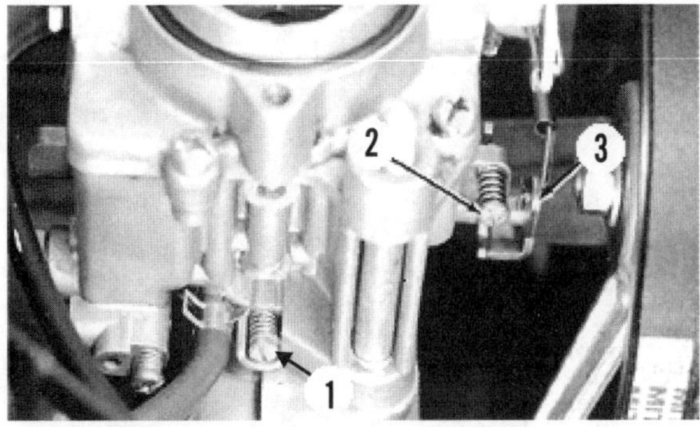

Fig. JD7-16–View showing location of idle mixture screw (1), idle speed stop screw (2) and throttle lever (3) on Model 425 carburetor.

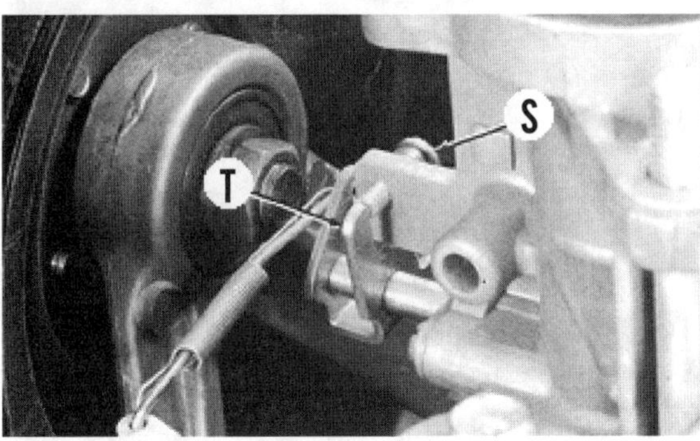

Fig. JD7-17–To adjust idle speed on Model 445, hold throttle lever (T) against idle speed screw (S) and turn screw to obtain desired speed. Idle speed should be approximately 1450 rpm.

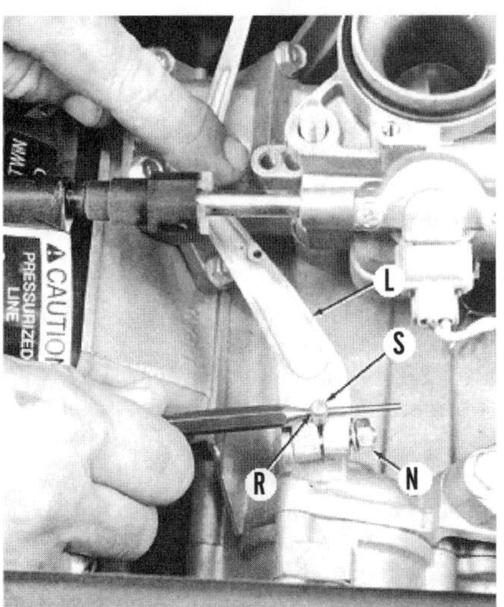

Fig. JD7-18–To adjust governor linkage on Models 425 and 445, loosen governor lever clamp (N). Pull governor lever (L) counterclockwise as far as possible and hold lever. Rotate governor shaft (S) as far as possible counterclockwise.

the fast idle stop, pull the throttle cable tight and tighten the cable clamp. Move the throttle lever through the full range and make sure the governor control lever moves fully to the slow and fast idle positions.

Fuel Shutoff Solenoid (Model 455)

The fuel shutoff solenoid holds the fuel injection pump linkage in a closed position until the battery voltage energizes the solenoid. The solenoid then moves the pump linkage so the fuel pump delivers fuel to the engine. Also refer to the ELECTRICAL SYSTEM section.

Adjustment

The shutoff solenoid must be adjusted so the plunger retracts fully while also providing full rack travel on the fuel injection pump.

To adjust, loosen the locknut (A—Fig. JD7-15) and detach the link (B) from the rod end (E). Push the solenoid plunger (F) in until bottomed. Push the injection pump shutoff lever (D) as far as possible toward the solenoid. Rotate the rod end (E) so it aligns with the hole in link (B), then turn the rod end (E) two turns counterclockwise. Reattach the link to the rod end. Check for free movement. Linkage must return to the stop position when the key switch is rotated to the OFF position.

Fuel Transfer Pump (Model 455)

The fuel transfer pump is located in the fuel tank. To test the pump for the correct operation, connect a suitable pressure gauge to the fuel tank output fitting. Turn the ignition switch on, but don't start the engine. The minimum allowable fuel pump pressure is 172 kPa (25 psi) at a fuel temperature of 59-77°F (15-25°C).

Direct a hose from the fuel line into a container. The fuel pump volume should be at least 450 mL (15 oz.) during 15 seconds of operation.

Carburetor (Model 425)

Model 425 is equipped with a float carburetor.

The initial setting of the idle mixture screw (1—Fig. JD7-16) is $1\frac{3}{8}$ turns out from a lightly seated position. Start and run the engine until the normal operating temperature is reached. Turn the idle mixture screw to obtain the highest idle speed (lean mixture), then turn the screw out counterclockwise an additional $\frac{1}{4}$ turn. Adjust the idle stop screw (2) so the engine idles at 1450 rpm. Recheck the throttle cable adjustment.

A fixed jet controls the main fuel mixture. The main jet is not adjustable, but different size main jets are available for high altitude operation.

The carburetor uses a vent solenoid (4—Fig. JD7-11) in conjunction with an ignition delay module to prevent backfire when the ignition switch is turned off. The vent solenoid equalizes the pressure on the upper and lower sides of the carburetor venturi when de-energized. With the pressure equalized, no vacuum is present at the venturi to draw fuel out of the main nozzle, and fuel flow to the engine is stopped immediately.

Fuel Injection (Model 445)

Model 445 is equipped with an electronically controlled, throttle body fuel injection system. Fuel mixture settings are not adjustable.

Slow idle speed is adjusted by turning the slow idle stop screw (S—Fig. JD7-17) while holding the throttle lever (T) in the slow speed position. The slow idle speed should be 1350-1550 rpm.

To adjust maximum unloaded engine speed (fast idle), run the engine with the throttle control lever in the maximum speed position. Using an accurate tachometer, check the engine rpm. Engine speed should be 3450-3650 rpm. Loosen the throttle control plate retaining screws (5—Fig. JD7-14) and move the control plate (6) to adjust the fast idle speed. Retighten screws.

Refer to the REPAIRS section for fuel injection service information.

Governor (Models 425 and 445)

To adjust the governor linkage, loosen the governor lever clamp nut (N—Fig. JD7-18). Pull the governor lever (L) counterclockwise as far as possible and hold the lever. Insert a small diameter rod (R) though the hole in the governor shaft (S) and rotate the governor shaft as far as possible counterclockwise. Retighten nut.

Ignition System (Models 425 and 445)

A breakerless, solid-state ignition system is used. Ignition timing is not adjustable. If a malfunction is suspected, refer to the REPAIRS section for the service procedure.

Valve Adjustment

Models 425 and 445

The engine must be cold when checking the valve stem end clearance. Remove the rocker arm cover and unscrew the spark plugs. Rotate the crankshaft so the piston for the cylinder being checked is at top dead center on the compression stroke. Both the intake and exhaust valves should be seated and the rocker arms loose. If not, the piston is not on the compression stroke and the crankshaft must be turned one complete revolution. Piston is at TDC when "1" or "2" mark with the triangle on the flywheel is aligned with the embossed triangle on the top side of the crankcase.

Use a feeler gauge to measure the clearance (A—Fig. JD7-19) between the valve stem and rocker arm. The specified clearance is 0.25 mm (0.010 in.). To adjust, loosen the jam nut (B) and turn the adjusting screw (C) to obtain the desired clearance. Tighten the jam nut to 9 N·m (79 in.-lb.) and recheck the clearance. Tighten spark plug to 25 N·m (221 in.-lb.).

Model 455

Adjust the valve clearance with the engine cold. The specified clearance is 0.2 mm (0.008 in.) for both the intake and exhaust valves.

To adjust the valves, remove the rocker arm cover. The number 1 cylinder is at the flywheel end of the engine. Turn the crankshaft in the normal direction of rotation (clockwise facing the flywheel) so the number 1 piston is at top dead center on the compression stroke. Adjust the intake and exhaust valves on the number 1 cylinder. Adjust the valve clearance (A—Fig. JD7-19) by loosening the locknut (B) and turning the adjusting screw (C) at the push rod end of the rocker arm until a 0.2 mm (0.008 in.) thick feeler gauge is a tight slip fit between the end of valve stem and rocker arm pad.

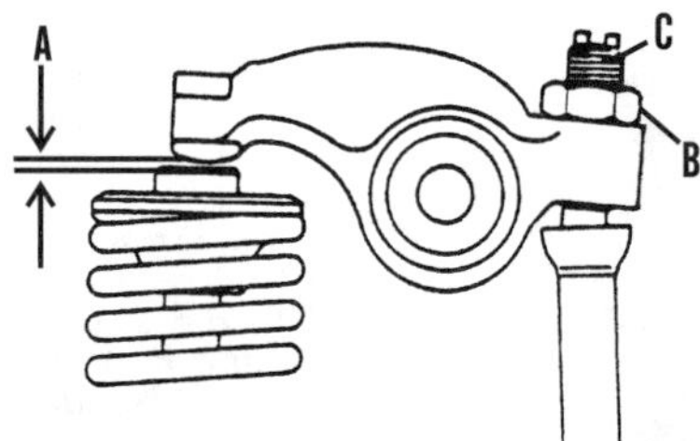

Fig. JD7-19–Loosen jam nut (B) and turn adjusting screw (C) to obtain desired clearance (A) between valve stem and rocker arm. Refer to text.

Continue to turn the crankshaft until the next piston in the firing order (1-3-2) is at top dead center on the compression stroke and adjust the valves for that cylinder in the same manner. Repeat the procedure for each cylinder in order.

Oil Pressure

To check oil pressure, remove the oil pressure sender and connect a suitable gauge to the port. On Model 455, remove the fuel filter to gain access to the oil pressure sender.

Run the engine until the normal operating temperature is reached, then record the oil pressure reading. The minimum allowable oil pressure with the engine running at fast idle is 276 kPa (40 psi) for Models 425 and 445. The specified oil pressure for Model 455 is 294-440 kPa (43-64 psi).

If the oil pressure is below specification, stop the engine and determine the cause.

Compression Pressure

When checking compression pressure, make sure the battery is fully charged. Minimum cranking speed is 250 rpm.

For Models 425 and 445, the minimum allowable compression pressure is 1171 kPa (170 psi). Maximum allowable difference between cylinders is 97 kPa (14 psi).

For Model 455, the minimum allowable compression pressure is 2448 kPa (355 psi). Maximum allowable difference between cylinders is 490 kPa (71 psi).

ENGINE REMOVAL AND INSTALLATION

Models 425 and 445

Disconnect the negative battery cable. Disconnect the tube to the air restriction indicator. Remove the front grille panel. Unscrew the fasteners securing the muffler shield to the front

Fig. JD7-20–On Model 445, turn fuel pressure relief screw (C) one-half turn counterclockwise to relieve fuel pressure before disconnecting fuel lines.

A. Fuel supply hose
B. Throttle control cable
C. Fuel system relief screw
D. Engine mounting bolts
E. Ground cable

support. The front support is secured to the frame by carriage bolts on both sides. Remove the upper carriage bolt on each side, then loosen the lower carriage bolts and tilt the front support forward. Unscrew and remove the muffler with the shield. Reinstall the engine lift bracket after removing the muffler. Disconnect the drive shaft from the engine pulley. Drain the coolant and disconnect radiator hoses. Disconnect the choke and throttle cables from the engine.

NOTE: On Model 445, turn the fuel pressure relief screw (C—Fig. JD7-20) one-half turn counterclockwise to relieve the fuel pressure in the fuel injection system before disconnecting fuel lines or hoses.

Disconnect all cables, wires and hoses that will interfere with engine removal. Unscrew the engine mounting bolts (D). Attach a suitable hoist to the engine lifting bracket. Carefully lift out the engine toward the front of the tractor to prevent damage to the radiator.

Reverse the removal procedure to install the engine. Be sure there is sufficient slack in the ground cable after attachment. Refer to the COOLING SYSTEM when refilling the cooling system. Bleed air from the fuel system as previously outlined in the FUEL FILTER section.

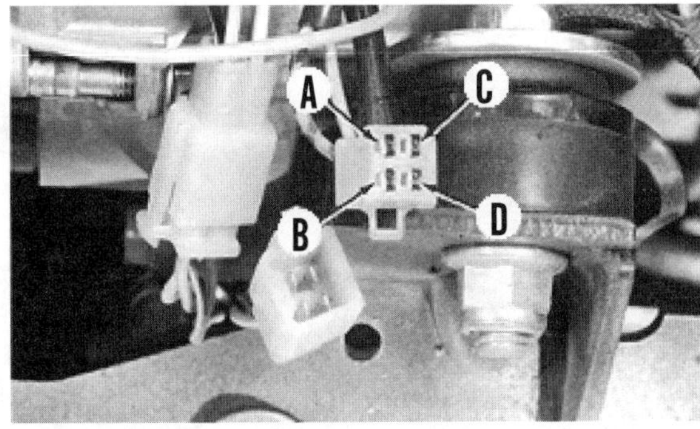

Fig. JD7-21–Disconnect 4-pin pulser connector to test pulser coil windings. Refer to text.

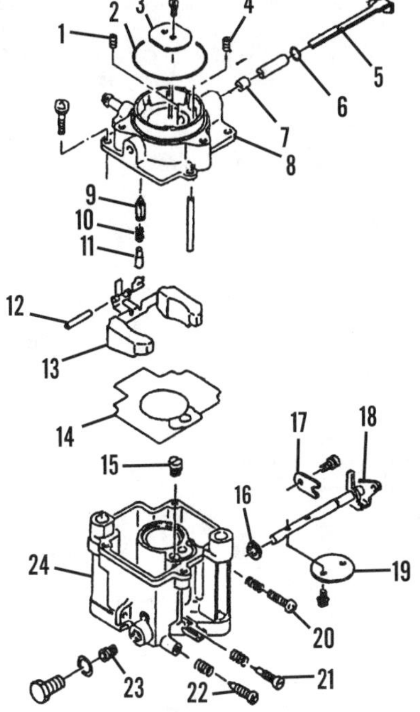

Fig. JD7-22–Exploded view of carburetor used on Model 425.

1. Air jet
2. Gasket
3. Choke plate
4. Air jet
5. Choke shaft
6. Seal
7. Bushing
8. Air horn
9.
10. Fuel inlet vlave
11. Spring
12. Pin
13. Float
14. Gasket
15. Pilot jet
16. Seal
17. Retainer
18. Throttle shaft
19. Throttle plate
20. Idle speed screw
21. Idle mixture screw
22. Drain screw
23. Main jet
24. Body

Model 455

Disconnect the negative battery cable. Remove the air cleaner assembly. Remove the front grille panel. The front support is secured to the frame by carriage bolts on both sides. Remove the upper carriage bolt on each side. Loosen the lower carriage bolts and tilt the front support forward. Remove the muffler assembly.

Disconnect the drive shaft from the engine pulley. Drain the coolant and disconnect the radiator hoses. Remove the coolant reservoir and the fan shroud. Disconnect all cables, wires and hoses that will interfere with engine removal. Identify wiring as it is disconnected so it can be correctly reconnected. Plug all fuel hoses to prevent dirt from entering the fuel system.

Reposition the lift eye on the left front side of the engine so the loop is up for lifting. Attach a suitable hoist to the engine lift brackets. Unscrew the engine mounting bolts. Carefully lift out the engine toward the front of the tractor to prevent damage to the radiator.

Reverse the removal procedure to install the engine. Be sure there is sufficient slack in the ground cable after attachment.

REPAIRS

The following engine repair section covers Models 425 and 445. For Model 455, refer to the YANMAR section in the ENGINE REPAIR section of this manual for repair procedures.

Tightening Torque

The recommended special tightening torque specifications are as follows:

Carburetor	17 N·m (12 in.-lb.)
Connecting rod	21 N·m (186 in.-lb.)
Crankcase cover	21 N·m (186 in.-lb.)
Cylinder head	21 N·m (186 in.-lb.)
Flywheel	110 N·m (80 ft.-lb.)
Intake manifold	6 N·m (52 in.-lb.)
Muffler	7 N·m (62 in.-lb.)
Rocker arm nut	9 N·m (79 in.-lb.)
Spark plug	20 N·m (180 in.-lb.)

IGNITION SYSTEM

The ignition system consists of an ignition module, two pulser coils (Model 445 uses one pulser coil) and two ignition coils. On Model 445, the ignition module is a part of the fuel injection module. The 12-volt battery supplies current to the ignition system. A safety switch operated by weight on the tractor seat disconnects current to the ignition system if the operator leaves the seat while the engine is running.

Refer to wiring diagrams at the end of this section for the ignition system components. Before testing the ignition system, be sure the safety circuit components are functioning correctly and not affecting the performance of the ignition system.

To check the pulser coil, turn the key switch OFF and disconnect the 4-pin pulser coil connector (Fig. JD7-21). Measure the resistance between the white/blue wire (A) and pink wire (B), then between the green/white wire (C) and yellow wire (D) at the pulser side of the connector. Resistance should be 85-270 ohms on Model 425 and 190-290 ohms on Model 445.

To test the ignition coil, disconnect the spark plug cable, positive wire (wide terminal) and negative wire (narrow terminal). To check the primary coil resistance, connect the ohmmeter test leads between the positive and negative wire terminals. The primary coil resistance should be 3.4-4.6 ohms. To measure the secondary coil resistance, remove the spark plug cap from the spark plug wire. Connect the ohmmeter leads to the spark plug wire and positive terminal. Secondary coil resistance should be 10.4k-15.5k ohms. Measure resistance between the spark plug wire and coil core. Reading should be infinity. If readings vary significantly from the specifications, replace the ignition coil.

Satisfactory tests are not available to check the ignition module other than replacing the ignition module with a good unit and checking performance.

CARBURETOR (Model 425)

Model 425 is equipped with the float carburetor shown in Fig. JD7-22. The

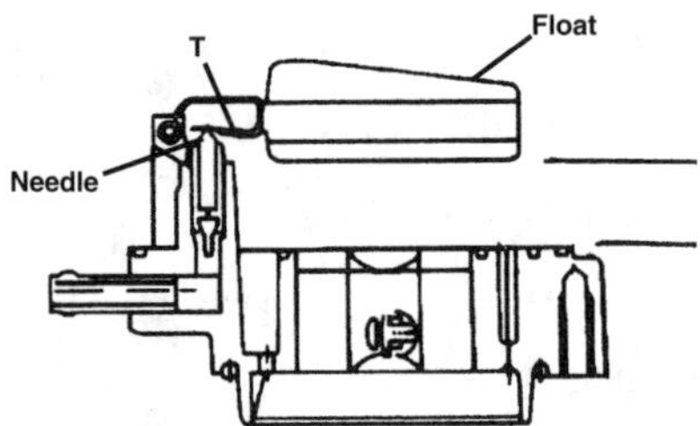

Fig. JD7-23–Float should be parallel with air horn surface. Adjust float level by bending float tab (T).

initial setting of the idle mixture screw (21) is 1$\frac{3}{8}$ turns out from lightly seated. Main fuel mixture is controlled by a fixed jet (23). Different size main jets are available for high altitude operation.

To disassemble carburetor, remove attaching screws and separate the air horn (8—Fig. JD7-22) from the carburetor body (24). Remove the float (13) and fuel inlet valve assembly (9, 10 and 11). Remove idle jet (15), idle mixture screw (21) and main jet (23). It is not necessary to remove the choke or throttle shafts unless wear or damage is evident.

Clean carburetor parts (except plastic components) using carburetor cleaner. Do not clean jets or passages with drill bits or wire as enlargement of passages could affect the carburetor's calibration. Rinse parts in warm water to neutralize the carburetor cleaner's corrosive action and dry with compressed air.

When assembling the carburetor, note the following. Install choke plate (2) with metering hole toward the fuel inlet side of the carburetor. To check the float level, invert air horn and position float so tab (T—Fig. JD7-23) just contacts the fuel inlet valve pin. Don't allow the float to compress the spring in fuel inlet valve. The float should be parallel with the air horn when inverted as shown in Fig. JD7-23. Bend tab (T) to adjust float position.

FUEL INJECTION SYSTEM (Model 445)

The engine is equipped with a throttle body fuel injection system. Refer to Fig. JD7-24 for a diagram indicating the location of the fuel injection components. Refer to Fig. JD7-25 for the fuel injection electrical circuit wiring diagram.

Operation

The fuel injection system is an electronically controlled, throttle body system. The system is divided into two subsystems, fuel delivery and control.

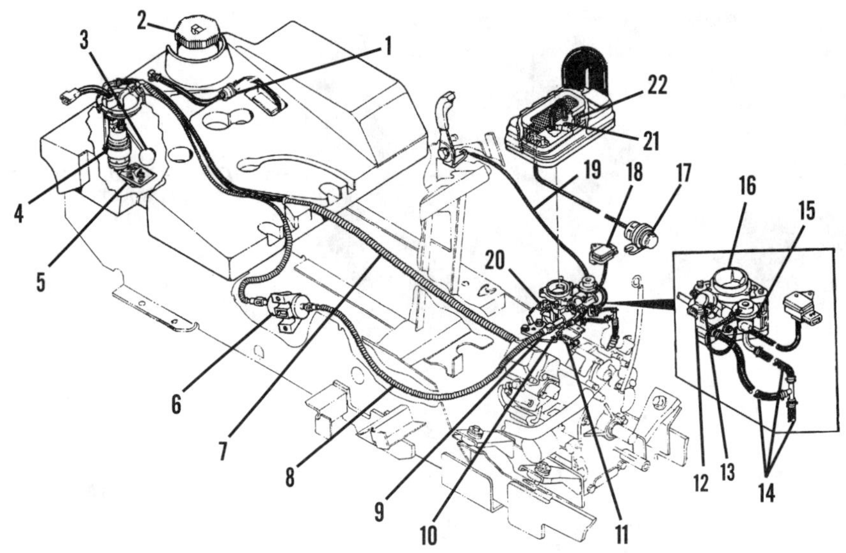

Fig. JD7-24–Drawing showing fuel system components on Model 445.

1. Tank relief/check valve
2. Fuel tank cap
3. Fuel gauge sensor
4. Fuel pump
5. Screen
6. Fuel filter
7. Fuel return hose
8. Fuel delivery hose
9. Throttle control plate
10. Throttle control lever
11. Governor lever
12. Fuel pressure relief screw
13. Fuel injector
14. Fuel return hose
15. Fuel pressure regulator
16. Throttle body
17. Air restriction indicator
18. Sensor
19. Throttle cable
20. Slow idle stop screw
21. Secondary filter element
22. Primary filter element

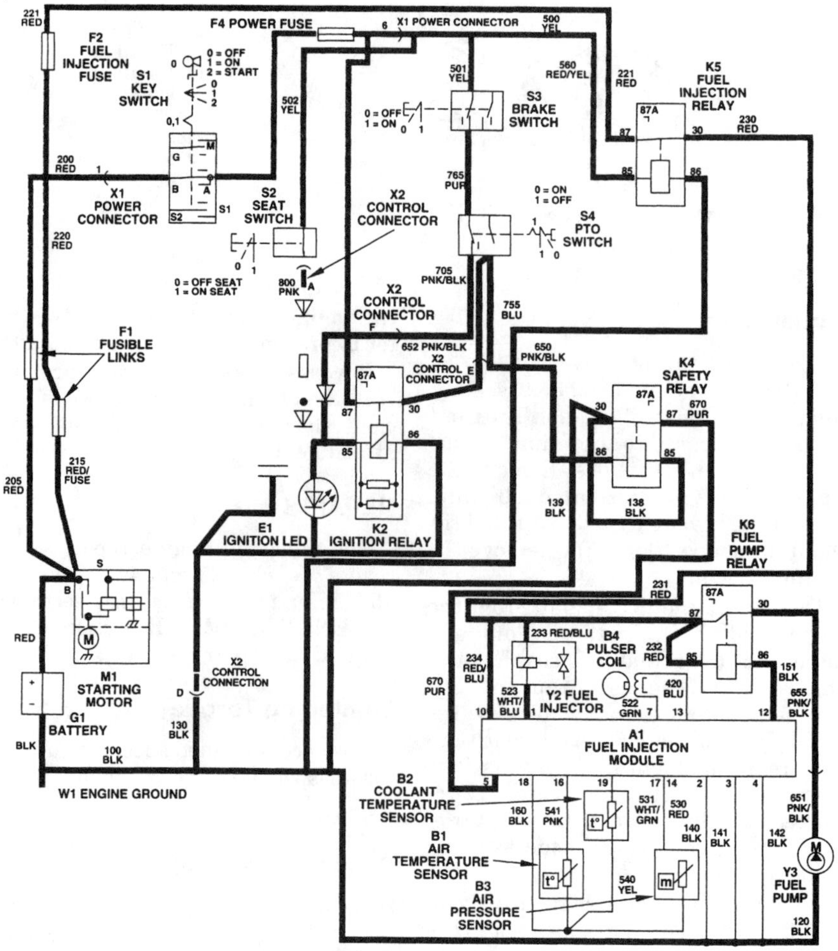

Fig. JD7-25–Wiring schematic for Model 445 fuel circuit.

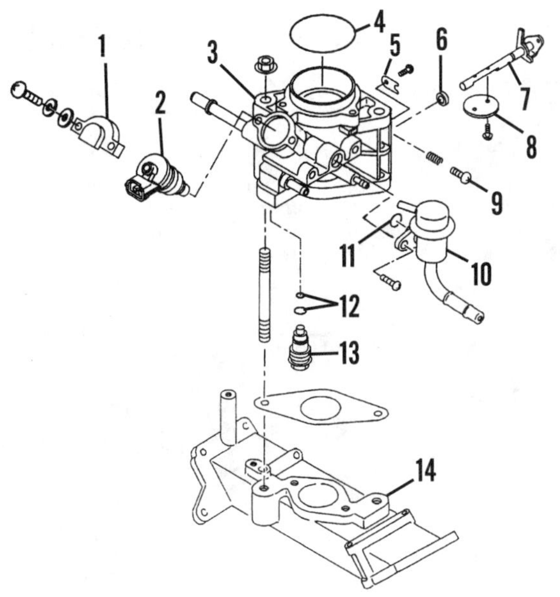

Fig. JD7-26–Exploded view of throttle body used on Model 445.

1. Retainer
2. Fuel injector
3. Throttle body
4. Gasket
5. Retainer
6. Seal
7. Throttle shaft
8. Throttle plate
9. Idle speed screw
10. Fuel pressure regulator
11. O-ring
12. O-ring
13. Fuel pressure relief plug
14. Intake manifold

The fuel delivery system consists of the fuel pump (4—Fig. JD7-24) mounted inside the fuel tank, fuel filter (6), fuel injector (13) and pressure regulator (15). The fuel pump forces fuel from the fuel tank through the filter to the fuel injector. The fuel injector is located in the throttle body, which is attached to the intake manifold. Excess fuel is routed from the injector to the pressure regulator, which maintains system pressure. See the FUEL PRESSURE REGULATOR section. Leak-off fuel from the regulator is directed back to the fuel tank.

A relief/check valve (1) opens to allow air to enter the fuel tank to prevent a vacuum, but closes to prevent gas fumes from escaping into the atmosphere. The relief valve opens and allows air to escape from the tank if tank pressure exceeds 3 kPa (0.4 psi). The fuel tank cap is not vented.

The control system consists of the fuel injection control module, fuel injection relay, fuel pump relay and several sensors. The sensors provide the control module with voltage readings related to air pressure, coolant temperature and air temperature. The control module also senses engine speed through pulses from the ignition pulser coil.

The fuel injection relay directs current to the control module when the ignition key switch is ON. The control module energizes the fuel pump relay when output from the fuel pump is required. The control module controls the time and duration of fuel injector output. Activation of the injector by the control module is determined by input from sensors and related circuits. Note the two fusible links are located in the system to protect system components.

Troubleshooting

If the fuel injection module recognizes a problem during operation, an LED on the instrument panel will flash a trouble code identifying the malfunctioning circuit. Note that the trouble codes only identify problem areas, not specific components. A problem may lie with a sensor, faulty wiring, bad connection or internal module circuit. The module only identifies problems tied electrically to the ECU. Other problems, such as fuel delivery problems, will not trigger a trouble code. Trouble codes and related problem areas are:

Code Flashes	Problem
Long, short, short	Air temperature sensor circuit
Long, short, short, short	Coolant sensor circuit
Long, long, short	Air pressure sensor circuit
Long, long, short, short	Air pressure sensor circuit*
Short, long continuously	Multiple sensor malfunction

*Turning key switch to start position before light is off will also trigger this code.

Refer to fuel system wiring diagram shown in Fig. JD7-25, and use normal troubleshooting techniques to isolate the faulty component. Voltage readings specified in the following paragraphs are taken with connectors connected. Be sure the battery is fully charged and all ground connections are good.

The following fuel system circuits may prevent the engine from starting if a malfunction occurs (including starter and ignition circuits):

- Fuel injection module.
- Fuel pump circuit.
- Fuel injector circuit.
- Engine speed circuit.
- Starter sensing circuit.

A rough running engine may be caused by a malfunction in the following:

- Air temperature sensor circuit.
- Air pressure sensor circuit.
- Coolant temperature sensor circuit.
- Engine speed circuit.

Note the following when performing voltage checks:

The fuel injection module must provide 5 V to sensors for the proper operation. Less voltage may be due to a faulty module.

FUEL PUMP CIRCUIT: When the ignition key switch is turned to the RUN position there should be 0.1-0.2 V for 2 seconds at thhe fuel injection module terminal 12 (Fig. JD7-25). Replace the module if voltage exceeds 0.2 V. With the key held in the start position, there should be 0.1-0.2 V at the fuel injection module terminal 12. Replace the module if voltage exceeds 0.2 V.

With the transmission in NEUTRAL, the PTO switch off, the park brake engaged, the seat switch depressed and the key switch in the RUN position, battery voltage should be read at the following locations: Fuel pump for two seconds, brake switch, seat switch, PTO switch, fuel injection module terminal 10, fuel pump relay terminals 85 and 87, safety relay terminal 86, and fuel injection relay terminals 30, 85 and 87.

THROTTLE BODY. An exploded view of the throttle body and associated components is shown in Fig. JD7-26. Note the following when servicing the throttle body. Loosen fuel pressure relief plug (13) before removing any fuel lines or components. To remove the injector (2—Fig. JD7-26), remove the cover (1) and unplug wire connector. Twist and pull the injector from the throttle body (3). It is not necessary to remove the throttle shaft (7) unless excessive wear is evident. If throttle shaft bore in throttle body is worn, throttle body must be replaced.

If removed, install the throttle shaft seal (6) with the lip out. If the throttle shaft was removed, apply a suitable thread-locking compound to the throttle plate screws when installing. The throttle plate (8) plate must be centered in the throttle body bore when closed and it must move freely when shaft retainer (5) screw is tightened. Tighten the pressure relief plug (13) to 15 N·m (133 in.-lb.).

FUEL INJECTION MODULE. Ignition module is a part of the fuel injection module. Satisfactory tests are not available to check the fuel injection module other than replacing module with a good unit and checking performance.

AIR PRESSURE SENSOR. The sensor monitors air pressure in the throttle body and adjusts voltage output to fuel injection module. Disconnect the connector to the sensor, then looking at the sensor with the air tube pointing down, measure the resistance between all connectors. Refer to the following:

Left to center terminal . . . 2986-3034 ohms
Right to center terminal . . 3774-3798 ohms
Left to right terminal. . . . . . . 773-787 ohms

Reconnect the sensor wire connector. Disconnect the air hose from the throttle body. Connect the voltmeter positive lead to the red/blue wire and negative voltmeter lead to black wire. With the key switch in the ON position, the voltmeter should read approximately 5 V. Connect the voltmeter positive lead to the white/brown wire. The voltmeter should read less than less than 5 V. Apply a slight vacuum to the air hose and the voltage should decrease.

AIR TEMPERATURE SENSOR. The air temperature sensor is located in the base of the air cleaner. To test the sensor, the key switch must be in the OFF position. Detach the air temperature sensor connector. The resistance reading between the sensor connector terminals at 68° F (20° C) should be 2.21k-2.69k ohms. At a temperature range of 32-86° F (0-30° C) resistance readings should be in range of 5.88k-1.65k ohms. Resistance should decrease as temperature increases.

COOLANT TEMPERATURE SENSOR. The specified temperatures and resistance readings are the same as for air temperature sensor.

FUEL INJECTOR. To test the injector, detach the injector wire connector. The resistance between the injector pins should be 13.8 ohms at a temperature of 68° F (20° C). Apply negative battery voltage to one injector pin and tap a wire from the positive battery terminal to the other injector pin. The injector should "click" each time a connection is made. If not, replace the injector.

FUEL PRESSURE REGULATOR (Model 445)

A vacuum-controlled fuel pressure regulator (10—Fig. JD7-26) is located on the throttle body of fuel injected engines. The regulator varies the fuel pressure according to the air pressure in the intake manifold. A vacuum hose connects the regulator to the intake

Fig. JD7-27–Connect pressure gauge (B) to fuel return fitting (F) to check fuel pump pressure. Refer to text.

manifold. This allows the air pressure in the regulator spring chamber and intake manifold to be equal. When the manifold pressure decreases, the fuel pressure is increased, and vice versa when the manifold pressure increases. The fuel pressure regulator must be serviced as a unit assembly.

FUEL PUMP (Model 445)

The fuel pump is located in the fuel tank. The fuel injection module actuates the electric fuel pump electronically. The fuel pressure regulator (10—Fig. JD7-26) controls the fuel pressure.

Testing

This test checks the fuel pressure, which indicates the condition of the fuel pump, fuel pressure regulator, fuel filters and hoses. Before testing the fuel pressure be sure the fuel filter and fuel line are in good condition and the fuel flow to the pump is unimpeded.

NOTE: Turn the fuel pressure relief screw (13—Fig. JD7-26) counterclockwise one-half turn and loosen the fuel tank cap to relieve the fuel system pressure before disconnecting the fuel lines.

Disconnect the fuel return hose (A—Fig. JD7-27) from the throttle body fitting (F) and plug the hose. Connect a suitable pressure gauge (B) to the return fitting. Loosen fuel pressure relief

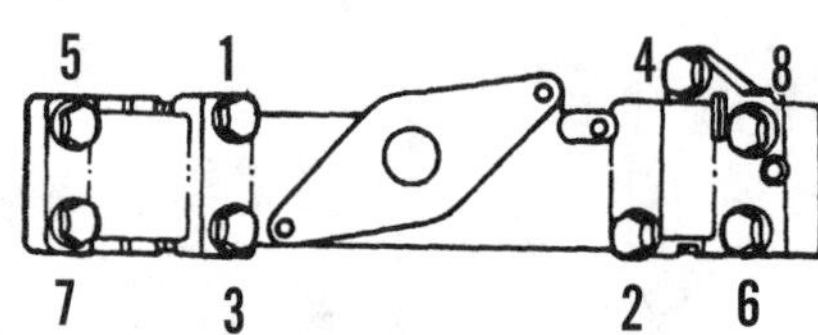

Fig. JD7-28–Loosen and tighten intake manifold bolts in sequence shown to help avoid distortion of manifold.

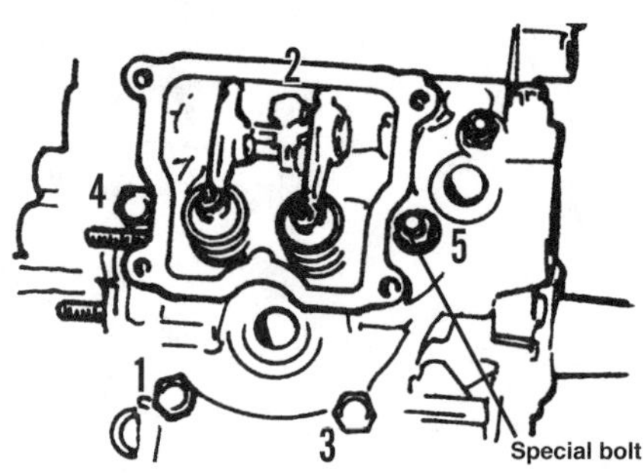

Fig. JD7-29–Loosen and tighten cylinder head bolts in sequence shown to help avoid distorting the cylinder head. Note location of special cylinder head bolt.

screw one-half turn. Turn ignition switch on, but don't start the engine, and observe the pressure gauge reading. Note the fuel pump will only operate for 2 seconds. The minimum allowable fuel pump pressure is 172-186 kPa (25-27 psi). Close the fuel pressure relief screw, and reconnect the fuel return hose.

If the fuel pressure is low, check the fuel pump screen (5—Fig. JD7-24), fuel filter (6) and hoses for restrictions. If no problem is found, replace the fuel pressure regulator or fuel pump.

If the fuel pressure is above specifications, check the fuel tank return line for restrictions and check fuel pressure regulator vacuum hose for leaks. If no problem is found, replace the pressure regulator.

CYLINDER HEAD

To remove the cylinder head, first drain the cooling system. Remove the air cleaner assembly, carburetor or throttle body assembly, intake manifold and muffler.

NOTE: Loosen intake manifold bolts and cylinder head bolts ¼ turn at a time in the sequence shown in Fig. JD7-28 and Fig. JD7-29 to prevent distortion of the manifold or cylinder head.

Rotate crankshaft so the piston is at top dead center on the compression stroke. Remove the rocker arm cover

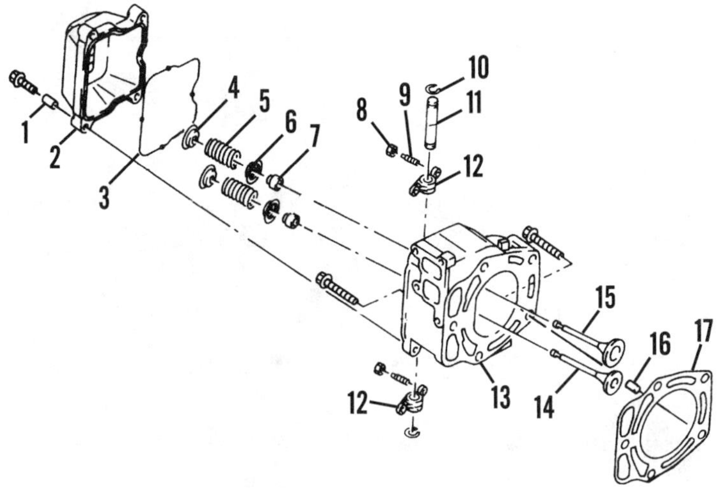

Fig. JD7-30–Exploded view of cylinder head and valve system components for Model 425 and 445.

1. Spacer
2. Rocker cover
3. Gasket
4. Valve spring retainer
5. Valve spring
6. Valve spring seat
7. Seal
8. Nut
9. Adjusting screw
10. Snap ring
11. Rocker shaft
12. Rocker arms
13. Cylinder head
14. Exhaust valve
15. Intake valve
16. Dowel pin
17. Head gasket

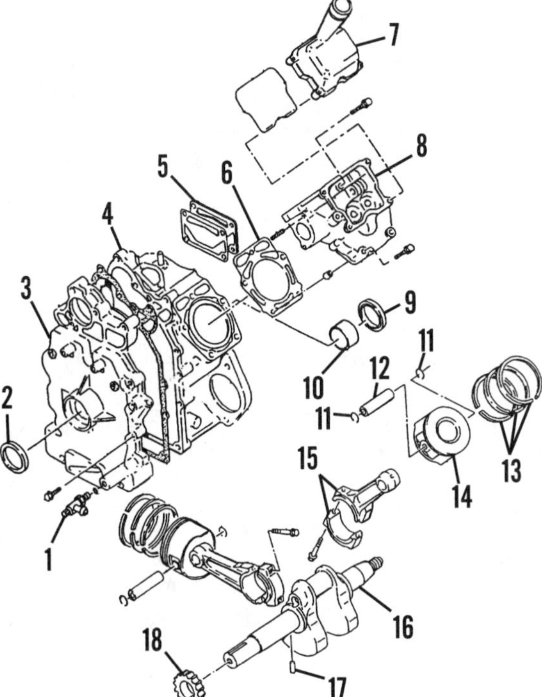

Fig. JD7-31–Exploded view of crankshaft, piston and rod assemblies used on Models 425 and 445.

1. Oil drain valve
2. Oil seal
3. Crankcase cover
4. Cylinder block
5. Breather
6. Head gasket
7. Rocker cover
8. Cylinder head
9. Oil seal
10. Main bearing
11. Snap ring
12. Piston pin
13. Piston rings
14. Piston
15. Connecting rod & cap
16. Crankshaft
17. Pin
18. Crankshaft gear

(2—Fig. JD7-30) Unscrew the cylinder head screws and remove the cylinder head.

Mark the position of all valve train components so they can be installed in their original position. Detach the snap rings (10—Fig. JD7-30) on the rocker shaft, withdraw the rocker shaft (11) and remove the rocker arms (12). Compress the valve springs (5) and disengage the spring retainers (4) from the valve stems. Remove the valve springs, spring seats (6), seals (7) and valves from the cylinder head. Identify all parts during disassembly so they can be returned to their original positions. Install new valve seals (7) when reassembling.

Remove the cylinder head gasket and thoroughly clean the cylinder head surface and combustion chamber. Be careful not to scratch or damage the cylinder head. Inspect the head for damage. Check the head for distortion using a straightedge and feeler gauge. Repair or replace the cylinder head if a 0.05 mm (0.002 in.) feeler gauge can be inserted between the straightedge and gasket surface of the head.

Install the cylinder head using a new head gasket. The new head gasket is treated with a sealing compound and should be installed dry. No additional sealant should be applied. Note the position of the special bolt in Fig. JD7-29. Follow the sequence shown in Fig. JD7-29 when tightening the cylinder head screws. Tighten the screws in steps of 3 N·m (27 in.-lb.) until a final torque of 21 N·m (186 in.-lb.) is attained. Follow the sequence shown in Fig. JD7-28 when tightening the intake manifold bolts. Tighten the intake manifold screws in steps of 3 N·m (27 in.-lb.) until a final torque of 6 N·m (52 in.-lb.) is attained.

Valve System

The valves (14 and 15—Fig. JD7-30) are located in the cylinder head. Clean carbon from the valve face and stem. Inspect valves for damage and replace when necessary.

Valve seats and guides are not replaceable. Valve face and seat angles should be 45°. The valve seat width should be 0.80 mm (0.031 in.). The minimum valve margin is 0.60 mm (0.024 in.).

Minimum valve stem diameter is 5.94 mm (0.234 in.) for intake and 5.92 mm (0.233 in.) for exhaust. Maximum allowable valve guide inside diameter is 6.05 mm (0.238 in.). Maximum valve stem runout measured with valve supported at ends is 0.03 mm (0.001 in.).

Maximum push rod runout measured with the push rod supported at the ends is 0.30 mm (0.012 in.). Minimum rocker shaft diameter is 11.95 mm (0.470 in.). Maximum rocker arm inner diameter is 12.07 mm (0.475 in.).

Inspect the valve springs for damage or evidence of overheating and replace when necessary. Minimum valve spring free length is 29.70 mm (1.170 in.).

Piston, Pin, Rings and Rod

Drain the engine coolant, and remove the cylinder heads (8—Fig. JD7-31) as previously described. Drain the engine oil. Remove the crankshaft pulley, water pump and crankcase cover (3) for access to the piston and rod assemblies. Mark the connecting rods and caps (15) so they can be installed in their original position. Remove carbon or ridge from the top of the cylinder before removing the piston to prevent damage to the ring lands. Unscrew the connecting rod cap screws, detach the rod cap and remove piston and rod assembly through the top of the cylinder bore.

Clean deposits from the top of the piston and piston ring grooves. Be sure the oil return passages in the ring groove are open. Inspect the piston for damage and replace when necessary.

Specified piston clearance in cylinder bore is 0.030-0.170 mm (0.0012-0.0067 in.). The standard piston diameter is 75.935-75.950 mm (2.9896-2.9902 in.). Measure the piston diameter 11 mm (0.43 in.) from the bottom of the piston perpendicular to the piston pin. Maximum allowable pin bore in piston is 17.04 mm (0.671 in.). Minimum allowable piston pin diameter is 16.98 mm (0.668 in.).

Install each piston ring squarely in the cylinder bore and measure ring end gap with a feeler gauge. Maximum allowable piston ring end gap is 1.20 mm (0.050 in.). If the end gap is excessive, check cylinder for wear.

Insert new compression rings in the ring grooves and measure the side clearance between the ring and ring land with a feeler gauge. Maximum allowable piston ring side clearance is 0.14 mm (0.006 in.) for top compression ring and 0.12 mm (0.005 in.) for the second compression ring. Pistons and rings are available in standard size and 0.5 mm (0.020 in.) oversize. Refer to the CYLINDER BLOCK section if oversize pistons are required.

The connecting rod rides directly on the crankpin. Maximum allowable inside diameter at big end of rod is 34.06 mm (1.341 in.). Minimum allowable crankpin journal diameter is 33.93 mm (1.336 in.). Maximum allowable inside diameter at pin end of rod is 17.05 mm (0.671 in.). The connecting rod is available with the standard size big end diameter as well as with 0.50 mm (0.020 in.) undersize big end diameter.

Assemble the piston and connecting rod as follows: On the number one piston and rod assembly, align the arrow match mark on the piston crown (Fig. JD7-32) with the "MADE IN JAPAN" marking on the connecting rod. On number two piston and rod assembly, align arrow match mark on piston crown opposite the "MADE IN JAPAN" marking on the connecting rod.

NOTE: Do not reuse piston pin retainers (11—Fig. JD7-31). Install new retainers if removed from the piston.

Install piston rings with the lettered side towards the piston crown. See Fig. JD7-33. Position piston rings so ring gaps are 180° apart. Lubricate the piston and rings with engine oil prior to installing in the cylinder bore.

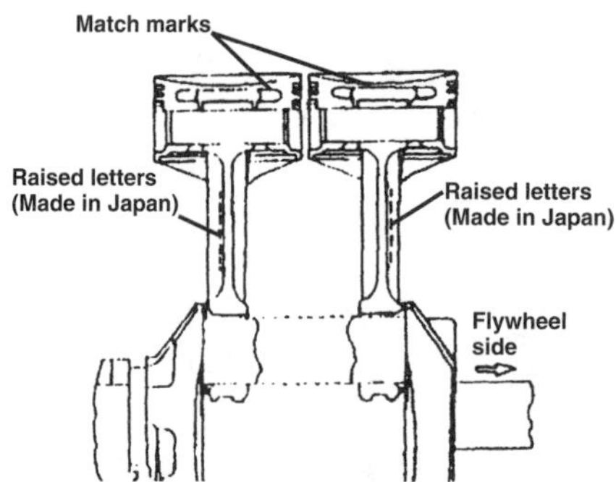

Fig. JD7-32–On Models 425 and 445, note the location of arrow marks on top of pistons in relation to "MADE IN JAPAN" on connecting rods. No. 1 piston is opposite that of No. 2 piston. Refer to text.

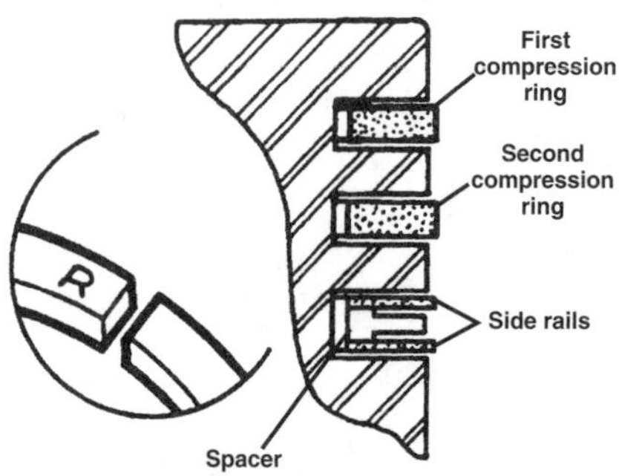

Fig. JD7-33–Cross section of piston and rings showing correct installation on Models 425 and 445. Be sure that "R" or "NPR" mark on end of top ring and second ring faces up. Oil ring can be installed either way.

Install piston and rod assemblies on crankshaft so the arrow mark on both pistons is pointing toward the flywheel as shown in Fig. JD7-32. Note the "MADE IN JAPAN" side of the connecting rods should be facing away from each other and the large chamfer side of each rod big end is next to the crankshaft web. Make sure the rod cap matches the connecting rod. Tighten rod cap screws to 21 N·m (186 in.-lb.). Tighten crankcase cover screws to 21 N·m (186 in.-lb.) in the sequence shown in Fig. JD7-34. Install cylinder head as previously outlined.

Camshaft

The camshaft is accessible after removing the crankcase cover. Rotate the crankshaft to align the timing marks (M—Fig. JD7-35) on camshaft and crankshaft gears prior to removing the camshaft.

The camshaft rides in nonreplaceable bushings in the cylinder block and crankcase cover. Replace the cylinder block or cover if the bushing diameter is greater than 16.07 mm (0.633 in.).

Fig. JD7-34–On Models 425 and 445, tighten oil pan screws in sequence shown above.

Fig. JD7-35–On Models 425 and 445, align timing marks (M) on crankshaft and camshaft gears when installing camshaft.

Minimum allowable camshaft bearing journal diameter is 15.91 mm (0.626 in.). Minimum allowable camshaft lobe height is 25.21 mm (0.992 in.) for intake lobe and 25.46 mm (1.002 in.) for exhaust lobe. Minimum fuel pump lobe height is 19.50 mm (0.768 in.).

When installing camshaft, be sure to align the timing marks (M—Fig. JD7-35) on the camshaft and crankshaft gears. Tighten the crankcase cover screws to 21 N·m (186 in.-lb.) in the sequence shown in Fig. JD7-34. Note the cap screw located at top center of the water pump attaches the crankcase cover to the crankcase and should be tightened to 21 N·m (186 in.-lb.). The remainder of the water pump mounting screws should be tightened to 8 N·m (70 in.-lb.).

Crankshaft and Main Bearings

To remove the crankshaft, first drain the coolant and engine oil. Remove the

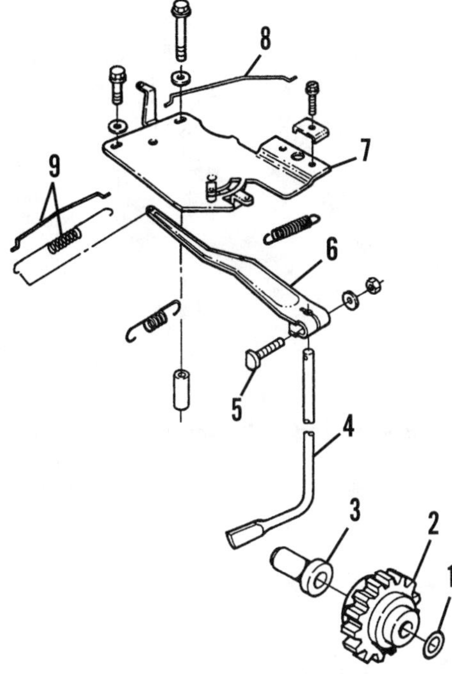

Fig. JD7-36–Exploded view of governor linkage used on Models 425 and 445.

1. Thrust washer
2. Governor gear
3. Sleeve
4. Governor arm
5. Clamp bolt
6. Governor lever
7. Control plate
8. Throttle link
9. Governor link & spring

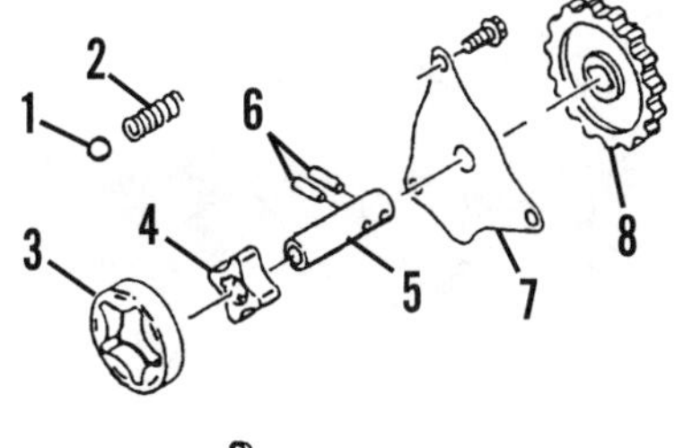

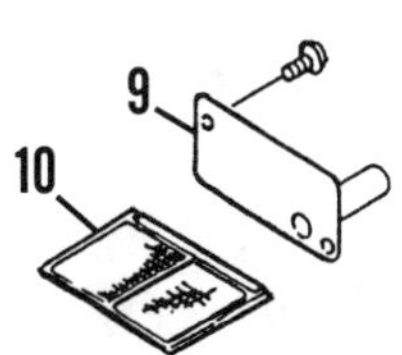

Fig. JD7-37–Exploded view of engine oil pump used on Models 425 and 445.

1. Oil pressure relief ball
2. Spring
3. Outer rotor
4. Inner rotor
5. Shaft
6. Pins
7. Cover
8. Oil pump gear
9. Screen retainer
10. Screen

engine from the tractor. Remove the flywheel, crankshaft pulley, water pump and crankcase cover. Rotate the crankshaft to align the timing marks on the camshaft and crankshaft gear, then remove the camshaft. Remove the connecting rod cap screws and push pistons to top of the cylinders. Withdraw the crankshaft.

The crankshaft rides in a replaceable bushing (10—Fig. JD7-31) in the cylinder block and a nonreplaceable bushing in the crankcase cover (3). Maximum allowable bushing diameter in block is 34.11 mm (1.343 in.). Maximum allowable bushing diameter in crankcase cover is 34.07 mm (1.341 in.). Minimum allowable crankshaft main bearing journal diameter is 33.91 mm (1.335 in.).

Minimum allowable crankpin diameter is 33.93 mm (1.336 in.). The crankpin may be reground to accept a connecting rod with a 0.50 mm undersize big end. Maximum allowable crankshaft runout is 0.05 mm (0.002 in.) measured at the main bearing journals with the crankshaft supported at ends.

When installing the crankshaft, be sure timing marks (M—Fig. JD7-35) on crankshaft and camshaft gears are aligned. Tighten the crankcase cover screws to 21 N·m (186 in.-lb.) in the sequence shown in Fig. JD7-34. Install new crankshaft oil seals with the lip facing inward.

Cylinder Block

The cylinders may be bored to accept oversize pistons. The standard bore diameter is 75.98-76.00 mm (2.994-2.995 in.) and the maximum wear limit is 76.07 mm (2.997 in.). Be sure to check the bore diameter when the cylinder is cold.

After honing the cylinder bore, clean the cylinder thoroughly using soap and warm water. Do not use gasoline, kerosene or other commercial solvents to clean the cylinder bores. Solvents will not remove all the abrasives from the cylinder wall.

Governor

A flyweight governor (2—Fig. JD7-36) is located in the crankcase cover. The governor gear is driven by the camshaft gear. Remove the crankcase cover for access to the governor assembly. The governor components must move freely without binding.

The governor is serviced as an assembly. Remove the governor assembly by prying or pulling off the shaft. The shaft must protrude above the boss 32.2-32.8 mm (1.27-1.29 in.). Install the governor by pushing down until it snaps onto the locating groove. Tighten the crankcase cover screws to 21 N·m (186 in.-lb.) in the sequence shown in Fig. JD7-34.

To adjust the governor linkage, loosen the clamp bolt (5—Fig. JD7-36) Pull the governor lever (6) counterclockwise as far as possible and hold the lever. Rotate the governor arm (4) as far as possible counterclockwise and tighten the clamp bolt.

Oil Pump

A gerotor oil pump (Fig. JD7-37) is located in the crankcase cover. The pump provides pressurized oil that is directed to the crankshaft main bearing journals and crankpin. Drilled passages in the connecting rods squirt oil on the underside of the pistons. A screen prevents foreign matter from entering the pump.

To check oil pressure, remove the oil pressure switch in the side of the cylinder block adjacent to the oil filter and connect an oil pressure gauge. With the engine at its operating temperature and running at the fast throttle setting, the oil pressure should be no less than 276 kPa (40 psi).

Remove the crankcase cover for access to the pump. Note the oil pump cover (7—Fig. JD7-37) holds the relief valve ball (1) and spring (2) in place. Remove and clean the oil pick-up screen (10).

Replace the relief valve spring (2) if the length is less than 19.50 mm (0.768 in.). Maximum inner rotor-to-outer rotor clearance is 0.3 mm (0.012 in.). Minimum allowable rotor shaft diameter is 10.92 mm (0.430 in.). Rotors (3 and 4) and rotor shaft (5) are renewed as a kit. Maximum allowable bore diameter in oil pan and pump cover is 11.07 mm (0.436 in.). Maximum rotor bore diameter in crankcase cover is 40.80 mm (1.606 in.). Replace the crankcase cover if wear is excessive.

When assembling the oil pump, fill the rotor housing with engine oil to provide initial lubrication. Be sure the hole in the cover (7) is centered over the relief valve.

COOLING SYSTEM

Radiator

Radiator cap pressure rating is 90 kPa (13 psi).

WARNING: The coolant in the radiator is pressurized. Remove radiator cap only when the engine is cold.

To remove the radiator, drain the coolant. Disconnect the hydraulic lines to the radiator and drain the hydraulic fluid from the radiator. Disconnect the coolant hoses. Remove the radiator screen and coolant reservoir. Unscrew the fan shroud and move it out of the way. Disconnect the choke control cable, if so equipped, and throttle control cable. Remove the radiator mounting fasteners and remove radiator.

Coolant system capacity is approximately 2.8 liters (3.0 qt.). The recommended coolant is a 50/50 mixture of clean water and permanent antifreeze. Antifreeze must be suitable for use in aluminum engines.

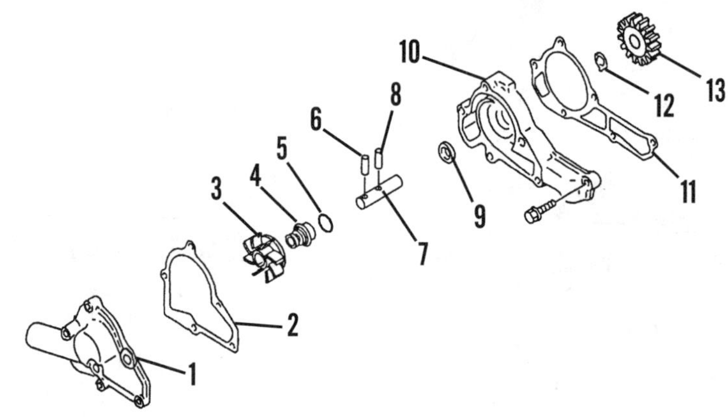

Fig. JD7-38–Exploded view of water pump used on Models 425 and 445.

1. Cover
2. Gasket
3. Impeller
4. Seal
5. O-ring
6. Pin
7. Shaft
8. Pin
9. Seal
10. Housing
11. Gasket
12. Washer
13. Gear

Water Pump (Models 425 and 445)

To remove the water pump, first drain the coolant. Disconnect the hoses from the pump. Unbolt and remove the pump assembly, noting the position and length of the cap screws.

Refer to Fig. JD7-38 for an exploded view of the water pump. Use a suitable puller to remove the pump drive gear (13). The impeller (3), shaft (7) and pin (6) are available as a unit assembly only. The minimum allowable diameter of shaft is 9.94 mm (0.391 in.). The maximum allowable diameter of housing bore is 10.09 mm (0.397 in.). Install the seal (4) using the driver provided in the seal kit.

When assembling the pump, coat the impeller (3) and seal (4) mating surfaces with clean water to provide lubrication. Install the pump. Tighten the 6 mm mounting screws to 8 N·m (71 in.-lb.) and 8 mm mounting screw to 21 N·m (186 in.-lb.).

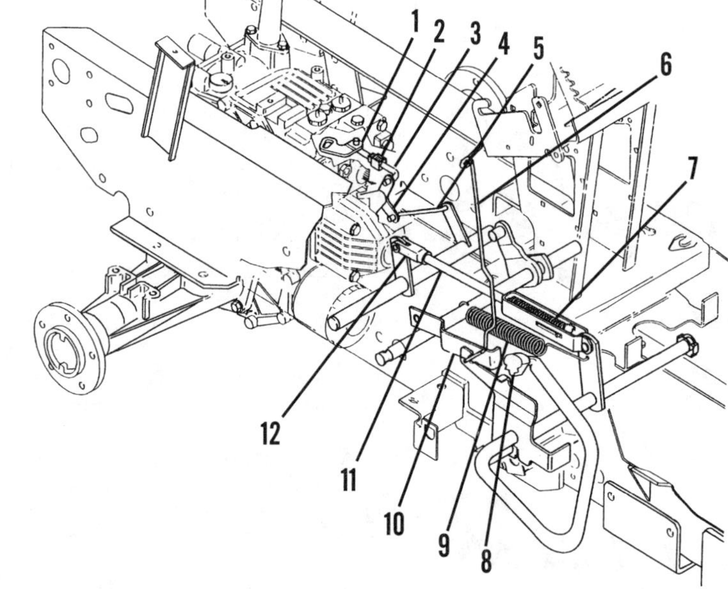

Fig. JD7-39–Drawing of brake linkage. Refer to text for brake adjustment.

1. Differential lock arm
2. Turnbuckle
3. Link
4. Brake arm
5. Brake link
6. Park brake rod
7. Brake spring
8. Brake pedal
9. Return spring
10. Park brake rod
11. Brake rod
12. Turnbuckle

BRAKES

All models are equipped with a disc brake contained in a compartment on the transaxle. Brake discs are located on the transaxle reduction shaft. When the brake pedal is depressed, brake linkage also actuates the differential lock mechanism so the axles are locked together to provide braking to both rear wheels.

ADJUSTMENT

Adjust differential lock linkage as follows: Disconnect the link (5—Fig. JD7-39) from the brake lever (4). Loosen jam nut on the turnbuckle (2). Pull the lower leg of the brake lever (4) to the front so the brake is engaged. Rotate the turnbuckle (3) so the differential lock arm (1) just contacts the differential lock shaft. Lengthen the turnbuckle by rotating $2\frac{1}{2}$ turns, then tighten the jam nut. Connect the link (5) to the brake lever (4). If the brake lever has two holes, place the link end in the higher hole.

Adjust brake linkage as follows: There should be no free play in the brake linkage with the pedal released. To adjust, disconnect the brake rod clevis (12) from the brake cross shaft. Rotate the clevis to remove free play in the linkage, but do not preload the brakes or excessive wear will result.

OVERHAUL

To gain access to the brake assembly, remove the transaxle as described in the TRANSAXLE section. An exploded view of the brake assembly is shown in Fig. JD7-40.

NOTE: Be prepared to catch loose balls (8) when removing cover (3).

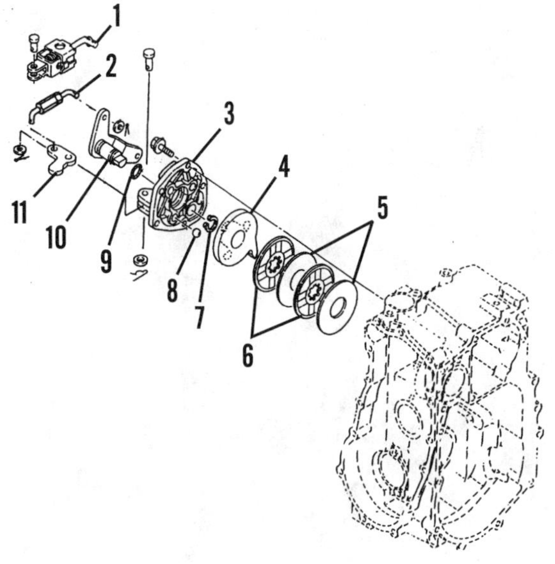

Fig. JD7-40–Exploded view of brake assembly.

1. Interlock linkage
2. Link
3. Brake cover
4. Actuator plate
5. Steel plate
6. Friction plates
7. Snap ring
8. Ball (3)
9. O-ring
10. Brake cam lever
11. Interlock arm

Disconnect the brake linkage (1 or 2). Unscrew the fasteners and remove the brake cover (3). Remove the actuator (4), brake discs (6) and plates (5). Detach the snap ring (7) and remove the brake lever (10) from the cover.

Inspect brake components for damage. Replace the brake discs (6) if the radial grooves are worn away.

Reassemble the brake by reversing the disassembly procedure. Lubricate the seal (9) before installing the brake lever. Use petroleum jelly to hold the balls (8) in the cover. Apply gasket-forming sealer to the mating surfaces of cover and transaxle. Tighten the cover screws to 25 N·m (221 in.-lb.) on a used transaxle case or to 30 N·m (22 ft.-lb.) on a new transaxle case.

HYDROSTATIC TRANSMISSION

MAINTENANCE

Periodically inspect the transmission for leakage. Oil for the transmission is routed from the oil sump in the final drive housing. A spin-on filter mounted on the final drive housing protects the hydrostatic transmission and other hydraulic components.

Refer to the FINAL DRIVE section for the oil change procedure. Change oil filter after first 50 hours of operation and every 200 hours thereafter.

SYSTEM OPERATION

The charge pump (6—Fig. JD7-41) mounted on the front of the hydrostatic transmission provides pressurized oil for the transmission, PTO, hydraulic lift and power steering systems. The hydraulic system uses oil contained in the final drive housing (1).

Oil from the housing sump passes through a filter (3), then to the charge pump. Pressurized oil in the charge pump passes through a flow control valve (7) blocking the outlet flow if the pressure falls below 1965 kPa (285 psi). When the flow control valve closes, oil must flow to the lube reduction valve (12) to insure lubricating oil will flow to the transmission. The lube reduction valve maintains the lubrication pressure at 586 kPa (85 psi) as well as directing oil to the PTO circuit (19). The implement relief valve (16) protects the system from the pressure exceeding 6371-7350 kPa (923-1065 psi).

Outlet oil from the charge pump travels to the power steering control valve and hydraulic lift circuits. Also refer to the POWER STEERING and HYDRAULIC LIFT sections.

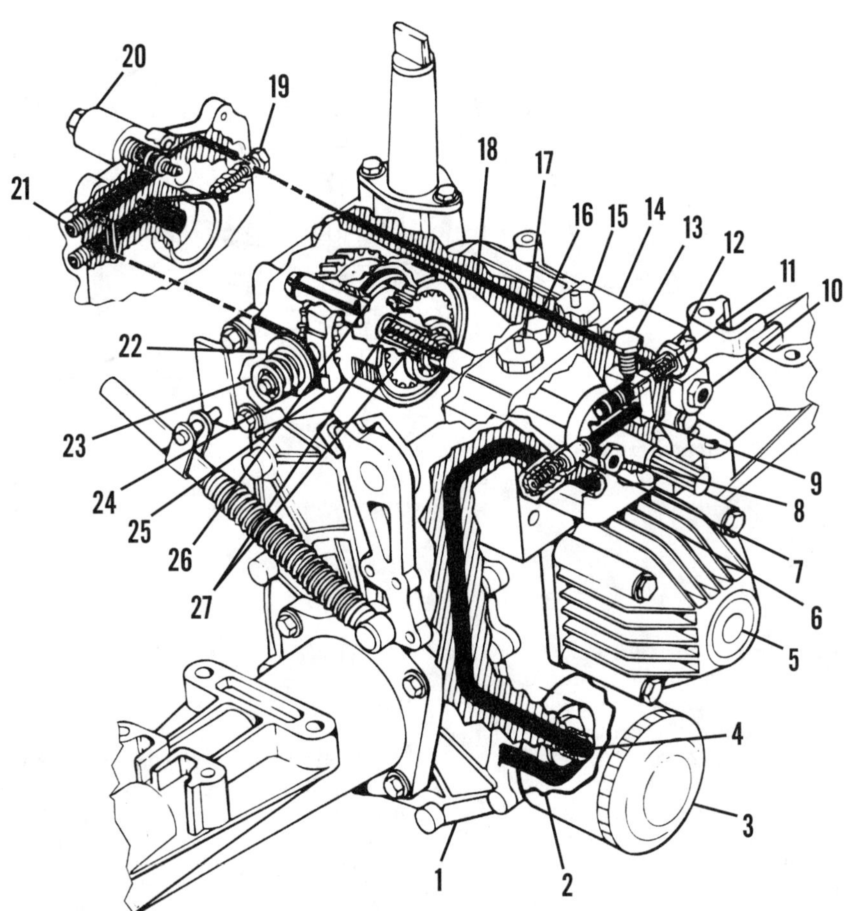

Fig. JD7-41–Drawing of hydrostatic drive showing fluid flow and location of components.

1. Transaxle case
2. Inlet from case
3. Filter
4. To charge pump
5. Hydrostatic motor
6. Charge pump
7. Charge pressure control valve
8. Outlet to steering
9. Lube passage.
10. Return from cooler
11. PTO flow orifice
12. Lube reduction valve
13. Charge pressure test port
14. Center section
15. Reverse directional valve
16. Implement relief valve
17. Forward directional valve
18. Passage to solenoid
19. PTO pressure control valve
20. PTO solenoid
21. Clutch & brake pressure test port
22. PTO brake
23. Brake spring
24. Brake piston
25. Brake shoe
26. Clutch piston
27. Clutch lube passage

Directional valves (15 and 17—Fig. JD7-41) in the valve block are check valves that open to allow pressurized oil from the charge pump to enter the hydrostatic transmission. Depressing the freewheeling pins on the directional valves unseats the check valves to vent oil pressure, thereby allowing the tractor to be pushed when the engine is stopped.

Anti-cavitation valves are located in the internal fluid passages of the transmission. The valves prevent motor cavitation by allowing the sump oil into the circuit when the motor is the driving element, such as when the freewheeling or traveling downhill.

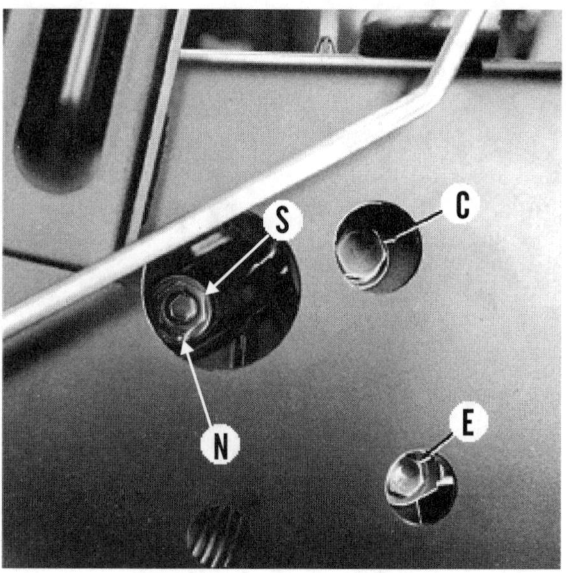

Fig. JD7-42–When adjusting transmission neutral position, loosen nut (N) and turn eccentric screw (S).

ADJUSTMENTS

Neutral Adjustment

Raise and block up the rear of the tractor so the wheels clear the ground. Start the engine and run at idle speed. With the transmission foot controls released, the rear wheels should not rotate.

NOTE: A cutout section of the frame on the tractor's right side provides access to the neutral adjustment screw.

If the wheels rotate, loosen the nut (N—Fig. JD7-42). Start the engine and run at idle speed. Rotate the eccentric screw (S) in one direction until the wheels just begin to turn, then rotate screw in the opposite direction until the wheels just begin to turn again. Position the screw at the midpoint, then tighten the nut (N). Run the engine at idle speed, and depress and release both the forward and reverse pedals. If the wheels rotate with the pedals released, repeat adjustment.

NOTE: If the eccentric screw (S) will not hold the adjustment, rotate the eccentric screw 180° and repeat adjustment.

If neutral adjustment is not possible, check for a faulty linkage, and if necessary, perform the adjustment with the linkage disconnected.

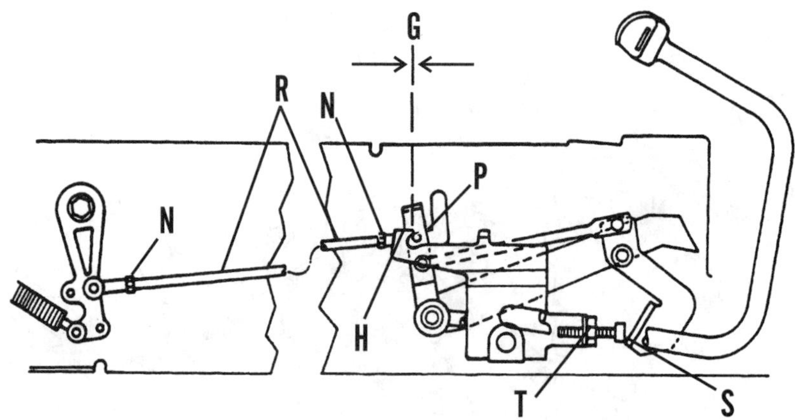

Fig. JD7-43–Refer to text for control linkage adjustment.

G. Gap
H. Hook
N. Nuts
P. Pin
R. Control rod
S. Screw
T. Nut

Control Linkage Adjustment

The transmission control linkage should be adjusted so the transmission returns to NEUTRAL and the control pedals are locked in NEUTRAL when the parking brake is set.

To adjust, first perform the transmission neutral adjustment as previously described. Loosen nuts (N—Fig. JD7-43) on the swash plate control rod. Fully depress the brake pedal. Looking from the inside right frame, measure the gap (G) between the hook (H) and pin (P). Rotate the control rod (R) so the gap is 1-2 mm (0.04-0.08 in.). Loosen the nut (T). With the brake pedal fully depressed, adjust the screw (S) so it just contacts the ramp on the neutral return linkage. Retighten the nuts.

Pedal Height Adjustment

The forward pedal height should be adjusted to insure the full travel speed can be attained. The pedal is threaded onto the top of the control rod. Loosen the jam nut and rotate the pedal on the rod so the pedal contacts the footrest panel when the control rod reaches the full down position.

TESTING

Flow Test

Attach a suitable thermometer to the spin-on filter to monitor the oil temperature. It may be necessary to block the airflow through the radiator to raise the oil temperature.

Remove the rear deck and move, but do not disconnect the fuel lines or fuel tank. Disconnect hydraulic lines from the charge pump and connect a flowmeter to the charge pump ports. Connect the flowmeter inlet to the charge pump outlet port (5—Fig. JD7-44) and the flowmeter outlet to the charge pump inlet (3). Check the oil flow with the engine running at full throttle and the oil temperature at 110° F (43° C). Normal oil flow is 17.0 L/m

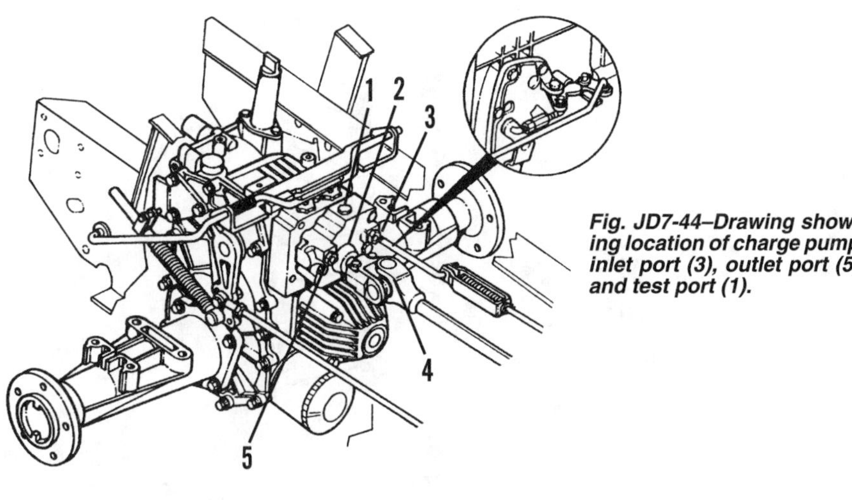

Fig. JD7-44–Drawing showing location of charge pump inlet port (3), outlet port (5) and test port (1).

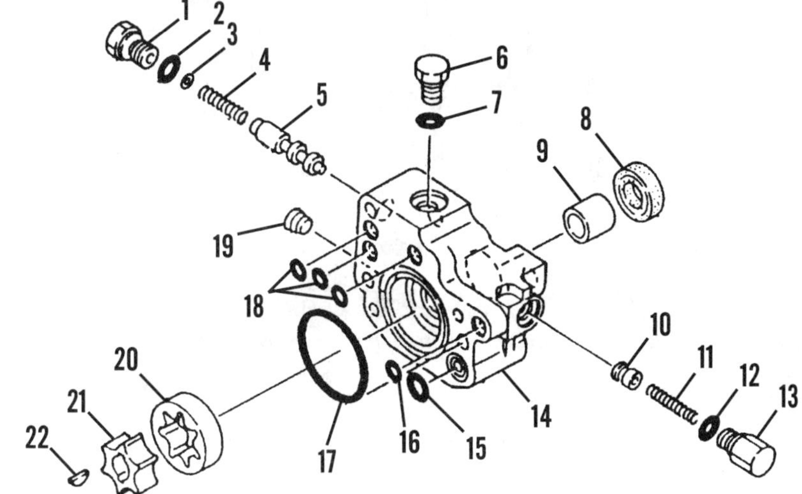

Fig. JD7-45–Exploded view of charge pump.

1. Lube reduction valve plug
2. Packing
3. Shim
4. Spring
5. Spool
6. Plug
7. O-ring
8. Seal
9. Bushing
10. Poppet valve
11. Spring
12. O-ring
13. Charge pressure control valve plug
14. Pump housing
15. Packing
16. Packing
17. Packing
18. Packing
19. Plug
20. Outer rotor
21. Inner rotor
22. Woodruff key

(4.5 gpm). The minimum allowable oil flow is 13.0 L/m (3.5 gpm).

NOTE: The flow test may be performed at the hydraulic couplers (see HYDRAULIC SYSTEM), but the results will not isolate the problems.

If the oil flow is nonexistent, check the following: the input shaft not turning; the charge pump drive key sheared; the charge pressure control valve stuck closed; plugged lube reduction valve modulation orifice.

If the oil flow is below specification, erratic or foamy, check the following: hydraulic oil level; restricted oil filter; plugged transaxle vent; leaking filter seal; oil ring at charge pump inlet; leakage between filter and charge pump in housing; loose dipstick or damaged O-ring; damaged or stuck open implement relief valve; faulty pump.

Pressure Test

Pressure may be tested either using a flowmeter connected as described in a previous flow test or with a pressure gauge. To check pressure with a pressure gauge, unscrew the plug (1—Fig. JD7-44) on top of the transmission and connect a suitable gauge to the port. An alternate method for checking the system pressure is described in the HYDRAULIC SYSTEM section.

Run the engine at full throttle. If using a pressure gauge, move the hydraulic lift control lever to the raise or lower position so the relief valve operates. Maximum pressure should be 6371-7350 kPa (924-1065 psi).

Inadequate pressure may indicate a maladjusted relief valve, faulty charge pump, plugged modulation orifice in the lube reduction valve, or excessive leakage in transmission pump.

CHARGE PUMP

Removal and Installation

The charge pump (2—Fig. JD7-44) may be removed without removing the transmission. Drain oil from the final drive housing. Remove the fuel tank. Thoroughly clean the charge pump and surrounding area to prevent dirt from entering the hydraulic system. Loosen the clamp screws at the rear of the drive shaft (4). Unscrew the retaining screws at the drive shaft's front end. Remove the drive shaft. Disconnect hydraulic lines from the charge pump.

NOTE: When removing the charge pump, be careful not to drop the pump components as they are easily damaged.

Unscrew the charge pump retaining screws and remove the pump from the transmission.

Install the charge pump by reversing the removal procedure. Be careful not to damage the oil seal or disturb the O-rings during installation. Tighten the short lower retaining screws to 25 N·m (221 in.-lb.) and the long upper retaining screw to 39 N·m (29 ft.-lb.).

Overhaul

Refer to Fig. JD7-45 for an exploded charge pump view. Remove the plug (1) and withdraw the pressure reducing valve spool (5), spring (4) and shim (3). Remove plug (13), spring (11) and charge pressure relief valve (10).

Inspect components for damage, including scratches, burrs and nicks. Replace the valve block if the block surface is scored. Be sure the small orifice in the lube reduction valve spool (5) is open. Lube reduction valve components are available only as a unit assembly. Pump rotors (20 and 21) and pump body (14) are available only as a unit assembly.

If the bushing (9) is removed, drive the bushing into the pump body until bottomed. Install the seal (8) into the bore with closed side out. Push the seal in until bottomed in the bore. Lubricate bushing and seal with clean hydraulic oil. Replace all O-rings (15-19).

MOTOR AND VALVE BLOCK

Overhaul

Remove the final drive from the tractor as described in a following section.

NOTE: When removing the charge pump, be careful not to drop pump components.

Unscrew the charge pump retaining screws and remove the pump from the transmission. Unscrew the three screws retaining the valve block, and remove the motor and valve block as a unit from the final drive case. Detach the snap ring and slide the pinion gear off the output shaft. Unscrew the motor retaining screws and separate motor from the valve block while being careful not to drop the valve plate (26—Fig. JD7-46).

Valve Block

Remove the directional check valves (1 and 3—Fig. JD7-46). The plunger pin and internal valve must move freely when the directional valves are shaken. Be sure the orifice (G) in the reverse check valve is open. Remove the implement relief valve components (12-19) and anticavitation valve assembly (27-34).

Thoroughly clean and inspect all components. Check the suction screen (27) for blockage. Note that the screen may be located in a bore in the transaxle housing. Inspect the surfaces of valve block (14) and valve plates (20 and 26) for scoring or scratches. When scratches can be detected by feel using a lead pencil or fingernail, the part must be replaced.

Directional check valves are similar but not identical. The reverse check valve (1) is identified by a small orifice (G) located in a land between the two valve passageways. The reverse check valve must be installed in the left port (marked "R") on the valve block.

Install needle bearings (21 and 24) with the stamped end out. The bearing must protrude 3 mm (0.12 in.) above the surface of the valve block.

Valve plates (20 and 26) are similar but not identical. The slotted ports on the pump valve plate (20) have feathering grooves into two ports. Feathering grooves are absent on motor valve plate. Replace either valve plate if damaged. When assembling, use petroleum jelly to hold the valve plate in position. Be sure the bronze surface faces away from the valve block and the locating pin in valve block engages the notch in valve plate.

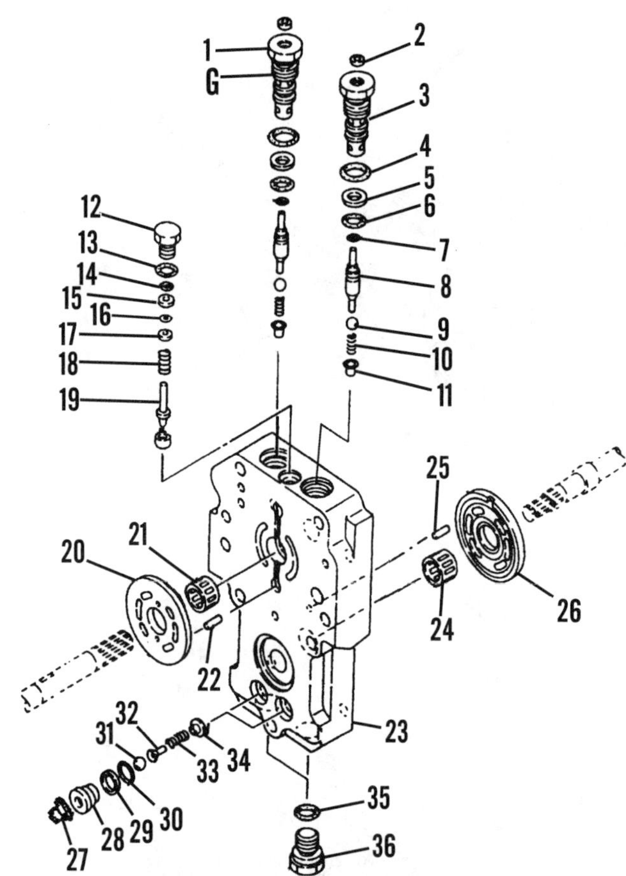

Fig. JD7-46–Exploded view of hydrostatic transmission valve block.

1. Directional valve (reverse)
2. Nut
3. Directional valve (forward)
4. O-ring
5. Backup ring
6. O-ring
7. Packing
8. Spool
9. Ball
10. Spring
11. Seat
12. Implement relief valve plug
13. O-ring
14. O-ring
15. Washer
16. Shims
17. Washer
18. Spring
19. Plunger
20. Valve plate
21. Bearing
22. Dowel pin
23. Valve block
24. Bearing
25. Dowel pin
26. Valve plate
27. Strainer
28. Anti-cavitation valve body
29. Backup ring
30. O-ring
31. Ball
32. Seat
33. Spring
34. Retainer
35. O-ring
36. Plug

Motor

Refer to Fig. JD7-47 when disassembling and reassembling the motor components. Mark the pistons (11) so they can be reinstalled in their original cylinder bores. Use care when removing the seal cap (24) to prevent damage to the bearing (22). Remove the snap ring (23) and withdraw the motor shaft (12).

Thoroughly clean and inspect the components. Check the machined surface of the cylinder block for scratches or grooves. The cylinder block must be replaced if scratches or grooves can be detected by feel. Check pistons for scoring or discoloration indicating overheating. The pistons must move freely in the cylinder bores.

NOTE: If any pistons (11) slide out of the cylinder, return them to their original bores.

Motor components (6-11) are available only as an assembly. Bushing (15), thrust washer (16) and housing (19) are available only as an assembly.

Reassemble Valve Block and Motor

When assembling the valve block and motor, note the following: Thoroughly lubricate components with clean transmission oil. Tighten direction check valves (1 and 3—Fig. JD7-46) to 35 N·m (26 ft.-lb.). Tighten bottom suction plug (36) to 50 N·m (37 ft.-lb.). Tighten implement relief valve plug (12) to 25 N·m (221 in.-lb.). Install the valve plates (20 and 26) on valve block using petroleum jelly to hold each in place. Position plate with bronze face out. The notch in the plate must fit around the pin on the valve block.

Apply gasket-forming sealer to the cap (24—Fig. JD7-47) and push the cap in until it is 4 mm (0.16 in.) below the

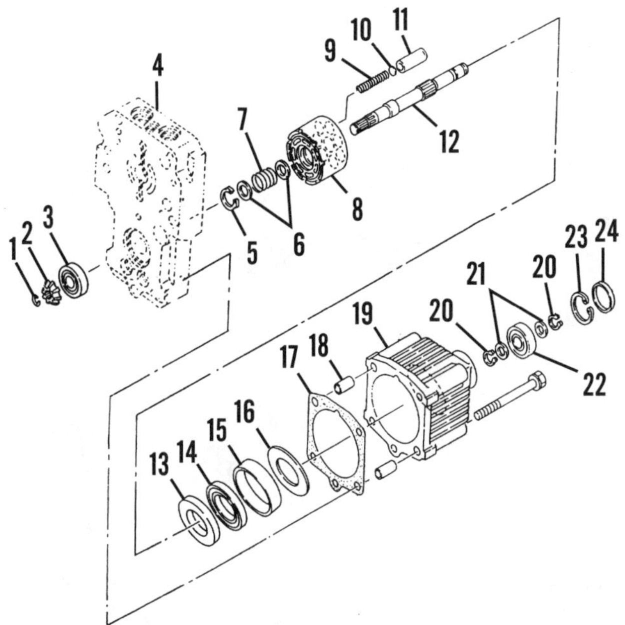

Fig. JD7-47–Exploded view of hydrostatic transmission motor.

1. Snap ring
2. Bevel pinion gear
3. Bearing
4. Valve block
5. Snap ring
6. Washers
7. Spring
8. Cylinder block
9. Spring
10. Shim
11. Piston
12. Shaft
13. Thrust plate (thick)
14. Thrust bearing
15. Bushing
16. Thrust plate (thin)
17. Gasket
18. Dowel pins
19. Motor housing
20. Snap ring
21. Washer
22. Bearing
23. Snap ring
24. Cap

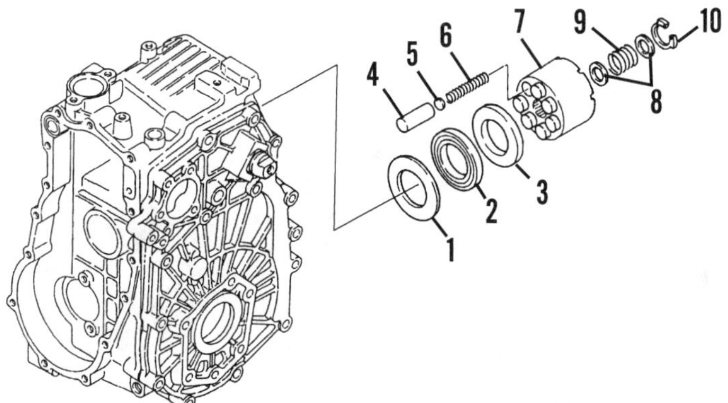

Fig. JD7-48–Exploded view of hydrostatic transmission pump.

1. Swashplate shaft
2. Thrust bearing
3. Thrust plate (thick)
4. Piston
5. Shim
6. Spring
7. Cylinder block
8. Washers
9. Spring
10. Snap ring

housing surface. Tighten the motor-to-valve block retaining screws to 39 N·m (29 ft.-lb.).

PUMP

Overhaul

The transmission pump is contained in a compartment in the final drive housing and rides on the input shaft. To remove the pump, remove the motor and valve block as described in the previous section. Remove the pump from the input shaft while being careful not to drop the pistons from the cylinder.

NOTE: If any pistons (4—Fig. JD7-48) slide out of the cylinder, return them to their original bores.

Refer to the FINAL DRIVE section to remove the swashplate and input shaft. Refer to Fig. JD7-48 when disassembling and reassembling pump components. Mark pistons so they can be reinstalled in their original cylinder bores.

Thoroughly clean and inspect components. Replace the pump assembly if scratches can be detected by feel on the machined surface of motor block. Pistons must move freely in cylinder block bores.

Pump components (4-9) are available only as an assembly.

FINAL DRIVE AND REAR AXLES

MAINTENANCE

The recommended oil is John Deere Low Viscosity Hy-Gard (J20D) transmission oil. Using other oils may cause chattering in the PTO or brake units. Oil capacity is 5.6 liter (6 qt.) for 2-wheel steering tractors and 6.6 liters (7 qt.) for 4-wheel steering tractors.

DRIVE SHAFT OVERHAUL

To remove the drive shaft, remove the fuel tank. Loosen clamp screws at the rear of the drive shaft. Unscrew the retaining screws at the front end of the drive shaft. Remove drive shaft.

Inspect for damage. The drive shaft and joint are available only as a unit assembly.

Reverse the removal procedure to reinstall the drive shaft. Install the front isolator plate so the bosses are toward the drive shaft.

REMOVAL AND INSTALLATION

To remove the final drive housing with axles, drain the transmission oil. Remove the rear fender and fuel tank. Disconnect the hydraulic lines from the charge pump. Loosen clamp screws at the rear of the drive shaft. Unscrew the retaining screws at the front end of the drive shaft. Remove drive shaft.

Remove the rear PTO shield and disconnect the rear PTO control rod. Disconnect the interfering electrical connectors. Remove the rear hitch plate. Disconnect the brake linkage and differential lock linkage. On 4-wheel steering models, disconnect the intermediate link connecting the rear steering arm to the rear pivot plate. Disconnect transmission control rod.

Support the rear of the tractor with suitable stands and remove the rear wheels. Disconnect the lift cylinder from the rockshaft. Remove the snap rings and bushings at each end of the rockshaft and remove the rockshaft. Support the final drive unit with a suitable hoist, unscrew the retaining screws at the axle housings and remove the unit.

Reinstall by reversing the removal procedure. Tighten the retaining screws to 88 N·m (65 ft.-lb.). Refill with transmission oil.

REAR AXLES OVERHAUL

2-Wheel-Steering Models

Remove the final drive housing and axles as previously described. Unscrew the axle housing retaining screws and separate the axle housing assembly from the final drive housing.

To remove the axle from the axle housing, detach the snap ring (2—Fig. JD7-49) from the axle housing. Press the axle assembly out of the axle housing. Detach the snap ring (8) and remove the bearings and spacers from the axle shaft.

To assemble the axle, install the bearing (6), seal (5) and snap ring (A) in the axle housing. Be sure the seal (5) is installed with the open side in. Apply petroleum jelly to the inside diameters of the seal and sleeve (4). Use a piece of pipe with the inside diameter that will fit over the axle shaft to push the washer (3) and sleeve (4) against shoulder on the shaft.

NOTE: Care must be used when pressing the axle into the housing to prevent damage to the housing.

Press the axle shaft into the housing. Install washer (7) and snap ring (8) on the axle shaft, using a piece of pipe to push them into place.

Apply gasket-forming sealer to the axle housing mating surface. Install the axle housing and tighten the retaining screws to 54 N·m (40 ft.-lb.).

4-Wheel-Steering Models

Remove the final drive housing and axles as previously described. Unscrew the steering pivot plate (2—Fig. JD7-50) from the axle housing. Disconnect the tie rod (3) from the steering arm (4). Unscrew the axle housing retaining screws and separate the axle housing assembly from the final drive housing.

Detach the steering arm (24—Fig. JD7-51) from the steering knuckle (18). Remove the upper kingpin (17) and separate the knuckle, hub and U-joint assembly from the axle. Inspect the bushing (3), bearing (4) and seal (5) for damage and replace when necessary.

To remove the axle (6) from the housing, remove the seal (10) and snap ring (8). Press the axle with the bearing out

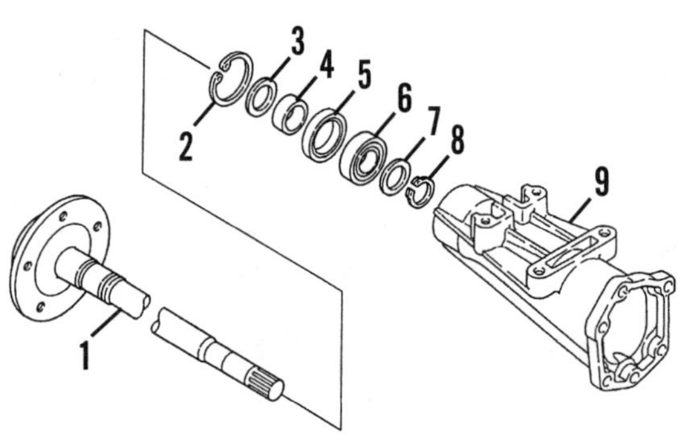

Fig. JD7-49–Exploded view of rear axle assembly used on 2-wheel-steering tractors.

1. Axle
2. Snap ring
3. Washer
4. Sleeve
5. Seal
6. Bearing
7. Washer
8. Snap ring
9. Axle housing

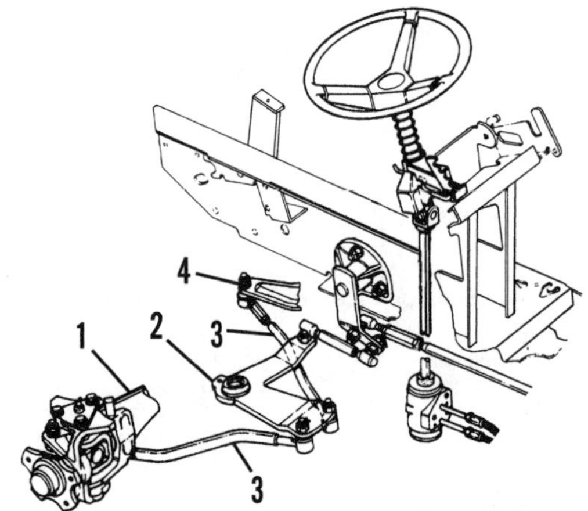

Fig. JD7-50–Drawing of steering linkage used for rear-wheel steering models

1. Axle housing
2. Rear steering pivot
3. Tie rod
4. Steering arm

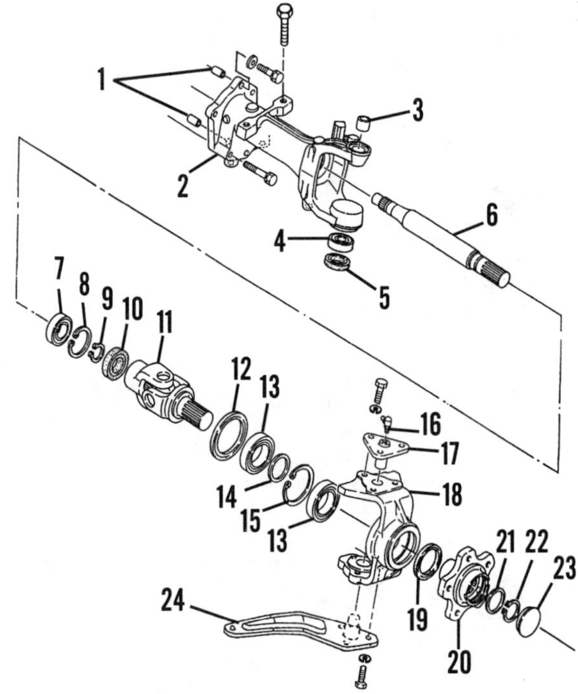

Fig. JD7-51–Exploded view of right rear axle assembly used on 4-wheel steering tractors. Left rear axle assembly is similar

1. Dowel pins
2. Axle housing
3. Bushing
4. Bearing
5. Seal
6. Axle
7. Bearing
8. Snap ring
9. Snap ring
10. Seal
11. Universal joint
12. Seal
13. Bearing
14. Washer
15. Snap ring
16. Grease fitting
17. King pin
18. Steering knuckle
19. Seal
20. Hub
21. Washer
22. Snap ring
23. Cap
24. Steering arm

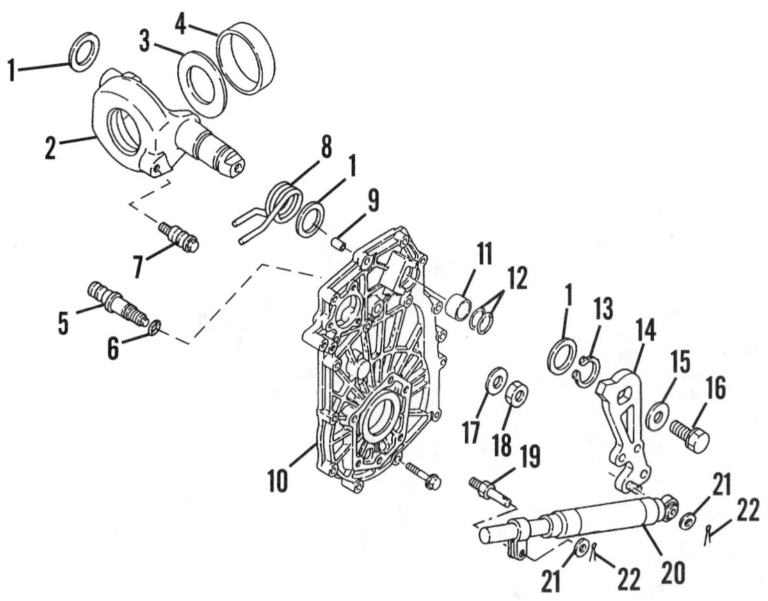

Fig. JD7-52–Exploded view of final drive right cover assembly.

1. Washer
2. Swashplate
3. Thrust plate
4. Bushing
5. Eccentric adjust fulcrum
6. O-ring
7. Fulcrum screw
8. Spring
9. Dowel pin
10. Cover
11. Bushing
12. O-rings
13. Snap ring
14. Control arm
15. Washer
16. Screw
17. Washer
18. Nut
19. Stud
20. Damper
21. Washer
22. Cotter pin

of the housing. Reverse the procedure to install the axle in the housing. Install the seal (10) with the open side toward the bearing (7).

To disassemble the hub and knuckle assembly, remove the seal cap (23—Fig. JD7-51). Detach the snap ring (22) and remove the universal joint (11). Remove the outer seal (19). Remove the inner seal (12), bearing (13), snap ring (15) and bearing (13).

Thoroughly clean all parts and inspect for damage.

To assemble, push the bearing (4) into its bore until bottomed. Install the seal (5) with the open side out. Push the bushing (3) into the bore until flush with the surface. Lubricate the bushing with multipurpose grease.

When assembling the knuckle and hub, push the outer bearing (13) in until bottomed in the knuckle. Fill the bearing cavity with multipurpose grease. Force the spacer (14) and inner bearing (13) against the outer bearing. Install seals (12 and 19) with the open side in. Push the seal (19) in until flush with the surface. Push the seal (12) in until bottomed. Install the wheel hub (20) in the knuckle housing. Apply grease to the splines on the universal joint shaft, then slide it into the knuckle housing. Install the washer (21), snap ring (22) and seal cap (23).

Apply Loctite to the kingpin (17) and steering arm (24) retaining screws. Tighten screws to 54 N·m (40 ft.-lb.). Inject multipurpose grease into the kingpin fitting until grease appears at the upper joint.

Reverse the removal procedure to install the axle housing. Apply gasket-forming sealer to the axle housing mating surface. Note that three lower axle housing retaining screws are longer than the upper screws. Tighten axle housing retaining screws to 54 N·m (40 ft.-lb.).

FINAL DRIVE OVERHAUL

Remove the final drive and axles as previously described. Remove the brake, axle housings, PTO brake, PTO clutch, PTO gears and hydrostatic transmission as described in related sections. Remove the control damper (20—Fig. JD7-52).

Remove the snap ring (17—Fig. JD7-53), then remove the input shaft (14) and bearing (18). Position the final drive housing on its left side, then remove the right cover (10—Fig. JD7-52) assembly. Lift the differential assembly (42-49—Fig. JD7-53) and differential lock shaft (37) as an assembly from the housing (7). Remove the bevel pinion shaft (29) and gear (26).

NOTE: Carefully disassemble the differential fork shaft assembly. Spring (35) is compressed.

Use a suitable puller to remove the bearing (42) from the differential case (44). Unscrew the differential case cap screws and remove the case, differential gears (46 and 49) and pinion gears (47).

Inspect components for damage. The swashplate (2—Fig. JD7-52), washer (3) and bushing (4) are available only as an assembly. The bevel gears (26 and 28—Fig. JD7-53) are available only as a set. Gear shaft (29) and ring gear (45) are available only as a set.

Note the following during assembly: The shallow side of the ring gear (45) must contact the differential case (44). The notched side gear (46) fits in the differential case. Install the differential lock fork (33) so the long end of the hub points toward the spring (35). Install bushing (11—Fig. JD7-52) so the end is flush with the inside cover surface. Position the spring (8) on the swashplate shaft so the spring ends are crossed and the spring ends fit the grooves on the eccentric stud (7). Install the seal (12—Fig. JD7-53) with the open side facing in.

Apply gasket-forming sealer to the cover and housing mating surfaces. Be sure all components remain in place when positioning the cover on the housing. Tighten the cover screws to 25 N·m (221 in.-lb.) on a used housing or to 30 N·m (22 ft.-lb.) on a new housing.

POWER TAKE-OFF (PTO)

All models are equipped with a power-take-off that uses a multiple disc, hydraulically actuated clutch to engage the PTO drive train. The PTO shaft extends forward on the final drive housing underside to connect with the mower drive. The PTO clutch transfers power from the hydrostatic transmission input shaft to the PTO drive train. A hydraulically actuated brake prevents PTO movement when the PTO is disengaged.

All models may be equipped with a 540 rpm PTO in addition to the standard PTO. The 540 rpm PTO coupler points to the rear of the tractor and derives power from the standard PTO drive train. A selector fork directs power to the standard PTO, 540 rpm PTO or both.

HYDRAULIC CIRCUIT

Operation

A small orifice in the hydrostatic transmission lube reduction valve routes oil to the PTO hydraulic circuit. A pressure control valve maintains cir-

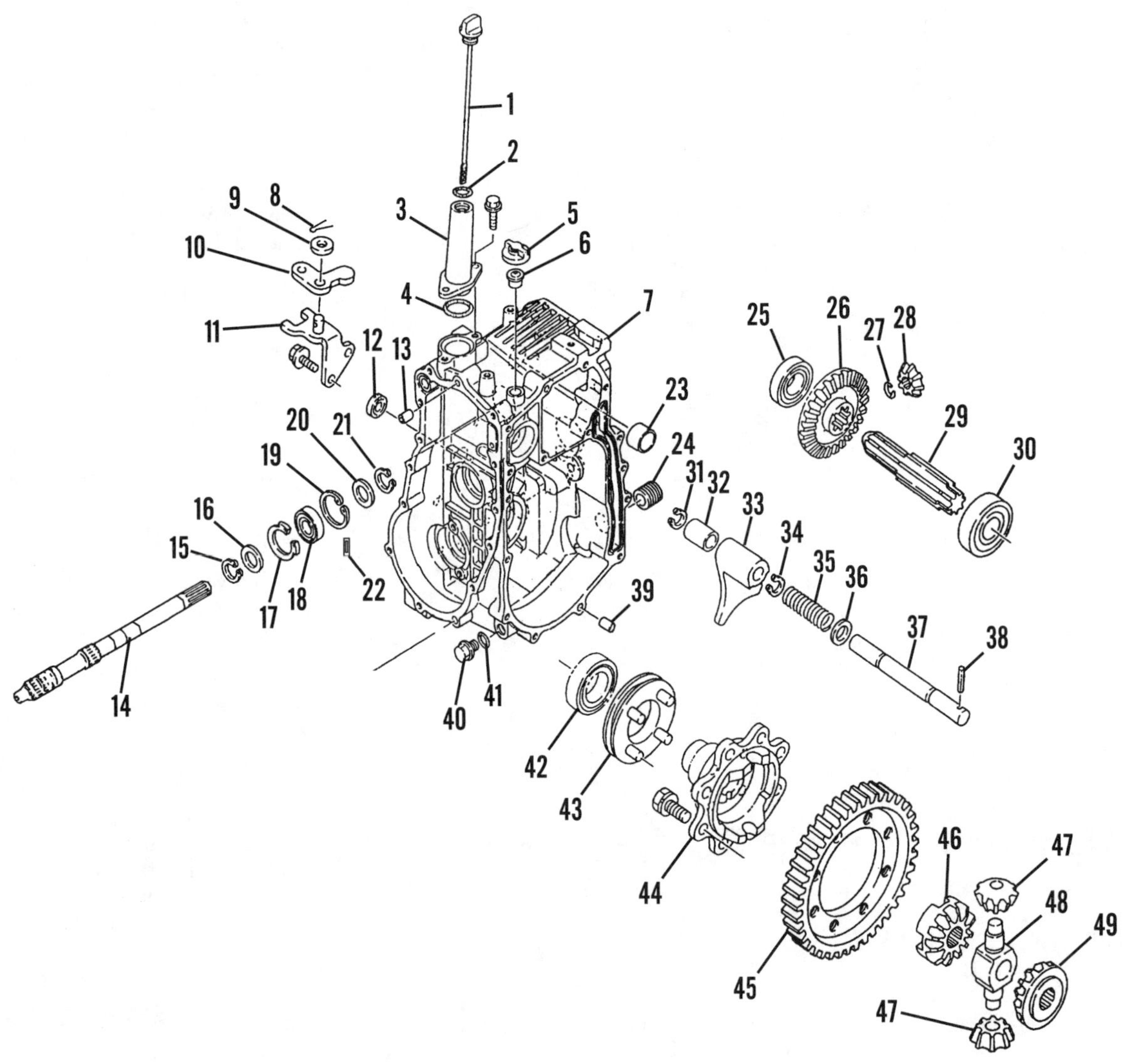

Fig. JD7-53–Exploded view of final drive.

1. Dipstick	10. Lever	19. Snap ring	28. Bevel pinion gear	36. Washer	44. Differential case
2. O-ring	11. Bracket	20. Washer	29. Pinion shaft	37. Shaft	45. Ring gear
3. Tube	12. Seal	21. Snap ring	30. Bearing	38. Roll pin	46. Notched side gear
4. O-ring	13. Dowel pin	22. Packing	31. Snap ring	39. Dowel pin	47. Pinion gear
5. Cap	14. Input shaft	23. Bushing	32. Sleeve	40. Drain plug	48. Pinion shaft
6. Vent	15. Snap ring	24. Oil filter adapter	33. Differential lock fork	41. O-ring	49. Side gear
7. Housing	16. Washer	25. Bearing	34. Snap ring	42. Bearing	
8. Cotter pin	17. Snap ring	26. Bevel gear	35. Spring	43. Differential lock collar	
9. Washer	18. Bearing	27. Snap ring			

cuit pressure. An electrically controlled solenoid controls oil flow to the PTO clutch and PTO brake. Oil pressure engages the PTO clutch while simultaneously releasing the PTO brake. A drop in oil pressure disengages the clutch and allows the brake spring to actuate the brake.

Testing

To check pto circuit pressure, unscrew plug (6A—Fig. JD7-54) from the upper right-hand port on the transaxle case and connect a suitable gauge to the port. With the brake engaged and the operator sitting on the seat, run the engine at wide-open throttle and actuate the PTO switch. The gauge should read 1420-1517 kPa (206-220 psi).

If the gauge indicates the specified pressure, but the clutch malfunctions, check the clutch assembly.

If the gauge indicates no pressure or low pressure, remove the plug (6B—Fig. JD7-54) and check the pressure at that port. If the pressure is higher at the port (B), check the operation of the solenoid control valve. If the pressure is low at both ports, check the pressure control valve. Also check the charge pump pressure and flow as described in the HYDROSTATIC TRANSMISSION section.

ELECTRICAL CIRCUIT

Hydraulic power to the PTO clutch is controlled by an electrical solenoid. The electrical circuit includes the seat switch, ignition relay and PTO relay, which interrupt the current flow to the PTO switch and stop the PTO if the operator leaves the seat while the PTO is engaged. The circuit also includes a brake switch that will disconnect the circuit and stop the PTO when the brake pedal is depressed.

Prior to engaging the PTO, the operator must be in the seat, the PTO switch must be OFF and the brake pedal must be released. To engage the PTO, turn

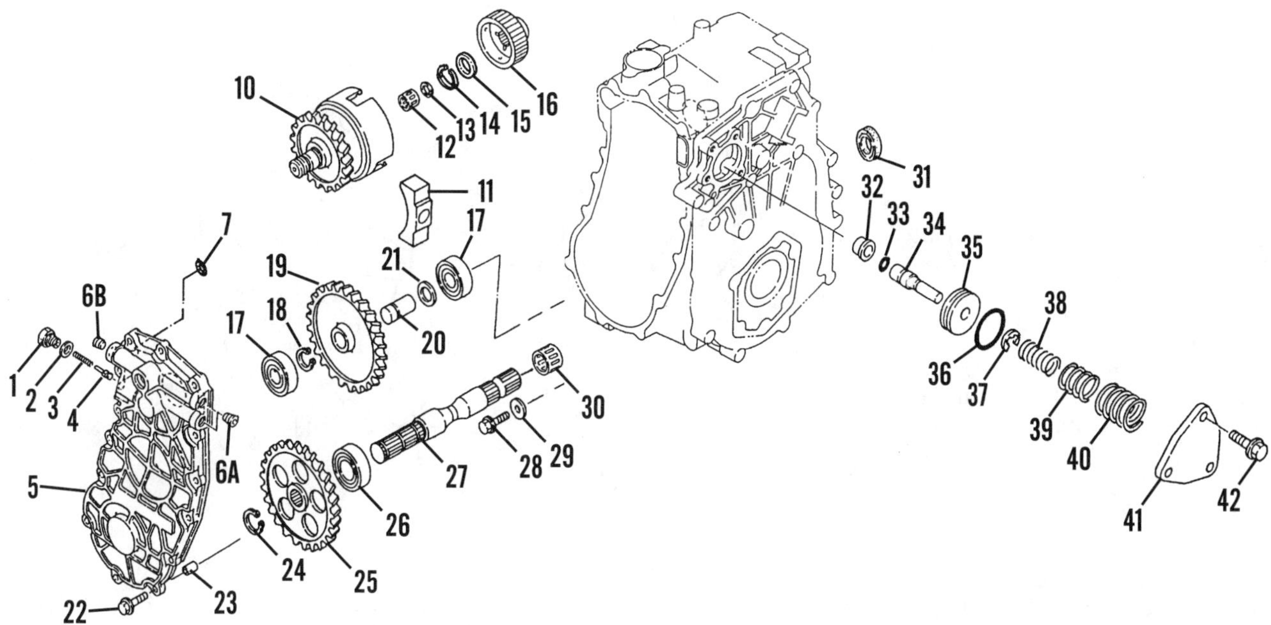

Fig. JD7-54–Exploded view of PTO brake and drive train. Refer to Fig. JD7-56 for exploded view of PTO clutch.

1. Relief valve
2. Gasket
3. Spring
4. Plunger
5. Cover
6A. Plug
6B. Plug
7. O-ring
10. Clutch assy.
11. Brake shoe
12. Bearing
13. Washer
14. Snap ring
15. Washer
16. Drive hub
17. Bearing
18. Snap ring
19. Gear
20. Shaft
21. Washer
22. Screw
23. Dowel pin
24. Snap ring
25. Gear
26. Bearing
27. PTO shaft
28. Screw
29. Washer
30. Bearing
31. Seal
32. Bushing
33. O-ring
34. Shaft
35. Piston
36. O-ring
37. Snap ring
38. Spring
39. Spring
40. Spring
41. Cover
42. Screw

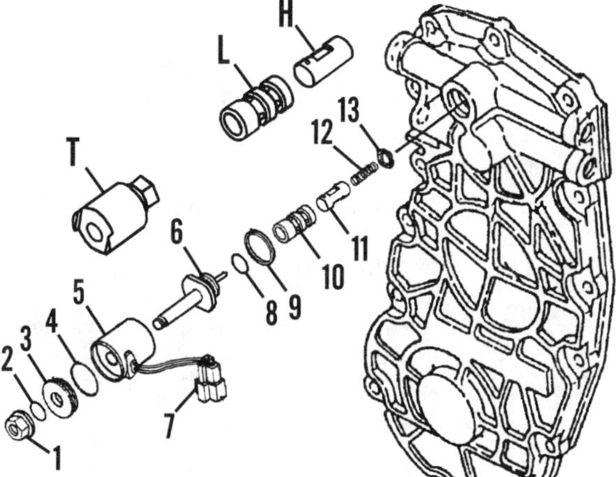

Fig. JD7-55–Exploded view of PTO solenoid valve. Assemble spool and sleeve with small hole (H) in spool toward large land (L) end of sleeve.

1. Nut
2. O-ring
3. Cover
4. O-ring
5. Solenoid coil
6. Solenoid armature
7. Electrical connector
8. O-ring
9. Gasket
10. Sleeve
11. Valve spool
12. Spring
13. Wave washer

the key switch to RUN, then turn the PTO switch ON.

When current is available to the PTO relay, an LED lights on the control/fuse module (see the ELECTRICAL SYSTEM section).

Also refer to the wiring schematic at the end of this section.

PTO Solenoid

To test the solenoid, detach the electrical connector (7—Fig. JD7-55). Connect an ohmmeter to the solenoid connector. The ohmmeter should indicate a maximum resistance of 0.1 ohms.

To remove the solenoid, disconnect the wiring connector (7) and unscrew the nut (1). Remove the solenoid cover (3) and coil (5). Be careful not to bend, twist or damage the solenoid armature (6), sleeve (10) or spool (11). A special socket tool JDG757A (T) is available for removing the solenoid armature assembly.

Clean and inspect parts for damage. The PTO may not function or function erratically if the spool, sleeve or armature is damaged. The solenoid coil (5) and armature (6) and the solenoid valve (10 and 11) are available only as assemblies.

When assembling, be sure the wave washer (13—Fig. JD7-55) is installed in the bottom of the bore in the PTO cover. Insert the spool (11) into the sleeve (10) so the end of the spool with the small hole (H) is toward the large land (L) on the sleeve. Install the sleeve (10) with the spool and spring (12) into the cover so the end of the sleeve with the smaller lands goes in first. Use a JDG757A socket tool to tighten the solenoid armature (6) to 22 N·m (195 in.-lb.). Position the solenoid coil onto the armature so the coil leads are facing towards the right side of the transaxle case cover.

NOTE: Tighten the plastic nut (1) to EXACTLY 4.9 N·m (43 in.-lb.). Overtightening the nut will damage the armature and/or coil.

PTO Relay

The PTO relay is part of the control/fuse module (see ELECTRICAL SYSTEM section). If the voltage checks indicate the PTO relay is faulty, the control/fuse module must be replaced.

PTO BRAKE OVERHAUL

Both the brake and the PTO clutch must be removed due to engagement of the brake shoe with the PTO clutch. Drain oil from the final drive housing. Remove the rear fender and fuel tank. Remove the rear hitch plate. Disconnect the electrical connector from the PTO solenoid on the rear cover. On models with 540 rpm PTO, remove the rear PTO assembly as described in the 540 RPM PTO section. On models without a 540 rpm PTO, remove the rear cover (5—Fig. JD7-54).

NOTE: The cover (41) is spring-loaded by brake springs.

Unscrew the brake cover (41) screws evenly to release spring tension on the cover. Remove brake components (32-40). Remove the PTO clutch (10) with the brake shoe (11). Be careful not to lose the needle bearing and washer on the input shaft.

Inspect components for damage. Check the piston (35) and rod (34) for scoring and burrs. Replace the brake shoe if the grooves on the contact surface are worn smooth. Piston, rod and springs are available only as a unit.

Reverse the disassembly procedure to reassemble the brake. Apply gasket-forming sealer to the cover and housing mating surfaces. Before tightening the screws, be sure the brake cover is properly aligned. Tighten the cover screws evenly to prevent cocking. Tighten brake cover screws to 25 N·m (18 ft.-lb.) on a used housing or to 30 N·m (22 ft.-lb.) on a new housing.

PTO CLUTCH AND GEARS OVERHAUL

Models Without 540 rpm PTO

Both the brake and PTO clutch must be removed due to engagement of the brake shoe with the PTO clutch. Remove the PTO brake, as well as the PTO clutch (10—Fig. JD7-54), as described in the PTO BRAKE section. Remove the PTO idler gear assembly (17-21) and PTO gear (25).

NOTE: Left axle passes over the necked section of the PTO output shaft (27). Remove the left axle before withdrawing the output shaft from the housing.

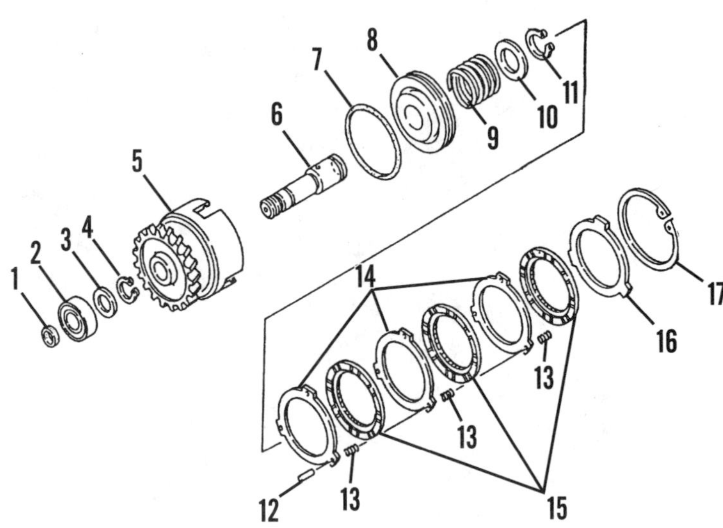

Fig. JD7-56–Exploded view of PTO clutch.

1. Seal ring
2. Bearing
3. Washer
4. Snap ring
5. Clutch housing
6. Shaft
7. O-ring
8. Piston
9. Spring
10. Washer
11. Snap ring
12. Pin (3)
13. Spring (9)
14. Steel plates
15. Friction plates
16. Steel plate (thick)
17. Snap ring

Inspect components for damage. The idler (19) and shaft (20) are available only as a unit.

Push against the lettered end of the bearing (30) during installation. Install the seal (31) with the open side toward the inside of the housing. Install the gear (25) with the wide side of the hub toward the bearing (26).

Refer to Fig. JD7-56 for an exploded view of the clutch assembly. To disassemble the clutch, detach the snap ring (17), then remove the clutch plates. Use a suitable compressor to compress the spring (9), then detach the snap ring (11) and remove the remainder of the clutch components. To measure the clutch plate wear, place the clutch discs (14, 15 and 16) and snap ring (17) in the clutch housing (5). Position the clutch housing on a flat surface so the gear end is up. Measure the gap between the top clutch plate and closed end of the slot in the side of the housing as shown in Fig. JD7-57. Replace the clutch plates if the gap is 2.7 mm (0.10 in.) or more. The clutch plate components (12-16—Fig. JD7-56) are only available as a set.

Apply gasket-forming sealer to the cover and housing mating surfaces. Be sure all components fit properly in the housing and rear cover before tightening the cover retaining screws. Tighten the rear cover screws to 25 N·m (18 ft.-lb.) on a used housing or to 30 N·m (22 ft.-lb.) on a new housing.

Models With 540 rpm PTO

The tractor may be equipped with a manually operated 540 rpm PTO mounted on the final drive housing rear cover. A shift collar selects the power flow to the front PTO, 540 rpm PTO or both.

Fig. JD7-57–Measure gap between top clutch and closed end of slot in side of PTO housing. Replace clutch plates if gap is 2.7 mm (0.10 in.) or more.

Drain oil from the final drive housing. Remove the rear fender and fuel tank. Disconnect the PTO manual control rod. Remove the rear hitch plate. Disconnect the electrical connectors from PTO solenoid and switches. Remove the final drive rear cover (47—Fig. JD7-58), on which the 540 PTO unit is mounted.

NOTE: Four long screws around the 540 PTO cover (30) also secure the rear cover to the final drive housing.

Remove the PTO cover (30). Refer to Fig. JD7-58 and disassemble as needed. Note the detent ball (39) is spring-loaded and will be free when the shift fork (41) is removed from the shift

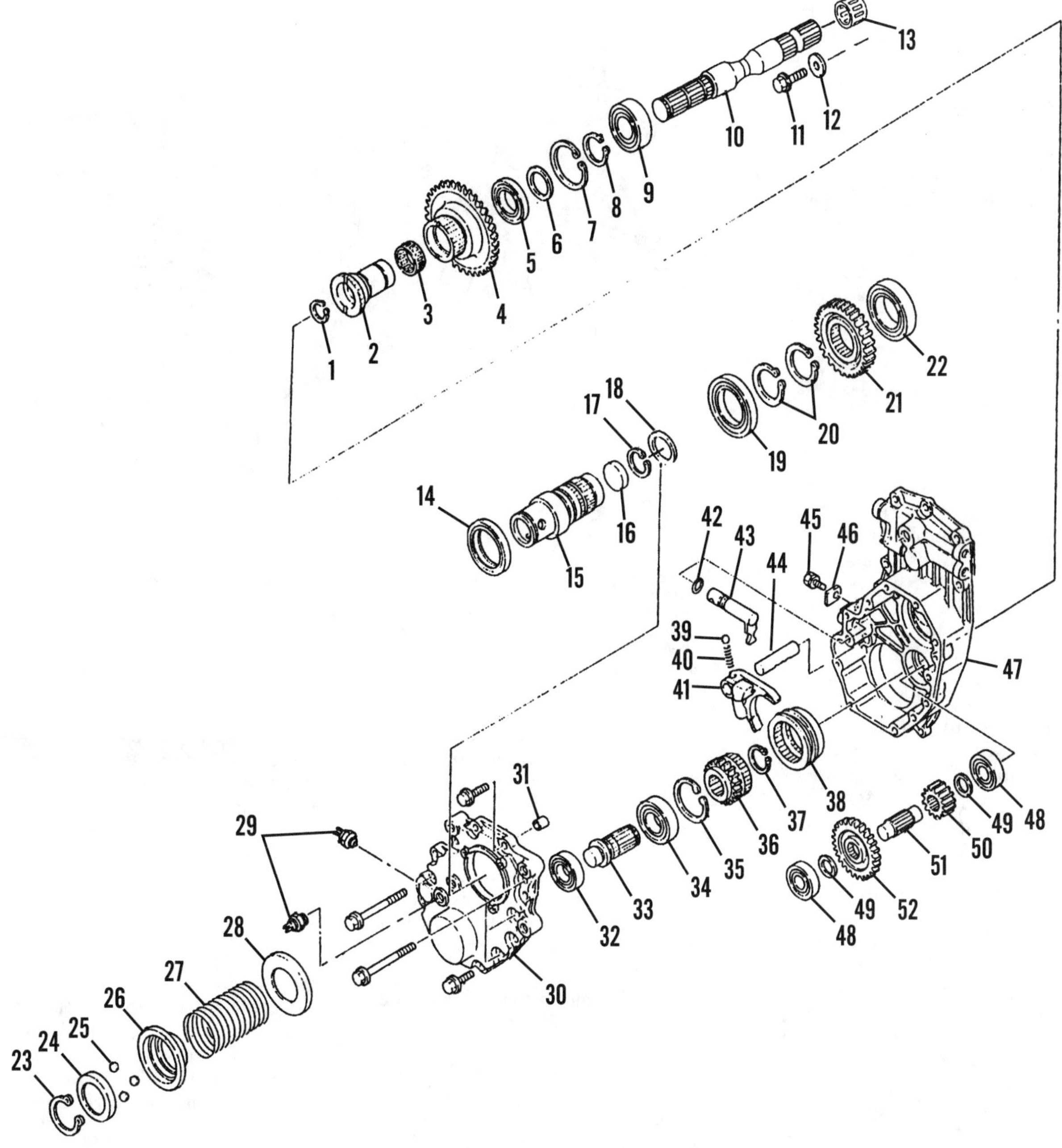

Fig. JD7-58–Exploded view of 540-rpm PTO assembly.

1. Snap ring
2. Splined sleeve
3. Bearing
4. Gear
5. Bearing
6. Spacer
7. Snap ring
8. Snap ring
9. Bearing
10. Front PTO shaft
11. Screw
12. Washer
13. Bearing
14. Seal
15. Coupler
16. Cap
17. Snap ring
18. Washer
19. Ball bearing
20. Snap ring
21. Gear
22. Bearing
23. Snap ring
24. Washer
25. Balls (3)
26. Bushing
27. Spring
28. Washer
29. Switches
30. Cover
31. Bushing
32. Bearing
33. Shaft
34. Bearing
35. Snap ring
36. Gear
37. Snap ring
38. Shift collar
39. Detent ball
40. Spring
41. Shift fork
42. O-ring
43. Shift lever
44. Shaft
45. Screw
46. Plate
47. Housing
48. Bearing
49. Washer
50. Gear
51. Shaft
52. Gear

shaft (44). The PTO clutch and remaining PTO drive components are the same as used on units not equipped with a 540 rpm PTO. Refer to the previous section.

Inspect components for damage. The rear PTO input gear (36), shift collar (38) and PTO idler gear (50) are serviced as a set. The rear PTO gear (21) and PTO idler pinion (52) are available only as a set.

Install the shift collar (38) so the end with the outer groove will be toward the cover (30). Be sure the detent ball (39) properly engages the grooves on the shift shaft (44). Install the seal (14) with the open side toward the inside of the cover (30). Push the bearings (32 and 34) against the shoulder on the shaft (33). Install the gear (21) so the wide side of the hub is toward the bearing (22).

Apply gasket-forming sealer to the mating surfaces of the PTO cover (30) and the final drive housing cover (47). Be sure all components fit properly in the housing and cover before tightening the cover retaining screws. Tighten the rear cover screws to 25 N·m (18 ft.-lb.) on a used housing or to 30 N·m (22 ft.-lb.) on a new housing.

Apply gasket-forming sealer to the final drive housing and housing cover (47) mating surfaces. Be sure all components fit properly in the housing and cover before tightening cover retaining screws. Tighten screws to 25 N·m (221 in.-lb.) on a used housing or to 30 N·m (22 ft.-lb.) on a new housing.

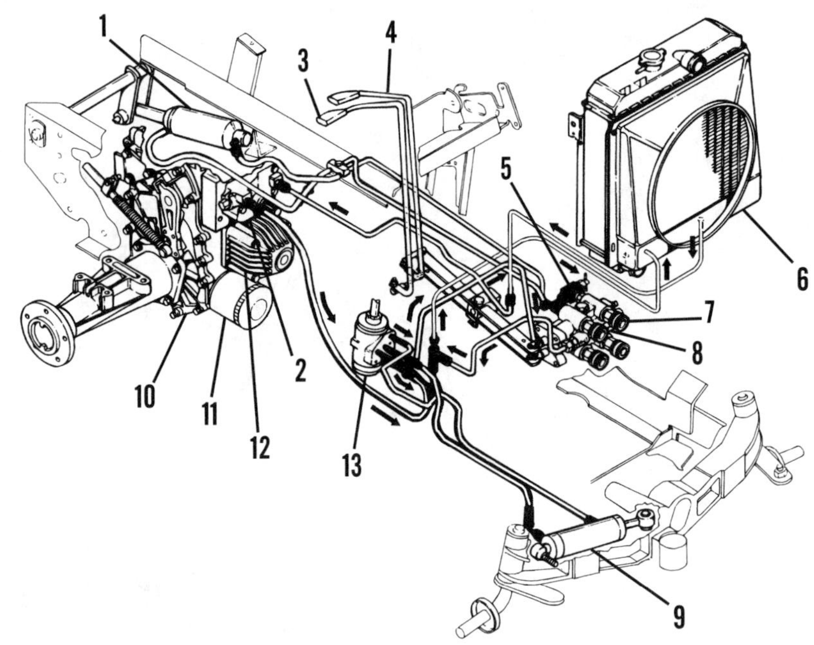

Fig. JD7-59–Diagram showing hydraulic system components and hydraulic oil flow.

1. Lift cylinder
2. Charge pump
3. Auxiliary control lever
4. Lift control lever
5. Shutoff valve
6. Radiator/oil cooler
7. Hydraulic couplers
8. Lift control valve
9. Power steering cylinder
10. Final drive
11. Oil filer
12. Hydrostatic transmission
13. Power steering control valve

HYDRAULIC SYSTEM

SYSTEM OPERATION

All models are equipped with a hydraulic system shown in Fig. JD7-59. The charge pump mounted on the front of the hydrostatic transmission provides pressurized oil for the transmission, PTO, hydraulic lift and power steering systems. The hydraulic system uses oil contained in the final drive housing. Oil from the housing sump passes through a filter, then to the charge pump. Pressurized oil from the charge pump travels internally to the transmission and PTO. An implement relief valve on top of the transmission valve block protects the system from excessive pressure.

Outlet oil from the charge pump travels to the power steering control valve and hydraulic lift circuits. Hydraulic oil at the control valve may be directed to operate the hydraulic lift cylinder or to power accessories through hydraulic couplers. Return oil from the steering valve and hydraulic control valve passes through an oil cooler in the radiator. Some models are equipped with a shutoff valve isolating the lift cylinder circuit for more positive action from accessories connected to hydraulic couplers.

Also refer to the POWER STEERING and TRANSMISSION sections.

TESTING

Pressure Testing

To check system pressure, connect a pressure gauge to a hydraulic coupler. Run the engine at full throttle. Move the hydraulic lift control lever to raise or lower the position so the relief valve operates. Maximum pressure should be 6371-7350 kPa (924-1065 psi).

Inadequate pressure may indicate a maladjusted relief valve, faulty charge pump, plugged modulation orifice in lube reduction valve, or excessive leakage in transmission pump. Refer to the TRANSMISSION section and perform charge pump tests.

Flow Test

Attach a suitable thermometer to the spin-on filter to monitor oil temperature. It may be necessary to block the airflow through the radiator to raise oil temperature.

Connect a flowmeter to the hydraulic couplers. Check the oil flow with the engine running at full throttle and oil temperature at 110° F (43° C). Move the hydraulic control lever to raise or lower position to obtain proper oil flow direction on gauge. Normal oil flow is 17.0 L/m (4.5 gpm). The minimum allowable oil flow is 13.0 L/m (3.5 gpm).

Note the test does not isolate the specific problem, which may be in the charge pump, power steering or hydraulic lift circuit.

HYDRAULIC CONTROL VALVE

Leak Test

To check the control valve for leakage, operate unit until oil reaches normal temperature. Operate the hydraulic control lever to fully extend the piston rod (raise position), then stop the engine. Disconnect the return hydraulic line from the control valve. Hold the lift control valve in raise position and start engine.

NOTE: Do not move the hydraulic control lever to neutral with the engine running because full hydraulic flow will discharge from control valve port.

There should be no more than a drip from the control valve port. Reconnect the return line.

Operate the hydraulic control lever to fully retract the piston rod (lower position), then stop engine. Disconnect the return hydraulic line from the control valve. Hold the lift control valve in the lower position and start engine.

NOTE: Do not move the hydraulic control lever to NEUTRAL with the engine running because the full hydraulic flow will discharge from the control valve port.

There should be no more than a drip from the control valve port. Reconnect return line.

Replace the control valve if leakage is excessive in either test.

Overhaul

Remove the radiator as previously described. Remove the footrest/console panel. Detach and remove the control valve (8—Fig. JD7-59). Rotate the valve as necessary to disconnect the

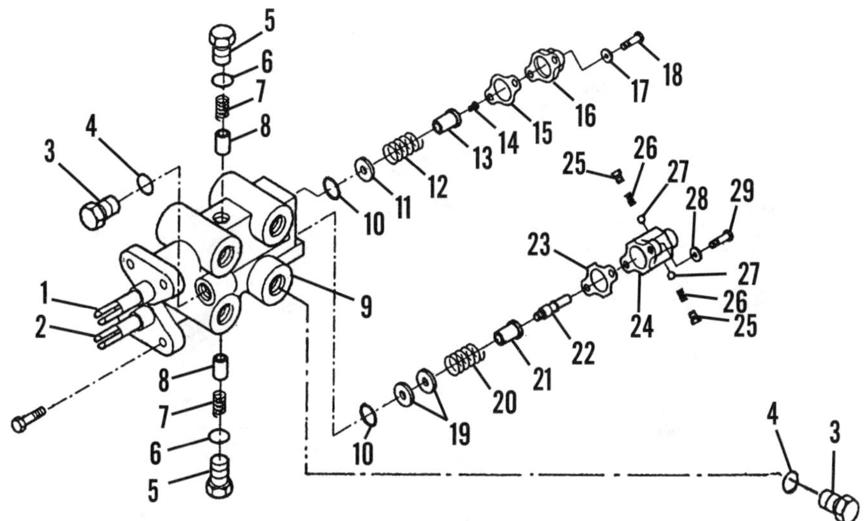

Fig. JD7-60–Exploded view of selective control valve.

1. Lift spool
2. Auxiliary spool
3. Plug
4. O-ring
5. Check valve cap
6. O-ring
7. Spring
8. Poppet
9. Housing
10. O-ring
11. Washer
12. Spring
13. Retainer
14. Screw
15. Gasket
16. Cap
17. Washer
18. Screw
19. Washers
20. Spring
21. Retainer
22. Spool detent
23. Gasket
24. Cap
25. Plug
26. Spring
27. Check ball
28. Washer
29. Screw

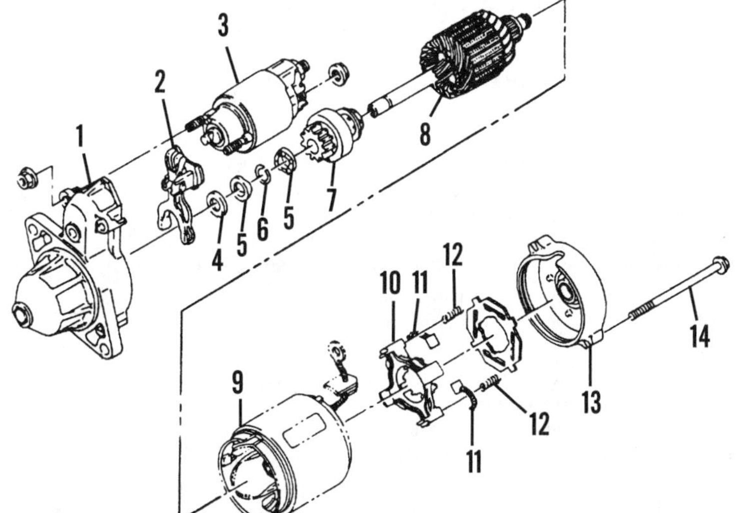

Fig. JD7-61–Exploded view of starter used on Models 425 and 445.

1. Drive housing
2. Fork
3. Solenoid
4. Washer
5. Pinion stop
6. Snap ring
7. Clutch assy.
8. Armature
9. Frame
10. Brush plate
11. Brushes
12. Springs
13. End cap
14. Through-bolt

links. Plug or cap the openings to prevent contamination.

To disassemble, remove the load check valves (5-8—Fig. JD7-60). The load check valves are serviced as an assembly kit. Remove the detent springs (26) and balls (27) before removing the end cap (24). Spools (1 and 2) are matched to the bores in the valve body and must be used in the original bores. Spools and valve body are available only as a unit assembly.

Apply multipurpose grease to detent springs and balls during assembly. Apply multipurpose grease to springs (12 and 20) during assembly. Apply Loctite to the end cap retaining screws and tighten screws to 4 N·m (36 in.-lb.). Tighten spool detent (22) to 4 N·m (36 in.-lb.).

Reinstall control valve by reversing the removal procedure.

HYDRAULIC CYLINDER

To check cylinder seals for internal leakage, first fully extend the piston rod (raise position), then stop the engine. Disconnect the hydraulic line at control valve connecting to the rod end of the cylinder. Hold the lift control valve in the raised position and start engine.

NOTE: Do not move hydraulic control lever to NEUTRAL while the engine is running because the full hydraulic flow will discharge from the control valve port.

There may be an initial flow of oil out the open hydraulic line, then the oil flow should stop. If oil continues to flow, the cylinder piston seal is faulty.

Hydraulic cylinder is a welded assembly and no service parts are available. Replace the cylinder if internal or external leakage is apparent.

ELECTRICAL SYSTEM

Some engine electrical components are covered in the engine service section. If service information is not found in this section, refer to the appropriate engine service section.

BATTERY

The tractor is equipped with a 12 volt, group U1 battery. On Models 425 and 445, the cold cranking amp rating is 342 amps with a reserve capacity of 44 minutes. On Model 455, the cold cranking amp rating is 470 amps with a reserve capacity of 76 minutes.

ELECTRIC STARTER

Models 425 and 445

An exploded view of electric starter is shown in Fig. JD7-61. Place alignment marks on the pinion housing (1), field coil frame (9) and end cover (13) before disassembly so they can be reinstalled in its original position. Remove the solenoid (3). Unscrew the through-bolts (14) and separate drive housing, end cover and brush holder (10) from the field coil frame (9).

Replace the brushes (11) if the length is less than 6 mm (0.24 in.). The starter no-load current draw should be 50 amps at starter speed of 6000 rpm. Starter current draw under load should be 72 amps at starter speed of 500 rpm.

Model 455

Refer to the Yanmar ENGINE SERVICE section for the starter motor service instructions.

ALTERNATOR

Models 425 and 445

The alternator stator is located under the flywheel. To check alternator, disconnect stator from the regulator/rectifier (Fig. JD7-62), and check the voltage reading at the stator leads. With the engine running at full speed, the minimum voltage reading is 26 volts AC.

Model 455

Refer to the Yanmar ENGINE SERVICE section for the alternator service instructions.

REGULATOR/RECTIFIER TESTING

Models 425 and 445

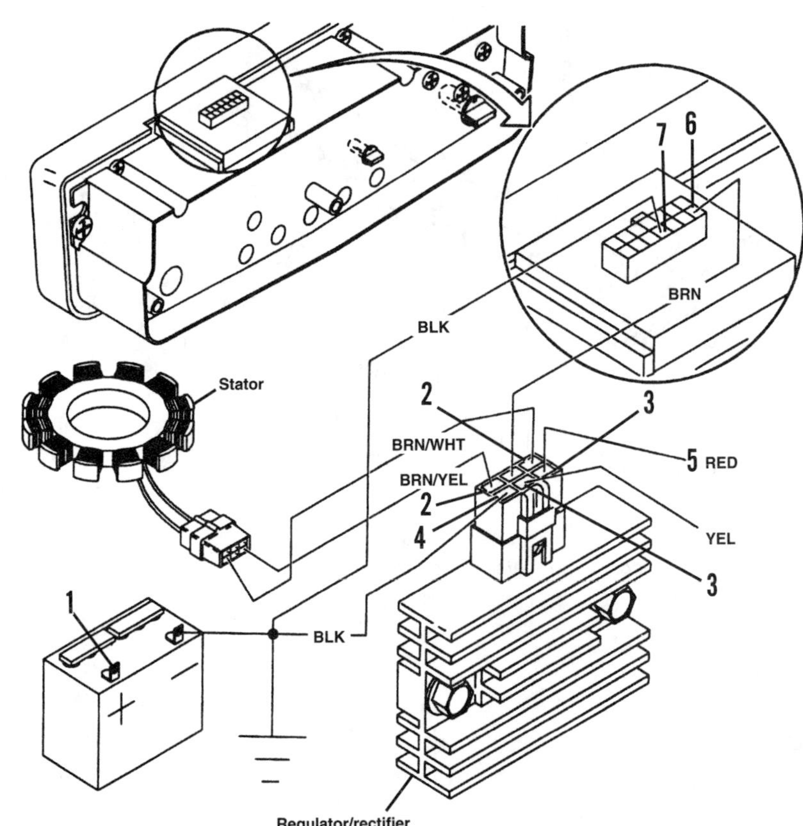

Fig. JD7-62–Refer to text to test regulator/rectifier used on Models 425 and 445.

The following tests are performed with the wire connector attached to the regulator/rectifier. When performing voltage tests, connect the negative voltmeter lead to the negative battery terminal. Insert the voltmeter positive lead into the specified wire connector (do not disconnect wire). Run the engine at the fast idle. Battery voltage must be 11.8-13.2 V. Battery voltage must be present at the red connector wire 5—Fig. JD7-62).

Check voltage at the brown/white connector wire (2). The voltmeter should read 26 V AC, if not check the alternator.

Check voltage at the black connector wire (4). The voltage should be greater than 0 but less than 0.2 V. If the voltage is greater than 0.2 V, check the ground circuit. If the voltage is zero, the regulator/rectifier is faulty.

Check the current at the red connector wire (5) using an ammeter. If the amperage is less than 13 amps, the regulator/rectifier is faulty.

Model 455

The following tests are performed with the wire connectors attached. When performing voltage tests, connect the negative voltmeter lead to the negative battery terminal. Insert the voltmeter positive lead into the specified wire connector (do not disconnect wire). Battery voltage must be 11.8-13.2 V. Battery voltage must be present at each of the number 3 (Fig. JD7-63) terminals.

Turn the key switch ON and check the voltage at the dash panel module terminal 4 (yellow wire). Voltage should be greater than 0 but less than 0.2 V. If voltage is greater than 0.2, check the charge lamp ground circuit. If voltage is zero, check the charge indicator bulb. If the bulb is not faulty, replace the dash panel module.

To determine whether the regulator/rectifier or alternator is faulty, conduct the following tests. If the unit fails voltage test and passes the amperage test, the regulator/rectifier is faulty. If the unit fails both tests, the alternator is faulty (regulator/rectifier may be faulty as well).

To check regulated voltage, partially discharge the battery. Run the engine at fast idle and monitor the voltage at the alternator red wire.

NOTE: To prevent damage, do not allow battery voltage to exceed 15.5 V.

Regulated voltage should be 12.2-14.7 V. If voltage is less than specified, alternator or regulator is faulty. If voltage exceeds 14.7 V, replace the regulator. Note that the regulator is contained in the alternator housing on Model 455.

To check the alternator unregulated amperage output, connect the ammeter to the red output wire (A—Fig. JD7-64). The alternator must be properly grounded and the battery voltage must present at the alternator regulator terminal.

NOTE: To prevent damage, do not perform the test longer than 10 seconds.

Start the engine. While running engine at 3350 rpm, insert a Phillips screwdriver through the rear hole (B) in the alternator rear cover as shown in Fig. JD7-64 and ground the regulator. The ammeter should indicate as least 35 amps, otherwise the alternator is faulty. If the voltage is less than specified, either the alternator or regulator is faulty. If the voltage exceeds 14.7 V, replace the regulator. The regulator is contained in the alternator housing on Model 455.

CONTROL/FUSE MODULE

All models are equipped with a control/fuse module serving as the mounting base for the fuses, relays, LEDs and associated circuitry. No components are

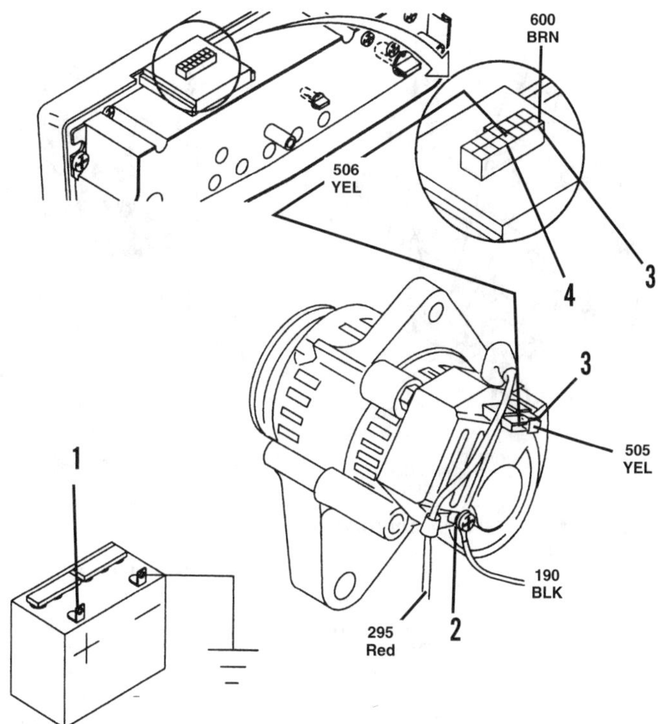

Fig. JD7-63–Refer to text to test regulator/rectifier used on Model 455.

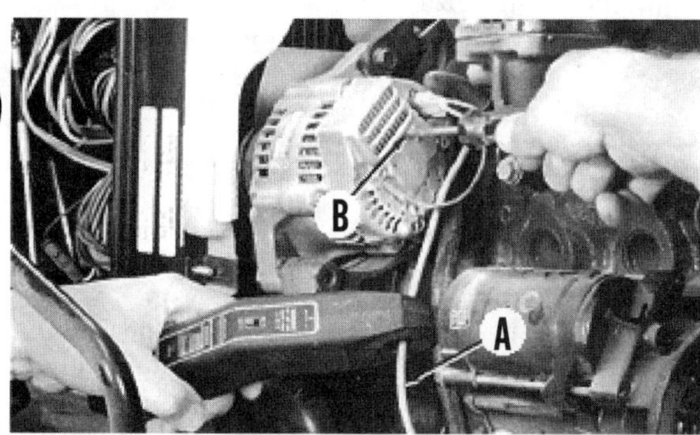

Fig. JD7-64–Refer to text to test unregulated amperage output of alternator used on Model 455.

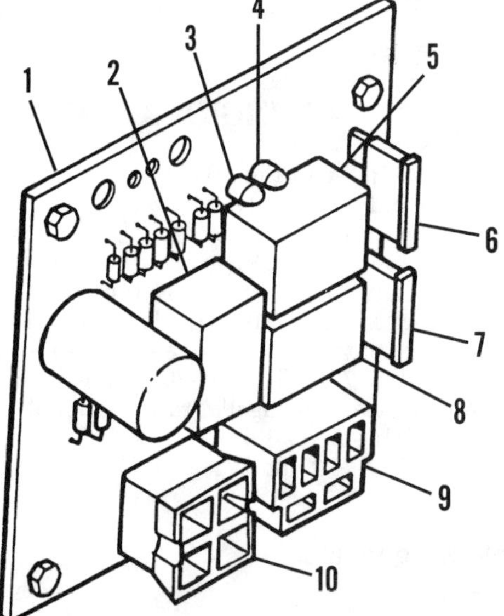

Fig. JD7-65–Drawing of control/fuse relay.

1. Module
2. Start relay
3. PTO LED
4. Ignition LED (Models 425-445)
4. Hold-in LED (Model 455)
5. Ignition relay (Models 425-445)
5. Hold-in relaty (Model 455)
6. Power circuit fuse (15 amp)
7. Headlight circuit fuse (15 amp)
8. PTO relay
9. Power connector
10. Control connector

available separately, except fuses. Major components mounted on the module include the following:

An LED (4—Fig. JD7-65) lights when power is available to the ignition relay (5) on Models 425 and 445. On Model 455, LED (4) indicates power is available to the hold-in relay (5), which holds the plunger of fuel shutoff solenoid in operating position.

The LED (3) lights when power is available to the PTO relay (8).

NOTE: Unlit LEDs are not an indication of a faulty module, only that current is not reaching the LED.

The start relay (2) directs current to starter motor when key switch and safety switches are closed.

The fuse (6) is rated 15 amps and protects the main power circuit. The fuse (7) is rated 15 amps and protects the headlight circuit.

Testing

The following tests will help determine if a module component or the associated circuit is causing an electrical problem.

Before conducting tests, be sure ground connections are good (terminal D—Fig. JD7-66 is ground) and the battery is fully charged. The fuses must be good. Turn the key switch OFF, disengage the PTO, shift the transmission to NEUTRAL, and engage the parking brake. Defeat the seat switch by jumping connector wires or by placing a weight on the seat.

Connect the negative voltmeter lead to the negative battery terminal. Connect the positive voltmeter lead to the terminals indicated in the following table. In each test, the voltmeter should indicate battery voltage. Conduct the tests with the key switch in the ON position. Refer to Fig. JD7-66.

Terminal	Fault
2 (red wire)	Power circuit
3 (red wire)	Power circuit
3 (red/black wire-Model 455)	Power circuit
4 (yellow wire)	Module (if fuses OK)
5 (pink/black wire)	Neutral start circuit
6 (pink wire)	Seat switch circuit
7 (pink/black wire)	Module
8 (yellow/blue wire)	Module

Disengage the parking brake for the next tests.

Terminal	Fault
9 (purple wire)	Pto relay engagement circuit
10 (blue wires)	Module

Engage the parking brake. Disconnect the starter solenoid wire. Turn the key switch to the START position. Measure the voltage at terminal 11 (purple wire). If the voltmeter indicates battery voltage, replace the module.

DIESEL CONTROL MODULE

In addition to the control/fuse module, Model 455 is equipped with a diesel control module. Two relays, the fuel shutoff pull-in relay (A—Fig. JD7-67) and the glow plug relay (B), are mounted on the module printed circuit board.

The pull-in relay energizes the fuel shutoff solenoid pull-in winding for 1 second. Refer to the FUEL SHUTOFF SOLENOID section.

The glow plug relay routes current to the engine glow plugs for 45 seconds.

Diesel control module must be serviced as a unit assembly.

Condition of the relays may be checked by referring to the wiring schematic and performing voltage tests, as well as listening for clicking sound when relay operates.

Testing

The following tests will help determine if an electrical problem is caused by a module component or the associated circuit.

Before conducting tests, be sure the grounds connections are good and the battery is fully charged. Fuses on control/fuse module must be good. Turn the key switch OFF, disengage the PTO, shift the transmission to NEUTRAL and engage the parking brake. Defeat the seat switch by jumping the connector wires or by placing a weight on the seat.

Connect the negative voltmeter lead to the negative battery terminal. Connect the positive voltmeter lead to the terminals in the following table. In each test, the voltmeter should indicate battery voltage. Conduct the tests with the key switch ON. Refer to Fig. JD7-67. The letter after the terminal number indicates left (L) or right (R) connector.

Terminal	Fault
2L (pink and brown wires)	Control/fuse module power circuit
3L (pink/blue and blue wires)	Fuel shutoff solenoid relay hold-in circuit
4R (red wire)	Power circuit
5R (red wire)	Power circuit
6R (red/black wire)	Power circuit

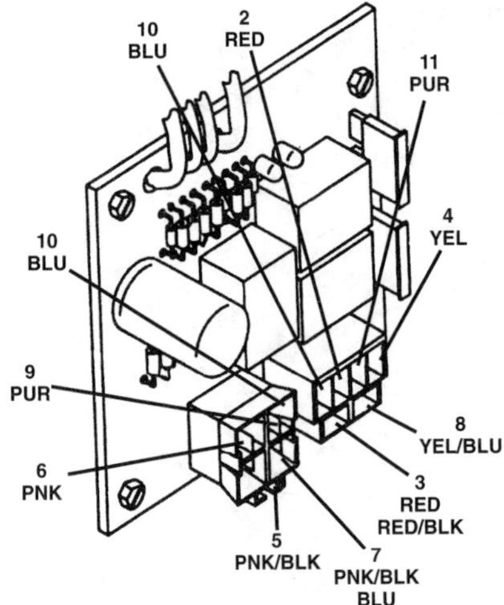

Fig. JD7-66–Refer to text for control/fuse module test procedure.

Turn the key switch OFF and ON repeatedly while performing the following tests. At terminals 7 and 8, the voltmeter should indicate battery voltage for up to 45 seconds. At terminal 9, the voltmeter should indicate battery voltage for up to 1 second.

Terminal	Fault
7R (white wire)	Module
8R (red/white wire)	Module
9R (white wire)	Module

Check voltage at terminal 10 (grey and orange/white wires) while turning key switch OFF and ON repeatedly. The voltmeter should indicate voltage greater than zero but less than 1 V for up to 20 seconds. If voltage exceeds 1 V, replace the diesel control module.

FUEL SHUTOFF SOLENOID (MODEL 455)

The fuel shutoff solenoid holds the fuel injection pump linkage in the closed position until the battery voltage energizes the solenoid. The solenoid then moves the pump linkage so the fuel pump delivers fuel to the engine. A pull-in winding moves the solenoid plunger, and a hold-in winding holds the plunger in position.

Separate relays control current to solenoid windings. Current for hold-in winding must pass through safety switches to the hold-in winding relay before reaching the solenoid. Current from the hold-in winding relay also travels to a pull-in winding relay timer, which sends current for 1 second to the pull-in winding relay. The pull-in relay energizes the solenoid pull-in winding for 1 second, the hold-in winding maintains the plunger position and the pull-in timer stops current to the pull-in relay.

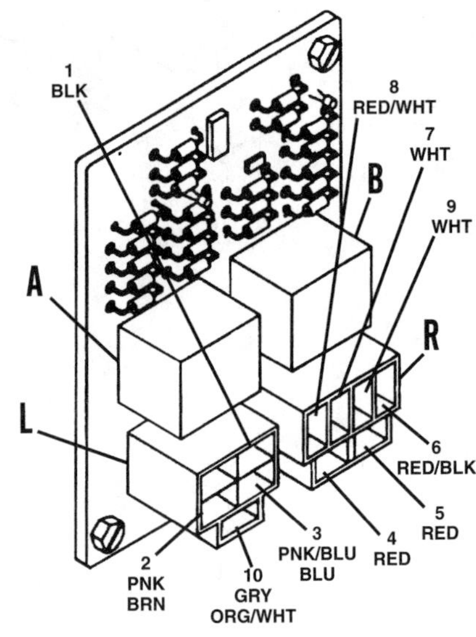

Fig. JD7-67–Refer to text for diesel control test procedure.

An LED on control/fuse module (Fig. JD7-65) lights when the current is available to the hold-in winding relay.

To check the fuel shutoff solenoid and linkage, measure amperage through the wires for the pull-in and hold-in windings with the solenoid installed. Be sure the voltage reaches the solenoid. Maximum amperage readings are 1 amp continuous for the red hold-in winding wire and 50 amps for $\frac{1}{2}$ second for the pull-in winding wire (white). Excessive readings indicate faulty windings or binding.

WIRING DIAGRAMS

Refer to Fig. JD7-68 for Models 425 and 445 electrical system component location. Refer to Fig. JD7-69 for Model 455 electrical system component location. The electrical system wiring diagram for Models 425 and 445 is illustrated in three sections (Fig. JD7-70A-Fig. JD7-70C). The electrical system wiring diagram for Model 455 is illustrated in two sections (Fig. JD7-71A and Fig. JD7-71B).

Fig. JD7-68 through JD7-71C are on the following pages.

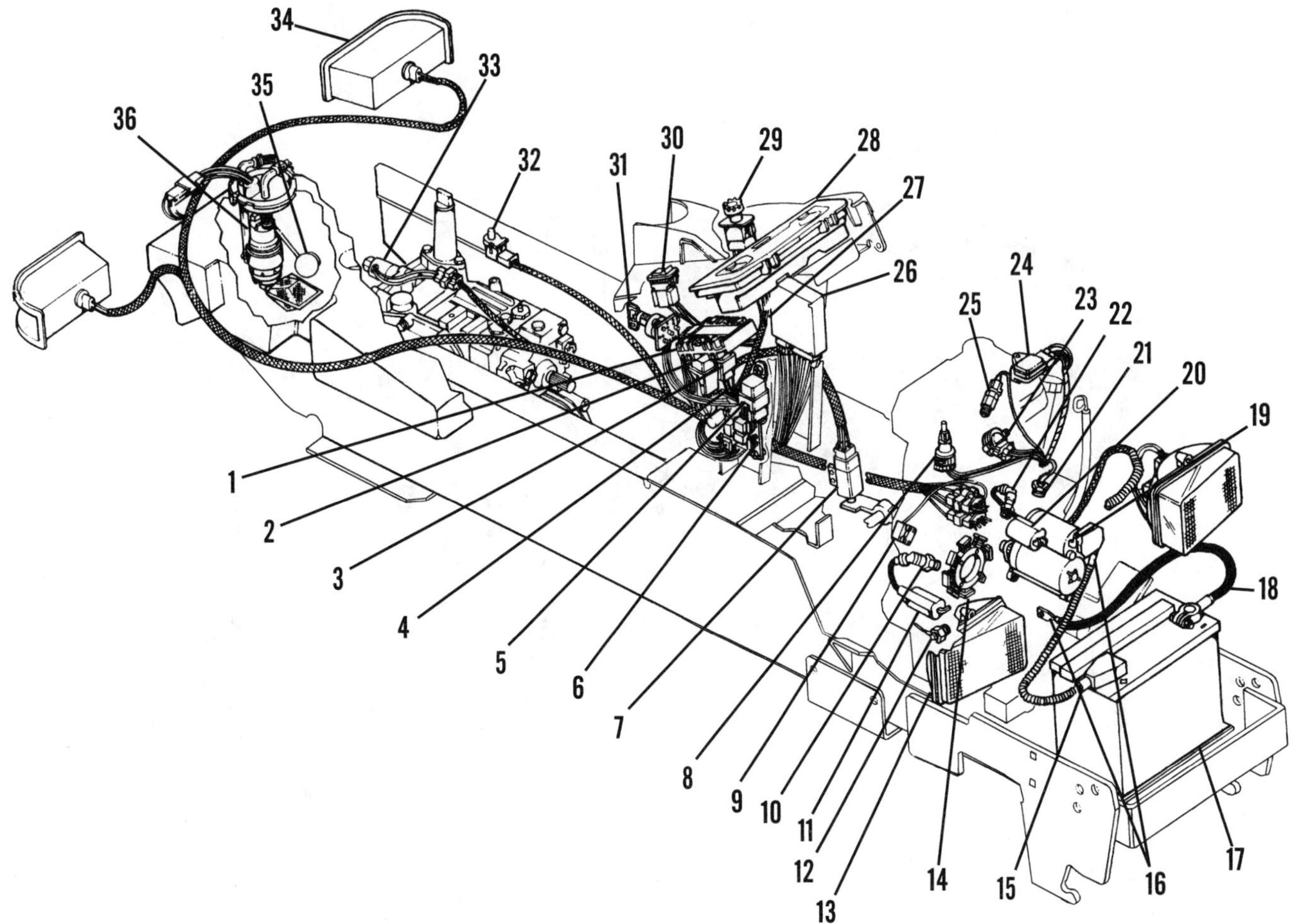

Fig. JD7-68–Drawing showing electrical system component location for Model 445. Model 425 is similar except for fuel injection components.

1. Regulator/rectifier
2. Fule pump relay
3. Fuel injection relay
4. Fuel injection fuse
5. Safety relay
6. Control/fuse module
7. Brake switch
8. Air temperature sensor
9. Pulser coil
10. Spark plug, R.H.
11. Ignition coil, R.H.
12. Oil pressure switch
13. Headlight
14. Stator
15. Positive battery cable
16. Engine ground
17. Battery
18. Negative battery cable
19. Starting motor
20. Ignition coil, L.H.
21. Coolant temperature switch
22. Spark plug, L.H.
23. Fuel injector
24. Air pressure sensor
25. Coolant temperature sensor
26. Fuel injection module
27. Dash panel connector
28. Dash panel module
29. PTO switch
30. Light switch
31. Key switch
32. Seat switch
33. PTO solenoid
34. Tailight
35. Fuel gauge sensor
36. Fuel pump

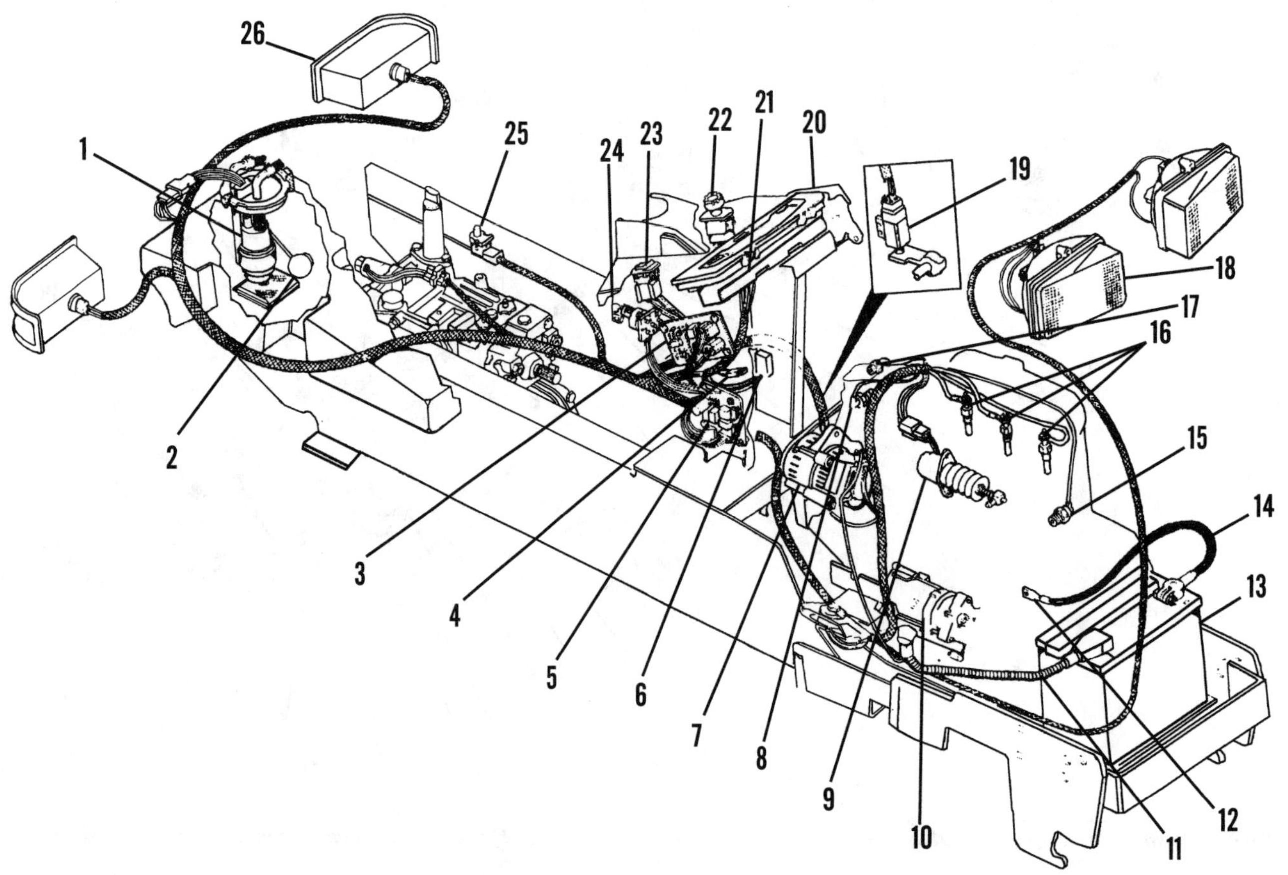

Fig. JD7-69–Drawing showing Model 455 electrical system component location.

1. Fuel pump
2. Fuel gauge sender
3. Diesel control module
4. Fuel pump fuse
5. Control/fuse module
6. Engine high temperature relay
7. Alternator
8. Coolant temperature switch
9. Fuel shutoff solenoid
10. Starting motor
11. Positive battery cable
12. Engine ground
13. Battery
14. Negative battery cable
15. Oil pressure switch
16. Glow plugs
17. Coolant temperature sensor
18. Headlight
19. Brake switch
20. Dash panel module
21. Dash panel connector
22. PTO switch
23. Light switch
24. Key switch
25. Seat switch
26. Taillight

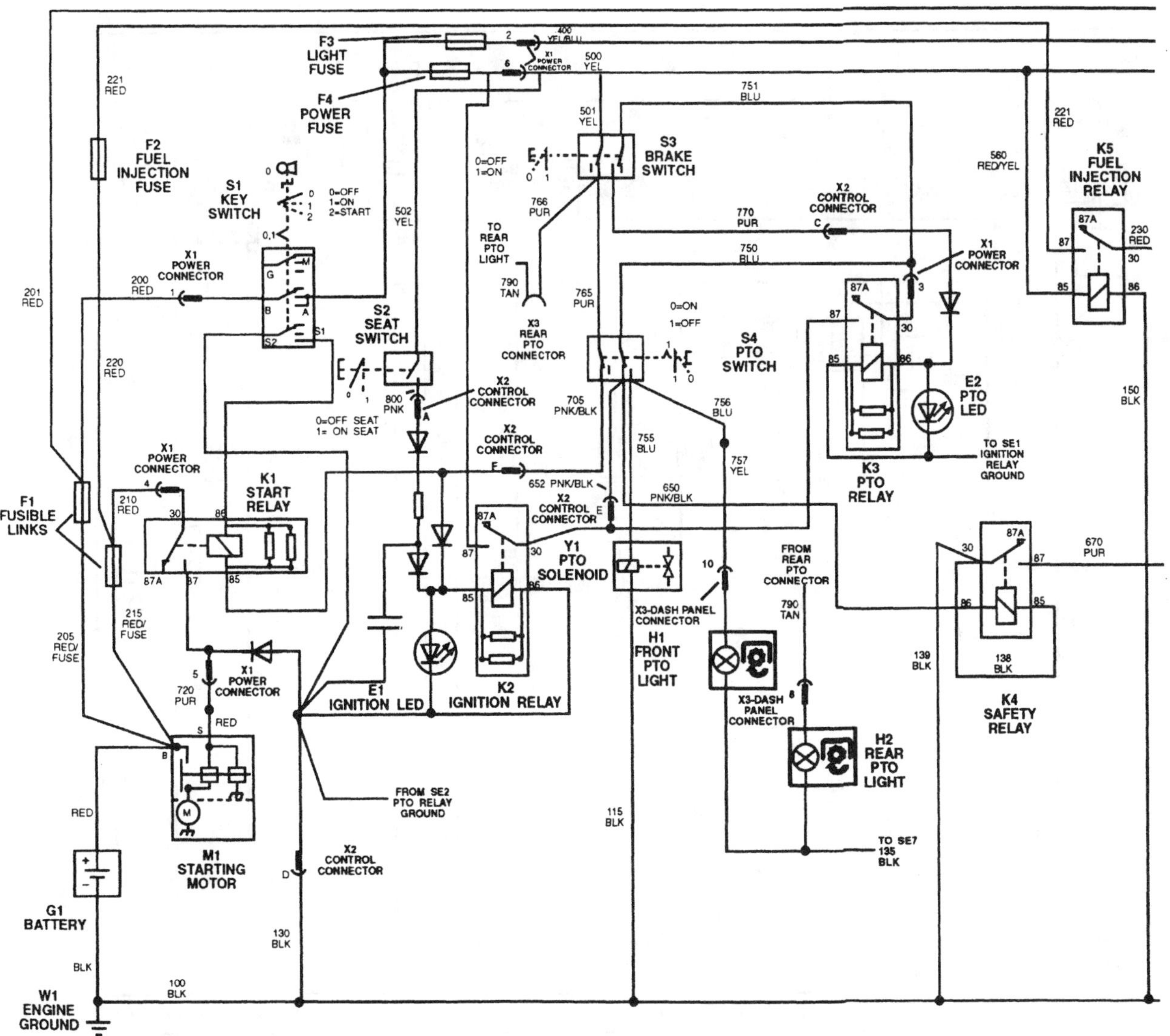

Fig. JD7-70A–Partial wiring schematic for Model 445. Model 425 is similar. Refer to Fig. JD7-70B and Fig. JD7-70C.

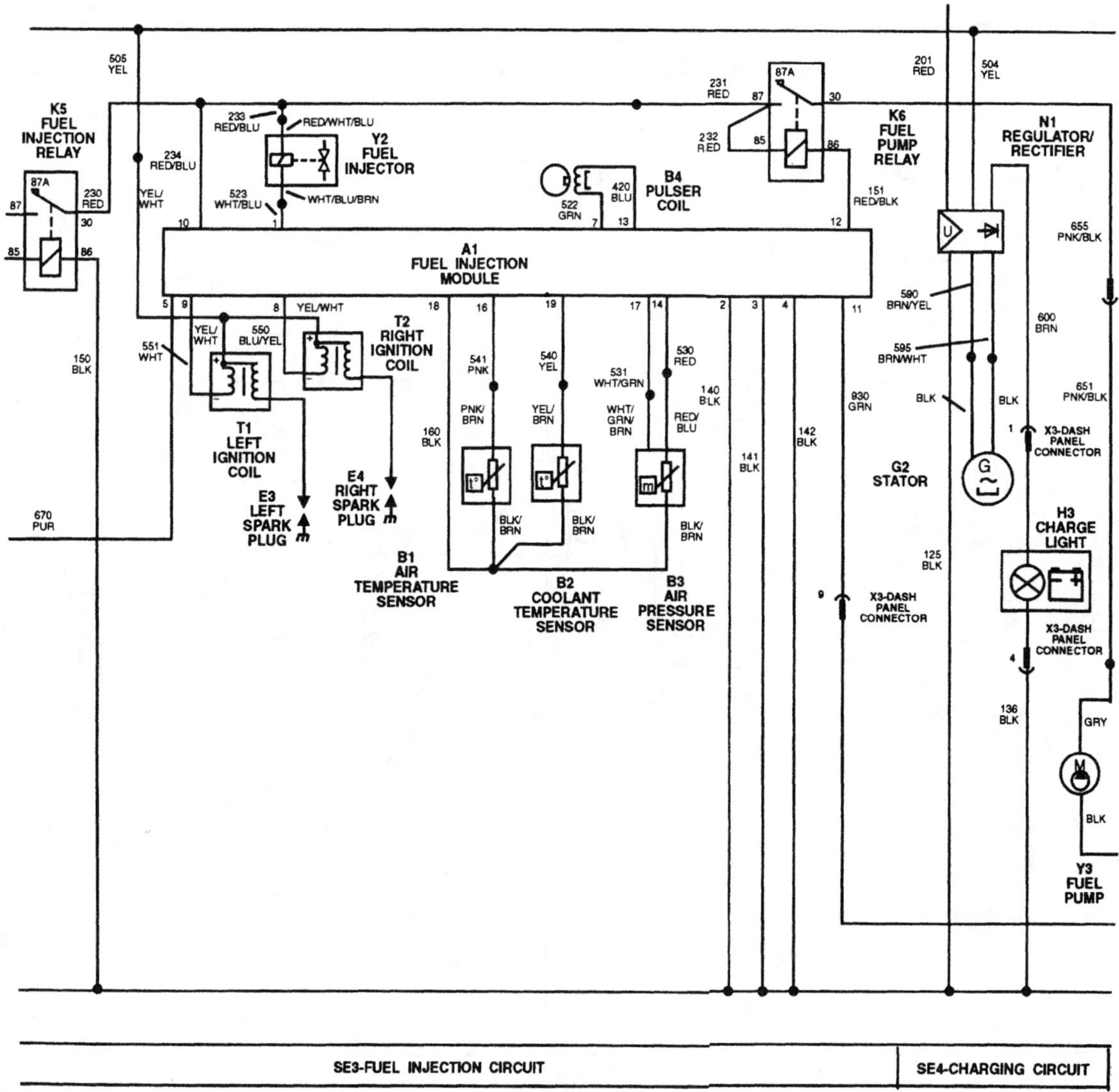

Fig. JD7-70B–Partial wiring schematic for Model 445. Model 425 is similar.

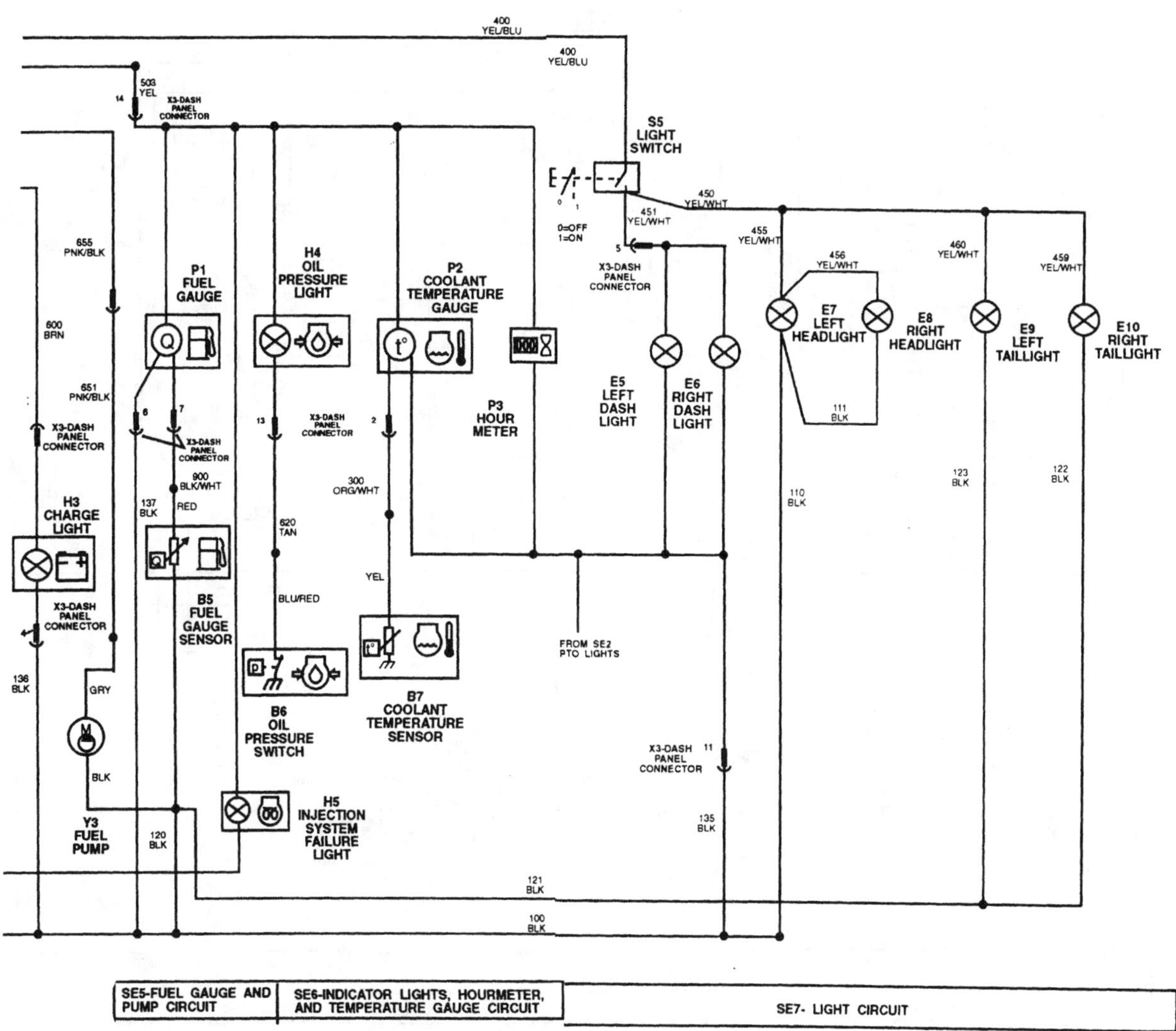

Fig. JD7-70C–Partial wiring diagram for Model 445. Model 425 is similar.

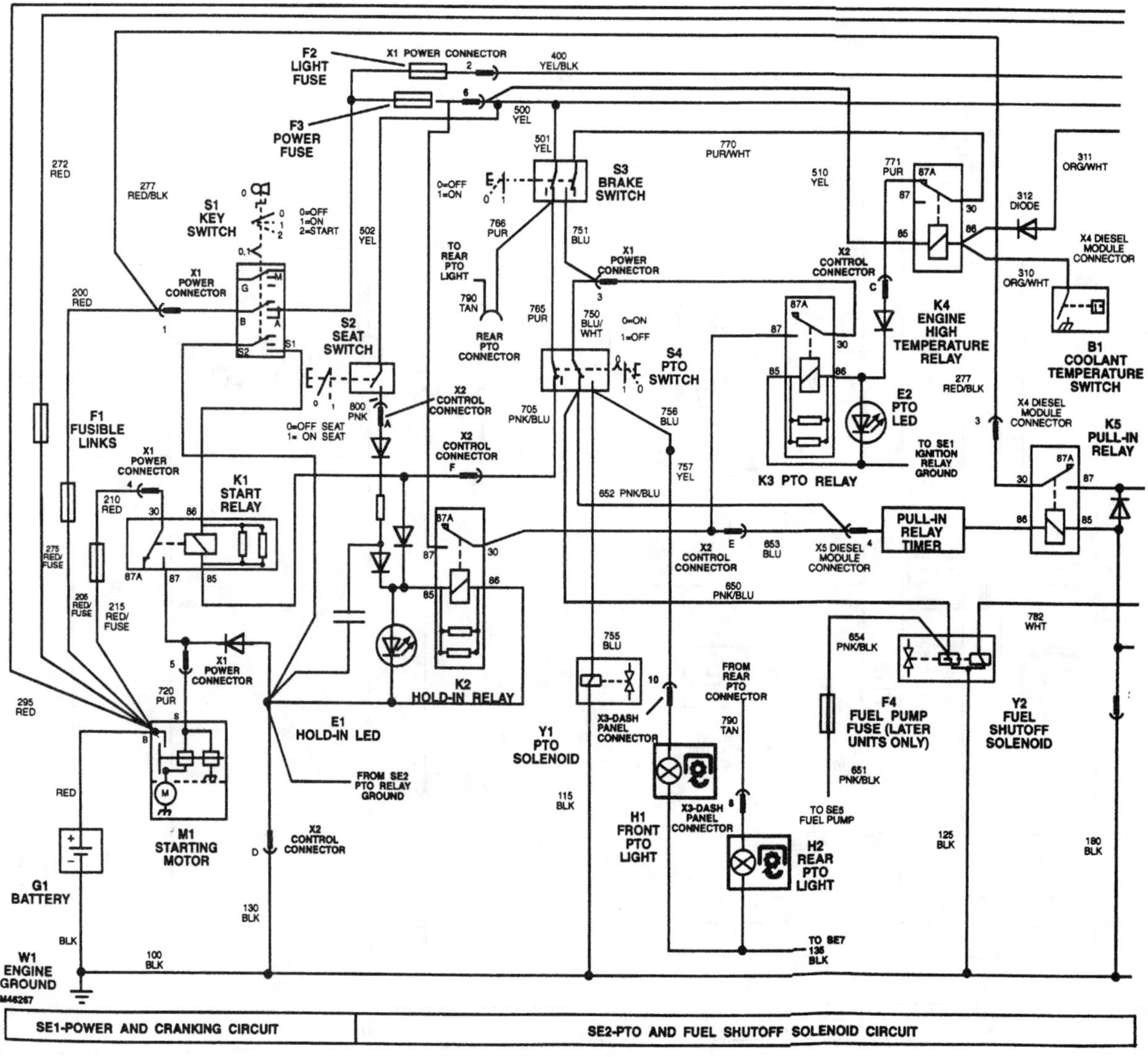

Fig. JD7-71A–Partial wiring schematic for Model 455. Refer also to Fig. JD7-71B and Fig. JD7-71C.

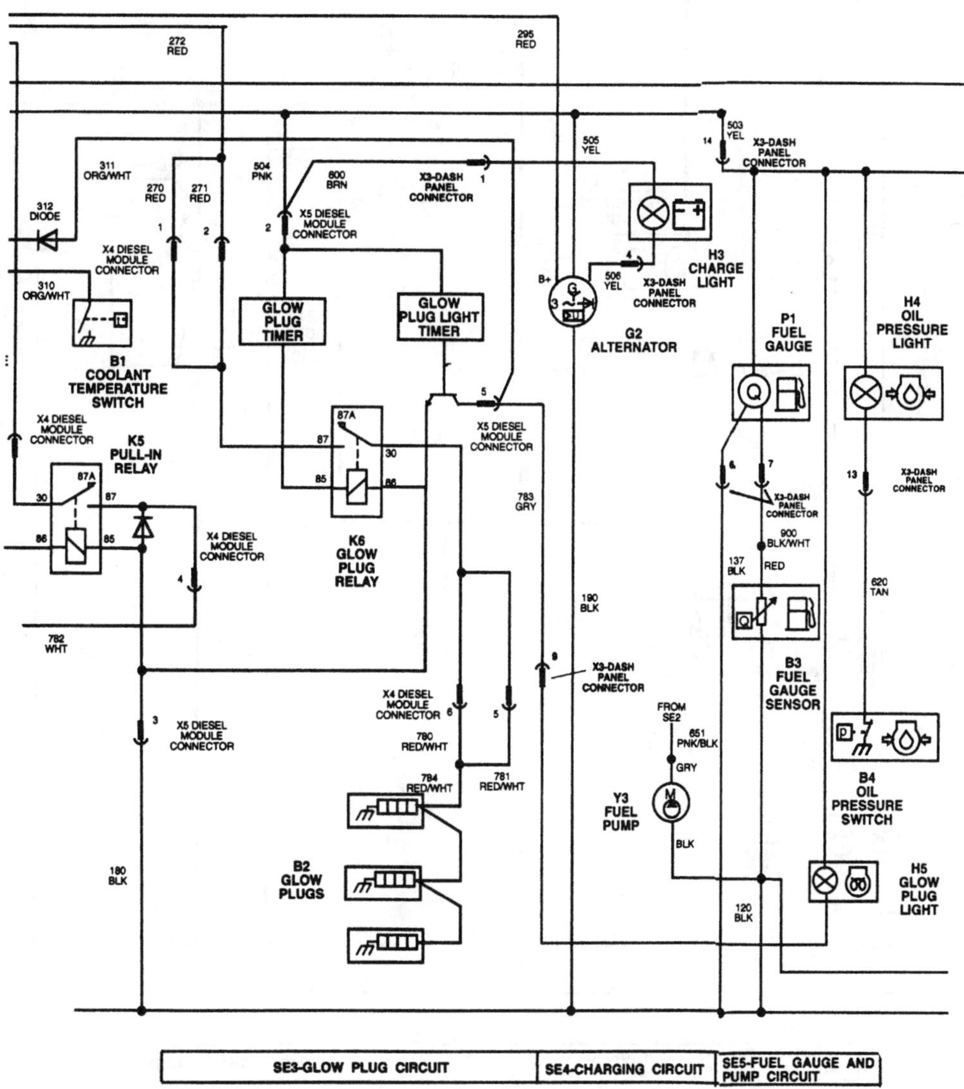

Fig. JD7-71B–Partial wiring diagram for Model 455.

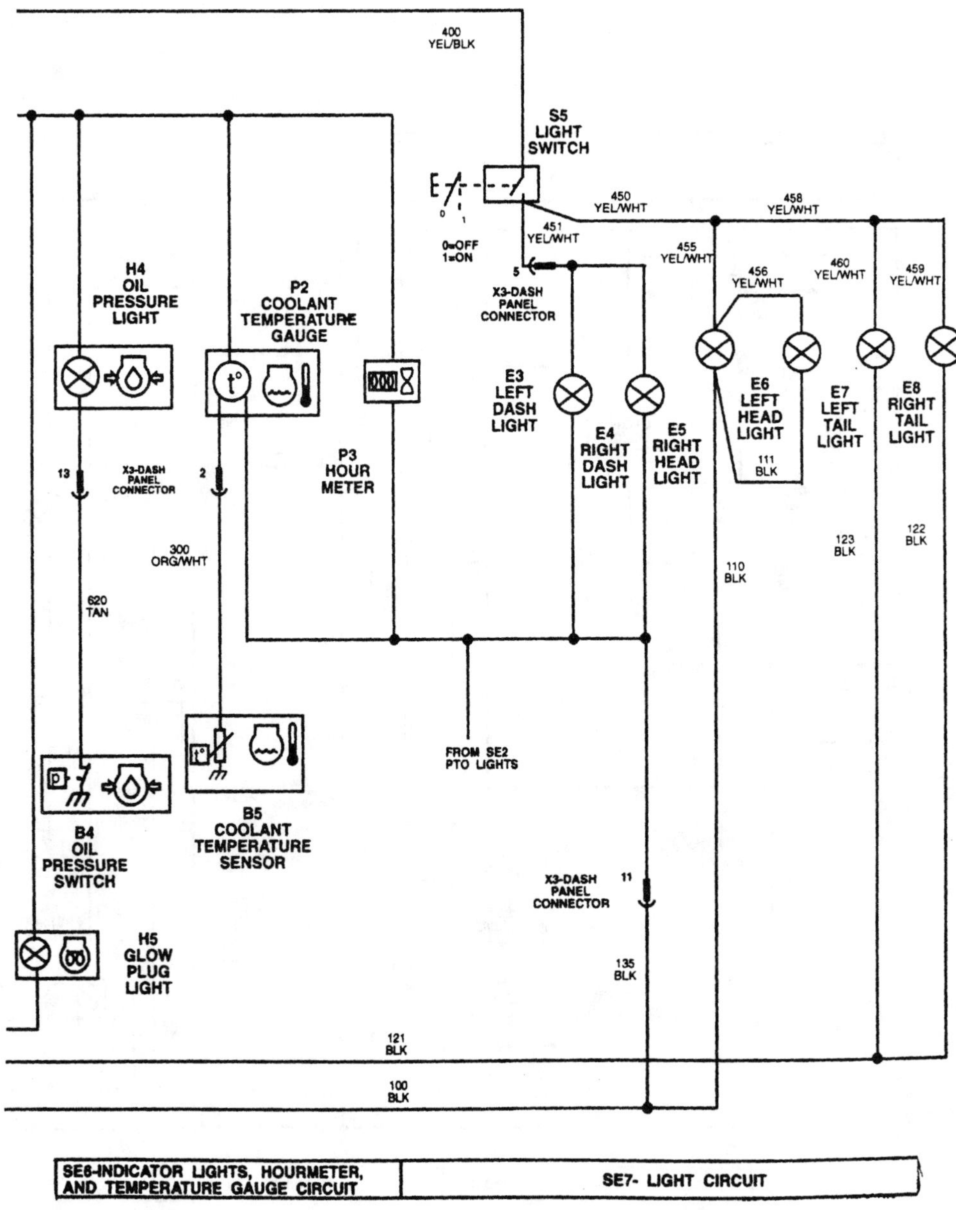

Fig. JD7-71C–Partial wiring schematic for Model 455.

FORD

CONDENSED SPECIFICATIONS

Models	LT10	LT12, LT12H	LT12.5, LT12.5H
Engine Make	B&S	B&S	B&S
Model	220000	281707	285000
Number of cylinders	1	1	1
Bore	3.438 in. (87.3 mm)	3.438 in. (87.3 mm)	3.438 in. (87.3 mm)
Stroke	2.375 in. (60.3 mm)	3.06 in. (77.7 mm)	3.06 in. (77.7 mm)
Displacement	22.04 cu. in. (361 cc)	28.04 cu. in. (465 cc)	28.04 cu. in. (465 cc)
Power Rating	10 hp (7.5 kW)	12 hp (9 kW)	12.5 hp (9.4 kW)
Slow Idle	1750 rpm	1750 rpm	1750 rpm
High Speed (No-Load)	3600 rpm	3600 rpm	3600 rpm
Crankcase Capacity	3 pt. (1.4 L)	3 pt. (1.4 L)	3 pt. (1.4 L)
Transmission Capacity	See text	See text	See text

Models	YT12.5	YT14	YT16, YT16H	YT18H
Engine Make	Kohler	Kohler	Kohler	Kohler
Model	CV12.5	CV14	MV16	MV18
Number of cylinders	1	1	2	2
Bore	87 mm (3.43 in.)	87 mm (3.43 in.)	3.12 in. (79.2 mm)	3.12 in. (79.2 mm)
Stroke	67 mm (2.64 in.)	67 mm (2.64 in.)	2.75 in. (69.85 mm)	2.75 in. (69.85 mm)
Displacement	398 cc (24.3 cu. in.)	398 cc (24.3 cu. in.)	42.18 cu. in. (691 cc)	42.18 cu. in. (691 cc)
Power Rating	9.33 kW (12.5 hp)	10.5 kW (14 hp)	16 hp (11.9 kW)	18 hp (13.4 kW)
Slow Idle	1750 rpm	1750 rpm	1750 rpm	1750 rpm
High Speed (No-Load)	3600 rpm	3600 rpm	3600 rpm	3600 rpm
Crankcase Capacity	See text	See text	See text	See text
Transmission Capacity	See text	See text	See text	See text

FRONT AXLE AND STEERING SYSTEM

MAINTENANCE

Steering spindles, tie rod ends, axle pivot, wheel bearings/bushings and steering gear should be lubricated at 25-hour intervals. Recommended lubricant is multipurpose, lithium base grease. Clean all pivot points and linkages and lubricate with SAE 30 oil. Check for looseness and wear, and repair when needed.

FRONT WHEELS

The front wheel bushings (15—Fig. F1-1) are pressed into wheel hubs. Replace the bushings as needed to correct excessive looseness. Lubricate with multipurpose, lithium base grease.

TIE BAR AND TOE-IN

Inspect the tie bar (1—Fig. F1-1) and bushings (2) for damage. Replace when excessive looseness is evident. Toe-in is not adjustable.

STEERING SPINDLES REMOVAL AND INSTALLATION

Raise and support the front of the tractor. Remove front wheel. Remove

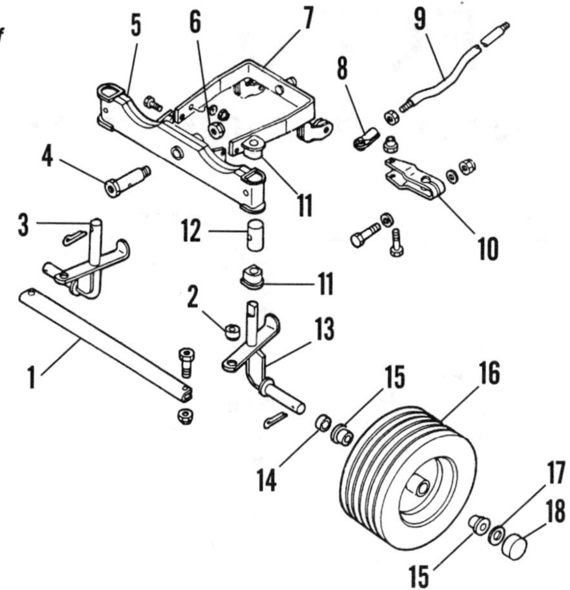

Fig. F1-1—Exploded view of front axle assembly.

1. Tie bar
2. Pivot bushing
3. Spindle (R)
4. Pivot bolt
5. Axle main member
6. Nut
7. Pivot bracket
8. Drag link end
9. Drag link
10. Steering arm
11. Bushing
12. Spacer
13. Spindle (L)
14. Spacer
15. Bushing
16. Wheel & tire
17. Washer
18. Hub cap

tie bar (1—Fig. F1-1). Remove the steering arm (10) from the left spindle (13) or cotter pin from the right spindle (3). Slide the spindle down out of the axle main member.

Inspect bushings (11) and spindles for damage, and replace components when needed.

Reinstall by reversing removal procedure. Lubricate spindles with multipurpose grease.

AXLE MAIN MEMBER REMOVAL AND INSTALLATION

The complete front axle assembly may be removed as a unit. Raise and support the front of the tractor. Disconnect drag link end (8—Fig. F1-1) from steering arm (10). Disconnect any implement attached to the pivot bracket (7). Support the axle and remove the bolts connecting the pivot bracket (7) to the main member (5). Remove pivot bolt (4) and remove main member assembly, then remove pivot bracket.

Install by reversing the removal procedure.

Prior to connecting the steering drag link 9—Fig. F1-1), first moving the front wheels to the left until there is a $\frac{1}{8}$ inch (3 mm) gap between the left spindle stop and the axle rear as shown in Fig. F1-2. Turn the steering wheel fully to the left so the sector gear is at the end of its travel. Adjust the drag link ball joint as needed so the hole in the ball joint aligns with the hole in the spindle steering arm. Attach the drag link to the steering arm with the nut and bolt, with the bolt coming from the bottom up.

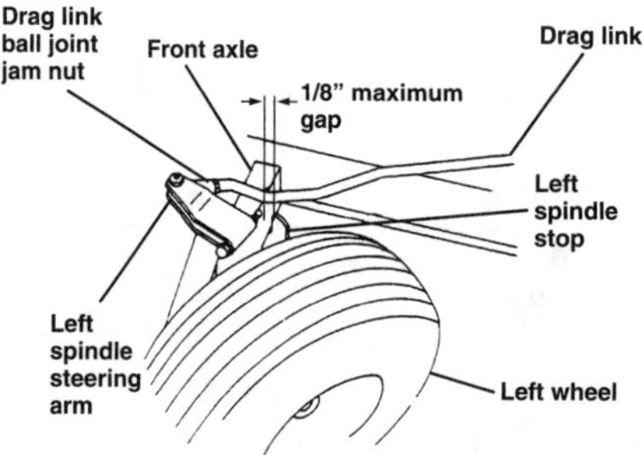

Fig. F1-2—With wheels turned fully to the left, there should be a 1/8 inch (3 mm) gap between left spindle stop and rear of axle. Refer to text for adjustment procedure.

STEERING GEAR OVERHAUL

To remove steering gear, first remove the mower deck if so equipped. Disconnect battery cables and remove the battery. Disconnect drag link (17—Fig. F1-3) from the sector gear (18). Remove the cotter pin (12) and spacer (16) from the lower end of the steering shaft. Loosen but do not remove the two cap screws attaching the lower bearing to the frame (Fig. F1-4). Compress the bellows (7—Fig. F1-3) and remove the bolt (9). Lift the steering wheel (4) and adapter (5) off the steering shaft. Remove the bellows (7) and sleeve (8).

Remove the bolts (19) attaching the upper bearing to the instrument panel shroud. Disconnect the speed control rod clevis from the speed control bellcrank. Remove the knobs from the parking brake link and the gearshift lever. Unbolt and remove the throttle control from the instrument panel. Disconnect the wires from the ammeter and remove the ammeter out the front

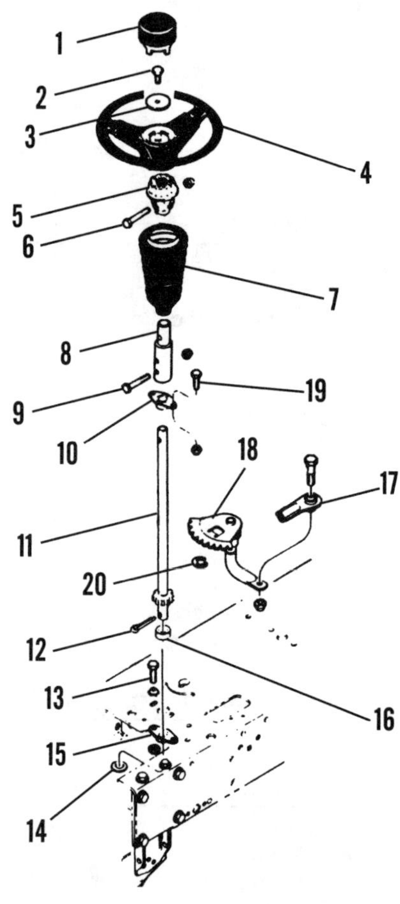

Fig. F1-3—Exploded view of steering mechanism typical of all models.

1. Dust cover
2. Bolt
3. Washer
4. Steering wheel
5. Adapter
6. Bolt
7. Bellows
8. Sleeve
9. Bolt
10. Flange bearing
11. Steering shaft
12. Cotter key
13. Bolt
14. Washer
15. Flange bearing
16. Spacer
17. Drag link end
18. Steering sector
19. Bolt
20. E-ring

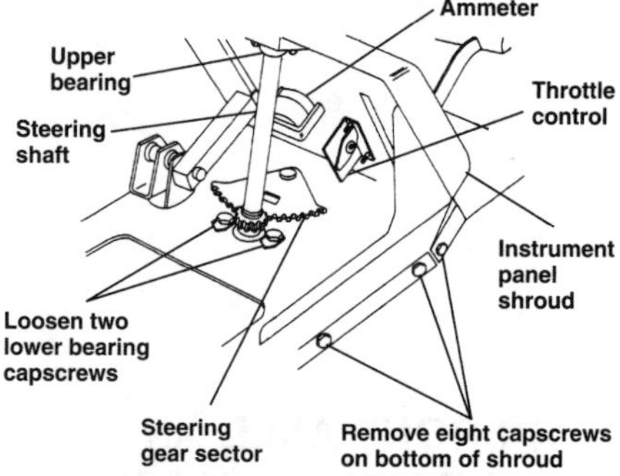

Fig. F1-4—Steering shaft gear and sector gear must mesh evenly and smoothly with minimum amount of backlash.

of the panel. Remove the eight screws along the bottom side edges of instrument panel (Fig. F1-4). Lift and pivot the instrument panel over the steering

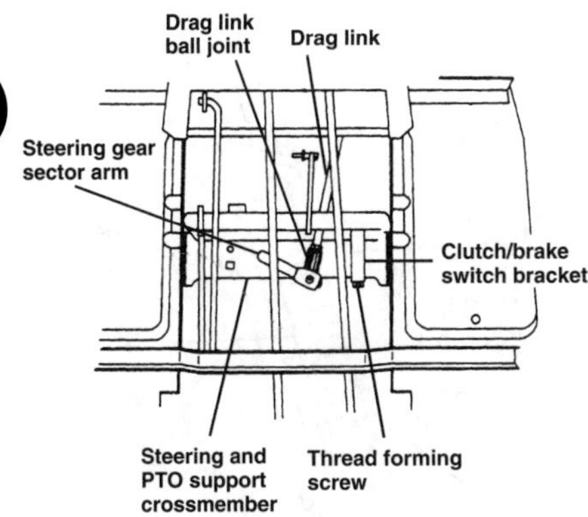

Fig. F1-5—Underside view of steering and PTO support crossmember.

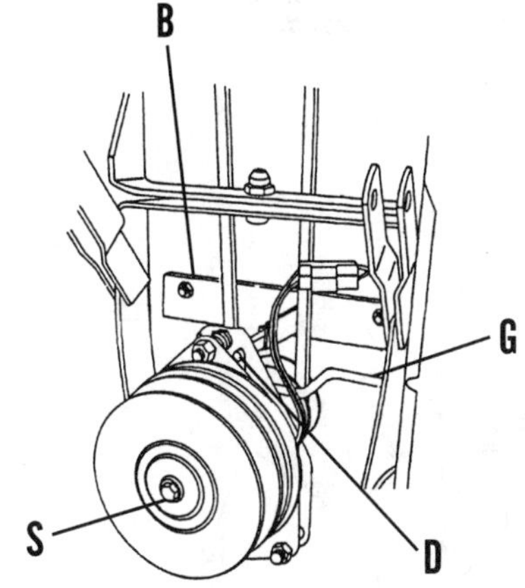

Fig. F1-6—View of electric PTO clutch on models so equipped.

B. Torque bracket
D. Stud
G. Belt guide
S. Cap screw

shaft. Pull the steering shaft (11) upward and out of the lower bearing.

To remove the steering sector (18—Fig. F1-3), disconnect the drag link (17) from the sector arm. Remove the screw attaching the clutch/brake switch bracket to the crossmember (Fig. F1-5). Remove the E-ring (20—Fig. F1-3) from the sector arm. Pry the plastic split bushing out of the crossmember. Remove four mounting cap screws from the steering support crossmember (Fig. F1-5). Rotate the crossmember 90° and work it off the sector arm. and steering sector (18). Work the steering sector up and out of the hole in the frame.

To install the steering gears, reverse the removal procedure and note the following special instructions. The locating tab on the steering sector split bushing must be aligned in slot in the crossmember. Lubricate the steering gear teeth with lithium base EP grease. Push steering shaft and flange bearing at lower end of steering shaft toward sector gear to provide full gear mesh before tightening lower bearing cap screws (13—Fig. F1-3). Tighten both cap screws to torque of 10-15 ft.-lb. (13.5-20.3 N·m). Steering shaft should rotate smoothly with minimum backlash. If binding is encountered, loosen cap screws (13) and move the shaft away from the sector gear (18) a small amount.

ENGINE

MODELS LT10, LT12, LT12.5, YT12.5, YT14 AND YT16

Maintenance

Regular engine maintenance is required to maintain peak performance and long engine life.

Check oil level daily. Inspect air cleaner element daily or periodically depending on operating conditions.

Refer to the engine section when servicing air cleaner or changing oil.

Refer to the engine section for service information concerning tune-up and adjustments.

Removal and Installation

Remove the mower deck, if so equipped. Loosen, but do not remove, screws retaining left and right transaxle pulley belt guides, then swing guides away from the pulley. Disconnect the battery cables. Disconnect the PTO clutch electrical connector. Remove the belt guide from the upper engine pulley. Depress the clutch/brake pedal and set the parking brake. Work the drive belt off the transaxle pulley and engine pulley. Disconnect the green headlight wire at connector clipped to right side of engine shroud. Remove hood. Identify and disconnect all interfering wiring from the engine. Disconnect throttle and choke cables from the engine. Disconnect the fuel line from fuel filter. Turn the steering wheel until front wheels are as far right as possible. Remove the four cap screws retaining the engine to the engine base assembly, then lift engine out of tractor.

Install the engine by reversing the removal procedure.

Overhaul

Engine make and model are listed in the specifications table at the beginning of this section. Refer to the appropriate engine section in this manual for service information on the engine and associated accessories.

MODELS LT12H, LT12.5H, YT16H AND YT18H

Maintenance

Regular engine maintenance is required to maintain peak performance and long engine life.

Check the oil level daily. Inspect air cleaner element daily or periodically depending on operating conditions.

Refer to the engine section when servicing the air cleaner or changing oil.

Refer to the engine section for service information concerning tune-up and adjustments.

Removal and Installation

Remove the mower deck, if so equipped. Disconnect the battery cables. On models equipped with an electric PTO clutch, disconnect the PTO clutch connector. Work the primary drive belt off the engine pulley. Remove hood. Identify and disconnect all interfering wiring from the engine. Disconnect the throttle and choke cables from engine. Disconnect the fuel line from the carburetor. On models equipped with an electric PTO clutch, unscrew the PTO clutch center retaining screw (S—Fig. F1-6) and pull the PTO clutch assembly off the engine crankshaft. Remove the torque bracket (B). Remove cap screws retaining the engine to the engine base assembly, then lift engine out of tractor.

Install the engine by reversing the removal procedure. On models equipped with an electric PTO clutch, apply an antiseize compound to the crankshaft before reinstalling the clutch. The clutch plate slot must align with the stud (D—Fig. F1-6) on the torque bracket (B). Tighten the clutch retaining screw to 50 ft.-lb. (68 N·m).

OVERHAUL

Engine make and model are listed in specifications table at beginning of this section. Refer to the appropriate engine section in this manual for service information on the engine and associated accessories.

CLUTCH AND BRAKE

MODELS LT10, LT12, LT12.5, YT14 AND YT16

Adjustment

The clutch idler pulley is spring loaded and does not require adjustment. If belt slippage occurs, inspect drive belt for excessive wear or stretching and replace if necessary.

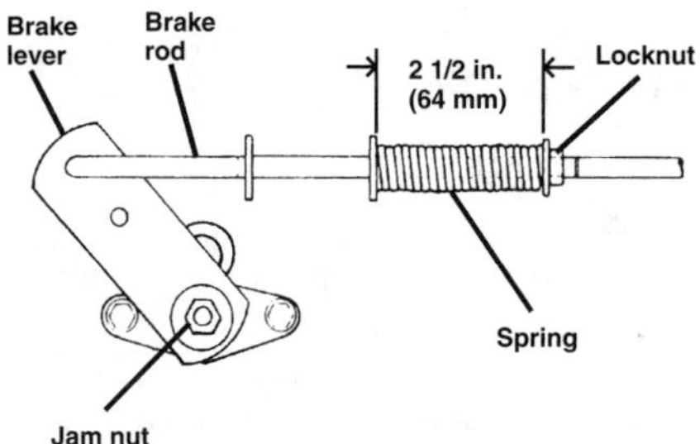

Fig. F1-7—On Models LT10, LT12, LT12.5, YT12.5, YT14 and YT16, brake spring should measure 2 1/2 inches (64 mm) when brake pedal is depressed fully. Refer to text.

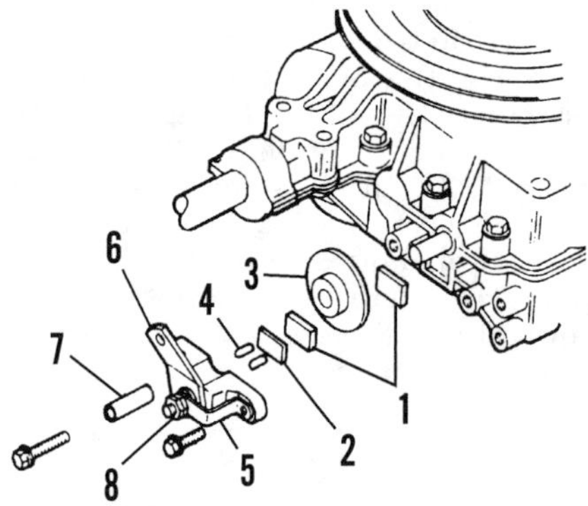

Fig. F1-8—Exploded view of disc brake assembly used on Models LT10, LT12, LT12.5, YT12.5, YT14 and YT16.

1. Brake pads
2. Back plate
3. Brake disc
4. Actuating pins
5. Brake pad holder
6. Brake lever
7. Spacer
8. Adjusting nuts

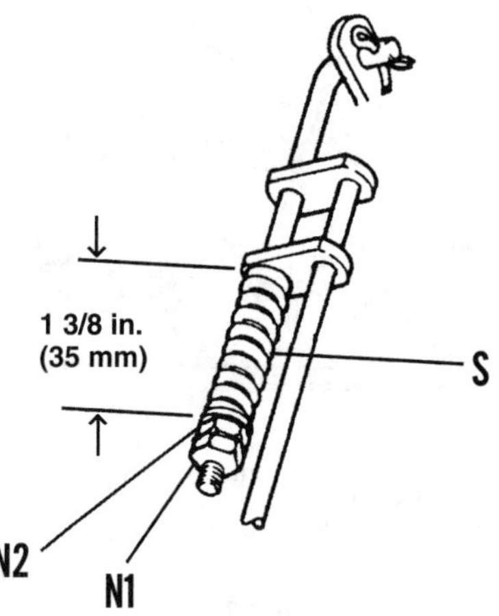

Fig. F1-9—On Models LT12H, LT12.5H, YT16H and YT18H, brake spring (S) length should be 1 3/8 inches (35 mm) when brake pedal is depressed.

To adjust the brake, fully depress the brake pedal and set the parking brake. The spring on the brake rod (Fig. F1-7) should be compressed to $2\frac{1}{2}$ inches (64 mm). Adjust by turning the locknut. With the spring correctly adjusted, depress the brake pedal and try to push the tractor in forward. If the brake does not stop rear wheels, release the brake pedal and loosen the jam nut at the brake lever. Tighten the inner adjustment nut until the rear wheels cannot be turned when the pedal is depressed. Rear wheels should turn easily with brake pedal in UP position. If the brake pad drags against the brake disc when the pedal is UP, loosen the adjusting nut slightly. Hold the adjusting nut and tighten the jam nut against it. If the correct brake adjustment cannot be obtained, replace the brake pads.

Overhaul

To replace the brake pads, raise and support the rear of the tractor. Remove the E-ring from the axle and remove the right rear wheel and tire assembly. Disconnect the brake rod from the brake lever. Remove two screws retaining the brake pad holder (5—Fig. F1-8) to the transaxle case. Remove outer brake pad, back-up plate (2) and actuator pins (4) from holder. Withdraw brake disc (3) from transaxle shaft and remove inner brake pad.

Reassembly is the reverse of disassembly. Adjust the brake as previously outlined.

MODELS LT12H, LT12.5H, YT16H AND YT18H

Adjustment

When depressed, the brake pedal is designed to return the hydrostatic transmission control lever to NEUTRAL. If the tractor creeps forward or backward after pedal is fully depressed, adjust linkage as outlined in the HYDROSTATIC TRANSMISSION section.

To adjust the brake, depress brake pedal and set the parking brake. Measure the length of the spring (S—Fig. F1-9) on the brake rod. If the spring length is not $1\frac{3}{8}$ inches (35 mm), loosen the outer jam nut (N1) and rotate the inner nut (N2) to adjust the spring length. Hold the inner jam nut and tighten the outer jam nut against the inner jam nut.

Overhaul

Brake components are contained in the transmission. Refer to HYDROSTATIC TRANSMISSION section for service.

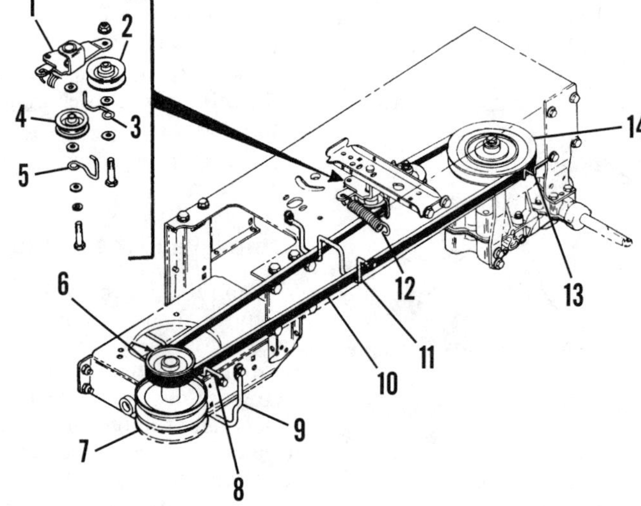

Fig. F1-10—Typical view of traction drive belt and pulleys used on Models LT10, LT12, LT12.5, YT12.5, YT14 and YT16.

1. Clutch pivot bracket
2. "V" idler pulley
3. Belt guide
4. Flat idler pulley
5. Belt guide
6. Engine pulley (traction drive)
7. Engine pulley (PTO)
8. Belt retainer, upper
9. Belt retainer, lower
10. Traction belt
11. Belt guide
12. Idler spring
13. Belt guide
14. Transaxle pulley

DRIVE BELT REMOVAL AND INSTALLATION

MODELS LT10, LT12, LT12.5, YT12.5, YT14 AND YT16

To remove the transaxle drive belt, first remove the mower deck. Depress clutch/brake pedal and set parking brake. Note the position of the belt guides (Fig. F1-10), then remove screws retaining the flat idler pulley (4) and

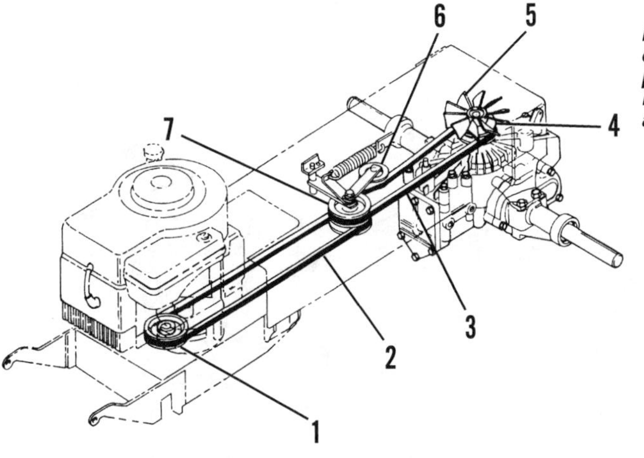

Fig. F1-11—Typical view of traction drive belt and pulleys used on Models LT12H, LT12.5H, YT16H and YT18H.

1. Engine pulley
2. Primary traction belt
3. Secondary traction belt
4. Transmission drive pulley
5. Fan
6. Spring-loaded idler
7. Jackshaft pulley

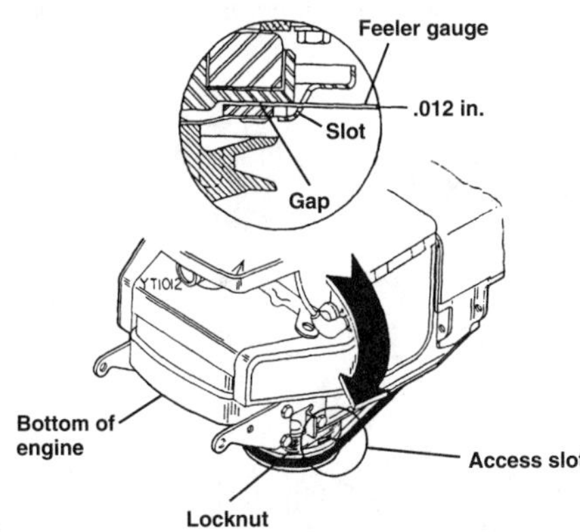

Fig. F1-12—With PTO clutch disengaged, clearance between clutch rotor and armature should be 0.012 inch (0.30 mm). Refer to text for adjustment.

V-idler pulley (2) to the clutch pivot bracket (1). Loosen screws retaining the left and right transaxle belt guides (13). Do not remove the belt guide retaining screws. Swing belt guides out of way. Remove belt guide (8) from the engine upper drive pulley (6). Lift the drive belt up and off the transaxle pulley. If equipped with an electric PTO clutch, disconnect the wire connector to the clutch. Slip the drive belt down and off both engine pulleys and through the lower belt guide (9).

When installing new belt, guides must be positioned ⅛ inch (3.2 mm) from the belt and pulley when the belt is tight. The spring-loaded clutch idler pulleys do not require adjustment.

MODELS LT12H, LT12.5H, YT16H AND YT18H

To remove the primary drive belt (2—Fig. F1-11), first remove the mower deck. If equipped with an electric PTO clutch, disconnect the wire connector to the clutch. Work the belt off the engine pulley (1) while turning the pulley clockwise by hand. Remove the belt from the jackshaft pulley (7), then pull the belt forward through the belt guide.

To install the primary belt, reverse the removal procedure. No adjustment of belt tension is necessary.

The secondary drive belt (3) can be removed after the primary belt has been removed. Pull the spring-loaded idler (6) to relieve belt tension. Remove the belt from the jackshaft and transmission pulleys. Work the belt around the fan blades and remove from the tractor.

To install the secondary belt, reverse the removal procedure. Be sure the spring-loaded idler pulley (6) is positioned on the backside of the belt. No adjustment of belt tension is necessary.

PTO CLUTCH

Some models may be equipped with an electric PTO clutch located on the engine crankshaft.

MODELS SO EQUIPPED

Adjustment

Clutch should be adjusted if clutch has been disassembled or if operation becomes erratic. The PTO and ignition switches must be off when performing the adjustment.

With the clutch disengaged, insert a feeler gauge through each slot in the clutch plate (Fig. F1-12) and measure the clearance between the clutch rotor and armature. Clearance should be 0.012 inch (0.30 mm).

To adjust, tighten the adjusting nut next to the slot until the feeler gauge begins to bind. Do not overtighten. Repeat adjustment at each of the slots in clutch plate. All slots must be adjusted equally.

Testing

Turn the ignition switch ON and actuate the PTO control switch. If the clutch does not engage, disconnect the wiring connector at the PTO clutch. Use a 12-volt test light to check for current to the connector. If the test light comes on, either the PTO or the wiring connection at clutch field coil is defective.

To check the field coil, disconnect the wiring connector at the PTO clutch. Using an ohmmeter set on the low scale, check the resistance between the PTO connector terminals. Specified resistance is 2.31-3.12 ohms. A reading other than the specified reading indicates the field coil is faulty and unit should be replaced.

Removal and Installation

To remove the PTO clutch, remove the mower deck and disconnect the wire connector. Unscrew the clutch retaining screw and pull clutch off crankshaft adapter.

Inspect the bearings in the field housing and armature for damage. Inspect the contact surfaces of rotor and armature for damage.

Apply an antiseize compound to the crankshaft before reinstalling the clutch. The slot in clutch plate must align with the stud (D—Fig. F1-6) on the torque bracket (B). Tighten the clutch retaining screw to 50 ft.-lb. (68 N·m). Adjust the clutch as previously outlined.

If a new clutch is installed, burnish the clutch friction surfaces: Start the engine and run at full speed. Actuate the PTO control switch on and off six times. Allow the mower to stop completely before turning the switch back on. Recheck adjustment.

TRANSAXLE (MODELS LT10, LT12, LT12.5, YT12.5, YT14 AND YT16)

LUBRICATION

The transaxle is filled at the factory with 30 ounces (0.9 L) of lithium base grease. Periodic lubrication is not required. Leakage indicates faulty seals or gaskets.

REMOVAL AND INSTALLATON

Remove the secondary drive belt as outlined in the previous DRIVE BELT section. Disconnect the gear selector lever from the transaxle. Disconnect the brake control rod from the brake lever. Raise and support rear of tractor. Remove screws attaching the axle mounting brackets to the frame. Roll the transaxle assembly back from the tractor. Remove the wheels.

To install the transaxle, reverse the removal procedure.

OVERHAUL

The tractor is equipped with a Peerless 801 series transaxle. Refer to the appropriate Peerless section in the TRANSAXLE SERVICE section for overhaul information.

HYDROSTATIC TRANSMISSION (MODELS LT12H, LT12.5H, YT16H AND YT18H

LUBRICATION

The hydrostatic transmission and transaxle unit share a common oil reservoir. Be sure to clean any dirty residue on or around the cap before removing the oil cap. Check oil level with transmission at normal operating temperature and engine stopped. Transmission reservoir is located under the hood on early models (Fig. F1-13) or at the rear of the tractor (Fig. F1-14) on later models.

On early models, the oil level should be even with the appropriate mark on the reservoir (Fig. F1-13). On later models, the oil level in the reservoir should be approximately 1/4 inch (6.4 mm) above the mold parting line on the reservoir tank. The recommended lubricant is SAE 20 engine oil.

Later models are equipped with a spin-on oil filter mounted on the transmission. Install a new filter after the first 10 hours of operation then after every 500 hours of operation. Recheck the oil level after installing the new filter and operating the transmission for a short time.

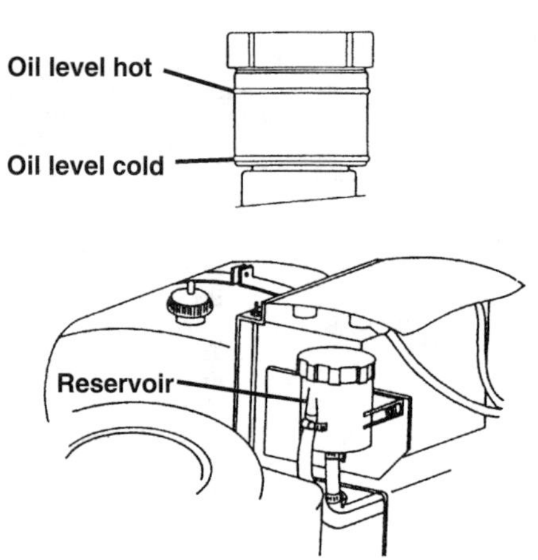

Fig. F1-13—On some models equipped with a hydrostatic transmission, transmission oil reservoir is located under hood. Desired oil levels are marked on reservoir.

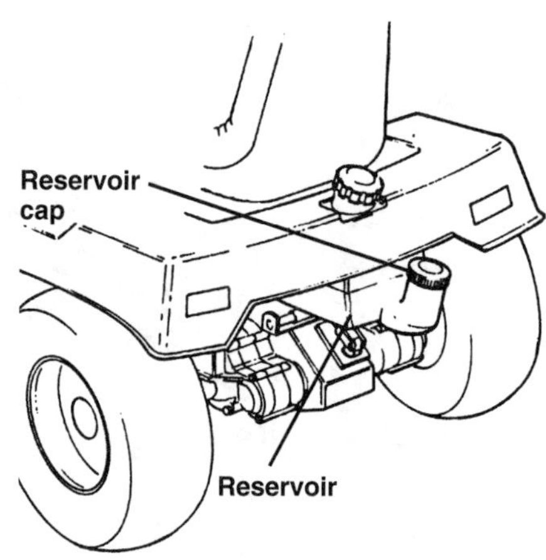

Fig. F1-14—On some models equipped with a hydrostatic transmission, transmission oil reservoir is located at rear of tractor.

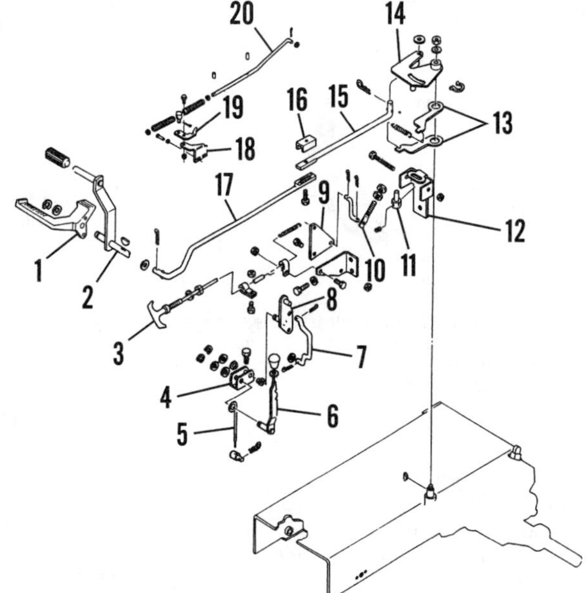

Fig. F1-15—Typical view of hydrostatic transmission control linkage used on Models LT12H, LT12.5H, YT16H and YT18H.

1. Speed control foot pedal
2. Brake pedal
3. Tow valve cable
4. Pivot bracket
5. Cruise release rod
6. Cruise release lever
7. Speed control link
8. Speed control arm
9. Pivot lever
10. Tow valve link
11. Neutral trunnion
12. Trunnion support
13. Neutral straps
14. Transmission control assy.
15. Speed control rear rod
16. Clamp
17. Speed control front rod
18. Lock bracket
19. Neutral control lock
20. Neutral lock rod

NEUTRAL ADJUSTMENT

To check transmission neutral adjustment, depress the foot control pedal (1—Fig. F1-15) to drive the tractor forward. Depress the brake pedal (2) all the way down, then release the pedal. Repeat the test in reverse. If the tractor creeps in either direction after the pedal is released, adjust the control linkage.

Position the tractor on a level surface and block the front wheels to prevent the tractor from rolling. Raise and support the tractor's rear so the rear wheels clear the ground. Loosen the neutral lock pivot bracket (18) mounting bolts and move the bracket in the slotted holes until the transmission is in neutral position.

To adjust the speed control pedal linkage, fully depress the pedal (1), then release the pedal. Loosen the speed control rod clamp (16) and adjust the length of the speed control rods (15 and 17) as required to place transmission in NEUTRAL. Tighten the clamp screw and check for proper operation. Repeat adjustment if necessary.

REMOVAL AND INSTALLATION

To remove the hydrostatic transmission and transaxle assembly, first remove the mower deck from the tractor. Remove the primary and secondary drive belts as previously outlined. Disconnect the brake control linkage and transmission control linkage. Disconnect and remove the reservoir oil lines from the transmission. Remove the screws attaching the transmission to the tractor frame. Support the transmission assembly with a jack to prevent tipping. Raise the rear of tractor until clear of the transmission and move to one side.

To install the transmission, reverse the removal procedure.

OVERHAUL

Models LT12H and LT12.5H are equipped with an Eaton 750 hydrostatic transmission. Models YT16 and YT18H are equipped with an Eaton 850 or 851 hydrostatic transmission. Refer to the appropriate Eaton section in the HYDROSTATIC TRANSMISSION SERVICE section for overhaul information.

ELECTRICAL SYSTEM

Refer to Figs. F1-16, F1-17 and F1-18 for wiring schematics. Engine related electrical components, such as the starter, are covered in the appropriate engine section at the rear of this manual.

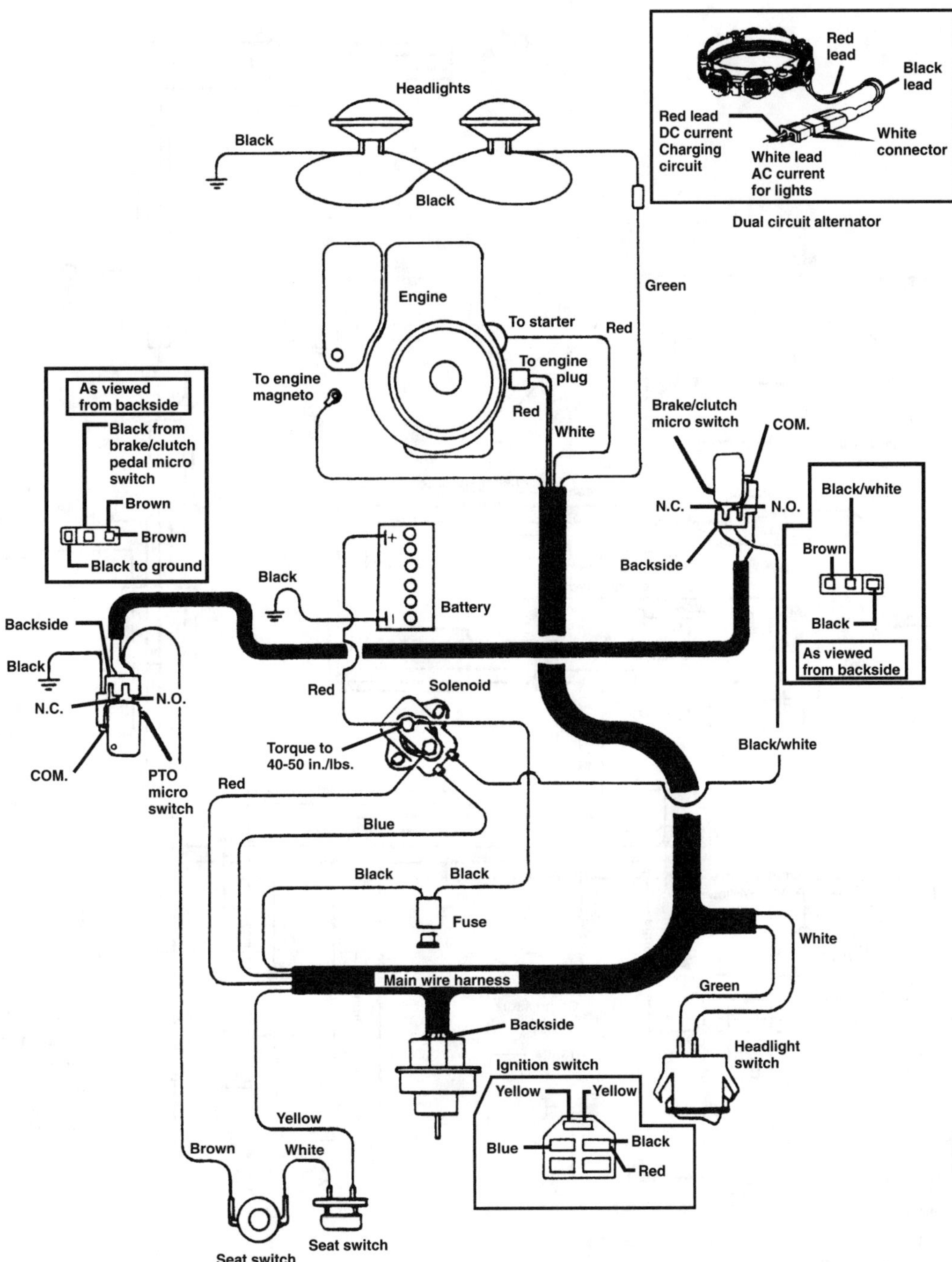

Fig. F1-16—Electrical wiring schematic for Model LT12.

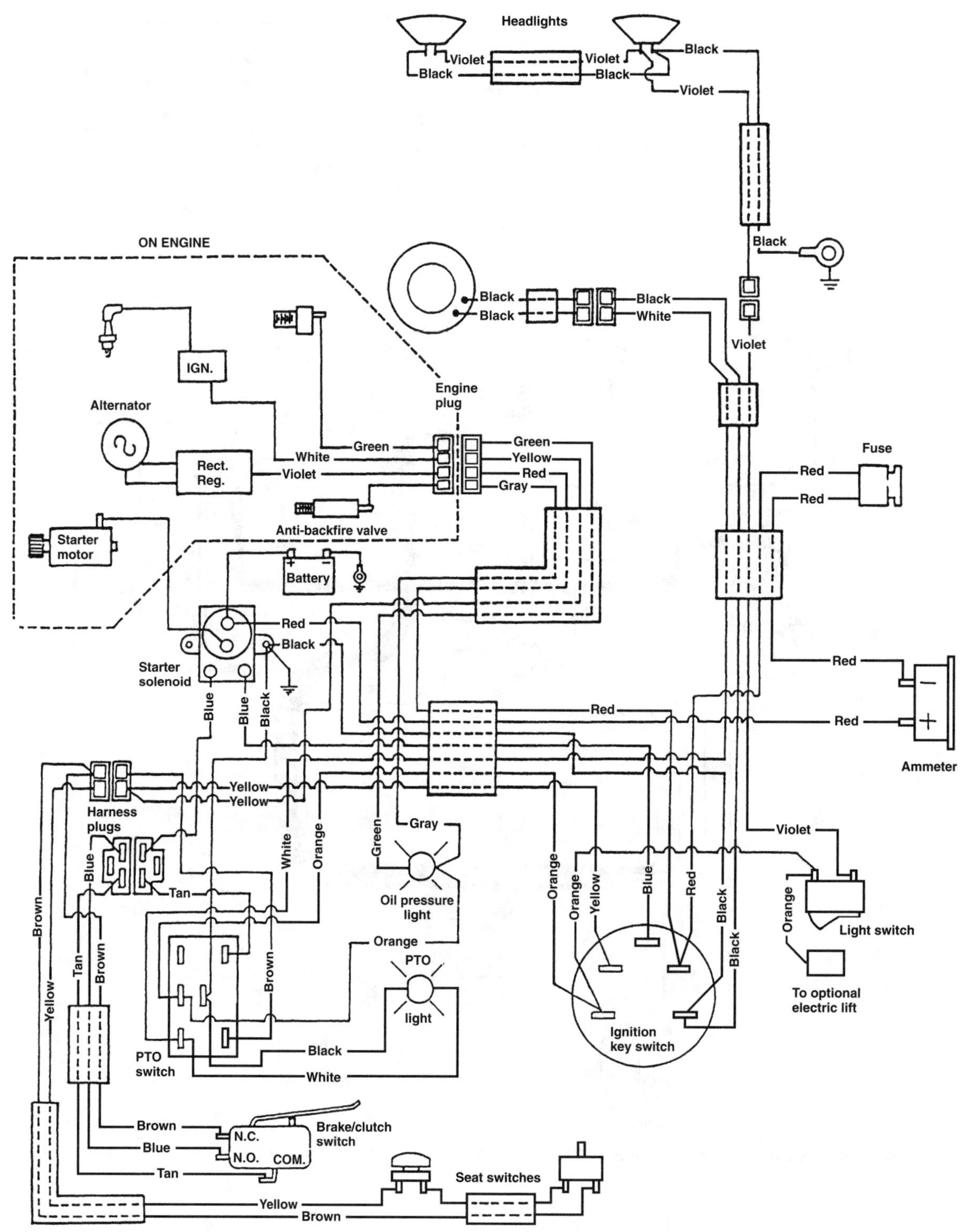

Fig. F1-17—Electrical wiring schematic for Models YT12.5 and YT14.

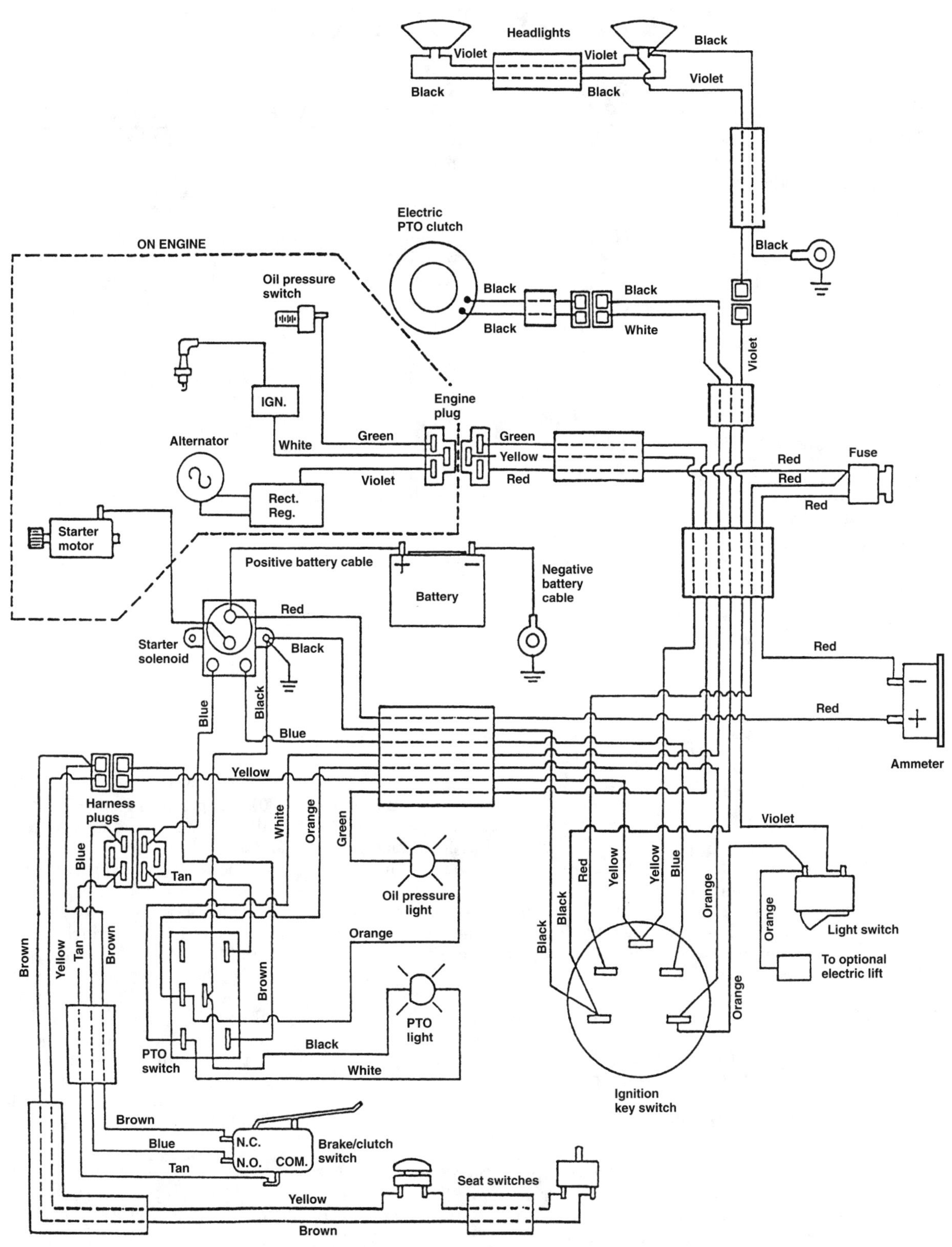

Fig. F1-18—Electrical wiring schematic for Models YT16, YT16H and YT18H.

FORD

CONDENSED SPECIFICATIONS

Models	GT65, LGT14D	GT75, LGT16D	GT85	GT95
Engine Make	Shibaura	Shibaura	Kohler	Kohler
Model	E643	E673	M18	M20
Number of cylinders	3	3	2	2
Bore	64 mm (2.52 in.)	67 mm (2.64 in.)	3.12 in. (79.2 mm)	3.12 in. (79.2 mm)
Stroke	64 mm (2.52 in.)	64 mm (2.52 in.)	2.75 in. (69.85 mm)	3.06 in. (78.0 mm)
Displacement	617 cc (37.7 cu. in.)	676 cc (41.2 cu. in.)	42.18 cu. in. (691 cc)	46.98 cu. In. (769.8 cc)
Power Rating	10.4 kW (14 hp)	11.9 kW (16 hp)	18 hp (13.4 kW)	20 hp (14.9 kW)
Slow Idle	1450 rpm	1450 rpm	1750 rpm	1750 rpm
High Speed (No-Load)	3400 rpm	3400 rpm	3400 rpm	3400 rpm
Crankcase Capacity	2.5 L* (2.6 qt.)	2.5 L* (2.6 qt.)	3.0 pt.** (1.4 L)	3.0 pt.** (1.4 L)
Transmission Capacity	See text	See text	See text	See text

*With filter—3.0 liter (3.2 qt.).
**With filter—3.5 pt.(1.7 L).

FRONT AXLE ASSEMBLY

MAINTENANCE

Inject grease into the grease fittings found on the axle and steering components at 50-hour intervals. Recommended lubricant is a multipurpose, lithium base grease. Clean all pivot points and linkages and lubricate with SAE 30 oil. Check for looseness and wear, and repair when needed.

FRONT WHEELS

Front wheel bearings are pressed into wheel hubs. Replace bearings when needed to correct excessive looseness. Lubricate with multipurpose, lithium base grease.

SPINDLES

Raise and support the side to be serviced. Remove the wheel and tire. Disconnect the tie rod end, and if needed, the drag link end. If removing the right spindle, detach the E-ring (2—Fig. F2-1 or Fig. F2-2) securing the top of the spindle and withdraw the spindle from the axle. If removing the left spindle, remove the clamp bolt, remove the steering arm and withdraw the spindle from the axle.

Inspect components for damage. Replaceable bushings are located in the axle. The bushing inside diameter wear limit is 1.002 in. (25.45 mm) for all models.

New bushing inside diameter is 0.984 inch (25.0 mm). It may be necessary to hone new bushings after installation so the spindle will turn freely. Lubricate the components with multipurpose, lithium base grease.

AXLE MAIN MEMBER OVERHAUL

Models GT65, GT75, GT85 and GT95

The axle pivot tube (30—Fig. F2-1) and PTO drive shaft (28) must be removed as a unit. Remove the mower deck and mower drive shaft, if so equipped. Remove the PTO belts as outlined in the PTO service section. Remove the sleeve (22), snap ring (23) and hub (24) with pulley (25).

Support the front of the tractor. Detach the drag link or power steering cylinder from the steering arm (14). Unscrew the pivot tube nut (27). Remove the screws retaining the axle pivot tube (30). Support the front axle, then carefully drive the pivot tube with the PTO shaft out of the frame. Lower and roll the axle assembly away from the tractor.

The specified radial clearance between the pivot tube (30) and axle (7) bore is 0.0004-0.0030 inch (0.010-0.076 mm). Maximum allowable radial clearance is 0.020 inch (0.51 mm). Replace the pivot tube and/or axle if worn.

Reverse the removal procedure to install the front axle. Apply Loctite to the pivot tube nut (27) during assembly, then tighten the nut so axle side play is 0.004 in. (0.1 mm). Maximum allowable side play is 0.04 in. (1.0 mm).

Models LGT14D and LGT16D

Refer to the PTO section and remove the PTO shaft (27—Fig. F2-2). Detach the drag link or power steering cylinder from the steering arm (14). Support the front of the tractor. Remove screws retaining the axle pivot tube (28). Support the front axle and withdraw the pivot tube (28) while noting the position of the spacer (31) and shims (32). Lower

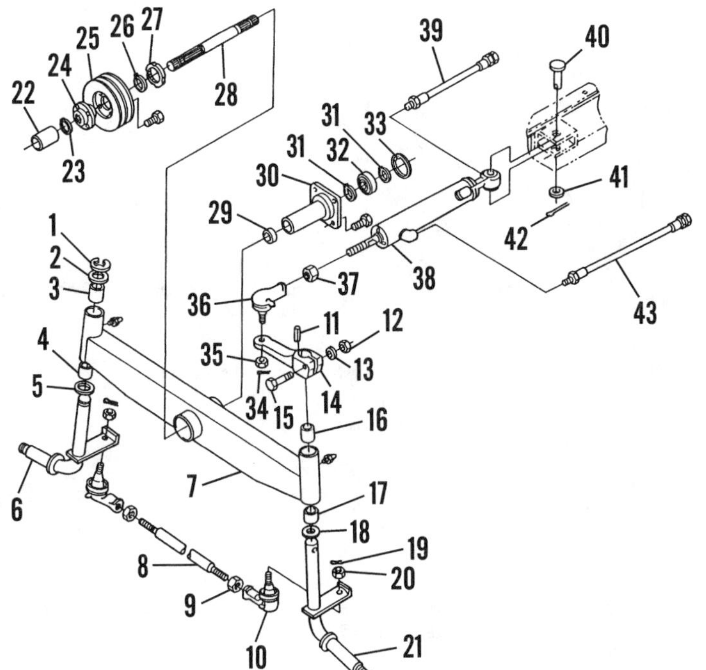

Fig. F2-1—Exploded view of front axle and PTO shaft assemblies used on Models GT65, GT75, GT85 and GT95. Hydraulic cylinder (38) is only used on models equipped with power steering.

1. E-ring
2. Washer
3. Bushing
4. Bushing
5. Washer
6. Steering spindle (right)
7. Axle main member
8. Tie rod
9. Nut
10. Tie rod end
11. Key
12. Nut
13. Washer
14. Steering arm
15. Bolt
16. Bushing
17. Bushing
18. Washer
19. Cotter pin
20. Nut
21. Spindle (left)
22. Sleeve
23. Snap ring
24. Hub
25. Pulley
26. Snap ring
27. Nut
28. PTO shaft
29. Bearing
30. Pivot tube
31. Snap rings
32. Bearing
33. Snap ring
34. Cotter pin
35. Nut
36. Rod end
37. Nut
38. Steering cylinder
39. Hydraulic hose
40. Clevis pin
41. Washer
42. Cotter pin
43. Hydraulic hose

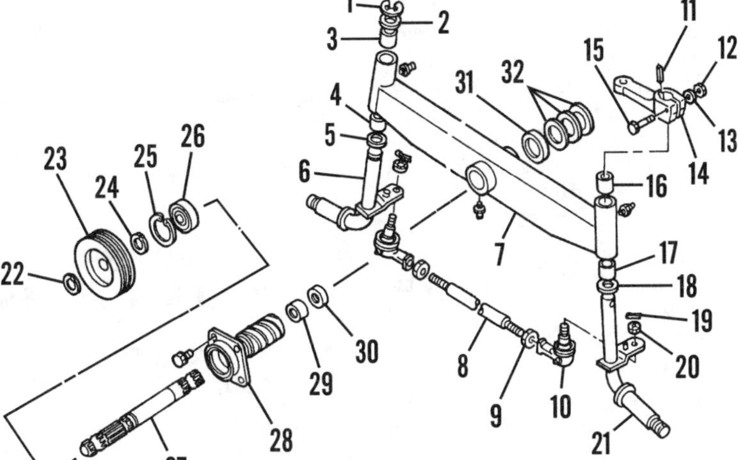

Fig. F2-2—Exploded view of front axle and PTO shaft assemblies used on Models LGT14D and LGT16D.

1. E-ring
2. Washer
3. Bushing
4. Bushing
5. Washer
6. Steering spindle (right)
7. Axle main member
8. Tie rod
9. Nut
10. Tie rod end
11. Key
12. Nut
13. Washer
14. Steering arm
15. Bolt
16. Bushing
17. Bushing
18. Washer
19. Cotter pin
20. Nut
21. Spindle (left)
22. Snap ring
23. Pulley
24. Snap ring
25. Snap ring
26. Bearing
27. PTO shaft
28. Pivot tube
29. Bearing
30. Seal
31. Spacer
32. Shims

the axle assembly and roll it away from the tractor.

The specified radial clearance between the pivot tube (28) and axle (7) bore is 0.0004-0.0030 in. (0.010-0.076 mm). Maximum allowable radial clearance is 0.020 in. (0.51 mm). Replace the pivot tube or axle if worn excessively.

The desired axle side play on the pivot tube is 0.0-0.012 in. (0.0-0.30 mm). Maximum allowable side play is 0.020 inch (0.51 mm). Adjust axle side play by installing shims (32).

Reverse the removal procedure to install the front axle.

MANUAL STEERING SYSTEM

TIE ROD AND TOE-IN ADJUSTMENT (ALL MODELS SO EQUIPPED)

With wheels set straight ahead, measure toe-in at hub height at the front and rear of the wheel rims. Adjust tie rod length to obtain toe-in of 0-$^{13}/_{64}$ in. (0-5.2 mm). Tighten jam nuts after adjustment.

DRAG LINK ADJUSTMENT (ALL MODELS SO EQUIPPED)

Models without power steering are equipped with an adjustable drag link between the steering arm on the left spindle and the pitman arm. Adjust the drag link length so the front wheels point straight ahead when the steering wheel is centered.

STEERING GEAR OVERHAUL

Models GT65, GT75, GT85,GT95 So Equipped

Disconnect the battery cables. Disconnect the throttle cable from the fuel injection pump. Loosen the PTO control cable nuts at the PTO end to increase the cable slack. Detach the lower and upper PTO idler springs. Disconnect the PTO cable.

Remove the steering wheel (1—Fig. F2-3). Drive out roll pins and remove the PTO and speed control levers. Remove the center panel below the dash panel. Remove the air intake screens on both sides of the control console.

Disconnect electrical wiring from the temperature sender, starter motor, alternator, oil pressure sender, glow plug, injection pump solenoid and headlamps. Drain coolant from the radiator and engine. Refer to ENGINE REMOVAL AND INSTALLATION for detailed instructions.

Remove the air intake horn. Remove both radiator hoses. Remove the pins

(1—Fig. F2-4) from the speed control overcenter link. Remove snap ring and slide spring shaft (3) inward so it clears the vertical control rod (5). Rotate shaft (3) back to relieve spring tension and detach spring (4).

Remove the nut and lockwasher from the lower end of the steering shaft (16—Fig. F2-3). Remove the screw (12) and rectangular holder (13) on each side of the sub frame. Lift out the steering column (4) and shaft (2) assembly while holding the tilt lever (11). Remove the snap ring (9), and drive out the pin (8) from the universal joint (10) Remove the snap ring (7) and drive out the steering shaft (2) with bearing (6).

Remove the two cap screws attaching the radiator/console sub frame (15) to the frame and lift the support with radiator off the tractor frame.

Disconnect the steering drag link from the pitman arm (17—Fig. F2-3). Remove the nut (18) attaching the pitman arm to the steering gear sector (14). Observe the alignment marks on the sector gear shaft and pitman arm. If marks are not present, make alignment marks on the shaft and pitman arm. Separate and remove the pitman arm and sector gear.

Inspect all parts for damage. Replace when necessary.

Reassemble by reversing the removal procedure. Align the marks on the sector gear shaft (14—Fig. F2-3) and pitman arm (17). Tighten the pitman arm retaining nut (18) to 67-84 ft.-lb. (91.1-114.6 N·m).

Models LGT14D and LGT16D So Equipped

Disconnect the battery cables. Disconnect the proofmeter cable from the proofmeter. Disconnect the throttle cable from the fuel injection pump. Loosen the PTO control cable nuts at the PTO end to increase the cable slack. Detach the lower and upper PTO idler springs. Disconnect the PTO cable.

Remove the steering wheel. Drive out roll pins and remove the PTO and speed control levers. Remove the panel around the ignition switch. Remove the air intake screens on both sides of the control console. Disconnect the electrical wiring from the temperature sender, starter motor, alternator, oil pressure sender, glow plug, injection pump solenoid and headlamps.

Drain coolant from the radiator and engine. Remove the alternator. Remove the air intake horn. Remove both radiator hoses. Remove the pins (1—Fig. F2-4) from the speed control overcenter link. Remove snap ring and slide spring shaft (3) inward so it clears the vertical control rod (5) Rotate shaft (3) back to relieve spring tension and detach spring (4).

Detach the cotter pin (9—Fig. F2-5), unscrew nut (8) and remove the washer (7) at the end of the steering shaft (3). Pull up the steering shaft so it clears the support plate (6). Remove the radiator/console support mounting screws and lift the support with the radiator off the tractor frame. Disconnect the drag link from the sector gear arm. Unscrew the pivot bolt (10—Fig. F2-5) and remove the sector gear (14).

Check for damage. Remove and replace bushings (5—Fig. F2-5) in the support plate if worn. Remove and replace bushings (13—Fig. F2-5) in the sector gear if worn.

Reassemble by reversing the removal procedure. After installing the steering shaft, but before installing the panels, check and, if necessary, adjust steering gear backlash. Install the steering wheel and check gear backlash by measuring wheel free play at the wheel rim. Desired wheel free play is ¾ to 1¼ in. (19-31 mm). Maximum allowable free play is 2¼ inches (57 mm). Adjust gear backlash by loosening the retaining bolts for the support plate (6—Fig. F2-5) and relocating the support plate.

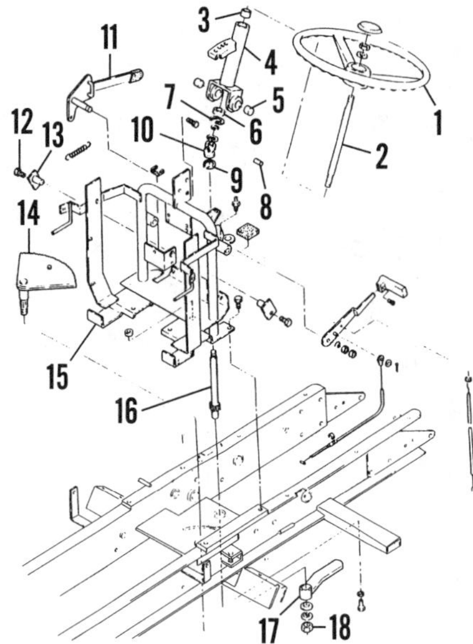
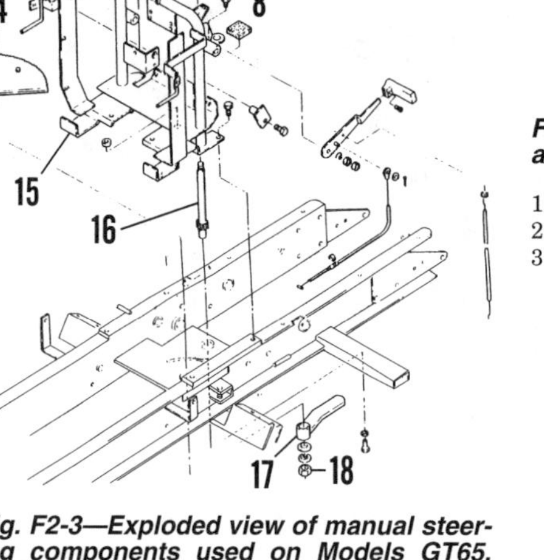

Fig. F2-3—Exploded view of manual steering components used on Models GT65, GT75, GT85 and GT95.

1. Steering wheel	10. Universal joint
2. Steering shaft	11. Tilt lever
3. Dust seal	12. Bolt
4. Steering column	13. Holder
5. Sleeve	14. Steering gear sector
6. Bearing	15. Sub frame
7. Snap ring	16. Steering gear shaft
8. Pin	17. Pitman arm
9. Snap ring	18. Nut

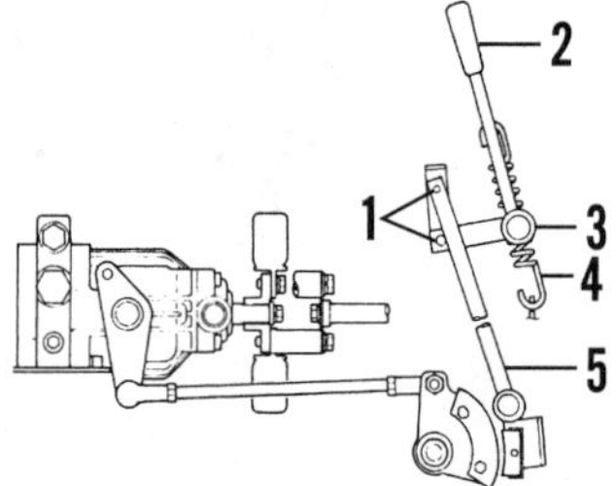

Fig. F2-4—Drawing of speed control lever assembly.

1. Pins	4. Spring
2. Speed control lever	5. Control rod
3. Shaft	

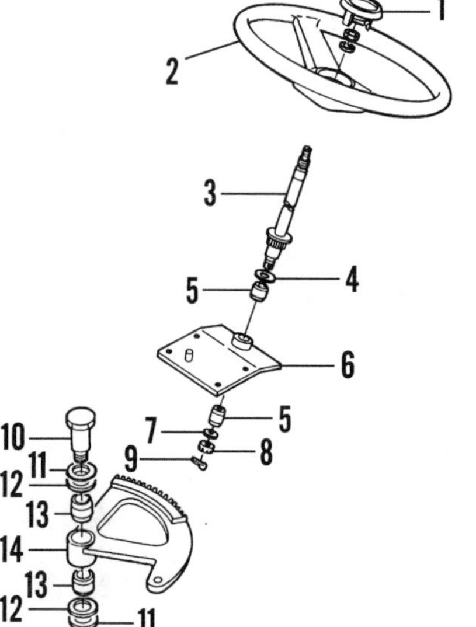

Fig. F2-5—Exploded view of manual steering gear assembly used on Models LGT14D and LGT16D.

1. Cap	8. Nut
2. Steering wheel	9. Cotter pin
3. Steering shaft & gear	10. Pivot pin
4. Thrust washer	11. Washers
5. Bushing	12. Spacers
6. Plate	13. Bushings
7. Washer	14. Sector gear

POWER STEERING SYSTEM

SYSTEM OPERATION (ALL MODELS SO EQUIPPED)

On models equipped with power steering, pressurized oil from the hydrostatic drive unit is supplied to a steering control valve. Movement of the steering wheel turns elements in the control valve directing the pressurized oil to either the right or left turn output ports on the control valve.

Hydraulic hoses connect the control valve ports to the steering cylinder attached to the left spindle steering arm. During right turns, pressurized oil

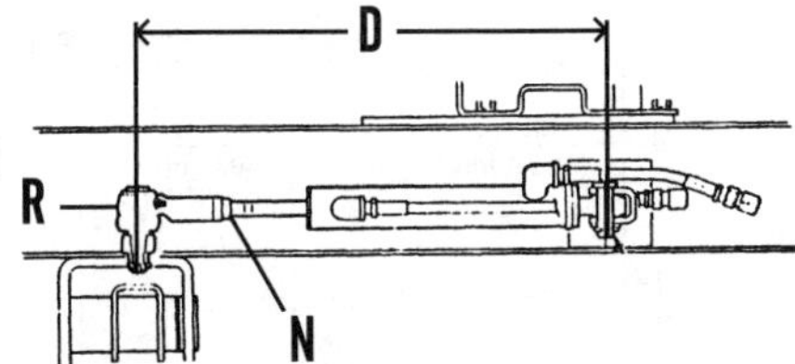

Fig. F2-6—With steering cylinder rod fully retracted, distance (D) should be 15.8 inches (402 mm). To adjust distance, loosen jam nut (N) and rotate rod end (R).

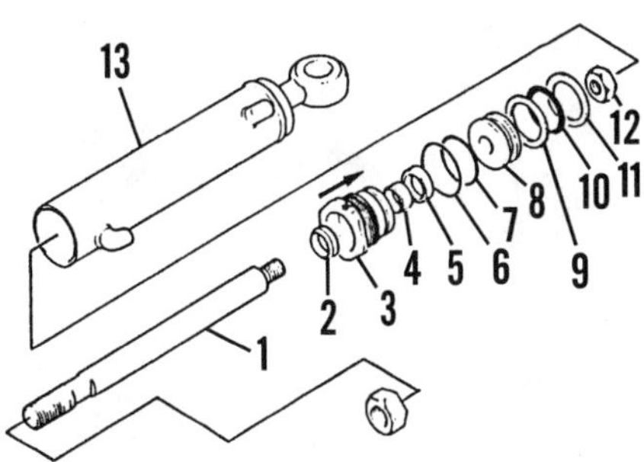

Fig. F2-7—Exploded view of power steering cylinder.

1. Rod
2. Wiper ring
3. Cylinder head
4. Bushing
5. U-ring
6. O-ring
7. O-ring
8. Piston
9. Backup ring
10. O-ring
11. Backup ring
12. Nut
13. Cylinder

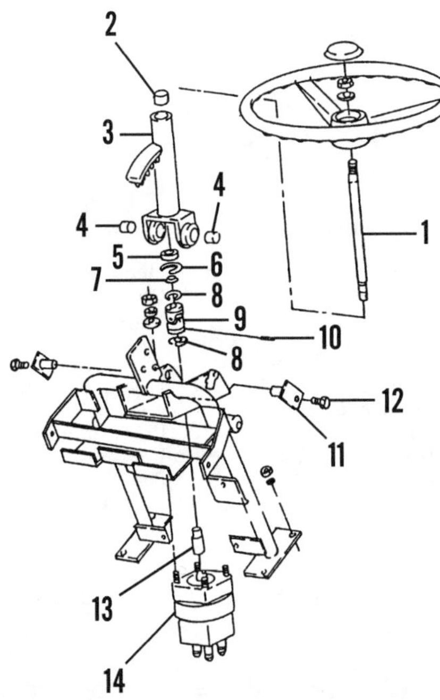

Fig. F2-8—Exploded view of power steering column assembly.

1. Steering shaft
2. Rubber
3. Steering column
4. Bushing
5. Bearing
6. Snap ring
7. Snap ring
8. Pin
9. Universal joint
10. Pin
11. Holder
12. Screw
13. Input shaft
14. Steering control valve

travels to the front steering cylinder hose (43—Fig. F2-1). During left turns, pressurized oil enters the cylinder through the rear hose (39).

If hydraulic flow to the steering control valve is interrupted, the steering control valve acts as a pump to maintain steering control.

Refer to the TRANSMISSION section for maintenance and service information for the hydrostatic drive unit.

Testing

Use the following procedure to check system pressure. Disconnect the steering cylinder right-turn hose (43—Fig. F2-1) from the elbow on the tractor frame. Connect a 0-2000 psi (0-14000 kPa) gauge to the elbow.

Run engine at high idle. Slowly turn steering wheel clockwise and observe the gauge reading. The pressure reading at full right turn should be 845-935 psi (5830-6451 kPa).

An incorrect reading may indicate a faulty steering control valve relief valve or a malfunction in the hydrostatic drive unit.

TIE ROD AND TOE-IN ADJUSTMENT (ALL MODELS SO EQUIPPED)

Measure toe-in at hub height at the front and rear of the wheel rims. Adjust tie rod length to obtain toe-in of 0-13/64 inch (0-5.2 mm). Tighten jam nuts after adjustment.

POWER STEERING CYLINDER (ALL MODELS SO EQUIPPED)

Length Adjustment

The effective length of the steering cylinder must be correct to provide proper steering geometry.

To check or adjust cylinder length, detach the rod end from the steering arm (14—Fig. F2-1). Retract the cylinder rod to its fully retracted position.

Measure from the center of the rear attachment pin to the center of the rod end as shown in Fig. F2-6. Distance (D) should be 15.8 in. (402 mm).

To adjust the distance, loosen the jam nut (N) and rotate the rod end (R). Retighten the jam nut and reattach the rod end to the steering arm.

Overhaul

Disconnect the neutral switch connector and remove the seat and seat support assembly. Pull up with a twisting motion and remove the transmission range and hydraulic lift control knobs.

Unscrew four fender-to-seat support screws. Unscrew fender-to-step plate screws and lift off the fender.

Unscrew the parking brake lever knob. Drive out the roll pin securing the speed control pedal and remove the pedal.

Remove the step plate over the steering cylinder. Disconnect the steering cylinder hydraulic hoses. Detach the steering cylinder from the spindle steering arm. Remove the steering cylinder from the tractor frame.

An exploded view of the steering cylinder is shown in Fig. F2-7. To disassemble cylinder, straighten the staked tab at the head end of the cylinder. Unscrew the cylinder head (3) and extract the rod and piston assembly. Unscrew the nut (12) and slide components off the rod toward the piston end of the rod.

Clean and inspect parts. Maximum allowable clearance between piston and cylinder bore is 0.0118 in. (0.300 mm). Maximum allowable clearance between bushing surface in cylinder head (3) and rod (1) is 0.0118 in. (0.300 mm).

Reassemble by reversing the disassembly procedure. Install the head (3) by sliding it onto the rod from the piston end of the rod.

Apply Loctite to piston retaining nut (12) and tighten nut to 18-23 ft.-lb. (24.5-31.3 N·m). Apply Loctite to the cylinder head (3) and tighten head to 29-43 ft.-lb. (39.4-58.5 N·m).

POWER STEERING CONTROL VALVE (ALL MODELS SO EQUIPPED)

Removal and Installation

Disconnect the battery cables. Disconnect neutral switch connector and remove the seat and seat support assembly. Pull up with a twisting motion and remove the transmission range and hydraulic lift control knobs. Unscrew four fender-to-seat support screws. Unscrew fender-to-step plate screws and lift off the fender.

Unscrew the parking brake lever knob. Drive out the roll pin securing the speed control pedal and remove the pedal. Remove the step plates.

Remove the steering wheel. Drive out the roll pins and remove the PTO and speed control levers. Remove the center panel below the dash panel. Remove the air intake screens on both sides of the control console.

Disconnect the instrument panel wiring. Remove grips from the throttle and steering wheel tilt lever. Mark, then disconnect the oil lines from the steering control valve. Cap or plug all openings.

Mark the steering control valve so it can be returned to its original position in the bracket. Refer to Fig. F2-8, unscrew the nuts securing the steering control valve in the bracket and remove the steering control valve.

Install by reversing the removal procedure. After installation is completed, start the engine and turn the steering wheel from full left to full right several times to bleed air from the system.

Overhaul

Before disassembling the steering control valve, note the alignment grooves (G—Fig. F2-9) machined in the unit's side. Thoroughly clean the outside of the unit and take necessary precautions to prevent dirt from entering the unit.

NOTE: Do not clamp the steering control valve in a vise for service work. Fabricate a holding fixture as shown in Fig. F2-10.

Place the steering valve in a holding fixture with the steering shaft down and secure with 5/16-24 NF nuts. Remove the four nuts securing the port cover (6—Fig. F2-11) and remove the cover.

Remove the sealing ring (8) and five O-rings (7). Remove the relief valve plug (1), spring (3) and cartridge (4). Remove the O-ring (2) from the plug.

Remove the port manifold (9) and the three springs (10). Remove the valve ring (12) and discard sealing rings (8 and 11).

Remove the valve plate (14) and the three springs (13) from the isolation manifold pockets. Remove the hex drive and pin assembly (16), then the isolation manifold (18).

Remove the drive link (20), seal (19), metering ring (21) and seal (22). Lift off the metering assembly and remove the seal (24).

Remove the 11 Allen head screws (23) and lift off the commutator cover (25). Remove the commutator ring (26), and carefully remove commutator (27) and the five alignment pins (28).

Remove the drive link spacer (29) and separate rotor (30) from stator (31). Remove the drive plate (32), spacer (33), thrust bearing (34), seal spacer (36) and face seal (35).

Separate the upper cover plate (37) and upper cover (38). Remove the steering input shaft (40) and service the upper bearing seat, washer and retaining ring as necessary.

Clean and inspect all parts and replace any showing signs of damage. Springs (10) should have a free length of 0.75 inch (19 mm) and springs (13) should have a free length of 0.50 inch (12.7 mm). Springs must be replaced as sets only.

The commutator (27) and commutator ring (26) are a matched set and must be replaceded as an assembly.

Check the rotor-to-stator clearance using a feeler gauge as shown in Fig. F2-12. If the clearance exceeds 0.003 in. (0.08 mm) replace the stator assembly.

Replace O-rings and lubricate all parts with clean hydraulic fluid prior to installation.

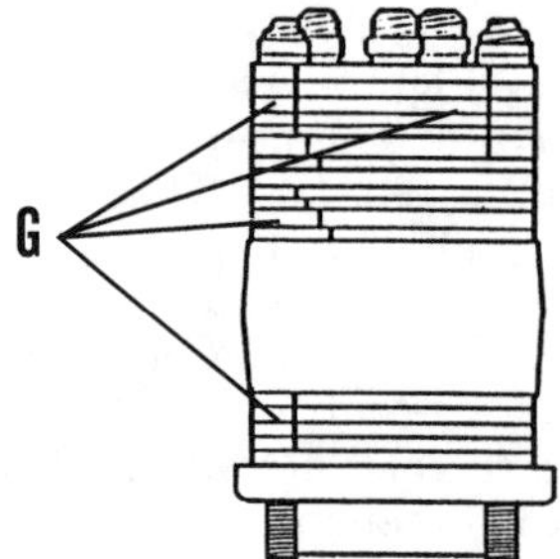

Fig. F2-9—Grooves (G) on side of control valve should be aligned as shown.

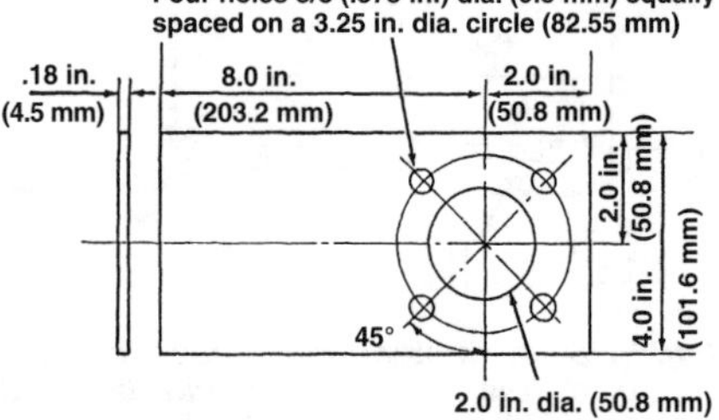

Fig. F2-10—Fabricate a holding fixture using the dimensions shown to secure control valve during overhaul.

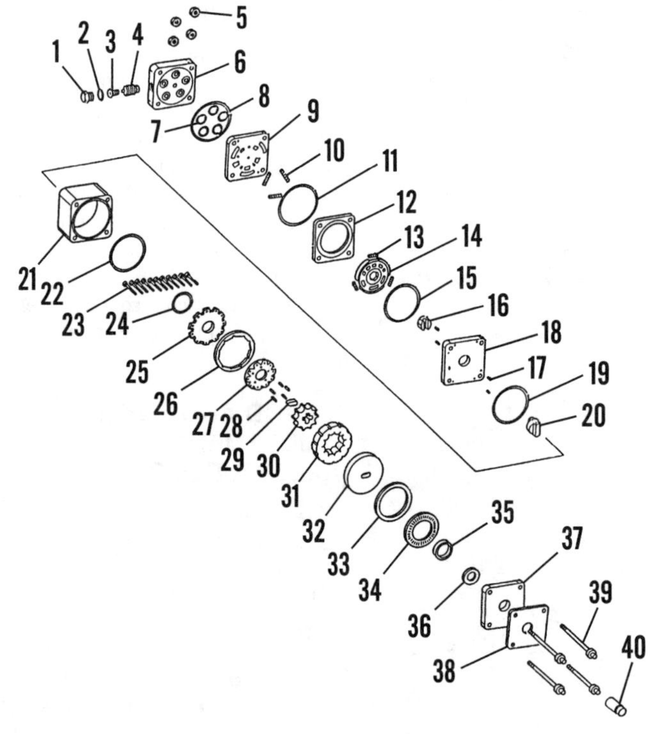

Fig. F2-11—Exploded view of power steering control valve.

1. Plug
2. O-ring
3. Spring
4. Relief valve cartridge
5. Nut
6. Port cover
7. O-rings
8. Seal ring
9. Port manifold
10. Springs
11. Seal ring
12. Valve ring
13. Springs
14. Valve plate
15. Seal ring
16. Hex drive assy.
17. Alignment pins (2)
18. Isolation manifold
19. Seal ring
20. Drive link
21. Metering ring
22. Seal ring
23. Screws (11)
24. Commutator seal
25. Commutator cover
26. Commutator ring
27. Commutator
28. Alignment pins (5)
29. Drive link spacer
30. Rotor
31. Stator
32. Drive plate
33. Spacer
34. Thrust bearing
35. Face seal
36. Face seal back-up ring
37. Upper cover plate
38. Upper cover
39. Bolts
40. Input shaft

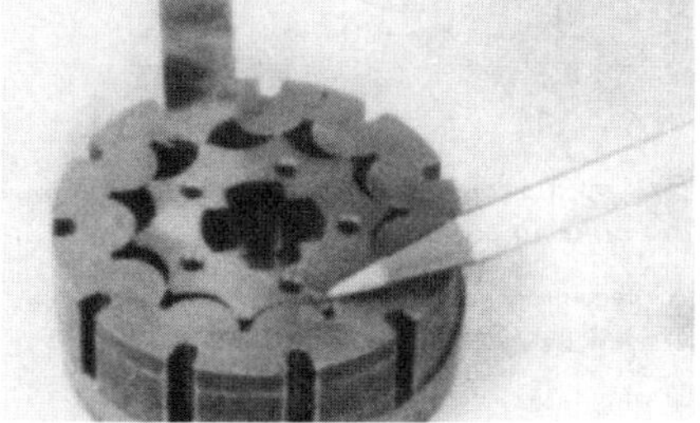

Fig. F2-12—Use a feeler gauge to check rotor to stator clearance. Refer to text.

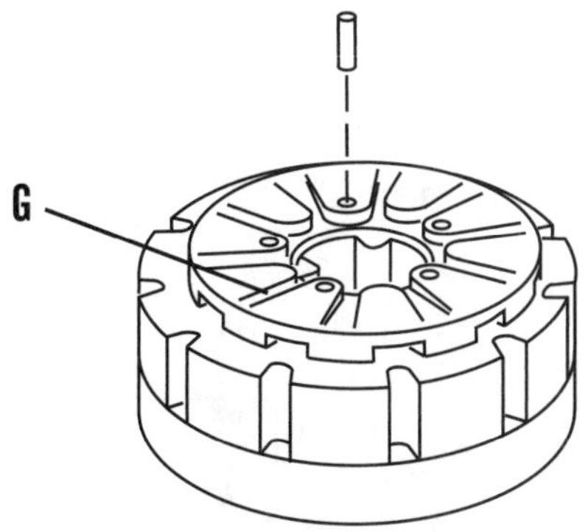

Fig. F2-13—Install commutator so long grooves (G) are out.

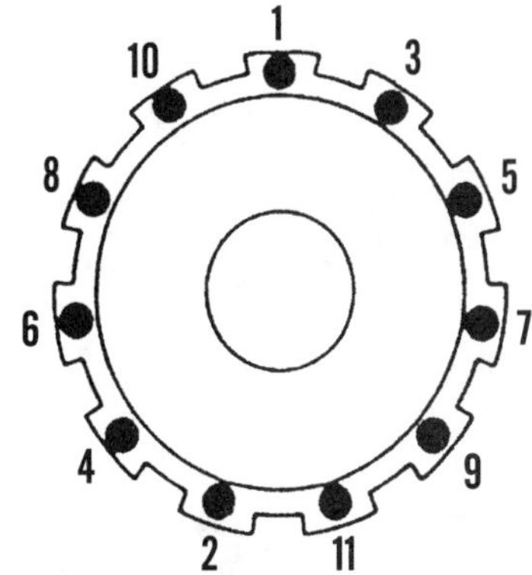

Fig. F2-14—Tighten the 11 Allen head screws to 11-13 in.-lb. (1.24-1.47 N•m) in sequence shown. Refer to text.

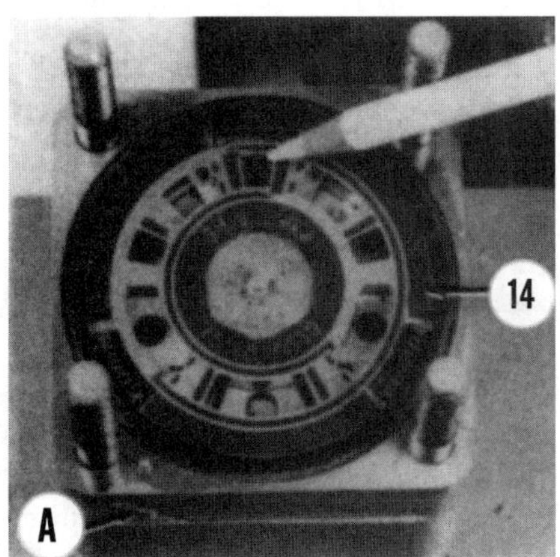

Fig. F2-15—Install valve plate (14) so "PORT SIDE" on plate is opposite from alignment grooves (A) on isolation manifold.

Reassemble by reversing the disassembly procedure and referral to the following notes: Be sure all parts with alignment grooves are aligned as shown in Fig. F2-9. Install the rotor (30—Fig. F2-11) so pin holes are out. Install the commutator so the long grooves are out as shown in Fig. F2-13. When installed, pins (28—Fig. F2-11) must not protrude above the commutator face.

Apply low strength thread-locking solution to the screw's threads (23) and install the screws finger tight. Insert the metering valve assembly in the metering ring (21) with the commutator cover (25) facing downward. Place a suitable size wood block under the metering valve assembly so the drive plate (32) is partially out of the metering ring.

Make six shims that are 0.007 in. thick, ½-inch wide and 1½ inches long. Insert one shim between the drive plate and metering ring in three equal distant place. Place another set of 3 shims between the drive plate and each of the 3 shims already in place. Remove the wood block and push metering valve down until the drive plate is flush with the metering ring surface. Tighten screws (23) to 11-13 in.-lb. (1.24-1.47 N·m) using the sequence shown in Fig. F2-14.

Commutator ring (26—Fig. F2-11) should now be concentric within 0.005 in. (0.127 mm) of the drive plate (32). Insert the large tang end of the drive link (20) into the slot in the rotor (30) and rotate the metering assembly to make certain parts do not bind. Install the commutator seal (24) so the yellow mark is toward the commutator cover (25).

Be sure ½ in. (13 mm) springs (13) are installed in the isolation manifold (18) and ¾ in. (19 mm) springs (10) are installed in the port manifold (9).

Install the valve plate (14) so the spring slot with the smallest cavity and the words "PORT SIDE" is opposite from alignment grooves on the isolation manifold (A) as shown in Fig. F2-15. Tighten valve assembly nuts in a crossing pattern to 18-22 ft.-lb. (27-33 N·m).

Install the relief valve spring (3—Fig. F2-11) so the small diameter is toward the cartridge (4). Make sure all parts with alignment grooves are aligned as shown in Fig. F2-9, otherwise the unit will not operate properly.

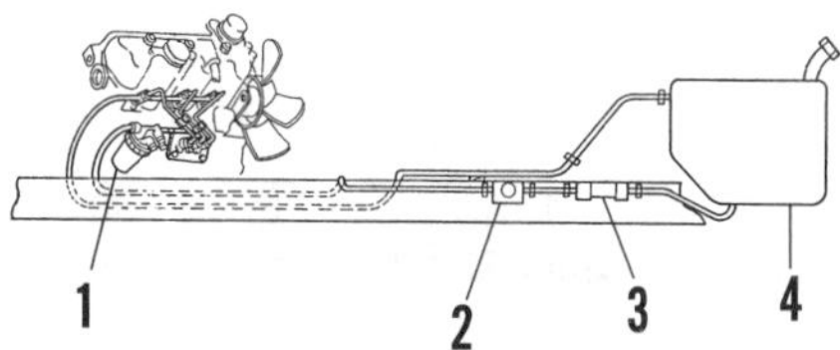

Fig. F2-16—Diagram of fuel system used on Models GT65, GT75, LGT14D and LGT16D.

1. Filter
2. Fuel pump
3. Filter
4. Fuel tank

ENGINE

MODELS GT65, GT75, LGT14D AND LGT16D

Maintenance

Check oil level daily. Inspect air cleaner element daily or periodically depending on operating conditions.

Refer to the Shibaura ENGINE SERVICE section in this manual for service information concerning tune-up and adjustments.

Lubrication

For new and reconditioned engines, the lubricating oil and filter should be changed after the first 50 hours of operation. The recommended oil change interval thereafter is every 100 hours of use. The recommended oil filter interval is after every 200 hours of use. Change the oil and filter more frequently when severe operating conditions are encountered.

Drain the oil while the engine is warm from operation. The oil will flow freely and carry away more impurities.

Oil filter is a spin-on paper element cartridge.

Use oil meeting the API classification CD. Select oil viscosity depending on expected ambient temperature range.

Air Filter

The air filter should be cleaned after every 25 hours of operation or more frequently when operating in extremely dusty conditions. Remove dust from filter element by tapping lightly with your hand, not on a hard surface.

Compressed air at pressure under 30 psi (210 kPa) may also be directed inside the filter element, but be careful not to damage the element. Replace the filter once a year or as necessary.

Fuel Filter

Check for water in the fuel filter sediment bowl (1—Fig. F2-16) prior to operating the tractor. If water is visible, close the fuel valve, unscrew the retaining nut (6—Fig. F2-17), and remove and clean the fuel bowl. Check the filter (3) for water damage.

NOTE: A clean, water-free supply of diesel fuel is essential for satisfactory engine performance. If water or sediment accumulates excessively in the fuel bowl, locate the source of contamination and correct it.

The fuel system is equipped with two filters. A cartridge filter is contained in the fuel bowl (1—Fig. F2-16) located adjacent to the fuel injection pump. An inline filter (3) is located in the fuel line along the tractor frame.

The following fuel filter change interval is recommended for normal conditions. Change the filters sooner if the engine has a noticeable loss of power.

Install a new filter (3—Fig. F2-17) in fuel bowl after every 200 hours of operation. Close the fuel shutoff valve, then remove the ring nut (6) and sediment bowl (5). Discard the old filter element and install a new element. Be sure the O-rings (2 and 4) are installed properly. Bleed the air from the system.

Install a new inline filter (3—Fig. F2-16) after every 600 hours of operation. To replace the filter either drain the fuel tank or pinch the fuel line on the inlet side of the pump to prevent fuel leakage. To drain the fuel, place a container under the fuel pump (2—Fig. F2-16) and disconnect the hose from the fuel inlet side of the pump. Remove the filter and discard. Install a new filter and bleed air from the system.

NOTE: After replacing the filters, or whenever any portion of the fuel system has been disconnected, bleed air from the system as outlined in the following paragraph. If fuel tank runs dry, bleed the fuel system.

Bleeding Fuel System

Be sure there is fuel in the tank. Open the fuel shutoff valve (Fig. F2-18). Loosen the bleed screw located on the fuel injection pump.

Turn the key start switch ON, but do not start the engine. When air-free fuel flows freely from the bleed screw, tighten the screw. Move the hand throttle to the high-speed position and crank the engine to pressurize the injector lines.

If the tractor fails to start at this time or if the fuel injector lines have been disconnected, bleed the injector lines. Loosen the injector line fittings at the injectors. Move the hand throttle to the high-speed position. Crank the engine until fuel flows from each fitting. Tighten the fittings to 18-22 ft.-lb. (24-29 N·m) and start the tractor.

Engine Removal and Installation

Raise the hood and disconnect the headlight wire. Remove the hood. Disconnect the battery cables.

Drain coolant from the radiator and engine. Drain the engine oil. Detach and remove the exhaust pipe. Detach and remove the air cleaner assembly. Remove the upper radiator hose.

Remove the fuel injector return tube. Pinch the fuel line to prevent fuel loss, and disconnect the fuel line from the fuel shutoff valve.

Disconnect the proofmeter cable from the engine. Mark then disconnect the electrical wiring from the glow plug terminal, injection pump solenoid, oil pressure sensor, coolant temperature sensor, alternator and starter motor.

Detach the throttle control cable from the fuel injection pump. Unscrew three grill support bolts on each side and remove front grill.

Remove the PTO drive belts as outlined in the PTO service section. Remove the battery and battery stand.

Working from the tractor's underside, detach the drive shaft from the transmission drive coupling. Slide the drive shaft back and remove.

Remove the air baffle. Unscrew two screws retaining the fan shroud. On Models LGT14D and LGT16D, remove engine side screen pin brackets. On all models, move the shroud out of the way.

Unscrew the engine mounting bolts. Note the location of the ground cable terminal. Lift the engine out of the tractor while being careful not to damage the fan or shroud.

Reverse the removal procedure to install engine.

Overhaul

Engine make and model are listed in the specifications table at the beginning of this section. Refer to the appropriate ENGINE SERVICE section in this manual for service information on the engine and associated accessories.

MODELS GT85 AND GT95

Maintenance

Regular engine maintenance is required to maintain peak performance and long engine life.

Check the oil level daily. Inspect air cleaner element daily or periodically depending on operating conditions.

Refer to the Kohler ENGINE SERVICE section in this manual for service information concerning tune-up and adjustments.

Lubrication

For new and reconditioned engines, the lubricating oil and filter should be changed after first 5 hours of operation. The recommended oil change interval thereafter is every 50 hours of use when using SAE 30 weight oil. The oil change interval should be shortened to every 25 hours of use when the tractor is being used continuously in heavy-duty operation or if multiviscosity oil is being used. The recommended oil filter change interval is every other oil change.

Drain the oil while the engine is warm from operation. The oil will flow freely and carry away more impurities.

The oil filter is a spin-on paper element cartridge. Coat the gasket of the new filter with clean engine oil. Screw the filter on until the gasket contacts the filter base, then turn the filter an additional ¾ turn.

Use oil meeting the latest API classification. Select oil viscosity depending on expected ambient temperature range.

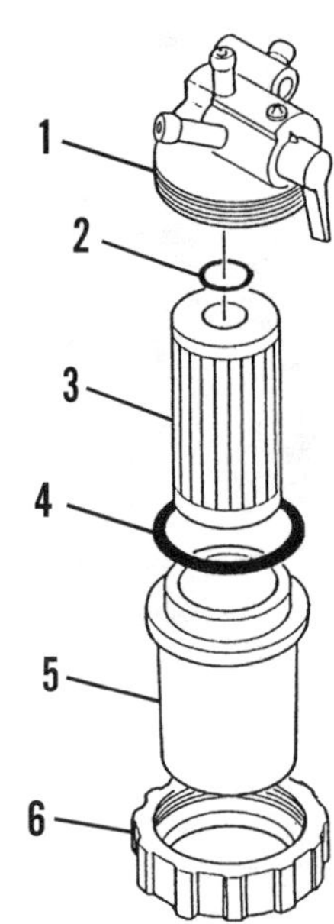

Fig. F2-17—Exploded of engine-mounted fuel filter/shutoff valve used on Models GT65, GT75, LGT14D and LGT16D.

1. Valve body
2. O-ring
3. Filter
4. O-ring
5. Bowl
6. Nut

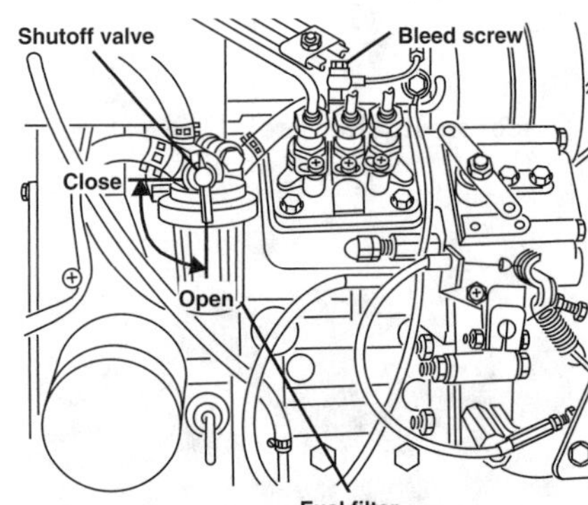

Fig. F2-18—View of diesel fuel system bleed screw. Refer to text to bleed air from the fuel system.

Air Filter

Models GT85 and GT95 are equipped with a paper filter element surrounded by a foam precleaner. The air filter should be checked for accumulation of dirt every 10 hours of operation.

The foam precleaner should be removed and washed in warm water with detergent after every 25 operating hours or more frequently if operating in extremely dusty conditions. Allow the precleaner to thoroughly dry. When dry, saturate the precleaner with clean engine oil and squeeze out excess oil.

Check the paper element every 100 hours for accumulation of dirt. Remove dust from filter element by tapping lightly with your hand, not on a hard surface. Do not wash the paper element or use pressurized air to clean it, as this will damage the element. Replace the element if it dirty or damaged.

Engine Removal and Installation

Raise the hood and disconnect the headlight wire. Remove the hood. Disconnect the battery cables.

Drain the engine oil. Remove the cover above the exhaust pipe, and remove exhaust pipe.

Disconnect the fuel line. Detach throttle and choke control wires. Disconnect the electric wire connector. Remove the PTO drive belts as outlined in the PTO SERVICE section.

Working from the tractor's underside, detach the drive shaft from the transmission drive coupling. Slide the drive shaft back and remove.

Unscrew the engine mounting bolts. Note the location of the ground cable terminal. Lift the engine out of the tractor approximately 3 inches, then detach the battery cable from the starter motor. Remove the engine.

Reverse the removal procedure to install engine.

Overhaul

Engine make and model are listed in the specifications table at the beginning of this section. Refer to the appropriate ENGINE SERVICE section in this manual for service information on the engine and associated accessories.

FUEL SYSTEM (MODELS GT65, GT75, LGT14D AND LGT16D)

Also refer to the fuel system information in the Shibaura ENGINE SERVICE section in this manual.

FUEL PUMP

The tractor is equipped with an electric fuel pump (2—Fig. F2-16) attached to the left frame rail. A 15-amp fuse located in fuse box protects the fuel pump and the headlight circuit.

The fuel pump is accessible after removing the left rear wheel. If fuel pump fuel lines are disconnected, bleed air from the system as outlined in the BLEEDING FUEL SYSTEM.

To test the fuel pump, disconnect the fuel hose from the fuel pump outlet. Connect a jumper hose to the fuel pump outlet and place the hose's open end in a one gallon container. Connect a 12-volt battery to fuel pump. Connect the positive battery terminal to the red pump wire and the negative battery terminal to the black pump wire. Operate the pump for exactly five minutes, then stop and measure the amount of fuel output. The fuel pump output must be at least 2.1 quarts (2 L) within 5 minutes. Replace the pump if output is below minimum.

COOLING SYSTEM (MODELS GT65, GT75, LGT14D AND LGT16D)

Also refer to cooling system information in the Shibaura ENGINE SERVICE section in this manual.

MAINTENANCE

Coolant system capacity is approximately 2.7 qt. (2.6 L). Radiator cap pressure rating is 13 psi (90 kPa).

Periodically clean debris from radiator screen. Check coolant in radiator after every 100 hours of operation.

WARNING: Coolant in the radiator is pressurized. Remove the radiator cap only when the engine is cold.

Coolant level should be 1½ to 2 inches (38-51 mm) below the bottom of the filler neck. The recommended coolant is a 50:50 mixture of clean water and permanent antifreeze.

Flush the cooling system after every 12 months. Drain the coolant by opening the engine coolant drain valve, located next to the oil filter and the radiator drain valve. Flush the system by running clean water through the radiator fill opening until clean water flows out of the drain valves. Refill with a 50:50 mixture of clean water and permanent antifreeze. Run the engine and recheck coolant level.

Periodically inspect the coolant hoses between the radiator and engine water pump. Replace damaged hoses.

RADIATOR

To remove the radiator, remove the hood and drain coolant from the radiator. Drive out the roll pins and remove the PTO and speed control levers. Remove the center panel below dash panel. Remove the air intake screens on both sides of the control console.

Detach the upper radiator hose. Remove the alternator. Detach the lower radiator hose. Remove the radiator debris screen. Remove the air cleaner air intake tube. Remove the three screws securing the air baffle to the radiator. Detach the fan shroud from the radiator, but don't remove the shroud.

Unscrew the bolts securing the radiator to the side frame and bottom base while noting the location of the rubber washers. Lift the radiator up past the fan shroud and out of the tractor.

Install the radiator by reversing the removal procedure. Initially install bottom base retaining bolts loose, then tighten after radiator is in final position.

FRONT COUPLER (MODELS GT65, GT75, LGT14D AND LGT16D)

The screws retaining the front drive shaft coupler on the engine drive flange have a special coating. If the screws are removed, new screws must be installed. Tighten the screws to 212-230 in.-lb. (24-26 N·m).

DRIVE SHAFT REMOVAL AND INSTALLATION

To remove the drive shaft, unbolt the rear coupler. Note the location of coupler spacer sleeves on diesel models. Move the drive shaft rearward to disengage the splines in the front universal joint and remove the drive shaft.

When installing the drive shaft on diesel models, place spacer sleeves in front of the transmission cooling fan on Models LGT14D and LGT16D. On GT65 and GT75 models, spacer sleeves must be behind the transmission cooling fan.

BRAKE

A disc brake is mounted on a transmission shaft that extends to the rear. An electrical switch actuated by the brake linkage prevents engine starting unless the brake is engaged. Refer to ELECTRICAL SYSTEM for brake switch adjustment procedure.

ADJUSTMENT

Loosen the outer jam nut (4—Fig. F2-19), then detach spring (1) from the end nut (2). Adjust the end nut (2) and inner jam nut (3) position so the brake pedal travel is 1-1⁹⁄₁₆ in. (25-40 mm). Retighten the outer jam nut (4) and reattach the spring (1).

OVERHAUL

The brake disc is accessible after removing the operator's seat, fender assembly, seat support, fuel tank and saddle. Detach the spring (1—Fig. F2-19) from the anchor bracket. Detach the brake neutral switch spring. Remove the nut (2) and spring from the brake rod (5).

Remove the brake actuating arm and the moveable (outer) brake pad. Remove the shield covering the disc. Detach the snap ring on the transmission shaft and withdraw the brake disc. The fixed brake pad is located behind the brake disc.

New pad thickness is 0.118 in (3.00 mm) for the fixed pad and 0.216 in (5.49 mm) for the moveable pad. Replace either pad if worn more than 0.02 in. (0.51 mm).

Replace the brake disc if wear on either face exceeds 0.012 in. (0.3 mm).

TRANSMISSION CONTROL LINKAGE

NEUTRAL ADJUSTMENT

The hydrostatic control linkage should return to NEUTRAL when the foot pedal is released. If the tractor creeps when the pedal is released, adjust as follows by first raising and blocking up the rear of the tractor so the wheels clear the ground. Start the engine and run at idle speed. With the transmission in NEUTRAL and range shift lever in high or low gear, the rear wheels should not rotate.

If the wheels rotate, loosen the screw (4—Fig. F2-20) and turn the eccentric nut (3). Rotate the nut in one direction until the wheels just begin to turn, then rotate the nut in opposite direction until the wheels just begin to turn again. Turn the nut to the midpoint position and tighten the screw (3).

SPEED CONTROL LEVER ADJUSTMENT

The speed control lever uses a brake pad and overcenter mechanism to hold

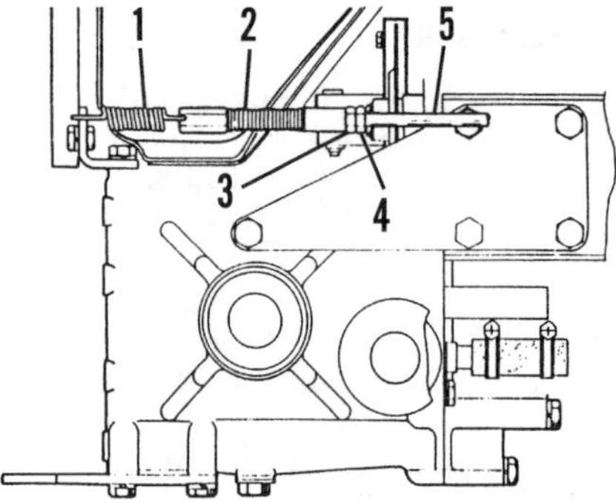

Fig. F2-19—Refer to text for brake adjustment procedure.

1. Spring
2. Nut
3. Jam nut
4. Jam nut
5. Brake rod

the speed pedal in a selected position. The speed pedal can then be released and the tractor will run at the selected speed.

To adjust the speed control lever, move the lever to the engaged position. Loosen the brake plate retaining screws (1—Fig. F2-21). Position the brake plate (2) so the distance (D) from the hole centerline shown in Fig. F2-21 to the back of the brake shoe (3) is 2.99 inches (76 mm). Retighten the screws (1).

If the speed control lever will not hold the speed linkage in position, readjust using a dimension up to 3.068 inches (77.93 mm). Be sure the brake shoe pad is not excessively worn.

If the speed control lever will not release when the brake pedal is depressed, loosen the nut (1—Fig. F2-22). Rotate the turnbuckle (2) so the lever (3) contacts the rod (4) on the brake lever (5). Retighten the nut (1) and check operation. Speed control lever must disengage when the brake pedal is depressed.

OVERHAUL

Inspect the components for damage. Replace the speed control brake pad (2—Fig. F2-21) if brake pad thickness at the narrowest point is less than 0.51 in. (13 mm).

HYDROSTATIC TRANSMISSION

MAINTENANCE

Periodically inspect the transmission for oil leakage. An oil level dipstick/filler cap is located below the tractor seat. Check the oil level with the tractor on a level surface with the engine off. Maintain the oil level between the marks on the dipstick. The recommended lubricant is Ford 134 transmission/hydraulic oil.

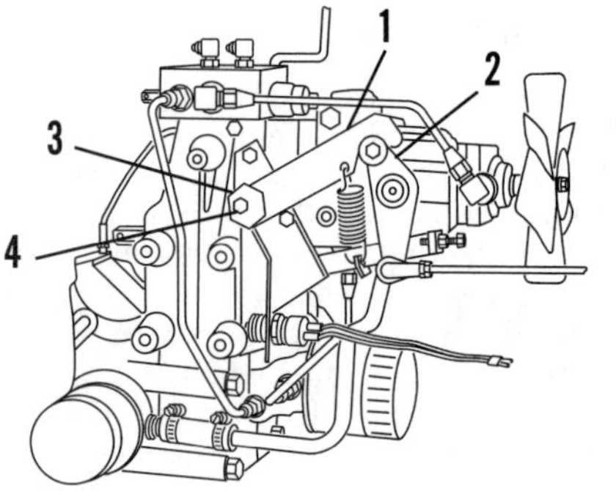

Fig. F2-20—Loosen screw (4) and turn eccentric nut (3) to adjust transmission neutral position. See text.

1. Centering arm
2. Actuating arm
3. Eccentric
4. Screw

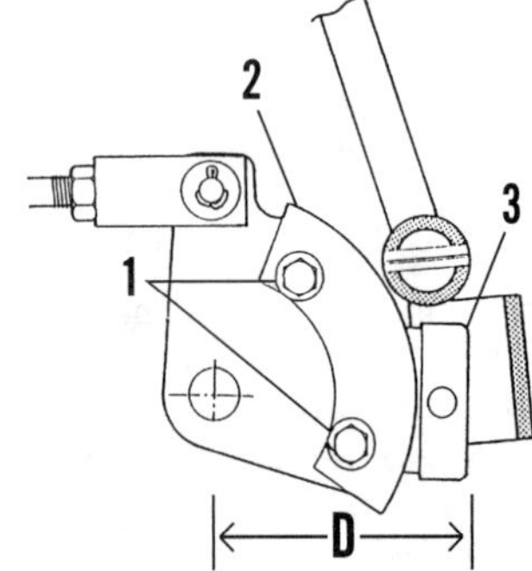

Fig. F2-21—When adjusting speed control lever, distance from centerline of brake disc to back of brake shoe should be 2.99 inches (76 mm) when speed control lever is engaged. Refer to text.

1. Cap screws
2. Brake lining
3. Brake shoe

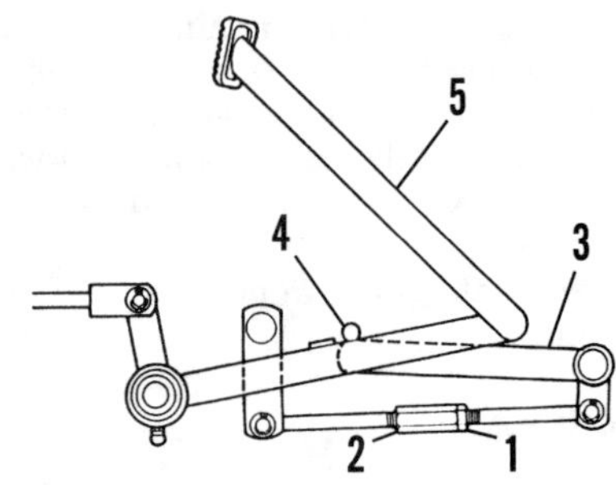

Fig. F2-22—If engaged speed control lever will not release when brake pedal is depressed, loosen nut (1). Rotate turnbuckle (2) so lever (3) contacts rod (4) on brake pedal (5).

Oil for the transmission is routed from the oil sump in the final drive housing. Spin-on filters mounted on range transmission and final drive housing protect the hydrostatic transmission and other hydraulic components.

The filter on the final drive housing's side filters the inlet oil to the charge

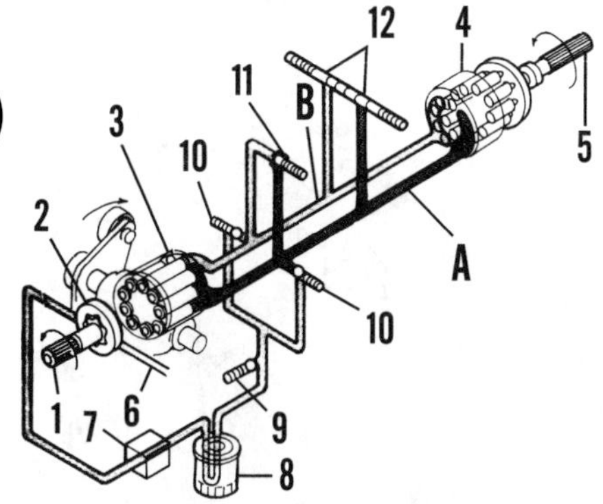

Fig. F2-23—Hydrostatic transmission consists of a charge pump (2), variable displacement piston pump (3) and fixed displacement piston motor (4).

1. Input shaft
2. Charge pump
3. Piston pump
4. Piston motor
5. Output shaft
6. Suction line
7. Hydraulic system control valve
8. Pressure filter
9. Charge pressure regulating valve
10. Feed valves
11. High pressure relief valve
12. Neutral valves

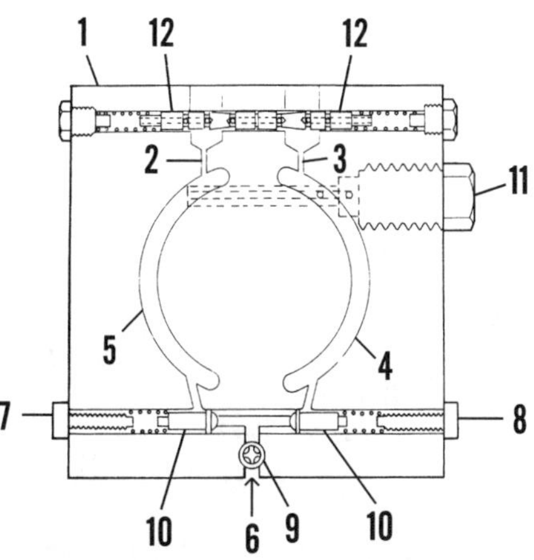

Fig. F2-24—A port block located between the piston pump and motor contains the pressure regulating valve (8), feed valves (10), neutral valves (12) and high pressure relief valve (11).

1. Port block
2. Orifice
3. Orifice
4. Pump to motor passage
5. Pump to motor passage
6. Inlet connector
7. Plug
8. Plug
9. Charge pressure regulator
10. Feed valves
11. High pressure relief valve
12. Neutral valves

Fig. F2-25—To perform pressure test, unscrew either plug (P) and connect a pressure gauge.

1. Charge pressure regulator valve
2. Feed valves
3. Neutral valves
4. Port block
5. Shims
6. High pressure relief valve

pump. The filter on the range transmission's front filters pressurized oil from the charge pump.

Refer to the RANGE TRANSMISSION section for oil change procedure. Change both oil filters after the first 50 hours of operation. Change the inlet filter after every 200 hours of operation. Change the pressure filter after every 100 hours of operation. Note that filters are not interchangeable.

SYSTEM OPERATION

The charge pump mounted on the hydrostatic transmission's front provides pressurized oil for the transmission, hydraulic lift system and, if so equipped, the power steering system. The hydraulic system uses oil contained in the common sump of the range transmission and final drive housing.

The hydrostatic circuit (A and B—Fig. F2-23) between the piston pump (3) and motor (4) is a closed system containing the feed valves (10), high pressure relief valve (11) and neutral valves (12).

Oil from the final drive passes through a filter, The charge pump (2—Fig. F2-23) draws oil from the final drive housing through a filter and suction tube (6). Pressurized oil from the charge pump travels to the power steering system, if so equipped, then to the hydraulic lift system control valve (7). Oil travels from the control valve, through the pressure filter (8), then to the hydrostatic transmission pump (3). A pressure regulating valve (9) limits the pressure in the charge system.

Feed valves (10) in the valve block (1—Fig. F2-24) are check valves that open to allow pressurized oil from the charge pump, via the power steering and hydraulic lift systems, to enter the hydrostatic transmission. A low pressure valve (9) maintains charge pump pressure and bypasses excess oil into the range transmission.

The neutral valves (12) control the oil flow between the pump and motor during starting and stopping to obtain smooth operation. A high pressure relief valve (11) protects the hydrostatic system from overload.

TROUBLESHOOTING

Some problems that might occur during operation of hydrostatic transmission and their possible causes are as follows:

1. No output power in either direction.
   a. Faulty charge pump or low pressure regulator valve.
   b. Low oil level.
   c. Plugged inlet filter.
   d. Faulty high pressure relief valve.
   e. Faulty feed valves.
   f. Faulty piston pump or motor.
   g. Faulty range transmission or differential.
2. Tractor fails to stop with speed control in NEUTRAL.
   a. Maladjusted control linkage.
   b. Faulty neutral valves.
3. Cannot attain maximum speed.
   a. Maladjusted control linkage.
   b. Faulty piston pump or motor.
   c. Leakage through feed valves.
4. External oil leakage.
   a. Worn seals or shafts.
   b. Plugged breather.

PRESSURE TESTING

If the tractor appears to lose power during operation, but engine performance is normal, check the hydrostatic transmission for hydraulic pressure loss. Pressure testing can help to determine if transmission has an internal problem.

Raise and block up the rear of tractor so the wheels clear the ground. Note location of test port plugs (P—Fig. F2-25) on underside of transmission port block (4) on either side of the transmission inlet tube fitting.

High Pressure

Pressure is regulated by the transmission relief valve (6—Fig. F2-25). To check the high pressure setting, unscrew either test port plug (P) and connect a gauge that reads 0-4000 psi (0-28000 kPa). Perform the test with the transmission cold, then repeat the test with the transmission at normal operating temperature.

Place the speed range lever in the high position. Start the engine. Depress the speed pedal 1/3 of its travel in direction that will produce gauge reading and increase engine speed to full throttle.

NOTE: Pressure reading will be low while in NEUTRAL and increase to high pressure in only one pedal direction, depending on to which port the gauge is connected.

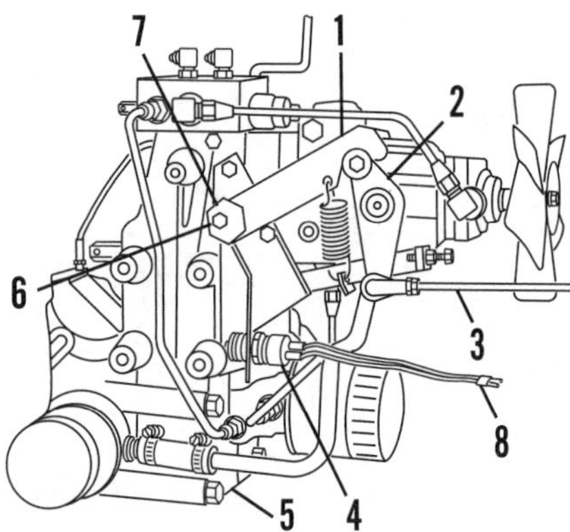

Fig. F2-26—View of transmission control linkage.

1. Neutral arm
2. Transmission control arm
3. Speed control rod
4. Neutral switch
5. Stop bracket
6. Screw
7. Eccentric nut

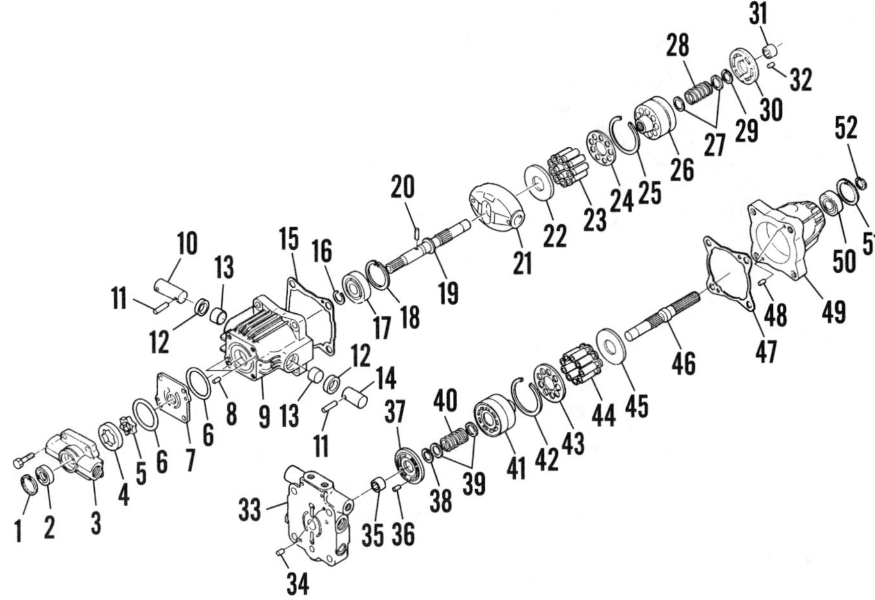

Fig. F2-27—Exploded view of hydrostatic transmission. Refer to Fig. F2-28 for exploded view of valve block (33) and valves.

1. Snap ring
2. Oil seal
3. Charge pump body
4. Outer rotor
5. Inner rotor
6. O-ring
7. Plate
8. Pin
9. Pump housing
10. Control shaft
11. Roll pin
12. Oil seal
13. Bushing
14. Trunnion shaft
15. Gasket
16. Snap ring
17. Bearing
18. Snap ring
19. Input shaft
20. Pin
21. Swashplate
22. Thrust plate
23. Pistons
24. Retainer plate
25. Snap ring
26. Cylinder block
27. Washers
28. Spring
29. Snap ring
30. Valve plate
31. Bearing
32. Pin
33. Valve block
34. Pin
35. Needle bearing
36. Locating pin
37. Valve plate
38. Snap ring
39. Washers
40. Spring
41. Cylinder block
42. Snap ring
43. Retainer plate
44. Pistons
45. Thrust plate
46. Output shaft
47. Gasket
48. Pin
49. Motor housing
50. Bearing
51. Snap ring
52. Snap ring

Depress the brake pedal and observe the gauge reading. Gauge should indicate 2773-3200 psi (19134-22080 kPa).

CAUTION: Do not maintain high pressure for longer than 2-3 seconds or transmission may overheat.

Adjust the relief valve pressure setting by adding or remove shims (5—Fig. F2-25). The relief valve (6) is located on the transmission's left side in the control block (4).

If pressure readings are the same during cold and hot tests and significantly lower than specified pressure reading, the relief valve is faulty and must be replaced.

A large drop in pressure when the transmission is hot indicates internal leakage due to worn parts.

Charge Pressure

Pressure is regulated by the low pressure regulating valve (1—Fig. F2-25). To check the charge pressure setting, unscrew either test port plug (P—Fig. F2-25) and connect a gauge that reads 0-400 psi (0-2800 kPa). Perform the test with the transmission cold, then repeat the test with the transmission at normal operating temperature.

Place the speed range lever and speed control pedal in NEUTRAL. Start the engine. Note gauge reading. Gauge should indicate 57-85 psi (394-586 kPa).

A pressure reading other than the specified pressure range may indicate system leakage due to excessive wear or faulty components, including the charge pressure regulator valve and spring (1—Fig. F2-25). The transmission must be disassembled for access to the charge pressure regulator valve.

REMOVAL AND INSTALLATION

Lift the seat, disconnect the seat switch connector and remove the seat and support assembly. Remove the control lever knobs for the range transmission and hydraulic system. Unscrew and remove the fender panel.

Detach the drive shaft from the transmission drive coupling. Slide the drive shaft back and remove. Detach hydraulic lines from transmission. Plug or cap all openings.

On Models LGT14D and LGT16D, disconnect wires from the transmission neutral switch (4—Fig. 2-26), then remove the switch. Detach the speed control rod (3) from the transmission control arm (2).

On GT series tractors, detach the damper from the transmission control arm. On all models, unscrew the eccentric screw (6) and nut (7). Detach the neutral arm (1) and spring. Remove the stop bracket (5). Drive out the roll pin and remove the control arm (2).

Remove the fan and hub. Unscrew the upper right and lower left retaining screws and remove the transmission as a unit from the range transmission.

NOTE: Shims may be located on the output shaft. Be sure to install the shims before installing the transmission on the range transmission.

Reverse the removal procedure to install the transmission. Be sure to install the O-ring between the hydrostatic transmission and range transmission. After installation, perform neutral adjustment as previously described.

On Models LGT14D and LGT16D, adjust the position of the transmission neutral switch (4—Fig. 2-26) so the switch is closed when the transmission is in NEUTRAL.

OVERHAUL

Disassembly

Prior to disassembly, thoroughly clean the outside of the transmission. Unscrew the charge pump mounting screws and remove the charge pump components (3 through 7—Fig. F2-27).

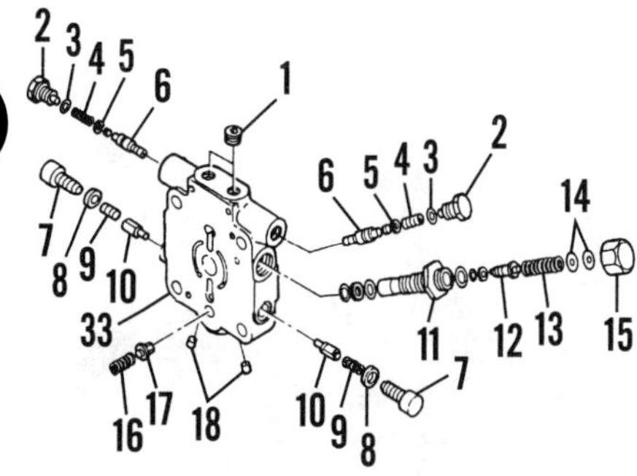

Fig. F2-28—Exploded view of valve block assembly.

1. Plug	12. High pressure relief valve
2. Neutral valve plug	13. Spring
3. O-ring	14. Shims
4. Spring	15. Cap
5. Washer	16. Spring
6. Spool	17. Charge pressure relief valve
7. Feed valve plug	18. Plugs
8. Seal washer	33. Valve body
9. Spring	
10. Poppet valve	
11. Valve body	

Fig. F2-29—Install locating pin in valve body so split side (S) is positioned as shown.

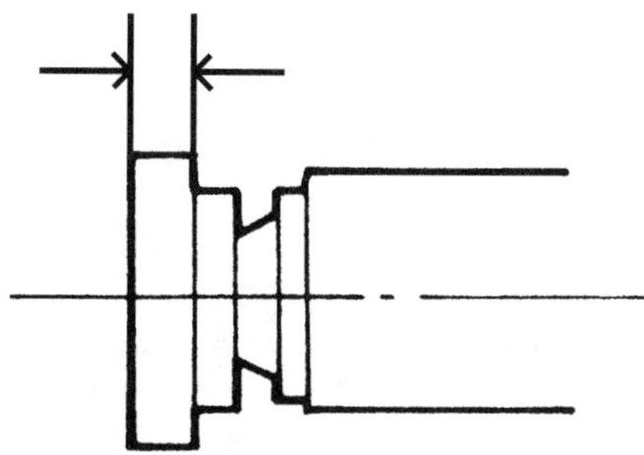

Fig. F2-30—Minimum allowable slipper thickness is 0.114 inch (2.90 mm).

Note the identification marks on the forward face of the charge pump rotors.

Place alignment marks on the pump housing (9), valve block (33) and motor housing (49) so they can be reassembled in its original position. Unscrew two Allen screws securing the housings together and carefully separate pump housing, valve block and motor housing. Valve plate (30) may adhere to either the valve block (33) or pump cylinder block (26).

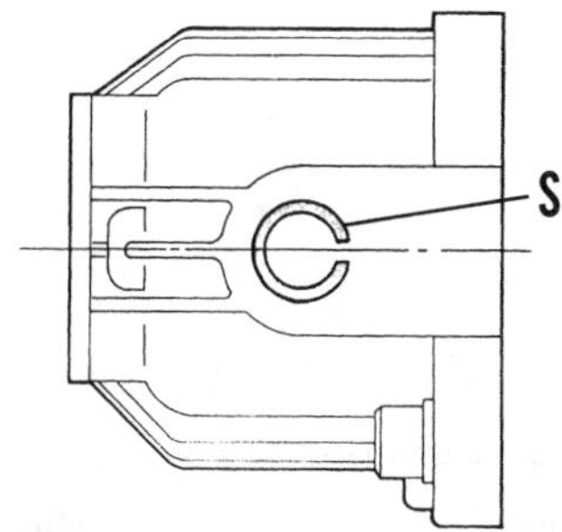

Fig. F2-31—Install bushings so split side (S) is toward flanged end of pump housing.

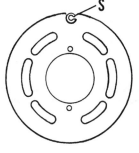

NOTE: The pump cylinder block, charge pressure regulating valve spring (16—Fig. F2-28) and the valve (17) can fall out when separating the pump housing from the valve block. Position the transmission so parts cannot fall out or hold parts in place during separation.

NOTE: If any of the pistons (23 or 44—Fig. F2-27) slide out of their cylinders, return them to the original bores.

Disengage the snap ring (25) from the groove in the swashplate (21), then remove the snap ring, pistons and cylinder block (26) as an assembly from the pump housing.

Insert a small rod or wire with a hook on one end against the thrust plate's (22) inside diameter and pull the thrust plate from the swashplate (21).

Drive roll pins (11) through the swashplate (21) and shafts (10 and 14) until the pins contact the housing. Pull out the longer shaft (10), then drive out the opposite shaft (14) from the inside. Remove the swashplate (21).

Remove the snap ring (18). Use a soft-faced hammer and gently drive the input shaft (19) and bearing (17) toward the inside of the pump housing. Bearing (17) may be pressed off the input shaft (19) after removing the snap ring (16).

Remove the large snap ring (51). Use a soft-faced hammer and gently drive the output shaft (46) and bearing (50) toward the outside of the motor housing. Disengage the snap ring (42) from the motor housing (49), then remove the snap ring, pistons and cylinder block (41) as an assembly from the motor housing.

Pull out the thrust plate (45). Bearing (50) may be pressed off the output shaft (46) after removing the snap ring (52).

Disassemble and reassemble valve block components after referring to the exploded view in Fig. F2-28. Identify all parts as they are removed for reassembly in their original locations. Do not interchange components.

Inspection and Repair

Thoroughly clean all parts and inspect for damage.

Use a press to remove the needle bearing (35—Fig. F2-27). When installing the bearing, press the bearing in until the bearing protrudes 0.138 in. (3.5 mm) above valve body face.

Valve plate locating pins (32 and 36) must protrude 0.157 inch (4.0 mm) above the valve body face. Position the pin so the split side is located as shown in Fig. F2-29 when the valve plate is installed. Tighten the neutral valve plugs (2—Fig. F2-28) to 27 ft.-lb. (36.7 N·m). Tighten the feed valve plugs (7) to 33 ft.-lb. (44.9 N·m). Tighten the high pressure relief valve cap (15) to 27 ft.-lb. (36.7 N·m).

Inspect the charge pump components (1 through 7—Fig. F2-27) for damage. Minor wear patterns may be removed by polishing on a surface plate. Excessive damage may cause low pressure. See TESTING.

Mark the piston retainer plate (24 or 43—Fig. F2-27) and cylinder block (26 or 41) so they can be reassembled in the original position. Mark the pistons so they can be reinstalled in their original cylinder bores. Thoroughly clean all components in solvent. Inspect the pump and motor components for damage.

Specified piston to cylinder bore clearance is 0.0008 inch (0.020 mm) with a maximum wear limit of 0.0016 inch (0.041 mm). Maximum allowable end play of slipper on piston is 0.008 inch (0.20 mm). Minimum allowable slipper thickness (Fig. F2-30) is 0.114 inch (2.90 mm). Pistons and cylinder blocks must be replaced as complete assemblies.

Check the valve plates (30 and 37—Fig. F2-27) for damage or evidence of overheating. Replace the valve plate if there is doubt about its serviceability. If a scratch or groove can be felt when sliding your fingernail or the point of a soft lead pencil over the surface of either plate, it must be replaced.

Use a press to remove the bushings (13—Fig. F2-27). Install new bushings so the split side is toward the flanged end of the pump housing as shown in Fig. F2-31. Install oil seals (12—Fig. F2-27) flush with outer surface of pump housing.

Reassembly

Reassemble the transmission by reversing the disassembly procedure. Care must be taken to prevent dirt or grit from contaminating the machined surfaces of the transmission. Even a small scratch

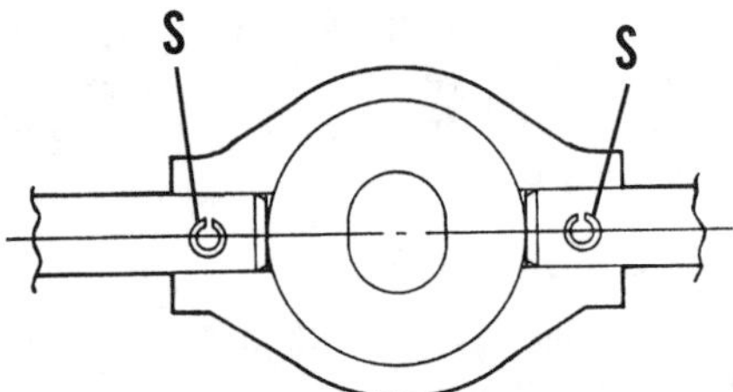

Fig. F2-32—Install roll pins so split side (S) is located as shown. Roll pins should protrude 0.059 inch (1.5 mm) above surface of swashplate.

or nick can result in internal oil leakage and poor performance. Be sure to liberally lubricate all parts during assembly.

Install roll pins (11) so the split side is located as shown in Fig. F2-32. Roll pins should protrude 0.059 inch (1.5 mm) above the surface of the swashplate.

NOTE: Installing roll pins in too deep may cause interference between pin and pump housing.

Install the valve plates (30 and 37—Fig. F2-27) with brass face away from the valve block (33).

Install the rotors (4 and 5) so the punch mark on each rotor face is toward the plate (7). Tighten pump housing-to-motor housing Allen screws evenly, then tighten to a final torque of 42 ft.-lb. (57 N·m). Tighten the charge pump mounting screws to 20 ft.-lb. (27.2 N·m).

RANGE TRANSMISSION

LUBRICATION

The range transmission is lubricated by oil contained in both the range transmission and the final drive. To determine oil level use the dipstick located under the tractor seat. Check the oil level with tractor sitting level and engine off.

If the oil level is low, add Ford 134 transmission/hydraulic oil through the dipstick tube opening to maintain the oil level between the two marks on the dipstick. Do not overfill.

Oil should be changed after first 50 hours of operation and after every 200 hours of operation thereafter. To drain the oil, place a container under the transmission housing and remove the drain plug on the underside of the final drive housing. Fill with Ford 134 transmission/hydraulic oil. Capacity is approximately 9.1 U.S. quarts (8.6 L).

Spin-on filters mounted on the range transmission and the final drive housing protect the hydrostatic transmission and other hydraulic components. The filter on the side of the final drive housing filters inlet oil to charge pump.

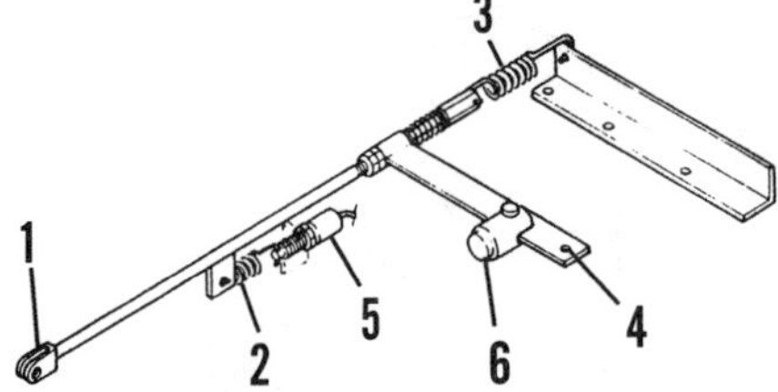

Fig. F2-33—View of brake actuating linkage.

1. Brake rod
2. Spring
3. Spring
4. Actuating arm
5. Brake switch
6. Brake pad

The filter on the front of the range transmission filters pressurized oil from the charge pump.

Change both oil filters after first 50 hours of operation. Change the inlet filter after every 200 hours of operation. Change the pressure filter after every 100 hours of operation. Note that filters are not interchangeable.

REMOVAL AND INSTALLATION

Drain the oil from the transmission housing. Remove the hydrostatic transmission as previously described.

Detach brake rod return spring (3—Fig. F2-33). Detach brake switch spring (2). Remove clevis pin at the brake rod's (1) forward end. Remove the pivot pin at the brake actuating arm's (4) left end. Remove the brake rod and the brake actuating arm assembly. Remove the rear shield and the brake disc.

Remove the rear panel behind the fuel tank. Unscrew the bolts retaining the seat support brackets and remove the brackets. Disconnect the fuel lines and remove the fuel tank. Remove the fuel tank support saddle.

Mark and disconnect the hydraulic lines from the hydraulic lift control valve. Plug all openings to prevent entry of dirt.

Raise the tractor's rear, place supports under the tractor frame and remove the rear wheels. Position a floor jack under the final drive. Unscrew the frame-to-transmission housing retaining screws. Unscrew the frame-to-rear axle housings screws. Lower and remove the range transmission and final drive assembly. Unscrew the retaining screws and separate the range transmission from the final drive housing (2—Fig. F2-34).

Reverse the removal procedure to install the range transmission.

OVERHAUL

To disassemble, withdraw the countershaft (5—Fig. F2-34) and fixed gear cluster.

Pry the sliding gear countershaft oil seal (9—Fig. F2-35) from the housing bore and remove the snap ring (8). Expand the snap ring (3) and move it forward on the countershaft (5).

Remove the shift rod retainer plate (2—Fig. F2-36). Slide the shift rod (4) forward, being careful not to lose the

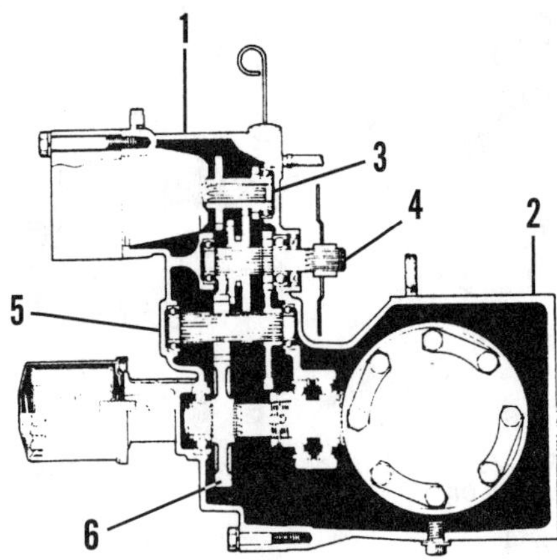

Fig. F2-34—Cross-sectional view of range transmission.

1. Hydrostatic transmission
2. Differential housing
3. Motor drive gear cluster
4. Countershaft & sliding gear assy.
5. Countershaft & fixed gear assy.
6. Pinion drive gear

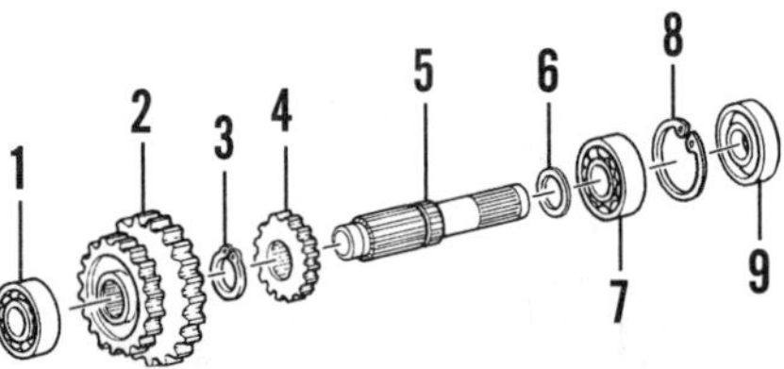

Fig. F2-35—Exploded view of sliding gear and shaft assembly.

1. Bearing
2. Cluster gear
3. Snap ring
4. Gear
5. Shaft
6. Shim
7. Bearing
8. Snap ring
9. Oil seal

Fig. F2-36—Exploded view of shift assembly.

1. Screw
2. Plate
3. O-ring
4. Shift shaft
5. Ball
6. Spring
7. Shift fork

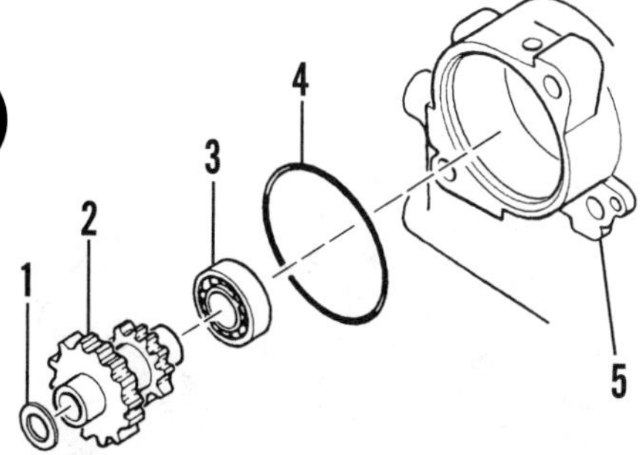

Fig. F2-37—Exploded view of drive gear cluster assembly.

1. Shim
2. Gear cluster
3. Bearing
4. O-ring
5. Housing

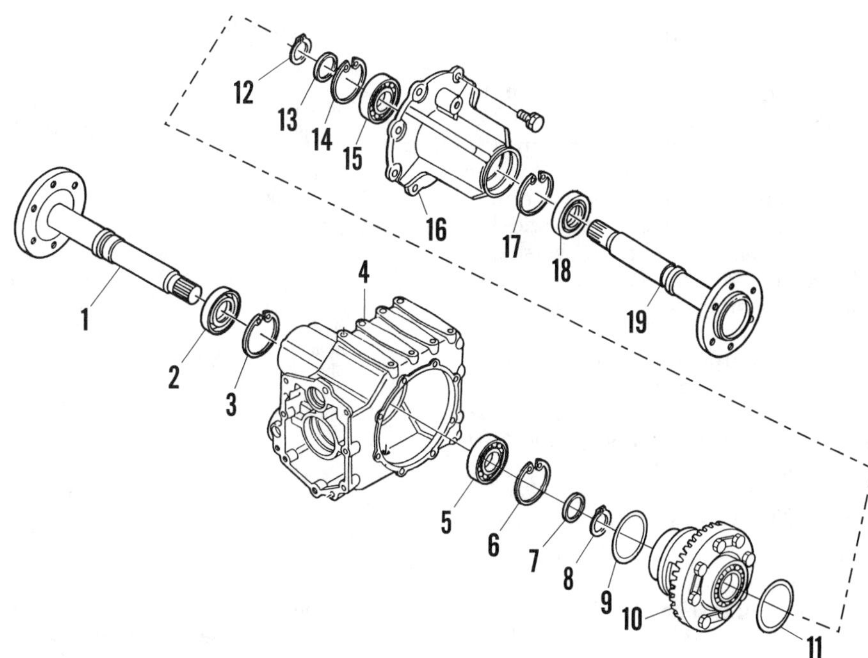

Fig. F2-40—Exploded view of final drive. Also refer to Figs. F2-41 and F2-42.

1. Axle (right)
2. Oil seal
3. Snap ring
4. Final drive housing
5. Bearing
6. Snap ring
7. Spacer
8. Snap ring
9. Shim
10. Differential assy.
11. Shim
12. Snap ring
13. Spacer
14. Snap ring
15. Bearing
16. Axle housing
17. Snap ring
18. Oil seal
19. Axle (left)

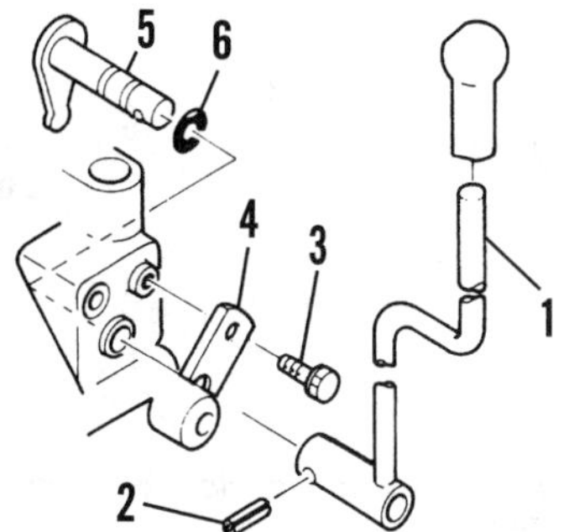

Fig. F2-38—Exploded view of shift control arm assembly.

1. Shift lever
2. Roll pin
3. Bolt
4. Stop plate
5. Shifter arm
6. Snap ring

Fig. F2-39—Maximum allowable side clearance (C) between shift fork (2) and gear (1) is 0.04 inch (1.0 mm).

detent ball (5) and spring (6) when sliding the shift fork (7) off the shift rod.

Pull the countershaft (5—Fig. F2-37) back while removing the bearing (1) and sliding gears (2 and 4) from the front of shaft. Remove the motor drive gear cluster (2), shim (1) and bearing (3). Remove and discard the O-ring (4). Drive out the roll pin (2—Fig. 2-38) and remove range shift lever (1). Remove the stop plate (4) and withdraw the shifter arm (5) from inside the case.

Inspect all components for damage. Maximum allowable side clearance (C—Fig. F2-39) between shift fork (2) and gear (1) is 0.04 inch (1.0 mm). Replace gears if gear backlash exceeds 0.02 in. (0.5 mm). Replace all O-rings and seals.

Assemble the components in reverse of disassembly. Install the larger diameter fixed gear on the countershaft (3—Fig. F2-34) so the extended hub's side is toward the rear of the housing. Apply gasket forming compound to the housing mating surfaces before assembly.

FINAL DRIVE

LUBRICATION

The final drive and range transmission share a common sump. Refer to the RANGE TRANSMISSION section for lubrication information.

REMOVAL AND INSTALLATION

Refer to the RANGE TRANSMISSION for removal and separation procedure.

DISASSEMBLY

Note the left-hand axle housing and the differential assembly must be removed in order to service the right-hand axle assembly.

Remove the cap screws attaching the left-hand axle housing to the differential housing. Separate the axle housing (16—Fig. F2-40) from the differential housing (4).

Note that liquid gasket making compound is applied to the axle housing flange during assembly. Do not damage the mating surfaces of final drive housing (4) and axle housing when removing the old gasket compound.

Identify and save the differential shims (11).

To disassemble the left axle assembly, first pry the seal (18) from the axle housing. Disengage the snap ring (17) from housing bore. Use a soft-faced hammer and gently drive the axle (19) with the bearing out of the housing (16). Remove the snap ring (12) and spacer (13). Press or pull the bearing (15) off the axle.

Lift the differential assembly (10) out of the housing (4). Identify and save the shims (9), which may remain in the housing or adhere to the differential bearing. Remove snap ring (8) and spacer (7). Use a soft-faced hammer and gently drive the axle out of the bearing and housing. Extract the seal (2) and remove the snap ring (3). Pull out the bearing (5).

To disassemble the differential, remove the cap screws from the case cover (2) and withdraw the cover. Remove the side gear (4) and thrust washer (3). Remove the pinion shaft retaining ring (8), and push the pinion shaft (9) out of the differential case. Remove the pinion gears (6), thrust washers (5) and the other side gear (4) and thrust washer.

To remove the pinion gear assembly, remove the snap ring (1—Fig. F2-41), spacer (2), bearing (3), gear (4) and snap ring (5) from the pinion shaft (15). Bend back the tabs on the tab washer (7) and unscrew the nuts (6 and 8). Remove the bearing (4) and pinion (15). Do not lose shims (13).

Fig. F2-41—Exploded view of pinion shaft and input gear assemblies.

1. Snap ring
2. Spacer
3. Bearing
4. Input gear
5. Snap ring
6. Nut
7. Tab washer
8. Nut
9. Bearing
10. Snap rings
11. Housing
12. Bearing
13. Shim
14. Washer
15. Pinion shaft

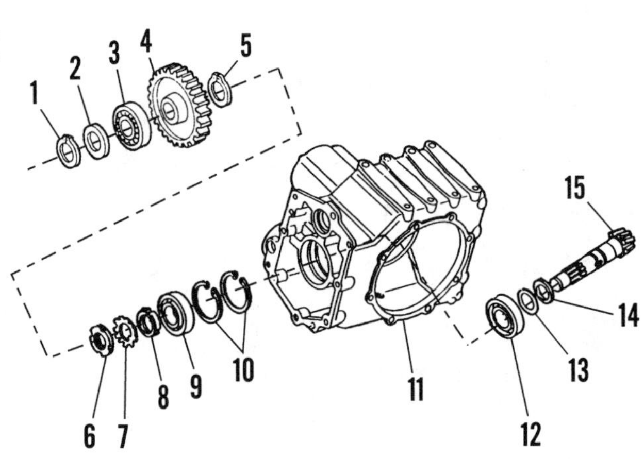

INSPECTION AND REPAIR

If the ring gear (7—Fig. F2-42) is worn or damaged, remove the mounting screws and separate the gear from the case (10). Examine the case bearings (1 and 11) for excessive damage. Use a suitable puller to remove the bearings if replacement is necessary.

The thickness of new side gear thrust washers (3) is 0.079 in. (2.00 mm) with a wear limit of 0.067 in. (1.70 mm). The thickness of new pinion gear thrust washers (5) is 0.047 in. (1.20 mm) with a wear limit of 0.035 in. (0.90 mm).

The specified clearance between the differential pinion shaft (9—Fig. F2-42) and pinion gears (6) is 0.0008-0.004 in. (0.02-0.114 mm). Replace the shaft and the gears if clearance exceeds 0.02 in. (0.5 mm).

The pinion (15—Fig. F2-41) and the ring gear (7—Fig. F2-42) are available only as a matched set. Tighten ring gear retaining screws to 36-46 ft.-lb. (49-62 N·m). Bend the locking tabs to prevent the bolts from loosening.

ASSEMBLY

If the ring gear and pinion, final drive housing, differential case bearings, pinion bearings, differential case or left axle housing are replaced, gear and bearing adjustment is required. If the components were not replaced, reassemble the final drive using the same shims in their original locations.

Drive Pinion Preload Adjustment

If a new ring gear and pinion are being installed, note that the gear and pinion are stamped with a value of error number (Fig. F2-43). The number is prefixed with a + or - to indicate the amount of error from zero adjustment.

If the value of error number on the new parts is greater than on the old parts, additional shims (13—Fig. F2-41) will be required. If the number on the new parts is less, the number of shims must be decreased. For example if the value of error number is -0.2 on the on the replaced pinion and the number on the new pinion is -0.1, the difference is –0.1. Decrease the shims (13) by 0.1 mm (0.004 in.).

Install the thrust washer (14—Fig. F2-41), correct the thickness shims (13) and the bearing (12) on the pinion shaft (15). Insert the pinion shaft from the rear, and install the front bearing (9) and inner locknut (8).

Wrap a strong cord around the pinion shaft (Fig. F2-44) and use a pull scale to measure the force required to rotate the pinion shaft (differential not installed). Tighten the nut (8—Fig. F2-41) until a constant pull of 2.4-3.6 pounds (5.3-8.0 kg) is required to rotate pinion shaft. Install tab washer (7) and nut (6). Tighten the nut (6) without disturbing nut (8), and bend tabs into slots on both nuts.

Differential Carrier Bearing Preload Adjustment

Assemble the differential gears, thrust washers and shaft in the differential case. Install the case cover with new lock plates. Tighten the case bolts, and bend the lock plates to prevent the bolts from loosening.

If removed, install the ring gear using new lock plates. Tighten the ring gear bolts to 36-46 ft.-lb. (49-62 N·m). Bend the locking plate tabs to prevent the bolts from loosening.

Position the differential assembly in the case using two equal shim packs (9 and 11—Fig. F2-40) that are thicker than will be required.

NOTE: Check to be sure there is no interference between the ring gear and pinion gear. There must be some backlash between the gear teeth to correctly set the preload.

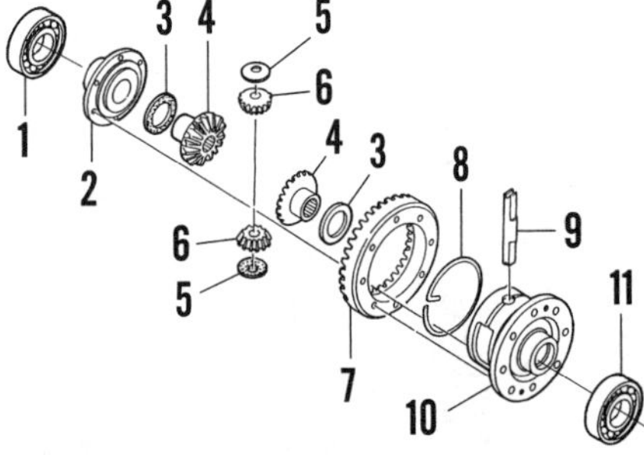

Fig. F2-42—Exploded view of differential assembly.

1. Bearing
2. Cover
3. Thrust washer
4. Side gear
5. Thrust washer
6. Pinion
7. Ring gear
8. Retainer ring
9. Pinion shaft
10. Case
11. Bearing

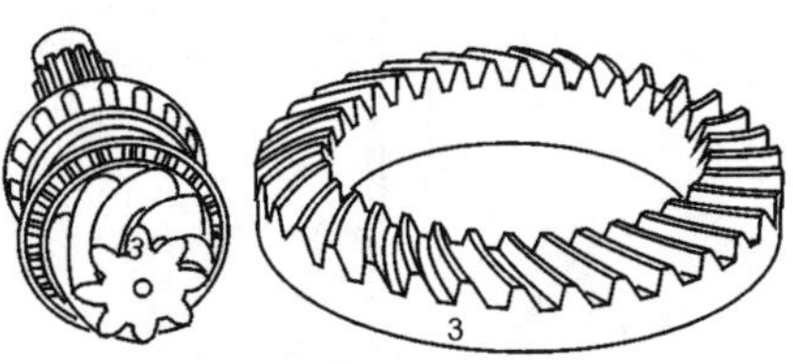

Fig. F2-43—Ring gear and pinion tolerance identification number.

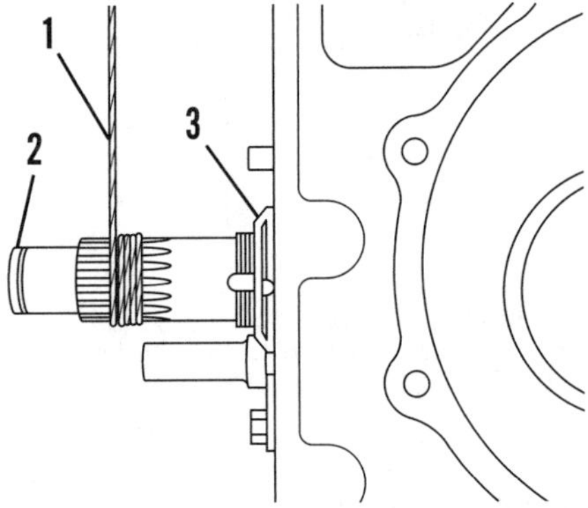

Fig. F2-44—Drive pinion preload adjustment. Refer to text.

1. Cord
2. Pinion shaft
3. Nut

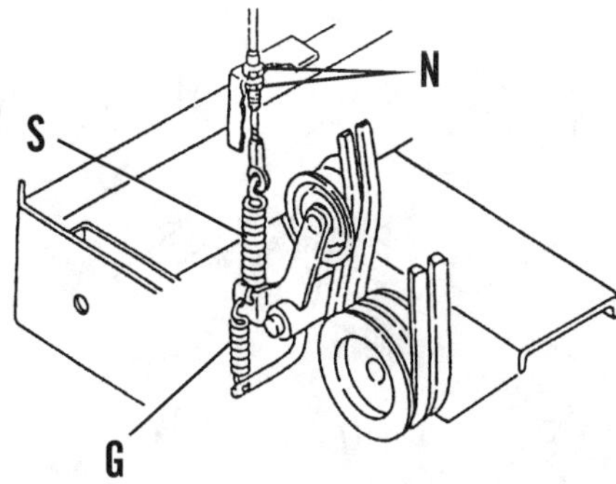

Fig. F2-45—Spring (S) length should be 3-7/8 to 4 in. (98-102 mm). Adjust position of nuts (N) to adjust spring length.

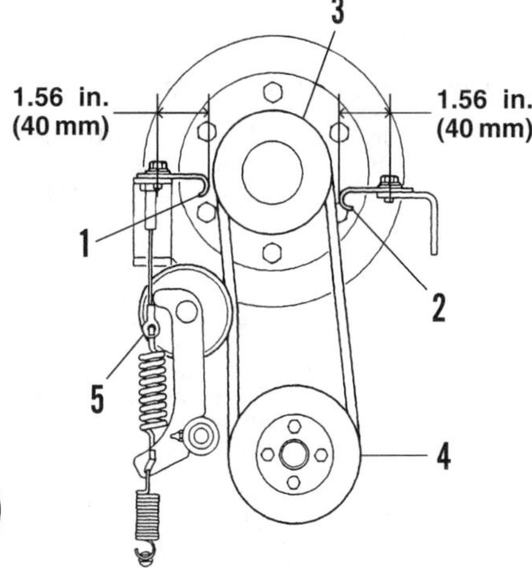

Fig. F2-46—Drawing of PTO belt guide installation.

1. Belt guide
2. Belt guide
3. Flywheel pulley
4. Drive pulley
5. Belt tightener pulley

Install the left axle housing to the differential case. Be sure the left-hand carrier bearing is fully seated in the axle housing. Install four of the axle housing mounting bolts equally spaced around the axle housing, and tighten the bolts finger tight.

Using a feeler gauge, measure the gap between the final drive housing and axle housing at three locations around the axle housing and average the measurements. Remove the axle housing and remove shims equal to the average measured gap. This will establish the desired zero preload for the carrier bearings.

Ring Gear to Pinion Backlash Adjustment

Install the left axle housing and tighten the retaining screws. Use a dial indicator to measure the backlash between the ring gear and pinion. The desired gear backlash is 0.006-0.008 inch (0.15-0.4 mm).

If backlash is not within the specified range, remove the axle housing and move the shims (9 and 11—Fig. F2-40) from one side of the differential to the other as needed to obtain the desired backlash. Do not change combined thickness of all shims, this would change the bearing preload.

Complete the assembly of the transmission and differential case assemblies. Apply liquid gasket sealant to all casting mating surfaces.

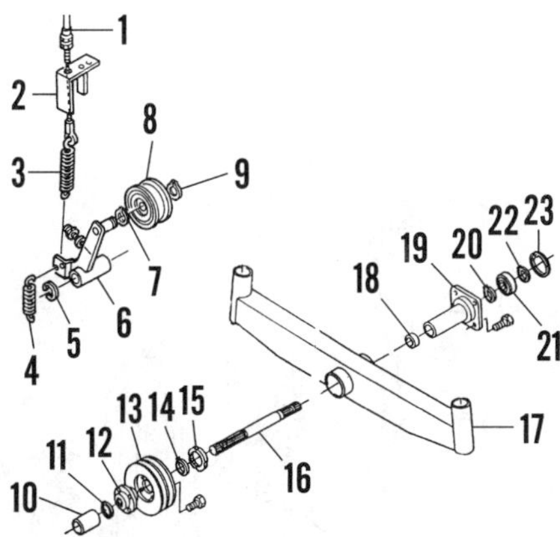

Fig. F2-47—Exploded view of PTO assembly used on Models GT65, GT75, GT85 and GT95.

1. Control cable
2. Bracket
3. Spring
4. Spring
5. Snap ring
6. Idler arm
7. Snap ring
8. Idler pulley
9. Snap ring
10. Sleeve
11. Snap ring
12. Hub
13. Pulley
14. Snap ring
15. Nut
16. PTO shaft
17. Axle main member
18. Bearing
19. Pivot tube
20. Snap ring
21. Bearing
22. Snap ring
23. Snap ring

PTO

Implements are driven by the power take-off (PTO) mechanism located at the front of the tractor. The PTO is belt driven by a pulley attached to the engine flywheel. A pair of drive belts transfers power from the engine to the PTO drive shaft.

An electrical switch actuated by the PTO control lever prevents engine starting unless the PTO is disengaged. Refer to the ELECTRICAL SYSTEM for PTO switch adjustment procedure.

DRIVE BELTS

Adjustment

Adjust belt tension after the first 25 hours of operation following the installation of new belts, then check adjustment periodically.

To adjust belt tension, be sure the ignition switch is OFF. Place the PTO control lever in the engaged position. Raise the hood and measure the length of the upper spring (S—Fig. F2-45). Spring length should be 3⅞ to 4 inches (98-102 mm). Adjust the position of the cable jam nuts (N) to adjust the spring length. Retighten the nuts. Check operation.

Removal and Installation

Remove the hood, then remove the upper and lower belt shields. Remove the cover. Loosen the belt guide fasteners and move the guides (1 and 2—Fig. F2-46) out of the way. Loosen the adjusting nuts (N—Fig. F2-45) to decrease spring tension. Detach the lower spring (G). Remove the drive belts from the pulleys.

Install the drive belts by reversing the removal procedure. Position the belt guides 1.56 in. (40 mm) from the belts (Fig. F2-46). Adjust belt tension as previously described.

PTO SHAFT ASSEMBLY OVERHAUL

Models GT65, GT75, GT85 and GT95

Remove the drive belts as previously described. Remove the snap ring (11—Fig. F2-47), and withdraw the hub (12) and pulley (13) from the drive shaft. If not previously removed, disconnect the implement drive shaft U-joint from the rear of the PTO drive shaft.

Raise and support the front of the tractor and the front axle so the front axle cannot drop when the axle pivot tube (19) is removed. Unscrew the pivot tube nut (15). Remove the bolts from the axle pivot tube (19), and carefully drive the pivot tube with the PTO shaft (16) out of the frame.

Remove the snap rings (14 and 23). Carefully drive the PTO shaft and bearing out of the pivot tube toward the flanged end of the tube. If necessary, remove the needle bearing (18).

Clean the bearings and repack with multipurpose lithium based grease. Note that the needle bearing (18—Fig. F2-47) has a wider flange on one end, and it must be installed with the wide flange facing inward.

Reverse the disassembly procedure to reassemble the components. Apply Loctite to the pivot tube nut (15) prior to assembly, then tighten the nut so the axle side play is 0.004 in. (0.1 mm). The maximum allowable side play is 0.04 in. (1.0 mm). Install the belts and adjust belt tension as previously described.

Models LGT14D and LGT16D

Remove the drive belts as previously described. Remove the snap ring (10—Fig. F2-48) and withdraw the pulley (12) and hub (13) from the drive shaft.

If not previously removed, disconnect the implement drive shaft U-joint from the rear of the PTO drive shaft (17).

Remove the snap ring (14). Carefully drive the PTO shaft (17) and bearing (15) out of pivot tube (18) toward the front of the tractor. If necessary, remove the seal (20) and needle bearing (19) from the pivot tube.

Clean the bearings and repack with multipurpose lithium based grease. Inspect all components for damage and replace as necessary.

Reverse disassembly procedure to reassemble the components. Install the belts and adjust belt tension as previously described.

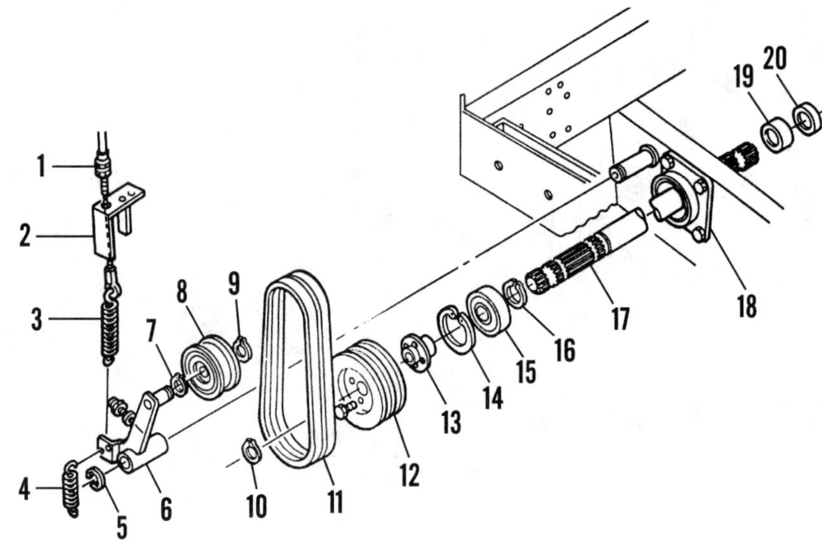

Fig. F2-48—Exploded view of PTO assembly used on Models LGT14D and LGT16D.

1. Control cable
2. Bracket
3. Spring
4. Spring
5. Snap ring
6. Idler arm
7. Snap ring
8. Idler pulley
9. Snap ring
10. Snap ring
11. Belt
12. Pulley
13. Hub
14. Snap ring
15. Bearing
16. Snap ring
17. PTO shaft
18. Pivot tube
19. Bearing
20. Seal

HYDRAULIC LIFT

HYDRAULIC LIFT SYSTEM

Operation

The transmission charge pump supplies the pressurized oil to operate the hydraulic implement lift. A single spool, open center control valve directs the pressurized fluid to a double-acting hydraulic cylinder. The control valve is equipped with an adjustable relief valve limiting system pressure.

Relief Valve Setting

When checking the relief valve pressure setting, hydraulic fluid must be at normal operating temperature. Shut off the engine and relieve the hydraulic pressure in system.

Disconnect the hydraulic lift hose from the control valve and cap or plug hose end. Lift the hose connects to the rear valve port. Connect a 0-800 psi (0-5500 kPa) pressure gauge to the control valve lift port.

Run the engine at high idle. Move the lift control lever to the RAISE position while observing the gauge.

CAUTION: Do not hold lift control lever in the RAISE position any longer than needed to read the pressure gauge, otherwise, hydraulic fluid will overheat.

Gauge should read 570-640 psi (3900-4400 kPa) on Models GT65, GT75, GT85 and GT95 or 426-497 psi (3000-3500 kPa) on Models LGT14D and LGT16D.

To adjust the relief valve pressure setting, loosen the nut (N—Fig. F2-49) and rotate the adjusting screw (S). Tighten the nut, and recheck pressure reading.

When the desired pressure setting is obtained, remove the gauge and reconnect lift cylinder hose to control valve.

CONTROL VALVE

Removal and Installation

To remove the valve, lift the seat and disconnect seat switch connector. Remove the seat and seat support as an assembly.

Remove knobs from the range shift lever and hydraulic lift control lever. Remove the four bolts attaching the seat support to the fenders and the two bolts attaching the fender to the step plates. Remove the fender assembly.

Remove the rear panel behind the fuel tank. Unscrew the bolts retaining seat support brackets and remove brackets.

Disconnect the hydraulic lines from the control valve. Plug or cap all openings. Provide support to control valve spool and gently drive out roll pin securing operating lever to spool end. Unscrew and remove lift operating lever assembly. Unscrew control valve retaining screws and remove control valve.

Reverse the removal procedure to install the control valve. Check hydraulic oil level. Start the engine and operate the lift control lever several times to purge air from the system.

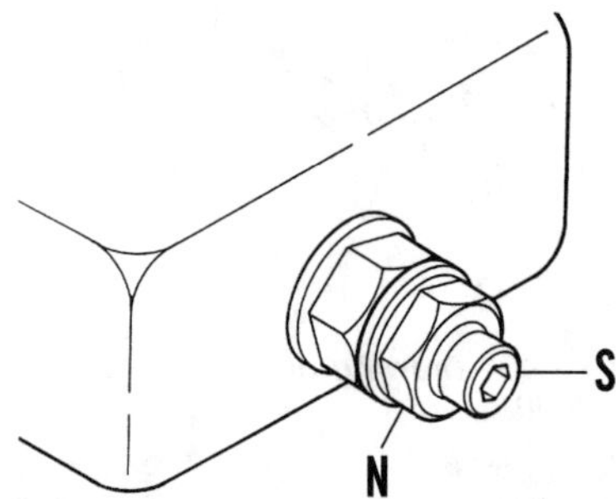

Fig. F2-49—To adjust hydraulic lift relief valve, loosen nut (N) and rotate adjusting screw (S).

Overhaul

Models GT65, GT75, GT85 and GT95

Clean the valve body before disassembly. To disassemble, remove the screws from the cap (2—Fig. F2-50) and withdraw the spool (13) and cap as an assembly from valve body. Detach snap ring (1) and remove cap (2).

CAUTION: Use care when disengaging the spool from the holder. Balls and spring can fly out with considerable force. Enclose the holder and spool with a shop towel to prevent uncontrolled ejection of the balls and spring.

Carefully separate the holder (3) from the spool assembly. Do not remove

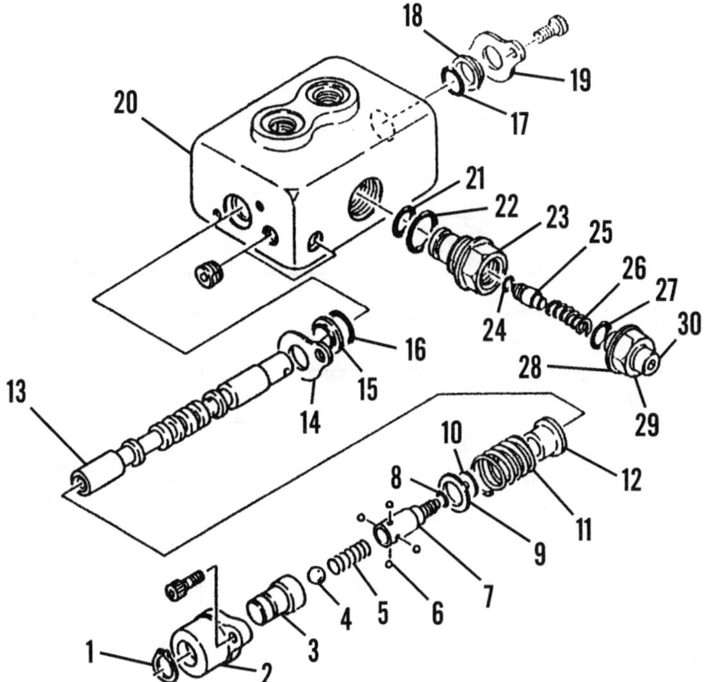

Fig. F2-50—Exploded view of hydraulic lift control valve used on Models GT65, GT75, GT85 and GT95.

1. Snap ring
2. Cap
3. Holder
4. Ball
5. Spring
6. Balls (4)
7. Stopper
8. O-ring
9. Spacer
10. Spacer
11. Spring
12. Spring seat
13. Spool
14. Seal plate
15. Wiper
16. O-ring
17. O-ring
18. Wiper
19. Seal plate
20. Body
21. O-ring
22. O-ring
23. Relief valve body
24. O-ring
25. Relief valve
26. Spring
27. O-ring
28. Washer
29. Nut
30. Screw

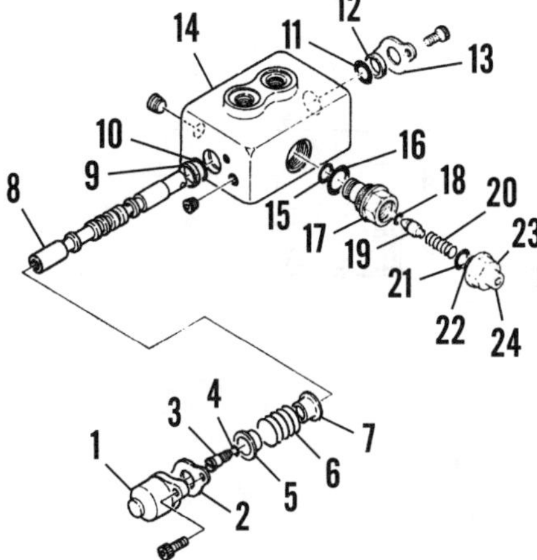

Fig. F2-51—Exploded view of hydraulic lift control valve used on Models LGT14D and LGT16D.

1. Cap
2. Seal plate
3. Screw
4. O-ring
5. Spring seat
6. Spring
7. Spring seat
8. Spool
9. Wiper
10. O-ring
11. O-ring
12. Wiper
13. Seal plate
14. Body
15. O-ring
16. O-ring
17. Relief valve body
18. O-ring
19. Relief valve
20. Spring
21. O-ring
22. Washer
23. Nut
24. Screw

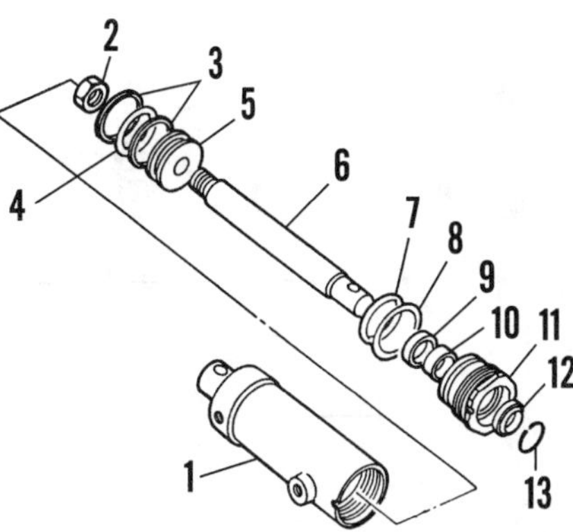

Fig. F2-52—Exploded view of hydraulic lift cylinder.

1. Cylinder
2. Nut
3. Backup rings
4. O-ring
5. Piston
6. Rod
7. O-ring
8. O-ring
9. Seal
10. Bushing
11. Gland nut
12. Wiper
13. Snap ring

the stopper (7) and spring assembly from the spool.

Remove the seal plate (19), O-rings and wipers from the valve body. Remove the relief valve assembly (21-30) from the valve body.

NOTE: To prevent damage, do not clamp the relief valve in a vise.

Using two wrenches, unscrew the adjustment locknut (29—Fig. F2-50) and disassemble the relief valve.

Clean and inspect components. Replace the control valve assembly if the valve spool or valve body bore damaged. Replace the relief valve as an assembly if faulty. Replace all O-rings and wipers. Lubricate before assembly.

When assembling the control valve, tighten the relief valve (23) to 29-36 ft.-lb. (39-49 N·m). To assemble the spool spring and balls, proceed by placing the spring (5), ball (4) and balls (6) at the end of the stopper (7) and hold in place with grease. Install the holder (3) over the stopper (7). Insert the holder in the cap (2). Install the snap ring (1) after installing the spool assembly in the valve body. Flat side of the snap ring must be toward end of holder.

Install the control valve on the tractor and adjust relief valve setting as previously outlined.

Models LGT14D and LGT16D

Clean the valve body before disassembly. To disassemble valve, remove the cap (1—Fig. F2-51) and seal plate (13). Withdraw the valve spool (8) from the valve body.

Unscrew the relief valve body (17) from the valve body. Using two wrenches, unscrew the adjusting locknut (23) from the valve body (17) and disassemble the relief valve.

Clean all components and inspect for damage. The valve spool and body must be replaced as an assembly if either is damaged. Replace the relief valve as an assembly if it is faulty.

Lubricate components before assembly. Install new O-rings and seals when assembling. Tighten the relief valve (17) to 29-36 ft.-lb. (39-49 N·m).

HYDRAULIC LIFT CYLINDER OVERHAUL

The hydraulic lift cylinder can be removed from underneath the tractor without removing sheet metal. Disconnect the hydraulic hoses and plug all openings. Remove the pins from each end of the cylinder and remove the cylinder from the tractor.

To disassemble the cylinder, unscrew the gland nut (11—Fig. F2-52) and pull internal components out of cylinder. Remove piston from rod. Remove and discard all seals.

NOTE: Do not clamp the rod or piston in a vise. Be careful not to scratch or mar the rod.

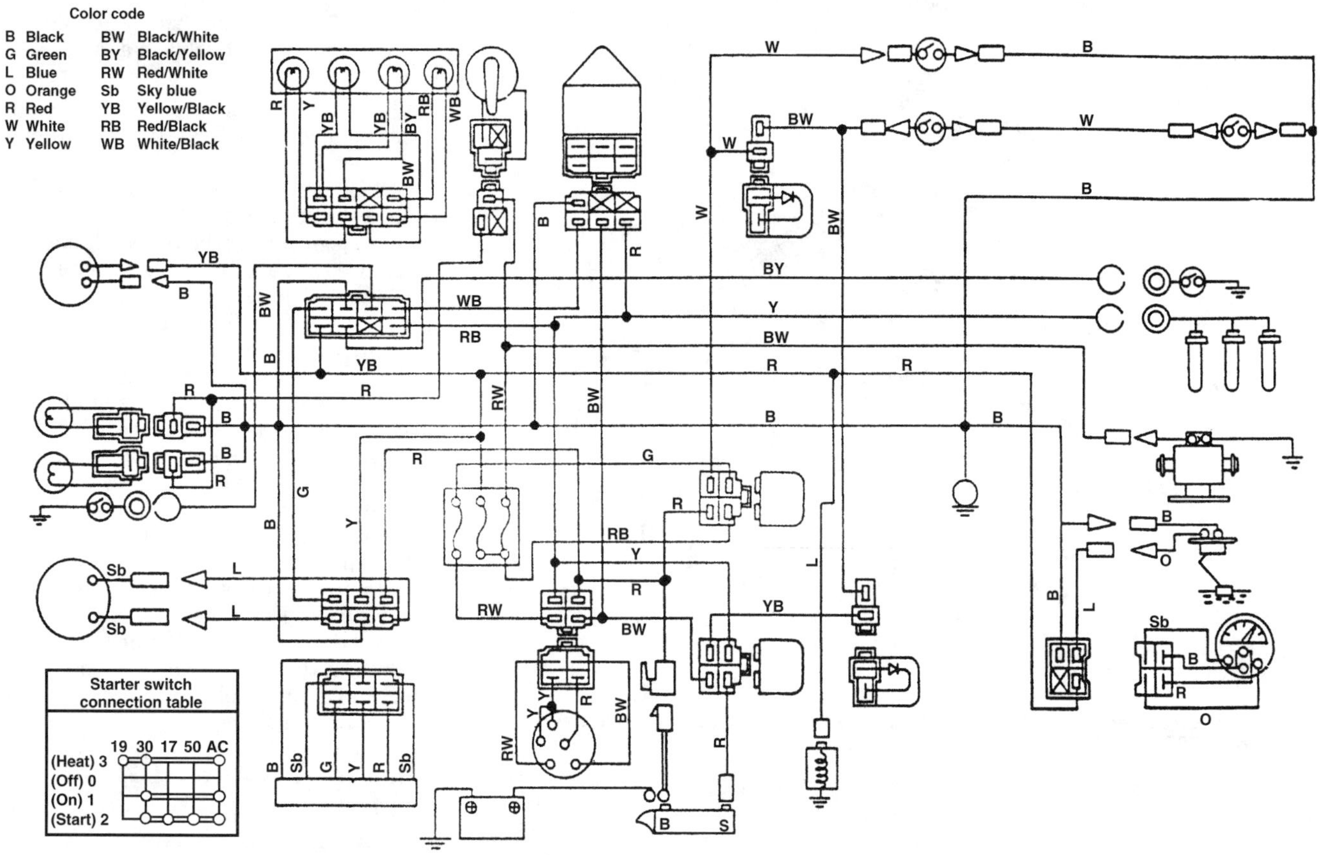

Color code

B	Black	BW	Black/White
G	Green	BY	Black/Yellow
L	Blue	RW	Red/White
O	Orange	Sb	Sky blue
R	Red	YB	Yellow/Black
W	White	RB	Red/Black
Y	Yellow	WB	White/Black

Starter switch connection table

	19	30	17	50	AC
(Heat) 3					
(Off) 0					
(On) 1					
(Start) 2					

Fig. F2-53—Wiring diagram for Models GT65 and GT75.

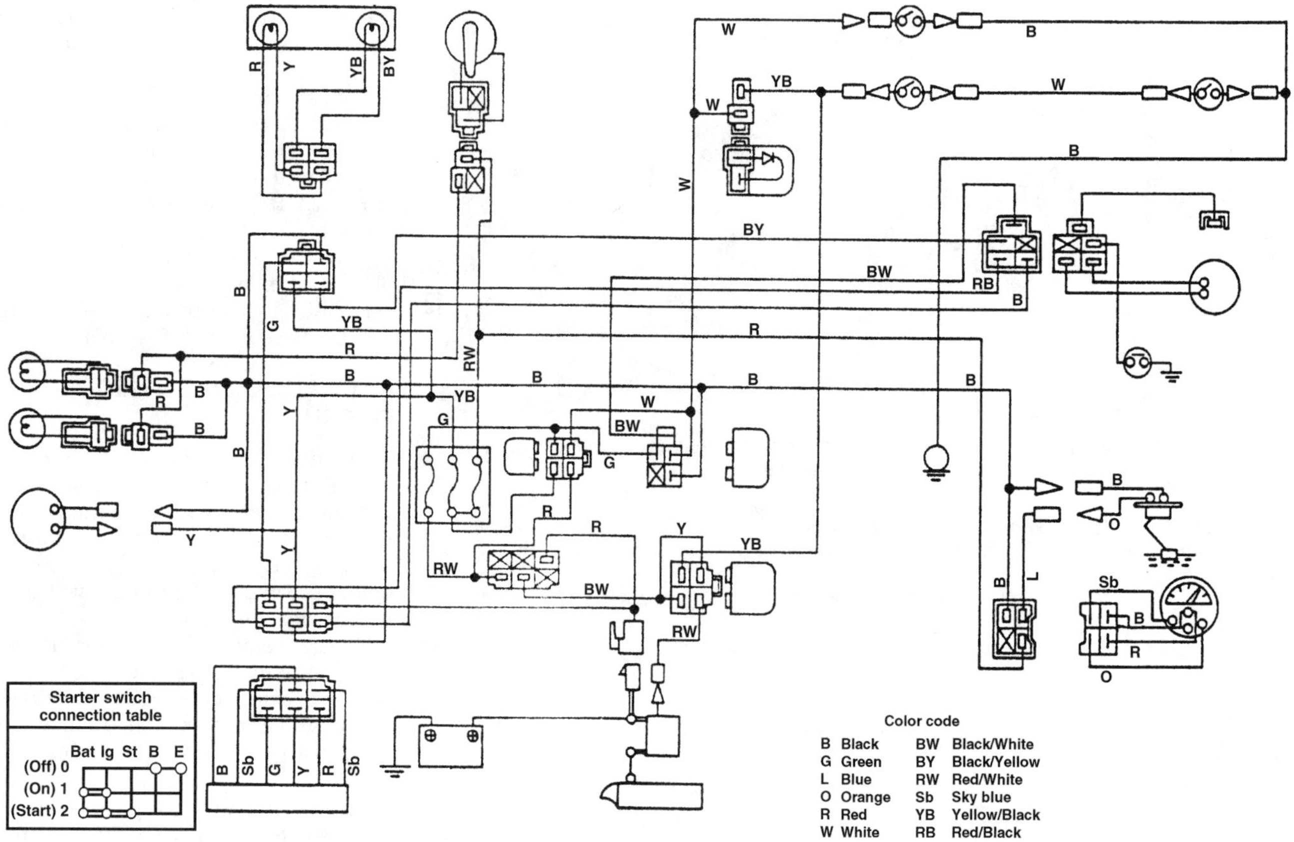

Starter switch connection table

	Bat	Ig	St	B	E
(Off) 0					
(On) 1					
(Start) 2					

Color code

B	Black	BW	Black/White
G	Green	BY	Black/Yellow
L	Blue	RW	Red/White
O	Orange	Sb	Sky blue
R	Red	YB	Yellow/Black
W	White	RB	Red/Black

Fig. F2-54—Wiring diagram for Models GT85 and GT95.

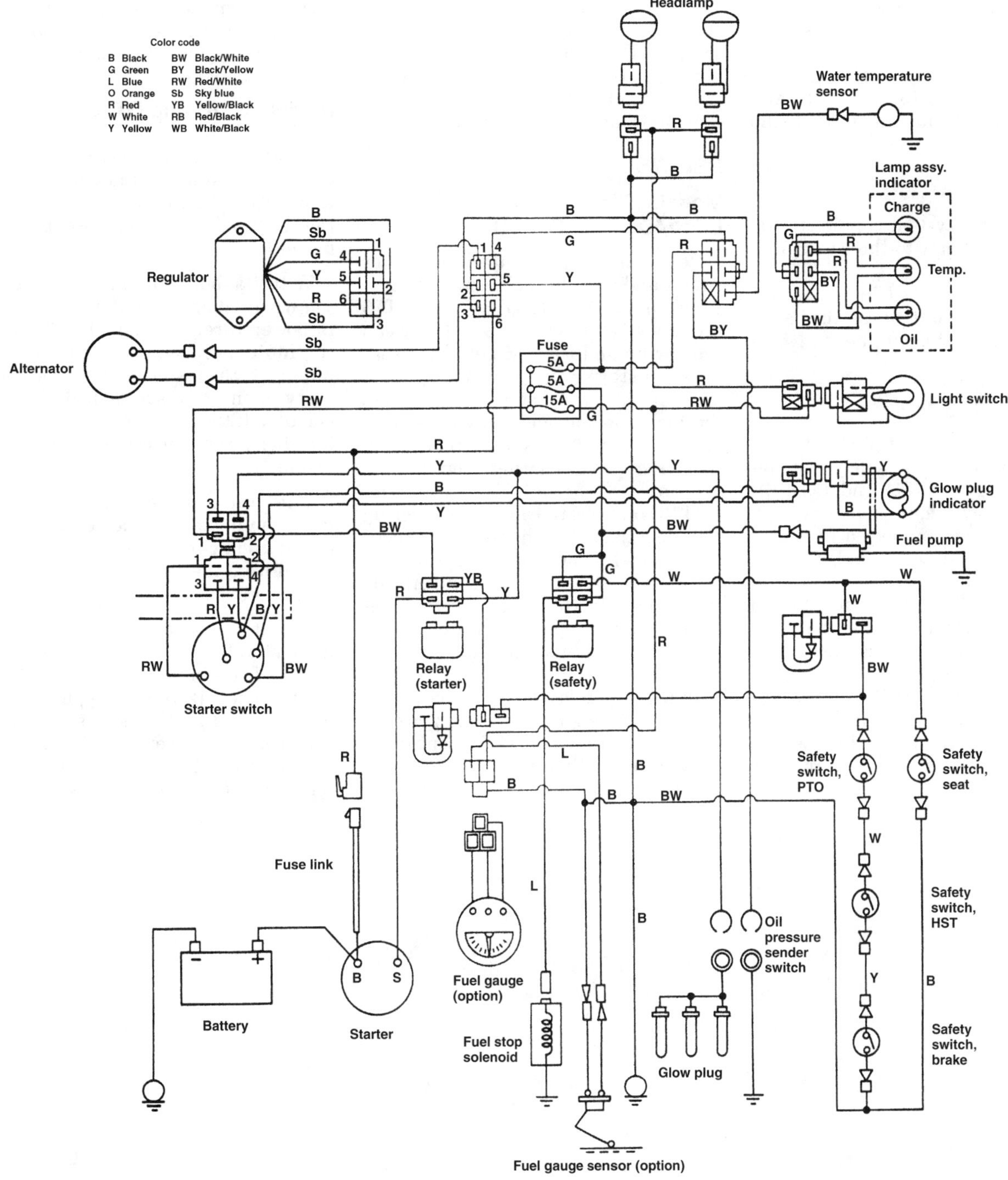

Fig. F2-55—Wiring diagram for Models LGT14D and LGT16D.

Inspect the rod, piston and cylinder bore for damage and replace if necessary. The maximum allowable clearance between the piston and cylinder bore is 0.010 in. (0.25 mm). The maximum allowable clearance between the rod and gland nut bushing is 0.012 in. (0.30 mm). The bushing (10) is replaceable. Replace all O-rings and backup rings.

Coat parts with clean oil during assembly. Be careful not to twist or cut the O-rings when assembling.

Install the cylinder on the tractor and check the hydraulic oil level. Start the engine and cycle the cylinder several times to purge air from the cylinder.

ELECTRICAL SYSTEM

Refer to Figs. F2-53, F2-54 and F2-55 for the wiring diagrams. Service procedures for engine related electrical components, such as the starter, are covered in the appropriate Shibaura or Kohler engine section at the rear of this manual.

BATTERY

The tractor is equipped with a 12-volt battery. Specified rating is 390 CCA for Model GT95 and 332 CCA for all other models.

REGULATOR/RECTIFIER

The regulator/rectifier is located adjacent to the steering column and can be identified by the fins on the body. The regulator/rectifier maintains a circuit voltage of 14-15 volts while regulating alternator output to 14 amps on Models GT65, GT75, LGT14D and LGT16D or to 22 amps on Models GT85 and GT95.

FUSES

The electrical system is protected by a fusible link. Refer to the wiring diagram for location.

Fuses are contained in a fuse box attached to the front side of the baffle panel between the engine and battery.

SAFETY SWITCHES

Models GT65, GT75, GT85 and GT95 are equipped with three safety switches while Models LGT14D and LGT16D are equipped with four safety switches. The switches are connected in series. Each switch must be closed before the engine can be started.

On Models GT65, GT75, GT85 and GT95, safety switches are located at the operator seat, PTO control lever and brake actuating rod. On Models LGT14D and LGT16D, the safety switches are located at the operator seat, PTO control lever, hydrostatic transmission control arm and brake actuating rod.

Close the switches so the engine will start only if operator is in the operator's seat, the PTO control lever is in disengaged position, brake is applied and on Models LGT14D and LGT16D, speed control pedal is in NEUTRAL.

RELAYS

Models GT65, GT75, LGT14D and -LGT16D

Relays are used to control the starter circuit and fuel stop solenoid circuit.

Relays on Models GT65 and GT75 are located on the baffle panel between the engine and battery. Left relay controls the starter circuit while right relay controls the fuel stop solenoid. Note the fuel stop solenoid relay only operates if the neutral start circuit functions. Refer to the wiring diagram.

Relays on Models LGT14D and LGT16D are located above the steering column adjacent to the regulator/rectifier. Left relay controls the fuel stop solenoid while right relay controls the starter circuit. Note the fuel stop solenoid relay only operates if the neutral start circuit functions. Refer to the wiring diagram.

To test the relay, refer to the wiring diagram and apply 12 volts to powered terminals of relay. Check for continuity between two other relay terminals. If the tester indicates no continuity when 12 volts is applied, the relay is faulty. If the tester indicates continuity when no voltage is applied, the relay is faulty.

Models GT85 and GT95

Relays are used to control the fused circuits, the starter circuit and the ignition circuit. The relays are located on the baffle panel between the engine and battery.

To test a four-terminal relay, refer to the wiring diagram and apply 12 volts to powered relay terminals. Check for continuity between two other relay terminals. If the tester indicates no continuity when 12 volts is applied, the relay is faulty. If the tester indicates continuity when no voltage is applied, the relay is faulty.

The ignition control relay is a five-terminal relay. The relay grounds the ignition circuit if voltage is not received from the safety switches and ignition switch.

To test the switch, connect a continuity tester between relay terminals 3 and 4. If continuity exists, the relay is faulty. When 12 volts is applied to terminals 1 and 2, the tester should indicate continuity between terminals 3 and 4. If the tester does not indicate continuity, the relay is faulty.

FORD NEW HOLLAND

CONDENSED SPECIFICATIONS

Model	LGT18H
Engine Make	Kohler
Model	M18
Number of cylinders	2
Bore	3.12 in. (79.2 mm)
Stroke	2.75 in. (69.85 mm)
Displacement	42.18 cu. in. (691 cc)
Power Rating	18 hp (13.4 kW)
Slow Idle	1750 rpm
High Speed (No-Load)	3600 rpm
Crankcase	3.0 pt.* (1.4 L)
Transmission	See text

*With filter—3.5 pt.(1.7 L).

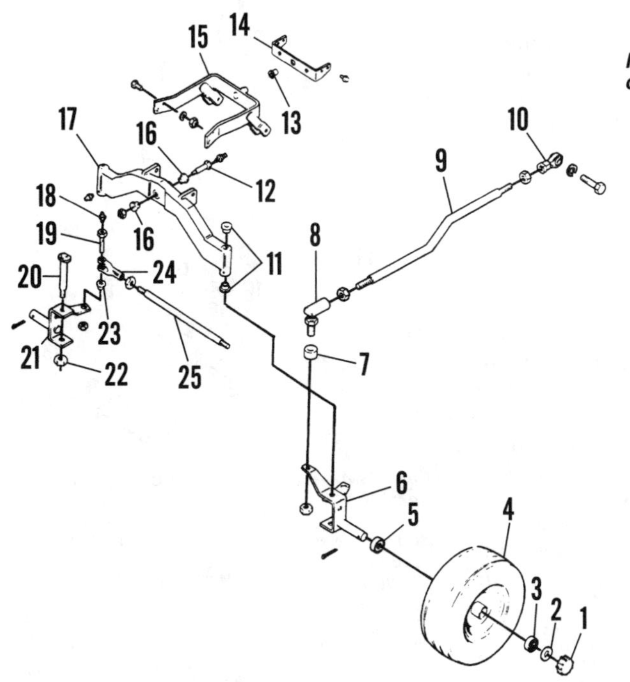

Fig. F3-1—Exploded view of front axle assembly.

1. Hubcap
2. Washer
3. Bearing
4. Wheel
5. Bearing
6. Left spindle
7. Spacer
8. Ball joint
9. Drag link
10. Rod end
11. Spindle bushings
12. Axle pivot bolt
13. Bushing
14. Pivot bracket
15. Axle pivot support
16. Bushings
17. Axle main member
18. Grease fitting
19. Special bolt
20. Spindle king pin
21. Right spindle
22. Locknut
23. Pivot bushing
24. Tie rod clevis
25. Tie rod

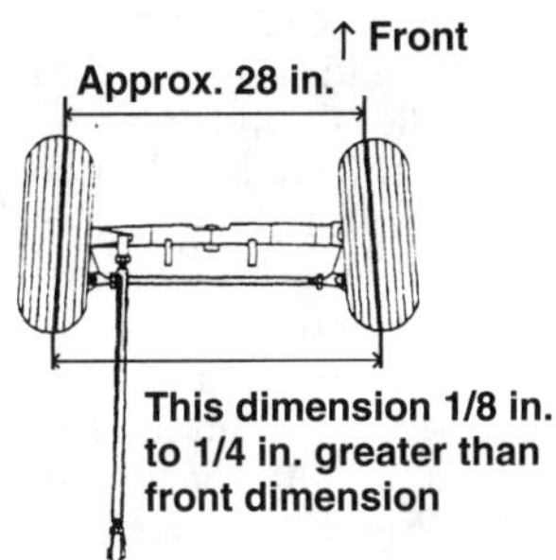

Fig. F3-2—Refer to text for front wheel toe-in setting.

FRONT AXLE AND STEERING SYSTEM

MAINTENANCE

Steering spindles, tie rod ends, axle pivot, wheel bearings and steering gear should be lubricated at 25-hour intervals. The recommended lubricant is multipurpose, lithium base grease.

Clean all pivot points and linkages and lubricate with SAE 30 oil. Check for looseness and wear, then repair when needed.

FRONT WHEELS

Front wheel bearings (3 and 5—Fig. F3-1) are pressed into the wheel hubs. Replace bearings when needed to correct excessive looseness. Lubricate with multipurpose, lithium base grease.

TIE ROD AND TOE-IN

Tie rod ends (24—Fig. F3-1) are available for service. Remove the locknuts from the special tie rod bolts (19). Remove the special bolts from the tie rod ends and remove the tie rod.

Check the condition of the pivot bushings (23) located in the spindle arms. Replace the bushings if worn.

Total length of the tie rod assembly is normally 23 in. (58.4 cm).

With the front wheels in straight-ahead position, measure between the front tires in the fourth tread groove from the inside of each tire (Fig. F3-2). Measure between the rear of the front tires in the same tread grooves and at the same height as the front measurement. This measurement should be $\frac{1}{8}$ to $\frac{1}{4}$ inch greater than the front dimension.

To adjust toe-in, detach the tie rod end from the left spindle. Loosen the jam nuts on the tie rod ends, and turn the tie rod ends equally to obtain recommended toe-in. Tighten jam nuts after adjustment and reconnect the tie rod end to the spindle.

STEERING SPINDLES REMOVAL AND INSTALLATION

Raise and support the front of the tractor. Remove the front wheel. Disconnect tie rod (25—Fig. F3-1) from the spindle to be serviced. If removing left spindle (5), disconnect the drag link (9). Remove the locknut (22) and spindle bolt (20). Remove the spindle.

Replaceable spindle bushings (11) are located in the front axle.

Inspect components for damage, and replace components when needed.

Install by reversing removal procedure.

DRAG LINK ADJUSTMENT

A drag link (9—Fig. F3-1) with replaceable ends is located between the left spindle (6) and the steering sector gear. The initial drag link length is approximately 24.25 in. (61.6 cm) with the front ball joint (8) and rod end (10) threaded equally onto the drag link.

Adjust the drag link length so the following occurs: When the steering wheel is turned full left, the tie rod arm on left spindle (Fig. F3-3) contacts axle before the steering sector gear contacts its stop. Turn the steering wheel full right. The right spindle should contact the axle or be within $\frac{1}{8}$ inch (3 mm) away from the axle before the sector gear contacts its stop.

If these conditions are not met, adjust the drag link as follows: Loosen the jam nut on the drag link rod end (10—Fig. F3-1). Detach the drag link rod end from the pitman arm. Manually turn the front wheels to the left until the left spindle contacts the axle (Fig. F3-3).

Turn the steering wheel to the left until the sector gear contacts its stop, then turn the steering wheel about 1 inch (25 mm) to the right. Adjust the drag link rod end until the rod end cap screw will thread into the sector gear pitman arm without disturbing the position of the steering wheel. Tighten the jam nut and check for correct steering travel.

AXLE MAIN MEMBER REMOVAL AND INSTALLATION

The complete front axle assembly may be removed as a unit. Raise and support the front of the tractor. Disconnect the drag link (9—Fig. F3-1) from the left spindle (5). Disconnect any implement attached to the pivot support bracket (15). Support the axle and remove bolts connecting the pivot bracket (15) to the main member (17). Remove the pivot bolt (12) and remove the axle main member (17). Remove the pivot bracket (15).

Install by reversing removal procedure.

STEERING GEAR OVERHAUL

Raise the hood and set in an upright position. Disconnect the battery cables and remove the battery. Disconnect the throttle and choke cables from the engine. Remove the seven screws at the bottom of the instrument panel attaching the panel to the frame. Remove the two screws from the fuel tank strap and remove the strap and fuel tank.

Disconnect the drag link rod end from the sector gear pitman arm (19—Fig. F3-4). Compress the bellows (9) to expose the bolt in the steering shaft sleeve (7). Remove the nut and bolt (8) and lift the steering wheel assembly and bellows off the steering shaft.

Remove the cap screws attaching the flange bearing (11) to the instrument panel. Remove the handle from the transmission drive control lever. Work the instrument panel back and over the steering shaft.

Remove the four screws attaching the steering mechanism to the steering support channel (17—Fig. F3-4). Remove the cap screw from the support brace (16), and lift the steering mechanism out of the tractor.

To disassemble, remove the nut from the end of the shaft (14) and withdraw the shaft and sector gear (19). Remove the cover (13). Drive out the roll pin (23) and withdraw the steering shaft (12). Catch the gear (22) and bushings (24 and 21) as the shaft is removed.

Clean and inspect all components. Replace the bearings, bushings and gears as needed.

When reassembling the steering mechanism, apply multipurpose grease to sector gear and pinion gear teeth. Lubricate bushings and pivot points with SAE 30 engine oil. Note the choke cable must be routed under the steering mechanism when reassembled. Adjust steering wheel free play when necessary.

Steering Wheel Free Play Adjustment

Steering wheel free play should not exceed $1\frac{1}{2}$ inches (38) measured at the steering wheel's outer diameter. If the steering gear was disassembled for service or if free play is excessive, adjust the steering gear as follows:

The steering adjustment nut can be adjusted through the hole in the left

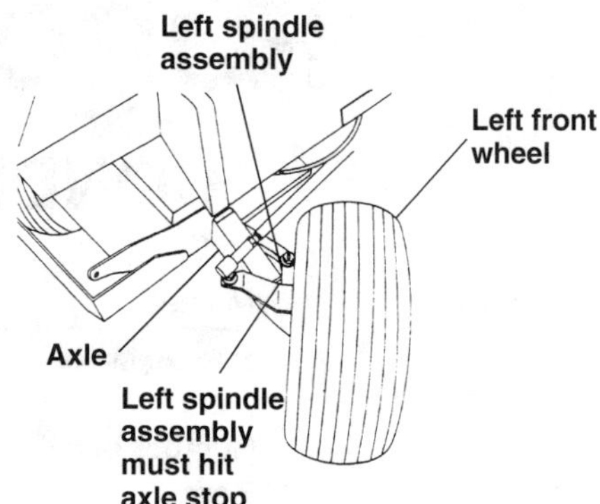

Fig. F3-3—Left spindle must contact axle before steering mechanism reaches full left stop.

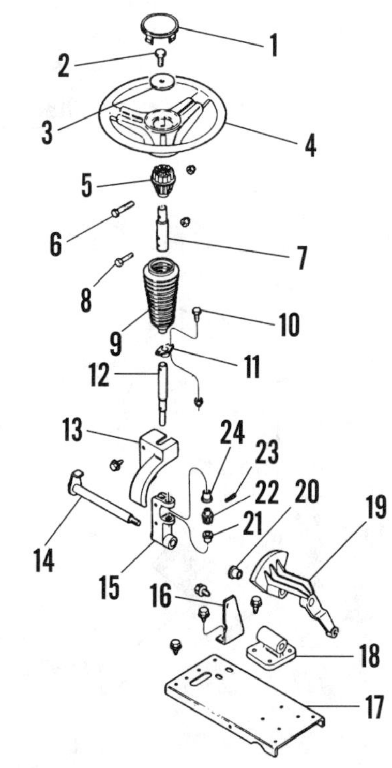

Fig. F3-4—Exploded view of steering assembly.

1. Dust cover
2. Bolt
3. Washer
4. Steering wheel
5. Adapter
6. Bolt
7. Sleeve
8. Bolt
9. Bellows
10. Bolt
11. Flange bearing
12. Steering shaft
13. Sector & pinion cover
14. Shaft
15. Support
16. Brace
17. Support channel
18. Support
19. Sector gear
20. Bushing
21. Bushing
22. Gear
23. Roll pin
24. Bushing

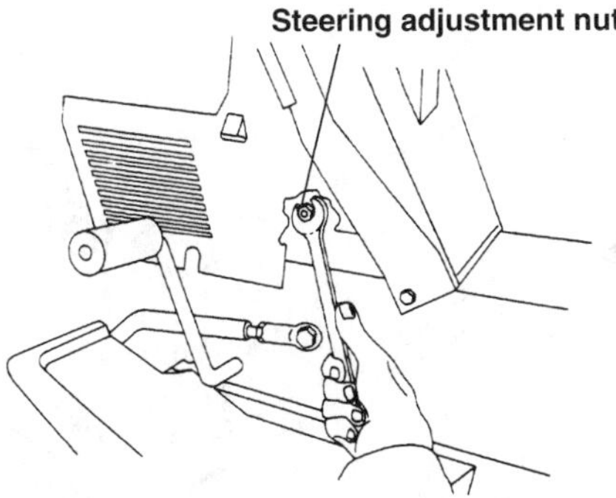

Fig. F3-5—Adjust steering through hole in left side of instrument panel.

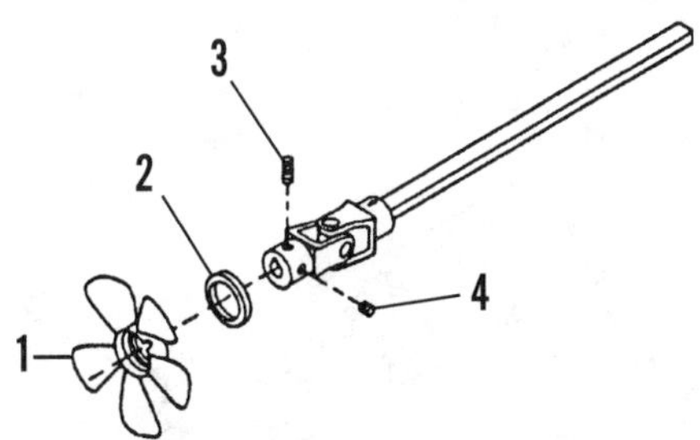

Fig. F3-6—Exploded view of transmission end of drive shaft. Drive shaft is a balanced assembly and must be reassembled the same as it was removed.

1. Fan
2. Spacer
3. Long setscrew
4. Short setscrew

side of the instrument panel (Fig. F3-5). Tighten the nut to reduce steering wheel free play, or loosen it to increase free play.

The steering shaft end play is also adjusted by tightening the steering adjustment nut. Pull up on the steering wheel until end play is removed. Hold the steering wheel in this position and tighten the adjustment nut until no end play is present.

ENGINE

MAINTENANCE

Check oil level daily. Inspect air cleaner element daily or periodically depending on operating conditions.

Refer to the engine section for service information concerning tune-up and adjustments.

LUBRICATION

For new and reconditioned engines, lubricating oil and filter should be changed after first 5 hours of operation. The recommended oil change interval thereafter is every 50 hours of use. The recommended oil filter change interval is after every 100 hours of use. Change oil and filter more frequently when severe operating conditions are encountered.

Drain the oil while the engine is warm from operation. The oil will flow freely and carry away more impurities.

The oil filter is a spin-on paper element cartridge.

Use oil meeting the latest API classification. Select oil viscosity depending on expected ambient temperature range.

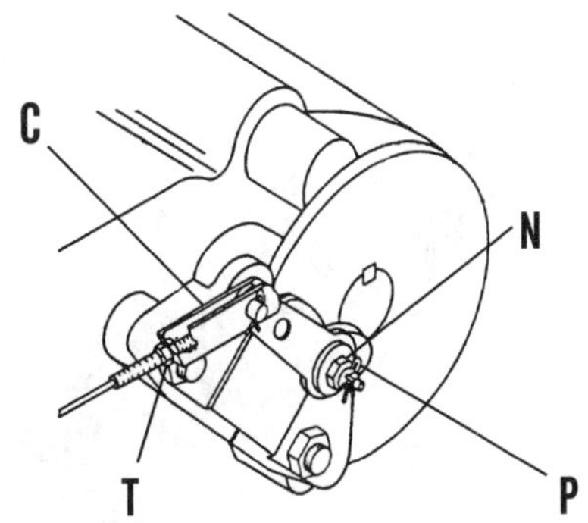

Fig. F3-7—Refer to text for brake adjustment procedure.

AIR FILTER

The air filter should be cleaned after every 100 hours of operation or more frequently if operating in extremely dusty conditions. Remove dust from the filter element by tapping lightly with your hand, not on a hard surface.

Do not wash the paper element or use compressed air as this will damage the element. Replace the filter if it is dirty or damaged.

Make sure the air filter base, cover and seals fit properly and are not damaged. Replace all damaged components.

REMOVAL AND INSTALLATION

Remove any remaining attachments from the tractor. Remove the hood and side panels.

Disconnect the negative battery cable. Disconnect the wire from the electric PTO clutch. Disconnect the starter wire at the solenoid. Disconnect the remaining wires at the connector plug at the rear of engine.

Disconnect the PTO belts and drive shaft, as equipped. Remove the exhaust system and deflectors as needed. Disconnect the fuel line at the fuel filter. Detach throttle and choke cables. Refer to the DRIVE SHAFT section and remove drive shaft.

Remove engine mounting bolts and remove engine.

Install by reversing removal procedure. Be sure to align the marks on the drive shaft during assembly. Refer to the DRIVE SHAFT section. Attach and adjust the throttle and choke cables as follows:

Move the throttle control lever to the FAST position. Attach the throttle cable end to the throttle arm. Move the cable towards the rear until throttle is fully open and tighten cable clamp.

Push the choke knob on the instrument panel in all the way. Attach the cable end to the choke lever. Move the cable until the choke plate is open fully. Tighten the cable clamp.

OVERHAUL

Engine make and model are listed in the specifications table at beginning of this section. Refer to the appropriate Kohler engine section in this manual for service information on the engine and associated accessories.

DRIVE SHAFT

REMOVAL AND INSTALLATION

Remove the mower deck, if so equipped. Unscrew long and short setscrews in the rear universal joint (Fig. F3-6). Move the drive shaft toward the engine so the rear universal joint disengages from transmission shaft. Remove spacer (2).

Make alignment marks on the front universal joint and drive shaft so the joint and drive shaft can be properly matched during assembly. Pull the drive shaft away from the front universal joint and extract the drive shaft through the bottom of the tractor.

NOTE: Drive shaft and universal joints are a balanced assembly. If any components are damaged or assembly is out-of-balance, the complete assembly must be replaced.

Reverse the removal procedure to install the drive shaft. Be sure to align the marks made during disassembly. Lubricate with SAE 30 oil.

BRAKE

ADJUSTMENT

Brake assembly is located on left side of transaxle.

To adjust the brake, remove the cotter pin (P—Fig. F3-7) and tighten the nut (N) until a light drag is felt as tractor is pushed forward by hand. Loosen the nut slightly and install the cotter pin.

With the brake/clutch pedal fully released, brake cable should have a slight amount of slack. To adjust cable slack, detach the brake cable clevis (C) from brake arm. Loosen the jam nut (T). Rotate the clevis clockwise to shorten the cable and remove slack or counterclockwise to lengthen the cable. Tighten the cable jam nut, and reattach clevis to the brake arm.

REMOVAL & INSTALLATION BRAKE PADS

Disconnect the brake cable clevis from the brake arm. Remove two screws retaining the brake pad holder (7—Fig. F3-8) to the transaxle case. Remove the outer brake pad (3), back-up plate (4) and actuator pins (6) from the holder. Withdraw the brake disc (2) from the transaxle shaft and remove the inner brake pad (1).

Reassembly is the reverse of disassembly. Adjust the brake as previously outlined.

HYDROSTATIC TRANSMISSION

LUBRICATION

The hydrostatic transmission and transaxle unit share a common oil reservoir. To check the oil level, the engine must be off. Unscrew the oil plug (P—Fig. F3-9). The oil level should be even with the oil plug opening. Fill the transmission with SAE 20 engine oil.

A spin-on oil filter is mounted on right side of tractor (Fig. F3-10). Install a new filter after the first 25 hours of operation then after every 100 hours of operation. Recheck the oil level after installing the filter and running the transmission for a short time.

ADJUSTMENT

If tractor creeps forward or backward after the foot control pedal returns to NEUTRAL, the NEUTRAL position should be adjusted.

Remove the mower deck if not previously done. Block the front and rear wheels to prevent tractor movement. Raise the left rear wheel so the tire clears the ground. Be sure the transaxle range control lever is in HI position. Disconnect the brake cable at the brake lever. Depress the clutch/brake pedal and apply the parking brake. Loosen the pivot bracket screw (2—Fig. F3-11). Do not remove the screw. Start the engine and run at full speed.

CAUTION: Do not make adjustments while engine is running.

With the foot pedal in NEUTRAL, the wheel should not rotate. If the wheel is rotating, stop the engine and insert a screwdriver blade into the adjustment notch (3—Fig. F3-11). Twist the screwdriver as necessary to position the control linkage in NEUTRAL. If rear wheel rotates forward, turn the screwdriver clockwise until the wheel stops turning. If wheel rotation is backward, turn the screwdriver counterclockwise. Tighten the retaining screw bracket.

Start the engine and check that the rear wheel does not turn. Depress the forward drive pedal fully, then release the pedal. The left rear wheel must come to a complete stop. Repeat the procedure with the reverse drive pedal. If the wheel continues to rotate in either direction, stop the engine and repeat adjustment.

When adjustment is correct, reconnect the brake cable to the brake arm.

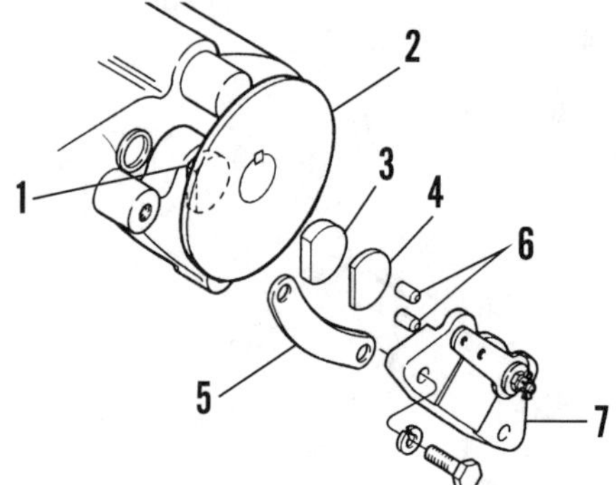

Fig. F3-8—Exploded view of brake assembly.

1. Rear brake pad
2. Brake disc
3. Outer brake pad
4. Backing plate
5. Spacer
6. Actuating pins
7. Brake caliper

REMOVAL AND INSTALLATION

Remove the mower deck, if so equipped. Raise and support the rear of the tractor. Loosen the setscrews and slide the fan hub assembly toward the transmission. Place a mark on the front universal joint and a matching mark on the rectangular drive shaft so they can be properly matched when reassembled. Refer to the DRIVE SHAFT section for details. Disconnect the drive shaft at the transmission end.

Disconnect the brake cable (4—Fig. F3-12) from the brake lever. Disconnect the rear speed control rod (11) from the transmission control arm (12). Disconnect the neutral return rod (6) from the neutral return lever (13).

Unbolt and remove the rear wheels. Lower the tractor until the transaxle rests on the floor. Raise the seat and disconnect the hydraulic hose from the top of the charge pump. Remove the cap screw attaching the hydraulic hose clamp to the main frame.

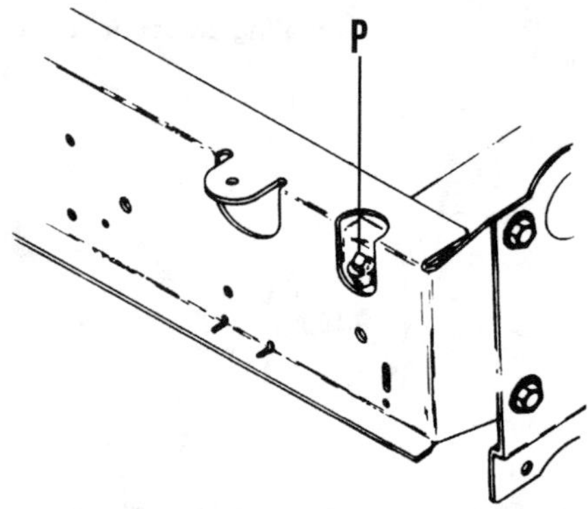

Fig. F3-9—Unscrew plug (P) to determine transmission oil level.

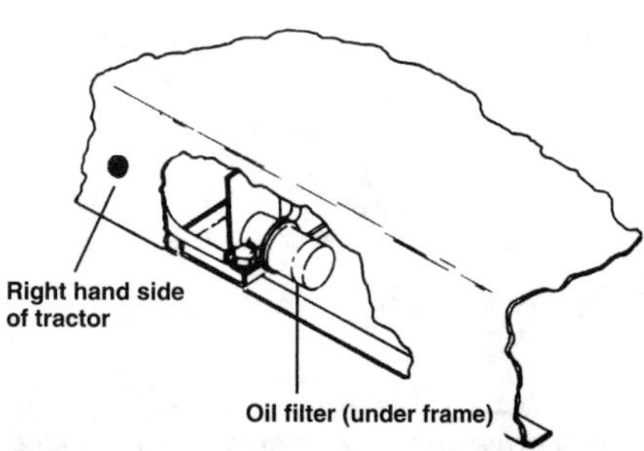

Fig. F3-10—Transmission oil filter is located adjacent to ride side tractor frame rail.

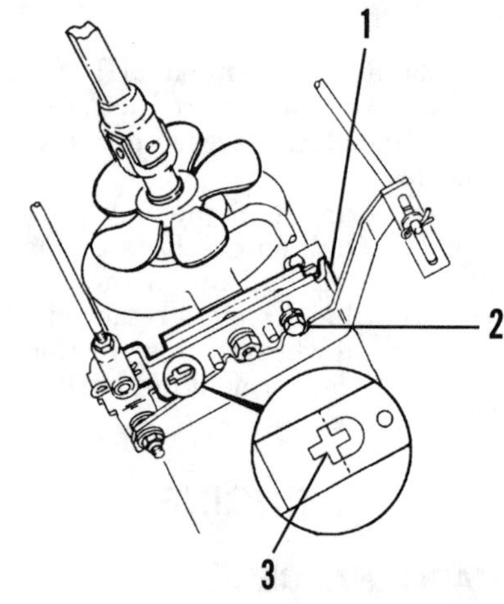

Fig. F3-11—Drawing of hydrostatic control linkage. Insert a screwdriver into slot (3) and turn to adjust neutral setting. Refer to text.

Support the front of the transmission to prevent tipping, then remove the screws attaching the transaxle to the main frame. Raise the rear of the tractor up far enough to disconnect the hydraulic return hose from the transmission. Raise the tractor's rear to clear the transmission and move to one side.

Rotate the transaxle until the transmission faces upward. Disconnect the

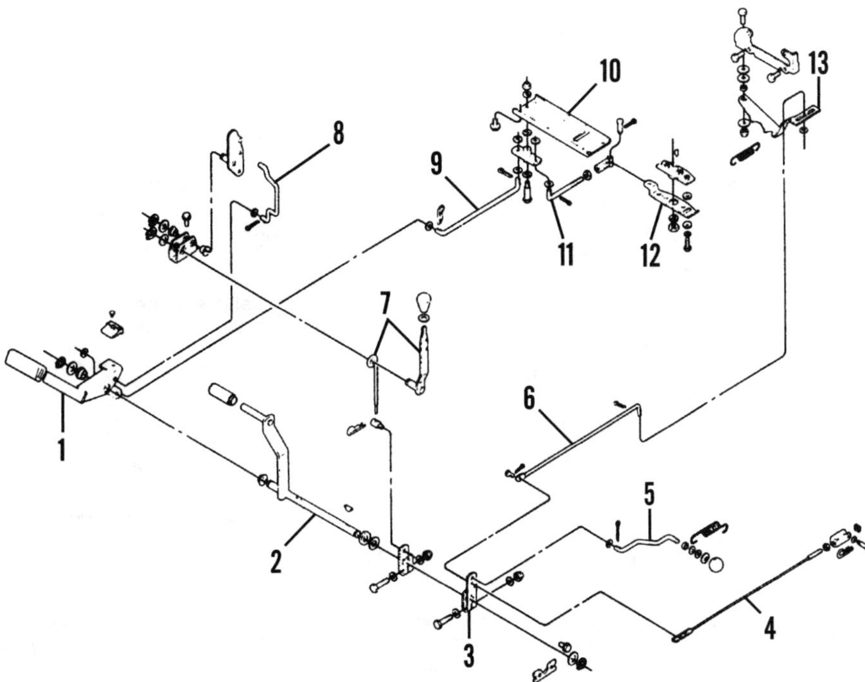

Fig. F3-12—Exploded view of transmission control linkage.

1. Forward/reverse pedal
2. Clutch/brake pedal
3. Brake arm
4. Brake cable
5. Park brake link
6. Neutral return rod
7. Speed control release lever
8. Speed control link
9. Speed control rod
10. Support plate
11. Speed control rod
12. Transmission control lever
13. Neutral return lever

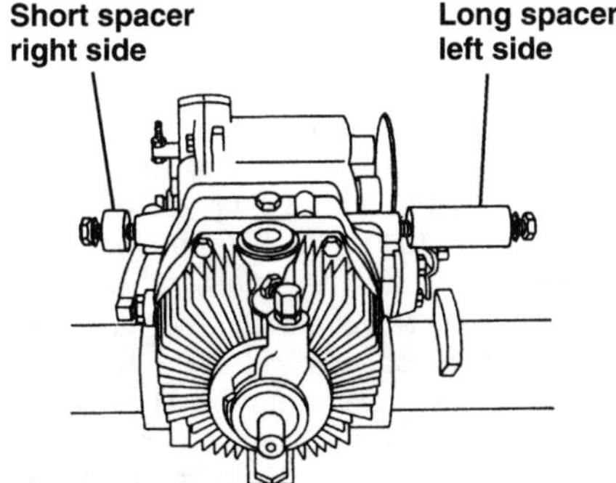

Fig. F3-13—Install spacers on transaxle mounting bolts as shown.

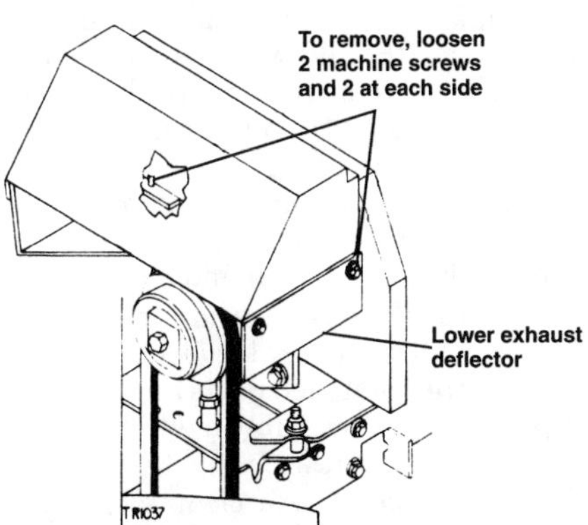

Fig. F3-14—Remove lower exhaust deflector for access to PTO clutch.

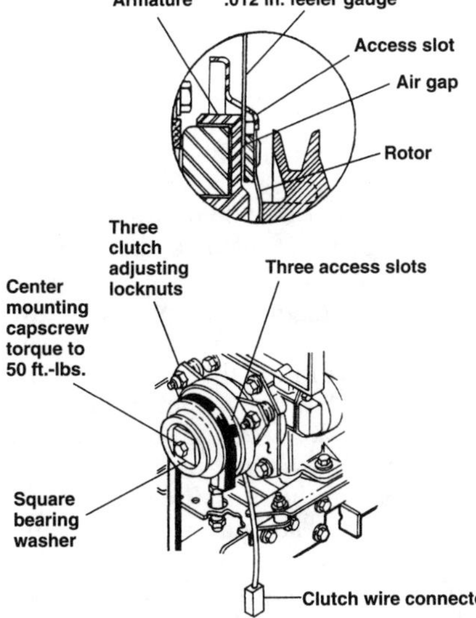

Fig. F3-15—Drawing of PTO clutch. Refer to text for adjustment.

oil inlet tube at the charge pump and transaxle housing. Remove the four cap screws attaching the transmission to the transaxle and remove the transmission assembly.

Install by reversing the removal procedure and noting the following: When lowering the main frame over the transaxle, be sure to align the Hi/Lo range control shaft stud on the transaxle's right side into the slotted hole of the Hi/Lo shift lever. Install the long spacer (Fig. F3-13) first on the transaxle's left side. Install the screw through the spacer and tighten to pull the transaxle to the left to make the right spacer's installation easier. Insert the short spacer (Fig. F3-13) on the transaxle's right side.

Refill the transmission with SAE 20 engine oil. Position the hydrostatic control lever in NEUTRAL and start and run the engine at idle speed. Operate the transmission in FORWARD and REVERSE direction for short distances. Stop the engine and check fluid level. Repeat the procedure until all air has been bled from the system.

Adjust the hydrostatic transmission control linkage as outlined in the ADJUSTMENT section. Adjust the brake.

OVERHAUL

The transmission is an Eaton Model 11 hydrostatic transmission. Refer to the appropriate Eaton section in the HYDROSTATIC TRANSMISSION SERVICE section for overhaul information.

FINAL DRIVE

REMOVAL AND INSTALLATION

Refer to the HYDROSTATIC TRANSMISSION section and follow the removal and installation procedure. Detach the hydrostatic transmission from the final drive housing to service the final drive.

OVERHAUL

The final drive is a Peerless 2500 series unit. Refer to the FINAL DRIVE section in this manual for overhaul information.

PTO CLUTCH

ADJUSTMENT

The PTO clutch should be adjusted when the clutch has been disassembled or when operation becomes erratic. The PTO switch and ignition switch must be OFF when performing the adjustment. Remove the lower exhaust deflector (Fig. F3-14) to gain access to the clutch.

With the clutch disengaged, insert a feeler gauge through one of the three slots in the clutch plate (Fig. F3-15) and measure clearance between the clutch rotor and armature. Clearance should be 0.012 inch (0.30 mm).

To adjust, tighten the adjusting nut next to the slot until the feeler gauge just begins to bind. Do not overtighten. Repeat the adjustment at each of the clutch plate slots. All slots must be adjusted equally.

TESTING

Turn the ignition switch ON but do not start the engine. Engage the PTO control switch.

If the clutch does not engage, disconnect the wiring connector at the PTO clutch. Use a 12-volt test light to check for current to the connector. If the test light comes on, the PTO is either defective or the wiring connection at the clutch field coil is poor.

To check the clutch field coil, disconnect the wiring connector at the PTO clutch. Use an ohmmeter set on low scale to check the coil resistance. Connect one probe to the PTO clutch connector. Scrape a small amount of paint off the clutch flange to expose bare metal and connect the other probe there. The specified resistance is 2.05-2.77 ohms. A reading other than the one specified indicates the field coil is faulty and unit should be replaced.

REMOVAL AND INSTALLATION

To remove the PTO clutch, remove the mower deck. Remove the lower exhaust deflector (Fig. F3-14). Disconnect the clutch wire connector (Fig. F3-15). Unscrew the clutch retaining screw and pull the clutch off the crankshaft adapter.

Inspect the bearings in the field housing and armature for wear or damage. Inspect contact surfaces of the rotor and armature for damage.

Apply antiseize compound to the crankshaft before installing the clutch. Tighten the clutch retaining screw to 50 ft.-lb. (68 N·m). Adjust the clutch as previously outlined.

If a new clutch is installed, burnish clutch friction surfaces as follows: Start the engine and run at full speed. Actuate the PTO control switch on and off six times. Allow the mower to stop completely before turning the switch back on. Recheck adjustment.

HYDRAULIC LIFT

HYDRAULIC LIFT SYSTEM

Operation

The hydraulic implement lift receives hydraulic power supply from the hydrostatic transmission charge pump (see Fig. F3-16). A single-spool, open-center control valve directs fluid to a double-acting hydraulic cylinder. The control valve is equipped with an adjustable relief valve limiting the system pressure at approximately 600 psi (4137 kPa).

Seal repair kits are the only service parts available for the control valve and hydraulic cylinder.

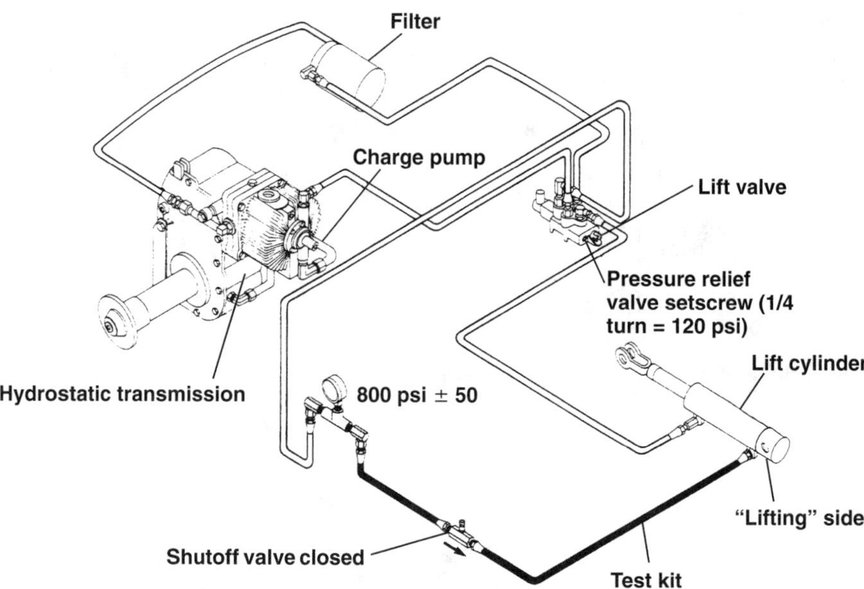

Fig. F3-16—Diagram of hydraulic lift system on tractors so equipped. To check lift system relief pressure, install a pressure gauge and shut-off valve in the line between lift control valve and piston side of cylinder. Refer to text.

Testing

When checking the relief valve pressure setting, hydraulic fluid must be at normal operating temperature. Shut off the engine and relieve the system's hydraulic pressure. Using a ¼-inch tee fitting, install a 0-1000 psi (0-7000 kPa) pressure gauge in piston end of hydraulic cylinder (Fig. F3-12).

Start the engine and operate at full speed. With the shut-off valve open, move the hydraulic lift lever back and forth several times to purge air from the system. Close the shut-off valve and hold the lift lever in the RAISE position. Observe the pressure gauge reading. Pressure should be 750-850 psi (5170-5860 kPa).

If necessary, adjust the system relief valve setscrew, located in the lift control valve, to obtain the desired system pressure.

If the specified operating pressure cannot be obtained, check the following: low hydraulic fluid level, hydraulic filter plugged, defective relief valve, charge pump worn.

If the specified operating pressure is obtained in the preceding test, but the system does not lift properly, test the cylinder for leakage. Open the tester shut-off valve. Start the engine and operate at full speed. Hold the lift lever in the RAISE position and observe pressure gauge reading. If gauge does not indicate 750-850 psi (5170-5860 kPa), the seal rings in the cylinder are probably faulty. Remove the cylinder and repair if necessary.

CONTROL VALVE OVERHAUL

The hydraulic lift system includes a single-spool, open-center control valve equipped with an integral pressure relief valve. Refer to Fig. F3-17 for an exploded view of the control valve assembly.

To remove the control valve, raise the seat and tag the control valve hoses to ensure proper reassembly. Disconnect the hydraulic hoses from the valve. Disconnect the control linkage from the valve spool. Remove the valve mounting bolts and remove the valve assembly.

Clean the outside of the valve prior to disassembly. Remove the screw (1—Fig. F3-17) from the end of the valve spool (8) and withdraw the spool from the valve body. Remove the washers (3), spacer (4) and spring (5). Unscrew the adjusting screw (9) while counting the number of turns required to remove screw from body. Remove the relief valve spring (10) and ball (11).

Inspect all parts for wear or damage. Replace all seals. Valve body (6) and spool (7) are matched parts and must be replaced as an assembly if either part is worn or damaged.

Coat all parts with clean oil during reassembly. Thread the relief valve adjusting screw (9) into body the same amount of turns as required for re-

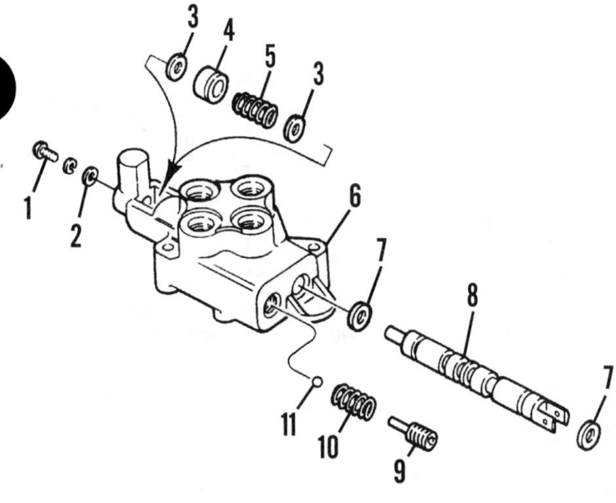

Fig. F3-17—Exploded view of lift control valve.

1. Screw
2. Washer
3. Washers
4. Spacer
5. Centering spring
6. Valve body
7. Seals
8. Spool
9. Adjusting screw
10. Relief valve spring
11. Relief valve ball

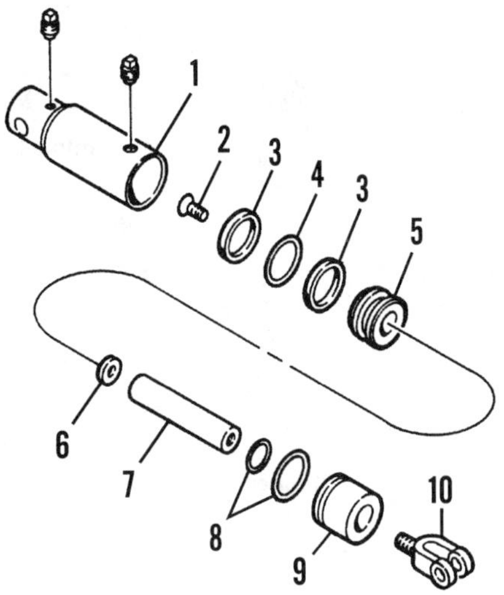

Fig. F3-18—Exploded view of hydraulic lift cylinder.

1. Cylinder tube
2. Screw
3. Back-up rings
4. O-ring
5. Piston
6. Rubber disc
7. Piston rod
8. O-rings
9. Rod guide
10. Clevis

moval. Install the valve assembly and adjust pressure setting as outlined in the TESTING paragraph.

HYDRAULIC CYLINDER

To check cylinder seals for internal leakage, first fully extend the piston rod. Disconnect the hydraulic hose from the rod end of the cylinder. Start the engine and operate the lift control valve to extend rod. There may be an initial flow of oil out the open cylinder port, then the oil flow should stop. If oil continues to flow from the cylinder port, the cylinder piston seal is faulty.

Before removing the lift cylinder, remove the attachment from the tractor. Disconnect the hydraulic lines from the cylinder and plug all openings. Remove the cotter pins and slide the cylinder off the mounting pins.

To disassemble the cylinder, first remove the hydraulic fitting from the rod end of the cylinder. Pull the rod (7—Fig. F3-18), rod guide (9) and piston (5) out of the cylinder. Remove the piston from the rod and remove and discard all seals.

NOTE: Do not clamp the rod or piston in a vise. Be careful not to scratch or mar the rod.

Inspect the rod, piston and cylinder bore for wear or other damage and replace as necessary. Replace all O-rings and back-up rings.

Coat parts with clean oil during assembly. Be careful not to damage O-rings when assembling. Align the tapped port in the rod guide with hole in cylinder tube.

Install the cylinder on tractor and check hydraulic oil level. Start the engine and cycle the cylinder several times to purge air from the cylinder.

ELECTRICAL SYSTEM

Refer to Fig. F3-19 for the wiring schematic. Engine related electrical components, such as the starter, are covered in the appropriate engine section at the rear of this manual.

The tractor is equipped with switches and relays preventing inadvertent starting of the tractor engine or operation if the operator leaves the tractor seat. The tractor engine should start only if the operator is in the tractor seat, the clutch/brake is depressed fully and the PTO control switch is in the OFF position.

The clutch/brake switch is attached to the left inside wall of the main frame. To test the switch for continuity, remove and tag all wires at the switch terminals.

With the switch leaf not depressed, there should not be continuity between any of the terminals (Fig. F3-20).

With the leaf depressed until one click is heard, there should be continuity between C and D terminals only.

With the leaf depressed until two clicks are heard, there should be continuity between A and B and between C and D terminals.

To test the PTO switch for continuity, remove and tag all wires at the switch terminals (Fig. F3-21).

With the switch in the OFF position, attach one test lead to terminal C and touch each of the other terminals with the other test lead. Continuity should exist only between terminals A and C. Repeat the test procedure starting with terminal D. Continuity should only exist between terminals D and F.

With the switch in the ON position, attach one test lead to terminal C and touch each of the other terminals with the other test lead. Continuity should exist only between terminals C and E. Repeat the test starting with terminal D. Continuity should only exist between terminals D and F.

The seat switch is located under the seat pan. There should be 1/32 to 1/16 inch (0.8-1.5 mm) gap between the plunger's end and the seat support bracket without the operator on the seat (Fig. F3-22).

There should not be continuity between switch terminals when the plunger is up. With the switch plunger depressed, continuity should exist.

Figures F3-19 through F3-22 are on the following page.

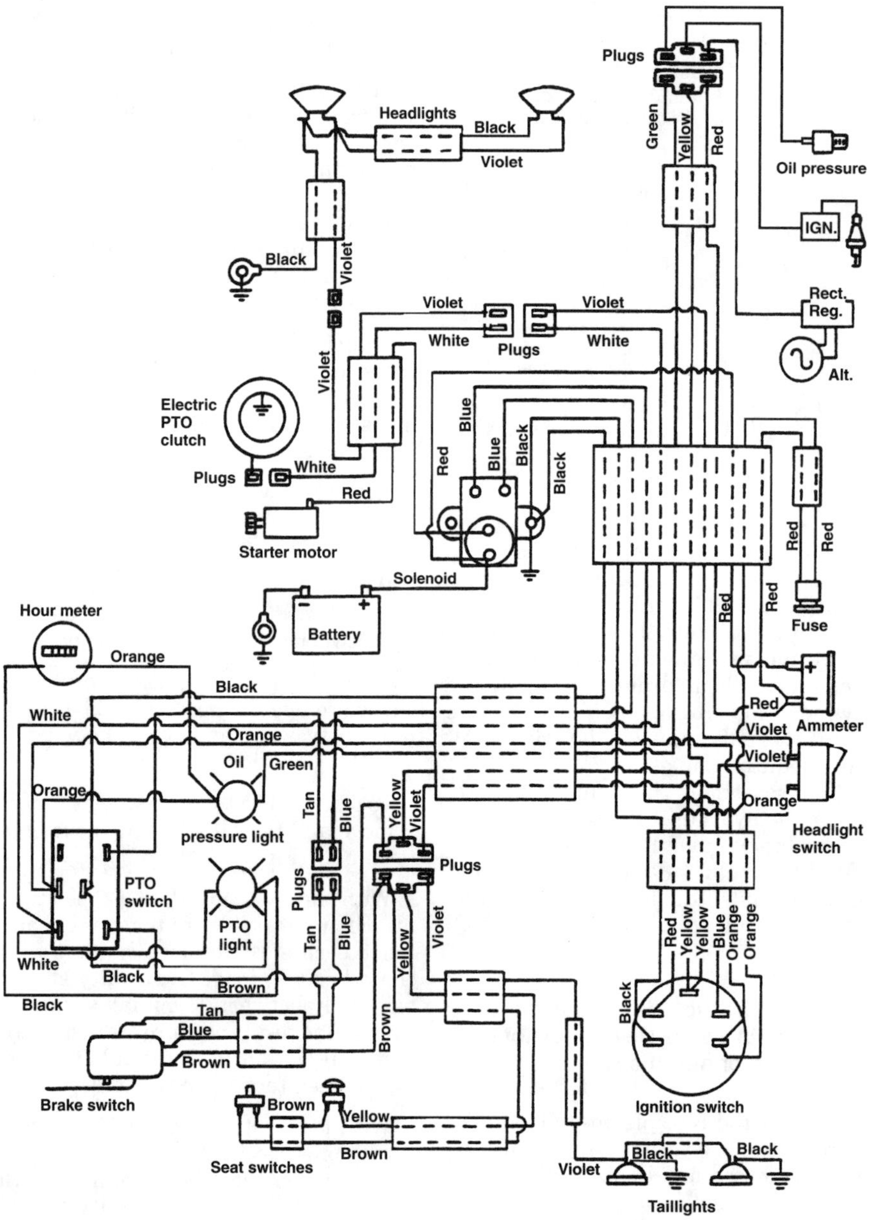

Fig. F3-19—Wiring schematic for Model LGT18H.

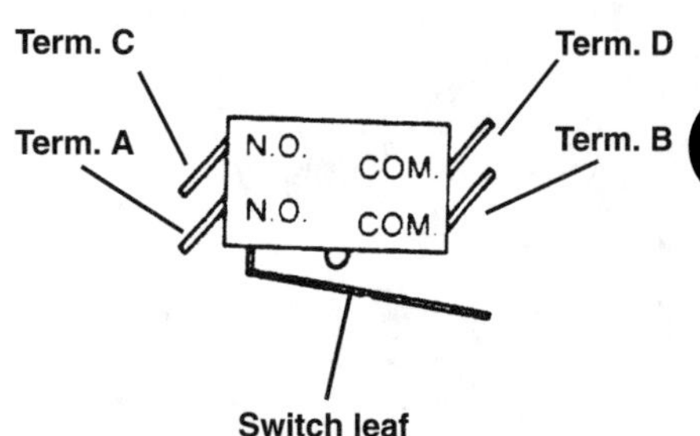

Fig. F3-20—Drawing of clutch/brake switch. Refer to text for continuity test.

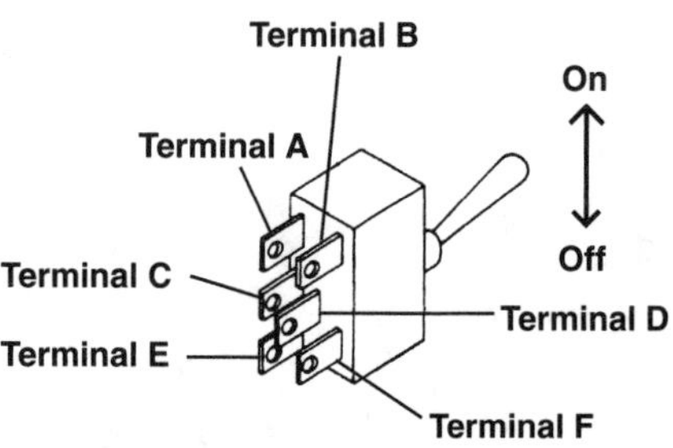

Fig. F3-21—Drawing of PTO switch. Refer to text for continuity test.

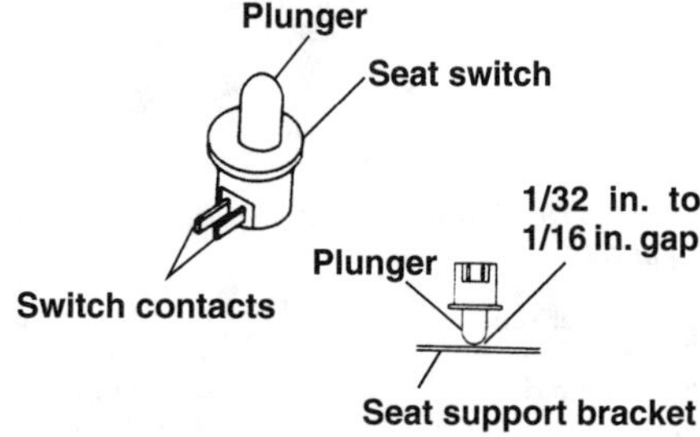

Fig. F3-22—Drawing of seat switch. Refer to text for continuity test.

GRAVELY

CONDENSED SPECIFICATIONS

Models	1232G, 1238G	1232H	1238H	1238H	GEM 12.5	GEM 14
Engine Make	B&S	B&S	B&S	Kawasaki	Kohler	Kohler
Model	281707	281707	281707	FB460V	CV12.5	CV14
Bore	3.44 in. (87.3 mm)	3.44 in. (87.3 mm)	3.44 in. (87.3 mm)	89 mm (3.50 in.)	3.43 in. (87 mm)	3.43 in. (87 mm)
Stroke	3.06 in. (77.7 mm)	3.06 in. (77.7 mm)	3.06 in. (77.7 mm)	74 mm (2.91 in.)	2.64 in. (67 mm)	2.64 in. (67 mm)
Piston Displacement	28.4 cu. in. (465 cc)	28.4 cu. in. (465 cc)	28.4 cu. in. (465 cc)	460 cc (28.1 cu. in.)	24.3 cu. in. (398 cc)	24.3 cu. In. (398 cc)
Rated Power	12 hp (8.9 kW)	12 hp (8.9 kW)	12 hp (8.9 kW)	12.5 hp (9.3 kW)	12.5 hp (9.3 kW)	14 hp (10.5 kW)
Slow Idle Speed—Rpm	1200	1200	1200	1200	1200	1200
High Idle Speed (No-Load)—Rpm	3300	3300	3300	3300	3600	3600
Crankcase Capacity	3 pts. (1.4 L)	3 pts. (1.4 L)	3 pts. (1.4 L)	3 pts. (1.4 L)	4 pts. (1.9 L)	4 pts. (1.9 L)
Transmission Capacity	24 oz. (0.7 L)	4.8 pts. (2.3 L)	4.8 pts. (2.3 L)	4.8 pts. (2.3 L)	6 qt. (5.7 L)	6 qt. (5.7 L)
Weight Capacity	Grease	SAE 20W-20	SAE 20W-20	SAE 20W-20	SAE 20W-20	SAE 20W-20

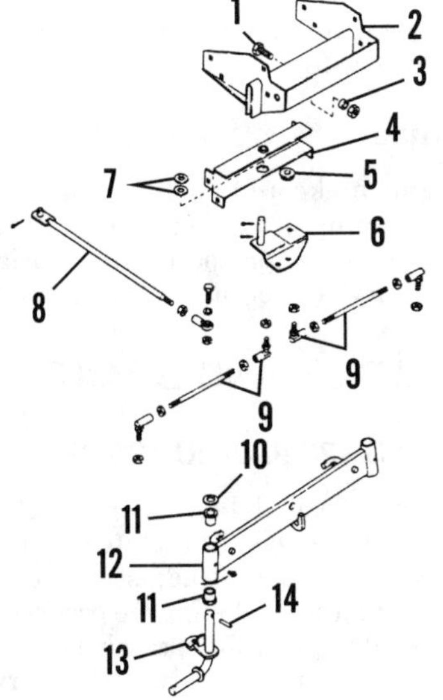

Fig. GR1-1—Exploded view of front axle assembly used on Models 1232G-1232H-1238G-1238H.

1. Pivot bolt
2. Axle support
3. Spacer
4. Steering pivot channel
5. Flange bushing
6. Steering pivot
7. Washers
8. Drag link
9. Tie rods
10. Washer
11. Flange bushings
12. Axle main member
13. Spindle
14. Spring pin

FRONT AXLE AND STEERING SYSTEM

AXLE MAIN MEMBER

The axle main member (12—Fig. GR1-1) is center mounted directly to the main frame and pivots on the bolt (1).

To remove the front axle, disconnect the tie rod ends (9) from the spindles (13). Support the front of the tractor and remove the front wheels. Remove the pivot bolt (1) and lower axle from the tractor.

Install the axle by reversing the removal procedure. Lubricate with multipurpose grease.

TIE RODS AND TOE-IN

A front wheel toe-in of $\frac{1}{16}$ to $\frac{1}{8}$ inch (1.6-3.2 mm) is recommended. To check toe-in, measure the distance between the front wheels at the wheel hub height at the front and back of the wheels. The front of the wheels should be closer together (toed in) than the rear.

To adjust the toe-in, loosen the tie rod jam nuts and turn each tie rod (9—Fig. GR1-1) an equal amount clockwise to decrease toe-in or counterclockwise to increase toe-in.

Replace worn tie rod ball joints.

STEERING SPINDLES

To remove the steering spindles (13—Fig. GR1-1), raise and support the front of the tractor. Remove the front wheels. Disconnect tie rod ends from the spindles. Drive out the spring pin (14) and lower the spindle from the axle.

Inspect the spindles and bushings (11) for excessive wear and replace when necessary. Lubricate with multipurpose grease.

Install the spindle by reversing the removal procedure.

STEERING GEAR

To remove the steering gear assembly, disconnect the fuel line and remove the fuel tank. Remove the bolts attaching the steering shaft flange bearing (2—Fig. GR1-2) to the instrument panel. Drive the spring pin (6) out of the pinion gear (7) and withdraw the steering wheel (1) and shaft (5) from the tractor.

Disconnect the drag link from the steering arm (18). Remove the cotter pin (17) from the steering arm shaft. Remove the clamp bolts (10) from the sector gear (9), then pull the steering

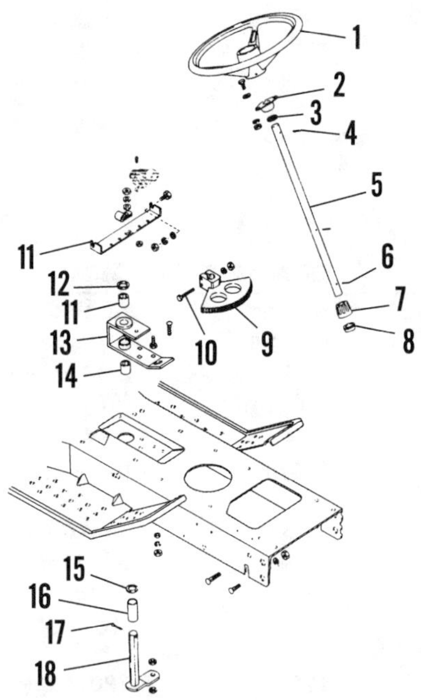

Fig. GR1-2—Exploded view of steering gear assembly used on Models 1232G, 1232H, 1238G and 1238H. Steering gear assembly used on GEM (Gravely Estate Mower) tractor is similar.

1. Steering wheel
2. Flange bearing
3. Washer
4. Spring pin
5. Steering shaft
6. Pin
7. Pinion gear
8. Bearing
9. Sector gear
10. Clamp bolt
11. Support bracket
12. Washer
13. Bushings
14. Steering support
15. Washer
16. Spacer
17. Cotter pin
18. Steering arm

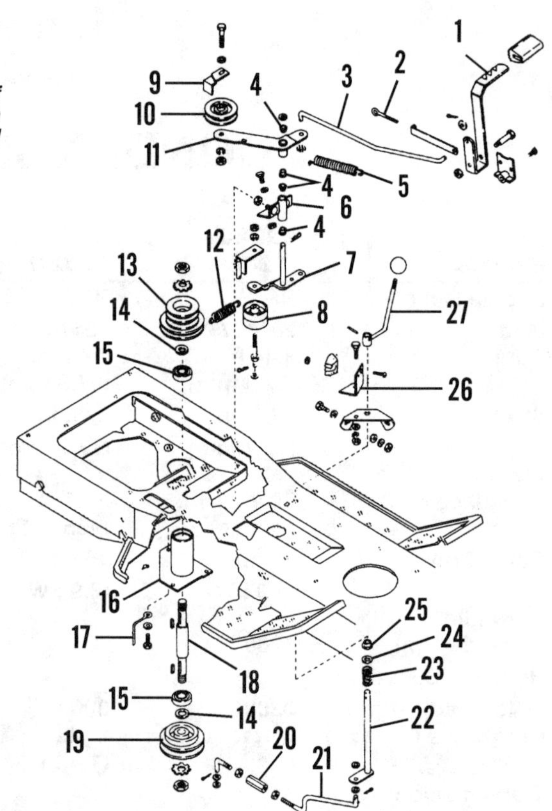

Fig. GR1-3—Exploded view of spring-loaded belt idler clutch used on Models 1232G and 1238G.

1. Clutch pedal
2. Eyebolt
3. Clutch rod
4. Flange bushings
5. Tension spring
6. Idler pivot
7. Idler arm
8. Idler
9. Belt guide
10. Idler pulley
11. Idler arm
12. Spring
13. Double groove pulley
14. Washer
15. Bearing
16. Spindle housing
17. Belt guide
18. Jackshaft
19. Jackshaft pulley
20. Turnbuckle
21. Idler link
22. PTO lever
23. Spring
24. Washer
25. Flange bushing
26. Safety switch bracket
27. PTO lever

arm out of the sector gear and remove the gear from the support (14).

To remove the steering pivot (6—Fig. GR1-1), disconnect the tie rods (9) and drag link (8) from the pivot. Remove the cotter pins from the pivot shaft and withdraw the pivot, washers (7) and flange bushing (5) from the steering pivot channel (4).

Inspect bearings (2, 8 and 13—Fig. GR1-2) for damage and replace when necessary. Check pinion gear and sector gear teeth for damage. Lubricate the gear teeth with multipurpose grease prior to reassembly.

Reassembly is the reverse of the disassembly procedure.

ENGINE

MODELS 1232G, 1232H, 1238G AND 1238H

Removal and Installation

To remove the engine, first remove the mower deck from the tractor. Remove the hood and grille assembly.

Remove the ground cable from the battery. Disconnect the throttle control cable from the engine. Disconnect the fuel line. Disconnect the wires from the starter. Disconnect the engine wiring harness connector.

Move the belt idler to relieve tension on the drive belt and slip the belt off the engine pulley. Remove the engine mounting bolts and lift the engine out of the tractor.

To install the engine, reverse the removal procedure.

Overhaul

Engine make and model are listed at the beginning of this section. To overhaul engine, refer to the appropriate engine service section in this manual.

MODELS GEM 12.5 AND GEM 14

Removal and Installation

To remove the engine, first remove the mower deck from the tractor. Remove the hood and grille assembly.

Disconnect the ground cable from the battery. Disconnect the throttle control cable from the engine. Disconnect the fuel line. Disconnect the wires from the starter and engine wiring harness.

Disconnect the springs from the jackshaft drive belt idler arm and transmission drive belt idler arm. Disconnect the electrical wire to the electric PTO clutch. Unbolt and remove the PTO clutch torque arm, then remove the belt from the PTO clutch. Remove the center bolt from the PTO clutch and remove clutch assembly.

Remove the transmission drive belt from the engine pulley. Remove the engine mounting bolts and lift engine from tractor.

To install the engine, reverse the removal procedure.

Overhaul

Engine make and model are listed at the beginning of this section. To overhaul engine, refer to the appropriate engine service section in this manual.

CLUTCH AND BRAKES

MODELS 1232G AND 1238G

A spring-loaded belt idler clutch is used on all models. The clutch is operated by a foot pedal. No adjustment of the clutch is required. If slippage occurs, inspect the drive belt for excessive wear or stretching and replace when necessary.

Refer to Fig. GR1-3 for an exploded view of the clutch linkage and jackshaft drive assembly. To replace the primary drive belt, first remove the mower or front mounted attachment from the tractor.

Disconnect the spring (5) from the traction clutch idler arm (11). Disconnect the PTO actuating rod (21) from the PTO idler arm (7), then disconnect the spring (12) from the idler arm. Loosen

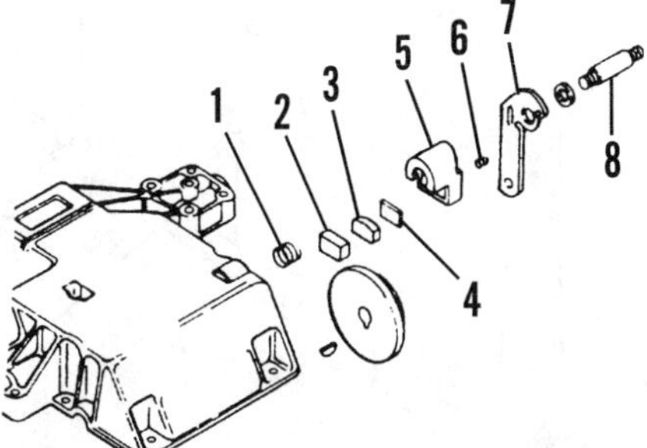

Fig. GR1-4—Exploded view of disc brake assembly used on Models 1232G and 1238G.

1. Spring
2. Brake pad, inner
3. Brake pad, outer
4. Back-up plate
5. Brake jaw assy.
6. Setscrew
7. Brake actuating lever
8. Shoulder bolt

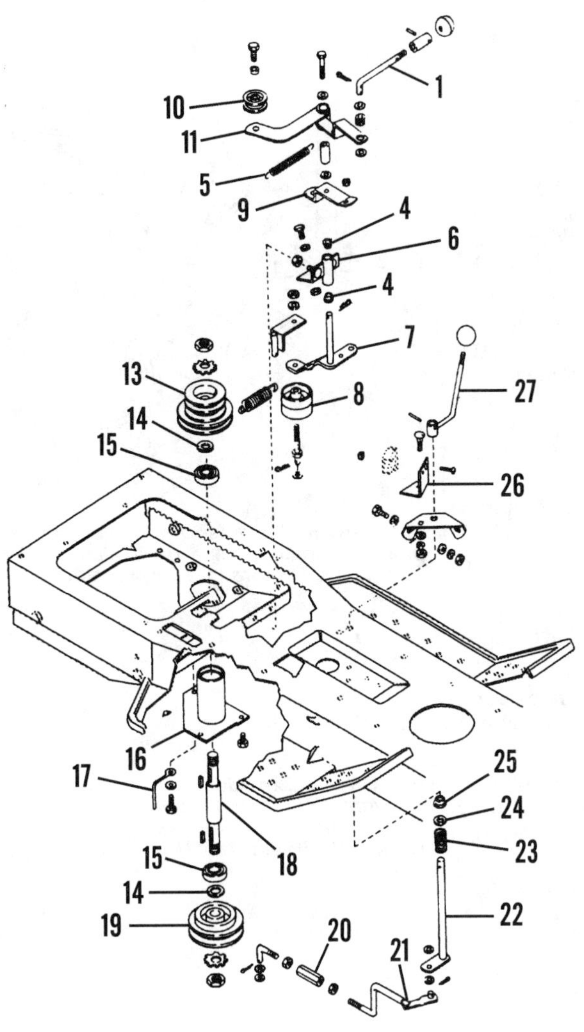

Fig. GR1-5—Exploded view of spring-loaded belt idler clutch used on Models 1232H and 1238H.

1. Clutch handle
4. Flange bushings
6. Pivot bracket
7. Idler arm
8. Idler
9. Idler bracket
10. Idler pulley
11. Clutch arm
12. Spring
13. Double groove pulley
14. Washer
15. Bearing
16. Spindle housing
17. Belt guide
18. Jackshaft
19. Jackshaft pulley
20. Turnbuckle
21. Idler link
22. PTO lever
23. Spring
24. Washer
25. Flange bushing
26. Safety switch bracket
27. PTO lever

the cap screws retaining the jackshaft housing (16) to the transaxle mount.

Disconnect the tension spring from the primary drive belt idler arm, then remove the belt from the engine pulley. Rotate the PTO idler (7) until the hairpin at the top of the idler pivot shaft can be removed. Lower the idler assembly until the pivot shaft is free from the traction clutch idler arm (11). Slide the drive belt between the upper and lower idler arms and remove from the tractor.

To install the belt, reverse the removal procedure.

To replace the transaxle drive belt, loosen the belt guide retaining cap screws and move guides away from belt. Depress the clutch pedal to relieve belt tension and work the belt off the pulleys.

Install new belt by reversing the removal procedure. Adjust the belt guides to provide $\frac{1}{16}$ to $\frac{1}{8}$ inch (1.6-3.2 mm) clearance between the belt and guides.

Models 1232G and 1238G are equipped with a disc brake mounted on the right side of transaxle housing (Fig. GR1-4). To adjust the brake, position the tractor on a level surface and place the gearshift lever in NEUTRAL so the tractor can be pushed by hand to check brake action.

With the brake pedal released, turn setscrew (6) in the brake pad holder clockwise until the brake starts to lock. Then, turn setscrew counterclockwise $\frac{1}{2}$ turn.

Push the tractor by hand to check brake action and to make sure the brake pads (2 and 3) do not drag on the brake disc (9) when the brake is released.

To replace the brake pads, disconnect the brake rod from the brake lever (7—Fig. GR1-4). Remove the shoulder bolt (8) and withdraw the lever, brake jaw (5) and outer brake pad (3). Remove the brake disc (9) from the transaxle shaft and remove the inner brake pad (2) and spring (1) from the transaxle housing.

To reassemble, reverse the disassembly procedure. Adjust brake as previously outlined.

MODELS 1232H AND 1238H

A spring-loaded belt idler clutch is used on all models. The clutch is operated by a hand lever (1—Fig. GR1-5). No adjustment is required. If slippage occurs, inspect the drive belt for excessive wear or stretching and replace when necessary.

To replace the main drive belt, first remove the mower deck or front mounted equipment from the tractor. Disconnect the clutch control lever (1—Fig. GR1-5) from the idler arm (11).

Disconnect the main idler pulley tension spring from frame, then remove the drive belt from the engine pulley. Remove the belt from the jackshaft pulley and remove from the tractor.

Install the new belt in the reverse order of removal.

To replace the traction drive belt, first remove the main drive belt as outlined above. Loosen the belt guide retaining screws and move the belt guides away from the belt. Move the idler arm (11) to relieve drive belt spring tension, then work belt off the jackshaft and transmission pulleys.

Install the new belt and adjust the belt fingers to provide $\frac{1}{16}$ to $\frac{1}{8}$ inch (1.6-3.2 mm) clearance between belt and fingers.

Models 1232H and 1238H are equipped with a disc brake located inside the transmission unit. When the brake pedal is depressed, the hydrostatic transmission control linkage is returned to NEUTRAL and then the brake is applied.

To adjust the parking brake, depress the brake pedal and measure the gap (G—Fig. GR1-6) between the clutch rod collar (2) and rod pivot (1). The gap should be $\frac{1}{16}$ inch (1.6 mm).

To adjust the gap, loosen the jam nut at the brake clevis pivot (4) and turn the pivot bolt (3) until the recommended gap between the rod collar and pivot is obtained. Release the parking brake, then depress brake pedal and recheck for proper gap.

Refer to the HYDROSTATIC TRANSMISSION SERVICE section in this manual for brake repair procedures.

MODELS GEM 12.5 AND GEM 14

A spring-loaded belt idler is used on all tractors and no adjustment is required. If slippage occurs, inspect the drive belt for excessive wear or stretching and replace when necessary.

To replace the transmission drive belt, remove the mower deck from the tractor. Disconnect springs from the jackshaft drive belt idler arm and transmission drive belt idler arm.

Disconnect the electrical wire to the PTO clutch. Unbolt and remove the torque arm from the PTO clutch, then slip the belt off the PTO clutch pulley. Remove the center bolt from the PTO clutch and remove clutch assembly. Slip the transmission drive belt off the engine pulley and then the transmission pulley.

Install the new belt in the reverse order of removal.

GEM tractors are equipped with a disc brake located inside the transmission unit. When the brake pedal is depressed, hydrostatic transmission control linkage is returned to NEUTRAL and then the brake is applied.

To adjust the parking brake, depress the brake pedal and set the parking brake rod. Measure the gap (G—Fig. GR1-7) between the clutch rod collar (1) and rod pivot (2). Gap should be 1/16 inch (1.6 mm).

To adjust gap, loosen the jam nut at the brake clevis pivot (4) and turn the pivot bolt (5) until the recommended gap between rod collar and pivot is obtained. Release the parking brake, then depress brake pedal and recheck for proper gap.

Refer to the HYDROSTATIC TRANSMISSION SERVICE section in this manual for brake repair procedures.

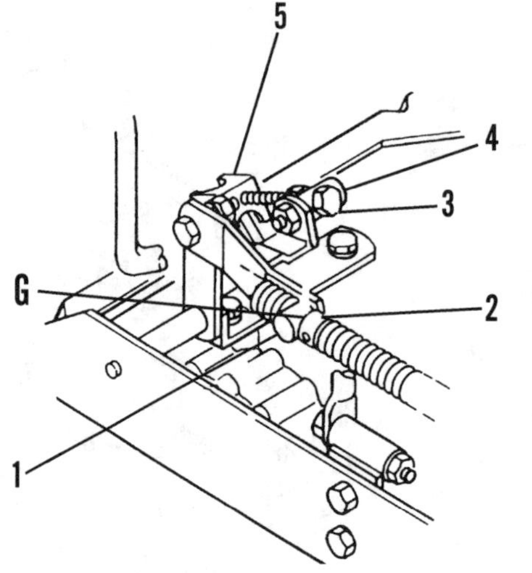

Fig. GR1-6—View showing adjustment point for brake linkage on Models 1232H and 1238H. Refer to text for procedure.

1. Pivot
2. Collar
3. Brake adjusting bolt
4. Pivot
5. Brake clevis

Fig. GR1-7—View showing adjustment point for brake linkage on GEM 12.5 and GEM 14 tractors. Refer to text for procedure.

1. Washer
2. Pivot
4. Pivot
5. Brake adjusting bolt

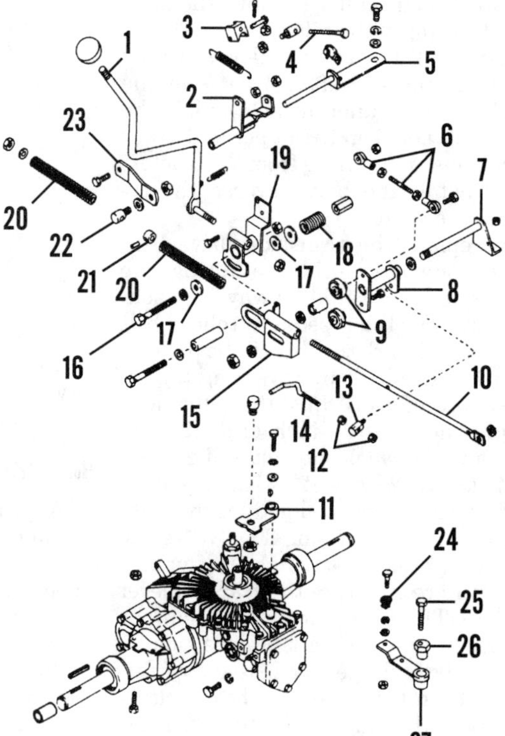

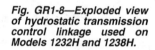

Fig. GR1-8—Exploded view of hydrostatic transmission control linkage used on Models 1232H and 1238H.

1. Shift lever
2. Brake tube
3. Brake clevis
4. Brake adjusting bolt
5. Brake bracket
6. Link
7. Brake pivot
8. Shift control arm
9. Ball bearings
10. Brake rod
11. Speed control arm
12. Jam nuts
13. Pivot
14. Speed control link
15. Brake bracket
16. Friction adjusting bolt
17. Friction washer
18. Compression spring
19. Shift bracket
20. Spring
21. Collar
22. Pivot
23. Brake link
24. Ball bearing
25. Cap screw
26. Eccentric
27. Neutral detent arm

HYDROSTATIC TRANSMISSION

MODELS 1232H AND 1238H

Lubrication

The transaxle housing serves as a common reservoir for the hydrostatic transmission and gear reduction unit. An expansion tank and dipstick are located at the rear of unit.

To check the oil level, raise the rear deck and clean the expansion tank cap, then remove the cap and dipstick. When the transmission is cold, the oil level should be at the mark indicated on the dipstick. If low, add SAE 20W-20 detergent oil. DO NOT use multiviscosity oil.

If oil appears to be milky or black, it is possible the oil is contaminated or has been overheated and the unit should be drained and refilled. Capacity is approximately 4.8 pints (2.3 L).

Adjustment

If the tractor continues to creep forward or backward when the shift control handle is moved to NEUTRAL or when the brake pedal is fully depressed then released, the hydrostatic control linkage should be adjusted.

Raise and support the rear of the tractor so the rear wheels are off the ground. Remove the rear wheels. Block the front wheels to prevent the tractor from rolling.

Raise the seat and seat deck and start the engine.

Loosen cap screw (25—Fig. GR1-8) and turn the eccentric (26) until the rear axles stop turning and the pump whine stops. If neutral adjustment is correctly obtained, tighten the eccentric cap screw being careful not to move the eccentric.

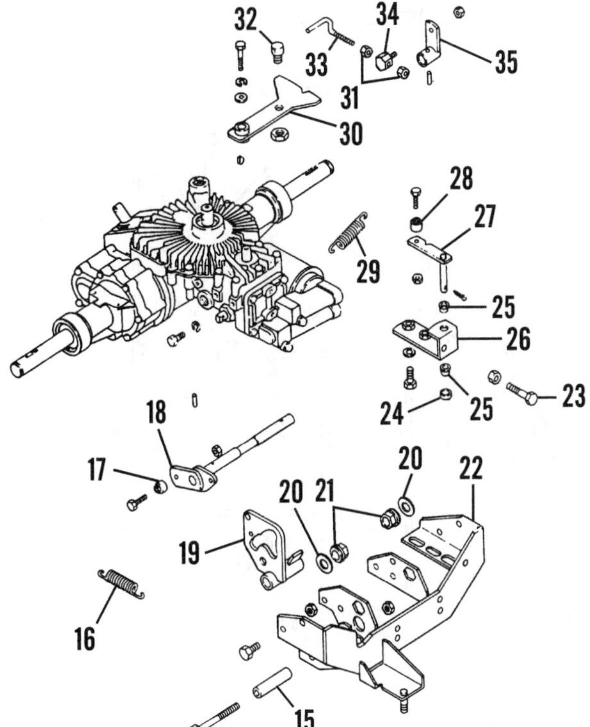

Fig. GR1-9—Exploded view of hydrostatic transmission control linkage used on GEM tractors.

15. Sleeve
16. Spring
17. Ball bearing
18. Cross shaft
19. Cam
20. Washer
21. Flange bushing
22. Torque bracket
23. Adjusting bolt
24. Bushing
25. Flange bushing
26. Pivot bracket
27. Neutral detent arm
28. Ball bearing
29. Spring
30. Speed control arm
31. Jam nuts
32. Pivot
33. Control link
34. Pivot
35. Control arm

Fig. GR1-10—Exploded view of hydrostatic transmission control linkage used on GEM tractors.

1. Locknut
2. Belleville washers
3. Flange bushing
4. Shift lever
5. Outer arm
6. Spring
7. Inner arm
8. Washer
9. Bushing
10. Brace
11. Flange bushing
12. Shift arm
13. Shift rod

If wheel creep or pump whine cannot be adjusted by turning the eccentric, turn the jam nuts (12) to move the pivot (13) on the control rod (14) until the rear axles stop turning and the whine stops. Readjust the eccentric (26) so the neutral arm bearing (24) is positioned in the speed control arm (11) notch.

If the speed control lever (1—Fig. GR1-8) will not remain in position when released, turn the friction adjusting bolt (16) clockwise to increase the control lever friction spring (18) tension. If the lever is too hard to move, turn friction adjusting bolt counterclockwise.

Removal and Installation

To remove the transaxle assembly, first remove the mower deck from the tractor. Disconnect the hydraulic oil expansion tank hoses, then unbolt and remove the drawbar and expansion tank from the rear of the frame.

Disconnect the brake control linkage. Slip the primary drive belt off the jackshaft pulley. Disconnect the clutch control lever from the clutch idler arm. Remove the knob from the transmission speed control lever.

Raise and support the rear of the tractor. Remove the cap screws attaching the transaxle mounting plate to main frame, and roll the transaxle assembly from the tractor.

Remove the transmission drive pulley and fan. Disconnect the speed control link from the transmission control arm. Remove the cap screws attaching the transaxle housing to the mounting plate and separate the transaxle from the plate.

To install the transaxle, reverse the removal procedure.

Overhaul

Models 1232H and 1238H are equipped with an Eaton 750 series hydrostatic transaxle. Refer to the Eaton section of the HYDROSTATIC TRANSAXLE service section in this manual for overhaul procedure.

MODELS GEM 12.5 AND GEM 14

Lubrication

The transaxle housing serves as a common reservoir for the hydrostatic transmission and the gear reduction unit. An oil expansion tank is located below the instrument panel, directly below the battery.

To check oil level, raise the hood and clean the area around the expansion tank cap/dipstick, then remove dipstick. When the transmission is cold, oil level should be at mark indicated on the dipstick. If low, add SAE 20W-20 oil. DO NOT use multiviscosity oil.

If the oil appears to be milky or black, it is possible the oil is contaminated or has been overheated. The unit should be drained and refilled. Capacity is approximately 6 quarts (6.7 L).

The transmission oil filter should be changed after the first 10 hours of operation and after every 400 hours of operation thereafter or yearly, whichever comes first.

Adjustment

If the tractor creeps forward or backward with the speed control lever in NEUTRAL, the control linkage should be adjusted as follows:

Support the rear of the tractor and remove the rear wheels. Loosen the two bolts on the bottom side of the torque bracket (22—Fig. GR1-9) retaining the cam follower pivot bracket (26). Start the engine and operate at approximately $\frac{1}{3}$ full throttle.

Turn the pivot bracket adjusting bolt (23) as necessary until the axles stop turning and the pump whine has stopped. Note that no more than 3 or 4 turns of adjusting bolt should be required to obtain neutral position.

If neutral position is correctly obtained, tighten the pivot bracket mounting bolts being careful not to disturb the bracket adjustment.

If unable to obtain neutral position by turning the adjusting bolt, proceed with the additional adjustment procedure outlined below.

Remove the knob from the speed control lever and remove the tractor's rear deck. Remove the fuel tank and use a suitable length of fuel line so the tank can be connected to the engine, but positioned in a remote location.

Loosen the two bolts and nut retaining the speed selector lever (4—Fig. GR1-10) to arm (7) and the two bolts retaining the pivot bracket (26—Fig. GR1-9) to the torque bracket (22). Depress the brake pedal and check that the ball bearing cam follower (17) is located in the center of the neutral cam (19). If not, adjust the brake linkage as previously outlined in the CLUTCH AND BRAKES section.

Make sure the ball bearing (28) is located in the control arm (30) detent. If not, loosen the jam nuts (31) and adjust the neutral arm (33) as necessary.

Start the engine and operate at about 1/3 full throttle. Depress the brake pedal and adjust the pivot bracket adjusting bolt (23) until the rear axles do not creep and there is no pump whine. Be sure the cam follower bearing (28) remains in the control arm (30) detent, readjust the neutral arm (33) if necessary.

Stop the engine and tighten the neutral arm jam nuts and the two bolts retaining the pivot bracket to the torque bracket. Be careful not to disturb the control linkage setting when tightening fasteners.

Install the fuel tank and rear deck. Hold the speed selector lever (4—Fig. GR1-10) in the neutral slot and tighten the center nut and two bolts attaching the lever to the arm, being careful not to move the inner arm (7). The center nut (1) should be tightened as necessary to obtain desired friction on the control lever.

Removal and Installation

To remove the transaxle assembly, first remove the mower deck from the tractor. Disconnect the hydraulic oil expansion tank hoses from the hydrostatic unit. Disconnect the brake control linkage and speed control linkage.

Remove the jackshaft drive belt and transmission drive belt. Remove the mounting bolts attaching the transaxle assembly to the frame. Support the tractor's rear and remove the transaxle from the tractor.

To install transaxle, reverse the removal procedure.

Overhaul

GEM models are equipped with an Eaton 850 series hydrostatic transaxle. Refer to the Eaton section of the HYDROSTATIC TRANSAXLE service section in this manual for the overhaul procedure.

TRANSAXLE (MODELS 1232G AND 1238G)

REMOVAL AND INSTALLATION

To remove the transaxle, first remove the mower deck from the tractor. Unbolt and remove the drawbar from the rear of the frame. Remove the knobs

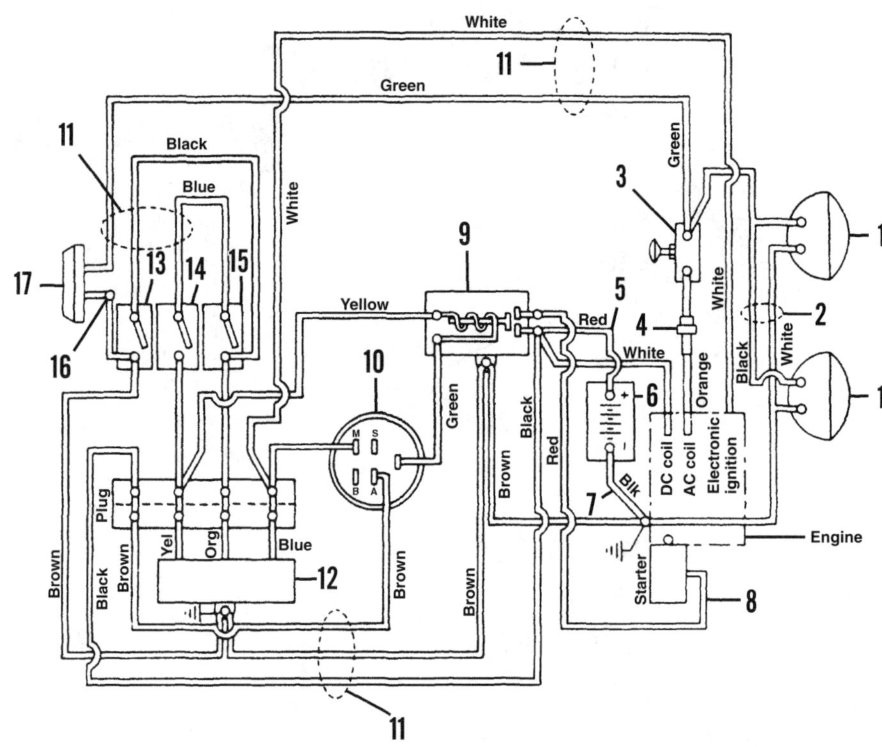

Fig. GR1-11—Wiring diagram for 1200 series tractors equipped with Briggs & Stratton engine.

1. Headlight
2. Wiring harness
3. Light switch
4. Fuse
5. Starter cable
6. Battery
7. Ground cable
8. Cable
9. Solenoid
10. Ignition switch
11. Wiring harness
12. Module
13. Seat switch
14. Interlock switch
15. Switch
16. Connector
17. Tail light

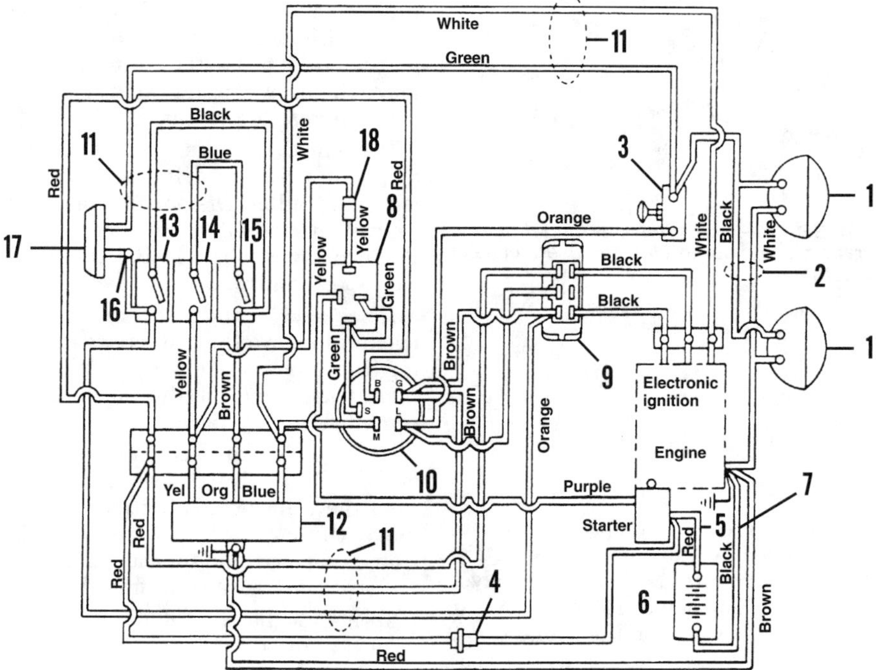

Fig. GR1-12—Wiring diagram for 1238H tractors equipped with Kawasaki engine.

1. Headlight
2. Wiring harness
3. Light switch
4. Fuse
5. Starter cable
6. Battery
7. Ground cable
8. Relay
9. Regulator
10. Ignition switch
11. Wiring harness
12. Module
13. Seat switch
14. Interlock switch
15. Switch
16. Connector
17. Tail light

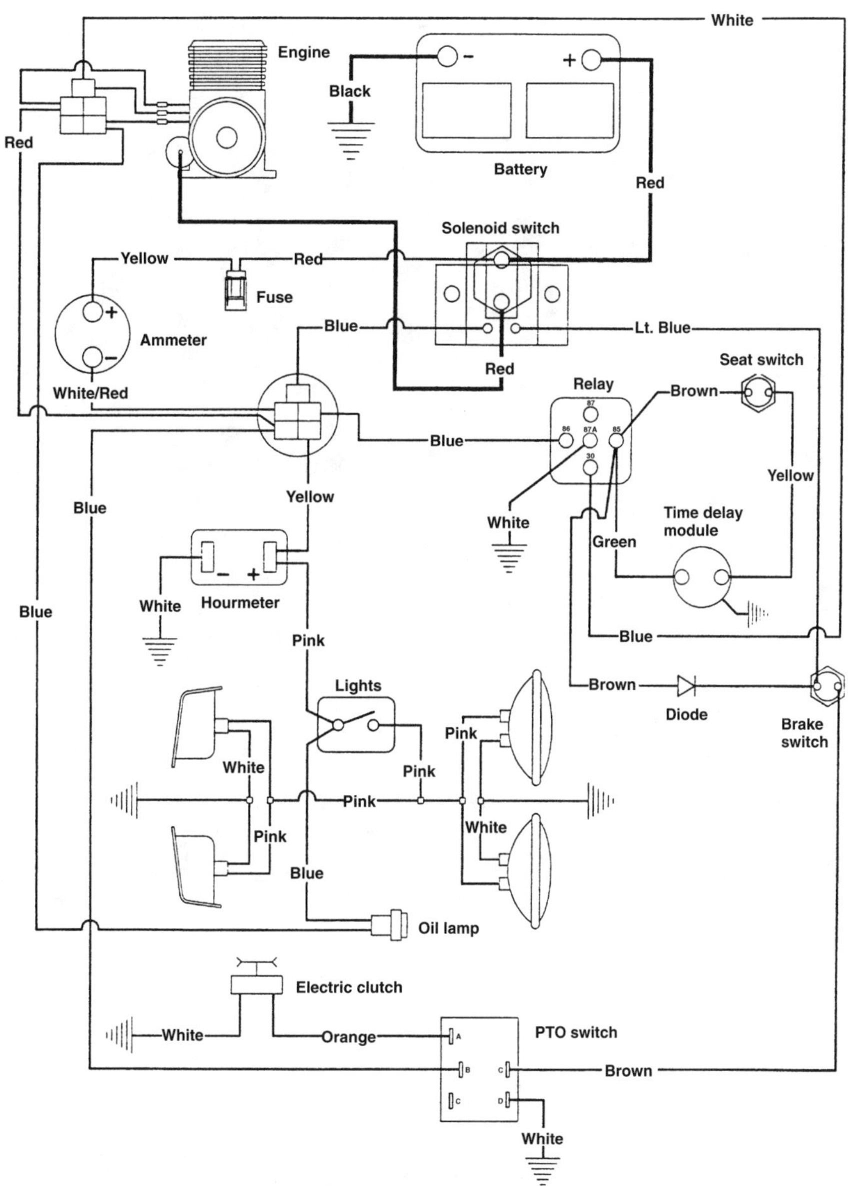

Fig. GR1-13—Wiring diagram for Gravely Estate Mower (GEM) tractors.

from the gear selector lever and range selector lever.

Loosen the transaxle belt guards and move them away from the drive belt. Depress the clutch pedal to relieve tension on the belt and remove the transaxle pulley belt. Slip the primary drive belt off the jackshaft pulley. Disconnect the brake control rod and spring from the brake lever.

Raise and support the tractor's rear. Remove the cap screws attaching the transaxle mounting plate to the main frame and roll the transaxle assembly backward from the tractor.

OVERHAUL

Models 1232G and 1238G are equipped with a Foote 4000 series transaxle. Refer to the Spicer (Foote) section in the TRANSAXLE service section in this manual for the overhaul procedure.

WIRING DIAGRAMS

Refer to Fig. GR1-11, GR1-12, and GR 1-13 for wiring diagrams typical of all models.

NOTES

HONDA

CONDENSED SPECIFICATIONS

Models	HT3813, HT4213
Engine Make	Honda
Model	GX360
Number of cylinders	2
Bore	58 mm (2.28 in.)
Stroke	68 mm (2.68 in.)
Displacement	359 cc (21.9 cu. in.)
Power Rating	9.7 kW (13 hp.)
Slow Idle	1300 rpm
High Speed (No-Load)	3300 rpm
Crankcase Capacity	1.4 L* (1.5 qt.)
Transaxle Capacity	2.9 L (3.1 qt.)
Coolant Capacity	1.35 L (1.4 qt.)

*If installing new filter, check oil level after running engine for a few minutes.

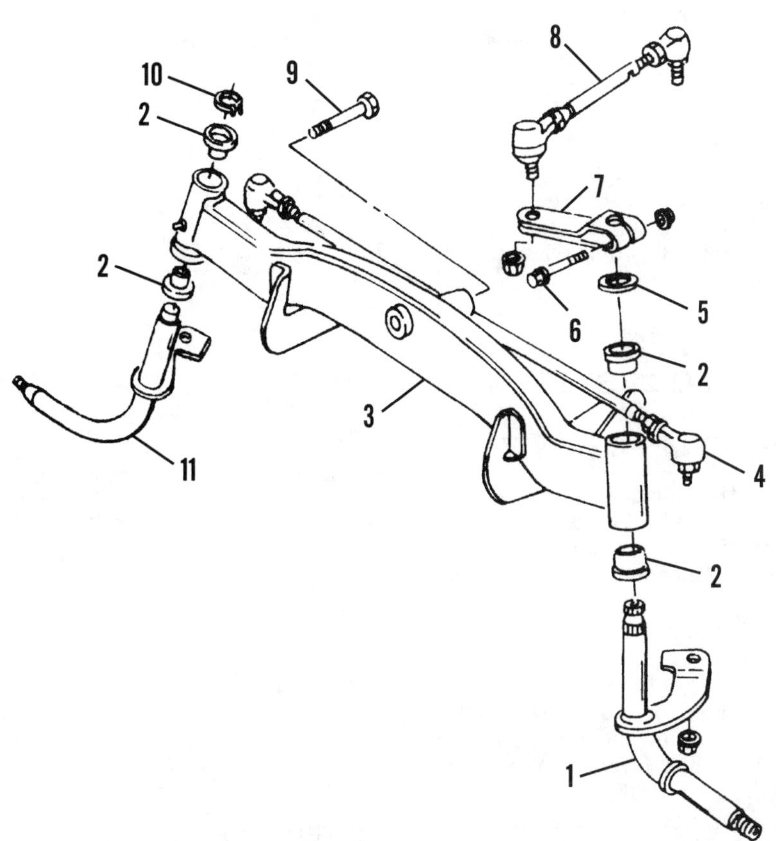

Fig. HN1-1—Exploded view of front axle assembly.

1. Spindle (left)
2. Bushing
3. Axle main member
4. Tie rod
5. Washer
6. Bolt
7. Steering lever
8. Drag link
9. Bolt
10. Snap ring
11. Spindle (right)

NOTE: Honda special tools may be required for some procedures and are indicated in the text. Read the text completely before attempting procedure.

FRONT AXLE AND STEERING SYSTEM

MAINTENANCE

Lubricate the steering spindles annually or after 100 hours of operation. Inject multipurpose grease into the grease fittings at the axle's outer ends. Clean the grease fittings before and after lubrication.

FRONT WHEELS AND BEARINGS

Each front wheel is supported by two sealed ball bearings not requiring periodic lubrication.

Replace the bearings if they are loose or do not spin smoothly. Tighten the bearing retaining nut to 55-65 N·m (40-47 ft.-lb.). Secure the nut with a cotter pin.

TIE ROD AND TOE-IN

The tie rod (4—Fig. HN1-1) is equipped with threaded ends at each end. Replace the tie rod if the ends are damaged.

The recommended front wheel toe-in is 6-14 mm (0.24-0.55 in.). Measure the

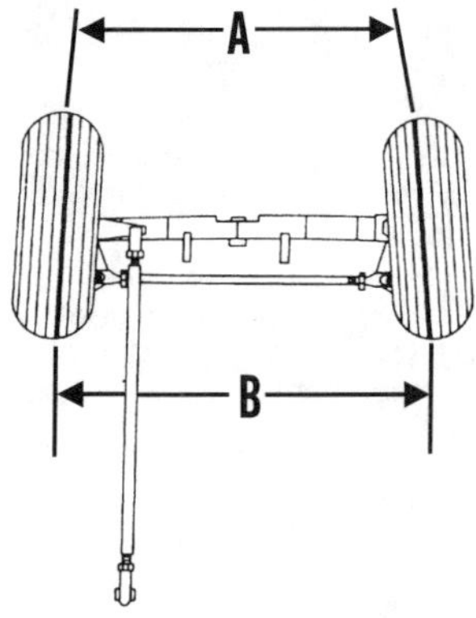

Fig. HN1-2—Measure distance "A" and "B" at front and rear of front wheels to determine front wheel toe-in.

distance (A—Fig. HN1-2) between the front of the front wheels at hub height and the distance (B) between the rear of the front wheels. The front distance (A) should be smaller than the rear distance (B).

To adjust toe-in, loosen the locknut at each tie rod end and rotate the tie rod.

NOTE: Left tie rod end and nut have left-hand threads.

STEERING SPINDLES REMOVAL AND INSTALLATION

To remove the steering spindle, raise and support the front of the tractor. Remove the front wheel. Disconnect tie rod end from spindle.

To remove the left spindle (1—Fig. HN1-1), remove the clamp bolt (6) and detach the steering arm (7) from the spindle. Slide spindle out of the axle.

When installing the steering lever, align the punch mark on the spindle end with the punch mark on the steering arm (Fig. HN1-3).

To remove the right spindle (11—Fig. HN1-1), detach the snap ring (10) and slide the spindle out of the axle.

AXLE MAIN MEMBER REMOVAL AND INSTALLATION

The complete front axle assembly may be removed as a unit. To remove the axle main member (3—Fig. HN1-1), raise and support the front of the tractor. Disconnect the drag link's (8) outer end.

Support the axle main member and remove the axle retaining bolt (9). Lower the axle main member from the mainframe pivot point and roll the axle out from under the tractor.

When installing the axle main member, tighten the axle retaining bolt to 45-55 N·m (33-40 ft.-lb.).

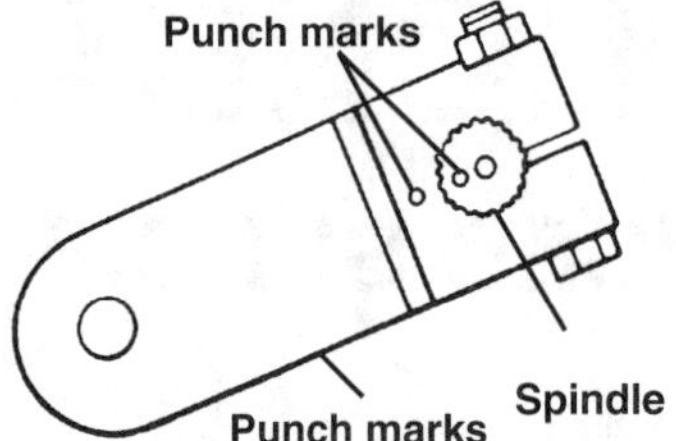

Fig. HN1-3—Align punch marks on steering lever and spindle during assembly.

STEERING GEAR OVERHAUL

To remove the steering shaft and gear assembly, remove the cover (1—Fig. HN1-4) and nut (2). Remove the steering wheel (3) and flat washer (4). Disconnect the drag link end and steering arm (15).

Remove the cap screws retaining the steering plate (8). Remove the three cap screws retaining the steering gear holder (17). Remove the nut (11) and pull the steering shaft (6) out of the tractor.

Remove the gear (9) and washer (10). Remove the steering gear (14) and washers (13 and 16). Replace the bushings (5, 7 and 12) as required.

Reverse the removal procedure for reassembly. Make certain the front wheels are straight ahead, the larger opening in the steering wheel is toward the top and the steering gears are meshed in the center of the gear (14) during reassembly. Tighten the three bolts retaining the steering gear holder (17) to 23-30 N·m (17-22 ft.-lb.) and nuts (2 and 11) to 45-54 N·m (33-40 ft.-lb.).

SAFETY INTERLOCK SYSTEM

The tractor is equipped with switches and relays preventing inadvertent starting of the tractor engine or operation if the operator leaves the tractor seat. The tractor engine should not start if the following occurs (engage parking brake):

- Operator in the tractor seat, shift lever in NEUTRAL and the PTO clutch lever in the ON position.
- Operator in the tractor seat, PTO clutch lever in the OFF position and the shift lever in a position other than NEUTRAL.
- Operator not in the seat when starting the engine.

The seat switch should kill the engine if the operator is not in the seat or leaves the seat when the PTO clutch is engaged or the tractor is in gear.

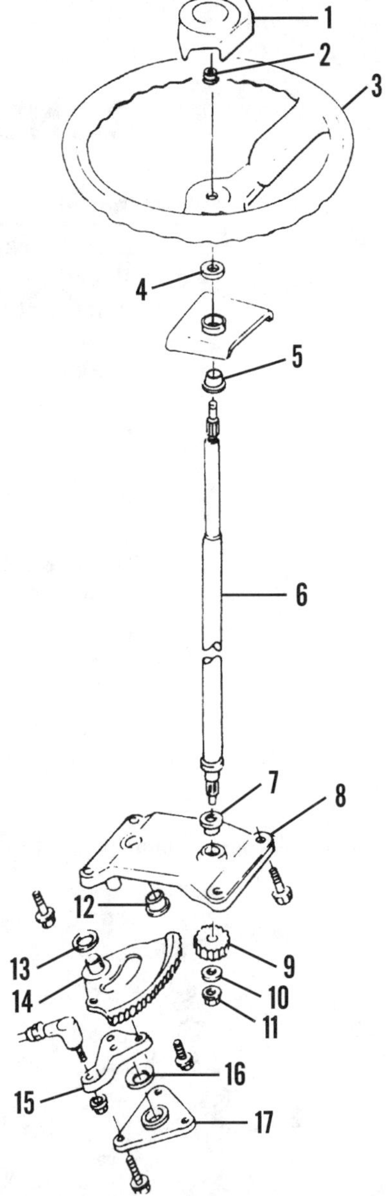

Fig. HN1-4—Exploded view of steering gear assembly.

1. Cover
2. Nut
3. Steering wheel
4. Washer
5. Bushing
6. Steering shaft
7. Bushing
8. Steering plate
9. Gear
10. Washer
11. Nut
12. Bushing
13. Washer
14. Sector gear
15. Steering arm
16. Washer
17. Steering gear holder

Refer to the wiring schematics at end of this section.

ENGINE

MAINTENANCE

The engine is equipped with a dry air filter that should be cleaned and inspected after every 50 hours of operation.

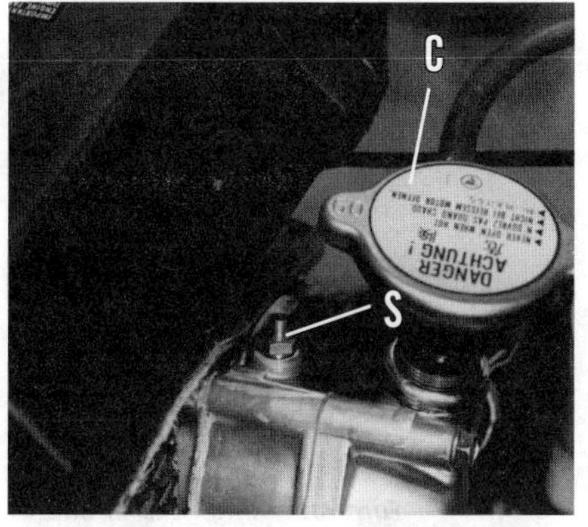

Fig. HN1-5—To bleed cooling system, open air bleed screw (S) and proceed as described in text.

Remove the foam and paper air filter elements from the air filter housing. Wash the foam element in a mild detergent and water solution. Rinse in clean water and allow to air dry.

After the foam element is dry, soak it in clean engine oil. Squeeze out excess oil.

Paper element may be cleaned by directing low pressure compressed air stream from inside the filter toward the outside.

Replace the paper element if it cannot be cleaned satisfactorily, or if it is damaged.

The engine oil level should be checked prior to operating engine. Check the oil level with the oil cap not screwed in, but just touching the opening's threads.

Oil should be changed after the first 20 hours of engine operation and after every 100 hours thereafter. Change the oil filter after every 300 hours of operation or after two years.

Use oil meeting the latest API service classification. Use SAE 10W-30 or 10W-40 oil; use SAE 10W-40 if the temperature is above 90°F (32°C).

Crankcase capacity is 1.4 liters (1.5 qt.).

REMOVAL AND INSTALLATION

Raise the hood and disconnect the battery cables. Disconnect the headlight wiring connector and remove bolt from the ground lead. Remove the hood hinge bolts and remove the hood.

Drain the coolant. Detach the radiator hoses and remove the radiator. Loosen the PTO belt tension knob and remove the mower drive belt.

Detach the engine ground cable from the front frame crossmember. Disconnect the throttle cable. Disconnect the fuel hoses.

Disconnect the wiring from the starting motor, charge coil and ignition coil. Remove regulator/rectifier bracket assembly from the engine. Separate the wiring from the engine.

Remove the cooling fan. Remove the PTO clutch as described in the PTO CLUTCH section. Detach the PTO cable from the brackets.

Remove the engine mounting bolts and nuts. Lift the engine and move it forward to separate the engine from the drive shaft and remove it from the tractor.

Reverse the removal procedure to install engine. Tighten front engine retaining nuts to 35-40 N·m (26-29 ft.-lb.).

OVERHAUL

Engine make and model are listed in specifications table at the beginning of this section. Refer to the appropriate Honda engine section in this manual for service information on the engine and associated accessories.

FUEL SYSTEM

Refer to ENGINE and ELECTRICAL SYSTEM sections for fuel system related components not covered here.

FUEL FILTER MAINTENANCE

A fuel filter is located in the fuel line between the fuel tank and the fuel pump. The fuel filter is visible through a hole in the rear hitch plate.

Inspect the fuel filter annually or after every 100 hours of operation. Replace the filter if it is dirty or damaged.

FUEL PUMP

The fuel pump is located on a bracket below the fuel tank.

Testing

Before testing the fuel pump be sure the fuel filter and fuel line are in good condition and the fuel flow to the pump is unimpeded.

Connect a suitable pressure gauge to the fuel pump output port. Turn the ignition switch ON, but do not start the engine. Fuel pump pressure should be 6.9-14.2 kPa (1.0-2.0 psi).

Direct a hose from pump output port into a container. Turn the ignition switch ON, but do not start the engine. Fuel pump volume should be at least 350 cc (11.8 oz.) during one minute of operation.

COOLING SYSTEM

Cooling components on the engine, such as the water pump and thermostat, are covered in the appropriate Honda engine section at rear of this manual.

MAINTENANCE

Maintain the coolant level between the reservoir tank's MIN and MAX marks. The recommended coolant is a 50:50 mixture of clean water and permanent antifreeze.

Periodically clean debris from the radiator screen. Periodically inspect coolant hoses between the radiator and engine water pump. Replace damaged hoses.

WARNING: Coolant in the system is pressurized. Remove the pressure cap only when engine is cold.

Change the coolant at least every two years. Flush the cooling system at least every three years. Coolant system capacity is approximately 1.35 liters (1.4 qt.).

CHANGE COOLANT

Remove the engine's pressure cap (C–Fig. HN1-5). Drain coolant by opening radiator drain valve.

WARNING: Coolant in the radiator is pressurized. Remove pressure cap only when the engine is cold.

Empty the reservoir tank. Close the radiator drain valve. Open the air bleed screw (S—Fig. HN1-5). Refill with a 50:50 mixture of clean water and permanent antifreeze. Pour coolant into the fill hole until air-free coolant runs out of bleed screw hole, then reinstall the bleed screw.

Position the pressure cap on the filler neck, but do not tighten the cap. Run the engine until the upper radiator hose becomes warm. Stop the engine and add coolant through the filler neck as needed. Install and tighten the pressure cap.

Fill the reservoir tank with coolant to proper level. Run the engine, while monitoring the engine temperature to be sure the engine does not overheat. Allow the engine to cool and recheck the coolant level.

HOSE ROUTING

The left radiator hose connects to the thermostat housing. The right radiator hose connects to a spigot on the right side of the cylinder block. Bypass hose attaches to a spigot at the right rear of

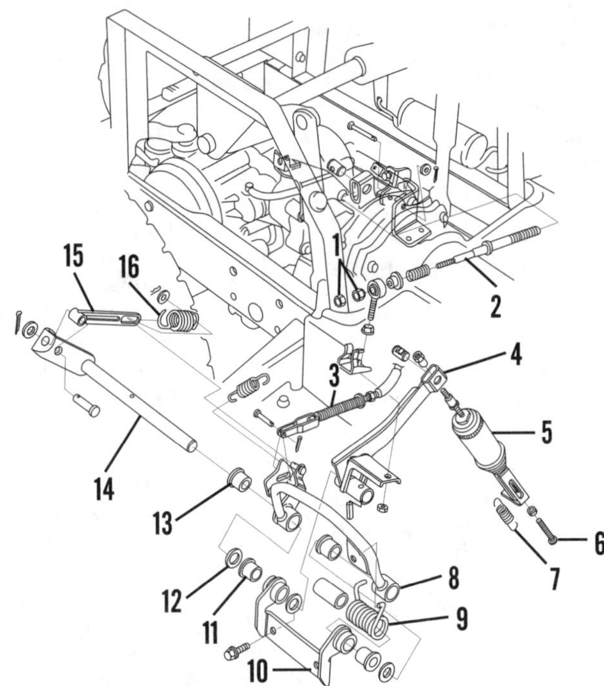

Fig. HN1-6—Exploded view of clutch linkage. Adjust clutch rod (2) length by turning nuts (1) at rod end.

1. Adjusting nuts
2. Clutch rod
3. Clutch cable
4. Damper arm
5. Damper
6. Adjustment bolt
7. Damper spring
8. Clutch arm
9. Spring
10. Change arm bracket
11. Bushing (2)
12. Washer (2)
13. Bushing (2)
14. Clutch arm shaft
15. Stopper arm
16. Spring

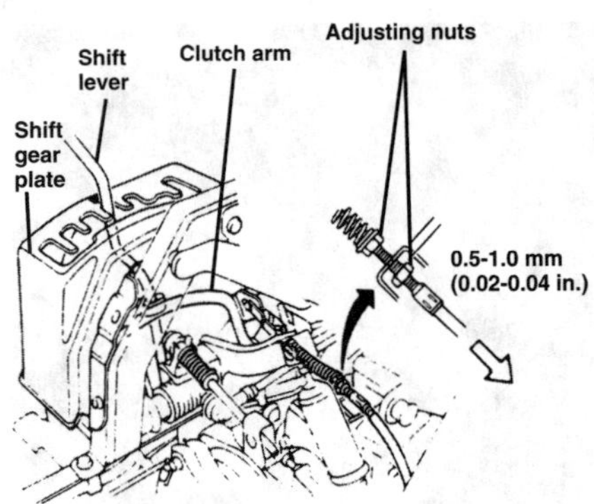

Fig. HN1-7—Turn adjusting nuts at end of clutch cable to adjust cable free play. Refer to text.

the cylinder block and connects to the thermostat housing.

CLUTCH

The clutch is a disc that is actuated by linkage connected to the shift lever and clutch/brake pedal. The clutch is disengaged when the shift lever is moved to another slot or the brake is applied. A hydraulic cylinder (damper) attached to the clutch linkage regulates clutch engagement speed.

ADJUSTMENT

Be sure the clutch is not worn excessively before attempting clutch adjustment. See INSPECTION section.

With the shift lever in the second gear slot, measure the lever free play between the side of the lever and the closed end of the slot. The permissible range for lever free play is 3-12 mm (0.12-0.47 in.); desired free play is 7-8 mm (0.27-0.31 in.).

Adjust the shift lever free play by altering length of clutch rod (2—Fig. HN1-6). Turn the adjusting nut (1) clockwise to increase free play or counterclockwise to decrease free play.

NOTE: Shift lever free play affects clutch engagement time. Less free play will slow the clutch engagement time; more free play will make the clutch engage faster.

Start the engine and shift the transmission into first gear. Note the clutch engagement time; it should be less than one second. If necessary, adjust shift lever free play to obtain desired clutch engagement action. If proper clutch engagement cannot be obtained by adjusting the shift lever free play within the permissible range, the clutch may be faulty.

Clutch cable free play should be 0.5-1.0 mm (0.02-0.04 in.). To adjust, remove the seat and rear fenders. Shift the transmission into second gear. Push the clutch arm towards the shift lever and hold it there. Adjust the nuts (Fig. HN1-7) at the rear end of the clutch cable to obtain the desired cable free play.

Hold the shift lever all the way toward the seat. Adjust position of the stopper bolt (1—Fig. HN1-8) so the end of the clutch rod lightly contacts the head of the stopper bolt.

INSPECTION

To check the clutch's condition, place the gearshift lever in the second speed slot. Raise the seat and remove inspection hole cover. The indicator mark on

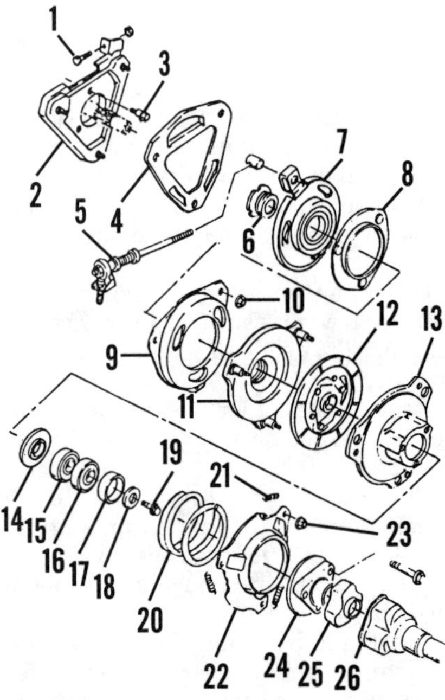

Fig. HN1-8—Exploded view of drive clutch assembly.

1. Stop bolt
2. Clutch plate
3. Bolt
4. Dust seal plate
5. Clutch rod
6. Bearing locknut
7. Ramp
8. Ball retainer
9. Rear clutch housing
10. Nut
11. Lifter plate
12. Clutch disc
13. Pressure plate
14. Special washer
15. Bearing
16. Bearing
17. Collar
18. Washer
19. Cap screw
20. Spring
21. Clutch setting spring
22. Clutch cover
23. Nut
24. Damper hub
25. Damper
26. Drive shaft

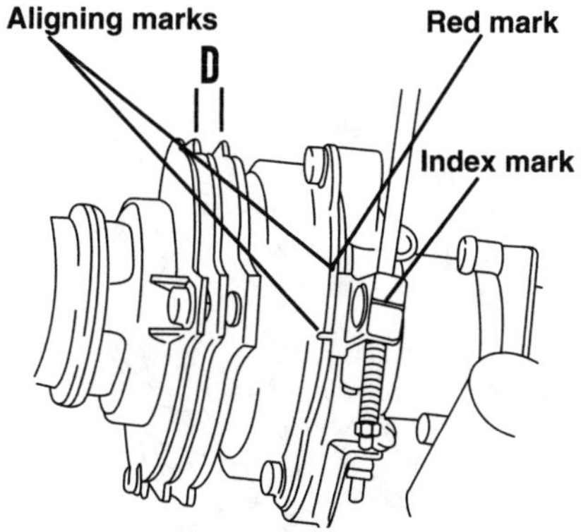

Fig. HN1-9—Measure the distance "D" between lifter plate and pressure plate to determine clutch disc thickness.

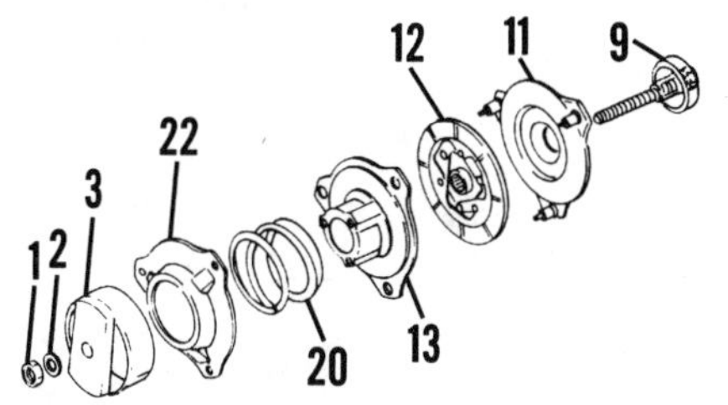

Fig. HN1-10—Exploded view of spring-loaded clutch pack with special spring compressor tool 07960-75000A.

1. Nut
2. Washer
3. Special tool
9. Special tool
11. Lifter plate
12. Clutch disc
13. Pressure plate
20. Spring
22. Clutch cover

the clutch lever should be between the two notches on the clutch housing (Fig. HN1-9). If the indicator mark is past the red notch on the clutch housing, clutch disc must be replaced.

Measure the distance (D) between the lifter plate and pressure plate. The permissible range is 4.5-6.1 mm (0.18-0.24 in.). If the measurement is less than 4.5 mm (0.18 in.), clutch disc is excessively worn. If distance is more than 6.1 mm (0.24 in.), clutch is out of adjustment.

OVERHAUL

Remove the seat and rear fenders. Remove the drive shaft. Disconnect all clutch linkage.

Remove three screws retaining the damper hub (24—Fig. HN1-8) and remove the hub. Remove the cap screw (19) and washer (18). Remove the three nuts (10) and slide the clutch assembly off the transaxle input shaft.

Use a spanner wrench or special tool 07916-3710100 to remove the left-hand thread bearing locknut (6). Use special

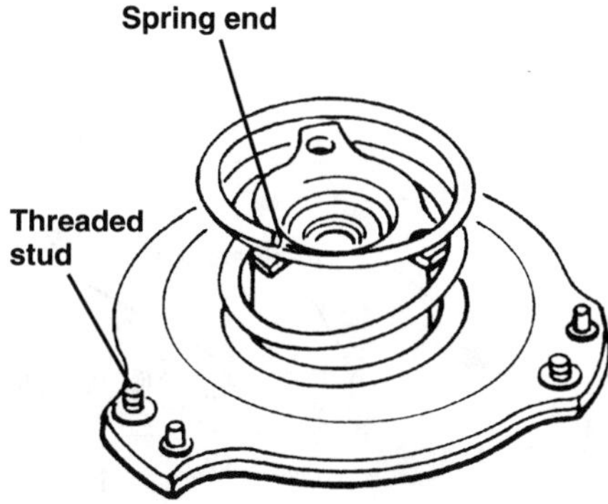

Fig. HN1-11—Align end of clutch spring with threaded stud prior to assembly.

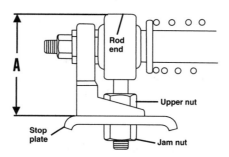

Fig. HN1-12—Adjust upper nut so clutch rod end height "A" is between 37-39 mm (1.45-1.53 in.).

spring compressor tool 07960-750000A or other suitable tool to compress the spring (20) in clutch pack (Fig. HN1-10). With the tool compressing the clutch pack, remove the three nuts (23—Fig. HN1-8). Slowly unscrew the spring compressor tool and disassemble the clutch pack.

The thickness of the clutch facing on the disc (12—Fig. HN1-8) should be 5.9-6.1 mm (0.232-0.240 in.). Replace the clutch disc if worn to a thickness of 4.5 mm (0.177 in.) or less.

The spring (20) free length should be 58.2 mm (2.29 in.). Replace the spring if the free length is less than 56.2 mm (2.21 in.).

Replace the clutch damper rubber (25) if damaged.

When reassembling the clutch, refer to Fig. HN1-8. Align the spring end with one of the three threaded studs on the pressure plate (Fig. HN1-11). Install the clutch disc (12—Fig. HN1-8) with the splined hub's long side toward the lifter plate (11).

Tighten the nuts (23 and 10—Fig. HN1-8) to 10-13 N·m (88-115 in.-lb.). Tighten the screw (19) to 24-30 N·m (18-22 ft.-lb.). Make certain the dust plate (4) is mounted on the clutch plate (2) and that the clutch plate studs are through the dust plate holes.

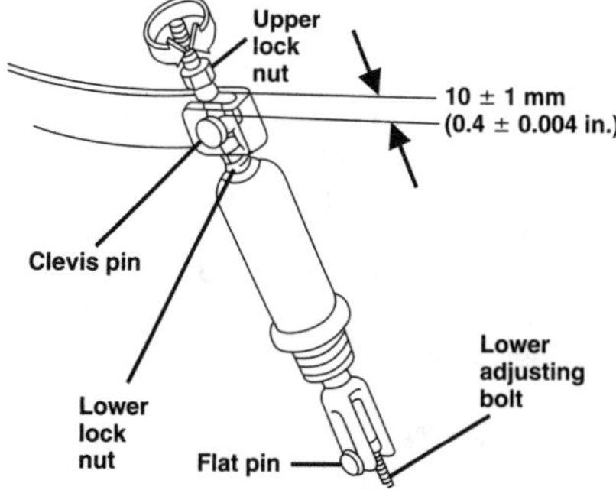

Fig. HN1-13—Adjust locknut on upper end of damper until there is 10 mm (0.4 in.) clearance between bottom of nut and the clevis pin.

If removed, reinstall the clutch rod end (Fig. HN1-12) so the top of rod end is 37-39 mm (1.46-1.53 in.) above the stop plate. Adjust the upper nut to obtain the desired height, and tighten the jam nut.

To determine if the clutch damper is functioning properly, remove the damper and suspend a 3.5 kg (7.7 lb.) weight from the bolt end of damper. After fully compressing the damper, measure the time required for the weight to fully extend the damper.

A normally functioning damper should extend in 3.4-4.3 seconds on Models HT3813K0 or 2.7-3.4 seconds on Models HT3813K1 and HT4213. Allowable limit is 3.2-4.5 seconds on Models HT3813K0 or 2.4-3.8 seconds on Models HT3813K1 and HT4213.

Before installing the damper, adjust the bolt position at the damper's lower end. The end of the adjusting bolt should be 25-27 mm (0.98-1.06 in.) from the upper end of slot in the damper bracket. Tighten jam nut to hold the bolt's position.

Install the damper. Move the shift lever to NEUTRAL. Thread the lower locknut (Fig. HN1-13) onto the damper as far as it will go toward the damper body. Compress, then release the damper. Be sure the lower adjusting bolt is seated against the flat pin in the damper bracket (Fig. FN1-13).

Turn the damper upper locknut so it is 9-11 mm (0.35-0.43 in.) above the clevis pin (Fig. HN1-13). Hold the upper nut so it cannot turn, then rotate the lower nut so the clevis pin is forced up against the upper nut.

BRAKE

The tractor is equipped with a drum brake located in the transaxle case. The brake drum is mounted on the transaxle countershaft.

The brake may be actuated either with the clutch/brake pedal or the parking brake lever. The clutch/brake pedal actuates both the clutch and brake.

When the parking brake lever is engaged, an indicator lamp lights. If the parking brake is engaged when the transmission is shifted into gear, a warning buzzer sounds.

ADJUSTMENT

Depressing the brake pedal disengages the drive clutch and applies the brake. Brake pedal rod must be adjusted so there is no clearance (Fig. HN1-14) between the end of operating rod and the front end of the brake pedal slot when the brake pedal is released. To adjust, loosen the jam nuts (2) and turn the brake rod (4) to remove any clearance.

When new brake shoes are installed, turn the cam plate rod adjusting nut (6—Fig. HN1-14) so there is a slight clearance between the rod end and the bottom end of the slot in the cam arm plate (5) when the brake pedal is released.

To check for proper parking brake cable adjustment, pull the parking brake lever up until the ratchet locks. The end of the parking brake cable should be aligned with the punch mark on the spring sleeve (Fig. HN1-15). To adjust, loosen the cable adjuster locknut and turn the adjuster as required.

OVERHAUL

To check brake shoe wear, depress the brake pedal and note position of the brake wear indicator (N—Fig. HN1-16) located near the brake assembly on the transaxle. If the indicator is near the wear limit point (P), replace the brake shoes.

To remove the brake shoes, remove the seat, rear fender and wire protector. Raise the tractor's right side so the transaxle oil will not flow out. Remove the screw (1—Fig. HN1-17), washer (2) and brake drum (3). Remove the brake spring (4) and shoes (5).

Brake lining thickness wear limit is 2.35 mm (0.093 in.). If the brake cam (6) is removed, reinstall the cam in the brake arm (11) so the punch marks on the cam and arm are aligned.

Adjust the brake linkage as previously described.

SHIFT CONTROL LINKAGE

ADJUSTMENT

The operator gearshift lever and transaxle gear selector arm must be synchronized for proper gear selection. Loosen jam nuts on the rod and rotate the rod end to adjust the rod length.

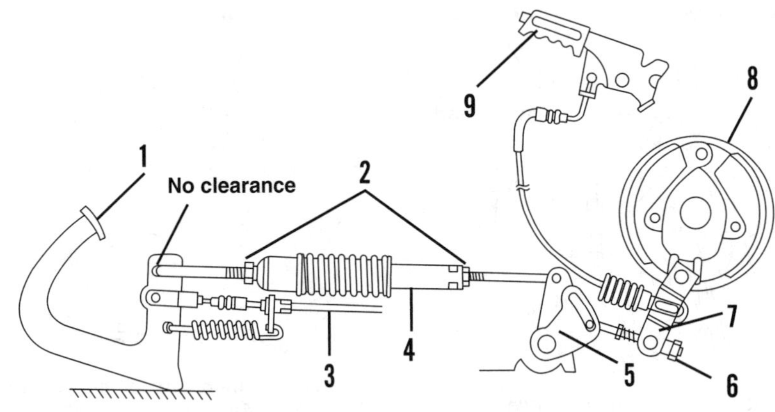

Fig. HN1-14—Adjust brake rod (4) so there is no clearance between the end of the brake rod and front end of brake pedal slot.

1. Brake pedal
2. Jam nuts
3. Clutch cable
4. Brake rod
5. Cam plate
6. Adjusting nut
7. Cam arm
8. Brake drum
9. Parking brake lever

NOTE: Rear jam nut has left-hand threads.

The punch marks (P–Fig. HN1-18) on the shift lever shaft (12) and shifter arm (16) must be aligned.

Move the shift lever to NEUTRAL. Check the punch mark on the transaxle shifter shaft (19) aligns with the index mark cast in the top of the transaxle case. Adjust the shift rod (17) length so the shift lever (6) is centered in the N-notch of the shifter console.

Move the shift lever to each gear position on the console and check that the proper gear is engaged in transaxle. Tighten the shift rod jam nuts.

REMOVAL AND INSTALLATION

To remove the shift linkage, remove the shift lever knob (1—Fig. HN1-18), seat and rear fenders. Remove the pivot bolt (11) and withdraw the shift lever (6). Remove the snap rings (2 and 3) and thrust washer (4). Pull the clutch roller (7) and bearing (5) off the shift lever.

Detach the shift rod (17) from the shifter arm (16). Remove the clamp bolt (18) and withdraw the shift lever shaft (12) from the shifter arm (16).

Inspect all parts for wear or damage and replace when necessary.

When installing the shift linkage, align the punch marks on the shift lever shaft (12) and shifter arm (16). Adjust the linkage as previously described.

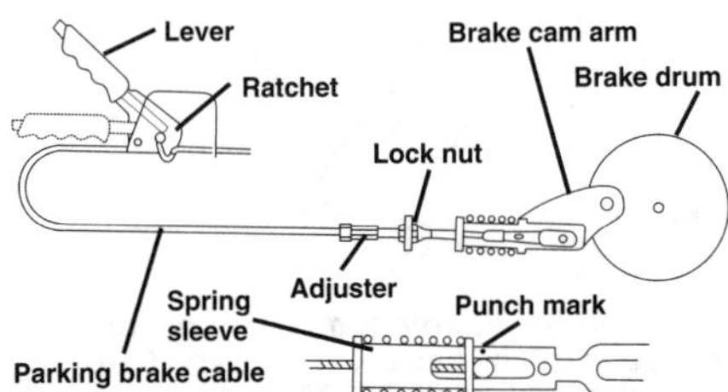

Fig. HN1-15—The end of the parking brake cable must align with the punch mark on the spring sleeve when the parking brake is engaged. Refer to text.

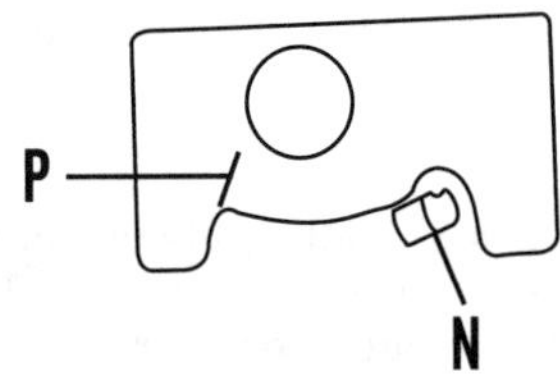

Fig. HN1-16—If brake wear indicator (N) is near wear limit point (P), replace brake shoes.

TRANSAXLE

The tractor is equipped with a five-speed transaxle. The transaxle also provides a reverse gear.

A drum brake is attached to the transaxle mainshaft and is located in a compartment on the right side of the transaxle. Refer to previous sections for service information on brake and clutch assemblies.

LUBRICATION

The transaxle oil level should be checked annually or after every 100 hours of operation. The transaxle oil should be level with the bottom edge of the fill cap opening located at the rear

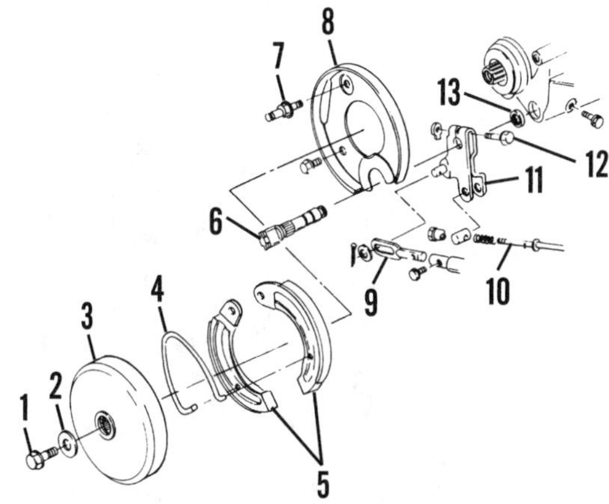

Fig. HN1-17—Exploded view of brake assembly.

1. Screw
2. Washer
3. Brake drum
4. Brake spring
5. Brake shoes
6. Cam
7. Stud
8. Backing plate
9. Parking brake rod
10. Brake rod
11. Brake arm
12. Bolt
13. Seal

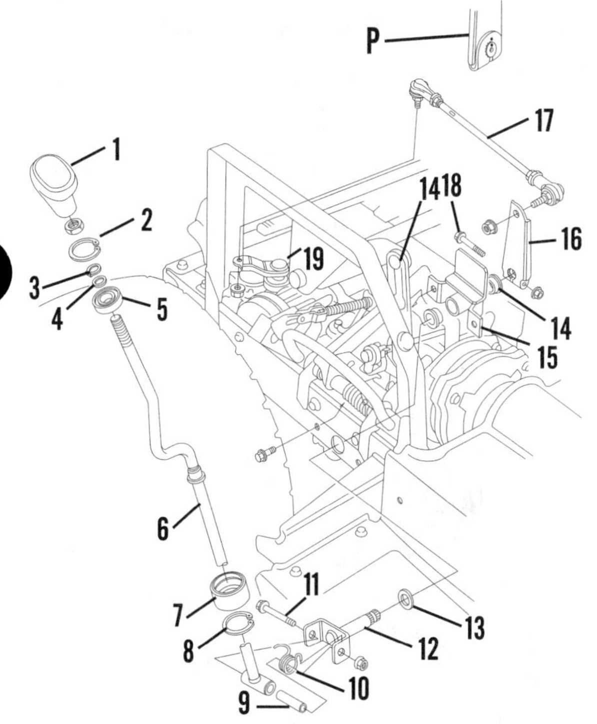

Fig. HN1-18—Exploded view of shift linkage.

1. Knob
2. Snap ring
3. Snap ring
4. Thrust washer
5. Ball bearing
6. Shift lever
7. Clutch roller
8. Snap ring
9. Sleeve
10. Spring
11. Bolt
12. Change lever shaft
13. Thrust washer
14. Bushings
15. Bracket
16. Shifter arm
17. Shift rod
18. Clamp bolt
19. Transaxle shifter shaft

of the transaxle. Be sure the machine is on a level surface when checking the oil level. Oil capacity is 2.9 liters (3.1 qt.). Recommended oil is SAE 10W-40 engine oil.

REMOVAL AND INSTALLATION

Raise and support the rear of the tractor. Remove the left and right wheels. Remove drive shaft and drive clutch. Disconnect shift rod from transaxle shift lever.

Disconnect all interfering electrical wires. Remove the fuel pump. Disconnect brake rod from the brake lever.

Support the transaxle and remove transaxle mounting bolts. Lower the transaxle assembly out of the frame and pull the transaxle from the tractor.

Reinstall by reversing the removal procedure. Tighten transaxle retaining screws to 24-30 N·m (18-22 ft.-lb.).

Refill transaxle with oil as described in the LUBRICATION paragraph. Adjust brake, clutch and shift linkage as previously described.

OVERHAUL

Remove the drain screw and drain the oil from the transaxle. Remove the brake assembly. Unscrew and remove the input shaft bearing housing (3—Fig. HN1-19).

Break or bend back the staked area of nut (6). Using Honda tool 07916-7500000, unscrew the nut (6) and remove the input shaft (9). The old nut should be discarded.

If bearing (8) must be removed, use Honda tool 07916-7500000 to unscrew the nut (7). Remove seal (1) and drive or press out the bearing (5).

Unscrew and separate the transaxle case halves (11 and 19). Remove the left axle shaft (14), bearings and seals as needed from the left housing (19).

Remove the countershaft gear (1—Fig. HN1-20) and shaft (2), differential assembly (23) and mainshaft and sliding gear shaft as an assembly (4) from the right hou Remove the setscrew (9) from the shift arm (10) and pull the shift shaft (16) out of the housing. Remove bearings and seals from the housing as needed.

Separate the gears from the mainshaft (6—Fig. HN1-21) and sliding gear shaft (24). Be careful not to lose the detent balls (21) and springs (20) when separating the gear selector (23) and sliding gear shaft (24).

NOTE: Ring gear (3—Fig. HN1-22) retaining screws have left-hand threads.

To disassemble the differential, remove the bearings (2—Fig. HN1-22) from the differential case (4). Unscrew the ring gear screws (left-hand threads) and separate the ring gear (3) from the case. Drive out the spring pin (7) and remove the pinion shaft (10), side gears (6) and pinion gears (9) and thrust washers (5 and 8).

Inspect all parts for damage and replace when necessary. Install new oil seals and gaskets when assembling.

When reassembling transaxle, note the following: If input shaft (9—Fig. HN1-19), input shaft bearing, bevel gear, main shaft (6—Fig. HN1-21), shims or transaxle cases were replaced, refer to the following section for the shimming procedure.

Washers (11—Fig. HN1-21) are 2 mm (0.080 in.) thick and the washer (19) is 1 mm (0.039 in.) thick. Install a Belleville washer (7) so the cup side is toward the gear (6). Install countershaft drive gear (8) so the extended hub is toward end of sliding gear shaft (24). Install the countershaft driven gear (1—Fig. HN1-20) so the extended hub is facing away from the countershaft gear teeth.

Tighten the ring gear (3—Fig. HN1-22) retaining screws (left-hand threads) to 45-55 N·m (33-40 ft.-lb.).

Tighten the inner pinion gear nut (7—Fig. HN1-19) to 70-80 N·m (52-58 ft.-lb.) and outer nut (6) to 90-110 N·m (67-80 ft.-lb.). During final assembly, stake the outer nut (6) into the slot in the transaxle case. Tighten the input shaft housing (3—Fig. HN1-19) cap screws to 20-24 N·m (15-17 ft.-lb.). Tighten the transaxle case cap screws to 8-14 N·m (6-10 Tighten the axle shaft-to-rear wheel nut to 550-65 N·m (40-47 ft.-lb.). Tighten the neutral switch to 16-20 N·m (12-15 ft.-lb.).

Gear Shimming Procedure

Input shaft gear and bevel gear contact pattern and backlash must be checked if the input shaft (9—Fig. HN1-19), input shaft bearing, bevel gear, gear shaft (6—Fig. HN1-21), shims or transaxle cases have been replaced or changed.

Coat the input bevel gear (9—Fig. HN1-19) with Prussian Blue or other suitable compound. Make a trial assembly by installing the input shaft assembly and the mainshaft and bevel gear assembly in the transaxle cases using the original pinion shaft shim (10—Fig. HN1-19) and mainshaft shim (1—Fig. HN1-21). Assemble the case halves.

Rotate the input shaft in the normal direction, then remove the shaft and check the contact pattern on the input gear teeth. Contact area should be centered on the tooth surface.

If the contact area is toward the outer edge of tooth, install a thinner shim (10—Fig. HN1-19). If contact area is toward base of tooth, install a thicker shim (10).

After correctly adjusting the bevel gear teeth contact, reassemble the transaxle. Check the bevel gear backlash.

Attach a hose clamp or other device to the mainshaft to provide a reading point. Position a dial indicator on the mainshaft (Fig. HN1-23). Prevent the input shaft from turning using the clutch or other device. Gently rotate the mainshaft back and forth while observing the dial indicator reading.

Backlash should be 0.016-0.026 mm (0.0006-0.0010 in.). If backlash is insufficient, decrease the thickness of the mainshaft shim (1—Fig. HN21). If backlash is excessive, increase the shim's thickness.

PTO BELT

ADJUSTMENT

Adjust belt tension by turning the tension knob at front of tractor. Belt tension is correct when the mark on the

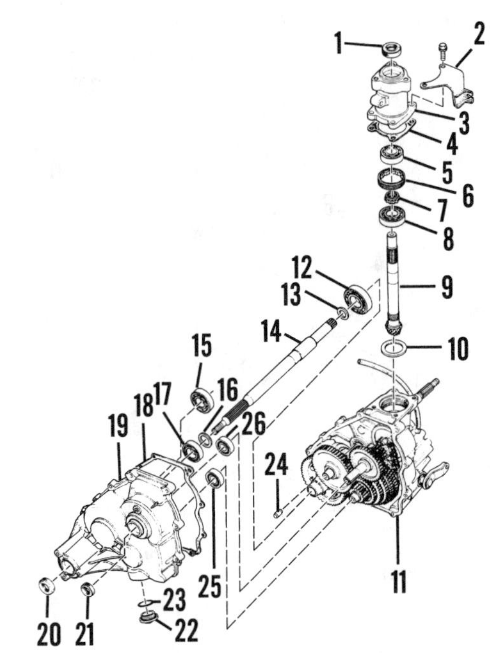

Fig. HN1-19—Exploded view of transaxle pinion shaft assembly and left axle shaft.

1. Seal
2. Bracket
3. Bearing housing
4. Gasket
5. Bearing
6. Outer nut
7. Inner nut
8. Bearing
9. Pinion shaft
10. Shim
11. Transaxle case half
12. Bearing
13. Washer
14. Axle shaft, left
15. Bearing
16. Washer
17. Bearing
18. Gasket
19. Transaxle case half
20. Oil seal
21. Oil seal
22. Fill plug
23. O-ring
24. Dowel
25. Bearing
26. Bearing

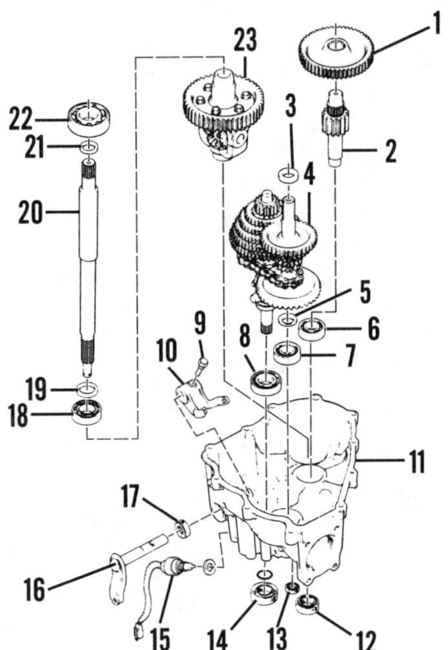

Fig. HN1-20—Exploded view of transaxle. Also refer to Fig. HN1-19 and HN1-21.

1. Countershaft driven gear
2. Countershaft
3. Washer
4. Mainshaft and change shaft assembly
5. Washer
6. Bearing
7. Bearing
8. Bearing
9. Setscrew
10. Shifter arm
11. Transaxle case, right
12. Oil seal
13. Oil seal
14. Oil seal
15. Neutral switch
16. Shifter shaft
17. Oil seal
18. Bearing
19. Washer (25 mm)
20. Axle shaft, right
21. Washer (20 mm)
22. Bearing

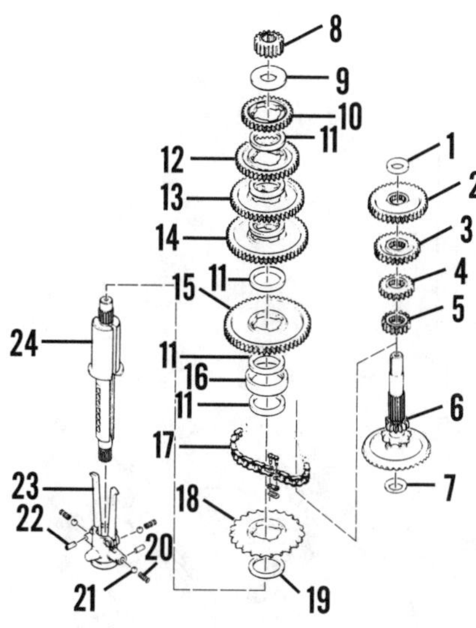

Fig. HN1-21—Exploded view of transaxle mainshaft and change shaft.

1. Shim
2. Main 5th gear (37T)
3. Main 4th gear (28T)
4. Main 3rd gear (21T)
5. Main 2nd gear (16T)
6. Mainshaft & bevel pinion gear
7. Belleville washer
8. Countershaft drive gear
9. Thrust washer
10. Change 5th gear (32T)
11. Spacer (2 mm)
12. Change 4th gear (41T)
13. Change 3rd gear (48T)
14. Change 2nd gear (53T)
15. Change 1st gear (56T)
16. Neutral positioner
17. Reverse chain
18. Reverse gear
19. Spacer (1 mm)
20. Detent spring (3)
21. Detent ball (3)
22. Spring pin (2)
23. Key holder
24. Change shaft

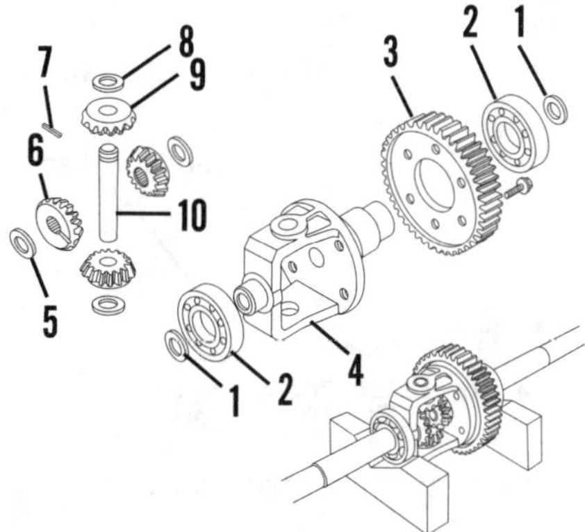

Fig. HN1-22—Exploded view of differential assembly.

1. Washer
2. Bearing
3. Ring gear
4. Differential case
5. Thrust washer (2)
6. Side gear (2)
7. Spring pin
8. Shim washer
9. Pinion gear (2)
10. Pinion shaft

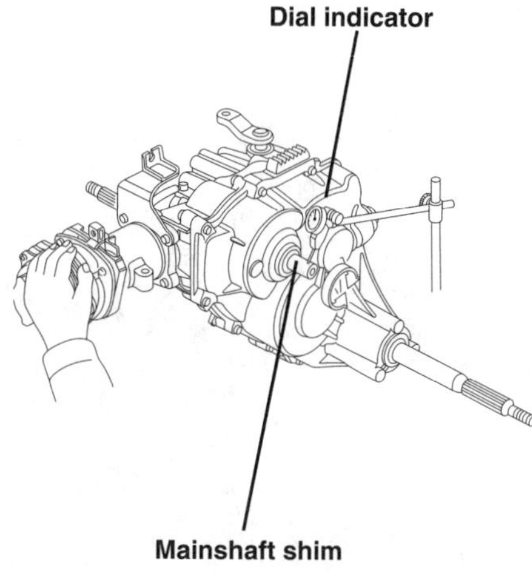

Fig. HN1-23—Use a dial indicator to measure bevel gear backlash. Refer to text.

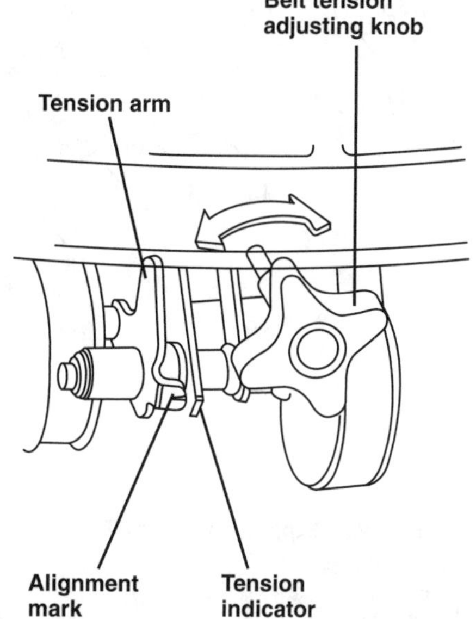

Fig. HN1-24—Turn belt tension adjusting knob to adjust PTO belt tension. Refer to text.

idler bracket aligns with the mark on the tension bracket (Fig. HN1-24).

REMOVAL AND INSTALLATION

To remove the PTO belt, lower the mower deck. Loosen the belt tension knob. Raise the idler pulley and remove the belt from pulleys and mower deck.

Open the hood and detach the belt guide. Open the upper radiator shroud and remove the belt from the top by routing it past the radiator.

Install the belt by reversing the removal procedure. Position the belt guide 3-6 mm (0.12-0.18 in.) from pulley. Adjust belt tension as described in previous section.

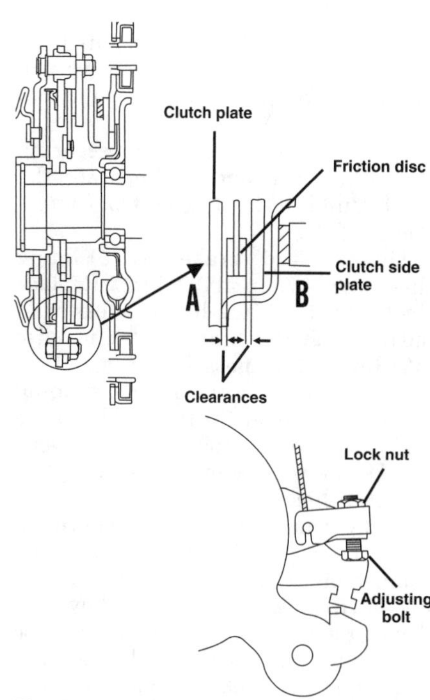

Fig. HN1-25—Use a feeler gauge to measure the PTO clutch plate clearances "A" and "B". Refer to text.

PTO CLUTCH

A cable-actuated disc clutch is attached to the end of the engine crankshaft. A switch prevents the engine starting if the PTO operating lever is in the engaged position.

ADJUSTMENT

To adjust the PTO clutch, open the hood and move the PTO clutch lever to the OFF position. Using a feeler gauge, measure the clearance (A—Fig. HN1-25) between the clutch plate and friction disc and clearance (B) between the friction disc and the clutch side plate. Add the two measured clearances together. Loosen the locknut and turn the adjusting bolt as necessary so the total (A plus B) clearance is 0.6 mm (0.02 in.).

The PTO operating lever free play should be 1-3 mm (0.04-0.1 in.) measured at the lever's outer end. To adjust free play, raise the hood and rotate adjusting nuts at the end of the clutch cable housing. Tighten the nuts and recheck free plaOVERHAUL

Before removing the PTO clutch, disconnect the negative battery cable. Remove the hood, radiator, fan and mower drive belt. Disconnect the PTO clutch cable (4—Fig. HN1-26).

Detach the clutch return spring (2—Fig. HN1-26). Unscrew the retaining screw (24), and remove the fan hub (22) and clutch assembly from the engine crankshaft. Remove the nuts from the special bolts (3) and remove the brake disc (5), ball retainer (9) and ball control plate (7).

Unscrew the nuts and bolts securing the clutch components. Separate the drive pulley (18) and clutch components (12-17).

The standard brake disc (5) lining thickness is 7.0 mm (0.28 in.). Replace the brake disc if the lining is less than 5.0 mm (0.20 in.). Standard friction disc (13) lining thickness is 6.0 mm (0.24 in.). Replace the brake disc if the lining is less than 3.0 mm (0.12 in.). The brake and friction discs must be replaced as a set. Do not replace one without replacing the other.

To determine the correct shim thickness (11–Fig. HN1-26), assemble the components (12-20). Place the assembly on a bench with the pulley (18) down. Push down on the friction disc hub so it contacts the pulley bearing (Fig. HN1-27). Measure the height (H) of the friction disc hub above the back face of the clutch bracket. Install shim thickness based on hub height above the bracket face as specified in the following table:

Hub Height	Shim Thickness
Over 6.00 mm (0.236 in.)	1.10 mm (0.043 in.)
5.90-6.00 mm (0.232-0.236 in.)	1.20 mm (0.047 in.)
5.80-5.90 mm (0.228-0.232 in.)	1.30 mm (0.051 in.)
5.70-5.80 mm (0.224-0.228 in.)	1.40 mm (0.055 in.)
5.60-5.70 mm (0.220-0.224 in.)	1.50 mm (0.059 in.)
Under 5.60 mm (0.220 in.)	1.60 mm (0.062 in.)

After assembly, measure the clearance between the side plate (Fig. HN1-25) and friction disc, then measure the clearance between the friction disc and clutch plate. Add the clearances together. Total clearance should be 0.6 mm (0.024 in.). Rotate the adjusting screw to obtain the specified clearance.

Adjust the PTO control cable as described in the previous section. With the engine stopped, move the PTO control lever to the engaged position. Measure the gap between the brake pad on the brake disc (5—Fig. HN1-26) and the back face of the bracket (12). The gap should be 1.5-2.3 mm (0.060-0.090 in.). If the gap is not correct, repeat adjustments.

ELECTRICAL SYSTEM

Engine related electrical components, such as the starter, are covered in the appropriate Honda engine section at the rear of this manual.

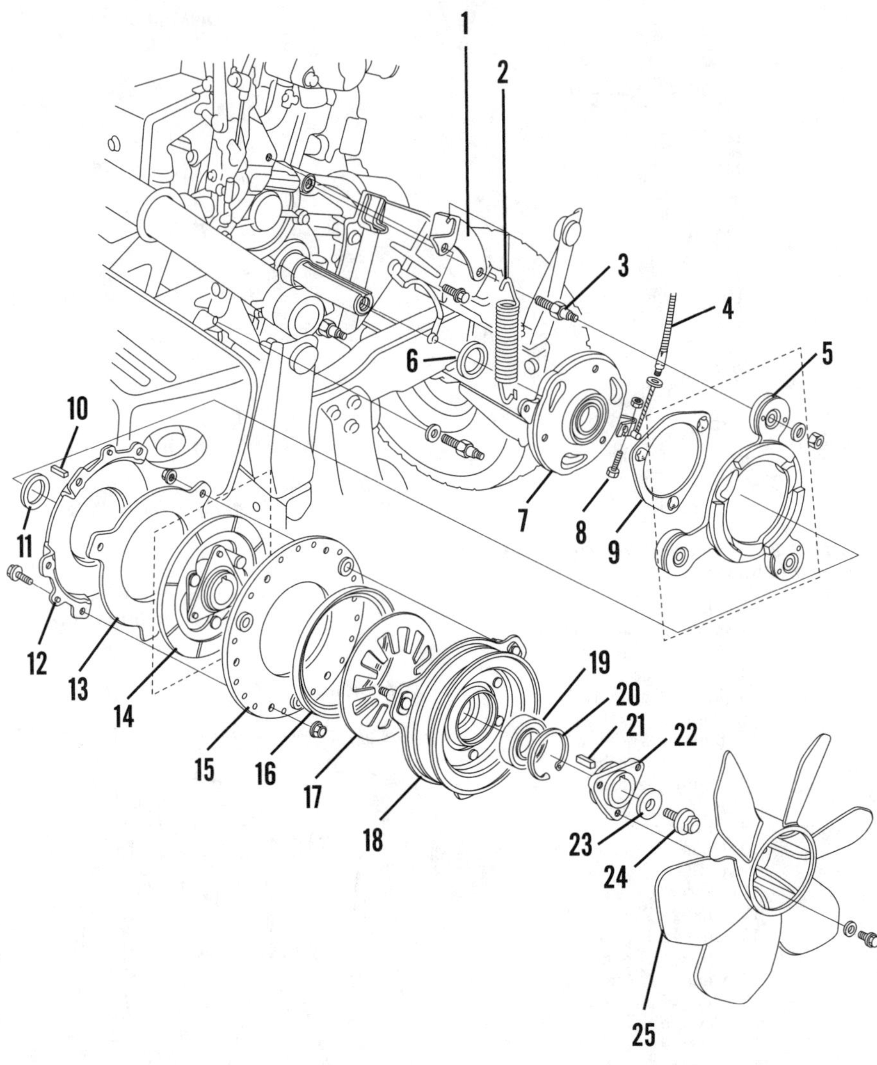

Fig. HN1-26—Exploded view of PTO clutch.

1. Spring bracket
2. Spring
3. Special bolt
4. PTO cable
5. Brake disc
6. Spacer
7. Ball control plate
8. Adjusting bolt
9. Ball retainer
10. Key
11. Shim
12. Clutch cover
13. Side plate
14. Friction disc
15. Clutch plate
16. Spring seat
17. Spring
18. Pulley
19. Bearing
20. Snap ring
21. Key
22. Fan hub
23. Washer
24. Screw
25. Fan

REGULATOR/RECTIFIER

The regulator/rectifier is attached to a bracket on the left side of the engine and can be identified by the fins on the body (Fig. HN1-28).

To test the unit, connect an ohmmeter to the terminals of the regulator/rectifier (Fig. HN1-29) as indicated in the chart in Fig. HN1-30. Replace the regulator/rectifier if the specified values are not obtained.

DIODE

The tractor is equipped with a six-terminal diode in the fuel control circuit. The diode is located below the PTO control lever.

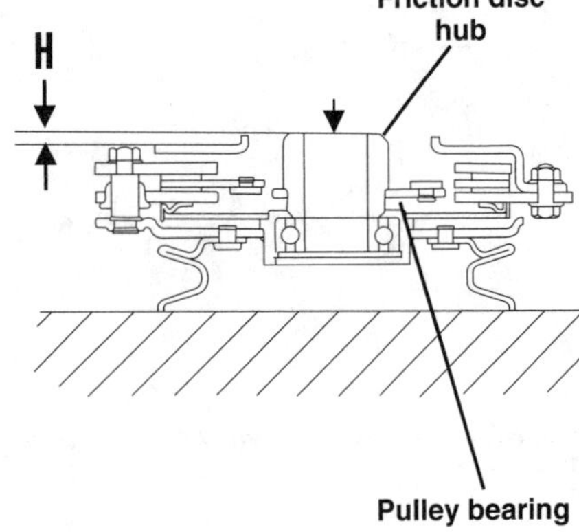

Fig. HN1-27—Measure clutch disc hub height (H) to determine adjusting shim thickness. Refer to text.

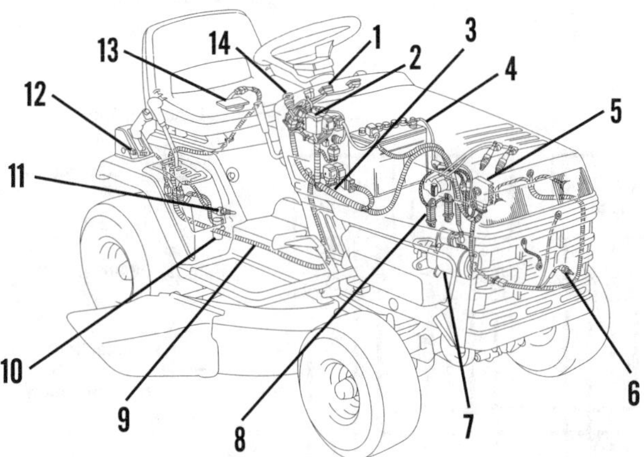

Fig. HN1-28—Drawing showing wiring harness routing.

1. Headlight switch
2. Fuse box
3. Main wire harness
4. Ground cable
5. Regulator/rectifier
6. Thermoswitch
7. Starter motor
8. Charge coil
9. Rear wire harness
10. Fuel pump
11. Neutral switch
12. Parking brake switch
13. Seat switch
14. Combination switch

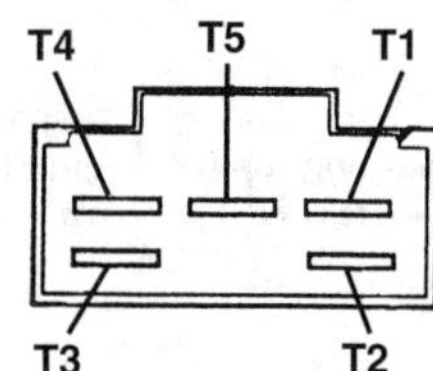

Fig. HN1-29—Connect ohmmeter to regulator/rectifier terminals and refer to regulator/rectifier test procedure in text. Refer to test table (Fig. HN1-30) for test values.

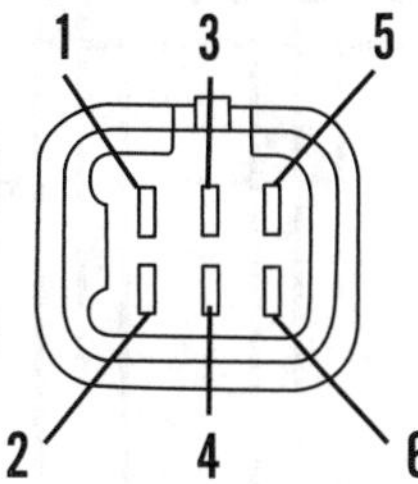

Fig. HN1-31—Connect ohmmeter to diode terminals and refer to diode test procedure in text. Refer to test table (Fig. HN1-32) for test values.

1. Green/Yellow I
2. Green/White
3. Green/Yellow II
4. Green
5. Green/Red
6. White/Black

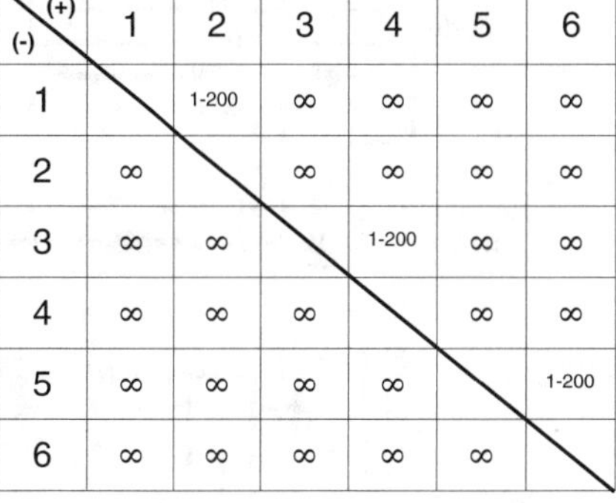

(-) \ (+)	1	2	3	4	5	6
1		1-200	∞	∞	∞	∞
2	∞		∞	∞	∞	∞
3	∞	∞		1-200	∞	∞
4	∞	∞	∞		∞	∞
5	∞	∞	∞	∞		1-200
6	∞	∞	∞	∞	∞	

Fig. HN1-32—Diode test table. Refer to Fig. HN1-31 for terminal identification.

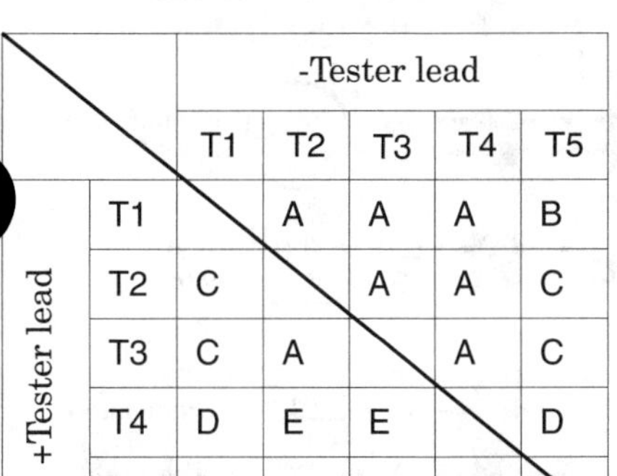

		-Tester lead				
		T1	T2	T3	T4	T5
+Tester lead	T1		A	A	A	B
	T2	C		A	A	C
	T3	C	A		A	C
	T4	D	E	E		D
	T5	B	A	A	A	

Fig. HN1-30—Regulator/rectifier test table. Refer to Fig. HN1-28 for terminal identification.

A. Infinity
B. 0.2k-5k ohms
C. 0.5k-20k ohms
D. 1k-50k ohms
E. 0.5k-10k ohms

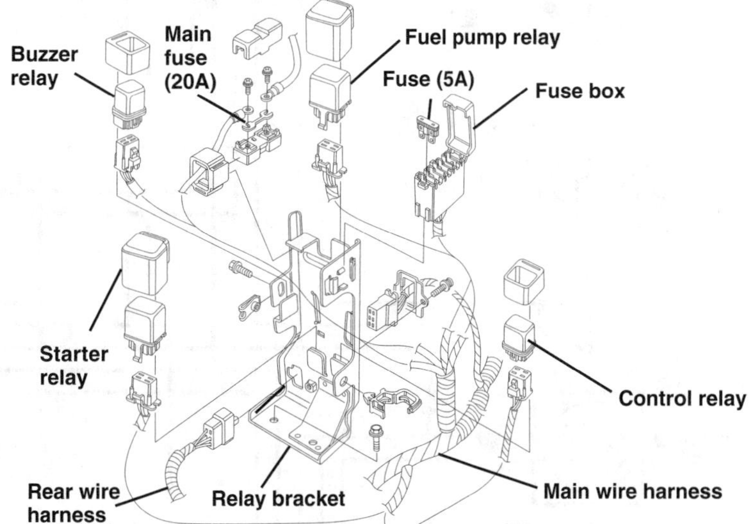

Fig. HN1-33—Electrical system relays are mounted on the relay bracket located next to the battery.

To test the diode, disconnect wire connector from diode and use an ohmmeter set on R×1. Refer to Fig. HN1-31.

In three separate tests, connect the positive ohmmeter lead to terminal 2 and the negative lead to terminal 1, the positive ohmmeter lead to terminal 4 and the negative lead to terminal 3, the positive ohmmeter lead to terminal 6 and the negative lead to terminal 5. In the foregoing tests, the ohmmeter should read 1-200 ohms (Fig. HN1-32).

Connect the ohmmeter to all other terminal combinations. Ohmmeter should read infinity except in the three tests where 1-200 ohms should be found.

FUSES

A 20 amp main fuse (Fig HN1-33) protects the electrical system. Three 5 amp fuses are also used to protect some circuits. The fuses are located on a bracket adjacent to the battery.

WIRING DIAGRAM

The wiring schematic for the tractor is shown in Fig. HN1-34.

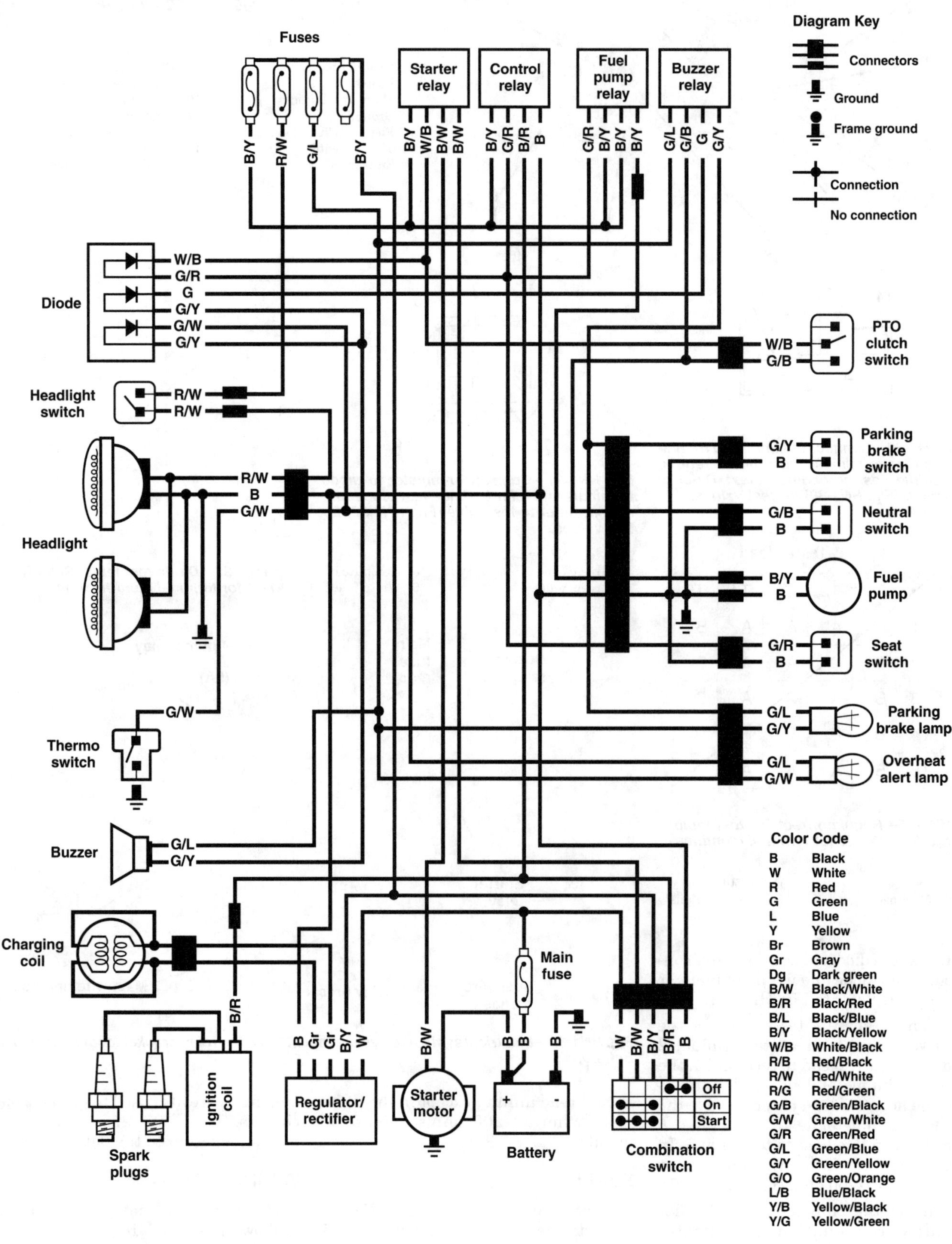

Fig. HN1-34—Wiring schematic.

HONDA

CONDENSED SPECIFICATIONS

Model	H4013
Engine Make	Honda
Model	GXV390
Number of cylinders	1
Bore	88 mm (3.46 in.)
Stroke	64 mm (2.52 in.)
Displacement	389 cc (23.7 cu. in.)
Power Rating	9.7 kW (13 hp.)
Slow Idle	1750 rpm
High Speed (No-Load)	3300 rpm
Crankcase Capacity	1.1 L (1.2 qt.)
Transaxle Capacity	2.6 L (2.8 qt.)

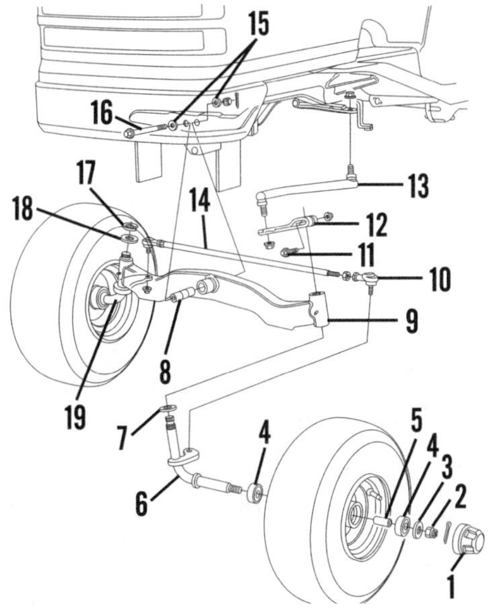

1. Hub cap
2. Nut
3. Washer
4. Bearing
5. Sleeve
6. Spindle (left)
7. Thrust washer
8. Bushing
9. Axle main member
10. Tie rod end
11. Clamp bolt
12. Steering arm
13. Drag link
14. Tie rod
15. Washers
16. Bolt
17. Snap ring
18. Thrust washer
19. Spindle (right)

Fig. HN2-1—Exploded view of front axle assembly.

NOTE: Honda special tools may be required for some procedures and are indicated in the text. Read the text completely before attempting the procedure.

FRONT AXLE AND STEERING SYSTEM

MAINTENANCE

Lubricate the steering spindles annually or after 100 hours of operation. Inject multipurpose grease into the grease fittings at the axle's outer ends. Clean the grease fittings before and after lubrication.

FRONT WHEELS AND BEARINGS

Each front wheel is supported by two sealed ball bearings (4—Fig. HN2-1). A spacer (5) is located between the bearings.

When installing a wheel, note that the washer (3) must be installed so the OUTSIDE marking on the washer is toward the nut. Tighten the retaining nut to 60 N·m (44 ft.-lb.). Secure the nut with a cotter pin.

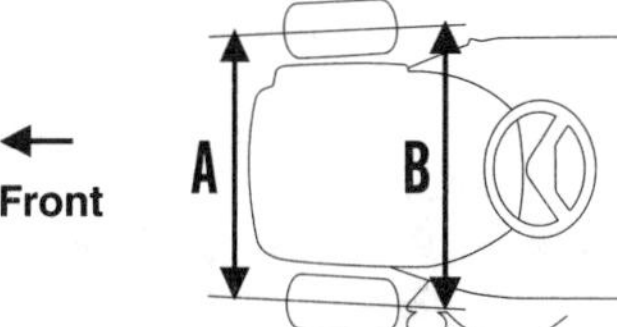

Fig. HN2-2—Set front wheel toe-in so distance "A" is 2-10 mm (0.08-0.40 in.) smaller than distance "B".

TIE ROD AND TOE-IN

The tie rod (14—Fig. HN2-1) is equipped with threaded ends (10). The tie rod's initial length should be 537.2-538.8 mm (21.15-21.21 in.) as measured from the tie rod end studs centerline with the studs perpendicular to the tie rod.

The recommended toe-in is 2-10 mm (0.08-0.40 in.). To check toe-in, set the front wheels straight ahead. Measure the distance between the front and rear of the front wheels (A and B—Fig. HN2-2) at hub height. Subtract measurement A from measurement B to determine toe-in.

To adjust toe-in, loosen the locknut at each rod end (10—Fig. HN2-1) and rotate the tie rod (14) if necessary.

NOTE: Left tie rod end and nut have left-hand threads.

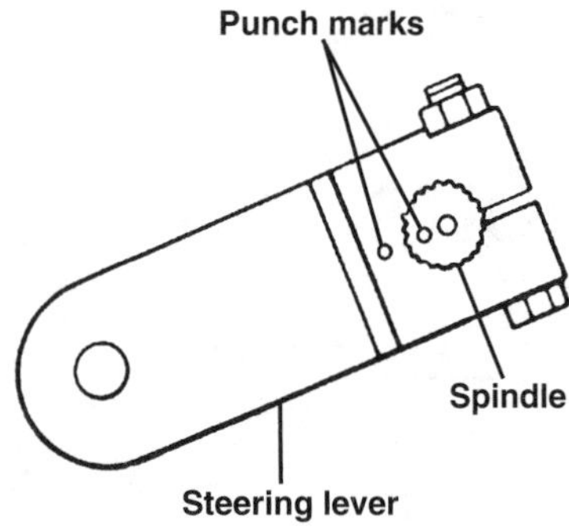

Fig. HN2-3—Align punch marks on steering lever and spindle during assembly. Also align punch marks on steering arm (9—Fig. HN2-4) and sector gear (6) shaft during assembly.

STEERING SPINDLES REMOVAL AND INSTALLATION

To remove steering spindles, raise and support the front of the tractor. Remove the front wheel. Disconnect the tie rod ends (10—Fig. HN2-1) from the spindle.

To remove left spindle (6), remove the clamp bolt (11), then detach the steering arm (12) from the spindle. Slide the spindle out of the axle. Note that a single thrust washer (7) is used at the bottom of the left spindle.

When installing the steering arm, align the punch mark on the spindle end with the punch mark on the steering arm (Fig. HN2-3).

To remove the right spindle, detach the snap ring (17—Fig. HN2-1) and slide the spindle out of the axle. Note that a thrust washer (18) is used at both the top and bottom of the right spindle.

AXLE MAIN MEMBER REMOVAL AND INSTALLATION

The complete front axle assembly may be removed as a unit. To remove the axle main member (9—Fig. HN2-1), raise and support the front of the tractor.

Disconnect the outer end of the drag link (13). Support the main member and remove the axle retaining bolt (16). Lower the complete axle main member from the main frame pivot point and roll the axle out from the under tractor.

When installing the axle main member, tighten the axle retaining bolt to 120 N·m (87 ft.-lb.).

STEERING GEARS

The hood and the engine must be removed for access to the steering gears. Remove the mower deck.

Disconnect the drag link from the steering arm (9—Fig. HN2-4). Remove

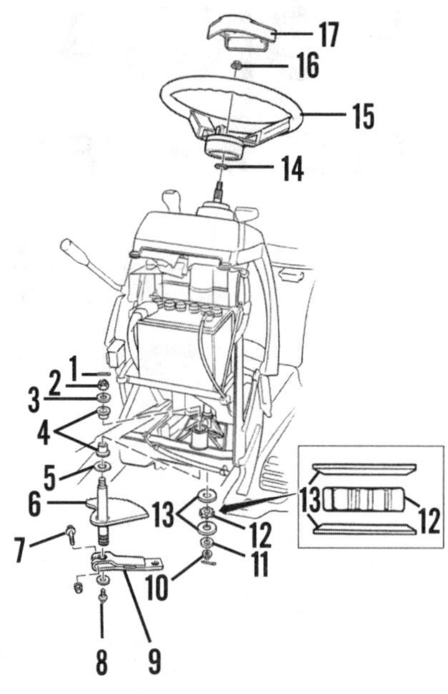

Fig. HN2-4—Exploded view of steering gear assembly.

1. Cotter pin
2. Nut
3. Washer
4. Bushing
5. Washer
6. Sector gear
7. Clamp bolt
8. Screw
9. Steering arm
10. Nut
11. Washer
12. Steering gear
13. Washers
14. Washer
15. Steering wheel
16. Nut
17. Cover

the nut (2) and lower the steering sector gear (6) from the tractor. Remove the clamp bolt (7) and retaining screw (8) and separate the steering arm from the gear shaft.

Unscrew the nut (10) and remove the washers (11 and 13) and steering drive gear (12).

Inspect components for damage and replace when necessary.

When assembling, install the two washers (13) so the convex sides are next to the steering gear (12) as shown in the inset in Fig. HN2-4. Tighten steering drive gear nut (10) to 40 N·m (29 ft.-lb.).

Align the punch mark on the steering arm (9) with the mark on the end of the sector gear shaft (6). Mesh the steering drive gear (12) with the center teeth of the steering sector gear (6). Tighten the sector gear shaft nut (2) to 55 N·m (40 ft.-lb.).

Attach the drag link to the steering arm (9).

STEERING SHAFT

The hood, steering wheel and instrument panel must be removed for access to the steering shaft assembly. Remove steering yoke clamp bolts (8 and 9—Fig. HN2-5) and withdraw upper steering shaft (5) and steering joint (7).

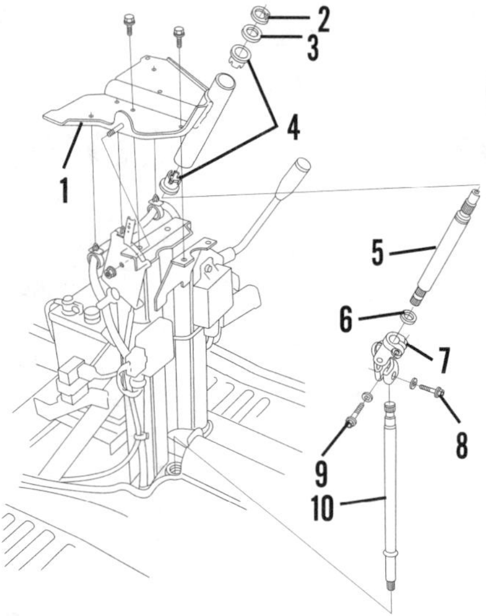

Fig. HN2-5—Exploded view of steering shaft assembly.

1. Steering support
2. Snap ring
3. Washer
4. Bushings
5. Upper steering shaft
6. Washer
7. Steering joint
8. Clamp bolt
9. Clamp bolt
10. Lower steering shaft

The steering drive gear (12—Fig. HN2-4) must be removed prior to removing the lower steering shaft (10—Fig. HN2-5).

Inspect the steering shaft bushings (4) for excessive wear and replace when needed.

When assembling, tighten the universal joint bolts to 22 N·m (16 ft.-lb.). The steering shaft must rotate without binding. If steering shaft binds, loosen the steering support column (1) mounting screws and relocate the support until shaft turns smoothly.

Position the front wheels straight ahead, then install the steering wheel so the two spokes in the steering wheel are centered.

SAFETY INTERLOCK SYSTEM

The tractor is equipped with switches and relays preventing inadvertent starting of the tractor engine or operation if the operator leaves the tractor seat. The tractor engine should not start if the following occurs (engage parking brake):

- Operator in the tractor seat, the shift lever in NEUTRAL and the

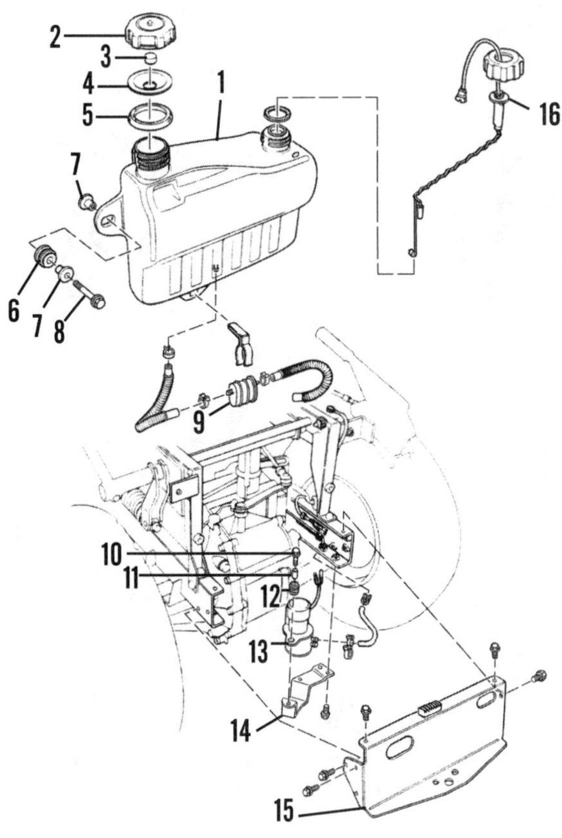

Fig. HN2-6—Remove the seat and rear fender for access to the fuel tank.

1. Fuel tank
2. Cap
3. Breather
4. Packing
5. Seal
6. Rubber bushing
7. Collar
8. Bolt
9. Fuel filter
10. Bolt
11. Collar
12. Rubber bushing
13. Fuel pump
14. Bracket
15. Hitch plate
16. Low fuel sensor

PTO clutch lever in the ON position.

- Operator in the tractor seat, the PTO clutch lever in the OFF position and the shift lever in a position other than NEUTRAL.
- Operator not in the seat when starting the engine.

The seat switch should kill the engine if the operator is not in the seat or leaves the seat when the PTO clutch is engaged or the tractor is in gear.

Refer to the wiring schematics at the end of this section.

TESTING

Use an ohmmeter or battery-powered continuity tester to test the switches for correct operation.

There should be continuity between the wire leads of the PTO clutch switch when the switch is depressed and no continuity when the switch is released.

There should be continuity between the wire leads of the seat switch when the switch is depressed and no continuity when the switch is released.

There should be continuity between the wire terminal on the neutral switch and the tab on the other end of the switch. There should not be continuity between the tab and switch body.

ENGINE

MAINTENANCE

Engine is equipped with a dry air filter that should be cleaned and inspected after every 50 hours of operation.

Remove foam and paper air filter elements from the air filter housing. The foam element should be washed in a mild detergent and water solution, rinsed in clean water and allowed to air dry. When dry, soak the foam element in clean engine oil. Squeeze out excess oil.

The paper element may be cleaned by directing low-pressure compressed air stream from inside the filter toward the outside. Replace the paper element if it cannot be satisfactorily cleaned or if it is damaged. Reinstall the elements.

The engine oil level should be checked prior to operating the engine. Check the oil level with the oil cap not screwed in, but touching the opening.

Oil should be changed after the first 20 hours of engine operation and after every 100 hours thereafter.

Use oil meeting the latest API service classification. Use SAE 10W-30 or 10W-40 oil; use SAE 10W-40 if temperature is above 90°F (32°C).

Crankcase capacity is 1.1 liters (1.16 qt.).

REMOVAL AND INSTALLATION

The engine sits on a removable plate that attaches to the frame. To remove the engine, remove the mower deck, if so equipped. Disconnect the battery cables from the battery.

Remove the hood. Remove the screen from the front of the engine air intake tube, then remove the intake tube.

Detach the clutch cable from the control plate on underside of tractor. Release belt tension by moving the tension pulley to the side, then disengage the belt.

Disconnect the engine charge coil leads, ignition coil lead, starter solenoid connector and engine ground wire. Detach the electric starter lead from the retainer clip.

Drain the engine oil. Disconnect the fuel and vent hoses from the engine. Remove the fuel shutoff solenoid. Detach the throttle cable from the control panel.

Remove the muffler. Remove the lower heat shield under the cylinder. Unscrew the four screws attaching the engine mounting plate to the frame and lift the engine with plate out of the tractor.

Remove the PTO clutch and drive pulley from the engine crankshaft, then unscrew the engine retaining screws and separate the engine from the mounting plate.

Install the engine by reversing the removal procedure. If removed, install the engine pulley so the long end of hub is toward the end of the crankshaft.

Tighten the mounting plate-to-tractor retaining screws to 22 N·m (16 ft.-lb.). Tighten the oil drain plug to 45 N·m (33 ft.-lb.). Adjust the PTO clutch cable.

OVERHAUL

Engine make and model are listed in specifications table at beginning of this section. Refer to the appropriate Honda engine section in this manual for service information on the engine and associated accessories.

FUEL SYSTEM

Also refer to ENGINE and ELECTRICAL SYSTEM for other fuel system related components.

FUEL FILTER MAINTENANCE

A fuel filter (9—Fig. HN2-6) is located in the fuel line between the fuel tank and the fuel pump.

The fuel filter is visible through a hole in the rear hitch plate (14). Inspect the fuel filter annually or after every 100 hours of operation. Replace the filter if it is dirty or damaged.

FUEL TANK REMOVAL AND INSTALLATION

Remove the seat and rear fender for access to the fuel tank (1—Fig. HN2-6). Drain the fuel from the tank.

Disconnect the fuel line from the tank. Disconnect the wire connector from the fuel reserve sensor (16). Remove the tank mounting bolt (8), collars (7) and rubber bushing (6). Remove the tank from the tractor.

Be sure the vent hole in the fuel tank cap (2) is clean.

To install the fuel tank, reverse the removal procedure. If the low-fuel warning sensor (16) was removed, align the projection of the fuel tank with the concave portion of the sensor when installing.

LOW-FUEL WARNING SENSOR

When the fuel level in the fuel tank drops to a certain level, the low-fuel warning sensor closes and turns on the instrument panel's fuel warning lamp. Unscrew the cap on the top right side of the fuel tank for access to the low-fuel warning sensor (16—Fig. HN2-6).

WARNING: Do not use gasoline or a low flash point solvent when testing the sensor.

To test the sensor, remove the sensor and submerge the tip of the sensor in solvent with a high flash point. Connect the negative terminal of a 12-volt battery to the black lead of the sensor cable. Connect a 12v 3.4W lamp to the positive terminal of the battery, then connect the lamp to the green sensor lead.

The test lamp should remain off when the sensor is submerged. When the sensor is lifted out of the solvent, the lamp should light after approximately 30 seconds.

When installing the sensor, align the projection of the fuel tank with the concave portion of the sensor.

FUEL PUMP

The fuel pump (13—Fig. HN2-6) is located on a bracket below the fuel tank.

Testing

Before testing the fuel pump, be sure the fuel filter and fuel line are in good condition and fuel flow to pump is unimpeded.

Connect a pressure gauge to the fuel pump output port. Turn the ignition switch ON, but do not start the engine. Fuel pump pressure should be 6.9-14.2 kPa (1.0-2.0 psi).

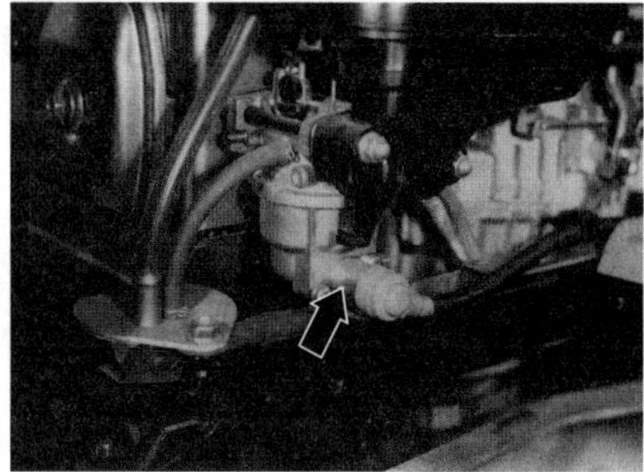

Fig. HN2-7—The carburetor is equipped with a fuel shutoff valve attached to the fuel bowl.

Direct a hose from the pump output port into a container. Fuel pump volume should be at least 350 cc (11.8 oz.) during one minute of operation.

FUEL SHUTOFF VALVE

The carburetor is equipped with a solenoid-operated valve attached to the fuel bowl (Fig. HN2-7).

CAUTION: On tractors with serial numbers prior to 1002969, applying voltage to the valve longer than 15 seconds may damage the solenoid.

To test the fuel shutoff valve, disconnect the control lead and remove the valve from the carburetor. Connect a 12-volt battery to the valve control lead.

On tractors with serial numbers prior to 1002969, the valve pin should extend 3.5 mm (0.14 in.) when battery voltage is applied. On tractors with serial numbers above 1002968, the valve pin should withdraw when battery voltage is applied and extend when voltage is removed.

TRACTION DRIVE BELT

A spring-loaded idler maintains tension on the drive belt between the engine pulley and transaxle pulley (Fig. HN2-8). Tension is not adjustable. If belt slippage occurs and all components are in good operating condition, a new belt must be installed.

REMOVAL AND INSTALLATION

Remove the mower deck, if so equipped. Detach the PTO clutch cable from the control plate on the tractor's underside. Disconnect the drag link from the steering gear lever.

Release belt tension by moving the spring-loaded idler pulley to the side (Fig. HN2-8), then disengage the belt

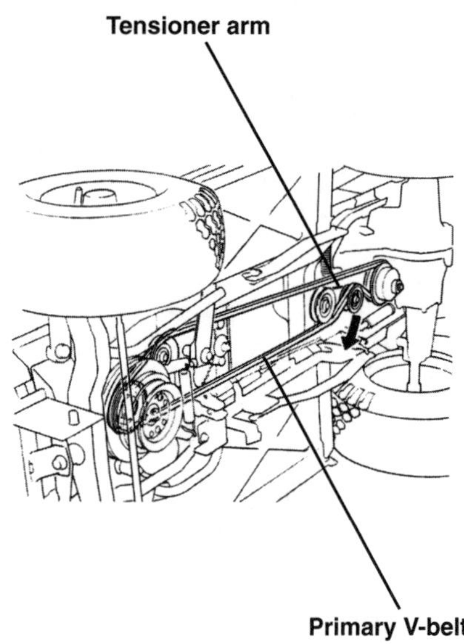

Fig. HN2-8—A spring-loaded idler maintains tension on the traction drive belt. No adjustment is necessary.

from the pulleys. Detach the idler spring. Remove the belt.

Reverse the removal procedure to install the belt. Adjust the PTO clutch cable.

BRAKE

The tractor is equipped with a brake drum located in the transaxle case. The brake drum is mounted on the transaxle countershaft. The brake may be actuated either with the clutch/brake pedal or the parking brake lever. The clutch/brake pedal actuates both the clutch and brake.

When the parking brake lever is engaged, an indicator lamp lights. If the parking brake is engaged when the transaxle is shifted into gear, a warning buzzer sounds. If the parking brake is not disengaged with the transaxle in gear, the engine should stop.

INSPECTION AND ADJUSTMENT

A wear indicator is attached to the brake camshaft (Fig. HN2-9). To determine brake shoe thickness, apply the brake fully and note the brake indicator pointer's position. Replace brake shoes if pointer aligns with or passes the brake housing's triangle wear mark.

To adjust foot brake, place shift lever in NEUTRAL and release parking brake. Measure the brake pedal's (Fig. HN2-10) free play. Specified free play is 6-11 mm (0.24-0.43 in.).

To adjust pedal free play, remove the mower deck for access to the brake linkage. With the brake pedal in the re-

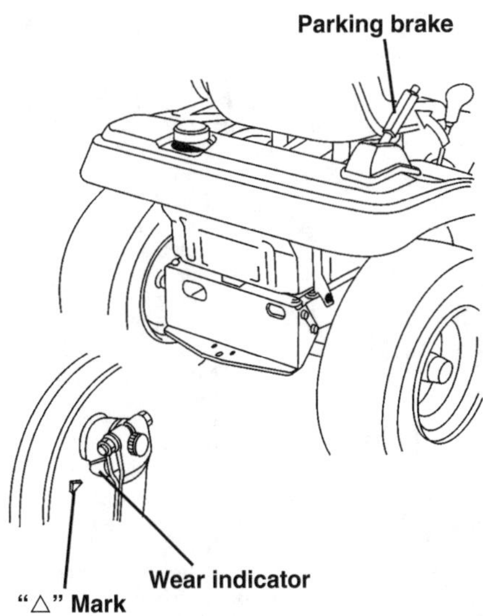

Fig. HN2-9—Replace brake shoes if wear indicator aligns with mark on brake panel. Refer to text.

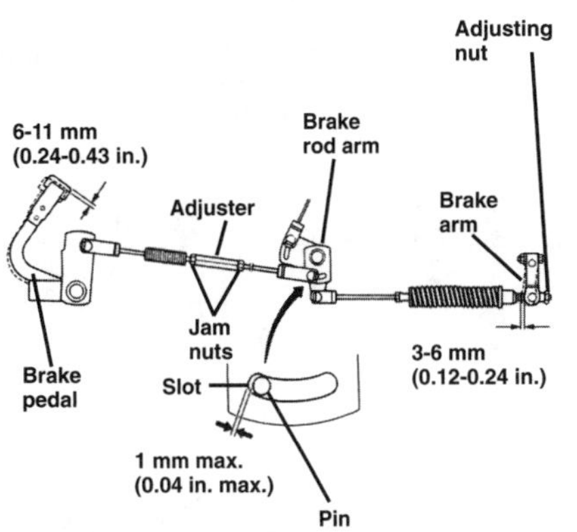

Fig. HN2-10—Drawing of brake operating linkage. Refer to text for adjustment procedure.

leased position, the brake rod arm must contact the frame.

The brake rod clevis pin (Fig. HN2-10) should not contact the end of the slot, but the gap should not exceed 1 mm (0.04 in.). To adjust the location of the pin in the slot, loosen the jam nuts and rotate the adjuster.

NOTE: Front jam nut has left-hand threads.

After adjusting the brake pedal free play, rotate the adjuster nut at the brake arm end of the brake actuating rod so there is 3-6 mm (0.12-0.24 in.) free play at brake lever with the brake disengaged (Fig. HN2-10).

To check or adjust the parking brake lever, position the parking brake lever in the disengaged position then push the brake rod arm (Fig. HN2-10) against the frame. The clevis pin should not contact the end of the slot in

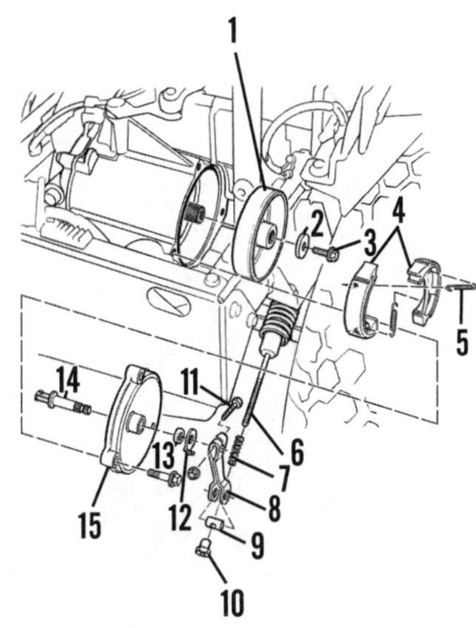

Fig. HN2-11—Exploded view of brake components.

1. Brake drum
2. Washer
3. Cap screw
4. Brake shoes
5. Spring
6. Brake rod
7. Spring
8. Brake arm
9. Sleeve
10. Adjusting nut
11. Clamp bolt
12. Wear indicator
13. Seal
14. Brake cam
15. Brake cover

the brake rod arm, but the gap should not exceed 1 mm (0.04 in.).

To adjust the location of the pin in the slot, rotate nuts at the parking brake lever end of the cable housing. The parking brake lever will emit 2-4 clicks during engagement when it is adjusted properly.

OVERHAUL

The brake assembly is accessible after removing the seat and rear fender and the fuel tank. Support the rear of the tractor and remove the right rear wheel.

Remove the brake rod adjusting nut (10—Fig. HN2-11) and detach the brake actuating rod (6) from the rear brake arm (8). Remove the three bolts attaching the brake housing (15) to the transmission and withdraw the housing.

Remove the brake arm clamp bolt (11), and remove the brake arm (8), wear indicator (12) and seal (13). Remove the brake shoes (4), springs (5) and brake cam (14). Remove the cap screw (3) and pull the brake drum (1) off the transaxle shaft.

Maximum allowable brake drum inner diameter is 96.5 mm (3.80 in.). With brake shoes installed on the brake housing, the minimum outer diameter of brake shoe linings is 93.0 mm (3.66 in.).

During assembly, apply a light coating of grease to the shaft and cam surface of the brake cam. Do not allow grease on the brake lining surfaces. Install the brake lever (8—Fig. HN2-11) on the brake cam shaft so the punch marks are aligned.

Apply a light coating of grease to the transaxle countershaft splines. Install the brake drum (1) and tighten the cap screw (3) to 22 N·m (16 ft.-lb.).

Install the rear wheel outer washer so the OUTSIDE lettering on the washer faces out. Tighten the rear wheel retaining nut to 60 N·m (44 ft.-lb.).

Adjust the brake as previously outlined.

CLUTCH

The clutch is a multiple-disc type actuated by linkage connected to the clutch/brake pedal. The clutch is disengaged when the brake is applied. An internal hydraulic cylinder (damper) attached to the clutch arm regulates clutch engagement speed.

ADJUSTMENT

Unscrew the brake adjusting nut (10—Fig. HN2-11) until the brake rod is loose in the brake lever. With the shift lever in second gear, measure clutch/brake pedal free play. Free play should be 15-25 mm (0.59-0.98 in.).

To adjust the pedal free play, rotate the nuts at the end of the clutch cable. Readjust the brake.

To determine if the clutch damper is functioning properly, position the shift lever in fifth gear with the engine running but the tractor stationary. Release the clutch/brake pedal and measure the elapsed time from clutch pedal release to tractor movement. Time lapse should be ½ second.

The clutch damper adjusting screw can be accessed through the inspection hole located beneath the operator's seat. To adjust the clutch damper, loosen the locknut (N—Fig. HN2-12) and rotate the adjusting screw (S). Rotating the screw clockwise increases engagement time while rotating the screw counterclockwise decreases engagement time. Retighten the locknut.

OVERHAUL

Remove the transaxle from the tractor as outlined in the TRANSAXLE section. Remove the belt pulley from the transaxle input shaft.

When unscrewing the retaining screws for the clutch cover, note the different lengths and location of the screws. Detach the clutch cover (1—Fig. HN2-13). Remove the push rod (10) and shim (11). Loosen the bearing

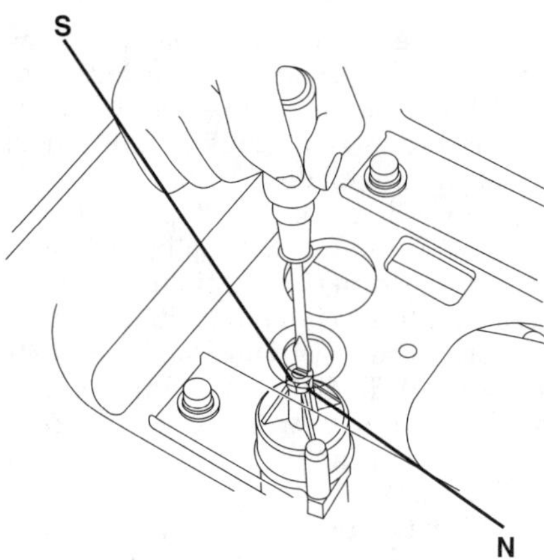

Fig. HN2-12—To adjust clutch damper, loosen locknut (N) and rotate stud (S). See text.

plate retaining screws (13) evenly in a crossing pattern and remove the plate (14) and springs (15).

Secure the clutch hub (18—Fig. HN2-13) with Honda tool 07HGB-001000A and unscrew the center nut (16) using Honda tool 07716-0020100 (Fig. HN2-14).

Clutch components (18-26—Fig. HN2-13) can now be removed from the clutch drum (27).

NOTE: The transaxle input shaft prevents removal of clutch drum (27). If it is necessary to remove the clutch drum, refer to the TRANSAXLE section for input shaft removal procedure.

To disassemble the clutch cover, remove the bolt (2—Fig. HN2-15) and withdraw the clutch shaft (5) from damper arm (1). Remove and discard the oil seal (4). Install the new seal with the seal lip's open side facing inward.

Stack all friction plates (23—Fig. HN2-13) and metal plates (24), plus the metal plate (21), together. Measure the thickness of the stack. Minimum total stack thickness is 21.2 mm (0.83 in.). Replace plates when needed.

Place the metal plates on a flat surface and check each plate for distortion using a feeler gauge. Replace metal plates if warped more than 0.10 mm (0.004 in.).

Inspect the clutch hub (18—Fig. HN2-13) for grooves or abnormal wear from the clutch plates and replace if necessary. A worn or damaged clutch hub can cause transmission noise.

The standard length of clutch springs (15) is 34.4 mm (1.35 in.) with a minimum allowable length of 33.4 mm (1.31 in.). Replace the springs as a set if any fail to meet the minimum length.

To check hydraulic damper (5—Fig HN2-13), position the damper with the stud end down. Apply 3.5 kg (7.7 lb.) force against the flanged end of damper and note the amount of time required to compress the damper. The damper should compress 5.5 mm (0.22 in.) within the specified time of 2.7-4.0 seconds. If otherwise, replace the damper.

Fig. HN2-13—Exploded view of clutch. Transaxle input shaft and gear must be removed before clutch drum and gear (27) can be removed.

1. Clutch cover
2. Gasket
3. Dowel pins
4. Clutch assy.
5. Damper
6. O-ring
7. Gasket
8. Damper housing
9. Nut
10. Push rod
11. Washer
12. Bearing
13. Cap screw
14. Bearing plate
15. Springs
16. Nut
17. Belleville washer
18. Clutch hub
19. Spring seat
20. Anti-chatter spring
21. Metal plate (1.2 mm)
22. Snap ring
23. Composition plates
24. Metal plates (1.4 mm)
25. Pressure plate
26. Washer
27. Clutch drum and gear
28. Sleeve
29. Shim

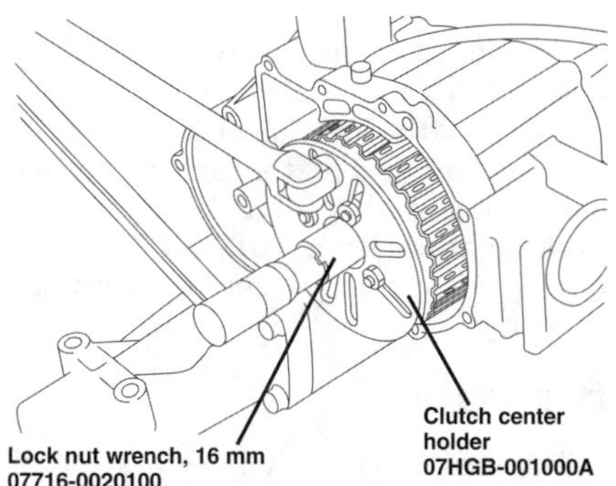

Fig. HN2-14—Special tools are used to remove and install the clutch.

If the clutch drum (27—Fig. HN2-13) has been removed, check the following: Specified inside diameter of the clutch drum hub is 26.020-26.041 mm (1.0244-1.0252 in.). Specified inside diameter of the sleeve (28) is 20.000-20.035 mm (0.7874-0.7888 in.) and outside diameter is 25.959-25.980 mm (1.0220-1.0228 in.). Specified outer diameter of the transaxle mainshaft at the mainshaft collar contact area is 19.980-19.993 mm (0.7866-0.7871 in.).

Reverse the disassembly procedure to assemble the clutch while noting the following:

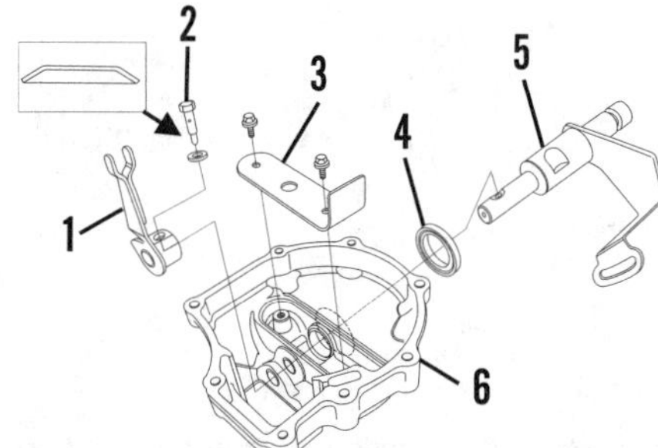

Fig. HN2-15—Exploded view of clutch cover.

1. Damper arm
2. Shoulder bolt
3. Oil guide
4. Oil seal
5. Damper shaft
6. Clutch cover

If removed, reinstall the mainshaft shim (29—Fig. HN2-13) so the stepped side is toward the inside of the transaxle. If the clutch drum and ring gear assembly (27) is replaced, check the input gear backlash and mesh position as outlined in the TRANSAXLE section.

Nominal thickness of each of the five metal plates (24) is 1.4 mm (0.055 in.). Nominal metal plate (21) thickness is 1.2 mm (0.047 in.).

Install an antichatter spring (20) with the tapered surface facing the spring seat (19) as shown in Fig. HN2-13.

Install a Belleville washer (17—Fig. HN2-13) so the OUTSIDE stamped on the washer faces away from the clutch hub (18). Install the locknut (16) so the chamfered side is toward the clutch as

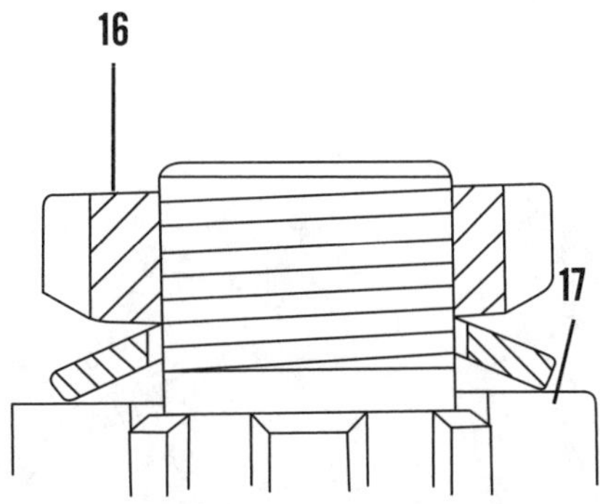

Fig. HN2-16—Install Belleville washer (17) so "OUTSIDE" stamped on face of washer faces away from clutch hub. Install clutch nut (16) so chamfered side is toward clutch assembly.

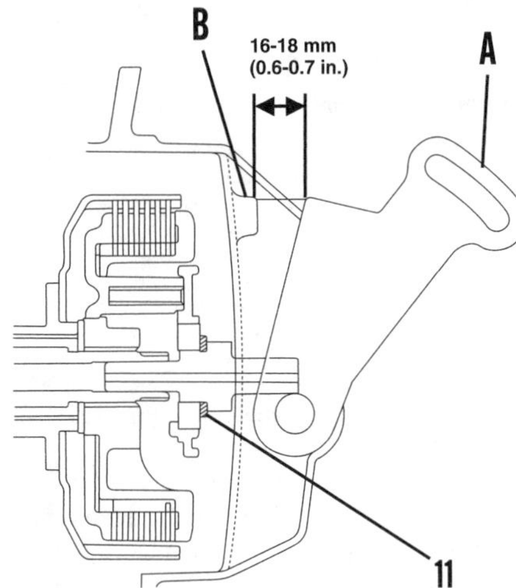

Fig. HN2-17—Select shim (11) thickness so gap between clutch damper arm (A) and boss (B) on clutch cover is 16-18 mm (0.6-0.7 in.).

shown in Fig. HN2-16. Tighten the nut to 60 N·m (44 ft.-lb.).

Tighten the bearing plate retaining screws (13—Fig. HN2-13) in a crossing pattern in three steps to a final torque of 10 N·m (88 in.-lb.).

If removed, assemble the clutch actuating arm (5—Fig. HN2-15) to the damper arm (1). Make sure the conical spring washer is positioned as shown. Be sure the damper arm engages the groove on the lower end of the clutch damper (5—Fig. HN2-13) when installing the cover. Be sure the clutch cover bolts are installed in the correct location according to their length. Tighten the bolts to 10 N·m (7.2 ft.-lb.)

After assembly, determine the appropriate thickness of the clutch lifter rod shim (11—Fig. HN2-13) as follows: With the clutch actuating arm (A—Fig. HN2-17) in outermost position, measure the distance from the arm to boss (B) on the clutch cover. Distance should be 16-18 mm (0.6-0.7 in.).

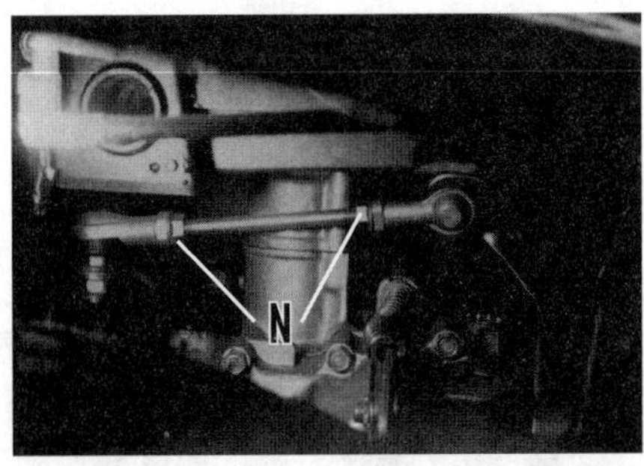

Fig. HN2-18—Adjust length of shift rod by loosening jam nuts (N) and rotating rod. Note that rear rod end marked "L" and adjacent jam nut have left-hand threads.

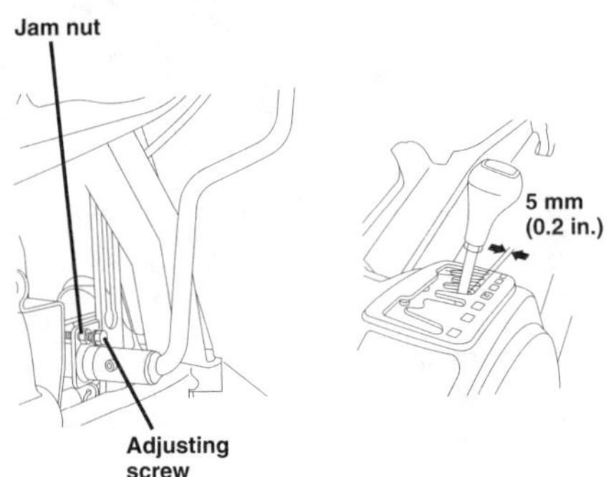

Fig. HN2-19—Loosen jam nut and rotate adjustment screw to adjust shift lever free play.

To adjust, remove the clutch cover (1—Fig. HN2-13), lifter rod (10) and shim (11). Reduce the thickness of shim (11) if the clearance is larger than specified distance. Install a thicker shim if clearance is less than specification. Note that changing the shim thickness 0.2 mm (0.008 in.) changes the clearance approximately 1.2 mm (0.047 in.).

If a new damper (5—Fig. HN2-13) was installed or the damper stud was rotated, rotate the stud until the distance from the top of the stud to the boss on the damper housing (8) is 20 mm (0.8 in.). Tighten the jam nut (9).

After transaxle installation, perform clutch and damper adjustments previously outlined.

SHIFT CONTROL LINKAGE ADJUSTMENT

The operator gear shift lever and transaxle gear selector arm must be synchronized for proper gear selection.

Shift the transmission into second gear and check that the shift lever is centered in the shift guide slot. If not, loosen the jam nuts (N—Fig. HN2-18) on the rod and rotate the rod end to adjust the length of the rod.

NOTE: Rear jam nut has left-hand threads.

Check gear selection in all gears. The shift lever should move smoothly into each shift position.

With the gear selector in the second gear slot of the gear indicator panel, there should be 0.5 mm (0.2 in.) between the selector shaft and the end of the slot. Loosen jam nut and rotate the adjustment screw (Fig. HN2-19) to adjust the gap. Retighten the jam nut.

TRANSAXLE

The tractor is equipped with a five-speed transaxle. The transaxle also provides a reverse gear.

A brake drum is attached to the transaxle mainshaft and is located in a compartment on the right side of the transaxle. A multiple plate clutch is also located on the right side of the transaxle.

Refer to previous sections for service information on the brake and clutch assemblies.

LUBRICATION

Transaxle oil level should be checked annually or after every 100 hours of operation. Be sure the tractor is on level surface when checking the oil level.

To check the oil level, remove the oil filler cap located at the rear of the transaxle. Oil should be level with the bottom edge of the filler cap opening.

Oil capacity is 2.6 liters (2.7 qt.). Recommended oil is SAE 10W-30 engine oil.

REMOVAL AND INSTALLATION

Remove mower deck, if so equipped. Remove the cover for the parking brake lever on the rear fender. Remove the cover for the mower height adjusting lever on the rear fender. Remove the fuel tank cap. Remove the shift lever knob. Raise seat and disconnect the seat switch wire connector. Unscrew the rear fender retaining bolts and lift off the rear fender and seat assembly.

Release the drive belt tension by moving the spring-loaded idler pulley to the side, then disengage the belt from the transaxle pulley. Disconnect the wires from the transaxle. Detach the clutch cable from the clutch actuating arm on the transaxle.

Detach the lower end of each mower deck lift strut, then disconnect the upper end of struts from the mower deck height levers.

Disconnect rear ball joint of shift rod from shift lever on the transaxle (Fig. HN2-20). Detach the spring from the shift mechanism. Unscrew the special bolt from the bottom of the shift bellcrank, and slide the bellcrank off

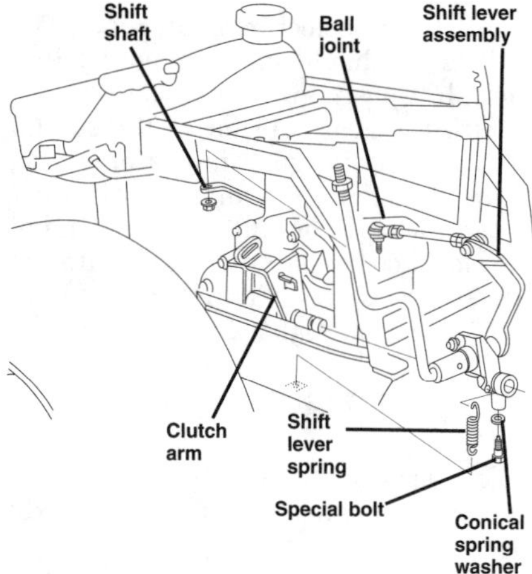

Fig. HN2-20—Drawing of shift linkage.

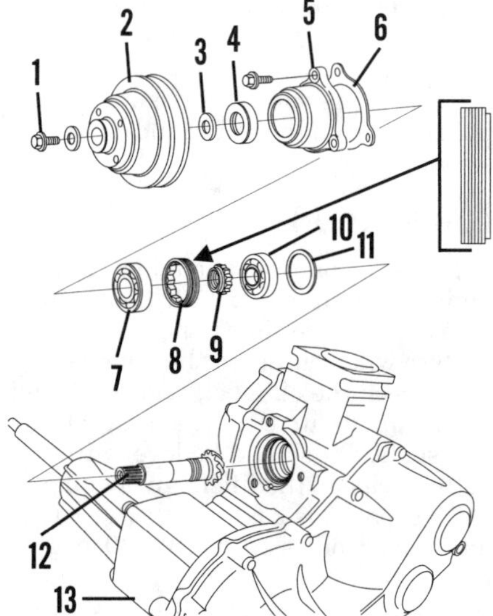

Fig. HN2-21—Exploded view of transaxle input shaft assembly.

1. Screw
2. Pulley
3. Washer
4. Oil seal
5. Bearing housing
6. Gasket
7. Bearing
8. Nut
9. Nut
10. Bearing
11. Shim
12. Input shaft
13. Transaxle housing

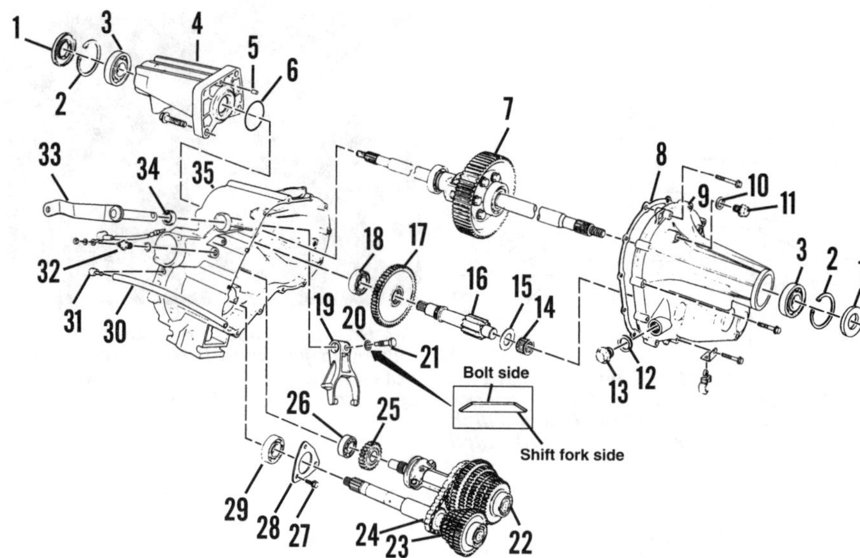

Fig. HN2-22—Exploded view of transaxle. Also refer to Figs. HN2-21 and HN2-23.

1. Oil seal
2. Snap ring
3. Bearing
4. Axle housing
5. Dowel pin
6. O-ring
7. Differential and axles
8. Gasket
9. Transaxle case half
10. Washer
11. Drain plug
12. Gasket
13. Fill plug
14. Roller bearing
15. Thrust washer
16. Countershaft
17. Countershaft driven gear
18. Ball bearing
19. Shift fork
20. Belleville washer
21. Setscrew
22. Change shaft
23. Mainshaft
24. Reverse chain
25. Countershaft drive gear
26. Ball bearing
27. Cap screw
28. Bearing retainer plate
29. Ball bearing
30. Breather tube
31. Breather joint
32. Neutral switch
33. Shift arm
34. Oil seal
35. Transaxle case half

the clutch actuating arm. Remove the shift control mechanism.

Block the front wheels. Raise and support the rear of the tractor. Remove the rear wheels.

Remove the brake rod adjusting nut (10—Fig. HN2-11) and detach the brake rod (6) from the brake lever (8).

Position a jack under the transaxle. Remove the two screws and retainer plate from the front of the transaxle. Unscrew two retaining screws for each axle housing. Carefully lower the transaxle to prevent damage to the fuel tank, then remove the transaxle.

Reinstall the transaxle by reversing the removal procedure while noting the following: Install all transaxle mounting bolts before final tightening.

Install the rear wheel outer washer so the OUTSIDE on the washer faces out. Tighten the rear wheel retaining nut to 60 N·m (44 ft.-lb.).

Install the Belleville washer on the shift bellcrank retaining screw so the concave side is toward the bellcrank (Fig. HN2-20). Tighten the bellcrank retaining screw to 22 N·m (16 ft.-lb.). Install the mower deck lift struts so the "OUTSIDE" mark on the strut faces outward.

Adjust the brake as previously outlined. Adjust the clutch cable as previously outlined.

OVERHAUL

To disassemble the transaxle, remove the brake and clutch assemblies as previously outlined. Clutch drum and bevel gear assembly (27—Fig. HN2-13) must remain in the housing until the input shaft is removed.

Unscrew the retaining screw (1—Fig. HN2-21) and remove the transmission pulley (2). Remove the cap screws attaching the input shaft bearing housing (5) to the transaxle housing and remove the bearing housing. Using Honda tool 07916-7500000 with attachment 07FPA-7510110, unscrew the locknut (8) and remove the input shaft (12).

If the bearing (10) must be removed, clamp the input shaft in a soft-jawed vise. Unstake the nut (9) and use Honda tool 07916-7500000 to unscrew the nut. The old nut should be discarded. Use a press and suitable tools to remove the bearings from the input shaft and bearing housing.

When unscrewing the retaining screws for transaxle case halves note the different lengths and location of the screws. Separate the transaxle case halves. Remove the differential and axles (7—Fig. HN2-22). Pry out the oil seals (1). Remove the snap rings (2) and press the bearings (3) out of the axle housings.

Remove the countershaft (16) and countershaft driven gear (17). Lift out the change shaft (22) and mainshaft (23) as an assembly. Remove the reverse chain (24). Separate the bearings, washers and gears from the mainshaft and change shaft (Fig. HN2-23). Do not lose the spring-loaded shift detent ball (4) when separating the gear selector (1) from the change shaft (2).

Remove the setscrew (21—Fig. HN2-22) and withdraw the shift shaft (33) and shift arm (19). Pry the seal (34) from the case.

Inspect all components for wear or damage and replace when necessary. Replace all O-rings, gaskets and seals.

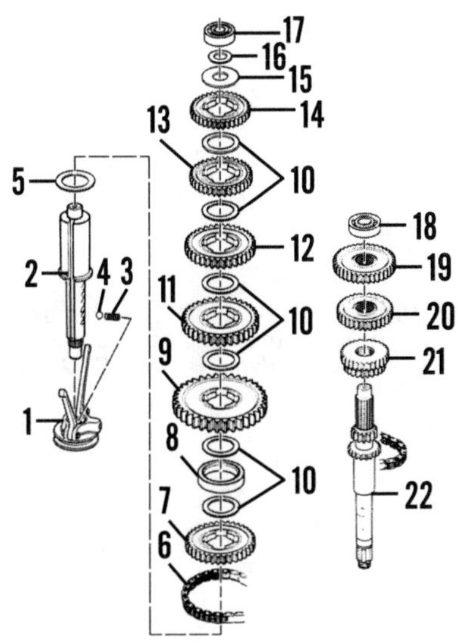

Fig. HN2-23—Exploded view of mainshaft and change shaft assemblies.

1. Gear selector
2. Change shaft
3. Washer (1 mm)
4. Spring
5. Detent ball
6. Reverse chain
7. Reverse sprocket (41T)
8. Neutral positioner
9. Change 1st gear (59T)
10. Washers (2 mm)
11. Change 2nd gear (50T)
12. Change 3rd gear (43T)
13. Change 4th gear (39T)
14. Change 5th gear (36T)
15. Thrust washer
16. Thrust washer
17. Ball bearing
18. Ball bearing
19. Mainshaft 5th gear (37T)
20. Mainshaft 4th gear (37T)
21. Mainshaft 2nd and 3rd gears (30/23T)
22. Mainshaft and 1st gear

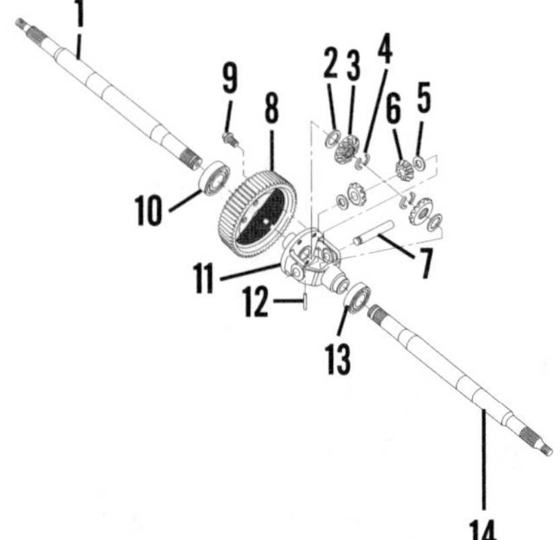

Fig. HN2-24—Exploded view of differential and axles.

1. Left axle shaft
2. Thrust washer
3. Side gear
4. Retainers
5. Thrust washer
6. Pinion gear
7. Pinion shaft
8. Final drive gear
9. Cap screw
10. Ball bearing
11. Differential case
12. Spring pin
13. Ball bearing
14. Right axle shaft

To reassemble transaxle, reverse the disassemble procedure and note the following:

Tighten bearing retainer (28—Fig. HN2-22) screws (27) to 12 N·m (106 in.-lb.). Install the shift fork (19) and shaft (33), being careful not to damage the oil seal (34) lip. Install Belleville washer (20) so the cup side is toward the shift fork (19). Tighten the shift fork retaining screw (25) to 30 N·m (22 ft.-lb.).

Install the spring (3—Fig. HN2-23) and detent ball (4) in the gear selector (1), then push the selector onto the change shaft (2) so the detent ball engages the second notch on the shaft.

Install components (5 through 14—Fig. HN2-23) onto the change shaft (2) so the stepped side of the shift lugs on the gears are toward the transaxle's left side. Note that washers are either 2 mm (0.080 in.) thick (10) or 1 mm (0.039 in.) thick (5).

Assemble the gears on the mainshaft (22). Install the reverses chain (6) on the change shaft and mainshaft assembly. Install the change shaft and mainshaft as an assembly into the transaxle case (Fig. HN2-22). Be sure that the shift fork (19—Fig. HN2-22) properly engages the change gear selector.

Wrap the axle spline with tape to prevent damage to the oil seals (1—Fig. HN2-22) when assembling the case halves. Tighten the case retaining screws to 10 N·m (88 in.-lb.).

NOTE: If transaxle case (13—Fig. HN2-21) or input shaft components (5 through 12—Fig. HN2-14) were replaced, or if the clutch drum (27—Fig. HN2-13) or shim (29) were replaced, refer to following section for the shimming procedure.

If input shaft shimming is not required, install the clutch components before installing the input shaft assembly. Clamp the input shaft (12—Fig. HN2-21) in a soft-jawed vise, and tighten the input shaft nut (9) to 75 N·m (55 ft.-lb.). Stake the nut to the shaft at the notch on shaft. Install the nut (8) with stepped face toward the gear and tighten to 90 N·m (66 ft.-lb.). Tighten the input shaft bearing housing (5) retaining screws to 22 N·m (195 in.-lb.).

Gear Shimming Procedure

Input shaft gear and clutch bevel gear contact pattern and the backlash must be checked if the transaxle case (13—Fig. HN2-21) or input shaft components (5-12) were replaced, or if clutch drum (27—Fig. HN2-13) or shim (29) were replaced.

After the transaxle has been assembled with original shims, but before the clutch is installed, coat the input gear (12—Fig. HN2-21) with Prussian Blue. Install the clutch components but do not install the clutch cover.

Install the input shaft components (8 through 12—Fig. HN2-21). Tighten the input shaft bearing nut (9) to 75 N·m (55 ft.-lb.)—DO NOT stake the nut to the shaft. Install the nut (8) with the stepped face toward the gear and tighten to 90 N·m (66 ft.-lb.).

Rotate the input shaft in the normal direction. Remove the input shaft and check contact pattern on the input gear teeth. Contact area should be centered on the tooth surface.

If the contact area is toward the outer edge of tooth, install a thinner shim (11—Fig. HN2-21). If contact area is toward base of tooth, install a thicker shim (11). If a proper contact area is not obtainable by shimming input shaft, change shim thickness (29—Fig. HN2-13) and repeat the procedure.

Check gear backlash by measuring the movement of clutch drum (27—Fig. HN2-13). Position a dial indicator on the clutch drum's outer diameter. Hold the input shaft to prevent it from turning. Push in against the clutch drum and rotate clutch drum back and forth while observing the dial indicator reading.

Backlash should be 0.12-0.20 mm (0.005-0.008 in.). If backlash is insufficient, decrease shim thickness (29). If backlash is excessive, increase shim thickness (29).

Complete assembly as previously outlined, while being sure to stake nut to the input shaft at the notch on the shaft.

DIFFERENTIAL OVERHAUL

To remove the differential, remove the transaxle from the tractor as outlined in the TRANSAXLE section. Separate the left case half (9—Fig. HN2-22) from the right case half (35). Remove the differential (7) and axles from the transaxle case.

Drive the spring pin (12—Fig. HN2-24) out of the differential case (11). Push the pinion shaft (7) out of the case. Remove the retainers (4) from axle shafts. Remove the pinion gears (6), side gears (3) and washers.

Pull the bearings (10 and 13) off the differential case. Remove the bolts (9) and separate the final drive gear (8) from the case.

Inspect all components for wear or damage and replace when necessary. Minor scuff marks can be removed from the pinion shaft (7) using fine emery paper.

If the final drive gear was removed, install the gear and tighten the retaining bolts (9) to 55 N·m (40 ft.-lb.). Install the axle shafts, side gears, pinion gears and washers. Select washers (5) of a thickness permitting smooth axle rotation without excessive play. Both washers (5) must be equal thickness.

Install the retainers (4) on the axle before inserting the pinion shaft (7). Drive in the split pin (12) so the split in the pin is facing away from the pinion shaft.

Install the axles and differential assembly in the transaxle case as outlined in the TRANSAXLE section.

PTO CLUTCH

A cable-actuated cone clutch is attached to the end of the engine crankshaft. A switch prevents engine starting if the PTO operating lever is in the engaged position.

ADJUSTMENT

The PTO operating lever free play should be 1-3 mm (0.04-0.12 in.). To adjust free play, raise the hood and rotate the adjusting nuts (N—Fig. HN2-25) at the end of the cable housing. Tighten the nuts and recheck free play.

Move the PTO clutch lever to the engaged position and measure the gap (G—Fig. HN2-26) between the PTO clutch brake plate (B) and the driven disc flange (F) with a feeler gauge. If the gap is less than 0.6 mm (0.024 in.), readjust lever free play. If the gap is less than 0.1 mm (0.004 in.), replace the driven disc.

OVERHAUL

Before removing the PTO clutch, disconnect the negative battery cable. Remove the mower deck. Remove the drive belt (19—Fig. HN2-27) as previously outlined. Detach spring (11). Unscrew retaining screw (1), and remove the driven disc pulley (4) and drive plate (6). Unscrew the flange nuts (7) and remove the brake plate (8), ball retainer (9) and ball control plate (13). Remove the clevis pin (12) and base plate (16).

Replace excessively worn or damaged components. Check the wear surfaces on flange and cone of driven pulley (4). Replace the driven pulley if the clutch material on the flange (F—Fig. HN2-26) is worn to the flange surface. Measure worn and unworn portions of clutch material on the cone surface (C) of driven pulley. Replace the driven pulley if the wear material on the cone surface has worn more than 1.0 mm (0.04 in.).

Reassemble by reversing the disassembly procedure while observing the following special instructions:

Hole in base plate (16—Fig. HN2-27) must index on the pin of the engine mounting plate. Be sure to install the retaining clip (12). Before attaching the return spring (11), rotate the control plate (13) clockwise and measure gap

Fig. HN2-25—Adjust PTO clutch lever free play by rotating nuts (N) on clutch cable.

between the stop on the control plate and the face of the adjusting screw. Rotate the screw so the gap is 14-16 mm (0.55-0.63 in.), then tighten jam nut.

After installation, check adjustment as previously outlined.

If the PTO clutch operating lever and clutch lever are separated, install the arm on the clutch lever shaft so the punch marks on the shaft end and arm are aligned.

ELECTRICAL SYSTEM

Engine related electrical components, such as the starter, are covered in the appropriate Honda engine section at the rear of this manual.

BATTERY

The tractor is equipped with a 12-volt 30 amp-hour battery. Standard battery is Yusa NX60-N24T(S).

FUSES

The electrical system is protected by a 20 amp main fuse. On early models, three 5 amp fuses are also used to protect some circuits. On later models, one 5 amp fuse is used in addition to the 20 amp main fuse. Refer to the appropriate wiring schematic.

On early models, the 20 amp main fuse holder is incorporated in the positive battery terminal connector. The three 5 amp fuses are located in a fuse holder beneath the PTO clutch lever.

On later models, the 20 amp main fuse and 5 amp auxiliary fuse are located in a fuse holder beneath the PTO clutch lever.

REGULATOR/RECTIFIER

The regulator/rectifier is located to the left of the steering shaft joint and can be identified by the fins on the body.

To test the unit, connect an ohmmeter to the terminals of the regulator/rectifier identified in Fig. HN2-28 and

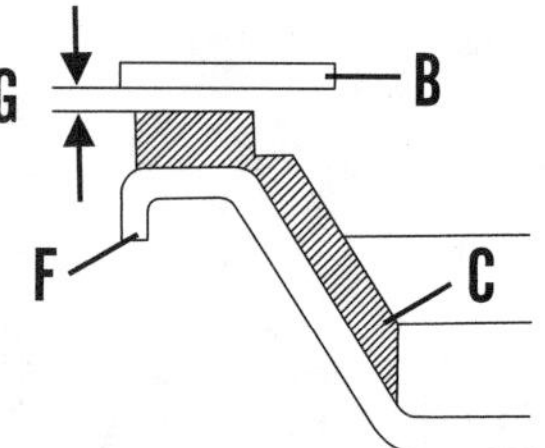

Fig. HN2-26—To check PTO clutch adjustment, engage clutch and measure gap (G) between brake plate (B) and PTO driven disc flange (F). See text.

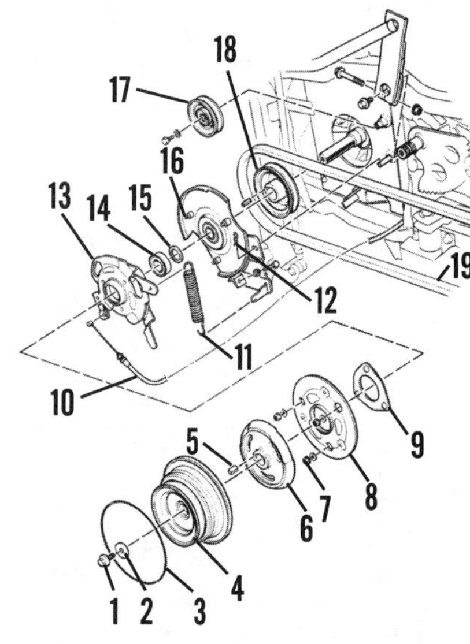

Fig. HN2-27—Exploded view of PTO clutch.

1. Screw
2. Washer
3. Ring
4. Pulley
5. Key
6. Drive plate
7. Nut
8. Brake plate
9. Ball retainer
10. PTO cable
11. Return spring
12. Clevis pin
13. Control plate
14. Bearing
15. Thrust washer
16. Base plate
17. Tensioner pulley
18. Engine pulley
19. Belt

refer to the chart in Fig. HN2-29 or HN2-30.

COMBINATION RELAY

The combination relay is located behind the instrument panel to the right of the steering shaft. The combination relay routes battery voltage to several components.

Refer to the following tests to determine if the combination relay is operating properly. Disconnect and remove the combination relay to perform the tests. The voltage source for the tests is a 12-volt battery.

Ignition Relay

Connect 12-volt battery positive lead to terminal Lo and negative lead to terminal PT (Fig. HN2-31) on the combination relay. Connect a continuity

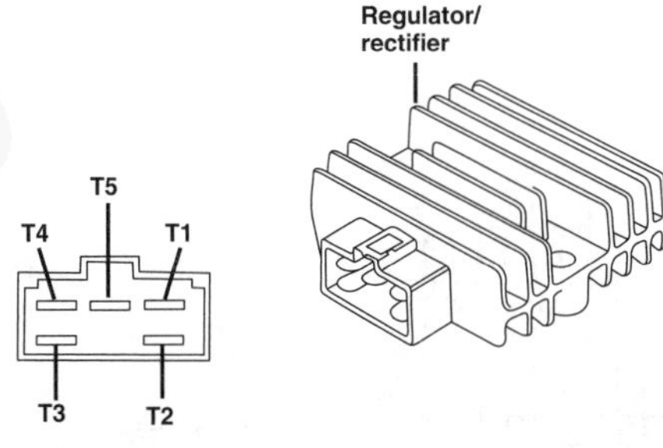

Fig. HN2-28—Use an ohmmeter to test regulator/rectifier as outlined in text. Refer to table (Fig. HN2-29 or Fig. HN2-30) for test values.

		-Tester lead				
		T1	T2	T3	T4	T5
+Tester lead	T1		A	A	D	A
	T2	B		A	C	A
	T3	B	A		C	A
	T4	A	A	A		A
	T5	A	A	A	A	

Fig. HN2-29—Test values for regulator used on tractors prior to serial number 1002451.

A. Infinity
B. 0.1k-50k ohms
C. 1k-200k ohms
D. 0.5k-1000k ohms

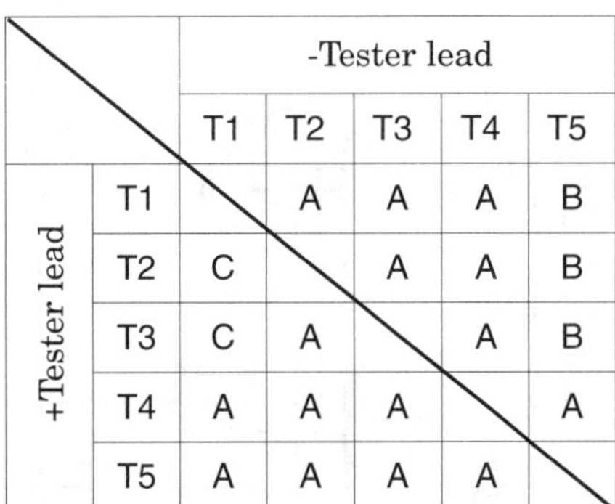

		-Tester lead				
		T1	T2	T3	T4	T5
+Tester lead	T1		A	A	A	B
	T2	C		A	A	B
	T3	C	A		A	B
	T4	A	A	A		A
	T5	A	A	A	A	

Fig. HN2-30—Test values for regulator used on tractors after serial number 1002450.

A. Infinity
B. 1k-50k ohms
C. 0.5k-20k ohms

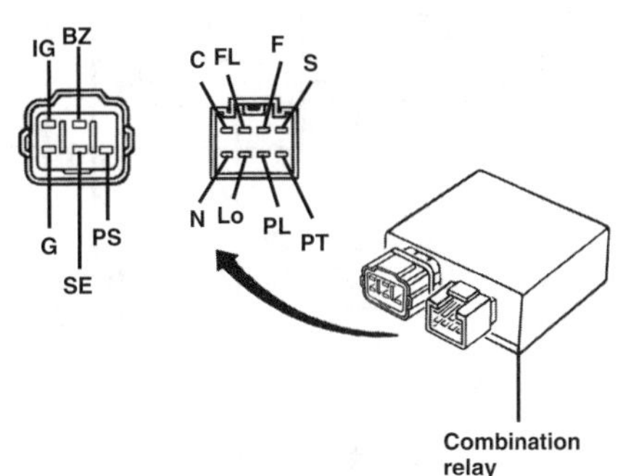

Fig. HN2-31—Refer to text for combination relay test procedure.

tester or ohmmeter between terminals IG and G on the combination relay.

If the combination relay is operating properly, there should be no continuity when the battery is connected and continuity when the battery is disconnected.

Starter Relay

Connect 12-volt battery positive lead to terminal C and negative leads to terminals G and PT (Fig. HN2-31). Connect negative voltmeter lead to negative battery terminal and positive voltmeter lead to relay terminal S.

If the combination relay is operating properly, voltmeter reading should indicate 12 volts when the battery is connected and zero volts when the battery is disconnected.

Parking Brake System

Connect the buzzer and warning light (12v 3.4W) in series between the relay terminals Bz and PL (Fig. HN2-31). Connect 12-volt battery positve lead to terminal Lo and negative leads to terminals G, SE and PS. Connect a continuity tester or ohmmeter between terminals IG and G on combination relay.

When the negative battery terminal is connected to terminal PS, there should be no continuity, the light should be out and the buzzer should be off. A few seconds after disconnecting negative terminal from terminal PS, the buzzer and light should come on.

Safety Interlock

Connect 12-volt battery positive lead to terminal Lo and negative leads to terminals G, SE and N (Fig. HN2-31). Connect a continuity tester or ohmmeter between terminals IG and G on combination relay.

When the negative battery terminal is connected to terminal SE, there should be no continuity. When the negative battery terminal is disconnected from terminal SE, there should be continuity.

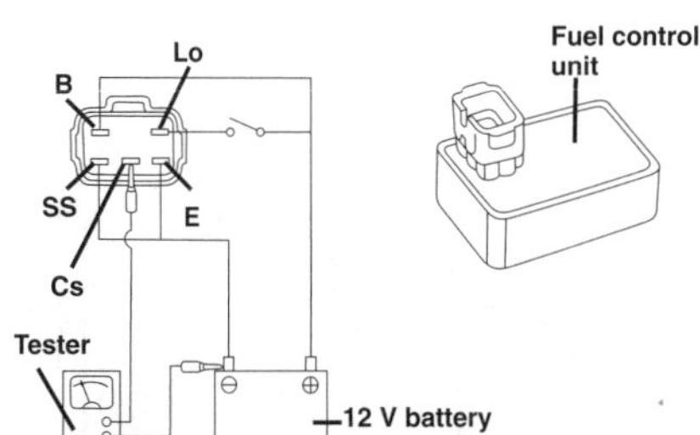

Fig. HN2-32—Refer to text for fuel control unit test procedure.

FUEL CONTROL UNIT

Tractors prior to serial number 1002451 are equipped with a fuel control unit that is mounted on a bracket behind the left side of the engine.

To test the fuel control unit, disconnect the connector from the unit. Connect 21-volt battery positive lead to terminal B (Fig. HN2-32). Connect positive 12 volts with a switch to terminal Lo. Connect negative leadss to terminals SS and E. Connect negative voltmeter lead to negative battery terminal and positive voltmeter lead to relay terminal Cs.

The voltmeter should indicate zero volts when the switch to terminal Lo is ON. When the switch to terminal Lo is OFF, the voltmeter should indicate approximately 12 volts for 9 seconds, then decrease to zero volts.

DIODE

Tractors prior to serial number 1002451 are equipped with a diode in the fuel control circuit.

To test the diode, disconnect the wire connector from the diode. With an ohmmeter set on Rx1, the meter should read low resistance when connected to the diode terminals in one test, then infinity when the ohmmeter connections to the diode terminals are reversed. Readings may be reversed (infinity then low resistance) depending on the connection sequence.

If ohmmeter readings are both low or both infinity, then the diode is faulty.

WIRING DIAGRAMS

The wiring diagram for tractors produced prior to serial number 1002451 is shown in Fig. HN2-33. The wiring diagram for tractors produced after serial number 1002450 is shown in Fig. HN2-34.

Figure HN2-33 and Figure HN2-34 are on the following page.

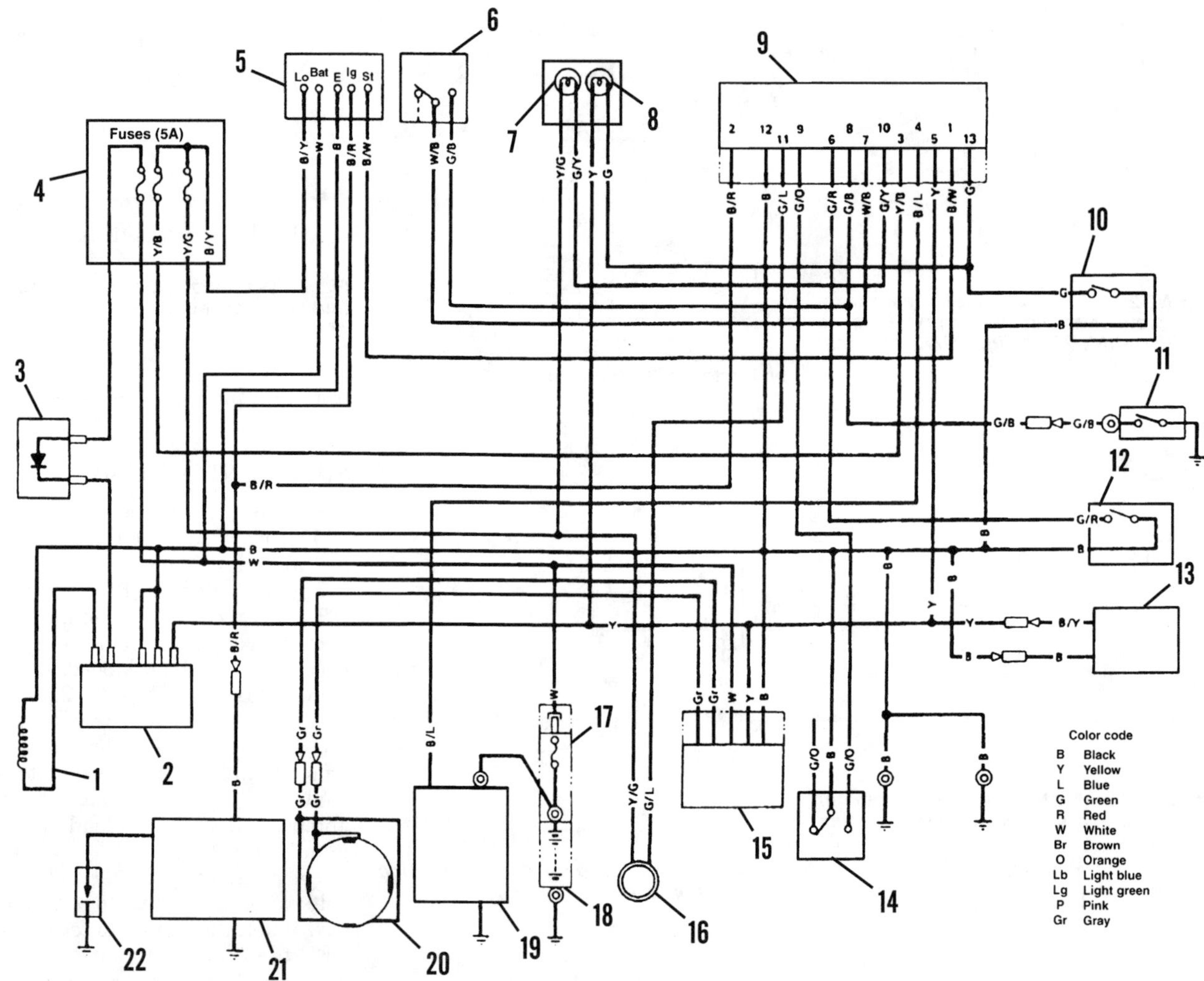

Fig. HN2-33—Wiring schematic for tractors prior to serial number 1002451.

1. Fuel control unit
2. Fuel shutoff solenoid
3. Diode
4. Fuse
5. Combination switch
6. PTO clutch switch
7. Parking brake lamp
8. Fuel reserve lamp
9. Combination relay
10. Fuel reserve switch
11. Neutral switch
12. Seat switch
13. Fuel pump
14. Parking brake switch
15. Regulator/rectifier
16. Buzzer
17. Battery
18. Main fuse
19. Starter
20. Charge coil
21. Ignition coil
22. Spark plug

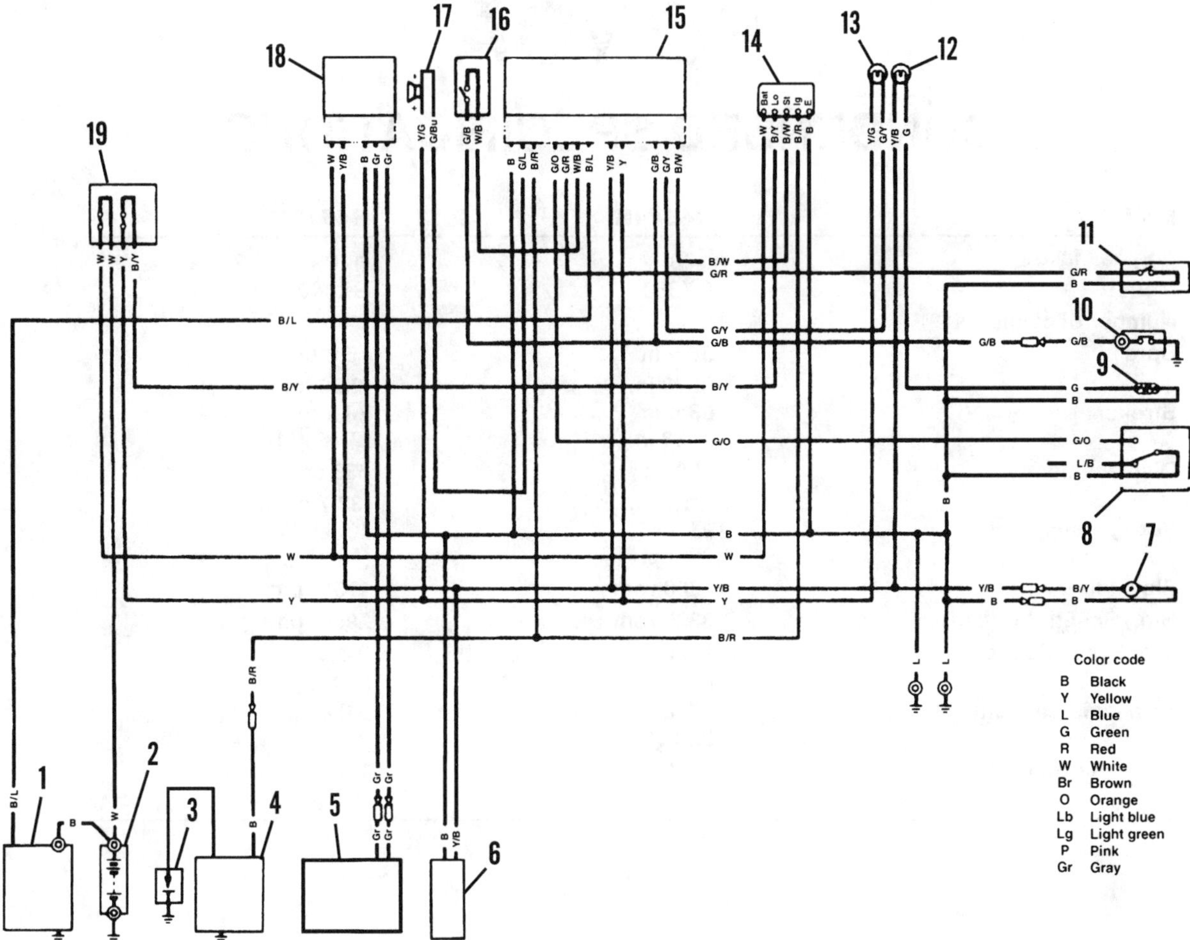

Fig. HN2-34—Wiring schematic for tractors after serial number 1002450.

1. Starter
2. Battery
3. Spark plug
4. Ignition coil
5. Charge coil
6. Fuel shutoff solenoid
7. Fuel pump
8. Parking brake switch
9. Fuel reserve lamp
10. Neutral switch
11. Seat switch
12. Fuel reserve lamp
13. Parking brake lamp
14. Combination switch
15. Combination relay
16. PTO clutch switch
17. Warning buzzer
18. Regulator/rectifier
19. Fuse

HONDA

CONDENSED SPECIFICATIONS

Model	H4514H	H4518H
Engine Make	Honda	Honda
Model	GX360	GX640
Number of cylinders	2	2
Bore	58 mm (2.28 in.)	76 mm (2.99 in.)
Stroke	68 mm (2.68 in.)	70 mm (2.76 in.)
Displacement	359 cc (21.9 cu. in.)	635 cc (38.7 cu. in.)
Power Rating	9.7 kW (13 hp.)	13.4 kW (18 hp.)
Slow Idle	1300 rpm	1750 rpm
High Speed (No-load)	3300 rpm	2950 rpm
Crankcase Capacity	1.4 L (1.5 qt.)	2.0 L (2.2 qt.)
Transaxle Capacity	5.0 L (5.3 qt.)	5.0 L (5.3 qt.)
Coolant Capacity	2.0 L (2.1 qt.)	1.8 L (1.9 qt.)

NOTE: Honda special tools may be required for some procedures and are indicated in the text. Read the text completely before attempting procedure.

FRONT AXLE AND STEERING SYSTEM

MAINTENANCE

Lubricate the steering spindles annually or after 100 hours of operation. Inject multipurpose grease into the grease fittings at the axle's outer ends. Clean the grease fittings before and after lubrication.

FRONT WHEELS AND BEARINGS

Each front wheel is supported by two sealed ball bearings (4—Fig. HN3-1). A spacer is located between the bearings.

When installing a wheel, note that the washer (3) must be installed so the OUTSIDE marking on the washer is facing the nut. Tighten the retaining nut to 60 N·m (44 ft.-lb.). Secure the nut with a cotter pin.

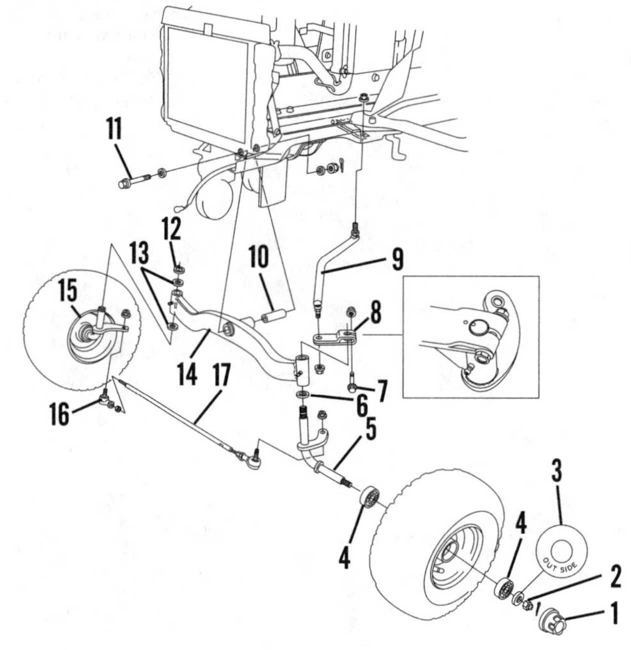

Fig. HN3-1—Exploded view of front axle assembly.

1. Hub cap
2. Nut
3. Washer
4. Bearings
5. Spindle (left)
6. Thrust washer
7. Clamp bolt
8. Steering lever
9. Drag link
10. Sleeve
11. Pivot bolt
12. Snap ring
13. Thrust washers
14. Axle main member
15. Spindle (right)
16. Tie rod end
17. Tie rod

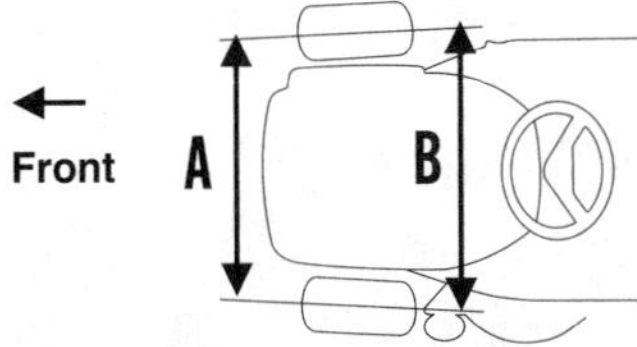

Fig. HN3-2—Subtract measurement "A" from measurement "B" to determine front wheel toe-in.

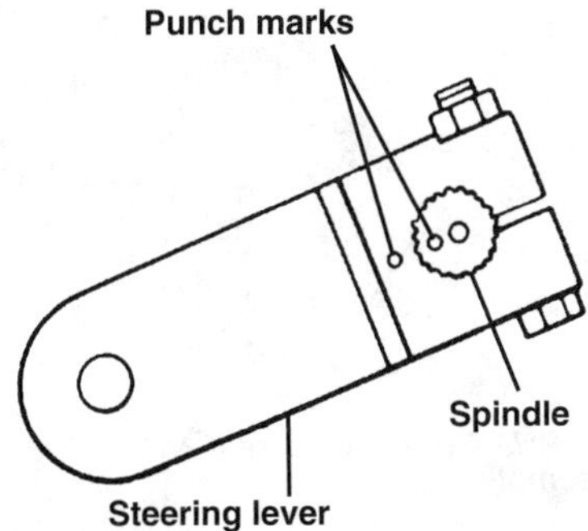

Fig. HN3-3—Align punch marks on steering lever and spindle during assembly. Also align punch marks on steering arm (19—Fig. HN3-4) and sector gear (21) shaft during assembly.

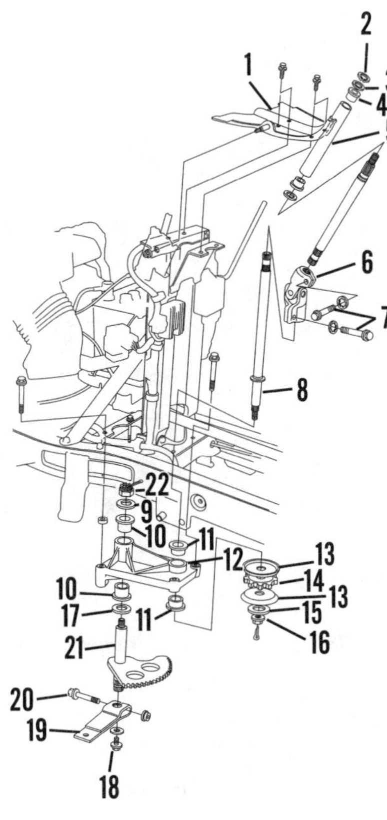

Fig. HN3-4—Exploded view of steering shaft and gears.

1. Steering support
2. Snap ring
3. Washer
4. Bushing
5. Upper steering shaft
6. Steering joint
7. Bolts
8. Lower steering shaft
9. Washer
10. Bushings
11. Bushings
12. Steering gear housing
13. Washers
14. Steering drive gear
15. Washer
16. Nut
17. Wave washer
18. Screw
19. Steering arm
20. Clamp bolt
21. Steering sector gear
22. Nut

TIE ROD AND TOE-IN

The tie rod (16—Fig. HN3-1) is equipped with threaded ends at each end. The initial tie rod length should be 537.2-538.8 mm (21.15-21.21 in.) as measured from the centerline of the tie rod end studs with the studs perpendicular to the tie rod.

The recommended toe-in is 2-10 mm (0.08-0.40 in.). To check toe-in, set the front wheels straight ahead. Measure the distance between the front and rear of the front wheels (A and B—Fig. HN3-2) at hub height. Subtract measurement A from measurement B to determine toe-in.

To adjust toe-in, loosen the locknut at each rod end (16—Fig. HN3-1) and rotate the tie rod (17) if necessary.

NOTE: The left tie rod end and nut have left-hand threads.

STEERING SPINDLES REMOVAL AND INSTALLATION

To remove the steering spindles, raise and support the front of the tractor. Remove the front wheel. Disconnect the tie rod end from the spindle.

To remove the left spindle (5—Fig. HN3-1), remove the clamp bolt (7) and detach the steering arm (8) from the spindle. Slide the spindle out of the axle. When reinstalling the steering arm, align the spindle end punch mark with the steering arm (Fig. HN3-3) punchmark.

To remove the right spindle, detach the snap ring (12—Fig. HN3-1) and slide the spindle (15) out of the axle. Note that two thrust washers (13) are used on the right spindle, while the left spindle is equipped with a single thrust washer (6).

AXLE MAIN MEMBER REMOVAL AND INSTALLATION

The complete front axle assembly may be removed as a unit. To remove the axle main member (14—Fig. HN3-1), raise and support the front of the tractor.

Disconnect the outer end of the drag link (9). Support the axle main member and remove the axle retaining bolt (11). Lower the axle main member (14) from the main frame pivot point and roll axle out from under the tractor.

When installing the axle main member, tighten the axle retaining bolt to 120 N·m (87 ft.-lb.).

STEERING GEARS AND SHAFTS

To remove the steering gears and shafts, first remove the mower deck. Open the hood and disconnect the battery cables. Remove the shift lever knob, parking brake lever cover, mower height adjusting lever cover and fuel tank cap. Remove the screws attaching the seat and fenders to the frame. Disconnect the neutral switch wire connector and the seat switch connector. Remove the seat and fender assembly.

Remove the steering wheel and throttle lever knob. Remove the instrument panel mounting screws. Disconnect wiring connectors as needed and remove the instrument panel and the steering column lower cover.

Remove the brake pedal. Remove the floor plate mounting screws and remove the floor/foot rest.

Remove the clamp bolts (7—Fig. HN3-4) and withdraw the upper steering shaft (5) and the steering joint (6).

Unscrew the steering gear nut (16) and remove the steering gear (14) and washers. Withdraw the lower steering shaft (8).

Remove the clamp bolt (20) and separate the drag link arm (19) from the steering sector gear (21). Remove the bolts attaching the steering housing (12) to the frame and remove the housing with the sector gear. Unscrew the nut (22) and remove the sector gear (21), washers (9 and 17) and bushings (12).

Inspect all components for excessive wear and damage and replace when necessary.

To install the steering gears and shafts, reverse the removal procedure while noting the following special instructions:

When installing the sector gear (21—Fig. HN3-4), be sure that the wave washer (17) is located at the bottom of the steering housing and thrust washer (9) is at the top. Tighten the sector gear shaft nut (22—Fig. HN3-4) to 55 N·m (40 ft.-lb.). When installing the drag link arm (19), align the punch mark on the end of the sector gear shaft with the steering arm (Fig. HN3-3) punch mark. Install the washers (13—Fig. HN3-4) so convex sides are next to the steering gear (14). Tighten the steering gear retaining nut (16) to 40 N·m (29 ft.-lb.).

Tighten the steering shaft universal joint screws (7—Fig. HN3-4) to 22 N·m (16 ft.-lb.). Steering shaft must rotate without binding. If shaft binds, loosen steering support (1) mounting screws and relocate the steering support until shaft rotates smoothly.

SAFETY INTERLOCK SYSTEM

The tractor is equipped with switches and relays preventing inadvertent starting of the tractor engine or operation if the operator leaves the tractor seat. The tractor engine should not start if the following occurs (engage parking brake):

- Operator in the tractor seat, shift lever in NEUTRAL and the PTO clutch lever in the ON position.
- Operator in the tractor seat, the PTO clutch lever in the OFF position and the shift lever in a position other than NEUTRAL.
- Operator not in the seat when starting the engine.

The seat switch should kill the engine if the operator is not in the seat or leaves the seat when the PTO clutch is engaged or the tractor is in gear.

Refer to the wiring schematics at end of this section.

TESTING

Use an ohmmeter or battery-powered continuity tester to test the switches for correct operation.

There should be continuity between the wire leads of the PTO clutch switch when the switch is depressed and no continuity when the switch is released.

There should be continuity between the seat switch wire leads when the switch is depressed and no continuity when the switch is released.

There should be continuity between the neutral switch wire leads when the switch is depressed and no continuity when the switch is released.

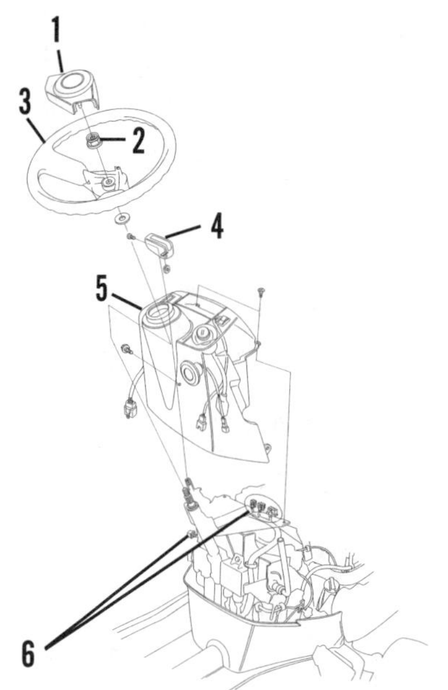

Fig. HN3-5—Drawing of instrument panel.

1. Cover
2. Nut
3. Steering wheel
4. Throttle lever knob
5. Instrument panel
6. Wiring connectors

SHEET METAL REMOVAL AND INSTALLATION

To remove the hood, raise the hood and disconnect the headlight wire connector. Unscrew the mounting screw and remove the front bumper. Unscrew the hood pivot screws and remove the hood.

When installing the hood and bumper, tighten the hood pivot bolts to 22 N·m (16 ft.-lb.) and bumper screws to 9 N·m (7 ft.-lb.).

To remove the instrument panel, remove the steering wheel cover (1—Fig. HN3-5), nut (2) and steering wheel (3). Remove the instrument panel mounting screws. Disconnect the electrical connectors (6) and remove the instrument panel (5).

When installing the instrument panel, tighten the mounting screws to 9 N·m (7 ft.-lb.). Tighten the steering wheel nut (2) to 60 N·m (43 ft.-lb.).

To remove the seat and fender assembly (1—Fig. HN3-6), remove the shift lever knob (2) and fuel tank cap (4). Remove screws attaching the parking brake lever cover (3) and height adjuster lever cover (5) to the fenders and remove the covers.

Remove the fender mounting screws. Raise the seat and fender assembly, disconnect the seat switch connector (6) and the neutral switch connector (7),

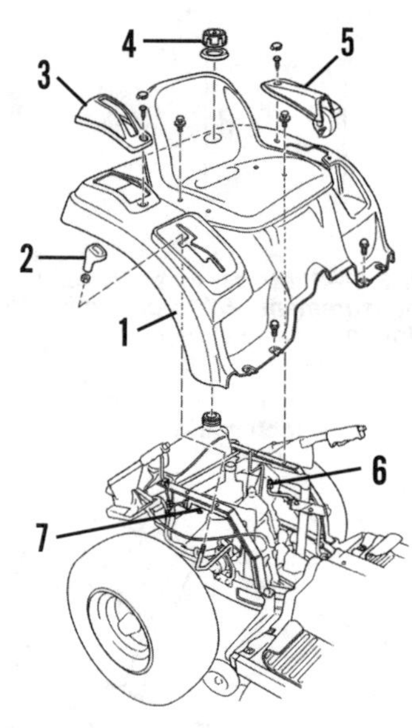

Fig. HN3-6 Drawing of seat and rear fender assembly.

1. Rear fenders
2. Shift lever knob
3. Parking brake lever cover
4. Fuel tank cap
5. Height adjuster lever cover
6. Seat switch connector
7. Neutral switch connector

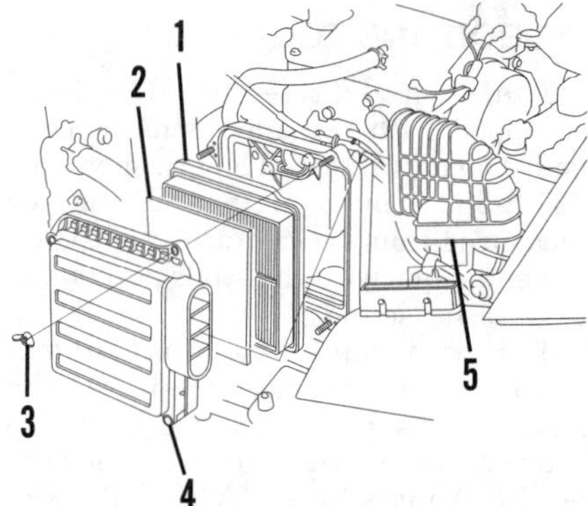

Fig. HN3-7—Exploded view of engine air cleaner assembly used on Model H4518H. Model H4514H is similar.

1. Paper element
2. Foam element
3. Wing nut
4. Air cleaner cover
5. Air duct

and remove the seat and fenders as an assembly.

Installation is the reverse of removal. Be sure the height adjuster cover tabs (5) are positioned inside the fender before tightening the mounting screw.

ENGINE

MAINTENANCE

The engine is equipped with a dry air filter that should be cleaned and inspected after every 50 hours of operation. Clean air filter more frequently when operating the tractor in dusty conditions.

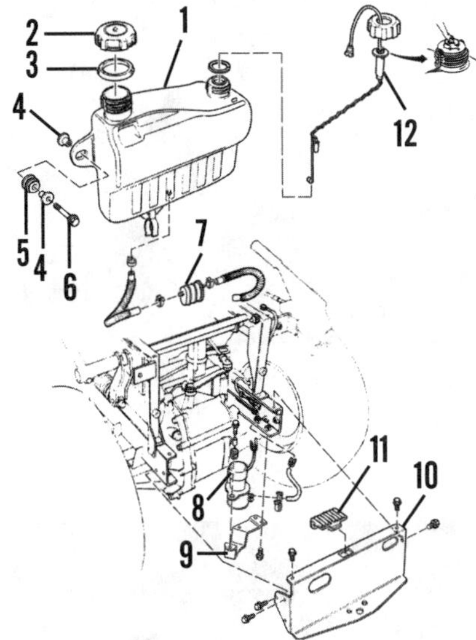

Fig. HN3-8—Exploded view of fuel tank and related components.

1. Fuel tank
2. Cap
3. Gasket
4. Collars
5. Rubber mount
6. Screw
7. Fuel filter
8. Fuel pump
9. Pump bracket
10. Hitch plate
11. Rubber cushion
12. Fuel level sensor

Remove the duct (5—Fig. HN3-7) and cover (4) for access to the filter elements. Remove foam and paper air filter elements from air filter housing.

The foam element (2) should be washed in a mild detergent and water solution, rinsed in clean water and allowed to air dry. When the foam element is completely dry, soak it in clean engine oil. Squeeze out excess oil.

Tap the paper element (1) lightly on a hard surface to remove dust and dirt. The element may also be cleaned by directing a low-pressure compressed air stream from inside the filter toward the outside. DO NOT wash the paper element in water or solvent as it will be damaged.

Inspect the filter elements for damage. A damaged filter element must be replaced to prevent dirt from entering the engine.

The engine oil level should be checked prior to operating the engine. Check the oil level with the oil cap not screwed in, but just touching the opening's threads.

Oil should be changed after the first 20 hours of engine operation and after every 100 hours thereafter. Change the oil filter after every 300 hours of operation or after two years, whichever occurs first.

Use engine oil meeting the latest API service classification. Use SAE 10W-30 or 10W-40 oil; use SAE 10W-40 if temperature exceeds 90°F (32°C).

Crankcase capacity is 1.4 liters (1.5 qt.) on Model H4514H and 2.0 liters (2.2 qt.) on Model H4518H.

REMOVAL AND INSTALLATION

Model H4514H

To remove the engine, first remove the hood. Disconnect the battery cables and remove the battery.

Drain the coolant, detach the radiator hoses and remove the radiator. Unscrew the fan mounting screws and remove the fan. Remove the PTO clutch as described in the PTO CLUTCH section in this manual.

Disconnect the fuel and vent hoses from the carburetor. Remove the muffler bracket bolt. Detach the throttle cable from the control plate and disengage the cable from the retainer bracket on the air cleaner case cover.

Remove the steering wheel. Remove the instrument panel mounting screws, disconnect electrical wire connectors as necessary and remove the instrument panel/steering column cover. Disconnect electrical wires from the starter solenoid relay, the ignition coil and charge coil. Remove the ground wires from the left side of the engine and the left front engine mount.

Remove drive shaft covers from the engine rear. Unscrew the three screws attaching the drive shaft front coupling to the engine Prevent crankshaft rotation by installing two screws in the fan mounting flange and inserting a bar between the screws.

Remove the engine mounting bolts. Support the engine with a hoist. Move the engine forward and remove it from the tractor.

Reverse the removal procedure to install the engine. Tighten the drive shaft coupler screws to 27 N·m (20 ft.-lb.). Refer to the GOVERNOR section to adjust throttle cable. Refer to the PTO CLUTCH section when installing PTO clutch.

Note the fan hub index tab; it must align with the notch in the fan bracket. Refer to COOLING SYSTEM when refilling the cooling system.

Model H4518H

To remove the engine, first remove the hood. Disconnect the negative battery lead.

Remove the heat shields and muffler. Drain coolant, detach radiator hoses and remove radiator. Note the lower coolant hose is retained by a clip on the left engine mount plate. Remove the cooling fan mounting screws and remove the fan.

Remove the PTO clutch as outlined in the PTO CLUTCH section. Remove the steering wheel. Remove the instrument panel mounting screws, disconnect electrical connectors if necessary and remove the instrument panel. Remove the lower steering column cover and air intake tube.

Disconnect the wiring connectors from the pulser coil, charging coil and ignition coil. Disconnect the starter solenoid connector and the starter cable from the starter solenoid. Detach the two ground cables from the front and rear of the engine. Disconnect the fuel cutoff solenoid connector and the decompressor solenoid connector. Remove the wire harness from the harness clips.

Detach the throttle cable from the control plate and release the cable from the cable holder on the air cleaner case cover. Disconnect the fuel hose from the carburetor. Detach the vent hose from the clip on the frame.

Bend back the lock tab, and unscrew the drive shaft coupler retaining screw. Remove the engine mounting screws. Note that the rear screws are longer than the front screws. Support the engine with a suitable hoist. Move the engine forward to disengage the drive shaft, and lift the engine out of the tractor.

If the engine mount brackets must be removed, mark the bracket's location for proper reassembly. Rubber motor mounts are interchangeable.

Reverse the removal procedure to install the engine. Lubricate the drive shaft and crankshaft splines with grease. Tighten the drive shaft coupler retaining screw to 22 N·m (16.2 ft.-lb.), then bend the lock tab against the screw.

Be sure there is at least 6.4 mm (0.25 inch) space at end of vent tube for free air movement. Refer to the GOVERNOR section to adjust throttle cable. Refer to the PTO CLUTCH section when installing the PTO clutch. Refer to COOLING SYSTEM when refilling the cooling system.

OVERHAUL

Refer to appropriate Honda engine section in this manual for service information on the engine and associated accessories.

FUEL SYSTEM

The carburetor is covered in the appropriate Honda engine section at the rear of this manual. Also refer to ELECTRICAL SYSTEM for other fuel system related components.

FUEL FILTER MAINTENANCE

A fuel filter (7—Fig. HN3-8) is located in the fuel line from the fuel tank to the fuel pump. The fuel filter is visible through a hole in the rear hitch plate (10).

Inspect the fuel filter annually or after every 100 hours of operation. Replace the filter if it is dirty or damaged.

FUEL TANK REMOVAL AND INSTALLATION

To remove the fuel tank (1—Fig. HN3-8), first remove the seat and rear fender assembly as previously outlined. Disconnect the fuel line and drain the fuel into a container.

Disengage the fuel filter (7) from its mounting clip. Disconnect the low-fuel sensor wire connector. Remove the two mounting bolts (6) and lift the tank from the tractor.

When installing the tank, make certain that the rubber bushings (5) and the rubber tank cushion (11) are in place.

FUEL PUMP TESTING

Before testing fuel pump be sure the fuel filter and fuel line are in good condition and fuel flow to the pump is unimpeded. Remove the hitch plate (10—Fig. HN3-8) for access to the fuel pump (8).

To check fuel pump pressure, disconnect the fuel discharge hose and connect a suitable pressure gauge to the fuel pump output port. Turn the ignition switch ON but do not start the engine. Fuel pump pressure should be 6.9-14.2 kPa (1.0-2.0 psi).

To check pump output, direct a hose from the pump output port into a container. Turn the ignition switch ON but do not start the engine. Fuel pump volume should be at least 350 cc (11.8 oz.) during one minute of operation.

If the fuel pump fails either test, replace the pump.

LOW-FUEL WARNING SENSOR

When the fuel level in the fuel tank drops to a certain level, the low-fuel warning sensor closes and turns on the fuel warning lamp on the instrument panel. Unscrew the cap on the top right side of the fuel tank for access to the low-fuel warning sensor (12—Fig. HN3-8).

WARNING: Do not use gasoline or a low flash point solvent when testing the sensor.

To test the sensor, remove the sensor and submerge the sensor tip in solvent with a high flash point. Connect the negative terminal of a 12-volt battery to the black lead of the sensor cable. Connect a 12v 3.4W lamp to the positive terminal of the battery, then connect the lamp to the green sensor lead.

The test lamp should remain off when the sensor is submerged. When the sensor is lifted out of the solvent, the lamp should light after approximately 30 seconds.

FUEL SHUTOFF VALVE

Models H4514H

The carburetor is equipped with a solenoid-operated valve attached to the fuel bowl (Fig. HN3-9).

CAUTION: On tractors with serial numbers prior to 1006847, applying voltage to the valve longer than 15 seconds may damage the solenoid.

To test the fuel shutoff valve, disconnect the control lead and remove the valve from the carburetor. Connect a 12-volt battery to the valve control lead.

On tractors with serial numbers prior to 1006847, the valve pin should extend 3.5 mm (0.14 in.) when battery voltage is applied.

On tractors with serial numbers above 1006846, the valve pin should withdraw when battery voltage is applied and extend when voltage is removed.

Models H4518H

The carburetor is equipped with a solenoid-operated valve attached to the fuel bowl (Fig. HN3-9).

CAUTION: Applying voltage to the valve longer than 15 seconds may damage solenoid.

To test the fuel shutoff valve, disconnect the control lead and remove the valve from the carburetor. Connect a 12-volt battery to the valve control lead. The valve pin should extend 3.5 mm (0.14 in.) when battery voltage is applied.

COOLING SYSTEM

Cooling components on the engine, such as the water pump and thermostat, are covered in the appropriate Honda engine section at the rear of this manual.

MAINTENANCE

Maintain coolant level between MIN and MAX marks on the reservoir tank. The recommended coolant is a 50:50 mixture of clean water and permanent antifreeze.

Fig. HN3-9—The carburetor is equipped with a fuel shutoff valve attached to the fuel bowl.

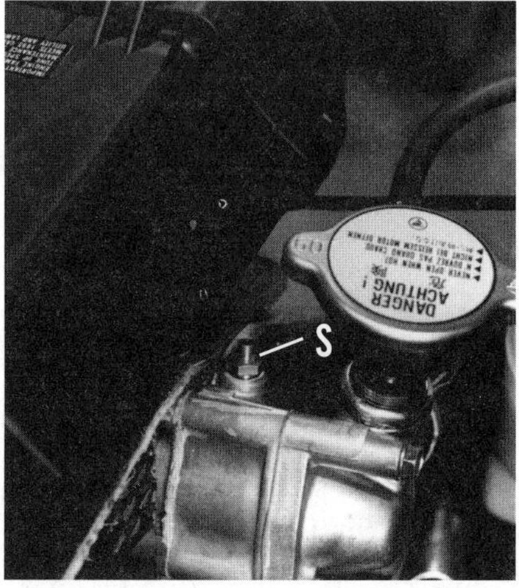

Fig. HN3-10—To bleed air from cooling system on Model H4514H, open air bleed screw (S) and proceed as described in text.

Periodically clean debris from radiator screen. Periodically inspect the coolant hoses between the radiator and engine water pump. Replace damaged hoses.

WARNING: Coolant in the system is pressurized. Remove the pressure cap only when the engine is cold.

Change coolant at least every two years. Flush the cooling system at least every three years. The coolant system capacity is approximately 2.0 liters (2.1 qt.) for Model H4514H or 1.8 liters (1.9 qt.) for Model H4518H.

The pressure cap pressure rating is 13 psi (90 kPa).

CHANGE COOLANT

Model H4514H

Remove the cooling system pressure cap. Drain the coolant by opening the radiator drain valve.

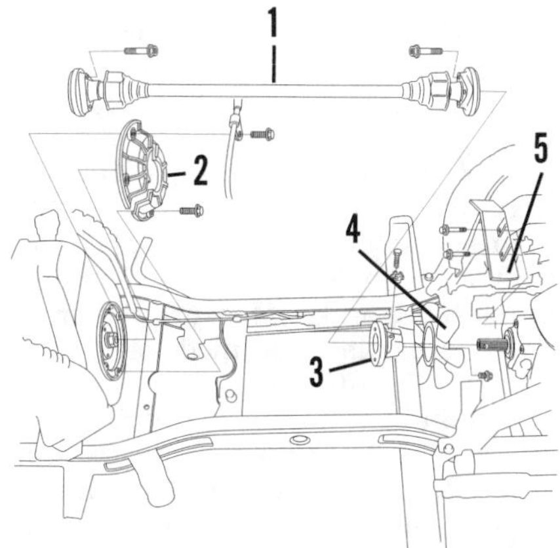

Fig. HN3-11—Drawing of drive shaft used on Model H4514H.

1. Drive shaft assembly
2. Cover
3. Hub
4. Cooling fan
5. Fan cover

WARNING: Coolant in the radiator is pressurized. Remove pressure cap only when the engine is cold.

Empty the reservoir tank. Close the radiator drain valve. Open the air bleed screw (S—Fig. HN3-10). Refill with a 50:50 mixture of clean water and permanent antifreeze. Pour coolant into the fill hole until air-free coolant runs out of the bleed screw hole, then install the bleed screw.

Position the pressure cap on the filler neck, but do not tighten the cap. Run the engine until the upper radiator hose becomes warm. Stop the engine and add coolant through the filler neck as needed.

Install and tighten the pressure cap. Fill the reservoir tank with coolant to the proper level. Run the engine, monitor engine temperature to be sure the engine does not overheat. Allow the engine to cool and recheck the coolant level.

Model H4518H

Remove the cooling system pressure cap. Drain coolant by opening the radiator drain valve.

WARNING: Coolant in the radiator is pressurized. Remove pressure cap only when the engine is cold.

Empty the reservoir tank. Close radiator drain valve. Refill with a 50:50 mixture of clean water and permanent antifreeze. Pour coolant into the fill hole until the coolant reaches the top of the filler neck.

Position pressure cap on the filler neck, but do not tighten cap. Run the engine until the upper radiator hose becomes warm. Stop the engine and add coolant through the filler neck as needed.

Install and tighten the pressure cap. Fill reservoir tank with coolant to the proper level. Run the engine, monitor engine temperature to be sure the engine does not overheat. Allow the engine to cool and recheck the coolant level.

HOSE ROUTING

Model H4514H

The left radiator hose connects to the thermostat housing. The right radiator hose connects to a spigot on the right side of the cylinder block. The bypass hose attaches to a spigot at the right rear of the cylinder block and connects to the thermostat housing.

Model H4518H

The left radiator hose connects to the thermostat housing on the cylinder block's left side. The right radiator hose connects to the spigot on the governor housing at the cylinder head's front.

DRIVE SHAFT OVERHAUL

MODEL H4514H

Remove the steering wheel and instrument panel/steering column cover. Remove the seat, seat frame and rear fender assembly. Remove the front floor cover and the floor. Remove the steering shaft and gear assembly as previously described.

Unbolt and remove the drive shaft cover (2—Fig. HN3-11). Use a strap wrench or other suitable tool to prevent the shaft from rotating, and unscrew the coupler screws at each end of drive shaft. Remove the drive shaft (1).

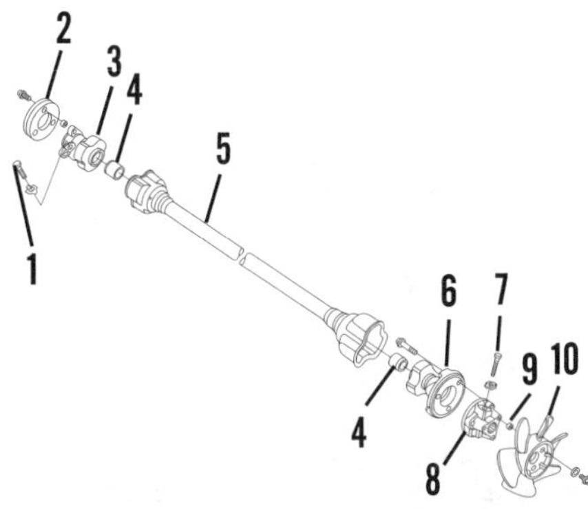

Fig. HN3-12—Drawing of drive shaft used on Model H4518H.

1. Screw
2. Dust cover
3. Damper
4. Centering bushings
5. Drive shaft
6. Damper
7. Screw
8. Hub
9. Fan collar (3)
10. Cooling fan

The drive shaft rear yoke (3) is mounted on the transaxle input shaft. The transaxle cooling fan (4) is mounted on the yoke. Bend back the lock tab, then unscrew the yoke retaining screw. Pull the yoke off the transmission input shaft.

Inspect dampers for damage.

Reverse the removal procedure to install the drive shaft. Lubricate the drive shaft splines with grease. Install the rear yoke so the retaining screw will mesh with the spline notches. Tighten the rear drive shaft yoke retaining screw to 22 N·m (16.2 ft.-lb.), then bend the lock tab against the screw. Tighten the coupler screws to 27 N·m (20 ft.-lb.).

MODEL H4518H

Remove the steering wheel and instrument panel. Remove the seat, seat frame and rear fender assembly. Remove the steering column lower cover and the floor. Move the steering gear as needed for clearance.

Bend back the lock tab and unscrew the special bolts (1 and 7—Fig. HN3-12) from the drive shaft yokes. Use a strap wrench or other suitable tool to prevent rotation of the drive shaft (5). Unscrew the coupler screws at the transaxle end of the drive shaft, then remove the screws from the engine end of the drive shaft.

Disengage the rear end of the drive shaft, then move the drive shaft back to disengage the front end from the crankshaft splines. Remove the drive shaft and dampers (3 and 6).

The drive shaft rear yoke (8) is mounted on the transaxle input shaft. The transaxle cooling fan (10) is mounted on the yoke. Bend back the lock tab, then unscrew the yoke retaining screw. Pull the yoke off the transmission input shaft.

Inspect dampers for damage. Install the bushing in the damper so the chamfered end is inserted first.

Reverse the removal procedure to install the drive shaft. Lubricate the drive shaft coupler, crankshaft and transaxle splines with grease. Install the centering bushing (4—Fig. HN3-12) so the chamfered end of the bushing is toward the transmission input shaft.

Install the rear coupler so the index line on the fan and punch mark on the end of the transaxle shaft are aligned (Fig. HN3-13).

Tighten the rear drive shaft yoke retaining screw (7—Fig. HN3-12) to 22 N·m (16.2 ft.-lb.), then bend the lock tab against the screw. Tighten the rear cou-

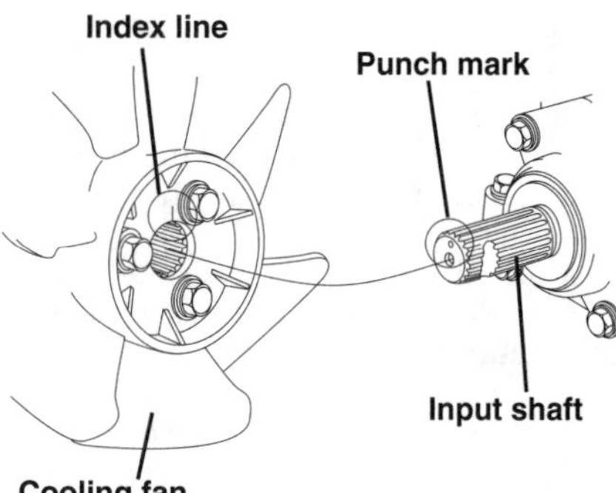

Fig. HN3-13—Align the punch mark on the transmission input shaft with the index mark on the cooling fan.

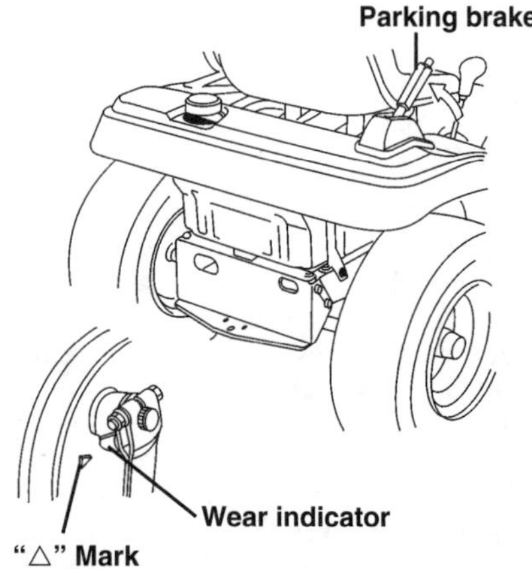

Fig. HN3-14—The brake wear indicator may be viewed through the inspection hole in the hitch plate.

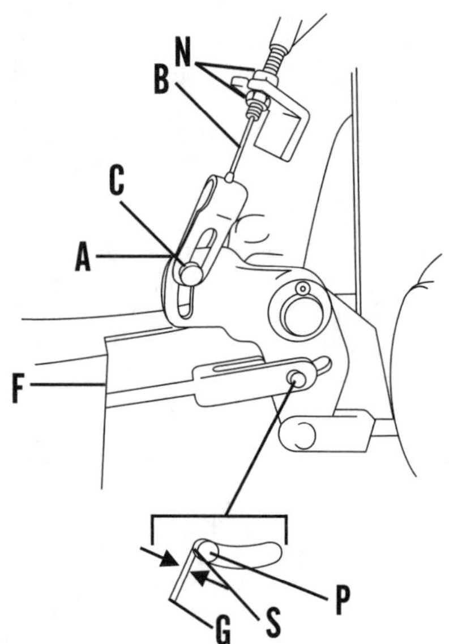

Fig. HN3-15—Drawing of brake operating linkage. Gap (G) should not exceed 1 mm (0.04 in.) when adjusting foot brake or parking brake.

A. Brake rod arm
B. Parking brake cable
C. Pin
F. Frame
G. Gap
N. Jam nuts
P. Pin
S. Slotted end

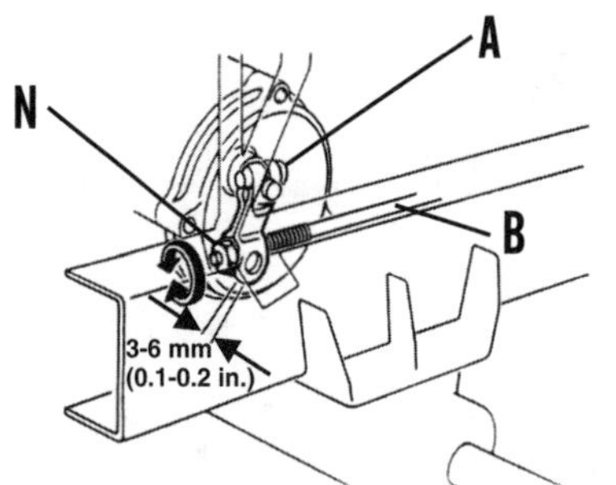

Fig. HN3-16—Adjust nut (N) on end of brake rod (B) to obtain brake arm (A) free play of 3-6 mm (0.1-0.2 in.).

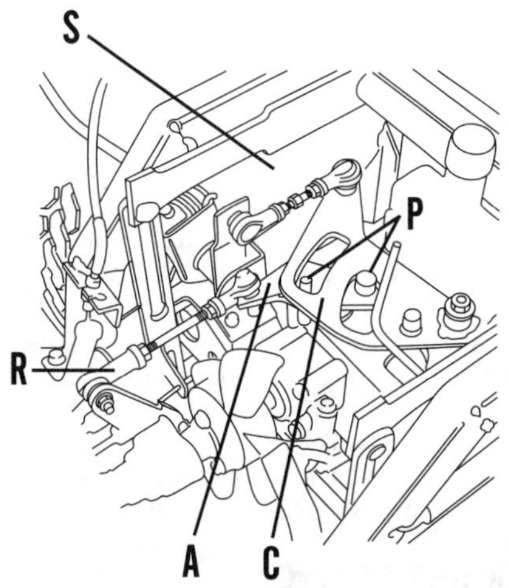

Fig. HN3-17—Adjust shift rod (S) length to obtain neutral position. Adjust return rod (R) length so pins (P) just contact the ends of slots in control arm (C). Refer to text.

pler screws to 27 N·m (20 ft.-lb.). Tighten the front drive shaft coupler retaining screw (1) to 22 N·m (16.2 ft.-lb.), then bend the lock tab against the screw.

BRAKE

The tractor is equipped with a brake drum brake located in the transaxle case. The brake drum is mounted on the transaxle countershaft.

The brake may be actuated either with the brake pedal or the parking brake lever. Depressing the brake pedal should return the transaxle shift lever to NEUTRAL.

When the parking brake lever is engaged, an indicator lamp lights. If the parking brake is engaged when the transaxle is shifted into gear, a warning buzzer sounds. If the parking brake is not disengaged with the transaxle in gear, the engine should stop.

INSPECTION AND ADJUSTMENT

A wear indicator is attached to the brake camshaft. To determine brake shoe thickness, set the parking brake and note the position of the brake indicator pointer (Fig. HN3-14). Replace brake shoes if the pointer aligns with or passes the brake housing's triangle wear mark.

To adjust the foot brake, place the shift lever in NEUTRAL and release the parking brake. Measure the brake pedal's free play. Specified free play is 6-11 mm (0.24-0.43 in.).

To adjust pedal free play, remove mower deck for access to the brake linkage. With the brake pedal in the released position, the brake arm (A—Fig. HN3-15) must contact the frame (F). The pin (P) should not contact the end of the slot (S), but the gap (G) should not exceed 1 mm (0.04 in.).

To adjust the location of the pin in the slot, loosen jam nuts on the brake rod and turn the adjuster to obtain proper clearance.

NOTE: Front jam nut has left-hand threads. Do not twist spring assembly on adjuster.

After adjusting brake pedal free play, rotate adjuster nut (N—Fig. HN3-16) at the brake end of the brake actuating rod (B) so there is 3-6 mm (0.12-0.24 in.) free play at the brake lever (A) with the brake disengaged.

To check or adjust the parking brake lever, position the parking brake lever in the disengaged position. Push the brake arm (A—Fig. HN3-15) against the frame (F). The clevis pin (C) should not contact the end of the slot in the brake rod arm (A), but the gap should not exceed 1 mm (0.04 in.).

To adjust the location of the pin in the slot, rotate the nuts (N—Fig. HN3-15) at the parking brake lever end of the cable housing. When the parking brake lever adjustment is correct, there will be 2-4 clicking sounds heard when the brake lever is pulled with a force of 10 kg (22 lb.).

Depressing the brake pedal must return the transaxle to NEUTRAL. To adjust brake return linkage, lift the seat and inspection cover under the seat.

Detach the return rod (R—Fig. HN3-17) from the return arm (A). Rotate the return arm counterclockwise until both pins (P) contact end of the slots in control arm (C). The pins should contact the control arm simultaneously.

If not, loosen the screws retaining the return arm bracket (21—Fig. HN3-18), and move the bracket so both pins contact the control arm simultaneously. Retighten the screws to 40 N·m (29.4 ft.-lb.).

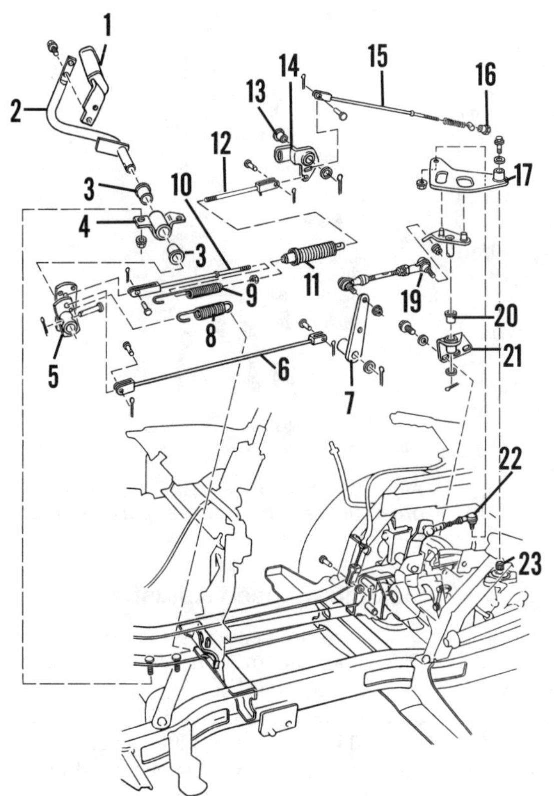

Fig. HN3-18—Drawing of transaxle control linkage.

1. Brake pedal
2. Brake pedal arm
3. Bushings
4. Pivot bracket
5. Pedal arm
6. Brake return rod
7. Return arm
8. Spring
9. Spring
10. Brake rod
11. Brake pipe
12. Brake rod
13. Bushing
14. Brake rod arm
15. Rear brake rod
16. Adjusting nut
17. Transmission control arm
18. Return arm
19. Return rod
20. Bushing
21. Return arm bracket
22. Shift rod
23. Transmission control shaft

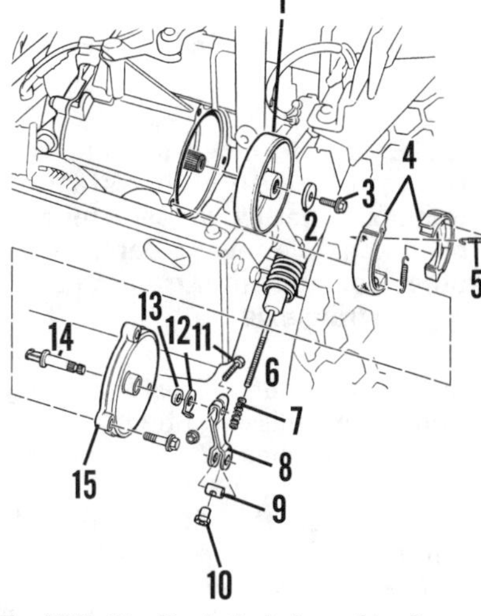

Fig. HN3-19—Exploded view of brake components.

1. Brake drum
2. Washer
3. Screw
4. Brake shoes
5. Return spring (2)
6. Brake rod
7. Spring
8. Brake arm
9. Sleeve
10. Adjusting nut
11. Clamp bolt
12. Wear indicator
13. Seal
14. Brake cam
15. Brake cover

Reattach the return rod (R—Fig. HN3-17) to the return arm (A). Fully depress the brake pedal. Loosen the jam nuts on the return rod, then rotate the rod so pins (P) just contact the ends of the slots. Tighten the jam nuts.

Release the brake pedal, then fully depress the pedal and recheck adjustment.

OVERHAUL

To remove the brake assembly, first remove the seat and rear fender assembly. Remove the rear hitch plate and fuel tank.

Remove the adjusting nut (10—Fig. HN3-19) and detach the brake actuating rod (6) from the brake arm (8). Remove the three screws from the brake cover (15) and withdraw the cover. Remove the clamp bolt (11) from the brake arm and remove the arm, wear indicator (12), seal (13) and brake cam (14).

Remove the brake shoes (4) and return springs (5). Remove center bolt (3) and withdraw the brake drum (1) from the transaxle shaft.

Maximum allowable brake drum inside diameter is 96.5 mm (3.80 in.). With the brake shoes installed on the brake cover, the minimum specified outer diameter between the brake shoe linings is 93.0 mm (3.66 in.).

During assembly apply grease to the brake cam and contact surface with the brake shoes. Do not allow grease on brake lining surfaces.

Tighten brake drum mounting bolt (3—Fig. HN3-19) to 22 N·m (16 ft.-lb.).

Install the brake lever (8—Fig. HN3-19) on the brake camshaft (14) so the punch marks on the arm and end of shaft are aligned.

Adjust the brake as previously outlined.

SHIFT CONTROL LINKAGE ADJUSTMENT

To adjust shift control linkage, place blocks against the front wheels to prevent movement. Support the right rear of the tractor and remove the right wheel. The left wheel must contact the ground.

Disconnect the seat safety switch and attach a jumper wire to the main circuit leads. Place the shift lever in the center of NEUTRAL position. Start the engine. Set the throttle at intermediate speed. Right rear axle should not rotate.

If the axle rotates, adjust the length of the shift rod (S—Fig. HN3-17) to obtain the NEUTRAL setting as follows: Loosen the jam nuts on the rod. Note that the jam nut adjacent to the rod end marked L has left-hand threads. Start the engine and move the throttle to the halfway position.

Rotate the left rod until the rear wheel begins to rotate. While counting turns, rotate the shift rod in the opposite direction until the rear wheel begins to rotate in the opposite direction. Determine half the number of turns and rotate the shift rod in the original direction that number of turns.

Tighten the shift rod jam nuts. Reconnect the seat safety switch.

HYDROSTATIC TRANSAXLE

Operation

The hydrostatic transaxle provides a variable selection of forward and reverse speeds from stop to full speed. The transaxle utilizes a hydraulic pump that is driven through a set of bevel gears from the input shaft, which is shaft-driven from the engine.

A control lever, which is linked to the operator's speed control panel, on the side of the transaxle determines pump output thereby setting machine speed and direction of travel.

Pressurized oil is directed from the pump to a hydraulic motor that is connected to the differential through a set of gears. Both the pump and motor are multiple-piston types using a swashplate to vary the stroke of the pistons.

Pump and motor assemblies are constructed to close tolerances and clean oil is a requirement to obtain a long service life.

Lubrication

The transaxle oil level should be checked prior to use of machine. The transaxle oil is contained in a reservoir on top of the transaxle.

To check the oil level, raise the seat and clean dirt from around the dipstick area. Remove the dipstick and note the oil level on the dipstick. Oil level should be maintained between the marks on the dipstick.

NOTE: Due to close tolerances present in the hydrostatic transaxle, particular care must be taken to prevent debris or other contaminants from entering the transaxle.

The recommended oil is Honda Hydrostatic Transmission Fluid.

Transaxle oil should be changed after every five years or 500 hours of operation. To change the oil, unscrew the drain plug on the bottom of the transaxle and drain the oil.

Tighten the drain plug to 40 N·m (29 ft.-lb.). Fill the reservoir to the proper level. Transaxle oil capacity is 5.0 liters (5.3 qt.).

Air Bleeding

Transaxle in Tractor

Air must be bled from the hydrostatic unit after draining and replacing the hydraulic fluid.

To bleed air with the transaxle installed in the tractor, the tractor must be on level ground. Remove the mower drive belt and engine spark plugs. Place blocks at the front wheels and support the rear of the machine so the rear wheels are off the ground.

Move the transaxle release lever to the engaged position, next to the green dot. Unscrew the plug in the port (B—Fig. HN3-20) and install Honda adapter 07KPJ-VD6010A and a hose fitting. Attach a clear hose to the fitting and direct the hose end into a container.

Place the PTO control lever in the engaged position. Route the mower drive belt or other V-belt around PTO drive pulley on the engine front so the pulley can be rotated. Rotate the PTO drive pulley counterclockwise as viewed from front until air-free fluid passes through the hose. Install the port (B) plug and tighten to 17 N·m (150 in.-lb.).

Place blocks against the right rear wheel so it cannot rotate. Attach a clear hose to the port (C) using the same procedure as just outlined for port (B). Attach another clear hose to port (A) with a reservoir (funnel or similar container) at the end of the hose.

Fill the reservoir with Honda hydrostatic transaxle fluid and hold the reservoir above the port so fluid will flow into the transaxle. Fluid must flow without interruption during the procedure. There should be no air bubbles.

Slowly rotate the left rear wheel counterclockwise until air-free fluid flows from the port (C). Place the shift control lever in REVERSE and rotate the PTO drive pulley counterclockwise until air-free fluid flows from the port (C). Remove the hoses. Install the port plugs and tighten to 17 N·m (150 in.-lb.).

With the shift control lever in the transport position, the left rear wheel should rotate counterclockwise when the transaxle pulley is rotated counterclockwise. With shift control lever in reverse position, the left rear wheel should rotate clockwise when the transaxle pulley is rotated counterclockwise. If not, repeat the bleeding procedure.

Reinstall the mower drive belt.

Transaxle Removed From Tractor

Air must be bled from the hydrostatic unit after servicing the unit.

To bleed air with the transaxle removed from the tractor, the brake drum must be installed. Shift control arm on top of the transaxle must be installed. Position the transaxle so bleed ports (A, B and C—Fig. HN3-20) face up. Install the drive shaft yoke on the input shaft so the shaft can be rotated.

Move the transaxle release lever to the engaged position (pull out). Unscrew the plug in the port (B—Fig. HN3-20) and install a Honda adapter 07KPJ-VD6010A and a hose fitting. Attach a clear hose to the fitting and direct the hose end into a container. Rotate the input shaft counterclockwise until air-free fluid passes through the hose. Reinstall the port (B) plug and tighten to 17 N·m (150 in.-lb.).

Attach a clear hose to the port (C) using the same procedure as just outlined for the previous port (B). Attach another clear hose to port (A) with a reservoir (funnel or similar container) at the end of the hose.

Fill the reservoir with Honda hydrostatic transaxle fluid and hold the reservoir above the port so fluid will flow into the transaxle. Fluid must flow without interruption during the procedure. There should be no air bubbles.

Slowly rotate the brake drum retaining screw clockwise until air-free fluid flows from the port (C—Fig. HN3-20). Place the shift control arm in reverse position (down) and rotate the input shaft counterclockwise until air-free fluid flows from the port (C). Remove the hoses. Install the port plugs and tighten to 17 N·m (150 in.-lb.).

Rotate input shaft while moving shift control arm through the shift positions. Axle shafts should rotate in both directions. If not, repeat bleeding procedure.

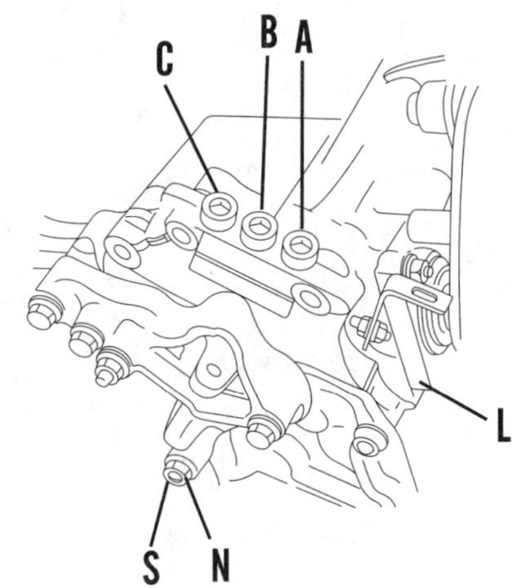

Fig. HN3-20—View showing location of hydrostatic transmission test ports (A, B and C) on transaxle.

Maximum Speed Adjustment

Maximum speed may be adjusted on the transaxle. To correctly adjust maximum speed, the tires must be at the recommended pressures (front—14 psi, rear—11 psi), tires must be original size, and maximum engine speed must be adjusted properly. See the engine section.

The machine should traverse a distance of 15 meters (49.2 ft.) on a level, hard surface in 7.0-7.9 seconds. To adjust maximum speed, loosen the nut (N—Fig. HN3-20) and turn the adjusting screw (S). Rotating the screw (S) clockwise will decrease maximum speed.

Pressure Tests

To check charge pump pressure, first be sure the transaxle fluid level is full. Raise seat and be sure the transaxle release lever is in the released position, next to the red dot.

Unscrew the plug in port (B—Fig. HN3-20) and install Honda adapter 07KPJ-VD6010A and a 0-700 kPa (0-100 psi) gauge. Position the shift control lever in NEUTRAL and run engine at full throttle. The charge pump pressure should be 196-392 kPa (29-57 psi).

To check drive pressure, first be sure transaxle fluid level is full and the engine maximum speed is adjusted correctly. The transaxle should be at normal operating temperature. Position the machine on a level paved surface with the front wheels contacting an immovable object that they cannot roll over. Liberally wet the area under the rear tires so the tires can rotate without moving the machine.

Place the transaxle release lever in the engaged position, next to the green dot. Unscrew plug in the port (A) and install Honda adapter 07KPJ-VD6010A and a pressure gauge that will read at least 35,000 kPa (5000 psi).

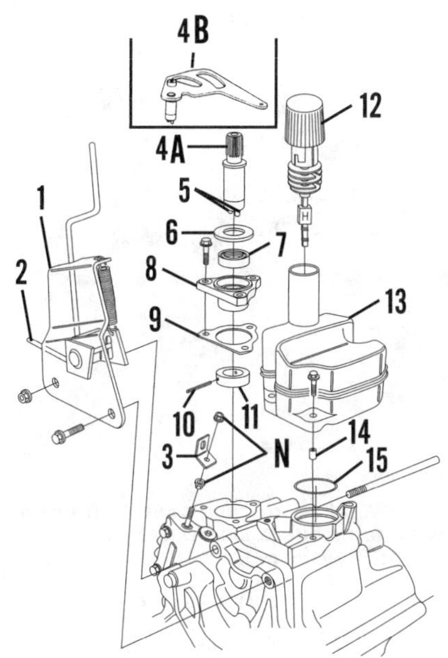

Fig. HN3-21—Exploded view of hydrostatic transmission control shaft assembly. Note the two different types of control shafts (4A and 4B).

1. ransmission release lever assembly
2. Release lever
3. Release valve bracket
4A. Control shaft
4B. Control shaft
5. Pins
6. Washer
7. Oil seal
8. Cover
9. Gasket
10. Pin
11. Collar
12. Tank cap
13. Fluid reservoir
14. Collar
15. O-ring

Run the engine at maximum speed with the speed control lever in NEUTRAL. Slowly move the speed control lever toward mowing position. Note he location on the control panel when the rear wheels begin to spin and observe the gauge reading. The shift control lever should be approximately 35 mm (1.38 in.) from NEUTRAL when the rear wheels slip. The gauge reading should be 15,680 kPa (2273 psi) if the operator weighs 151-200 pounds. Add 1570 kPa (227 psi) for each 50 pounds of additional operator weight, or subtract a like amount for less operator weight.

CAUTION: Transaxle may be damaged if wheels are allowed to spin continuously for longer than 5 seconds.

If the speed control lever must be moved more than 35 mm, or the wheels do not spin, internal leakage may be the cause.

Removal and Installation

Detach the battery cables. Remove the mower deck and deck lift rods. Remove the seat and rear fender assembly. Remove the 6 mm screws at the rear of the floorboards.

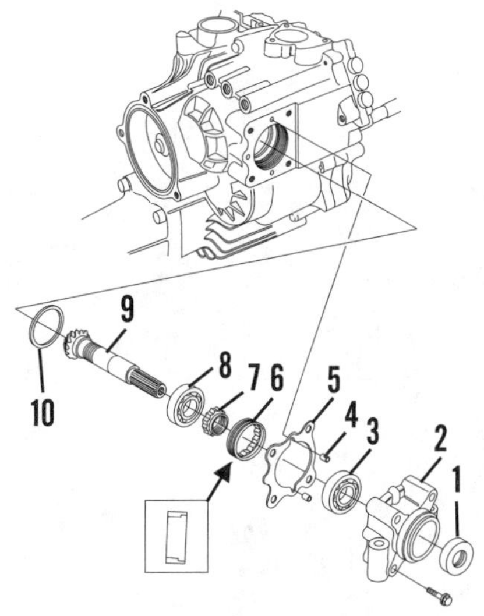

Fig. HN3-22—Exploded view of transmission input shaft assembly.

1. Oil seal
2. Bearing housing
3. Bearing
4. Dowel pin (2)
5. Gasket
6. Locknut
7. Nut
8. Bearing
9. Input shaft
10. Shim

Remove the rear hitch plate. Detach the fuel sensor wire from the retaining clip. Drain the fuel and remove the fuel tank. Remove the fuel pump and bracket.

Raise and support the rear of the tractor frame. Remove rear wheels. Remove screw securing the frame stiffener to right rear frame. Unscrew and remove the left rear frame and height adjusting lever assembly.

Detach the brake actuating rod from the brake lever. Detach the shift rod and return rod from the shift mechanism on the top of the transaxle. Use a strap wrench to prevent rotation of the drive shaft, and unscrew coupler screws at the transaxle end of the drive shaft.

Position a floor jack under the transaxle. Unscrew the retaining screws at the rear axles and the front of the transaxle. Lower and remove the transaxle.

Reverse the removal procedure to install the transaxle. Tighten the retaining screws at the axle housings to 40 N·m (29.4 ft.-lb.). Tighten the retaining screws at the front of the transaxle to 24 N·m (17.6 ft.-lb.). Tighten the drive shaft rear coupler screws to 27 N·m (20 ft.-lb.).

When installing the rear wheels, note the washer must be installed so the OUTSIDE marking on the washer is toward the retaining nut. Tighten the retaining nut to 60 N·m (44 ft.-lb.). Secure the nut with a cotter pin.

Adjust the brake and shift linkage as previously described.

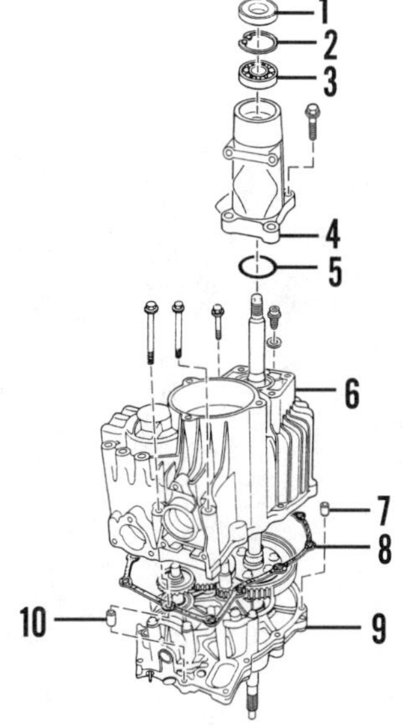

Fig. HN3-23—Drawing of transaxle housing components.

1. Oil seal
2. Snap ring
3. Bearing
4. Axle housing
5. O-ring
6. Transaxle center housing
7. Dowel pin
8. Gasket
9. Distributor plate
10. Dowel pin

Overhaul

Remove the drain screw and drain oil from transaxle. Remove the fluid reservoir (13—Fig. HN3-21). Unbolt and remove the transmission release valve linkage (1).

Note that the transmission control arm is attached to the control shaft (4A) with a cap screw on some models, and on some models the arm and shaft are an integral unit (4B). If a two-piece assembly is used, remove the cap screw and separate the arm from the shaft.

On all models, remove the cap screws attaching the control shaft cover (8) to the transmission case and withdraw the control shaft assembly. Drive out the spring pin (10) and remove the retaining collar (11) and control shaft from the shaft cover. Pry the oil seal (7) out of the cover.

Remove drive shaft yoke from input shaft. Unscrew the input shaft bearing housing (2—Fig. HN3-22) retaining screws and withdraw the input shaft assembly from transaxle case. Save the shim (10) for use in reassembly.

Using Honda tool 07916-7500000 with attachment 07FPA-7510110 or other suitable tool, unscrew the nut (6) and remove the input shaft (9) from the bearing housing. If the bearing (8) must be removed, grind away the staked area of nut (7) and use Honda tool 07916-7500000 or other suitable tool to unscrew the nut. The old nut should be discarded. Remove the oil seal (1) and drive or press out the bearing (3).

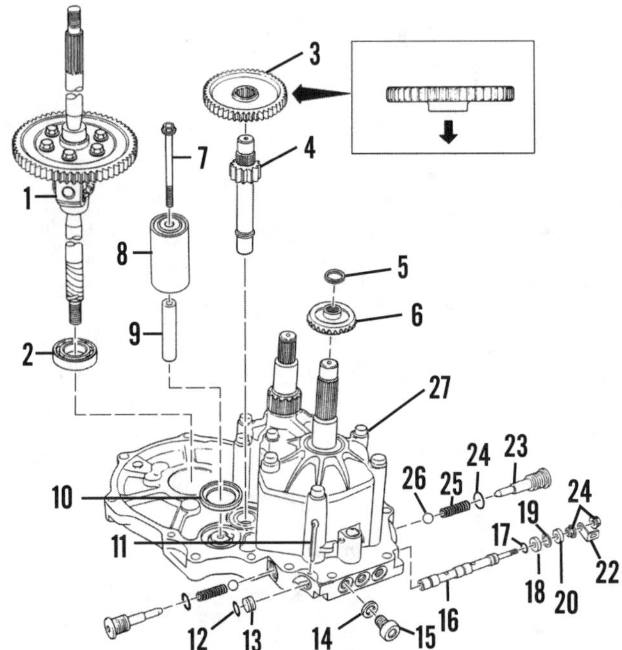

Fig. HN3-24—Exploded view of hydrostatic transmission control valves and transaxle gears.

1. Differential and axles
2. Bearing
3. Countershaft gear
4. Countershaft
5. Shim
6. Bevel gear
7. Bolt
8. Suction filter
9. Sleeve
10. Guide cap
11. Cotter pin
12. O-ring
13. Cap
14. Seal washer
15. Plug
16. Release valve
17. O-ring
18. Collar
19. Snap ring
20. Seal
21. Nuts
22. Release bracket
23. Check valve plug (2)
24. O-ring (2)
25. Check valve spring (2)
26. Ball (2)
27. Hydrostatic pump housing

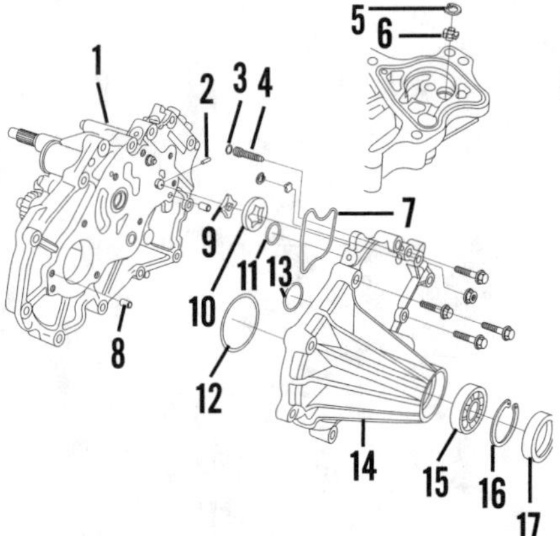

Fig. HN3-25—Exploded view of transmission charge pump. On Model H4518H, a ball is used in place of the spring guide (6).

1. Distributor plate
2. Pin
3. O-ring
4. Speed adjusting bolt
5. Snap ring
6. Spring guide
7. Seal ring
8. Dowel pin (2)
9. Inner rotor
10. Outer rotor
11. O-ring
12. O-ring
13. O-ring
14. Charge pump case
15. Bearing
16. Snap ring
17. Oil seal

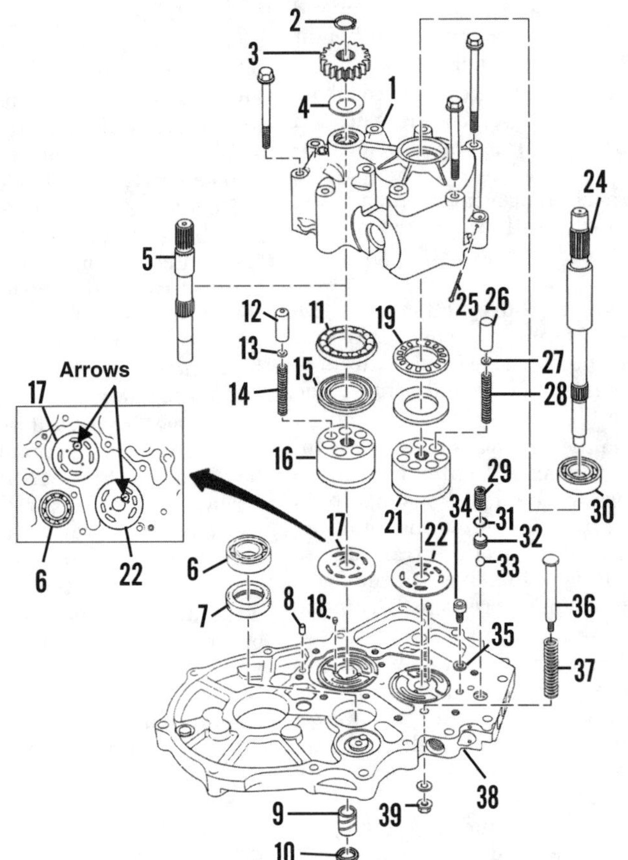

Fig. HN3-26—Exploded view of the hydrostatic transmission pump and motor. The motor and pump valve plates (17 and 22) must be installed with arrows facing up and pointing away from the ball bearing (6).

1. Pump housing
2. Snap ring
3. Drive gear
4. Thrust washer
5. Motor shaft
6. Bearing
7. Oil seal
8. Dowel pin
9. Bushing
10. Snap ring
11. Thrust bearing
12. Motor piston
13. Washer
14. Spring
15. Bearing plate
16. Motor cylinder
17. Valve plate
18. Dowel pin
19. Thrust bearing
20. Bearing plate
21. Pump cylinder
22. Valve plate
23. Dowel pin
24. Pump shaft
25. Pin
26. Pump piston
27. Washer
28. Spring
29. Charge relief spring
30. Bearing
31. O-ring
32. Spring guide
33. Charge relief ball
34. Special bolt
35. Seal washer
36. Return shaft
37. Spring
38. Distributor plate
39. Nut

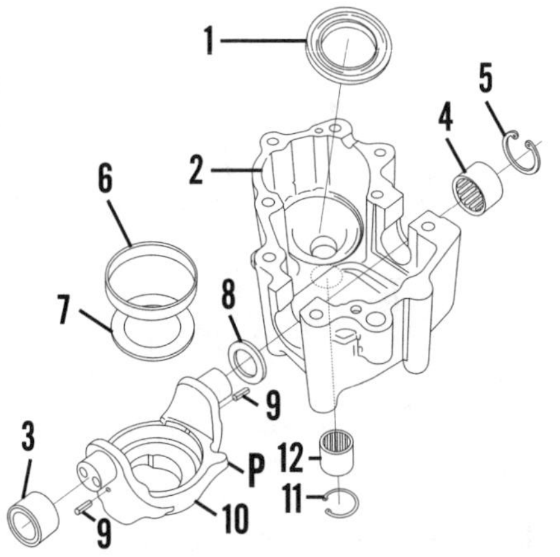

Fig. HN3-27—Exploded view of hydrostatic transmission pump swashplate.

1. Bearing plate
2. Pump housing
3. Collar
4. Bearing
5. Snap ring
6. Ring
7. Bearing plate
8. Washer
9. Pins
10. Swashplate
11. Snap ring
12. Bearing

Outer bearing plate
Beveled edge
Thrust ball bearing
Inner bearing plate
Pump case

Fig. HN3-28—Refer to text for correct assembly of inner and outer bearing plates. Thrust ball bearing must be installed with beveled edge toward the inner bearing plate.

Position the transaxle so the left axle points down. Unscrew the retaining screws from the right axle housing (4—Fig. HN3-23) and remove the axle housing. Pry out the seal (1) and remove the snap ring (2). Press or drive out the bearing (3).

Remove retaining screws from transaxle case (6—Fig. HN3-23) and lift off transaxle case. Remove rear axle and differential assembly (1—Fig. HN3-24). Remove countershaft gear (3) and shaft (4). Remove bevel gear (6) and shim (5). Save the shim for reassembly.

Unscrew the retaining screws from the charge pump case (14—Fig. HN3-25) and separate the case/axle

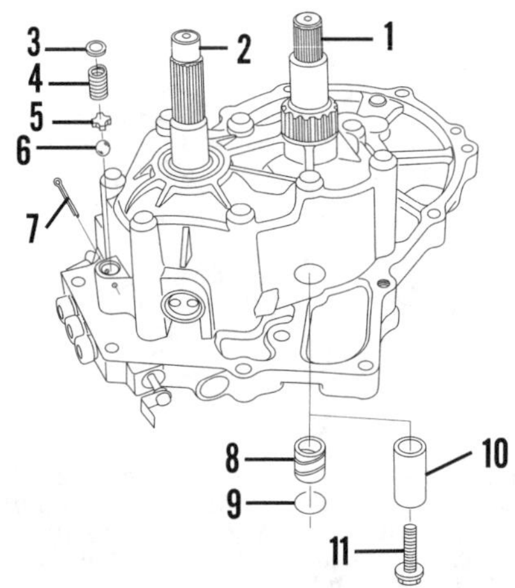

Fig. HN3-29—Use a sleeve (10) and bolt (11) to retain the motor in the pump housing during assembly of the housing to the distributor plate. Refer to text.

1. Motor shaft
2. Pump shaft
3. Washer
4. Charge relief valve spring
5. Spring guide
6. Ball
7. Cotter pin
8. Bushing
9. Snap ring

housing from the distributor plate (1). Remove the charge pump rotors (9 and 10) and drive pin (2) from the pump shaft. Remove and discard all O-rings.

Unscrew the mounting bolt (7—Fig. HN3-24) and remove the filter (8), sleeve (9) and guide cap (10). Remove the check valve plugs (23), springs (25) and balls (26). Remove the flange nuts (21) and bracket (22) from the release valve (16). Remove the cotter pin (11) and push the release valve (16) and cap (13) from the distributor plate.

Remove pin (2—Fig. HN3-25) from the end of the pump shaft if not previously removed. Remove the snap ring (10—Fig. HN3-26) and bushing (9) from the motor shaft (5). Remove the retaining screws and separate the pump housing (1) from the distributor plate (38).

Remove the pump assembly and motor assembly from the pump housing. Be careful not to damage the motor valve plate (17) or pump valve plate (22). Keep all pump and motor components in their original positions for reassembly.

To remove pump swashplate (10—Fig. HN3-27), remove the snap ring (5), needle bearing (4) and collar (3). Lift the swashplate (10) out of the pump housing (2). Pins (9) must be driven out to release the control yoke ring (6) and bearing plate (7). To remove the needle bearing (12), detach the snap ring (11) and drive out the bearing; the bearing will be damaged during disassembly and must be discarded.

Inspect components for excessive wear and damage. Pump and motor cylinder assemblies must be replaced as sets. Replace the valve plates (17 and 22—Fig. HN3-26) if they are damaged.

To reassemble transaxle, install bearings, bushings, seals and dowel pins in the cases and housings as required. Do not install bushing (9—Fig. HN3-26) at this point. Lubricate components with Honda hydrostatic transaxle oil during assembly.

Install the check valve balls (26—Fig. HN3-24) and springs (25), and tighten plugs (23) to 33 N·m (24 ft.-lb.). Install the release valve (16), but leave the nuts (21) loose.

Install the return shaft (36—Fig. HN3-26), spring (37), washer and locknut (39) on the distributor plate (38). The shaft must slide freely. Install the special screw (34) with seal washer (35) and tighten the screw to 25 N·m (118 ft.-lb.).

Install dowel pins (18 and 23), motor valve plate (17) and pump valve plate (22) on the distributor plate. Position the valve plates so the arrow mark (Fig. HN3-26) is facing up and pointing away from the bearing (6).

If removed, install the piston assemblies (26, 27 and 28) in the pump cylinder (21). Note the pump pistons heads are round, while the motor piston heads are indented. Position the pump cylinder assembly on the distributor plate (38). Install the bearing plate (20) and bearing (19) on the cylinder.

Install bearing plate (7—Fig. HN 3-27) and ring (6) in the swashplate (10), then insert the roll pins (9) so the split in pin is away from the ring (6) and the inner end of the pin does not extend past the ring's inside diameter. Install the washer (8) onto the swashplate trunnion located next to the projection (P) on the swashplate.

Install the swashplate in the pump housing (2). Install the needle bearing onto the trunnion on which the washer was installed. Secure the bearing with the snap ring (5). Install the bushing (3) onto the other trunnion so the cutout in bushing is toward the gap in the housing.

Install the motor shaft (5—Fig. HN3-26) with thrust washer (4) and drive gear (3) into the pump housing (1). Note the inner bearing plate (Fig. HN3-28) has a thinner inner ridge than the outer bearing plate and are not interchangeable. The thrust ball bearing plate must be installed so the beveled side is toward the inner bearing plate as shown in Fig. HN3-28.

If removed, install the piston assemblies (12, 13 and 14—Fig. HN3-26) into the motor cylinder (16). Install the motor cylinder assembly onto the motor shaft in the pump housing (1).

Install a sleeve (10—Fig. HN3-29) that is slightly smaller in diameter than the shaft bore into the distributor plate and a 6×2.5 mm bolt (11) onto the end of the motor shaft (1). The sleeve will hold the motor cylinder in place while assembling the pump housing assembly onto the distributor plate.

Assemble the pump housing to the distributor plate. Note the different length screws and their locations (Fig. HN3-30) in the housing. Tighten the retaining screws loosely. Install the bearing (30—Fig. HN3-26) on pump shaft (24) and install the shaft into the case. Rotate the shafts and check for binding.

Tighten the pump housing screws gradually in the sequence shown in Fig. HN3-30 to 25 N·m (18 ft.-lb.). Look through the check hole in the side of the pump housing and check for the correct positioning of the motor bearing plates and bearing (Fig. HN3-28).

Remove the bolt and sleeve from the motor shaft end and install bushing (8—Fig. HN3-29) and snap ring (9). On Model H4514H, install the relief valve assembly (3-6) with the flat side of the guide (5) next to the spring (4) and secure with a cotter pin (7). On Model H4518H, the washer (3) is not used and a plug equipped with an O-ring is used in place of the guide (5).

Install the suction filter (8—Fig. HN3-24) and tighten the retaining bolt (7) to 10 N·m (7 ft.-lb.).

On Model H4514H, install the spring seat (6—Fig. HN3-25) so the concave side is toward snap ring (5). On Model H4518H, a ball is used in place of the seat (6). Install the charge pump assembly and housing (14). Tighten the charge pump housing retaining screws to 25 N·m (18 ft.-lb.).

Assemble remainder of transaxle by reversing disassembly while noting the following: Install countershaft gear (3—Fig. HN3-24) so long end of hub is toward gear on countershaft (4). Tighten transaxle case (6—Fig. HN3-23) retaining screws to 25 N·m (18 ft.-lb.).

Install the input shaft (9—Fig. HN3-22) with the original shim (10). Install the input shaft bearing nut (7—Fig. HN3-22) so the end with outer ridges is toward the gear. Tighten the nut (7) to 75 N·m (55 ft.-lb.) and stake the nut to the shaft at the notch on the shaft. Install the nut (6) so the end with inner ridges is toward the gear and tighten to 90 N·m (66 ft.-lb.). Tighten the input shaft bearing housing retaining screws to 21 N·m (185 in.-lb.).

Lubricate the control shaft (4—Fig. HN3-21) with lithium grease before inserting in the cover (8). Install the collar (11) on the shaft and retain with pin (10). Install the control shaft assembly onto the transmission, aligning the two

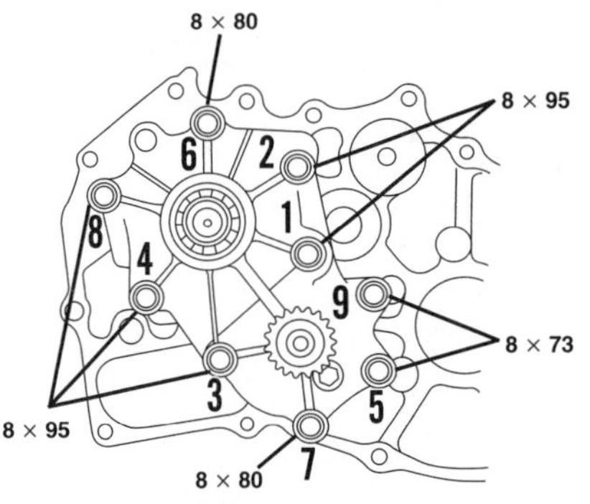

Fig. HN3-30—Note the different length screws and their location in the pump housing. Tighten screws gradually in the sequence indicated in the above drawing to 25 N• m (18 ft.-lb.).

pins (5) with the holes in the pump swashplate. On models equipped with type-A control shaft (4A), the punch mark on the splined end of the shaft must face forward and away from the reservoir tank after installation. Install the control arm on type-A control shaft so the punch mark on the shaft end and mark on the control arm are aligned.

Check for control arm free play. If the control arm free play is not 5-10 mm (0.2-0.4 in.) at the end of the control arm, loosen the cover (8) retaining screws and relocate holder.

If not installed when assembling the transaxle, attach the transaxle release lever assembly (1—Fig. HN3-21) to transaxle. Insert the release rod (2) through the slot in the release arm (3) before attaching the lever assembly. Adjust the position of nuts (N) after the transaxle is installed in the tractor.

Fill the transaxle with Honda Hydrostatic Transmission Fluid and bleed air from the unit as previously outlined.

Shift Lever

To check the friction preload on the shift lever, tie a cord on the shift lever 20 mm (0.79 in.) below the top of the lever and attach a spring scale to the other end of the cord. Pull the spring scale and measure the force required to move the lever. It should be between 1.9-2.5 kg (4.2-5.5 lb.).

To adjust friction preload, remove the shift lever assembly and adjust the number of shim washers (9—Fig. HN3-31). One washer changes the preload by about 0.15 kg (0.33 lb.).

To remove the shift lever assembly, first remove the seat and rear fenders. Disconnect the shift rod (1—Fig. HN3-31) from the shift lever arm (2). Remove the screws attaching the shift lever housing (17) to the frame and remove shift lever assembly.

Remove the cover (14). Unscrew the nut (12) and withdraw the friction

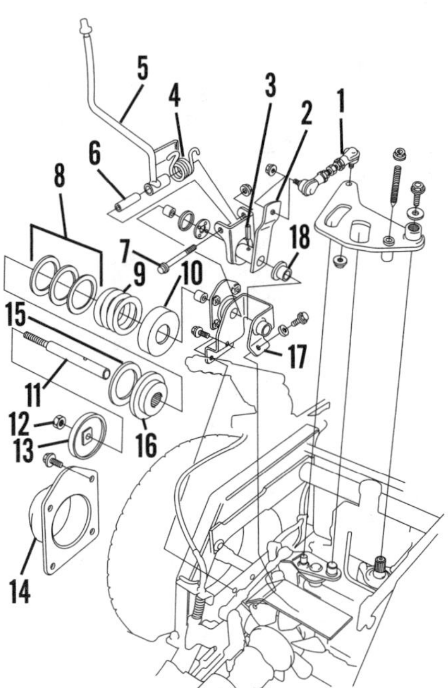

Fig. HN3-31—Exploded view of shift linkage. To adjust shift lever preload friction, add or remove washers (8).

1. Shift rod
2. Shift lever arm
3. Spring pin
4. Spring
5. Shift lever
6. Sleeve
7. Pivot bolt
8. Washers
9. Friction spring
10. Spring seat
11. Friction shaft
12. Nut
13. End cap
14. Cover
15. Friction washer
16. Collar
17. Shift lever holder

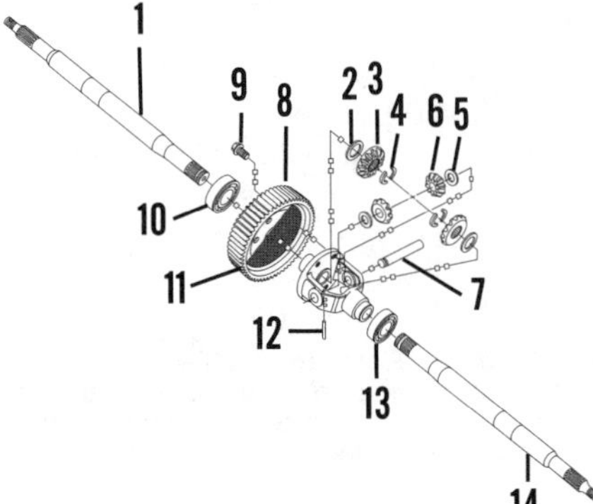

Fig. HN3-32—Exploded view of differential and axles.

1. Axle shaft, left
2. Washer
3. Differential gear
4. Split retainer
5. Washer
6. Pinion gears
7. Pinion shaft
8. Final drive gear
9. Bolt
10. Bearing
11. Differential case
12. Spring pin
13. Bearing
14. Axle shaft, right

washers and spring from the friction lever shaft (11). Remove nut and bolt (7) and remove the shift lever (5) and spring (4) from the lever arm (2). Drive out the spring pin (3) and remove the friction shaft (11) and the shift lever arm from the shift lever housing (17).

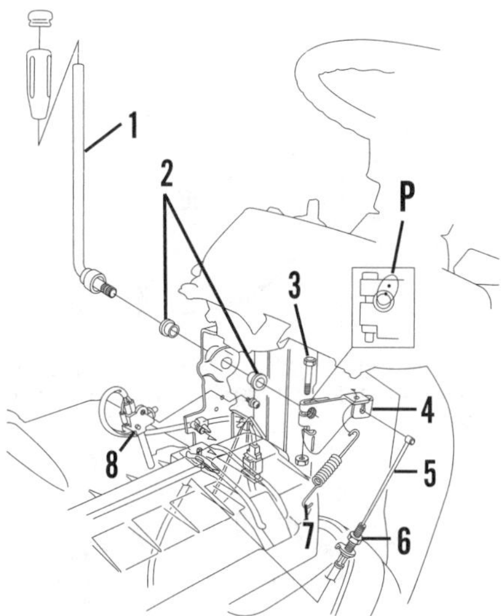

Fig. HN3-33—Exploded view of PTO clutch control lever.

1. Clutch lever
2. Bushings
3. Clamp bolt
4. PTO clutch arm
5. Clutch cable
6. Adjusting nut
7. Spring
8. PTO clutch switch

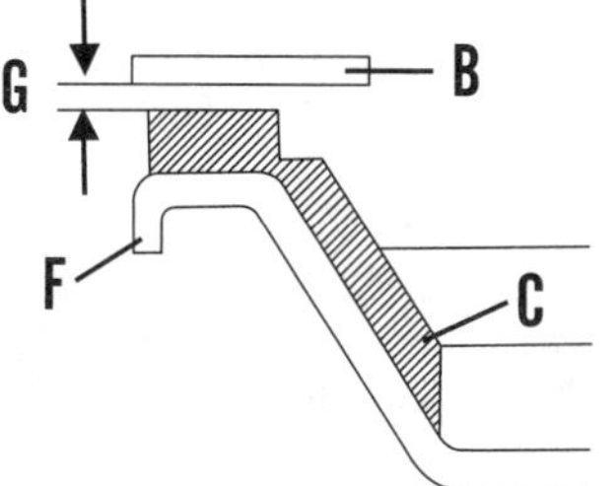

Fig. HN3-34—To check PTO clutch adjustment, engage clutch and measure gap (G) between brake plate (B) and PTO driven disc flange (F). Refer to text.

To reassemble the shift lever, reverse the disassembly procedure while noting the following special instructions. Hook the longer end of the spring (4) around the shift lever. Tighten the nut (12) to 40 N·m (30 ft.-lb.).

DIFFERENTIAL AND REAR AXLES OVERHAUL

To remove the differential and axles, remove the transaxle from the tractor as previously outlined. Drain the oil from the transaxle housing. Separate the transaxle case halves (6 and 9—Fig. HN3-23. Remove the differential and axles as an assembly (1—Fig. HN3-24) from the housing.

To disassemble, drive the spring pin (12—Fig. HN3-32) out of the differential case (11). Push the pinion shaft (7) out of the case. Remove the retainers (4) from the axle shafts. Remove the pinion gears (6), side gears (3) and washers.

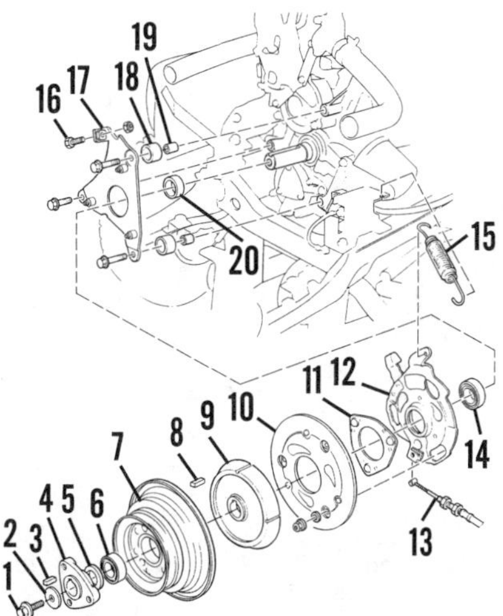

Fig. HN3-35—Exploded view of PTO clutch used on Model H4514H.

1. Screw
2. Washer
3. Key
4. Fan hub
5. Spacer
6. Bearing
7. Pulley
8. Key
9. Drive plate
10. Brake plate
11. Ball retainer
12. Control plate
13. PTO clutch cable
14. Bearing
15. Return spring
16. Stop bolt
17. Base plate
18. Spacer
19. Dowel pin
20. Collar

Pull the bearings (10 and 13) off the differential case. Remove the bolts (9) and separate the final drive gear (8) from the case.

Inspect all components for wear or damage and replace when necessary. Minor scuff marks can be removed from the pinion shaft (7) using fine emery paper.

If the final drive gear was removed, install the gear and tighten the retaining bolts (9) to 55 N·m (40 ft.-lb.). Install the axle shafts, side gears, pinion gears and washers. Select washers (5) of a thickness permitting smooth axle rotation without excessive play. Both washers (5) must be equal thickness.

Install the retainers (4) on the axle before inserting the pinion shaft (7). Drive in the split pin (12) so the split in the pin is facing away from the pinion shaft.

Install the axles and differential assembly in the transaxle case as outlined in the TRANSAXLE section.

PTO CLUTCH

A cable-actuated cone clutch is attached to the end of the engine crankshaft. A switch prevents engine starting if the PTO operating lever is in the engaged position.

ADJUSTMENT

PTO operating lever free play should be 1-3 mm (0.04-0.12 in.) measured at

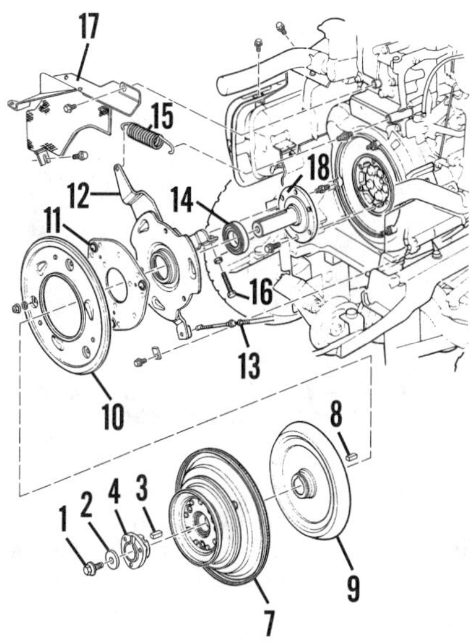

Fig. HN3-36—Exploded view of PTO clutch used on Model H4518H.

1. Screw
2. Washer
3. Key
4. Fan hub
7. Pulley
8. Key
9. Drive plate
10. Brake plate
11. Ball retainer
12. Control plate
13. PTO clutch cable
14. Bearing
15. Spring
16. Stop bolt
17. Muffler heat shield
18. Spindle

the top of the lever. To adjust free play, raise the hood and rotate the adjusting nuts (6—Fig. HN3-33) at the end of the cable housing. Tighten nuts and recheck free play. Be sure that the punch marks (P) on the end of the clutch lever (1) and clutch arm (4) are aligned.

Move the PTO clutch lever to the engaged position and measure the gap (G—Fig. HN3-34) between the PTO clutch brake plate (B) and the driven disc flange (F). If the gap is less than 0.6 mm (0.024 in.), readjust the lever free play. If the gap is less than 0.1 mm (0.004 in.), replace the driven disc.

OVERHAUL

Before removing the PTO clutch, disconnect the negative battery cable. Remove the hood and drain the engine coolant. Remove the radiator, cooling fan and mower drive belt.

Detach the spring (15—Fig. HN3-35 or HN3-36) and PTO cable (13). Unscrew the retaining screw (1) and remove the fan hub (4), drive pulley (7) and drive plate (9). Unscrew the brake plate nuts and remove the brake plate (10), ball retainer (11) and control plate (12).

Replace excessively damaged components. Check the wear surfaces on flange and cone of the driven pulley (7). Replace the driven pulley if the wear material on the flange (F—Fig. HN3-34) is worn to the flange surface. Measure worn and unworn portions of

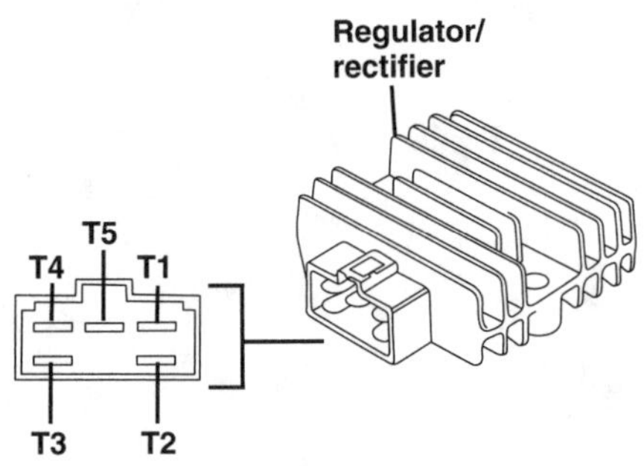

Fig. HN3-37—Drawing of regulator/rectifier. Refer to text for test procedure.

the wear material on the cone surface (C) of the driven pulley. Replace the driven pulley if the wear material on the one surface has worn more than 1.0 mm (0.04 in.).

Reassemble by reversing the disassembly procedure. Before attaching spring (15—Fig. HN3-35 or Fig. HN3-36), rotate the control plate (12) clockwise and measure the gap between stop and screw (16). Rotate the screw so the gap is 12-14 mm (0.47-0.55 in.), then tighten the jam nut. After installation, check the adjustment as previously outlined.

If the PTO clutch operating lever (1—Fig. HN3-33) and clutch arm (4) are separated, install the arm on the clutch lever shaft so the punch marks (P) on the shaft end and arm are aligned.

ELECTRICAL SYSTEM

Wiring schematics are located at the end of this section. Engine related electrical components, such as the starter, are covered in the appropriate Honda engine section at the rear of this manual.

REGULATOR/RECTIFIER

The regulator/rectifier is located to the left of the steering shaft joint and can be identified by the fins on the body. To test the unit, connect an ohmmeter to the terminals of the regulator/rectifier identified in Fig. HN3-37 then refer to chart in Fig. HN3-38 or HN3-39.

FUSES

A 20 amp main fuse protects the electrical system. On early H4514H models, three 5 amp fuses are also used to protect some circuits. On Model H4518H and later H4514H models, one 5 amp fuse is used in addition to the 20 amp main fuse. Refer to the appropriate wiring schematic.

On early H4514H models, the 20 amp main fuse holder is incorporated in the positive battery terminal connector.

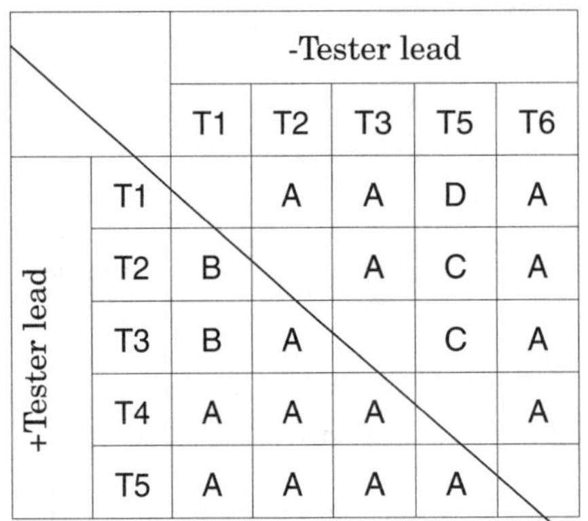

+Tester lead \ -Tester lead	T1	T2	T3	T5	T6
T1		A	A	D	A
T2	B		A	C	A
T3	B	A		C	A
T4	A	A	A		A
T5	A	A	A	A	

Fig. HN3-38—Test values for regulator used on Model H4514H tractors prior to serial number 1006847.

A. Infinity
B. 0.1k-50k ohms
C. 1k-200k ohms
D. 0.5-1000k ohms

+Tester lead \ -Tester lead	T1	T2	T3	T4	T5
T1		A	A	A	B
T2	C		A	A	B
T3	C	A		A	B
T4	A	A	A		A
T5	C	A	A	A	

Fig. HN3-39—Test values for regulator used on Model H4518H and Model H4514H tractors after serial number 1006846.

A. Infinity
B. 1k-50k ohms
C. 0.5k-20k ohms

The three 5 amp fuses are located in a fuse holder near the right end of the battery.

On Model H4518H and later H4514H models, the 20 amp main fuse and 5 amp auxiliary fuse are located in a fuse holder near the right end of the battery.

COMBINATION RELAY

The combination relay is located behind the instrument panel to the right of the steering shaft. The combination relay routes battery voltage to several components. Refer to the following tests to determine if the combination relay is operating properly in a given circuit. Disconnect and remove the combination relay to perform the tests. The voltage source for the tests is a 12-volt battery.

Ignition Relay

Connect 12-volt battery positive lead to terminal Lo and negative leads to

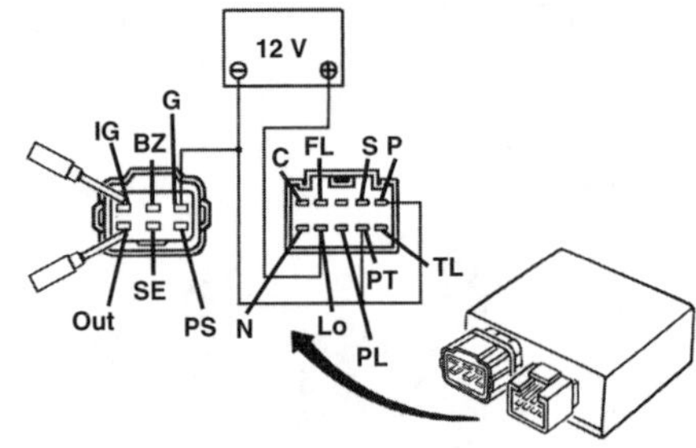

Fig. HN3-40—A 12-volt power source is needed to test the combination relay. Refer to text.

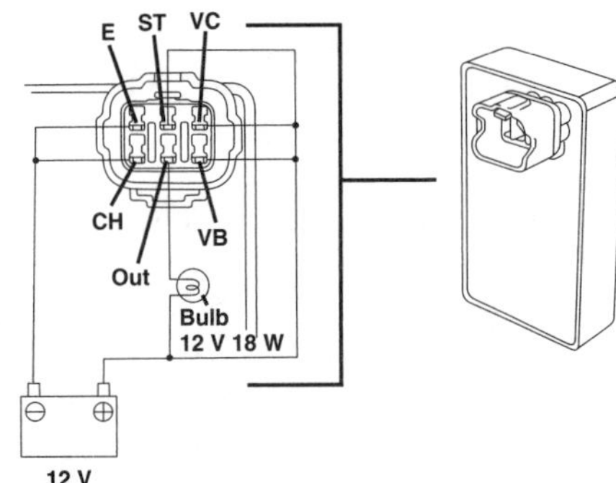

Fig. HN3-41—Refer to text to test the engine control unit used on Model H4518H.

terminals PT, P and G (Fig. HN3-40). Connect a continuity tester or ohmmeter between terminals IG and OUT on the combination relay. If the combination relay is operating properly, there should be no continuity when the battery is disconnected and continuity when the battery is connected.

Starter Relay

Connect 12-volt battery positve lead to terminals C and Lo. Connect negative leads to terminals G, P and PT (Fig. HN3-40). Connect negative voltmeter lead to negative battery terminal and positive voltmeter lead to relay terminal S. If the combination relay is operating properly, voltmeter reading should indicate 12 volts when the battery is connected and zero volts when the battery is disconnected.

Parking Brake System

Connect the buzzer and warning light (12v 3.4W) between terminals BZ and PL (Fig. HN3-240). Connect 12-volt battery positive lead to terminal Lo and negative leads to terminals G, SE and PS. Connect a continuity tester or ohmmeter between terminals IG and OUT on the combination relay. When the negative battery terminal is connected to terminal PS, there should be no continuity between terminals IG and OUT, the light should be out and the buzzer

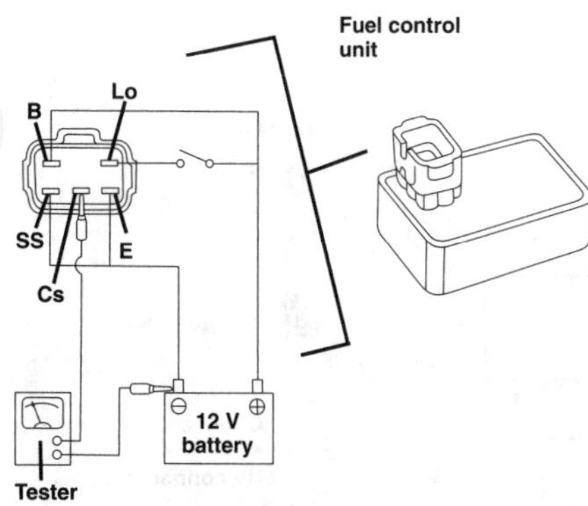

Fig. HN3-42—Refer to text to test the fuel control unit used on Model H4514H tractors prior to serial number 1006847.

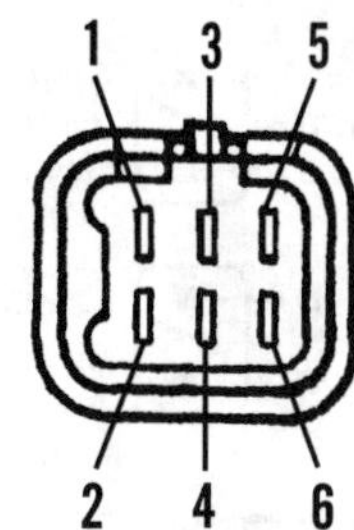

Fig. HN3-43—Connect ohmmeter to numbered terminals shown above while referring to diode test procedure in text.

should be off. A few seconds after disconnecting negative terminal from terminal PS, the buzzer and light should come on.

Safety Interlock

Connect12-volt battery positive lead to terminal Lo and negative leads to terminals G, SE and N (Fig. HN3-40). Connect a continuity tester or ohmmeter between terminals IG and OUT on the combination relay. When the negative battery terminal is connected to terminal SE, there should be no continuity. When the negative battery terminal is disconnected from terminal SE, there should be continuity.

ENGINE CONTROL UNIT (MODEL H4518H)

The engine control unit is mounted on a bracket near the left end of the battery. The engine control unit is a rectangular box with a single six-wire connector (Fig. HN3-41).

To test the engine control unit, disconnect the connector from the unit and use a 12-volt battery for the following test. Connect a 12 v 18 W bulb between positive terminal on battery and the OUT terminal. Connect battery positve lead to terminals VB, VC and ST. Connect negative leads to terminals CH and E. Disconnect voltage from terminal ST. Bulb should light for a few seconds then go out.

FUEL CONTROL UNIT (MODEL H4514H— PRIOR TO SERIAL NUMBER 1006847)

Tractors prior to serial number 1006847 are equipped with a fuel control unit. The fuel control unit is mounted on a bracket near the left end of the battery. The engine control unit is a rectangular box with a single five-wire connector (Fig. HN3-42).

To test the fuel control unit, disconnect the connector from the unit. Connect 12-volt battery positive lead to terminal B. Connect positive 12-volt lead with a switch to terminal Lo. Connect negative leads to terminals SS and E. Connect the negative voltmeter lead to the negative battery terminal and positive voltmeter lead to relay the terminal Cs. The voltmeter should indicate zero volts when the switch to terminal Lo is on. When switch to terminal Lo is off, voltmeter should indicate approximately 12 volts for 9 seconds, then decrease to zero volts.

DIODE (MODEL H4514H—PRIOR TO SERIAL NUMBER 1006847)

Tractors prior to serial number 1006847 are equipped with a six-terminal diode in the fuel control circuit. The diode is located below the regulator/rectifier.

To test diode, disconnect the connector from the diode and use an ohmmeter set on R×1. Refer to Fig. HN3-43.

In three separate tests, connect the positive ohmmeter lead to terminal 2 and the negative lead to terminal 1, the positive ohmmeter lead to terminal 4 and the negative lead to terminal 3, the positive ohmmeter lead to terminal 6 and the negative lead to terminal 5. In the foregoing tests, the ohmmeter should read 1-200 ohms.

Connect the ohmmeter to all other terminal combinations. The ohmmeter should read infinity except in the three tests where 1-200 ohms should be found.

WIRING SCHEMATICS

The wiring schematic for Model H4514H (serial number 1000001-1006846) is shown in Fig. HN3-44. Wiring schematic for Model H4514H (serial number 1006846-on) is shown in Fig. HN3-45. The wiring schematic for Model H4518H is shown in Fig. HN3-46.

Figure HN3-44, Figure HN3-45 and Figure HN3-46 are on the following pages.

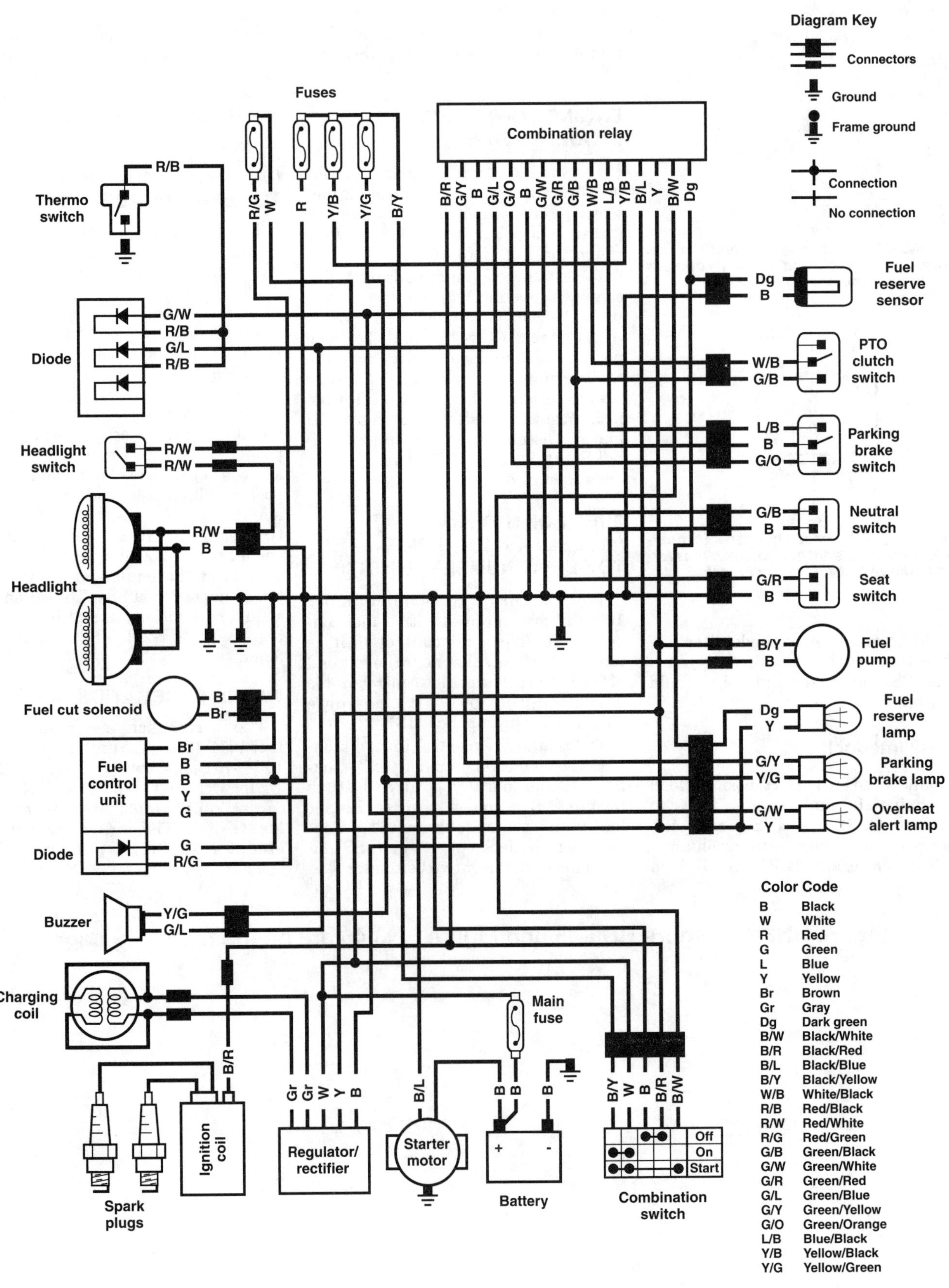

Fig. HN3-44—Wiring schematic for Model H4514H tractors prior to serial number 1006847.

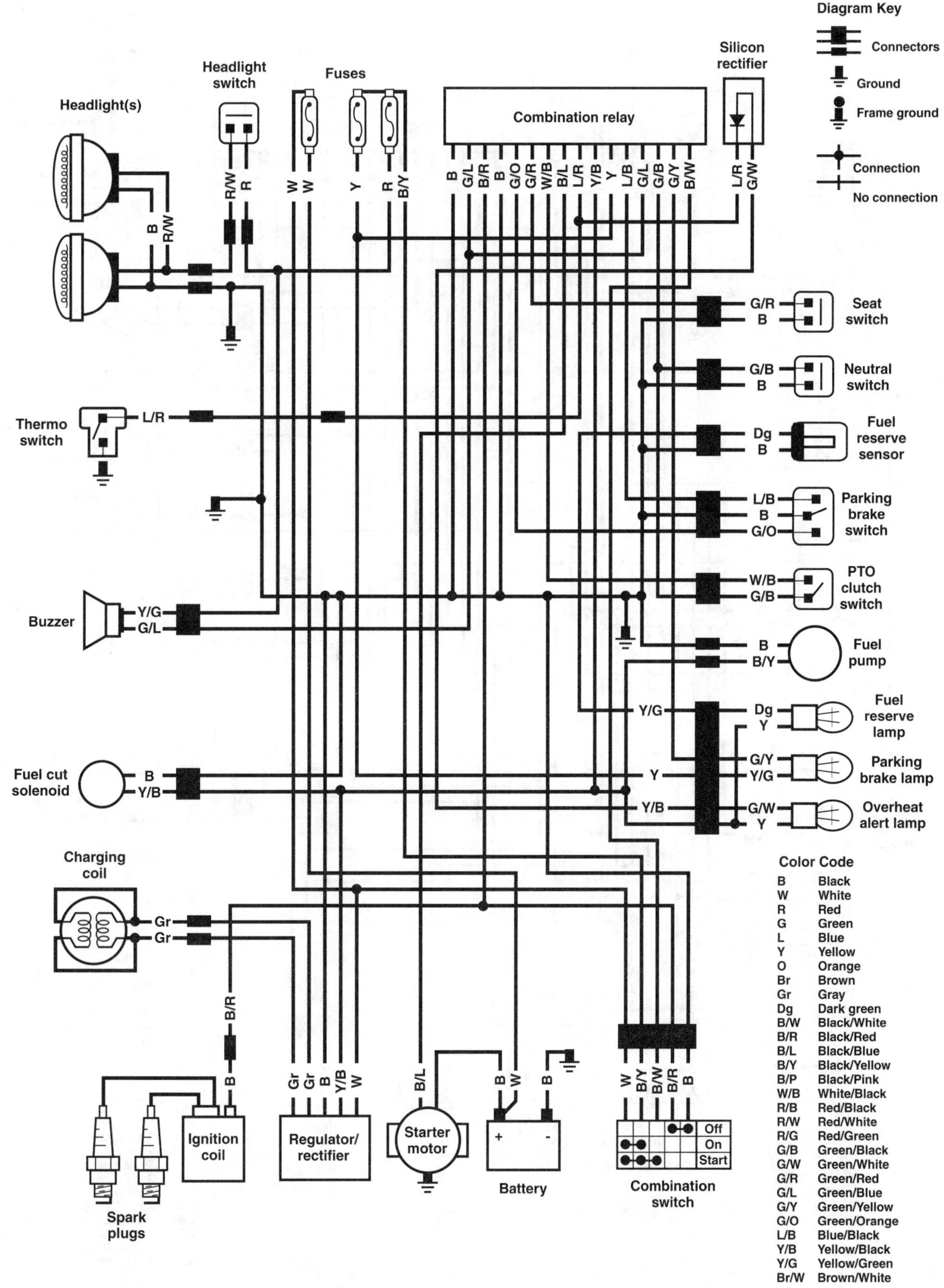

Fig. HN3-45—Wiring schematic for Model H4514H tractors after serial number 1006846.

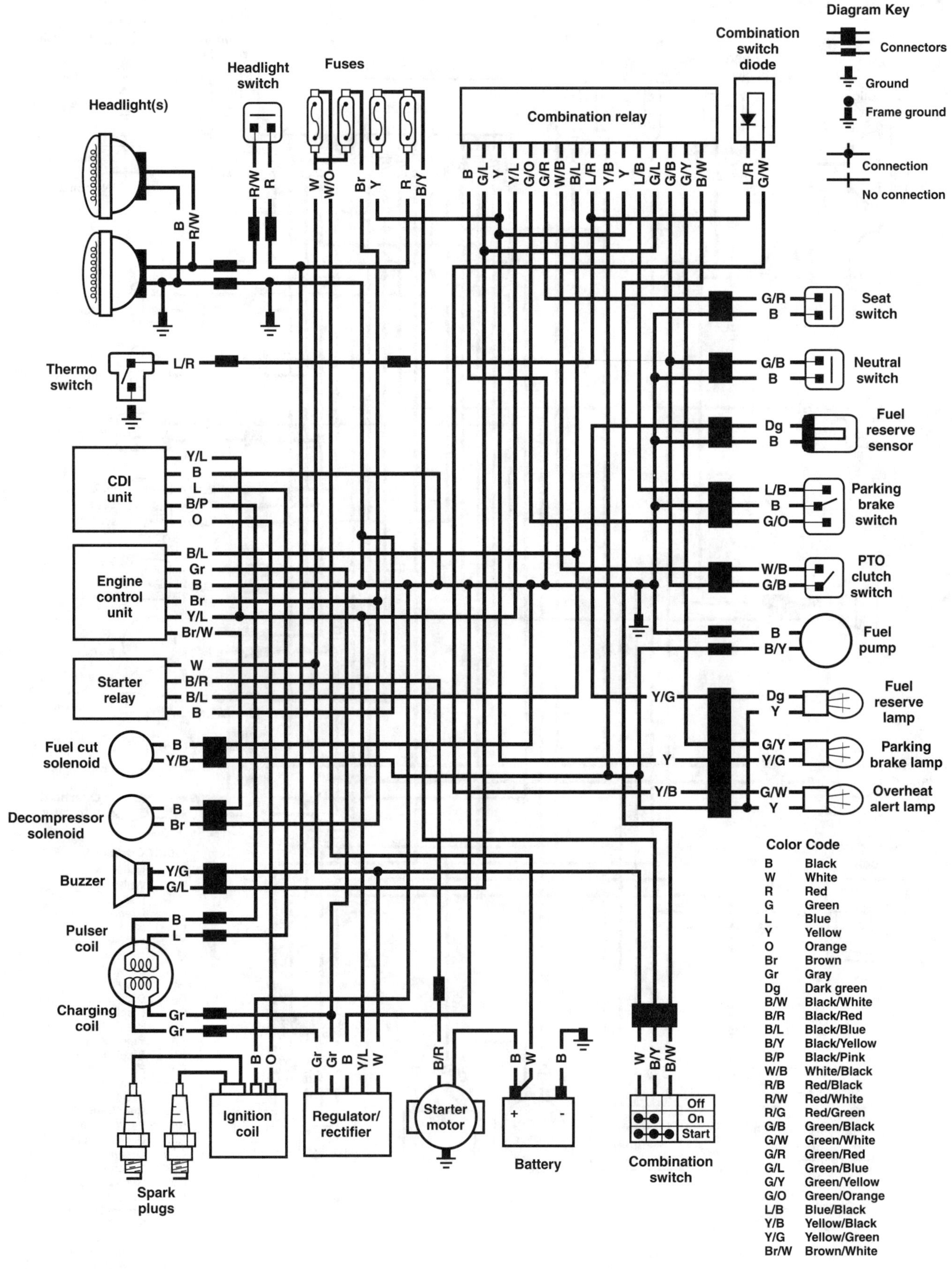

Fig. HN3-46—Wiring schematic for Model H4518H.

INGERSOLL

CONDENSED SPECIFICATIONS

Models	1112G	1112H	1114AWS	1212G	1212H	1214AWS
Engine Make	B&S	B&S	B&S	B&S	B&S	B&S
Model	283707	283707	294777	283707	283707	261777
Number of cylinders	1	1	2	1	1	1
Bore	3.438 in. (87.3 mm)	3.438 in. (87.3 mm)	68 mm (2.68 in.)	3.438 in. (87.3 mm)	3.438 in. (87.3 mm)	87 mm (3.43 in.)
Stroke	3.06 in. (77.7 mm)	3.06 in. (77.7 mm)	66 mm (2.60 in.)	3.06 in. (77.7 mm)	3.06 in. (77.7 mm)	73 mm (2.86 in.)
Displacement	28.04 cu. in. (465 cc)	28.04 cu. in. (465 cc)	480 cc (29.3 cu. in.)	28.04 cu. in. (465 cc)	28.04 cu. in. (465 cc)	435 cc (26.5 cu. In.)
Power Rating	12 hp (9 kW)	12 hp (9 kW)	14 hp (10.5 kW)	12 hp (9 kW)	12 hp (9 kW)	14 hp (10.5 kW)
Slow Idle	1750 rpm	1750 rpm	1400 rpm	1750 rpm	1750 rpm	1400 rpm
High Speed (No-load)	3600 rpm	3600 rpm	3600 rpm	3600 rpm	3600 rpm	3600 rpm
Crankcase Capacity	3 pt. (1.4 L)	3 pt. (1.4 L)	3.5 pt.* (1.65 L)	3 pt. (1.4 L)	3 pt. (1.4 L)	4.4 pt.* (2.1 L)
Transmission Capacity	30 oz. (890 mL)	See text	30 oz. (890 mL)	30 oz. (890 mL)	See text	30 oz. (890 mL)

*Includes oil filter.

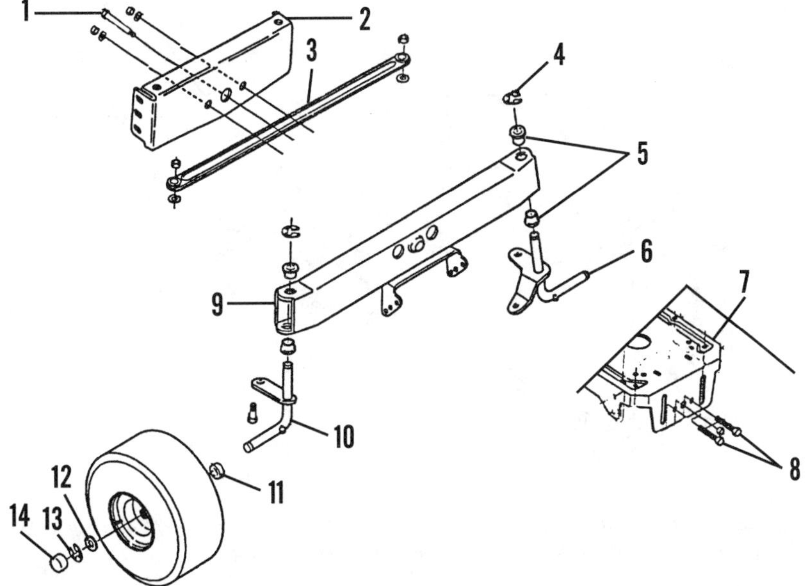

Fig. IN1-1—Exploded view of front axle assembly used on Models 1112G, 1112H and 1114AWS.

1. Pivot bolt
2. Bracket
3. Tie rod
4. E-ring
5. Bushings
6. Spindle (left)
7. Frame
8. Bolts
9. Axle main member
10. Spindle (right)
11. Bearing
12. Washer
13. E-ring
14. Hub cap

FRONT AXLE ASSEMBLY

MAINTENANCE

Inject grease into the grease fittings located on the axle and steering components at 25-hour intervals. The recommended lubricant is multipurpose, lithium-base grease.

Clean all pivot points and linkages and lubricate with SAE 30 oil. Check for looseness and wear. Repair as needed.

SPINDLES

Models 1112G, 1112H and 1114AWS

Raise the front of the tractor and support with suitable stands. Remove the wheel and tire. Disconnect tie rod end, and if needed, drag link end. Detach E-ring (4—Fig. IN1-1) securing the top of the spindle and withdraw the spindle from the axle.

Inspect components for damage. Replaceable bushings (5) are located in the axle.

Install the spindle by reversing the removal procedure.

Models 1212G, 1212H and 1214AWS

Raise the front of tractor and support with suitable stands. Remove the wheel and tire. Disconnect tie rod end, and if needed, drag link end. Remove the roll pin (10—Fig. IN1-2) securing the top of the spindle and withdraw the spindle from the axle.

Inspect components for damage. Replace the spindle (6 or 14) and/or axle if damaged.

Install spindle by reversing the removal procedure.

AXLE MAIN MEMBER REMOVAL AND INSTALLATION

Models 1112G, 1112H and 1114AWS

To remove the axle main member (9—Fig. IN1-1), raise and support the front of the tractor. Remove the front wheels. Remove the spindles as previously described. Unscrew the axle travel limiting bolts (8). Unscrew the pivot bolt (1) and remove the axle from the tractor.

Reassemble by reversing removal procedure.

Models 1212G, 1212H and 1214AWS

The complete front axle assembly may be removed as a unit. Raise and support the front of the tractor. Disconnect the drag link end from the left spindle (6—Fig. IN1-2). Support the axle and remove the pivot bolt (1) and pivot bracket (11), then remove the main member assembly (4).

Install by reversing the removal procedure.

FRONT STEERING SYSTEM

Models 1112G, 1112H, 1212G and 1212H are equipped with a 2-wheel steering system, while Models 1114AWS and 1214AWS are equipped with a 4-wheel steering system. The front wheel steering mechanism is similar for all models.

On the 4-wheel steering system, a rear drag link attached to the steering sector gear transfers steering motion to the rear wheel steering mechanism. Refer to the REAR STEERING SYSTEM section for related service information.

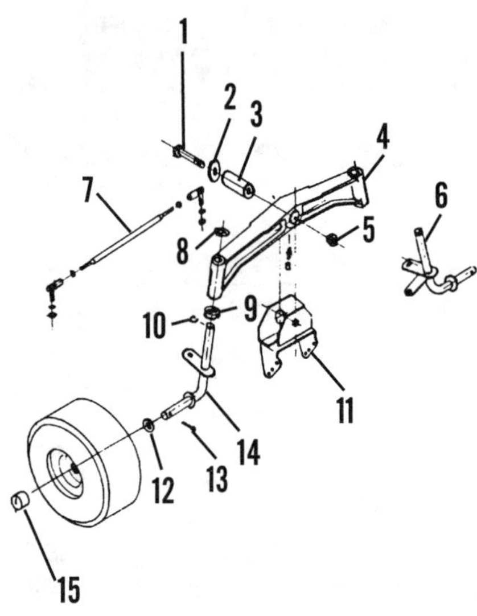

Fig. IN1-2—Exploded view of front axle assembly used on Models 1212G, 1212H and 1214AWS.

1. Bolt
2. Washer
3. Pivot pin
4. Axle main member
5. Nut
6. Spindle (left)
7. Tie rod
8. Washer
9. Thrust washer
10. Roll pin
11. Pivot bracket
12. Washer
13. Cotter pin
14. Spindle (right)
15. Hub cap

Fig. IN1-3—Exploded view of steering gear assembly Models 1112G, 1112H, 1212G and 1212H.

1. Steering wheel
2. Roll pin
3. Boot
4. Pedestal
5. Steering shaft
6. Roll pin
7. Steering gear
8. Thrust washer
9. Nut
10. Washer
11. Washer
12. Sector gear
13. Bushing
14. Pivot bolt
15. Drag link
16. Special washer
17. Washer
18. E-ring

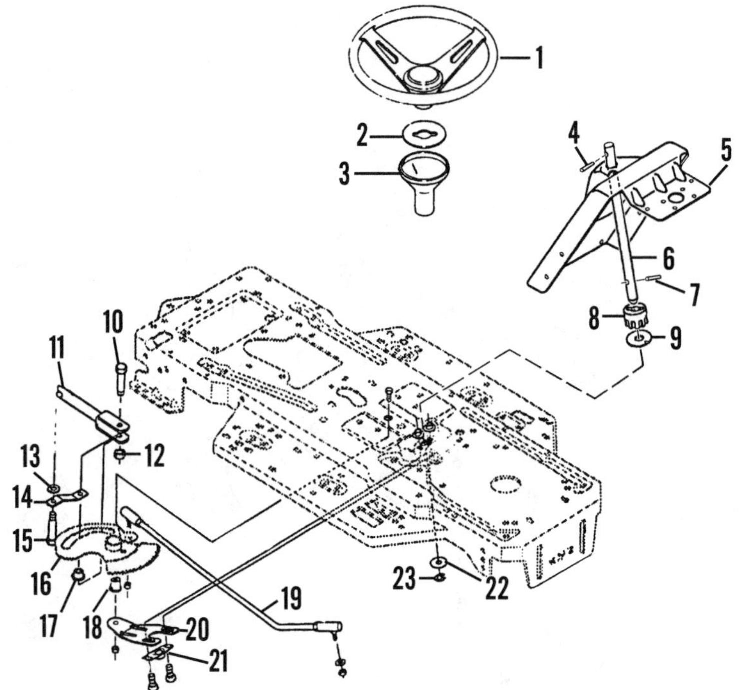

Fig. IN1-4—Exploded view of steering gear assembly Models 1114AWS and 1214AWS. Refer to Fig. IN1-11 for exploded view of rear steering components.

1. Steering wheel
2. Insert
3. Boot
4. Roll pin
5. Pedestal
6. Steering shaft
7. Roll pin
8. Steering gear
9. Thrust washer
10. Pivot pin
11. Rear drag link
12. Nut
13. Washer
14. Link
15. Pivot bolt
16. Sector gear
17. Roller
18. Bushing
19. Drag link
20. Bracket
21. Flange bearing
22. Washer
23. E-ring

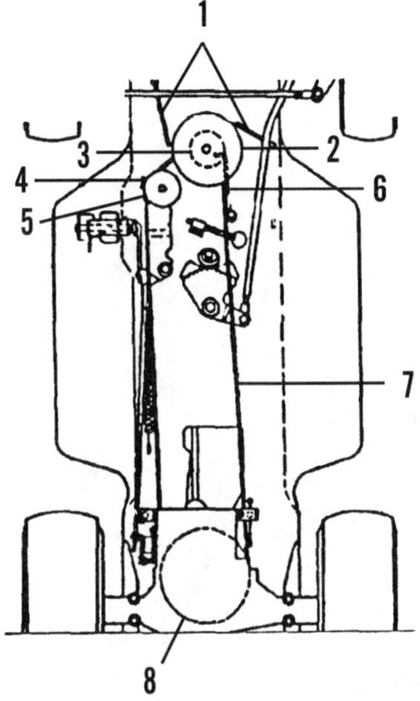

Fig. IN1-5—Drawing of traction drive belt routing.

1. Belt guides
2. Lower engine pulley
3. Upper engine pulley
4. Belt guide
5. Idler pulley
6. Belt guide
7. Traction drive belt
8. Transaxle/final drive pulley

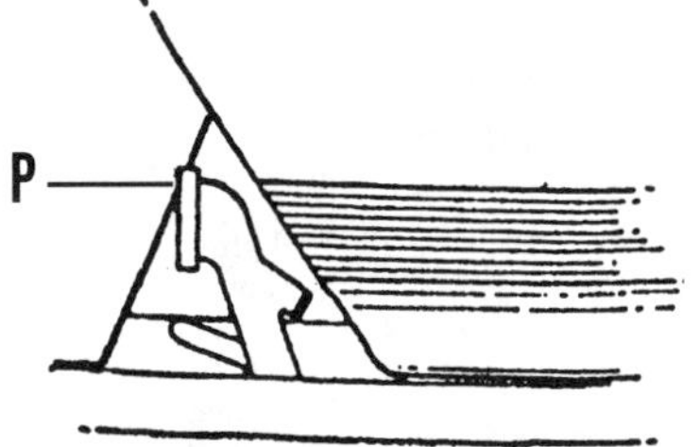

Fig. IN1-6—When drive belt is properly adjusted, clutch/brake should appear in position shown when released.

STEERING GEAR REMOVAL AND INSTALLATION

Models 1112G, 1112H, 1212G and 1212H

Remove the mower deck, if so equipped. Drive out the roll pin (2—Fig. IN1-3) and remove the steering wheel. Drive out the roll pin (6), pull up the steering shaft, and remove the steering gear (7). Remove the steering shaft.

Detach the drag link from the sector gear (12). Unscrew the pivot bolt (14) and remove the sector gear.

Install by reversing the removal procedure.

Models 1114AWS and 1214AWS

Remove the mower deck, if so equipped. Drive out the roll pin (4—Fig. IN1-4) and remove the steering wheel. Drive out the roll pin (7), pull up the steering shaft, and remove the steering gear (8). Remove the steering shaft.

Detach the front and rear drag links from the sector gear (16). Unscrew the sector gear pivot bolt, then unscrew and remove the bracket (20). Remove the sector gear.

Install by reversing the removal procedure.

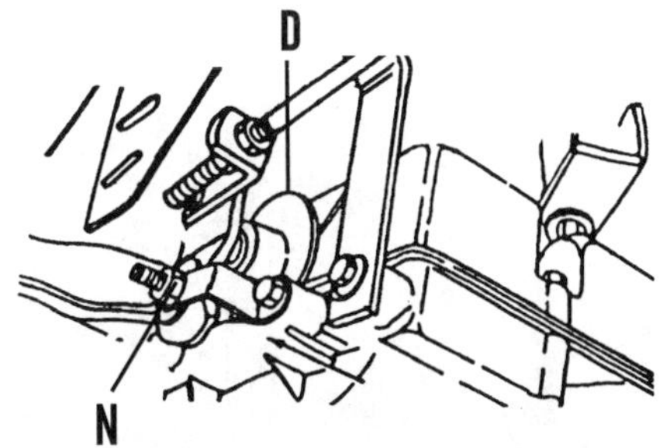

Fig. IN1-7—On Models 1112G, 1212G, 1114AWS and 1214AWS turn nut (N) to adjust brake. Clearance between brake disc (D) and pad should be 0.020 inch (0.5 mm).

ENGINE

REMOVAL AND INSTALLATION

Remove the hood, side panels and grille. Disconnect the battery cables, starter wires and all necessary electrical connections at engine. Disconnect the fuel line. Disconnect the engine control cable from the engine.

Remove the drive belts from the engine pulleys. On Models 1114AWS and 1214AWS remove the muffler heat shield and muffler. Remove the engine pulley. Remove the engine mounting bolts and lift the engine from the tractor.

Install by reversing the removal procedure.

OVERHAUL

Refer to the appropriate Briggs & Stratton engine section in this manual for tune-up specifications, engine overhaul procedures and engine maintenance.

TRACTION BELTS REMOVAL AND INSTALLATION

Remove the mower deck and mower drive belt, if so equipped. Push down the clutch/brake pedal and engage the parking brake.

Loosen the clutch idler pulley (5—Fig. IN1-5) screw and remove the traction drive belt from the pulley. Remove the drive belt from the engine pulley (3) and the transaxle or final drive pulley (8).

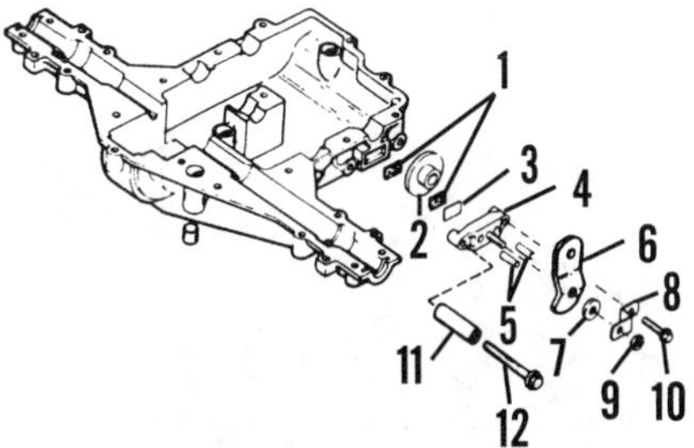

Fig. IN1-8—Exploded view of disc brake assembly used on Models 1112G, 1212G, 1114AWS and 1214AWS. Disc brake on Models 1112H and 1212H is similar.

1. Brake pads
2. Brake disc
3. Back plate
4. Brake holder
5. Actuating pins
6. Brake lever
7. Washer
8. Bracket
9. Adjusting nut
10. Cap screw
11. Spacer
12. Screw

Reinstall the traction drive belt by reversing the removal procedure. The belt must be positioned inside the upper engine pulley belt guide. Position the belt guides so the gap between the guide and pulley is $\frac{1}{16}$ inch (1.6 mm).

CLUTCH/BRAKE

MODELS 1112G, 1212G, 1114AWS AND 1214AWS

Adjustment

When the clutch is properly adjusted, the clutch/brake pedal should be positioned as shown in Fig. IN1-6 when the pedal is released. Clutch and brake mechanisms should be adjusted together for proper operation.

Remove the mower deck, if so equipped. Push down the clutch/brake pedal and engage the parking brake.

Loosen the clutch idler pulley (5—Fig. IN1-5) screw and move the idler pulley to obtain the desired clutch/brake pedal position.

Move the idler pulley away from the engine pulley to move the pedal forward. Move the idler pulley toward the engine pulley to move the pedal rearward. Retighten the idler pulley screw.

Note that the belt guide (4) adjacent to the idler pulley should be toward the forward juncture of the tractor frame and running board.

Check brake operation. Attempt to push the tractor with the parking brake engaged in the second notch and the transaxle shift lever in NEUTRAL. If the tractor cannot be pushed, the brake is too tight.

Push down the clutch/brake pedal and engage the parking brake in the fourth notch. If the tractor can be pushed, the brake is too loose.

To adjust the brake, depress the clutch/brake pedal sufficiently so the

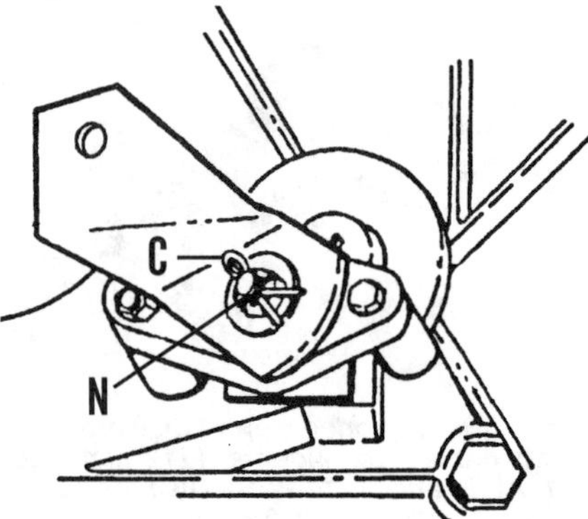

Fig. IN1-9—To adjust brake on Models 1112H and 1212H, remove cotter pin (C) and rotate adjustment nut (N).

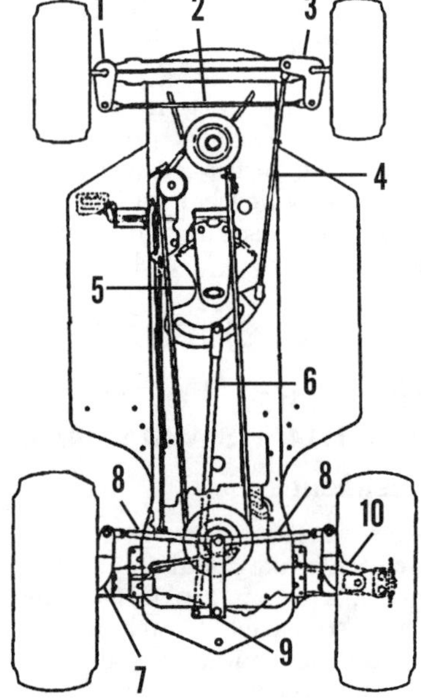

Fig. IN1-10—Drawing showing steering components on Models 1114AWS and 1214AWS.

1. Front spindle (right)
2. Tie rod
3. Front spindle (left)
4. Front drag link
5. Sector gear
6. Rear spindle (right)
7. Tie rods
8. Rear pivot arm
9. Rear spindle (left)

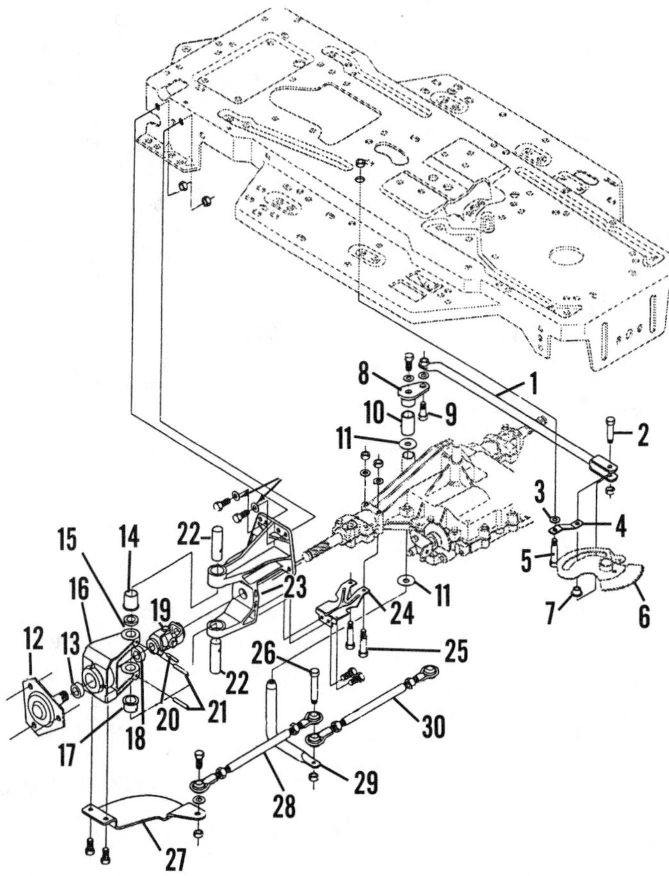

Fig. IN1-11—Exploded view of rear steering system used on Models 1114AWS and 1214AWS.

1. Rear drag link
2. Pivot bolt
3. Washer
4. Link
5. Pivot bolt
6. Sector gear
7. Roller
8. Steering lever
9. Pivot bolt
10. Spacer
11. Washer
12. Outer axle
13. Bearing
14. Bushing
15. Washer
16. Spindle
17. Bushing
18. Bearing
19. Universal joint
20. Roll pin
21. Roll pin
22. Kingpin
23. Axle mounting bracket
24. Bracket
25. Shoulder bolt
26. Pivot bolt
27. Steering arm
28. Tie rod (right)
29. Pivot arm
30. Tie rod (left)

parking brake can be engaged. Use a feeler gauge to measure the clearance between the brake disc (D—Fig. IN1-7) and pad. Clearance should be 0.020 inch (0.5 mm). Turn the nut (N) to obtain the correct clearance. Recheck brake adjustment.

Brake Pads

To remove the brake assembly, first raise and support the rear of the tractor. Remove the right rear wheel. Disconnect the brake rod from the brake lever (6—Fig. IN1-8). Remove the brake mounting cap screws and withdraw the brake holder (4), disc (2) and pads (1).

To reinstall the brake, reverse the removal procedure. Adjust the brake as previously outlined.

MODELS 1112H AND 1212H

Adjustment

When the clutch is properly adjusted, the clutch/brake pedal should be positioned as shown in Fig. IN1-6 when the pedal is released. Clutch and brake mechanisms should be adjusted together for proper operation.

Remove the mower deck, if so equipped. Push down the clutch/brake pedal and engage the parking brake. Loosen the clutch idler pulley (5—Fig. IN1-5) screw and move the idler pulley to obtain the desired clutch/brake pedal position.

Move the idler pulley away from the engine pulley to move the pedal forward. Move the idler pulley toward the engine pulley to move the pedal rearward. Retighten the idler pulley screw.

Note that the belt guide (4) adjacent to the idler pulley should be toward the forward juncture of the tractor frame and running board.

Check brake operation. Attempt to push the tractor with the transmission release control rod engaged and the shift control lever in NEUTRAL. If the tractor cannot be pushed, the brake is too tight.

Push down the clutch/brake pedal and engage the parking brake in the fourth notch. If the tractor can be pushed, the brake is too loose.

To adjust the brake, remove the cotter pin (C—Fig. IN1-9) and rotate the adjustment nut (N) in small increments. Rotate the nut clockwise to tighten the brake.

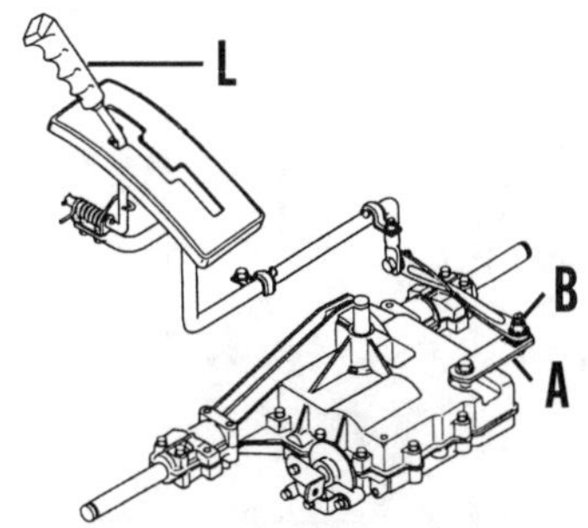

Fig. IN1-12—To adjust neutral of shift linkage on Models 1112G, 1212G, 1114AWS and 1214AWS, refer to text and drawing.

Reinstall the cotter pin. Recheck brake adjustment.

Brake Pads

To remove the brake assembly, first raise and support the rear of the tractor. Remove the right rear wheel. Disconnect the brake rod from the brake lever (6—Fig. IN1-8). Remove the brake mounting cap screws and withdraw the brake holder (4), disc (2) and pads (1).

To reinstall the brake, reverse the removal procedure. Adjust the brake as previously outlined.

REAR-WHEEL STEERING SYSTEM

Models 1114AWS and 1214AWS are equipped with a 4-wheel steering system (see Fig. IN1-10). Movement of the steering sector gear (5) provides directional force for the rear steering system.

Linkage transfers the steering motion to the rear pivot arm (9). Tie rods connected between the rear pivot arm force the rear steering knuckles (7 and 10) to turn in the desired direction.

MAINTENANCE

Inject grease into the grease fittings located on the axle and steering components at 25-hour intervals. The recommended lubricant is multipurpose, lithium-base grease.

Clean all pivot points and linkages and lubricate with SAE 30 oil. Check for looseness and wear. Repair as needed.

TIE RODS AND TOE-IN

Tie rods (28 and 30—Fig. IN1-11) are adjustable. Note the outer tie rod end and adjacent jam nut have left-hand threads.

When the front wheels point straight ahead, the rear wheels should point straight ahead and rear wheel toe-in should be ⅛ inch (3.2 mm). Loosen the jam nuts and rotate the tie rods as needed to obtain proper toe-in.

Tie rods are unequal lengths. Right tie rod (28) nominal length is 8.0 inches (203.2 mm), while left tie rod (30) nominal length is 9.5 inches (241.3 mm).

OUTER AXLES OVERHAUL

To remove the outer axle (12—Fig. IN1-11), support the rear of the tractor and remove the rear wheel. Drive out the roll pin (20) and remove the axle (12). Inspect the bearings (13 and 18) and remove if necessary.

Reinstall by reversing the removal procedure.

STEERING SPINDLE OVERHAUL

To remove the spindle (16—Fig. IN1-11), support the rear of the tractor and remove the rear wheel. Detach the outer steering arm (27) from the spindle (16).

Drive out the roll pins (21), extract the kingpins (22) and remove the spindle assembly. Drive out the roll pin (20) to remove the universal joint (19) and outer axle (12).

Replace the kingpins and bushings if they are damaged.

Reinstall by reversing the removal procedure.

AXLE MOUNTING BRACKET OVERHAUL

Remove the steering spindle as previously described. Support the transaxle. Remove the universal joint if not removed with the spindle. Unbolt and remove the axle mounting bracket (23—Fig. IN1-11).

Reinstall by reversing the removal procedure.

SHIFT CONTROL LINKAGE

MODELS 1112G, 1212G, 1114AWS AND 1214AWS

Neutral Adjustment

Position the shift control lever (L—Fig. IN1-12) so the transmission is in NEUTRAL. Without disturbing the position of the transaxle shift arm (A), loosen the bolt (B) that secures the shift link to the transaxle shift arm. Move the shift control lever to the neutral slot in the shift quadrant. Retighten the bolt (B). Check operation.

MODELS 1112H AND 1212H

Neutral Adjustment

The tractor should not creep in either direction when the shift control lever is in the neutral position.

To adjust control lever neutral position, loosen the mounting bolts of the shift control lever bracket (2—Fig. IN1-13) located under the right rear fender. Relocate the bracket as needed so the control lever is positioned in the neutral slot of the shift quadrant when the transmission is in NEUTRAL.

Tension Adjustment

The shift control lever should not move out of a set position during operation. If the lever moves, rotate the nut (6—Fig. IN1-13) to adjust the spring (8) tension.

TRANSAXLE

MODELS 1112G AND 1212G

Lubrication

The transaxle is filled at the factory with Bentonite grease and does not require periodic checking of the lubricant level. If an oil leak develops, the leak should be repaired and unit refilled with gear lubricant. Transaxle capacity is approximately 30 ounces (890 mL).

Removal and Installation

Remove the mower deck and mower drive belt, if so equipped. Push down the clutch/brake pedal and engage the parking brake. Loosen the clutch idler pulley (5—Fig. IN1-5) screw and remove the traction drive belt from the idler pulley. Remove the drive belt from the transaxle pulley (8).

Raise and support the rear of the tractor. Remove the rear wheels. Disconnect the transaxle shift linkage and brake linkage. Remove the cap screws attaching the transaxle to the frame and lower the transaxle from the tractor.

To install the transaxle, reverse the removal procedure. Adjust the drive belt tension as previously outlined.

Overhaul

Tractor is equipped with a Peerless Model 930 transaxle. Refer to the Peerless section in the TRANSAXLE SERVICE section for overhaul procedure.

MODELS 1114AWS AND 1214AWS

Lubrication

The transaxle is filled at the factory with Bentonite grease and does not require periodic checking of the lubricant level. If an oil leak develops, the leak should be repaired and the unit refilled with gear lubricant. Transaxle capacity is approximately 30 ounces (890 mL).

Removal and Installation

Remove the mower deck and mower drive belt, if so equipped. Push down the clutch/brake pedal and engage the parking brake. Loosen the clutch idler pulley (5—Fig. IN1-5) screw and remove the traction drive belt from the idler pulley. Remove the drive belt from the transaxle pulley (8).

Disconnect the transaxle shift linkage and brake linkage. Remove the tie rods. Detach the rear drag link from the rear steering pivot arm. Remove the rear axle mounts. Remove the transaxle from the tractor.

To install the transaxle, reverse the removal procedure. Adjust the drive belt tension as previously outlined.

Overhaul

The tractor is equipped with a Peerless Model 930 transaxle. Refer to the Peerless section in the TRANSAXLE SERVICE section for overhaul procedure.

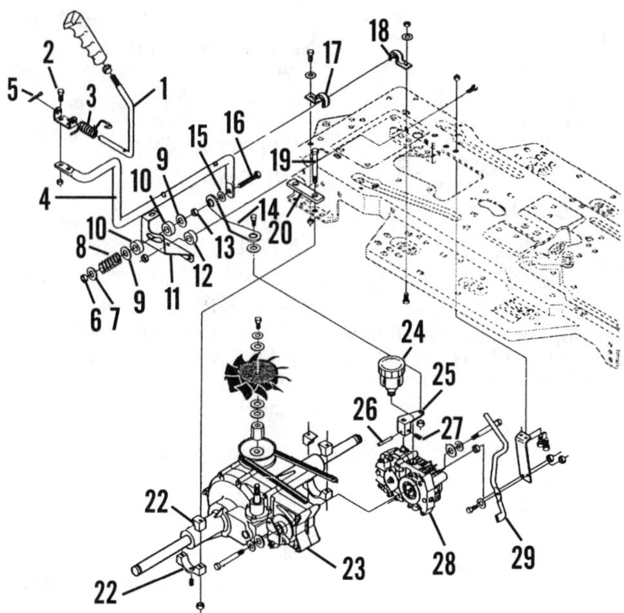

Fig. IN1-13—Exploded view of transmission shift control linkage on Models 1112H and 1212H.

1. Control lever
2. Bracket
3. Spring
4. Shift rod
5. Cotter pin
6. Nut
7. Washer
8. Spring
9. Washer
10. Washer
11. Bracket
12. Spacer
13. Flange nut
14. Link
15. Washer
16. Bolt
17. Retainer
18. Retainer
19. Shoulder bolt
20. Plate
21. Lower mounting block
22. Upper mounting block
23. Final drive
24. Oil reservoir
25. Control arm
26. Roll pin
27. Setscrew
28. Hydrostatic transmission
29. Release valve rod

HYDROSTATIC TRANSMISSION (MODELS 1112H AND 1212H)

LUBRICATION

The hydrostatic transmission is equipped with an integral reservoir located under the tractor seat. The transmission is factory-filled with oil.

The oil level should be at the lower or COLD mark on the reservoir with the unit cold. Recommended oil is SAE 10W30 engine oil with an SF rating.

NOTE: On early models, the reservoir cap has left-hand threads.

If contamination is observed in the reservoir tank or the color of the fluid has changed (black or milky), fluid should be drained and replaced.

To drain fluid from the Sundstrand transmission, unscrew the hex drain plug on the transmission underside.

Fill the transmission until oil reaches the lower mark on the reservoir.

REMOVAL AND INSTALLATION

Remove the mower deck and mower drive belt, if so equipped. Push down the clutch/brake pedal and engage the parking brake. Loosen the clutch idler pulley (5—Fig. IN1-5) screw and remove the traction drive belt from the idler pulley. Remove the drive belt from the final drive pulley (8).

Disconnect the transmission speed control linkage from the transmission. Disconnect the brake actuating rod from the brake lever. Remove the final drive housing mounting bolts and the axle housing clamp bolts, then remove the transmission and final drive housing from the tractor. Unbolt and separate the hydrostatic transmission from the final drive housing.

To install the hydrostatic unit, reverse the removal procedure. Refill unit with the recommended fluid and the adjust control linkage as previously outlined.

OVERHAUL

The tractor is equipped with a Hydro-Gear BDU-10 transmission. Refer to the HYDROSTATIC TRANSMISSION section at the rear of this manual for overhaul information.

FINAL DRIVE (MODELS 1112H AND 1212H)

LUBRICATION

The final drive is lubricated with grease at the factory and should not require additional lubrication. Capacity is 16 ounces (473 mL) of Shell Darina #0 grease.

REMOVAL AND INSTALLATION

To remove and reinstall the final drive, follow the procedure described in the HYDROSTATIC TRANSMISSION section.

OVERHAUL

The tractor is equipped with a Hydro-Gear 210-1010 final drive. Refer to the Hydro-Gear section in the FINAL DRIVE service section for overhaul procedure.

MTD

450 and 472 Series

Due to the numerous number of MTD models and the wide variety of engines installed, an accurate cross-reference and specification table is not available. Determine the manufacturer and model number of the engine being serviced and refer to the appropriate engine section in the rear of this manual for service information.

FRONT AXLE AND STEERING SYSTEM

MAINTENANCE

Lubricate the steering spindles and the steering gear periodically with a lithium based, multipurpose grease. Clean away excess grease.

STEERING SPINDLES

To remove the steering spindles (31 and 37—Fig. MT1-1), raise and support the front of the tractor. Remove the front wheels.

Detach the tie rod (40) and drag link (15) from the steering spindle or steering arm. Detach the steering arm (32) from the upper end of the left spindle (37) Remove the cap (24) from the right spindle (31). Pull the spindle down out of axle main member.

Inspect all parts for wear and damage. New spindle bushings (26) are available for service.

Reinstall by reversing the removal procedure. Apply lithium based, multipurpose grease to the bushings before installing the spindles. Inject grease into the grease fitting after assembly.

TIE ROD AND TOE-IN

Some models are equipped with an adjustable tie rod (40—Fig. MT1-1). Inspect the ball joints (38) for excessive wear and looseness and replace if needed.

Adjust the length of the tie rod to obtain front wheel toe-in of 1/8 inch (3.2

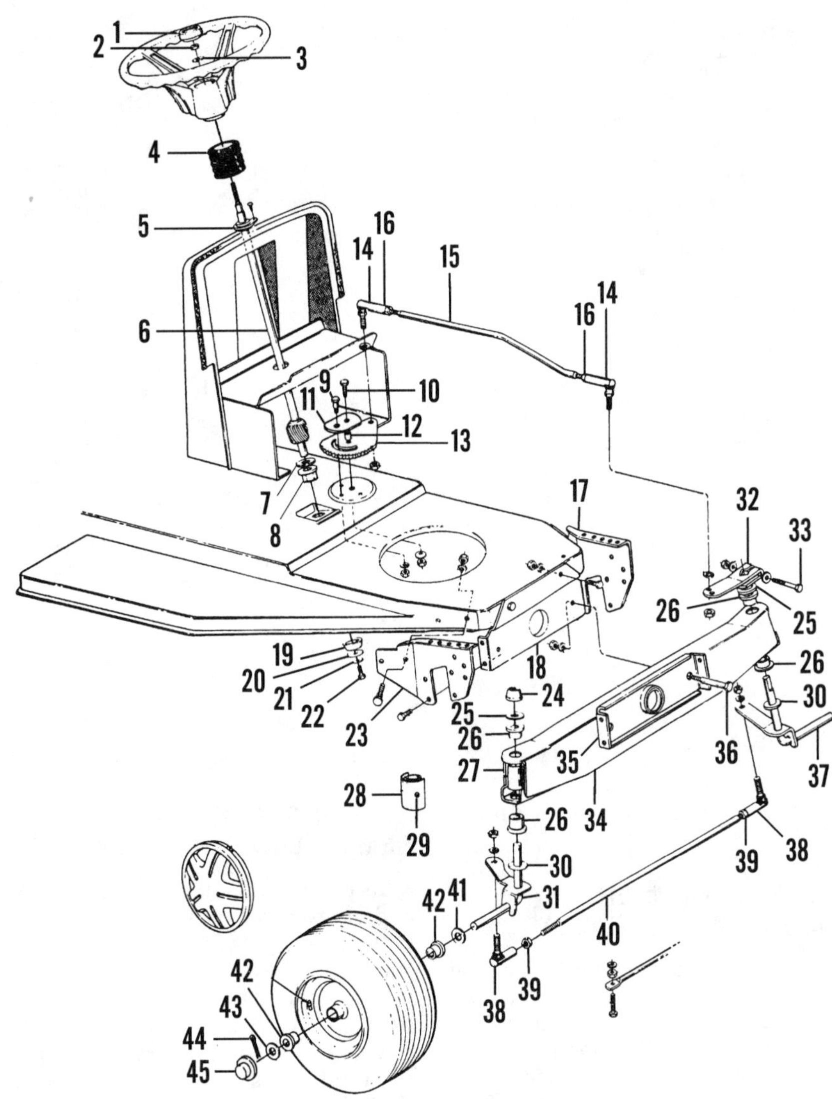

Fig. MT1-1—Exploded view of front axle and steering system.

1. Cap
2. Nut
3. Belleville washer
4. Bellow
5. Flange bearing
6. Steering shaft
7. Washer
8. Flange bushing
9. Shoulder bolt
10. Screw
11. Retainer plate
12. Spacer
13. Sector gear
14. Rod end
15. Drag link
16. Jam nut
17. Left side plate
18. Rear axle pivot bracket
19. Spacer
20. Washer
21. Lockwasher
22. Screw
23. Right side plate
24. Push cap
25. Washer
26. Flange bushings
27. Plastic tube
28. End cap
29. Grease fitting
30. Washer
31. Spindle (right)
32. Steering arm
33. Clamp bolt
34. Axle main member
35. Front axle pivot bracket
36. Pivot stop bolt
37. Spindle (left)
38. Rod end
39. Jam nut
40. Tie rod
41. Washer
42. Wheel bearings
43. Washer
44. Cotter pin
45. Hub cap

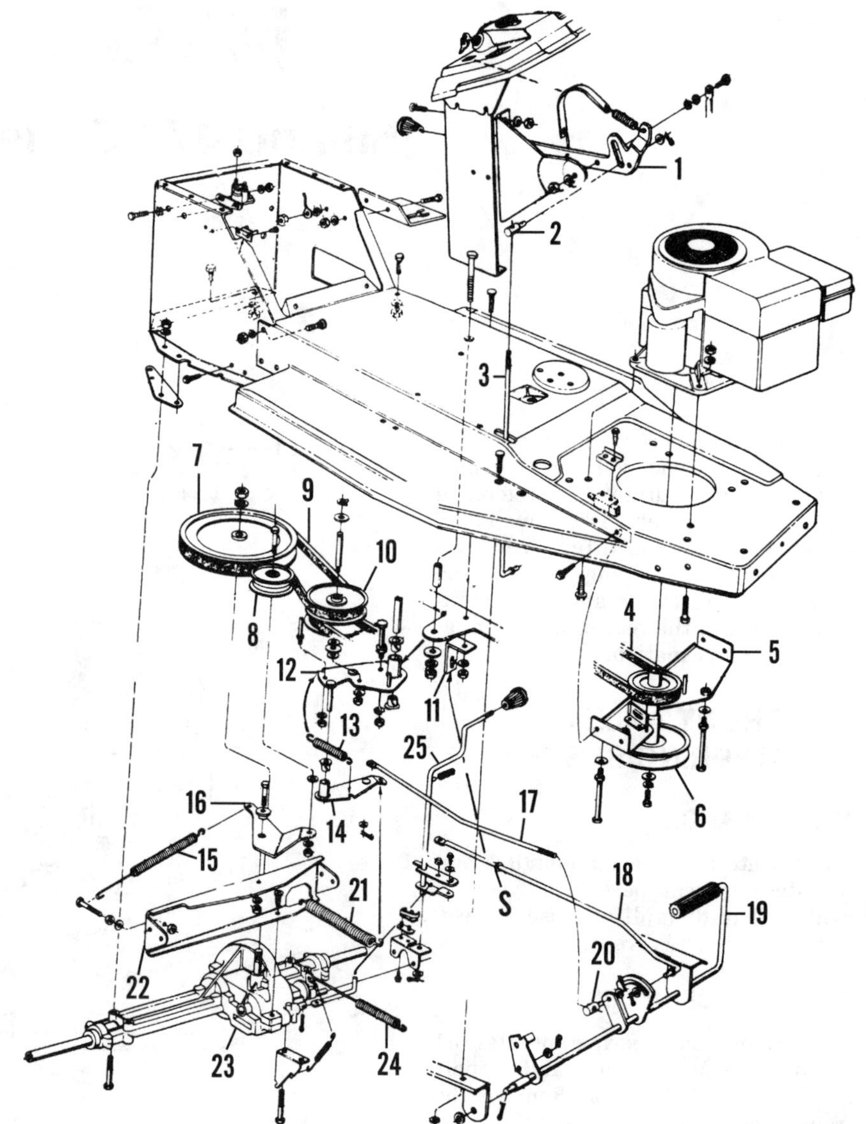

Fig. MT1-2—Exploded view of variable speed drive system.

1. Speed control lever
2. Ferrule
3. Speed control rod
4. Front drive belt
5. Pulley guard
6. Engine pulley
7. Transaxle pulley
8. Idler pulley
9. Rear drive belt
10. Variable speed pulley assembly
11. Rod bracket
12. Variable speed bracket
13. Spring
14. Variable speed torque bracket
15. Spring
16. Idler bracket
17. Speed control rod
18. Brake rod
19. Clutch/brake pedal
20. Ferrule
21. Tension spring
22. Transaxle support bracket
23. Transaxle
24. Brake spring
25. Shift rod

mm). Secure the tie rod ends with jam nuts.

AXLE MAIN MEMBER REMOVAL AND INSTALLATION

To remove the axle main member (34—Fig. MT1-1), raise and support the front of the tractor frame and remove the front wheels. Disconnect the drag link (15) from the steering arm (32). Disconnect the tie rod (40) from both spindles.

Detach the steering arm (32) from the left spindle and withdraw the spindle. Remove the cap (24) from the left spindle and withdraw the spindle.

Support the axle main member (34), remove the rear (18) and front (35) pivot brackets and remove the axle from the tractor.

Install by reversing the removal procedure.

STEERING GEAR REMOVAL AND INSTALLATION

To remove the steering gears, raise and support the hood. Disconnect the battery cables.

Remove the steering wheel cap (1—Fig. MT1-1), retaining nut (2) and Belleville washer (3), then lift off the steering wheel and bellow (4). Remove the retaining screw from the steering shaft flange bushing (5) and remove the bushing from the shaft.

Disconnect the drag link (15) from the sector gear (13). Remove the mounting bolt and shoulder bolt (9) from the sector retainer plate (11) and withdraw the sector gear.

Remove the retaining screw (22) from the lower end of the steering shaft (6) and remove the steering shaft, thrust washer (7) and bushing (8).

Inspect all parts for excessive wear or damage and replace when necessary. Install by reversing the removal procedure. Lubricate the flange bushings with SAE 30 oil. Apply a light coat of multipurpose grease to the teeth of the steering gears.

ENGINE

REMOVAL AND INSTALLATION

Remove the mower deck if so equipped. Remove the hood, grille brace, or side panels, and grille. Disconnect the battery cables and starter wires. Identify and disconnect all necessary electrical connections from the engine. Disconnect the fuel line from the carburetor. Disconnect choke and throttle control cables from the engine.

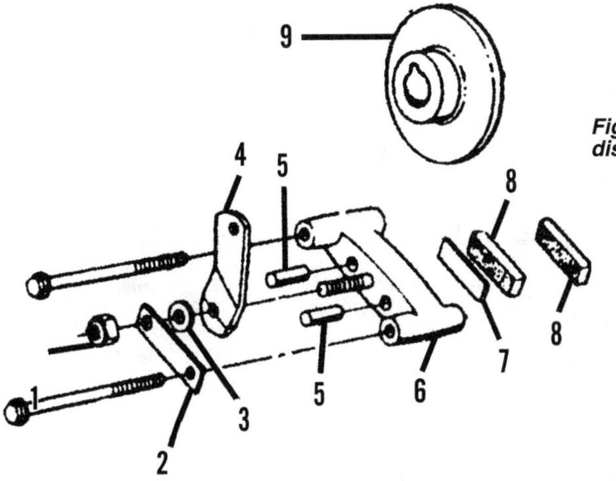

Fig. MT1-3—Exploded view of disc brake.

1. Adjusting nut
2. Bracket
3. Washer
4. Brake lever
5. Actuating pins
6. Brake pad holder
7. Back-up plate
8. Brake pads
9. Brake disc

Remove the belt guide (5—Fig. MT1-2). Disconnect the spring from the clutch idler bracket to relieve the tension on the traction drive belt. Work the drive belts off the engine pulleys. Remove the muffler heat shield, if so equipped. Remove the engine mounting bolts and lift the engine from the tractor.

Install by reversing the removal procedure.

OVERHAUL

Refer to the appropriate engine section in this manual for tune-up specifications, engine overhaul procedures and engine maintenance.

CLUTCH AND BRAKE ADJUSTMENT

A continuously variable drive pulley is used on these models. Depressing the clutch/brake pedal part way disengages the clutch. Depressing the pedal all the way down disengages the clutch and engages the disc brake.

To adjust the clutch and speed control linkage, first adjust the speed control lever linkage as follows: Push the clutch/brake pedal forward until there is ⅛ to ¼ inch (3.2-6.3 mm) clearance between the stop (S—Fig. MT1-2) on the brake rod (18) and the variable speed pulley bracket (11) and hold the pedal in this position.

Position the speed control shift lever (1) in the parking brake position. Remove the hairpin clip from the speed control rod ferrule (2), and adjust the ferrule on the rod so the upper end of the rod (3) contacts the bottom of the slot in the speed shift lever (1). Reinstall the hairpin clip.

Adjust the speed control link (17) to obtain the correct neutral adjustment as follows: Place the transmission shift lever in the neutral position and start the engine. Move the speed control lever (1) to the full speed position. Release the clutch/brake pedal completely, then fully depress the pedal and hold it in this position.

Shut off the engine, and after the engine completely stops, release the clutch/brake pedal. Move the speed control lever to the first position. Disconnect the speed control link (17) from the variable speed torque bracket (14). Move the clutch/brake pedal as far up as it will go. While holding the pedal in this position, thread the speed control link in or out of the ferrule (20) until the rod lines up with the hole in the torque bracket. Install the cotter pin to secure the speed control link to the torque bracket.

The disc brake is located on the left side of the final drive housing. To adjust the brake, remove the cotter pin and adjust the castle nut (1—Fig. MT1-3) so the brake starts to engage when the brake lever (4) is ¼ to 5/16 inch (6.4-7.9 mm) away from the axle housing. Make sure that the brake does not drag when the pedal is released.

TRACTION DRIVE BELTS REMOVAL AND INSTALLATION

To remove the rear drive belt (9—Fig. MT1-2), first remove the mower deck from underneath the tractor. Start the engine. Place the shift lever in NEUTRAL and the speed control lever in high speed position, then shut off the engine.

Disconnect the tension spring (21) from the final drive support bracket (22). Note that a hole is provided in the rear of the frame for access to the tension spring. Disconnect the small spring (15) from the right side of frame. Move the brake rod (18) out of the variable speed pulley bracket (11). Loosen, but do not remove, the bolts securing the variable speed pulley bracket. Work the drive belt off the top of the variable speed pulley (10), then remove the belt from the final drive pulley (7) and idler pulley (8).

Reverse the removal procedure to install the new belt. The clutch idler pulley is spring loaded and no adjustment is necessary.

To remove the front drive belt (4), first remove the rear drive belt as outlined above. Unbolt and remove the engine pulley belt guard (5). Slip the drive belt off the engine pulley and remove it from the variable speed pulley.

Reverse the removal procedure to install the new belt. Be sure that the belt is not twisted and that it is positioned inside all the belt guides.

FINAL DRIVE

LUBRICATION

Final drive is lubricated with grease at the factory and should not require additional lubrication. Capacity is 10 ounces (296 mL) of lithium based grease.

REMOVAL AND INSTALLATION

To remove the final drive assembly, first remove the mower deck from underneath the tractor. Remove the traction drive belt from the final drive pulley as previously outlined. Disconnect the shift linkage and brake linkage at final drive.

Support the rear of tractor and remove all fasteners securing the final drive to the frame. Raise the rear of tractor and roll the final drive assembly out from under the tractor.

Install by reversing the removal procedure. Adjust the brake as previously outlined.

OVERHAUL

All models are equipped with a MTD final drive. Refer to the MTD section in the FINAL DRIVE section of this manual for overhaul procedure.

SAFETY INTERLOCK SYSTEM

Before the engine will start, the key must be turned on and both of the safety switches must be activated. One switch (6—Fig. MT1-4) is activated when the clutch/brake pedal is depressed and the other (6) is activated when the blade is disengaged. When the two safety switches are activated, the circuit is completed between the battery and the

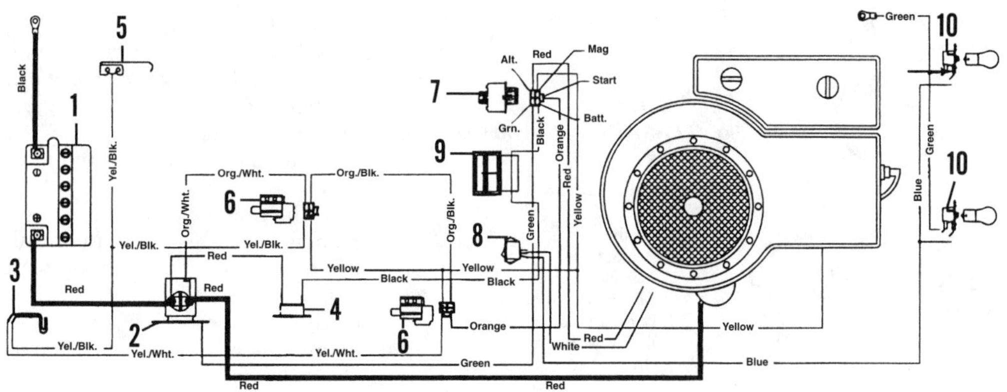

Fig. MT1-4—Wiring diagram for Series 450-470 models.

1. Battery
2. Solenoid
3. Seat switch
4. Circuit breaker
5. Spring switch
6. Safety switches
7. Ignition switch
8. Light switch
9. Ammeter (optional)
10. Headlight

starter solenoid, allowing the starter motor to crank the engine.

Some models are equipped with a seat safety switch (3) and a reverse safety switch (5). However, these switches are not involved in the starting circuit. The seat safety switch is designed to stop the engine if the operator leaves the seat with the blades or PTO engaged. The blades must be in the disengaged position when shifting into reverse or the engine will shut off.

To test the two safety start switches, first check the two switches to see if the switch plungers are depressed a minimum of $\frac{1}{8}$ inch (3 mm) when the blade is disengaged and the clutch/brake pedal is depressed. If the switch plunger is correctly depressed, use a continuity checker to determine if there is continuity across the switch terminals when the switches are activated (plunger depressed). If continuity is not indicated when the plunger is depressed, replace the switch.

To check for correct operation of the seat safety switch, start the engine and set the parking brake. Place the shift lever in NEUTRAL and engage the PTO or blades. Raise up off the seat. The engine should stop running.

WIRING DIAGRAM

The wiring diagram illustrated in Fig. MT1-4 is typical of all models.

MTD

600, 700 and 800 Series (2-Wheel Steering)

Due to the numerous number of MTD models and the wide variety of engines installed, an accurate cross-reference and specification table is not available. Determine the manufacturer and model number of the engine being serviced and refer to the appropriate engine section in the rear of this manual for service information.

FRONT AXLE AND STEERING SYSTEM

MAINTENANCE

On models equipped with grease fitting at the end of the axle main member, periodically inject grease into the grease fitting. If not equipped with a grease fitting, lubricate the steering spindles periodically with lithium-based, multipurpose grease.

Periodically lubricate steering gear with a lithium-based, multipurpose grease. Clean away excess grease.

STEERING SPINDLES REMOVAL AND INSTALLATION

600 and 700 Series

Raise and support the front of the tractor. Remove the front wheels. Detach the tie rod (30—Fig. MT2-1) from the spindles.

To remove the left spindle (29), detach the drag link (15) from the steering arm (26). Remove the clamp bolt (27) and separate the steering arm from the spindle. Lower the spindle from the axle.

To remove the right spindle (38), remove the retaining cap (20) and washer (21). Pull the spindle down out of the axle main member.

NOTE: On early models, a roll pin is used in place of the cap (20) to hold the spindle in the axle.

Inspect the parts for wear and damage. Replace the spindle bushings

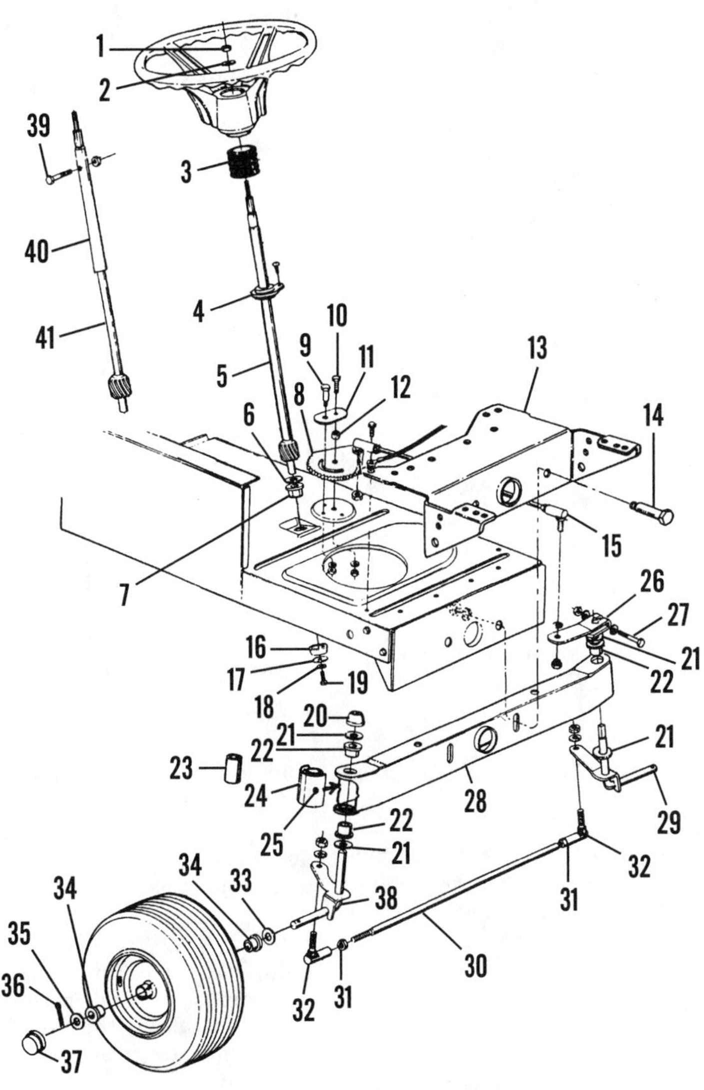

Fig. MT2-1—Exploded view of front axle and steering system used on Series 600 and 700 tractors.

1. Nut
2. Belleville washer
3. Bellow
4. Flange bearing
5. Steering shaft
6. Washer
7. Flange bushing
8. Sector gear
9. Shoulder bolt
10. Screw
11. Retainer plate
12. Spacer
13. Axle pivot bracket
14. Pivot stop bolt
15. Drag link
16. Spacer
17. Washer
18. Lockwasher
19. Screw
20. Push cap
21. Washer
22. Flange bushings
23. Plastic tube
24. End cap
25. Grease fitting
26. Steering arm
27. Clamp bolt
28. Axle main member
29. Spindle (left)
30. Tie rod
31. Jam nut
32. Rod end
33. Washer
34. Wheel bearings
35. Washer
36. Cotter pin
37. Hub cap
38. Spindle (right)
39. Bolt
40. Upper steering shaft
41. Lower steering shaft

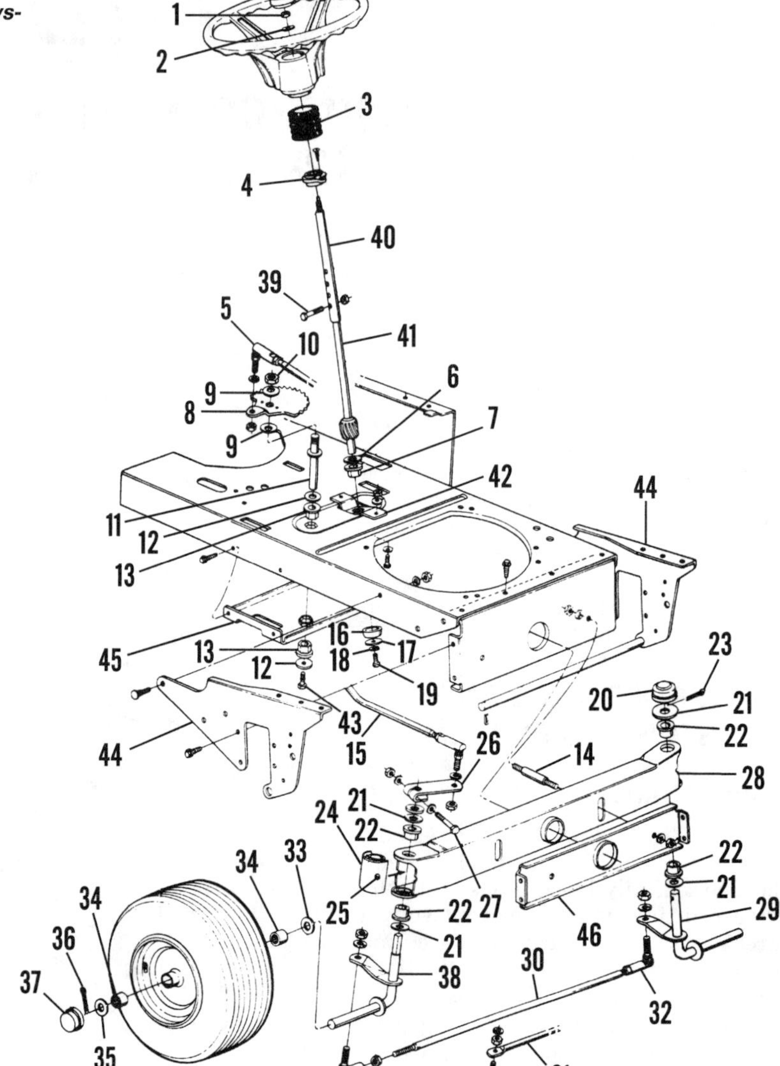

Fig. MT2-2—Exploded view of front axle and steering system used on 800 series tractors.

1. Nut
2. Belleville washer
3. Bellow
4. Flange bearing
5. Drag link end
6. Washer
7. Flange bushing
8. Sector gear
9. Belleville washer
10. Nut
11. Sector shaft
12. Washers
13. Flange bushings
14. Pivot stop bolt
15. Drag link
16. Spacer
17. Washer
18. Lockwasher
19. Screw
20. Push cap
21. Washer
22. Flange bushings
23. Cotter pin
24. End cap
25. Grease fitting
26. Steering arm
27. Clamp bolt
28. Axle main member
29. Spindle (left)
30. Adjustable tie rod
31. Non-adjustable tie rod
32. Rod end
33. Washer
34. Wheel bearings
35. Washer
36. Cotter pin
37. Hub cap
38. Spindle (right)
39. Bolt
40. Upper steering shaft
41. Lower steering shaft
42. Bearing retainer
43. Screw
44. Pivot bar assembly
45. Idler support bracket
46. Front pivot bracket

(22—Fig. MT2-1) and/or spindles if excessive wear is evident.

Install by reversing the removal procedure. Apply lithium-based, multipurpose grease to the bushings before installing the spindles. Inject grease into the grease fitting (25) after assembly.

800 Series

Raise and support the front of the tractor. Remove the front wheels. Detach the tie rod (30 or 31—Fig. MT2-2) from the spindles.

To remove the right spindle (38), disconnect the drag link (15) from the steering arm (26). Remove the clamp bolt (27) and detach the steering arm (26) from the upper end of the spindle. Remove the spindle and washers from the axle (28).

To remove the left spindle (29), remove the cap (20) and cotter pin (23) from the top of the spindle. Pull the spindle down out of the axle main member and remove the washers (21).

Inspect the parts for wear and damage. Replace the spindle bushings (22) and/or spindles if excessive wear is evident.

Install by reversing the removal procedure. Apply lithium based, multipurpose grease to the spindle bushings before installing the spindles. Inject grease into the grease fitting (25) after assembly.

TIE ROD AND TOE-IN

Some models are equipped with an adjustable tie rod (30—Fig. MT2-1 or Fig. MT2-2). Inspect the ball joints (32) for excessive wear and looseness and replace if needed.

Adjust the length of the tie rod to obtain front wheel toe-in of ⅛ inch (3.2 mm). Secure the tie rod ends with the jam nuts.

AXLE MAIN MEMBER REMOVAL AND INSTALLATION

600 and 700 Series

To remove the axle main member (28—Fig. MT2-1), raise and support the front of the tractor and remove the front wheels. Remove the hood and grille.

Remove the spindles as previously described. Unscrew the axle travel limiting bolts (14). Remove the screws attaching the pivot bracket (13) to the frame, and remove the bracket and axle.

Reassemble by reversing the removal procedure.

800 Series

To remove the axle main member (28—Fig. MT2-2), first detach the mower deck from the front pivot bracket (46). Raise and support the front of the tractor frame and remove the front wheels. Remove the hood and grille. Remove the heat shield and muffler.

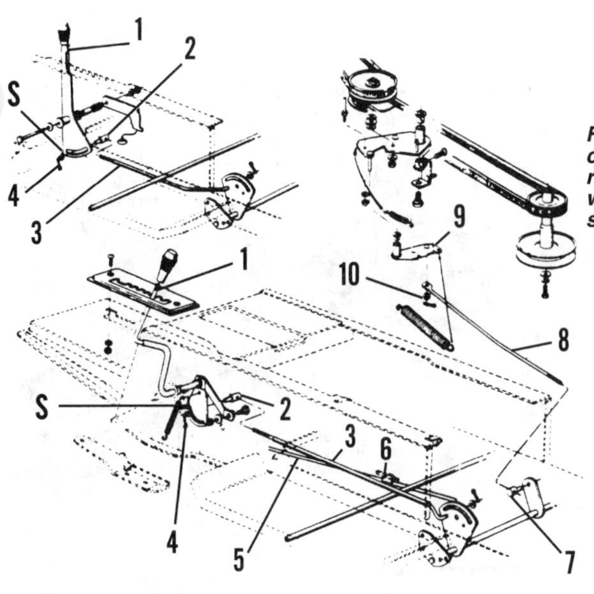

Fig. MT2-3—Exploded view of control linkage used on Series 600 and 700 equipped with variable speed transmission.

1. Speed control lever
2. Ferrule
3. Speed control rod
4. Clip
5. Brake rod
6. Stop
7. Ferrule
8. Speed control link
9. Variable speed torque bracket
10. Cotter pin

Remove the spindles as previously described. Support the axle main member (28). Remove the retaining nuts from the studs (14) that limit the axle travel. Unbolt and remove the axle front pivot bracket (46). Lower the axle from the tractor.

Reinstall by reversing the removal procedure.

STEERING GEAR REMOVAL AND INSTALLATION

600 and 700 Series

To remove the steering gears, first remove the mower deck. Raise and support the hood. Disconnect the battery cables. Remove the fuel tank.

Remove the steering wheel cap, retaining nut (1—Fig. MT2-1) and Belleville washer (2). Lift off the steering wheel and bellow (3). Remove the retaining screw from steering shaft flange bushing (4) and remove the bushing from the shaft.

Disconnect the drag link (15) from the sector gear (8). Remove the mounting bolt and shoulder bolt (9) from the sector retainer plate (11) and withdraw the sector gear. Remove the retaining screw (19) from the lower end of the steering shaft (5) and remove the steering shaft, thrust washer (6) and bushing (7).

Inspect all parts for damage and replace if necessary. Install by reversing the removal procedure. Lubricate flange bushings with SAE 30 oil. Apply a light coat of multipurpose grease to the steering gear teeth.

800 Series

To remove the steering gear, first remove the mower deck from the tractor. Raise and support the hood. Disconnect the battery cables. Remove the fuel tank.

Remove the steering wheel cap, retaining nut (1—Fig. MT2-2) and Belleville washer (2). Lift off the steering wheel and bellow (3). Remove the retaining screw from the steering shaft flange bushing (4) and remove the bushing from the shaft.

Unscrew the steering shaft coupling bolt (39). Detach the drag link end (5) from the sector gear (8). Unscrew the retaining nut (10) and remove the sector gear (8) from the sector shaft (11). Unscrew the retaining screw (43) at the bottom of the sector shaft and remove the shaft (11), bushings (13) and washers (12).

Unscrew the retaining screw (19) at the bottom of steering shaft (41) and remove the washer (17) and spacer (16). Remove the retaining bolts from the lower bearing retainer (42). Move the lower steering shaft (41) up out of the retainer (42), remove the retainer and withdraw the steering shaft down out of the tractor.

Reassemble by reversing the disassembly procedure.

ENGINE

REMOVAL AND INSTALLATION

Remove the hood, grille brace, or side panels, and grille. Disconnect the battery cables and starter wires. Identify and disconnect the electrical connections from the engine.

Disconnect the fuel line from the carburetor. Disconnect the choke and throttle control cables from the engine. Remove the drive belts from the engine pulleys. Remove the heat shield, if so equipped, and the muffler. Remove the engine mounting bolts and lift the engine from the tractor.

Install by reversing the removal procedure.

OVERHAUL

Refer to the appropriate engine section in this manual for tune-up specifications, engine overhaul procedures and engine maintenance.

SPEED CONTROL LINKAGE

600 AND 700 SERIES (WITH VARIABLE SPEED TRANSMISSION)

Some models are equipped with a continuously variable drive pulley that provides infinite travel speeds. Depressing the clutch/brake pedal partway disengages the clutch. Depressing the pedal all the way down disengages the clutch and engages the disc brake.

Adjustment

Before adjusting the clutch rod, adjust the brake as described in the BRAKE section. To adjust the clutch and speed control linkage, first adjust the speed control lever (1—Fig. MT2-3) as follows:

Push the clutch/brake pedal forward until the stop (6) on the brake rod (5) contacts the frame. While holding the pedal in this position, place the speed control lever (1) in the park position. The ferrule (2) on the speed control rod should contact the back end of the slot (S) of the speed control lever. If not, remove the cotter pin (4) and adjust the ferrule on the rod so it contacts the back end of the slot. Then lengthen the rod one additional turn.

Next, adjust the clutch rod (8) to obtain the correct neutral setting as follows: Start the engine and place the shift lever in the NEUTRAL position. Move the speed control lever (1) to the high-speed position. Release the clutch/brake pedal, then slowly depress the pedal to the fully down (park) position. Hold the pedal in the park position, stop the engine and after the engine stops, release the clutch/brake pedal.

Position the speed control lever as follows: On models with seven-speed selector, place the lever in the second-speed position. On models with six-speed selector, position and hold the lever between the first- and second-speed position. On models with five-speed selector, place the lever in first-speed position.

Detach the clutch rod from the torque bracket (9). Using light hand pressure, push the clutch/brake pedal rearward as far as possible and hold in this position. Thread the clutch rod (8) into or out of the ferrule (7) so the rod end fits easily onto the pin on the torque bracket (9). Reattach the rod end to the bracket.

800 SERIES (WITH VARIABLE SPEED TRANSMISSION)

Some 800 series models are equipped with a continuously variable drive pulley that provides infinite travel speeds. Engine power is transferred through the variable speed transmission to either a single-speed or two-speed transaxle.

Depressing the clutch/brake pedal partway disengages the clutch. Depressing pedal all the way down disengages the clutch and engages the disc brake.

Adjustment

To adjust the speed control linkage, run the engine and position the shift lever in the NEUTRAL position. Move the speed control lever to the seventh-speed position. Release the clutch/brake pedal, then slowly depress the pedal to the fully down (park) position. Hold the pedal in park position, stop the engine and after the engine stops, release the clutch/brake pedal.

Detach the rear speed control link (Fig. MT2-4) from the torque bracket. Move the speed control lever to the first-speed position. Detach the front speed control link (Fig. MT2-4) from the torque bracket. On 1990 models, position a $\frac{5}{8}$ inch (16 mm) shim under the point on the bracket of the clutch/brake shaft as shown in Fig. MT2-4. On later models, position a $1\frac{1}{2}$ inch (38 mm) shim under the point on the bracket of the clutch/brake shaft (Fig. MT2-4). Thread the front speed control link into or out of the ferrule so the rod end fits easily onto the pin on the torque bracket. Reattach the rod end to the torque bracket.

Using light hand pressure, push rear speed control link rearward as far as possible and hold in this position. Thread the rear speed control link into or out of its ferrule so the rod end fits easily onto the pin on the torque bracket. Rotate the link two additional turns clockwise (lengthen the link), and reattach the rod end to the torque bracket. Remove the shim.

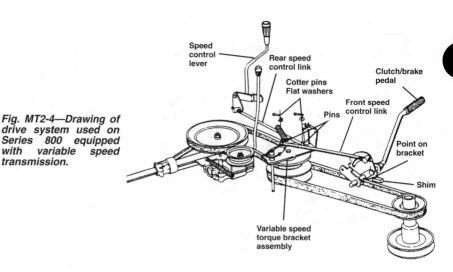

Fig. MT2-4—Drawing of drive system used on Series 800 equipped with variable speed transmission.

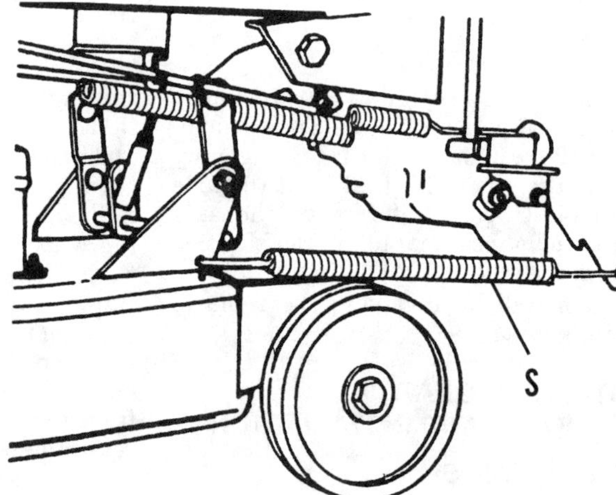

Fig. MT2-5—Detach the spring (S) from transmission support bracket to relieve tension on the front drive belt on Series 600 and 700 with variable speed transmission and electric PTO.

DRIVE BELTS

NOTE: The tractor does not need to be tipped to remove the drive belts. If the tractor is tipped, remove the battery and drain the fuel tank or place a piece of plastic wrap over the neck of the fuel tank and screw on the cap to prevent leakage.

FRONT DRIVE BELT REMOVAL AND INSTALLATION

600-700 Series (With Variable Speed Transmission)

Without Electric PTO

Remove the mower deck. Remove the rear drive belt as described in the following section.

Position the lift lever in the disengaged position. Detach the spring (S—Fig. MT2-5) from the transmission support bracket. Raise and support the front of the tractor. Unscrew the belt guide bolts around the engine drive pulley. Detach the mower deck belt from the engine pulley. Remove the belt guard for the engine pulley.

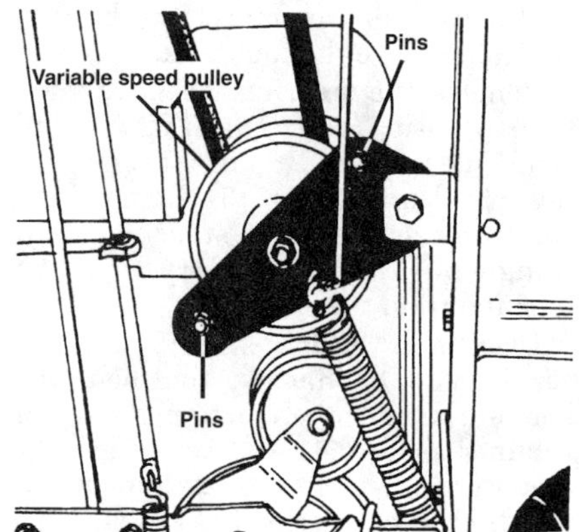

Fig. MT2-6—On Series 600 and 700 tractors with variable speed transmission, push forward on variable speed pulley and remove belt from engine pulley. It may be necessary to remove guide pins for access to the belt.

Move the clutch/brake pedal to park position. Push the variable speed pul-

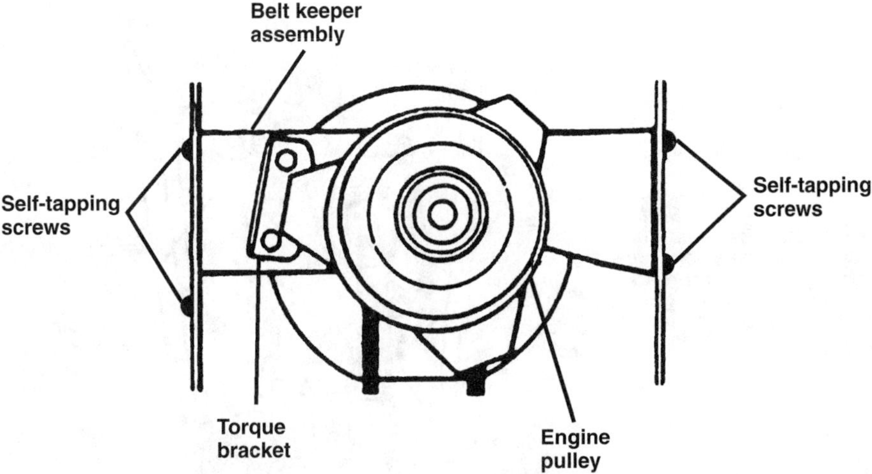

Fig. MT2-7—On Series 600 and 700 tractors with variable speed transmission and electric PTO, remove PTO torque bracket and belt keeper assembly to remove the front drive belt.

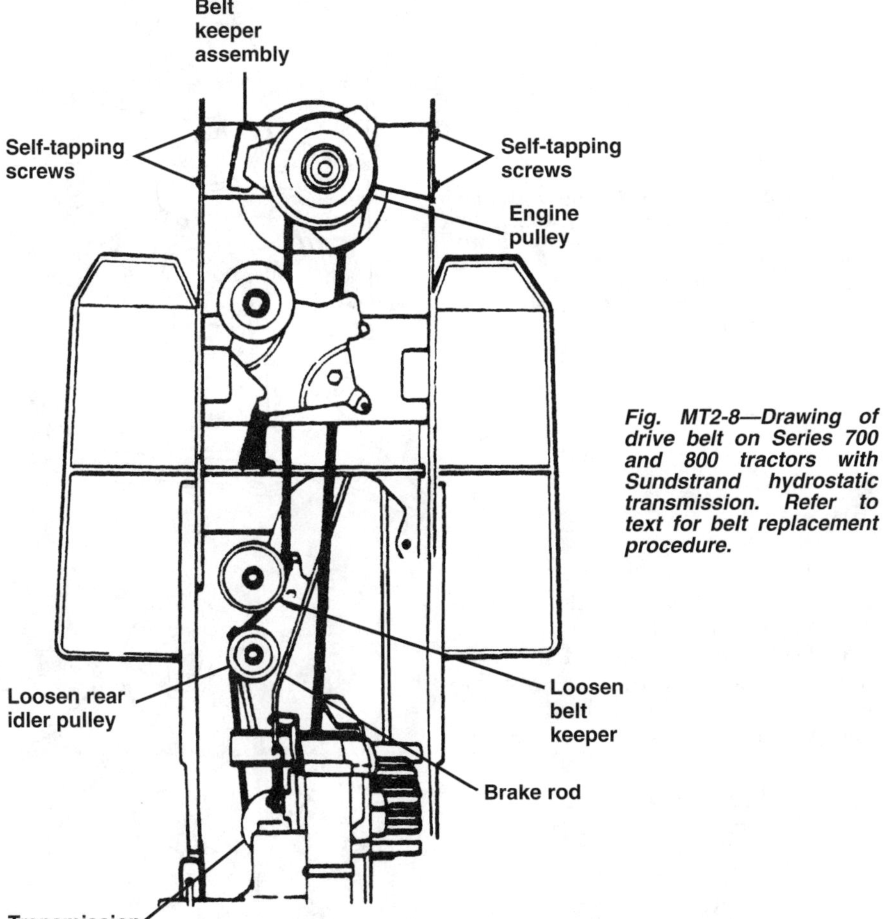

Fig. MT2-8—Drawing of drive belt on Series 700 and 800 tractors with Sundstrand hydrostatic transmission. Refer to text for belt replacement procedure.

ley (Fig. MT2-6) towards the front of the tractor and detach the traction belt from the engine pulley. If necessary, remove the belt guide pins. Move the clutch/brake pedal as needed to disengage the belt from the variable speed pulley.

Reverse the removal procedure to install the belt.

Equipped With Electric PTO

Remove the mower deck. Remove the rear drive belt as described in the following section.

Position the lift lever in the disengaged position. Detach the spring (S—Fig. MT2-5) from the transmission support bracket. Raise and support the front of the tractor. Disconnect the PTO clutch electrical connector. Remove the PTO torque bracket (Fig. MT2-7) and belt keeper assembly. Loosen the pin at the idler pulley and remove the PTO clutch.

Move the clutch/brake pedal to park position. Push the variable speed pulley (Fig. MT2-6) toward the right side of the tractor and detach the traction belt from the engine pulley. If necessary, remove the belt guide pins. Move the clutch/brake pedal as needed to disengage the belt from the variable speed pulley.

Reverse the removal procedure to install the belt.

700-800 Series (With Sundstrand Hydrostatic Transmission)

To remove the belt, first remove the mower deck. Depress the clutch/brake pedal and set the parking brake. Raise and support the front of the tractor.

Remove the mounting screws from the engine pulley belt guard, and move it forward out of the way. Remove the belt guard at the transmission pulley. Unscrew the hex bolt serving as a belt guide near the front idler pulley (Fig. MT2-8). Loosen the center bolt in the rear idler pulley and move the belt off both idler pulleys.

Detach the PTO clutch electrical connector. Work the belt out of the engine pulley onto the pulley hub. Lift the belt off the transmission pulley and over the fan, and then remove the belt from the engine pulley.

Block the tractor so it cannot move. Disengage the parking brake. Detach the brake rod from the clutch/brake pedal and pass the belt through the opening.

Reverse the removal procedure to reinstall the belt.

800 Series (With Variable Speed Transmission)

Remove the mower deck from the tractor. Depress the clutch/brake pedal and engage the parking brake. Raise and support the front of the tractor.

Remove the four screws attaching the engine pulley belt keeper to the frame. Move the belt keeper forward out of the way. Unscrew the belt guide pins around the variable speed pulley (Fig. MT2-9). Work the belt off the variable speed pulley and remove it from the engine pulley.

Reverse the removal procedure to install the belt.

REAR DRIVE BELT REMOVAL AND INSTALLATION

600-700-800 Series (With Variable Speed Transmission)

Remove the front drive belt as instructed in the previous section. Remove the transmission cover. Disconnect the idler pulley spring. Detach the speed control rod from variable speed pulley. Move the belt idler pulley away from the belt and move the belt over the idler pulley. Detach the belt from the variable speed pulley.

Install belt by reversing the removal procedure.

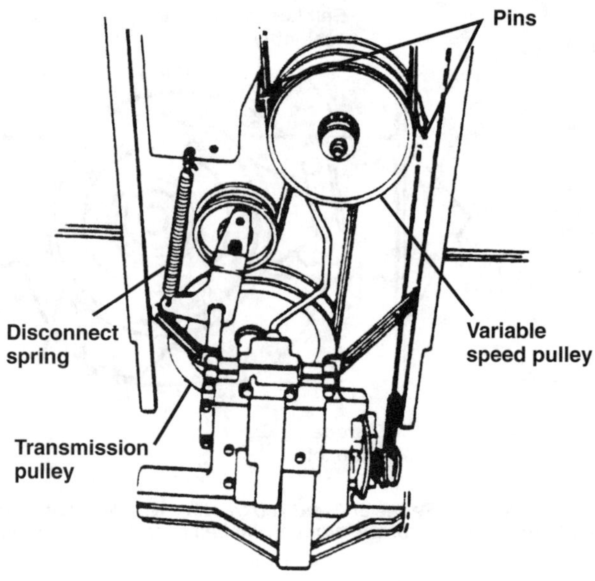

Fig. MT2-9—On Series 800 tractors with variable speed transmission, detach the idler spring and remove the belt guide pins to remove the drive belts.

BRAKE

MODELS 600, 609, 690 AND 699

Adjustment

These models are equipped with a Hydro-Gear hydrostatic transaxle that is equipped with brake discs inside the transaxle housing. Check for correct brake adjustment by inserting a feeler gauge (F—Fig. MT2-10) between the two brake discs through the opening on underside of the housing. The gap between the brake discs should be 0.015-0.025 inch (0.4-0.6 mm). Turn the nut (N) that retains the brake lever to obtain the specified gap.

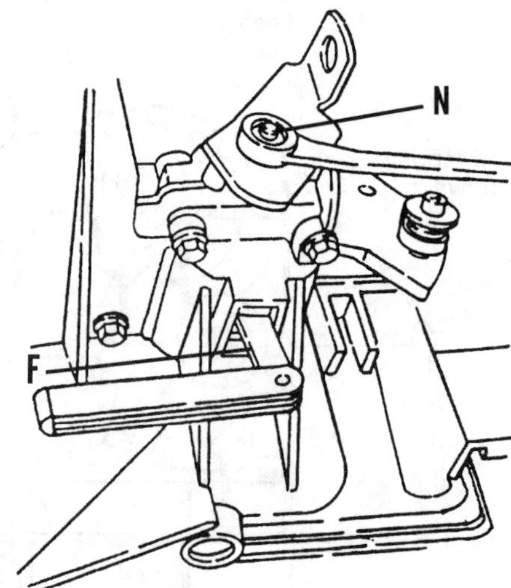

Fig. MT2-10—On Models 600, 609, 690 and 699, check for correct brake adjustment by inserting a feeler gauge (F) between two brake discs. Gap between brake discs should be 0.015-0.025 inch (0.4-0.6 mm). Rotate brake lever retaining nut (N) to obtain specified gap.

Overhaul

Transaxle housing halves must be separated for access to the brake discs. Refer to the Hydro-Gear section in the HYDROSTATIC TRANSAXLE section at the rear of this manual.

ALL OTHER MODELS

Adjustment

This adjustment applies to the disc brakes equipped with a castle nut (1—Fig. MT2-11 or MT2-12). To adjust the disc brake, detach the cotter pin and turn the castle nut so that brake engagement begins when the brake lever is ¼-⁵⁄₁₆ inch (6.4-7.9 mm) away from the axle housing. Reinstall the cotter pin.

Brake Pads

Refer to Figs. MT2-11 and MT2-12. Disconnect the brake linkage from the cam lever. Unbolt and remove the brake pad holder. Slide the brake disc off the transaxle shaft and remove the inner brake pad from the holder slot in the transaxle housing.

Replace worn or damaged parts as needed. Reassemble by reversing the disassembly procedure. Adjust as previously outlined.

HYDROSTATIC TRANSAXLE (600-800 SERIES WITH HYDRO-GEAR HYDROSTATIC TRANSAXLE)

LUBRICATION

Recommended oil is SAE 20W50 with an API rating of SG. To check or fill the transaxle, first clean the area around the breather plug (P—Fig. MT2-13), and then unscrew the breather plug. To

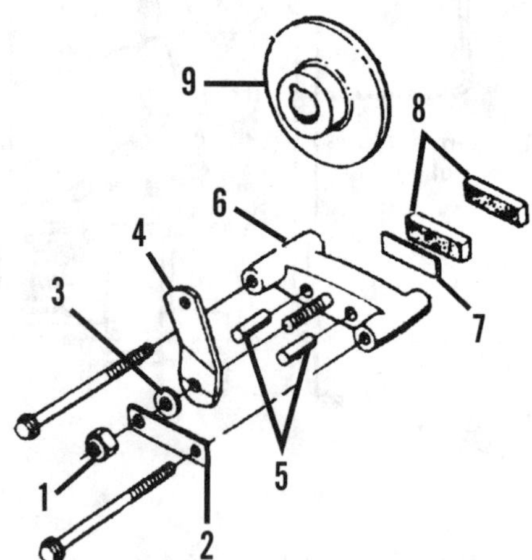

Fig. MT2-11—Exploded view of disc brake used on some models.

1. Adjusting nut
2. Bracket
3. Washer
4. Brake lever
5. Actuating pins
6. Brake pad holder
7. Back-up plate
8. Brake pads

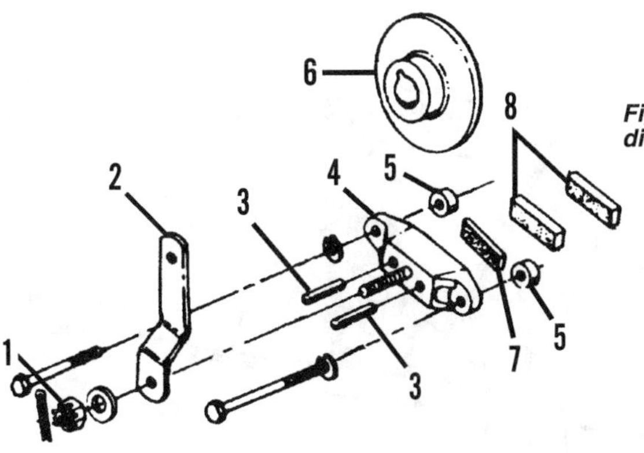

Fig. MT2-12—Exploded view of disc brake used on some models.

1. Adjusting nut
2. Brake lever
3. Actuating pins
4. Brake pad holder
5. Spacers
6. Brake disc
7. Back-up plate
8. Brake pads

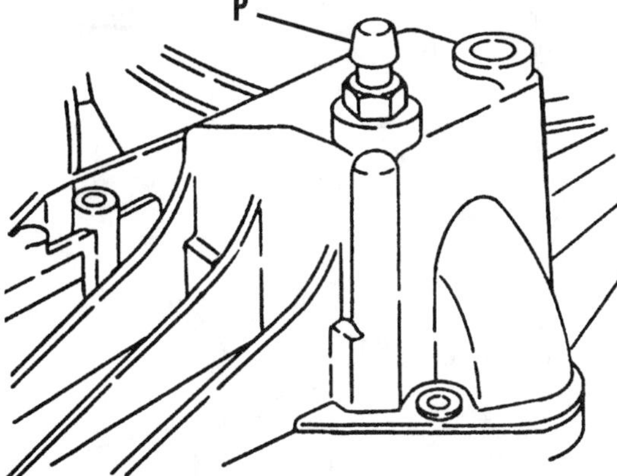

Fig. MT2-13—Unscrew breather plug (P) to check oil level or add oil on the Hydro-Gear hydrostatic transaxle.

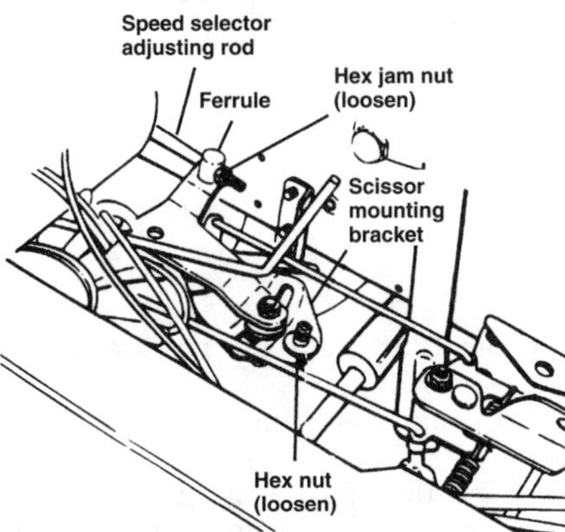

Fig. MT2-14—Drawing of Series 600 and 800 Hydro-Gear hydrostatic transmission control linkage showing adjustment points. Refer to text.

check the oil level, measure from the boss surface to the oil. Oil level on Model 310-0500 transaxle should be 1.75-2.00 inches (44-51 mm) the boss surface. Oil level on Model 310-0750 transaxle should be 1.00-1.25 inches (25-32 mm) below the boss.

LINKAGE ADJUSTMENT

Raise and securely support the rear of the tractor so the wheels are clear of the ground. Start and run the engine. With the transmission in neutral, the wheels should not rotate. If the wheels rotate, stop the engine and remove the transmission cover plate. Loosen the nut on the scissor mounting bracket (Fig. MT2-14). Loosen the jam nut on the speed selector rod (Fig. MT2-14).

CAUTION: Be careful of the transmission cooling fan and the drive belt when the engine is running.

Start the engine and run at full throttle. Move the hydrostatic control lever until the wheels do not rotate in either direction. Depress the clutch/brake pedal and shut off the engine. Tighten the nut on the scissor mounting bracket. Adjust the length of speed control rod so the hydrostatic control lever is aligned with the neutral position on the speed control bracket. Tighten the control rod jam nut.

REMOVAL AND INSTALLATION

To remove the hydrostatic transaxle, proceed as follows: Remove the seat and fenders. Remove the final drive belt. Disconnect the transaxle speed control linkage from the transaxle. Disconnect the brake actuating rod and the return spring from the transaxle brake lever. Support the transaxle and remove the mounting bolts and the axle housing clamp bolts. Remove the transaxle from the tractor.

To install the hydrostatic transaxle, reverse the removal procedure. Refill unit with recommended fluid and adjust the control linkage as previously outlined.

OVERHAUL

Refer to the Hydro-Gear section in the HYDROSTATIC TRANSAXLE in the rear of this manual for service information.

HYDROSTATIC TRANSMISSION (700-800 SERIES EQUIPPED WITH SUNDSTRAND HYDROSTATIC TRANSMISSION)

LUBRICATION

Models Prior to 1993

The hydrostatic transmission is equipped with an integral reservoir located under the tractor seat. The transmission is factory-filled with oil. The oil level should be at the lower or COLD mark on the reservoir with the unit cold. Recommended oil is SAE 10W30 engine oil with an SF rating.

If contamination is observed in the reservoir tank or the color of the fluid has changed (black or milky), the fluid should be drained and replaced.

NOTE: Reservoir tank cap has left-hand threads.

To drain fluid from the Sundstrand transmission, unscrew the hex drain plug located on the underside of the transmission housing.

Fill the transmission with new oil until the oil reaches the lower mark on the reservoir.

Models After 1992

On models after 1992, the transmission uses oil contained in the final drive housing. A spin-on oil filter is located on the left side of the final drive housing. Refer to the FINAL DRIVE section in this manual for oil filling or draining information.

LINKAGE ADJUSTMENT

Remove the mower deck from the tractor. Raise and securely support the rear of tractor so the wheels clear the ground. Start and run the engine. With the transmission control in neutral, the wheels should not rotate.

If the wheels rotate, perform the neutral adjustment as follows: Loosen the locknut on the neutral return rod and disconnect the ferrule from the speed selector handle bracket (Fig. MT2-15). Depress the clutch/brake pedal and move the hydrostatic control lever to the neutral position on the speed control bracket. Adjust the ferrule on the neutral return rod until it lines up with the hole in the speed selector handle bracket. Attach the ferrule to the bracket and tighten the locknut.

The tractor should not move when the hydrostatic control lever is in the NEUTRAL position. To adjust the control lever, remove the transmission panel. Loosen the bolt attaching the control lever bracket to the control link (Fig. MT2-16). Loosen the bolt attaching the pintle arm extension to the pintle arm (Fig. MT2-17).

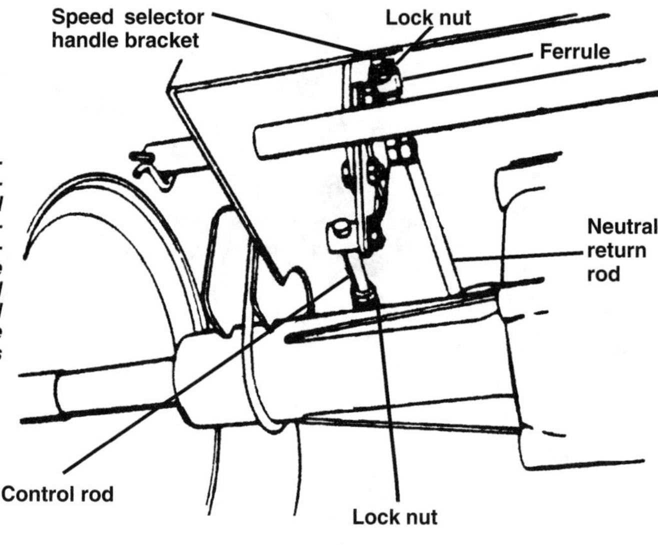

Fig. MT2-15—On Series 700 and 800 tractors with Sundstrand hydrostatic transmission, adjust the neutral return rod so the hydrostatic control lever is in the neutral position when the clutch/brake pedal is depressed.

CAUTION: Be careful of the transmission cooling fan and drive belt when the engine is running.

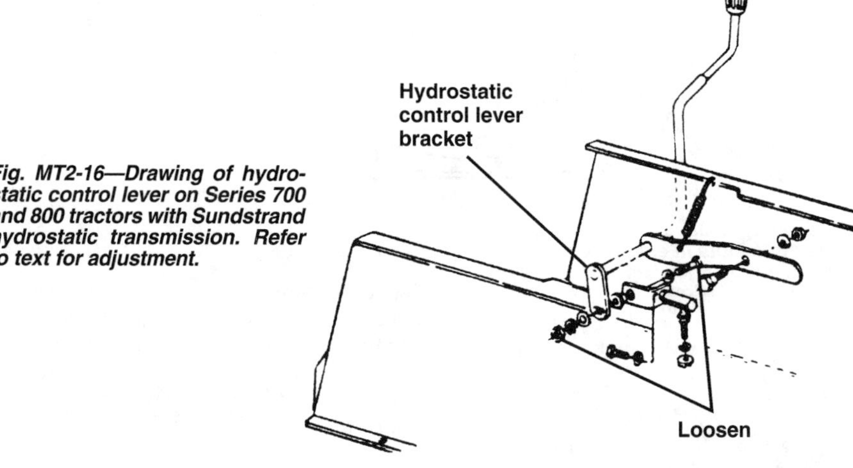

Fig. MT2-16—Drawing of hydrostatic control lever on Series 700 and 800 tractors with Sundstrand hydrostatic transmission. Refer to text for adjustment.

Depress the clutch/brake pedal and set the parking brake. Start the engine and run at full speed. Move the hydrostatic control lever to move the pintle arm until the rear wheels do not turn in either direction. Tighten the bolt securing the pintle arm to the pintle arm extension. Release the clutch/brake pedal. The wheels should not turn. If they do, repeat the adjustment.

Stop the engine and adjust the position of the hydrostatic control lever as follows: Depress the clutch/brake pedal and set the parking brake. Move the hydrostatic control lever to the NEUTRAL position on the quadrant. Tighten the nut and bolt on the hydrostatic control lever bracket (Fig. MT2-16).

REMOVAL AND INSTALLATION

To remove the hydrostatic transmission, proceed as follows: Remove the seat and fenders. Remove the final drive belt. Disconnect the transmission speed control linkage from the transmission. Disconnect the brake actuating and return springs from the brake lever and remove the brake caliper. Remove the final drive housing mounting bolts and the axle housing clamp bolts, then remove the transmission and final drive housing from the tractor. Unbolt and separate the hydrostatic transmission from the final drive housing.

To reinstall the hydrostatic unit, reverse the removal procedure. Refill the unit with recommended fluid and adjust the control linkage as previously outlined.

OVERHAUL

Models prior to 1993 are equipped with a Sundstrand BDU-10S transmission while models after 1992 are equipped with a Sundstrand BDU-10L transmission. Refer to the HYDROSTATIC TRANSMISSION section at the rear of this manual for overhaul information.

TRANSAXLE (MODELS EQUIPPED WITH VARIABLE SPEED TRANSMISSION)

LUBRICATION

The transaxle used on 600 and 700 series tractors with variable speed transmission is lubricated with grease at the factory and should not require additional lubrication. Capacity is 10 ounces (296 mL) of lithium-based grease.

Transaxle used on 800 series tractors with variable speed transmission is lubricated with grease at the factory and should not require additional lubrication. Capacity is 16 ounces (473 mL) of Benalene 372-0 grease.

REMOVAL AND INSTALLATION

To remove the transaxle assembly, first remove the mower deck from the tractor. Remove the drive belt from the transaxle pulley as previously outlined. Disconnect the shift linkage and brake linkage from the transaxle. Support the rear of the tractor and remove all fasteners securing the transaxle to the frame. Raise the rear of the tractor and roll the transaxle assembly out from under the tractor.

Install by reversing the removal procedure. Adjust the brake as previously outlined.

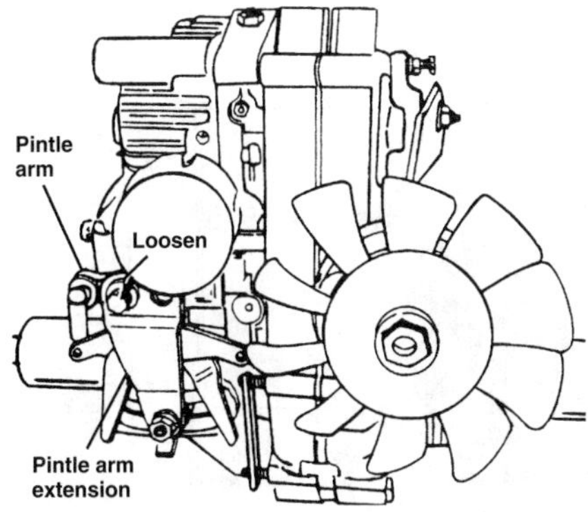

Fig. MT2-17—Adjust the Sundstrand hydrostatic transmission controls as outlined in the text.

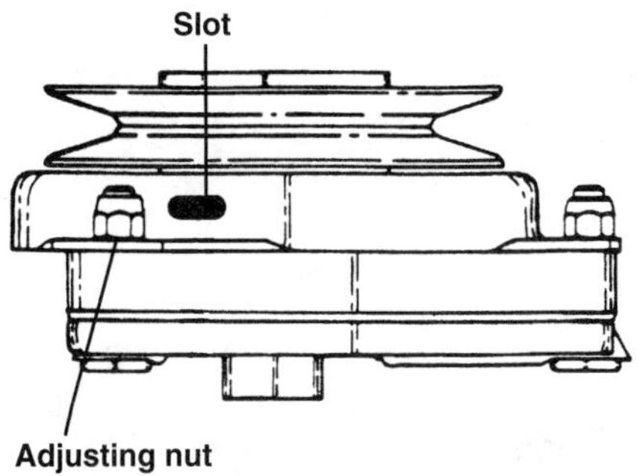

Fig. MT2-18—Measure the air gap at each of the three slots in electric clutch housing with a feeler gauge. Turn the adjusting nut to adjust the gap.

OVERHAUL

Refer to the MTD section in the TRANSAXLE service section in this manual for overhaul procedure.

FINAL DRIVE (MODELS EQUIPPED WITH SUNDSTRAND HYDROSTATIC TRANSMISSION)

LUBRICATION

Models Prior to 1993

The final drive used on tractors with a Sundstrand hydrostatic transmission is lubricated with grease at the factory and should not require additional lubrication. Capacity is 16 ounces (473 mL) of Shell Darina #0 grease.

Models After 1992

On models after 1992, the hydrostatic transmission uses oil contained in the final drive housing. A spin-on oil filter is located on the left side of the final drive housing.

Recommended oil is SAE 20W-50 engine oil for temperatures above 15° F (-9° C). Use SAE 10W-40 engine oil for temperatures from -5° F () to 100° F (-20° C). Synthetic oil rated SAE 15W-50 may be used from -35° F (-37° C) to 100° F (-20° C). Oil should meet API classification SH/CD.

The oil and oil filter should be changed annually or after 200 hours of operation, whichever occurs first. Change the oil and filter more frequently if the tractor is operated in severe conditions.

REMOVAL AND INSTALLATION

To remove the final drive, first remove the mower deck from the tractor. Remove the seat and fenders. Remove the final drive belt as previously outlined.

Disconnect the transmission speed control linkage from the transmission. Disconnect the brake actuating and return springs from the brake lever and remove the brake caliper.

Remove the final drive housing mounting bolts and axle housing clamp bolts, then remove the transmission and final drive housing from the tractor. Unbolt and separate the hydrostatic transmission from the final drive housing.

To reinstall the final drive, reverse the removal procedure.

OVERHAUL

Models prior to 1993 are equipped with a Hydro-Gear Model 210-1010 final drive unit. Models after 1992 are equipped with a Hydro-Gear Model 210-3000 final drive unit. Refer to the Hydro-Gear section in the FINAL DRIVE service section in this manual for overhaul procedure.

PTO CLUTCH

ADJUSTMENT

The PTO clutch should be adjusted if the clutch has been disassembled or if operation becomes erratic. The PTO and ignition switches must be off when performing the adjustment.

With the clutch disengaged, insert a feeler gauge through one of the slots (Fig. MT2-18) in the clutch housing and measure the clearance between the clutch rotor and armature. Clearance should be 0.010-0.025 inch (0.25-0.64 mm).

To adjust, tighten the adjusting nut next to the slot until the feeler gauge just begins to bind. Do not over tighten. Repeat the adjustment at each of the slots in the clutch housing. All slots must be adjusted equally.

TESTING

Turn the ignition switch ON and actuate the PTO control switch. If the clutch does not engage, check for voltage to the clutch. If voltage is present, use an ammeter to check the current in one of the PTO wires. Clutch should draw 3.5 amps or more when engaged.

To check the field coil, disconnect the wiring connector from the PTO clutch. Using an ohmmeter set on low scale, check the resistance between the terminals of the PTO connector. Specified resistance is 2.40-3.40 ohms. A reading not within the specified range indicates that the field coil is faulty and the clutch should be replaced.

REMOVAL AND INSTALLATION

To remove the PTO clutch, first remove the mower deck. Disconnect the wire connector from the clutch lead. Unscrew the clutch retaining screw and pull the clutch off the crankshaft.

Inspect the bearings in the field housing and armature for wear or damage. Inspect the contact surfaces of the rotor and armature for scoring, grooves or other damage. Replace the clutch when necessary.

Apply an antiseize compound to the crankshaft before installing the clutch. Adjust the clutch as previously outlined.

If a new clutch is installed, burnish the clutch friction surfaces as follows: Start the engine and run at half speed. Actuate the PTO control switch on and off six times. Increase engine speed to three-quarter speed and repeat the procedure. Allow the mower to stop completely before turning the switch back on. Recheck the clutch adjustment.

SAFETY INTERLOCK SYSTEM

Before the engine will start, the key must be turned ON and both of the safety switches must be activated. One switch is activated when the clutch/brake pedal is depressed and the other is activated when the blade is disengaged. When the two safety switches are activated, the circuit is completed between the battery and the starter solenoid, allowing the starter motor to crank the engine.

Some models are equipped with a seat safety switch and a reverse safety switch. However, these switches are not involved in the starting circuit. The seat safety switch is designed to stop the engine if the operator leaves the seat with the blades or PTO engaged. The blades must be in the disengaged

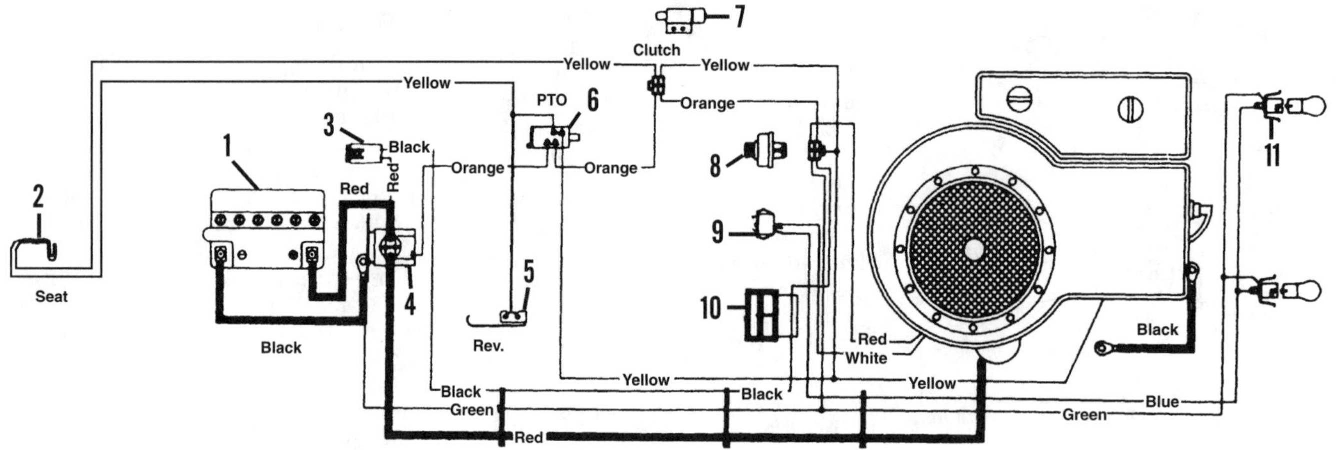

Fig. MT2-19—Typical wiring diagram for models with single-cylinder engine.

1. Battery
2. Seat safety switch
3. Fuse
4. Solenoid
5. Reverse safety switch
6. PTO safety switch
7. Clutch safety switch
8. Ignition switch
9. Light switch
10. Ammeter
11. Headlights

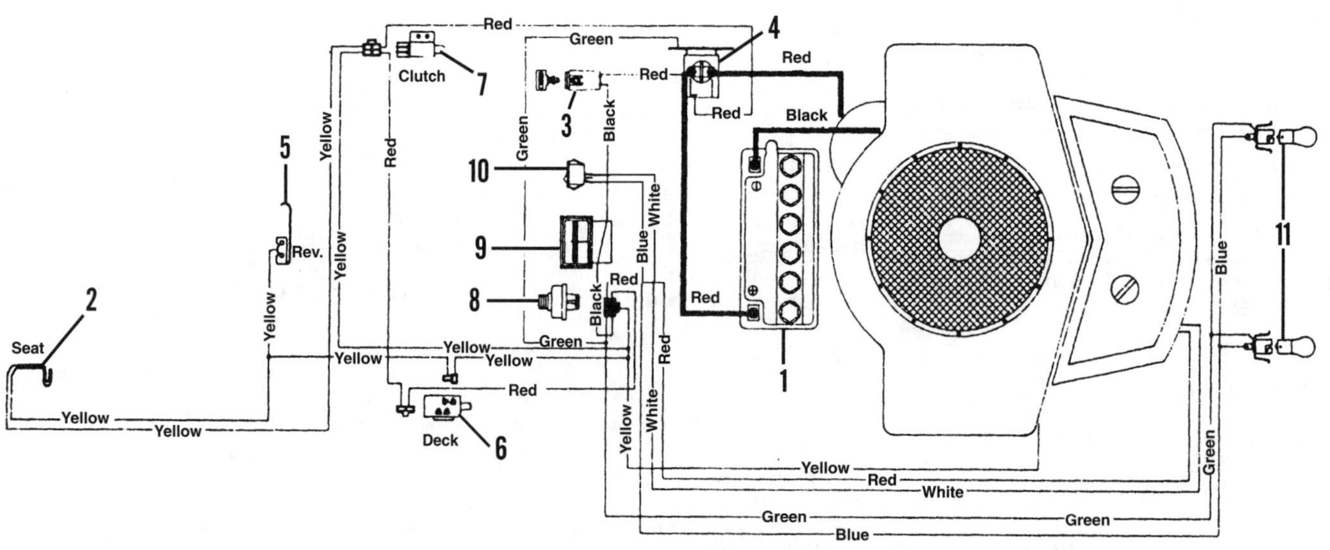

Fig. MT2-20—Typical wiring diagram for models with two-cylinder engine not equipped with an electric PTO clutch.

1. Battery
2. Seat safety switch
3. Fuse
4. Solenoid
5. Reverse safety switch
6. PTO safety switch
7. Clutch safety switch
8. Ignition switch
9. Ammeter
10. Light switch
11. Headlights
12. Indicator lights
13. Relays
14. PTO switch
15. Taillights

position when shifting into reverse or the engine will shut off.

To test the two safety start switches, first check the two switches to see if the switch plungers are depressed a minimum of $\frac{1}{8}$ inch (3 mm) when the blade is disengaged and the clutch/brake pedal is depressed. If the switch plunger is correctly depressed, use a continuity checker to determine if there is continuity across the switch terminals when the switches are activated (plunger depressed). If continuity is not indicated when the plunger is depressed, replace the switch.

To check for correct operation of the seat safety switch, start the engine and set the parking brake. Place the shift lever in NEUTRAL and engage the PTO or blades. Raise up off the seat. The engine should stop running.

WIRING DIAGRAMS

Wiring diagrams typical of all models are illustrated in Fig. MT2-19, MT2-20 and MT2-21.

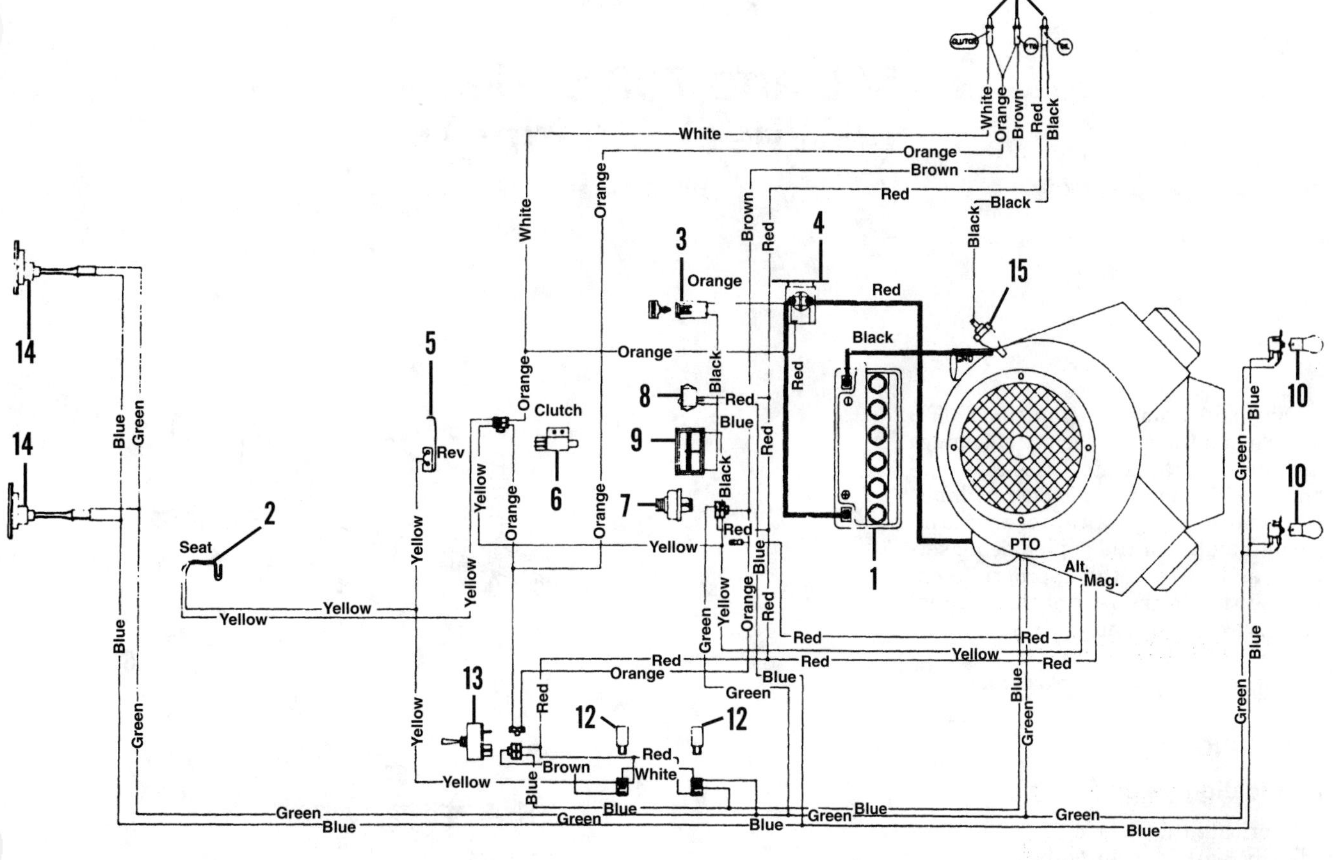

Fig. MT2-21—Typical wiring diagram for models with two-cylinder engine and equipped with an electric PTO clutch.

1. Battery
2. Seat safety switch
3. Fuse
4. Solenoid
5. Reverse safety switch
6. Clutch safety switch
7. Ignition switch
8. Light switch
9. Ammeter
10. Headlights
11. Indicator lights
12. Relays
13. PTO switch
14. Taillights
15. Oil pressure switch

MTD

600 and 700 Series (4-Wheel Steering)

Due to the numerous number of MTD models and the wide variety of engines installed, an accurate cross-reference and specification table is not available. Determine the manufacturer and model number of the engine being serviced and refer to the appropriate engine section in the rear of this manual for service information.

FRONT AXLE SYSTEM

STEERING SPINDLES

Lubrication

Lubricate the steering spindles periodically with a lithium-based, multipurpose grease. Clean away any excess grease.

Removal and Installation

Remove the mower deck from the tractor. Raise and support the front of the tractor. Remove the front wheels. Detach the tie rod (12—Fig. MT3-1) and the drag link (2) from the steering spindle or steering arm.

To remove the left spindle (8), loosen the clamp bolt (5) and remove the steering arm (4). Lower the spindle from the axle. To remove the right spindle (15), remove the roll pin (13) in right spindle. Pull the spindle down out of the axle main member.

Inspect the spindles and bushings (7) for wear or damage and replace when needed.

Install by reversing the removal procedure. Apply lithium-based, multipurpose grease to the bushings before installing the spindles.

AXLE MAIN MEMBER REMOVAL AND INSTALLATION

Remove the axle main member (9—Fig. MT3-1) as follows: Remove the mower deck from the tractor. Raise and support the front of the tractor and remove the front wheels. Remove the spindles as previously described.

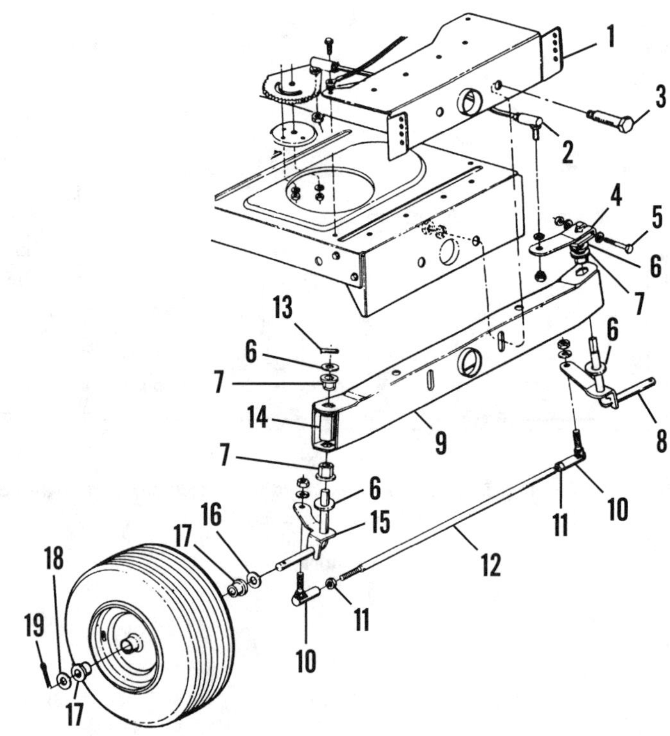

Fig. MT3-1—Exploded view of front axle assembly.

1. Axle pivot bracket
2. Drag link
3. Pivot stop bolt
4. Steering arm
5. Clamp bolt
6. Washer
7. Flange bushings
8. Spindle (left)
9. Axle main member
10. Rod end
11. Jam nut
12. Tie rod
13. Roll pin
14. Plastic tube
15. Spindle (right)
16. Washer
17. Wheel bearings
18. Washer
19. Cotter pin

Remove the grille for access to the front axle pivot bracket (1). Unscrew the bolts (3) that limit the axle travel. Unscrew the bolts attaching the pivot bracket (1) to the frame. Support the axle main member and remove the bracket and axle.

Reassemble by reversing the removal procedure.

STEERING SYSTEM

All models are equipped with a 4-wheel-steering system. A cam-type steering gearbox (6—Fig. MT3-2) on the steering shaft transfers steering motion to the rear wheel steering mechanism. A gear at the bottom of the steering shaft actuates the front steering system. Rear wheels turn in the opposite direction to the front wheels to decrease the steering radius. The rear wheels do not turn until the front wheel steering angle exceeds 45°.

ALIGNMENT ADJUSTMENT

Adjust the length of the tie rod (12—Fig. MT3-1) to obtain front wheel

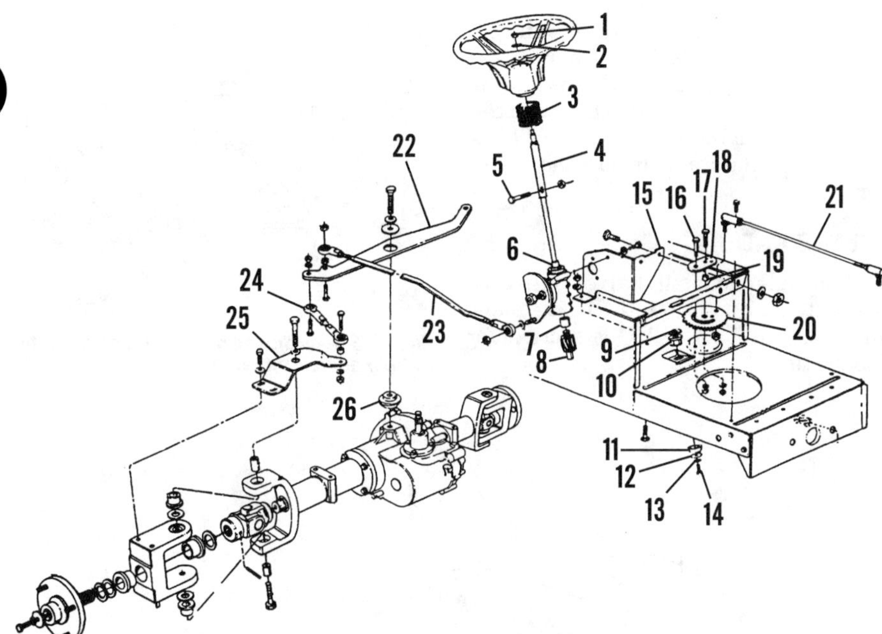

Fig. MT3-2—Exploded view of steering system.

1. Nut
2. Belleville washer
3. Bellow
4. Upper steering shaft
5. Bolt
6. Steering gearbox
7. Splined coupler
8. Steering gear
9. Washer
10. Flange bushing
11. Spacer
12. Washer
13. Lockwasher
14. Screw
15. Bracket
16. Shoulder bolt
17. Screw
18. Retainer plate
19. Spacer
20. Sector gear
21. Drag link
22. Center steering arm
23. Rear steering link
24. Tie rod
25. Outer steering arm
26. Pivot

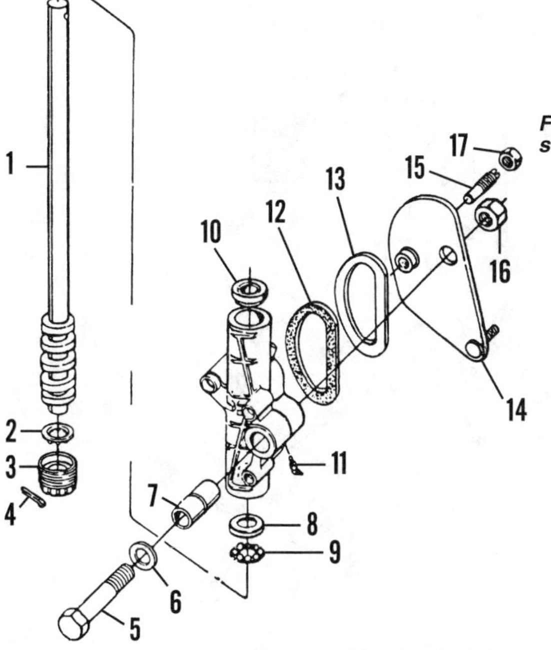

Fig. MT3-3—Exploded view of steering gearbox.

1. Steering shaft
2. Bearing
3. Adjustment plug
4. Cotter pin
5. Pivot bolt
6. Washer
7. Bushing
8. Bearing cup
9. Bearing
10. Oil seal
11. Grease fitting
12. Seal
13. Seal retainer
14. Steering arm
15. Cam follower
16. Locknut
17. Jam nut

toe-in of $\frac{1}{8}$ inch (3.2 mm). Secure the tie rod ends with the jam nuts.

Rotate the steering wheel so the holes in the sector gear (20—Fig. MT3-2) and the retainer plate (18) are aligned. Insert a suitable size pin so the holes remain aligned. Adjust the length of the drag link (21) so the front wheels point straight ahead.

Note the hole in the steering gear housing under the grease fitting (11—Fig. MT3-3). Rotate the steering wheel 16° in each direction so a pin inserted in the hole will lock the steering worm. Adjust the length of the rear steering link (23—Fig. MT3-2) so the rear wheels point forward. Adjust the length of each tie rod (24) to adjust the position of each rear wheel so they point straight ahead.

STEERING GEAR AND GEARBOX

Removal and Installation

Remove the steering gear assembly as follows: Disconnect the battery cables. Remove the mower deck from the tractor. Remove the fuel tank.

Remove the steering wheel cover, retaining nut (1—Fig. MT3-2) and Belleville washer (2). Pull the steering wheel off the shaft and remove the bellow (3). Unscrew the steering shaft coupling bolt (5) and remove the upper steering shaft (4).

Disconnect the drag link (21) from the sector gear (20). Remove the mounting bolt (17) and shoulder bolt (16) from the sector retainer plate (18) and withdraw the sector gear.

Remove the retaining screw (14) from the lower end of the steering gear (8) shaft and remove the lower steering gear, thrust washer (9) and bushing (10). Disconnect the rear steering link (23) from the steering gearbox. Remove the steering gearbox from the tractor.

Inspect all parts for excessive wear or damage and replace when necessary.

Install by reversing the removal procedure. Apply a light coat of multipurpose grease to the teeth of the steering gears.

Overhaul Steering Gearbox

Disassemble the steering gear as follows: Clamp the steering arm plate (14—Fig. MT3-3) in a vise and remove the nut (16) and jam nut (17). Separate the gearbox from the steering arm plate. Remove the cotter pin (4) and adjustment plug (3). Remove the steering shaft and cam assembly (1) and bearings from the gearbox.

Inspect the cam follower for flat spots. Inspect the ends of the cam (1), the ball bearings and bearing cups for roughness or pitting. Check the cam grooves for wear, roughness and galling.

During reassembly, coat the cam, bearing balls and races with lithium-base grease. Install the steering shaft and cam, balls and races into the gearbox. Make certain that the races enter the gearbox squarely and are not cocked. Thread the adjustment plug (3) into the gearbox until the end play of the cam is removed but the shaft still turns freely. Insert the cotter pin (4) into the nearest hole in the adjustment plug.

Fill the housing with lithium-base grease. Loosen the jam nut (17) and back the cam follower (15) out two turns. Install the seal (12), retainer (13) and steering arm plate (14). Install the nut (16). Tighten the nut until there is 3/32 inch (2.4 mm) clearance between the steering arm plate and gearbox. Install a jam nut against the nut (16) and tighten the jam nut to 40 ft.-lb. (54 N·m).

Inject grease into the fitting (11) until grease begins to appear between the steering arm plate (14) and gearbox.

Center the steering cam by rotating the steering shaft halfway between full right and full left turn. Turn the cam follower (15) inward to eliminate backlash, then tighten the jam nut (17) to 40 ft.-lb. (54 N·m). The steering shaft should rotate smoothly with minimum backlash.

ENGINE

REMOVAL AND INSTALLATION

Remove the hood, grille brace, or side panels, and grille. Disconnect the battery cables, starter wires and all necessary electrical connections from the engine. Disconnect the fuel line. Disconnect the choke and throttle control cables from the engine.

Remove the drive belts from the engine pulleys. Remove the muffler heat shield, if so equipped. Remove the engine mounting bolts and lift the engine from the tractor.

Install by reversing the removal procedure.

OVERHAUL

Refer to the appropriate engine section in this manual for tune-up specifications, engine overhaul procedures and engine maintenance.

CLUTCH AND BRAKE

All models are equipped with a continuously variable drive pulley that provides infinite travel speeds. Depressing the clutch/brake pedal partway disengages the clutch. Depressing the pedal all the way down disengages the clutch and engages the disc brake.

ADJUSTMENT

Remove the cotter pin in the castle nut (N—Fig. MT3-4) on the transaxle brake lever. Hand-tighten the nut so the brake lever is trapped against the transaxle bracket. Detach the clutch rod (2—Fig. MT3-5) from the torque bracket (1).

Depress the clutch/brake pedal until resistance is felt. Rotate the clutch rod (2) so the rod end fits easily onto the pin on the torque bracket (1). Shorten the clutch rod by rotating two turns and reattach the rod end to the bracket. Loosen the castle nut (N—Fig. MT3-4) one or two flats and insert the cotter pin.

BRAKE PADS

Transaxle housing halves must be separated for access to the brake pads. Refer to the TRANSAXLE section for instructions.

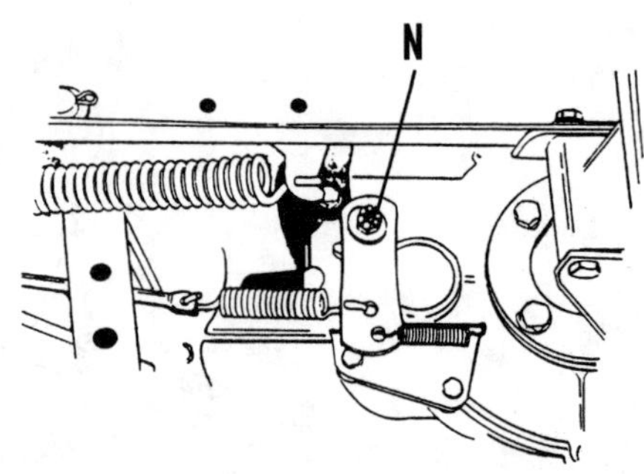

Fig. MT3-4—Adjust brake by turning castle nut (N) as described in text.

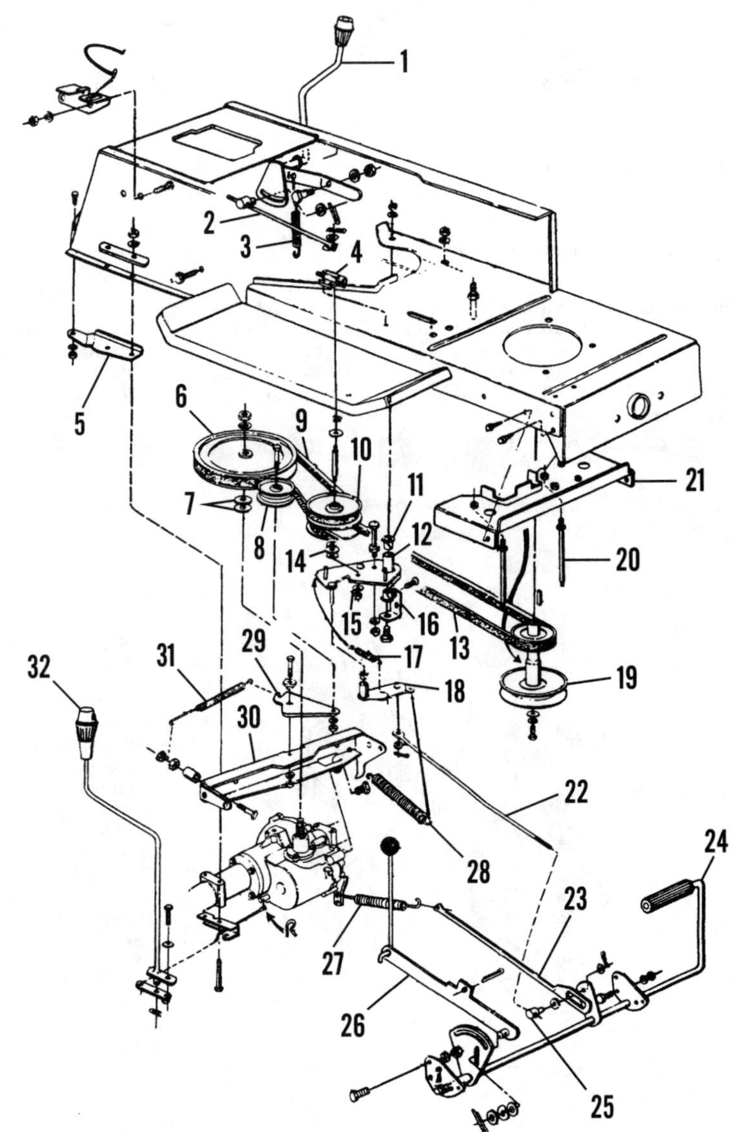

Fig. MT3-5—Exploded view of variable speed drive components.

1. Speed selector lever
2. Speed selector rod
3. Spring
4. Clutch safety switch
5. Axle support bracket
6. Transaxle pulley
7. Washers
8. Idler pulley
9. Rear drive belt
10. Variable speed pulley
11. Bearing
12. Variable speed bracket
13. Front drive belt
14. Washers
15. Belleville washers
16. Bearing bracket
17. Spring
18. Torque bracket
19. Engine pulley
20. Guide bolt (2)
21. Belt guard
22. Speed control link
23. Brake rod
24. Clutch/brake pedal assy.
25. Ferrule
26. Parking brake rod
27. Brake spring
28. Spring
29. Idler bracket
30. Transaxle support bracket
31. Spring
32. Shift lever

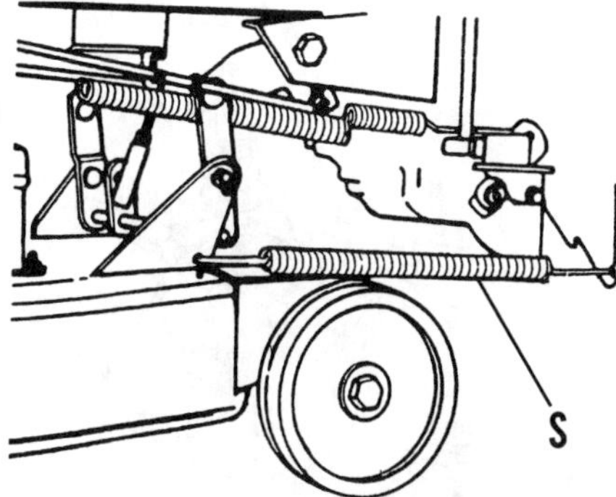

Fig. MT3-6—Detach spring (S) from transmission support bracket to relieve tension on the drive belts for belt removal.

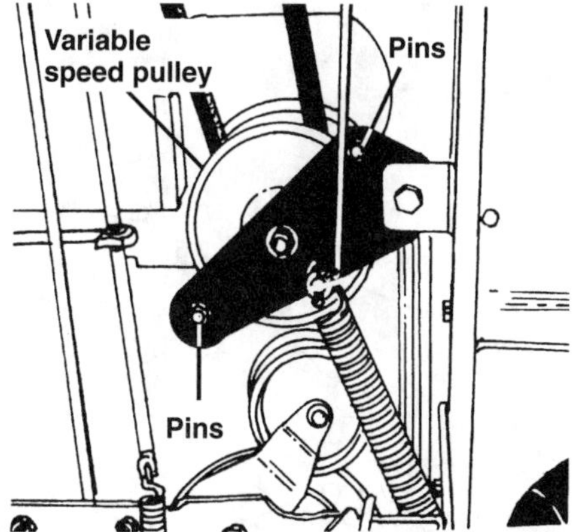

Fig. MT3-7—Push forward on variable speed pulley and remove belt from engine pulley. It may be necessary to remove guide pins for access to belt.

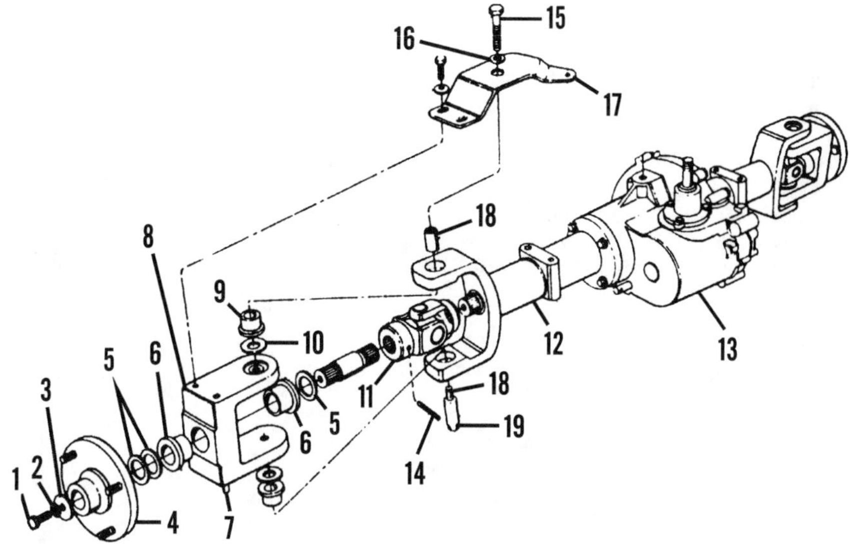

Fig. MT3-8—Exploded view of rear axle assembly.

1. Screw
2. Lockwasher
3. Washer
4. Outer axle
5. Washers
6. Bushing
7. Grease fitting
8. Steering knuckle
9. Bushing
10. Washer
11. Universal joint
12. Axle housing
13. Transaxle
14. Pin
15. Screw
16. Washer
17. Steering arm
18. Pivot sleeve
19. Screw

DRIVE BELTS

REAR DRIVE BELT REMOVAL AND INSTALLATION

Disconnect the battery cables. Remove the mower deck from the tractor. Remove the transmission cover.

NOTE: It is not necessary to tip the tractor to remove the belts. If the tractor is tipped, remove the battery and drain the fuel tank or place a piece of plastic wrap over the neck of the tank and screw on the cap to prevent leakage.

Detach the speed selector rod (2—Fig. MT3-5) from the variable speed pulley (10). Move the belt idler pulley (8) away from the belt to relieve tension on the belt and move the belt over the idler pulley. Remove the belt from the variable speed pulley (10) and the transaxle pulley (6).

Install the belt by reversing the removal procedure.

FRONT DRIVE BELT REMOVAL AND INSTALLATION

Remove the rear drive belt as described in the previous section. Position the lift lever in the disengaged position. Detach spring (S—Fig. MT3-6) from the transmission support bracket. Raise and support the front of the tractor.

Unscrew the belt guide bolts (20—Fig. MT3-5) located around the engine drive pulley. If so equipped, detach the mower deck belt from the engine pulley. Remove the bolts attaching the engine pulley belt guard (21) to the frame. Slide the belt guard rearward and to the right to remove it. Move the clutch/brake pedal to the park position. Push the variable speed pulley (Fig. MT3-7) forward and detach the belt from the engine pulley. If necessary, remove the belt guide pins. Move the clutch/brake pedal as needed to disengage the belt from the variable speed pulley.

Reverse the removal procedure to install the belt. Be sure that the belt is positioned inside the guide pins.

REAR AXLE PIVOT ASSEMBLY

LUBRICATION

Lubricate the rear wheel outer axle bushings periodically by injecting lithium-based, multipurpose grease into the grease fitting (7—Fig. MT3-8) located on the underside of each steering knuckle (8). Clean away any excess grease.

OVERHAUL

Remove the mower deck from the tractor. Raise and support the rear of the tractor. Remove the rear wheel.

Detach the tie rod from the steering arm (17—Fig. MT3-8). Remove the upper (15) and lower (19) pivot screws. Separate the steering knuckle (8) from the axle housing. Drive out the roll pin (14), then separate and remove the axle flange (4) and universal joint (11).

Inspect components for damage. Also inspect the outer end of the transaxle axle for wear. Replace the bushings (6 and 9) if damaged. Reassemble by reversing the disassembly procedure.

TRANSAXLE

LUBRICATION

Transaxle lubricant level does not require periodic checking. The recommended lubricant is Shell Darina grease. Capacity is 32 ounces (947 mL).

REMOVAL AND INSTALLATION

To remove the transaxle and axle pivot assemblies as a unit, proceed as follows. Remove the mower deck from the tractor. Remove the rear drive belt as previously outlined. Raise and support the rear of the tractor. Remove the rear wheels.

Disconnect the rear steering link (23—Fig. MT3-2) from the center steering arm (22). Detach the brake actuating spring (28—Fig. MT3-5) from the brake lever. Detach the shift lever (32) from the transaxle shift shaft.

Support the transaxle, remove the mounting bolts and remove the transaxle and axle assembly. If necessary, remove the outer axle pivot assemblies from the transaxle as previously outlined.

Install by reversing the removal procedure.

OVERHAUL

Remove the axle pivot assemblies as previously outlined before disassembling transaxle. Refer to Fig. MT3-9 for an exploded view of the transaxle.

To disassemble, unbolt and remove the input shaft (33) and housing (4) assembly. Remove the snap rings (2 and 38) and withdraw the bevel gear (37), thrust bearing (35 and 36) and shaft from the housing.

Unbolt and remove the axle housings (12—Fig. MT3-8) on each side. Remove the cap screws retaining the housing cover (10—Fig. MT3-9) and separate the cover from the transaxle housing (5).

Withdraw the axle shafts (39 and 51—Fig. MT3-9) and differential assembly from the housing. Unbolt and separate the differential case (49) from the differential gear (42). Remove the nuts (45) and side gears (43) from the axles. To remove the spider gears (44), detach the snap ring (47) and withdraw the cross shaft (50) from the differential case.

Slide the brake disc (15—Fig. MT3-9) off the drive shaft (16). Unbolt and remove the brake pad holder (13). Withdraw the drive shaft (16) and bevel gear (22) as an assembly. Remove the bolts retaining the spring retainer plate (19) to the bevel gear. Separate the retainer plate, springs (20) and drive pins (21) from the bevel gear.

Unscrew the setscrew (27) located in the bottom of the transaxle case to release the detent spring and ball (25) before removing the shift fork (24). Lift up on the shift assembly and rotate to remove it from the case.

Inspect the splines in the shift collar for wear or damage. Check the drive shaft splines and gear teeth for wear. Replace worn or damaged components as needed.

Backlash between the pinion gear (37—Fig. MT3-9) and bevel gear (28) should be 0.006-0.010 inch (0.15-0.25 mm). Adjust backlash by adding or deleting 0.010 inch shims (30).

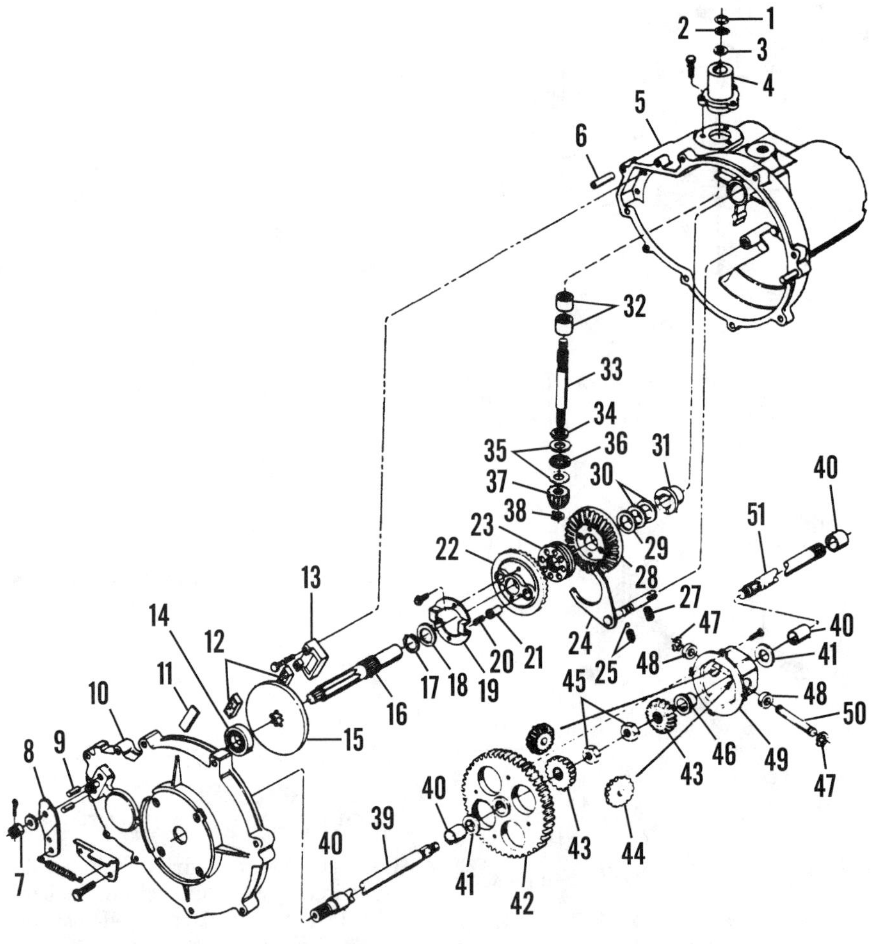

Fig. MT3-9—Exploded view of transaxle.

1. Wire ring
2. Snap ring
3. Washer
4. Input shaft housing
5. Case
6. Dowel pin
7. Nut
8. Brake arm
9. Brake actuator pin
10. Cover
11. Plate
12. Brake pads
13. Brake holder
14. Bearing
15. Brake disc
16. Drive shaft
17. Snap ring
18. Washer
19. Spring retaining plate
20. Spring
21. Pin
22. Bevel gear
23. Shift collar
24. Shift fork
25. Detent spring & ball
27. Set screw
28. Bevel gear
29. Washer
30. Shims
31. Bushing
32. Bearing
33. Input shaft
34. Seal
35. Thrust washer
36. Thrust bearing
37. Gear
38. Snap ring
39. Axle shaft
40. Bushing
41. Washer
42. Gear
43. Side gear
44. Pinion
45. Nut
46. Bushing
47. Snap ring
48. Spacer
49. Differential case
50. Shaft
51. Axle

Reassemble by reversing the disassembly procedure. Fill the housing with 32 ounces (947 mL) of Shell Darina grease. Adjust the castle nut (7—Fig. MT3-9) so there is ¼ to 3/8 inch (6.5-9.5 mm) clearance between the brake stop bracket and the brake cam (8).

SAFETY INTERLOCK SYSTEM

Before the engine will start, the key must be turned on and both of the safety switches must be activated. One switch (7—Fig. MT3-10) is activated when the clutch/brake pedal is depressed and the other switch (6) is activated when the blade is disengaged. When the two safety switches are activated, the circuit is completed between the battery and the starter solenoid, allowing the starter motor to crank the engine.

Some models are equipped with a seat safety switch (2) and a reverse safety switch (5). However, these switches are not involved in the starting circuit. The seat safety switch is designed to stop the engine if the operator leaves the seat with the blades or PTO engaged. The blades must be in the disengaged position when shifting into reverse or the engine will shut off.

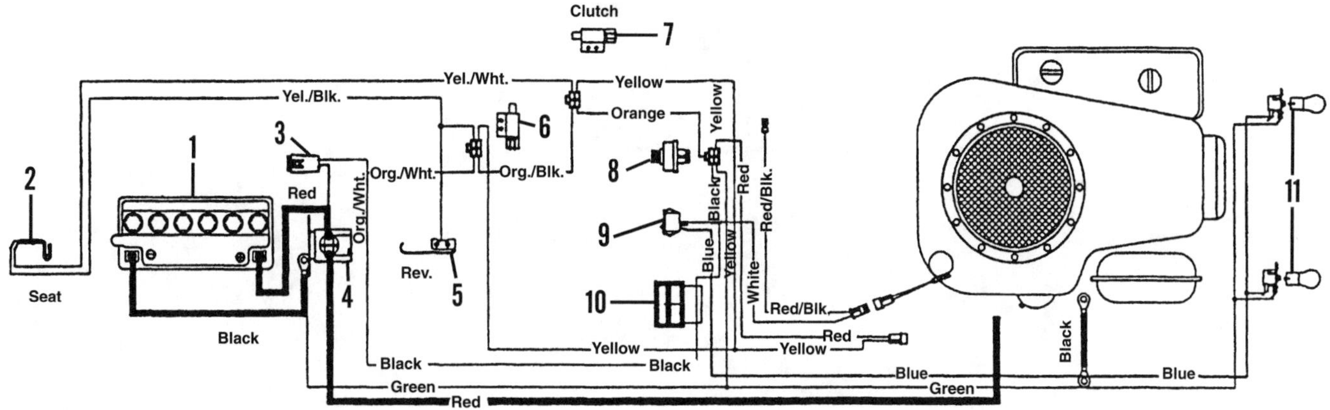

Fig. MT3-10—Typical wiring diagram.

1. Battery
2. Seat safety switch
3. Fuse
4. Solenoid
5. Reverse safety switch
6. PTO safety switch
7. Clutch safety switch
8. Ignition switch
9. Light switch
10. Ammeter
11. Headlights

To test the two safety start switches, first check the two switches to see if the switch plungers are depressed a minimum of 1/8 inch (3 mm) when the blade is disengaged and the clutch/brake pedal is depressed. If the switch plunger is correctly depressed, use a continuity checker to determine if there is continuity across the switch terminals when the switches are activated (plunger depressed). If continuity is not indicated when the plunger is depressed, replace the switch.

To check for correct operation of the seat safety switch, start the engine and set the parking brake. Place the shift lever in NEUTRAL and engage the PTO or blades. Raise up off the seat. The engine should stop running.

WIRING DIAGRAM

The wiring diagram illustrated in Fig. MT3-10 is typical of all models.

MTD

900 Series

Due to the numerous number of MTD models and the wide variety of engines installed, an accurate cross-reference and specification table is not available. Determine the manufacturer and model number of the engine being serviced and refer to the appropriate engine section in the rear of this manual for service information.

FRONT AXLE AND STEERING SYSTEM

MAINTENANCE

Periodically inject lithium-based, multipurpose grease into the grease fittings located at the ends of the axle main member. Periodically lubricate the steering gear with lithium-based, multipurpose grease. Clean away any excess grease.

STEERING SPINDLES

Raise and support the front of the tractor. Remove the front wheels. Detach the tie rod (20—Fig. MT4-1) and drag link (19) from the steering spindle.

Remove the dust cap (13) and withdraw the cotter pin (12) to free the steering spindles (7 and 17). Pull the spindle down out of the axle main member.

Inspect the spindles and bushings (10) for wear and replace when necessary.

Reinstall by reversing the removal procedure. Apply lithium-based, multipurpose grease to the spindle bushings before installing the spindles.

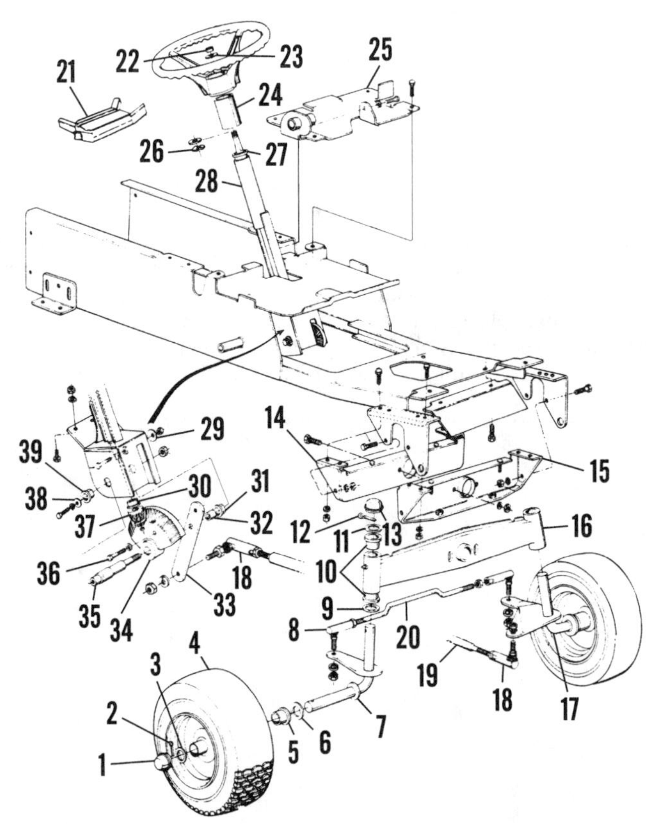

Fig. MT4-1—Exploded view of front axle and steering gear assembly.

1. Dust cap
2. Cotter pin
3. Washer
4. Tire & hub assy.
5. Bushing
6. Washer
7. Spindle
8. Tie rod end
9. Thrust washer
10. Bushings
11. Washer
12. Cotter pin
13. Cap
14. Rear pivot bracket
15. Axle main member
16. Front pivot bracket
17. Spindle
18. Drag link end
19. Drag link
20. Tie rod
21. Cap
22. Nut
23. Steering wheel
24. Sleeve
25. Dash panel base plate
26. Wave washer
27. Bushing
28. Steering column
29. Belleville washer
30. Bushing
31. Nut
32. Spacer
33. Steering arm
34. Sector gear
35. Steering shaft
36. Cap screw
37. Pinion gear
38. Cap screw
39. Bushing

TIE ROD AND TOE-IN

Some models are equipped with an adjustable tie rod (20—Fig. MT4-1). Inspect the ball joints (8) for excessive wear and looseness and replace if needed.

Adjust the length of the tie rod to obtain front wheel toe-in of 1/8 inch (3.2 mm). Secure the tie rod ends with jam nuts.

AXLE MAIN MEMBER REMOVAL AND INSTALLATION

To remove the axle main member (16—Fig. MT4-1), remove the hood and grille. Remove the PTO drive shaft as outlined in the PTO Section.

Raise and support the front of tractor frame and remove the front wheels. Disconnect the drag link end (18) from the left spindle (17). Disconnect the tie rod (20) from both spindles. Remove the cap (13) and cotter pin (12) and withdraw the spindles from the axle.

Support the axle main member (16). Remove the front (15) and rear (14) pivot brackets and remove the axle from the tractor.

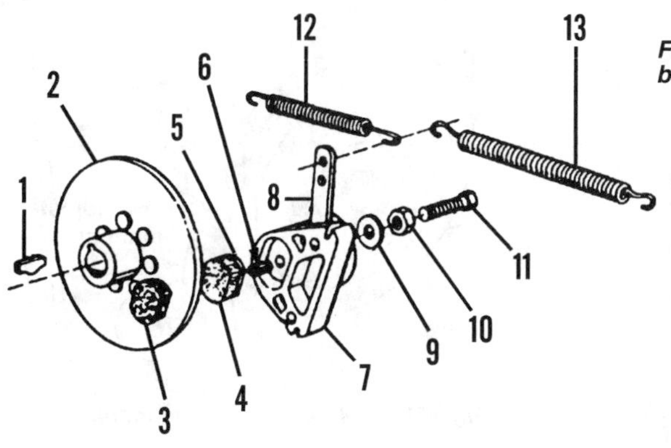

Fig. MT4-2—Exploded view of brake components.

1. Key
2. Disc
3. Brake pad
4. Brake pad
5. Metal backing plate
6. Pin
7. Caliper
8. Brake lever
9. Washer
10. Jam nut
11. Adjustment bolt
12. Spring
13. Spring

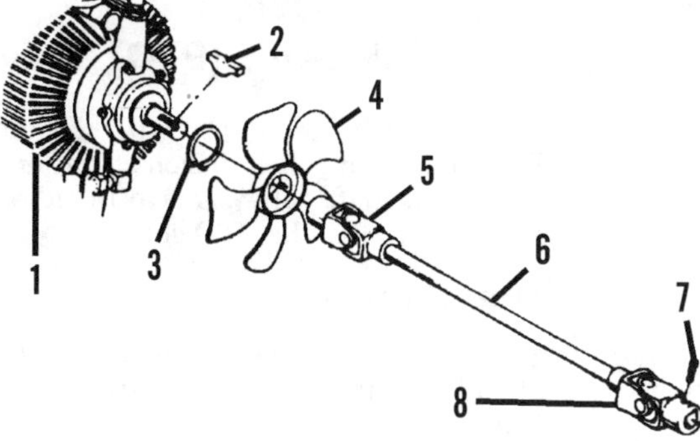

Fig. MT4-3—Exploded view of drive shaft assembly typical of all models.

1. Hydrostatic transmission
2. Key
3. Snap ring
4. Cooling fan
5. Rear universal joint & yoke
6. Drive shaft
7. Setscrew
8. Front universal joint & yoke

Install by reversing the removal procedure.

STEERING GEAR

To remove the steering gear, first disconnect the battery cables. Disconnect the drag link end (18—Fig. MT4-1) from the steering arm (33). Remove the steering wheel insert (21) and unscrew the nut (22) that retains the steering wheel. Remove the steering wheel (23), bellows or sleeve (24), wave washer (26) and upper bearing (27) from the steering shaft.

Remove the nut from the lower end of the steering shaft and pull the steering shaft up and out of the pinion gear (30).

Remove the cap screw (38) and nut (31). Drive the sector shaft (35) out of the steering bracket and sector gear (34). Remove the spacer (32) and gear (34).

Reinstall by reversing the removal procedure. Make certain the sector shaft (35) goes through the steering lever (33).

ENGINE

REMOVAL AND INSTALLATION

Remove the hood, grille brace, or side panels, and grille. Disconnect the battery cables, starter wires and all necessary electrical connections from the engine. Disconnect the fuel line. Disconnect the choke and throttle control cables from the engine.

Remove the engine shrouds. Disconnect the drive shaft from the rear of the engine. Detach the PTO pulley from the front of the engine.

Remove the bolts securing the engine to the frame and lift the engine from the tractor.

Install by reversing the removal procedure.

OVERHAUL

Refer to the appropriate engine section in this manual for tune-up specifications, engine overhaul procedures and engine maintenance.

BRAKE

ADJUSTMENT

The brake is located on the left side of the final drive. The brake adjustment access hole is located above the left rear axle mounting bracket.

To adjust the brake, loosen the jam nut (10—Fig. MT4-2) and use a 7/16-inch socket and extension to tighten the adjustment bolt (11) until the pads (3 and 4) are pushed against the brake disc (2). Loosen the adjustment bolt ½ turn and check the brake operation. When satisfactory, tighten the jam nut (10).

BRAKE PADS

Disconnect the brake rod and springs (12 and 13—Fig. MT4-2) from the brake lever (8). Remove the bolts securing the caliper (7) to the final drive. Remove the brake pad (4), metal backing plate (5) and actuating pin (6) from the caliper (7). Remove the disc (2) and inner pad (3).

Reinstall by reversing the removal procedure. Adjust the brake as previously outlined.

DRIVE SHAFT REMOVAL AND INSTALLATION

The drive shaft connects the engine to the hydrostatic drive unit. To remove the drive shaft, loosen the setscrew (7—Fig. MT4-3) and slide the drive shaft assembly (6) forward until the rear universal joint yoke slips off the hydrostatic drive unit. Lift the drive shaft and pull the front universal joint and yoke (8) from the crankshaft.

Install by reversing the removal procedure

SPEED CONTROL LINKAGE ADJUSTMENT

Raise and support the rear of the tractor so the tires are off the ground. Disconnect the rod end (13—Fig. MT4-4) from the control rod (16). Loosen the jam nut (12) and the two cap screws (10). Move the slide mounting plate (6) until the alignment hole (5) is aligned with the cam plate (7) alignment hole. Insert a 5/16-inch screw through the alignment holes. Start the engine and run at idle speed.

CAUTION: Exercise caution when working around the spinning wheels and drive components.

Rotate the cam plate (7) until all wheel rotation stops. Tighten the cap screws (10). Shut off the engine and engage the parking brake. Adjust the length of the rod (9) until the rod end (13) can be inserted into the control rod plate. Secure with the lock washer and nut. Tighten the jam nut (12) and remove the 5/16-inch screw from the alignment holes.

HYDROSTATIC TRANSMISSION

LUBRICATION

The hydrostatic drive unit and two-speed final drive share a common

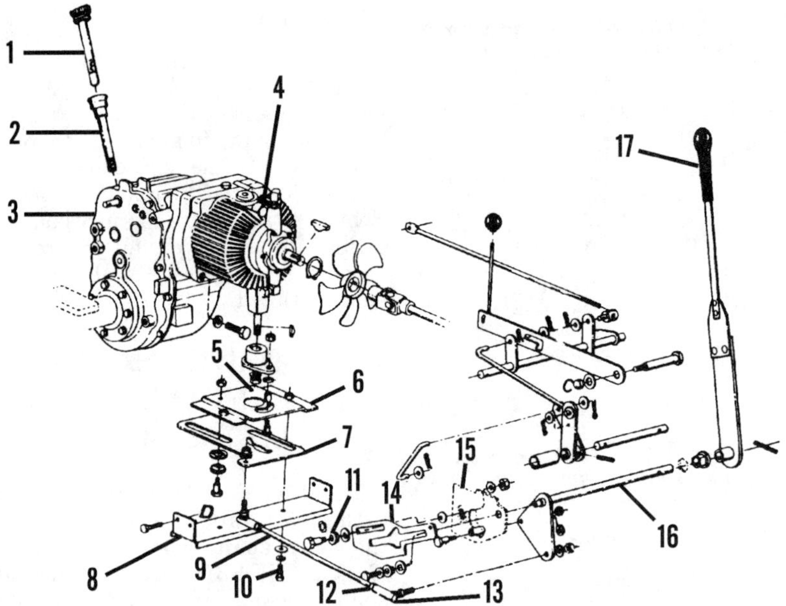

Fig. MT4-4—Exploded view of hydrostatic transmission control linkage.

1. Dipstick
2. Dipstick tube
3. Transaxle
4. Hydrostatic transmission
5. Alignment hole
6. Slide mounting plate
7. Cam plate
8. Support channel
9. Speed control rod
10. Cap screws
11. Shoulder bolt
12. Jam nut
13. Rod end
14. Neutral control slide
15. Frame piece
16. Control rod
17. Hydrostatic control lever

fluid reservoir located in the final drive housing. Check the fluid level with the dipstick (1—Fig. MT4-4) located just below the seat and deck assembly at the rear of the tractor. Check the fluid level when the fluid is cold. Maintain the fluid level at the "FULL" mark on the dipstick.

Change the fluid and filter at 100-hour intervals. Approximate fluid capacity is 6 quarts (5.7 L). Recommended fluid is SAE 20W engine oil with service classification SF.

REMOVAL AND INSTALLATION

To remove the hydrostatic transmission, remove the seat, fenders and drive shaft. Disconnect the hydraulic hoses and plug or cap the openings to prevent dirt from entering the system. Disconnect the hydrostatic drive control linkage. Remove the bolts retaining the hydrostatic unit to the final drive and remove the unit from the tractor.

To install the hydrostatic unit, reverse the removal procedure. Fill with recommended fluid and adjust the control linkage as previously outlined.

OVERHAUL

Tractor is equipped with an Eaton Model 11 hydrostatic transmission. Refer to the HYDROSTATIC TRANSMISSION section at the rear of this manual for transmission overhaul information.

FINAL DRIVE

LUBRICATION

Refer to the previous Hydrostatic Transmission section for lubrication information.

REMOVAL AND INSTALLATION

To remove the final drive, first remove the hydrostatic transmission as previously outlined. Raise and support the rear of the tractor.

Disconnect the brake rod from the brake lever. Detach the two-speed shift linkage from the differential. Support the differential and remove bolts retaining the differential to the frame. Lower the differential and roll the assembly away from the tractor. Drain the fluid from the unit and remove the brake assembly.

To install the final drive, reverse the removal procedure.

OVERHAUL

The tractor is equipped with a Peerless Model 2500 final drive. Refer to the FINAL DRIVE section at the rear of this manual for final drive overhaul information.

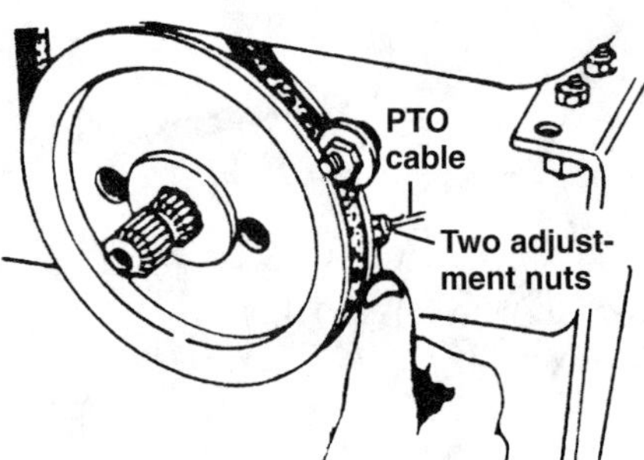

Fig. MT4-5—PTO cable adjustment.

POWER TAKE-OFF (PTO)

The tractor is equipped with a front PTO shaft that is belt driven off the engine crankshaft pulley. A pivoting idler system actuates the PTO clutch.

LUBRICATION

Lubricate the PTO engagement lever at 25-hour intervals. Use multipurpose, lithium-based grease.

ADJUSTMENT

Adjust the PTO cable at either end until the idler depresses the safety switch plunger within 1/8 inch (3.2 mm) of bottoming out in the switch with the PTO in the "OFF" position. Refer to Fig. MT4-5.

PTO BELT

To replace the PTO belt, move the PTO lever (5—Fig. MT4-6) to the OFF position. Remove the four screws from the PTO belt guard (12) and remove the guard.

Loosen the two screws attaching the PTO belt guard (3) to the frame. Remove the belt from the pulleys.

Install the new belt and adjust as previously outlined.

REMOVAL AND INSTALLATION

To remove the PTO shaft (9—Fig. MT4-6), first remove the mower deck from the tractor. Remove the PTO belt as previously outlined.

Remove the snap ring (15) and withdraw the pulley (14) from the PTO shaft. Unbolt and remove the bearing flanges (7), bearings (8) and shaft (9) from the tractor.

To reinstall the PTO shaft, reverse the removal procedure.

HYDRAULIC SYSTEM

LUBRICATION

Pressurized oil from the hydrostatic drive unit is utilized for the hydraulic

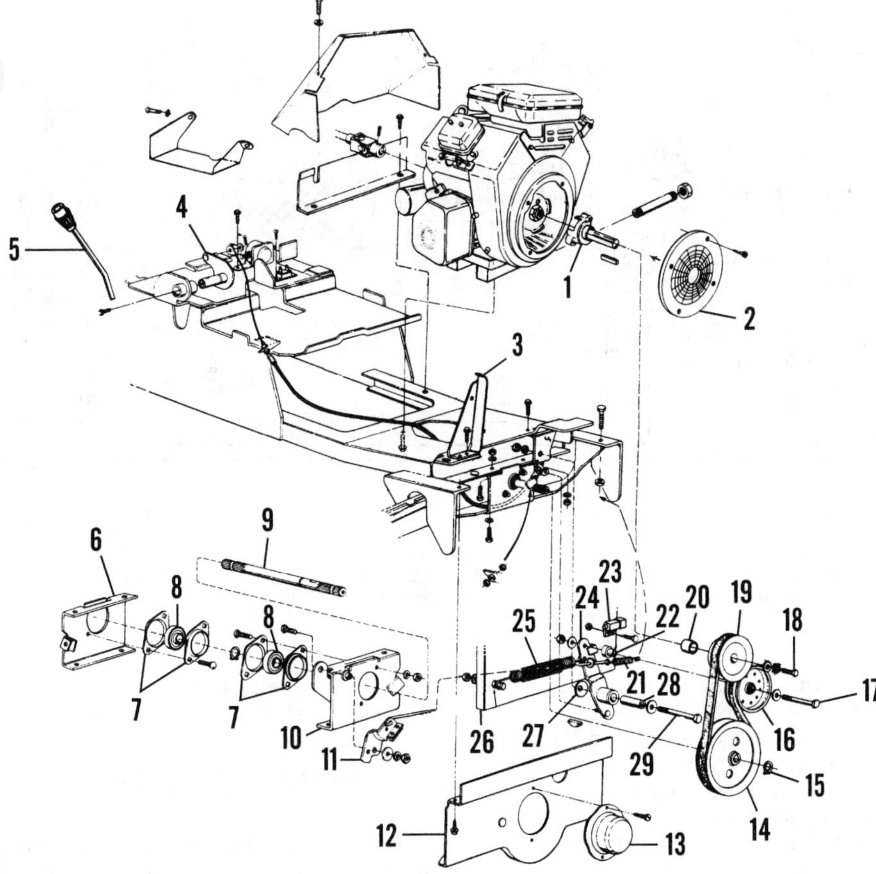

Fig. MT4-6—Exploded view of PTO system. Crankshaft extension (1) and spacer (20) are not used on all models.

1. Crankshaft extension
2. Cover
3. Belt guide
4. PTO actuator lever
5. PTO handle
6. Bearing retainer bracket
7. Bearing flanges
8. Bearings
9. PTO drive shaft
10. Bearing retainer bracket
11. PTO brake assy.
12. Belt guard
13. PTO cup
14. PTO pulley
15. Snap ring
16. Idler pulley
17. Bolt
18. Bolt
19. Engine pulley
20. Spacer
21. Spring
22. Idler adapter
23. PTO safety switch
24. Idler bracket
25. Spring
26. Heat shield
27. Belleville washer
28. Spacer
29. Bolt

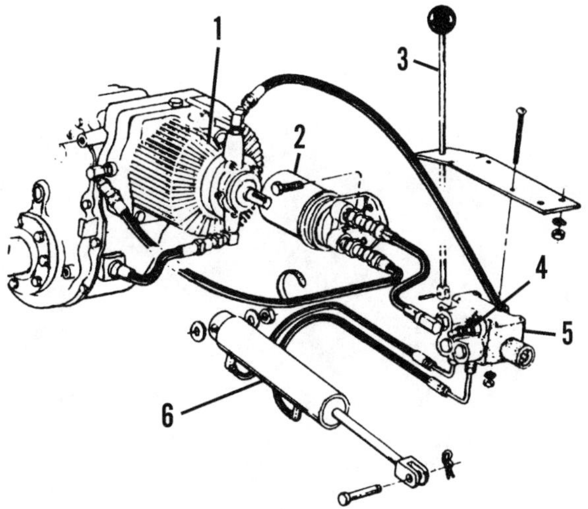

Fig. MT4-7—View showing locations of various components of hydraulic lift system.

1. Hydrostatic drive unit
2. Filter
3. Control valve lever
4. Pressure adjustment screw
5. Control valve
6. Cylinder

system. Refer to the HYDROSTATIC TRANSMISSION section for lubrication information.

TESTING AND ADJUSTMENT

To check and adjust the hydraulic system pressure, install a 0-1000 psi (0-7000 kPa) test gauge in line with the lift cylinder (6—Fig. MT4-7). Start and run the tractor engine at 3600 rpm.

Work the control valve lever (3) in the direction that provides a reading on the test gauge. Hold the control lever in this direction to fully extend or retract the lift cylinder. When the cylinder reaches the end of the stroke, the gauge should read approximately 700 psi (4827 kPa). Pressure may be adjusted by turning the adjustment screw (4) on the control valve in or out as necessary.

CAUTION: Do not exceed 700 psi (4827 kPa) pressure as damage to the hydrostatic drive unit may occur.

Hydraulic system control valve (5) and cylinder (6) are serviced as complete assemblies only.

SAFETY INTERLOCK SYSTEM

Before the engine will start, the key must be turned ON and both of the safety switches must be activated. One switch (4—Fig. MT4-8) is activated when the clutch/brake pedal is depressed and the other switch (5) is activated when the blade is disengaged. When the two safety switches are activated, the circuit is completed between the battery and the starter solenoid, allowing the starter motor to crank the engine.

Some models are equipped with a seat safety switch (2) and a reverse safety switch (3). However, these switches are not involved in the starting circuit. The seat safety switch is designed to stop the engine if the operator leaves the seat with the blades or PTO engaged. The blades must be in the disengaged position when shifting into reverse or the engine will shut off.

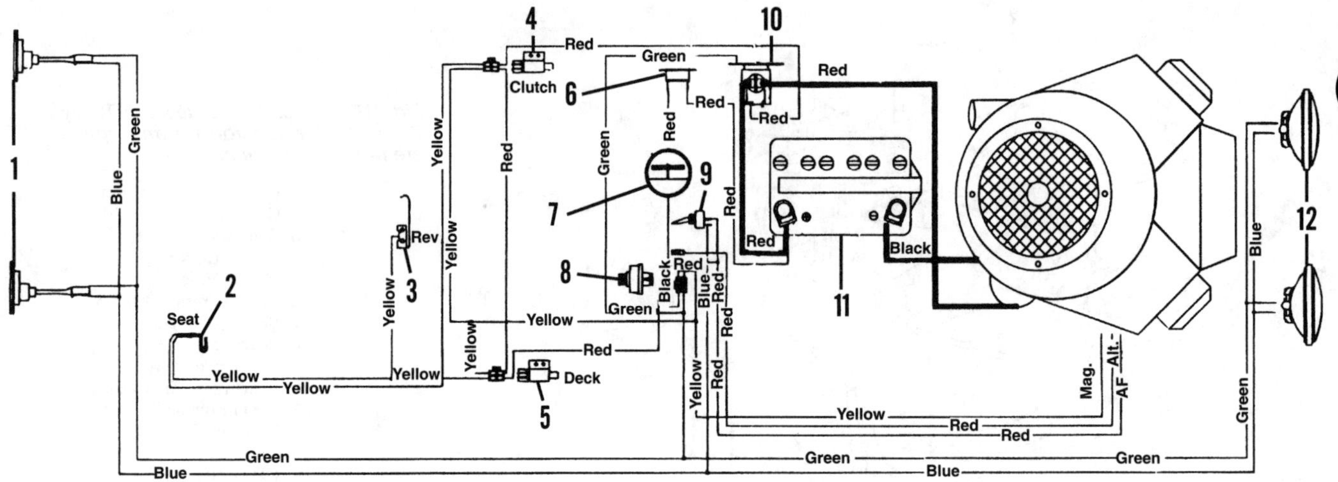

Fig. MT4-8—Typical wiring diagram for Series 900 models.

1. Taillights
2. Seat safety switch
3. Reverse safety switch
4. Clutch safety switch
5. PTO switch
6. Circuit breaker
7. Ammeter
8. Ignition switch
9. Light switch
10. Solenoid
11. Battery
12. Headlights

To test the two safety start switches, first check the two switches to see if the switch plungers are depressed a minimum of $\frac{1}{8}$ inch (3 mm) when the blade is disengaged and the clutch/brake pedal is depressed. If the switch plunger is correctly depressed, use a continuity checker to determine if there is continuity across the switch terminals when the switches are activated (plunger depressed). If continuity is not indicated when the plunger is depressed, replace the switch.

To check for correct operation of the seat safety switch, start the engine and set the parking brake. Place the shift lever in NEUTRAL and engage the PTO or blades. Raise up off the seat. The engine should stop running.

WIRING DIAGRAM

The wiring diagram illustrated in Fig. MT4-8 is typical of all models.

POWER KING

CONDENSED SPECIFICATIONS

Models	1212G	1214H	1218G	1218H
Engine Make	Kohler	Kohler	Kohler	Kohler
Model	K301	M14	M18	M18
Number of cylinders	1	1	2	2
Bore	3.375 in. (85.725 mm)	3.50 in. (88.9 mm)	3.12 in. (79.2 mm)	3.12 in. (79.2 mm)
Stroke	3.25 in. (82.55 mm)	3.25 in. (82.55 mm)	2.75 in. (69.85 mm)	2.75 in. (69.85 mm)
Displacement	29.07 cu. in. (476.5 cc)	31.27 cu. in. (512 cc)	42.18 cu. in. (691 cc)	42.18 cu. in. (691 cc)
Power Rating	12 hp. (8.9 kW)	14 hp. (10.4 kW)	18 hp. (13.4 kW)	18 hp. (13.4 kW)
Slow Idle	1000 rpm	1200 rpm	1200 rpm	1200 rpm
High Speed (No-load)	3600 rpm	3600 rpm	3600 rpm	3600 rpm
Crankcase Capacity	2 qt. (1.9 L)	2 qt. (1.9 L)	3.5 pt. (1.7 L)	3.5 pt. (1.7 L)
Transmission Capacity	See text	See text	See text	See text
Final Drive Capacity	See text	See text	See text	See text

Models	1218HV	1220HV	1614G	1618G
Engine Make	Kohler	Kohler	Kohler	Kohler
Model	CH18	CH20	M14	M18
Number of cylinders	2	2	1	2
Bore	3.03 in. (77 mm)	3.03 in. (77 mm)	3.50 in. (89 mm)	3.12 in. (79.2 mm)
Stroke	2.64 in. (83 mm)	2.64 in. (83 mm)	3.25 in. (82.5 mm)	2.75 in. (69.8 mm)
Displacement	38 cu. in. (624 cc)	38 cu. in. (624 cc)	31.27 cu. in. (512 cc)	42.18 cu. in. (691 cc)
Power Rating	18 hp. (13.4 kW)	20 hp. (14.9 kW)	14 hp. (10.4 kW)	18 hp. (13.4 kW)
Slow Idle	1000 rpm	1200 rpm	1200 rpm	1200 rpm
High Speed (No-load)	3600 rpm	3600 rpm	3600 rpm	3600 rpm
Crankcase Capacity	2 qt. (1.9 L)	2 qt. (1.9 L)	3.5 pt. (1.7 L)	3.5 pt. (1.7 L)
Transmission Capacity	See text	See text	See text	See text
Final Drive Capacity	See text	See text	See text	See text

Model	1618GV	1618H	1620GV	1620HV
Engine Make	Kohler	Kohler	Kohler	Kohler
Model	CH18	M18	CH18	CH20
Number of cylinders	2	2	2	2
Bore	3.03 in. (77 mm)	3.12 in. (79.2 mm)	3.03 in. (77 mm)	3.03 in. (77 mm)
Stroke	2.64 in. (83 mm)	2.75 in. (69.85 mm)	2.64 in. (83 mm)	2.64 in. (83 mm)
Displacement	38 cu. in. (624 cc)	42.18 cu. in. (691 cc)	38 cu. in. (624 cc)	38 cu. in. (624 cc)
Power Rating	18 hp. (13.4 kW)	18 hp. (13.4 kW)	20 hp. (14.9 kW)	20 hp (14.9 kW)
Slow Idle	1200 rpm	1200 rpm	1200 rpm	1200 rpm
High Speed (No-load)	3600 rpm	3600 rpm	3600 rpm	3600 rpm
Crankcase Capacity	2 qt. (1.9 L)	3.5 pt. (1.7 L)	2 qt. (1.9 L)	2 qt. (1.9 L)
Transmission Capacity	See text	See text	See text	See text
Final Drive Capacity	See text	See text	See text	See text

Models	1620H	1622HV	2414G	2418H
Engine Make	Kohler	Kohler	Kohler	Kohler
Model	M20	CH22	M14	M18
Number of cylinders	2	2	1	2
Bore	3.12 in. (79.2 mm)	3.03 in (77 mm)	3.50 in. (88.9 mm)	3.12 in. (79.2 mm)
Stroke	3.06 in. (78.0 mm)	2.64 in. (83 mm)	3.25 in. (82.55 mm)	2.75 in. (69.85 mm)
Displacement	47 cu. in. (769.8 cc)	38 cu. in. (624 cc)	31.27 cu. in. (512 cc)	42.18 cu. In. (691 cc)
Power Rating	20 hp. (14.9 kW)	22 hp. (16.4 kW)	14 hp. (8.9 kW)	18 hp. (13.4 kW)
Slow Idle	1200 rpm	1200	1200 rpm	1200 rpm
High Speed (No-Load)	3600 rpm	3600	3600 rpm	3600 rpm
Crankcase Capacity	3.5 pt. (1.7 L)	2.0 qt. (1.9 L0	2 qt. (1.9 L)	3.5 pt. (1.7 L)
Transmission Capacity	See text	See text	See text	See text
Final Drive Capacity	See text	See text	See text	See text

FRONT AXLE AND STEERING SYSTEM

MAINTENANCE

Lubricate the steering spindles, tie rod ends, drag link ends, axle pivot and front wheel bearings at 50-hour intervals. Use multipurpose, lithium-base grease. Clean all grease fittings before and after lubrication.

FRONT WHEEL BEARINGS REMOVAL AND INSTALLATION

Models 1212G, 1214H, 1218G and 1218H

The bearings (29 and 31—Fig. E1-1) are a press fit in the wheel hub (30). To remove the bearings, first remove the hub from the spindle; then use a hammer and punch to drive the bearings outward from inside of hub.

Replace or repair the hub (30) if the bearings are a loose fit in the hub. Press the new bearings into the wheel hub. Install the wheel and secure with the cotter pin (33).

All Other Models

Raise and support the side to be serviced. Remove the dust cap (22—Fig. E1-2). Remove and discard the cotter pin from the castellated nut (21). Un-

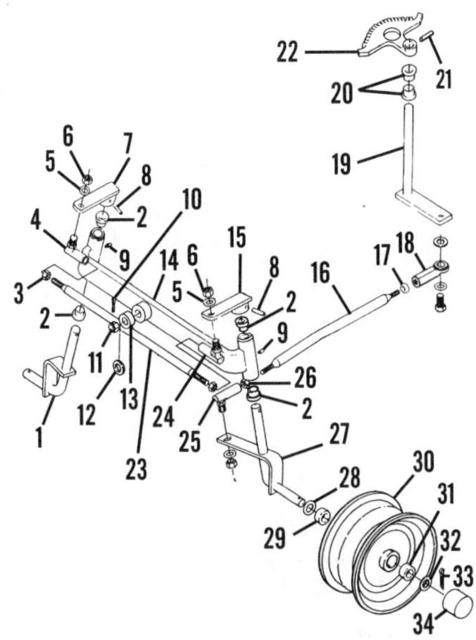

Fig. E1-1—Exploded view of front axle and steering system used on some models.

1. Spindle
2. Bushings
3. Jam nut
4. Tie rod end
5. Washer
6. Nut
7. Steering arm
8. Pin
9. Grease fitting
10. Cotter pin
11. Nut
12. Washer
13. Bushing
14. Axle main member
15. Steering arm
16. Drag link
17. Jam nut
18. Drag link end
19. Steering lever shaft
20. Bushings
21. Pin
22. Steering sector
23. Tie rod
24. Tie rod end
25. Drag link end
26. Jam nut
27. Spindle
28. Spacer
29. Bearing
30. Wheel and hub assembly
31. Bearing
32. Washer
33. Cotter pin
34. Dust cap

screw the nut and remove the outer bearing (19), wheel (18) and hub (17).

Pry the seal (15) out of the wheel hub and remove the inner bearing (16). Use a punch to carefully drive the bearing cups out of the hub if bearing replacement is necessary.

Clean and repack or replace the bearings. Install by reversing the removal procedure. Adjust the nut (21) so the bearings turn freely with a slight amount of end play. Install a new cotter pin.

TIE ROD AND TOE-IN

To remove tie rod (23—Fig. E1-1 or 7—Fig. E1-2), disconnect the tie rod ends from each steering arm.

Check the tie rod ends for wear and replace the ends if necessary. Reinstall by reversing the removal procedure.

Adjust the length of the tie rod to obtain ⅛-inch (3.2 mm) front wheel toe-in (Fig. E1-3). Tighten the jam nuts against the rod ends.

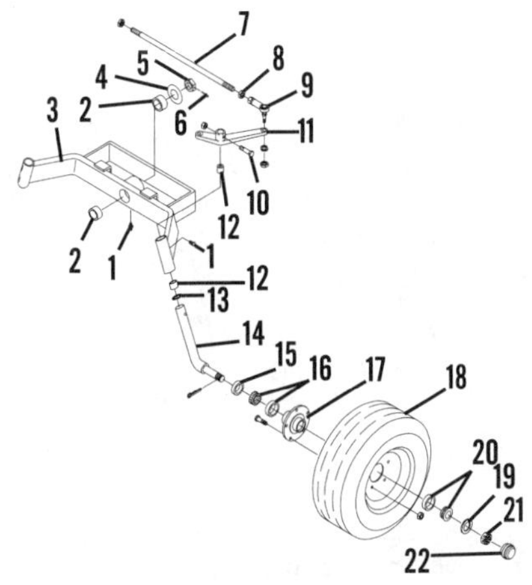

Fig. E1-2—Exploded view of front axle used on some models.

1. Grease fitting
2. Bushings
3. Axle main member
4. Thrust washer
5. Nut
6. Pin
7. Tie rod
8. Jam nut
9. Ball joint
10. Shoulder bolt
11. Steering arm
12. Bushing
13. Thrust washer
14. Spindle
15. Seal
16. Bearing assembly
17. Wheel hub
18. Wheel
19. Washer
20. Nut
22. Hub cap

STEERING SPINDLES REMOVAL AND INSTALLATION

Models 1212G, 1214H, 1218G and 1218H

Raise and support the front of the tractor. Remove the dust cap (34—Fig. E1-1), cotter pin (33) and tire and wheel assembly from each side. Disconnect the drag link end (25) from the steering spindle (27). Remove the tie rod (23). Drive out the pins (8) and remove the steering arms (7 and 15). Lower the spindles (1 and 27) from the axle main member.

Replace the bushings (2) and/or spindles (1 and 27) as necessary. Install by reversing the removal procedure and adjust toe-in.

All Other Models

Raise and support the front of the tractor. Remove the tire and wheel. Remove the dust cap (22—Fig. E1-2), nut (21), bearing (20) and hub (17) from each side. Disconnect the drag link end (9) from the steering lever (11).

Remove the tie rod (7). Drive out the pins or unscrew the bolts (10—Fig. E1-2) from the left and right steering arms (11). Lower the spindles (14) out of the steering arms and the axle main member.

Replace the bushings (12) and/or spindles as necessary. Install by reversing the removal procedure. Adjust the

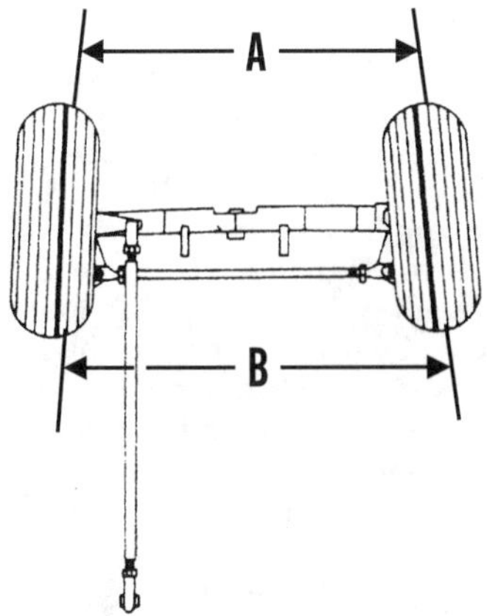

Fig. E1-3—To check front wheel toe-in, measure distance (A) between front of tires and distance (B) between rear of tires at the same height. Distance (A) should be 1/8 inch (3.2 mm) less than distance (B).

front wheel toe-in as previously outlined.

AXLE MAIN MEMBER REMOVAL AND INSTALLATION

Models 1212G, 1214H, 1218G and 1218H

Raise and support the front of the tractor. Disconnect the drag link end (18—Fig. E1-1) from the steering lever (19). Support the axle main member (14). Remove the cotter pin (10), nut (11) and washer (12). Pull the axle main member forward off the pivot pin and lower the axle to the ground. Roll the axle assembly away from the tractor.

Replace the bushing (13) as necessary. Install by reversing the removal procedure.

All Other Models

Raise and support the front of the tractor. Disconnect the drag link end from the steering lever (11—Fig. E1-2). Support the axle main member (3). Remove the cotter pin (6), nut (5) and washer (4). Slide the axle assembly forward off the pivot pin. Lower the axle to the ground and roll the axle assembly away from the tractor.

Replace the bushings (2) if necessary. Install by reversing the removal procedure.

MANUAL STEERING GEAR

Models 1212G, 1214H, 1218G and 1218H

Overhaul

Disconnect the battery cables. Disconnect the seat safety switch, then remove the seat and seat mounting bracket. Remove all bolts and nuts securing the rear fender/body assembly. Remove the shift lever knobs and place the transmission shift lever in reverse position. Remove the fuel tank gauge and cap assembly. Tilt the entire fender/body assembly forward far enough to clear the shift lever and lift the assembly from the tractor. Reinstall the fuel gauge and cap assembly.

Raise the hood and remove the six nuts, retaining clips and screws and lift the firewall off the tractor. Remove the battery and battery support shelf. Identify and disconnect the wiring harness connectors from the back of the dash panel. Disconnect the choke and throttle cables.

Drive out the pin (12—Fig. E1-4) and remove the steering wheel. Remove the washer (10) and bushing (9) from the steering shaft. If there is a snap ring (2) on the shaft, remove it. Remove the screws securing the console to the side panels and lift the console (13) and steering support bracket (3) off the tractor.

Turn the front wheels all the way to the left. Remove the screw attaching the drag link end (18—Fig. E1-1) to the steering arm (19). Drive the pin (21—Fig. E1-1) out of the steering sector (22). Lift the sector off the steering lever shaft (19).

Replace the steering shaft bushings if excessively worn.

Reassemble as follows: Position the steering sector (22—Fig. E1-1) on the steering lever shaft (19) and secure with the pin (21). Slide the thrust washer (7—Fig. E1-4) onto the steering shaft (1) so it rests on the gear at the bottom of the shaft. Slide the bushing (8) down the shaft approximately 6 in. (15 cm).

If equipped with a snap ring (2), install the ring in the groove in the shaft. If not equipped with a snap ring. Wrap tape around the shaft about 2 in. (5 cm) down from the top to prevent the bushing (9) and grommet (10) from falling into the steering tube. Insert the steering shaft (1) into the steering tube from the bottom.

Install the bushing (9) and grommet (10) on the top of the tube. Install the console and steering shaft assembly onto the tractor making sure the lower end of the steering shaft is inserted in the bushing (5) in the steering support bracket (3) and the spiral gear engages the sector gear (22—Fig. E1-1) at its center. Install the mounting screws in the steering support bracket and console.

Install the steering wheel on the steering shaft. Set the front wheels straight ahead. Attach the drag link to the steering arm. Turn the steering wheel left and right to be sure the front wheels turn equally in each direction. If adjustment is needed, disconnect the drag link from the steering arm and turn the drag link to adjust its length as necessary.

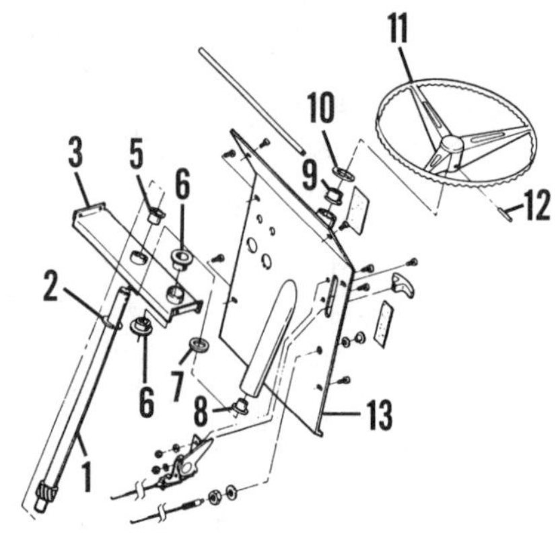

Fig. E1-4—Exploded view of steering column components for 1200 series tractors.

1. Steering shaft
2. Snap ring
3. Support bracket
5. Bushing
6. Bushings
7. Thrust washer
8. Bushing
9. Bushing
10. Grommet
11. Steering wheel
12. Pin
13. Console

All Other Models

Removal and Installation

Raise and remove the hood. Disconnect the battery cables and remove the battery and battery support shelf. Disconnect the choke and throttle cable from the engine. Disconnect the engine wiring harness, the starter-to-solenoid wire and all electrical connections from the dash panel. Remove both heat shields from between the engine and console. If equipped with a hydraulic lift, remove the hydraulic pump and drive belt.

Place match marks on the driveshaft and engine so the driveshaft can be installed in its original position. Remove the four cap screws securing the driveshaft to the engine and slide the driveshaft back on the clutch input shaft.

Remove the pin (18—Fig. E1-5) and use a suitable puller to remove the steering arm (17) from the steering gear output shaft. Remove the steering wheel and dust seal from the steering shaft. Remove the mounting bracket (6) and slide the steering gear assembly to the left, out of bushing (15) and frame bracket. Raise the steering column and slide it forward out of the console sheet metal.

Install by reversing the removal procedure. Make certain the steering wheel is in the mid-position and the front wheels are set straight ahead when attaching the steering drag link (16). Locate and align the match marks on the driveshaft and engine grass shield that were made during removal, and connect the driveshaft to the engine.

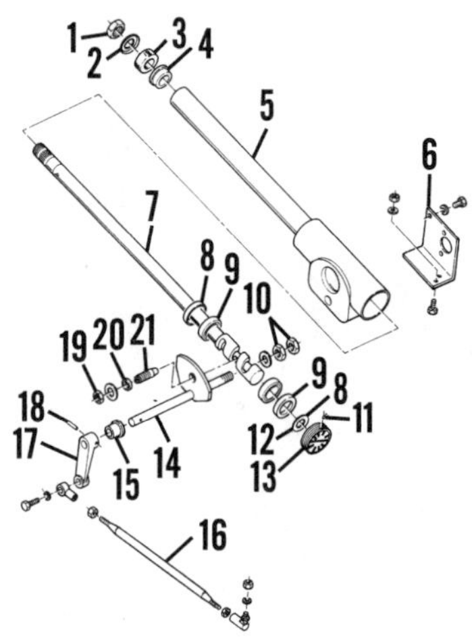

Fig. E1-5—Exploded view of steering gear assembly used on all models except Models 1212G, 1214H, 1218G and 1218H.

1. Nut
2. Washer
3. Seal
4. Bushing
5. Housing
6. Bracket
7. Shaft
8. Bearing cup
9. Bearing
10. Adjustment nuts
11. Cotter pin
12. Washer
13. Adjustment plug
14. Steering lever
15. Bushing
16. Drag link
17. Pitman arm
18. Pin
19. Jam nut
20. Adjusting nut
21. Stud

Overhaul

Remove the adjustment nuts (10—Fig. E1-5) from the steering lever (14). Pull the steering lever from the steering housing (5). Remove the cotter pin (11), adjustment plug (13) and washer (12). Press the steering shaft (7) and bearing assemblies out of the housing (5). Remove the bearings (9) from the shaft (7) and the bearing cup (8) from the housing (5) as necessary.

Inspect all parts for damage and replace when necessary. Pack the steering housing with multipurpose grease during assembly.

Install the bearing cup (8) in the steering housing (5), making certain it seats squarely in the bore. Install the bearings (9) on the steering shaft (7) and install the assembly in the housing (5). Install the bearing cup (8) squarely in the housing bore, install the washer (12) and adjustment plug (13), but do not tighten the adjustment plug at this time. Turn the adjustment stud (21) counterclockwise two full turns, and install the steering lever (14) on the steering housing (5).

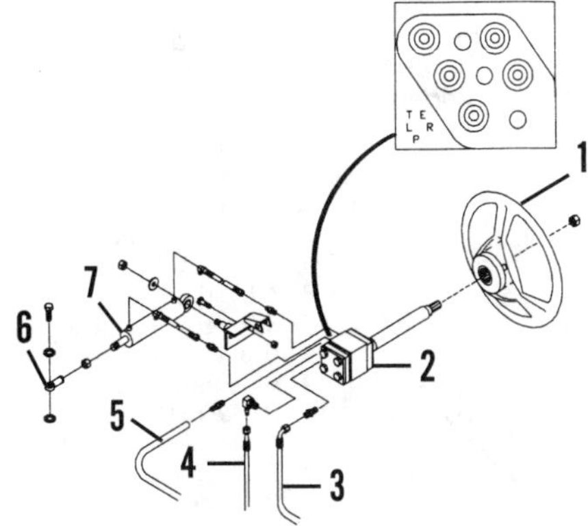

Fig. E1-6—Exploded view of power steering components.

1. Steering wheel
2. Steering gear
3. Pump pressure hose
4. Hose to hydraulic control valve
5. Return hose
6. Rod end
7. Steering cylinder

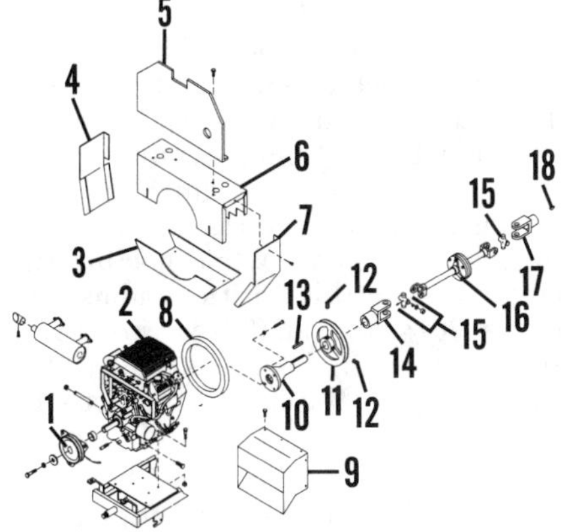

Fig. E1-7—Exploded view of engine baffles and drive shaft components used on Model 1620GV.

1. PTO clutch
2. Engine
3. Bottom intake baffle
4. Intake screen
5. Heat shield
6. Top intake baffle
7. Intake screen
8. Foam
9. Muffler shroud
10. Driveshaft adapter
11. Pulley
12. Setscrews
13. Key
14. Coupler
15. Universal joint
16. Driveshaft
17. Coupler

Adjust the steering gear as follows: Steering gear must be free of all load when adjusting. Tighten the adjustment plug (13) to 10-14 ft.-lb. (13-19 N·m) and install the cotter pin (15). When correctly adjusted, the steering wheel should turn freely with only a slight drag.

Turn the steering wheel to the mid-position of its travel. The adjustment of the steering lever (14) controls the backlash at the steering worm and free travel at the steering wheel. To adjust, insert a 0.100 inch (2.54 mm) feeler gauge or shim between the steering lever plate and the housing. Tighten the steering lever adjustment nut (10) until there is a slight drag as the gauge or shim is withdrawn. Install the jam nut (10) and tighten to 40 ft.-lb. (54 N·m). Tighten the adjustment stud (21) until a slight drag is felt as the steering shaft (7) is turned past mid-position. Secure with the jam nut (19).

POWER STEERING (MODELS SO EQUIPPED)

A belt-driven hydraulic pump supplies pressurized fluid to the power steering control valve (2—Fig. E1-6). The steering control valve directs pressurized oil to the power steering cylinder (7) to turn the wheels to the left or right, depending on the direction the steering wheel is turned.

At the time of printing of this manual, service parts were not available for the hydraulic pump or steering control valve. Refer to the Hydraulic System section for additional information.

ENGINE

MODELS 1212G, 1214H, 1218G AND 1218H

Maintenance

Regular engine maintenance is required to maintain peak performance and long engine life.

Check the oil level daily or after five hours of operation. Inspect the air cleaner element periodically depending on operating conditions.

Clean and re-oil the foam precleaner at 25-hour intervals and clean or replace the dry filter element at 100-hour intervals.

Removal and Installation

Remove any front-mounted equipment connected to the front PTO. Remove the hood and disconnect the negative battery cable.

On models prior to serial number 59658, remove the battery and battery mounting plate.

On all models, disconnect the wire from the PTO clutch at the front of the engine. Disconnect the electrical wires from the engine. Remove the air cleaner assembly, and disconnect the choke and throttle cables.

On models after serial number 59657, detach the cotter pins and remove the front footrest rod. Detach the grass screen from the underside of the tractor.

Disconnect the flexible driveshaft coupler from the engine crankshaft adapter. Perform this step from above on models prior to serial number 59658 or from underneath on models after serial number 59657.

Close the fuel shutoff valve at fuel tank, then disconnect the fuel line from the engine. Unscrew the bolts retaining the engine to the frame. Slide the engine forward and lift it off the frame.

Reinstall by reversing the removal procedure.

Overhaul

Engine make and model are listed at the beginning of this section. For tune-up specifications, engine overhaul procedures and engine maintenance, refer to the appropriate Kohler engine section in this manual.

ALL OTHER MODELS

Maintenance

Regular engine maintenance is required to maintain peak performance and long engine life.

Check the oil level daily or after five hours of operation. Inspect the air cleaner element periodically depending on operating conditions.

Clean and re-oil the foam precleaner at 25-hour intervals and clean or replace the dry filter element at 100-hour intervals.

Removal and Installation

Remove the hood and disconnect battery cables. Disconnect electrical leads from the PTO clutch and the starter motor. Disconnect the engine wiring harness connector. Detach the choke and throttle cables from the engine.

Close the fuel shutoff valve and disconnect the fuel line from the fuel pump. Remove the baffles and heat shroud (4 through 7—Fig. E1-7) located between the engine and dash console. If equipped with a hydraulic lift, remove the hydraulic pump belt.

Remove the four screws that attach the driveshaft adapter (10) to the engine flywheel and disconnect the driveshaft from the engine. Remove the bolts retaining the engine to the frame and lift the engine out of the tractor.

Install by reversing the removal procedure. Note that the driveshaft must be installed so the keyway in the rear universal joint yoke is 90° to the right of the engine flywheel key position (Fig. E1-8).

Overhaul

Engine make and model are listed at the beginning of this section. For tune-up specifications, engine overhaul procedures and engine maintenance,

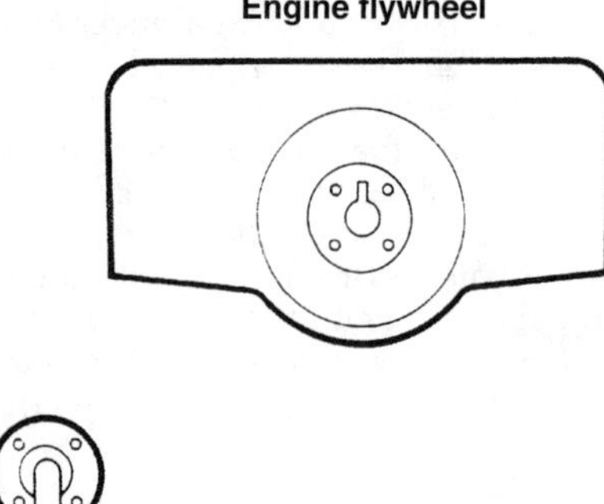

Fig. E1-8—When installing the driveshaft, position the engine flywheel key at 12 o'clock and rear U-joint key at 3 o'clock.

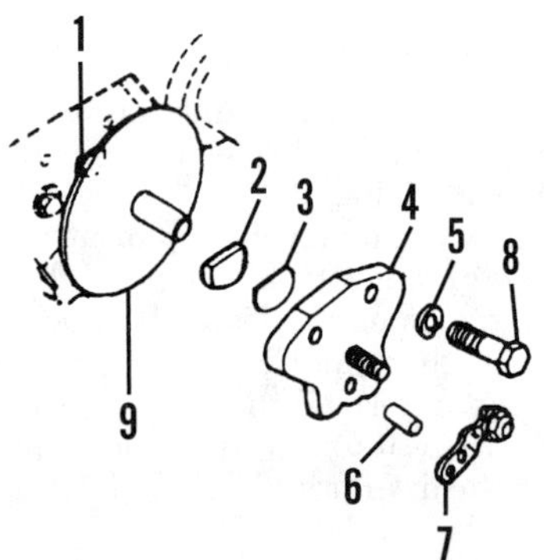

Fig. E1-9—Exploded view of disc brake system.

1. Inner brake pad
2. Outer brake pad
3. Metal backing plate
4. Caliper
5. Cap screw
6. Pin
7. Brake lever
8. Adjustment nut
9. Brake disc

refer to the appropriate Kohler engine section in this manual.

BRAKES

BRAKE DISC MODELS

Adjustment

Pull the brake pedal all the way back so there is no tension on the brake extension spring. Remove the cotter pin from the brake adjustment nut (8—Fig. E1-9). Push the brake disc (9) towards the transaxle housing and insert a 0.020 inch (0.51 mm) feeler gauge between the outer friction pad (2) and disc (9). Finger tighten the adjustment nut until the pad is firmly against the feeler gauge. Back the nut off so the cotter pin can be inserted through the nut.

Removal and Installation

Disconnect the brake rod from the brake lever (7—Fig. E1-9). Remove the cap screws (5), caliper (4), pin (6), outer brake pad (2) and metal plate (3). Remove the brake disc (9) and inner pad (1).

Install by reversing the removal procedure. Adjust the brake as previously outlined.

Fig. E1-10—Exploded view of clutch/brake linkage used on Models 1212G and 1214G.

1. Brake shoe
2. Pin
3. Pin
4. Actuating arm
5. Brake shaft
6. Adjusting nut
7. Spring
8. Brake clevis
9. Adjustning nut
10. Brake rod
11. Brake pedal, right
12. Brake pedal, left
13. Bushing
14. Return spring
15. Bracket
16. Brake shaft
17. Parking brake lever

BRAKE BAND MODELS

Adjustment

Brake pedals must have ½ inch (12.7 mm) of free travel before resistance is encountered. Adjust each wheel brake individually.

To adjust, loosen the clevis jam nut and turn the adjusting nut (9—Fig. E1-10) to obtain the desired pedal free travel. Tighten the jam nut against the adjusting nut.

Adjust the nut (6) at the rear of the spring (7) until the spring is compressed to 2¼ inches (57 mm). Perform the same adjustment on the brake on the other side of the tractor.

Removal and Installation

Raise and support the rear of the tractor. Remove the tire and wheel assemblies. Remove the fenders as necessary to obtain additional working space.

Use a hammer and punch to drive the pins (4—Fig. E1-10) out of the cams (3). Remove the cam and brake band (1) assemblies. Drive the pins (2) out of the brake bands and separate the cams from the brake bands.

Install the brake bands by reversing the removal procedure. Adjust the brakes as previously outlined.

CLUTCH (GEAR DRIVE MODELS)

ADJUSTMENT

A safety switch on the clutch housing prevents the engine from starting unless the clutch pedal is depressed. To adjust the switch, depress the clutch pedal fully. Adjust the position of the switch so the gap between the switch plunger and the clutch actuating arm is 0-1/16 inch (0.0-1.6 mm).

The clutch pedal should have approximately ¼ inch (6.3 mm) of free travel. To adjust the clutch, detach the clevis (26—Fig. E1-11) from the clutch actuating arm (25). Move the clutch arm (25) forward until it contacts the throwout bearing and stops. While holding the clutch arm in this position, adjust the clevis (26) so the pin (30) can just be inserted through the clevis and clutch arm, then turn the clevis out exactly 1½ additional turns.

Reassemble the linkage. Check the clutch pedal free travel. Adjust the clutch switch as previously described.

REMOVAL AND INSTALLATION

Disconnect the battery cables. Disconnect the seat safety switch, and remove the seat and seat mounting bracket. Remove all the bolts and nuts securing the rear fender/body assembly. Remove the shift lever knobs and place the transmission shift lever in reverse position. Remove the fuel tank gauge and cap assembly. Tilt the entire fender/body assembly forward far enough to clear the shift lever and lift the assembly from the tractor. Reinstall the fuel gauge and cap assembly.

Move the transmission shift lever to the first gear position. Remove the bolts and spacers from the clutch side of driveshaft coupler. Relocate the driveshaft slightly to one side, unscrew two set screws in the coupler and disengage the coupler from the clutch input shaft.

Detach the clutch return spring (31—Fig. E1-11) from the clutch arm (25). Disengage the clevis (26) from the clutch arm. Disconnect the wires and

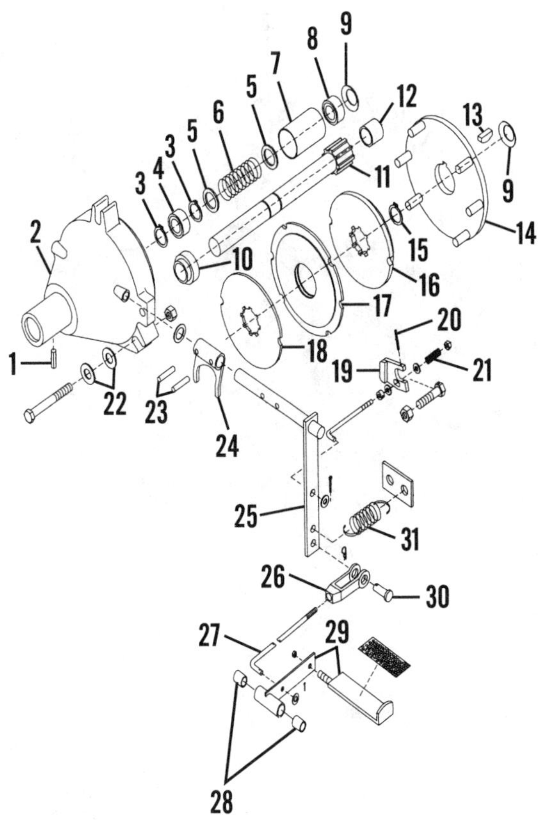

Fig. E1-11—Exploded view of clutch used on Model 1620GV. Six-pin plate (14) attaches to transmission input shaft.

1. Roll pin
2. Clutch housing
3. Snap rings
4. Bearing
5. Washer
6. Clutch spring
7. Collar
8. Bearing
9. Belleville washer
10. Throwout sleeve
11. Clutch shaft
12. Bushing
13. Woodruff key
14. Six-pin plate
15. Snap ring
16. Drive disc
17. Driven disc
18. Pressure plate
19. Clutch brake
20. Pin
21. Spring
22. Washer
23. Pins
24. Throwout fork
25. Clutch arm and shaft
26. Clevis
27. Clutch rod
28. Bushings
29. Clutch pedal
30. Clevis pin
31. Return spring

remove the clutch safety switch from the left side of the clutch housing.

Install a 1/2-20 × $1\frac{1}{2}$ inch screw in the hole for the switch in the clutch housing. Rotate the screw so it contacts the clutch arm, and continue to turn the screw until pressure from the internal clutch spring is felt. Installing the screw will relieve spring pressure against the clutch plates.

Unscrew the fasteners holding the clutch housing on the transmission. Slide the clutch assembly forward and remove it from the tractor. Note that the six-pin plate (14—Fig. E1-11), and possibly the clutch plates, will remain on the transmission. Remove the temporary $1\frac{1}{2}$-inch long screw.

To install the clutch, install the $1\frac{1}{2}$-inch long screw in the lug on the clutch housing to relieve spring pressure. Line up the six-pin plate (14) with the slotted plate (17) in the clutch housing and install the clutch housing on the transmission. The clutch housing must bottom in the grooves on the transmission housing.

NOTE: Tighten the clutch retaining bolts progressively in stages around the housing. Tightening one bolt until tight may cause the clutch plates to bind.

Tighten the three clutch housing bolts to 22 ft.-lb. (30 N·m). Complete the reassembly and adjust the clutch as previously outlined.

OVERHAUL

Remove the clutch as previously outlined. Using a $\frac{5}{32}$-inch punch, drive the retaining pins (25—Fig. E1-11) out of the throwout fork (24) and clutch arm (25). Withdraw the clutch arm and shaft from the housing and remove the fork (16). Lift out the clutch input shaft (11) with the bearings, washers, spring and sleeve.

Use a bearing puller to remove the front bearing (4), then slide the washers, spring (6) and sleeve (7) off the shaft. Force the rear bearing (8) off toward the front of the shaft and remove the throwout collar (10). If the bushing (12) is worn, use a bearing puller to remove it from the end of the shaft..

If removed, install a new bushing (12) and ream the inside diameter to 0.516 inch (13.16 mm). Slide the throwout bearing collar (10) over the forward end of the shaft (11). Install the Belleville washer (if used), rear bearing (8) and sleeve (7), pressing them into position on the shaft. Install the washers (5) and spring (6).

On models equipped with snap rings (3), install the rear snap ring on the shaft. Press the front bearing (4) onto the shaft until it is seated against the snap ring. Install the front snap ring in its groove. If snap rings are not used, press the front bearing onto the shaft until the forward face of the bearing is 2 $\frac{11}{16}$ inches (68.26 mm) from the forward end of shaft.

Install the input shaft assembly in the clutch housing. Install the clutch arm shaft (17) and fork (16), then secure the fork on shaft with pins (15). Install the clutch plates in the order shown in Fig. E1-11.

Reinstall the clutch as previously outlined.

HYDROSTATIC TRANSMISSION (SERIES 1200)

MAINTENANCE

Check the fluid level and clean the grass clippings, leaves, grease and dirt from the transmission cooling fins before each use.

The hydrostatic transmission uses oil contained in the final drive reservoir. Maintain the fluid level at the lower edge of the check plug located at the right rear corner of the transaxle housing.

Change the transmission oil filter at 100-hour intervals and change the fluid and filter at 500-hour intervals. The oil drain plug is located at the lower right corner of the transaxle housing. The oil fill plug is located at the upper right corner of the housing. Recommended fluid is a premium grade hydraulic fluid. Approximate hydrostatic transmission and final drive fluid capacity is 4 quarts (3.8 L).

NEUTRAL ADJUSTMENT

Forward or reverse tractor motion should stop when the brake is applied and the hydrostatic transmission control lever is moved to the neutral position. If the tractor creeps when the transmission control lever is in the neutral position, adjustment is required.

CAUTION: Exercise care when working around rotating parts.

Raise and securely support the rear of tractor so the rear wheels are off the ground. Remove the left rear wheel to provide access to the control linkage. Start and run the engine at $\frac{3}{4}$ throttle. Loosen both nuts (8—Fig. E1-12) on the eccentric adjusting screw (6) located under the tractor in the pivot bracket (5). Insert an Allen wrench in the bottom of the eccentric adjusting screw

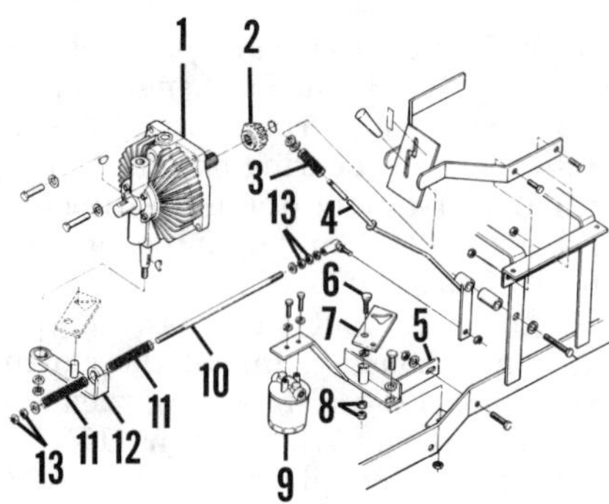

Fig. E1-12—Exploded view of hydrostatic transmission control linkage used on 1200 series.

1. Hydrostatic transmission
2. Bevel gear
3. Spring
4. Control lever
5. Bracket
6. Eccentric bolt
7. Cam plate
8. Jam nuts
9. Hydraulic filter
10. Control rod
11. Spring
12. Control arm
13. Adjusting nuts

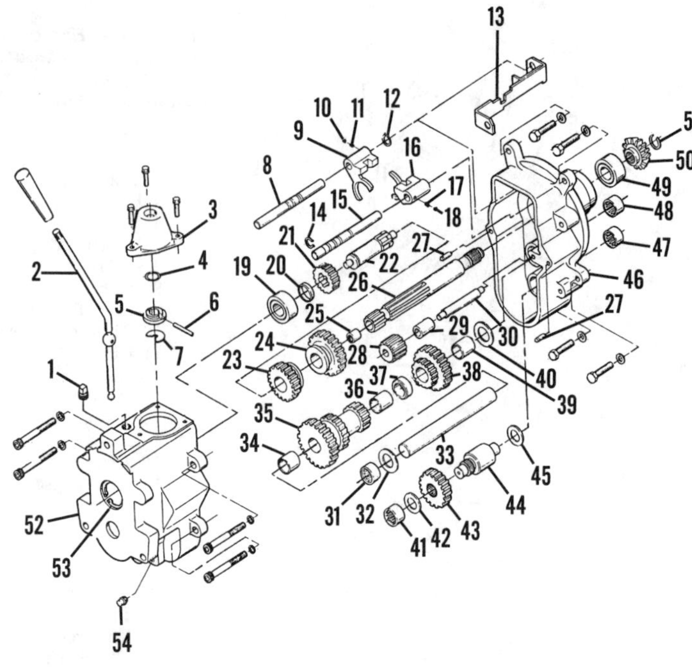

Fig. E1-13—Exploded view of 4-speed transmission used on some models. A dipstick or vent may be used in place of fill plug (1) on some units.

1. Fill plug
2. Shift lever
3. Shift housing
4. O-ring
5. Retainer
6. Pin
7. Ring
8. Shift rail
9. Shift fork
10. Detent ball
11. Spring
12. Snap ring
13. Shift stop
14. Snap ring
15. Shift rail
16. Shift fork
17. Spring
18. Detent ball
19. Bearing
20. Spacer
21. Gear (16T)
22. Input shaft
23. Gear (20T)
24. Gear (26T)
25. Needle bearing
26. Output shaft
27. Dowel pin
28. Reverse idler gear
29. Spacer
30. Shaft
31. Needle bearing
32. Thrust washer
33. Countershaft
34. Bushing
35. Cluster gear
36. Bushing
37. Spacer
38. Cluster gear
39. Bushing
40. Thrust washer
41. Needle bearing
42. Thrust washer
43. Gear (22T)
44. Pinion shaft
45. Thrust washer
46. Rear housing
47. Needle bearing
48. Needle bearing
49. Bearing
50. Bevel gear
51. Snap ring
52. Front housing
53. Snap ring
54. Drain plug

and rotate the screw so the wheel does not rotate when the transmission control lever is in neutral. Tighten both nuts on the eccentric adjusting screw to lock the screw in position. Install the wheel and lower the tractor to the ground.

Check for creep with the tractor on level ground, engine running and the transmission in neutral. If the tractor creeps, adjust the position of the jam nuts (13) on the end of the transmission control arm rod (10).

REMOVAL AND INSTALLATION

Remove the rear fender and body assembly from the tractor. Drain the fluid from the final drive. Disconnect the hydraulic lines and cap the openings. Disconnect the driveshaft coupler from the transmission input shaft.

Disconnect the transmission control linkage. Unscrew the screws attaching the hydrostatic transmission to the final drive housing and carefully separate the transmission from the final drive.

Install the transmission by reversing the removal procedure. Note that the retaining screw in the upper right position is ¼ inch (6.4 mm) shorter than the other three retaining screws. Fill the final drive with new hydraulic fluid. Adjust the transmission control linkage as previously outlined in the NEUTRAL ADJUSTMENT section.

OVERHAUL

An Eaton Model 11 hydrostatic transmission is used. Refer to the appropriate Eaton section in the HYDROSTATIC TRANSMISSION service section for overhaul information.

GEAR TRANSMISSION

MAINTENANCE

Periodically check the four-speed transmission fluid level. If equipped with a dipstick, raise the hood and remove the dipstick from the transmission. Unfold the dipstick and wipe it clean. Insert the dipstick fully into the transmission housing. Remove the dipstick and note the oil level in relation to the notched markings on the dipstick.

IMPORTANT: If equipped with a folding dipstick, be sure the dipstick is folded before reinstalling it in the transmission. Otherwise, serious damage to the transmission can occur if the tractor is operated with the dipstick installed in the unfolded position.

Maintain the fluid level at the full (F) mark or at the round punch mark on the dipstick, if so equipped. Fluid level should be approximately 3⅜ inches (86 mm) below the oil fill hole on tractors not equipped with a dipstick.

Recommended oil is Power King Special Blend Fluid. Engineering Products specifies STP Oil Treatment as an acceptable alternative. Approximate oil capacity is 1½ pints (0.7 L).

REMOVAL AND INSTALLATION

Remove the clutch as previously outlined. Unscrew the drain plug on transmission housing and drain the oil. Unscrew the bolt located on the underside of the transmission that attaches the transmission to the tractor frame. Remove the screws retaining the transmission to the tractor frame. Rotate the transmission counterclockwise so it will clear the frame, and withdraw the transmission from the final drive.

Install the transmission by reversing the removal procedure. Apply gasket compound to the transmission-to-final drive mating surface. Note the retaining screw in the upper right position is ¼ inch (6.4 mm) shorter than the other

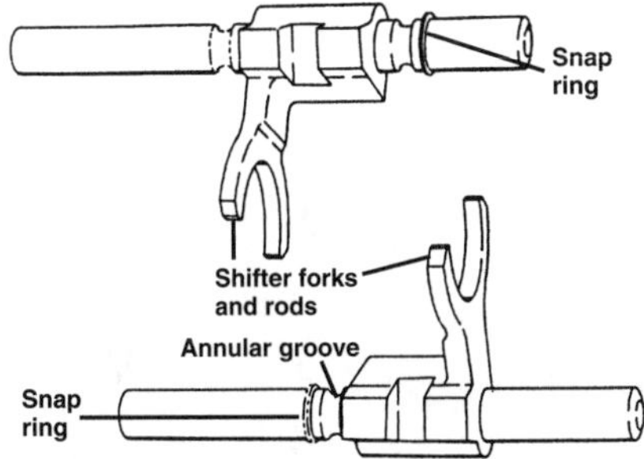

Fig. E1-14—Assemble the shift rails and forks as shown.

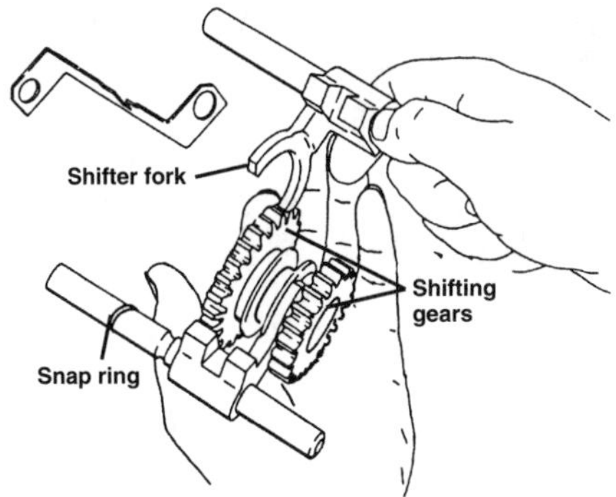

Fig. E1-15—Assemble the shift rails, forks, gears and shift stop as shown.

three retaining screws. Tighten the transmission mounting screws evenly to 20-22 ft.-lb. (27.2-30 N·m). Fill the transmission with the recommended fluid.

CAUTION: Failure to tighten the transmission mounting screws evenly and to the specified torque could result in cracking the transmission housing.

OVERHAUL

Position the transmission so the front housing is down and the transmission is supported on the six-pin clutch plate. Remove the three cap screws securing the shift lever housing (3—Fig. E1-13) and remove the complete shift lever assembly.

To disassemble the shift lever, remove the knob from the shift lever (2). Compress and remove the snap ring (7). Slide the housing (3) over the shift lever. Replace the roll pin (6) if it is bent or worn.

Pull the output shaft (26) along with bevel gear (50) and bearing (49) out of the transmission. Remove the snap ring (51) and remove the gear (50) and bearing (49) from the output shaft (26). If the needle bearing (25) is worn, use a blind bearing puller to remove it from the shaft.

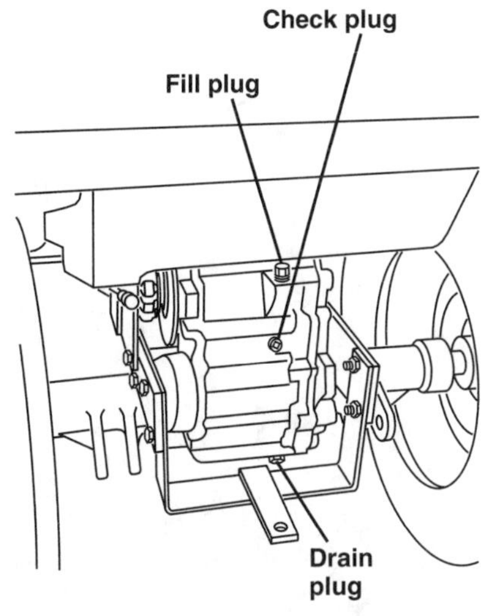

Fig. E1-16—View of rear of transaxle showing location of oil fill plug, oil level check plug and drain plug.

Position the transmission so the front housing (52) is down. Unscrew the four Allen screws holding the transmission housings together. Lift the rear housing (46) off the front housing (52). It may be necessary to tap the rear housing to separate the housings.

Remove the two thrust washers (40 and 45). Lift out the cluster gear (38). Lift out the pinion shaft (44) and 22-tooth gear (43). Lift out both the shift fork assemblies. Note the locations of the shift assemblies for reference during reassembly.

NOTE: Shift balls (10 and 18) and springs (11 and 17) will be loose when the shift forks and shift rails are separated.

Lift out the reverse idler shaft (30), spacer (29) and gear (28). Remove the countershaft and gear components (32-37).

Reposition the front housing and detach the snap ring (15—Fig. E1-11) from the transmission input shaft. Remove the six-pin clutch plate (14) and key (13). Adequately support the gear (21—Fig. E1-13) to prevent damage to the transmission housing, and gently drive the input shaft (22) through the bearing (19), spacer (20) and gear (21).

Extract the snap ring (53) and drive the bearing (19) out of the front housing. Use a suitable press to remove the bearings remaining in housings.

Reassemble by reversing the disassembly procedure while noting the following: Spacer (37) is pressed into position at the factory. The spacer should be 1¾ inches (44.45 mm) from end of countershaft (33). Adjust the spacer position if necessary.

Assemble the shift forks and rails as shown in Fig. E1-14 (be sure to install the detent balls and springs in the shift forks before installing on the rails). Position the shift forks on the gears (23 and 24—Fig. E1-13) as shown in Fig. E1-15, and install the shift stop (13) so the notches align with the notches on the shift forks.

FINAL DRIVE

1200 SERIES GEAR DRIVE

Lubrication

The manufacturer recommends using 80/90 gear oil in the final drive. Approximate capacity is 4 quarts (3.8 L). Less oil may be required to refill a drained unit due to some oil being trapped in the internal compartments. Fill the unit until oil reaches the check plug hole (Fig. E1-16).

Removal and Installation

Disconnect the battery cables. Disconnect the wires from the seat safety switch. Remove the seat mounting brackets. Remove the nut from the inside of the foot pedal arm and unscrew the long screw from the arm. Remove the screws attaching the fenders to the footrests. Remove the transmission shift lever knob and the fuel tank cap gauge. Place the shift lever in reverse position. Tilt the fender assembly up and forward to clear the shift lever. Lift the fender assembly off the tractor.

If so equipped, remove the brackets attached to the rear frame and final drive. Drain the oil from the final drive. Remove the fuel tank. Unscrew the two screws attaching the brake to the transaxle and remove the brake assembly. Detach the HI-LO shift arm from the final drive. Disconnect the electrical wire from the interlock safety switch.

Raise the rear of the tractor and place supports under the rear of the tractor frame. If equipped with an electric rear lift, detach any components that interfere with final drive removal.

Position a jack under the final drive housing. Unscrew screws retaining the transmission to the final drive. Remove the screws securing the final drive axle housings to the rear tractor frame, and separate the final drive the with rear wheels from the tractor. Lower the final drive and roll it away from the tractor.

Install the final drive by reversing the removal procedure while noting the following: Note that the axle housing retaining screws on the left side are longer than the right side screws. Apply gasket compound to the transmission-to-final drive mating surface. Note the retaining screw in the upper right position is ¼ inch (6.4 mm) shorter than the other three retaining screws. Tighten the screws attaching the transmission to the final drive evenly in a crossing pattern to 20-22 ft.-lb. (27.2-30 N·m).

CAUTION: Transmission housing may be damaged if the transmission retaining screws are over tightened.

Fill the final drive with oil as previously outlined. Adjust the brake as previously outlined.

Overhaul

Both models are equipped with a Peerless 2500 final drive. Refer to the FINAL DRIVE section for overhaul information.

1200 SERIES HYDROSTATIC

Lubrication

Oil in the final drive is also used in the hydrostatic transmission. Maintain the oil level at the lower edge of the check plug (Fig. E1-16) located on rear of the final drive. Change the transmission oil filter at 100-hour intervals and change the oil and filter at 500-hour intervals. Recommended oil is hydraulic oil. The approximate oil capacity for the hydrostatic transmission and final drive is 4 quarts (3.8 L).

Removal and Installation

Remove the hydrostatic transmission as previously outlined. If so equipped, remove the brackets attached to the rear frame and final drive. Drain the oil from the final drive. Remove the fuel tank. Unscrew the screws attaching the brake to the final drive housing and remove the brake assembly. Detach the HI-LO shift arm from the final drive. Disconnect the electrical wire from the interlock safety switch.

Raise the rear of the tractor and place supports under the rear of the tractor frame. If equipped with an electric rear lift, detach any components that interfere with final drive removal.

Position a jack under the final drive housing. Remove the screws securing the final drive axle housings to the rear tractor frame. Separate the final drive with rear wheels from the tractor. Lower the final drive and roll it away from the tractor.

Install the final drive by reversing the removal procedure while noting the following: Note that the axle housing retaining screws on the left side are longer than the right side screws. Adjust the brake as previously outlined.

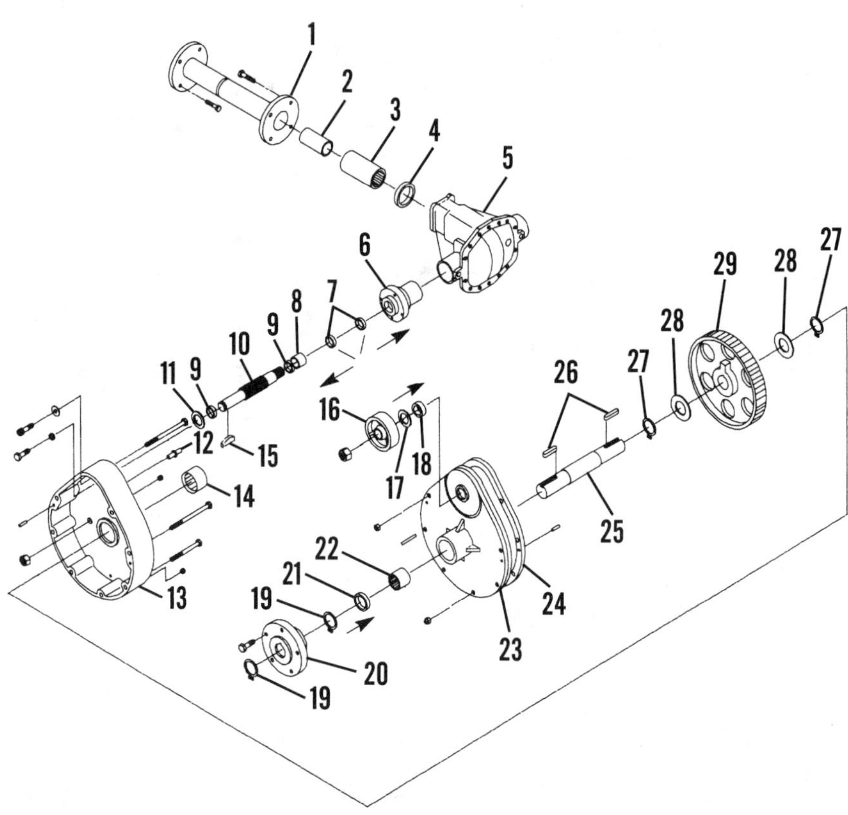

Fig. E1-17—Exploded view of final drive assembly used on Model 1620GV. Other models are similar.

1. Driveshaft tube
2. Spacer
3. Driveshaft coupling
4. Washer
5. Differential housing
6. Bearing housing
7. Oil seals
8. Bearing
9. Bearing race
10. Pinion shaft
11. Wave washer
12. Hitch pin
13. Final drive housing
14. Bearing
15. Key
16. Brake drum
17. Seal
18. Bearing
19. Snap rings
20. Wheel hub
21. Oil seal
22. Bearing
23. Cover
24. Gasket
25. Axle shaft
26. Keys
27. Snap rings
28. Thrust washers
29. Drive gear

Overhaul

Both models are equipped with a Peerless 2500 final drive. Refer to the FINAL DRIVE section for overhaul information.

1600 AND 2400 SERIES

Overhaul

Disconnect the battery cables. Disconnect the wires from the seat safety switch. Remove the two nuts attaching the rear of the fenders to the frame. Remove the screws retaining the fenders to the footrests. Remove the shift lever knob and the oil dipsitck. Remove the fuel tank cap and the hydraulic tank cap if so equipped. Tilt the fender assembly up and forward to clear the shift lever. Lift the fenders and seat off the tractor.

Raise the rear of the tractor and place support stands under the tractor frame. Remove the rear wheel and tire. Remove the drain plug from the bottom of the final drive housing and drain the oil into a suitable container.

Remove the nut retaining the brake drum (16—Fig. E1-17) on the pinion shaft (10), and pull the brake drum off the shaft. Remove the Woodruff key (15) from the pinion shaft.

Unbolt and remove the final drive cover (23) with the axle shaft (25) and drive gear (29). Remove the outer snap ring (19—Fig. E1-17) and pull the wheel hub (20) from the axle. Remove the inner snap ring (19) and key (26) from the axle. Pull the axle shaft from the cover. Remove and discard the seal (21). Remove the snap ring (27) and thrust washer (28) from the inner end of the axle, and press the drive gear (29) off the shaft.

Support the differential housing using a jack or blocks. Remove the pinion shaft (10) if it was not removed with the cover. Remove the cap screws securing

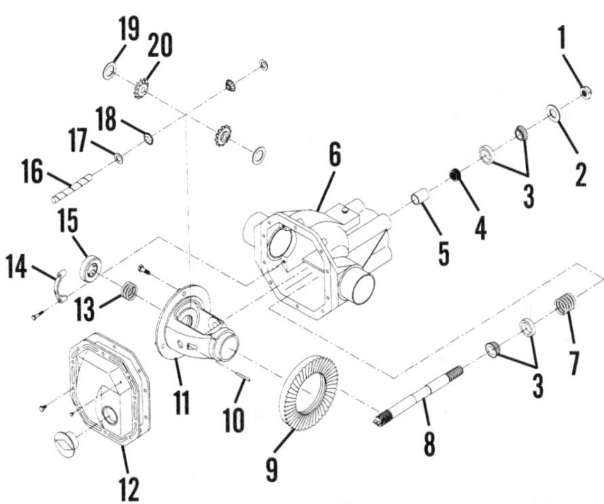

Fig. E1-18—Exploded view of differential assembly used on Model 1620GV. Other models are similar.

1. Nut
2. Washer
3. Bearing
4. Shims
5. Sleeve
6. Differential housing
7. Shims
8. Pinion shaft
9. Ring gear
10. Pin
11. Differential carrier
12. Cover
13. Shims
14. Bearing cap
15. Bearing
16. Differential pinion shaft
17. Thrust washers
18. Pinion gears
19. Thrust washers
20. Side gears

the final drive housing (13) to the tractor main frame and pull the final drive housing straight out from the differential housing (5).

Inspect all parts for damage and replace if necessary. Replace all oil seals, noting the proper direction of the seal lips as indicated in Fig. E1-17.

To reassemble, position the final drive housing (13—Fig. E1-17) on the tractor frame. Insert the brake actuating shaft from the inner side of the final drive housing through the housing. Install and tighten the screws attaching the final drive housing to the differential case and the tractor frame.

Install the pinion shaft (10) into the bearing housing (6), making sure that the shaft meshes with the splines in the differential.

If the tapered hitch pin (12) was removed, place a bead of gasket eliminator around the tapered surface of the pin. Install the pin in the final drive housing and secure with the nut.

Assemble the inner key (26), snap rings (27), thrust washers (28) and drive gear (29) on the axle shaft (25). Slide the cover (23) over the axle, and install a new oil seal (21) in the cover with the seal lip facing inward. Install the cover with the axle and drive gear onto the final drive housing. Install the snap rings (19) and wheel hub (20).

Install the key (15) on the pinion shaft (10). Slide the brake drum (16) onto the shaft and secure with the nut.

Complete the remainder of the reassembly in the reverse of the disassembly procedure.

DIFFERENTIAL (1600 AND 2400 SERIES)

REMOVAL AND INSTALLATION

To remove the differential assembly, first remove the clutch, transmission, brakes and final drives as outlined in previous sections. Remove the differential housing from the tractor.

To install, reverse the removal operations.

OVERHAUL

To disassemble the removed differential assembly, remove the drain plug and drain the oil from the differential housing. Thoroughly clean the outside of the housing and cover. Unbolt and remove the rear cover (12—Fig. E1-18).

Mark the bearing caps (14) so they can be reinstalled on the same side and in the position as they were before removal. The caps are a matched part of the housing and cannot be interchanged or replaced.. Remove the bearing caps and pry the differential carrier (11) loose with a bar and lift it from the housing.

NOTE: Observe the number and placement of the adjusting shims (13) as they will be needed in reassembly.

Drive the pin (10) out of the differential pinion shaft (16) and remove the shaft. Rotate the differential side gears (20) and remove the pinion gears (18), side gears and thrust washers (17 and 19).

Remove the nut (1) from the pinion shaft (8), and press the pinion rearward out of the housing. Remove the bearings (3), shims (4 and 7) and sleeve (5).

Inspect all parts for damage and replace when necessary. Replace the complete bearing if the cup or cone is damaged. Inspect the gear teeth for cracks, wear or other damage. The pinion (8—Fig. E1-18) and ring gear (9) must be replaced as a matched set. If the ring gear was removed from the carrier (11), install the gear and secure with the four retaining screws. Tighten the screws evenly to 45-65 ft.-lb. (61-88 N·m).

If neither the bearings nor the pinion and ring gear are being replaced, the differential can be assembled with the original shim packs.

If the differential carrier bearings (15—Fig. E1-18) were replaced, position the differential carrier in the housing and install the bearing caps (14) with the screws finger-tight. Position a dial indicator to measure the side play of the carrier. Shift the carrier from side-to-side and record the indicator reading. Assemble a shim pack (13) equal in thickness to the measured side play.

Install the pinion shaft (8—Fig. E1-18) and bearings in the housing and tighten the nut (1) to 50-70 ft.-lb. (68-94 N·m). With the pinion shaft in a vertical position, measure the torque required to continuously rotate the shaft. Disregard the torque required to start rotating the shaft. The torque should be between 4-15 in.-lb. (0.5-1.7 N·m). If the torque is greater than 15 in.-lb. (1.7 N·m), it will be necessary to increase the thickness of the shims to reduce the turning torque. If the turning torque is low, remove shims as necessary to bring the torque within specified limits.

If the differential carrier bearings were replaced, install shims (13—Fig. E1-18) as required to eliminate end play and to obtain slight backlash between the ring gear and pinion. Tighten the bearing cap screws to 35-50 ft.-lb. (48-67 N·m).

To complete reassembly, reverse the disassembly procedure. Refill the differential with two pints (0.9 L) of EP80-90 gear oil.

HYDRAULIC LIFT

Some models are equipped with a hydraulic lift system. A gear hydraulic pump is belt driven from a pulley on the engine crankshaft. Hydraulic oil or automatic transmission fluid (Dextron) should be used in the hydraulic system.

HYDRAULIC PUMP AND DRIVE BELT

Service parts are not available for the hydraulic pump. If service is necessary, replace the pump as a complete unit.

Pump drive belt tension is adjusted by adjusting the position of the nut (5—E1-19). Turn the nut to compress the tension spring (4) until there is approximately 0.060 inch (1.5 mm) gap between the spring coils.

To replace the drive belt, turn the adjusting nut (5) to relieve the spring tension. Loosen the set screws securing the driveshaft (10) to the flywheel adapter (7). Slide the drive shaft back on the clutch input shaft. Remove the belt (1) from the pulleys.

Install the new belt and reconnect the driveshaft to the adapter. Adjust the belt tension as previously outlined.

HYDRAULIC CONTROL VALVE

A single-spool, four-way valve is used with raise, lower, hold and float positions. The valve is serviced as a complete unit.

HYDRAULIC CYLINDER

A cylinder repair kit is available to replace the packing and O-rings. To disassemble the cylinder, remove the snap ring from the ram end of the cylinder. Withdraw the end cap and ram from the cylinder tube.

Be sure to clean all parts thoroughly and lubricate the packing and O-rings with clean hydraulic oil when assembling.

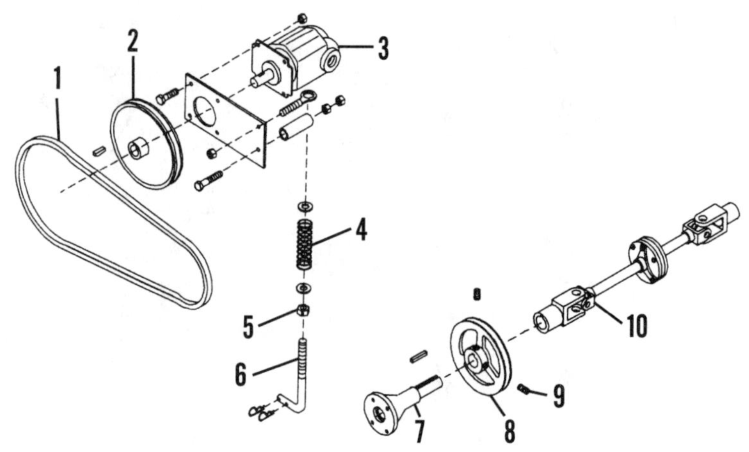

Fig. E1-19—Exploded view of hydraulic pump and pump drive components.

1. Belt
2. Pulley
3. Hydraulic pump
4. Spring
5. Adjusting nut
6. Rod
7. Adapter shaft
8. Pulley
9. Setscrews
10. Driveshaft assembly

POWER TAKE-OFF (PTO) ADJUSTMENT

The clutch portion of the electric clutch is self-adjusting. The brake portion of the clutch assembly requires periodic adjustment.

To adjust the brake, raise the hood and remove the side panels. Remove the belt from the clutch pulley. Insert a 0.015 inch (0.38 mm) feeler gauge into each of the three slots in the brake flange (Fig. E1-20). Turn the ignition switch to the RUN position, but do not start the engine. Engage the PTO. Turn the locknut adjacent to the slot with the feeler gauge until the brake flange bottoms against the feeler gauge. Repeat the adjustment at each of the three slots. The gap must be equal on all three slots. Do not overtighten the nuts.

Install the belt. Start the engine and check the clutch operation.

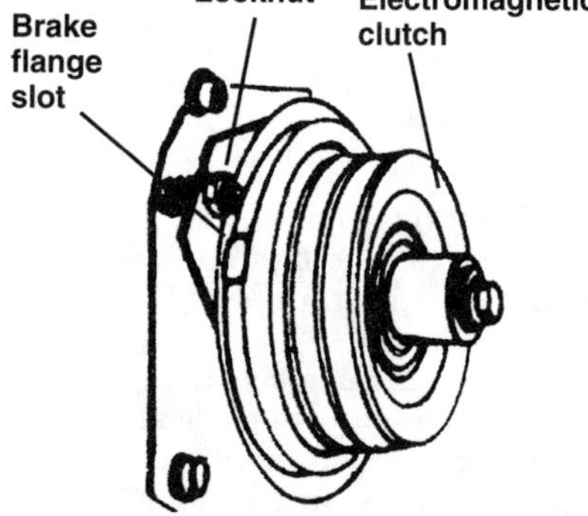

Fig. E1-20—View showing location of slots in brake flange of electric PTO clutch. Refer to text for adjustment procedure.

WIRING DIAGRAMS

Wiring diagrams typical of most models are shown in Figs. E1-21 and E1-22.

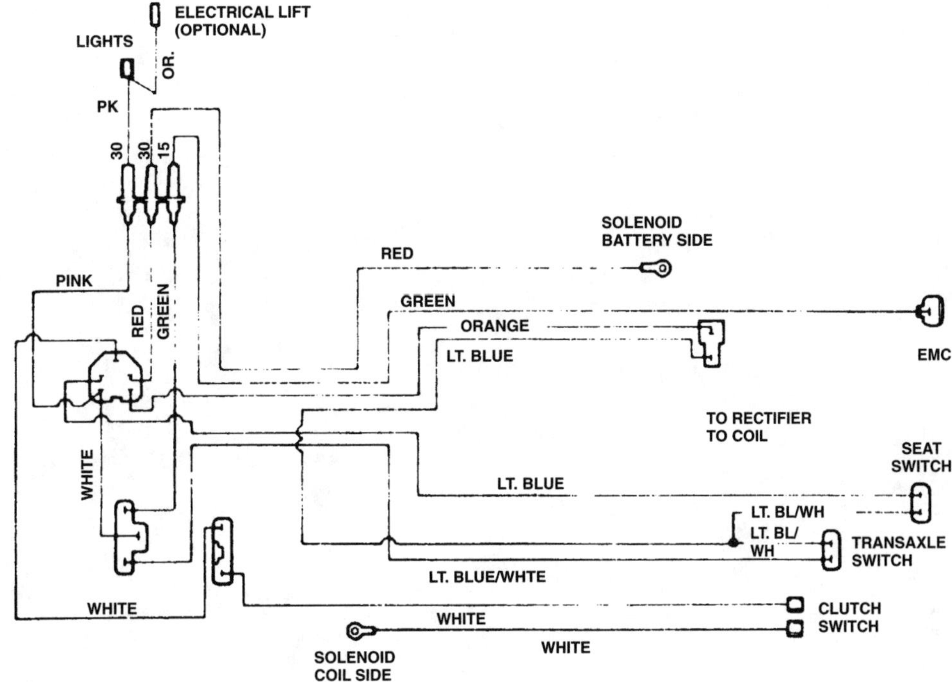

Fig. E1-21—Typical wiring diagram for 1200 series tractors.

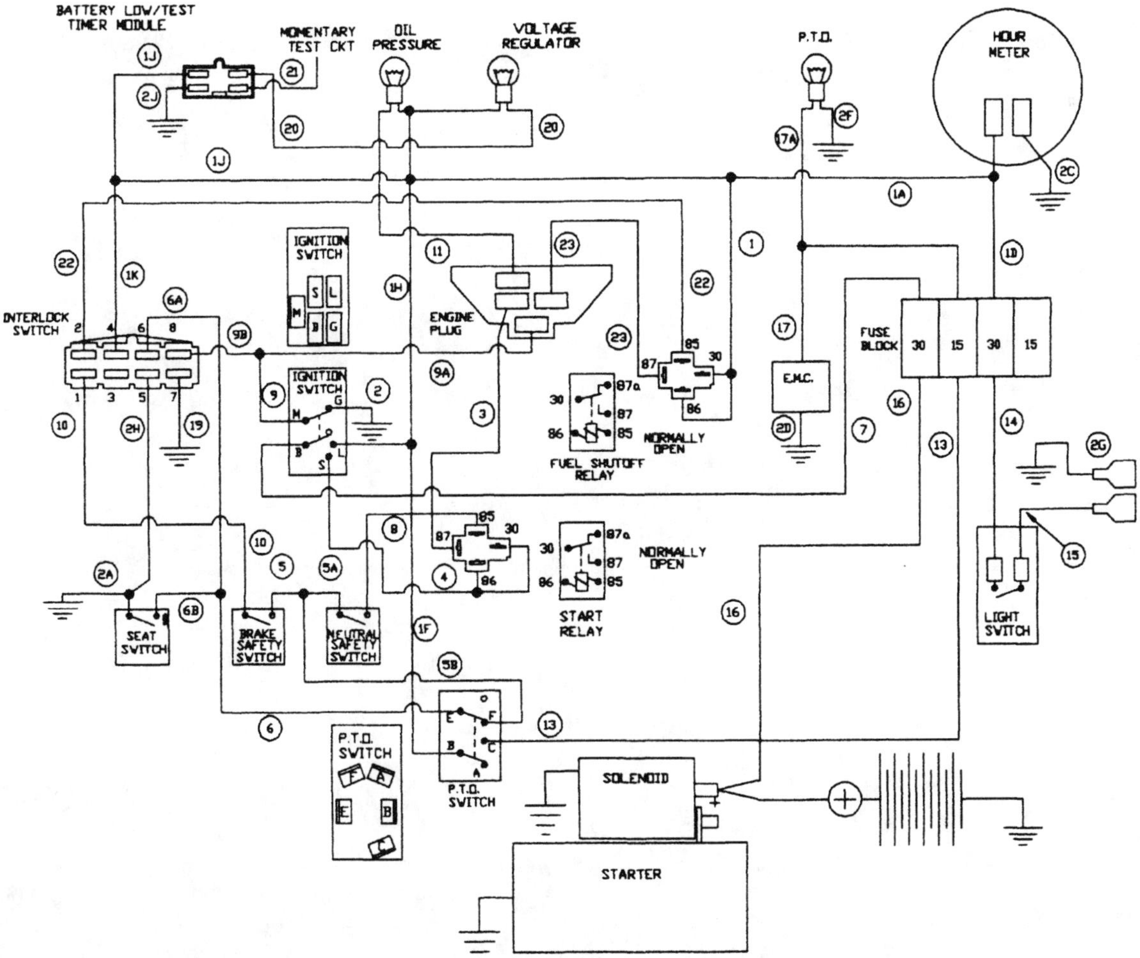

WIRES		
NO.	GA.	COLOR
1	16	WHITE
2	16	GREEN
3	16	GREEN
4	16	YELLOW
5	16	GREEN
6	16	BROWN
7	14	RED
8	16	PINK
9	16	RED
10	16	YELLOW
11	16	RED
12	16	DK BLUE
13	16	LT BLUE
14	16	RED
15	16	BROWN
16	14	RED
17	16	LT BLUE
18		
19	14	BLACK
20	16	BLUE
21	16	ORANGE
22	16	GREEN
23	16	WHITE

Fig. E1-22—Typical wiring diagram for 1600 and 2400 series tractors.

NOTES

SNAPPER

CONDENSED SPECIFICATIONS

Models	LT120G	LT125G, RLT125G	LT125G	LT140G
Engine Make	B&S	B&S	Kohler	B&S
Model	283707	289707	CV12.5S	287707
Bore	3.44 in. (87.3 mm)	3.44 in. (87.3 mm)	87 mm (3.43 in.)	3.44 in. (87.3 mm)
Stroke	3.06 in. (77.7 mm)	3.06 in. (77.7 mm)	64 mm (2.64 in.)	3.06 in. (77.7 mm)
Displacement	28.4 cu. in. (465 cc)	28.4 cu. in. (465 cc)	398 cc (24.3 cu. in.)	28.4 cu. In. (465 cc)
Power Rating	12 hp. (8.9 kW)	12.5 hp. (9.3 kW)	9.3 kW (12.5 hp.)	14 hp. (10.4 kW)
Slow Idle	1750 rpm	1750 rpm	1200 rpm	1200 rpm
High Speed (No-Load)	3600 rpm	3600 rpm	3600 rpm	3600 rpm
Crankcase Capacity	3 pt. (1.4 L)	3 pt. (1.4 L)	1.9 L (2 qt.)	3 pt. (1.4L)
Transmission Capacity	30 oz. (890 mL)	30 oz. (890 mL)	30 oz. (890 mL)	30 oz. (890 mL)

Models	LT140G	LT140H	LT150G	LT150H	LT155H
Engine Make	Kohler	B&S	Kohler	B&S	B&S
Model	CV14S	287707	CV15S	28Q777	28Q777
Bore	87 mm (4.43 in.)	3.44 in. (87.3 mm)	90 mm (3.60 in.)	3.44 in. (87.3 mm)	3.44 in. (87.3 mm)
Stroke	67 mm (2.64 in.)	3.06 in. (77.7 mm)	67 mm (2.64 in.)	3.06 in. (77.7 mm)	3.06 in. (77.7 mm)
Displacement	398 cc (24.3 cu. in.)	28.4 cu. in. (465 cc)	426 cc (26.0 cu. in.)	28.4 cu. in. (465 cc)	28.4 cu. in. (465 cc)
Power Rating	14 hp. (10.4 kW)	14 hp. (10.4 kW)	15 hp. (11.2 kW)	14 hp. (10.4 kW)	14 hp. (10.4 kW)
Slow Idle	1200 rpm	1200 rpm	1200 rpm	1200 rpm	1200 rpm
High Speed (No-Load)	3600 rpm	3600 rpm	3600 rpm	3600 rpm	3600 rpm
Crankcase Capacity	4 pt.* (1.9 L)	3 pt. (1.4 L)	4 pt.* (1.9 L)	3 pt. (1.4 L)	3 pt. (1.4 L)
Transmission Capacity	30 oz. (890 mL)	2.0 L (4.2 pt.)	30 oz. (890 mL)	2.0 L (4.2 pt.)	2.0 L (4.2 pt.)

*Add 1/2 pint (0.24 L) if changing oil filter.

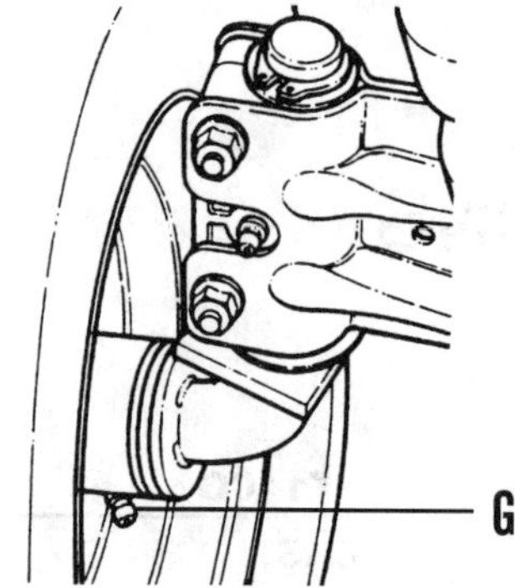

Fig. SN1-1—Inject multipurpose grease into grease fitting (G) on wheel hubs after every 25 hours of operation.

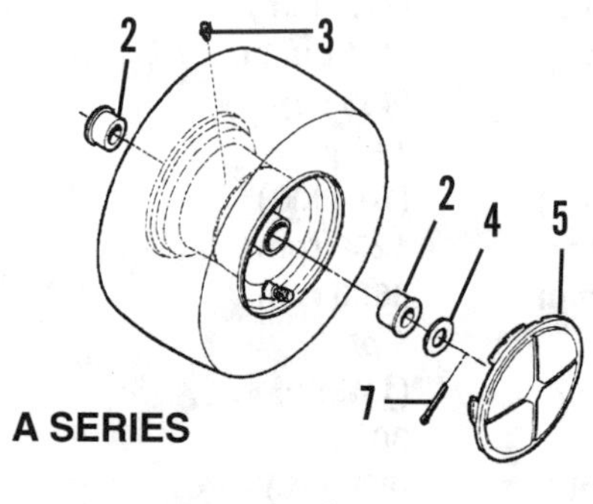

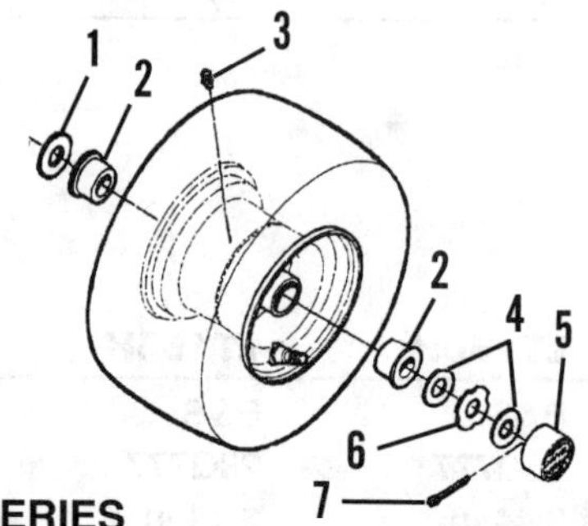

Fig. SN1-2—Exploded view of front wheel and bearings. Upper view is for Series A tractors and lower view is for Series B.

1. Washer
2. Bearings
3. Grease fitting
4. Washer
5. Hub cap
6. Retainer
7. Cotter pin

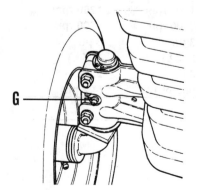

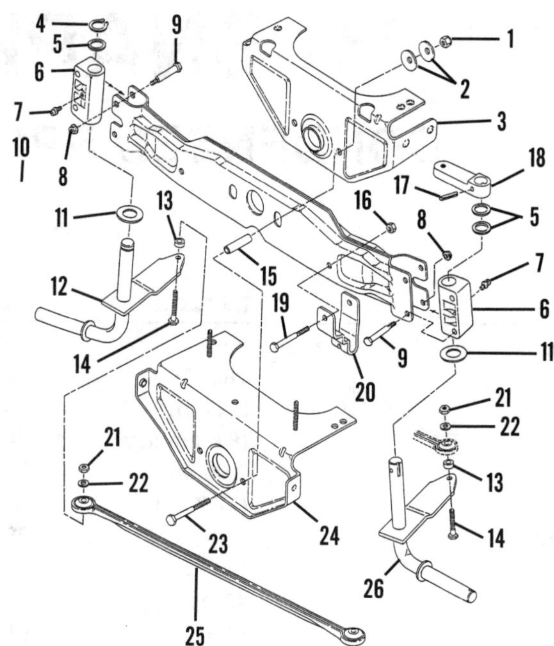

Fig. SN1-4—Exploded view of front axle assembly.

1. Locknut
2. Belleville washers
3. Bracket
4. Snap ring
5. Washer
6. Bearing block
7. Grease fitting
8. Locknut
9. Shoulder bolt
10. Axle main member
11. Thrust washer
12. Steering spindle (right)
13. Spacer
14. Bolt
15. Spacer (2)
16. Locknut
17. Roll pin
18. Steering arm
19. Bolt
20. Lift bracket
21. Nut
22. Lockwasher
23. Spacer
24. Bracket
25. Tie rod
26. Steering spindle (left)

FRONT AXLE SYSTEM

FRONT WHEELS AND BEARINGS

Lubricate the wheel bearings after every 25 hours of operation by injecting multipurpose grease into the grease fitting (G—Fig. SN1-1).

The front wheels are equipped with replaceable bearings (2—Fig. SN1-2). To remove the front wheels, raise and support the front of the tractor.

Remove the hub cap (5). Remove the cotter pin (7) and washers. Withdraw the wheel and bearings from the axle spindle.

Replace parts that are damaged. Reassemble by reversing the removal procedure. Lubricate the wheel bearings with multipurpose grease.

STEERING SPINDLES

Lubrication

Lubricate the spindles every 25 hours of operation by injecting multipurpose grease into the grease fitting (G—Fig. SN1-3) located in the spindle bearing block. Two shots from the grease gun usually provides sufficient lubrication.

Fig. SN1-3—Inject multipurpose grease into grease fitting (G) on axle bearing block after every 25 hours of operation.

Overhaul

Raise and support the front of the tractor. Remove the wheel and tire. Disconnect the tie rod end (25—Fig. SN1-4), and if needed, the steering drag link end.

If removing the right spindle (12), detach the snap ring (4) securing the top of the spindle and withdraw the spindle from the bearing block (6). If removing the left spindle (26), drive out the pin (17). Drive the spindle down out of the steering arm (18) and bearing block. Note the number of washers (5) so that the same number can be reinstalled.

Inspect components for damage. Replace the bearing block (6) and/or spindle if excessively worn.

When reassembling, be sure that the thrust washer (11) is located below the bearing block and that the correct number of shim washers (5) are installed at the top of the block. Inject grease into the bearing block grease fitting after assembly.

AXLE MAIN MEMBER REMOVAL AND INSTALLATION

To remove the axle main member (10—Fig. SN1-4), raise and support the front of the tractor and remove the front wheels. Remove the hood.

Detach the steering gear drag link from the steering arm (18). Detach the tie rod (25) from the spindles. Unscrew the shoulder bolts (9) and remove the bearing blocks (6) with the spindles as assemblies.

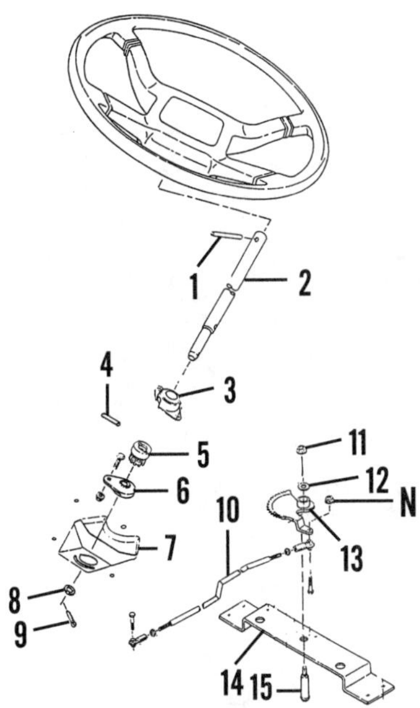

Fig. SN1-5—Exploded view of steering assembly. Sector gear (13) on some models is equipped with replaceable bushings.

1. Pin
2. Steering shaft
3. Bearing
4. Pin
5. Gear
6. Adjuster
7. Platform
8. Washer
9. Cotter pin
10. Drag link
11. Locknut
12. Washer
13. Sector gear
14. Support
15. Shoulder bolt

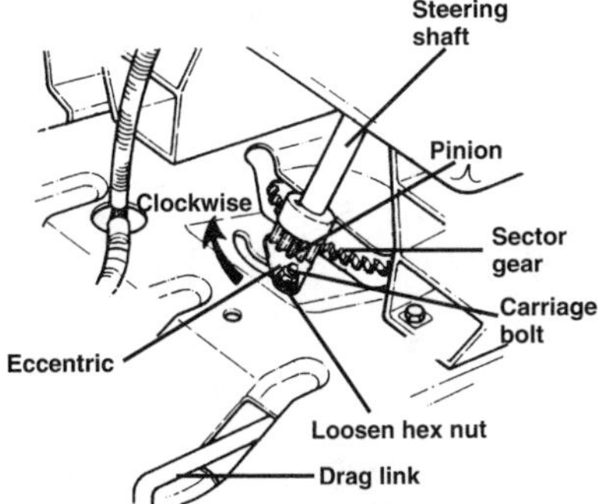

Fig. SN1-6—Loosen steering adjuster nut and move steering adjuster eccentric clockwise to remove free play.

Remove the nuts and washers from the engine mounting studs located on the front bracket (24). Remove the two hood mounting screws from each side of the frame. Unscrew the Torx head screws from each side of the frame.

Separate the axle with the front and rear brackets (3 and 24) as an assembly from the frame. Unscrew the bracket screws (23) and separate the axle and brackets.

Reassemble by reversing the removal procedure.

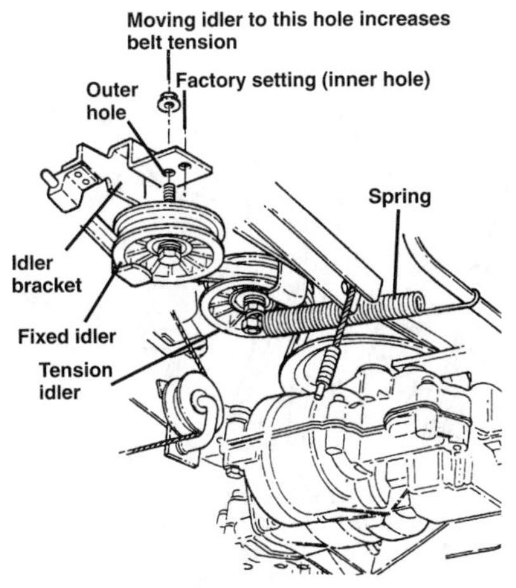

Fig. SN1-7—Detach the belt idler spring to relieve tension on traction drive belt.

STEERING SYSTEM

TIE ROD AND TOE-IN

The tie rod (25—Fig. SN1-4) is removed after unscrewing the retaining bolts at each end of tie rod.

Replace the tie rod if the tie rod is damaged or if the ends are excessively worn.

Front wheel toe-in is not adjustable.

DRAG LINK

A drag link (10—Fig. SN1-5) is located between the steering arm and the pitman arm. Inspect the drag link ends for looseness and replace when necessary.

Adjust the length of the drag link so that the front wheels turn equal distance in both directions when the steering wheel is turned lock-to-lock.

STEERING GEAR OVERHAUL

To remove the steering gear assembly, first remove the mower deck. Raise and support the front of the tractor.

Disconnect the drag link (10—Fig. SN1-5) from the sector gear (13). Remove the bolt securing the steering adjuster (6), and rotate the adjuster until the steering shaft gear (5) is separated from the sector gear teeth.

Unscrew the nut (11), withdraw the pivot bolt (15) and remove the sector gear (13).

Remove the cotter pin (9) and washer (8) from the bottom of the steering shaft. Drive out the roll pin (4) and remove the pinion gear (5) from the steering shaft. Pull the steering shaft upward until clear of the console.

Rotate the steering adjuster (6) until the locking tab on the adjuster aligns with the notch in the steering support, then lift and remove adjuster from steering support.

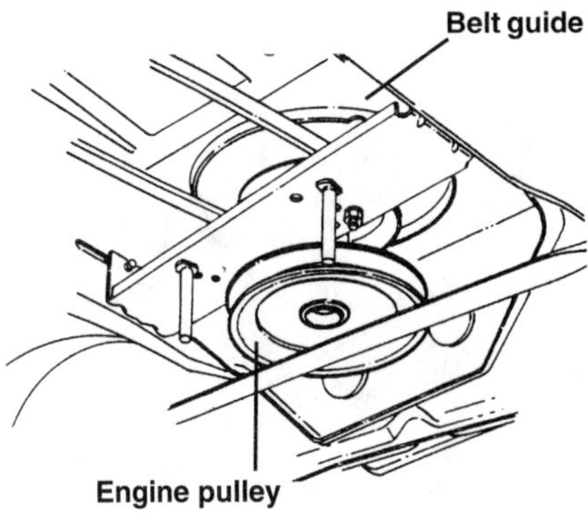

Fig. SN1-8—Remove the belt guide to provide clearance for belt removal.

NOTE: Early models were equipped with a flange nut (N—Fig. SN1-5) to secure the drag link to the sector gear. Discard the flange nut and install a locknut (Snapper part 9-0546).

Inspect all parts for excessive wear and replace when required.

To install the steering gear assembly, reverse the removal procedure. Lubricate the steering gear teeth with a light coat of multipurpose grease.

Adjust the steering gear "free play" as follows: Loosen the steering adjuster nut (Fig. SN1-6). Move the steering adjuster eccentric clockwise until free play is removed, but the steering wheel still turns freely without binding. Retighten the adjuster nut.

ENGINE

REMOVAL AND INSTALLATION

To remove the engine, first remove the mower deck from the tractor. Remove the deck drive belt from the engine pulley. Remove the hood and disconnect the battery cables.

Disconnect all interfering electrical wiring to the ignition coil, alternator and starter. Disconnect the throttle control cable and choke cable from the carburetor. Detach the fuel line from the carburetor.

Depress the clutch/brake pedal and set the park brake lever. Disconnect the belt idler spring (Fig. SN1-7). Unfasten and move the engine pulley belt guide (Fig. SN1-8) out of the way. Work the traction drive belt off the engine pulley. Remove the engine mounting bolts and lift the engine out of the tractor.

Install the engine by reversing removal procedure.

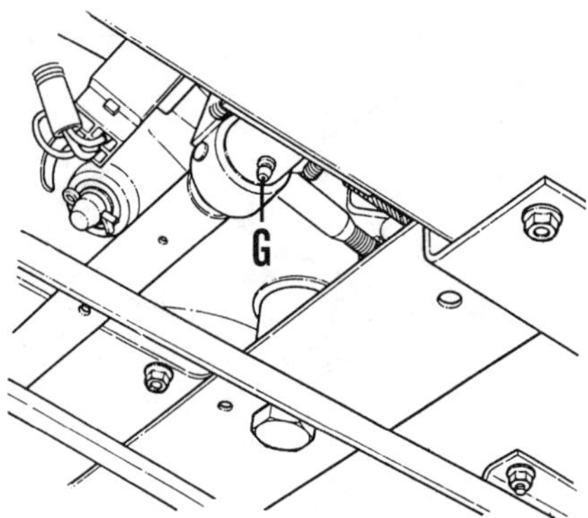

Fig. SN1-9—Inject one shot of multipurpose grease into grease fitting (G) on clutch/brake pivot shaft after every 25 hours of operation.

OVERHAUL

Engine make and model are listed at the beginning of this section. For tune-up specifications, engine overhaul procedures, and engine maintenance, refer to the appropriate engine section in this manual.

CLUTCH AND DRIVE BELT

LUBRICATION

After every 25 hours of operation, inject one shot of multipurpose grease into the grease fitting (G—Fig. SN1-9) on the pivot shaft.

ADJUSTMENT

The clutch idler pulley is spring-loaded and does not require adjustment. If clutch slippage occurs, inspect the drive belt for excessive wear and stretching which may indicate belt replacement is required. Some belt slack may be removed by moving the belt idler (Fig. SN1-7) to the outer hole on the idler bracket.

REMOVAL AND INSTALLATION

Depress the clutch/brake pedal and engage the parking brake. Remove the mower deck, and remove the mower drive belt from the engine pulley.

Disconnect the traction drive belt idler spring (Fig. SN1-7). Unfasten and move the belt guides out of way.

Remove the hairpin, and separate the control rod from the control crank as shown in Fig. SN1-10. Remove the traction drive belt from the engine pulley. Loosen the retaining nuts on the idler pulleys just enough to allow the belt to clear the belt guides. Remove the drive belt from the idler pulleys and the transaxle drive pulley.

Fig. SN1-10—When removing drive belt, disconnect control rod from control crank.

To install the traction drive belt, refer to Fig. SN1-11 and proceed as follows. Place the traction drive belt around the engine pulley (top groove).

NOTE: When installing a new belt, be sure the stationary idler is mounted in the hole closest to the left side of the tractor (Fig. SN1-11)

Route the belt as shown in Fig. SN1-11 and install the belt on the transaxle drive pulley. Be sure that the belt is positioned above the mower lift arms. Reposition the belt guides on the idler and tension pulleys and tighten the pulley mounting nuts.

Reattach the control rod to the control arm (Fig. SN1-10).

NOTE: If a notch (N—Fig. SN1-12) exists in the engine opening of the tractor frame, position the belt guide (B) so it rests in the notch.

BRAKE

MODELS WITH GEAR TRANSAXLE

Adjustment

When the brake is properly adjusted, the tractor should stop from top forward speed within six feet after the clutch/brake pedal has been fully depressed.

To increase or decrease the braking action, adjust the nut (N—Fig. SN1-13) on the brake rod located at the rear of the tractor behind the right wheel. Turn the nut clockwise to increase the braking action.

If satisfactory braking cannot be obtained by adjusting the brake rod nut, adjust the disc brake at the transaxle as follows:

Make sure that the park brake is disengaged. Loosen the brake rod adjusting nut (N—Fig. SN1-13) until the spring is loose.

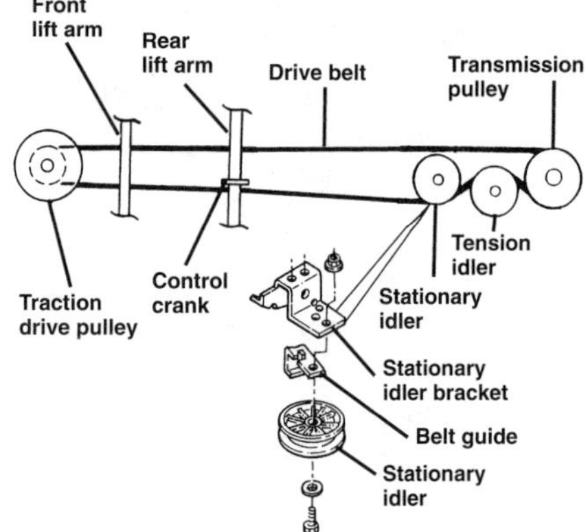

Fig. SN1-11—Install drive belt so it is routed as shown.

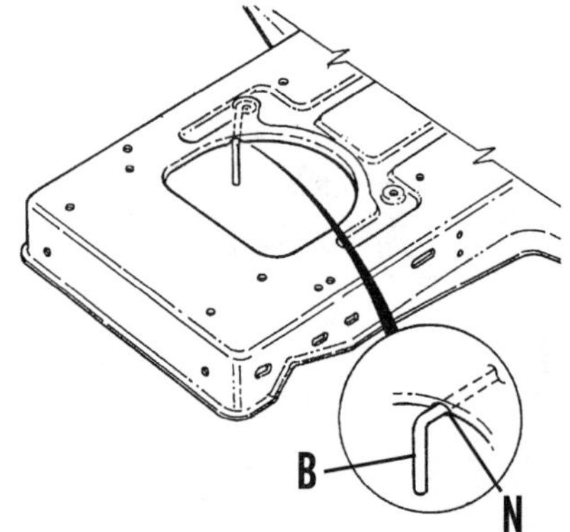

Fig. SN1-12—If a notch (N) exists in engine opening of tractor frame, position belt guide (B) so guide rests in notch.

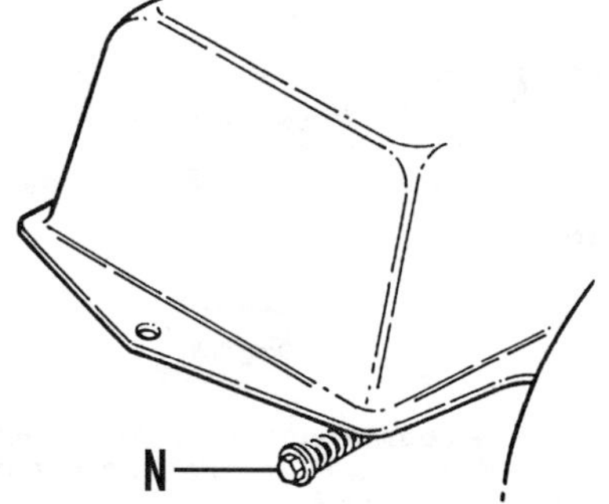

Fig. SN1-13—Adjust brake on models equipped with gear transaxle by rotating nut (N). Turn nut clockwise to increase brake action.

Use a feeler gauge to measure the clearance between the brake disc and pad (Fig. SN1-14). Clearance should be 0.010 inch (0.25 mm). Turn the nut on the brake assembly to obtain the correct clearance.

After adjusting the brake at the transaxle, adjust the brake rod nut (N—Fig. SN1-13) until it is snug against the spring. Check brake operation.

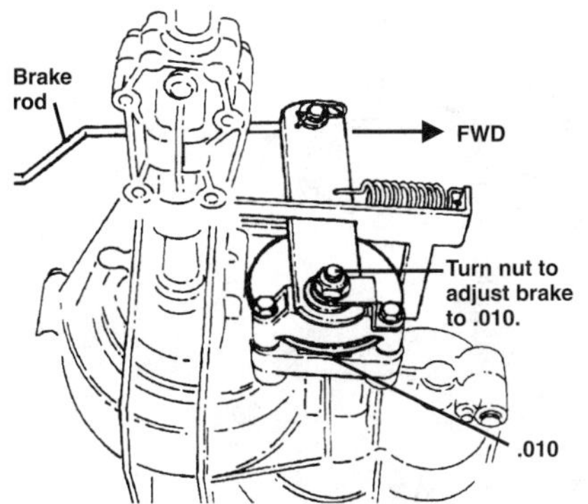

Fig. SN1-14—Clearance between brake disc and brake pad should be 0.010 inch (0.25 mm) with brake disengaged.

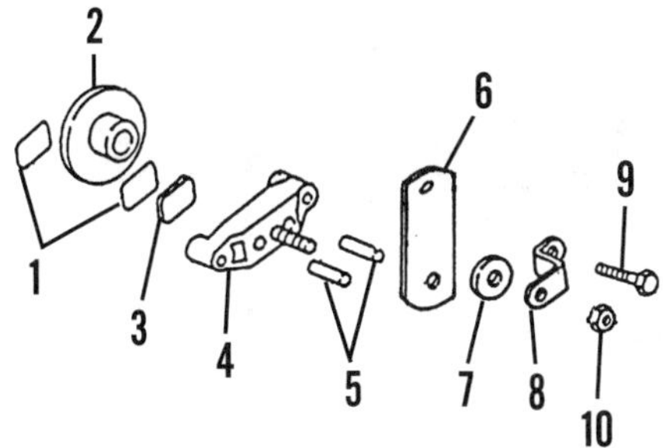

Fig. SN1-15—Exploded view of disc brake assembly used on models equipped with gear transaxle.

1. Brake pads
2. Brake disc
3. Back plate
4. Brake holder
5. Actuating pins
6. Brake lever
7. Washer
8. Bracket
9. Screw
10. Adjusting nut

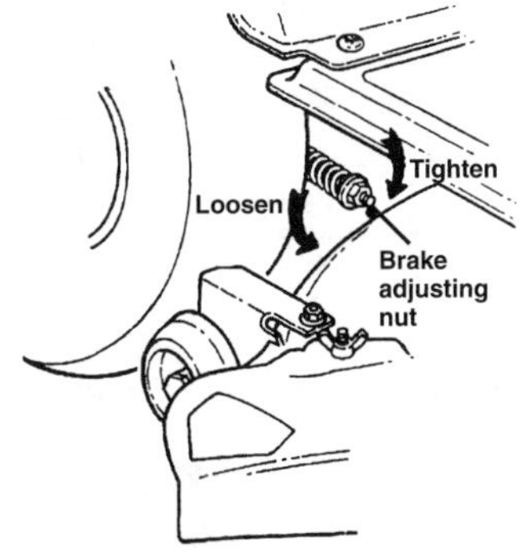

Fig. SN1-16—Adjust brake on models with hydrostatic transmission by rotating the brake rod nut. Turn the nut clockwise to increase brake action.

Removal and Installation

To remove the disc brake assembly, raise and support the rear of the tractor. Remove the right rear wheel.

Disconnect the brake rod from the brake lever (6—Fig. SN1-15). Remove the mounting cap screws (9) and withdraw the brake holder (4), disc (2) and pads (1).

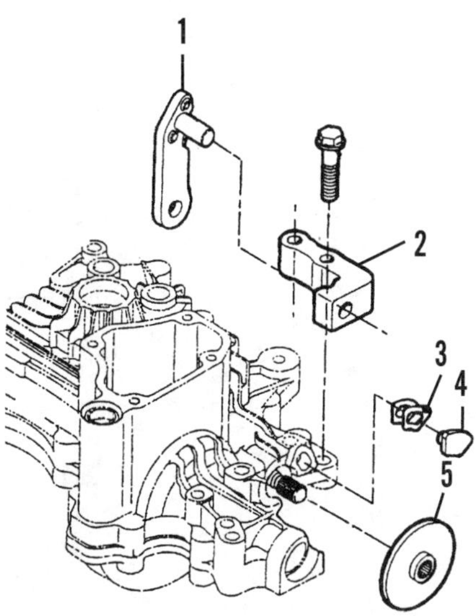

Fig. SN1-17—Exploded view of disc brake used on models equipped with hydrostatic transaxle.

1. Brake lever
2. Mounting bracket
3. Shims
4. Brake shoe
5. Brake disc

To reinstall the brake, reverse the removal procedure. Adjust the brake as previously outlined.

MODELS WITH HYDROSTATIC TRANSAXLE

Adjustment

When the brake is properly adjusted, the tractor should stop from the top forward speed within six feet after the brake pedal is fully depressed.

To adjust the braking action, turn the brake adjustment nut located in front of the right rear wheel (Fig. SN1-16). Turn the nut clockwise to increase the braking action or counterclockwise to reduce the braking action.

Removal and Installation

To remove the disc brake assembly, raise and support the rear of the tractor. Remove the right rear wheel.

Disconnect the brake rod from the brake lever (1—Fig. SN1-17). Remove the mounting cap screws from the brake lever bracket (2). Remove the mounting bracket, brake lever (1), brake disc (5), brake shoe (4) and shims (3).

Inspect all parts for damage and replace when needed.

To install the brake assembly, reverse the removal procedure. Install shims (3) as needed to adjust the air gap between the brake disc (5) and brake lever (1) to 0.03-0.05 inch (0.08-1.3 mm).

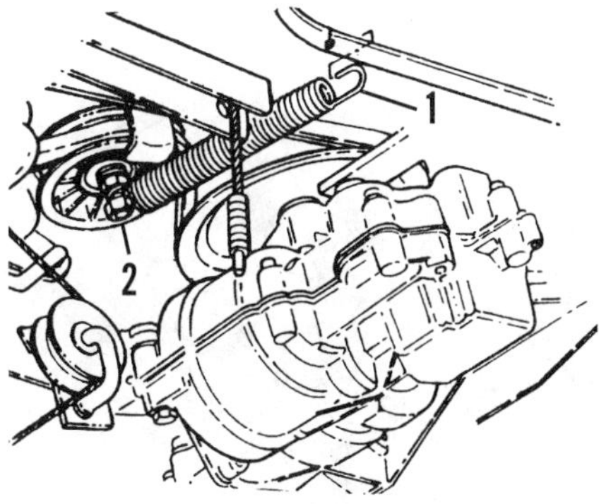

Fig. SN1-18—Disconnect idler pulley spring (1) to relieve tension on traction drive belt.

Tighten the mounting bracket cap screws to 33-43 ft.-lb. (44-59 N·m).

Adjust the brake rod nut as previously outlined.

GEAR TRANSAXLE (ALL MODELS SO EQUIPPED)

LUBRICATION

The transaxle is filled at the factory with SAE 90 GL5 gear lubricant and does not require periodic checking of lubricant level. If an oil leak develops, the leak should be repaired and unit refilled with gear lubricant. Transaxle capacity is approximately 890 mL (30 oz.).

The transaxle rear axle bearings should be lubricated with multipurpose grease after every 25 hours of operation. A grease fitting is located on each side of the transaxle housing.

REMOVAL AND INSTALLATION

To remove the transaxle, first remove the mower deck. Raise and support the rear of the tractor. Remove the rear wheels. Move the shift lever to the reverse position.

Depress the clutch/brake pedal and engage the parking brake. Disconnect the traction drive belt idler spring (1—Fig. SN1-18). Remove the drive belt from the transaxle pulley. Disconnect the shift linkage from the transaxle shift arm. Disconnect the brake rod from the disc brake lever. Disconnect the brake return spring from the pulley bracket.

Disconnect the wiring from the safety start switch located on top of the transaxle. Support the transaxle. Remove the cap screws attaching the transaxle to the frame and lower the transaxle from the tractor.

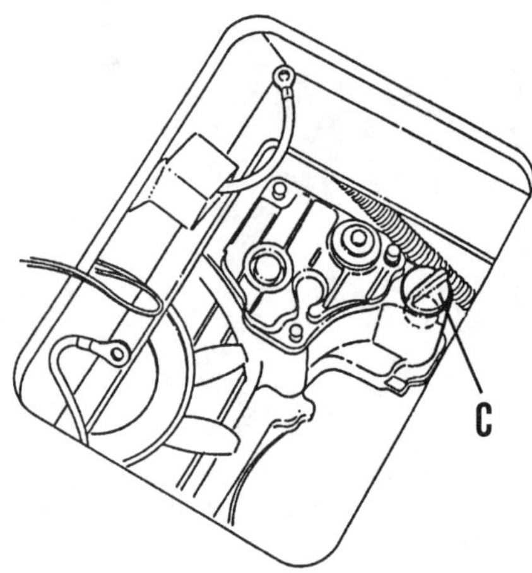

Fig. SN1-19—Remove cap (C) to check oil level on hydrostatic transaxle.

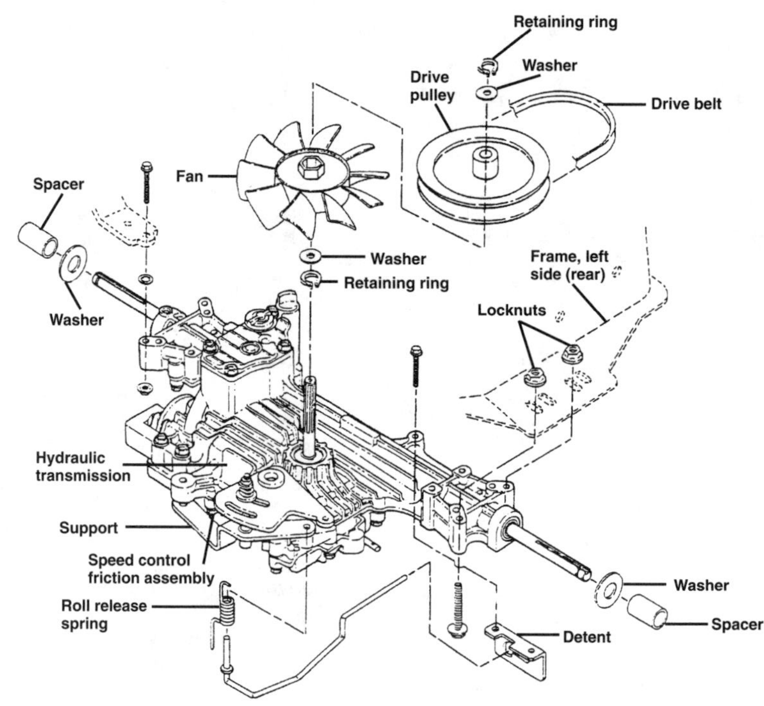

Fig. SN1-20—Drawing of hydrostatic drive transaxle.

To install the transaxle, reverse the removal procedure. Adjust the brake as previously outlined.

OVERHAUL

Tractor is equipped with a Peerless Model 930 transaxle. Refer to the Peerless section in the TRANSAXLE SERVICE section for overhaul procedure.

HYDROSTATIC TRANSAXLE (ALL MODELS SO EQUIPPED)

LUBRICATION

To check the oil level, unscrew the seat adjustment knobs and move the seat out of the way—do not damage the seat switch wires. Disconnect the battery leads and remove the battery. Remove the battery tray.

Thoroughly clean the area around the transaxle oil fill cap (C—Fig. SN1-19) before removing the oil fill cap. The oil level should be 1/2-1 inch (13-25 mm) below the oil fill opening. Recommended oil is SAE 10W-30 engine oil.

Reinstall the battery tray, battery and seat.

REMOVAL AND INSTALLATION

To remove the transaxle, first remove the mower deck. Raise and support the rear of the tractor. Remove the rear wheels. Remove any washers or spacers on the axles and mark them so they may be reinstalled in their original positions.

Remove the drive belt from the transaxle pulley. Disconnect the roll release spring and remove the detent (Fig. SN1-20). Disconnect the shift linkage and brake linkage from the transaxle.

Support the transaxle, unscrew the mounting bolts and remove the transaxle.

Reverse the removal procedure to install the transaxle.

OVERHAUL

Models equipped with a hydrostatic transaxle are equipped with a TUFF TORQ Model K50 transaxle manufactured by Kanzaki. Refer to the TUFF TORQ section in the TRANSAXLE SERVICE section for overhaul procedure.

ELECTRICAL SYSTEM

INTERLOCK START SYSTEM

Operation

All models are equipped with a safety interlock system containing three interlock switches; seat, mower blade and clutch/brake switch (Fig. SN1-21). The mower blade and clutch/brake switches must be closed before the engine can be started. The seat switch does not have to be closed to start the engine.

After the engine has been started, the mower blade and clutch/brake switch can be opened without "killing" the engine as long as the key switch is in the RUN position and the operator remains in the seat to keep the seat switch closed. Thus the mower drive may be engaged and the transmission gears selected.

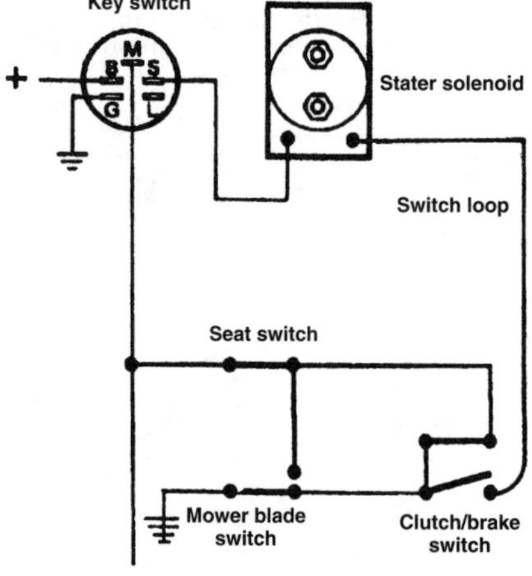

Fig. SN1-21—Safety interlock starting system wiring diagram.

The interlock system will "kill" the engine if the operator leaves the seat unless the mower blade lever has been moved to the OFF position, the shift lever placed in neutral, and the parking brake set.

Testing

The seat switch, clutch/brake switch, blade switch and key switch can be checked for the correct operation using a continuity light or an ohmmeter.

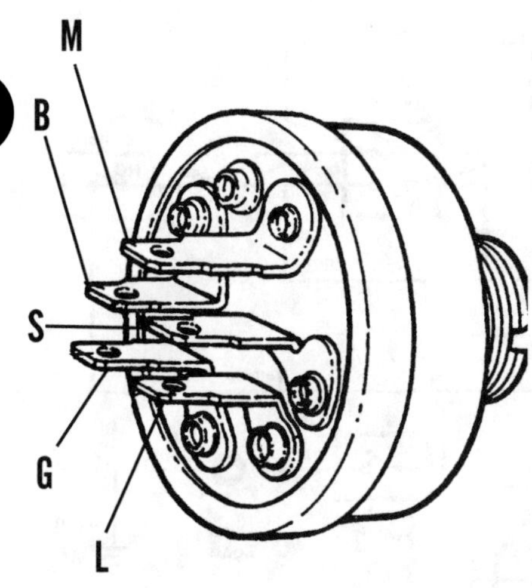

Fig. SN1-22—Drawing of key switch. Refer to text for testing procedure.

To test the seat switch, attach the tester leads to the switch terminals. There should be continuity when the switch is released, and there should not be continuity when the switch button is depressed.

To test the clutch/brake switch, attach the tester leads to the switch terminals. There should not be continuity when the switch button is released, and there should be continuity when the button is depressed.

The blade switch has four terminals; two terminals on one side are normally closed (continuity) and the two terminals on the other side are normally open (no continuity). When the switch button is depressed, the normally open terminals should indicate continuity.

To test the key switch (Fig. SN1-22), place the switch in the OFF position. There should be continuity between the "M" and "G" terminals only. Place the switch in the ON position. There should be continuity between the "B" and "S" terminals only. Hold the switch in the START position. There should be continuity between the "B" and "S" terminals only.

The LT series lawn tractors are equipped with a 20-amp fuse to protect the electrical system. The fuse holder is located in the wiring harness below the fuel tank.

WIRING SCHEMATICS

Refer to Fig. SN1-23 through SN1-25 for tractor wiring schematics.

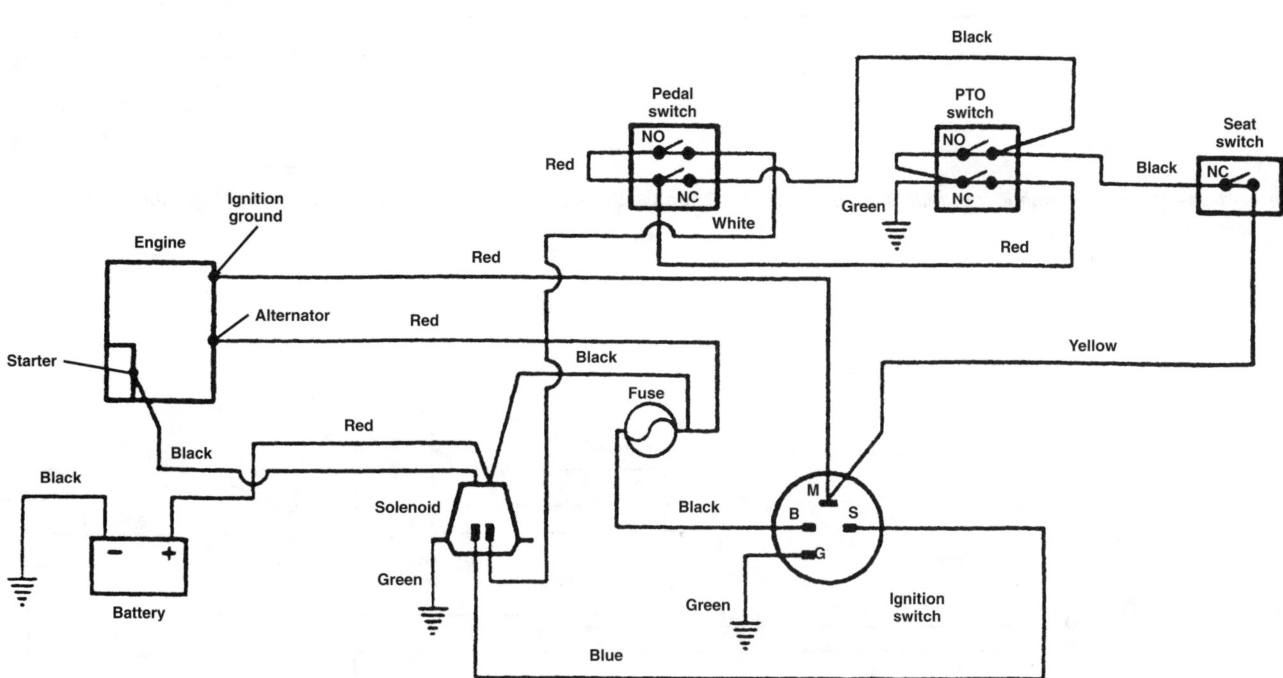

Fig. SN1-23—Wiring schematic for models equipped with a Briggs & Stratton engine without lights.

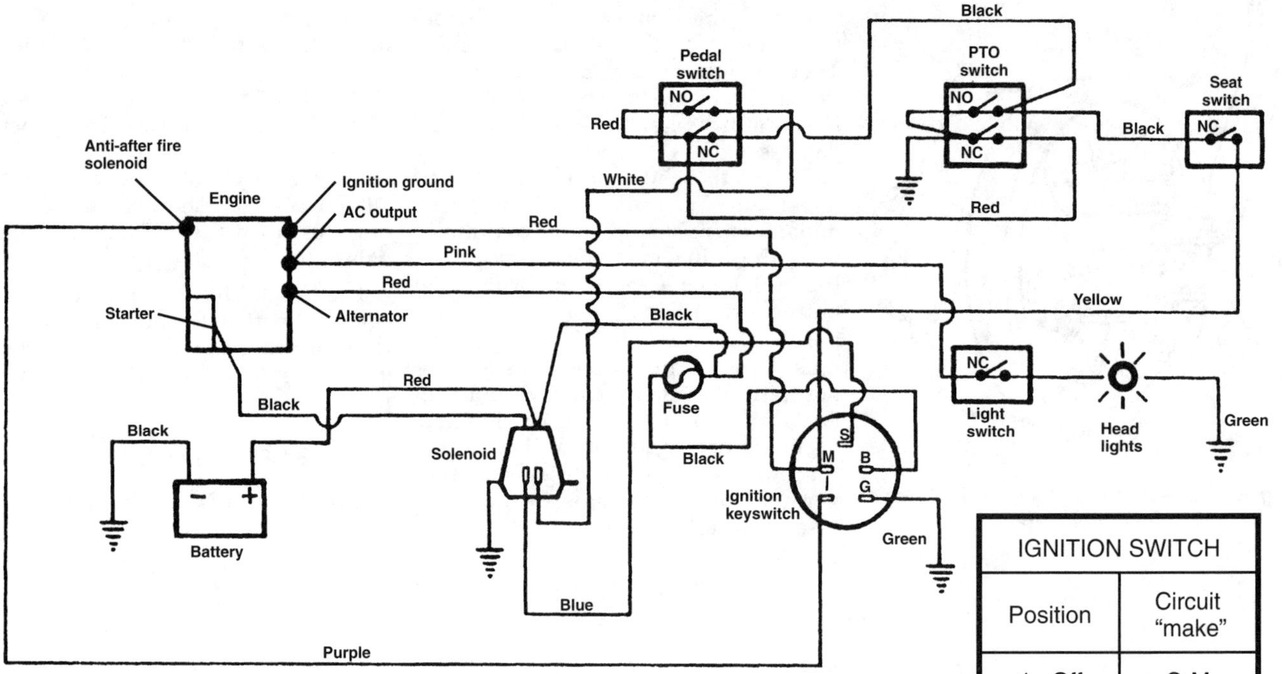

IGNITION SWITCH	
Position	Circuit "make"
1. Off	G-M
2. Run	B-L
3. Start	B-S-L

Fig. SN1-24—Wiring schematic for models equipped with a Briggs & Stratton engine with an anti-afterfire solenoid and lights.

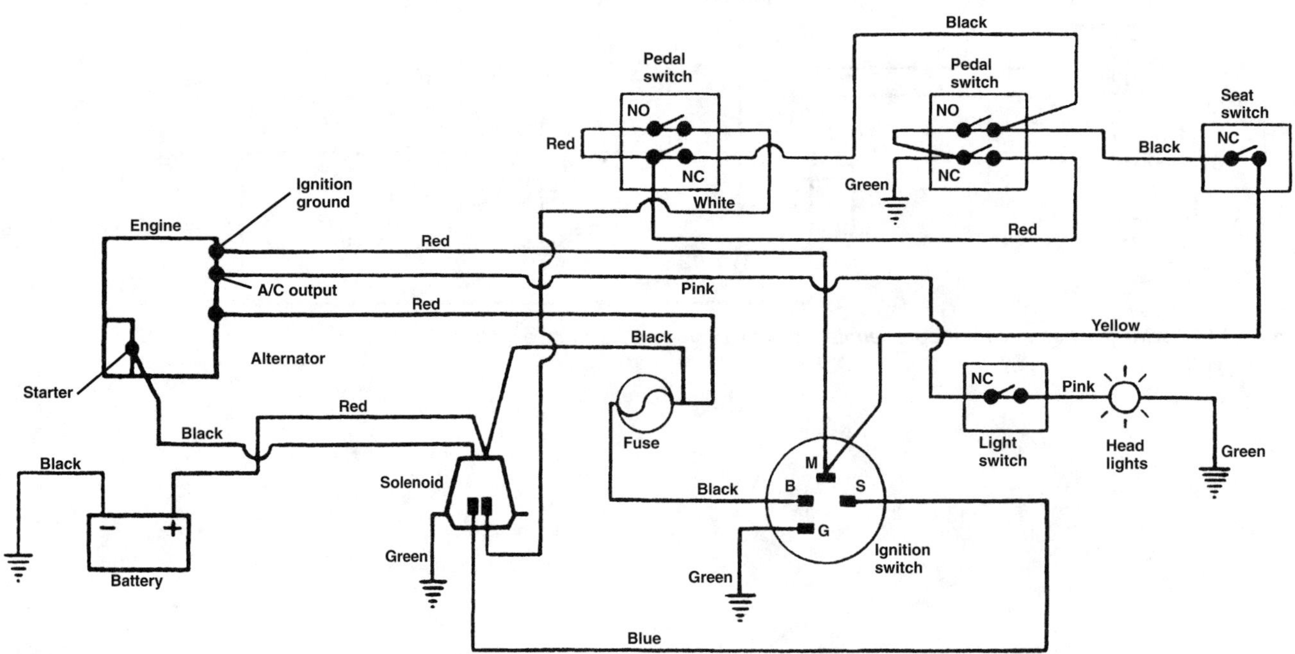

Fig. SN1-25—Wiring schematic for models equipped with a Kohler engine or a Briggs & Stratton engine not equipped with an anti-afterfire solenoid.

TORO

CONDENSED SPECIFICATIONS

Wheel Horse Models	310-8	312-8	312-H	314-8
Engine Make	Kohler	Kohler	Kohler	Kohler
Model	M10	M12	M12	M14
Number of cylinders	1	1	1	1
Bore	3.25 in. (82.5 mm)	3.38 in. (85.7 mm)	3.38 in. (85.7 mm)	3.50 in. (88.9 mm)
Stroke	2.88 in. (73.0 mm)	3.25 in. (82.5 mm)	3.25 in. (82.5 mm)	3.25 in. (82.5 mm)
Displacement	23.85 cu. in. (392 cc)	29.07 cu. in. (476 cc)	29.07 cu. in. (476 cc)	31.27 cu. In. (512 cc)
Power Rating	10 hp. (7.5 kW)	12 hp. (8.9 kW)	12 hp. (8.9 kW)	14 hp. (10.4 kW)
Slow Idle	1200 rpm	1200 rpm	1200 rpm	1200 rpm
High Speed (No-Load)	3600 rpm	3600 rpm	3600 rpm	3600 rpm
Crankcase Capacity	4 pt. (1.9 L)	4 pt. (1.9 L)	4 pt. (1.9 L)	4 pt. (1.9 L)
Transaxle Capacity	4 pt. (1.9 L)	4 pt. (1.9 L)	....	4 pt. (1.9 L)
Transmission Capacity	....	....	**	....
Final Drive Capacity	....	....	5 qt** (4.7 L)	....
Hydraulic System Capacity	....	....	**	....

**On Model 312-H, final drive contains oil for transmission and hydraulic system.

Wheel Horse Models	314-H	416-8	416-H	520-H
Engine Make	Kohler	Toro	Toro	Toro
Model	M14	P216	P216	P220
Number of cylinders	1	2	2	2
Bore	3.50 in. (88.9 mm)	3.25 in. (82.5 mm)	3.25 in. (82.5 mm)	3.25 in. (82.5 mm)
Stroke	3.25 in. (82.5 mm)	2.625 in. (66.68 mm)	2.625 in. (66.68 mm)	2.875 in. (73.03 mm)
Displacement	31.27 cu. in. (512 cc)	43.6 cu. in. (715 cc)	43.6 cu. in. (715 cc)	47.7 cu. in. (782 cc)
Power Rating	14 hp. (10.4 kW)	16 hp. (11.9 kW)	16 hp. (11.9 kW)	20 hp. (14.9 kW)
Slow Idle	1200 rpm	1100 rpm	1100 rpm	1100 rpm
High Speed (No-Load)	3600 rpm	3600 rpm	3600 rpm	3600 rpm
Crankcase Capacity	4 pt. (1.9 L)	1.7 qt.* (1.6 L)	1.7 qt.* (1.6 L)	1.7 qt.* (1.6 L)
Transaxle Capacity	....	4 pt. (1.9 L)	....	....
Transmission Capacity	**	....	**	**
Final Drive Capacity	5 qt** (4.7 L)	....	5 qt. (4.7 L)	5qt. (4.7 L)
Hydraulic System Capacity	**	....	**	**

*Add 0.3 quart (0.3 L) if changing oil filter.
**On Models 314-H, 416-H and 520-H, final drive contains oil for transmission and hydraulic system.

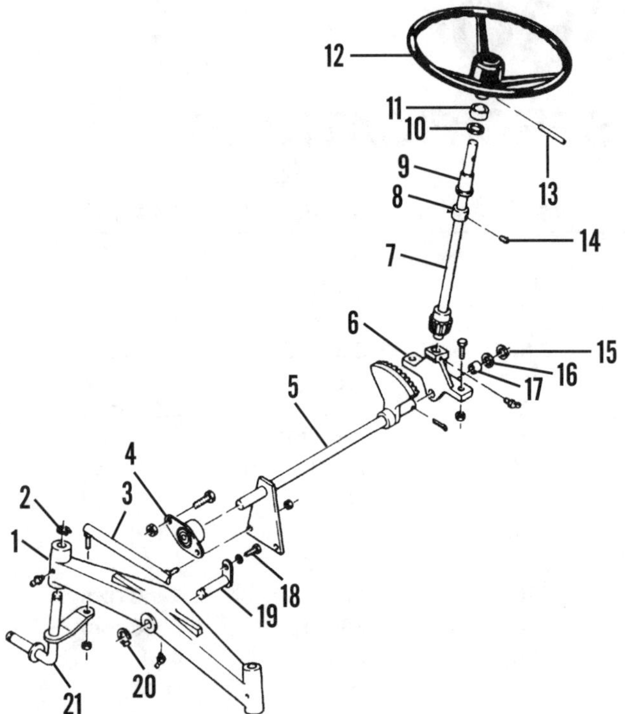

Fig. T1-1—Exploded view of typical front axle and steering assembly used on all models except Model 520-H. Later models are equipped with a nut that secures rear end of steering shaft in place of a cotter pin.

1. Axle main member
2. Snap ring
3. Tie rod
4. Flange bearing
5. Lower steering shaft
6. Steering support
7. Upper steering shaft
8. Collar
9. Bushing
10. Washer
11. Collar
12. Steering wheel
13. Roll pin
14. Setscrew
15. Shim washer
16. Shim washer
17. Bearing
18. Retaining bolt
19. Pivot pin
20. Snap ring
21. Spindle

FRONT AXLE SYSTEM

MAINTENANCE

Lubricate the steering gear, front wheel bearings, steering spindles and axle pivot after every 25 hours of operation. Recommended lubricant is multipurpose lithium base grease. Clean fittings before and after lubrication.

Clean all other pivot points and lubricate with SAE30 oil. Check for looseness and wear and repair when necessary.

FRONT WHEEL BEARINGS

Model 520-H is equipped with tapered roller bearings in the front wheel hubs. All other models are equipped with ball bearings. Replace the bearings and/or wheel hubs if excessive looseness is evident.

STEERING SPINDLES REMOVAL AND INSTALLATION

Raise and support the front of the tractor. Remove the front wheel and hub assembly. Disconnect the tie rod (3—Fig. T1-1 or Fig. T1-2) from the steering spindle (12 or 21). Remove the snap ring located on the upper end of the spindle. Slide the spindle out of the axle main member.

Install spindle by reversing the removal procedure. Lubricate the spindles with multipurpose grease.

TIE ROD AND TOE-IN

Some models are equipped with an adjustable tie rod. Inspect the tie rod ball joints for excessive wear and looseness and replace if needed.

Adjust the length of the tie rod to obtain front wheel toe-in of 1/8 inch (3.2 mm). Secure the tie rod ends with jam nuts.

AXLE MAIN MEMBER REMOVAL AND INSTALLATION

To remove the axle main member (1—Fig. T1-1 or T1-2), raise and support the front of the tractor frame and remove the front wheels. Disconnect the tie rods from both spindles. Remove the spindles.

Detach the snap ring (20) and unscrew the pivot pin retaining screw (18). Withdraw the pivot pin (19) and remove the axle.

Reinstall the axle by reversing the removal procedure.

STEERING GEAR OVERHAUL

Model 520-H

Refer to Fig. T1-2 for an exploded view of the steering assembly.

Detach the tie rod ends from the arm of the lower steering shaft (5). Unscrew and remove the bearing block (16), then remove the lower shaft (5). Drive out the roll pin (22) and remove the steering wheel. Remove the bolts securing the intermediate steering shaft support (28). Lift up the upper steering shaft (27), and remove the intermediate steering shaft and support assembly. Remove the upper steering shaft.

When assembling the steering shaft assemblies, install shims (15 and 24) so the steering gears rotate easily without binding or excessive play.

All Other Models

Remove the steering wheel retaining nut and use a suitable puller to remove the steering wheel. Drive out the roll pin (13—Fig. T1-1). Loosen the setscrew (14) and move the upper steering shaft (7) up to clear the support (6).

Disconnect the inner ends of the tie rods from the arm of the lower steering shaft (5). Remove the cotter pin or nut from the rear end of the lower shaft (5) and remove the shims (15 and 16).

Unbolt and remove the support (6). The upper shaft (7) and lower shaft (5) can now be pulled out from underneath the tractor. Unbolt and remove the flange bearing (4).

Inspect the parts for wear, scoring or other damage and replace when necessary.

Install by reversing the removal procedure. Before tightening the setscrew (14), apply downward pressure on the steering wheel, slide the collar (8) up against the bushing (9), and tighten the setscrew (14).

Adjust the steering gear mesh by adding or removing shims (15 and 16)

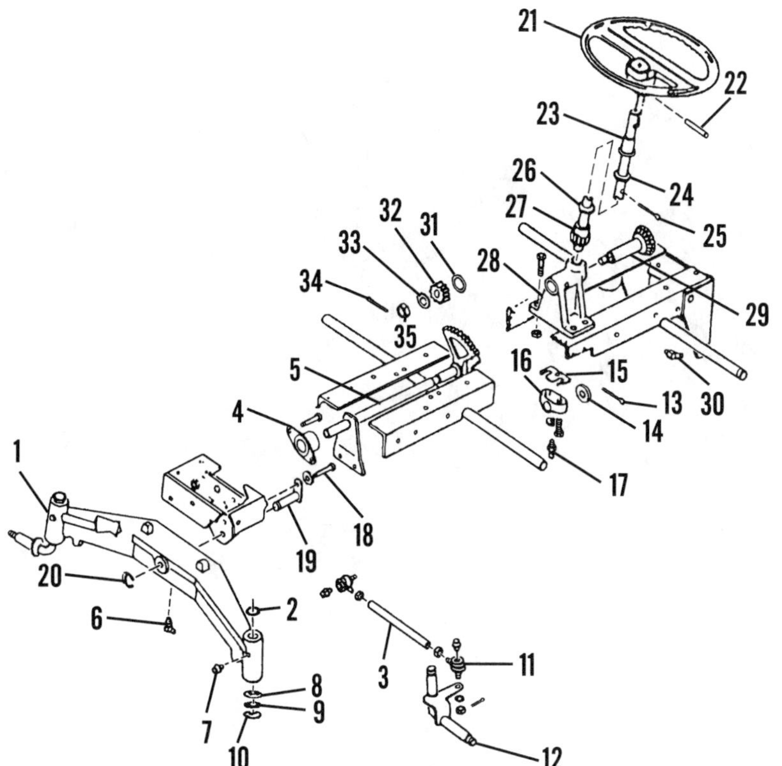

Fig. T1-2—Exploded view of front axle and steering assembly used on Model 520-H.

1. Axle
2. Snap ring
3. Tie rod
4. Flange bearing
5. Lower steering shaft
6. Grease fitting
7. Grease fitting
8. Washer
9. Thrust bearing
10. Washer
11. Tie rod end
12. Spindle
13. Cotter pin
14. Washer
15. Shim
16. Bearing block
17. Grease fitting
18. Bolt
19. Pivot pin
20. Retaining ring
21. Steering wheel
22. Pin
23. Flange bearing
24. Shim washer
25. Cotter pin
26. O-ring
27. Upper steering shaft
28. Steering support
29. Steering gear
30. Grease fitting
31. Washer
32. Pinion gear
33. Washer
34. Cotter pin
35. Nut

until 0.0-0.015 inch (0.0-0.4 mm) end play is present in the lower steering shaft (5).

ENGINE

MAINTENANCE

Regular engine maintenance is required to maintain peak performance and long engine life.

Check oil level daily or after five hours of operation. Inspect air cleaner element periodically depending on operating conditions. Clean the air cleaner as specified in the engine section.

REMOVAL AND INSTALLATION

Raise and support the hood. Disconnect the negative battery cable. Remove the mower deck.

Disconnect the choke and throttle cables. Disconnect the fuel line from the carburetor. Identify and disconnect all electrical connections from the engine.

Remove the belt guard. Disconnect the clutch rod and yoke as needed. Disengage the transmission drive clutch on hydrostatic drive models or depress the clutch and remove the drive belt from the engine pulley on standard transmission models.

Remove the bolts attaching the engine to the frame. Remove the engine from the tractor.

Install by reversing the removal procedure.

OVERHAUL

Engine make and model are listed at the beginning of this section. For tune-up specifications, engine overhaul procedures and engine maintenance, refer to the appropriate engine section in this manual.

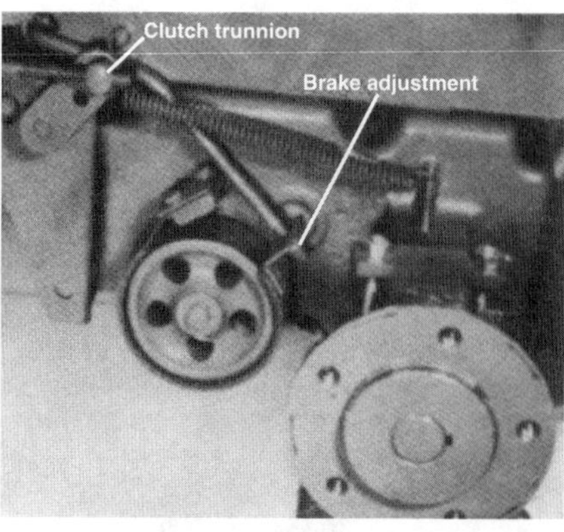

Fig. T1-3—View of clutch and brake adjustment points on Models 310-8, 312-8, 314-8 and 416-8. Refer to text.

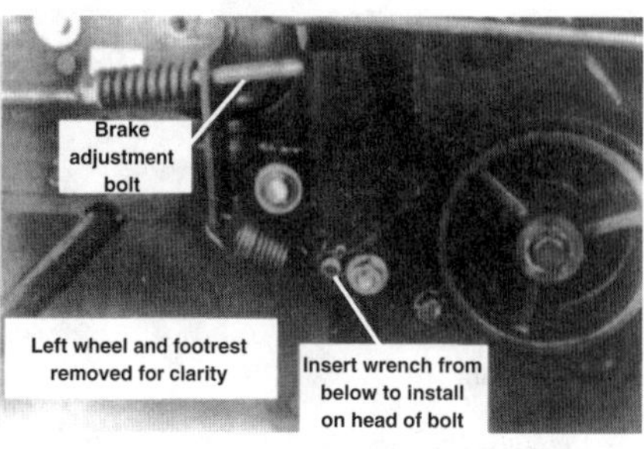

Fig. T1-4—View showing brake mechanism and adjustment nut on Models 312-H, 314-H, 416-H and 520-H.

BRAKE ADJUSTMENT

MODELS 310-8, 312-8, 314-8 AND 416-8

Depress the brake pedal and engage the park brake lever. Tighten the brake rod nut gradually against the flange of the brake band (Fig. T1-3) until both rear wheels of the tractor will skid when the tractor is pushed by hand. Tighten the nut another half turn so the pedal and parking brake are in proper adjustment.

Release the parking brake to check operation. The clutch must disengage before the brake is applied.

MODELS 312-H, 314-H, 416-H AND 520-H

Push the brake pedal down and engage the parking brake. Tighten the adjustment nut (Fig. T1-4) until both rear wheels skid when the tractor is pushed by hand. Release the brake and tighten the adjustment nut another half turn.

After adjustment, the parking brake lever should not travel to the rear end of the lever slot when engaged and the brake band should not drag on the

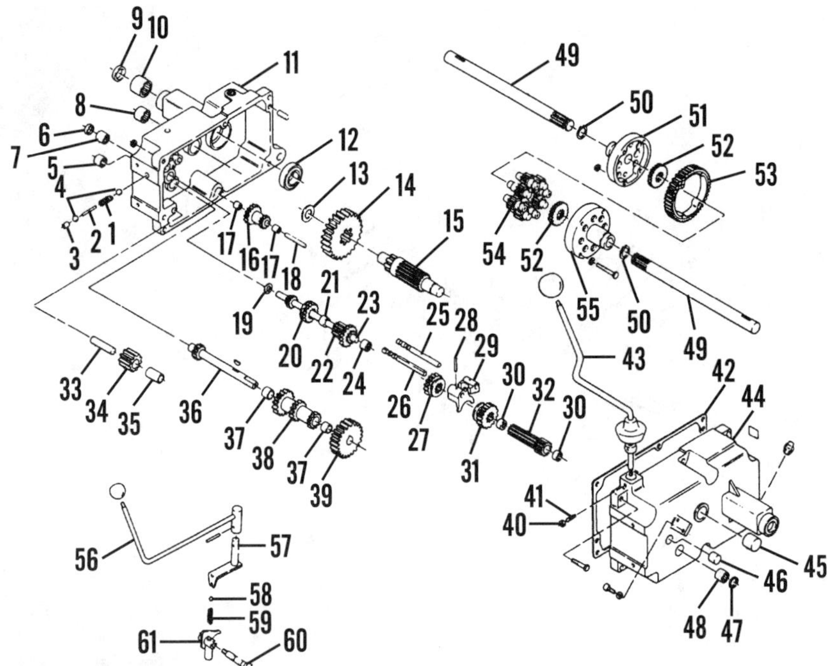

Fig. T1-5—Exploded view of eight-speed transaxle.

1. Detent spring
2. Detent pin
3. Plug
4. Detent balls
5. Needle bearing
6. Seal
7. Needle bearing
8. Needle bearing
9. Axle seal
10. Needle bearing
11. Case
12. Ball bearing
13. Thrust washer
14. Gear (44T)
15. Spline/gear
16. Reduction cluster
17. Needle bearings
18. Reduction shaft
19. Thrust washer
20. Sliding gear
21. Needle bearing
22. Gear and spline
23. Input shaft
24. Needle bearing
25. Rear shift rail
26. Front shift rail
27. High-2nd gear
28. Pin
29. Shift forks
30. Needle bearings
31. Low-reverse gear
32. Pinion and spline
33. Reverse idler shaft
34. Reverse idler gear
35. Bronze bushing
36. Brake/cluster shaft
37. Bearings
38. Cluster gear
39. Reduction gear
40. Jam nut
41. Setscrew
42. Gasket
43. Selector lever
44. Case
45. Bearing
46. Bearing
47. Seal (brake shaft)
48. Bearing
49. Axle shaft
50. Snap ring
51. Differential case half
52. Axle gear
53. Ring gear
54. Pinion gears
55. Differential case half
56. Range gear selector lever
57. Shift lever
58. Detent ball
59. Detent spring
60. Detent bolt
61. Shift fork

brake drum when the brake is fully released.

CLUTCH ADJUSTMENT (MODELS 310-8, 312-8, 314-8 AND 416-8

The clutch pedal is connected to a spring-loaded, pivoting idler pulley. Belt tension is maintained by spring pressure and no adjustment is required.

TRANSAXLE (MODELS 310-8, 312-8 AND 314-8, 416-8)

MAINTENANCE

The transaxle oil level should be checked after every 25 hours of operation. Maintain the oil level at the full mark on the dipstick.

Change the oil after every 200 hours of operation. Recommended oil is SAE 140 EP gear lube. Oil capacity is approximately 4 pints (1.9 L). Do not overfill.

REMOVAL AND INSTALLATION

To remove the transaxle, first remove the mower deck. Unbolt and remove the belt guard. Depress the clutch pedal and remove the drive belt from the transaxle pulley. Disconnect the brake rod linkage from the transaxle.

Remove the knobs from the gearshift lever and range selector lever. Raise and support the frame at a point forward of the transaxle. Remove the transaxle mounting screws, then lower and remove the entire unit from the tractor.

Reverse the removal procedure to install the transaxle. Adjust the brake as previously described.

OVERHAUL

Drain the oil and clean the exterior of the transaxle. Remove the wheel and hub assemblies. Clamp the transaxle housing in a holding fixture so the right axle points down.

Remove the brake band assembly and the brake drum. Remove the input pulley and back out the setscrew (41—Fig. T1-5) so the gearshift lever (43) can be removed.

Clean the exposed ends of axles and remove any burrs near the keyway edges. Unbolt the left transmission case and lift it off over the axle. Differential assembly and both axles can now be lifted out and set aside for later disassembly.

Pull out the spline shaft (32), low-reverse gear (31) and second-third gear (27). Lift out the cluster/brake shaft (36) with the cluster gear (38) and reduction gear (39). Remove the reverse idler gear (34) and idler shaft (33).

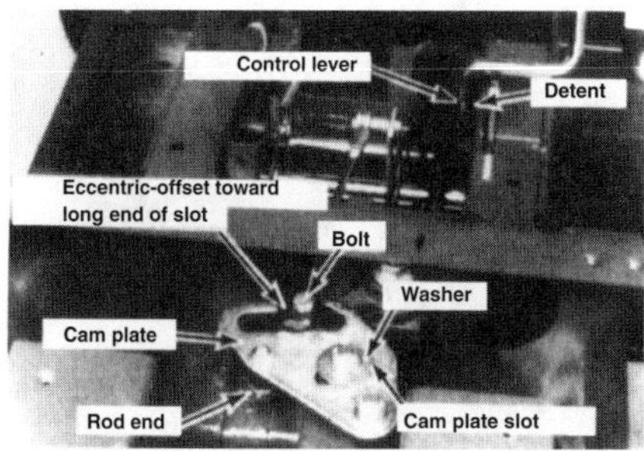

Fig. T1-6—View of neutral position adjustment points on Models 312-H, 314-H, 416-H and 520-H.

The first and reverse gear shift rail (26) and first shift fork should be removed using caution so the stop balls (4) are not dropped and lost as they are disengaged from the shift rail detents. The balls, spring (1) and guide pin (2) may be caught by holding a free hand over the case opening.

Remove the second and third gear (rear) shift rail (25) and fork. Remove the output gear drive set (15 and 14). Back out the detent bolt (60) and withdraw the input shaft (23) that carries the input gear and spline (22) and the range sliding gear (20). When moving these gears, watch for the stop spring (59) and detent ball (58) when the range shift fork (61) is dislodged. Remove the range cluster gear (16) and its shaft (18).

Disassemble the differential assembly by unbolting the through-bolts so the end caps (51 and 54) can be separated from the ring gear (53). Remove the differential pinions (54).

NOTE: Models equipped with a limited slip differential or spur gear differential will vary in construction. However, after removal of through-bolts, units may be disassembled.

After snap rings (50) have been removed, the axle shafts (49) can be pulled from the internal splines of the axle gears (52) and out of the end caps.

Inspect all parts for damage. Reassemble by reversing the disassembly procedure.

HYDROSTATIC TRANSMISSION (MODELS 312-H, 314-H, 416-H AND 520-H

MAINTENANCE

The hydrostatic transmission uses the oil contained in the final drive housing. Refer to the FINAL DRIVE section for recommended oil and oil change intervals.

NEUTRAL ADJUSTMENT

Operate the tractor until the transmission oil is at normal operating temperature. Raise and support the rear of the tractor so the wheels are off ground.

CAUTION: Use care when working near rotating parts.

Start and run the engine. Move the motion control lever to the forward position. Fully depress and release the brake pedal. The transmission should return to neutral and wheels should not rotate.

If the wheels continue to turn, loosen the bolt shown in Fig. T1-6 and turn the eccentric so the tires just stop rotating. Continue turning the eccentric until the wheels just begin to rotate in the opposite direction. Set the eccentric at midway position between these two points. Tighten the bolt and recheck the neutral position.

REMOVAL AND INSTALLATION

To remove the hydrostatic transmission, first remove the mower deck. Remove the seat, rear fender and control cover plate. Support the rear of the tractor. Drain the oil from the final drive housing. Remove the rear wheels.

Shut off the fuel and disconnect the fuel line. Unbolt the oil filter base. Remove the tube and bracket from the top of the final drive housing. Remove the two bolts securing the seat support bracket, and remove the fuel tank and seat support as an assembly.

Remove the transmission cooling fan and disengage the drive belt from the transmission pulley. Disconnect the speed control rod from the cam plate. Disconnect the hydraulic hoses. Unbolt and remove the transmission from the final drive housing.

Install by reversing the removal procedure. Tighten the transmission mounting screws to 30-35 ft.-lb. (41-47 N·m). Perform the neutral adjustment as previously described.

OVERHAUL

Models 312-H, 314-H, 416-H and 520-H are equipped with an Eaton 11 hydrostatic transmission. Refer to the appropriate Eaton section in the HYDROSTATIC TRANSMISSION service section for overhaul information.

FINAL DRIVE (MODELS 312-H, 314-H, 416-H AND 520-H)

MAINTENANCE

The final drive housing contains the oil that is used in the final drive, hydrostatic transmission and hydraulic system. A spin-on filter cleans the oil.

Maintain the oil level at the full mark on the dipstick. Recommended oil is SAE 10-30 oil. Oil and filter should be changed after every 100 hours of operation.

REMOVAL AND INSTALLATION

Remove the hydrostatic transmission as previously described. Disconnect any remaining hydraulic lines. Unscrew the final drive mounting bolts and remove final drive.

Reverse the removal procedure to install the final drive.

OVERHAUL

To disassemble the final drive, remove the axle hubs. Remove burrs and corrosion from the axle shaft. Remove the brake drum and remove burrs and corrosion from brake shaft. Remove eight retaining screws and lift off the left case half. A soft mallet may be used to break the gasket seal.

Withdraw the pinion shaft (17—Fig. T1-7) and the reduction gear (16), the brake shaft (6) and the gears (4 and 5), and the differential assembly from right case half (2).

Remove the axle seals (8) and the brake shaft seal (10). New seals are not installed until after transaxle is reassembled.

Inspect the bearings in the case halves and replace when as needed. Axle needle bearings (9) can be driven out from inside the case. All other bearings should be driven out from outside the case.

To remove the upper bearing in the right case, use a $\frac{1}{4}$-inch punch through the small opening behind the bearing.

The axle needle bearings (9) should be pressed in from the outside. All other bearings are pressed in from inside the case. All bearings should be flush with the machined surface on the inside of the case.

To disassemble the differential, remove the four bolts and separate the case halves (19—Fig. T1-7). Remove the pinion gears (21) and ring gear (22). Remove the snap rings (24), and separate the axles (18 and 23) from the end caps (19) and gears (20).

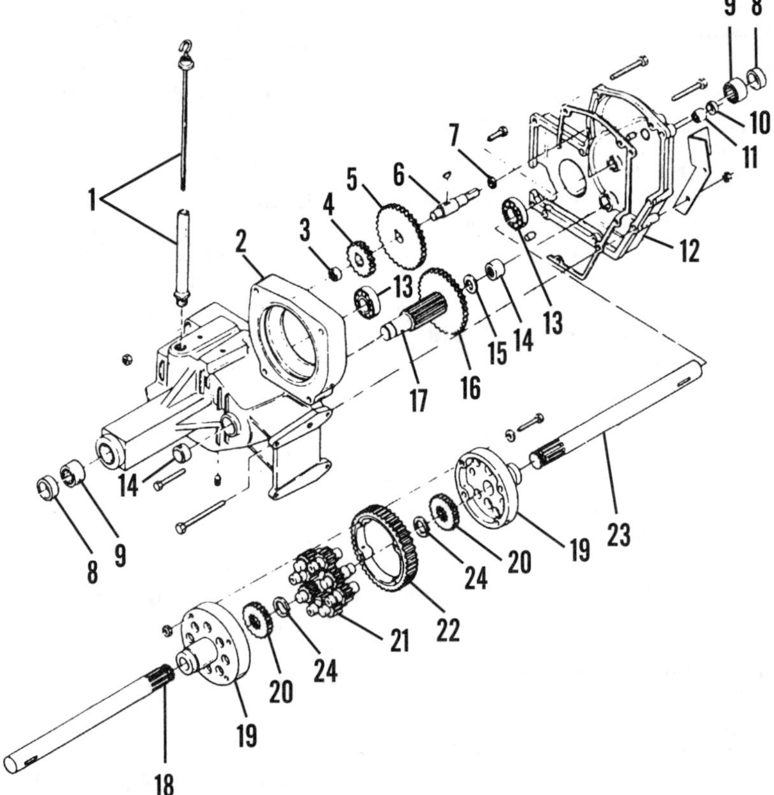

Fig. T1-7—Exploded view of final drive used on Models 312-H, 314-H, 416-H and 520-H.

1. Dipstick and filler tube
2. Case half (right)
3. Needle bearing
4. Gear
5. Gear
6. Brake shaft
7. Thrust washer
8. Axle seal
9. Needle bearing
10. Seal
11. Needle bearing
12. Case half (left)
13. Ball bearing
14. Needle bearing
15. Thrust washer
16. Reduction gear
17. Pinion gear
18. Axle (right)
19. End caps
20. Axle gears
21. Pinion gears
22. Ring gear
23. Axle (left)
24. Snap rings

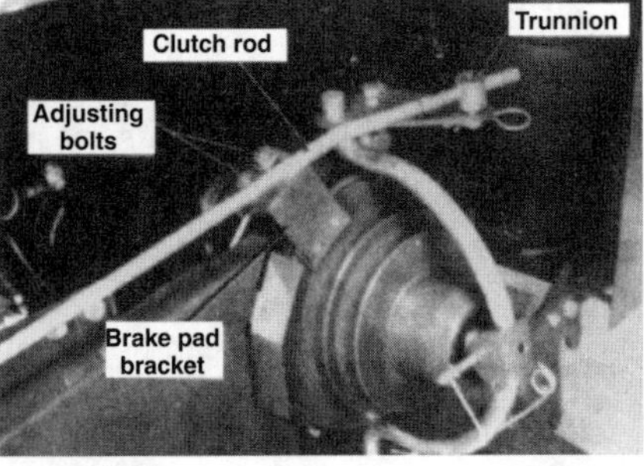

Fig. T1-8—View showing PTO linkage adjustment. Refer to text.

Clean and inspect all parts and replace when needed.

To reassemble, reverse the disassembly procedure while noting the following special instructions. The reduction gear (16) is a press fit on the pinion shaft (17). Be sure the differential pinions (21) are installed in the opposite directions (teeth up, teeth down, teeth up, etc.). Be sure the beveled edge of the axle gears face the end cap. Use new high-tensile nuts and grade 8 bolts when reassembling the differential, making sure the hardened washers are under the bolt heads and the nuts are on the same side as the long axle. Tighten the bolts to 30-35 ft.-lb. (41-47 N·m). Tighten the case retaining bolts to 30-35 ft.-lb. (41-47 N·m).

After assembling the case, install the new oil seals. Lubricate the seals with oil and protect from nicks. Use a suitable seal driver to install the seals flush with the outside of the case.

POWER TAKE-OFF (PTO)

MAINTENANCE

Periodically check the condition of the PTO drive belt and lubricate the pivots points on the linkage with SAE 30 oil.

ADJUSTMENT

If clutch slippage occurs, turn the trunnion (Fig. T1-8) farther onto the clutch rod until slippage ceases.

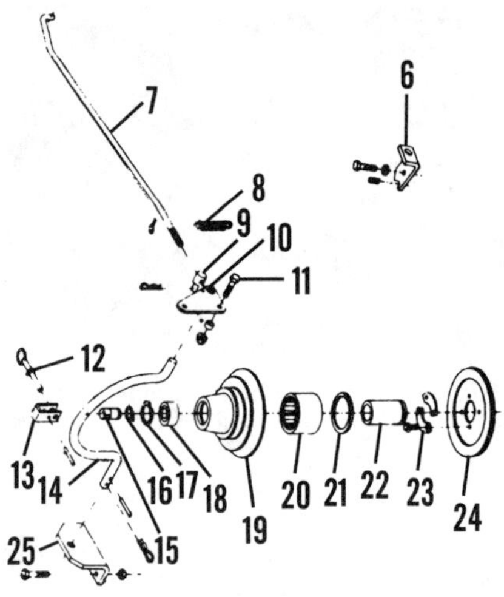

Fig. T1-9—Exploded view of manual PTO clutch assembly.

1. Lever
2. Spacer
3. Bushing (2)
4. Washer
5. E-ring
6. Bracket
7. Clutch rod
8. Spring
9. Trunnion
10. Plate
11. Pivot bolt
12. Pin
13. Clevis
14. Housing rod
15. Clutch shaft
16. Snap ring
17. Snap ring
18. Ball bearing
19. Pulley and housing
20. Bearing
21. Seal
22. Bearing race
23. Bearing race retainer (2)
24. Clutch plate
25. Support

To adjust the PTO clutch brake, engage the PTO clutch and loosen the two bolts holding the brake pad bracket to the support bracket. Place a 0.012 inch (0.3 mm) feeler gauge between the brake pad and the clutch pulley. Hold the brake pad against the feeler gauge and pulley and tighten the two brake bracket bolts. Remove the feeler gauge and check the PTO clutch for proper operation.

OVERHAUL

Disconnect the trunnion (9—Fig. T1-9) from the plate (10). Disconnect the pin (12) from the clevis (13). Press inward on the pulley assembly (19) and swing the housing rod (14) rearward so the drive belts can be removed. Remove the snap rings (16 and 17).

Note the sequence of parts and continue clutch disassembly. The clutch plate (24) will separate from the engine

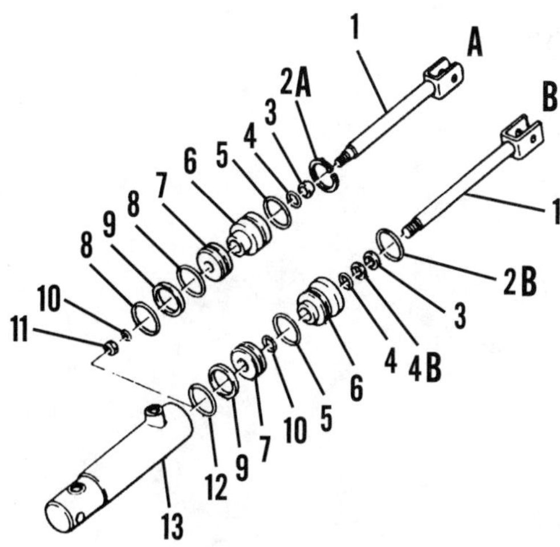

Fig. T1-10—Exploded view of two styles of hydraulic lift cylinders used on some models.

1. Piston rod
2A. Snap ring
2B. Wire retaining ring
3. Wiper
4A. O-ring
4B. Backup ring
5. O-ring
6. Rod guide bushing
7. Piston
8. Backup rings
9. Seal ring
10. O-ring
11. Retaining nut
12. O-ring
13. Cylinder tube

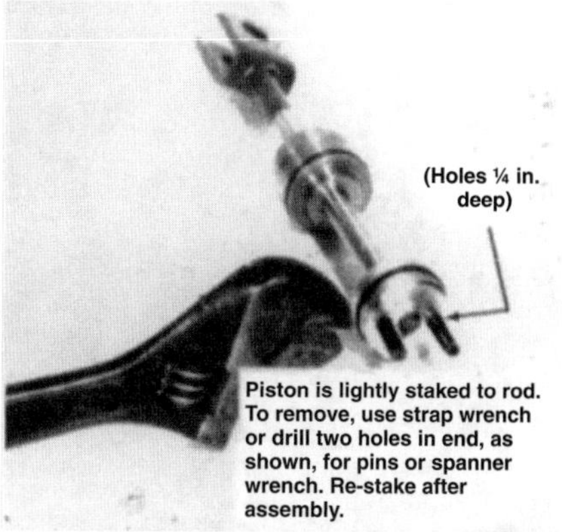

pulley when the bearing race retainers (23) are unbolted.

Reassemble by reversing the disassembly procedure.

HYDRAULIC SYSTEM (MODELS 312-H, 314-H, 416-H, AND 520-H)

MAINTENANCE

The hydraulic system uses oil contained in the final drive housing. Refer to the FINAL DRIVE section for recommended oil and oil change intervals.

CONTROL VALVE OVERHAUL

Clean the control valve before disconnecting the hydraulic hoses and removing the valve. A repair kit is available. Exercise care when handling parts to prevent damage.

LIFT CYLINDER OVERHAUL

To disassemble the cylinder, refer to Fig. T1-10 and remove the snap ring (2A) or wire retaining ring (2B) from the cylinder tube. Withdraw the cylinder tube from the piston and rod assembly.

On the A-style cylinder, unscrew the retaining nut (11) and withdraw the piston (7) and guide (6).

On the B-style cylinder, the piston is threaded to the rod and lightly staked. To remove the piston, use a strap wrench or drill two holes 1/4-inch (6 mm) deep in the end of the piston for a spanner wrench or pins as shown in Fig. T1-11. Be careful not to mar the piston or piston rod. Remove and discard all O-rings and seals.

Reassemble by reversing the disassembly procedure. Lubricate all parts with clean oil prior to assembly. Be careful not to cut the O-rings during installation. Be sure the rod guide bushing is seated against the retaining ring.

(Holes 1/4 in. deep)

Piston is lightly staked to rod. To remove, use strap wrench or drill two holes in end, as shown, for pins or spanner wrench. Re-stake after assembly.

Fig. T1-11—On "B" style cylinder (Fig. T1-10), remove piston as shown. Be careful not to mar piston or rod surfaces.

NOTES

YARDMAN

450 and 472 Series

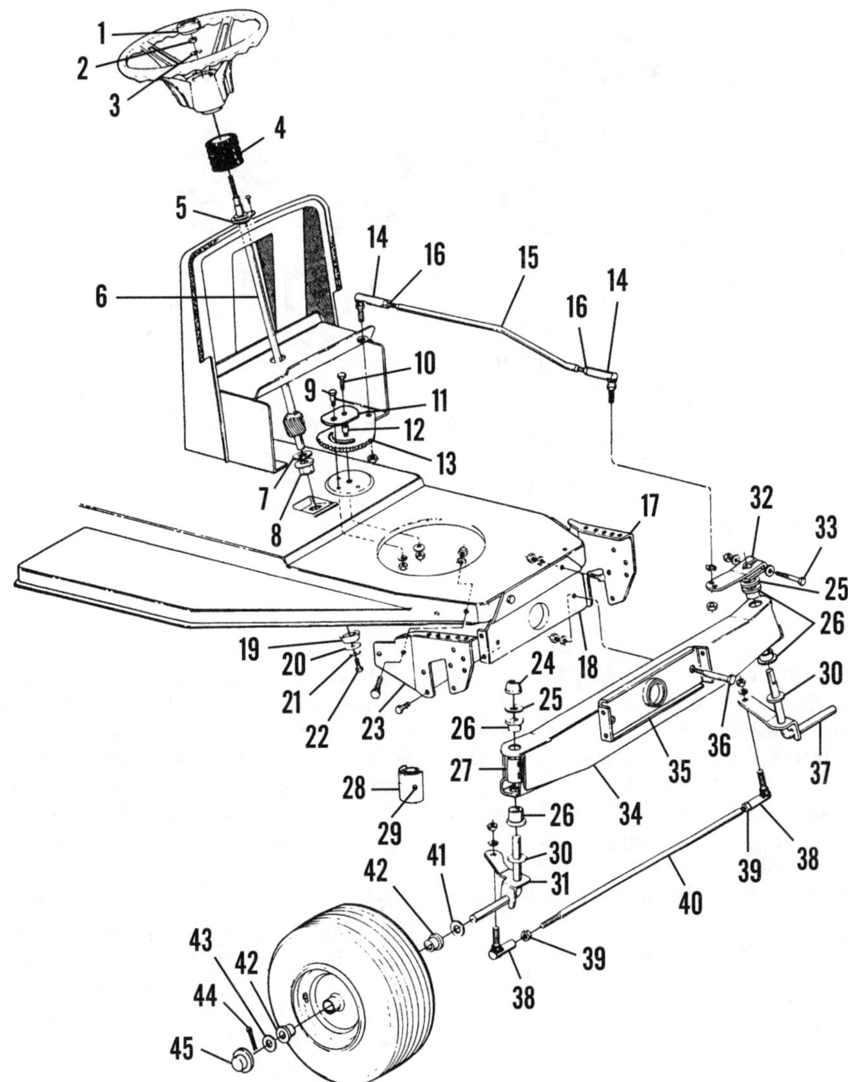

Fig. Y1-1—Exploded view of front axle and steering system.

1. Cap
2. Nut
3. Belleville washer
4. Bellow
5. Flange bearing
6. Steering shaft
7. Washer
8. Flange bushing
9. Shoulder bolt
10. Screw
11. Retainer plate
12. Spacer
13. Sector gear
14. Rod end
15. Drag link
16. Jam nut
17. Left side plate
18. Rear axle pivot bracket
19. Spacer
20. Washer
21. Lockwasher
22. Screw
23. Right side plate
24. Push cap
25. Washer
26. Flange bushings
27. Plastic tube
28. End cap
29. Grease fitting
30. Washer
31. Spindle (right)
32. Steering arm
33. Clamp bolt
34. Axle main member
35. Front axle pivot bracket
36. Pivot stop bolt
37. Spindle (left)
38. Rod end
39. Jam nut
40. Tie rod
41. Washer
42. Wheel bearings
43. Washer
44. Cotter pin
45. Hub cap

Due to the numerous number of Yardman models and the wide variety of engines installed, an accurate cross-reference and specification table is not available. Determine the manufacturer and model number of the engine being serviced and refer to the appropriate engine section in the rear of this manual for service information.

FRONT AXLE AND STEERING SYSTEM

MAINTENANCE

Lubricate the steering spindles and steering gear periodically with a lithium based, multipurpose grease. Clean away excess grease.

STEERING SPINDLES

To remove the steering spindles (31 and 37—Fig. Y1-1), raise and support the front of the tractor. Remove the front wheels.

Detach the tie rod (40) and drag link (15) from the steering spindle or steering arm. Detach the steering arm (32) from the upper end of the left spindle (37) Remove the cap (24) from the right spindle (31). Pull the spindle down out of axle main member.

Inspect all parts for wear and damage. New spindle bushings (26) are available for service.

Reinstall by reversing the removal procedure. Apply lithium based, multipurpose grease to the bushings before installing the spindles. Inject grease into the grease fitting after assembly.

TIE ROD AND TOE-IN

Some models are equipped with an adjustable tie rod (40—Fig. Y1-1). Inspect the ball joints (38) for excessive wear and looseness and replace if needed.

Adjust the length of the tie rod to obtain front wheel toe-in of 1/8 inch (3.2 mm). Secure the tie rod ends with jam nuts.

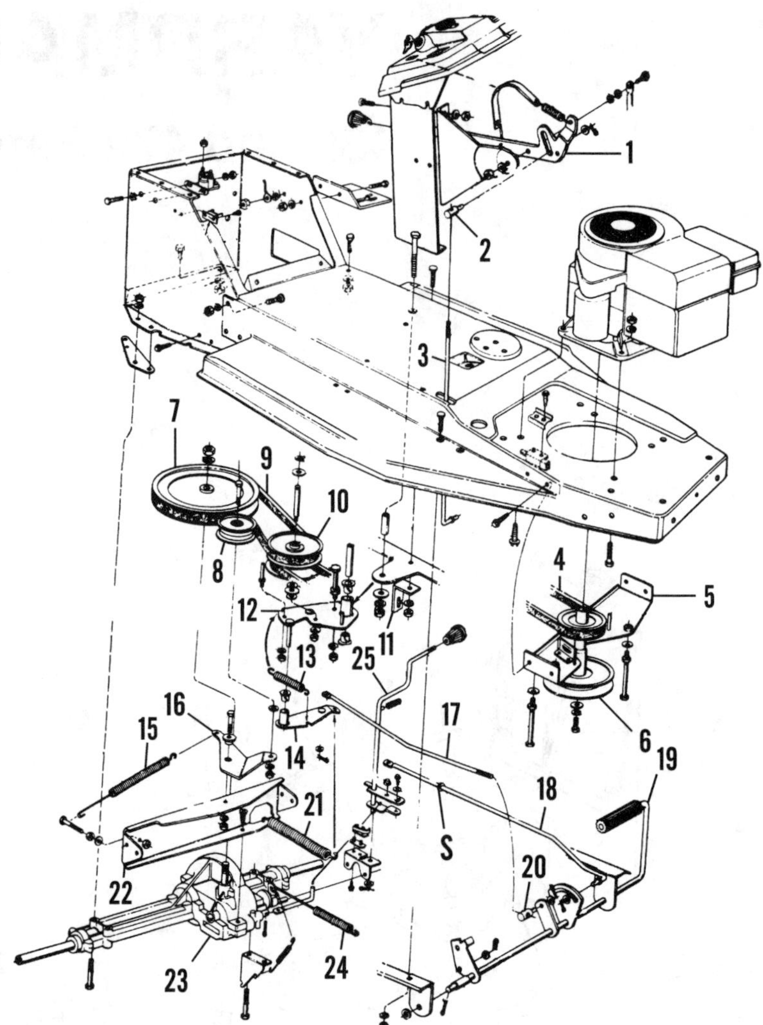

Fig. Y1-2—Exploded view of variable speed drive system.

1. Speed control lever
2. Ferrule
3. Speed control rod
4. Front drive belt
5. Pulley guard
6. Engine pulley
7. Transaxle pulley
8. Idler pulley
9. Rear drive belt
10. Variable speed pulley assy.
11. Rod bracket
12. Variable speed bracket
13. Spring
14. Variable speed torque bracket
15. Spring
16. Idler bracket
17. Speed control rod
18. Brake rod
19. Clutch/brake pedal
20. Ferrule
21. Tension spring
22. Transaxle support bracket
23. Transaxle
24. Brake spring
25. Shift rod

AXLE MAIN MEMBER REMOVAL AND INSTALLATION

To remove the axle main member (34—Fig. Y1-1), raise and support the front of the tractor frame and remove the front wheels. Disconnect the drag link (15) from the steering arm (32). Disconnect the tie rod (40) from both spindles.

Detach the steering arm (32) from the left spindle and withdraw the spindle. Remove the cap (24) from the left spindle and withdraw the spindle.

Support the axle main member (34), remove the rear (18) and front (35) pivot brackets and remove the axle from the tractor.

Install by reversing the removal procedure.

STEERING GEAR REMOVAL AND INSTALLATION

To remove the steering gears, raise and support the hood. Disconnect the battery cables.

Remove the steering wheel cap (1—Fig. Y1-1), retaining nut (2) and Belleville washer (3), then lift off the steering wheel and bellow (4). Remove the retaining screw from the steering shaft flange bushing (5) and remove the bushing from the shaft.

Disconnect the drag link (15) from the sector gear (13). Remove the mounting bolt and shoulder bolt (9) from the sector retainer plate (11) and withdraw the sector gear.

Remove the retaining screw (22) from the lower end of the steering shaft (6) and remove the steering shaft, thrust washer (7) and bushing (8).

Inspect all parts for damage and replace when necessary. Reinstall by reversing the removal procedure. Lubricate the flange bushings with SAE 30 oil. Apply a light coat of multipurpose grease to the teeth of the steering gears.

ENGINE

REMOVAL AND INSTALLATION

Remove the mower deck if so equipped. Remove the hood, grille brace, or side panels, and grille. Disconnect the battery cables and starter wires. Identify and disconnect all necessary electrical connections from the engine. Disconnect the fuel line from the carburetor. Disconnect choke and throttle control cables from the engine.

Remove the belt guide (5—Fig. Y1-2). Disconnect the spring from the clutch idler bracket to relieve the tension on the traction drive belt. Work the drive belts off the engine pulleys. Remove the muffler heat shield, if so equipped. Remove the engine mounting bolts and lift the engine from the tractor.

Install by reversing the removal procedure.

OVERHAUL

Refer to the appropriate engine section in this manual for tune-up specifications, engine overhaul procedures and engine maintenance.

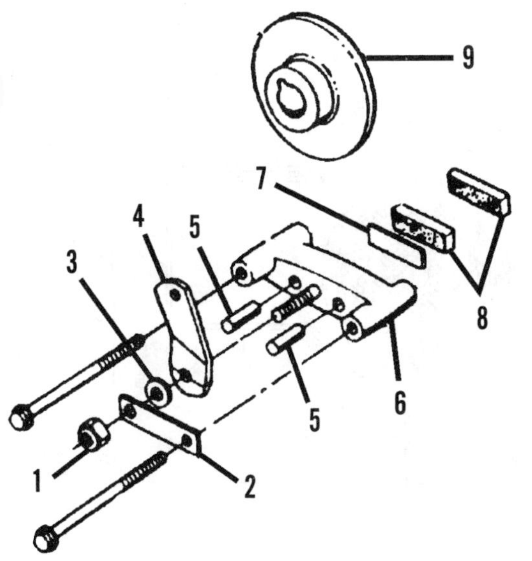

Fig. Y1-3—Exploded view of disc brake.

1. Adjusting nut
2. Bracket
3. Washer
4. Brake lever
5. Actuating pins
6. Brake pad holder
7. Back-up plate
8. Brake pads
9. Brake disc

To remove the front drive belt (4), first remove the rear drive belt as outlined above. Unbolt and remove the engine pulley belt guard (5). Slip the drive belt off the engine pulley and remove it from the variable speed pulley.

Reverse the removal procedure to install the new belt. Be sure that the belt is not twisted and that it is positioned inside all the belt guides.

CLUTCH AND BRAKE ADJUSTMENT

A continuously variable drive pulley is used on these models. Depressing the clutch/brake pedal part way disengages the clutch. Depressing the pedal all the way down disengages the clutch and engages the disc brake.

To adjust the clutch and speed control linkage, first adjust the speed control lever linkage as follows: Push the clutch/brake pedal forward until there is $\frac{1}{8}$ to $\frac{1}{4}$ inch (3.2-6.3 mm) clearance between the stop (S—Fig. Y1-2) on the brake rod (18) and the variable speed pulley bracket (11) and hold the pedal in this position.

Position the speed control shift lever (1) in the parking brake position. Remove the hairpin clip from the speed control rod ferrule (2), and adjust the ferrule on the rod so the upper end of the rod (3) contacts the bottom of the slot in the speed shift lever (1). Reinstall the hairpin clip.

Adjust the speed control link (17) to obtain the correct neutral adjustment as follows: Place the transmission shift lever in the neutral position and start the engine. Move the speed control lever (1) to the full speed position. Release the clutch/brake pedal completely, then fully depress the pedal and hold it in this position.

Shut off the engine, and after the engine completely stops, release the clutch/brake pedal. Move the speed control lever to the first position. Disconnect the speed control link (17) from the variable speed torque bracket (14). Move the clutch/brake pedal as far up as it will go. While holding the pedal in this position, thread the speed control link in or out of the ferrule (20) until the rod lines up with the hole in the torque bracket. Install the cotter pin to secure the speed control link to the torque bracket.

The disc brake is located on the left side of the final drive housing. To adjust the brake, remove the cotter pin and adjust the castle nut (1—Fig. Y1-3) so the brake starts to engage when the brake lever (4) is $\frac{1}{4}$ to $\frac{5}{16}$ inch (6.4-7.9 mm) away from the axle housing. Make sure that the brake does not drag when the pedal is released.

TRACTION DRIVE BELTS REMOVAL AND INSTALLATION

To remove the rear drive belt (9—Fig. Y1-2), first remove the mower deck from underneath the tractor. Start the engine. Place the shift lever in NEUTRAL and the speed control lever in high speed position, then shut off the engine.

Disconnect the tension spring (21) from the final drive support bracket (22). Note that a hole is provided in the rear of the frame for access to the tension spring. Disconnect the small spring (15) from the right side of frame. Move the brake rod (18) out of the variable speed pulley bracket (11). Loosen, but do not remove, the bolts securing the variable speed pulley bracket. Work the drive belt off the top of the variable speed pulley (10), then remove the belt from the final drive pulley (7) and idler pulley (8).

Reverse the removal procedure to install the new belt. The clutch idler pulley is spring loaded and no adjustment is necessary.

FINAL DRIVE

LUBRICATION

Final drive is lubricated with grease at the factory and should not require additional lubrication. Capacity is 10 ounces (296 mL) of lithium-based, multipurpose grease.

REMOVAL AND INSTALLATION

To remove the final drive assembly, first remove the mower deck from underneath the tractor. Remove the traction drive belt from the final drive pulley as previously outlined. Disconnect the shift linkage and brake linkage at final drive.

Support the rear of tractor and remove all fasteners securing the final drive to the frame. Raise the rear of tractor and roll the final drive assembly out from under the tractor.

Install by reversing the removal procedure. Adjust the brake as previously outlined.

OVERHAUL

All models are equipped with a Yardman final drive. Refer to the YARDMAN section in the FINAL DRIVE section of this manual for overhaul procedure.

SAFETY INTERLOCK SYSTEM

Before the engine will start, the key must be turned on and both of the safety switches must be activated. One switch (6—Fig. Y1-4) is activated when the clutch/brake pedal is depressed and the other (6) is activated when the blade is disengaged. When the two safety switches are activated, the circuit is completed between the battery and the starter solenoid, allowing the starter motor to crank the engine.

Some models are equipped with a seat safety switch (3) and a reverse safety switch (5). However, these switches are not involved in the starting circuit. The seat safety switch is designed to stop the engine if the operator leaves the seat with the blades or PTO

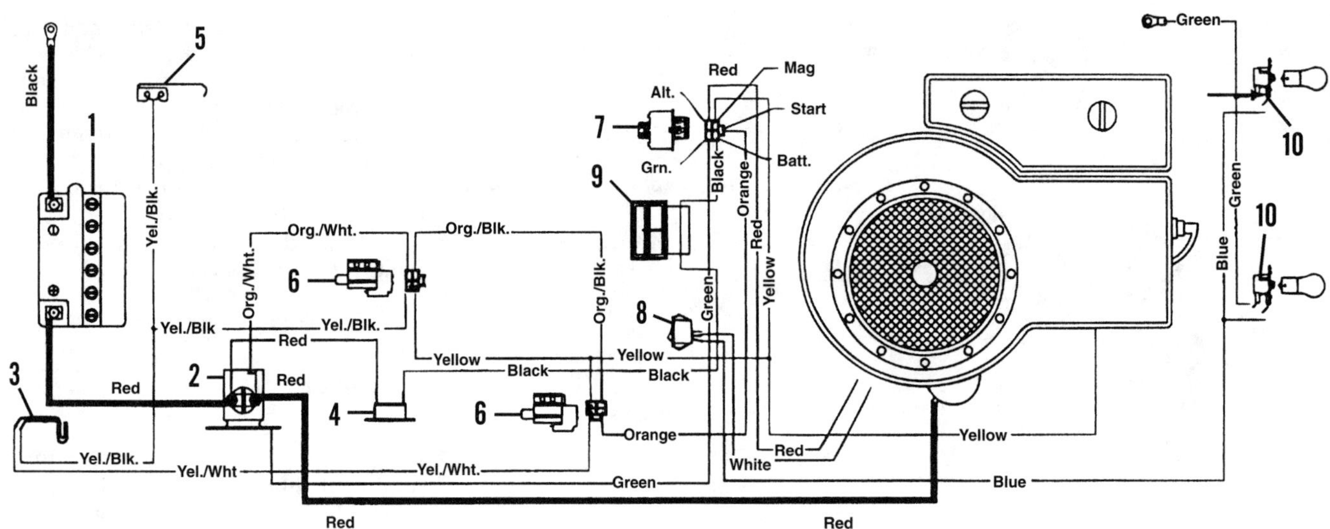

Fig. Y1-4—Wiring diagram for Series 450-470 models.

1. Battery
2. Solenoid
3. Seat switch
4. Circuit breaker
5. Spring switch
6. Safety switches
7. Ignition switch
8. Light switch
9. Ammeter (optional)
10. Headlight

engaged. The blades must be in the disengaged position when shifting into reverse or the engine will shut off.

To test the two safety start switches, first check the two switches to see if the switch plungers are depressed a minimum of 1/8 inch (3 mm) when the blade is disengaged and the clutch/brake pedal is depressed. If the switch plunger is correctly depressed, use a continuity checker to determine if there is continuity across the switch terminals when the switches are activated (plunger depressed). If continuity is not indicated when the plunger is depressed, replace the switch.

To check for correct operation of the seat safety switch, start the engine and set the parking brake. Place the shift lever in NEUTRAL and engage the PTO or blades. Raise up off the seat. The engine should stop running.

WIRING DIAGRAM

The wiring diagram illustrated in Fig. Y1-4) is typical of all models.

YARDMAN

600-700-800 Series (2-Wheel Steering)

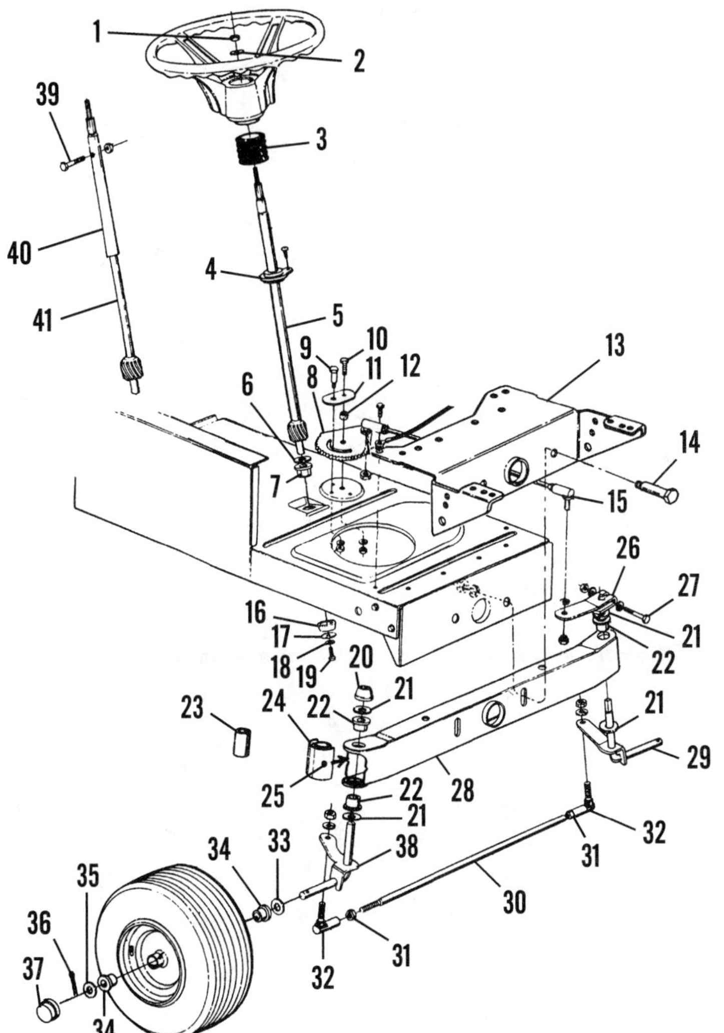

Fig. Y2-1—Exploded view of front axle and steering system used on 600 and 700 series tractors.

1. Nut
2. Belleville washer
3. Bellow
4. Flange bearing
5. Steering shaft
6. Washer
7. Flange bushing
8. Sector gear
9. Shoulder bolt
10. Screw
11. Retainer plate
12. Spacer
13. Axle pivot bracket
14. Pivot stop bolt
15. Drag link
16. Spacer
17. Washer
18. Lockwasher
19. Screw
20. Push cap
21. Washer
22. Flange bushings
23. Plastic tube
24. End cap
25. Grease fitting
26. Steering arm
27. Clamp bolt
28. Axle main member
29. Spindle (left)
30. Tie rod
31. Jam nut
32. Rod end
33. Washer
34. Wheel bearings
35. Washer
36. Cotter pin
37. Hub cap
38. Spindle (right)
39. Bolt
40. Upper steering shaft
41. Lower steering shaft

Due to the numerous number of Yardman models and the wide variety of engines installed, an accurate cross-reference and specification table is not available. Determine the manufacturer and model number of the engine being serviced and refer to the appropriate engine section in the rear of this manual for service information.

FRONT AXLE AND STEERING SYSTEM

MAINTENANCE

On models equipped with a grease fitting at the end of the axle main member, periodically inject grease into the grease fitting. If not equipped with a grease fitting, lubricate the steering spindles periodically with lithium-based, multipurpose grease.

Periodically lubricate the steering gear with a lithium-based, multipurpose grease. Clean away excess grease.

STEERING SPINDLES

600 and 700 Series Remove and Reinstall

Raise and support the front of the tractor. Remove the front wheels. Detach the tie rod (30—Fig. Y2-1) from the spindles.

To remove the left spindle (29), detach the drag link (15) from the steering arm (26). Remove the clamp bolt (27) and separate the steering arm from the spindle. Lower the spindle from the axle.

To remove the right spindle (38), remove the retaining cap (20) and washer (21). Pull the spindle down out of the axle main member.

NOTE: On early models, a roll pin is used in place of the cap (20) to hold the spindle in the axle.

Inspect the parts for wear and damage. replace the spindle bushings (22—Fig. Y2-1) and/or spindles if excessive wear is evident.

Reinstall by reversing the removal procedure. Apply lithium-based, multipurpose grease to the bushings before installing the spindles. Inject grease into the grease fitting (25) after assembly.

800 Series
Remove and Reinstall

Raise and support the front of the tractor. Remove the front wheels. Detach the tie rod (30 or 31—Fig. Y2-2) from the spindles.

To remove the right spindle (38), disconnect the drag link (15) from the steering arm (26). Remove the clamp bolt (27) and detach the steering arm (26) from the upper end of the spindle. Remove the spindle and washers from the axle (28).

To remove the left spindle (29), remove the cap (20) and cotter pin (23) from the top of the spindle. Pull the spindle down out of the axle main member and remove the washers (21).

Inspect the parts for wear and damage. replace the spindle bushings (22) and/or spindles if excessive wear is evident.

Reinstall by reversing the removal procedure. Apply lithium based, multipurpose grease to the spindle bushings before installing the spindles. Inject grease into the grease fitting (25) after assembly.

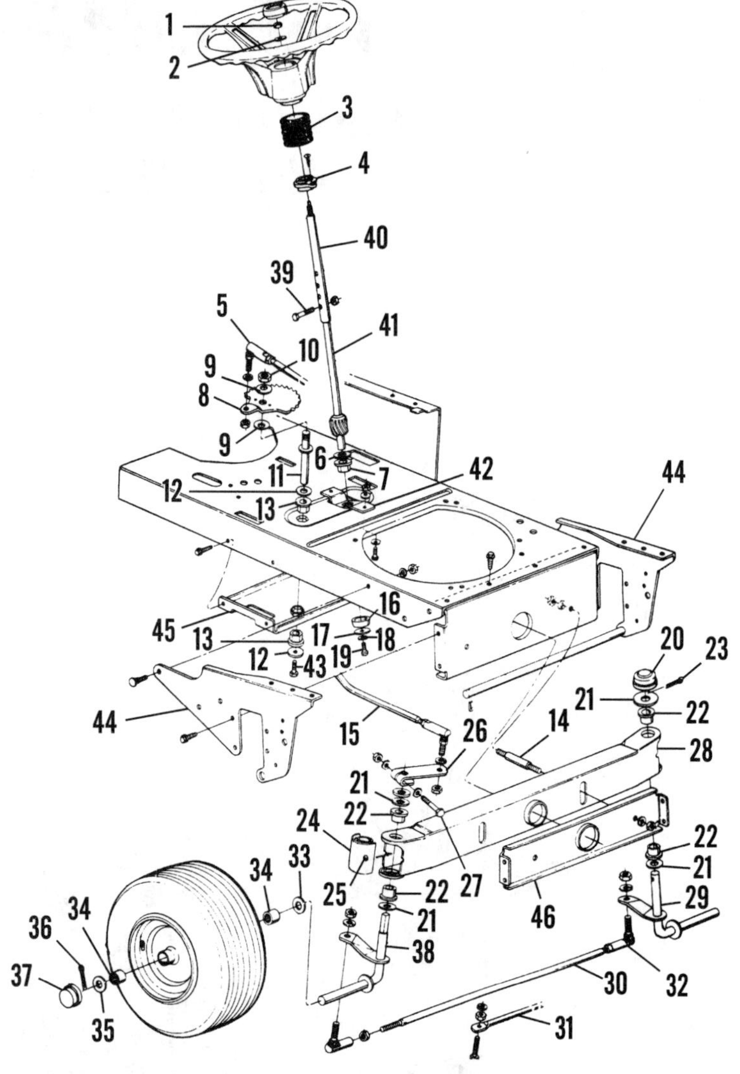

Fig. Y2-2—Exploded view of front axle and steering system used on 800 series tractors.

1. Nut
2. Belleville washer
3. Bellow
4. Flange bearing
5. Drag link end
6. Washer
7. Flange bushing
8. Sector gear
9. Belleville washer
10. Nut
11. Sector shaft
12. Washers
13. Flange bushings
14. Pivot stop bolt
15. Drag link
16. Spacer
17. Washer
18. Lockwasher
19. Screw
20. Push cap
21. Washer
22. Flange bushings
23. Cotter pin
24. End cap
25. Grease fitting
26. Steering arm
27. Clamp bolt
28. Axle main member
29. Spindle (left)
30. Adjustable tie rod
31. Non-adjustable tie rod
32. Rod end
33. Washer
34. Wheel bearings
35. Washer
36. Cotter pin
37. Hub cap
38. Spindle (right)
39. Bolt
40. Upper steering shaft
41. Lower steering shaft
42. Bearing retainer
43. Screw
44. Pivot bar assembly
45. Idler support bracket
46. Front pivot bracket

TIE ROD AND TOE-IN

Some models are equipped with an adjustable tie rod (30—Fig. Y2-1 or Fig. Y2-2). Inspect the ball joints (32) for excessive wear and looseness and replace if needed.

Adjust the length of the tie rod to obtain front wheel toe-in of $\frac{1}{8}$ inch (3.2 mm). Secure the tie rod ends with the jam nuts.

AXLE MAIN MEMBER REMOVAL AND INSTALLATION

600 and 700 Series

To remove the axle main member (28—Fig. Y2-1), raise and support the front of the tractor and remove the front wheels. Remove the hood and grille.

Remove the spindles as previously described. Unscrew the axle travel limiting bolts (14). Remove the screws attaching the pivot bracket (13) to the frame, and remove the bracket and axle.

Reassemble by reversing the removal procedure.

800 Series

To remove the axle main member (28—Fig. Y2-2), first detach the mower deck from the front pivot bracket (46). Raise and support the front of the tractor frame and remove the front wheels. Remove the hood and grille. Remove the heat shield and muffler.

Remove the spindles as previously described. Support the axle main member (28). Remove the retaining nuts from the studs (14) that limit the axle travel. Unbolt and remove the axle front pivot bracket (46). Lower the axle from the tractor.

Reinstall by reversing the removal procedure.

STEERING GEAR REMOVAL AND INSTALLATION

600 and 700 Series

To remove the steering gears, first remove the mower deck. Raise and support the hood. Disconnect the battery cables. Remove the fuel tank.

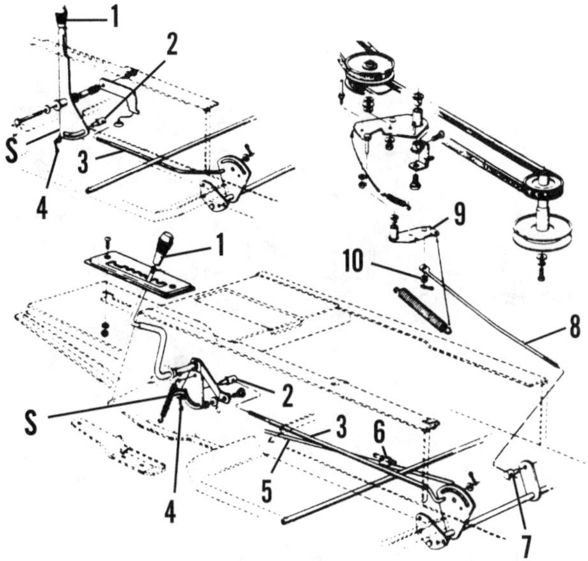

Fig. Y2-3—Exploded view of control linkage used on 600 and 700 series equipped with variable speed transmission.

1. Speed control lever
2. Ferrule
3. Speed control rod
4. Clip
5. Brake rod
6. Stop
7. Ferrule
8. Speed control link
9. Variable speed torque bracket
10. Cotter pin

Remove the steering wheel cap, retaining nut (1—Fig. Y2-1) and Belleville washer (2). Lift off the steering wheel and bellow (3). Remove the retaining screw from steering shaft flange bushing (4) and remove the bushing from the shaft.

Disconnect the drag link (15) from the sector gear (8). Remove the mounting bolt and shoulder bolt (9) from sector retainer plate (11) and withdraw the sector gear. Remove the retaining screw (19) from the lower end of the steering shaft (5) and remove the steering shaft, thrust washer (6) and bushing (7).

Inspect all parts for excessive wear or damage and replace as necessary. Reinstall by reversing the removal procedure. Lubricate flange bushings with SAE 30 oil. Apply light coat of multipurpose grease to teeth of steering gears.

800 Series

To remove the steering gear, first remove the mower deck from the tractor. Raise and support the hood. Disconnect the battery cables. Remove the fuel tank.

Remove the steering wheel cap, retaining nut (1—Fig. Y2-2) and Belleville washer (2). Lift off the steering wheel and bellow (3). Remove the retaining screw from the steering shaft flange bushing (4) and remove the bushing from the shaft.

Unscrew the steering shaft coupling bolt (39). Detach the drag link end (5) from the sector gear (8). Unscrew the retaining nut (10) and remove the sector gear (8) from the sector shaft (11). Unscrew the retaining screw (43) at the bottom of the sector shaft and remove the shaft (11), bushings (13) and washers (12).

Unscrew the retaining screw (19) at the bottom of steering shaft (41) and remove the washer (17) and spacer (16). Remove the retaining bolts from the lower bearing retainer (42). Move the lower steering shaft (41) up out of the retainer (42), remove the retainer and withdraw the steering shaft down out of tractor.

Reassemble by reversing the disassembly procedure.

ENGINE

REMOVE AND REINSTALL

Remove the hood, grille brace, or side panels, and grille. Disconnect the battery cables and starter wires. Identify and disconnect the electrical connections from the engine.

Disconnect the fuel line from the carburetor. Disconnect the choke and throttle control cables from the engine. Remove the drive belts from the engine pulleys. Remove the heat shield, if so equipped, and the muffler. Remove the engine mounting bolts and lift the engine from the tractor.

Reinstall by reversing the removal procedure.

OVERHAUL

Refer to the appropriate engine section in this manual for tune-up specifications, engine overhaul procedures and engine maintenance.

SPEED CONTROL LINKAGE

600 AND 700 SERIES EQUIPPED WITH VARIABLE SPEED TRANSMISSION

Some models are equipped with a continuously variable drive pulley that provides infinite travel speeds. Depressing the clutch/brake pedal partway disengages the clutch. Depressing the pedal all the way down disengages the clutch and engages the disc brake.

Adjustment

Before adjusting the clutch rod, adjust the brake as described in the BRAKE section. To adjust the clutch and speed control linkage, first adjust the speed control lever (1—Fig. Y2-3) as follows:

Push the clutch/brake pedal forward until the stop (6) on the brake rod (5) contacts the frame. While holding the pedal in this position, place the speed control lever (1) in the park position. The ferrule (2) on the speed control rod should contact the back end of the slot (S) of the speed control lever. If not, remove the cotter pin (4) and adjust the ferrule on the rod so it contacts the back end of the slot. Then lengthen the rod one additional turn.

Next, adjust the clutch rod (8) to obtain the correct neutral setting as follows: Start the engine and place the shift lever in the neutral position. Move the speed control lever (1) to the high-speed position. Release the clutch/brake pedal, then slowly depress the pedal to the fully down (park) position. Hold the pedal in the park position, stop the engine and after the engine stops, release the clutch/brake pedal.

Position the speed control lever as follows: On models with seven-speed selector, place the lever in the second-speed position. On models with six-speed selector, position and hold the lever between the first- and second-speed position. On models with five-speed selector, place the lever in first-speed position.

Detach the clutch rod from the torque bracket (9). Using light hand pressure, push the clutch/brake pedal rearward as far as possible and hold in this position. Thread the clutch rod (8) into or out of the ferrule (7) so the rod end fits easily onto the pin on the torque bracket (9), and reattach the rod end to the bracket.

800 SERIES EQUIPPED WITH VARIABLE SPEED TRANSMISSION

Some 800 series models are equipped with a continuously variable drive pulley that provides infinite travel speeds. Engine power is transferred through the variable speed transmission to either a single-speed or two-speed transaxle.

Depressing the clutch/brake pedal partway disengages the clutch. Depressing pedal all the way down disengages the clutch and engages the disc brake.

Adjustment

To adjust the speed control linkage, run the engine and position the shift lever in neutral position. Move the speed control lever to the seventh-speed position. Release the clutch/brake pedal, then slowly depress the pedal to the fully down (park) position. Hold the pedal in park position, stop the engine and after the engine stops, release the clutch/brake pedal.

Detach the rear speed control link (Fig. Y2-4) from the torque bracket. Move the speed control lever to the first-speed position. Detach the front speed control link (Fig. Y2-4) from the torque bracket. On 1990 models, position a 5/8 inch (16 mm) shim under the point on the bracket of the clutch/brake shaft as shown in Fig. Y2-4. On later models, position a 1½ inch (38 mm) shim under the point on the bracket of the clutch/brake shaft (Fig. Y2-4). Thread the front speed control link into or out of the ferrule so the rod end fits easily onto the pin on the torque bracket, and reattach the rod end to the torque bracket.

Using light hand pressure, push rear speed control link rearward as far as possible and hold in this position. Thread the rear speed control link into or out of its ferrule so the rod end fits easily onto the pin on the torque bracket. Rotate the link two additional turns clockwise (lengthen the link), and reattach the rod end to the torque bracket. Remove the shim.

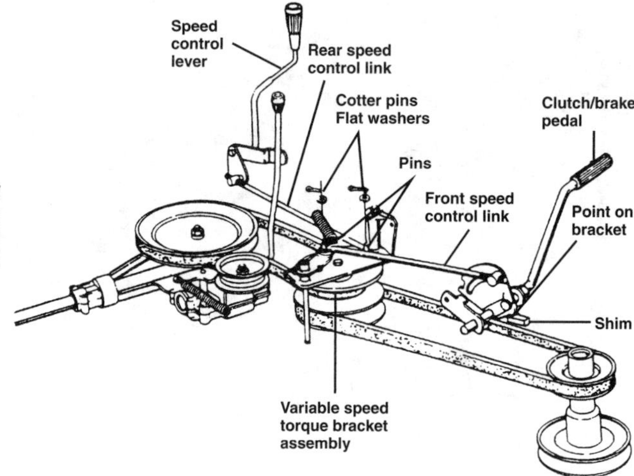

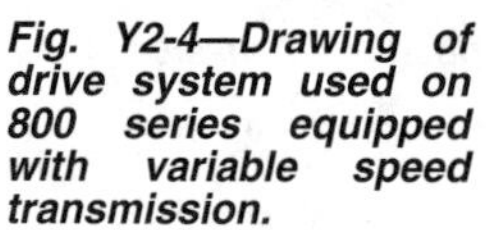
Fig. Y2-4—Drawing of drive system used on 800 series equipped with variable speed transmission.

DRIVE BELTS

NOTE: The tractor does not need to be tipped to remove the drive belts. If the tractor is tipped, remove the battery and drain the fuel tank or place a piece of plastic wrap over the neck of the fuel tank and screw on the cap to prevent leakage.

FRONT DRIVE BELT REMOVAL AND INSTALLATION

600-700 Series With Variable Speed Transmission

Without Electric PTO

Remove the mower deck. Remove the rear drive belt as described in the following section.

Position the lift lever in the disengaged position. Detach the spring (S—Fig. Y2-5) from the transmission support bracket. Raise and support the front of the tractor. Unscrew the belt guide bolts around the engine drive pulley. Detach the mower deck belt from the engine pulley. Remove the belt guard for the engine pulley.

Move the clutch/brake pedal to park position. Push the variable speed pulley (Fig. Y2-6) towards the front of the tractor and detach the traction belt from the engine pulley. If necessary, remove the belt guide pins. Move the clutch/brake pedal as needed to disengage the belt from the variable speed pulley.

Reverse the removal procedure to install the belt.

Equipped With Electric PTO

Remove the mower deck. Remove the rear drive belt as described in the following section.

Position the lift lever in the disengaged position. Detach the spring (S—Fig. Y2-5) from the transmission support bracket. Raise and support the front of the tractor. Disconnect the PTO clutch electrical connector. Remove the PTO torque bracket (Fig. Y2-7) and belt keeper assembly. Loosen the pin at the idler pulley and remove the PTO clutch.

Move the clutch/brake pedal to park position. Push the variable speed pulley (Fig. Y2-6) toward the right side of the tractor and detach the traction belt from the engine pulley. If necessary, remove the belt guide pins. Move the clutch/brake pedal as needed to disengage the belt from the variable speed pulley.

Reverse the removal procedure to install the belt.

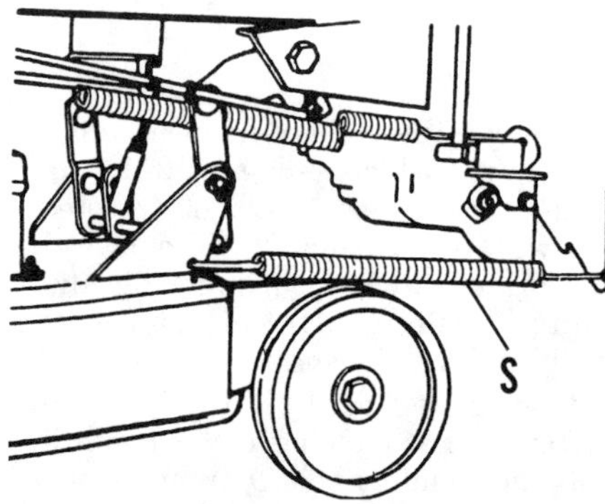

Fig. Y2-5—Detach the spring (S) from transmission support bracket to relieve tension on the front drive belt on 600 and 700 series with variable speed transmission and electric PTO.

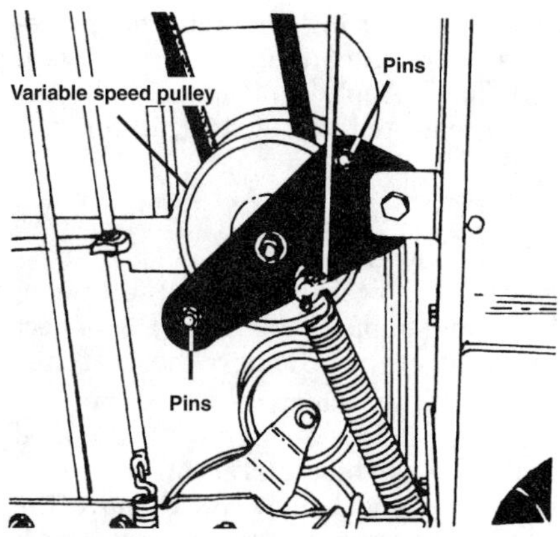

Fig. Y2-6—On Series 600 and 700 tractors with variable speed transmission, push forward on variable speed pulley and remove belt from engine pulley. It may be necessary to remove guide pins for access to the belt.

700-800 Series With Sundstrand Hydrostatic Transmission

To remove the belt, first remove the mower deck. Depress the

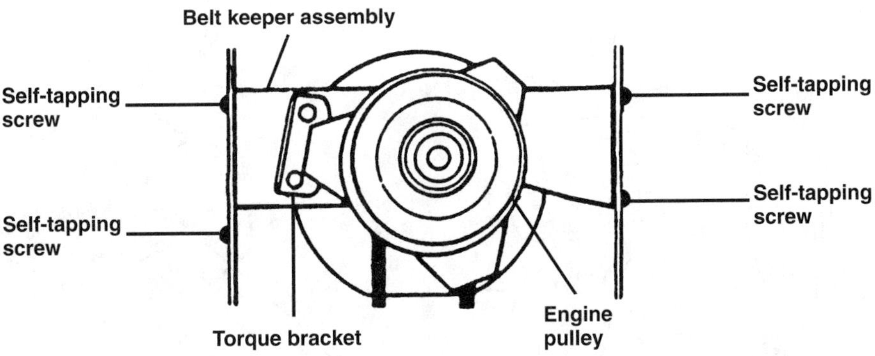

Fig. Y2-7—On Series 600 and 700 tractors with variable speed transmission and electric PTO, remove PTO torque bracket and belt keeper assembly to remove the front drive belt.

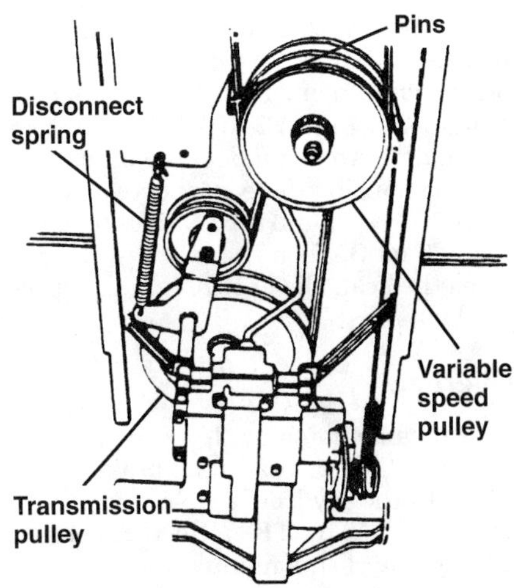

Fig. Y2-9—On 800 series tractors with variable speed transmission, detach the idler spring and remove the belt guide pins to remove the drive belts.

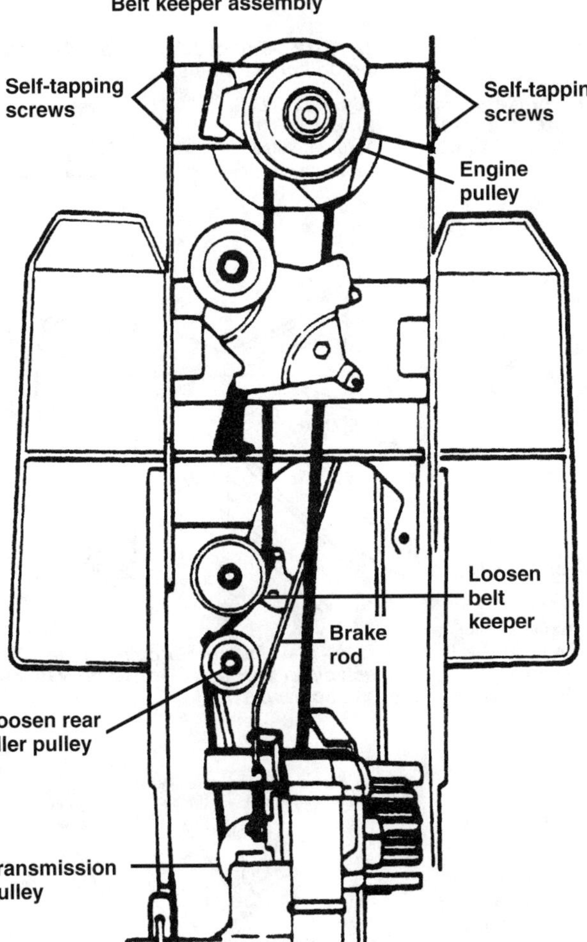

Fig. Y2-8—Drawing of drive belt on 700 and 800 series tractors with Sundstrand hydrostatic transmission. Refer to text for belt replacement procedure.

clutch/brake pedal and set the parking brake. Raise and support the front of the tractor.

Remove the mounting screws from the engine pulley belt guard, and move it forward out of the way. Remove the belt guard at the transmission pulley. Unscrew the hex bolt serving as a belt guide near the front idler pulley (Fig. Y2-8). Loosen the center bolt in the rear idler pulley and move the belt off both idler pulleys.

Detach the PTO clutch electrical connector. Work the belt out of the engine pulley onto the pulley hub. Lift the belt off the transmission pulley and over the fan, and then remove the belt from the engine pulley.

Block the tractor so it cannot move. Disengage the parking brake. Detach the brake rod from the clutch/brake pedal and pass the belt through the opening.

Reverse the removal procedure to reinstall the belt.

800 Series With Variable Speed Transmission

Remove the mower deck from the tractor. Depress the clutch/brake pedal and engage the parking brake. Raise and support the front of the tractor.

Remove the four screws attaching the engine pulley belt keeper to the frame. Move the belt keeper forward out of the way. Unscrew the belt guide pins around the variable speed pulley (Fig. Y2-9). Work the belt off the variable speed pulley and remove it from the engine pulley.

Reverse the removal procedure to install the belt.

REAR DRIVE BELT REMOVAL AND INSTALLATION

600-700-800 Series With Variable Speed Transmission

Remove the front drive belt as instructed in the previous section. Remove the transmission cover. Disconnect the idler pulley spring. Detach the speed control rod from variable speed pulley. Move the belt idler pulley away from the belt and move the belt over the idler pulley. Detach the belt from the variable speed pulley.

Reinstall belt by reversing removal procedure.

BRAKE

MODELS 600, 609, 690 AND 699

Adjustment

These models are equipped with a Hydro-Gear hydrostatic transaxle that is equipped with brake discs inside the transaxle housing. Check for correct brake adjustment by inserting a feeler gauge (F—Fig. Y2-10) between two brake discs through opening on underside of housing. The gap between the brake discs should be 0.015-0.025 inch (0.4-0.6 mm). Turn the nut (N) that retains the brake lever to obtain the specified gap.

Overhaul

Transaxle housing halves must be separated for access to the brake discs. Refer to the Hydro-Gear section in the HYDROSTATIC TRANSAXLE section at the rear of this manual.

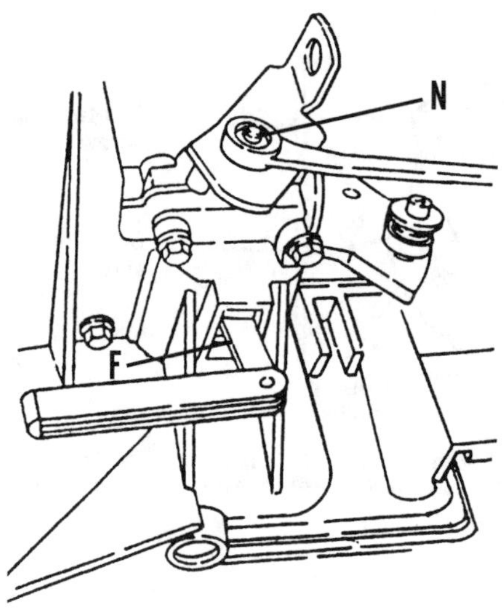

Fig. Y2-10—On Models 600, 609, 690 and 699, check for correct brake adjustment by inserting a feeler gauge (F) between two brake discs. Gap between brake discs should be 0.015-0.025 inch (0.4-0.6 mm). Rotate brake lever retaining nut (N) to obtain specified gap.

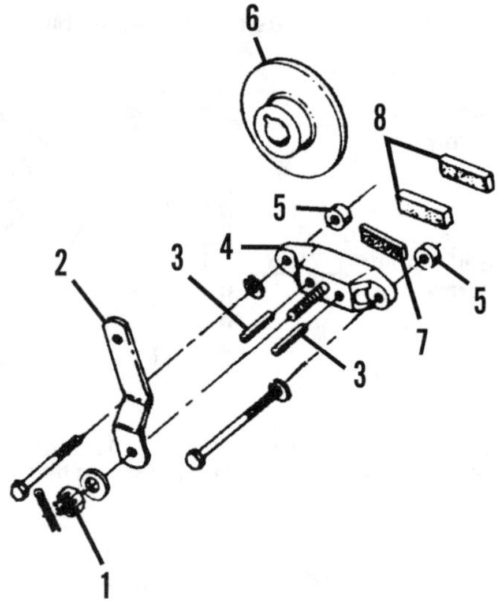

Fig. Y2-12—Exploded view of disc brake used on some models.

1. Adjusting nut
2. Brake lever
3. Actuating pins
4. Brake pad holder
5. Spacers
6. Brake disc
7. Back-up plate
8. Brake pads

ALL OTHER MODELS

Adjustment

This adjustment applies to the disc brakes equipped with a castle nut (1—Fig. Y2-11 or Y2-12). To adjust the disc brake, detach the cotter pin and turn the castle nut so that brake engagement begins when the brake lever is $\frac{1}{4}$-$\frac{5}{16}$ inch (6.4-7.9 mm) away from the axle housing. Reinstall the cotter pin.

Brake Pads

Refer to Figs. Y2-11 and Y2-12. Disconnect the brake linkage from the cam lever. Unbolt and remove the brake pad holder. Slide the brake disc off the transaxle shaft and remove the inner brake pad from the holder slot in the transaxle housing.

Replace worn or damaged parts as needed. Reassemble by reversing the disassembly procedure. Adjust as previously outlined.

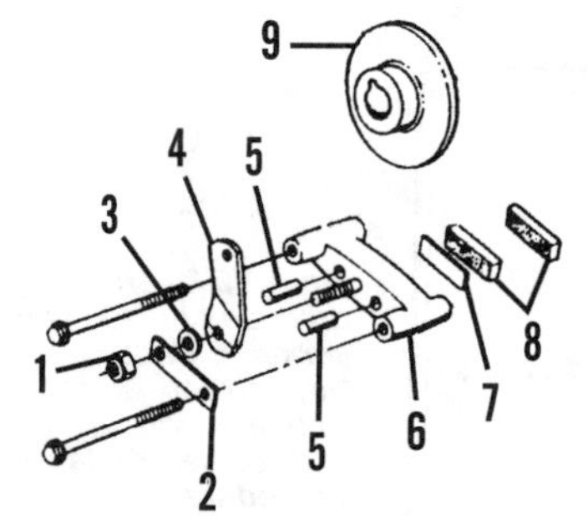

Fig. Y2-11—Exploded view of disc brake used on some models.

1. Adjusting nut
2. Bracket
3. Washer
4. Brake lever
5. Actuating pins
6. Brake pad holder
7. Back-up plate
8. Brake pads

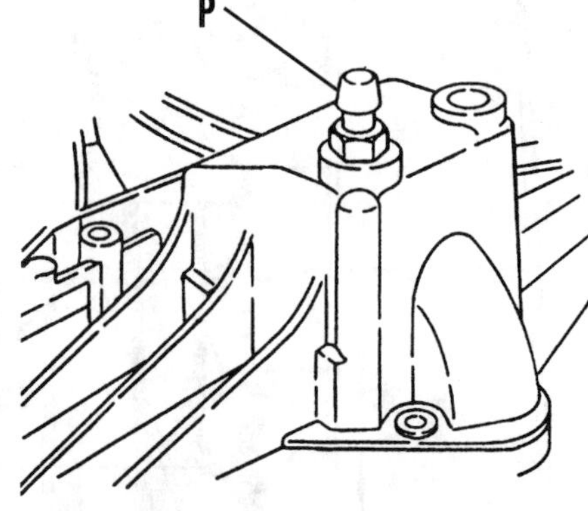

Fig. Y2-13—Unscrew breather plug (P) to check oil level or add oil on Hydro-Gear hydrostatic transaxle.

HYDROSTATIC TRANSAXLE

600 AND 800 SERIES EQUIPPED WITH HYDRO-GEAR HYDROSTATIC TRANSAXLE

Lubrication

Recommended oil is SAE 20W50 with an API rating of SG. To check or fill the transaxle, first clean the area around the breather plug (P—Fig. Y2-13), and then unscrew the breather plug. To check the oil level, measure from the boss surface to the oil. Oil level on Model 310-0500 transaxle should be 1.75-2.00 inches (44-51 mm) the boss surface. Oil level on Model 310-0750 transaxle should be 1.00-1.25 inches (25-32 mm) below the boss.

Linkage Adjustment

Raise and securely support the rear of the tractor so the wheels are clear of the ground. Start and run the engine. With the transmission in neutral, the wheels should not rotate. If the wheels rotate, stop the engine and remove the transmission cover plate. Loosen the nut on the scissor mounting bracket (Fig. Y2-14). Loosen the jam nut on the speed selector rod (Fig. Y2-14).

CAUTION: Be careful of the transmission cooling fan and the drive belt when the engine is running.

Start the engine and run at full throttle. Move the hydrostatic control lever until the wheels do not rotate in

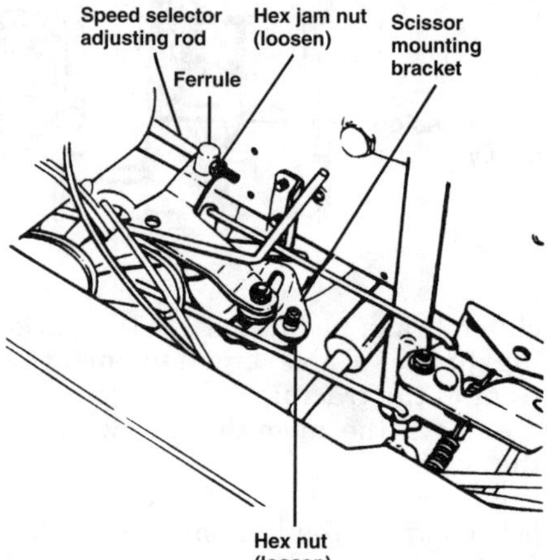

Fig. Y2-14—Drawing of 600 and 800 series Hydro-Gear hydrostatic transmission control linkage showing adjustment points. Refer to text.

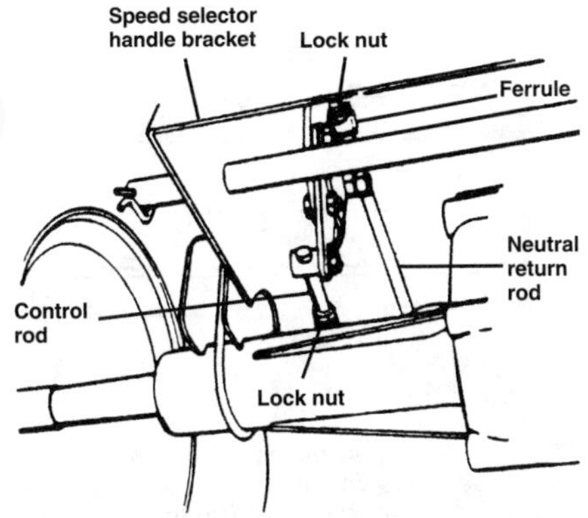

Fig. Y2-15—On 700 and 800 series tractors with Sundstrand hydrostatic transmission, adjust the neutral return rod so the hydrostatic control lever is in neutral position when clutch/brake pedal is depressed.

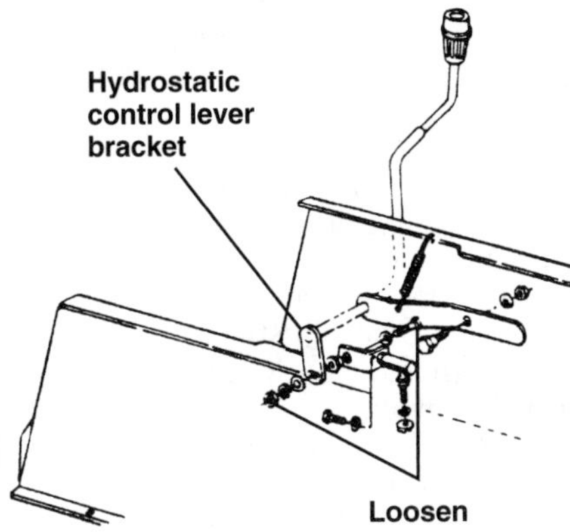

Fig. Y2-16—Drawing of hydrostatic control lever on 700 and 800 series tractors with Sundstrand hydrostatic transmission. Refer to text for adjustment.

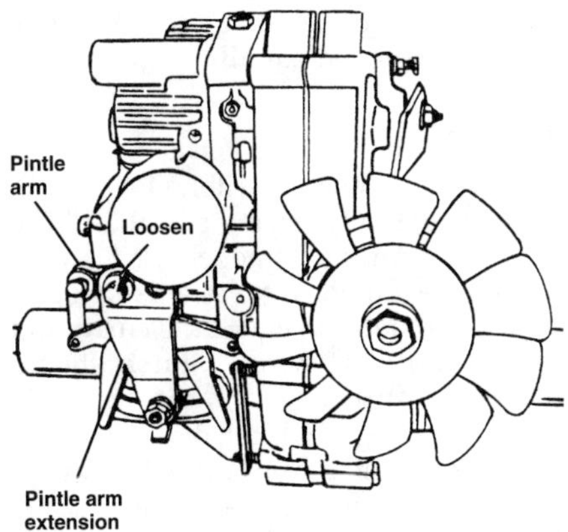

Fig. Y2-17—Adjust the Sundstrand hydrostatic transmission controls as outlined in the text.

either direction. Depress the clutch/brake pedal and shut off the engine. Tighten the nut on the scissor mounting bracket. Adjust the length of speed control rod so the hydrostatic control lever is aligned with the neutral position on the speed control bracket. Tighten the control rod jam nut.

Removal and Installation

To remove the hydrostatic transaxle, proceed as follows: Remove the seat and fenders. Remove the final drive belt. Disconnect the transaxle speed control linkage from the transaxle. Disconnect the brake actuating rod and the return spring from the transaxle brake lever. Support the transaxle and remove the mounting bolts and the axle housing clamp bolts. Remove the transaxle from the tractor.

To reinstall the hydrostatic transaxle, reverse the removal procedure. Refill the unit with recommended fluid and adjust the control linkage as previously outlined.

Overhaul

Refer to the Hydro-Gear section in the HYDROSTATIC TRANSAXLE in the rear of this manual for service information.

HYDROSTATIC TRANSMISSION (700-800 SERIES EQUIPPED WITH SUNDSTRAND HYDROSTATIC TRANSMISSION)

LUBRICATION

Models Prior to 1993

The hydrostatic transmission is equipped with an integral reservoir located under the tractor seat. The transmission is factory-filled with oil. The oil level should be at the lower or "COLD" mark on the reservoir with the unit cold. Recommended oil is SAE 10W30 engine oil with an SF rating.

If contamination is observed in the reservoir tank or the color of the fluid has changed (black or milky), the fluid should be drained and replaced.

NOTE: Reservoir tank cap has left-hand threads.

To drain fluid from the Sundstrand transmission, unscrew the hex drain plug located on the underside of the transmission housing.

Fill the transmission with new oil until the oil reaches the lower mark on the reservoir.

Models After 1992

On models after 1992, the transmission uses oil contained in the final drive housing. A spin-on type oil filter is located on the left side of the final drive housing. Refer to the FINAL DRIVE section in this manual for oil filling or draining information.

LINKAGE ADJUSTMENT

Remove the mower deck from the tractor. Raise and securely support the rear of tractor so the wheels are clear of the ground. Start and run the engine. With the transmission control in neutral, the wheels should not rotate.

If the wheels rotate, perform the neutral adjustment as follows: Loosen the locknut on the neutral return rod and disconnect the ferrule from the speed selector handle bracket (Fig. Y2-15). Depress the clutch/brake pedal and move the hydrostatic control lever to the neutral position on the speed control bracket. Adjust the ferrule on the neutral return rod until it lines up with the hole in the speed selector handle bracket. Attach the ferrule to the bracket and tighten the locknut.

The tractor should not move when the hydrostatic control lever is in the neutral position. To adjust the control lever, remove the transmission panel. Loosen the bolt attaching the control lever bracket to the control link (Fig. Y2-16). Loosen the bolt attaching the pintle arm extension to the pintle arm (Fig. Y2-17).

CAUTION: Be careful of the transmission cooling fan and drive belt when the engine is running.

Depress the clutch/brake pedal and set the parking brake. Start the engine and run at full speed. Move the hydrostatic control lever to move the pintle arm until the rear wheels do not turn in either direction. Tighten the bolt that secures the pintle arm to the pintle arm extension. Release the clutch/brake pedal. The wheels should not turn. If they do, repeat the adjustment.

Stop the engine and adjust the position of the hydrostatic control lever as follows: Depress the clutch/brake pedal and set the parking brake. Move the hydrostatic control lever to the neutral position on the quadrant. Tighten the nut and bolt on the hydrostatic control lever bracket (Fig. Y2-16).

REMOVAL AND INSTALLATION

To remove the hydrostatic transmission, proceed as follows: Remove the seat and fenders. Remove the final drive belt. Disconnect the transmission speed control linkage from the transmission. Disconnect the brake actuating and return springs from the brake lever and remove the brake caliper. Remove the final drive housing mounting bolts and the axle housing clamp bolts, then remove the transmission and final drive housing from the tractor. Unbolt and separate the hydrostatic transmission from the final drive housing.

To reinstall the hydrostatic unit, reverse the removal procedure. Refill the unit with recommended fluid and adjust the control linkage as previously outlined.

OVERHAUL

Models prior to 1993 are equipped with a Sundstrand BDU-10S transmission while models after 1992 are equipped with a Sundstrand BDU-10L transmission. Refer to the HYDROSTATIC TRANSMISSION section at the rear of this manual for overhaul information.

TRANSAXLE (MODELS EQUIPPED WITH VARIABLE SPEED TRANSMISSION)

LUBRICATION

The transaxle used on 600 and 700 series tractors with variable speed transmission is lubricated with grease at the factory and should not require additional lubrication. Capacity is 10 ounces (296 mL) of lithium-based grease.

Transaxle used on 800 series tractors with variable speed transmission is lubricated with grease at the factory and should not require additional lubrication. Capacity is 16 ounces (473 mL) of Benalene 372-0 grease.

REMOVAL AND INSTALLATION

To remove the transaxle assembly, first remove the mower deck from the tractor. Remove the drive belt from the transaxle pulley as previously outlined. Disconnect the shift linkage and brake linkage from the transaxle. Support the rear of the tractor and remove all fasteners securing the transaxle to the frame. Raise the rear of the tractor and roll the transaxle assembly out from under the tractor.

Reinstall by reversing the removal procedure. Adjust the brake as previously outlined.

OVERHAUL

Refer to the Yardman section in the TRANSAXLE service section in this manual for overhaul procedure.

FINAL DRIVE (MODELS EQUIPPED WITH SUNDSTRAND HYDROSTATIC TRANSMISSION)

LUBRICATION

Models Prior to 1993

The final drive used on tractors with a Sundstrand hydrostatic transmission is lubricated with grease at the factory and should not require additional lubrication. Capacity is 16 ounces (473 mL) of Shell Darina #0 grease.

Models After 1992

On models after 1992, the hydrostatic transmission uses oil contained in the final drive housing. A spin-on type oil filter is located on the left side of the final drive housing.

Recommended oil is SAE 20W-50 engine oil for temperatures above 15° F (-9° C). Use SAE 10W-40 engine oil for temperatures from -5° F () to 100° F (-20° C). Synthetic oil rated SAE 15W-50 may be used from -35° F (-37° C) to 100° F (-20° C). Oil should meet API classification SH/CD.

The oil and oil filter should be changed annually or after 200 hours of operation, whichever occurs first. Change the oil and filter more frequently if the tractor is operated in severe conditions.

REMOVAL AND INSTALLATION

To remove the final drive, first remove the mower deck from the tractor. Remove the seat and fenders. Remove the final drive belt as previously outlined.

Disconnect the transmission speed control linkage from the transmission. Disconnect the brake actuating and return springs from the brake lever and remove the brake caliper.

Remove the final drive housing mounting bolts and axle housing clamp bolts, then remove the transmission and final drive housing from the tractor. Unbolt and separate the hydrostatic transmission from the final drive housing.

To reinstall the final drive, reverse the removal procedure.

OVERHAUL

Models prior to 1993 are equipped with a Hydro-Gear Model 210-1010 final drive unit. Models after 1992 are equipped with a Hydro-Gear Model 210-3000 final drive unit. Refer to the Hydro-Gear section in the FINAL DRIVE service section in this manual for overhaul procedure.

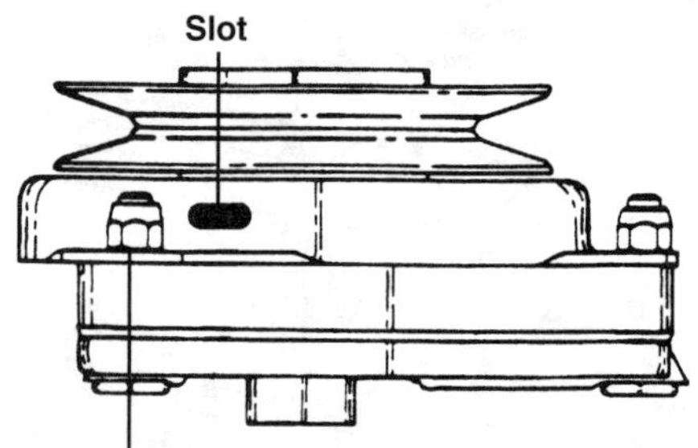

Fig. Y2-18—Measure the air gap at each of the three slots in electric clutch housing with a feeler gauge. Turn the adjusting nut to adjust the gap.

PTO CLUTCH

ADJUSTMENT

The PTO clutch should be adjusted if the clutch has been disassembled or if operation becomes erratic. PTO switch and ignition switch must be off when performing the adjustment.

With the clutch disengaged, insert a feeler gauge through one of the slots (Fig. Y2-18) in the clutch housing and measure the clearance between the clutch rotor and armature. Clearance should be 0.010-0.025 inch (0.25-0.64 mm).

To adjust, tighten the adjusting nut next to the slot until the feeler gauge just begins to bind. Do not over tighten. Repeat the adjustment at each of the slots in the clutch housing. All slots must be adjusted equally.

TESTING

Turn the ignition switch ON and actuate the PTO control switch. If the clutch does not engage, check for voltage to the clutch. If voltage is present, use an ammeter to check the current in one of the PTO wires. Clutch should draw 3.5 amps or more when engaged.

To check the field coil, disconnect the wiring connector from the PTO clutch. Using an ohmmeter set on low scale, check the resistance between the terminals of the PTO connector. Specified resistance is 2.40-3.40 ohms. A reading not within the specified range indicates that the field coil is faulty and the clutch should be replaceed.

REMOVAL AND INSTALLATION

To remove the PTO clutch, first remove the mower deck. Disconnect the wire connector from the clutch lead.

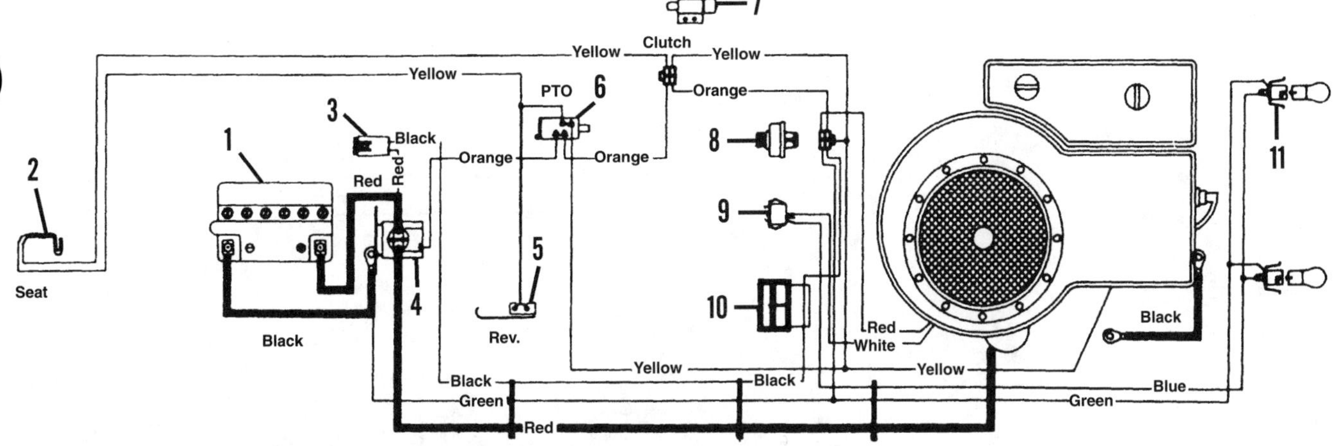

Fig. Y2-19—Typical wiring diagram for models with single-cylinder engine.

1. Battery
2. Seat safety switch
3. Fuse
4. Solenoid
5. Reverse safety switch
6. PTO safety switch
7. Clutch safety switch
8. Ignition switch
9. Light switch
10. Ammeter
11. Headlights

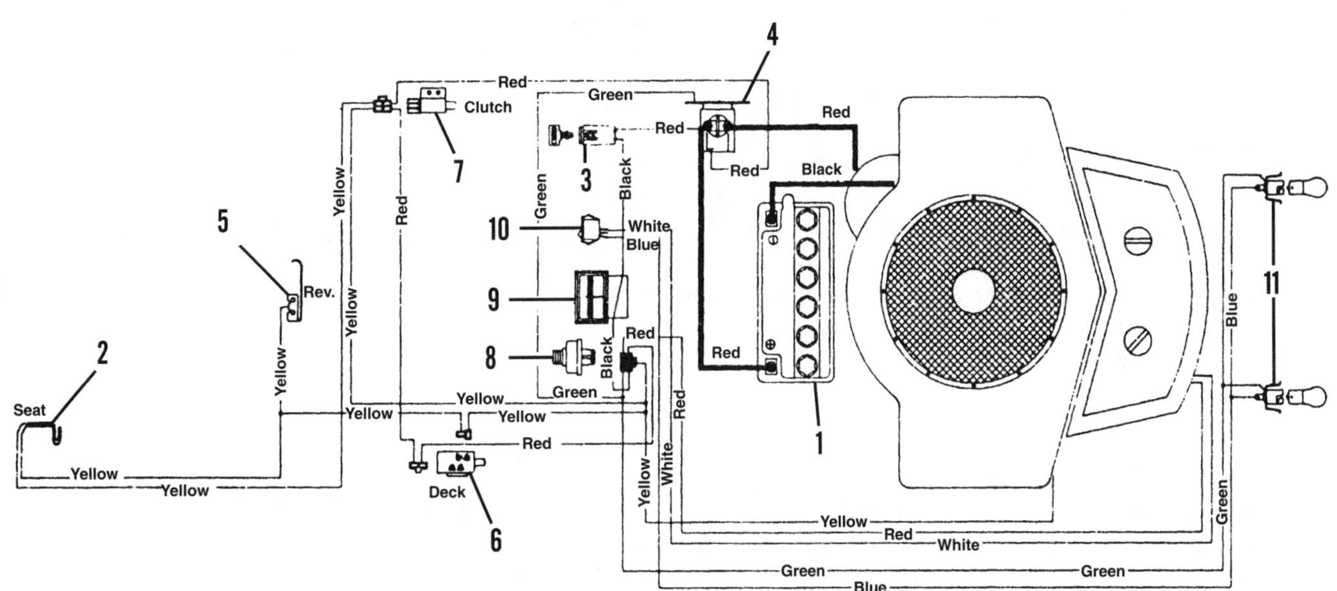

Fig. Y2-20—Typical wiring diagram for models with two-cylinder engine not equipped with an electric PTO clutch.

1. Battery
2. Seat safety switch
3. Fuse
4. Solenoid
5. Reverse safety switch
6. PTO safety switch
7. Clutch safety switch
8. Ignition switch
9. Ammeter
10. Light switch
11. Headlights
12. Indicator lights
13. Relays
14. PTO switch
15. Taillights

Unscrew the clutch retaining screw and pull the clutch off the crankshaft.

Inspect the bearings in the field housing and armature for wear or damage. Inspect the contact surfaces of the rotor and armature for scoring, grooves or other damage. replace the clutch as necessary.

Apply antiseize compound to the crankshaft before installing the clutch. Adjust the clutch as previously outlined.

If a new clutch is installed, burnish the clutch friction surfaces as follows: Start the engine and run at half speed. Actuate the PTO control switch on and off six times. Increase engine speed to three-quarter speed and repeat the procedure. Allow the mower to stop completely before turning the switch back on. Recheck the clutch adjustment.

SAFETY INTERLOCK SYSTEM

Before the engine will start, the key must be turned on and both of the safety switches must be activated. One switch is activated when the clutch/brake pedal is depressed and the other is activated when the blade is disengaged. When the two safety switches are activated, the circuit is completed between the battery and the starter solenoid, allowing the starter motor to crank the engine.

Some models are equipped with a seat safety switch and a reverse safety switch. However, these switches are not involved in the starting circuit. The seat safety switch is designed to stop the engine if the operator leaves the seat with the blades or PTO engaged. The blades must be in the disengaged

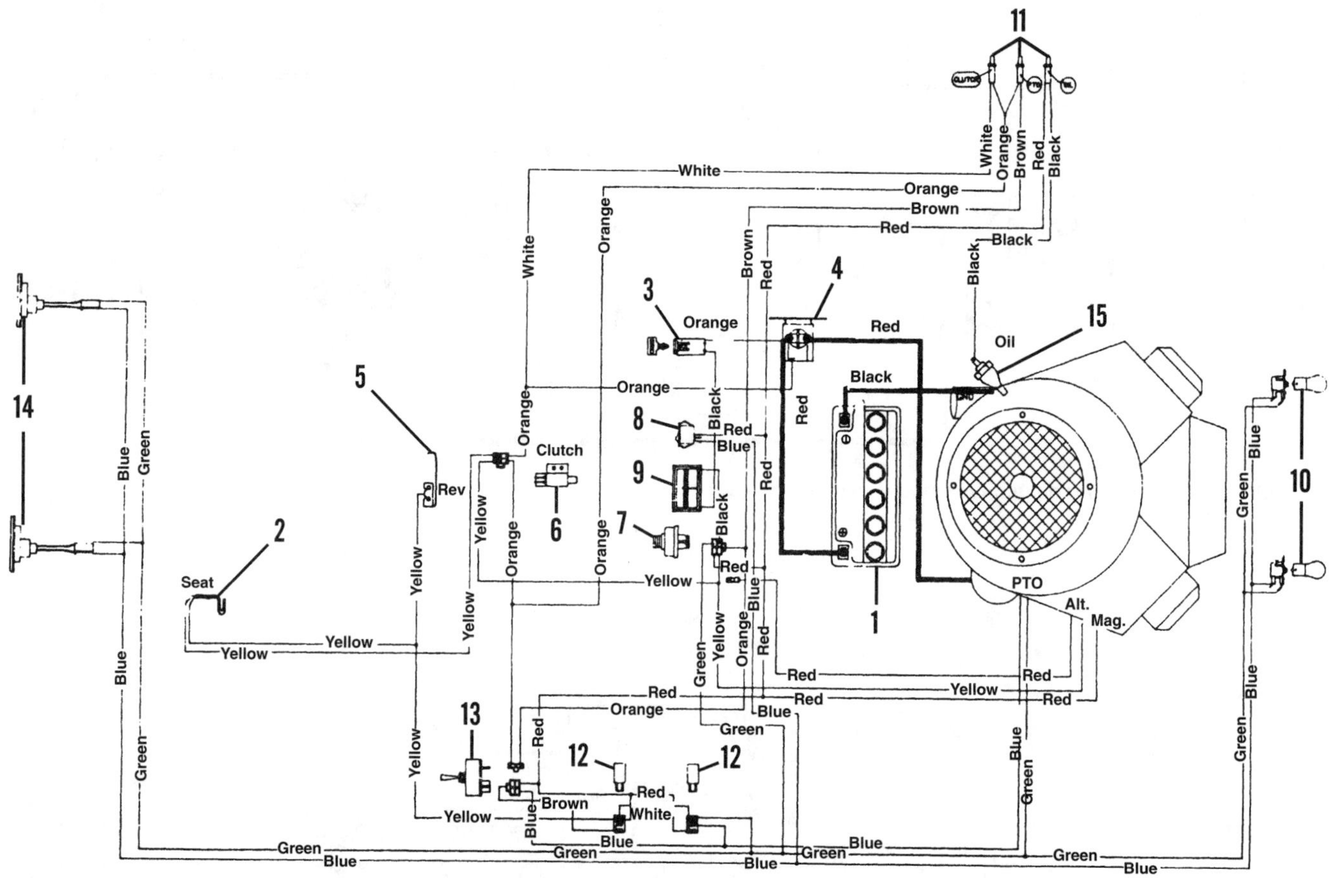

Fig. Y2-21—Typical wiring diagram for models with two-cylinder engine and equipped with an electric PTO clutch.

1. Battery
2. Seat safety switch
3. Fuse
4. Solenoid
5. Reverse safety switch
6. Clutch safety switch
7. Ignition switch
8. Light switch
9. Ammeter
10. Headlights
11. Indicator lights
12. Relays
13. PTO switch
14. Taillights
15. Oil pressure switch

position when shifting into reverse or the engine will shut off.

To test the two safety start switches, first check the two switches to see if the switch plungers are depressed a minimum of 1/8 inch (3 mm) when the blade is disengaged and the clutch/brake pedal is depressed. If the switch plunger is correctly depressed, use a continuity checker to determine if there is continuity across the switch terminals when the switches are activated (plunger depressed). If continuity is not indicated when the plunger is depressed, replace the switch.

To check for correct operation of the seat safety switch, start the engine and set the parking brake. Place the shift lever in neutral and engage the PTO or blades. Raise up off the seat. The engine should stop running.

WIRING DIAGRAMS

Wiring diagrams typical of all models are illustrated in Fig. Y2-19, Y2-20 and Y2-21.

YARDMAN

600 and 700 Series (4-Wheel Steering)

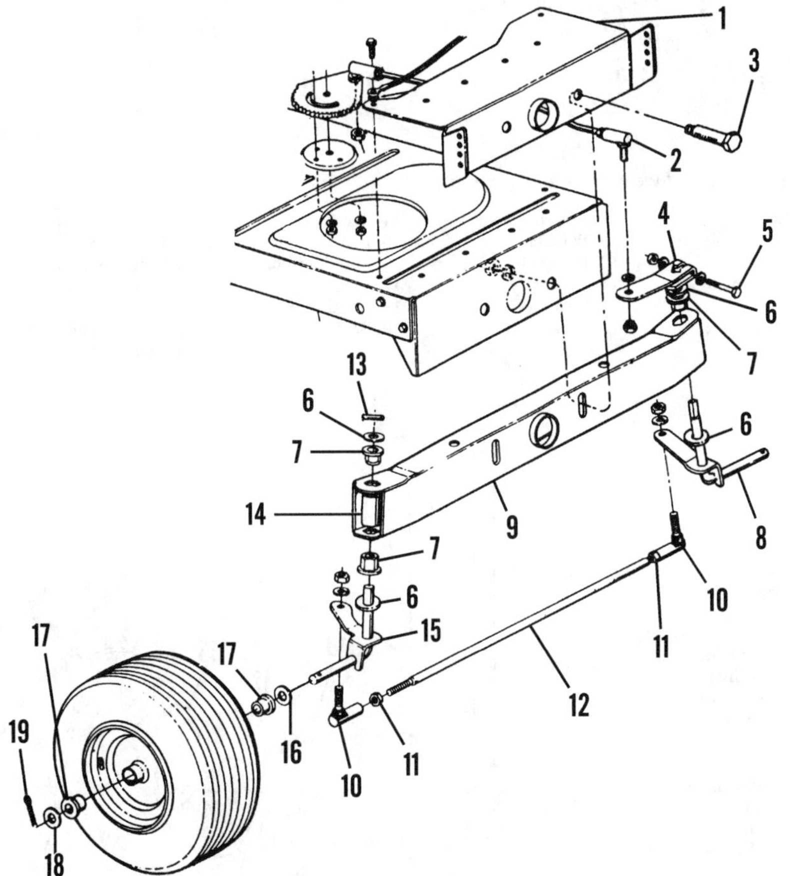

Fig. Y3-1—Exploded view of front axle assembly.

1. Axle pivot bracket
2. Drag link
3. Pivot stop bolt
4. Steering arm
5. Clamp bolt
6. Washer
7. Flange bushings
8. Spindle (left)
9. Axle main member
10. Rod end
11. Jam nut
12. Tie rod
13. Roll pin
14. Plastic tube
15. Spindle (right)
16. Washer
17. Wheel bearings
18. Washer
19. Cotter pin

Due to the numerous number of Yardman models and the wide variety of engines installed, an accurate cross-reference and specification table is not available. Determine the manufacturer and model number of the engine being serviced and refer to the appropriate engine section in the rear of this manual for service information.

FRONT AXLE SYSTEM

STEERING SPINDLES

Lubrication

Lubricate the steering spindles periodically with a lithium-based, multipurpose grease. Clean away any excess grease.

Removal and Installation

Remove the mower deck from the tractor. Raise and support the front of the tractor. Remove the front wheels. Detach the tie rod (12—Fig. Y3-1) and the drag link (2) from the steering spindle or steering arm.

To remove the left spindle (8), loosen the clamp bolt (5) and remove the steering arm (4). Lower the spindle from the axle. To remove the right spindle (15), remove the roll pin (13) in right spindle. Pull the spindle down out of the axle main member.

Inspect the spindles and bushings (7) for damage and replace when needed.

Install by reversing the removal procedure. Apply lithium-based, multipurpose grease to the bushings before installing the spindles.

AXLE MAIN MEMBER REMOVAL AND INSTALLATION

Remove the axle main member (9—Fig. Y3-1) as follows: Remove the mower deck from the tractor. Raise and support the front of the tractor and remove the front wheels. Remove the spindles as previously described.

Remove the grille for access to the front axle pivot bracket (1). Unscrew the bolts (3) limiting the axle travel. Unscrew the bolts attaching the pivot bracket (1) to the frame. Support the axle main member and remove the bracket and axle.

Reassemble by reversing the removal procedure.

STEERING SYSTEM

All models are equipped with a 4-wheel-steering system. A cam-type steering gearbox (6—Fig. Y3-2) on the steering shaft transfers steering motion to the rear wheel steering mechanism. A gear at the bottom of the steering shaft actuates the front steering system. Rear wheels turn in the opposite direction to the front wheels to decrease the steering radius. The rear wheels do not turn until the front wheel steering angle exceeds 45°.

ALIGNMENT ADJUSTMENT

Adjust the length of the tie rod (12—Fig. Y3-1) to obtain front wheel toe-in of 1/8 inch (3.2 mm). Secure the tie rod ends with the jam nuts.

Rotate the steering wheel so the holes in the sector gear (20—Fig. Y3-2) and the retainer plate (18) are aligned. Insert a suitable size pin so the holes remain aligned. Adjust the length of the drag link (21) so the front wheels point straight ahead.

Note the hole in the steering gear housing under the grease fitting (11—Fig. Y3-3). Rotate the steering wheel 16° in each direction so a pin inserted in the hole will lock the steering worm. Adjust the length of the rear steering link (23—Fig. Y3-2) so the rear wheels point forward. Adjust the length of each tie rod (24) to adjust the position of each rear wheel so they point straight ahead.

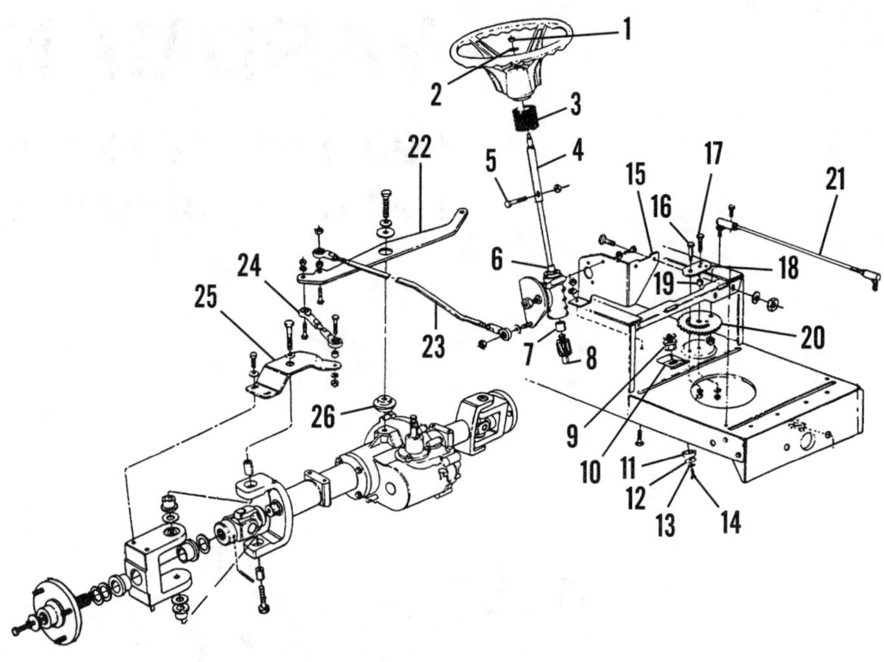

Fig. Y3-2—Exploded view of steering system.

1. Nut
2. Belleville washer
3. Bellow
4. Upper steering shaft
5. Bolt
6. Steering gearbox
7. Splined coupler
8. Steering gear
9. Washer
10. Flange bushing
11. Spacer
12. Washer
13. Lockwasher
14. Screw
15. Bracket
16. Shoulder bolt
17. Screw
18. Retainer plate
19. Spacer
20. Sector gear
21. Drag link
22. Center steering arm
23. Rear steering link
24. Tie rod
25. Outer steering arm
26. Pivot

STEERING GEAR AND GEARBOX

Removal and Installation

Remove the steering gear assembly as follows: Disconnect the battery cables. Remove the mower deck from the tractor. Remove the fuel tank.

Remove the steering wheel cover, retaining nut (1—Fig. Y3-2) and Belleville washer (2). Pull the steering wheel off the shaft and remove the bellow (3). Unscrew the steering shaft coupling bolt (5) and remove the upper steering shaft (4).

Disconnect the drag link (21) from the sector gear (20). Remove the mounting bolt (17) and shoulder bolt (16) from the sector retainer plate (18) and withdraw the sector gear.

Remove the retaining screw (14) from the lower end of the steering gear (8) shaft and remove the lower steering gear, thrust washer (9) and bushing (10). Disconnect the rear steering link (23) from the steering gearbox. Remove the steering gearbox from the tractor.

Inspect all parts for excessive wear or damage and replace when necessary.

Install by reversing the removal procedure. Apply a light coat of multipurpose grease to the teeth of the steering gears.

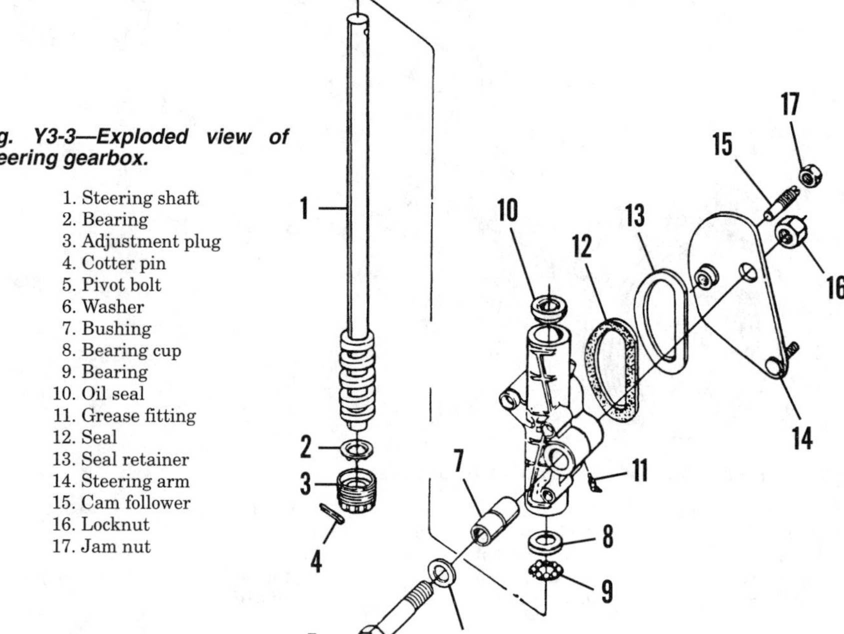

Fig. Y3-3—Exploded view of steering gearbox.

1. Steering shaft
2. Bearing
3. Adjustment plug
4. Cotter pin
5. Pivot bolt
6. Washer
7. Bushing
8. Bearing cup
9. Bearing
10. Oil seal
11. Grease fitting
12. Seal
13. Seal retainer
14. Steering arm
15. Cam follower
16. Locknut
17. Jam nut

Overhaul Steering Gearbox

Disassemble the steering gear as follows: Clamp the steering arm plate (14—Fig. Y3-3) in a vise and remove the nut (16) and jam nut (17). Separate the gearbox from the steering arm plate. Remove the cotter pin (4) and adjustment plug (3). Remove the steering shaft and cam assembly (1) and bearings from the gearbox.

Inspect the cam follower for flat spots. Inspect the ends of the cam (1),

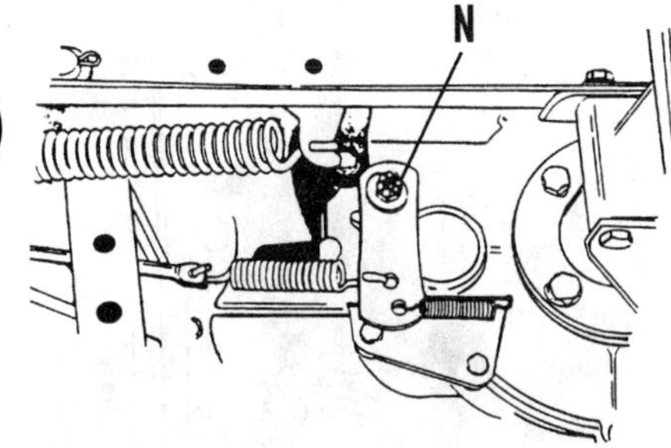

Fig. Y3-4—Adjust brake by turning castle nut (N) as described in text.

the ball bearings and bearing cups for roughness or pitting. Check the cam grooves for wear, roughness and galling.

During reassembly, coat the cam, bearing balls and races with lithium-base grease. Install the steering shaft and cam, balls and races into the gearbox. Make certain that the races enter the gearbox squarely and are not cocked. Thread the adjustment plug (3) into the gearbox until the end play of the cam is removed but the shaft still turns freely. Insert the cotter pin (4) into the nearest hole in the adjustment plug.

Fill the housing with lithium-base grease. Loosen the jam nut (17) and back the cam follower (15) out two turns. Install the seal (12), retainer (13) and steering arm plate (14). Install the nut (16). Tighten the nut until there is $\frac{3}{32}$ inch (2.4 mm) clearance between the steering arm plate and gearbox. Install a jam nut against the nut (16) and tighten the jam nut to 40 ft.-lb. (54 N·m).

Inject grease into the fitting (11) until grease begins to appear between the steering arm plate (14) and gearbox.

Center the steering cam by rotating the steering shaft halfway between full right and full left turn. Turn the cam follower (15) inward to eliminate backlash, then tighten the jam nut (17) to 40 ft.-lb. (54 N·m). The steering shaft should rotate smoothly with minimum backlash.

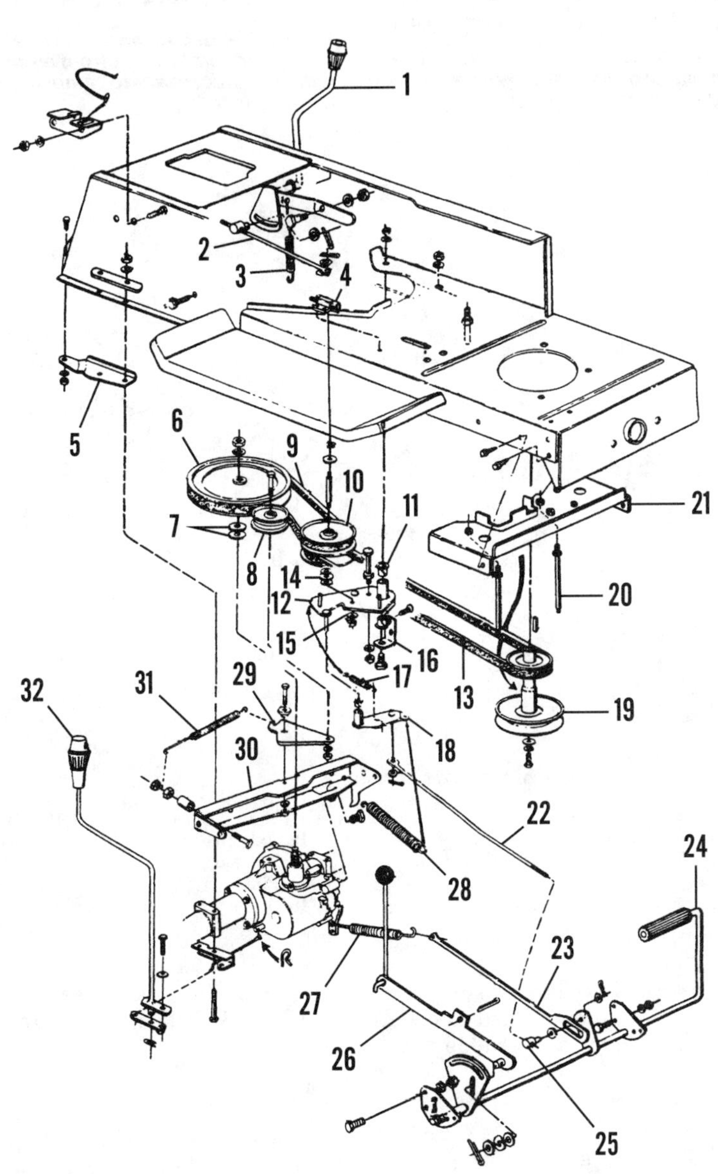

Fig. Y3-5—Exploded view of variable speed drive components.

1. Speed selector lever
2. Speed selector rod
3. Spring
4. Clutch safety switch
5. Axle support bracket
6. Transaxle pulley
7. Washers
8. Idler pulley
9. Rear drive belt
10. Variable speed pulley
11. Bearing
12. Variable speed bracket
13. Front drive belt
14. Washers
15. Belleville washers
16. Bearing bracket
17. Spring
18. Torque bracket
19. Engine pulley
20. Guide bolt (2)
21. Belt guard
22. Speed control link
23. Brake rod
24. Clutch/brake pedal assy.
25. Ferrule
26. Parking brake rod
27. Brake spring
28. Spring
29. Idler bracket
30. Transaxle support bracket
31. Spring
32. Shift lever

ENGINE

REMOVAL AND INSTALLATION

Remove the hood, grille brace, or side panels, and grille. Disconnect the battery cables, starter wires and all necessary electrical connections from the engine. Disconnect the fuel line. Disconnect the choke and throttle control cables from the engine.

Remove the drive belts from the engine pulleys. Remove the muffler heat shield, if so equipped. Remove the engine mounting bolts and lift the engine from the tractor.

Install by reversing the removal procedure.

OVERHAUL

Refer to the appropriate engine section in this manual for tune-up specifications, engine overhaul procedures and engine maintenance.

CLUTCH AND BRAKE

All models are equipped with a continuously variable drive pulley providing infinite travel speeds. Depressing the clutch/brake pedal partway disengages the clutch. Depressing the pedal all the way down disengages the clutch and engages the disc brake.

ADJUSTMENT

Remove the cotter pin from the castle nut (N—Fig. Y3-4) on the transaxle brake lever. Hand-tighten the nut so the brake lever is trapped against the transaxle bracket. Detach the clutch rod (2—Fig. Y3-5) from the torque bracket (1).

Depress the clutch/brake pedal until you feel resistance. Rotate the clutch rod (2) so the rod end fits easily onto the pin on the torque bracket (1). Shorten the clutch rod by rotating two turns and reattach the rod end to the bracket. Loosen the castle nut (N—Fig. Y3-4) one or two flats and insert the cotter pin.

BRAKE PADS

Transaxle housing halves must be separated for access to the brake pads. Refer to the TRANSAXLE section for instructions.

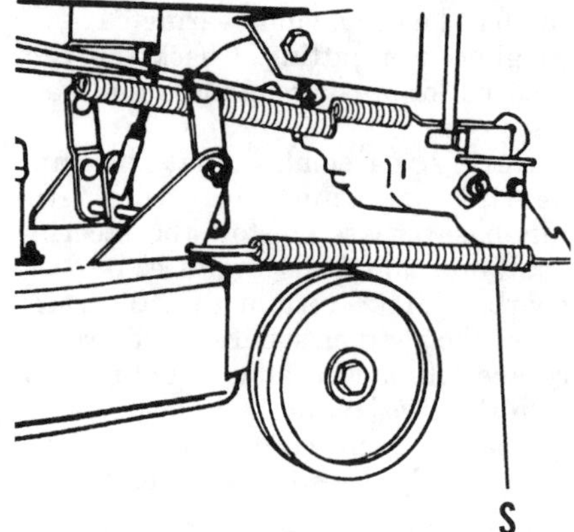

Fig. Y3-6—Detach spring (S) from transmission support bracket to relieve tension on the drive belts for belt removal.

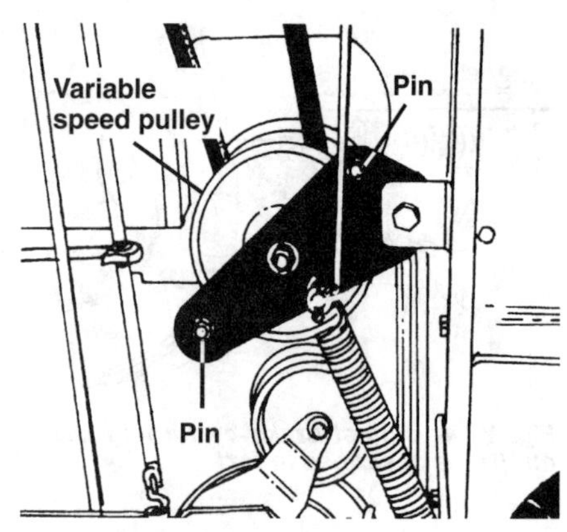

Fig. Y3-7—Push forward on variable speed pulley and remove belt from engine pulley. It may be necessary to remove guide pins for access to belt.

DRIVE BELTS

REAR DRIVE BELT REMOVAL AND INSTALLATION

Disconnect the battery cables. Remove the mower deck from the tractor. Remove the transmission cover.

NOTE: It is not necessary to tip the tractor to remove the belts. If the tractor is tipped, remove the battery and drain the fuel tank or place a piece of plastic wrap over the neck of the tank and screw on the cap to prevent leakage.

Detach the speed selector rod (2—Fig. Y3-5) from the variable speed pulley (10). Move the belt idler pulley (8) away from the belt to relieve tension on the belt and move the belt over the idler pulley. Remove the belt from the variable speed pulley (10) and the transaxle pulley (6).

Install the belt by reversing the removal procedure.

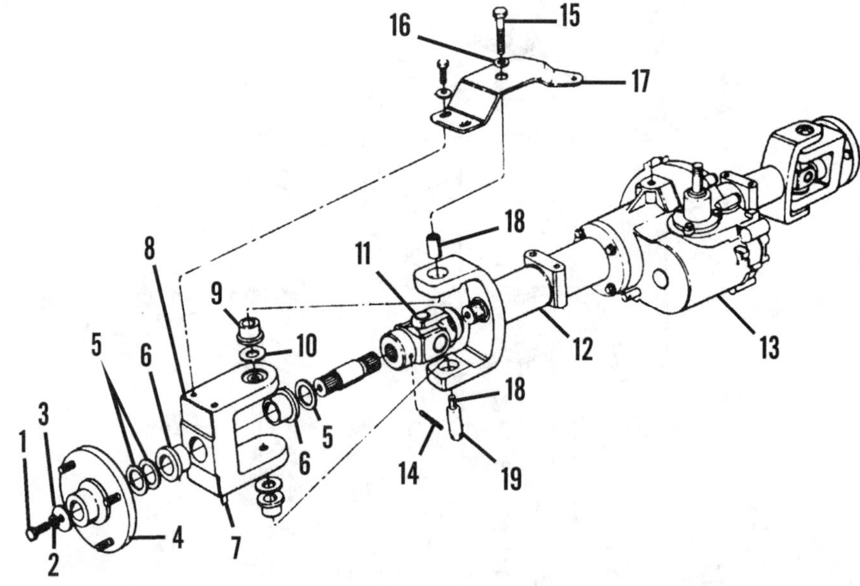

Fig. Y3-8—Exploded view of rear axle assembly.

1. Screw
2. Lockwasher
3. Washer
4. Outer axle
5. Washers
6. Bushing
7. Grease fitting
8. Steering knuckle
9. Bushing
10. Washer
11. Universal joint
12. Axle housing
13. Transaxle
14. Pin
15. Screw
16. Washer
17. Steering arm
18. Pivot sleeve
19. Screw

FRONT DRIVE BELT REMOVAL AND INSTALLATION

Remove the rear drive belt as described in the previous section. Position the lift lever in the disengaged position. Detach spring (S—Fig. Y3-6) from the transmission support bracket. Raise and support the front of the tractor.

Unscrew the belt guide bolts (20—Fig. Y3-5) located around the engine drive pulley. If so equipped, detach the mower deck belt from the engine pulley. Remove the bolts attaching the engine pulley belt guard (21) to the frame. Slide the belt guard rearward and to the right to remove it. Move the clutch/brake pedal to the park position. Push the variable speed pulley (Fig. Y3-7) forward and detach the belt from the engine pulley. If necessary, remove the belt guide pins. Move the clutch/brake pedal as needed to disengage the belt from the variable speed pulley.

Reverse the removal procedure to install the belt. Be sure that the belt is positioned inside the guide pins.

REAR AXLE PIVOT ASSEMBLY

LUBRICATION

Lubricate the rear wheel outer axle bushings periodically by injecting lithium-based, multipurpose grease into the grease fitting (7—Fig. Y3-8) located on the underside of each steering knuckle (8). Clean away any excess grease.

OVERHAUL

Remove the mower deck from the tractor. Raise and support the rear of the tractor. Remove the rear wheel.

Detach the tie rod from the steering arm (17—Fig. Y3-8). Remove the upper (15) and lower (19) pivot screws. Separate the steering knuckle (8) from the axle housing. Drive out the roll pin (14), then separate and remove the axle flange (4) and universal joint (11).

Inspect components for damage. Also inspect the outer end of the transaxle

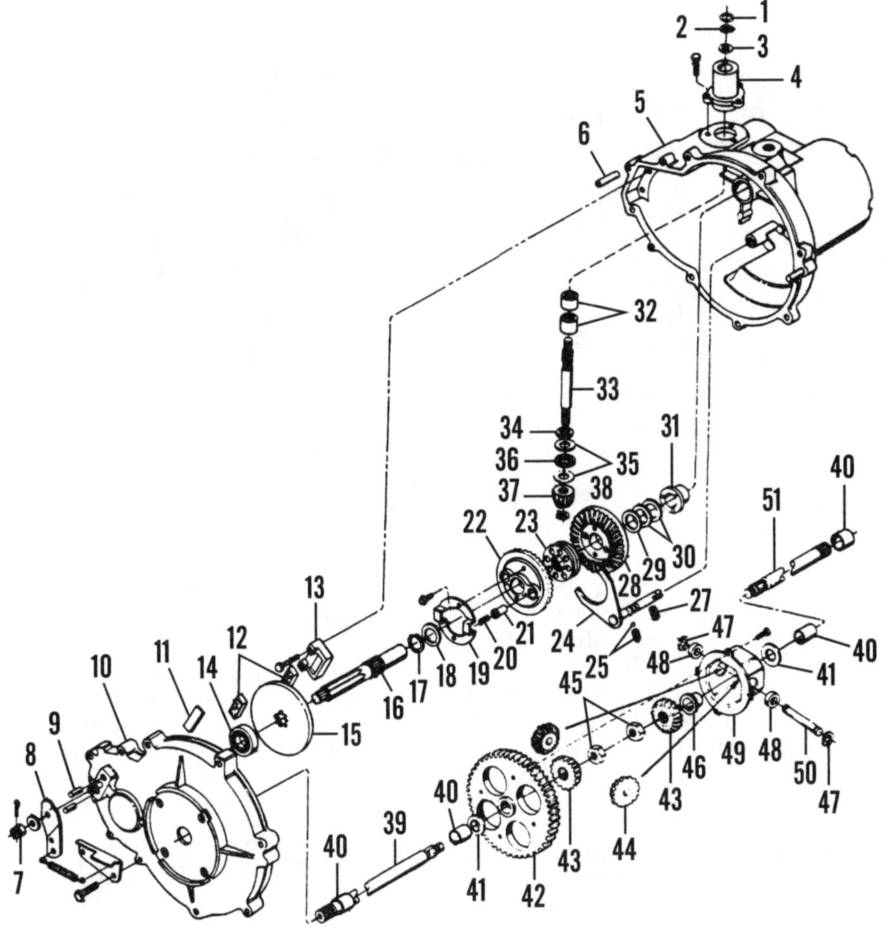

Fig. Y3-9—Exploded view of transaxle.

1. Wire ring	14. Bearing	27. Set screw	40. Bushing
2. Snap ring	15. Brake disc	28. Bevel gear	41. Washer
3. Washer	16. Drive shaft	29. Washer	42. Gear
4. Input shaft housing	17. Snap ring	30. Shims	43. Side gear
5. Case	18. Washer	31. Bushing	44. Pinion
6. Dowel pin	19. Spring retaining plate	32. Bearing	45. Nut
7. Nut	20. Spring	33. Input shaft	46. Bushing
8. Brake arm	21. Pin	34. Seal	47. Snap ring
9. Brake actuator pin	22. Bevel gear	35. Thrust washer	48. Spacer
10. Cover	23. Shift collar	36. Thrust bearing	49. Differential case
11. Plate	24. Shift fork	37. Gear	50. Shaft
12. Brake pads	25. Detent spring & ball	38. Snap ring	51. Axle
13. Brake holder		39. Axle shaft	

axle for wear. Replace the bushings (6 and 9) if damaged. Reassemble by reversing the disassembly procedure.

TRANSAXLE

LUBRICATION

Transaxle lubricant level does not require periodic checking. Recommended lubricant is Shell Darina grease. The capacity is 32 ounces (947 mL).

REMOVAL AND INSTALLATION

To remove the transaxle and axle pivot assemblies as a unit, proceed as follows. Remove the mower deck from the tractor. Remove the rear drive belt as previously outlined. Raise and support the rear of the tractor. Remove the rear wheels.

Disconnect the rear steering link (23—Fig. Y3-2) from the center steering arm (22). Detach the brake actuating spring (28—Fig. Y3-5) from the brake lever. Detach the shift lever (32) from the transaxle shift shaft.

Support the transaxle, remove the mounting bolts and remove the transaxle and axle assembly. If necessary, remove the outer axle pivot assemblies from the transaxle as previously outlined.

Install by reversing the removal procedure.

OVERHAUL

Remove the axle pivot assemblies as previously outlined before disassembling transaxle. Refer to Fig. Y3-9 for an exploded view of the transaxle.

To disassemble, unbolt and remove the input shaft (33) and housing (4) assembly. Remove the snap rings (2 and 38) and withdraw the bevel gear (37), thrust bearing (35 and 36) and shaft from the housing.

Unbolt and remove the axle housings (12—Fig. Y3-8) on each side. Remove the cap screws retaining the housing cover (10—Fig. Y3-9) and separate the cover from the transaxle housing (5).

Withdraw the axle shafts (39 and 51—Fig. Y3-9) and differential assembly from the housing. Unbolt and separate the differential case (49) from the differential gear (42). Remove the nuts (45) and side gears (43) from the axles. To remove the spider gears (44), detach the snap ring (47) and withdraw the cross shaft (50) from the differential case.

Slide the brake disc (15—Fig. Y3-9) off the drive shaft (16). Unbolt and remove the brake pad holder (13). Withdraw the drive shaft (16) and bevel gear (22) as an assembly. Remove the bolts retaining the spring retainer plate (19) to the bevel gear. Separate the retainer plate, springs (20) and drive pins (21) from the bevel gear.

Unscrew the setscrew (27) located in the bottom of the transaxle case to release the detent spring and ball (25) before removing the shift fork (24). Lift up on the shift assembly and rotate to remove it from the case.

Inspect the splines in the shift collar for wear or damage. Check the drive shaft splines and gear teeth for wear. Replace worn or damaged components as needed.

Backlash between the pinion gear (37—Fig. Y3-9) and bevel gear (28) should be 0.006-0.010 inch (0.15-0.25 mm). Adjust backlash by adding or deleting 0.010 inch shims (30) as necessary.

Reassemble by reversing the disassembly procedure. Fill the housing with 32 ounces (947 mL) of Shell Darina grease. Adjust the castle nut (7—Fig. Y3-9) so there is ¼ to ⅜ inch (6.5-9.5 mm) clearance between the brake stop bracket and the brake cam (8).

SAFETY INTERLOCK SYSTEM

Before the engine will start, the key must be turned on and both of the safety switches must be activated. One switch (7—Fig. Y3-10) is activated when the

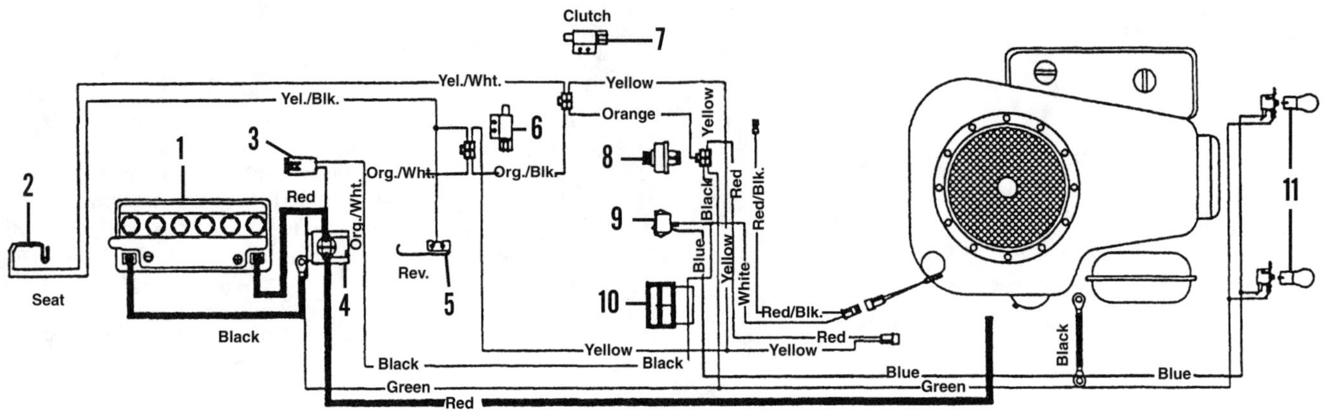

Fig. Y3-10—Typical wiring diagram.

1. Battery
2. Seat safety switch
3. Fuse
4. Solenoid
5. Reverse safety switch
6. PTO safety switch
7. Clutch safety switch
8. Ignition switch
9. Light switch
10. Ammeter
11. Headlights

clutch/brake pedal is depressed and the other switch (6) is activated when the blade is disengaged. When the two safety switches are activated, the circuit is completed between the battery and the starter solenoid, allowing the starter motor to crank the engine.

Some models are equipped with a seat safety switch (2) and a reverse safety switch (5). However, these switches are not involved in the starting circuit. The seat safety switch is designed to stop the engine if the operator leaves the seat with the blades or PTO engaged. The blades must be in the disengaged position when shifting into reverse or the engine will shut off.

To test the two safety start switches, first check the two switches to see if the switch plungers are depressed a minimum of $\frac{1}{8}$ inch (3 mm) when the blade is disengaged and the clutch/brake pedal is depressed. If the switch plunger is correctly depressed, use a continuity checker to determine if there is continuity across the switch terminals when the switches are activated (plunger depressed). If continuity is not indicated when the plunger is depressed, replace the switch.

To check for correct operation of the seat safety switch, start the engine and set the parking brake. Place the shift lever in NEUTRAL and engage the PTO or blades. Raise up off the seat. The engine should stop running.

WIRING DIAGRAM

The wiring diagram illustrated in Fig. Y3-10 is typical of all models.

YARDMAN

900 Series

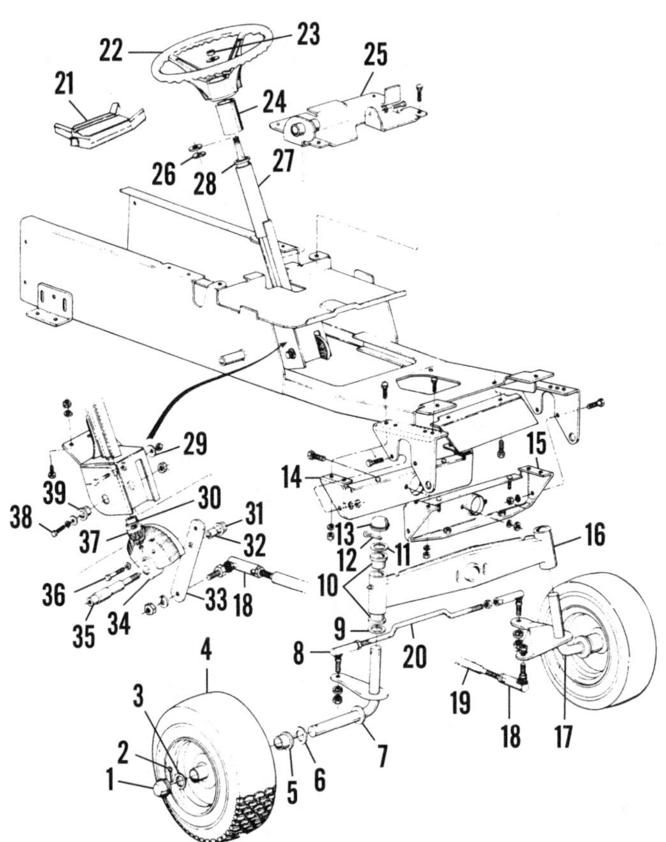

Fig. Y4-1—Exploded view of front axle and steering gear assembly.

1. Dust cap
2. Cotter pin
3. Washer
4. Tire & hub assy.
5. Bushing
6. Washer
7. Spindle
8. Tie rod end
9. Thrust washer
10. Bushings
11. Washer
12. Cotter pin
13. Cap
14. Rear pivot bracket
15. Axle main member
16. Front pivot bracket
17. Spindle
18. Drag link end
19. Drag link
20. Tie rod
21. Cap
22. Nut
23. Steering wheel
24. Sleeve
25. Dash panel base plate
26. Wave washer
27. Bushing
28. Steering column
29. Belleville washer
30. Bushing
31. Nut
32. Spacer
33. Steering arm
34. Sector gear
35. Steering shaft
36. Cap screw
37. Pinion gear
38. Cap screw
39. Bushing

Due to the numerous number of Yardman models and the wide variety of engines installed, an accurate cross-reference and specification table is not available. Determine the manufacturer and model number of the engine being serviced and refer to the appropriate engine section in the rear of this manual for service information.

FRONT AXLE AND STEERING SYSTEM

MAINTENANCE

Periodically inject lithium-based, multipurpose grease into the grease fittings located at the ends of the axle main member. Periodically lubricate the steering gear with lithium-based, multipurpose grease. Clean away any excess grease.

STEERING SPINDLES

Raise and support the front of the tractor. Remove the front wheels. Detach the tie rod (20—Fig. Y4-1) and drag link (19) from the steering spindle.

Remove the dust cap (13) and withdraw the cotter pin (12) to free the steering spindles (7 and 17). Pull the spindle down out of the axle main member.

Inspect the spindles and bushings (10) for wear and replace when necessary.

Reinstall by reversing the removal procedure. Apply lithium-based, multipurpose grease to the spindle bushings before installing the spindles.

TIE ROD AND TOE-IN

Some models are equipped with an adjustable tie rod (20—Fig. Y4-1). Inspect the ball joints (8) for excessive wear and looseness and replace if needed.

Adjust the length of the tie rod to obtain front wheel toe-in of 1/8 inch (3.2 mm). Secure the tie rod ends with jam nuts.

AXLE MAIN MEMBER REMOVAL AND INSTALLATION

To remove the axle main member (16—Fig. Y4-1), remove the hood and grille. Remove the PTO drive shaft as outlined in the PTO Section.

Raise and support the front of tractor frame and remove the front wheels. Disconnect the drag link end (18) from the left spindle (17). Disconnect the tie rod (20) from both spindles. Remove the cap (13) and cotter pin (12) and withdraw the spindles from the axle.

Support the axle main member (16). Remove the front (15) and rear (14) pivot brackets and remove the axle from the tractor.

Install by reversing the removal procedure.

STEERING GEAR

To remove the steering gear, first disconnect the battery cables. Disconnect the drag link end (18—Fig. Y4-1) from the steering arm (33). Remove the steering wheel insert (21) and unscrew the nut (22) retaining the steering wheel. Remove the steering wheel (23), bellows or sleeve (24), wave washer (26) and upper bearing (27) from the steering shaft.

Remove the nut from the lower end of the steering shaft and pull the steering shaft up and out of the pinion gear (30).

Remove the cap screw (38) and nut (31). Drive the sector shaft (35) out of the steering bracket and sector gear (34). Remove the spacer (32) and gear (34).

Reinstall by reversing the removal procedure. Make certain the sector shaft (35) goes through the steering lever (33).

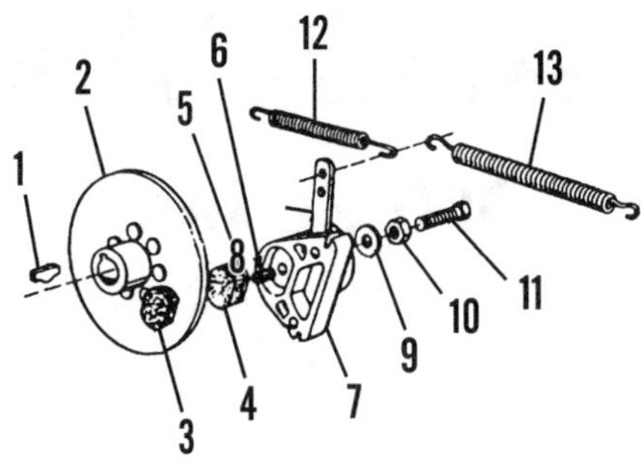

Fig. Y4-2—Exploded view of brake components.

1. Key
2. Disc
3. Brake pad
4. Brake pad
5. Metal backing plate
6. Pin
7. Caliper
8. Brake lever
9. Washer
10. Jam nut
11. Adjustment bolt
12. Spring
13. Spring

Fig. Y4-3—Exploded view of drive shaft assembly typical of all models.

1. Hydrostatic transmission
2. Key
3. Snap ring
4. Cooling fan
5. Rear universal joint & yoke
6. Drive shaft
7. Setscrew
8. Front universal joint & yoke

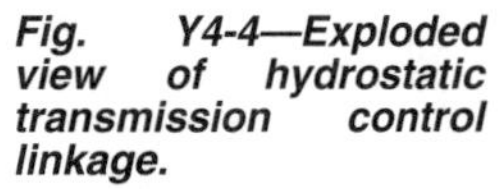

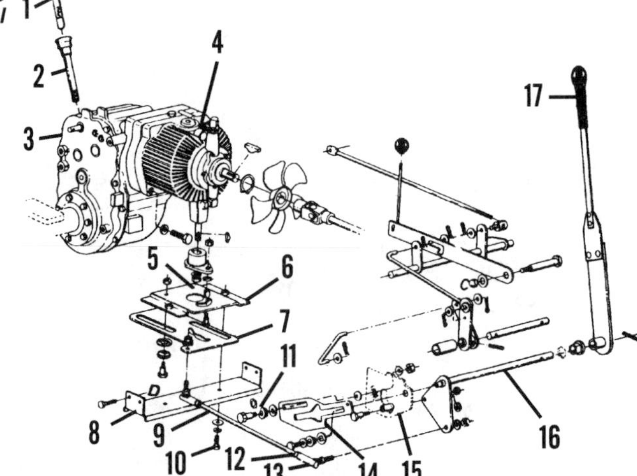

Fig. Y4-4—Exploded view of hydrostatic transmission control linkage.

1. Dipstick
2. Dipstick tube
3. Transaxle
4. Hydrostatic transmission
5. Alignment hole
6. Slide mounting plate
7. Cam plate
8. Support channel
9. Speed control rod
10. Cap screws
11. Shoulder bolt
12. Jam nut
13. Rod end
14. Neutral control slide
15. Frame piece
16. Control rod
17. Hydrostatic control lever

ENGINE

REMOVAL AND INSTALLATION

Remove the hood, grille brace, or side panels, and grille. Disconnect the battery cables, starter wires and all necessary electrical connections from the engine. Disconnect the fuel line. Disconnect the choke and throttle control cables from the engine.

Remove the engine shrouds. Disconnect the drive shaft from the rear of the engine. Detach the PTO pulley from the front of the engine.

Remove the bolts securing the engine to the frame and lift the engine from the tractor.

Install by reversing the removal procedure.

OVERHAUL

Refer to the appropriate engine section in this manual for tune-up specifications, engine overhaul procedures and engine maintenance.

BRAKE

ADJUSTMENT

The brake is located on the left side of the final drive. The brake adjustment access hole is located above the left rear axle mounting bracket.

To adjust the brake, loosen the jam nut (10—Fig. Y4-2) and use a 7/16-inch socket and extension to tighten the adjustment bolt (11) until the pads (3 and 4) are pushed against the brake disc (2). Loosen the adjustment bolt ½ turn and check the brake operation. When satisfactory, tighten the jam nut (10).

BRAKE PADS

Disconnect the brake rod and springs (12 and 13—Fig. Y4-2) from the brake lever (8). Remove the bolts securing the caliper (7) to the final drive. Remove the brake pad (4), metal backing plate (5) and actuating pin (6) from the caliper (7). Remove the disc (2) and inner pad (3).

Reinstall by reversing the removal procedure. Adjust the brake as previously outlined.

DRIVE SHAFT REMOVAL AND INSTALLATION

The drive shaft connects the engine to the hydrostatic drive unit. To remove the drive shaft, loosen the setscrew (7—Fig. Y4-3) and slide the drive shaft assembly (6) forward until the rear universal joint yoke slips off the hydrostatic drive unit. Lift the drive shaft and pull the front universal joint and yoke (8) from the crankshaft.

Install by reversing the removal procedure

SPEED CONTROL LINKAGE ADJUSTMENT

Raise and support the rear of the tractor so the tires are off the ground. Disconnect the rod end (13—Fig. Y4-4) from the control rod (16). Loosen the jam nut (12) and the two cap screws (10). Move the slide mounting plate (6) until the alignment hole (5) is aligned with the cam plate (7) alignment hole. Insert a 5/16-inch screw through the alignment holes. Start the engine and run at idle speed.

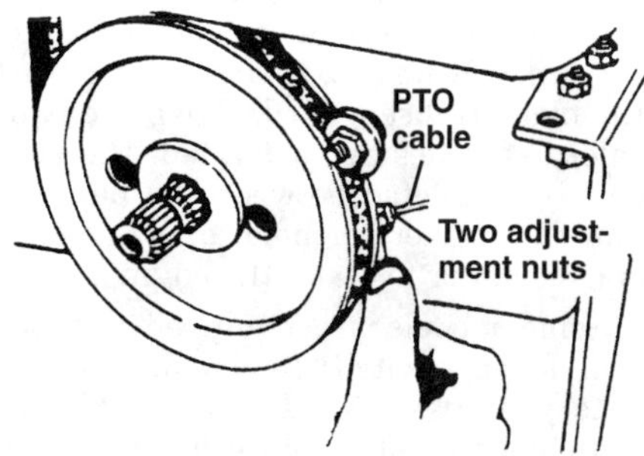

Fig. Y4-5—The PTO cable can be adjusted at either end. Refer to text for procedure.

CAUTION: Exercise caution when working around spinning wheels and drive components.

Rotate the cam plate (7—Fig. Y4-4) until all wheel rotation stops. Tighten the cap screws (10). Shut off the engine and engage the parking brake. Adjust the length of the rod (9) until the rod end (13) can be inserted into the control rod plate. Secure with the lock washer and nut. Tighten the jam nut (12) and remove the 5⁄16-inch screw from the alignment holes.

Fig. Y4-6—Exploded view of PTO system. Crankshaft extension (1) and spacer (20) are not used on all models.

1. Crankshaft extension
2. Cover
3. Belt guide
4. PTO actuator lever
5. PTO handle
6. Bearing retainer bracket
7. Bearing flanges
8. Bearings
9. PTO drive shaft
10. Bearing retainer bracket
11. PTO brake assy.
12. Belt guard
13. PTO cup
14. PTO pulley
15. Snap ring
16. Idler pulley
17. Bolt
18. Bolt
19. Engine pulley
20. Spacer
21. Spring
22. Idler adapter
23. PTO safety switch
24. Idler bracket
25. Spring
26. Heat shield
27. Belleville washer
28. Spacer
29. Bolt

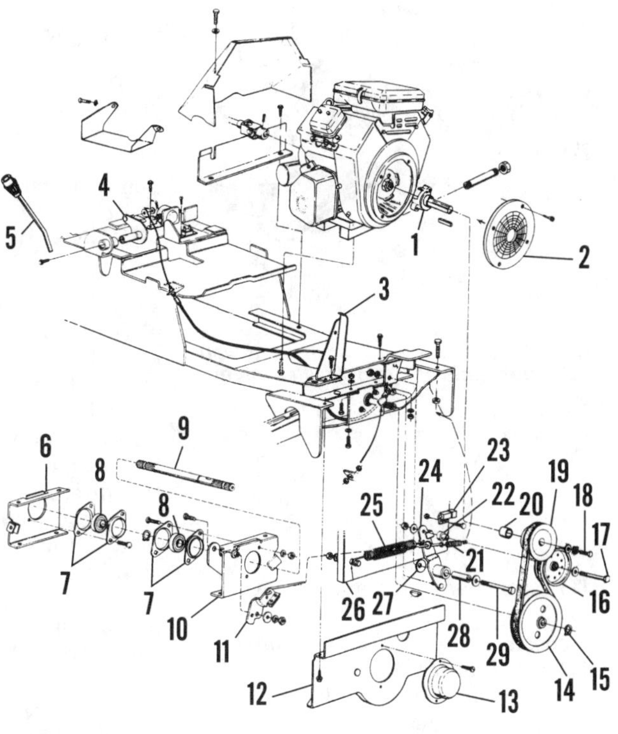

HYDROSTATIC TRANSMISSION

LUBRICATION

The hydrostatic drive unit and two-speed final drive share a common fluid reservoir located in the final drive housing. Check the fluid level with the dipstick (1—Fig. Y4-4) located just below the seat and deck assembly at the rear of the tractor. Check the fluid level when the fluid is cold. Maintain the fluid level at the "FULL" mark on the dipstick.

Change the fluid and filter at 100-hour intervals. Approximate fluid capacity is 6 quarts (5.7 L). Recommended fluid is SAE 20W engine oil with service classification SF.

REMOVAL AND INSTALLATION

To remove the hydrostatic transmission, remove the seat, fenders and drive shaft. Disconnect the hydraulic hoses and plug or cap the openings to prevent dirt from entering the system. Disconnect the hydrostatic drive control linkage. Remove the bolts retaining the hydrostatic unit to the final drive and remove the unit from the tractor.

To install the hydrostatic unit, reverse the removal procedure. Fill with the recommended fluid and adjust the control linkage as previously outlined.

OVERHAUL

The tractor is equipped with an Eaton Model 11 hydrostatic transmission. Refer to the HYDROSTATIC TRANSMISSION section at the rear of this manual for transmission overhaul information.

FINAL DRIVE

LUBRICATION

Refer to the previous Hydrostatic Transmission section for lubrication information.

REMOVAL AND INSTALLATION

To remove the final drive, first remove the hydrostatic transmission as previously outlined. Raise and support the rear of tractor.

Disconnect the brake rod from the brake lever. Detach the two-speed shift linkage from the differential. Support the differential and remove bolts retaining the differential to the frame. Lower the differential and roll the assembly away from the tractor. Drain the fluid from the unit and remove the brake assembly.

To install the final drive, reverse the removal procedure.

OVERHAUL

The tractor is equipped with a Peerless Model 2500 final drive. Refer to the FINAL DRIVE section at the rear of this manual for final drive overhaul information.

POWER TAKE-OFF (PTO)

The tractor is equipped with a front PTO shaft that is belt driven off the engine crankshaft pulley. A pivoting idler system actuates the PTO clutch.

LUBRICATION

Lubricate the PTO engagement lever at 25-hour intervals. Use multipurpose, lithium-based grease.

ADJUSTMENT

Adjust the PTO cable at either end until the idler depresses the safety switch plunger within 1⁄8 inch (3.2 mm) of bottoming out in the switch with the PTO in the OFF position. Refer to Fig. Y4-5.

PTO BELT

To replace the PTO belt, move the PTO lever (5—Fig. Y4-6) to the OFF position. Remove the four screws from the

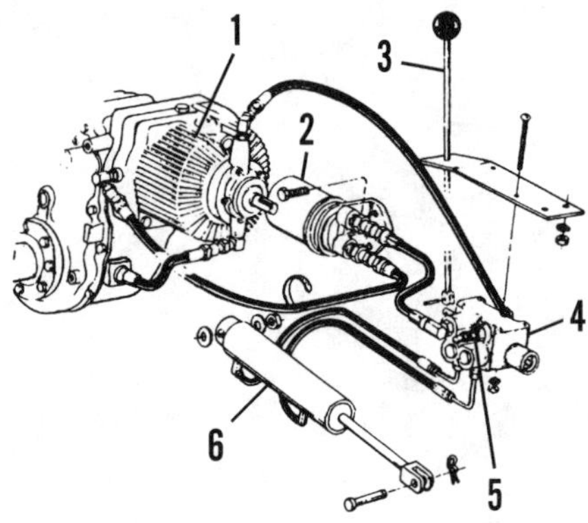

Fig. Y4-7—View showing locations of various components of hydraulic lift system.

1. Hydrostatic drive unit
2. Filter
3. Control valve lever
4. Control valve
5. Pressure adjustment screw
6. Cylinder

PTO belt guard (12) and remove the guard.

Loosen the two screws attaching the PTO belt guard (3) to the frame. Remove the belt from the pulleys.

Install the new belt and adjust as previously outlined.

REMOVAL AND INSTALLATION

To remove the PTO shaft (9—Fig. Y4-6), first remove the mower deck from the tractor. Remove the PTO belt as previously outlined.

Remove the snap ring (15) and withdraw the pulley (14) from the PTO shaft. Unbolt and remove the bearing flanges (7), bearings (8) and shaft (9) from the tractor.

To reinstall the PTO shaft, reverse the removal procedure.

HYDRAULIC SYSTEM

LUBRICATION

Pressurized oil from the hydrostatic drive unit is utilized for the hydraulic system. Refer to the HYDROSTATIC TRANSMISSION section for lubrication information.

TESTING AND ADJUSTMENT

To check and adjust the hydraulic system pressure, install a 0-1000 psi (0-7000 kPa) test gauge in line with the lift cylinder (6—Fig. Y4-7). Start and run the tractor engine at 3600 rpm.

Work the control valve lever (3) in the direction providing a reading on the test gauge. Hold the control lever in this direction to fully extend or retract the lift cylinder. When the cylinder reaches the end of the stroke, the gauge should read approximately 700 psi (4827 kPa). Pressure may be adjusted by turning the adjustment screw (5) on the control valve in or out as necessary.

CAUTION: Do not exceed 700 psi (4827 kPa) pressure as damage to the hydrostatic drive unit may occur.

Hydraulic system control valve (4—Fig. Y4-7) and cylinder (6) are serviced as complete assemblies only.

SAFETY INTERLOCK SYSTEM

Before the engine will start, the key must be turned on and both of the safety switches must be activated. One switch (4—Fig. Y4-8) is activated when the clutch/brake pedal is depressed and the other switch (5) is activated when the blade is disengaged. When the two safety switches are activated, the circuit is completed between the battery and the starter solenoid, allowing the starter motor to crank the engine.

Some models are equipped with a seat safety switch (2) and a reverse safety switch (3). However, these switches are not involved in the starting circuit. The seat safety switch is designed to stop the engine if the operator leaves the seat with the blades or PTO engaged. The blades must be in the disengaged position when shifting into reverse or the engine will shut off.

To test the two safety start switches, first check the two switches to see if the switch plungers are depressed a minimum of 1/8 inch (3 mm) when the blade is disengaged and the clutch/brake pedal is depressed. If the switch plunger is correctly depressed, use a continuity checker to determine if there is continuity across the switch terminals when the switches are activated (plunger depressed). If continuity is not indicated when the plunger is depressed, replace the switch.

To check for correct operation of the seat safety switch, start the engine and set the parking brake. Place the shift lever in NEUTRAL and engage the PTO or blades. Raise up off the seat. The engine should stop running.

WIRING DIAGRAM

The wiring diagram illustrated in Fig. Y4-8 is typical of all models.

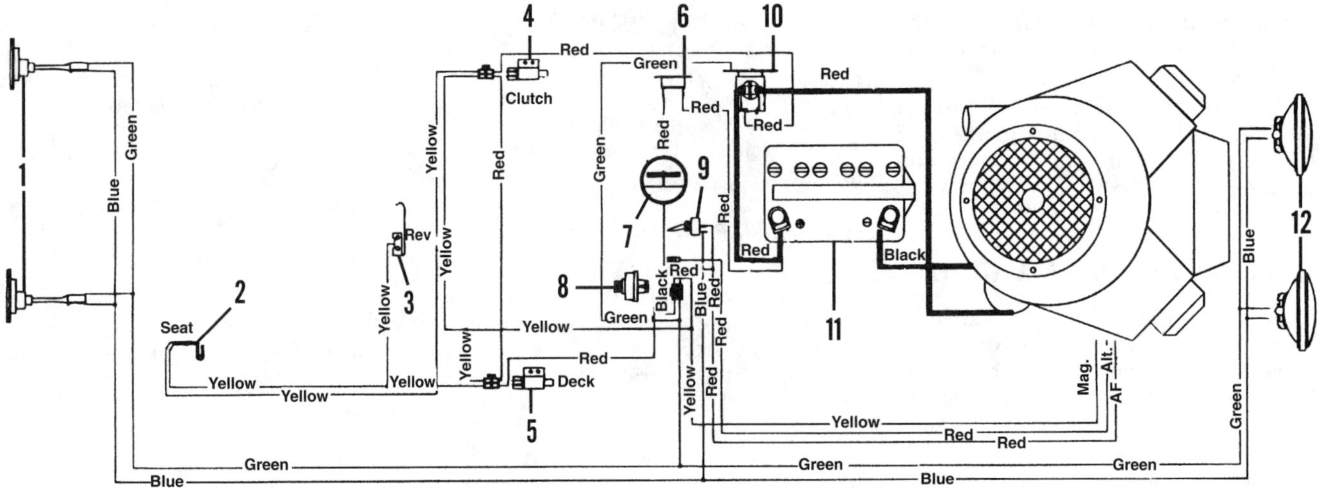

Fig. Y4-8—Typical wiring diagram for 900 series models.

1. Taillights
2. Seat safety switch
3. Reverse safety switch
4. Clutch safety switch
5. PTO switch
6. Circuit breaker
7. Ammeter
8. Ignition switch
9. Light switch
10. Solenoid
11. Battery
12. Headlights

TRANSAXLES

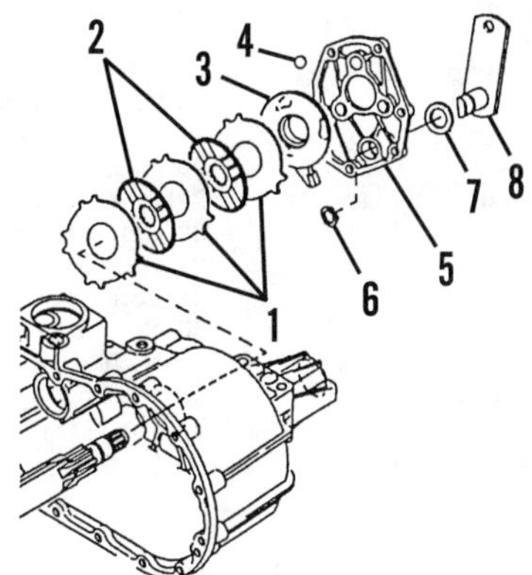

Fig. TR1-1–Exploded view of disc brake used on Tuff Torq Model K211.

1. Plates
2. Friction discs
3. Actuator
4. Balls (3)
5. Cover
6. Snap ring
7. Seal
8. Brake lever

KANZAKI

TUFF TORQ K210 AND K211

Models K210 and K211 are six-speed transaxles with a vertical input shaft. Model K210 is equipped with an external drum brake while Model K211 is equipped with an internal disc brake.

Overhaul

To disassemble the transaxle, drain the oil from the housing. On Model K210 remove the external brake components. On Model K211, remove the brake cover (5—Fig. TR1-1), then remove the remaining brake components shown in Fig. TR1-1.

Drive out the roll pin (2—Fig. TR1-2) and remove the shift interlock arm (1). Remove the cap screws securing the housing halves and separate the housing. Note the location of all thrust washers and shims as the gears and shafts are removed from the housing halves.

Drive out the pins (16 and 17—Fig. TR1-2) and remove the shift arm (18) and shift lever (24). Drive out the roll pin (12) and remove the detent spring (9) and ball (10). Remove the snap rings (15) and withdraw the shift fork (19) from the shift shaft (20).

Separate the gears from the reduction shaft (15—Fig. TR1-3) and shift shaft (34). Remove the shift collar assembly (3 through 8—Fig. TR1-2) from the shift shaft. Remove the spring ring (8) and drive out the pins (7) to disassemble the shift collar assembly.

Remove the E-ring (1—Fig. TR1-3), pulley (2), snap ring (3) and washer (4) from the input shaft (10). Carefully pry the oil seal (5) from the housing bore, then remove the snap ring (6) and tap the input shaft with bearings out of the housing.

Remove the snap rings (7—Fig. TR1-4) and press the axle shafts (1 and 17) and needle bearings (4) out of the housing halves. Remove the mounting bolts from the differential case halves and separate the ring gear (8) and differential components. Note that the bearing (9) must be pressed outward from the case half (10) if replacement is necessary.

Inspect all parts for damage and replace when necessary. Refer to the following specifications:

Shift arm OD . . . . **16.96-17.00 mm (0.668-0.669 in.)**
Shift fork shaft OD . . . . **16.96-17.00 mm (0.668-0.669 in.)**
Transaxle housing shifter bore ID . . . . **17.02-17.04 mm (0.670-0.671 in.)**
Shift collar groove width . . . . . . **6.1-6.2 mm (0.240-0.244 in.)**
Shift fork thickness . . . . **5.7-5.9 mm (0.224-0.232 in.)**
Differential thrust washer thickness— min. . . . . **0.5 mm (0.020 in.)**
Differential pinion gear ID . . . . **14.02-14.03 mm (0.552-0.553 in.)**

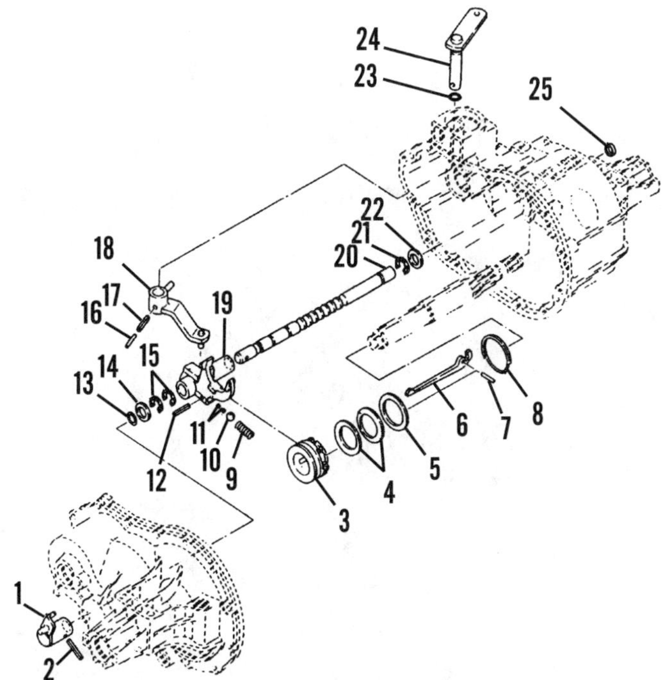

Fig. TR1-2–Exploded view of Tuff Torq transaxle shift components.

1. Shift interlock
2. Roll pin
3. Shift collar
4. Spring washers
5. Thrust washer
6. Shift key
7. Pin
8. Spring ring
9. Detent sprng
10. Ball
11. Balls
12. Roll pin
13. O-ring
14. Washer
15. Retainer rings
16. Pin
17. Pin
18. Shift arm
19. Shift fork
20. Shift shaft
21. Retainer ring
22. Washer
23. O-ring
24. Shift lever
25. Plug

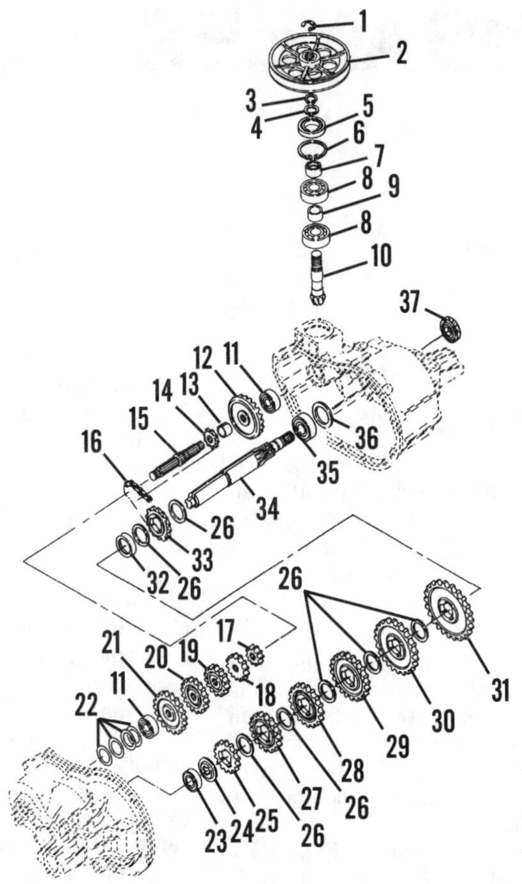

Fig. TR1-3–Exploded view of Tuff Torq transaxle assembly.

1. E-ring
2. Pulley
3. Snap ring
4. Washer
5. Oil seal
6. Snap ring
7. Sleeve
8. Bearings
9. Spacer
10. Input shaft
11. Bearing
12. Bevel gear
13. Bushing
14. Sprocket
15. Reduction shaft
16. Drive chaing
17. Gear (14 T)
18. Gear (18 T)
19. Gear (23 T)
20. Gear (26 T)
21. Gear (32 T)
22. Shims
23. Bearing
24. Washer
25. Gear (24 T)
26. Thrust washers
27. Gear (30 T)
28. Gear (34 T)
29. Gear (38 T)
30. Gear (49 T)
31. Gear (62 T)
32. Collar
33. Sprocket
34. Shift shaft
35. Bearing
36. Washer
37. Oil seal

Differential pinion shaft OD . . . . 13.97-13.98 mm (0.550-0.551 in.)
Pinion shaft-to-gear clearance—
Wear limit . . . . 0.4 mm (0.016 in.)
Axle shaft thrust washer thickness
Wear limit . . . . 1.5 mm (0.059 in.)
Brake lever shaft OD . . . . . 19.95-20.00 mm (0.785-0.787 in.)
Brake cover shaft bore . . . 20.02-20.05 mm (0.788-0.789 in.)

To check the tension of the shift keys (6—Fig. TR1-2), hold the two keys all the way into grooves in the shift shaft. Use a belt tension gauge to measure the pressure required to push the third key into the shaft groove. It should take a minimum of 2.7 kg (6 lb.) to push the key into the groove. Repeat the check with all three keys. Replace the keys if tension is less than specified.

To reassemble the transaxle, reverse the disassembly procedure while noting the following special instructions: When assembling the shift collar components, be sure that the spring washers (4—Fig. TR1-2) are installed with the outside edges away from each other. Install the thrust washers (26—Fig. TR1-3), sprocket (33) and collar (32) on the shifter assembly with the largest

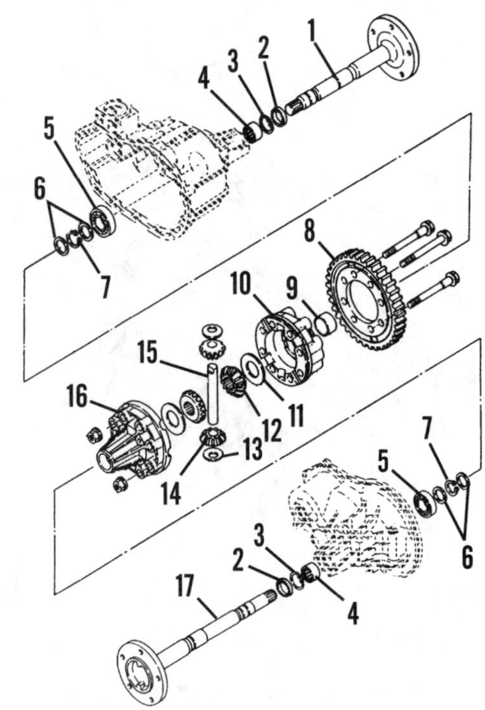

Fig. TR1-4–Exploded view of Tuff Torq axle shafts and differential assembly.

1. Axle (right)
2. Oil seal
3. Snap ring
4. Needle bearing
5. Ball bearing
6. Washers
7. Snap ring
8. Ring gear
9. Bushing
10. Differential case half
11. Thrust washer
12. Differential side gear
13. Thrust washer
14. Differential pinion gear
15. Pinion shaft
16. Differential case half
17. Axle (left)

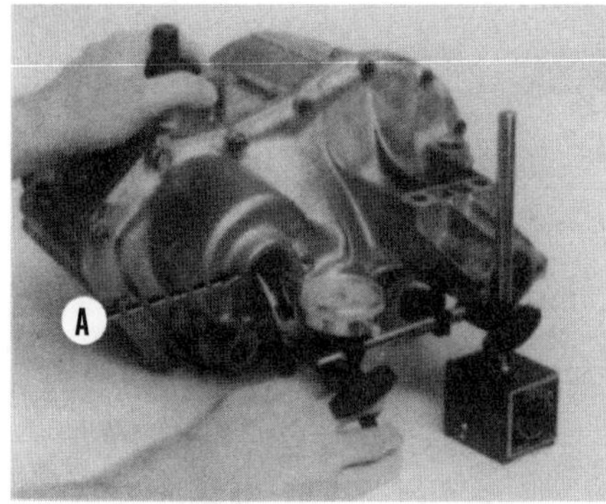

Fig. TR1-5–Use a dial indicator to measure reduction shaft end play. Refer to text for adjustment procedure.

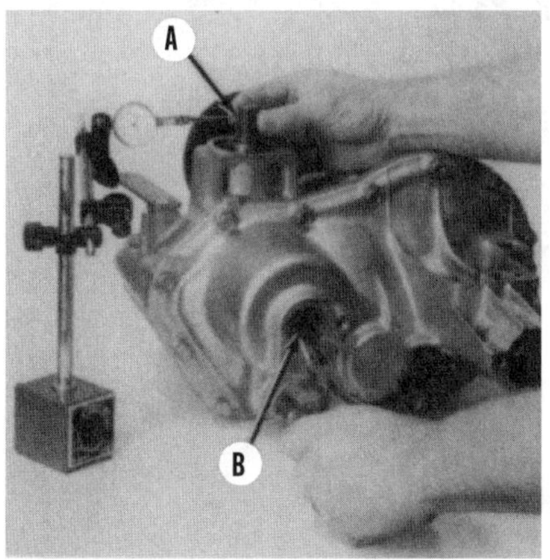

Fig. TR1-6–Use a dial indicator to measure backlash between reduction gear and input shaft bevel gear. Refer to text for adjustment procedure.

inside diameter of the collar (32) facing the sprocket (33).

When installing the dished tooth washer (24) on the shift shaft (34), the outer edge of the washer should contact the last shift shaft gear (25).

Bearings (11) are a press fit on the reduction shaft (15). When installing new axle shaft needle bearings (4—Fig. TR1-4), press the bearings into the housings with the printed side of the bearing facing outward. Apply grease to the lip of oil seals (2) before installing.

When assembling the differential, align the notch in the pinion shaft (15—Fig. TR1-4) with the offset inside the differential housing (16). Note that two holes in the ring gear (8) and housing (10) are larger for installation of the two shoulder bolts. Clean the threads of the differential housing bolts and apply Loctite 242 to the bolts, then tighten to 51 N·m (38 ft.-lb.).

Install the inner detent ball (11—Fig. TR1-2) and shift fork (19) on the shift shaft (20) first, then install the remainder of the shifter components. Make sure that the slot in the roll pin (12) faces away from the spring (9) when installing the roll pin. The shift lever (24) must be pointing toward the right-hand axle when installing the shift arm (18).

Assemble the gears and shafts in the housings and tighten the housing mounting screws to 29 N·m (22 ft.-lb.) if a new housing is used, or 24 N·m (18 ft.-lb.) if the original housing is reused. Use a dial indicator to measure the end play of the reduction shaft as shown in Fig. TR1-5. Install shims (22—Fig. TR1-3) between the left housing half and reduction shaft bearing until end play is less than 0.1 mm (0.004 in.).

To check backlash between the input shaft bevel gear and reduction shaft gear, position a dial indicator against the side of the input shaft splines as shown in Fig. TR1-6. Pull out and hold the reduction shaft while rotating the input shaft back and forth to measure the backlash. Specified backlash is 0.20-0.35 mm (0.008-0.014 in.). Add or remove reduction shaft shims (22—Fig. TR1-3) as necessary to obtain desired backlash.

Apply suitable gasket maker compound to the mating surfaces of the transaxle housing. Tighten the housing cap screws to 29 N·m (22 ft.-lb.) if a new housing is used, or 24 N·m (18 ft.-lb.) if the original housing is reused. Lubricate the lip of the input shaft oil seal (5—Fig. TR1-3) with grease, then install the seal in the housing bore. Install the transaxle pulley and secure with the E-ring (1). Install the shift interlock arm (1—Fig. TR1-2) on the shift shaft (20). Make certain that the gears can be shifted.

Install the brake assembly. Fill the transaxle with oil specified in the tractor service section.

MTD

MODELS 618-0002, 618-0024, 618-0073 AND 717-0542

These MTD transaxles provide forward and reverse motion. A belt drive couples the transaxle to the variable speed pulley. Depending on application, the brake assembly may be located on the right side of the transaxle or on the left side.

Thoroughly clean the exterior of the transaxle case. Remove the input pulley from the input shaft (6—Fig. TR1-7). Remove the brake caliper assembly, brake disc (24) and key (23). Remove all the cap screws retaining the upper case half (4) to the lower case half (44). Carefully separate the upper case half from the lower case half.

NOTE: Note the position of the washers so proper gear backlash can be maintained.

Remove the wire ring (1), if so equipped. Remove the snap rings (2 and 10), washer (3), gear (9), thrust washer (8) and square seal (7). Remove the input shaft (6) and bearings (5) as needed. Remove the shifter assembly (13). Lift the drive/brake shaft (18) and the gear assembly out as an assembly and disassemble as needed.

Lift the axle shafts and differential assembly out as an assembly. Remove the cap screws retaining the differential housing (38) to the differential gear (29). Remove the snap rings (36), cross shaft (39) and spider gears (30). Remove the nuts (32 and 33) and remove the side gears (31 and 34). Pull the axles out of the housing and gear assembly.

Reassemble by reversing the disassembly procedure. Apply grease to the gears and shafts during assembly to prevent galling. Backlash between the input gear (9) and bevel gear (19) should be 0.006-0.015 inch (0.15-0.38 mm). Adjust the thickness of the washers (15, 16 and 17) to obtain the desired backlash. Before installing the upper case half, pack the transaxle housing with 10 ounces (296 mL) of lithium based grease.

MODELS 618-0009, 618-0156 AND 717-1150

These MTD transaxles provide two speeds in forward and reverse. A belt drive couples the transaxle to the variable speed pulley.

Refer to Fig. TR1-8 for an exploded view of transaxle. Disassembly should be performed with the unit inverted (input shaft pointing down). Remove the plate (59) and extract the detent springs (58). Unbolt and remove the lower housing half (55). Locate and remove the four detent balls (60). Lift out the shifter forks (56 and 63).

NOTE: During disassembly, be sure to identify the shims and washers so they can be returned to their original location.

Roll the drive shaft (45) assembly back and remove the shim washers, bearings (37) and shift collar (38) from the ends of the drive shaft. Rotate the drive shaft down into the housing and rotate the output shaft (34) assembly up. Remove the shim washers and bearings (27) from each end of the shaft.

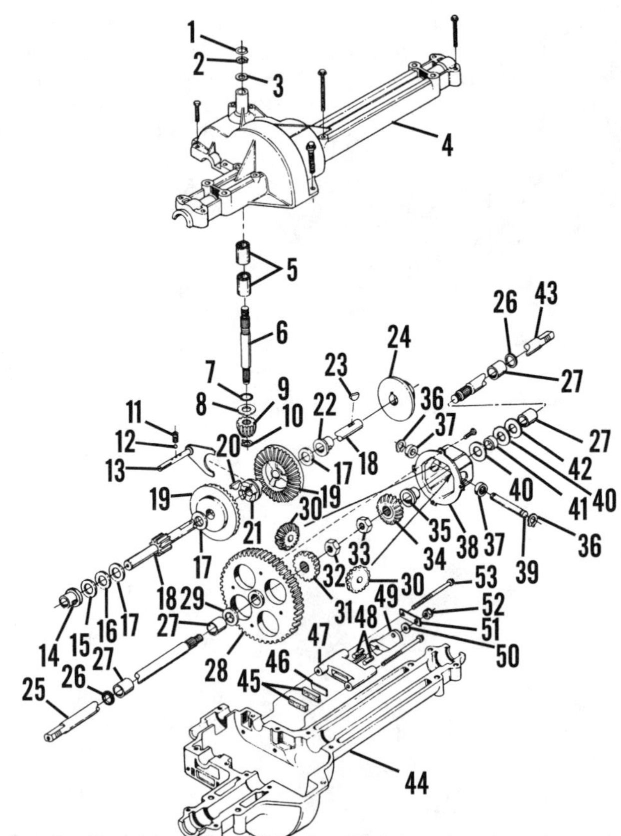

Fig. TR1-7–Exploded view of MTD 618-002 transaxle. Models 618-0024, 618-0073 and 717-0542 are similar. Shift key (20) is not used on later models. On later models brake disc (24) is secured by splines and key (23) is not used.

1. Wire ring
2. Snap ring
3. Washer
4. Upper case half
5. Bearings
6. Input shaft
7. Square seal
8. Thrust washer
9. Gear
10. Snap ring
11. Spring detent
12. Detent ball
13. Shifter
14. Flange bearing
15. Washer
16. Washer (0.020 in.)
17. Washer
18. Drive/brake shaft
19. Bevel gear
20. Key
21. Clutch collar
22. Flange bearing
23. Key
24. Brake disc
25. Axle shaft
26. Seal
27. Sleeve bearing
28. Washer
29. Differential gear
30. Spider gear
31. Side gear
32. Nut
33. Nut
34. Side gear
35. Flange bearing
36. Snap ring
37. Thrust bearing
38. Housing
39. Cross shaft
40. Washers
41. Spacer
42. Washer
43. Axle
44. Lower case half
45. Brake pads
46. Back-up plate
47. Brake pad holder
48. Acutating pins
49. Brake lever
50. Washer
51. Bracket
52. Adjusting nut
53. Bolt

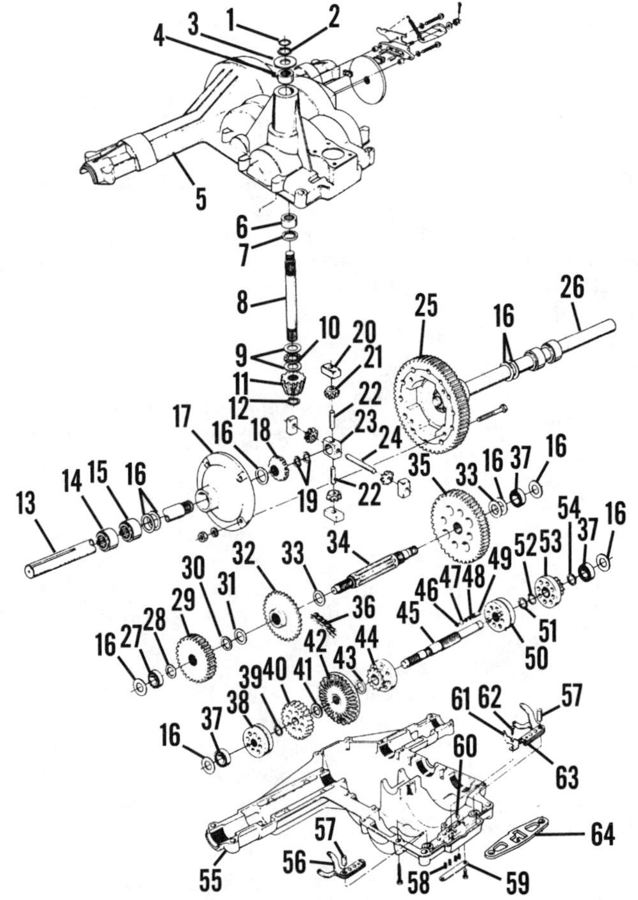

Fig. TR1-8–Exploded view of two-speed transaxle MTD model 717-1150 transaxle. Models 618-0009 and 618-0156 are similar. Lockout plate (64) is used instead of shift guide (61) on later models.

1. Wire ring
2. Snap ring
3. Thrust washer
4. Bearing
5. Upper case half
6. Bearing
7. Oil seal
8. Input shaft
9. Thrust washer
10. Thrust bearing
11. Gear
12. Snap ring
13. Axle shaft
14. Bearing
15. Bearing
16. Washer
17. Differential cover
18. Side gear
19. Retainers
20. Thrust block
21. Pinion gear
22. Shafts
23. Pinion block
24. Shaft
25. Ring gear
26. Axle shaft
27. Bearing
28. Washer
29. Gear (31 T)
30. Washer
31. Spacer
32. Sprocket
33. Washer
34. Output shaft
35. Gear (45 T)
36. Chain
37. Bearing
38. Forward shift collar
39. Retainer
40. Gear
41. Washer
42. Bevel gear
43. Washer
44. Sprocket
45. Drive shaft
46. Retainer
47. Plug
48. Spring
49. Pin
50. Creeper shift collar
51. Washer
52. Retainer
53. Plate assy.
54. Shim
55. Lower case half
56. Shift arm (right)
57. Pin
58. Detent spring
59. Plate
60. Detent ball
61. Shift
62. Screw
63. Shift arm (left)
64. Lockout plate

Remove the disc brake assembly from the output shaft. Remove the drive gear (29), spacer (30) and shim washer (31), and then pull the output shaft out of the sprocket (32). Lift the drive shaft assembly from the housing.

Remove the retaining rings (39 and 52) and withdraw the gears (40 and 53), clutch collar (50), bevel gear (42) and sprocket (44) from the drive shaft. Lift out the differential and axles.

Remove the cap screws holding the differential case (17) to the differential gear (25) and separate the differential components (16-24). Remove the snap rings (2 and 12) and pull the pinion gear (11), thrust bearing (9 and 10) and input shaft (8) from the housing.

Inspect components for damage. Pins (49) must move freely in the clutch collar (50). Replace the pins if broken or excessively rounded.

When assembling the unit, note the following: Apply grease to the gears and shafts during assembly to prevent galling. Outer axle bearings (14) must be installed with the sealed end towards the outer end of the axle. Hub side of the sprocket (32) must be toward the bevel gear (42).

Drive shaft (45) end play should be 0.004-0.007 inch (0.10-0.18 mm). Install shims as needed to obtain the desired end play.

Prior to fitting the case half, fill with 16 ounces (473 mL) of Benalene 372-0 grease.

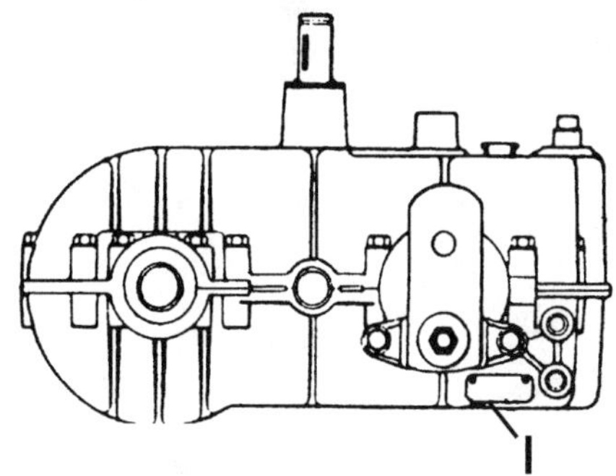

Fig. TR1-9–Peerless model and series numbers are located on a tag (I) attached to right side of transaxle near brake.

PEERLESS

SERIES 800/801

The 800/801 series transaxle may have 4 or 5 forward speeds and a single reverse speed. Oil impregnated bushings are used in the transaxle in addition to the needle bearings or ball bearings on the axles, input and output shaft.

The model number is located on a tag (I—Fig. TR1-9) attached to the transaxle case. Note that 800 series models do not have a suffix number, for instance, Model 834 is an 800 series transaxle. Series 801 models have a suffix number, for instance, Model 801-011 is an 801 series transaxle. Of particular note, Model 801 (no suffix number) is an 800 series transaxle.

Overhaul

To disassemble the transaxle, first remove the drain plug and drain the lubricant. Place the shift lever in NEUTRAL and remove the shift lever. Remove the set screw (2—Fig. TR1-10), spring (3) and index ball (4).

Remove the 17 cap screws retaining the cover (5). Push the shift fork assembly (12) in while removing the cover. Before removing the gear shaft assemblies, the shift fork (12) should be removed.

It will be difficult to keep parts from falling off. Note the position of parts before removal. Remove the gear and shaft assemblies from the case taking care not to disturb the drive chain (34). Remove the needle bearing (43), flat

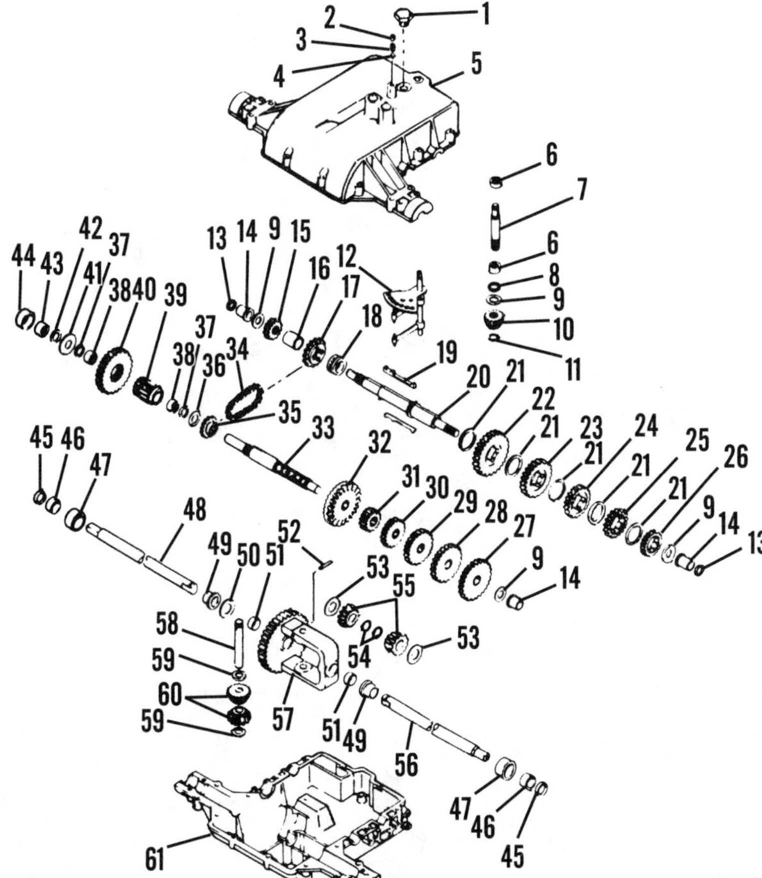

Fig. TR1-10–Exploded view of Peerless 800 series transaxle. Series 801 is similar

1. Plug
2. Setscrew
3. Spring
4. Ball
5. Cover
6. Needle bearing
7. Input shaft
8. Square cut ring
9. Thrust washer
10. Input pinion
11. Snap ring
12. Shift fork assy.
13. Square cut ring
14. Bushing
15. Spur gear (12 or 15 tooth)
16. Spacer
17. Sprocket (18 tooth)
18. Shift collar
19. Key
20. Brake shaft
21. Thrust washer
22. Spur gear (35 tooth)
23. Spur gear (30 tooth)
24. Spur gear (25 tooth)
25. Spur gear (22 tooth)
26. Spur gear (20 tooth)
27. Gear (30 tooth)
28. Gear (28 tooth)
29. Gear (25 tooth)
30. Gear (20 tooth)
31. Spur gear (12 or 15 tooth)
32. Bevel gear (42 tooth)
33. Countershaft
34. Drive chain
35. Sprocket (9 tooth)
36. Flat washer
37. Square cut ring
38. Needle bearing
39. Output pinion
40. Output gear
41. Flat washer
42. Square cut seal
43. Needle bearing
44. Spacer
45. Oil seal
46. Needle bearing
47. Spacer
48. Axle (short)
49. Bushing
50. Washer
51. Bushing
52. Pin
53. Thrust washer
54. Snap rings
55. Bevel side gears
57. Differential gear assy.
58. Drive pin
59. Thrust washer
60. Bevel case
61. Case

washer (41), square cut seals (42), output gear (40) and output pinion (39) from the countershaft. Angle the two shafts together (Fig. TR1-11). Mark the position of the chain on the sprocket collars and remove the chain. Remove the sprocket (35—Fig. TR1-10), bevel gear (32), gears (27, 28, 29, and 30), spur gear (31), thrust washer (9) and flange bushing (14). All gears mesh with the splines on the countershaft.

Disassembly of the brake shaft (20) is self-evident after inspection. Keep the gears and washers in order as they are removed to aid reassembly. Remove the snap ring (11), input pinion (10) and pull the input shaft (7) through the cover.

To disassemble the differential, drive the roll pin out of the drive pin (58) and remove the drive pin. Remove the pinion gears (60) by rotating the gears in opposite directions. Remove the snap rings (54), side gears (55), thrust washers (53) and slide the axles out.

Clean and inspect all parts for damage. When installing new inner input shaft needle bearings, press the bearing in to a depth of 0.135-0.150 inches (3.43-3.81 mm) below flush. When installing the thrust washers and shifting gears on the brake shaft, the 45° chamfer on the inside diameter of the thrust washers must face the shoulder on the brake shaft (Fig. TR1-12). The flat side of the gears must face the shoulder on the shaft.

Before installing the upper cover (5—Fig. TR1-10) on the case (61), pack EP lithium base grease into the case. The amount of grease is 30 ounces (887 mL) for 800 series and 36 ounces (1064 mL) for 801 series. Complete reassembly and tighten the case to cover screws to 80-100 in.-lb. (9-11 N·m).

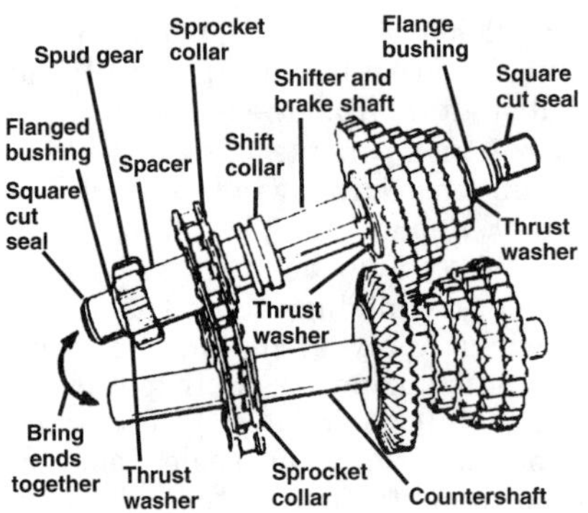

Fig. TR1-11–Mark position of chain on sprocket collars, angle shafts together and remove chain.

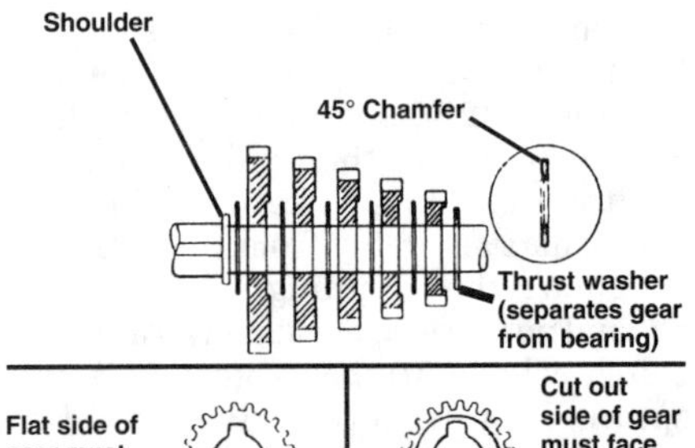

Fig. TR1-12–When installing thrust washers and gears on brake shaft, 45° chamfer on inside diameter of thrust washers must face shoulder on brake shaft.

SERIES 915 TRANSAXLE

The 915 series transaxle provides five forward speeds and one reverse speed. The transaxle model number is located on a tag (I—Fig. TR1-9) attached to the right side of the transaxle housing just below the brake assembly.

Overhaul

To disassemble the transaxle, first remove the wheel assemblies and brake components as outlined in the equipment section and drain the lubricant. Remove the pulley from the input shaft. Move the shift lever to the neutral position and remove the shift lever from the shift shaft. Remove the neutral switch, if so equipped, and remove any brackets attached to the cases. Unscrew and remove the upper case (4—Fig. TR1-13).

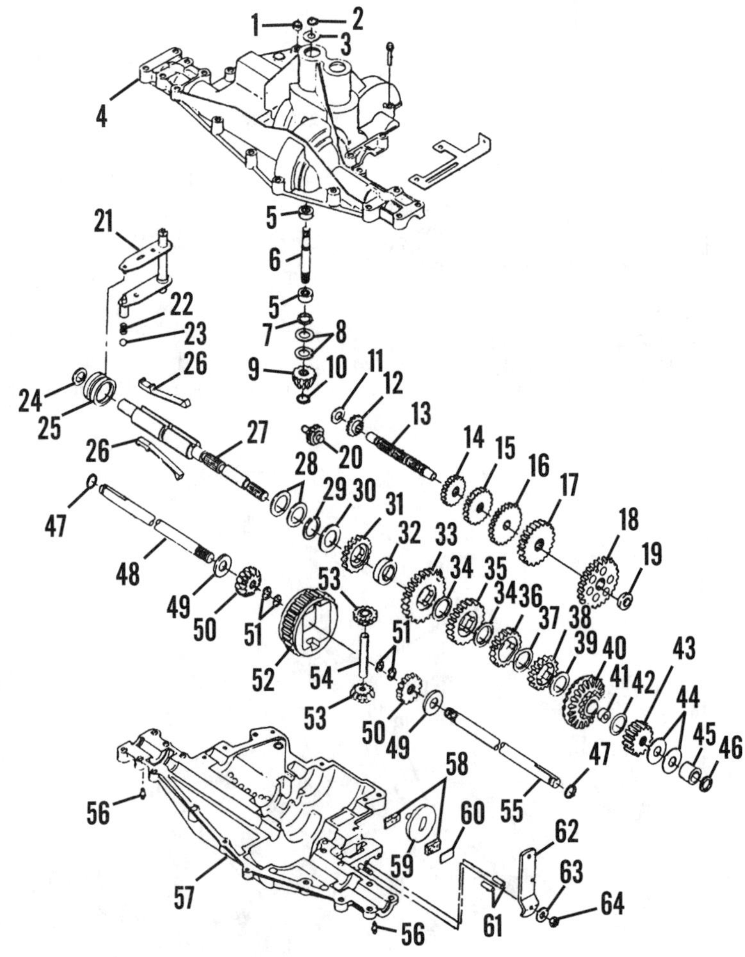

Fig. TR1-13–Exploded view of Peerless Model 915 transaxle.

1. Quad ring
2. Snap ring
3. Washer
4. Upper case half
5. Needle bearing
6. Input shaft
7. O-ring
8. Thrust washer
9. Pinion gear
10. Snap ring
11. Thrust washer
12. Gear
13. Countershaft
14. Geare
15. Gear
16. Gear
17. Gear
18. Bevel gear
19. Thrust washer
20. Reverse idler
21. Shift fork
22. Detent spring
23. Detent ball
24. Thrust washer
25. Shift collar
26. Shift key
27. Shift/brake shaft
28. Thrust washer
29. Snap ring
30. Washer
31. Gear
32. Spacer
33. Gear
34. Thrust washer
35. Gear
36. Gear
37. Thrust washer
38. Gear
39. Thrust washer
40. Bevel gear
41. Needle bearing
42. Thrust washer
43. Gear
44. Thrust washer
45. Bushing
46. Quad ring
47. Quad ring
48. Axle
49. Thrust washer
50. Side gear
51. Snap rings
52. Ring gear
53. Pinion gear
54. Pinion shaft
55. Axle
56. Grease fitting
57. Lower case half
58. Brake pads
59. Brake disc
60. Backup plate
61. Pins
62. Brake lever
63. Washer
64. Nut

Remove the differential and axle assembly from the case and disassemble as needed. Note that two snap rings (51) are used to secure the side gears (50) on the axles.

Remove the shift/brake shaft (27) assembly. Remove the brake disc (59), then refer to Fig. TR1-13 and separate the remainder of the components. The needle bearing (41) in the bevel gear (40) is renewable. Install new bearing so it is flush with the small gear side of the gear.

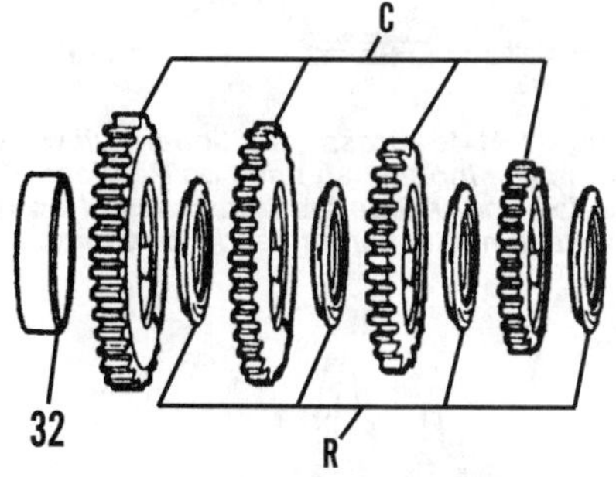

Fig. TR1-14–When assembling gears and thrust washers on shift/brake shaft, note location of spacer (32), cutout (C) side of gears and rounded side (R) of thrust washers.

Remove the countershaft (13) assembly. Refer to Fig. TR1-13 and disassemble the components. Withdraw the shift fork (21) while being careful not to lose the detent ball (23) and spring (22). Detach the snap ring (2) and remove the input shaft (6) assembly. Detach the snap ring (10) and separate the pinion gear (9) from the shaft.

The input shaft needle bearings (5) are renewable. Install the upper bearing so it is flush with the outer case surface and install the lower bearing so it is 0.135-0.150 inch (3.43-3.81 mm) from the inside case surface.

Inspect components for damage. Lubricate all internal components before assembly with Bentonite grease.

Assemble the unit by reversing the disassembly procedure while noting the following: Washer (11) is thicker than washer (19). When assembling gears (33, 35, 36 and 38) on the shift/brake shaft (27), place the rounded side of the thrust washers next to the cutout side of the gears as shown in Fig. TR1-14. Coat the brake disc splines on the shift/brake shaft (27) with Lubriplate before installing the brake disc (59) on the shaft. Install the brake pads (58) and backup plate (60) in the case before installing the shift/brake shaft assembly. Be sure the bushing (45) and quad ring (46) fit in the case properly.

With the gear assemblies installed in the lower case half, pack the lower case half around the gears and shafts with 18 ounces (533 mL) of Bentonite grease. Install the upper case half and tighten the screws to 100 in.-lb. (11.3 N·m). Using a hand-held grease gun, inject one or two shots of grease into the grease fittings (56) at the outer axle ends.

SERIES 920 AND SERIES 930

Both the 920 series and 930 series transaxles are available with 5, 6 or 7 speeds forward and one reverse speed. The transaxle model number is located on a tag (I—Fig. TR1-9) attached to the right side of the transaxle housing just below the brake assembly.

Overhaul

To disassemble the transaxle, place the shift lever in NEUTRAL. Remove the snap ring and drive pulley. Remove the neutral start switch. Remove the

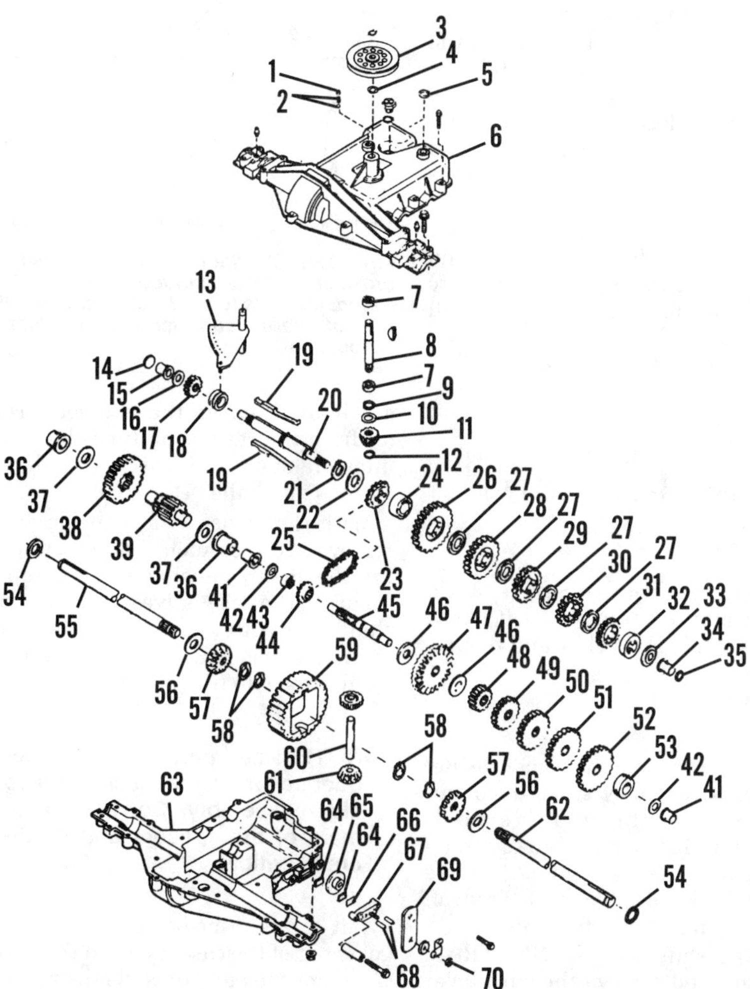

Fig. TR1-15–Exploded view of 930 series transaxle. Series 920 is similar.

1. Set screw
2. Detent ball & spring
3. Pulley
4. Thrust washer
5. Seal ring
6. Cover
7. Needle bearings
8. Input shaft
9. Seal ring
10. Thrust washer
11. Bevel pinion gear
12. Snap ring
13. Shifter assy.
14. Plug
15. Flanged bushing
16. Thrust washer
17. Gear
18. Shift collar
19. Shift keys
20. Shifter/brake shaft
21. Snap ring
22. Thrust washer
23. Reverse sprocket
24. Neutral collar
25. Chain
26. Gear
27. Washers (curved)
28. Gear
29. Gear
30. Gear
31. Gear
32. Spacer
33. Thrust washer (thick)
34. Flanged bushing
35. Square cut ring
36. Flanged bushing
37. Thrust washer
38. Output gear
39. Output shaft
41. Flanged bushing
42. Thrust washer
43. Spacer
44. Reverse sprocket
45. Countershaft
46. Thrust washer
47. Bevel gear
48. Gear
49. Gear
50. Gear
51. Gear
52. Gear
53. Spacer
54. Seal
55. Axle (left)
56. Thrust washer
57. Axle gear
58. Snap rings
59. Ring gear
60. Pinion shaft
61. Pinion gear
62. Axle (right)
63. Case
64. Brake pads
65. Brake disc
66. Back-up late
67. Brake pad holder
68. Actuating pins
69. Brake lever
70. Adjusting nut

set screw (1—Fig. TR1-15), spring and detent ball (2). Remove the mounting screws and separate the cover (6) from the case (63).

Unbolt and remove the disc brake assembly from the case. Remove the gear shifter assembly (13). Remove the upper bearing block from the differential gear, then lift out the axles and differential assembly.

Remove the countershaft (45) assembly, output shaft (39) assembly and shifter/brake shaft (20) assembly from the case as complete units if possible. Remove the snap ring (12) securing the bevel gear (11) on the input shaft (8), then pull the input shaft out of the case.

As parts are removed from the shafts, clean the grease from each part and arrange in order of removal to make reassembly easier. Inspect all parts for damage and replace when necessary.

Lubricate all parts with grease during reassembly. The input shaft upper needle bearing is pressed flush with the housing and the lower needle bearing is pressed into the housing 0.135-0.150 inch (3.4-3.8 mm) below flush as shown in Fig. TR1-16. The square cut seal ring must be replaced whenever the input shaft is removed. Lubricate the needle bearings (7—Fig. TR1-15) with grease before installing the input shaft (8).

Assemble the shifter/brake shaft and countershaft at the same time. Lubricate the keyways of the shifter/brake shaft, then slide the keys (19) and shift collar (18) on the shaft. Install the chain (25) on the reverse sprockets (23 and 44), making sure that the hub side of both sprockets faces the same direction.

Slide the larger sprocket (23) onto the shifter/brake shaft with the hub side of the sprocket facing away from the shifting keys and the shoulder on the shaft. Slide the keys through the sprocket and install the neutral collar (24) over the ends of the keys and pull the collar and sprocket against the shoulder of the shaft.

Insert the splined countershaft (45) into the smaller reverse sprocket (44). Install the thrust washer (46) next to the smaller reverse sprocket, then install the bevel gear (47) with bevel toward the reverse sprocket. Install another thrust washer (46) on the other side of the bevel gear.

Install the spur gears (48 through 52) on the countershaft, alternating with the mating gears (26 through 31) on the shifter/brake shaft. Note that the largest shifting gear (26) is installed first on the shifter/brake shaft and that the flat side of the gears must face the shoulder of the shaft (Fig. TR1-17).

Install the shifting washers (27) on the shifter/brake shaft with the rounded side of the washers toward the shifting keys. Install the spacers (43 and 53—Fig. TR1-15), thrust washers (42) and bronze bushings (41) on the countershaft.

Install the spacer (32), larger thrust washer (33), bronze bushing (34) and O-ring (35) on the end of the shifter/brake shaft. Install the spur gear (17), thrust washer (16) and bronze bushing (15) on the other end of the shifter/brake shaft. Assembly of the countershaft and shifter/brake shaft is complete.

Install the output gear (38) on the stepped end of the output pinion (39). Position the thrust washers (37) and flange bushings (36) on the output pinion. Lubricate the flange bearing mounting surfaces with grease.

Assemble the output shaft, countershaft and shifter/brake shaft assemblies in the transaxle case. Make sure that the tabs of all flange bushings fit into the V-notches of the case. Position the seal plug (14) in the case at the end of the shifter/brake shaft opposite the brake assembly. Install the shifter fork.

Before installing the differential into the case, insert four felt wicks in the case and lubricate the wicks and flange bearing surfaces with grease. Insert the lower bearing block into the case. Assemble the differential and axles and hold in position while the assembly is installed in the case.

Pack 30 ounces (887 mL) of Bentonite grease in the case. Install the cover and tighten the mounting cap screws to 90-100 in.-lb. (10.2-11.3 N·m). Reinstall the brake assembly making sure that the brake pads and disc are free of oil and grease.

SPICER (FORMERLY FOOTE)

SERIES 4000

The Spicer (Foote) Series 4000 transaxle may be equipped with two, three or six forward gears and one reverse gear.

Overhaul

Clean the exterior of the transaxle. Remove the drive pulley from the input shaft. Remove the shoulder bolt (76—Fig. TR1-18) from the brake assembly and remove the brake jaw (72), brake pads (69), brake disc (68) and Woodruff key from the intermediate shaft.

Place the shift lever in NEUTRAL, then unbolt and remove the shift lever

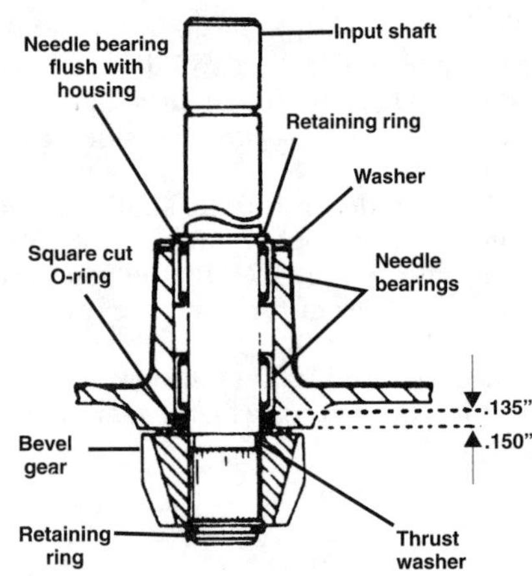

Fig. TR1-16–Cross sectional view of transaxle input shaft used on Peerless 920 series and 930 series transaxles showing correct installation of needle bearings.

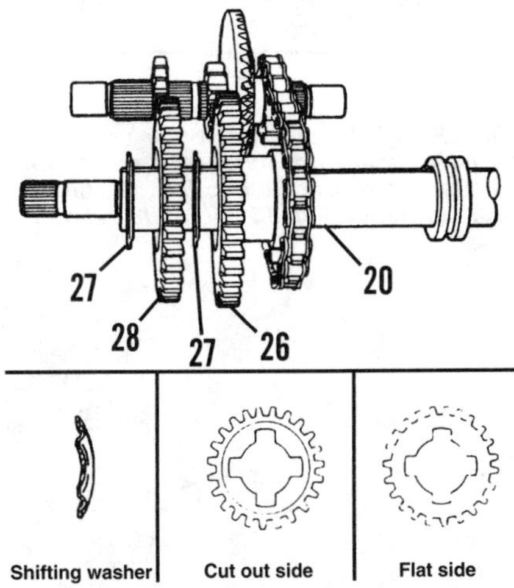

Fig. TR1-17–When assembling shifter/ brake shaft, install curved washers (27) so rounded side is toward shaft shoulder. Flat side of gears also must face shoulder on output shaft.

assembly. Remove the two set screws (3) from the case, then turn the transmission over and catch the detent springs and balls (4).

With the transmission upside down, remove the case mounting screws and lift the lower housing straight up to separate the case halves. Lift the drive shaft (53) with gears as an assembly from the case. All parts on the drive shaft are a slip fit.

NOTE: Keep parts in proper sequence when disassembling to aid reassembly. Correct placement of the spacers and washers is critical.

Lift the intermediate shaft (36) with gears out of the case. Remove the E-ring (23) from one end and slide the parts off

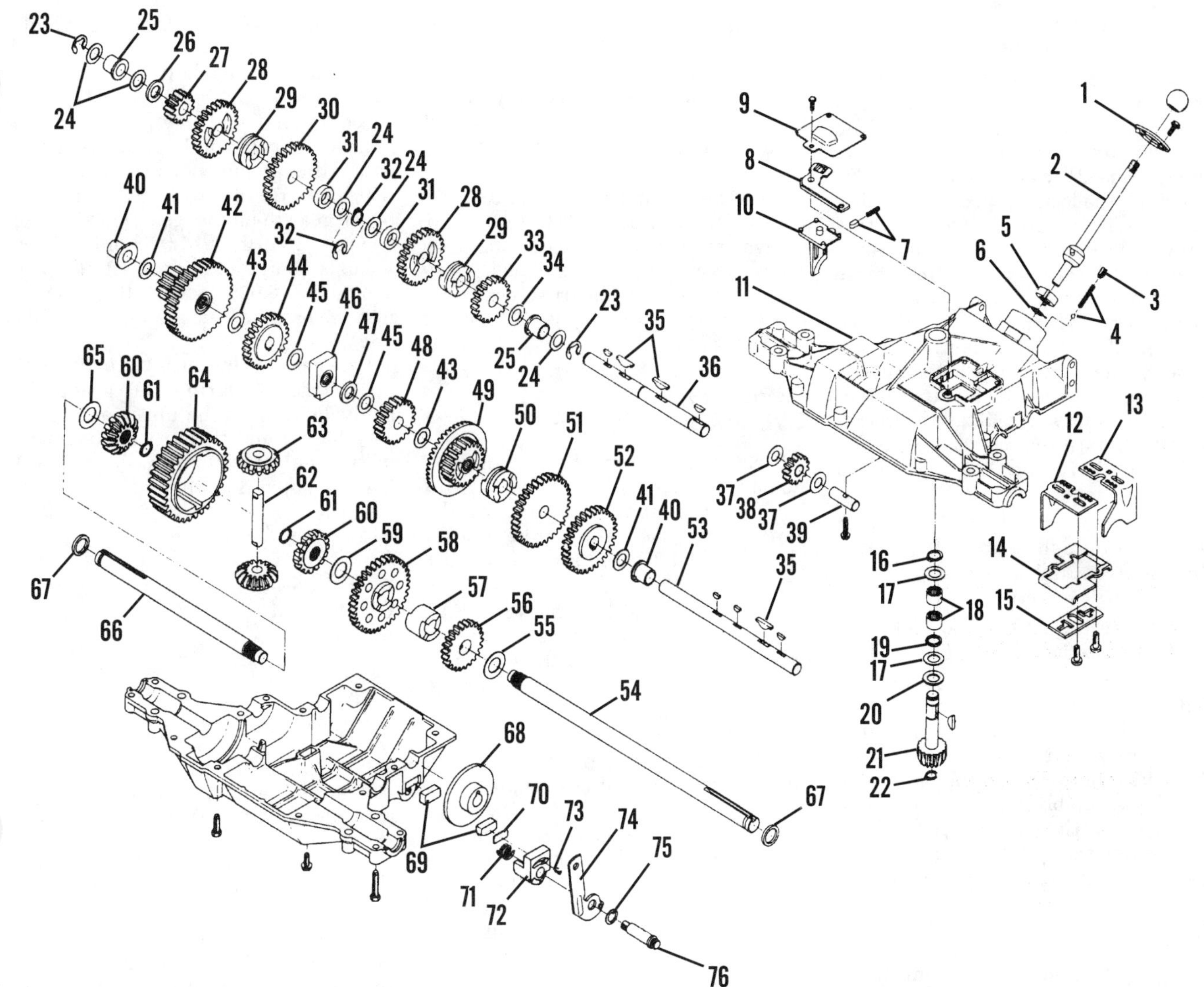

Fig. TR1-18–Exploded view of Spicer (Foote) 4000 series transaxle. Size of washers is listed in parenthesis as their correct placement on shafts is critical. Shim washers are installed as required to adjust end play.

1. Nylon cover
2. Shift lever
3. Set screw
4. Detent spring & ball
5. Nylon insert
6. Wave washer
7. Detent spring & pin
8. Hi-Lo shift lever
9. Cover
10. Hi-Lo shift fork
11. Upper housing
12. Shifter fork
13. Shifter fork
14. Support plate
15. Lock-out plate
16. Snap ring
17. Shim washer
18. Needle bearings
19. O-ring
20. Washer (.040)
21. Input shaft & pinion gear
22. Snap ring
23. E-ring
24. Shim washer
25. Flange bearing
26. Spacer (1.0 x .630 x .110)
27. Gear (13T)
28. Gear (25T)
29. Shift collar
30. Gear (30T)
31. Spacer (1.0 x .630 x .260)
32. Snap ring
33. Gear (20T)
34. Washer (.010)
35. Hi-pro key
36. Intermediate shaft
37. Washers (1.0 x .505 x .020)
38. Idler gear
39. Idler shaft
40. Bushing
41. Shim washer
42. Gear assy. (12 T & 37T)
43. Washer (.045)
44. Gear (25T)
45. Washer (.025)
46. Shaft support
47. Spacer (1.0 x .630 x .110)
48. Gear (20T)
49. Bevel gear assy.
50. Shift collar
51. Gear (33T)
52. Gear (30 T)
53. Drive shaft
54. Axle right
55. Washer (1.25 x .755 x .031)
56. Gear (22T)
57. Gear lock
58. Gear (35T)
59. Washer (1.25 x .755 x .031)
60. Axle gear
61. Axle gear
62. Cross shaft
63. Bevel gar
64. Differential gear
65. Shim washer
66. Axle (left)
67. Felt seal
68. Brake disc
69. Brake pads
70. Back-up plate
71. Spring
72. Brake jaw
73. Set screw
74. Brake lever
75. Washer
76. Shoulder bolt

shaft, being careful to keep the parts in order. Push the axles (54 and 66) toward the center of the differential and lift the assembly from the case. Disassemble each part from the differential unit as necessary. Remove the self-tapping screw from the idler shaft (39) and remove the shaft, gear (38) and thrust washers (37).

Remove the retaining ring (22) and press the input shaft (21) out of the housing. Press out the needle bearings (18), being careful not to damage the bore of the housing.

Remove the shifter fork mounting screws and remove the shifter forks (12 and 13), support plate (14) and lock-out plate (15). Unbolt and remove the cover plate (9), Hi-Lo shift lever (8) and Hi-Lo shift fork (10).

Clean and inspect all parts and replace any showing signs of damage.

To reassemble the input shaft, press one needle bearing in from the outside of the housing until flush with the outer surface of the housing. Press the other needle bearing in from the inside of the housing until the bearing is recessed 0.093 inch (2.36 mm) below the housing surface. Insert the O-ring (19) and original shim washers (17). Pack the needle bearings with grease and install the input shaft into the housing from the inside. Install snap rings (16 and 22), then check the shaft end play. Add or remove shim washers (17) as necessary to obtain the recommended end play of 0.005-0.015 inch (0.13-0.38 mm).

Install the Hi-Lo shifter mechanism and the gear shift mechanism in the case. Be sure that the flared ends of the fork support plate (14) face upward, and the raised tab of the shifter fork engages the the lock-out plate (15) T-slot. Turn the four shifter plate mounting screws clockwise as far as possible, then turn the screws counterclockwise ¼ turn to ensure free movement of the shifter forks. There should be a maximum of 0.012 inch (0.3 mm) clearance between the head of the bolts and the fork support plate. Install the detent balls and springs (4) and tighten the set screws (3) until the screws are flush to 0.030 inch (0.76 mm) below the top of the case.

Install the idler gear (38), thrust washers (37) and shaft (39). Tighten the shaft retaining screw to 80-90 in.-lb. (9.0-10.1 N·m).

Assemble the differential and axles and install in the case.

Assemble the gears (28, 30 and 33), shift collars (29), spacers and washers on the intermediate shaft (36). Be sure that the lug cavities in the gears face the shift collars. Install the intermediate shaft assembly in the housing, making sure that the legs of the shift forks engage the grooves of the shift collars. Use a feeler gage to check the end play of the gears on the intermediate shaft. End play should be 0.005-0.015 inch (0.13-0.38 mm) and is adjusted by changing the thickness of shims (24).

Assemble the components on the drive shaft (53) in the order shown in Fig. TR1-18. Note that the gear (44) has two different width keyways; use the narrow keyway during this assembly. The hub side of the gear (44) must face away from the spur gear (42). Install the shaft support (46) with the stepped side facing the hub side of the gear (44). Be sure the gears (49 and 51) are installed with the lug cavities toward the shift collar (50). Install the gear (52) with the large hub side facing outward.

Install the drive shaft assembly in the housing, making sure that the leg of the Hi-Lo shift fork engages the shift collar groove. Tabs on the flange bearings must engage the notches in the housing, and the shaft support (46) must be positioned upward. Use a feeler gauge to measure the gear end play on the drive shaft. End play should be 0.005-0.015 inch (0.13-0.38 mm) and is adjusted by changing the thickness of shims (41).

Pack the housing with 30 ounces (887 mL) of Shell Darina "O" grease or equivalent. Tighten the case mounting screws to 80-90 in.-lb. (9.0-10.1 N·m). Tighten the shaft support screw in the center of the case to 100-110 in.-lb. (11.3-12.4 N·m).

SERIES 4360 OVERHAUL

Clean the exterior of the transaxle. Remove the drive pulley and Woodruff key from the input shaft. Remove the cap screws from the brake holder (64—Fig. TR1-19) and remove the disc brake assembly.

Place the shift fork in the NEUTRAL position. Remove the two set screws (2) from the case, then turn the transmission over and catch the detent springs and balls (3).

With the transmission upside down, remove the case mounting screws and lift the lower housing straight up to separate the case halves. Lift the intermediate shaft (21) with gears and the drive shaft (43) with gears as an assembly from case. Remove the chain (22) from the sprockets. All parts on the intermediate shaft and drive shaft are a slip fit.

NOTE: Keep parts in proper sequence when disassembling to aid reassembly.

Lift out the idler shaft (37) and gear (35) assembly. Push the axles (53 and 59) toward the center of the differential and lift the assembly from the case. Remove the retaining ring (15) and press the input shaft (13) out of the housing. Press out the needle bearings (10), being careful not to damage the housing bore.

Clean and inspect all parts and replace any showing excessive wear or damage.

To reassemble, reverse the disassembly procedure. Before installing the input shaft assembly, pack the needle bearings (10) with grease.

Install the input shaft using the original shim washers (5 and 11), then check the shaft end play. Add or remove shim washers (5 and 11) as necessary to obtain the recommended shaft end play of 0.005-0.015 inch (0.13-0.38 mm) and bevel gear-to-pinion gear backlash of 0.005-0.015 inch (0.13-0.38 mm). Intermediate shaft and drive shaft end play should be 0-0.015 inch (0-0.38 mm). Adjust by changing thickness of shims (17 and 36).

Pack the housing with 15 ounces (445 mL) of Shell Darina "O" grease or equivalent. Mate the upper and lower case halves and tighten the mounting bolts evenly to 80-90 in.-lb. (9.0-10.1 N·m). Tighten the brake holder mounting bolts to 200-250 in.-lb. (22.6-28.2 N·m).

SERIES 4450 OVERHAUL

To disassemble the transaxle, remove the mounting screws and separate the case halves. Lift the drive shaft (35—Fig. TR1-20) and axles (19 and 26) with gears from the case. All parts are a slip fit on the shafts.

Remove the cap screw (49) retaining the idler shaft (48) and remove the shaft, gear (47) and thrust washers (46). Remove the snap ring (10) and press the input shaft (8) out of the upper case.

Inspect all parts for wear or damage and replace when necessary. To reassemble, reverse the disassembly procedure. Before installing the input shaft assembly, pack the needle bearings (6) with grease.

Install the input shaft using the original shim washers (5), then check the shaft end play. The recommended end play is 0.005-0.015 inch (0.13-0.38 mm). Change the thickness of the shim washer (5) to adjust end play. Recommended drive shaft end play is 0.005-0.015 inch (0.13-0.38 mm). Adjust by changing the thickness of shims (28).

Pack the housing with 14 ounces (414 mL) of Shell Darina "O" grease or equivalent. Join the housing halves and tighten the mounting cap screws to 80-90 in.-lb. (9.0-10.1 N·m).

Figures TR1-19 and TR1-20 are on the following pages.

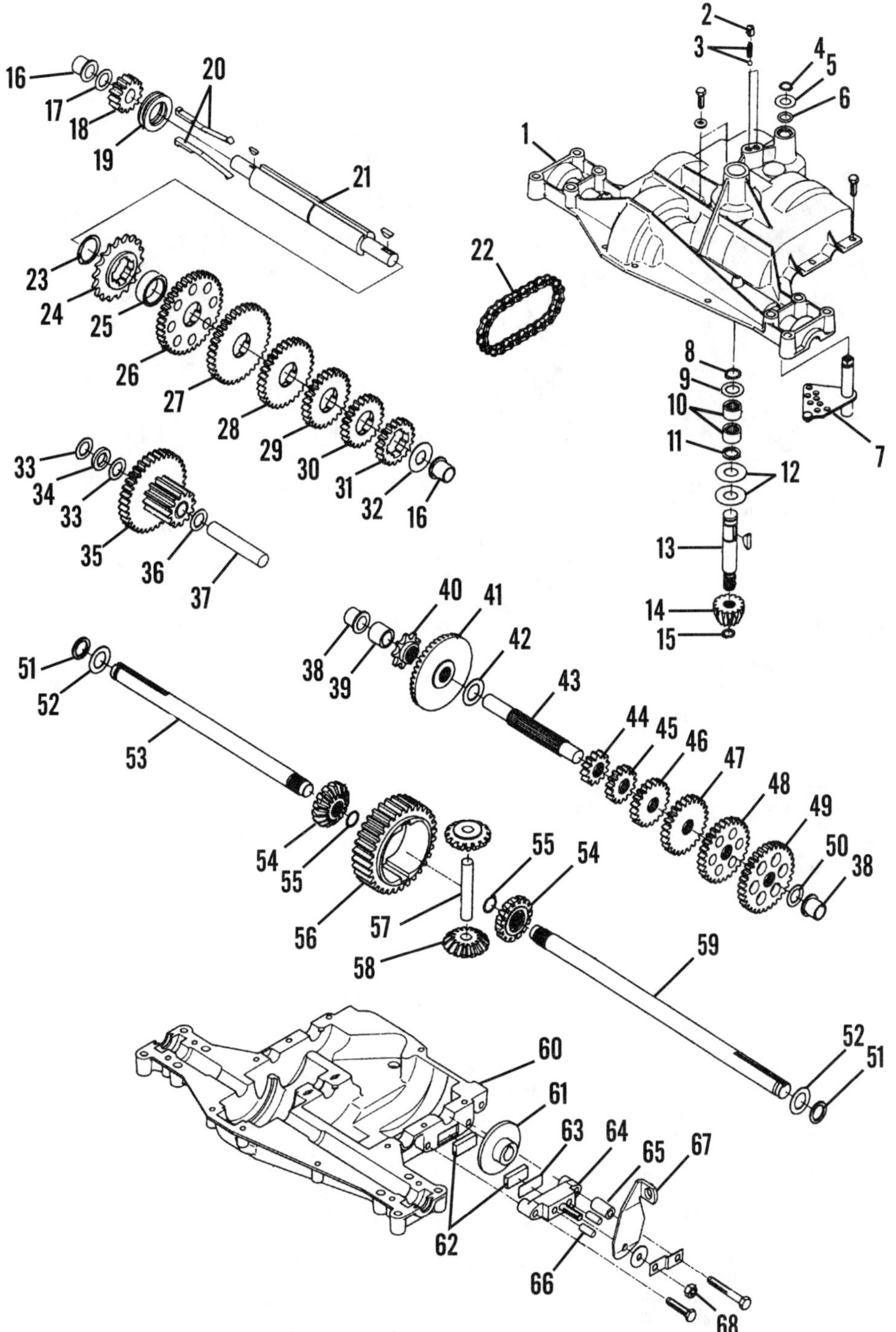

Fig. TR1-19–Exploded view of Spicer Series 4360 transaxle. Unit shown has six forward speeds and one reverse speed.

1. Upper housing
2. Set screw
3. Detent spring & ball
4. Snap ring
5. Shim washer
6. O-ring
7. Shifter
8. Snap ring
9. Shim
10. Needle bearings
11. O-ring
12. Washers
13. Input shaft
14. Bevel pinion
15. Snap ring
16. Flange bearing
17. Shim
18. Gear (14T)
19. Shift collar
20. Shift keys
21. Intermediate shaft
22. Chain
23. Snap ring
24. Sprocket
25. Spacer
26. Gear (37T)
27. Gear (35T)
28. Gear (30T)
29. Gear (25T)
30. Gear (22T)
31. Gear (19T)
32. Washer
33. Washers
34. Spacer
35. Gear assy.
26. Shim
37. Idler shaft
38. Flange bearing
39. Spacer
40 .Sprocket
41. Bevel gear
42. Shim washer
43. Drive shaft
44. Gear (12T)
45. Gear (15T)
46. Gear (20T)
47. Gear (25T)
48. Gear (28T)
49. Gear (31T)
50. Washer
51. Felt seal
52. Shim washer
53. Axle L.H.
54. Axle gear
55. Retaining ring
56. Differential gear
57. Cross shaft
58. Differential pinion
59. Axle (right)
60. Lower housing
61. Brake disc
62. Brake pads
63. Back-up plate
64. Brake holder
65. Spacer
66. Actuating pins
67. Actuating lever
68. Adjusting nut

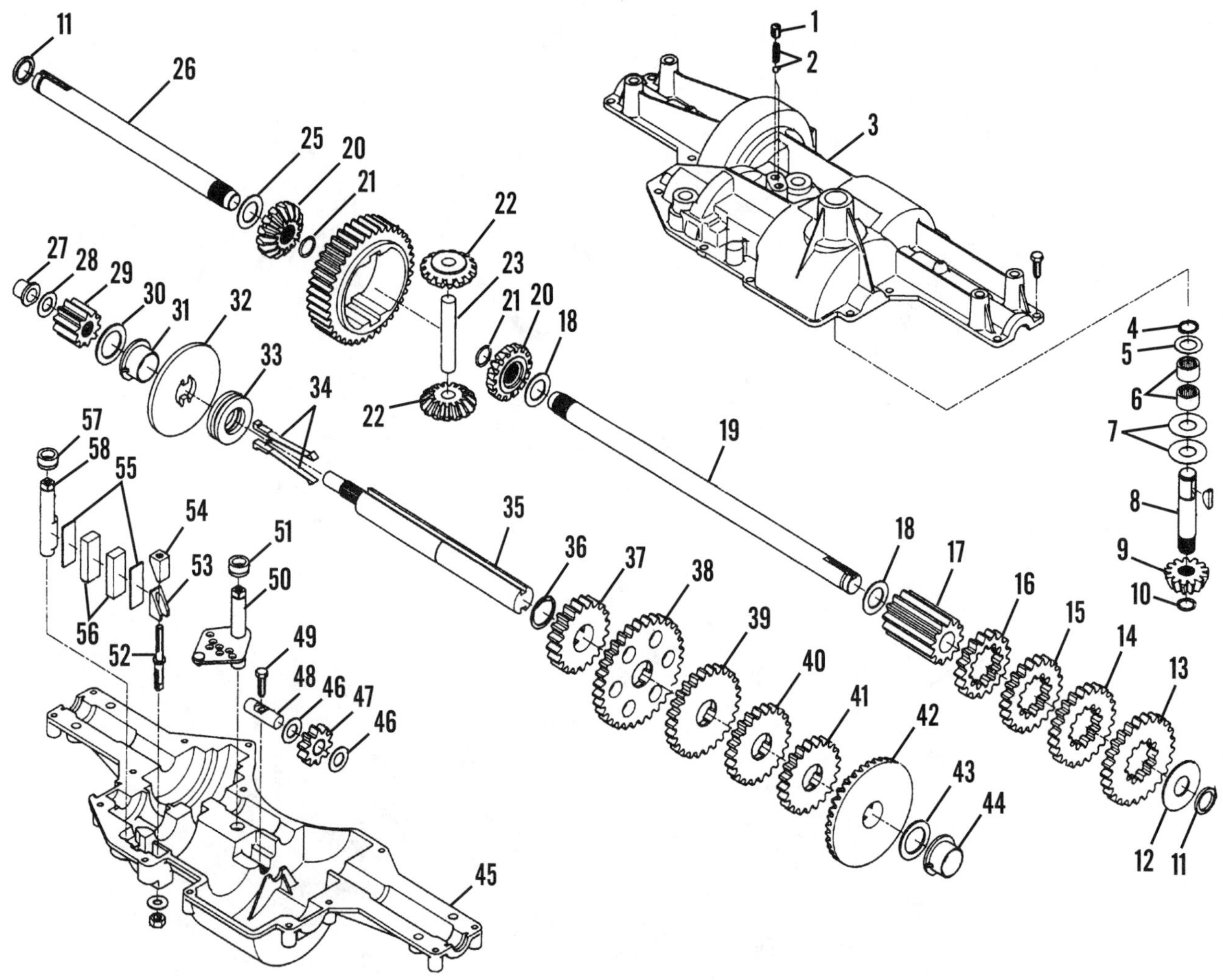

Fig. TR1-20–Exploded view of Spicer Series 4450 transaxle. Unit shown has five forward speeds and one reverse speed.

1. Set screw
2. Detent spring & ball
3. Upper housing
4. Snap ring
5. Shim
6. Needle bearing
7. Washer
8. Input shaft
9. Bevel pinion
10. Snap ring
11. Felt seal
12. Washer
13. Gear (25T)
14. Gear (23T)
15. Gear (21T)
16. Gear (17T)
17. Gear (12T)
18. Washer
19. Axle (right)
20. Axle gear
21. Retaining ring
22. Differential pinions
23. Cross shaft
24. Differential gear
25. Shim washer
26. Axle (left)
27. Flange bearing
28. Shim washer
29. Gear (10T)
30. Shim washer
31. Flange bearing
32. Brake disc
33. Shift collar
34. Shift keys
35. Drive shaft
36. Retaining ring
37. Gear (20T)
38. Gear (32T)
39. Gear (26T)
40. Gear (22T)
41. Gear (21T)
42. Bevel gear
43. Washer
44. Flange bearing
45. Lower housing
46. Thrust washer
47. Idler gear
48. Idler shaft
49. Cap screw
50. Shift
51. Seal
52. Brake adjustment stud
53. Adjustment cam
54. Brake cam
55. Spacers
56. Brake pads
57. Seal
58. Brake shaft

FINAL DRIVES

HYDRO-GEAR

SERIES 210-1010 OVERHAUL

Separate the hydrostatic unit from the transaxle housing. Note that the hydrostatic input and output shafts are coupled to the transaxle shafts with two sets of couplers (44—Fig. FD1-1) that are retained on the shafts with Loctite. It may be necessary to heat the couplers and use a suitable puller to remove the couplers from the shafts.

Remove the wheel and hub assemblies from the axles. Remove the park brake assembly from the brake shaft (22—Fig. FD1-1). Clean the axle shafts (10 and 36) and remove any burrs from the shafts. Remove the input pulley and fan from the input shaft (3). Remove the screws securing the input shaft housing (5) and remove the input shaft assembly. Remove the case screws while noting the length and location of the screws. Separate the case halves (9 and 37). It may be necessary to tap against the end of the drive shaft (18) to separate the case.

Clean grease from internal components and remove the reduction gears (33 and 39), differential and axle shafts, drive shaft (18), brake shaft (22) and bearings from the housing halves. Remove the snap rings (1 and 12) and pull the pinion gear (8), thrust bearing (6 and 7) and input shaft (3) from the housing (5). Unbolt and remove the differential housing (14) from the reduction gear (33) and remove the side gears (27), snap rings (32), pinion gears (30) and pinion shaft (29). Discard the snap rings (32) and differential housing bolts. Use a suitable puller to remove the ball bearings from the housings if bearing replacement is necessary.

Lubricate all components with type "O" grease when reassembling the transaxle. Apply Loctite 242 to all retaining nuts and bolts. Install new ball bearings in the housings using Loctite 609 Retaining Compound.

Install new snap rings (32) when assembling the differential assembly.

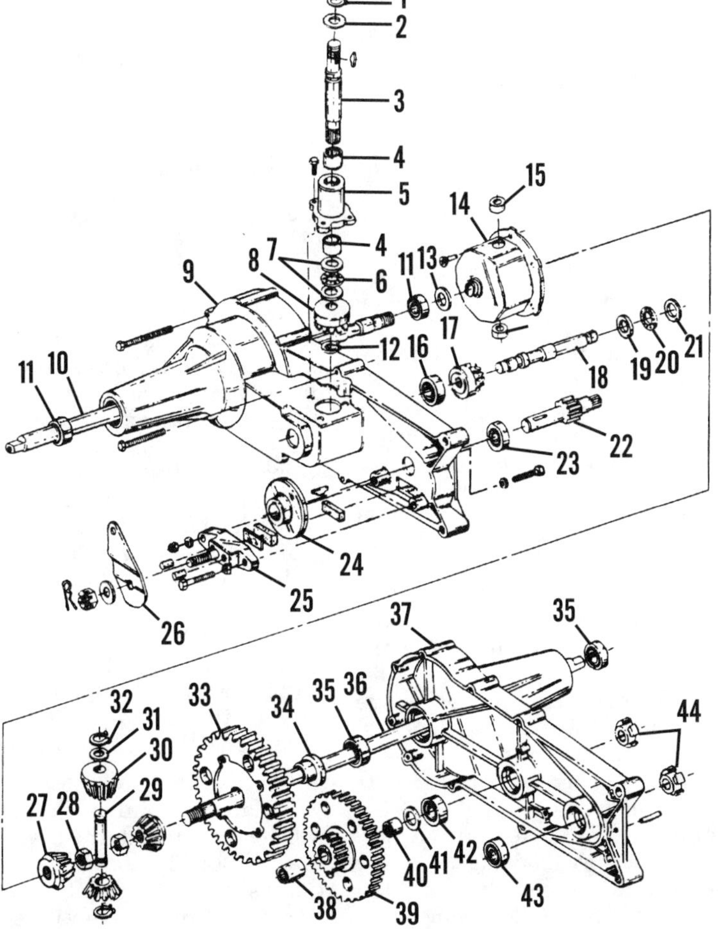

Fig. FD1-1–Exploded view of Hydro-Gear 210-1010 series final drive. Some units use a single needle bearing in reduction gear (39) in place of two bearings (38 and 40).

1. Snap ring
2. Washer
3. Input shaft
4. Needle bearings
5. Input shaft housing
6. Thrust bearing
7. Thrust washers
8. Input pinion gear
9. Housing half (right)
10. Axle shaft
11. Ball bearings
12. Snap ring
13. Thrust washer
14. Differential housing
15. Thrust bearings
16. Ball bearing
17. Drive pinion gear
18. Drive shaft
19. Washer (thick)
20. Thrust bearing
21. Washer (thin)
22. Brake shaft
23. Ball bearing
24. Brake disc
25. Brake caliper
26. Brake actuator arm
27. Differential side gear
28. Nut
29. Shaft
30. Differential pinion gear
31. Thrust washer
32. Snap ring
33. Differential gear
34. Flange bearing
35. Ball bearings
36. Axle shaft
37. Housing half (left)
38. Needle bearing (long)
39. Reduction gear
40. Needle bearing (short)
41. Washer
42. Ball bearing
43. Ball bearing
44. Couplers

Tighten the axle shaft nuts (28) to 40-55 ft.-lb. (55-74 N·m). Install new locking bolts attaching the differential housing (14) to the differential gear (33) and tighten to 180-205 in.-lb. (20.3-23.1 N·m).

When installing new needle bearing in the reduction gear (39), note that the numbered side of the bearing is installed toward the 60-tooth side of the reduction gear assembly and that the bearing must be 0.005-0.015 inch (0.13-0.38 mm) below the face of the 17-tooth side of the gear assembly.

If a new reduction gear (39) is being installed, the correct thickness washer (19) must be selected to obtain the recommended running clearance. To select the correct thickness washer, first install the 0.050 inch (1.27 mm) thick washer and thrust bearing (20) on the drive shaft (18) and assemble the shaft in the reduction gear. Position the reduction gear and drive shaft assembly in the housing. Place a straightedge across the housing surface and measure the distance between the face of the reduction gear (39) and the straightedge (S—Fig. FD1-2). Subtract 0.019 inch (0.74 mm) from the measured distance, the result must be within the range of 0.015-0.030 inch (0.38-0.76 mm).

If the gap is within this range, the 0.050 inch (1.27 mm) thick washer is correct size. If gap is too narrow, remove the reduction gear and replace the 0.050 inch (1.27 mm) washer with a 0.040 inch (1.0 mm) thick washer (19—Fig. FD1-1).

Fill the unit with 10 ounces (300 mL) of Shell Darina #0 type grease. Tighten the screws securing the case halves together to 80-120 in.-lb. (9.0-13.6 N·m). After the housings are bolted together, check for 0.015 to 0.030 inch (0.38-0.76 mm) minimum clearance between the thrust race and thrust bearing using a feeler gauge inserted through the opening in the housing for the input shaft as shown in Fig. FD1-3. If clearance is not within the specified range, repeat the thrust washer selection procedure.

When installing new needle bearings (4—Fig. FD1-1) in the input housing (5), press the bearings in until flush with both ends of the housing. Pack the bearings with grease before installing the input shaft (3). Input shaft end play is adjusted by installing the correct thickness washer (2). Maximum allowable end play is 0.010 inch (0.25 mm).

Pack five ounces (150 mL) of Shell Darina #0 type grease on the input gear. Mount the input shaft assembly in the housing. Apply Loctite 242 to the threads of the input housing retaining screws and tighten the screws to 80-120 in.-lb. (9.0-13.6 N·m).

Reinstall the couplings (44—Fig. FD1-1) using Loctite 609 to bond the couplings to the shafts. Allow the Loctite to cure for 24 hours before operating the unit. Assemble the hydrostatic unit on the reduction gear housing and tighten the mounting bolts to 80-120 in.-lb. (9.0-13.6 N·m).

SERIES 210-3000

The Hydro-Gear Series 210-3000 final drive is designed for use with a Hydro-Gear Series BDU-21L hydrostatic transmission. The final drive provides the oil reservoir for the transmission. A spin-on oil filter cleans oil routed from the final drive to the transmission.

Overhaul

Separate the hydrostatic unit from the transaxle housing. Disconnect the oil hoses and remove the oil filter (1—Fig. FD1-4). Drain the oil from the housing. Remove the brake components (31-40).

Mark the position of the axle housings and remove the axle housings (4) from both sides. Position the final drive so the brake shaft is up. Unscrew the bolts securing the cases together. Tap lightly on the brake shaft and lift off the upper case half. Refer to Fig. FD1-4 and lift out the gear and shaft assemblies. Note the location of any washers. It may be necessary to carefully pry out the input shaft assembly.

Inspect components for damage. The bearings in the case halves are not available separately. Case half and bearings must be replaced as a unit assembly. Input shaft, gear and bearings (26) must be replaced as a unit assembly.

Check the tightness of the differential (18) bolts. Specified torque is 25-32 ft.-lb. (34-43 N·m). The coupling on the brake shaft (13) is a press fit. Renew the brake shaft if the coupling is loose. Remove all old gasket material.

To assemble the unit, install a new oil seal (8) in the filter-side case half (11). Pack the axle opening of the case with Rykon grease or a suitable equivalent to hold the washers in place. Install the notched washer (7) so it aligns with the ribs on the case, then place the outer washer (6) on the notched washer. Be sure the notched washer does not dislodge during assembly.

Install the O-ring (5) onto the axle housing (4) and install the axle housing assembly on the case half. Apply Loctite to the axle housing retaining screws. Install the screws and tighten to 156-180 in.-lb. (17.6-20.3 N·m).

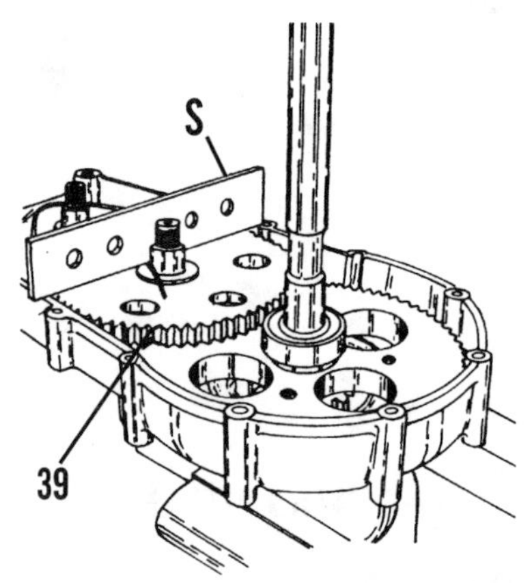

Fig. FD1-2–Place straightedge (S) across housing as shown and measure distance between hub of reduction gear (39) and straightedge. Use this measurement to select correct thickness washer to obtain desired gear end play. Refer to text for details.

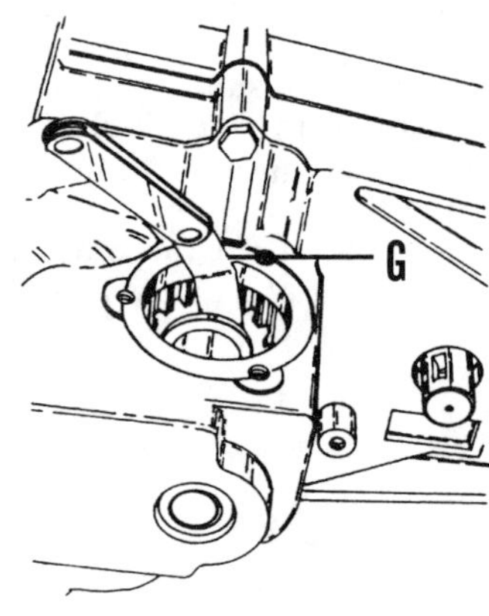

Fig. FD1-3–After reduction gear housing halves are bolted together, use a feeler gauge (G) to check for 0.015 to 0.030 inch (0.38-0.76 mm) clearance between thrust race and thrust bearing.

Position the case half so the axle points down. Place the tab washer (17) on the axle with the tabs up (toward the differential), then install the differential (18) on the axle. Install the brake shaft (13) in the case half with the keyway up. Position the washer (14) and gear (16) on the case half, then slide the jackshaft (15) through the gear and washer into the case half. Install the washer (14A).

NOTE: If the jackshaft does not slide easily through the gear, install the brake shaft with the jackshaft and gear as a unit.

Install the pinion shaft (19) and washer (20). Install the bevel gear and bearing (12). The bearing should enter the case bore using slight force and the gear should rotate freely in the bearing.

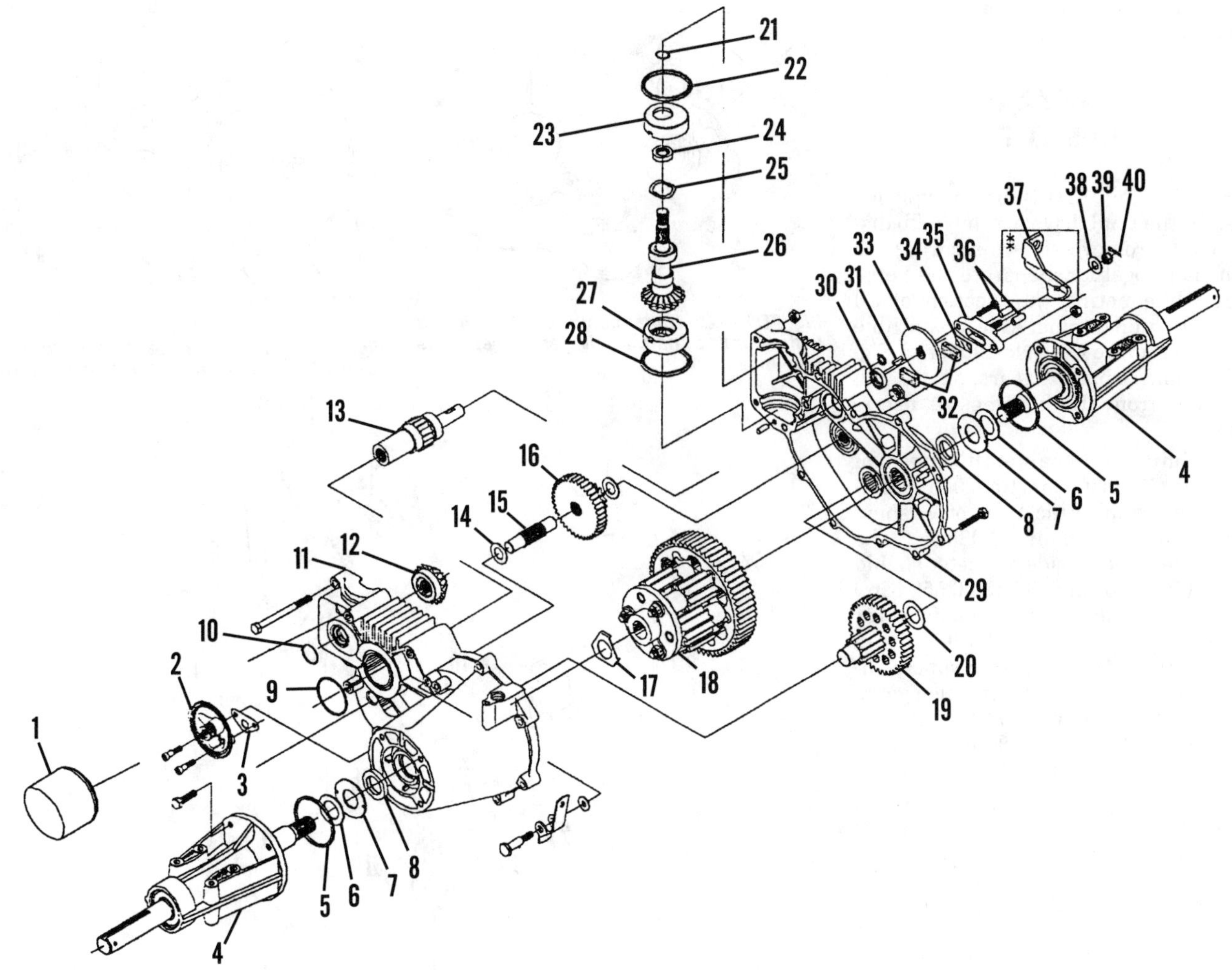

Fig. FD1-4–Exploded view of Hydro-Gear Series 210-3000 final drive.

1. Oil filter
2. Filter adapter
3. Gasket
4. Axle assy.
5. O-ring
6. Washer
7. Notched washer
8. Oil seal
9. O-ring
10. Quad ring
11. Case half
12. Input bevel gear
13. Brake shaft
14. Washer
15. Jackshaft
16. Gear
17. Tab washer
18. Differential
19. Pinion shaft
20. Washer
21. Retaining ring
22. Washer
23. Bearing retainer
24. Oil seal
25. Wave washer
26. Input shaft
27. Bearing retainer
28. Quad ring
29. Case half
30. Oil seal
31. Key
32. Brake pads
33. Brake disc
34. Backing plate
35. Brake caliper
36. Pins
37. Brake actuator arm
38. Washer
39. Castle nut
40. Cotter pin

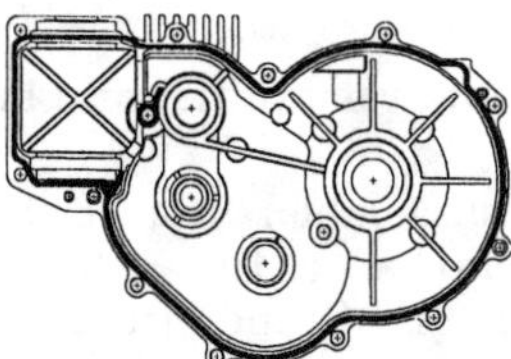

Fig. FD1-5–On transmissions equipped with an input shaft, apply gasket sealer as shown.

Be sure the bearing retainers (23 and 27) are clean and free of old gasket material. Bearing retainers are interchangeable. Install the seal (24) in the upper retainer (23). Place the wave washer (25) on the input shaft (26). Wrap cellophane or tape over the shaft end to prevent damage to the seal during installation. Lubricate the seal, then carefully insert the shaft through the seal. Install seal rings (22 and 28) on the bearing retainers (23 and 27).

NOTE: Use an O-ring if the bearing retainer has a machined groove. If no groove is present, install a quad ring.

Place the lower bearing retainer (28) on the shaft. Be sure the input shaft is properly positioned in the bearing retainers so the input shaft centers on the bevel gear (12). Apply a small amount of liquid gasket sealer on the case where the seal ring on the lower bearing retainer contacts the case. Force the bearing retainers inward to collapse the wave washer, then install the input shaft assembly in the case so the notches in the bearing retainers align with the tabs on the case.

Apply liquid gasket sealer to the remaining case half (29) mating surface as shown in Fig. FD1-5 or FD1-6. Do not apply excessive amount of sealer. Install the case half (29—Fig. FD1-4). Tighten the case screws to 16-21 ft.-lb. (21.8-28.6 N·m) using the sequence shown in Fig. FD1-7. Follow the installation procedure for the previously installed axle housing and install the remaining axle housing assembly. Install the brake assembly.

KANZAKI (TUFF TORQ)

Refer to Fig. FD1-8 for an exploded view of the final drive assembly. To disassemble, remove screws securing the housings together. Separate the housings while noting the location of all washers and shims. Use a suitable press to remove the axles. Refer to Fig. FD1-8 and separate gears, shafts and bearings from the housings as necessary.

Minimum allowable thickness of washers (14) is 0.5 mm (0.020 in.). Minimum allowable thickness of washers (28 and 31) is 2.16 mm (0.085 in.). The pinion gear (18) inside diameter should be 14.02-14.03 mm (0.5520-0.5524 in.) and pinion shaft outside diameter should be 13.97-13.98 mm (0.5500-0.5504 in.). The maximum allowable clearance between pinion gears and shaft is 0.4 mm (0.016 in.). The minimum allowable thickness of washers (11) is 1.5 mm (0.060 in.).

When assembling the differential, press the bearings (8) into the housings so the printed side is out. Insert the axles into the housings and press the bearings (10) onto the axles so the bearing is 4-5 mm (0.16-0.20 in.) below the snap ring groove on the axle. Place the washer and snap ring on the axle, and tap the inner (splined) end of the axle until the snap ring forces the washer against the bearing.

The bearing (3) must be pressed onto the pinion (4). The bearings (23 and 33) must be pressed onto the gear shaft (32). Install the gear (26) on the shaft (25) and press the bearings (24) onto the shaft. Washers (28 and 31) must be installed on the shaft (27) with oil grooves towards the bearing (29).

Be sure the pinion shaft (17) is properly centered within the ring gear (16) when assembling the differential housing components. Apply Loctite thread locking compound to the differential housing bolts and tighten to 27 N·m (20 ft.-lb.).

Assemble components in the right housing (9). Tap the idler shaft (27) to seat it in the housing. Install shims and washers in the left housing using grease to hold them in place. Apply sealer to the housing mating surface. If original housings are being installed, tighten the housing screws to 26 N·m (19 ft.-lb.). If new housings with untapped holes are being installed, tighten the screws to 30 N·m (22 ft.-lb.).

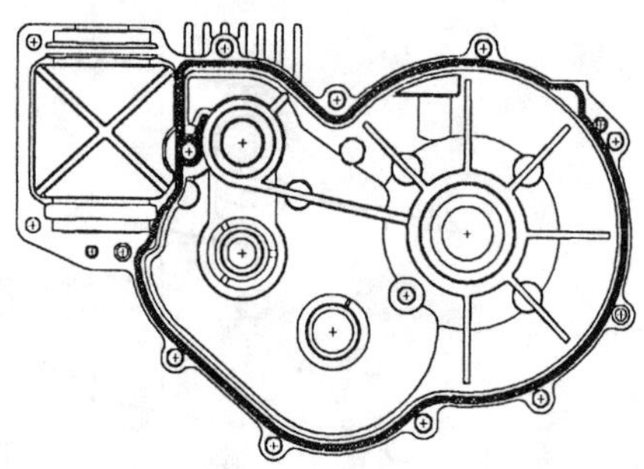

Fig. FD1-6–On transmissions not equipped with an input shaft, apply gasket sealer as shown.

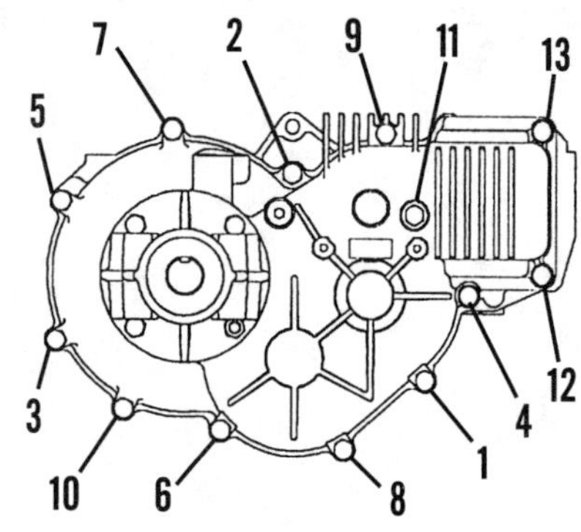

Fig. FD1-7–Tighten case screws to 16-21 ft.-lb. (21.8-28.6 N•m) in sequence shown.

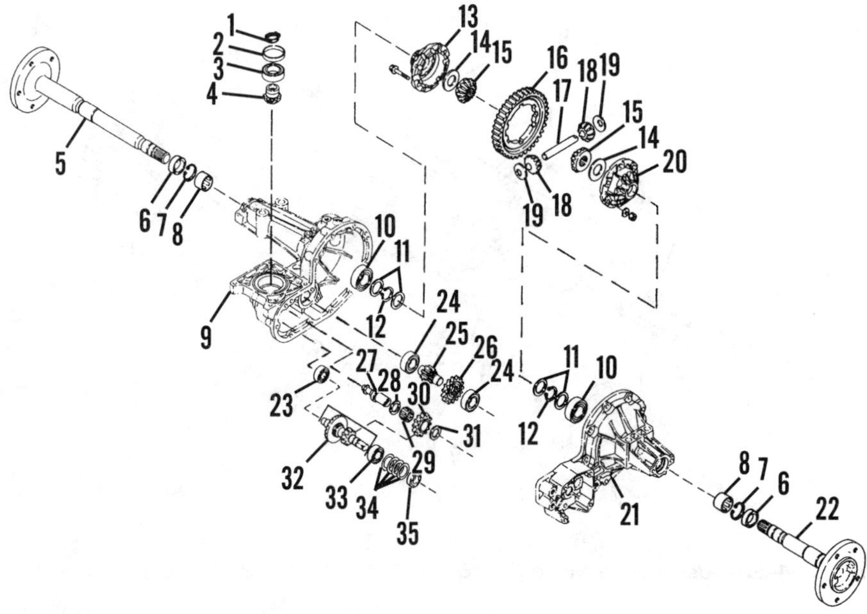

Fig. FD1-8–Exploded view of Kanzaki Tuff Torq final drive.

1. Snap ring
2. Bushing
3. Bearing
4. Pinion
5. Axle
6. Seal
7. Snap ring
8. Bearing
9. Housing
10. Housing
11. Washers
12. Snap ring
13. Carrier half
14. Washer
15. Side gear
16. Ring gear
17. Pinion shaft
18. Pinion
19. Washer
20. Carrier half
21. Housing
22. Axle
23. Bearing
24. Bearing
25. Gear
26. Gear
27. Shaft
28. Washer
29. Bearing
30. Gear
31. Washer
32. Brake shaft
33. Bearing
34. Shims
35. Seal

Measure the pinion (4) backlash while pulling out the splined brake end of the shaft (32). Backlash should be 0.06-0.24 mm (0.002-0.009 in.). Add or delete shims (34) as needed to obtain the desired backlash.

PEERLESS OVERHAUL

SERIES 2500

Clean the exterior of the unit prior to disassembly, Drain the lubricant and remove the hydrostatic transmission. Unbolt and remove the disc brake assembly.

To disassemble, first scribe alignment marks on the axle housings (15—Fig. FD1-9) and case (1) and cover (13) to aid reassembly. Remove burrs, rust and dirt from the axle shafts. Unbolt and remove the axle housings.

Position the unit with the cover (13) facing up, then unbolt and remove the cover. Lift out the differential and axle assembly (40-54). Remove the output shaft (36), gear (35) and thrust washers (37). Unscrew the set screw (2) and remove the spring (3) and ball (4). Remove the brake shaft (32), sliding gear

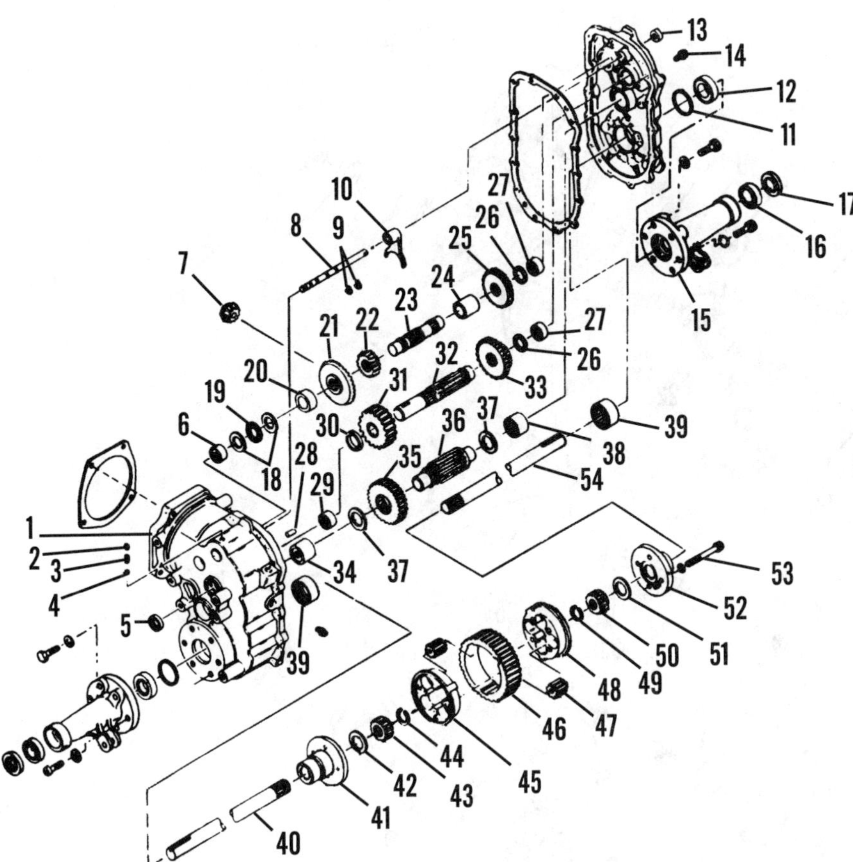

Fig. FD1-9–Exploded view of Peerless 2500 series two-speed final drive.

1. Case
2. Set screw
3. Spring
4. Ball
5. Seal
6. Needle bearing
7. Transmission output gear
8. Shift rail
9. Snap ring
10. Shift fork
11. Quad ring
12. Tapered roller bearing
13. Cover
14. Seal
15. Axle housing
16. Ball bearing
17. Oil seal
18. Thrust washer
19. Thrust bearing
20. Spacer
21. Bevel gear
22. Gear (16T)
23. Shaft
24. Spacer
25. Gear (23T)
26. Thrust washer
27. Needle bearing
28. Dowel pin
29. Needle bearing
30. Spacer
31. Gear
32. Brake shaft
33. Sliding gear
34. Needle bearing
35. Output gear
36. Output shaft
37. Thrust washer
38. Needle bearing
39. Needle bearing
40. Axle (left)
41. Differential carrier (Left)
42. Thrust washer
43. Axle gear
44. Snap ring
45. Body core
46. Ring gear
47. Pinion gears (8)
48. Body core
49. Snap ring
50. Axle gear
51. Thrust washer
52. Differential carrier (right)
53. Cap screw
54. Axle (right)

(33), shift fork (10) and shift rail (8). Remove the input shaft and gear components (18-26).

To disassemble the differential, remove the cap screws (53) and separate the differential carriers (41 and 52) and axles from the ring gear assembly. Remove the snap rings (44 and 49) and separate the axle gears (43 and 50), thrust washers (42 and 51) and axle shafts (40 and 54). Remove the pinions (47) and separate the body cores (45 and 48) from the ring gear (46).

Inspect components for damage. To reassemble, reverse the disassembly procedure. Apply Loctite 242 to the threads of the differential bolts (53). Install the differential bolts so the heads of the bolts are on the side of the shorter carrier (52) and tighten the bolts to 7 ft.-lb. (9 N·m).

Check the movement of the shift rail (8) when tightening the set screw (2).

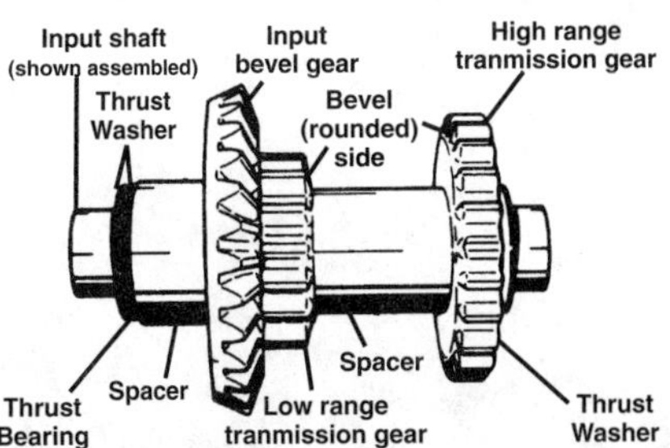

Fig. FD1-10–View of input shaft and gears. Note that beveled sides of gears face each other.

Install the gears (22 and 25) so bevels on the gear teeth face together as shown in Fig. FD1-10. Install the axle housings (15—Fig. FD1-9), aligning the match marks made prior to disassembly. Do not rotate the axle housings after the housings have been pressed tight against the seals (11) as the seals might be cut.

Install the unit in the tractor, then refill with the transmission fluid recommended by the equipment manufacturer.

SERIES 2600

To disassemble the final drive assembly, remove the hitch plate, if so equipped, and remove the six bolts securing each axle housing to the differential housing. Separate the differential housing and axle housings.

Remove the screws and separate the cover (13—Fig. FD1-11) from the case (39). Remove the differential, locking shifter rod, thrust washers and high range driven gear as an assembly. Remove the bolt (40), spring (41) and ball (42). Remove the shift rod (19), shift fork (20), sliding gear (22) and shaft (21) as an assembly. Remove the output shaft (49), thrust washers (47 and 50) and gear (48) as an assembly. Disassemble the gear and shaft assemblies and differential unit as needed.

Inspect all parts for wear, looseness or damage and replace when needed.

Reassemble by reversing the disassembly procedure. Replace all gaskets and seals. Apply Loctite 242 to the differential carrier (60) screws and tighten to 35-40 ft.-lb. (47-54 N·m).

Install the unit in the tractor, then refill with the transmission fluid recommended by the equipment manufacturer.

Figure FD1-11 is on the following page.

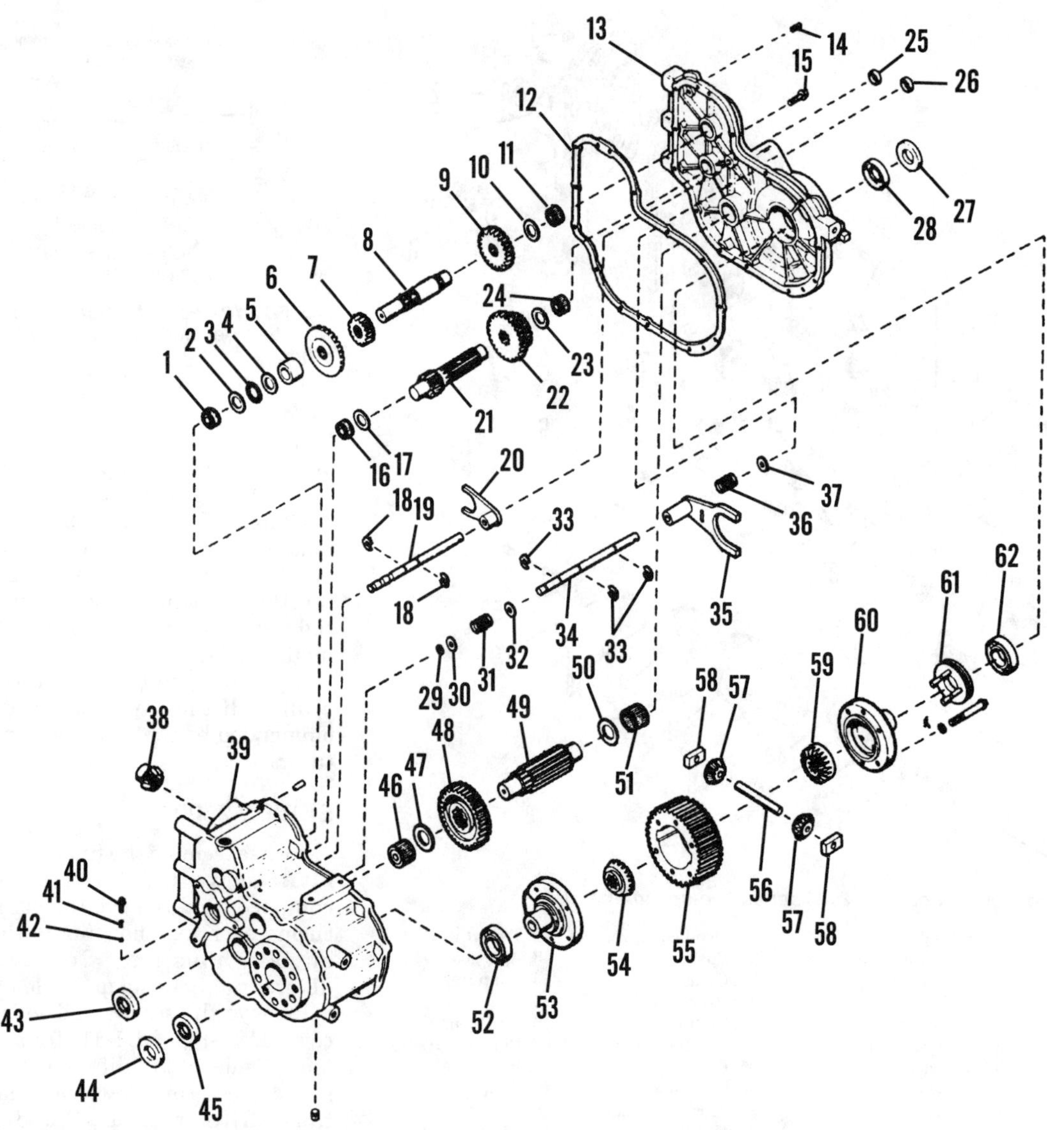

Fig. FD1-11–Exploded view of Peerless 2600 final drive.

1. Bearing
2. Thrust washer
3. Thrust bearing
4. Thrust washer
5. Spacer
6. Bevel gear
7. Spur gear
8. Countershaft
9. Spur gear
10. Thrust washer
11. Bearing
12. Gasket
13. Cover
14. Plug
15. Cap screw
16. Bearing
17. Thrust washer
18. Snap rings
19. Shift rod (range transmission)
20. Shift fork
21. Shaft & gear
22. Sliding gear
23. Thrust washer
24. Bearing
25. Seal (as equipped)
26. Seal (as equipped)
27. Spacer
28. Seal
29. Retaining ring
30. Thrust washer
31. Spring
32. Thrust washer
33. Snap rings
34. Shift rod (differential lock)
35. Shift fork
36. Spring
37. Thrust washer
38. Pinion gear
39. Case
40. Bolt
41. Detent spring
42. Detent ball
43. Seal (as equipped)
44. Spacer
45. Seal
46. Bearing
47. Thrust washer
48. Output gear
49. Output shaft
50. Thrust washer
51. Bearing
52. Bearing
53. Carrier
54. Axle gear
55. Ring gear
56. Cross shaft
57. Pinion gears
58. Pinion blocks
59. Axle gear
60. Carrier
61. Locking collar
62. Bearing

HYDROSTATIC TRANSAXLES

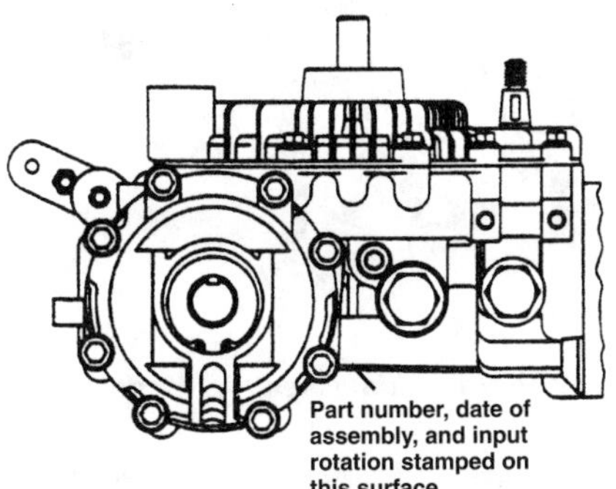
Part number, date of assembly, and input rotation stamped on this surface.

Fig. HX1-1–On Eaton Models 751 and 851 hydrostatic transaxles, the transaxle identification information is located opposite the input shaft, on the back of the housing.

EATON (MODELS 750, 751, 850 AND 851)

OPERATION

Eaton Models 750, 751, 850 and 851 hydrostatic transaxles use a variable displacement, reversible flow, ball piston pump and two fixed displacement, ball piston motors to provide infinite speed and torque output. The Models 850 and 851 are also equipped with a charge pump and an oil filter. Model 750 and 850 are equipped with an external disc brake, while Models 751 and 851 are equipped with internal type brakes.

On all models, changing the oil delivery of the variable displacement pump regulates tractor ground speed. This is accomplished by changing the position of the cam ring in which the pump ball pistons operate.

The system operates as a closed loop. Any oil that is lost from the closed loop is replaced by oil from the reservoir. On Models 750 and 751, the hydrostatic pump draws oil directly into the suction side of the loop from the reservoir through one of the directional check valves located in each side of the loop. On Models 850 and 851, the charge pump forces oil into the suction side of the loop through one of the directional check valves, depending on the direction of rotation.

The transaxle identification information is located opposite the input shaft, on the back of the transaxle housing (Fig. HX1-1).

TROUBLESHOOTING

The following problems and possible causes may be used as an aid in locating and correcting transmission problems.

1. Loss of power or transmission will not operate in either direction.
   a. Broken or slipping drive belt.
   b. Broken speed control linkage.
   c. Low transmission oil level.
   d. Wrong transmission oil or contaminated oil.
   e. Transmission oil temperature too hot.
   f. Transmission roll release valve in wrong position.
   g. Plugged oil filter.
   h. Faulty charge pump or charge pressure relief valve.
   i. Worn or damaged transmission pump and/or motor.
   j. Drive pulley slipping on the transmission input shaft.
   k. Internal damage to the reduction gear assembly.
2. Transmission operating too hot.
   a. Low transmission oil level.
   b. Wrong oil in transmission.
   c. Defective cooling fan.
   d. Blocked transmission cooling fins.
   e. Faulty roll release valve.
   f. Overloaded tractor.
   g. Worn transmission pump and/or motor.
3. Transmission jerks when starting or operates in one direction only.
   a. Faulty speed control linkage.
   b. Faulty charge check valve.
4. Tractor creeps when in NEUTRAL. Could be caused by a worn or misadjusted control linkage.

OVERHAUL

Models 750 and 850

Disassembly is similar for both models. However, Model 750 is not equipped with an oil filter assembly or charge pump.

Prior to disassembly, remove the fan, pulley, and all external brackets, levers and fittings. Thoroughly clean the outside of the unit.

Drain the oil from the unit, and if equipped, remove the oil filter and detach the oil filter base. During disassembly, mark components so they may be returned to their original position.

The axle housing assemblies must be removed to gain access to the hydrostatic motors (24—Fig. HX1-2). The service procedure is the same for either axle housing assembly. Remove the cap screws securing the axle housing (6) and withdraw the axle housing and planetary assembly (1-21) from the hydrostatic housing (29).

CAUTION: Be very careful not to dislodge the hydrostatic motor assembly. The spring-loaded balls (22) are a selective fit in the motor rotor (24) and must be installed in their matching bore in the rotor if removed.

To disassemble the axle assembly, remove the wear plate (21), first planetary assembly (16, 17 and 18), ring gear (19), brake gear (11) and second planetary assembly (13, 14 and 15). Remove the large thrust washer (9), snap ring (8) and small thrust washer (7) from the axle shaft. Remove the outer snap ring (1), and remove the axle shaft (4), oil seal (3) and bearing (2) from the axle housing (6) by tapping on the splined end of the shaft with a soft hammer.

Detach the brake housing (27) and remove the parking brake assembly (28) being careful not to move the brake lever. The brake is self-adjusting and moving the lever will expand the brake assembly, making installation more difficult. The brake assembly is available only as a unit and should not be disassembled.

To remove the hydrostatic motor, place a large rubber band or similar device around the motor rotor (24) to hold the spring-loaded ball pistons (22) in their bores. Carefully withdraw the motor assembly. Due to the selective fit, if the balls are removed they must be returned to their original rotor bore.

To disassemble the hydrostatic pump, unbolt and remove the oil filter base (53—Fig. HX1-3) from the housing on Model 850. On both models, unscrew the fasteners retaining the pump cover (35) to the housing (47). Note that there is a screw located in the drain hole. Separate the cover from the housing and remove the snap ring (30).

Tap or press the input shaft (32) and bearing (31) out of the cover by forcing the shaft towards the outside of the cover. The shaft and bearing assembly is available only as a unit assembly. Drive the input shaft seal (33) out of the cover bore.

Remove the charge pressure relief valve spring (45) and ball (46). Remove the buttons (36), control shaft (37) and cam ring insert (38) from the cam ring (40). Remove the pump rotor drive ring (41). Place a wide rubber band or similar device around the pump rotor (42) to hold the ball pistons (43) in their bores. The balls are a selective fit in the rotor and must be installed in their matching bore if removed from the rotor. Carefully lift the pump rotor from the housing.

The dump valve bracket (51) can be removed from the housing after removing the nut (48). The check valves (Fig. HX1-4) should be flushed with solvent, but not removed, and are available only with the housing. Removal of the dampening pistons (39—Fig. HX1-3) is also not recommended.

On Model 850, the charge pump assembly (1—Fig. HX1-5) may be removed from the housing for inspection after removing the pump plate (2). The charge pump components are available only with the housing (47) as an assembly.

Inspect components for damage. When removing the ball pistons from the pump and motor rotors, number the rotor bores and place the balls in a plastic ice cube tray or egg carton with cavities numbered to correspond to the rotor bores. Piston balls and rotor bores

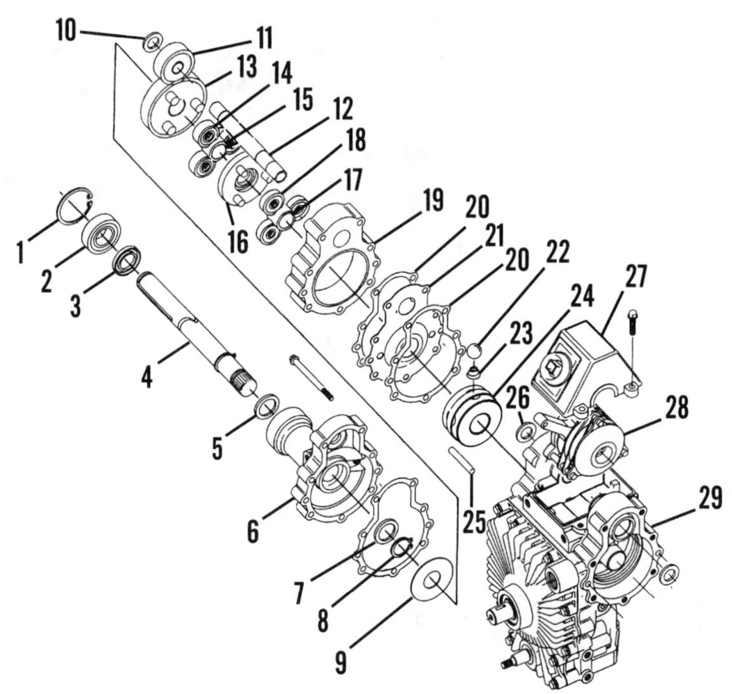

Fig. HX1-2–Exploded view of Eaton 850 hydrostatic transaxle assembly. Model 750 is similar.

1. Snap ring
2. Bearing
3. Seal
4. Axle shaft
5. Thrust washer
6. Axle housing
7. Thrust washer
8. Snap ring
9. Thrust washer
10. Spacer
11. Brake gear
12. Brake shaft
13. Planetary carrier
14. Planetary gear (2nd)
15. Sun gear (2nd)
16. Planetary carrier
17. Sun gear (1st)
18. Planetary carrier (1st)
19. Ring gear
20. Gaskets
21. Wear plate
22. Ball piston
23. Spring
24. Motor rotor
25. Dowel
26. Seal
27. Brake cover
28. Parking brake assy.
29. Transmission housing

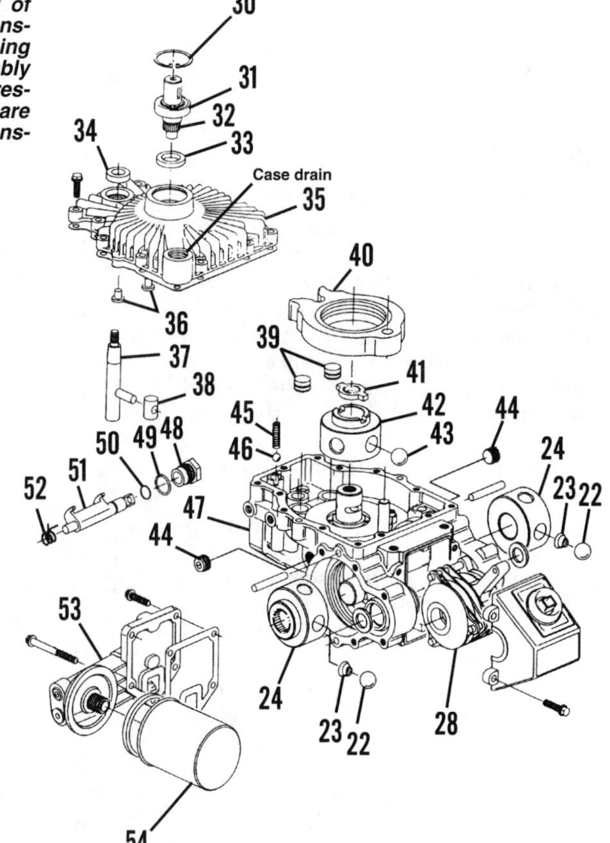

Fig. HX1-3–Exploded view of Eaton 850 hydrostatic transmission pumo and housing components. Filter assembly (53 and 54) and charge pressure relief valve (45 and 46) are not used on Model 750 transmission.

22. Ball piston
23. Spring
24. Motor rotor
28. Brake assy.
30. Snap ring
31. Bearing
32. Input shaft assy.
33. Oil seal
34. Oil seal
35. Cover
36. Buttons
37. Control shaft
38. Insert
39. Dampening pistons
40. Cam ring
41. Drive ring
42. Pump rotor
43. Ball piston
44. Plugs
45. Charge relief valve spring
46. Charge relief valve ball
47. Housing
48. Plug
49. O-ring
50. O-ring
51. Dump valve bracket
52. Spring
53. Oil filter base
54. Oil filter

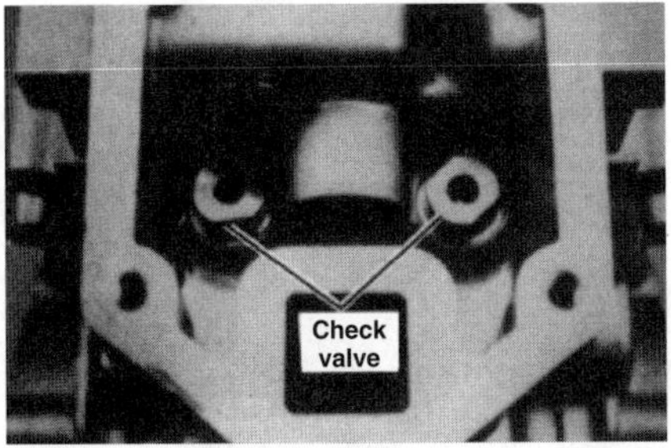

Fig. HX1-4–Check valves are available only with the hydrostatic housing and should be flushed, but not removed.

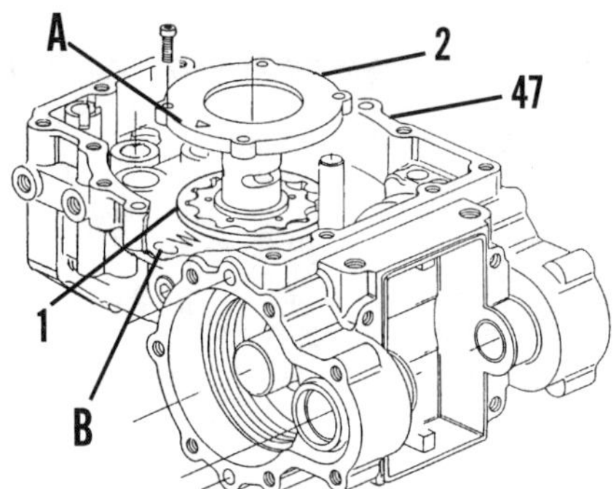

Fig. HX1-5–On Model 850, install the charge cover (2) so arrow (A) points toward "CW" mark on the housing.

must be smooth and free of any irregularities. Pump and motor rotors and balls are unit assemblies as balls are selectively fitted to the rotor bores.

Assemble by reversing the disassembly procedure while noting the following: Lubricate all assemblies with clean transmission oil. Install the dump valve spring (52—Fig. HX1-3) so the right angle bend points toward the O-ring (50). Tighten the dump valve nut (48) to 150 in.-lb. (17 N·m).

Install the charge pump cover (Model 850) so the arrow (A—Fig. HX1-5) points toward the CW on the housing. Do not tighten the cover screws until the pump rotor is installed. Note that the pins on the bottom of the pump rotor (42—Fig. HX1-3) must engage the holes in the charge pump inner rotor. Rotate the pump rotor clockwise to center the pump cover, then tighten the cover screws in a crossing pattern to 44 in.-lb. (5.0 N·m).

Install the cam ring (40—Fig. HX1-3) so the flush side is out. Install the seals (33 and 34) so the lip is to the inside of the cover. Be sure the snap ring (30) is firmly seated in the cover after installing the input shaft assembly (32). Hold the buttons (36) in place with petroleum jelly. Be sure the charge relief valve ball (46) is not dislodged when installing the cover assembly on the housing.

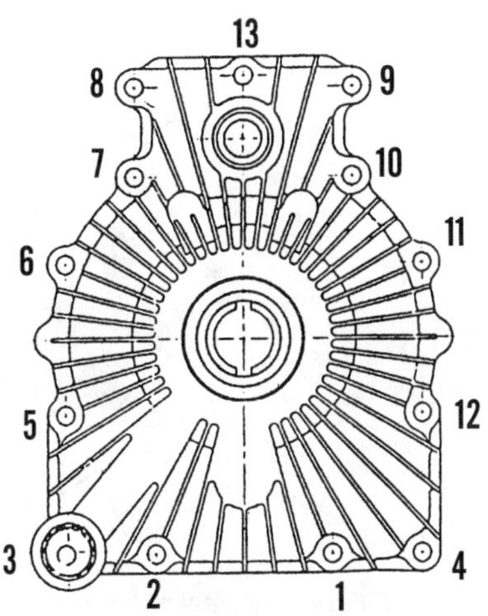

Fig. HX1-6–Tighten transmission cover screws to 105 in.-lb. (11.9 N•m) using the tightening sequence shown above

The splines on the input shaft must engage the splines of the drive ring (41); do not force the cover onto the housing. Tighten the cover screws to 105 in.-lb. (11.9 N·m) using the tightening sequence shown in Fig. HX1-6.

Carefully install the motor rotors in the housing and remove the rubber band used to retain the ball pistons in the rotors.

Install the brake assembly (28—Fig. HX1-2) so the lever is toward the cover side of the housing. Note that the axle housings and the sides of the transaxle housing are identified with an A or B as shown in Fig. HX1-7. The B-side of the transaxle should be assembled first. Note that the B-side brake shaft (12—Fig. HX1-2) is longer than the A-side shaft. Insert the B-side brake shaft into the brake assembly and rotate so the splines are engaged. Install the A-side brake shaft. When both shafts are properly installed, the shafts will rotate independently.

Install the axle components while noting the following: The inner sun gear (17—Fig. HX1-2) is taller than outer sun gear (15). Install the ring gear (19) so the side with the needle bearing mates with the axle housing (6). Install the outer sun gear (15) so the pointed convex end is towards the inner sun gear (17).

Install the axle housing seal (3) so the lip points inward. Install the wear plate (21) so the bowed side is facing the motor rotor. Tighten the axle housing screws to 125 in.-lb. (14 N·m). Tighten the oil filter base screws to 125 in.-lb. (14 N·m).

Models 751 and 851

Disassembly is similar for both models. However, Model 751 is not equipped with an oil filter assembly or charge pump.

Fig. HX1-7–Note that the axle housings and sides of transaxle housing are identified with an "A" or "B" as shown above. Refer to text.

Prior to disassembly, remove the fan, pulley, and all external brackets, levers and fittings. Thoroughly clean the outside of the unit. Drain the oil from the unit, and if equipped, remove the oil filter and detach the oil filter base. During disassembly, mark components so they may be returned to their original position.

The axle housing assemblies must be removed to gain access to the hydrostatic motors (18—Fig. HX1-8). The service procedure is the same for either axle housing assembly. Remove the cap screws securing the axle housing (7). Remove the axle housing assembly.

CAUTION: Be very careful not to dislodge the hydrostatic motor assembly. The spring-loaded balls (19) are a selective fit in the motor rotor (18) and must be installed in the matching bore in the rotor if removed.

To disassemble the axle assembly, remove the planetary unit from the axle housing. Remove the outer snap ring (1) and inner snap ring (5A). Tap on the splined end of the axle shaft with a soft hammer and force the axle with the bearing and seal out toward the outer end of the axle housing.

To disassemble the planetary unit, proceed as follows: Remove the secondary ring gear (11). Slightly squeeze the secondary planet gears (10) and remove the gears and carrier (9). Remove the sun gear (12) from the carrier (13). Disassemble the remaining components. Remove the sun gear (15) and brake friction plate (17) from the motor (18). Remove the brake pad (21).

NOTE: Disassembly of the brake actuating mechanism is generally not necessary.

To remove the hydrostatic motors, place a large rubber band or similar device around the motor rotor (18) to hold the spring-loaded ball pistons (19) in their bores. Carefully withdraw the motor assembly. Due to the selective fit, if the balls are removed they must be returned to their original rotor bore.

To disassemble the hydrostatic pump, unbolt and remove the oil filter base (52—Fig. HX1-9) from the housing on Model 851. On both models, unscrew the fasteners retaining the pump cover (35) to the housing (57). Note that there is a screw located in the drain hole. Separate the cover from the housing and remove the snap ring (31).

Tap or press the input shaft (32) and bearing out of the cover by forcing the shaft toward the outside of the cover. The shaft and bearing are available only as a unit assembly.

Drive the input shaft seal (33) out of the cover bore. Remove the charge pressure relief valve spring (46) and ball (47). Remove the buttons (37), control shaft (41) and cam ring insert (42) from the cam ring (43).

Remove the pump rotor drive ring (38). Place a wide rubber band or similar device around the pump rotor (39) to hold the ball pistons (40) in their bores. The balls are a selective fit in the rotor and must be installed in their matching bore if removed from the rotor. Carefully lift the pump rotor from the housing.

The dump valve bracket (55) can be removed from the housing after removing the nut (49). The check valves (Fig. HX1-4) should be flushed with solvent, but not removed, and are available only with the housing. Removal of the dampening pistons (48—Fig. HX1-9) is also not recommended.

On Model 851, the charge pump (45—Fig. HX1-9) may be removed from the housing for inspection after removing the pump plate (44). The charge pump components are available only with the housing (57) as an assembly.

Inspect components for damage. When removing the ball pistons from the pump and motor rotors, number the rotor bores and place the balls in a plastic ice cube tray or egg carton with the cavities numbered to correspond to the rotor bores.

The piston balls and rotor bores must be smooth and free of any irregularities. The pump and motor rotors and balls are unit assemblies as the balls are electively fitted to the rotor bores.

Assemble by reversing the disassembly procedure while noting the following: Lubricate all assemblies with clean transmission oil. Install the dump valve spring (54—Fig. HX1-9) so the

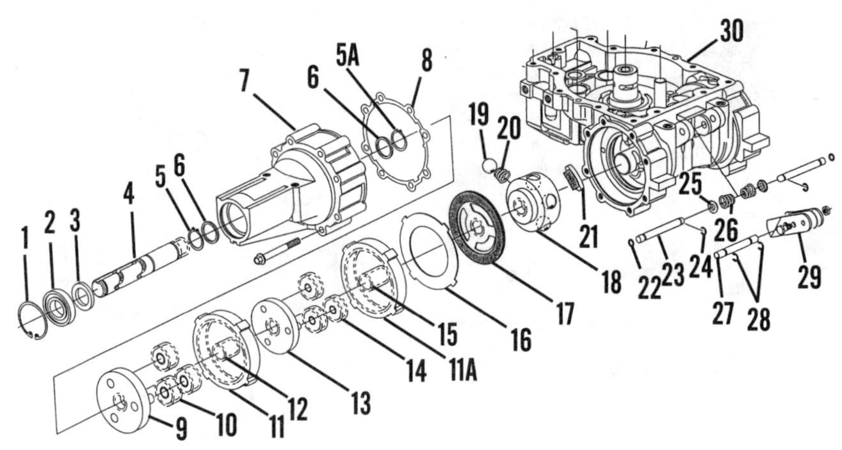

Fig. HX1-8–Exploded view of Eaton Model 851 hydrostatic transaxle assembly. Model 751 is similar.

1. Snap ring
2. Bearing
3. Oil seal
4. Axle shaft
5. Snap ring
5A. Inner snap ring
6. Thrust washer
7. Axle housing
8. Gasket
9. Planetary carrier (2nd)
10. Planet gears (2nd)
11. Ring gear (2nd)
11A. Ring gear (1st)
12. Sun gear (2nd)
13. Planetary carrier (1st)
14. Planet gears (1st)
15. Sun gear (1st)
16. Brake plate
17. Brake disc
18. Motor
19. Ball
20. Spring
21. Brake pad
22. O-ring
23. Brake shaft
24. Retaining ring
25. Spring retainer
26. Spring
27. Shaft
28. Retaining rings
29. Brake arm
30. Transmission housing

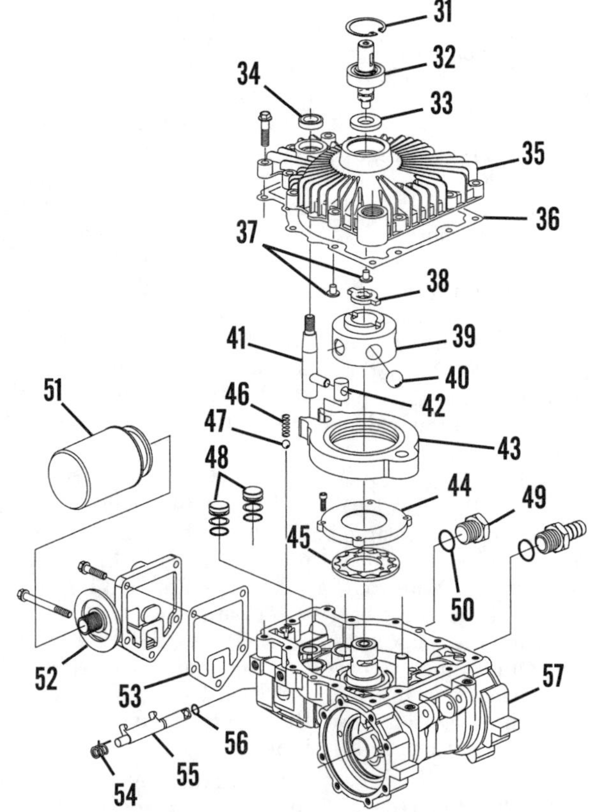

Fig. HX1-9–Exploded view of Eaton Model 851 hydrostatic transmission components. Model 751 is similar except filter assembly (51 and 52) and charge pump assembly (44 through 47) are not used.

31. Snap ring
32. Input shaft assy.
33. Oil seal
34. Oil seal
35. Housing cover
36. Gasket
37. Buttons
38. Drive plate
39. Pump
40. Ball
41. Control shaft
42. Insert
43. Cam ring
44. Charge pump cover
45. Charge pump rotor
46. Charge pressure relief spring
47. Ball
48. Dampening pistons
49. Plug
50. O-ring
51. Oil filter
52. Filter base
53. Gasket
54. Return spring
55. Dump valve bracket
56. O-ring
57. Transmission housing

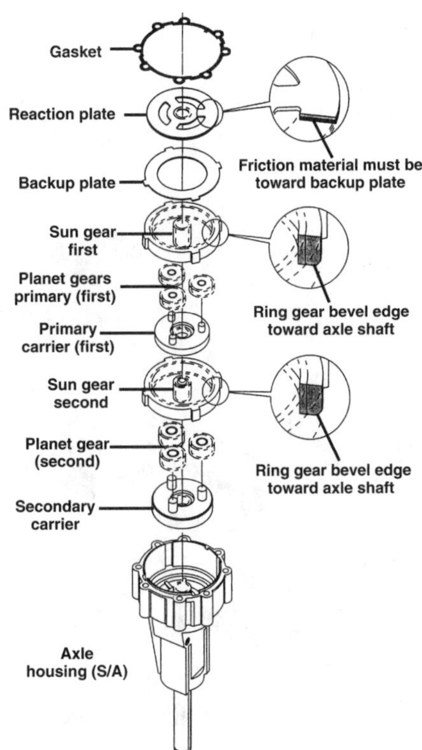

Fig. HX1-10–Exploded view of planetary and brake components. Refer to text for assembly instructions.

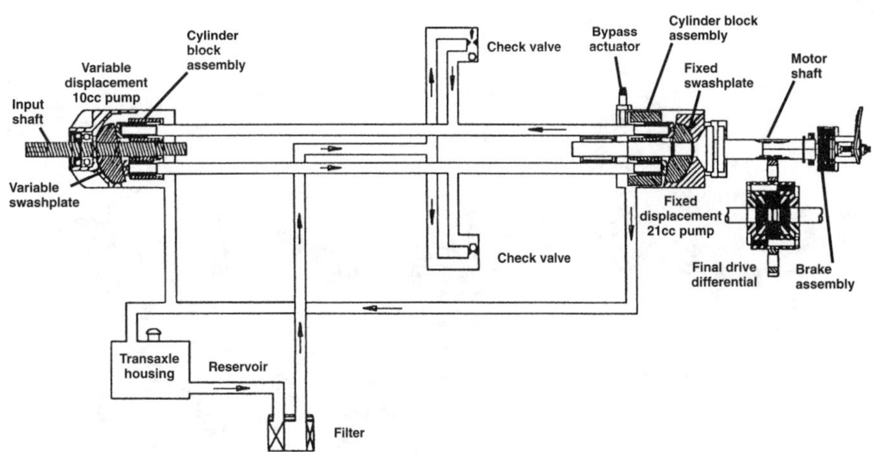

Fig. HX1-11–Exploded view of Hydro-Gear Model 31-0500 and 310-0750 hydrostatic transaxle

right angle bend points toward the O-ring (56). Tighten the dump valve nut (49) to 150 in.-lb. (17 N·m).

Install the charge pump cover (Model 851) so the arrow (A—Fig. HX1-5) points toward the CW on the housing. Do not tighten the cover screws until the pump rotor is installed. Note that the pins on the bottom of the pump rotor (39—Fig. HX1-9) must engage the holes in the charge pump inner rotor. Rotate the pump rotor clockwise to center the pump cover, then tighten the cover screws in a crossing pattern to 44 in.-lb. (5.0 N·m).

Install the cam ring (43) so the flush side is out. Install the seals (33 and 34) so the lip is to the inside of the cover. Be sure the snap ring (31) is firmly seated in the cover after installing the input shaft assembly (32). Hold the buttons (37) in place with petroleum jelly.

Be sure the charge relief valve ball (47) is not dislodged when installing the cover assembly on the housing. The splines on the input shaft must engage the splines of the drive ring (38); do not force the cover onto the housing. Tighten the cover screws to 125 in.-lb. (14 N·m) using the tightening sequence shown in Fig. HX1-6.

Carefully install the motor rotors in the housing and remove the rubber band used to retain the ball pistons in the rotors.

Install the axle components while noting the following: The inner sun gear (15—Fig. HX1-8) is taller than outer sun gear (12). On models with 16:1 ratio, the inner sun gear (15) is stepped. Install the brake friction plate (17) so the side with the friction material is toward the backup plate (Fig. HX1-10).

Install the ring gears (11 and 11A—Fig. HX1-8) so the beveled edge is toward the axle shaft (Fig. HX1-10). The ears on the backup plate (16—Fig. HX1-8) and ring gears (11 and 11A) must fit in the notches in the axle housing (7). Install the axle housing seal (3) so the lip points inward.

Tighten the axle housing screws to 125 in.-lb. (14 N·m). Tighten the oil filter base screws to 125 in.-lb. (14 N·m).

HYDROGEAR (MODELS 310-0500 & 310-0750)

OPERATION

The hydrostatic transaxle consists of a variable volume, reversible swashplate, axial piston pump connected in a closed loop to a fixed displacement, axial piston motor. Refer to Fig. HX1-11. The engine driven hydrostatic pump delivers high-pressure oil to the hydrostatic motor, causing the motor to rotate. The motor output shaft transfers the power to the differential ring gear. The differential is connected to the axle shafts, which transfer the power to the tractor wheels. A multi-disc brake is mounted on the motor shaft.

Hydrostatic motor speed is controlled by the hydrostatic pump rpm and the angle of pump swashplate. As the angle of pump swashplate is increased from the neutral zero degree position, the length of each pump piston stroke increases and more oil is pumped to the motor. Because the motor is a fixed displacement unit, it must turn faster in order to accept the increased flow from the pump. When the pump swashplate angle decreases, the opposite effect takes place and motor speed decreases.

The hydrostatic pump turns in the same direction all the time. The hydrostatic motor is capable of turning in both directions. Reversing the pump swashplate angle, which reverses the flow of oil being pumped to the motor, reverses motor direction of rotation. When the control lever is in the neutral position, there is no pump swashplate tilt and no pump piston stroke.

The hydrostatic pump inlet is connected to the internal reservoir (transaxle housing), allowing the pump to make-up any oil that is lost from the closed loop system during operation. Refer to Fig. HX1-11 for a circuit diagram. Make-up oil is drawn from the reservoir through an oil filter screen that is mounted in the transaxle housing. Reservoir oil will pass through a check valve when the transmission oil pressure is not sufficient to keep the check valve closed.

TROUBLESHOOTING

When troubleshooting the hydrostatic drive system, always check the easiest and most obvious items first. Some problems that may occur during operation of the hydrostatic transmission and their possible causes are as follows:

1. Lack of drive or limited speed in both directions.

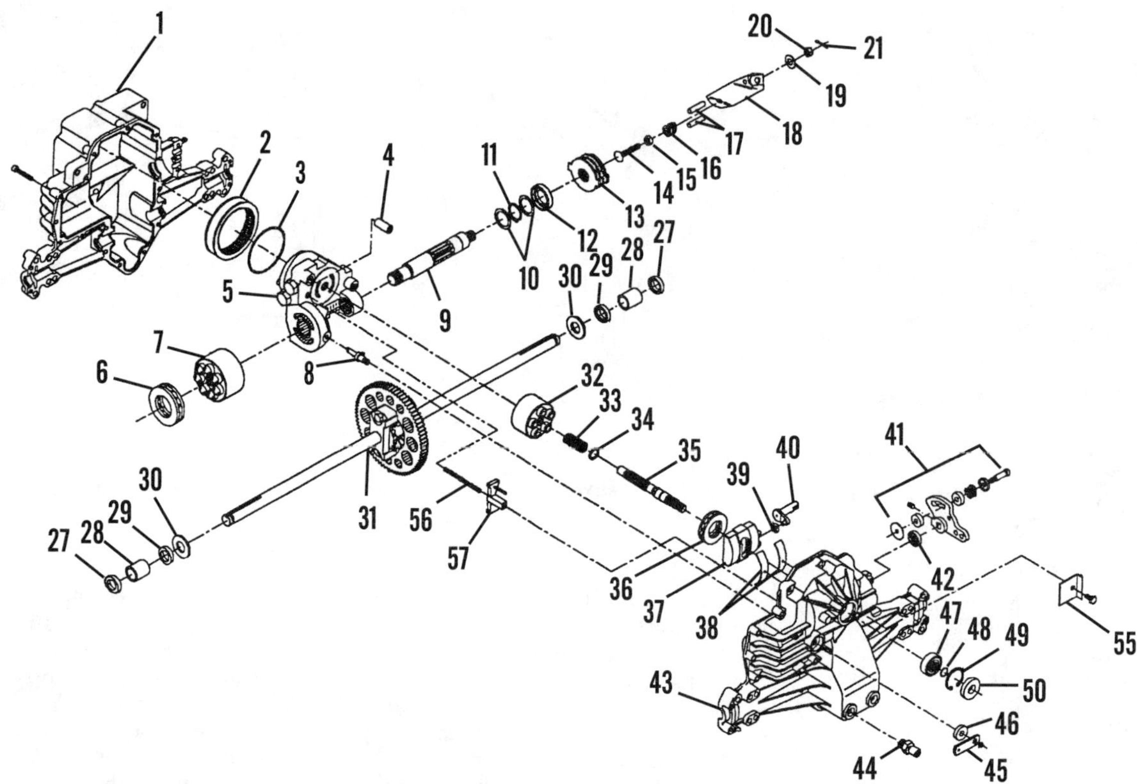

Fig. HX1-12–Exploded view of Hydro-Gear Model 310-0500 hydrostatic transaxle. Refer to Fig. HX1-13 for parts identifcation except for brake stop (55).

a. Broken or misadjusted control linkage.
b. Slipping or broken transmission drive belt (if used).
c. Stuck open or leaking bypass valve.
d. Low oil level.
e. Plugged oil filter.
f. Internal leakage of high pressure fluid due to excessive wear of pump and/or motor.
g. Failure of the final drive.

2. Lack of drive or limited speed in one direction.
   a. Damaged or binding control linkage.
   b. Movement of pump swashplate being restricted in one direction.
   c. Charge check valve not seating.
3. Noisy operation.
   a. Low oil level.
   b. Excessive loading.
   c. Misadjusted brake.
   d. Loose parts.
   e. Damage bypass valve linkage.
4. Hot operation.
   a. Debris buildup.
   b. Low oil level.
   c. Excessive loading.
   d. Misadjusted brake.

OVERHAUL

Before disassembling the transmission, thoroughly clean the exterior of the unit. Remove the breather and drain the oil from the transaxle.

Remove the input pulley and fan. Remove the control arm assembly (41—Fig. HX1-12 and HX1-13). Loosen the nut retaining the brake arm. Position the transaxle so the input shaft is down. Unscrew the twenty screws securing the case halves together, and separate the case halves. If necessary pry the case halves apart, but use care so the mating surfaces are not damaged.

NOTE: The differential assembly and axles (31) may stick to the removed case half.

Remove the differential assembly and axles. Remove the burrs from the axles before removing the bushings (28) from the axles. Remove the brake discs (13) from the motor shaft. Remove and discard the filter (2).

NOTE: The pump cylinder may stick to the center section during removal. Separate the pump cylinder from the center section while removing the center section.

Unscrew and remove the center section (5) with the motor cylinder (7).

NOTE: Springs will force the center section out of position. Do not allow the pistons to fall out of the motor cylinder.

Withdraw the motor cylinder (7) from the motor shaft (9), then remove the motor shaft from the center section. Remove the thrust bearing assembly (6). On Model 310-0750, unscrew the retaining screws (23) and remove the jackshaft (24) and pinion gear (25).

Remove the pump cylinder (32), spring (33), washer (34) and thrust bearing (36). Remove the swashplate (37), control lever (40) and thrust bearings (38). Remove the seal (50) and snap ring (49). Push out the input shaft (35) with the bearing (47) toward the outside of the case.

Do not remove the check valve plate from the center section (5). Check the check valve plate retaining screws for proper torque. If three screws secure the plate, the torque should be 135-185 in.-lb. (15.25-20.9 N·m). If four screws

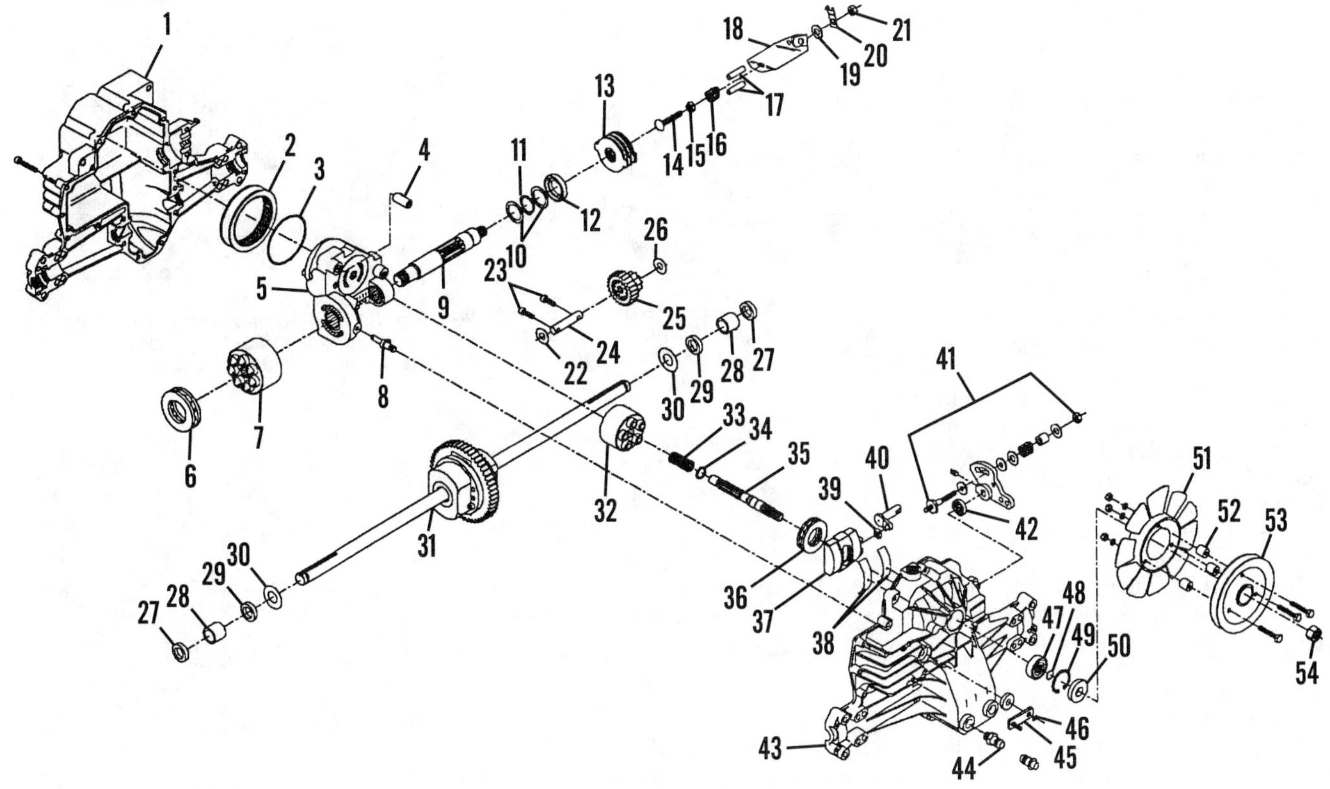

Fig. HX1-13–Exploded view of Hydro-Gear Model 310-0750 hydrostatic transaxle.

1. Lower housing
2. Oil filter
3. O-ring
4. Dowel pin
5. Center section
6. Thrust bearing assy.
7. Motor
8. By-pass actuator
9. Motor shaft
10. Washers
11. Retaining ring
12. Seal
13. Brake rotor
14. Bolt
15. Lock nut
16. Spring
17. Actuating pins
18. Brake arm
19. Washer
20. Nut
21. Cotter pin
22. Washer
23. Cap screws
24. Jack shaft
25. Pinion gear
26. Washer
27. Dust seal
28. Sleeve bearing
29. Oil seal
30. Washer
31. Differential assy.
32. Pump
33. Spring
34. Thrust washer
35. Input shaft
36. Thrust bearing assy.
37. Swashplate
38. Cradle bearings
39. Oil seal
40. Trunnion arm
41. Control arm assy.
42. Oil seal
43. Upper housing
44. Breather
45. By-pass arm
46. Oil seal
47. Bearing
48. Retaining ring
49. Snap ring
50. Oil seal
51. Fan
52. Spacer
53. Pulley
54. Nut

secure the plate, torque should be 170-240 in.-lb. (19.2-27.1 N·m).

Inspect the pistons and cylinder bores for damage. The specified motor piston diameter is 0.6767-0.6770 inch (17.188-17.196 mm). The specified motor cylinder bore diameter is 0.6776-0.6784 inch (17.211-17.231 mm). The specified pump piston diameter is 0.6288-0.6291 inch (15.972-15.979 mm). The specified pump cylinder bore diameter is 0.6295-0.6303 inch (15.989-16.010 mm). The pump and motor cylinder blocks are serviced as complete assemblies.

Remove old sealant from the mating surfaces on the case halves. Check the polished surfaces of the center section (5) and cylinder blocks for wear, scoring or scratches. The center section and cylinder blocks must be replaced if wear exceeds 0.0004 inch (0.01 mm).

On Model 310-0750, the jackshaft (24) diameter should be 0.4986-0.4996 inch (12.664-12.690 mm). The pinion gear (25) bore should be 0.5014-0.5024 inch (12.736-12.761 mm).

The specified axle shaft diameter at the bushing contact area should be 0.7486-0.7496 inch (19.014-19.040 mm). The specified bushing (28) diameter is 0.7535-0.7561 inch (19.139-19.205 mm).

Check for looseness in the differential bushings by moving the axles. If excessive wear is noted, the differential and axles must be replaced as a unit assembly. Check the differential housing retaining screws for proper torque. On Model 310-0500, torque should be 192-216 in.-lb. (20.6-24.4 N·m). On Model 310-0750, torque should be 144-168 in.-lb. (16.3-19 N·m).

Replace all O-rings and oil seals. Coat parts with oil during reassembly.

To reassemble, install the seal (42—Fig. HX1-12 or Fig. HX1-13) and control lever (40). Install the bearing (47) and retaining ring (48) on the input shaft (35), then install the input shaft into the case half. Install the snap ring (49) and seal (50). Install the thrust bearings (38), swashplate (37) and thrust bearing assembly (36).

Install the guide block (39) on the control lever (40) pin and into the notch in the swashplate (37). Install the thrust washer (34) and spring (33) on the input shaft. Use a rubber band to hold the pistons in the bores of the pump cylinder (32), then install the pump cylinder on the input shaft. Be sure the splines on the shaft and cylinder are properly engaged.

On Model 310-0750, install the jackshaft (24) and pinion gear (25). Tighten the retaining screws (23) to 120-170 in.-lb. (13.6-27.1 N·m).

Install the seal (46) and bypass actuator (8). On Model 310-0500, install the leveler (57—Fig. HX1-12) and spring (56). On both models, install the dowel pins (4—Fig. HX1-12 or HX1-13).

Install the washers (10), snap ring (11) and seal (12) on the motor shaft (9), then insert the shaft into the center section (5). Install the bypass actuator (8) into the center section (5) by inserting the small end first.

Install the motor cylinder (7) onto the motor shaft (9). While positioning washers (10) and seal (12) in the recess in the case half (43), install the center section (5) and motor shaft assembly into the case half (43). Push down the center section against spring pressure, and install the center section retaining screws. Tighten the screws to 44-58 ft.-lb. (60-79 N·m).

To install the thrust bearing (6) assembly, push the pistons in motor cylinder (7) inward against spring pressure using a flat-blade tool. Install the thrust bearing so the thick race is next to the pistons.

Install the brake discs (13) by assembling in this order: tanged disc, splined disc, tanged disc, splined disc, tanged disc, tanged disc. Install the splined discs with the hub to the inside. Install the brake bolt (14) in the recess in the case half. Install the O-ring (3) and filter (2).

Apply a bead of oil and heat resistant RTV sealant on the case mating surface as shown in Fig. HX1-14 or HX1-15. Install the case half onto the assembled case half. Tighten the case retaining screws in the tightening sequence shown in Fig. HX1-16 or HX1-17 to a torque of 135-165 in.-lb. (15.3-18.6 N·m). Install the remainder of the components.

To check the case for leaks, apply compressed air (no more than 10 psi) through the breather (44) hole in the case. Do not submerge the unit. Use soapy water to locate leaks.

Fill the transaxle with SAE 20W-50 oil with an API rating of SH. Pour oil through the breather (44) opening. To check the oil level, measure from the boss surface to the oil with the unit level. The oil level on Model 310-0500 transaxle should be 1.75-2.00 inches (44-51 mm). The oil level on Model 310-0750 transaxle should be 1.25-1.62 inches (32-41 mm).

After filling the transaxle, but before installation it in the tractor, purge air from the oil circuits using the following procedure. Rotate the input shaft clockwise at 1000-1500 rpm. Rotate the bypass lever to engage the bypass valve. Move the control arm back and forth to forward and reverse positions three times. Hold the control arm in forward or reverse position five seconds. Disengage the bypass lever. Once again move the control arm back and forth to forward and reverse positions three times. Hold the control arm in forward or reverse position five seconds. Recheck the oil level.

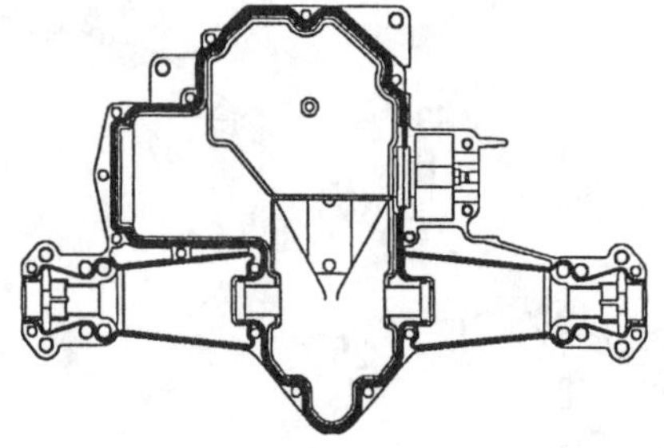

Fig. HX1-14–On Model 310-0500 transaxle, apply sealant to the housing mating surface indicated by the darker line.

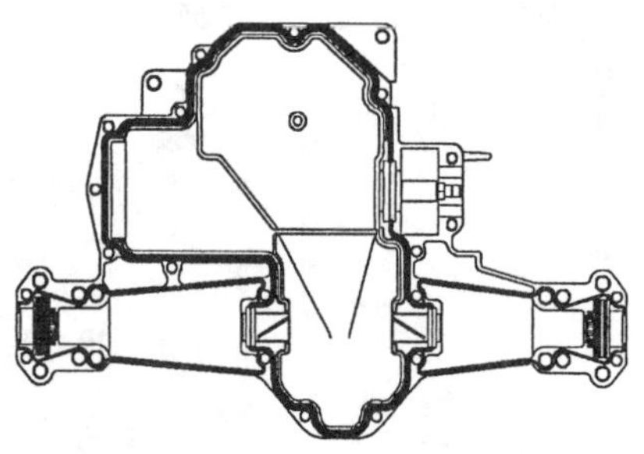

Fig. HX1-15–On Model 310-0750 transaxle, apply sealant to the housing mating surface indicated by the darker line.

Adjust the brake after installing the transaxle in the tractor.

KANZAKI

TUFF TORQ MODELS K50 AND K55

Operation

Tuff Torq Models K50 and K55 hydrostatic transmissions use a variable displacement, reversible flow, axial piston pump and a fixed displacement, axial piston motor to provide infinite speed and torque output.

Hydrostatic motor speed is controlled by hydrostatic pump rpm and the angle of pump swashplate. As the angle of pump swashplate is increased from the zero degree neutral position, the length of each pump piston stroke increases and more oil is pumped to the motor. Since the motor is a fixed displacement unit, it must turn faster in order to accept the increased flow from the pump. When pump swashplate angle decreases, the opposite effect takes place and motor speed decreases.

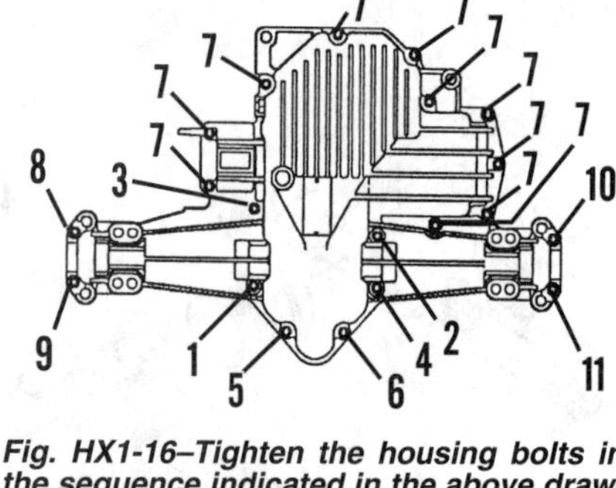

Fig. HX1-16–Tighten the housing bolts in the sequence indicated in the above drawing on Model 310-0500 transaxle.

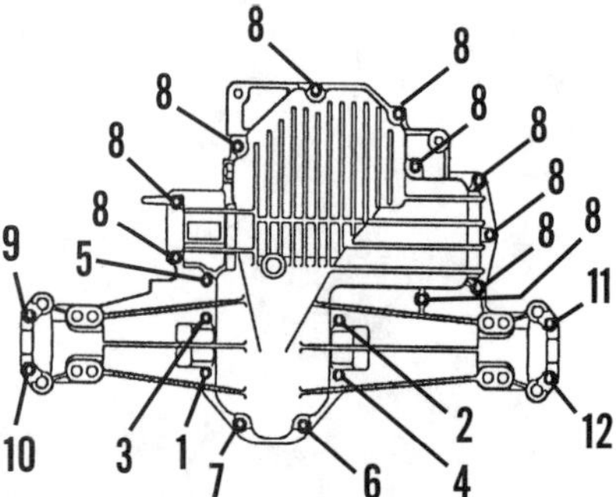

Fig. HX1-17–Tighten the housing bolts in the sequence indicated in the above drawing on Model 310-0750 transaxle.

The hydrostatic pump turns in the same direction all the time. The hydrostatic motor is capable of turning in either direction. Reversing the pump swashplate angle, which reverses the flow of oil being pumped to the motor, reverses motor direction of rotation. When the control lever is in NEUTRAL, there is no pump swashplate tilt and no pump piston stroke.

Power from the motor output shaft is transferred through reduction gears to the differential, which in turn rotates the axles. Brake pads grip a disc attached to the motor output shaft to provide brake action.

The hydrostatic pump inlet is connected to the reservoir (transaxle housing), allowing the pump to make up any oil that is lost from the closed loop system during operation. Make-up oil is drawn from the reservoir through an internal oil filter.

Overhaul

Remove the drain plug (D—Fig. HX1-18) and drain the oil.

NOTE: Do not remove plug (G—Fig. HX1-18). The plug is a factory-installed fill plug.

Remove the brake assembly (Fig. HX1-19). Unscrew the seventeen

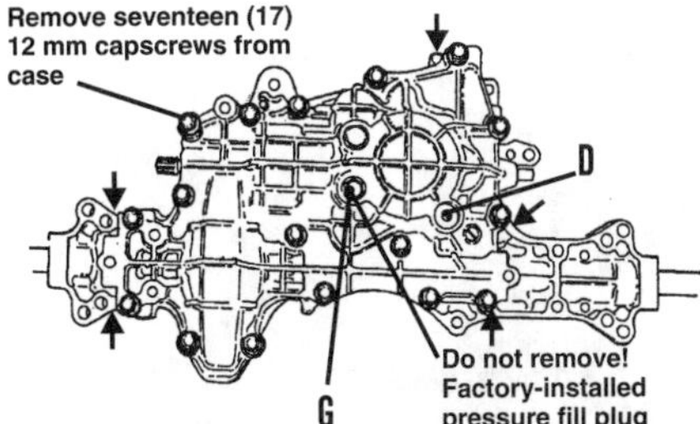

Fig. HX1-18–Do not remove the factory-installed fill plug (G). Insert a screwdriver at points indicated by arrows to pry apart the case halves.

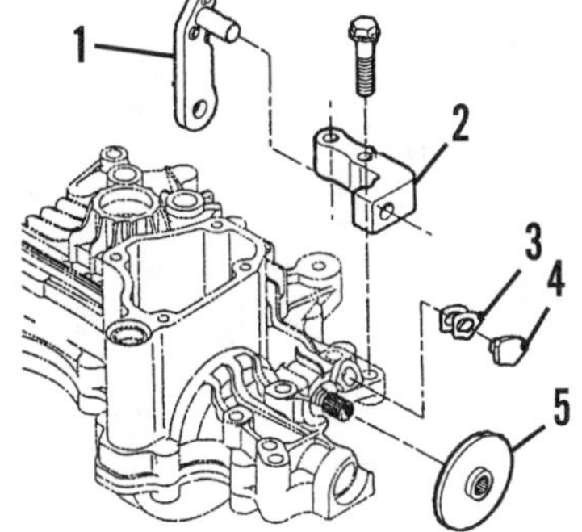

Fig. HX1-19–Exploded view of brake components.

1. Brake lever
2. Mounting bracket
3. Shims
4. Brake shoe
5. Brake disc

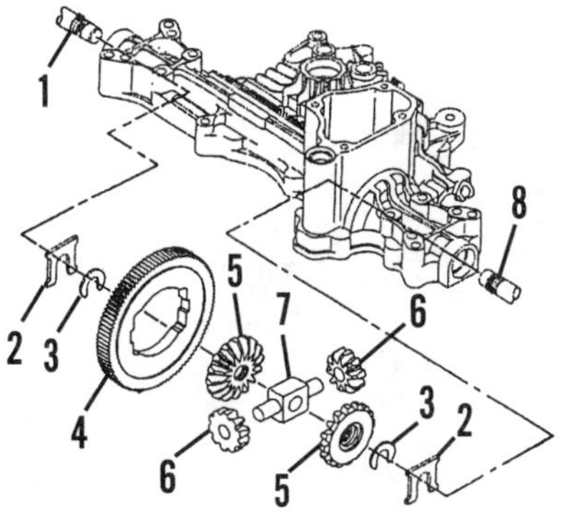

Fig. HX1-20–Exploded view of differential components.

1. Long axle
2. Thrust plates
3. Retainers
4. Ring gear
5. Side gears
6. Pinion gears
7. Pinion shaft
8. Short axle

screws securing the case halves and separate the case halves. A suitable tool may be inserted at the points identified by arrows in Fig. HX1-18 to pry apart the case halves.

Remove and clean the magnet located in the lower case half. Remove the thrust plates (2—Fig. HX1-20), retainers (3) and axles (1 and 8). Note that the

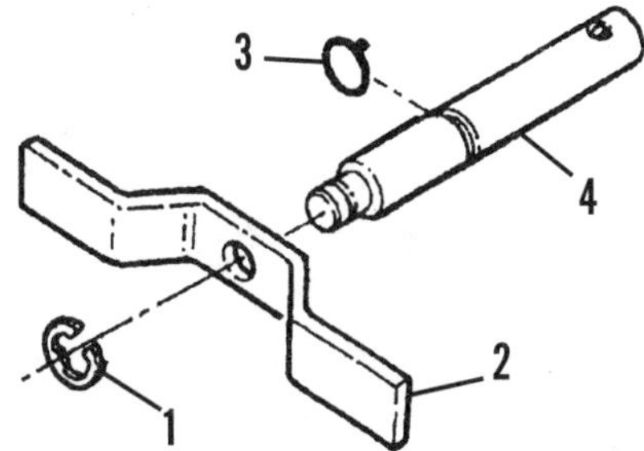

Fig. HX1-21–Drawing of freewheeling actuator.

1. Retaining ring
2. Actuating bracket
3. O-ring
4. Pin

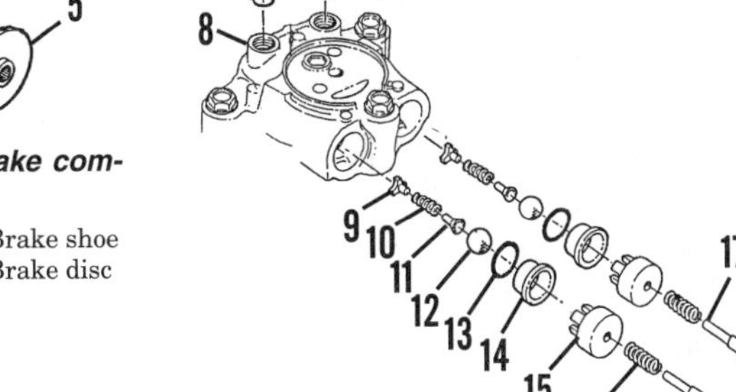

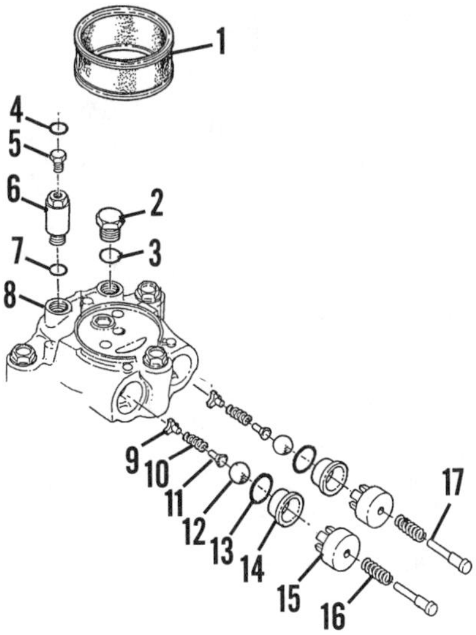

Fig. HX1-22–Exploded view of the pump and motor center section components.

1. Oil filter
2. Plug
3. O-ring
4. O-ring
5. Pipe plug
6. Bleed port
7. O-ring
8. Center section
9. Spring guide
10. Spring
11. Ball seat
12. Ball
13. O-ring
14. Valve body
15. Valve cap
16. Spring
17. Actuating plunger

retainers (3) can fall into the case after removal of the thrust plates (2).

Lift out the differential assembly. Remove the freewheeling actuator (Fig. HX1-21) from the lower case half. Remove the filter (1—Fig. HX1-22). Extract the valve components (15-17).

To remove the remaining components, attach the brake disc to the motor shaft and rotate the disc back and forth. If the valve ball and seat cannot be removed, unscrew the plug (5—Fig. HX1-22) and direct compressed air into the port to expel the parts (catch the parts with a cloth). Exchange positions of the connector (6) and plug (2) to expel the ball and seat from the remaining valve.

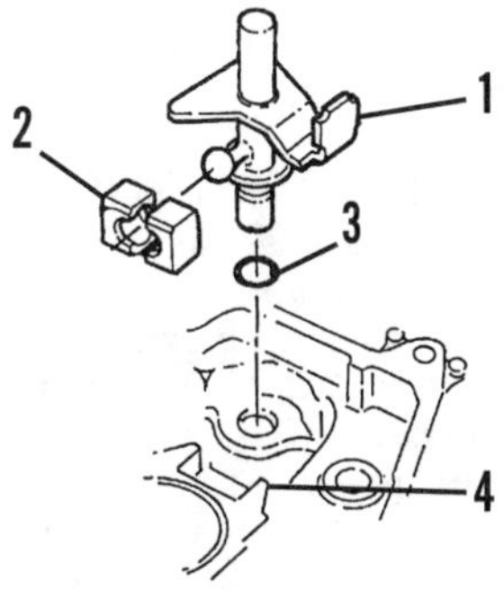

Fig. HX1-23–Exploded view of shifter components.

1. Shift shaft
2. Shift blocks
3. O-ring
4. Pump swashplate

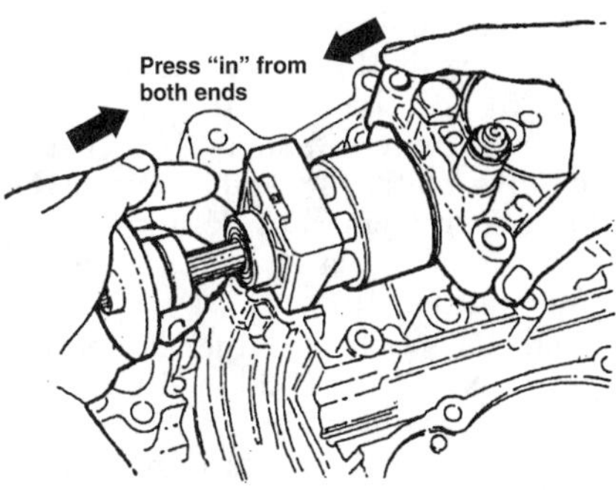

Fig. HX1-24–Push in against the motor shaft and the pump and center section to hold components together and lift and remove the motor, pump and center section as an assembly.

Before removing the shift shaft, measure the gap between the shift blocks (2—Fig. HX1-23) and the sides of the swashplate (4). If the gap is more than 0.15 mm (0.006 in.), renew the shift blocks. Remove the shift shaft assembly (1—Fig. HX1-23).

If not previously reinstalled, install the brake disc on the motor shaft. While holding down the center section (8—Fig. HX1-22), unscrew the cap screws retaining the center section (note spacers) and maintain pressure against the center section. Push in against the brake disc while pushing against the center section as shown in Fig. HX1-24, then lift and remove the center section, motor and pump assemblies. Releasing pressure will allow the assemblies (Fig. HX1-25) to separate. Remove the seal (1) and snap ring (2), then remove the input shaft and bearing.

NOTE: Note the location of the pump and motor pistons (13 and 24—Fig. HX1-25) if they are removed. The pistons must be installed in their original cylinder

bores from which they were removed.

Remove old sealant from the mating surfaces on the case halves. Inspect components for wear and damage. The minimum allowable thickness of bearings (7—Fig. HX1-25) is 1.30 mm (0.051 in.). The maximum allowable inner diameter of pinion gears (6—Fig. HX1-20) is 15.11 mm (0.595 in.). The minimum allowable diameter of pinion shafts (7) is 14.96 mm (0.589 in.). Minimum allowable diameter of axle shafts is 19.00 mm (0.748 in.).

Reassemble by reversing the disassembly procedure while noting the following: Lubricate all components during assembly with oil. Note the position of the thin thrust washer (10—Fig. HX1-25) and the thick thrust washer (12) in the pump swashplate (8). Install the valve plates (18 and 20) with the bronze side facing out. Use grease to hold the valve plates in place on the center section (19).

Note the position of the thin thrust washer (N—Fig. HX1-26) and the thick thrust washer (T) in the motor swashplate (26). Install the motor swashplate (26) so the side stamped "S" as shown in Fig. HX1-26 fits in the upper case half. Tighten the center section retaining screws to 44-58 N·m (33-42 ft.-lb.).

When installing valve components (Fig. HX1-27), the seat with 0.51 mm orifice (O) must be installed in the right-hand bore.

Apply a bead of RTV gasket sealer to the case mating surface as well as the two inner holes on the lower case half. After assembling the case halves, be sure the holes for the bleed port connector (6—Fig. HX1-22) are aligned. Tighten the two inner case retaining screws (S—Fig. HX1-28) first, then tighten the remaining screws in a crossing pattern to 23-27 N·m (17-20 ft.-lb.).

NOTE: If installing a new upper case half, tighten the case retaining screws to 27-31 N·m (20-23 ft.-lb.).

Tighten the drain plug to 20-24 N·m (177-212 in.-lb.). Install brake components and install the shims (3—Fig. HX1-19) so the clearance between the brake pad (4) and disc (5) is 0.08-1.3 mm (0.003-0.051 inch). Tighten the brake bracket retaining screws to 44-59 N·m (32-43 ft.-lb.).

With the transaxle assembled, use the following procedure to fill the transaxle with oil. Recommended oil is SAE 10W-30 oil with latest API classification. Position the transaxle with the input shaft down. Unscrew the bleed port plug (P—Fig. HX1-29). Rotate the brake disc and pour oil into the plug hole until oil reaches the bottom of the hole. Use Teflon tape on the plug threads. Tighten the plug to 8 N·m (71 in.-lb.).

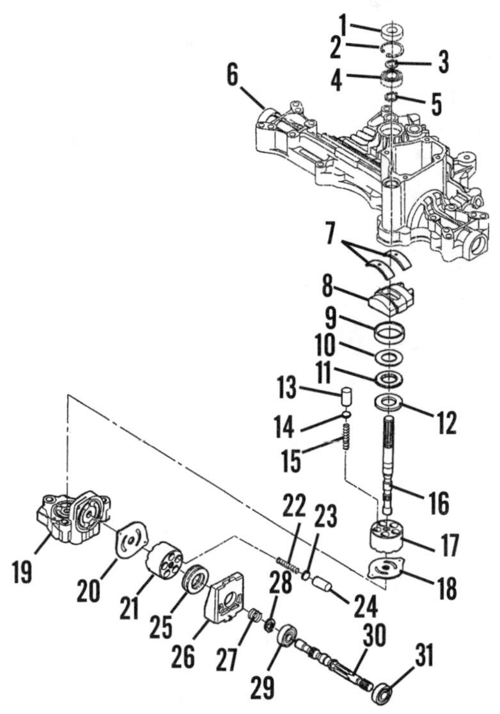

Fig. HX1-25–Exploded view of Tuff Torq K50 and K55 hydrostatic transmission components.

1. Seal
2. Snap ring
3. Snap ring
4. Bearing
5. Snap ring
6. Upper case half
7. Thrust bushings
8. Pump swashplate
9. Bushing
10. Thrust plate (thin)
11. Thrust bearing
12. Thrust plate (thick)
13. Pump piston
14. Washer
15. Spring
16. Pump input shaft
17. Pump cylinder block
18. Pump plate
19. Center section
20. Motor plate
21. Motor cylinder block
22. Spring
23. Washer
24. Motor piston
25. Thrust bearing assy.
26. Motor swashplate
27. Spring
28. Snap ring
29. Bearing
30. Motor output shaft
31. Bearing

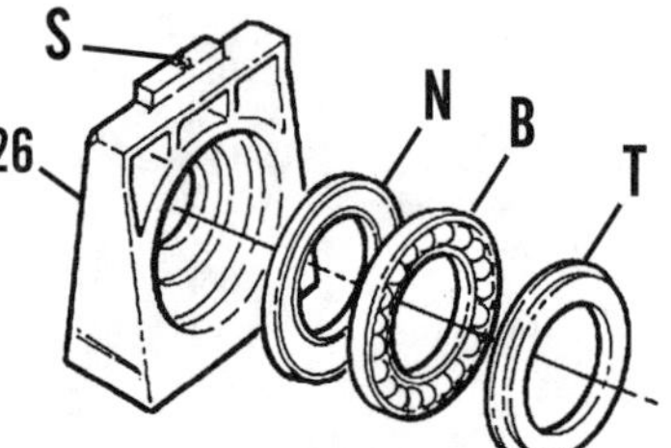

Fig. HX1-26–Note the position of the thin thrust (N) and thick thrust washer (T). Install the swashplate (26) so the "S" side fits in the upper case half.

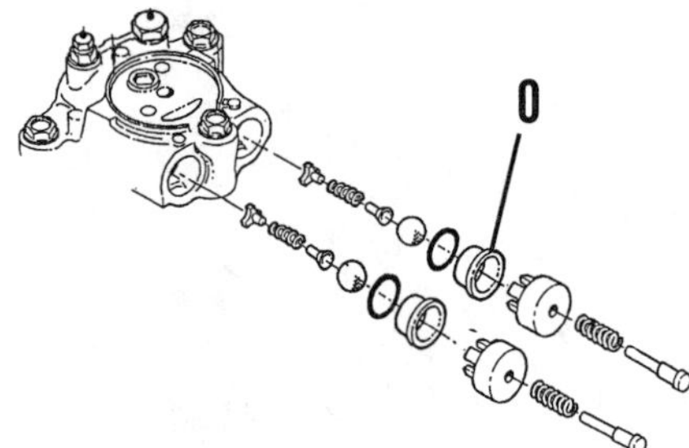

Fig. HX1-27–Exploded view of the check valves. The valve seat with the orifice (O) must be installed in the right-hand bore.

TUFF TORQ MODELS K60 AND K61

Operation

Tuff Torq Models K60 and K61 hydrostatic transmissions use a variable displacement, reversible flow, axial piston pump and a fixed displacement, axial piston motor to provide infinite speed and torque output.

Hydrostatic motor speed is controlled by hydrostatic pump rpm and the angle of pump swashplate. As the angle of pump swashplate is increased from the zero degree neutral position, the length of each pump piston stroke increases and more oil is pumped to the motor. Since the motor is a fixed displacement unit, it must turn faster in order to ac-

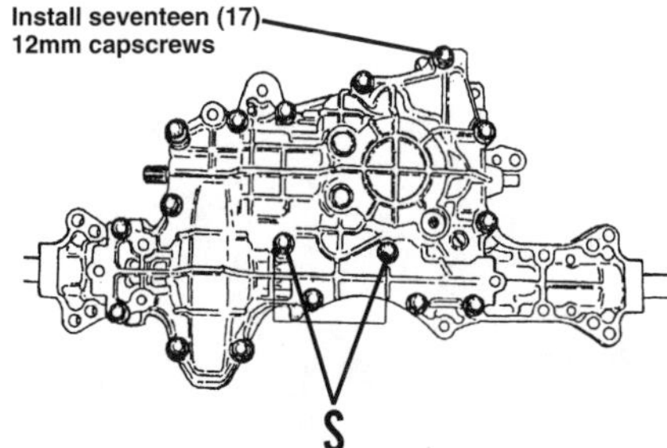

Fig. HX1-28–Tighten the housing cap screws in a criss-cross pattern, beginning with the two center cap screws (S).

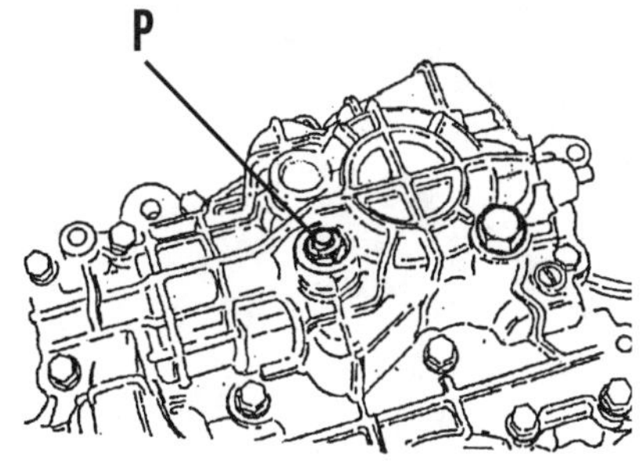

Fig. HX1-29–To fill the unit with oil, remove the pipe plug (P) from the bleed valve and pour oil into the plug hole

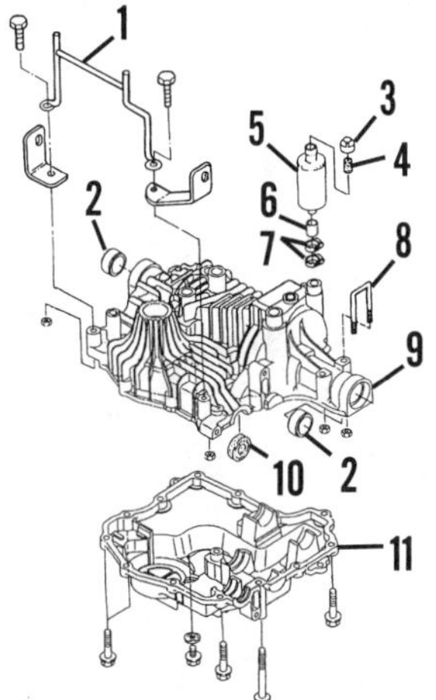

Fig. HX1-30–Exploded view of Tuff Torq K60 and K61 transaxle housing.

1. Belt guide
2. Bushings
3. Cap
4. Filter
5. Fill bottle
6. Hose
7. Clamps
8. U-bolt
9. Upper case half
10. Seal
11. Lower case half

cept the increased flow from the pump. When the pump swashplate angle decreases, the opposite effect takes place and motor speed decreases.

The hydrostatic pump turns in the same direction all the time. The hydrostatic motor is capable of turning in either direction. Reversing the pump swashplate angle, which reverses the flow of oil being pumped to the motor, reverses motor direction of rotation. When the control lever is in neutral position, there is no pump swashplate tilt and no pump piston stroke.

Power from the motor output shaft is transferred through reduction gears to the differential, which in turn rotates the axles. A brake band grips a drum attached to the motor output shaft to provide brake action.

The hydrostatic pump inlet is connected to the reservoir (transaxle housing), allowing the pump to make up any oil that is lost from the closed loop system during operation. Make-up oil is drawn from the reservoir through an internal oil filter.

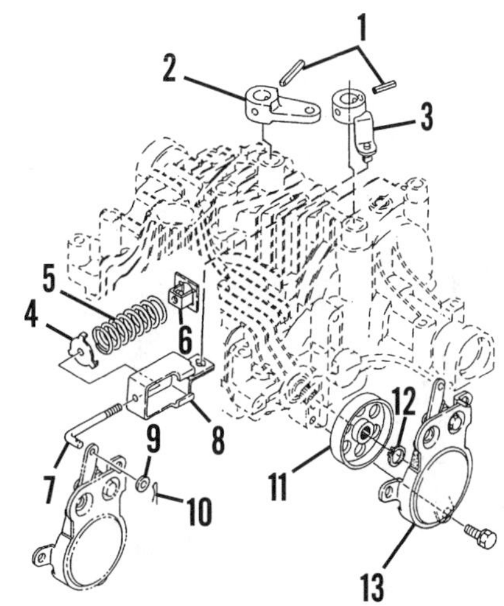

Fig. HX1-31–Exploded view of K60 and K61 brake components.

1. Roll pins
2. Brake arm
3. Brake arm
4. Spring seat
5. Spring
6. Adjuster
7. Brake rod
8. Holder
9. Washer
10. Cotter pin
11. Brake drum
12. Snap ring
13. Brake band

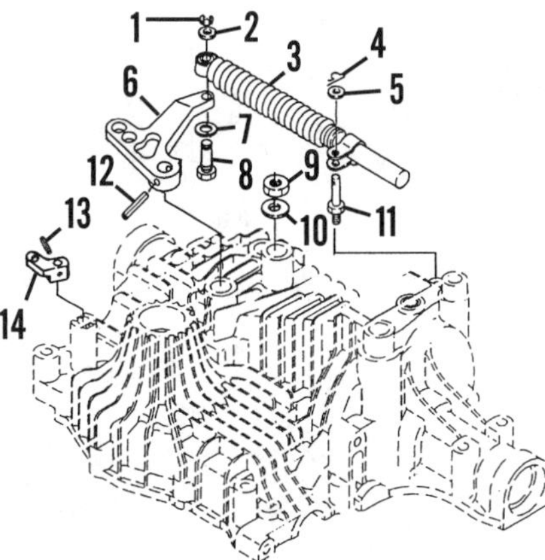

Fig. HX1-32–Exploded view of shifter components.

1. Retaining ring
2. Washer
3. Dampener
4. Cotter pin
5. Washer
6. Shift arm
7. Lockwasher
8. Shoulder bolt
9. Nut
10. Washer
11. Ball stud
12. Roll pin
13. Roll pin
14. Tow lever

Overhaul

Remove the drain plug and drain the oil. Remove the neutral switch and oil reservoir (5—Fig. HX1-30). Remove the brake assembly shown in Fig. HX1-31 and detach the control arm (3) from the shaft. Remove the belt guide and brackets.

Remove the shift damper (3—Fig. HX1-32). Remove the neutral adjustment nut (9) and washer (10). Detach the snap ring (3—Fig. HX1-33) from the input shaft. Remove the screws securing the transaxle halves together. Separate the halves.

On Model K60, both transaxle halves support the axles. Lift out the axle and differential assembly shown in Fig. HX1-34. Disassemble as necessary.

On Model K61, the axles are supported in the upper transaxle half. Note the position, then remove the snap ring (7—Fig. HX1-35) and collar (6) from each axle. While holding the differential assembly together, move the axles outward and remove the differential assembly. Disassemble as necessary.

Lift out the pinion shaft (12—Fig. HX1-34 or HX1-35) and reduction gear (13) assembly. Remove and discard the filter (72—Fig. HX1-33). Remove the check valve arm (12), plungers (43) and springs (44).

NOTE: Mark the valve components so they can be reinstalled in original bores. Mark the pump and motor pistons so they can be reinstalled in original bores. Do not damage the machined surfaces of the pump, motor or valve body.

NOTE: Do not allow the pistons to fall out of either the motor or pump cylinder block during removal.

Remove the center section/valve body (55—Fig. HX1-33) retaining screws and remove the center section and motor assembly. Remove the pump assembly.

Before removing the pump swashplate assembly, measure the side clearance (C—Fig. HX1-36) between the shift blocks (38) and swashplate (15). If clearance exceeds 0.30 mm (0.012 in.), replace the shift blocks and swashplate.

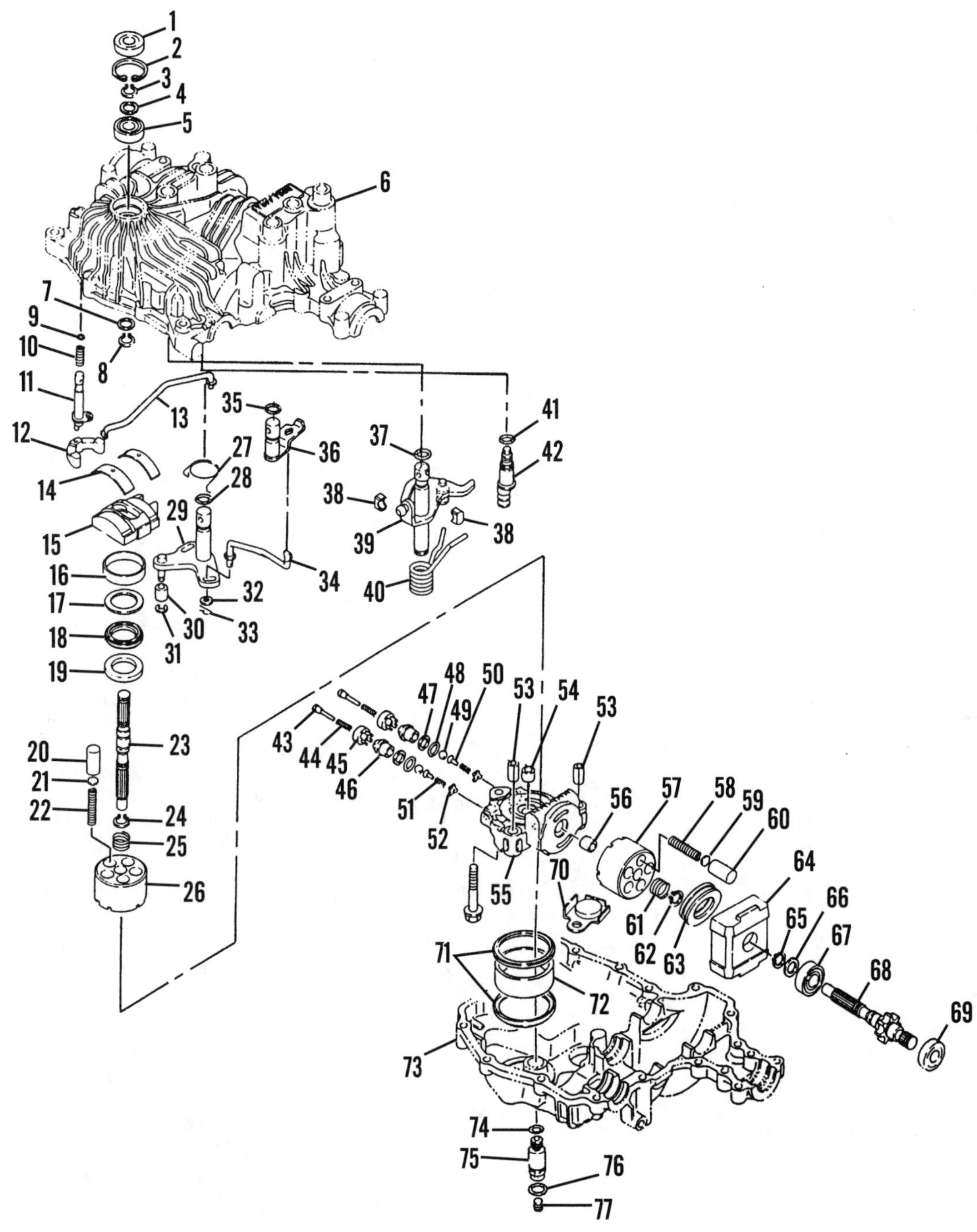

Fig. HX1-33–Exploded view of Tuff Torq K60 and K61 hydrostatic transaxle.

1. Seal
2. Snap ring
3. Snap ring
4. Washer
5. Bearing
6. Upper case half
7. Washer
8. Snap ring
9. O-ring
10. Spring
11. Tow lever shaft
12. Check valve arm
13. Rod
14. Bearing
15. Pump swashplate
16. Bushing
17. Thin plate
18. Thrust bearing
19. Thick plate
20. Pump piston
21. Disk
22. Spring
23. Pump input shaft
24. Snap ring
25. Spring
26. Pump cylinder block
27. Spring
28. O-ring
29. Brake lever
30. Roller
31. E-clip
32. Washer
33. Cotter pin
34. Brake rod
35. O-ring
36. Brake shaft
37. O-ring
38. Shoes
39. Swashplate control lever
40. Spring
41. O-ring
42. Neutral adjustment eccemtric
43. Actuating spring
44. Spring
45. Valve cap
46. Valve body
47. Back-up ring
48. O-ring
49. Ball
50. Seat
51. Spring
52. Spring guide
53. Locating pins
54. Bushing
55. Center section
56. Bushing
57. Motor cylinder block
58. Spring
59. Disk
60. Motor piston
61. Spring
62. Snap ring
63. Thrust bearing assy.
64. Motor swashplate
65. Snap ring
66. Washer
67. Bearing
68. Motor shaft
69. Seal
70. Magnet
71. Gaskets
72. Oil filter
73. Lower case half
74. O-ring
75. Fill port
76. O-ring
77. Pipe plug

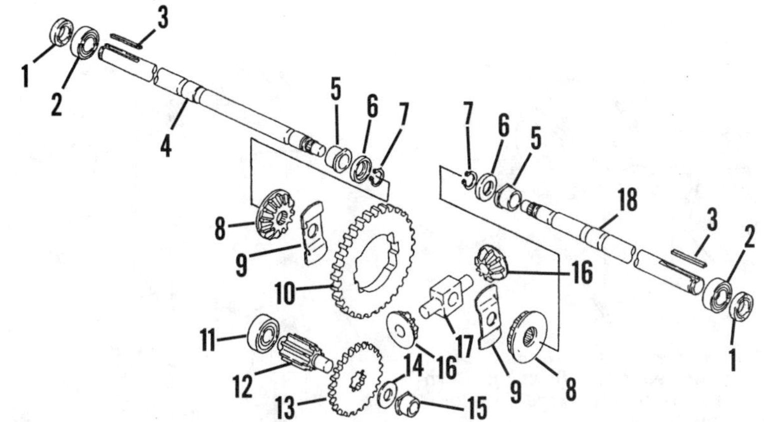

Fig. HX1-34–Exploded view of Tuff Torq K60 transaxle reduction gears and axles.

1. Seal
2. Bearing
3. Key
4. Axle shaft
5. Bushing
6. Locking collar
7. Snap ring
8. Side gears
9. Thrust plate
10. Ring gear
11. Bearing
12. Reduction shaft
13. Gear
14. Thrust washer
15. Bushing
16. Pinion gears
17. Pinion shaft
18. Axle shaft

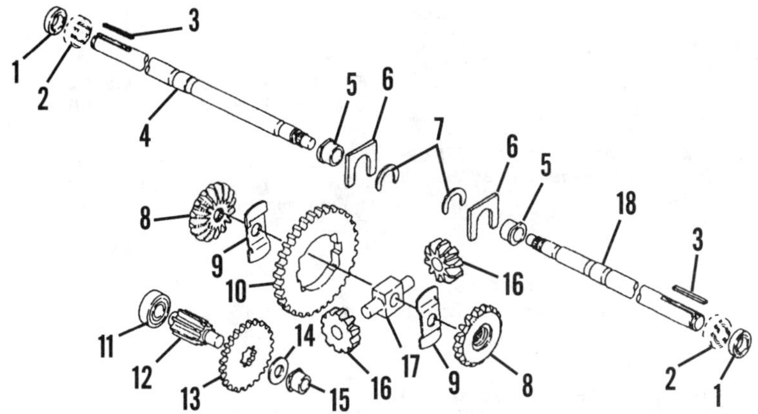

Fig. HX1-35–Exploded view of Tuff Torq K61 transaxle reduction gears and axles.

1. Seal
2. Bearing
3. Key
4. Axle shaft
5. Bushing
6. Thrust plate
7. Retainer
8. Side gears
9. Thrust plate
10. Ring gear
11. Bearing
12. Reduction shaft
13. Gear
14. Thrust washer
15. Bushing
16. Pinion gears
17. Pinion shaft
18. Axle shaft

Refer to Fig. HX1-33 and disassemble components when necessary. Note that the bearings (5 and 67) are a press fit on the pump shaft (23) and motor shaft (68).

Inspect components for wear and damage. Measure the thickness of the bearings (14—Fig. HX1-33). Minimum allowable thickness is 1.30 mm (0.051 in.). Refer to the following specifications for final drive components:

Final Drive Components (Fig. HX1-34 or HX1-35)

Pinion gear (16) max. ID .... 15.03 mm (0.592 in.)

Pinion shaft (17) min. OD ...... 14.99 mm (0.590 in.)

Pinion gear to shaft clearance, max. .... 0.50 mm (0.020 in.)

Axle inner end min. OD .... 21.98 mm (0.865 in.)

Axle bushing (5) max. ID .... 22.15 mm (0.872 in.)

Axle to bushing clearance, max. . 0.50 mm (0.020 in.)

Pinion shaft (12) outer end min. OD .... 14.97 mm (0.589 in.)

Pinion shaft bushing (15) max. ID .... 15.13 mm (0.596 in.)

Pinion shaft to bushing clearance, max. .... 0.50 mm (0.020 in.)

Reassemble by reversing the disassembly procedure while noting the following: Lubricate all components during assembly with oil. When installing the tow lever (14—Fig. HX1-32), insert the pin (13) in the hole of the shaft (11—Fig. HX1-33) that is nearer the case. When assembled correctly, the brake shaft (29) should protrude slightly above the brake control arm (2—Fig. HX1-31) bore.

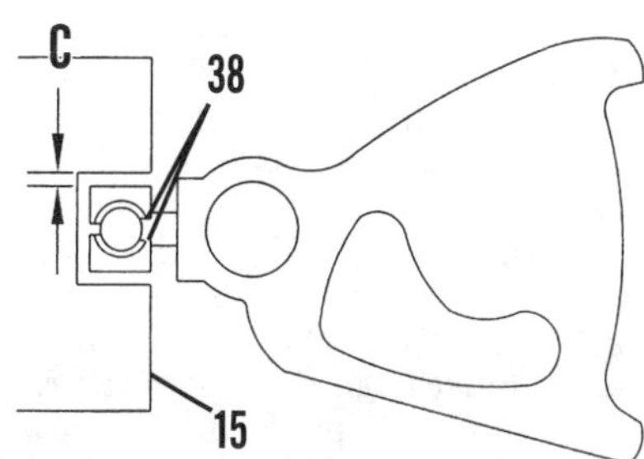

Fig. HX1-36–Clearance (C) between swashplate and shift blocks should not exceed 0.15 mm (0.006 in.)

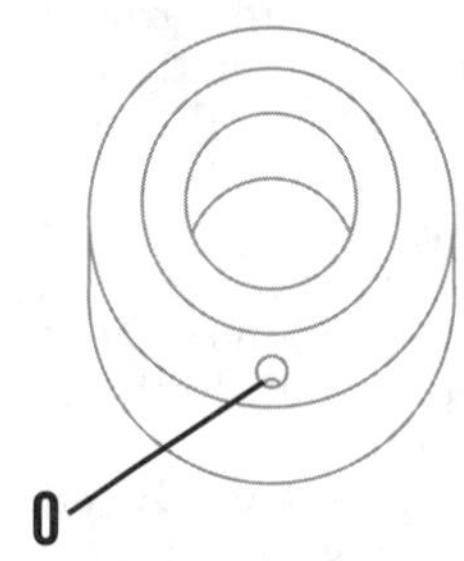

Fig. HX1-37–The check valve body with the orifice (O) must be installed in the right-hand (reverse) port in the center section.

Be sure the spring (27—Fig. HX1-33) is positioned properly. The outer spring end should be hooked on the brake lever arm that connects to the brake rod (34). Position the spring (40) ends around the eccentric shaft (42), then install the control cam (39), spring and eccentric shaft (42) as a unit into the case.

The bearings (14) fit on pegs in the case. Use petroleum jelly to hold the shoes (38) on the pivot ball of the control cam (39), and install components (15 through 19).

The valve (46) with orifice (O—Fig. HX1-37) must be installed in the right-hand (reverse) bore of the valve body when viewed with the pump surface up. Install the valves (43 through 52—Fig. HX1-33) in the center section. Apply pipe sealant to the threads of the pipe plug (77—Fig. HX1-33).

Install the seal (69—Fig. HX1-33) with the open side toward the gear. Install the thrust bearing assembly (63) in the motor swashplate as follows: Install the thin plate first with the flat side towards the swashplate. Install the ball bearing with the scalloped side facing the thin plate. Install the thick plate with the flat side facing away from the bearing. Assemble the motor shaft and motor assembly in the swashplate.

Note the boss (B—Fig. HX1-38) and indentations (I) on the motor swashplate (64). When installed, the boss (B) must fit in the slot of the case and the indentations (I) must be down. Install the motor and swashplate assembly in the case. Install the magnet (70—Fig. HX1-33) and cap screws. Tighten the cap screws evenly to draw the assembly into place. Tighten the cap screws to 43 N·m (32 ft.-lb.).

Install the actuating arm (12—Fig. HX1-33) with the slot in the arm facing the case. Install a new filter (72).

Install the reduction shaft (12—Fig. HX1-34 or Fig. HX1-35) and axle shaft assemblies in the case. The flats on the bushings (5 and 15) must face the case halves. Apply sealant to the outer circumference of the axle seals (1). Apply sealant to area (T—Fig. HX1-39). Apply sealer to case mating surfaces. Install the longer screws in holes (L and T—Fig. HX1-39). Tighten the case screws to 9 N·m (72 in.-lb.).

Refer to the tractor service section and fill and adjust the unit after installation.

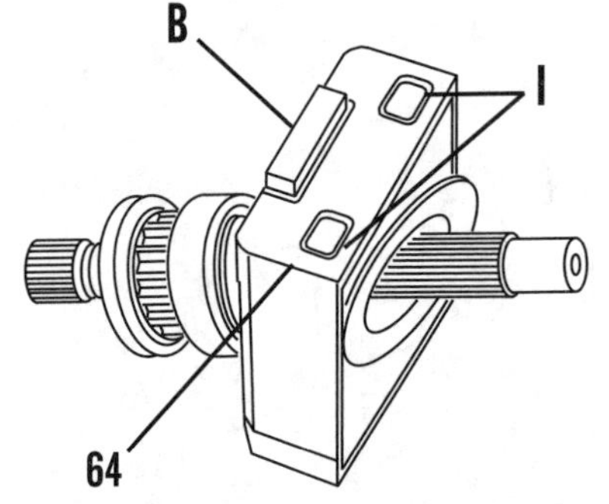

Fig. HX1-38–Motor swashplate must be installed with the recesses (I) facing downward. The tab (B) must engage the slot in the lower case half.

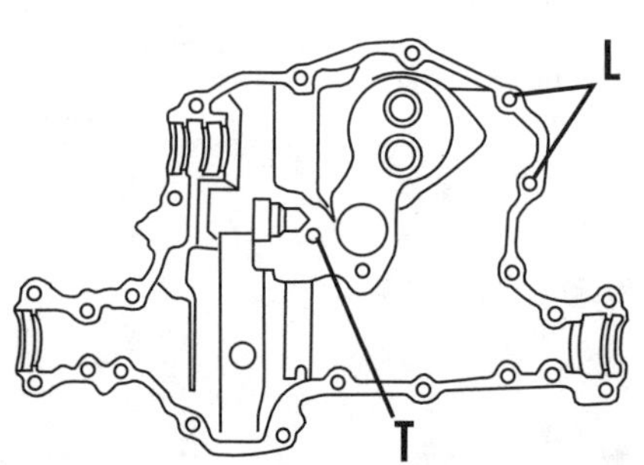

Fig. HX1-39–Apply sealant to area (T) before assembly. Install longer cap screws in holes (L and T).

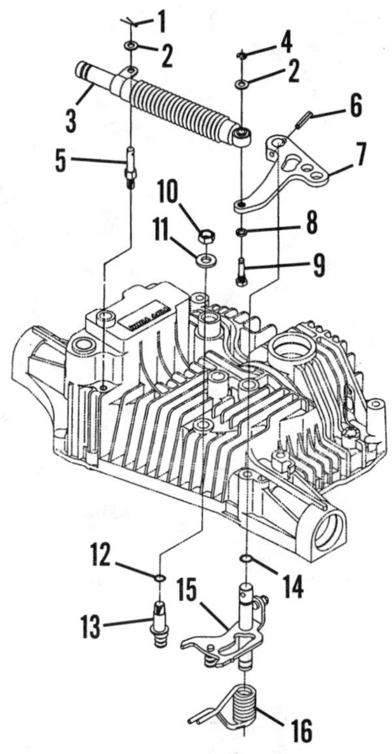

Fig. HX1-40–Exploded view of Tuff Torq Model K70 transmission controls.

1. Cotter pin
2. Washer
3. Dampener
4. Retaining ring
5. Stud
6. Roll pin
7. Shift control arm
8. Lock washer
9. Shoulder bolt
10. Nut
11. Washer
12. O-ring
13. Neutral adjustment eccentric
14. O-ring
15. Shift control shaft
16. Spring

TUFF TORQ MODEL K70

Operation

Tuff Torq Model K70 hydrostatic transmission uses a variable displacement, reversible flow, axial piston pump and a fixed displacement, axial piston motor to provide infinite speed and torque output.

Hydrostatic motor speed is controlled by hydrostatic pump rpm and the angle of pump swashplate. As the angle of the pump swashplate is increased from the zero degree (neutral) position, the length of each pump piston stroke increases and more oil is pumped to the motor. Since the motor is a fixed displacement unit, it must turn faster in order to accept the increased flow from the pump. When the pump swashplate angle decreases, the opposite effect takes place and motor speed decreases.

The hydrostatic pump turns in the same direction all the time. The hydrostatic motor is capable of turning in either direction. Reversing the pump swashplate angle, which reverses the flow of oil being pumped to the motor, reverses motor direction of rotation. When the control lever is in neutral position, there is no pump swashplate tilt and no pump piston stroke.

Power from the motor output shaft is transferred through reduction gears to the differential, which in turn rotates the axles. An internal disc type brake attached to the motor output shaft provides brake action.

The system operates as a closed loop type and any internal loss of oil from the loop is replaced by oil from the charge pump. Pressurized oil from the charge pump is forced into the loop circuit through the directional check valves, depending on the direction of travel. The charge pump inlet is connected to the reservoir (transaxle housing), allowing the pump to make up any oil that is lost from the closed loop system during operation. Make-up oil is drawn from the reservoir through an oil filter that is mounted in the lower transaxle housing. A pressure relief valve opens if pressure is excessive. A bypass valve opens to allow reservoir oil to enter the system if the charge pump fails or pressure drops below a critical level.

Overhaul

Remove the drain plug and drain the oil. Remove the neutral switch. Remove the cooling fan and pulley from the input shaft. Remove the shift damper (3—Fig. HX1-40) and control arm (7). Position the transaxle so the input shaft is down. Unscrew the screws securing the case halves together, and separate the case halves.

Lift out the pinion shaft (16—Fig. HX1-41) and reduction gear (15) assembly. Note the position, then remove the retaining ring (7) and collar (6) from each axle. While holding the differential assembly together, move the axles outward, then remove the differential assembly. Disassemble as necessary.

Remove the check valve arm (33—Fig. HX1-42) from the shaft (30). Remove the plungers (31—Fig. HX1-43) and springs (30).

NOTE: Mark the valve components so they can be reinstalled in their original bores. Mark the pump and motor components so they can be reinstalled in their original position. Do not damage the machined surfaces of the pump, motor, valve body or charge pump.

Unscrew the cap screws attaching the charge pump (38—Fig. HX1-43) to the valve body and remove the charge

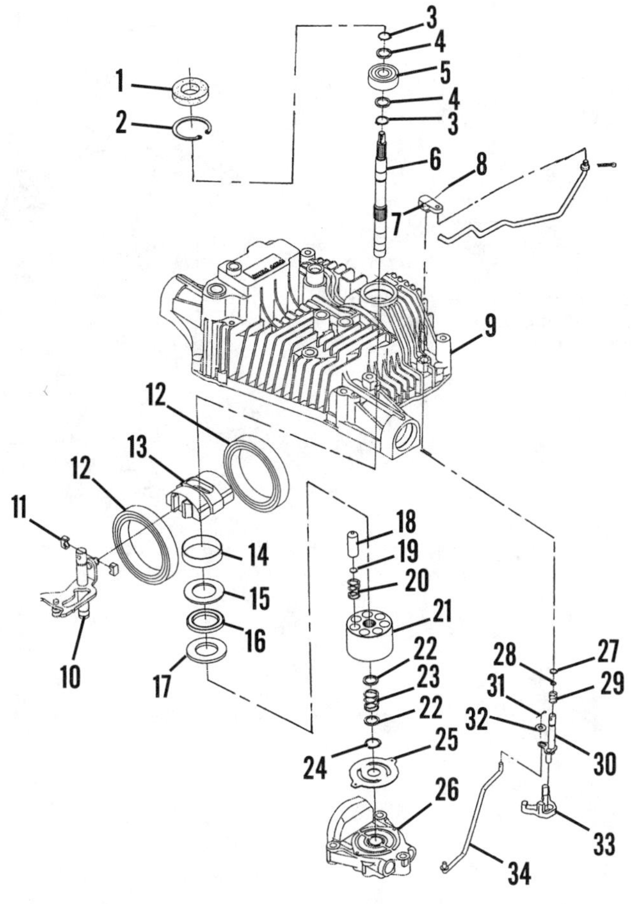

Fig. HX1-42–Exploded view of Tuff Torq K70 hydrostatic pump components.

1. Seal
2. Snap ring
3. Snap ring
4. Washer
5. Bearing
6. Pump input shaft
7. Free-wheel arm
8. Roll pin
9. Case upper half
10. Control shaft
11. Shift blocks
12. Bearings
13. Pump swashplate
14. Bushing
15. Thin plate
16. Thrust bearing
17. Thick plate
18. Pump piston
19. Disk
20. Spring
21. Pump cylinder block
22. Washers
23. Spring
24. Snap ring
25. Pump valve plate
26. Center section
27. O-ring
28. O-ring
29. Spring
30. Free-wheel shaft
31. Cotter pin
32. Washer
33. Free-wheel arm
34. Rod

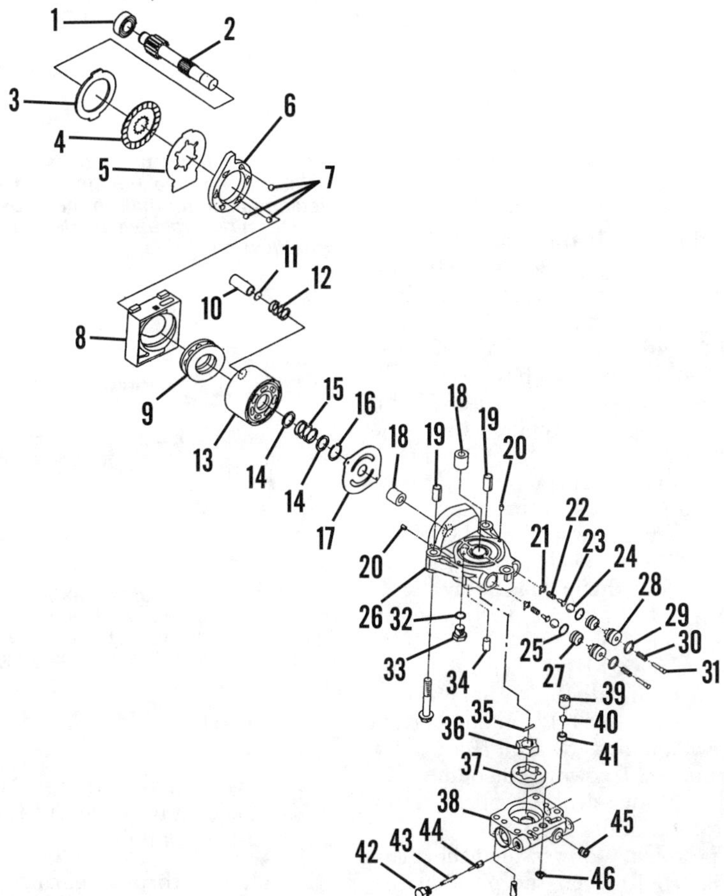

Fig. HX1-43–Exploded view of Tuff Torq K70 hydrostatic motor, transaxle brake and control valve assemblies.

1. Bearing
2. Motor shaft
3. Plate, thick
4. Brake friction disc
5. Plate, thin
6. Brake actuator
7. Balls (3)
8. Motor swashplate
9. Thrust bearing assy.
10. Motor piston
11. Washer
12. Spring
13. Motor cylinder block
14. Washers
15. Spring
16. Retaining ring
17. Motor valve plate
18. Bushing
19. Locating dowels
20. Pin
21. Spring guide
22. Spring
23. Seat
24. Ball
25. O-ring
26. Center section
27. By-pass valve
28. Valve body
29. O-ring
30. Spring
31. Actuating plunger
32. O-ring
33. Plug
34. Pin
35. Drive pin
36. Inner rotor
37. Outer rotor
38. Charge pump body
39. Orifice
40. Ball
41. Sleeve
42. Plug
43. Spring
44. Charge relief valve
45. Plug
46. Screen

pump. Remove the valve body (21) retaining screws. Push the swashplate (8) inward to relieve spring pressure, and remove the valve body and motor assembly as a unit.

NOTE: Do not allow the pistons to fall out of either the motor or pump cylinder block during removal.

Remove the pump assembly. Before removing the pump swashplate assembly, measure the side clearance (C—Fig. HX1-44) between the shift blocks (11) and swashplate (13). If clearance exceeds 0.15 mm (0.006 in.), replace the shift blocks and swashplate. Refer to Figs. HX1-45 and HX1-46 and disassemble remaining components when necessary.

Refer to the following specifications and inspect components for excessive wear and damage.

Final Drive Components (Figure HX1-41)

Pinion gear (11) ID .... 15.05-15.06 mm (0.592-0.593 in.)
Pinion shaft (12) OD ..... 14.96-14.98 mm (0.589-0.590 in.)
Pinion gear to shaft clearance .... 0.05-0.10 mm (0.002-0.004 in.)
Pinion gear to shaft clearance, max. .... 0.50 mm (0.020 in.)
Axle inner end OD .... 25.32-25.38 mm (0.997-1.000 in.)
Axle bushing (5) ID ..... 25.44-25.530 mm (1.001-1.005 in.)
Axle to bushing clearance .... 0.06-0.21 mm (0.002-0.008 in.)
Axle to bushing clearance, max. .... 0.50 mm (0.020 in.)
Pinion shaft (16) outer end OD .... 16.97-16.99 mm (0.668-0.669 in.)
Pinion shaft bushing (15) ID .... 17.05-17.13 mm (0.671-0.674 in.)
Pinion shaft to bushing clearance, max. .... 0.50 mm (0.020 in.)

Brake Components (Fig. HX1-43)

Steel plate (3) thickness .... 4.40-4.60 mm (0.173-0.180 in.)
Minimum .... 4.30 mm (0.170 in.)
Steel plate (5) thickness .... 1.10-1.30 mm (0.040-0.050 in.)
Minimum .... 1 mm (0.039 in.)
Friction plate (4) thickness .. 2.90-3.10 mm (0.110-0.120 in.)

To determine wear in the brake ball races, place a brake ball in each race on the swashplate (Fig. HX1-47) and measure the distance from the swashplate face to the ball. If the distance is not 34.125-34.325 mm (1.3435-1.3514 in.), replace the balls and swashplate. Place a brake ball in each race on the actuator (Fig. HX1-48) and measure the distance from the actuator face to the ball. If the distance is not 14.185-14.335 mm (0.5585-0.5644 in.), replace the balls and actuator.

Reassemble by reversing disassembly procedure while noting the following: Always use new seals and O-rings. Lubricate the seals and O-rings with petroleum jelly during assembly.

When installing roll pins, position the split as shown in Fig. HX1-49. When assembling the pump swashplate, install the thinner thrust plate (15—Fig. HX1-42) in the bottom of the swashplate (13) and the thicker thrust plate (17) toward the pump (21). The pump swashplate must move freely after installation.

Use petroleum jelly to hold the shoes (11—Fig. HX1-42) on the pivot ball of the control cam (10) during installation.

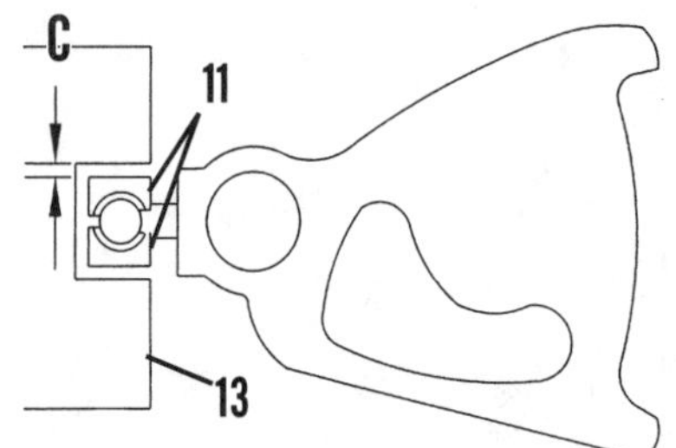

Fig. HX1-44–Clearance (C) between pump swashplate and shift blocks must not exceed 0.15 mm (0.006 in.)

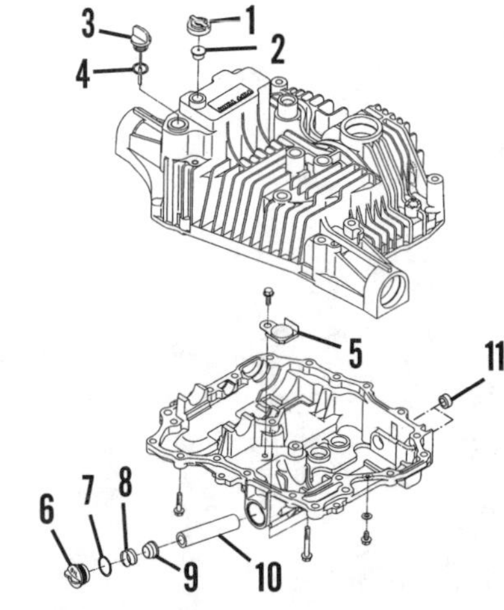

Fig. HX1-45–Drawing of Tuff Torq K70 transaxle case.

1. Dipstick
2. O-ring
3. Cap
4. Valve
5. Magnet
6. Cap
7. O-ring
8. Spring
9. Spacer
10. Oil filter
11. Cap

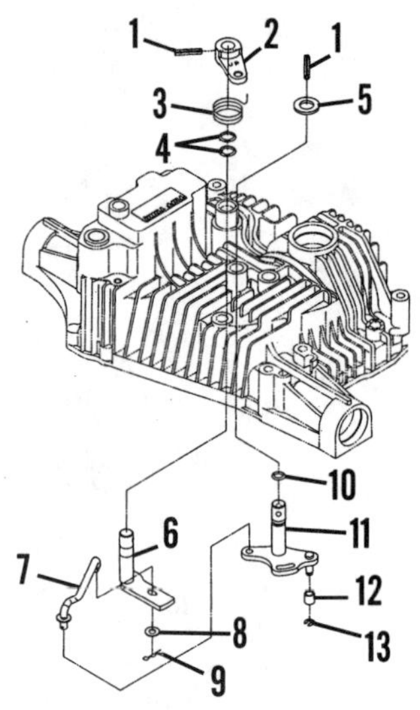

Fig. HX1-46–Exploded view of K70 transaxle brake linkage.

1. Roll pin
2. Brake arm
3. Spring
4. O-rings
5. Washer
6. Brake shaft
7. Rod
8. Washer
9. Cotter pin
10. O-ring
11. Brake interlock arm
12. Bushing
13. Retaining ring

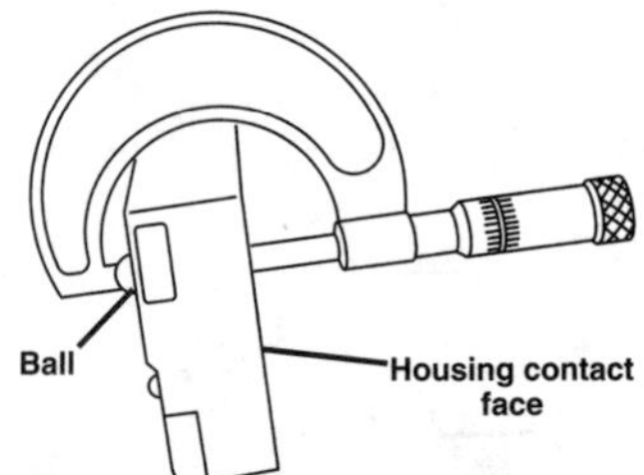

Fig. HX1-47–Place brake balls in each race in the swashplate housing and measure distance from the ball to the housing face to determine brake wear. Refer to text for specification.

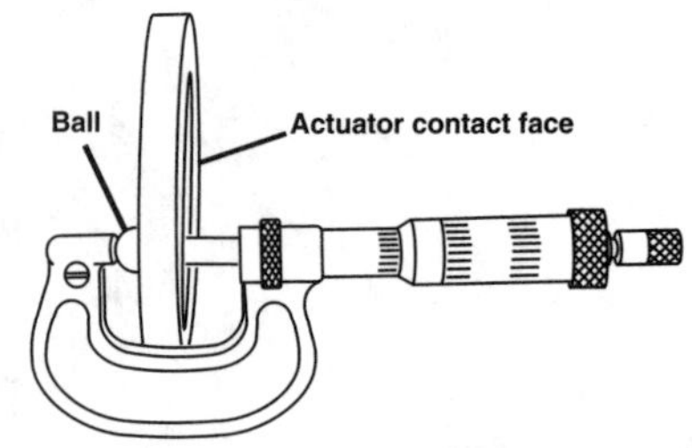

Fig. HX1-48–Place brake balls in each race in the brake actuator and measure distance from the ball to the actuator face to determine brake wear. Refer to text for specification.

Note that the spring (16—Fig. HX1-40) ends must cross and fit around the eccentric shaft (13).

Install the thrust bearing (9—Fig. HX1-43) so the side with the larger di-

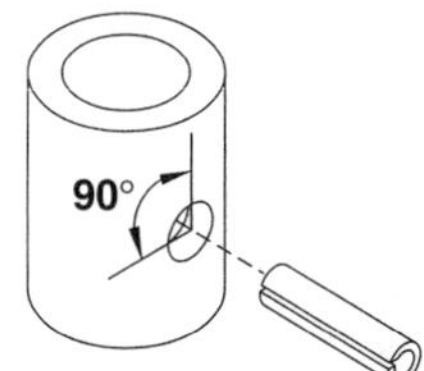

Fig. HX1-49–When installing roll pins, position the split as indicated in the above drawing.

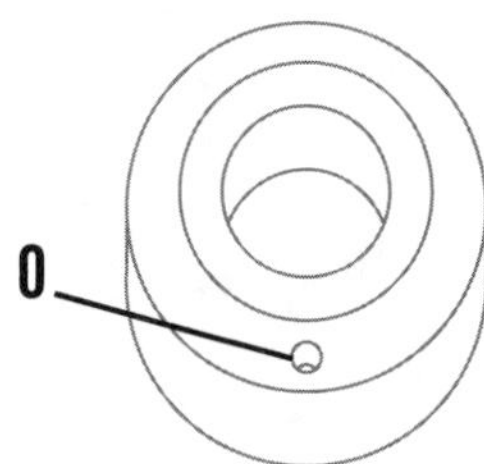

Fig. HX1-50–The check valve body with the orifice (O) must be installed in the right-hand (reverse) port in the center section

ameter fits against the swashplate (8). Use petroleum jelly to hold the balls (7) in the actuator (6). Install the actuator (6) so the outer arm is toward the B mark on the swashplate (8).

The by-pass valve (27) with an orifice (O—Fig. HX1-50) must be installed in right-hand reverse bore of the center section body when viewed with the charge pump surface down. The pump valve plate (25—Fig. HX1-42) can be identified by the ramps on one side. Install the plate so the ramped side is facing away from the center housing (26).

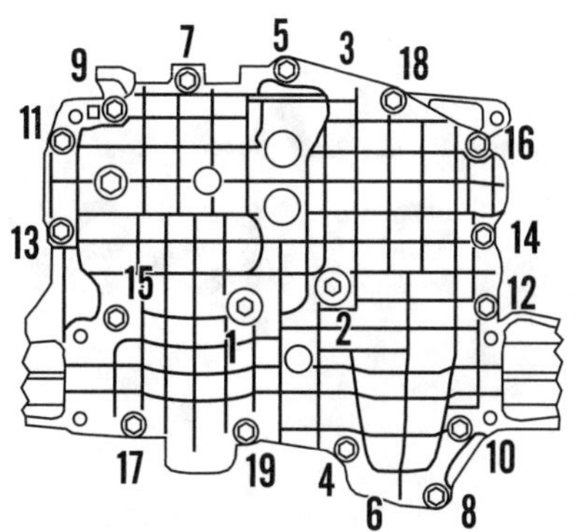

Fig. HX1-51–Tighten the case center cap screws (1 and 2) first, and then tighten the outside cap screws in the sequence shown.

When installing the motor, brake and center section unit, the B mark on the swashplate (8—Fig. HX1-43) must be toward the upper input case half. Tighten the center section retaining screws evenly to 54 N·m (40 ft.-lb.).

Be sure the locating dowels (34) are installed in the center section (26). Install the inner and outer rotors (36 and 37) in the center section. Install the charge pump by-pass valve, using petroleum jelly to hold the orifice (39) in place. Tighten the charge pump retaining screws to 23 N·m (204 in.-lb.). Install the relief valve and tighten the relief valve plug (42) to 22 N·m (195 in.-lb.). Install the charge pump body (38) on the valve body and tighten the four cap screws to 23 N·m (204 in. lb.).

Install axle seals (1—Fig. HX1-41) with the open side to the inside. The axle end should be taped prior to installation to prevent seal damage due to sharp edges. When installing the axles and differential, position the bushings (5) in case and insert the axles so they do not extend past the bushings. Assemble the differential and place it in the case, then push in the axles so they engage the side gears. Install the retaining rings (7), then insert the collars (6) between the bushings and retaining rings.

Install the pinion shaft assembly and remaining components. Apply flexible sealer to the case mating surfaces. Tighten the center case screws (1 and 2—Fig. HX1-51) first, then tighten the remaining screws in the sequence shown in Fig. HX1-51 to 23 N·m (204 in.-lb.).

HYDROSTATIC TRANSMISSIONS

EATON

MODEL 7

Operation

The Eaton Model 7 hydrostatic transmission uses a ball piston pump and motor as shown in the flow diagram (Fig. HT1-1). Two directional valves are used to maintain hydraulic pressure by allowing oil from the reservoir to enter the system. Transmission operation is as follows:

The ball piston pump output is reversible. The direction of high pressure oil to the ball piston motor is determined by the location of shift lever. The ball piston motor will rotate according to the direction of the high-pressure oil flow from the pump and transfer power to the final drive unit. When the shift lever is in NEUTRAL, oil pressure is equal on both sides of motor and it will not turn.

Directional valves open and close to allow oil from the reservoir to enter the low-pressure line to replace oil that is lost from the system due to oil seepage or excess pressure. When the directional valve (V2) is forced to close due to high pressure in the adjoining oil line, the other directional valve (V1) can open if low pressure in the adjoining line is not sufficient to keep it closed and oil from the reservoir can enter the system. If pump rotation is reversed, directional valve (V1) will be the high-pressure valve and directional valve (V2) will be the low pressure valve.

Troubleshooting

The following problems and possible causes may be used as an aid in locating and correcting transmission problems.

1. Loss of power or transmission will not operate in either direction.
   a. Broken or slipping drive belt.
   b. Broken speed control linkage.

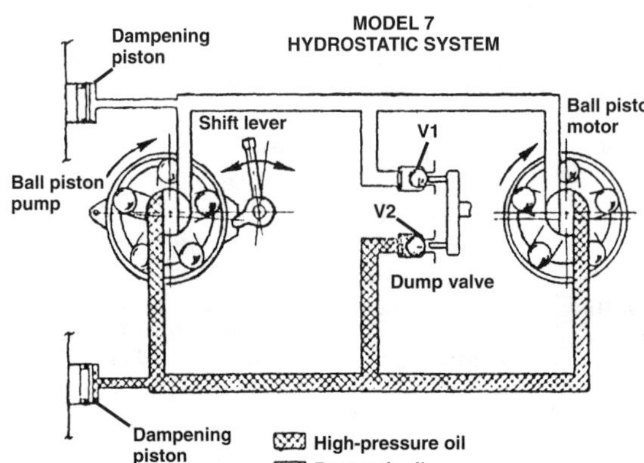

Fig. HT1-1—Flow diagram of Eaton Model 7 hydrostatic transmission.

   c. Low Transmission oil level
   d. Wrong transmission oil or contaminated oil.
   e. Transmission oil temperature too hot.
   f. Defective transmission dump valve.
   g. Worn or damaged transmission pump and/or motor.
   h. Internal damage to reduction gear unit.
2. Transmission operating too hot.
   a. Low transmission oil level.
   b. Wrong oil in transmission.
   c. Defective cooling fan.
   d. Blocked transmission cooling fins.
   e. Worn transmission pump and/or motor.
3. Transmission jerks when starting or operates in one direction only.
   a. Faulty control linkage.
   b. Faulty pintle assembly check valve.
   c. Faulty pintle assembly acceleration valve.
4. Tractor creeps when in NEUTRAL could be caused by a worn or misadjusted control linkage.

Overhaul

Place the transmission in a holding fixture (see Fig. HT1-2) with the input shaft pointing up. Remove the dust shield (1—Fig. HT1-3) and snap ring (3). Remove the cap screws from the charge pump body (7). Note that one cap screw is ½ inch (13 mm) longer than the others and must be installed in its original position.

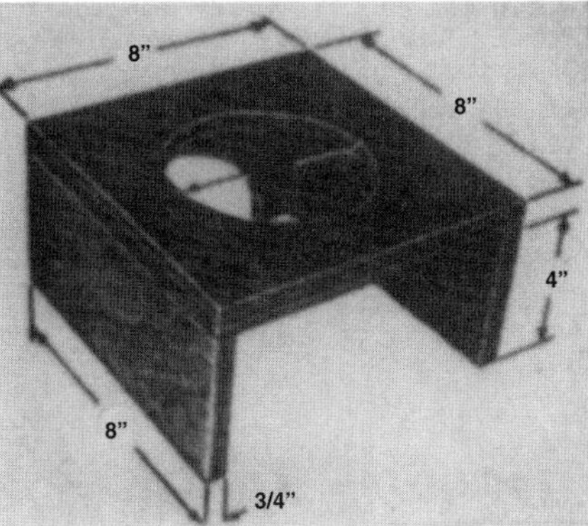

Fig. HT1-2–The wooden stand shown above is helpful when repairing an Eaton Model 7 or 11 hydrostatic transmission

Remove the charge pump body (7) with ball bearing (4). Ball bearing and oil seal (6) can be removed after removing the retaining ring (2). Remove the snap rings (5 and 8) and charge pump rotor assembly (9). Remove the O-rings (10) and pump plate (11).

Turn the hydrostatic unit over in the fixture and remove the output gear. Un-

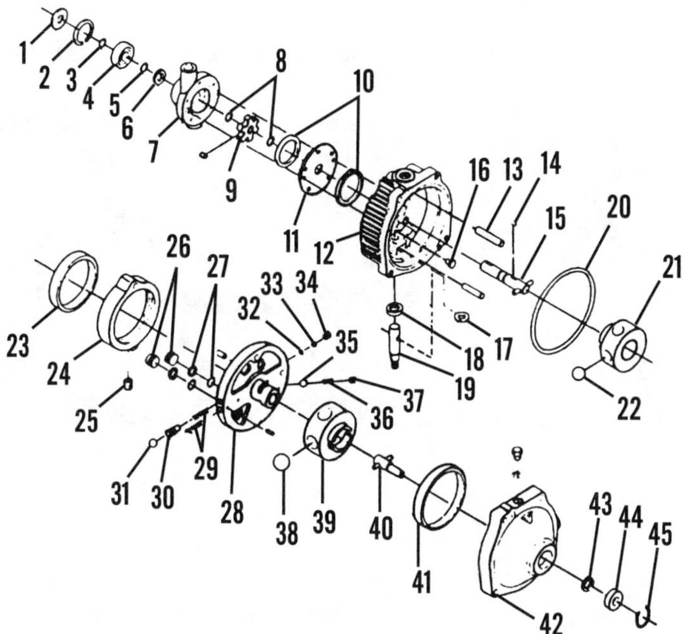

Fig. HT1-3–Exploded view of Eaton Model 7 hydrostatic transmission.

1. Dust shield
2. Retaining ring
3. Snap ring
4. Ball bearing
5. Snap ring
6. Oil seal
7. Charge pump body
8. Snap ring
9. Charge pump rotor assy,
10. Square cut seals
11. Pump plate
12. Housing
13. Cam pivot pin
14. Key
15. Input shaft
16. Neutral spring cap
17. Washer
18. Seal
19. Control shaft
20. O-ring
21. Pump rotor
22. Pump ball pistons
23. Pump race
24. Pump cam ring
25. Cam ring insert
26. Dampening pistons
27. O-ring
28. Pintle
29. Spring
30. Acceleration valve body
31. Acceleration valve ball
32. Retaining ring
33. Check vlave ball
34. Check valve body
35. Charge relief ball
36. Spring
37. Relief valve plug
38. Motor ball piston
39. Motor rotor
40. Output shaft
41. Motor race
42. Body
43. Oil seal
44. Ball bearing
45. Retainer

screw the two cap screws until two threads remain engaged. Raise the body (42) until it contacts the cap screw heads. Insert a fork tool (Fig. HT1-4) between the motor rotor (39—Fig. HT1-3) and pintle (28). Remove the cap screws, lift off the body and motor assembly with the fork tool and place the assembly on a bench or in a holding fixture with the output shaft pointing down.

Remove the fork and place a wide rubber band around the motor rotor to hold the ball pistons (38) in their bores. Carefully remove the motor rotor assembly and lay aside for later disassembly.

Remove the motor race (41) and output shaft (40). Remove the retainer (45), bearing (44) and oil seal (43). With the housing assembly (12) resting in the holding fixture, remove the pintle assembly (28).

CAUTION: Do not allow the pump to raise with the pintle as the ball pistons (22) may fall out of the rotor (21).

Hold the pump in position by inserting a finger through the hole in the pintle. Remove the plug (37), spring (36) and charge relief ball (35).

To remove the directional check valves, it may be necessary to drill through the pintle with a drill bit that will pass freely through the roll pins. Redrill the holes from the opposite side with a ¼ inch drill bit. Newer units are drilled at the factory. Press the roll pin from the pintle.

Using a 5/16-18 tap, thread the inside of valve bodies (34) then remove the valve bodies using a draw bolt or slide hammer puller. Remove the check valve balls (33) and retaining ring (32).

To remove the acceleration valves, first remove the retaining pin. Insert a $\frac{3}{16}$ inch (5 mm) diameter rod 8 inches (203 mm) long through the passage in the pintle and carefully drive out the spring (29), body (30) and ball (31).

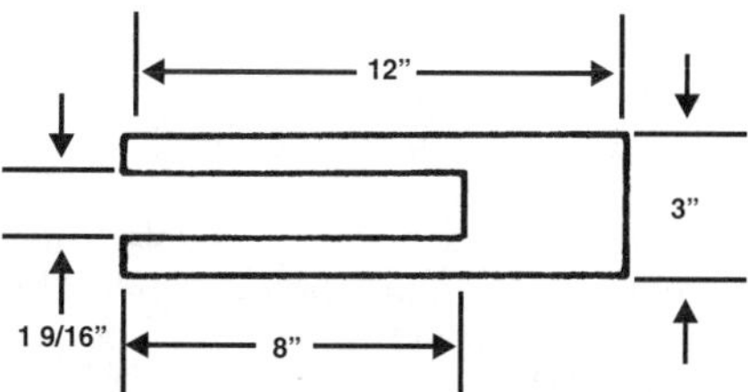

Fig. HT1-4–A special fork tool for Eaton hydrostatic transmission overhaul may be constructed from 1/8-inch flat stock using the dimensions shown above.

To remove the dampening pistons (26), carefully tap the outside edge of the pintle on a workbench to jar the pistons free.

NOTE: If the pintle journal is damaged, the pintle must be replaced.

Remove the pump cam ring (24) and pump race (23). Place a wide rubber band around the pump rotor to prevent the ball pistons (22) from falling out. Carefully remove the pump assembly and input shaft (15).

To remove the control shaft (19), drill an $\frac{11}{32}$-inch hole through the aluminum housing (12) directly in line with the centerline of the dowel pin. Press the dowel pin from the control shaft, and then withdraw the control shaft.

Remove the oil seal (18). Thread the drilled hole in the housing with a $\frac{1}{8}$-inch pipe tap. Apply a light coat of Loctite 680 to a $\frac{1}{8}$-inch pipe plug, install the plug and tighten until snug. Do not over tighten.

Number the piston bores (1-5) on the pump rotor and on the motor rotor. Use a plastic ice cube tray or equivalent and mark the cavities 1P through 5P for the pump ball pistons and 1M through 5M for the motor ball pistons. Remove the ball pistons (22) one at a time, from the pump rotor and place each ball in the correct cavity in the tray. Remove the ball piston (38) and springs from the motor rotor in the same manner.

Clean and inspect all parts and replace any showing excessive damage. Replace all gaskets, seals and O-rings. Ball pistons are a select fit to 0.0002-0.0006 inch (0.005-0.015 mm) clearance in the rotor bores and must be reinstalled in their original bores.

If the rotor bushing-to-pintle journal clearance is 0.002 inch (0.05 mm) or more, the pump rotor or motor rotor and/or pintle must be replaced.

Check the clearance between the input shaft (15) and housing bushing. Normal clearance is 0.0013-0.0033 inch (0.033-0.084 mm). If clearance is excessive, replace the input shaft and/or housing assembly.

Install the ball pistons (22) in the pump rotor (21), and the ball pistons (38) and springs in the motor rotor (39), then use wide rubber bands to hold the pistons in their bores.

Install the charge relief valve ball (35) and spring (36) in the pintle. Screw the plug (37) into the pintle until just below the outer surface of the pintle. Install the acceleration valve springs (29) and bodies (30) making sure the valves move freely. Tap the balls (31) into the pintle until the roll pins will go into place. Install the snap rings (32), check valve balls (33) and valve bodies (34) in the pintle and secure with new roll pins.

NOTE: When installing oil seals (6, 18 or 43), apply a light coat of Loctite 680 to seal the outer diameter.

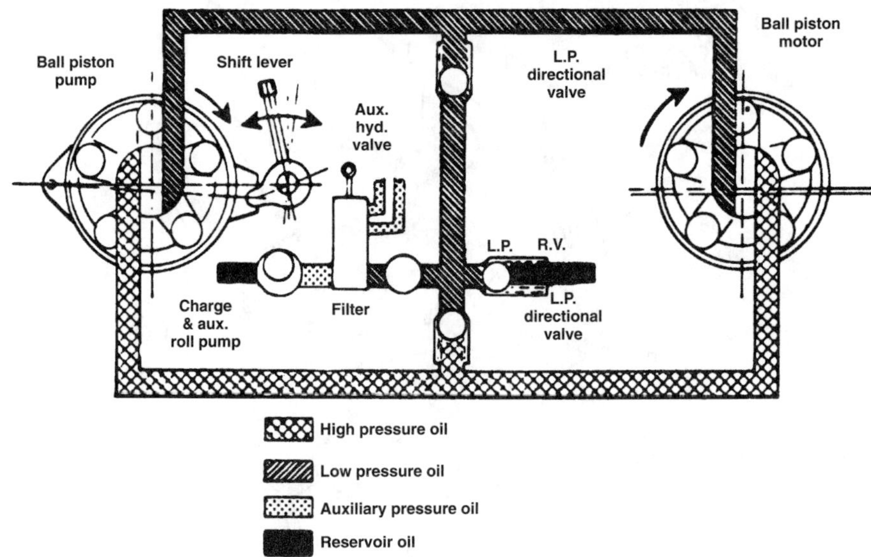

Fig. HT1-5–Flow diagram of Eaton Model 11 hydrostatic transmission.

Replace the oil seal (18) and install the control shaft (19) in the housing. Install the special washer (17), and press the dowel pin through the control shaft until the pin extends 1¼ inches (32 mm) from the control shaft. Renew the oil seal (43) and reinstall the output shaft (40), bearing (44), retainer (45), output gear and snap ring.

Insert the input shaft (15) in the housing (12). Install the snap ring (8) in its groove on the input shaft. Place the O-ring (10), pump plate (11) and O-ring in the housing, then install the charge pump drive key (14).

Apply light grease or Vaseline to the pump rollers and place the rollers in the rotor slots (9). Install the oil seal (6) and pump race in the charge pump body (7), then install the body assembly. Secure with the five cap screws, making certain the long cap screw is installed in its original location, the heavy section of the pump body. Tighten the cap screws to 28-30 ft.-lb. (38-41 N·m). Install the snap ring (5), bearing (4), retaining ring (2), snap ring (3) and dust shield (1).

Place the charge pump and housing assembly in a holding fixture with the input shaft pointing downward. Install the pump race (23) and insert (25) in the cam ring (24), then install the cam ring assembly over the cam pivot pin (13) and control shaft dowel pin. Turn the control shaft (19) back and forth and check movement of the cam ring. Cam ring must move freely from stop to stop. If not, check installation of the insert (25) in the cam ring.

Install the pump rotor assembly and remove the rubber band used to retain the pistons. Install the pintle assembly (28) over the cam pivot pin (13) and into the pump rotor. Place the O-ring (20) in position on the housing.

Place the body assembly (42) in a holding fixture with the output gear down. Install the motor race (41) in the body, then install the motor rotor assembly and remove the rubber band used to retain the pistons in the rotor.

Use a fork tool (Fig. HT1-4) to retain the motor assembly in the body, and carefully install the body and motor assembly over the pintle journal. Remove the fork tool, align the bolt holes and install the two cap screws. Tighten the cap screws to 15 ft.-lb. (20 N·m).

Place the hydrostatic unit on the holding fixture with the reservoir adapter opening and venting plug opening facing upward. Fill the unit with recommended fluid until fluid flows from the fitting hole in the body. Plug all openings to prevent dirt or other foreign material from entering the hydrostatic unit.

MODEL 11

Troubleshooting

Use the following problems and possible causes a guide to locate and correct transmission problems.

1. Loss of power or transmission will not operate in either direction.
   a. Broken or slipping drive belt.
   b. Broken speed control linkage.
   c. Low transmission oil level.
   d. Wrong transmission oil or contaminated oil.
   e. Transmission oil temperature too hot.
   f. Faulty relief valve.
   g. Worn or damaged transmission pump and/or motor.
   h. Internal damage in final drive unit.
   i. Faulty acceleration valve in pintle assembly.
   j. Faulty charge pump.
   k. Clogged oil filter.
2. Transmission operating too hot.
   a. Low transmission oil level.
   b. Wrong oil in transmission.
   c. Defective cooling fan.
   d. Blocked or damaged transmission cooling fins.
   e. Worn transmission pump and/or motor.
   f. Faulty relief valve.
   g. Faulty charge pump.
   h. Clogged oil filter.
3. Transmission jerks when starting or operates in one direction only.
   a. Faulty control linkage.
   b. Faulty check valve in pintle assembly.
   c. Faulty acceleration valve in pintle assembly.
4. Tractor creeps when in NEUTRAL could be caused by a worn or misadjusted control linkage.

Operation

The Eaton Model 11 hydrostatic transmission is composed of four major parts: (1) a reversible flow, variable displacement, ball piston pump, (2) a fixed displacement, ball piston motor (3) a system of valves located between the

Fig. HT1-6–Exploded view of Eaton Model 11 hydrostatic transmission.

1. Dust shield
2. Retaining ring
3. Snap ring
4. Ball bearing
5. Snap ring
6. Oil seal
7. Charge pump body
8. Charge pump race
9. Snap ring
10. Charge pump rotor
11. Snap ring
12. Pump roller (6 used)
13. Dowel pin
14. O-ring
15. Pump plate
16. O-ring
17. Bushing
18. Retainer
19. O-ring
20. Reservoir adapter
21. Screen
22. Housing
23. Bushing
24. Oil seal
25. Control shaft
26. Washer
27. Dowel pin
28. Insert
29. Insert cap
30. Drive pin
31. Cam pivot pin
32. Charge pump drive key
33. Input shaft
34. O-ring
35. Pump ball pistons
36. Pump rotor
37. Rotor bushing
38. Pump race
39. Pump cam ring
40. Plug (2 used)
41. Roll pings
42. Snap ring (2 used)
43. Check valve ball (2 used)
44. Direction check valve body (2 used)
45. Plug
46. Relief spring
47. Charge relief ball
48. Pintle
49. Needle bearing
50. Rotor bushing
51. Motor ball pistons
52. Springs
53. Motor rotor
54. Drive pin
55. Output shaft
56. Motor race
57. Body
58. Gasket
59. Venting plug
60. Cap screw
61. Oil seal
62. Ball bearing
63. Retainer
64. Output gear
65. Snap ring

pump and motor (4) a charge and auxiliary hydraulic supply pump.

Tractor ground speed is regulated by changing the amount of oil delivered by the variable displacement pump. Moving the speed control pedal in a forward direction regulates the forward ground speed. When the speed control pedal is moved in the reverse direction (depressed with the heel), the transmission output shaft reverses thereby reversing the tractor direction.

The system operates as a closed loop and any internal loss of oil from the loop is replaced by oil from the charge pump. See Fig. HT1-5. This oil is forced into the loop circuit through the directional check valves, depending on the direction of travel. The charge pump normally pumps more oil than is needed to make up losses, and all excess oil passes through the charge pressure relief valve and back into the reservoir.

Overhaul

Before disassembling the transmission, thoroughly clean the exterior of the unit. If so equipped, remove the venting plug (59—Fig. HT1-6) and reservoir adapter (18 through 21). Invert the assembly and drain the fluid. Place the unit in a holding fixture similar to one shown in Fig. HT1-2 so the input shaft is pointing up.

Remove the dust shield (1—Fig. HT1-6) and snap ring (3). Place an identifying mark across the joining edges of each section to aid in correct assembly. Remove the five cap screws from the charge pump body (7). Note that one cap screw is ½ inch (13 mm) longer than the others and must be installed in its original position, the heavy section of pump body.

Remove the charge pump body (7) with the ball bearing (4). Ball bearing and oil seal (6) can be removed after removing the retaining ring (2). Remove the six charge pump rollers (12), snap rings (5, 9 and 11) and charge pump rotor (10). Remove the O-rings (14 and 16) and pump plate (15).

Turn the hydrostatic unit over in the fixture and remove the output gear. Remove the snap ring (65) and output gear (64). Unscrew the two cap screws (60) until two threads remain engaged. Raise the body (57) until it contacts the cap screw heads. Insert a fork tool (Fig. HT1-4) between the motor rotor (53—Fig. HT1-6) and pintle (48). Remove the cap screws, lift off the body and motor assembly with the fork tool and place the assembly on a bench or in a holding fixture with the output shaft pointing down. Remove the fork and place a wide rubber band around the motor rotor to hold ball pistons (51) in their bores.

Carefully remove the motor rotor assembly and lay aside for later disassembly. Remove the motor race (56) and output shaft (55). Remove the retainer (63), bearing (62) and oil seal (61). With the housing assembly (22) resting in the holding fixture, remove the pintle assembly (48).

CAUTION: Do not allow the pump to raise with the pintle as the ball pistons (35) may fall out of the rotor (36).

Hold the pump in position by inserting your finger through the hole in the pintle. Remove the plug (45), spring (46) and charge relief ball (47). To remove the directional check valves, it may be necessary to drill through the pintle with a drill bit that will pass freely through the roll pins (41). Redrill the holes from the opposite side with a ¼-inch drill bit. Newer units are drilled at the factory.

Press the roll pin from the pintle. Using a 5/16-18 tap, thread the inside of the valve bodies (44), then remove the valve bodies using a draw bolt or slide hammer puller. Remove the check valve balls (43) and retaining ring (42). Do not remove the plugs (40).

Remove the pump cam ring (39) and pump race (38). Place a wide rubber band around the pump rotor to prevent the ball pistons (35) from falling out. Carefully remove the pump assembly and input shaft (33).

To remove the control shaft (25), drill a 11/32-inch hole through the aluminum housing (22) directly in line with the centerline of the dowel pin (27). Press the dowel pin from the control shaft, and then withdraw the control shaft. Remove the oil seal (24). Thread the drilled hole in the housing with a 1/8-inch pipe tap. Apply a light coat of Loctite 680 to a 1/8-inch pipe plug, install the plug and tighten until snug. Do not over tighten.

Number the piston bores (1-5) on the pump rotor and on the motor rotor. Use a plastic ice cube tray or equivalent and mark the cavities 1P through 5P for the pump ball pistons and 1M through 5M for the motor ball pistons. Remove the ball pistons (35) one at a time, from the pump rotor and place each ball in the correct cavity in the tray. Remove the ball piston (51) and springs (52) from the motor rotor in the same manner.

Clean and inspect all parts and replace any showing excessive wear or other damage. Replace all gaskets, seals and O-rings. Ball pistons are a select fit to 0.0002-0.0006 inch (0.005-0.015 mm) clearance in rotor bores and must be reinstalled in their original bores. If the rotor bushing-to-pintle journal clearance is 0.002 inch (0.051 mm) or more, the pump rotor or motor rotor must be replaced.

Check the clearance between the input shaft (33) and housing bushing. Normal clearance is 0.0013-0.0033 inch (0.033-0.084 mm). If clearance is excessive, replace the input shaft and/or housing assembly.

Install the ball pistons (35) in the pump rotor (36), and the ball pistons (51) and springs (52) in the motor rotor (53). Use wide rubber bands to hold the pistons in their bores.

Install the charge relief valve ball (47) and spring (46) in the pintle. Screw the plug (45) into the pintle until it extends just below the outer surface of the pintle. Install the snap rings (42), check valve balls (43) and valve bodies (44) in the pintle (48) and secure with new roll pins (41).

NOTE: When installing the oil seals (6, 24 or 61), apply a light coat of Loctite 680 to the seal outer diameter.

Replace the oil seal (24) and install the control shaft (25) in the housing. Install the special washer (26), and then press the dowel pin through the control shaft until 1¼ inches (32 mm) of the pin extends from the control shaft.

Replace the oil seal (61) and reinstall the output shaft (55), bearing (62), retainer (63), output gear (64) and snap ring (65).

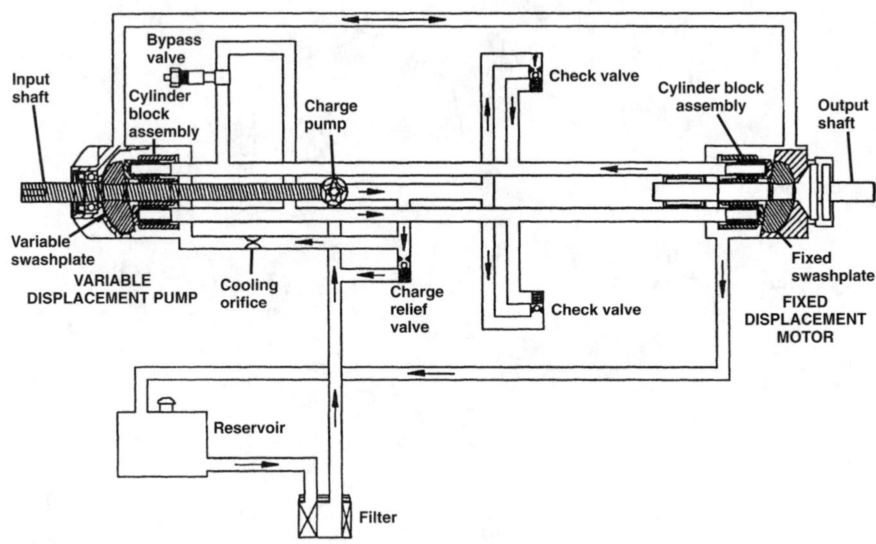

Fig. HT1-7–Circuit diagram of Hydro-Gear Series BDU-10L hydrostatic transmission.

Insert the input shaft (33) with the drive pin (30) through the bushing (17) in the housing. Install the snap ring (11) in its groove on the input shaft. Place the O-ring (16), pump plate (15) and O-ring (14) in the housing, and then install the charge pump drive key (32). Apply light grease or Vaseline to the pump rollers (12) and place the rollers in the rotor slots.

Install the oil seal (6) and pump race (8) in the charge pump body (7), then install the body assembly. Secure with the five cap screws, making certain the longer cap screw is installed in its original location, the heavy section of the pump body. Tighten the cap screws to 28-30 ft.-lb. (38-41 N·m). Install the snap ring (5), bearing (4), retaining ring (2), snap ring (3) and dust shield (1).

Place charge pump and housing assembly in a holding fixture with input shaft pointing downward. Install pump race (38), insert cap (29) and insert (28) in cam ring (39), then install cam ring assembly over cam pivot pin (31) and control shaft dowel pin (27). Turn control shaft (25) back and forth and check movement of cam ring. Cam ring must move freely from stop to stop. If not, check installation of insert (28) in cam ring.

Install pump rotor assembly and remove rubber band used to retain pistons. Install the pintle assembly (48) over the cam pivot pin (31) and into pump rotor. Place the O-ring (34) in position on the housing.

Place the body assembly (57) in a holding fixture with the output gear down. Install the motor race (56) in the body, then install the motor rotor assembly and remove the rubber band used to retain the pistons in the rotor.

Use the special fork tool (Fig. HT1-4) to retain the motor assembly in the body, and carefully install the body and motor assembly over the pintle journal. Remove the fork tool, align the bolt holes and install the two cap screws. Tighten the cap screws to 15 ft.-lb. (20 N·m).

Place the hydrostatic unit on the holding fixture with the reservoir adapter opening and venting plug opening facing upward. Fill the unit with the recommended fluid until the fluid flows from the fitting hole in the body. Install the venting plug (59—Fig. HT1-6) with the gasket (58), then install the reservoir adapter (20), screen (21), O-ring (19) and retainer (18). Plug all openings to prevent dirt or other foreign material from entering the hydrostatic unit.

HYDROGEAR/ SUNDSTRAND

SERIES BDU-10L AND BDU-10S

The BDU-10 hydrostatic transmission is constructed in two models that are identified by the suffix letters L and S.

The BDU-10L model is equipped with a charge pump that feeds oil from an external oil reservoir to the transmission pump. The transmission input shaft drives the charge pump. Oil from the reservoir is routed through an external filter before traveling to the charge pump.

The BDU-10S model is self-contained. Oil is contained in an internal reservoir and passes through an

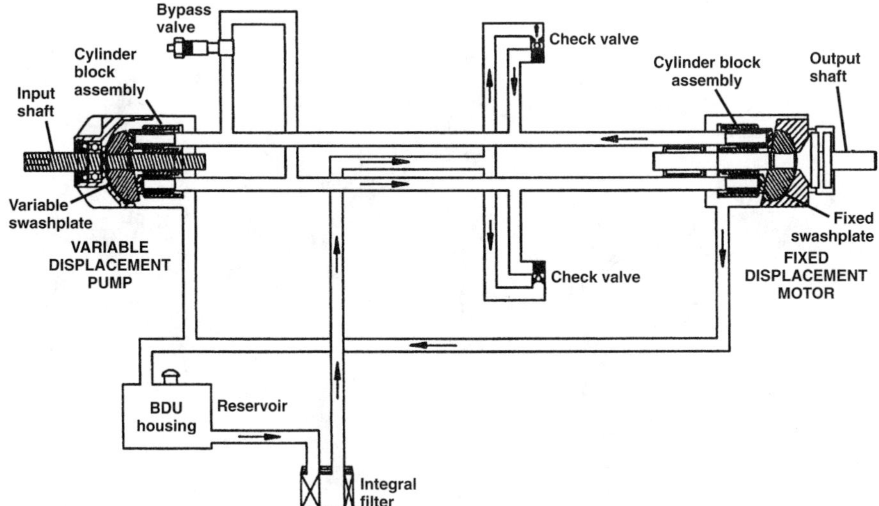

Fig. HT1-8–Circuit diagram of Hydro-Gear Series BDU-10S hydrostatic transmission.

internal filter before entering the transmission pump. No charge pump is used.

Operation

The hydrostatic transmission consists of a variable volume, reversible swashplate, axial piston pump connected in a closed loop to a fixed displacement, axial piston motor. The engine drives the hydrostatic pump, and the motor is connected to the final drive unit.

On the Model BDU-10L, the charge pump supplies oil to the transmission pump. Refer to Fig. HT1-7 for a circuit diagram. Oil in the external reservoir travels through the oil filter before entering the charge pump. The transmission input shaft drives the charge pump. A relief valve bypasses excess oil flow to prevent excessive pressure in charge pump circuit.

On Model BDU-10S, the hydrostatic pump inlet is connected to the internal reservoir (transmission housing), allowing the pump to make-up any oil that is lost from the closed loop system during operation. Refer to Fig. HT1-8 for a circuit diagram. Make-up oil is drawn from the reservoir through an oil filter screen mounted in the hydrostatic transmission housing.

Hydrostatic motor speed is controlled by hydrostatic pump rpm and the angle of the pump swashplate. As the angle of the pump swashplate is increased from the zero degree NEUTRAL position, the length of each pump piston stroke increases and more oil is pumped to the motor. Because the motor is a fixed displacement unit, it must turn faster in order to accept the increased flow from the pump. When the pump swashplate angle decreases, the opposite effect takes place and motor speed decreases.

The hydrostatic pump turns in the same direction all the time. The hydrostatic motor is capable of turning in both directions. Reversing the pump swashplate angle reverses the flow of oil from the pump to the motor, causing the motor rotation to reverse. When the control lever is in the neutral position, there is no pump swashplate tilt and no pump piston stroke.

Any oil lost internally from the closed loop system is replaced by oil from the internal oil reservoir on Model BDU-10S or from the charge pump on Model BDU-10L.

On Model BDU-10S, reservoir oil will pass through the check valve when the transmission oil pressure is not sufficient to keep the check valve closed.

On Model BDU-10L, the charge pump forces oil from the external reservoir through the check valve on the low-pressure side of the hydrostatic loop. On Model BDU-10L, all excess charge oil passes through the charge pressure regulator valve and is relieved to the suction side of the charge pump.

Troubleshooting

When troubleshooting the hydrostatic drive system, always check the easiest and most obvious items first. Some problems that may occur during operation of hydrostatic transmission and their possible causes are as follows:

1. Lack of drive or limited speed in both directions.
   a. Broken or misadjusted control linkage.
   b. Slipping or broken transmission drive belt (if used).
   c. Bypass valve stuck open or leaking.
   d. Low oil level.
   e. Plugged oil filter.
   f. Faulty charge pump or charge relief valve (Model BDU-10L).
   g. Internal leakage of high pressure fluid due to excessive wear of pump and/or motor.
   h. Failure of final drive.
2. Lack of drive or limited speed in one direction.
   a Movement of pump swashplate being restricted in one direction.
   b. Charge check valve not seating.

Overhaul

To disassemble the transmission, first remove the transmission control arm. If so equipped, remove the external reservoir (it may have left-hand threads). Drain the oil from the transmission housing.

NOTE: On Model BDU-10L, charge pump installation must match the direction of input shaft rotation. Mark the charge pump and spacer plate, if so equipped, before disassembly so they can be installed in their original position.

On Model BDU-10L, unscrew and remove the charge pump housing (3—Fig. HT1-9). Remove the pump rotors (4), charge relief valve (9) and drive pin (5). On both models, unscrew and separate the end cover (13) from the housing (39), being careful not to damage the machined surfaces of the end cover and pump and motor cylinder blocks. Remove the check valves (12) and bypass valve (11) from the end cover. Pry out the oil seal (1) on Model BDU-10S and the seal (10) on both models.

Position the housing (39) on its side and slide out the pump cylinder block (15) with the pistons and the motor cylinder block (27) with pistons. The motor shaft (26) should slide out with the motor cylinder block. Remove the motor thrust bearing assembly (33). Remove the spring (19), washer (20) and pump swashplate (22) with the thrust bearing assembly (21).

Remove the slot guide (24) and cradle bearings (25). On Model BDU-10S, remove the filter screen (35), washer (36) and spring (37). Remove the retaining ring (45) and pry out the oil seal (44), taking care not to damage the pump shaft or housing.

Tap the inner end of the pump shaft (40) with a soft hammer to remove the shaft and bearing (41) from the housing. Withdraw the trunnion arm (23) and remove the bearing (38) from the housing.

Inspect the pistons and cylinder bores for damage. The specified motor or pump piston diameter is 0.6288-0.6291 inch (15.972-15.979 mm). The specified motor or pump cylinder bore diameter is 0.6295-0.6303 inch (15.989-16.010 mm). Pump and motor cylinder blocks are serviced as complete assemblies.

Check the polished surfaces of the end cover (13) and cylinder blocks for wear, scoring or scratches. The end cover and cylinder blocks must be replaced if wear exceeds 0.0004 inch (0.01 mm). Inspect the check valve balls and their seats for damage or wear and replace when necessary.

Motor shaft (26) bearing diameter should be 0.4961-0.4998 inch (12.601-12.693 mm). Pump shaft (40) bearing diameter should be 0.4961-0.4998 inch (12.601-12.693 mm). Trunnion arm shaft (23) bearing diameter should be 0.4722-0.4733 inch (11.993-12.022 mm). Replace all O-rings and oil seals.

Coat parts with oil during reassembly. To reassemble, reverse the disassembly procedure while noting the following special instructions: The bearing (38) must be positioned so there is 0.020-0.060 inch (0.51-1.52 mm) end play of the trunnion arm (23) shaft with the swashplate (22) installed. Piston springs (16 and 28) must be centered in the cylinder bores. Be sure that the pistons are returned to their original bores in the cylinder blocks and that they slide freely in the cylinder block. Use a rubber band to hold the pistons in their bores. Tighten the end cover mounting screws evenly to 18-21 ft.-lb. (24.5-28.6 N·m). Tighten the charge pump housing screws to 84-120 in.-lb. (9.5-13.6 N·m).

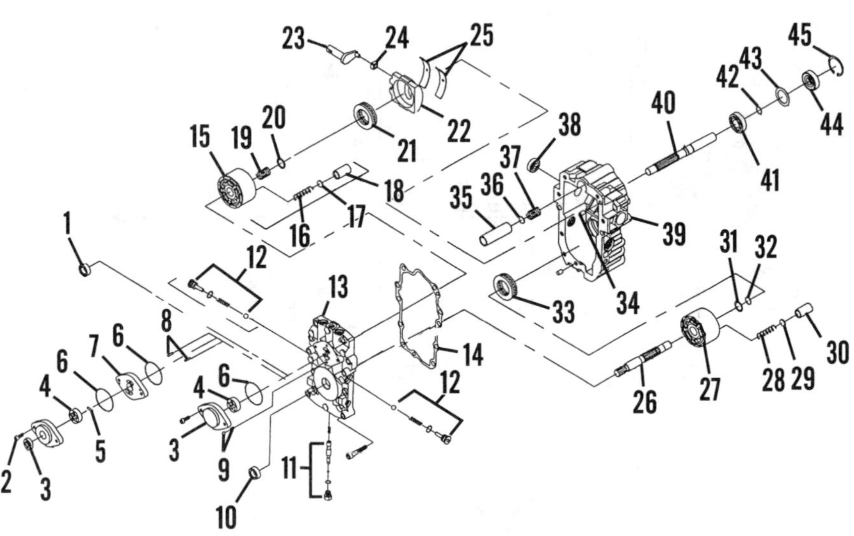

Fig. HT1-9–Exploded view of Hydro-Gear BDU-10 series hydrostatic transmission.

1. Oil seal
2. Oil seal
3. Charge pump Housing
4. Oil pump rotors
5. Drive pin
6. O-ring
7. Spacer
8. Dowel pins
9. Check valve
10. Oil seal
11. Bypass valve assy.
12. Check valves
13. End cover
14. Gasket
15. Pump cylinder block
16. Spring
17. Seat
18. Piston
19. Spring
20. Thrust washer
21. Thrust bearing
22. Swashplate
23. Trunnion arm
24. Slot guide
25. Bearings
26. Motor shaft
27. Motor cylinder block
28. Spring
29. Seat
30. Piston
31. Thrust washer
32. Retaining ring
33. Thrust bearing
34. Dowel pins
35. Filter
36. Washer
37. Spring
38. Bearing
39. Transmission housing
40. Pump shaft
41. Ball bearing
42. Retaining ring
43. Spacer
44. Oil seal
45. Retaining ring

SERIES BDU-21

Operation

The hydrostatic transmission consists of a variable volume, reversible swashplate, axial piston pump connected in a closed loop to a fixed displacement, axial piston motor. Any oil lost internally from the closed loop system is replaced by oil from the charge pump. See Fig. HT1-10. This make-up oil is drawn from the reservoir through an oil filter and is pumped through the check valve on the low pressure side of the hydrostatic loop. All excess charge oil passes through the charge pressure regulator valve and is relieved to the suction side of the charge pump.

Hydrostatic motor speed is controlled by hydrostatic pump rpm and the angle of the pump swashplate. As the angle of the pump swashplate is increased from the zero degree NEUTRAL position, the length of each pump piston stroke increases and more oil is pumped to the motor. Since the motor is a fixed displacement unit, it must turn faster in order to accept the increased flow from the pump. When the pump swashplate angle decreases, the opposite effect takes place and the motor speed decreases.

The hydrostatic pump turns in the same direction all the time. The hydrostatic motor is capable of turning in both directions. Reversing the pump swashplate angle reverses the flow of oil being pumped to the motor, causing the motor rotation to reverse. When the control lever is in NEUTRAL, there is no pump swashplate tilt and no pump piston stroke.

A free-wheeling valve is included in the system to allow oil to bypass the pump when the unit is moved without the engine running. The free-wheeling valve connects both sides of the closed loop together so there will not be a pressure build-up from the motor as it is turned by the final drive.

Some transmissions are equipped with ports that provide pressurized oil for use in the tractor hydraulic system, usually for a hydraulic lift. See Fig. HT1-10 for a circuit diagram.

Some transmissions may be equipped with Easy-Ride valves that suppress high pressure spikes when the transmission is shifted rapidly thereby preventing abrupt tractor movement.

Troubleshooting

When troubleshooting the hydrostatic drive system, always check the easiest and most obvious items first. Some problems that may occur during operation of hydrostatic transmission and their possible causes are as follows:

1. Lack of drive or limited speed in both directions.
   a. Broken or misadjusted control linkage.
   b. Slipping or broken transmission drive belt (if used).
   c. Free-wheeling valve stuck open or leaking.
   d. Low oil level.
   e. Plugged oil filter.
   f. Faulty charge pump or charge relief valve.

Fig. HT1-10–Circuit diagram of Hydro-Gear Series BDU-21 hydrostatic transmission equipped with implement circuit.

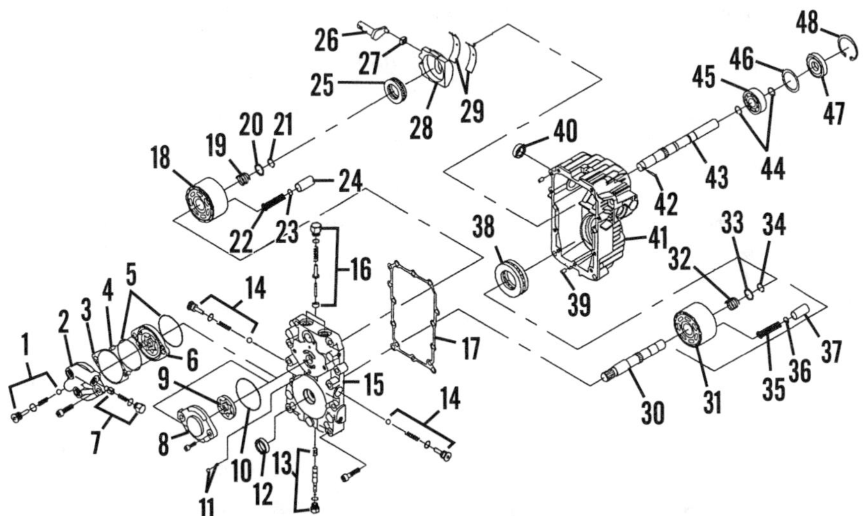

Fig. HT1-11–Exploded view of Hydro-Gear BDU-21 hydrostatic transmission. Bearings (29) are not used on later transmissions.

1. Check valve
2. Port plate
3. Gasket
4. Dowel pins
5. O-ring
6. Oil pump housing
7. Relief valve
8. Charge pump housing
9. Oil pump rotors
10. O-ring
11. Relief valve
12. Oil seal
13. Bypass valve assy,
14. Check vlaves
15. End cover
16. Easy ride valve
17. Gasket
18. Pump cylinder block
19. Spring
20. Thrust washer
21. Retaining rng
22. Spring
23. Seat
24. Piston
25. Thrust bearing
26. Trunnion arm
27. Slot guide
28. Swashplate
29. Bearings
30. Motor shaft
31. Motor cylinder block
32. Spring
33. Thrust washer
34. Retaining ring
35. Spring
36. Seat
37. Piston
38. Thrust bearing
39. Dowel pins
40. Bearing
41. Transmission housing
42. Oil pump drive pin
43. Pump shaft
44. Retaining ring
45. Ball bearing
46. Spacer
47. Oil seal
48. Retaining ring

g. Internal leakage of high pressure fluid due to excessive wear of pump and/or motor.

h. Failure of final drive.

2. Lack of drive or limited speed in one direction.

a. Movement of pump swashplate being restricted in one direction.

b. Charge check valve not seating.

Overhaul

Before disassembling the transmission, thoroughly clean the exterior of the unit. Scribe a line on the charge pump housing (8) and end cover (15) to ensure correct reassembly.

On transmissions equipped with an implement port plate (2—Fig. HT1-11), mark the port plate, charge pump housing (6) and end cover (15). Unscrew and remove the implement port plate (2), charge pump housing (6) and charge relief valve (11).

On all other transmissions, unscrew and remove the charge pump housing (8), pump rotors (9) and charge relief valve (11).

On all transmissions, remove the charge pump drive pin (42). Remove the screws securing the end cover (15) and separate the end cover from the housing (41). Remove the check valves (14), free-wheeling valve (13) and Easy Ride valves (16) as shown in Fig. HT1-11, being careful not to interchange the parts or lose the shims.

NOTE: Pump and motor pistons (24 and 37) must be identified prior to removal so they can be reinstalled in their original cylinder bore. Do not lose the ball in each piston.

Position the housing (41) on its side. Remove the pump cylinder block (18) and piston assembly. Remove the motor cylinder block (31) and piston assembly and shaft. Lay the cylinder block assemblies aside for later disassembly.

Remove the thrust bearing assembly (25) and swashplate (28). Early transmissions are equipped with removable bearings (29), while on later transmissions the swashplate is supported by a bearing surface in the housing (41).

NOTE: Early models are equipped with a four-piece thrust bearing assembly as shown in Fig. HT1-12. Later models are equipped with a three-piece bearing assembly (25).

Remove the snap ring (48—Fig. HT1-11) and extract the input shaft (43) assembly. Remove the control arm (26).

NOTE: Do not remove the needle bearings in the end cover (15) or housing (41). End cover or housing must be replaced if bearings are damaged.

Inspect components for damage and wear. Inspect the pistons and cylinder bores for scoring and scratches.

Specified motor or pump piston diameter is 0.6767-0.6770 inch (17.188-17.196 mm). Specified motor or pump cylinder bore diameter is

0.6776-0.6784 inch (17.211-17.231 mm). Pump and motor cylinder blocks are serviced as complete assemblies.

Inspect the mating surfaces of the end cover and the pump and motor cylinder blocks for scratches or excessive wear. If scratches or wear can be detected by moving your fingernail or a soft lead pencil across the mating surfaces, components should be replaced.

Check the bearing surface on the bearings (29) on early transmissions or in the housing (41) of later transmissions. If the bearing surface is excessively worn or damaged, replace the bearings (29) on early transmissions or the housing (41) on later transmissions.

Inspect the check valves for nicks and scratches. On transmissions equipped with Easy Ride valves (16), inspect the seats in the end cover (15). End cover must be replaced if the seats are damaged. Inspect the charge pump rotors and the face of the end cover for scoring and scratches.

Coat parts with transmission oil during assembly. Be sure the pistons are returned to their original bore in the cylinders. Use a rubber band to hold the pistons in their bores.

On transmissions equipped with four-piece thrust bearing (Fig. HT1-12), note that the thrust washer (52) is thinner than the thrust washer (50).

If normal pump shaft rotation is counterclockwise, install the charge pump cover so the flat edge on the cover ear is toward the control arm side of the transmission. If normal pump shaft rotation is clockwise, install the charge pump cover so the flat edge on the cover ear is opposite the control arm side of the transmission. Tighten the charge pump housing screws to 84-120 in.-lb. (9.5-13.6 N·m).

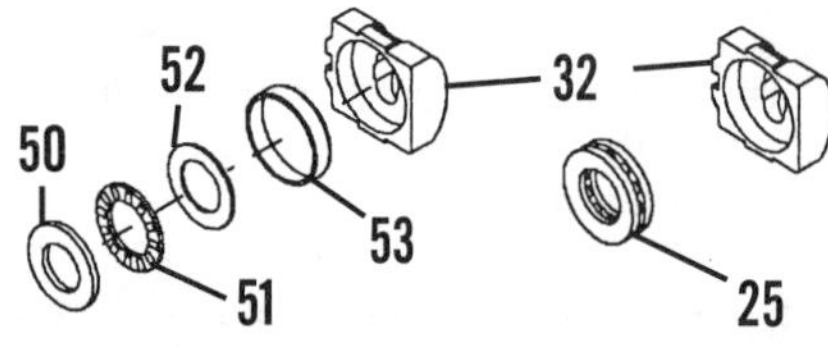

Fig. HT1-12–Early BDU-12 transmissions are equipped with a four-piece thrust bearing while later transmissions are equipped with a three-piece bearing assembly (25). Bearings and swashplates are not interchangeable.

25. 3-piece thrust bearing
32. Swashplate
50. Thrust washer (thick)
51. Thrust bearing
52. Thrust washer (thin)
53. Sleeve

SUNDSTRAND (SERIES 15 "U" TYPE)

OPERATION

The hydrostatic transmission consists of the following components: a variable volume, reversible swashplate, axial piston pump; a fixed displacement, axial piston motor; a gerotor charge pump; two check valves; a charge pressure regulator valve and an oil filter.

The system operates as a closed loop. See Fig. HT1-13. However, any oil lost internally from the closed loop circuit is replaced by oil from the charge pump. This make up oil is drawn from the reservoir (differential case) through the oil filter and is pumped into the loop through the check valve on the low pressure side at 70-120 psi (483-827 kPa). All excess charge oil passes through the charge pressure regulator valve and is dumped on the pump and motor, cooling and lubricating the units.

Motor speed is controlled by pump rpm and swashplate angle. Reversing the pump swashplate angle causes the motor direction of rotation to reverse.

During normal operation of the tractor, the operating pressure range is 750-1500 psi (5171-10342 kPa). When the control lever is in NEUTRAL, there is no pump swashplate tilt and no pump piston stroke. With no oil flowing through the pump, a dynamic braking action takes place and tractor motion is halted. Although braking is normally accomplished by use of the control lever, a foot brake is also provided.

A free-wheeling valve knob is located beneath the seat. When the valve knob is turned clockwise, both check valves are held open and oil is allowed to recirculate through the hydraulic motor while bypassing the pump. This allows manual movement of the tractor. Free-wheeling valve knob must be

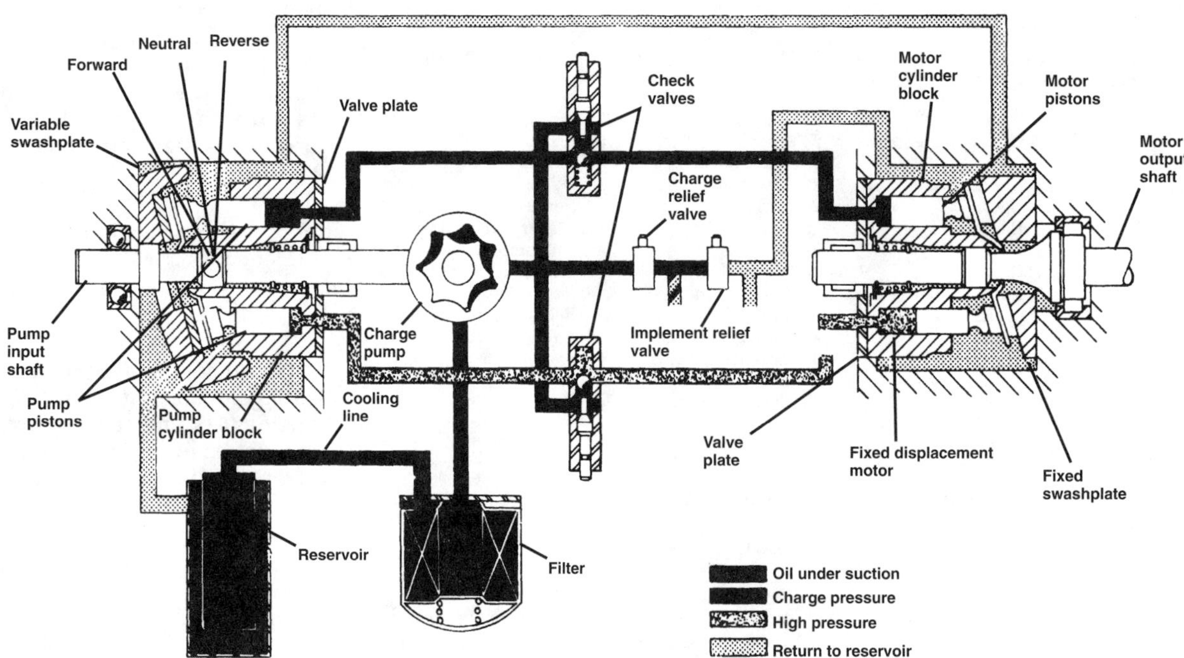

Fig. HT1-13–Circuit diagram of Sundstrand Series 15 U-type hydrostatic transmission.

turned fully counterclockwise for full power to be transmitted to the rear wheels.

OVERHAUL

To disassemble the hydrostatic unit, it is suggested that a wooden holding fixture be made from a piece of lumber 2 inches (50.8 mm) thick, 6 inches (152.4 mm) wide and 12 inches (304.8 mm) long as shown in Fig. HT1-14. Thoroughly clean the exterior of the unit, then place the unit in the holding fixture with the charge pump facing upward. Scribe a mark on the charge pump housing and center section to ensure correct reassembly.

Unbolt and remove the charge pump assembly. See Fig. HT1-15. Pry the oil seal (29—Fig. HT1-16) from the housing (28), then press the needle bearing (30) out the front of the housing. Remove the check valves (20) and relief valves (24 and 34). Unbolt and lift off the center section (33).

CAUTION: Valve plates (18 and 36) may stick to the center housing. Be careful not to drop them. Remove and identify the valve plates. Pump valve plate has two relief notches and motor valve plate has four notches. See Fig. HT1-17.

Tilt the housing (7—Fig. HT1-16) on its side. Identify and remove the cylinder block and piston assemblies from the pump and motor shafts. Lay the cylinder block assemblies aside for later assembly.

To remove the pump swashplate (12), tilt and hold the swashplate in the full forward position while driving the pins (13) out of the shafts (2 and 8). Be careful not to damage the housing when driving out the pins. When the pins are free of the shafts, withdraw the shafts and swashplate.

Withdraw the pump shaft (11) and bearing (10). Remove the cap screws securing the motor swashplate (40) to the housing, then lift out the swashplate and motor shaft (41).

Bearings (5 and 6) and oil seals (4 and 9) can now be removed from the housing. Remove the needle bearings (35) from the center section (33).

NOTE: Pump cylinder block and pistons are identical to the motor cylinder block and pistons and complete assemblies are interchangeable. However, since pistons or cylinder blocks are not serviced separately, it is advisable to keep each piston set with its original cylinder block.

Carefully remove the slipper retainer (16) with pistons (15) from the pump cylinder block (17) as shown in Fig. HT1-18. Check the cylinder block valve face and piston bores for scratches or other damage. Inspect the pistons for excessive wear or scoring. Check piston slippers for excessive wear, scratches or embedded material. Make certain the center oil passage is open in pistons.

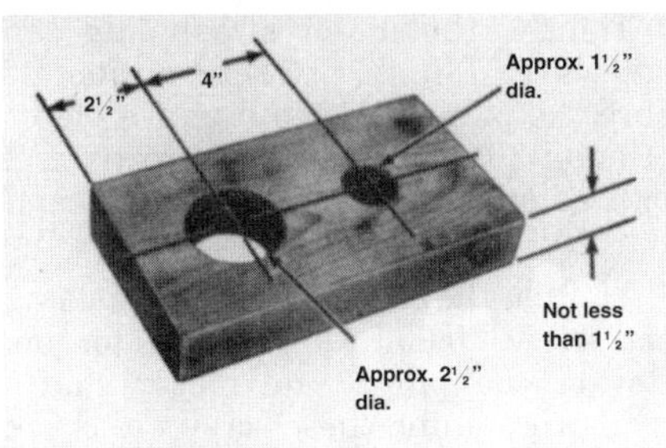

Fig. HT1-14–View showing dimensions of holding fixture used in disassembly and reassembly or Sunstrand Series 15 U-type hydrostatic transmission

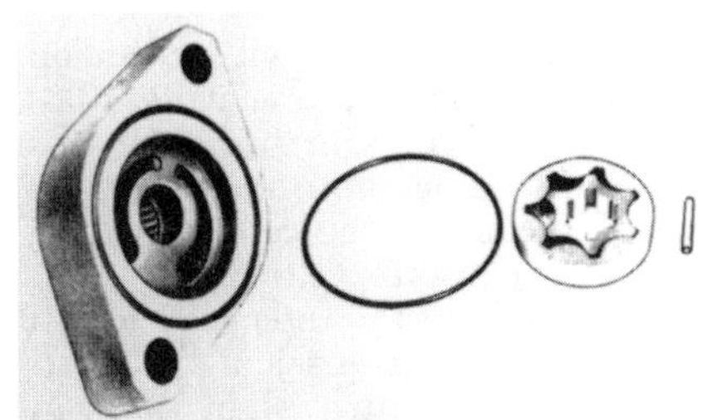

Fig. HT1-15–Exploded view of charge pump used on Sunstrand Series 15 U-type hydrostatic transmission

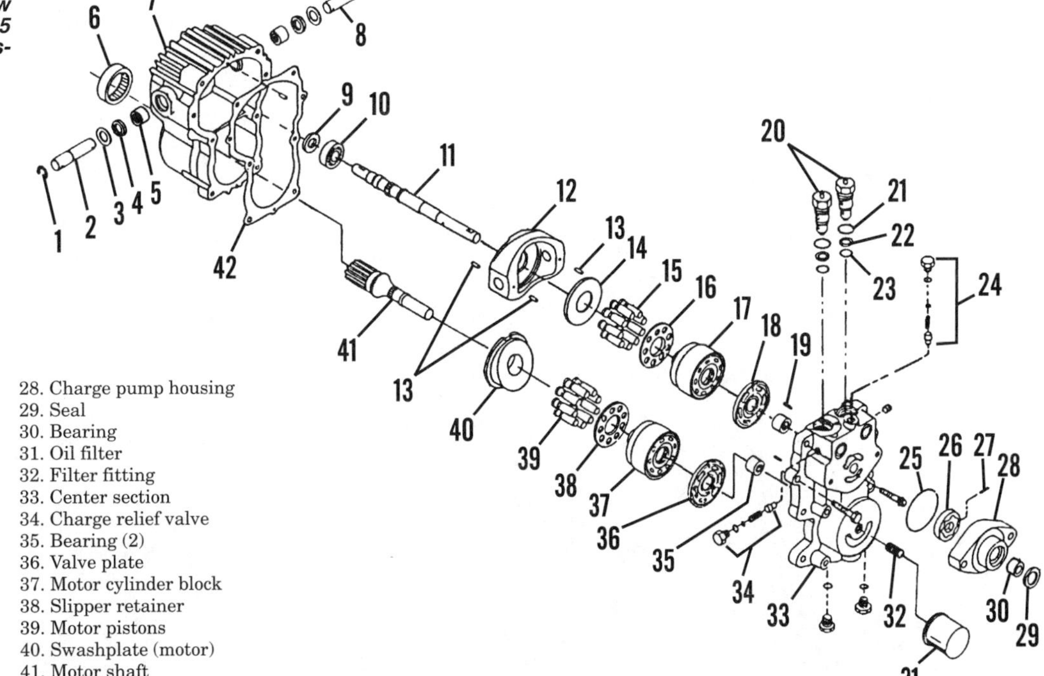

Fig. HT1-16–Exploded view of Sundstrand Series 15 U-type hydrostatic transmission.

1. Retaining ring (2)
2. Control shaft
3. Washer (2)
4. Seal (2)
5. Bearing (2)
6. Bearing
7. Transmission housing
8. Trunnion shaft
9. Oil seal
10. Bearing
11. Pump shaft
12. Swashplate (pump)
13. Spring pins
14. Thrust plate
15. Pump pistons
16. Slipper retainer
17. Pump cylinder blcck
18. Valve plate
19. Dowel pins (2)
20. Check valves
21. Backup washer
22. O-ring
23. O-ring
24. Implement lift relief valve
25. O-ring
26. Rotor assy.
27. Drive pin
28. Charge pump housing
29. Seal
30. Bearing
31. Oil filter
32. Filter fitting
33. Center section
34. Charge relief valve
35. Bearing (2)
36. Valve plate
37. Motor cylinder block
38. Slipper retainer
39. Motor pistons
40. Swashplate (motor)
41. Motor shaft
42. Gasket

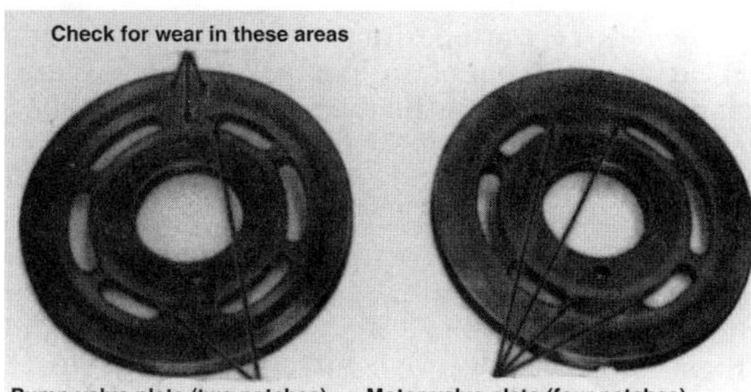

Fig. HT1-17–View of valve plates used in Sundstand Series 15 U-type hydrostatic transmissions. Note that pump valve plate has two notches and motor valve plate has four notches.

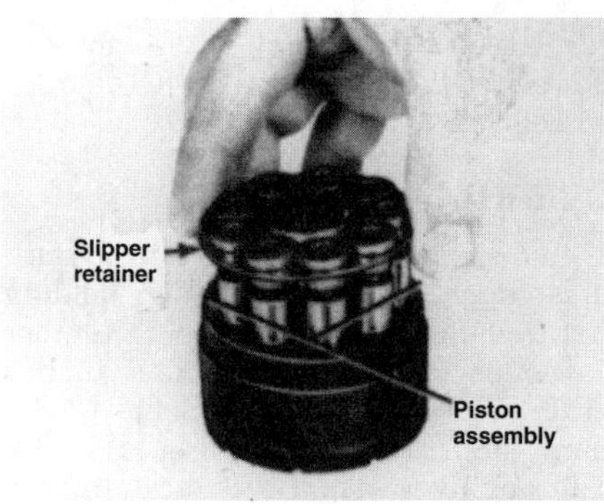

Fig. HT1-18–Withdraw slipper retainer with pistons from cylinder block. Pump and motor piston and cylinder block assemblies are identical and must be replaced as complete units.

If excessive wear or other damage is noted on the cylinder block or pistons, install a new cylinder block kit which includes the pistons, slipper retainer and new cylinder block assembly.

If original parts are serviceable, thoroughly clean the parts. Reassemble and wrap the cylinder block assembly in clean paper. Repeat the operation on the motor cylinder block assembly (37-39—Fig. HT1-16) using the same checks as used on the pump cylinder block assembly.

Check the pump valve plate (18) and motor valve plate (36) for damage and replace when necessary. Inspect the motor swashplate (40) and pump swashplate thrust plate (14) for wear, embedded material or scoring and replace when required.

Check the charge pump housing (28) and rotor assembly (26) for damage and replace when necessary. Charge pump relief valve cone should be free of nicks and scratches.

The check valves (20) are interchangeable and are serviced only as assemblies. Wash the check valves in clean solvent and air dry. Thoroughly lubricate the check valve assemblies with clean oil before installation.

Replace all O-rings, gaskets and seals and reassemble by reversing removal procedure, keeping the following points in mind:

Lubricate all parts with clean oil. When installing new bearings (35), press the bearings in until they are 0.100 inch (2.54 mm) above the machined surface of the center housing. Pump swashplate (12) must be installed with the thin stop pad toward the top of the transmission.

Be sure the control shaft (2) is installed on the correct side. Drive new pins (13) into the pump swashplate and shafts, using two pins on the control shaft (2). Pins should be driven in until they extend $\frac{1}{4}$ inch (6 mm) below the surface of the swashplate.

Tighten the motor swashplate cap screws to 67 in.-lb. (7.5 N·m) torque. Be sure the pump and motor valve plates (18 and 36) are installed correctly and located on the needle bearing (35) and pin (19).

Tighten the center section to housing cap screws to 30 ft.-lb. (41 N·m) torque. Rotate the pump and motor shafts while tightening these screws to check for proper internal assembly.

Reinstall the unit and prime with oil as previously outlined.

BRIGGS & STRATTON

Model Series	No. Cyls.	Bore	Stroke	Displacement	Power Rating
170000, 171000	1	3.00 in. (76.2 mm)	2.375 in. (60.3 mm)	16.8 cu. in. (275 cc)	7 hp (5.2 kW)
190000, 191000, 192000, 193000, 194000, 195000, 196000	1	3.00 in. (76.2 mm)	2.750 in. (69.85 mm)	19.44 cu. in. (318 cc)	8 hp (6 kW)
220000, 221000, 222000	1	3.438 in. (87.3 mm)	2.375 in. (60.3 mm)	22.04 cu. in. (361 cc)	10 hp (7.5 kW)
250000, 251000, 252000, 253000, 254000, 255000, 256000, 257000, 258000, 259000	1	3.438 in. (87.3 mm)	2.625 in. (66.68 mm)	24.36 cu. in. (399 cc)	11 hp (8.2 kW)
280000, 281000, 282000, 283000, 284000	1	3.438 in. (87.3 mm)	3.06 in. (77.7 mm)	28.4 cu. in. (465 cc)	12 hp (9 kW)
285000, 286000, 289000	1	3.438 in. (87.3 mm)	3.06 in. (77.7 mm)	28.4 cu. in. (465 cc)	12.5 hp (9.4 kW)

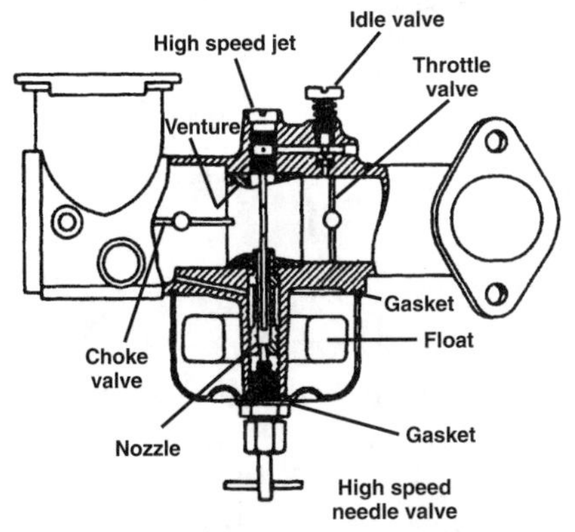

Fig. B501—Cross-sectional view of Flo-Jet I carburetor.

Engines in this section are four-stroke, single-cylinder engines with either a horizontal or vertical crankshaft. The crankshaft may be supported by main bearings that are an integral part of crankcase and crankcase cover/oil pan or by ball bearings pressed on the crankshaft. All engines are constructed of aluminum. Cylinder bore may be either aluminum or a cast iron sleeve that is cast in the aluminum.

A float carburetor is used on all models. A fuel pump is available as optional equipment for some models.

Refer to the BRIGGS & STRATTON ENGINE IDENTIFICATION INFORMATION section for engine identification. Engine model number as well as type number and serial number are necessary when ordering parts.

MAINTENANCE

LUBRICATION

Horizontal crankshaft engines have a splash lubrication system provided by an oil dipper attached to the connecting rod.

Vertical crankshaft engines are lubricated by an oil slinger wheel on the governor gear driven by the camshaft gear.

Engine oil should be changed after first eight hours of operation and after every 50 hours of operation or at least once each operating season. If equipment undergoes severe usage, change oil weekly or after every 25 hours of operation.

Use SAE 30 oil for temperatures above 40°F (4°C); use SAE 10W-30 oil for temperatures between 0°F (-18°C) and 100°F (38°C); below 0°F (-18°C) use petroleum based SAE 5W-20 or a suitable synthetic oil.

Crankcase oil capacity for 16.8 and 19.44 cubic-inch engines is 2.25 pints (1.1 L) for vertical crankshaft models and 2.75 pints (1.3 L) for horizontal crankshaft models.

Crankcase oil capacity for 22.04, 24.36 and 28.4 cubic-inch engines is 3 pints (1.4 L) for vertical crankshaft models and 2.5 pints (1.2 L) for horizontal crankshaft models.

SPARK PLUG

The recommended spark plug is J19LM Champion. The specified spark plug electrode gap is 0.030 inch (0.76 mm).

CAUTION: Briggs & Stratton does not recommend using abrasive blasting to clean the spark plug as this may introduce some abrasive material into the engine that could cause extensive damage.

CARBURETOR

Engines in this section may be equipped with one of three different Flo-Jet carburetors as well as a Walbro carburetor. The Flo-Jet carburetors are identified as either Flo-Jet I (Fig. B501), Flo-Jet II (Fig. B502) or Cross-Over Flo-Jet (Fig. B503). Refer to the appropriate service section for model being serviced.

Flo-Jet I Carburetor

Initial setting of idle mixture screw is one turn out and high speed needle valve is 1½ turns out. With the engine at normal operating temperature and equipment control lever in the SLOW position, adjust the idle speed screw so the engine idles at 1750 rpm. With the engine running at idle speed, turn the idle mixture screw clockwise until engine speed just starts to drop. Note the screw position. Turn the idle mixture screw counterclockwise until engine speed just starts to drop again. Note the screw position, then turn the screw to the midpoint between the noted screw positions.

Adjust the high-speed needle valve with speed control set to FAST using the same procedure. If the engine will not accelerate cleanly, slightly enrich the mixture by turning the high-speed needle valve counterclockwise. If necessary, readjust the idle speed screw.

To check the float level, remove the float bowl and invert the carburetor body. Refer to Fig. B504 for the proper float level dimensions. Adjust by bending the float lever tang that contacts the inlet valve.

Flo-Jet II Carburetor

Initial setting of the idle mixture screw is 1¼ turns out and high speed needle valve is 1½ turns out. With the engine at normal operating temperature and the equipment control lever in the SLOW position, adjust the idle speed screw so the engine idles at 1750 rpm. With the engine running at idle speed, turn the idle mixture screw clockwise until the engine speed just starts to drop. Note the screw position. Turn the idle mixture screw counterclockwise until the engine speed just starts to drop again. Note the screw position, then turn the screw to the midpoint between the noted screw positions.

Adjust the high-speed needle valve with the speed control set to FAST using the same procedure. If the engine will not accelerate cleanly, slightly enrich the mixture by turning the high-speed needle valve counterclockwise. If necessary, readjust the idle speed screw.

To check the float level, remove the float bowl and invert the carburetor body. The float should be parallel to the carburetor body as shown in Fig. B503. Adjust the float level by bending the float lever tang that contacts the inlet valve. Check the carburetor upper body

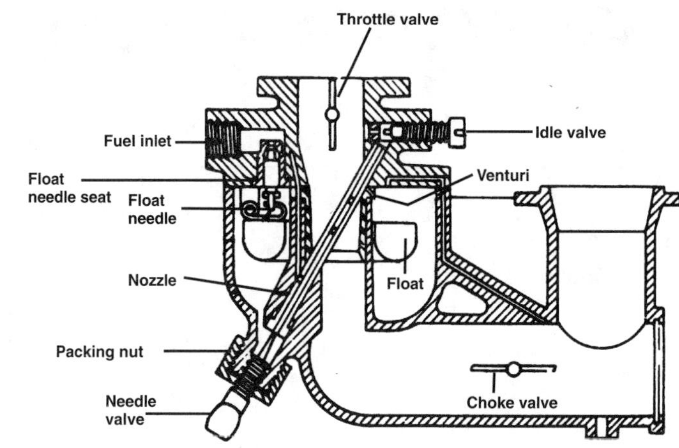

Fig. B502—Cross-sectional view of Flo-Jet II carburetor. Before separating upper and lower body section, loosen packing nut and power needle valve as a unit and use special screwdriver (tool 19062) to remove nozzle.

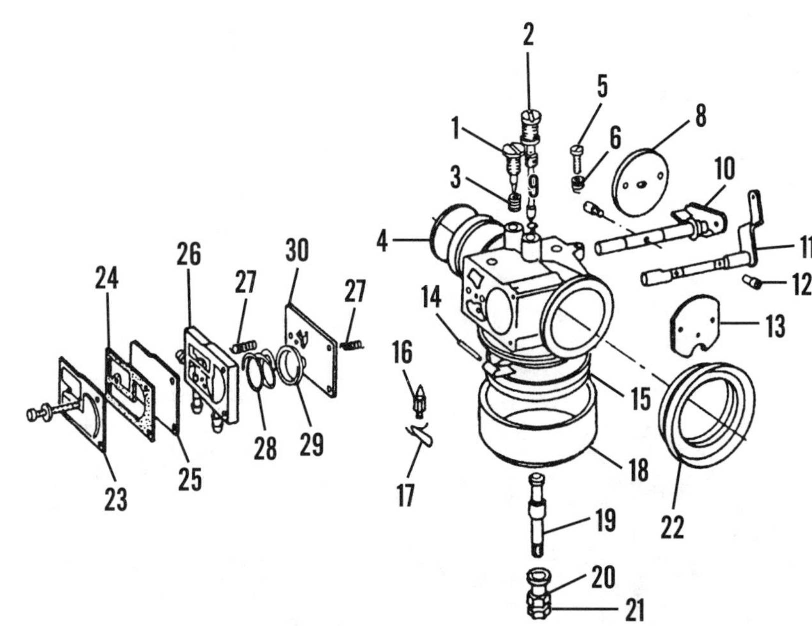

Fig. B503—Exploded view of Cross-Over Flo-Jet carburetor used on some models.

1. Idle mixture screw
2. High speed mixture screw
3. Spring
4. O-ring
5. Idle speed screw
6. Spring
7. Packing
8. Throttle plate
9. Screw
10. Throttle shaft
11. Choke shaft
12. Screw
13. Choke plate
14. Pin
15. Float
16. Fuel inlet valve
17. Clip
18. Fuel bowl
19. Nozzle
20. Washer
21. Screw
22. Gasket
23. Fuel pump cover
24. Gasket
25. Diaphragm
26. Fuel pump body
27. Spring
28. Spring
29. Spring cup
30. Diaphragm

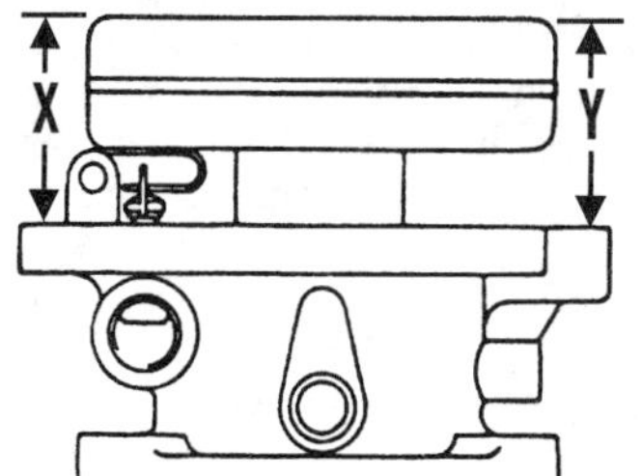

Fig. B504—Dimension (Y) must be the same as dimension (X) plus or minus 1/32 inch (0.8 mm).

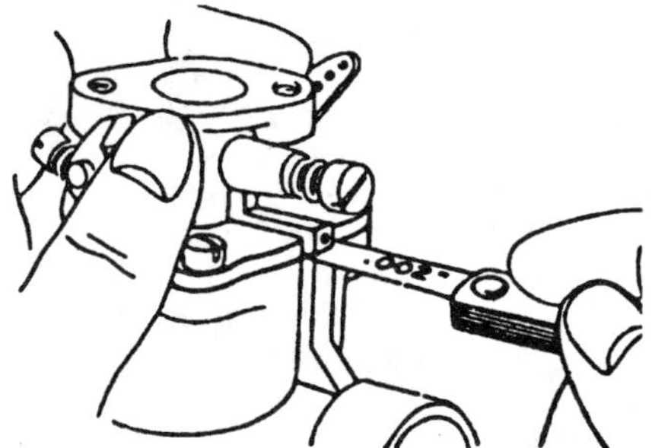

Fig. B505—Check upper body of Flo-Jet II carburetor for warpage as outlined in text.

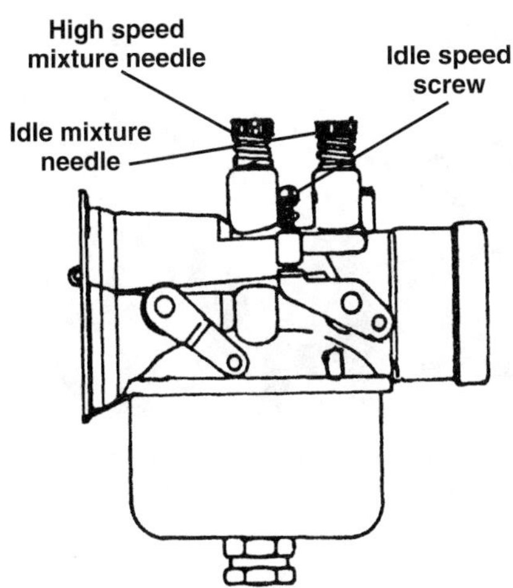

Fig. B506—View of adjustment screws on Cross-Over Flo-Jet carburetor.

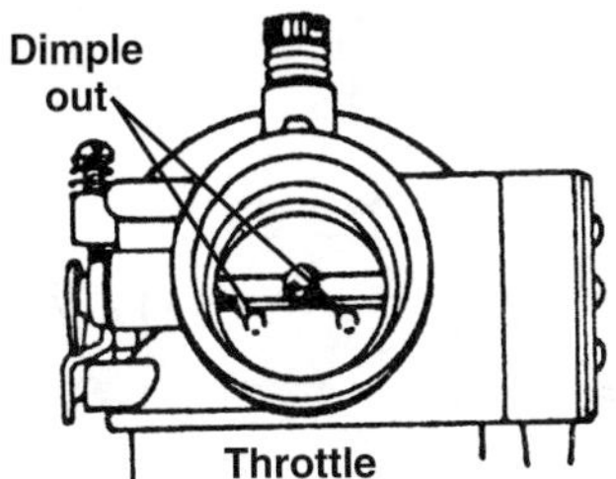

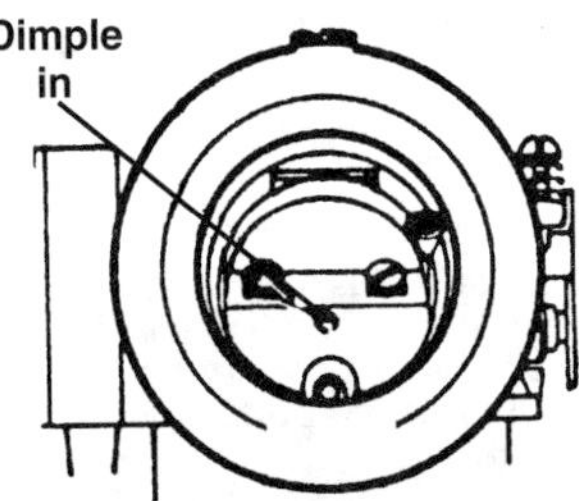

Fig. B507—Install throttle and choke plates on Cross-Over Flo-Jet carburetor so dimples are located as shown above when plates are closed.

for distortion using a 0.002 inch (0.05 mm) feeler gauge as shown in Fig. B505. The upper body must be renewed if warped more than 0.002 inch (0.05 mm).

Cross-Over Flo-Jet Carburetor

The Cross-Over Flo-Jet shown in Fig. B503 is equipped with an integral diaphragm type fuel pump.

Initial setting of idle mixture screw (Fig. B506) is one turn out and high-speed mixture screw is 1½ turns out. With the engine at normal operating temperature and the equipment control lever in the SLOW position, adjust the idle speed screw so the engine idles at 1750 rpm. With the engine running at idle speed, turn the idle mixture screw clockwise until the engine speed just starts to drop. Note the screw position. Turn the idle mixture screw counterclockwise until the engine speed just starts to drop again. Note the screw position, then turn the screw to the midpoint between the noted screw positions.

If equipped with a high-speed mixture screw, set the speed control to FAST and adjust the high-speed screw using the same procedure. If the engine will not accelerate cleanly, slightly enrich the mixture by turning the idle mixture screw counterclockwise. If necessary, readjust the idle speed screw.

Disassembly of the carburetor is evident after inspection of carburetor and referral to exploded view in Fig. B505. Clean and inspect components and discard any parts that are damaged or excessively worn.

When reassembling the carburetor, note the following: Install the choke and throttle plates so the indentations are located as shown in Fig. B507 when the choke or throttle plate is in the closed position. The fuel inlet valve seat is replaceable. Use a suitable screw-type puller to remove the seat. Install the inlet seat so it is flush with the carburetor body surface.

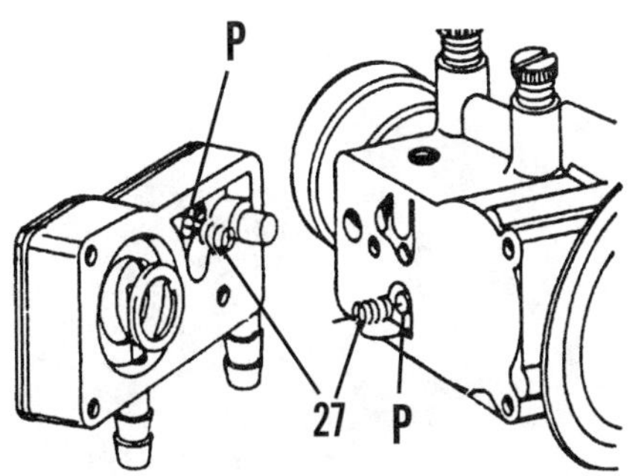

Fig. B508—When assembling fuel pump on Cross-Over Flo-Jet carburetor, install springs (27) on pegs (P) on pump body and carburetor body.

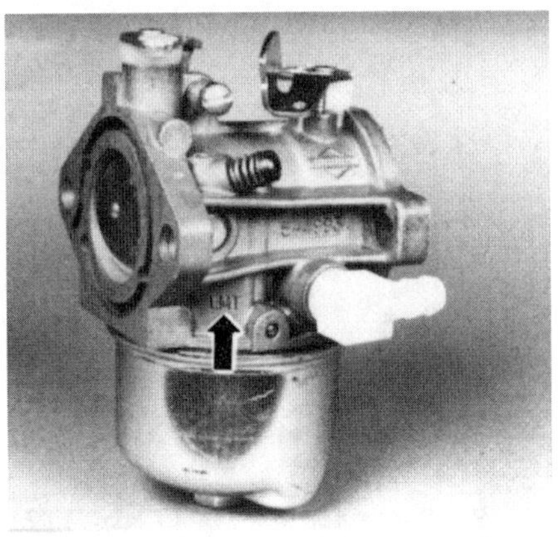

Fig. B509—Walbro LMT carburetor may be identified by "LMT" cast in side of body.

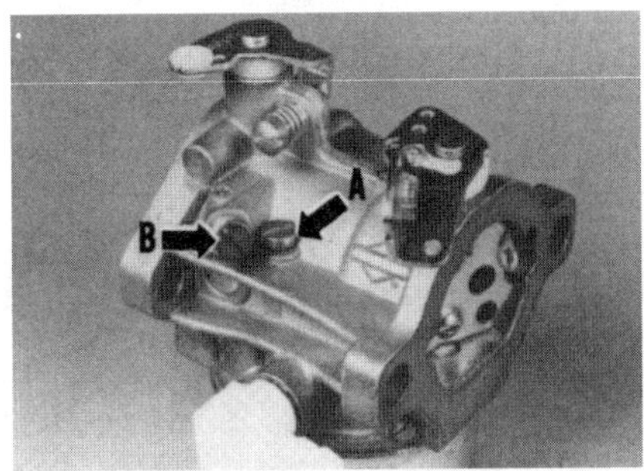

Fig. B510—View showing location of idle jet (A) and idle mixture screw (B).

To check the float level, invert the carburetor body and float assembly. The float should be parallel to carburetor body as shown in Fig. B503. Adjust the float level by bending the float lever tang that contacts the inlet valve.

When assembling the fuel pump, install the springs (27—Fig. B508) on the pegs (P) on the pump body and carburetor body.

Walbro Carburetor

The Walbro LMT carburetor can be identified by the letters LMT embossed on the side of the carburetor (Fig. B509). The Walbro carburetor is equipped with an adjustable idle mixture screw (B—Fig. B510) and a fixed main jet.

Initial setting of the idle mixture screw is 1½ turns out. With the engine at normal operating temperature and the equipment control lever in the SLOW position, adjust the idle speed screw so the engine idles at 1750 rpm. With the engine running at idle speed, turn the idle mixture screw clockwise until the engine speed just starts to drop. Note the screw position. Turn the idle mixture screw counterclockwise until the engine speed just starts to drop again. Note the screw position, then turn the screw to the midpoint between the noted screw positions. If the engine will not accelerate cleanly, slightly enrich the mixture by turning the idle mixture screw counterclockwise. If necessary, readjust the idle speed screw.

Optional main jets are available to accommodate various applications, such as high altitude operation.

To disassemble the carburetor for cleaning and inspection, unscrew the idle mixture screw (B—Fig. B510) and idle fuel jet (A). Unscrew the fuel bowl retaining screw and remove the fuel bowl and gasket. Remove the float pin, float and fuel inlet valve. Extract the

Fig. B511—Fuel inlet seat is recessed in body.

Fig. B512—Nozzle unscrews from center of body.

fuel inlet valve seat (Fig. B511) using a suitable tool. Unscrew the nozzle (Fig. B512).

If equipped with a metal choke, unscrew the choke plate retaining screws and remove the choke plate and choke shaft. If equipped with a plastic choke, insert a sharp tool between the choke shaft and choke plate and pull out the choke plate, then remove the choke shaft.

Unscrew the throttle plate retaining screws and remove the throttle plate and throttle shaft. To remove the Welch plug (Fig. B513), pierce the plug with a thin-blade screwdriver, then pry out the plug.

CAUTION: Insert a screwdriver into the plug only far enough to pierce the plug, otherwise, the underlying metal may be damaged.

NOTE: Two air bleed holes in carburetor bore (Fig. B514) are fitted with calibrated metal orifices. Do not attempt to remove the orifices or clean with wire. Clean the orifices only with compressed air.

Clean the carburetor in suitable carburetor cleaner. Some carburetor parts

Fig. B513—Remove and install Welch plug as described in text.

Fig. B514—Do not attempt to remove or clean with wire the orifices shown.

may be made of plastic and should not be soaked in carburetor cleaner.

Inspect the carburetor and components. The body must be replaced if there is excessive throttle or choke shaft play as bushings are not available.

Assemble the carburetor by reversing the disassembly procedure while noting the following: Install the Welch plug while being careful not to indent the plug; the plug should be flat after installation. Apply a nonhardening sealant around the plug. Use a $\frac{3}{16}$-inch rod to install the fuel inlet valve seat. The groove on the seat must be down, toward the carburetor bore. Push in the seat until it bottoms.

If equipped with a choke return spring, install the spring so spring tension tries to open the choke. Install the choke plate so the edge with a single notch is on the fuel inlet side of the carburetor (Fig. B515). The plate should be centered on the choke shaft. Install the throttle plate so the numbers are visible and toward the idle mixture screw when the throttle is closed.

The float level is not adjustable. If the float is not approximately parallel with body when carburetor is inverted, then float, fuel valve and/or valve seat

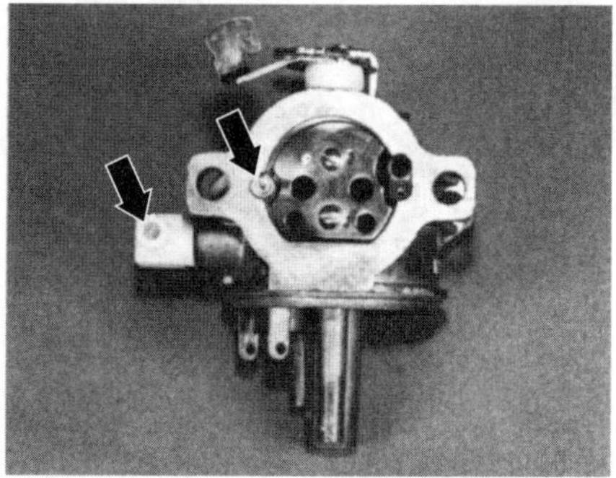

Fig. B515—Install choke plate so edge with a single notch is on fuel inlet side of carburetor.

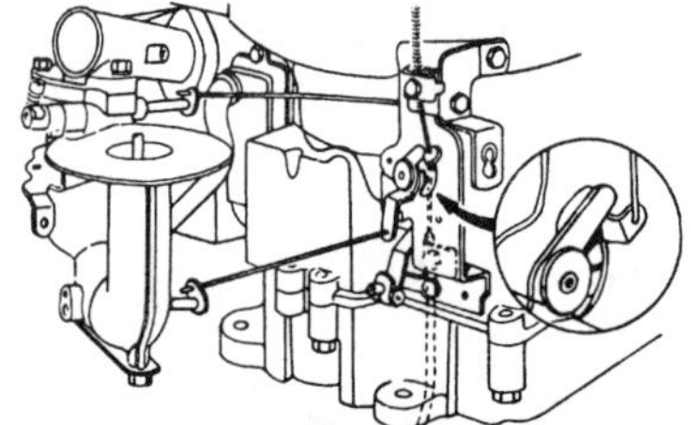

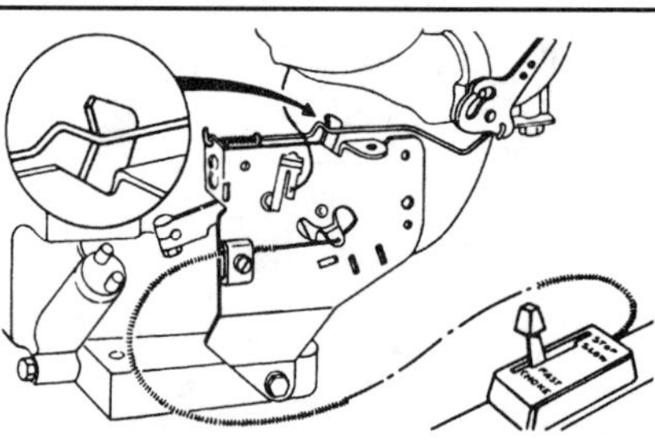

Fig. B516—On Choke-A-Matic controls shown, choke actuating lever (A) should just contact choke link or shaft (B) when control is at "FAST" position. If not, loosen screw (C) and move control wire housing (D) as required.

must be replaced. Tighten fuel bowl retaining screw to 40 in.-lb. (4.5 N·m).

CHOKE-A-MATIC CARBURETOR CONTROLS

Engines may be equipped with a control unit that operates the carburetor choke, throttle and magneto grounding switch from a single lever (Choke-A-Matic carburetors).

To check the operation of Choke-A-Matic controls, move the control lever to the CHOKE position; the carburetor choke slide or plate must be completely closed. Move the control lever to the STOP position; magneto grounding switch should be making contact. With the control in the RUN, FAST or SLOW position, the carburetor choke should be completely open. On units with remote controls, synchronize the movement of the remote lever to the carburetor control lever by loosening

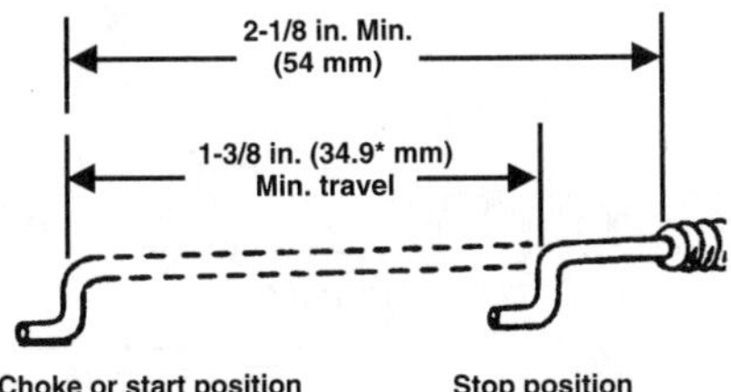

Fig. B517—For proper operation of Choke-A-Matic controls, remote control wire must extend to dimension shown and have a minimum travel of 1 3/8 inches (34.9 mm).

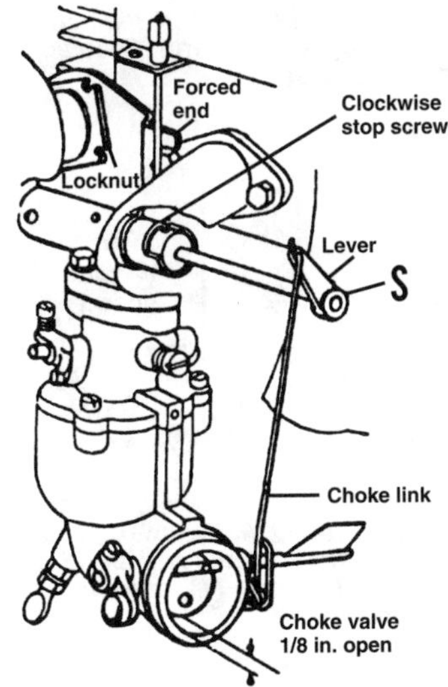

Fig. B518—Automatic choke used on some models equipped with Flo-Jet II carburetor showing unit in "HOT" position.

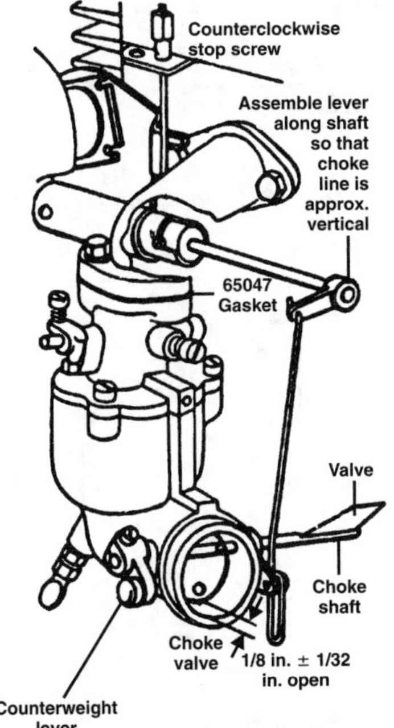

Fig. B519—Turn thermostat shaft counterclockwise until stop screw contacts thermostat stop as shown.

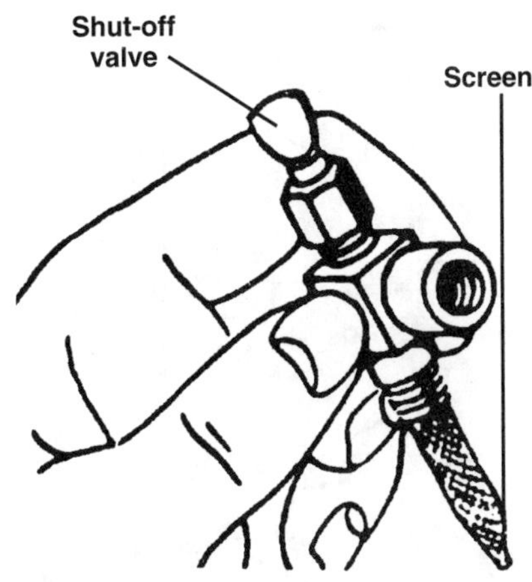

Fig. B520—Fuel tank outlet used on some B&S models.

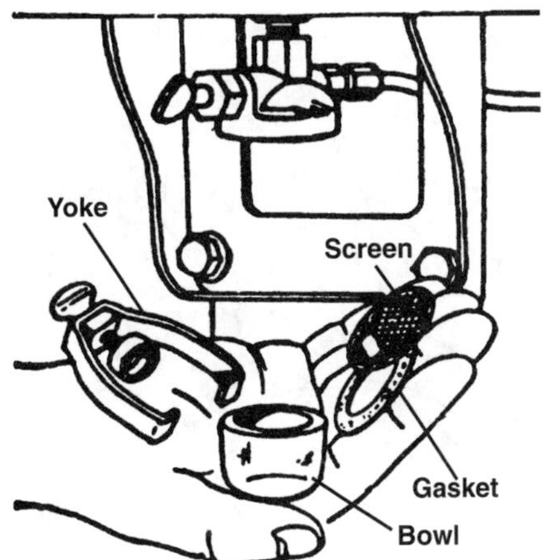

Fig. B521—Fuel sediment bowl and tank outlet used on some models.

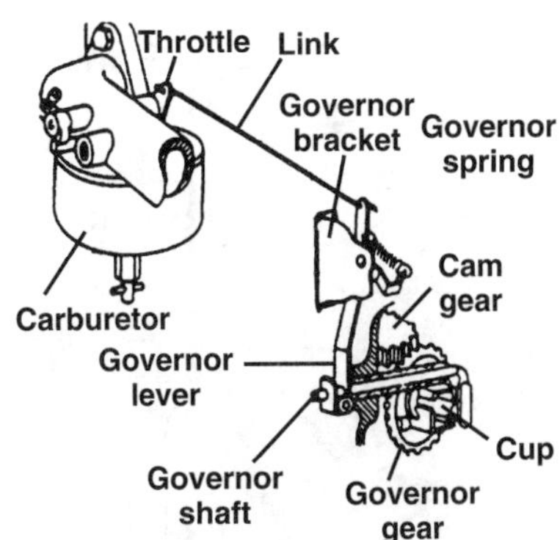

Fig. B522—View of typical governor assembly used on engines with vertical crankshaft.

the screw (C—Fig. B516) and moving the control wire housing (D) as required. Tighten the screw to clamp the housing securely. Refer to Fig. B517 to check the remote control wire movement.

AUTOMATIC CHOKE (THERMOSTAT TYPE)

A thermostat operated choke is used on some models equipped with Flo-Jet II carburetor. To adjust the choke linkage, hold the choke shaft so the thermostat lever is free. At room temperature, the stop screw in the thermostat collar should be located midway between the thermostat stops. If not, loosen the stop screw, adjust the collar and tighten the stop screw.

Loosen the set screw (S—Fig. B518) located on the thermostat lever. Slide the lever on the shaft to ensure free movement of the choke unit. Turn the thermostat shaft clockwise until the stop screw contacts the thermostat stop. While holding the shaft in this position, move the shaft lever until the choke is open exactly 1/8 inch (3 mm) and tighten the lever set screw.

Turn the thermostat shaft counterclockwise until the stop screw contacts the thermostat stop as shown in Fig. B519. Manually open the choke valve until it stops against the top of the choke link opening. At this time the choke should be open at least 3/32 inch (2.4 mm), but not more than 5/32 inch (4 mm). Hold the choke valve in wide-open position and check the position of the counterweight lever. The lever should be in a horizontal position with the free end towards the right.

FUEL TANK OUTLET

Some models are equipped with a fuel tank outlet as shown in Fig. B520. Other models may be equipped with a fuel sediment bowl that is part of the fuel tank outlet shown in Fig. B521.

Clean any debris or dirt from the tank outlet screens with a brush. Varnish or other gasoline deposits can be removed using a suitable solvent. Tighten the packing nut or remove the nut and shutoff valve, then replace the packing if leakage occurs around the shutoff valve stem.

GOVERNOR

All engines are equipped with a gear-driven mechanical governor attached to the crankcase cover or oil pan. The governor is driven by the camshaft gear. Governor and linkage must operate properly to prevent "hunting" or unsteady operation. The carburetor must be properly adjusted before performing governor adjustments.

To adjust the governor linkage, loosen the clamp bolt on the governor lever shown in Fig. B522 or B523. Move the link end of the governor lever so the carburetor throttle plate is in the wide-open position. Using a screw-

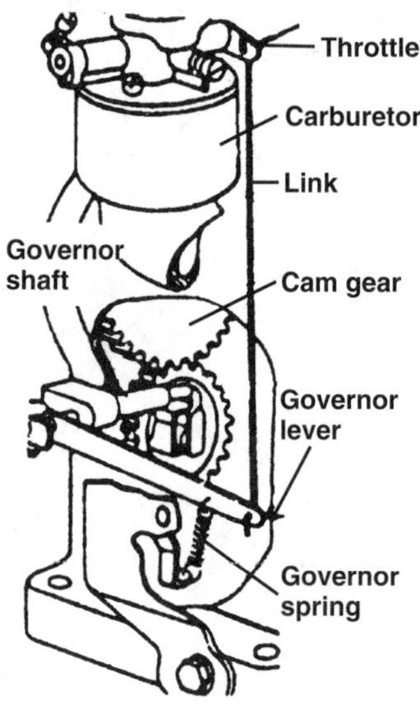

Fig. B523—View of typical governor assembly used on engines with horizontal crankshaft.

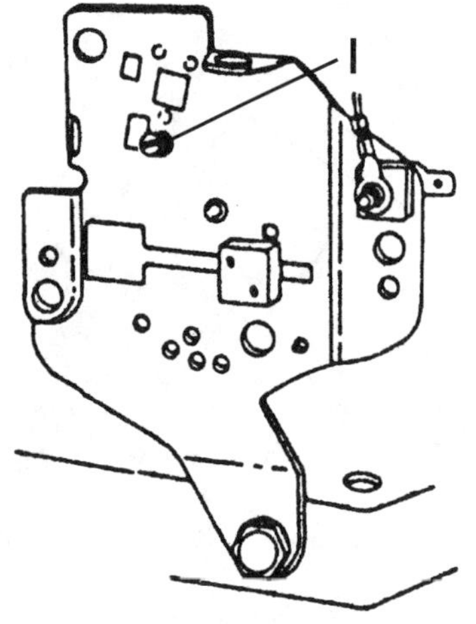

Fig. B524—On engines equipped with a governed idle adjustment screw (I), refer to text for adjustment procedure.

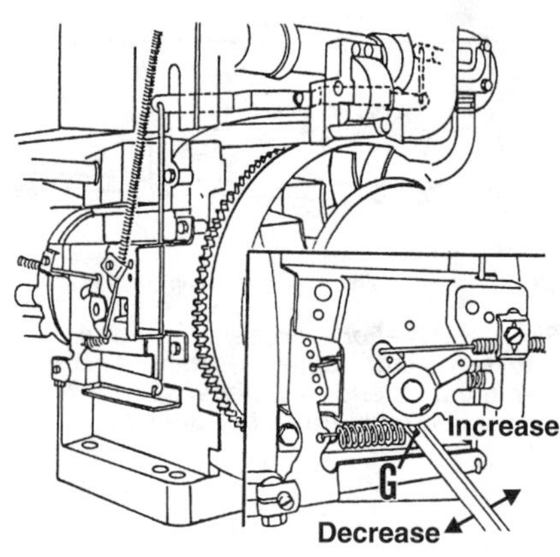

Fig. B526—On Models 253400 and 255400, bend spring anchor tang (G) to adjust governed idle speed.

driver, rotate the governor lever shaft clockwise as far as possible and tighten the clamp bolt.

On models equipped with a governed idle screw (I—Fig. B524), set the remote control to the idle position, then adjust the idle speed screw on the carburetor so the engine idles at 1550 rpm. Position the remote control so the engine idles at 1750 rpm, then rotate the governed idle screw (I) so the screw just contacts the remote control lever.

On models equipped with a governed idle stop (P—Fig. B525), set the remote control to the idle position, then adjust the idle speed screw on the carburetor so the engine idles at 1550 rpm. Loosen the governed idle stop screw (W). Position the remote control so the engine idles at 1750 rpm, then position the stop (P) so it contacts the remote control lever and tighten the screw (W).

On Models 253400 and 255400, set the remote control to idle position, then adjust the idle speed screw on the carburetor so the engine idles at 1550 rpm. Bend the tang (G—Fig. B526) so the engine idles at 1750 rpm.

IMPORTANT: Running an engine at a maximum speed other than the speed specified by the equipment manufacturer can be dangerous to the operator, harmful to the equipment and inefficient. Adjust the governed engine speed to the specification stipulated by equipment manufacturer.

To set maximum no-load speed on all models except 253400 and 255400,

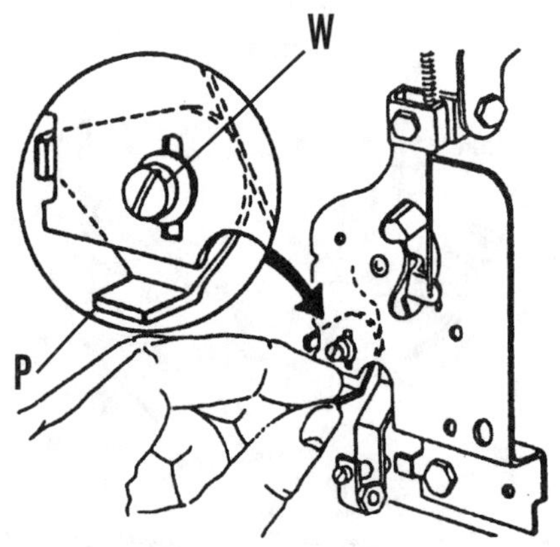

Fig. B525—On models equipped with a governed idle stop (P), refer to GOVERNOR section to adjust governed idle speed.

move the remote speed control to the maximum speed position. With the engine running, bend the governor spring anchor tang (T—Fig. B527) to obtain the desired maximum no-load speed.

To set the maximum no-load speed on Models 253400 and 255400, move the remote speed control to the maximum speed position. With the engine running, turn the screw (S—Fig. B528) to obtain the desired maximum no-load speed.

Some models are equipped with a top speed screw (T—Fig. B529) that determines maximum no-load speed according to which hole the screw occupies. There may be one, two, three or four numbered holes. If a screw is installed in a numbered hole, the maximum speed will be reduced. Installing the top speed screw (T) in a higher numbered hole will reduce top engine speed the most. For instance, installing the screw in hole "2" will reduce engine speed to

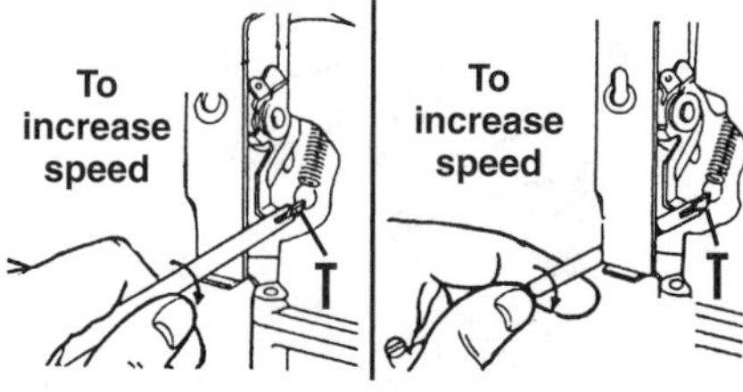

Fig. B527—Insert a suitable tool between cover and engine (left view) or through hole in cover (right view) and bend governor spring anchor tang (T) to adjust maximum governed speed.

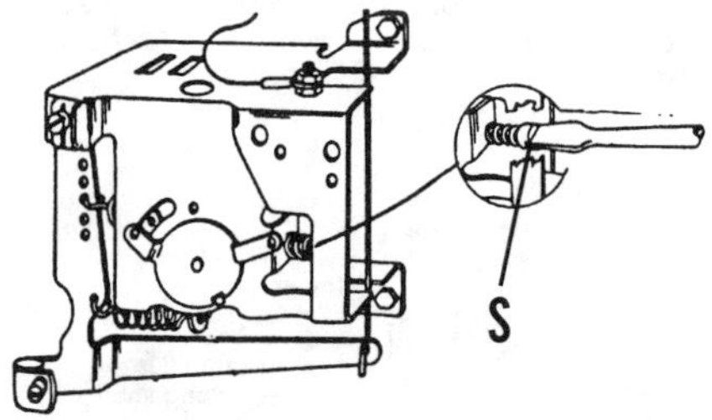

Fig. B528—On Models 253400 and 255400, rotate screw (S) to adjust maximum governor speed.

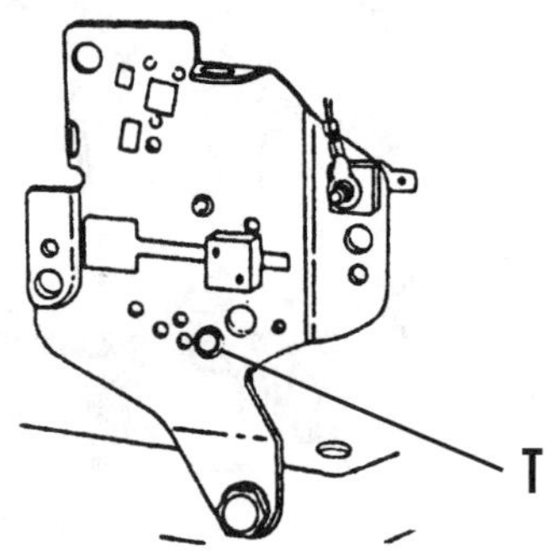

Fig. B529—Some engines may be equipped with a maximum governed speed limit screw (T). Location of screw in one of the numbered holes determines maximum governed speed. See text.

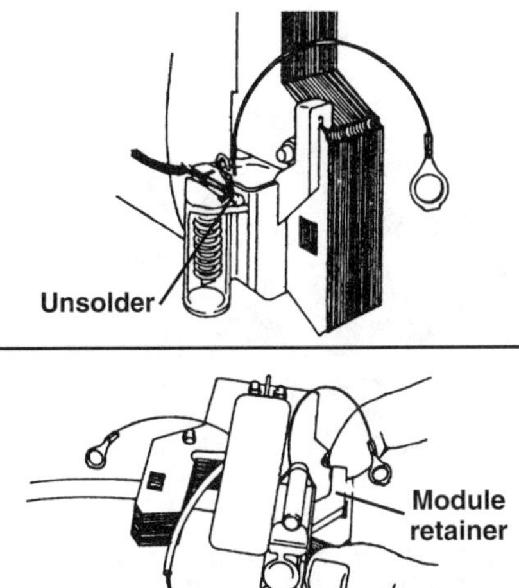

Fig. B530—Wires must be unsoldered to remove Magnetron module.

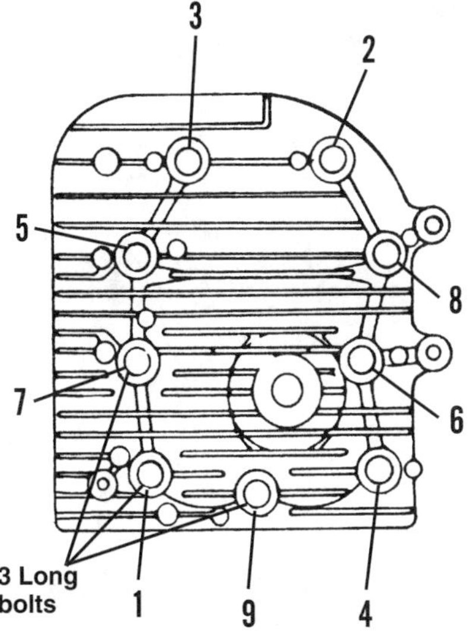

Fig. B531—Tighten cylinder head screws in sequence shown. Note location of three long screws.

3300 rpm while installing the screw in hole "4" will reduce engine speed to 2400 rpm. An accurate tachometer should be used to determine engine speed for specific holes.

IGNITION SYSTEM

The Magnetron ignition is a self-contained breakerless ignition system. Flywheel removal is not necessary except to check or service the keyways or crankshaft key.

To check for a spark, remove the spark plug. Connect the spark plug cable to B&S tester 19051 and ground the remaining tester lead on the engine cylinder head. Crank the engine at 350 rpm or more. If a spark jumps the 0.166 inch (4.2 mm) tester gap, the system is functioning properly.

The armature and module have been manufactured as either one-piece units or a two-piece assembly. Two-piece units are identified by the large rivet heads on one side of the armature laminations.

To remove the armature and Magnetron module, remove the flywheel shroud and armature retaining screws.

On one-piece units, disconnect the stop switch wire at the spade connector.

On two-piece units, use a 3/16 inch (4.8 mm) diameter pin punch to release the stop switch wire from the module. To remove the module on two-piece units, unsolder the wires, push the module retainer away from the laminations and remove the module. See Fig. B530.

When installing the two-piece unit, solder the module wires and use Permatex or equivalent to hold the ground wires in position.

Armature air gap should be 0.010-0.014 inch (0.25-0.36 mm) for two-leg armature or 0.012-0.016 inch (0.30-0.41 mm) for three-leg armature. Ignition timing is not adjustable on these models.

VALVE ADJUSTMENT

To correctly set the tappet clearance, remove the spark plug and rotate the crankshaft in normal direction (clockwise at flywheel) so the piston is at top dead center on the compression stroke. Continue to rotate the crankshaft so the piston is 1/4 inch (6.4 mm) down from top dead center. This position places the tappets away from the compression release devices on the cam lobes. Remove the tappet cover/breather assembly and use a feeler gauge to measure the clearance between the valve stem end and tappet.

Exhaust valve tappet clearance (cold) for all models is 0.009-0.011 inch (0.23-0.28 mm).

Intake valve tappet clearance (cold) on Series 253400 and 255400 engines with electric start should be 0.009-0.011 inch (0.23-0.28 mm). If a Series 253400 or 255400 engine is equipped with a manual starter and an electric starter, intake valve tappet clearance should be 0.005-0.007 inch (0.13-0.18 mm).

Intake valve tappet clearance (cold) on Series 286700 engines should be 0.004-0.006 inch (0.10-0.15 mm).

Intake valve tappet clearance (cold) for all models except Series 253400, 255400 and 286700 engines is 0.005-0.007 inch (0.13-0.18 mm).

Valve tappet clearance is adjusted on all models by carefully grinding the end of the valve stem to increase clearance or by grinding the valve seats deeper and/or renewing the valve or lifter to decrease clearance.

CRANKCASE BREATHER

A crankcase breather is built into the engine valve cover. A partial vacuum must exist in the crankcase to prevent oil seepage past the oil seals, gaskets, breaker point plunger or piston rings. Air can flow out of crankcase through the breather, but a one-way valve blocks return flow, maintaining the necessary vacuum. The breather mounting holes are offset one way. A vent tube connects the breather to the carburetor air horn for extra protection against dusty conditions.

CYLINDER HEAD

After 100 to 300 hours of engine operation, remove the cylinder head and remove any carbon or deposits.

REPAIRS

CYLINDER HEAD

When removing the cylinder head, note the location and lengths of the cylinder head retaining screws so they can be installed in their original positions.

Clean all deposits from the cylinder head, being careful not to damage the gasket sealing surface.

Always install a new cylinder head gasket. Do not apply sealer to the head gasket. Be sure the air baffle is in place on the cylinder head before tightening the cylinder head fasteners. Lubricate the cylinder head retaining screws with graphite grease and tighten the screws evenly in the sequence shown in Fig. B531 to 165 in.-lb. (19 N·m).

VALVE SYSTEM

To remove the engine valves, remove the cylinder head and tappet chamber/breather cover. Note that either a two-piece split collar or a one-piece slotted retainer retains the valves. Compress the valve springs and remove the valve spring retainers (Fig. B532). Remove the valves from the cylinder block.

Valve face and seat angle should be ground at 45°. replace the valve if margin is 1/64 inch (0.4 mm) or less. Seat width should be 3/64 to 1/16 inch (1.2-1.6 mm). All models are equipped with replaceable valve seat inserts.

Valve guides are replaceable. Use B&S tool 19204 to press in the new guide so the guide is flush with the top of the guide bore. Valve guide 230655 does not require reaming, however, other valve guides must be finish

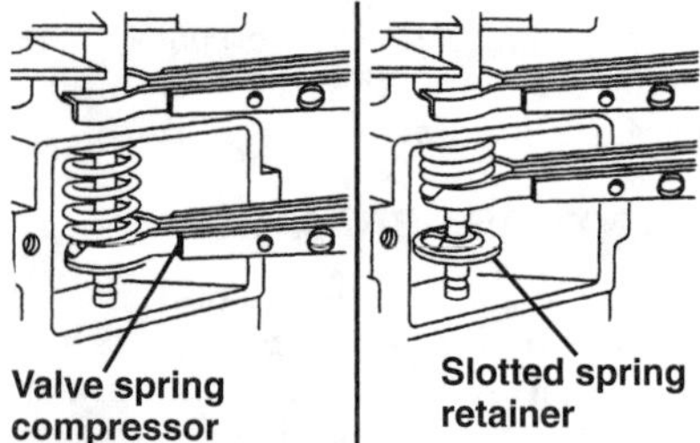

Fig. B532—To remove the engine valves, compress the valve spring with a suitable tool and remove the spring retainer.

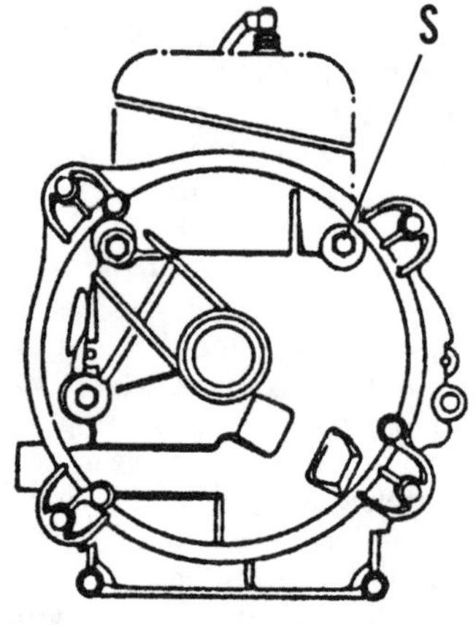

Fig. B533—On horizontal crankshaft engines without right-angle drive, apply nonhardening sealant to crankcase cover retaining screw (S).

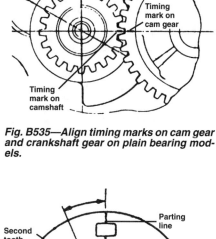

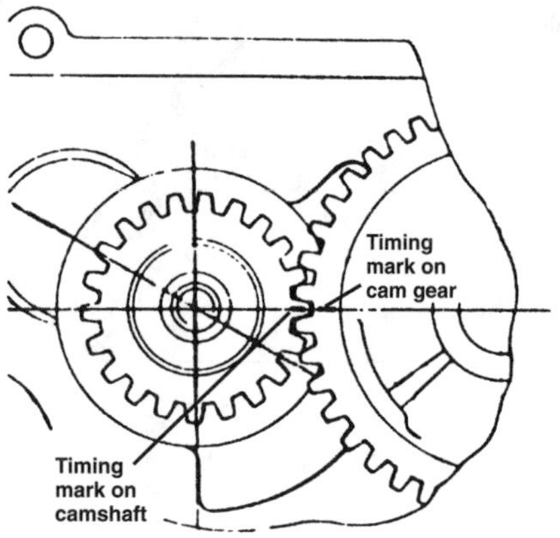

Fig. B535—Align timing marks on cam gear and crankshaft gear on plain bearing models.

reamed using B&S reamer 19233 and reamer guide 19234.

Some engines may be equipped with a Cobalite exhaust valve and exhaust seat insert as well as a rotocoil on the exhaust valve stem. These components are offered as replacement parts for engines used in severe engine service.

CRANKCASE COVER/OIL PAN

To remove the crankcase cover or oil pan, first drain the oil from the engine. Remove rust, dirt or burrs from the power take-off end of the crankshaft. Remove the fasteners and withdraw the crankcase cover or oil pan.

Tighten the crankcase cover or oil pan retaining screws to 140 in.-lb. (15.8 N·m). On horizontal crankshaft models not equipped with a right-angle drive, apply nonhardening sealant to screw (S—Fig. B533).

CAMSHAFT

To remove the camshaft, remove the crankcase cover or oil pan as previously outlined. Turn the crankshaft to align the crankshaft and camshaft gear timing marks. Remove the camshaft and gear assembly from the crankcase.

The camshaft is supported at both ends in bearing bores machined in the crankcase and crankcase cover or oil pan. The camshaft gear is an integral part of the camshaft.

The camshaft should be replaced if either journal is worn to a diameter of 0.498 inch (12.66 mm) or less or if cam lobes are worn or damaged.

Crankcase, crankcase cover or oil pan must be replaced if bearing bores are 0.506 inch (12.85 mm) or larger, or if tool 19164 enters bearing bore ¼ inch (6.4 mm) or more.

A compression release mechanism on the camshaft gear holds the exhaust valve slightly open at very low engine rpm as a starting aid. The mechanism should work freely and the spring should hold the actuator cam against the pin.

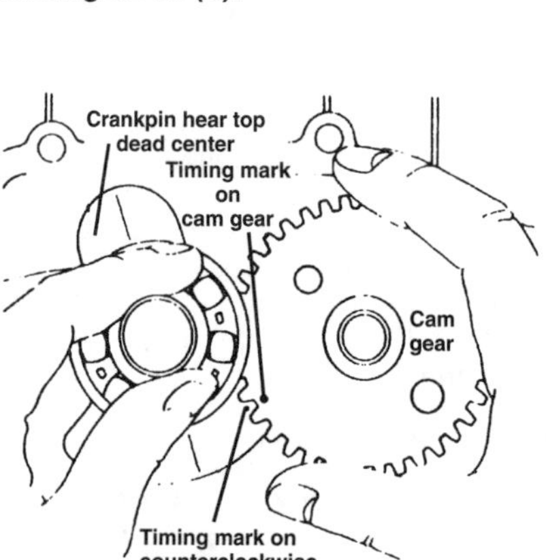

Fig. B534—Align timing mark on cam gear with mark on crankshaft counterweight on ball bearing equipped models.

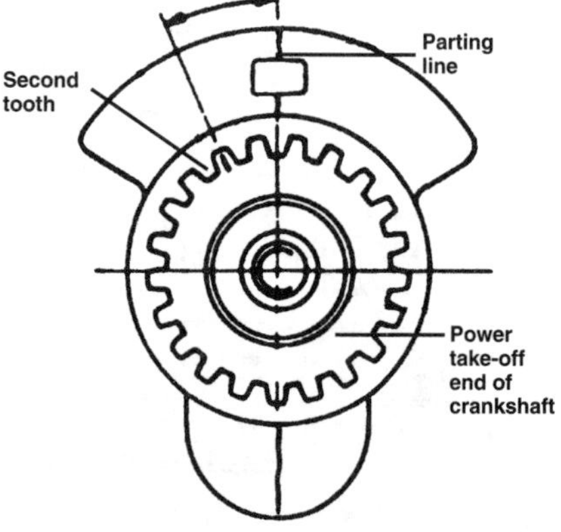

Fig. B536—Location of tooth to align with timing mark on cam gear if mark is not visible on crankshaft gear.

When installing the camshaft in engines with ball bearing main bearings, align the timing marks on the camshaft gear and crankshaft counterweight as shown in Fig. B534.

When installing camshaft in engines with integral type main bearings, align timing marks on camshaft and crankshaft gears as shown in Fig. B535.

If the timing mark is not visible on the crankshaft gear, align the camshaft gear timing mark with the second tooth to the left of the crankshaft counterweight parting line as shown in Fig. B536.

PISTON, PIN AND RINGS

The connecting rod and piston are removed from the cylinder head end of block as an assembly. Remove the cylinder head, crankcase cover or oil pan and camshaft to access the connecting rod. Remove carbon and ridge (if present) from top of cylinder before removing the piston. Remove the connecting rod cap and push the connecting rod and piston out of the cylinder block.

Cylinder bore may be aluminum or a cast iron sleeve, and pistons are designed to run in only one type of bore. Pistons designed for use in a cast iron bore have a dull finish and are stamped with an L on the piston's crown. Pistons designed for use in an aluminum cylinder bore are chrome plated (shiny finish). Pistons cannot be interchanged.

Reject pistons showing visible signs of wear, scoring and scuffing. If, after cleaning carbon from the top ring groove, a new top ring has a side clearance of 0.009 inch (0.23 mm), reject the piston. Reject the piston or hone the piston pin hole to 0.005 inch (0.13 mm) oversize if pin hole is 0.0005 inch (0.013 mm) or more out-of-round, or is worn to a diameter of 0.673 inch (17.09 mm) or more on 170000, 171000, 190000, 191000, 192000, 193000, 194000, 195000 and 196000 series engines, or 0.801 inch (20.34 mm) or more on all other engines.

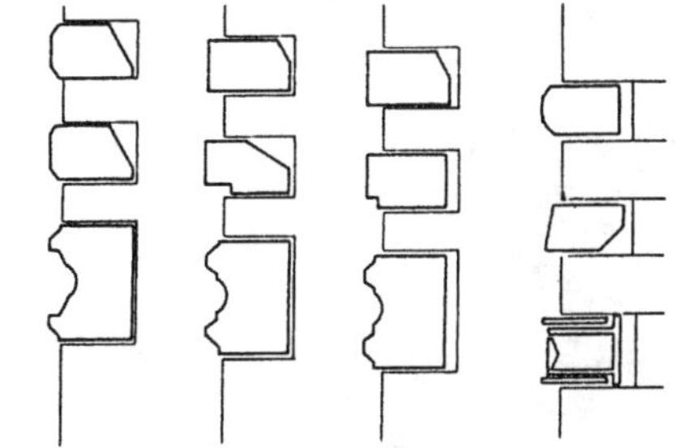

Fig. B537—Refer to above illustration for proper arrangement of piston rings used in engines with aluminum bore.

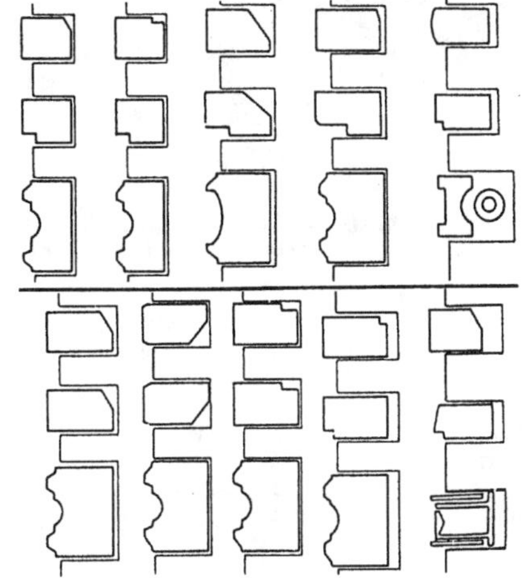

Fig. B538—Refer to above illustration for proper arrangement of piston rings used in engines with cast iron sleeve.

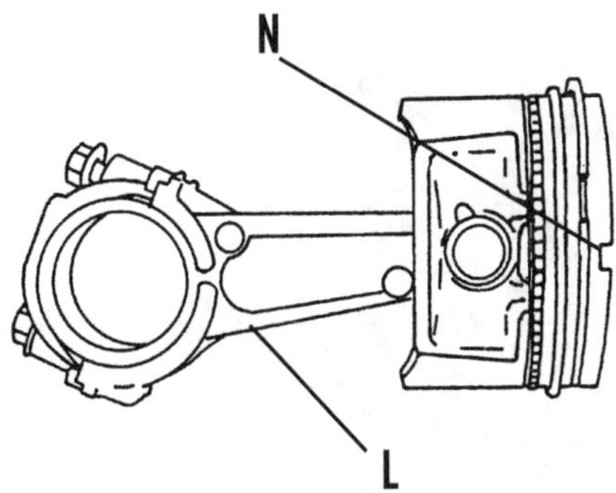

Fig. B539—If piston crown is notched (N), assemble connecting rod and piston as shown while noting relation of long side of rod (L) and notch (N) in piston crown.

If the piston pin is 0.0005 inch (0.013 mm) or more out-of-round, or is worn to a diameter of 0.671 inch (17.04 mm) or smaller on 170000, 171000, 190000, 191000, 192000, 193000, 194000, 195000 and 196000 series engines, or 0.799 inch (20.30 mm) or smaller on all other models, reject the pin.

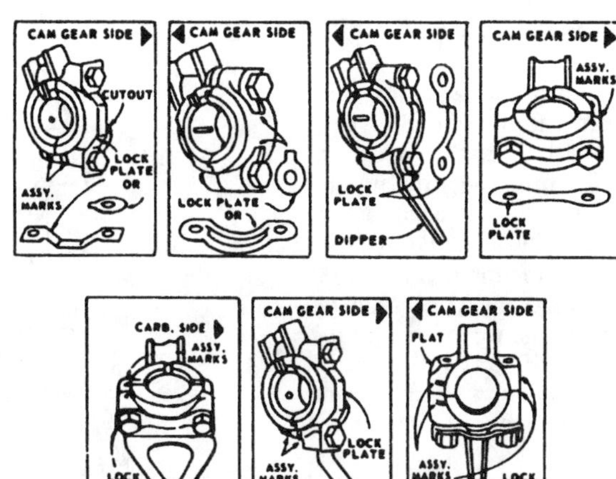

Fig. B540—Install connecting rod in engine as indicated according to type used. Note dipper installation on horizontal crankshaft engine connecting rod.

On aluminum bore engines, reject compression rings having an end gap of 0.035 inch (0.90 mm) or more and reject oil rings having an end gap of 0.045 inch (1.14 mm) or more. On cast iron bore engines, reject compression rings having an end gap of 0.030 inch (0.75 mm) or more and reject oil rings having an end gap of 0.035 inch (0.90 mm) or more.

Pistons and rings are available in several oversizes as well as standard. Refer to Figs. B537 and B538 for correct installation of piston rings.

A chrome piston ring set is available for slightly worn standard bore cylinders. No honing or cylinder deglazing is required for these rings. The cylinder bore can be a maximum of 0.005 inch (0.13 mm) oversize when using chrome rings.

If the piston has a notch (N—Fig. B539) in the piston crown, install the connecting rod in the piston as shown in Fig. B539. Install the piston and rod in the engine so the notch (N) is towards the flywheel.

CONNECTING ROD

Connecting rod and piston are removed from the cylinder head end of block as an assembly. The aluminum alloy connecting rod rides directly on an induction hardened crankshaft crankpin journal.

Rod should be rejected if the big end of the rod is scored or out-of-round more than 0.0007 inch (0.018 mm) or if the piston pin bore is scored or out-of-round more than 0.0005 inch (0.013 mm). Replace the connecting rod if either the crankpin bore or piston pin bore is worn to, or larger than, the sizes given in the table.

REJECT SIZES FOR CONNECTING ROD

Model Series	Crankpin Bore	Pin Bore*
170000, 171000.	1.095 in. (27.81 mm)	0.674 in. (17.12 mm)
190000, 191000, 192000, 193000, 194000, 195000, 196000.	1.127 in. (28.61 mm)	0.674 in. (17.12 mm)
All other models.	1.252 in. (31.8 mm)	0.802 in. (20.37 mm)

*Piston pins that are 0.005 inch (0.13 mm) oversize are available for service. The piston pin bore in the rod can be reamed to this size if the crankpin bore is within specifications.

Refer to Fig. B540, locate the type of connecting rod being serviced and note the installation instructions. If the piston has a notch (N—Fig. B539) in the piston crown, install the connecting rod in the piston as shown in Fig. B539. Install the piston and rod in the engine so the notch (N) is towards the flywheel.

Tighten the connecting rod screws to 165 in.-lb. (19 N·m) on 170000 and 171000 series engines and to 190 in.-lb. (22 N·m) on all other engines.

GOVERNOR

The governor gear and weight unit can be removed after removing the crankcase cover or oil pan. Refer to exploded views of the engines in Figs. B541, B542, B543 and B544.

The governor weight unit on horizontal crankshaft models rides on a shaft in the crankcase cover. The governor weight unit along with the oil slinger on vertical crankshaft models rides on the end of the camshaft as shown in Fig. B545.

Remove the governor lever, cotter pin and washer from the outer end of the governor lever shaft. Slide the governor lever out of the bushing towards the inside of the engine. The governor gear and weight unit can now be removed.

Replace the governor lever shaft bushing in the crankcase, if necessary, and ream the new bushing after installation to 0.2385-0.2390 inch (6.058-6.071 mm). Briggs & Stratton tool 19333 can be used to ream the bushing.

CRANKSHAFT AND MAIN BEARINGS

The crankshaft may be supported by bearing surfaces that are an integral part of crankcase, crankcase cover or oil pan, or by ball bearings at each end of the crankshaft. The ball bearings are a press fit on the crankshaft and fit into machined bores in the crankcase, crankcase cover or oil pan.

The crankshaft used in models with integral bearings should be replaced or reground if main bearing journals exceed service the limits specified in the following table.

CRANKSHAFT REJECT SIZES

Model	Magneto End Journal	PTO End Journal
170000, 171000, 190000, 191000, 192000, 193000, 194000, 195000, 196000	0.997 in.* (25.32 mm)	1.179 in. (29.95 mm)
All other models	1.376 in. (34.95 mm)	1.376 in. (34.95 mm)

*Models equipped with Synchro-Balancer have a main bearing rejection size for the main bearing at the magneto side of 1.179 inch (29.95 mm).

Crankshaft for models with ball bearing main bearings should be replaced if the new bearings are loose on the journals. Bearings should be a press fit.

Crankshaft for all models should be replaced or reground if the connecting rod crankpin journal diameter exceeds the service limit listed in the following table.

CRANKSHAFT REJECT SIZES

Model	Crankpin Journal
170000, 171000	1.090 in. (27.69 mm)
190000, 191000, 192000, 193000, 194000, 195000, 196000	1.122 in. (28.50 mm)

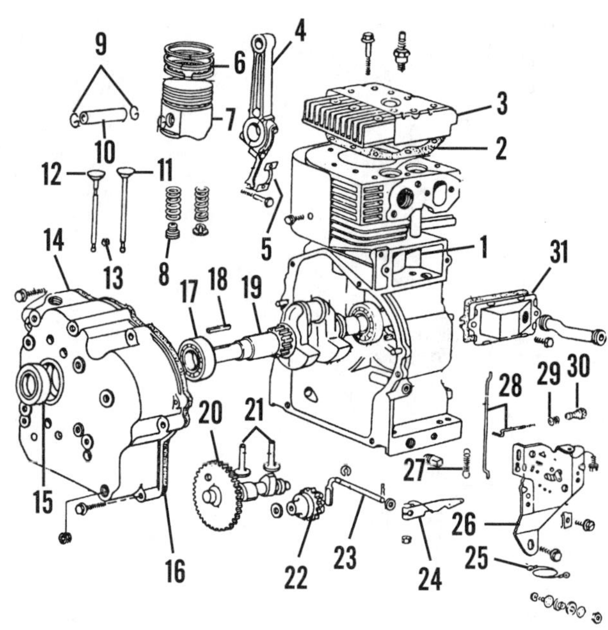

Fig. B541—Exploded view of Series 220000 or 221000 horizontal crankshaft engine assembly. Series 170000, 171000, 190000 and 195000 are similar. Series 222000 is similar but ball bearings (17) are not used.

1. Cylinder block/crankcase
2. Head gasket
3. Cylinder head
4. Connecting rod
5. Rod bolt lock
6. Piston rings
7. Piston
8. Rotocoil (exhaust valve)
9. Retainer clips
10. Piston pin
11. Intake valve
12. Exhaust valve
13. Retainers
14. Crankcase cover
15. Oil seal
16. Crankcase gasket
17. Main bearing
18. Key
19. Crankshaft
20. Camshaft
21. Tappet
22. Governor gear
23. Governor crank
24. Governor lever
25. Ground wire
26. Governor control plate
27. Spring
28. Governor rod
29. Spring
30. Nut
31. Breather assembly

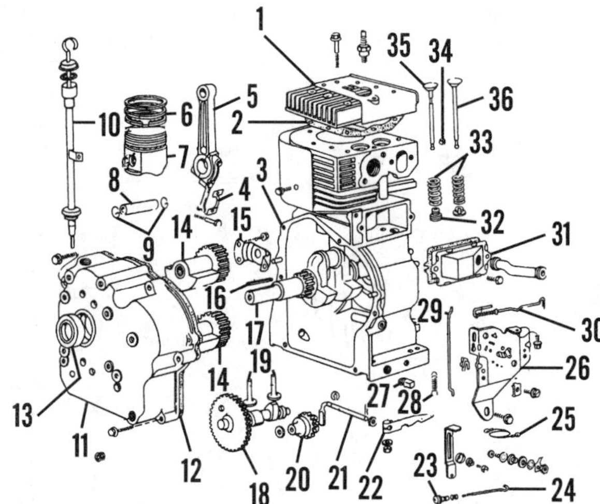

Fig. B542—Exploded view of Series 251000, 252000 or 254000 engine assembly. Series 253000 and 255000 are similar.

1. Cylinder head
2. Head gasket
3. Cylinder block/crankcase
4. Rod bolt lock
5. Connecting rod
6. Piston rings
7. Piston
8. Piston pin
9. Retainer clips
10. Dipstick
11. Crankcase cover
12. Crankcase gasket
13. Oil seal
14. Counterweight and bearing assembly
17. Crankshaft
18. Camshaft
19. Tappet
20. Governor gear
21. Governor crank
22. Governor lever
23. Governor nut & spring
24. Governor control rod
25. Ground wire
26. Governor control plate
27. Drain plug
28. Spring
29. Governor link
30. Choke link
31. Breather assy.
32. Rotocoil (exhaust valve)
33. Valve springs
34. Retainer
35. Exhaust valve
36. Intake valve

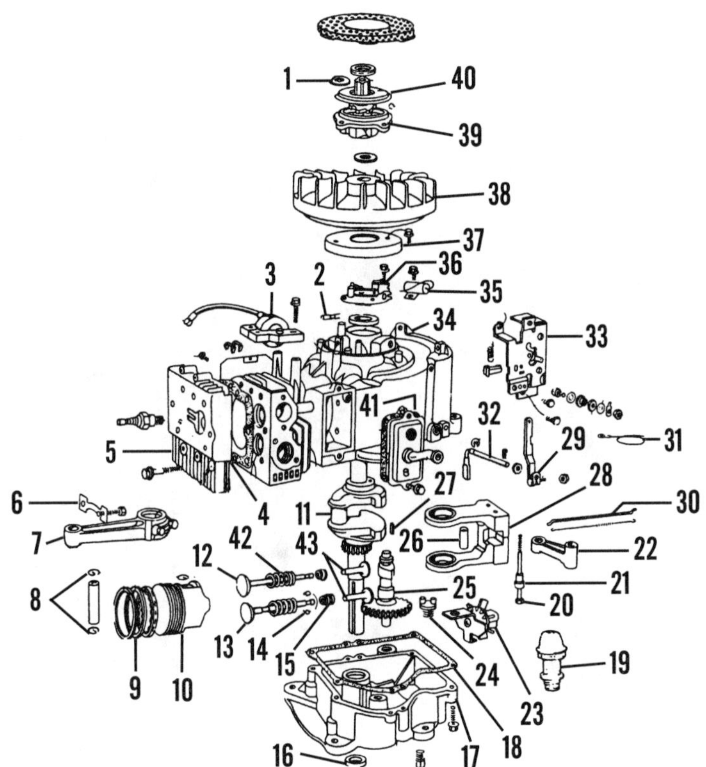

Fig. B543—Exploded view of typical vertical crankshaft engine equipped with Synchro-Balancer.

1. Thrust washer
2. Breaker point plunger
3. Armature assembly
4. Head gasket
5. Cylinder head
6. Rod bolt lock
7. Connecting rod
8. Piston pin and retaining clips
9. Piston rings
10. Piston
11. Crankshaft
12. Intake valve
13. Exhaust valve
14. Retainer
15. Rotocoil (exhaust valve)
16. Oil seal
17. Oil pan
18. Crankcase gasket
19. Oil minder
20. Cap screw (2)
21. Spacer (2)
22. Link
23. Governor and oil slinger
24. Plug
25. Camshaft
26. Dowel pin (2)
27. Key
28. Counterweight assembly
29. Governor lever
30. Governor link
31. Ground wire
32. Governor crank
33. Choke-A-Matic control
34. Cylinder block/crankcase
35. Condenser
36. Breaker points
37. Cover
38. Flywheel assembly
39. Clutch housing
40. Rewind starter clutch
41. Breather assembly
42. Valve springs
43. Tappet

All other models.................... 1.247 in. (31.67 mm)

A connecting rod with undersize big end diameter is available to fit a crankshaft that has had the crankpin journal reground to 0.020 inch (0.51 mm) undersize.

On models equipped with integral main bearings, crankcase, crankcase cover or oil pan must be renewed or reamed to accept service bushings if the service limits in the following table are exceeded.

MAIN BEARING REJECT SIZES

Model	Magneto End Bearing	PTO End Bearing
170000, 171000, 190000, 191000, 192000, 193000, 194000, 195000, 196000	1.004 in.* (25.50 mm)	1.185 in. (30.10 mm)
All other models	1.383 in. (35.13 mm)	1.383 in. (35.13 mm)

***Models equipped with Synchro-Balancer have a main bearing rejection size for the main bearing at the magneto side of 1.185 inch (30.10 mm).**

Install steel-backed aluminum service bushing as follows. After reaming the bearing bore to the proper size, place the new bushing against the reamed out bearing with the notch in the new bearing aligned with the notch or oil hole in the housing. Use a chisel and hammer to make an indentation in the reamed out bearing opposite the split in the new bushing (Fig. B546).

Install the new bushing so oil notches are properly aligned and bushing is flush with bore. Oil hole must be clear after installation. Stake the bushing into the previously made indentation and finish ream the bushing. Do not stake where the bushing is split.

When installing a DU type bushing, stake the bushing at the oil notches in the crankcase, but locate the bushing so the bushing split is not aligned with an oil notch.

On Series 170000 and 190000 models, bushing should be $^{3}/_{32}$ inch (2.4 mm) below the face of the crankcase bore and $^{1}/_{32}$ inch (0.8 mm) below the face of the crankcase cover or oil pan.

On Series 171000, 191000, 192000, 193000, 194000, 195000 and 196000 models, bushing should be $^{1}/_{64}$ inch (0.4 mm) below the face of the crankcase bore and $^{1}/_{32}$ inch (0.8 mm) below the face of the crankcase cover or oil pan.

On all other models, bushing should be $^{7}/_{64}$ inch (2.8 mm) below the face of the crankcase bore and $^{1}/_{8}$ inch (3.2 mm) below the face of the crankcase cover or oil pan.

Ball bearing mains are a press fit on the crankshaft and must be removed by pressing the crankshaft out of the bearing. Reject ball bearing if worn or rough. Expand a new bearing by heating it in oil and before installing it on the crankshaft. Be sure the seal side is towards the crankpin journal.

Crankshaft end play is 0.002-0.008 inch (0.05-0.20 mm). At least one 0.015 inch thick crankcase gasket must be in place when measuring end play. Additional gaskets in several sizes are available to aid in end play adjustment. If end play is excessive, place shims between the crankshaft gear and crankcase on plain bearing models, or on the flywheel side of the crankshaft if equipped with a ball bearing.

When installing the crankshaft, make certain the timing marks are aligned (Fig. B534 or B535). Refer to the Rotating Counterbalance System paragraph for balancer alignment procedure.

CYLINDER

If cylinder bore wear is 0.003 inch (0.08 mm) or more or is 0.0025 inch (0.06 mm) or more out-of-round, cylinder must be bored to next larger oversize or replaced.

Standard cylinder bore diameter is 2.9990-3.0000 inches (76.175-76.230 mm) for Series 170000, 171000, 190000, 191000, 192000, 193000, 194000, 195000 and 196000 models. Standard cylinder bore diameter is 3.4365-3.4375 inches (87.287-87.313 mm) for all other models.

Special stones are required to hone aluminum cylinder bore on models so equipped. Follow recommendations

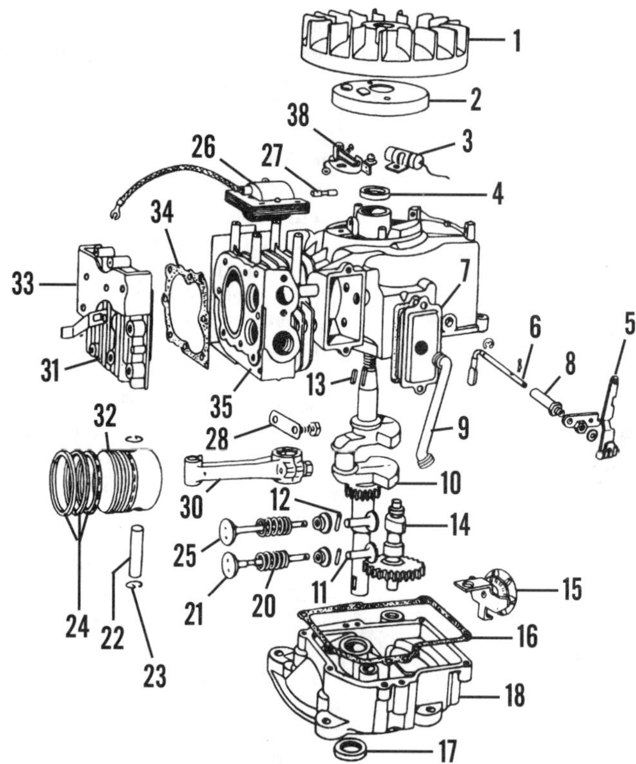

Fig. B544—Exploded view of typical vertical crankshaft engine not equipped with Synchro-Balancer.

1. Flywheel
2. Cover
3. Condenser
4. Oil seal
5. Governor lever
6. Governor crank
7. Breather assembly
8. Bushing
9. Breather vent tube
10. Crankshaft
11. Tappet
12. Valve retaining pins
13. Key
14. Camshaft
15. Governor and oil slinger
16. Crankcase gasket
17. Oil seal
18. Oil pan
19. Valve spring retainer
20. Valve springs
21. Exhaust valve
22. Piston pin
23. Retainer clip
24. Piston rings
25. Intake valve
26. Armature and coil assembly
27. Breaker point plunger
28. Rod bolt lock
30. Connecting rod
31. Cylinder head
32. Piston
33. Air baffle
34. Head gasket
35. Cylinder block/crankcase
38. Breaker points

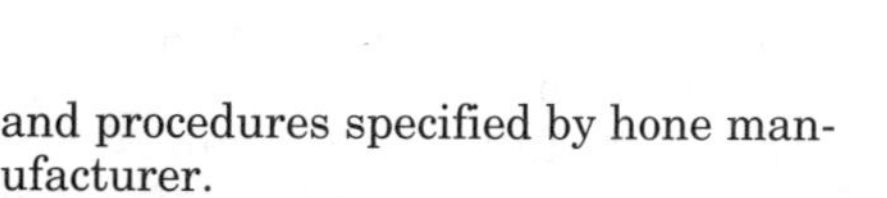

and procedures specified by hone manufacturer.

A chrome piston ring set is available for slightly worn standard bore cylinders. No honing or cylinder deglazing is required for these rings. The cylinder bore can be a maximum of 0.005 inch (0.13 mm) oversize when using chrome rings.

SYNCHRO-BALANCER

All vertical crankshaft engines, except Series 220000, 221000 and 222000 models, may be equipped with an oscillating Synchro-Balancer. Balance weight assembly rides on eccentric journals on the crankshaft and move in the opposite direction of the piston (Fig. B547).

To disassemble the balancer unit, first remove the flywheel, oil pan, cam gear, cylinder head and connecting rod and piston assembly. Carefully pry off the crankshaft gear and key. Remove the two cap screws holding the counterweight halves together. Separate the weights and remove the link, dowel pins and spacers. Slide the weights from the crankshaft (Fig. B548).

To reassemble, install the magneto side weight on the magneto end of the crankshaft. Place the crankshaft (PTO end up) in a vise (Fig. B549). Install both dowel pins and place the link on the pin as shown. Note the rounded

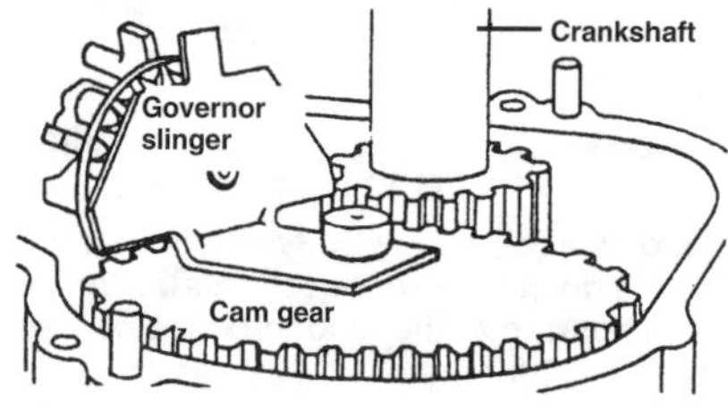

Fig. B545—View of governor weight assembly and oil slinger used on vertical crankshaft models.

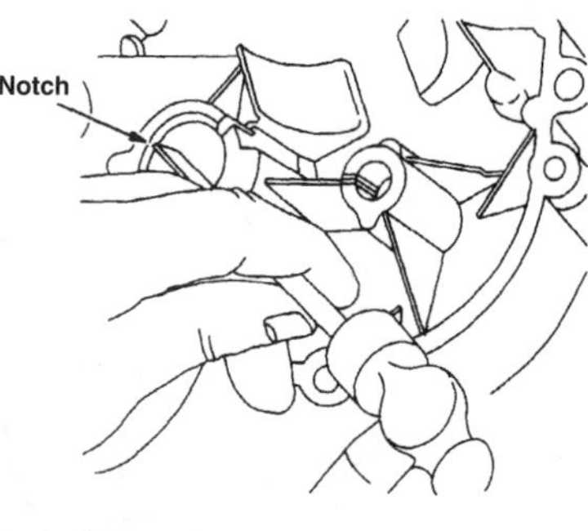

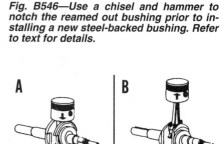

Fig. B546—Use a chisel and hammer to notch the reamed out bushing prior to installing a new steel-backed bushing. Refer to text for details.

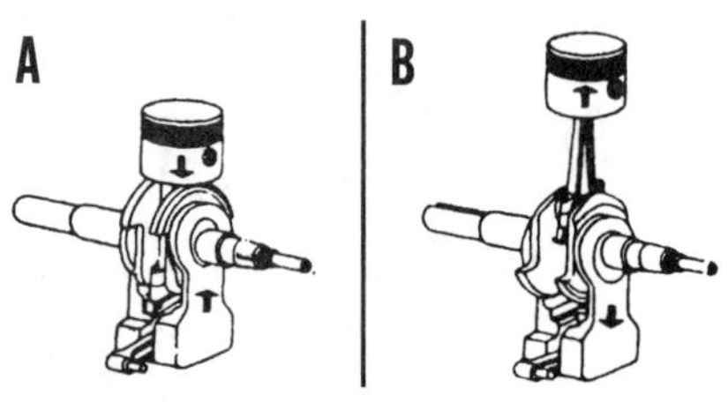

Fig. B547—View showing operating principle of Synchro-Balancer used on some vertical crankshaft engines. Counterweight oscillates in opposite direction of piston.

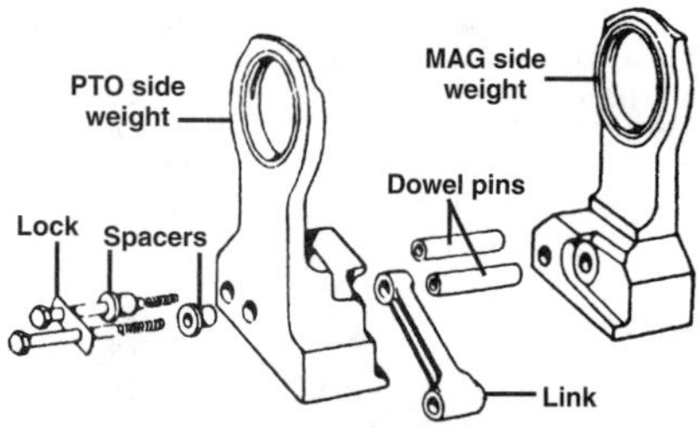

Fig. B548—Exploded view of Synchro-Balancer assembly. Counterweights ride on eccentric journals on crankshaft.

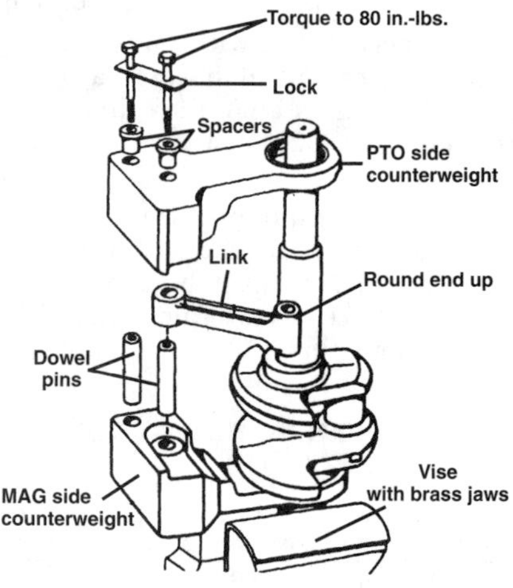

Fig. B549—Assemble balance units on crankshaft as shown. Install link with rounded edge on free end toward PTO end of crankshaft.

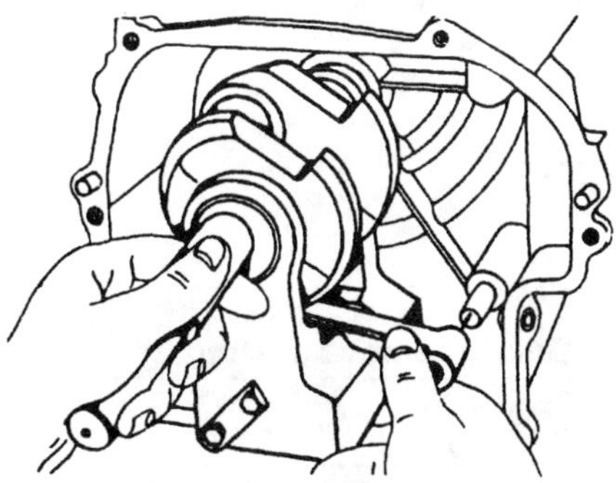

Fig. B550—When installing crankshaft and balancer assembly, place free end of link on anchor pin in crankcase.

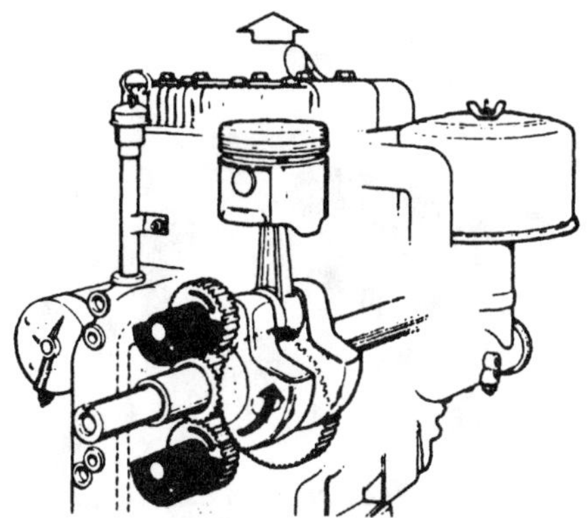

Fig. B551—View of rotating counterbalance system used on some models. Counterweight gears are driven by crankshaft.

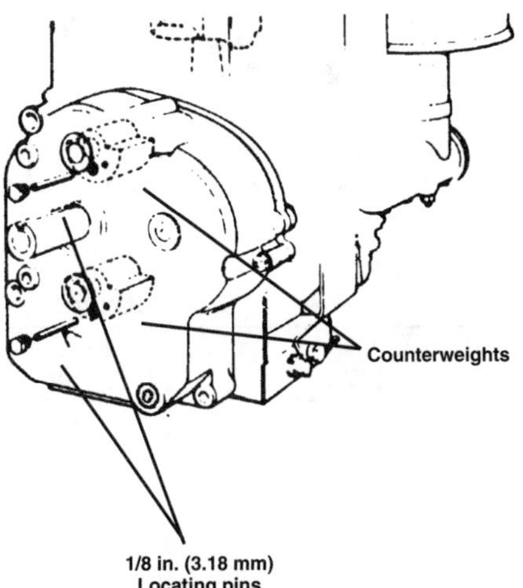

Fig. B552—To properly align counterweights, remove two small screws from crankcase cover and insert 1/8-inch (3.2 mm) diameter locating pins.

edge on the free end of the link must be up. Install the PTO side weight, spacers, lock and cap screws. Tighten the cap screws to 80 in.-lb. (9 N·m) and secure with lock tabs. Install the key and crankshaft gear with the chamfer on the inside of the gear facing the shoulder on the crankshaft.

Install the crankshaft and balancer assembly in the crankcase, sliding the free end of the link on the anchor pin as shown in Fig. B550. Reassemble the engine.

ROTATING COUNTERBALANCE SYSTEM

All horizontal crankshaft engines, except Series 220000, 221000 and 222000 models, may be equipped with two gear-driven counterweights in constant mesh with the crankshaft gear. Gears, mounted in the crankcase cover, rotate in the opposite direction of the crankshaft (Fig. B551).

To properly align the counterweights when installing the cover, remove the two small screws from the cover and insert 1/8-inch (3.2 mm) diameter locating pins through the holes in the cover and into the holes in the counterweights as shown in Fig. B552.

With the piston at TDC, install the cover assembly. Remove the locating pins, coat the threads of the timing hole screws with nonhardening sealer and install the screws with fiber sealing washers.

NOTE: If the counterweights are removed from the crankcase cover, exercise care in handling or cleaning to prevent loss of needle bearings.

BRIGGS & STRATTON

4-STROKE OHV ENGINES

Model Series	No. Cyls.	Bore	Stroke	Displacement	Power Rating
287700, 28Q700	1	3.44 in. (87.3 mm)	3.06 in. (77.7 mm)	28.4 cu. in. (465 cc)	14 hp (10.4 kW)

ENGINE INFORMATION

The 287700 and 28Q700 models are air-cooled, four-stroke, single-cylinder engines. The engine has a vertical crankshaft and utilizes an overhead valve system.

MAINTENANCE

LUBRICATION

Engine lubrication is accomplished by a rotor oil pump located in the bottom of the crankcase, as well as by an oil slinger wheel on the governor gear that is driven by the camshaft gear.

Change the oil after first eight hours of operation and after every 50 hours of operation or at least once each operating season. Change oil weekly or after every 25 hours of operation if equipment undergoes severe usage.

Engine oil level should be maintained at the full mark on dipstick. Engine oil should meet or exceed the latest API service classification. Use SAE 30 oil for temperatures above 40° F (4° C); use SAE 10W-30 oil for temperatures between 0° F (-18° C) and 100° F (38° C); below 20° F (-7° C) use petroleum based SAE 5W-20 or a suitable synthetic oil.

Crankcase capacity is 1.5 qt. (1.4 L). Fill the engine with oil so the oil level reaches, but does not exceed, the full mark on dipstick.

AIR CLEANER

The air cleaner consists of a canister and the filter element it contains. The filter element is made of paper. A foam precleaner surrounds the filter element.

The foam precleaner should be cleaned after every 25 hours of operation. The paper filter should be cleaned yearly or after every 100 hours of operation, whichever occurs first.

Tap the paper filter gently to dislodge accumulated dirt. The filter may be washed using warm water and nonsudsing detergent directed from inside the filter to the outside. DO NOT use petroleum-based cleaners or solvents to clean the paper filter. DO NOT direct pressurized air towards the filter. Let the filter air dry thoroughly. Inspect the filter and discard it if damaged.

Clean the filter canister. Inspect and, if necessary, replace any defective gaskets.

Clean the foam precleaner in soapy water and squeeze until dry. Inspect the filter for tears, holes or any other opening. Discard the precleaner if it cannot be cleaned satisfactorily or if the precleaner is torn or otherwise damaged. Pour clean engine oil into the precleaner, then squeeze to remove excess oil and distribute the oil throughout.

CRANKCASE BREATHER

The crankcase breather is built into the tappet cover. A fiber disc acts as a one-way valve.

Clearance between the fiber disc valve and the breather body should not exceed 0.045 inch (1.14 mm). If it is possible to insert a 0.045 inch (1.14 mm) wire (Fig. B651) between the disc and breather body, replace the breather assembly. Do not use excessive force when measuring the gap.

The disc should not stick or bind during operation. Replace the breather if the disc is distorted or damaged. Inspect the breather tube for leakage.

Fig. B651—Renew breather assembly if it is possible to insert a 0.045 inch (1.14 mm) diameter wire between disc and breather body. Do not use excessive force when measuring gap.

SPARK PLUG

Recommended spark plug is Champion RC12YC or Autolite 3924. Specified spark plug electrode gap is 0.030 inch (0.76 mm).

CAUTION: Briggs & Stratton does not recommend using abrasive blasting to clean spark plugs as this may introduce some abrasive material into the engine that could cause extensive damage.

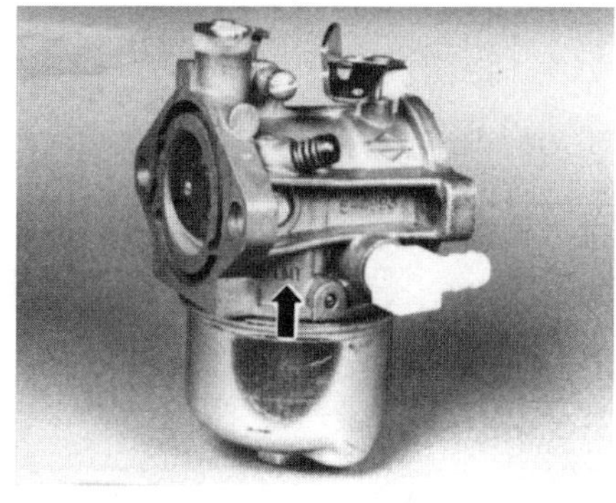

Fig. B652—Walbro LMT carburetor may be identified by "LMT" cast in side of body.

CARBURETOR

The engine is equipped with a Walbro LMT float type carburetor. The Walbro LMT carburetor can be identified by the letters LMT embossed on the side of the carburetor (Fig. B652). The Walbro

Fig. B653—View showing location of idle jet (A) and idle mixture screw (B).

Fig. B654—Fuel inlet seat is recessed in body.

carburetor is equipped with an adjustable idle mixture screw (B—Fig. B653) and fixed main jet.

For initial setting of the idle mixture screw, back the screw out counterclockwise and then turn it in until the head of the screw just contacts the spring. Start and run the engine until it reaches normal operating temperature. Place the equipment control lever in the SLOW position, and adjust the idle speed screw so the engine idles at 1750 rpm.

With the engine running at idle speed, turn the idle mixture screw clockwise until the engine speed just starts to drop. Note the screw position. Turn the idle mixture screw counterclockwise until the engine speed just starts to drop again. Note the screw position, then turn the screw to the midpoint between the noted screw positions.

If engine will not accelerate cleanly, slightly enrich the mixture by turning the idle mixture screw counterclockwise. If necessary, readjust the idle speed screw.

Optional main jets are available to accommodate various applications, such as high altitude operation.

To disassemble the carburetor for cleaning and inspection, unscrew the idle mixture screw (B—Fig. B653) and idle fuel jet (A). Unscrew the fuel bowl retaining screw and remove the fuel

Fig. B655—Nozzle unscrews from center of body.

Fig. B656—Remove and install Welch plug as described in text.

bowl and gasket. Remove the float pin, float and fuel inlet valve. Extract the fuel inlet valve seat (Fig. B654) using a suitable tool.

Unscrew the nozzle (Fig. B655). If equipped with a metal choke, unscrew the screws retaining the choke plate and remove the choke plate and choke shaft. If equipped with a plastic choke, insert a sharp tool between the choke shaft and choke plate and pull out the choke plate, then remove the choke shaft.

Unscrew the throttle plate screws and remove the throttle plate and throttle shaft.

To remove the Welch plug (Fig. B656), pierce the plug with a thin punch or awl, then pry out the plug.

CAUTION: Insert the punch into the Welch plug only far enough to pierce it, otherwise, the underlying metal may be damaged.

Fig. B657—Do not attempt to remove the orifices or clean them with wire.

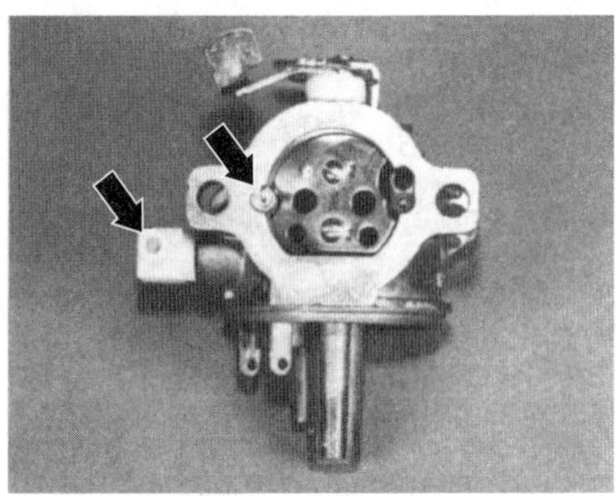

Fig. B658—Install choke plate so edge with a single notch is on fuel inlet side of carburetor.

NOTE: Two air bleed holes in the carburetor bore (Fig. B657) are fitted with calibrated metal orifices. Do not attempt to remove the orifices or clean with wire. Clean the orifices only with compressed air.

Clean the carburetor in suitable carburetor cleaner. Some carburetor parts may be made of plastic and should not be soaked in carburetor cleaner.

Inspect the carburetor and components. The body must be replaced if there is excessive throttle or choke shaft play as bushings are not available.

Assemble the carburetor by reversing the disassembly procedure while noting following: Install a new Welch plug while being careful not to indent plug; plug should be flat after installation. Apply a nonhardening sealant around the plug. Use a $\frac{3}{16}$-inch diameter rod to install the fuel inlet valve seat. The groove on the seat must be down (toward carburetor bore). Push in the seat until it bottoms.

If equipped with a choke return spring, install the spring so spring tension tries to open choke. Install the choke plate so the edge with a single notch is on the fuel inlet side of carburetor (Fig. B658). The plate should be centered on the choke shaft.

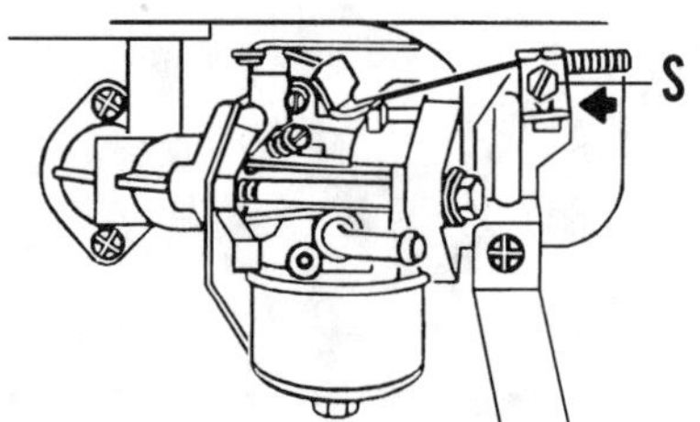

Fig. B659—Loosen clamp screw (S) to adjust position of control cable.

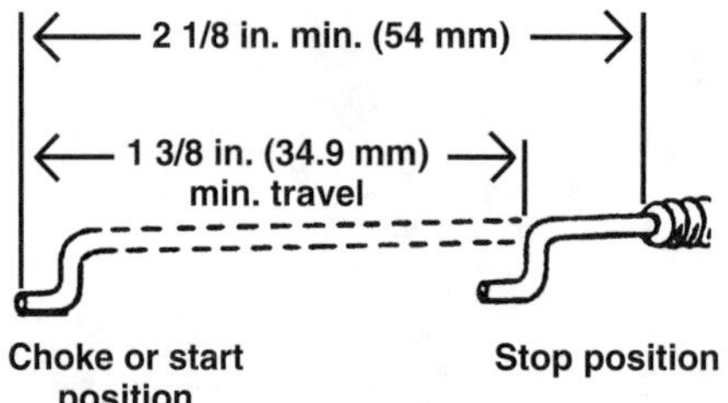

Fig. B660—For proper operation of Choke-A-Matic controls, remote control wire must extend to dimension shown and have a minimum travel of 1 3/8 inches (34.9 mm).

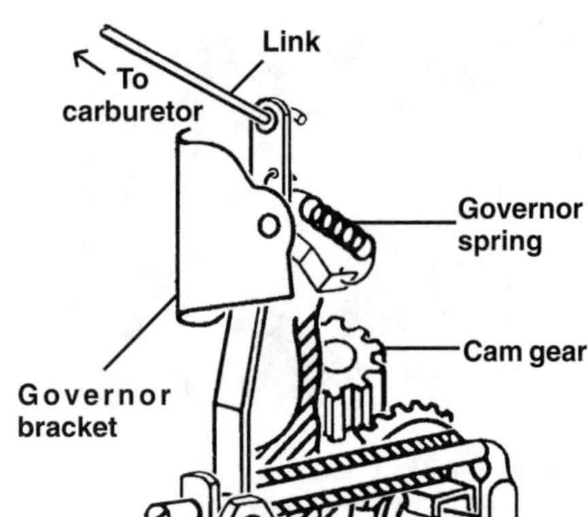

Fig. B661—Drawing of governor and linkage.

Install the throttle plate so numbers are visible and toward the idle mixture screw when the throttle is closed.

The float level is not adjustable. If the float is not approximately parallel with the body when the carburetor is inverted, replace the float, fuel valve and/or valve seat. Tighten the fuel bowl retaining screw to 40 in.-lb. (4.5 N·m).

FUEL PUMP

The engine may be equipped with a diaphragm fuel pump that uses engine vacuum to operate pump. Pump must be serviced as a unit assembly.

CHOKE-A-MATIC CARBURETOR CONTROLS

Engines may be equipped with a control unit that operates the carburetor choke, throttle and magneto grounding switch from a single lever (Choke-A-Matic carburetors).

To check operation of Choke-A-Matic controls, move equipment control lever to the CHOKE position. The carburetor choke slide or plate must be completely closed. Move the control lever to the STOP position. The magneto grounding switch should be making contact. With the control in the RUN, FAST or SLOW position, the carburetor choke should be completely open.

To synchronize the movement of the remote control lever to the carburetor control lever, loosen the screw (S—Fig. B659) and move the control wire housing as required. Tighten screw to clamp housing securely. Refer to Fig. B660 to check remote control wire movement.

GOVERNOR

Engine is equipped with a gear-driven mechanical governor located in the oil pan. The governor is driven by the camshaft gear (Fig. B661). Governor and linkage must operate properly to prevent "hunting" or unsteady operation. The carburetor must be properly adjusted before performing governor adjustments.

To adjust governor linkage, loosen the governor lever clamp bolt. Move the throttle link (Fig. B661) attached to the governor lever so the carburetor throttle plate is in wide-open position. Using a screwdriver, rotate the governor lever shaft clockwise as far as possible and tighten the clamp bolt.

On models equipped with governed idle, set the remote control to idle position, then adjust the idle speed screw on the carburetor so the engine idles at 1200 rpm. Place the remote control so the engine idles at 1750 rpm, then bend the governor idle tang (Fig. B662) so the tang just contacts the sliding block actuator.

To set maximum no-load speed, move the remote speed control to maximum speed position. With the engine running, insert a suitable tool between the governor control cover and the engine casting and bend the governor spring anchor tang (T—Fig. B663) to obtain desired maximum no-load speed.

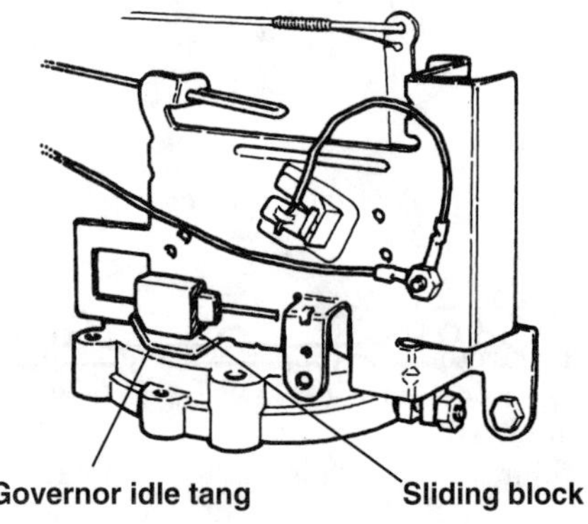

Fig. B662—Bend governor idle tang to adjust governed idle speed. Refer to text.

IGNITION SYSTEM

All models are equipped with a Magnetron ignition system.

To test the system for a spark, remove the spark plug and connect the spark plug cable to B&S tester 19051, and ground the remaining tester lead to the engine. Crank the engine at 350 rpm or more. If a spark jumps the 4.2 mm (0.166 in.) tester gap, the system is functioning properly.

To remove the armature and Magnetron module, remove the flywheel shroud and armature retaining screws. Disconnect the stop switch wire from the module.

Position the armature so air gap between armature legs and flywheel surface is 0.010-0.014 in. (0.25-0.36 mm).

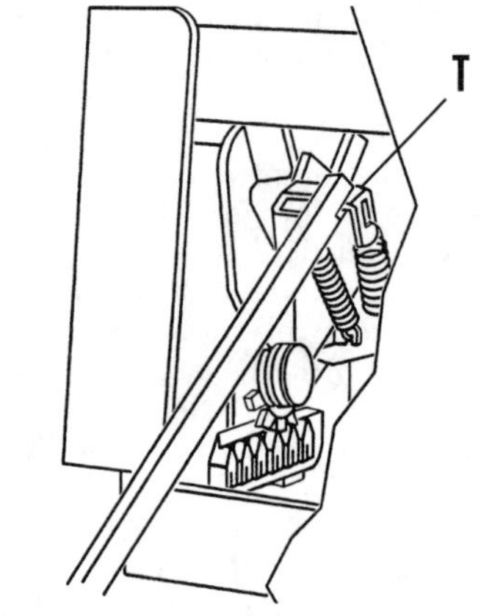

Fig. B663—Bend tang (T) to adjust maximum governed speed. See text.

VALVE ADJUSTMENT

Remove the rocker arm cover. Remove the spark plug. Rotate the crankshaft so the piston is at top dead center on compression stroke. Using a suitable measuring device inserted through the spark plug hole, rotate the crankshaft clockwise as viewed at flywheel end so the piston is 0.250 in. (6.35 mm) below TDC. This will prevent interference by the compression release mechanism with the exhaust valve.

Use a feeler gauge to measure the clearance between the rocker arm and

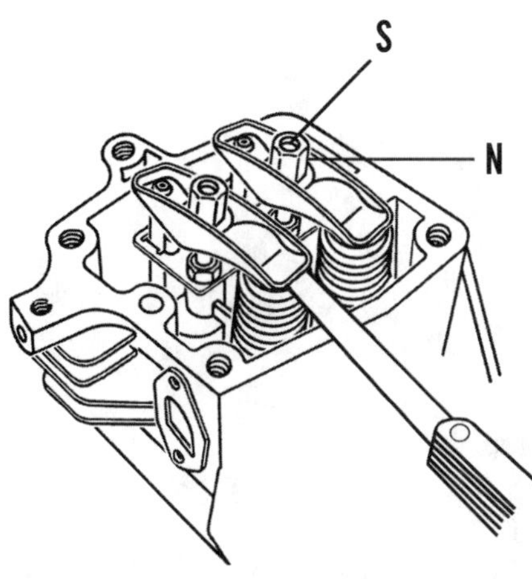

Fig. B664—Loosen Torx screw (S) and rotate pivot nut (N) to adjust valve clearance.

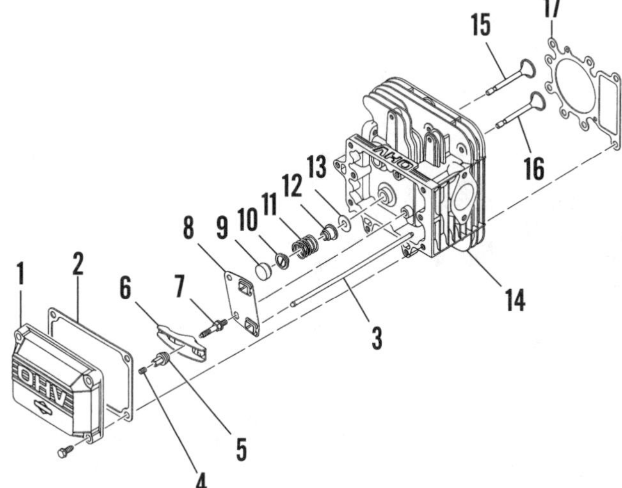

Fig. B665—Exploded view of cylinder head assembly.

1. Rocker arm cover
2. Gasket
3. Push rod
4. Torx screw
5. Pivot nut
6. Rocker arm
7. Rocker arm stud
8. Push rod guide
9. Valve cap
10. Retainer
11. Valve spring
12. Valve seal
13. Washer
14. Cylinder head
15. Exhaust valve
16. Intake valve
17. Head gasket

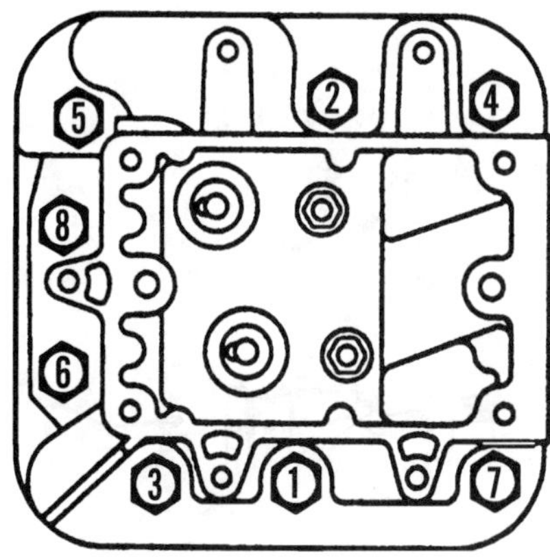

Fig. B666—Tighten cylinder head screws in sequence shown.

valve stem (Fig. B664). Valve clearance should be 0.003-0.005 in. (0.08-0.12 mm) for the intake valve and 0.005-0.007 in. (0.13-0.18 mm) for the exhaust valve.

To adjust clearance, loosen the Torx lock screw and turn the pivot nut (N—Fig. B664) to obtain desired clearance. Tighten the Torx lock screw to 50 in.-lb. (5.6 N·m). Tighten valve cover screws to 60 in.-lb. (6.8 N·m).

CYLINDER HEAD

After 100 to 300 hours of engine operation, remove the cylinder head and remove any carbon or deposits.

REPAIRS

TIGHTENING TORQUES

Recommended tightening torque specifications are as follows:

Carburetor/air cleaner nuts	**55 in.-lb. (6.2 N·m)**
Connecting rod	**185 in.-lb. (21.8 N·m)**
Cylinder head	**220 in.-lb. (24.8 N·m)**
Flywheel nut	**65 ft.-lb. (88 N·m)**
Oil pan	**140 in.-lb. (16 N·m)**
Rocker arm cover	**60 in.-lb. (6.8 N·m)**
Rocker arm lock screw	**50 in.-lb. (5.6 N·m)**
Rocker arm stud	**85 in.-lb. (9.6 N·m)**

CYLINDER HEAD AND VALVE SYSTEM

Always allow the engine to cool completely before loosening the cylinder head bolts. To remove the cylinder head, first locate the piston at top dead center of the compression stroke. Remove the air shrouds and intake and exhaust systems. Remove the rocker cover and breather assembly. Remove the cylinder head retaining screws and remove the cylinder head. Discard the cylinder head gasket.

Loosen the rocker arm screws (4—Fig. B665) and remove the rocker arm nuts (5) and rocker arms (6). Compress the valve spring (11) and remove the valve cap (9) and retainer (10). Remove the spring, valve seal (12), washer (13) and valve from the cylinder head.

Thoroughly clean the cylinder head and inspect for cracks or other damage. Position the cylinder head on a flat plate and use a feeler gauge to check flatness of the head gasket sealing surface. Replace the cylinder head if necessary.

Valve face and seat angles are 45° for intake and exhaust. Specified seat width is 0.031-0.078 in. (0.79-1.98 mm) for both valves. Minimum allowable valve margin is 0.015 in. (0.38 mm).

The cylinder head (14—Fig. B665) is equipped with replaceable valve guides for both valves. Maximum allowable inside diameter of guide is 0.240 in. (6.10 mm). Use B&S tools 19345 and 19346 to ream new valve guide to correct size.

Rocker arm studs are threaded into the cylinder head. When installing studs tighten to 85 in.-lb. (9.6 N·m). Lubricate the intake valve seal (12—Fig. B665) with engine oil prior to installation. Remove all lubricant from the valve stem ends and valve caps (9) before placing the caps on the valve stems.

Use a new head gasket when installing the cylinder head. Do not apply sealer to the head gasket. Note that the exhaust push rod has a red band. Lubricate the cylinder head retaining screws with graphite grease. Tighten the head bolts in 75 in.-lb. (8.5 N·m) increments following the sequence shown in Fig. B666 until reaching final torque of 220 in.-lb. (24.8 N·m).

CAMSHAFT

The camshaft (25—Fig. B667) is supported at both ends in bearing bores machined in the crankcase and oil pan. The camshaft gear is an integral part of the camshaft.

To remove the camshaft, first remove any rust, dirt or burrs from the PTO end of the crankshaft. Drain the engine oil and remove the oil pan for access to the camshaft. Rotate the crankshaft until the crankshaft and camshaft gear timing marks are aligned. Position the engine so the tappets will not fall out when removing camshaft. Remove the camshaft from the cylinder block. Identify the tappets if they are removed so they can be installed in their original position in the engine.

Replace the camshaft if either journal is worn to a diameter of 0.498 inch (12.66 mm) or less or if cam lobes are worn or damaged.

Crankcase, crankcase cover or oil pan must be replaced if the bearing bores are 0.504 inch (12.80 mm) or larger, or if B&S tool 19164 enters the bearing bore $\frac{1}{4}$ inch (6.4 mm) or more.

Compression release mechanism on the camshaft gear holds the exhaust valve slightly open at very low engine rpm as a starting aid. The mechanism should work freely and the spring should hold the actuator cam against the pin.

When installing the camshaft in the engine, align the timing marks on the camshaft and crankshaft gears as shown in Fig. B668.

NOTE: Do not force the oil pan onto the crankcase. The oil pump rotor must engage the drive pin. It may be necessary to rotate the crankshaft and camshaft to align the camshaft with the oil pump.

Install a seal protector or tape on the crankshaft end to help prevent damage to the oil seal. Install the oil pan. Note that the screw located at position (9—Fig. B669) was coated with sealant at the factory. If sealant is missing, coat the screw with a nonhardening sealant such as Permatex 2.

Note that two different types of oil pan screws have been used (Fig. B670). Tighten the early style screws to 140 in.-lb. (16 N·m). Tighten the late type screws to 200 in.-lb. (23 N·m). Follow the tightening sequence shown in Fig. B669 for both types of fasteners.

PISTON, PIN AND RINGS

The piston (21—Fig. B667) and connecting rod (24) are removed as an assembly after first removing the cylinder head, oil pan and connecting rod cap. Remove any carbon or ridge from the top of the cylinder to prevent damage to the piston or rings during removal. Push the connecting rod and piston out through the top of the cylinder.

To separate the piston from the connecting rod, remove one of the retaining rings (22—Fig. B667) and push out the pin (23) from the opposite side.

Reject the piston or hone the piston pin hole to 0.005 inch (0.13 mm) oversize if pin hole is 0.0005 inch (0.013 mm) or more out-of-round, or is worn to a diameter of 0.799 inch (20.29 mm) or more.

If the piston pin is 0.0005 inch (0.013 mm) or more out-of-round, or is worn to a diameter of 0.801 inch (20.34 mm) or smaller reject pin.

Reject compression rings having an end gap of 0.030 inch (0.75 mm) or more and reject oil rings having an end gap of 0.035 inch (0.90 mm) or more.

Pistons and rings are available in several oversizes as well as standard. Refer to Figs. B671 for correct installation of piston rings. Stagger the ring end gaps around the piston.

Assemble piston and rod so notch (A—Fig. B672) in piston crown is positioned relative to long side of rod (B) as shown. Compress the piston rings with a suitable tool. Lubricate the cylinder bore with engine oil. Rotate the crankshaft so the crankpin is at its lowest position. Install the piston and rod in the engine with the notch (A) toward the flywheel side of the engine.

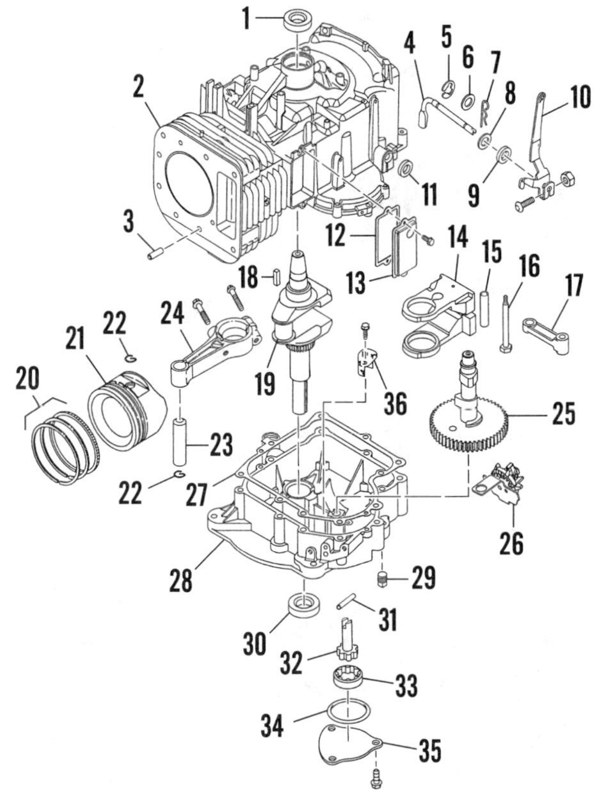

Fig. B667—Exploded view of engine.

1. Seal
2. Cylinder block/crankcase
3. Dowel pin (2)
4. Governor shaft
5. E-ring
6. Washer
7. Clip
8. Washer
9. Seal
10. Governor lever
11. Seal
12. Gasket
13. Breather assy.
14. Counterweight assy.
15. Dowel
16. Screw
17. Link
18. Key
19. Crankshaft
20. Piston rings
21. Piston
22. Retaining clips
23. Piston pin
24. Connecting rod
25. Camshaft
26. Governor & oil slinger
27. Gasket
28. Oil pan
29. Drain plug
30. Oil seal
31. Pin
32. Oil pump inner rotor
33. Outer rotor
34. O-ring
35. Cover
36. Oil pump screen

Fig. B668—Align timing marks on camshaft gear and crankshaft gear.

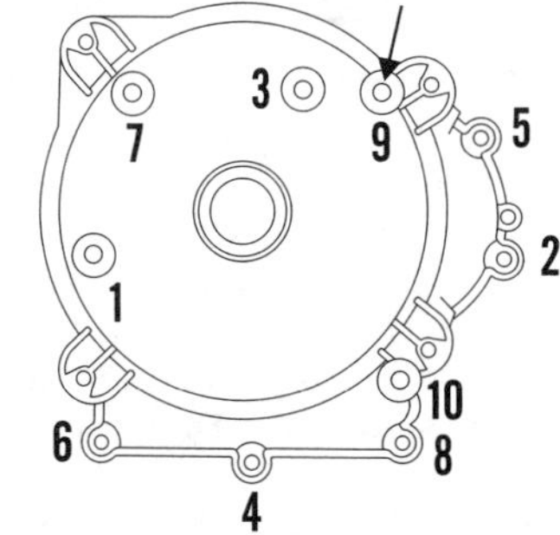

Fig. B669—Tighten oil pan screws in the sequence shown. Screw in position 9 should have sealant applied to the threads.

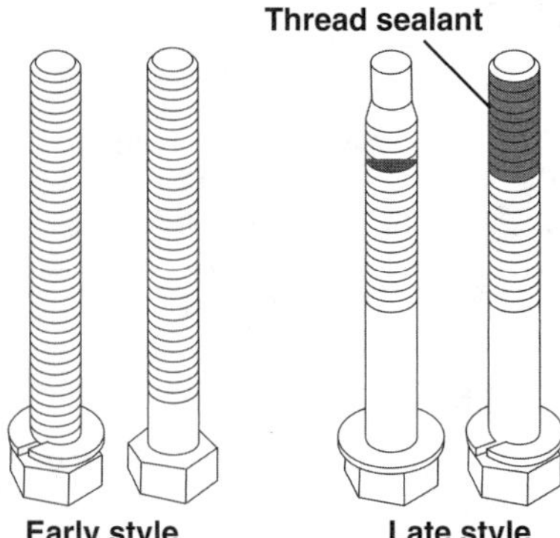

Fig. B670—Two different types of screws have been used to attach the oil pan to the engine.

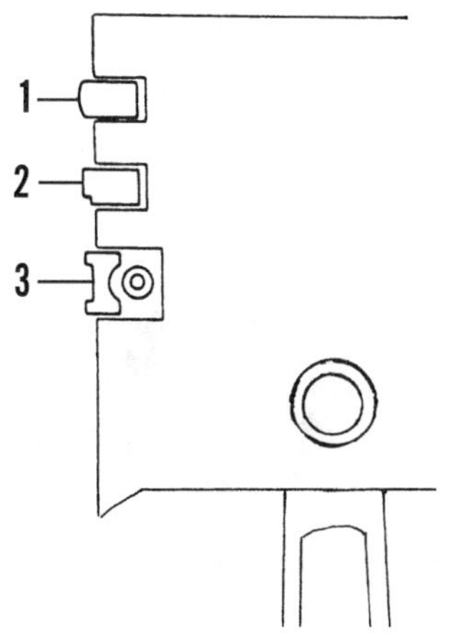

Fig. B671—Refer to above drawing for proper arrangement of piston rings.

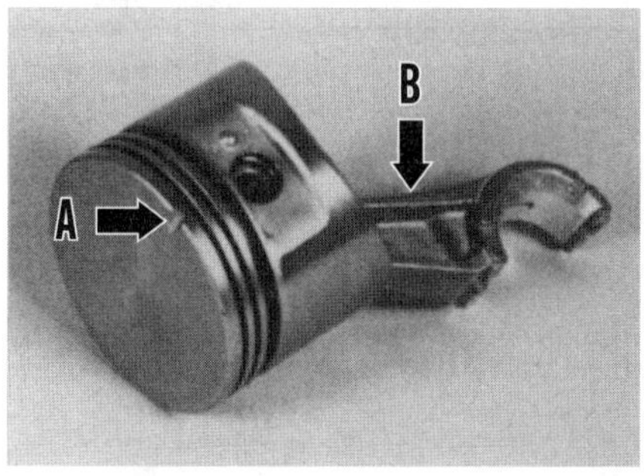

Fig. B672—Assemble connecting rod and piston as shown while noting relation of notch (A) in piston crown and long side of rod (B).

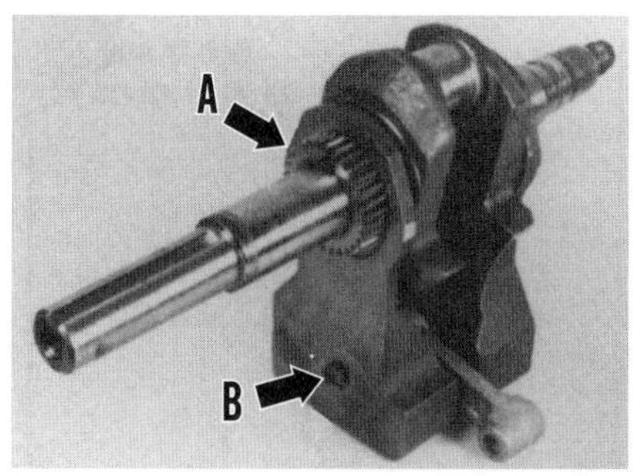

Fig. B673—View of crankshaft and balancer assembly.

Lubricate the crankpin with engine oil. Pull the connecting rod against the crankpin and install the rod cap with the match marks on the rod and cap aligned. Tighten the smaller connecting rod screw to 130 in.-lb. (14.7 N·m) and the larger screw to 260 in.-lb. (29.4 N·m).

CONNECTING ROD

The piston and connecting rod are removed as an assembly. Refer to PISTON, PIN AND RINGS for removal procedure.

Fig. B674—After separating balance weights, remove link.

The connecting rod rides directly on crankpin. Reject size for rod big end diameter is 1.252 in. (31.80 mm). Reject size for small end diameter is 0.802 in. (20.37 mm). A connecting rod with 0.020 in. (0.51 mm) undersize big end diameter is available to accommodate a worn crankpin (machining instructions are included with new rod).

Install the piston and rod assembly in the engine with notch (A—Fig. B672) in the piston crown toward flywheel. Be sure the match marks on the connecting rod and cap are aligned. Tighten the smaller connecting rod screw to 130 in.-lb. (14.7 N·m) and the larger screw to 260 in.-lb. (29.4 N·m).

Install the oil pan as previously outlined in the CAMSHAFT section.

GOVERNOR

The governor weight unit (26—Fig. B667) along with the oil slinger rides on the end of the camshaft. Remove the oil pan to access the governor unit. The governor is serviced as an assembly.

Replace the governor lever shaft bushing in crankcase, if necessary, and ream new bushing after installation to 0.2385-0.2390 inch (6.058-6.071 mm). Briggs & Stratton tool 19333 can be used to ream the bushing.

CRANKSHAFT AND MAIN BEARINGS

The crankshaft rides directly in the oil pan at the PTO end and in a replaceable bushing at the flywheel end. To remove the crankshaft, it is necessary to remove the flywheel, oil pan, camshaft and connecting rod cap. Rotate the crankshaft to position the piston at top dead center, then remove the crankshaft and balancer unit.

Replace the crankshaft if the main bearing journal at either end is 1.376 in. (34.95 mm) or less. Reject size for the crankpin is 1.247 in. (31.67 mm). A connecting rod with 0.020 in. (0.51 mm) undersize big end diameter is available to accommodate a worn crankpin (machining instructions are included with the new rod).

The reject size for the main bearing bore in the crankcase or oil pan is 1.383 in. (35.13 mm) or less. Replace the oil pan if the main bearing bore is excessively worn or damaged. A service bushing is not available for the oil pan. Crankcase is equipped with a replaceable DU bushing in the main bearing bore.

When installing a DU bushing, install the bushing so the oil hole in the bushing and crankcase are aligned. The bushing should be 7/64 inch (2.8 mm) below the face of the crankcase bore. The oil hole must be clear after installation. Stake the bushing into the notches and finish ream the bushing. Do not stake where the bushing is split.

Specified crankshaft end play is 0.002-0.023 inch (0.05-0.58 mm). At least one 0.015 inch crankcase gasket must be in place when measuring end play. Additional gaskets in several sizes are available to aid in end play adjustment.

When reinstalling the crankshaft, make certain the timing marks are aligned (Fig. B668).

NOTE: Do not force the oil pan onto the crankcase. Oil pump rotor must engage drive pin. It may be necessary to remove the oil pump before installing the oil pan.

CYLINDER

If cylinder bore wear is 0.003 inch (0.08 mm) or more or is 0.0015 inch (0.038 mm) or more out-of-round, the cylinder must be bored to the next larger oversize or replaced. Standard cylinder bore diameter is 3.4365-3.4375 inches (87.287-87.313 mm).

SYNCHRO-BALANCER

The engine may be equipped with an oscillating Synchro-Balancer (Fig. B673). Balance weight assembly rides on eccentric journals on the crankshaft and moves in the opposite direction of the piston.

To disassemble the balancer unit, first remove the flywheel, oil pan, camshaft, cylinder head and connecting rod and piston assembly. Carefully pry off the crankshaft gear (A—Fig. B673) and key. Remove the cap screw (B) holding the counterweight halves together. Separate the weights and remove the link (Fig. B674) and dowel pin. Slide the weights off the crankshaft.

Inspect the eccentrics (Fig. B675) on each side of the crankshaft. Replace the eccentrics if they are scored or discolored or otherwise damaged. Replace the eccentric if the outside diameter is equal or less than 2.202 inches (55.93 mm).

Inspect the bushings in the balance weights. Replace the balance weight set if the bushings are scored or discolored or otherwise damaged. Replace the balance weight set if the bushing inside diameter is equal or greater than 2.212 inches (56.18 mm).

To reassemble, install the magneto side weight on the magneto end of the crankshaft. Place the crankshaft (PTO end up) in a vise (Fig. B676). Install the dowel pin and place the link on the pin as shown. Note the rounded edge on the free end of the link must be up (B677). Install the pto side weight, spacers, lock and cap screw. Tighten the cap screw to 115 in.-lb. (13 N·m) and secure with lock tabs. Install the key and crankshaft gear with the chamfer on the inside of the gear facing the shoulder on the crankshaft.

Install the crankshaft and balancer assembly in the crankcase while attaching the free end of the link to the anchor pin in the crankcase. Reassemble the engine.

Fig. B675—Measure outside diameter of eccentric.

Fig. B676—Position balance weight and crankshaft as shown during assembly.

OIL PUMP

The rotor oil pump is located in the oil pan and is driven by the camshaft.

Remove the oil pump cover (35—Fig. B667) from the bottom of the oil pan for access to the oil pump. Extract the pump rotors (32 and 33). Replace any components that are damaged.

Fig. B677—Round side of link end must be toward PTO end of crankshaft.

BRIGGS & STRATTON

VANGUARD OHV ENGINES

Model	Bore	Stroke	Displacement	Power Rating
290400, 294400, 290700, 294700, 303400, 303700	68 mm (2.68 in.)	66 mm (2.60 in.)	480 cc (29.3 cu. in.)	11.9 kW (16 hp)

ENGINE INFORMATION

NOTE: Metric fasteners are used throughout the engine except the threaded hole in the PTO end of the crankshaft, flange mounting holes and flywheel puller holes, which are US threads.

The Vanguard models included in this section are air-cooled, four-stroke, twin-cylinder engines. Models 290400, 294400 and 303400 have a horizontal crankshaft while Models 290700, 294700 and 303700 have a vertical crankshaft. All models are equipped with an overhead valve system. The number 1 cylinder is nearer to the flywheel. The cylinder number is marked on the cylinder side nearest flywheel.

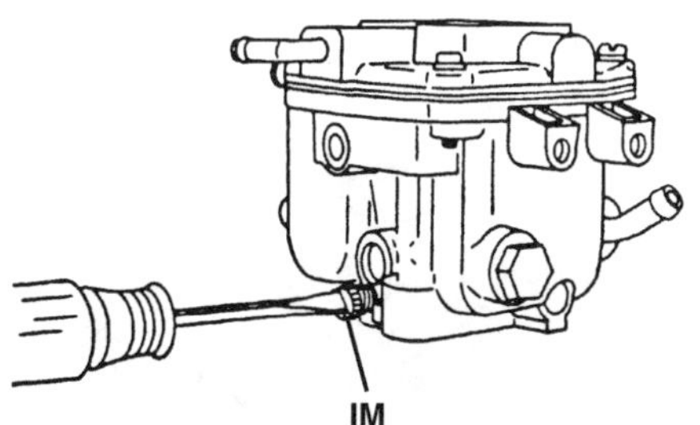

Fig. B201—View showing location of carburetor idle mixture screw (IM) on horizontal crankshaft models.

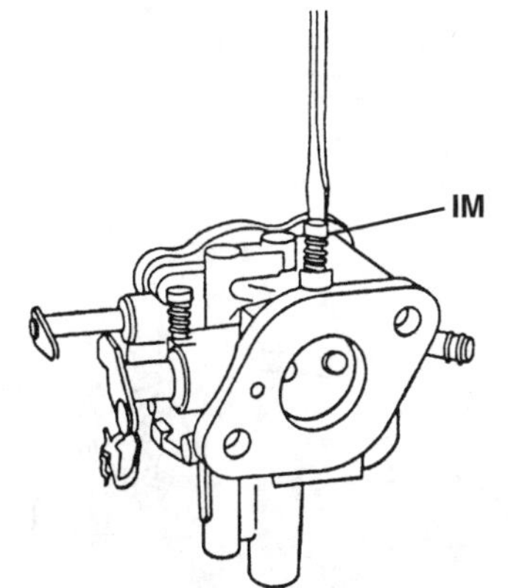

Fig. B202—View showing location of carburetor idle mixture screw (IM) on vertical crankshaft models.

MAINTENANCE

SPARK PLUG

The recommended spark plug is either an Autolite 3924 or Champion RC12YC. The specified spark plug electrode gap is 0.76 mm (0.030 in.). Tighten spark plug to 19 N·m (165 in.-lbs.).

CAUTION: Briggs & Stratton does not recommend using abrasive blasting to clean spark plugs as this may introduce some abrasive material into the engine that could cause extensive damage.

FUEL FILTER

The fuel tank is equipped with a filter at the outlet and an inline filter may also be installed. Check filters periodically during the operating season and clean or replace as necessary.

CARBURETOR

Adjustment

Initial adjustment of the idle mixture screw (IM—Fig. B201 or Fig. B202) is 1¼ turns out from the seated position. Remove the air cleaner, carburetor cover and valley cover, if so equipped, for access to the governor linkage. Place the remote speed control in the idle position. Bend the throttle restrictor tang shown in Fig. B203 so the throttle cannot open greater than ¼ open.

Start and run the engine until its operating temperature is reached. Place the remote speed control in the idle position. Hold the carburetor throttle lever against the idle speed adjusting screw and adjust the idle speed to 1400 rpm if the governor idle spring (S—Fig. B204) is red, or to 1100 rpm if the governor idle spring is white.

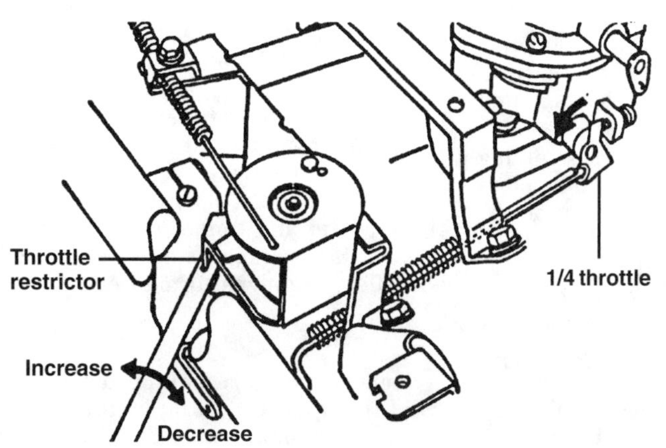

Fig. B203—When adjusting carburetor, bend throttle restrictor tang so throttle cannot open greater than ¼ open as outlined in text.

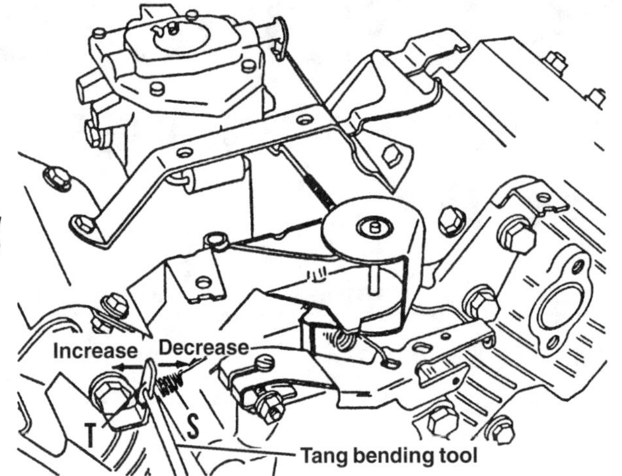

Fig. B204—Adjust governed idle speed as outlined in text.

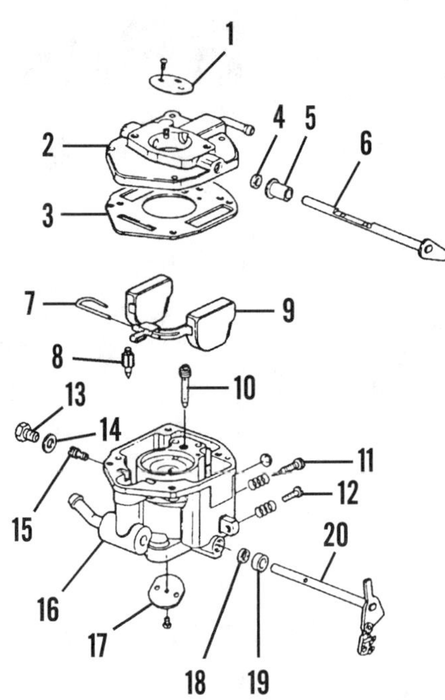

Fig. B205—Exploded view of carburetor used on horizontal crankshaft models.

1. Choke plate
2. Cover
3. Gasket
4. Seal
5. Collar
6. Choke shaft
7. Float pin
8. Fuel inlet valve
9. Float
10. Nozzle
11. Idle mixture screw
12. Idle speed screw
13. Plug
14. Gasket
15. Main jet
16. Body
17. Throttle plate
18. Seal
19. Collar
20. Throttle shaft

With the throttle lever against the idle speed adjusting screw, turn the idle mixture screw clockwise until there is a reduction in engine speed and note the screw position. Back out the idle mixture screw until engine speed lessens again and note the screw position. Rotate the screw so it is halfway between the lean and rich positions.

With the throttle lever against the idle speed screw, readjust idle speed to 1200 rpm if the governor idle spring is red, or to 900 rpm if the governor idle spring is white. Release the throttle lever.

With the remote control in idle position, bend the tab (T—Fig. B204), to obtain 1400 rpm if the governor idle spring is red, or to 1100 rpm if the governor idle spring is white.

All models are equipped with a fixed high-speed jet. An optional jet for high altitude operation is offered on vertical crankshaft models.

Overhaul

Horizontal Crankshaft Models

Refer to Fig. B205 for an exploded view of the carburetor. Clean the parts in a suitable carburetor cleaner. Do not use wire or drill bits to clean the fuel passages as carburetor calibration may be affected if the passages are enlarged. Inspect parts for wear or damage and replace when necessary.

Note the following when assembling the carburetor: Install the choke plate so the hole in the plate is towards the vent tube (Fig. B206). Install the throttle plate so the flat portion (not sharp edge) of the chamfers on the plate fit against the carburetor bore when the plate and shaft are installed in the carburetor.

With the fuel inlet valve and float installed in the carburetor body, press lightly against the fuel valve so it bottoms against its seat. The top of the float should be parallel with the gasket surface of the body (see Fig. B207). Adjust the float level by bending the float tang.

Note that the spacer between the carburetor and intake manifold has an indexing pin that must fit into the intake manifold. Tighten the carburetor mounting screws to 7 N·m (62 in.-lbs.).

Vertical Crankshaft Models

Refer to Fig. B208 for an exploded view of the carburetor. Clean parts in a suitable carburetor cleaner. Do not use wire or drill bits to clean the fuel passages as carburetor calibration may be affected if the passages are enlarged.

To check the float level, invert the carburetor body as shown in Fig. B209. The float should be parallel with the bowl mating surface. Bend the float tang to adjust the float level. Tighten the carburetor mounting screws to 7 N·m (62 in.-lbs.).

ANTI-AFTERFIRE SYSTEM

Some models are equipped with an anti-afterfire system that stops fuel flow through the carburetor when the ignition switch is in off position. A solenoid inserts a plunger into the main jet to stop fuel flow. Refer to Fig. B210 for a drawing of the anti-afterfire system.

To test solenoid operation, remove the solenoid and connect a 9-volt battery to the solenoid. A faulty solenoid will affect engine performance.

FUEL PUMP

Some models are equipped with a vacuum operated, diaphragm fuel pump. Individual components are not

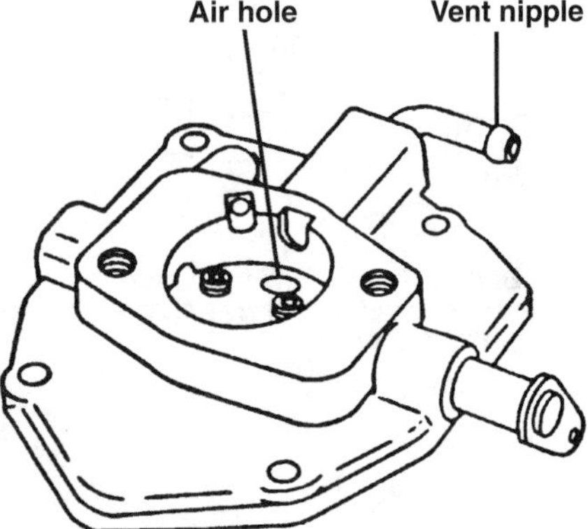

Fig. B206—Install choke plate so the hole in the plate is toward the vent.

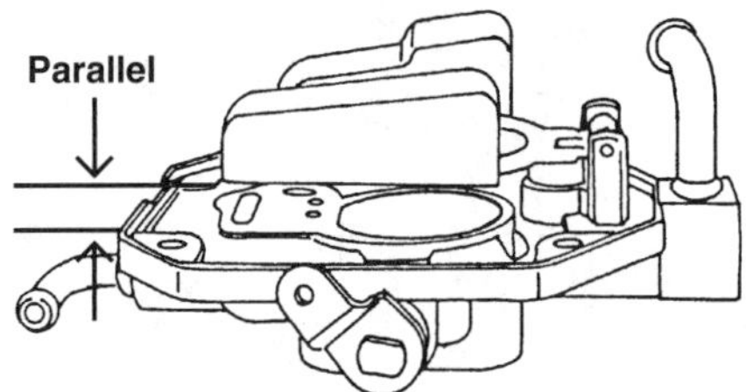

Fig. B207—Float must be parallel to body surface. Bend float tang to adjust.

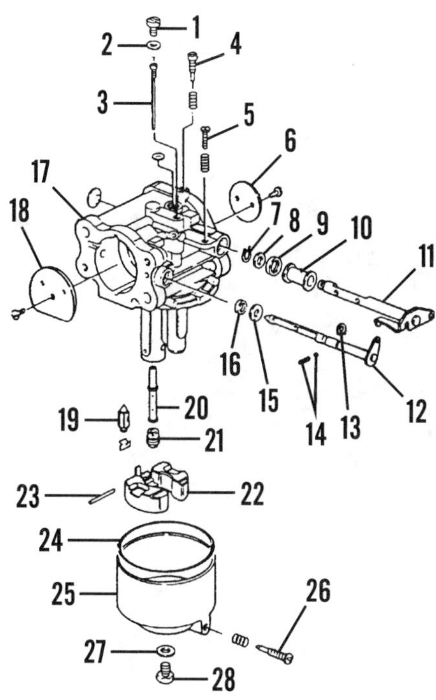

Fig. B208—Exploded view of carburetor used on vertical crankshaft models.

1. Plug
2. Washer
3. Idle jet
4. Idle mixture screw
5. Idle speed screw
6. Throttle plate
7. Clip
8. Washer
9. Seal
10. Collar
11. Throttle shaft
12. Choke shaft
13. Clip
14. Choke detent spring & ball
15. Washer
16. Seal
17. Body
18. Choke plate
19. Fuel inlet valve
20. Nozzle
21. Main jet
22. Float
23. Pin
24. Gasket
25. Fuel bowl
26. Drain screw
27. Gasket
28. Screw

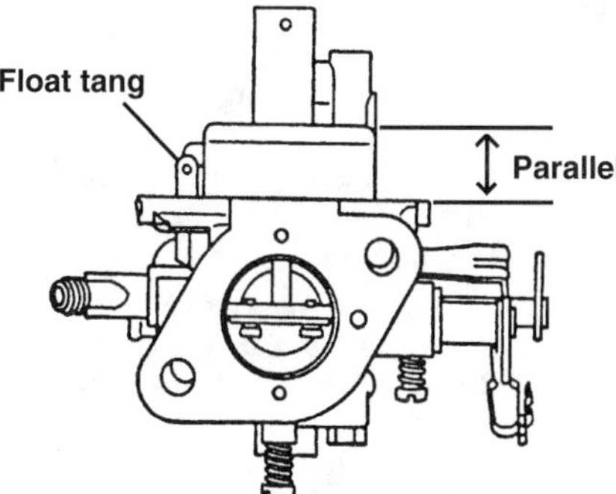

Fig. B209—Float must be level with body surface. Bend float tang to adjust.

available. If the pump is faulty, it must be serviced as a unit assembly.

CARBURETOR CONTROL MECHANISM

To assure proper speed control, measure the travel of the remote control wire with the remote control unit installed. Minimum wire travel is 1⅜ inches as shown in Fig. B211.

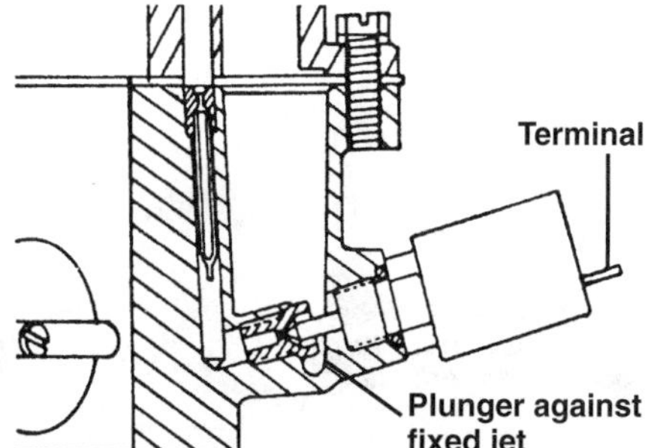

Fig. B210—Drawing of anti-afterfire solenoid used on some carburetors.

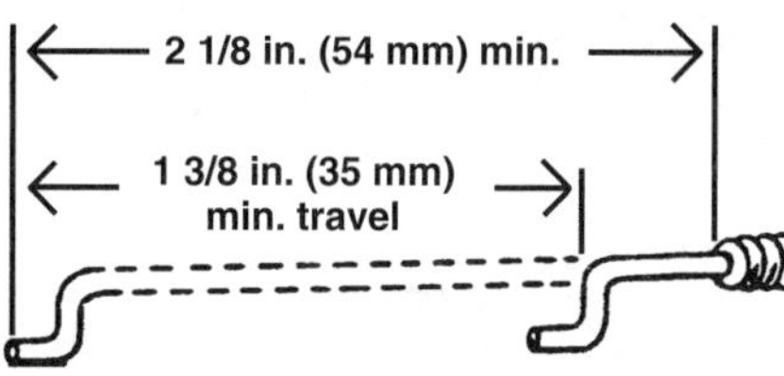

Fig. B211—Remote control wire must extend and travel to dimensions shown above.

To adjust the speed control cable, move the remote control lever to the idle position. The carburetor throttle lever should contact the idle speed screw. If not, loosen the cable housing clamp and reposition the cable housing.

The remote choke control should completely close the carburetor choke plate when the remote control is in the CHOKE position. If necessary, loosen the cable clamp and reposition the cable to synchronize the carburetor choke and remote control.

GOVERNOR

The engine is equipped with a mechanical, flyweight governor. To adjust governor linkage, proceed as follows: Remove the air cleaner for access to the governor linkage. Loosen the governor lever clamp nut (N—Fig. B212). Rotate the governor lever (L) so the throttle plate is fully open and hold the lever in place. Turn the governor shaft (S) counterclockwise as far as possible, then tighten the nut (N) to 8 N·m (71 in.-lbs.).

No-load governed top speed is adjusted by bending the tang at the end of the governor spring (G). Normal governed speed is 3600 rpm unless specified otherwise by the equipment manufacturer.

The governor flyweight assembly is mounted on the end of the camshaft. Refer to the CAMSHAFT and GOVERNOR SHAFT sections if internal service is required.

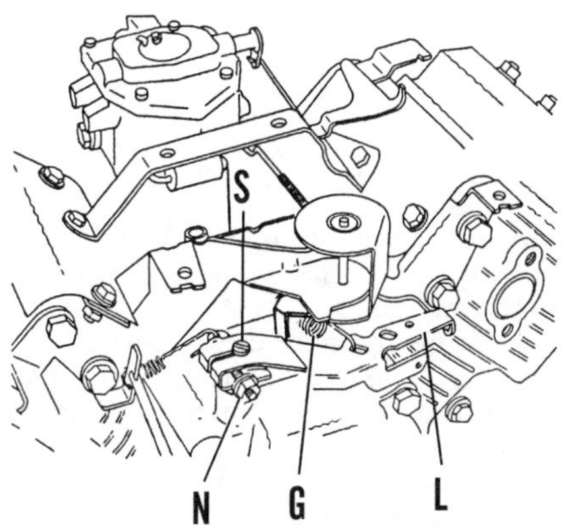

Fig. B212—To adjust governor, loosen governor lever clamp nut (N), rotate governor lever (L) so throttle plate is fully open and hold lever in place. Turn governor shaft (S) counterclockwise and retighten nut.

IGNITION SYSTEM

All models are equipped with a Magnetron ignition system.

To check for a spark, remove the spark plug and connect the spark plug cable to B&S tester 19051. Ground the remaining tester lead to the engine. Crank the engine at 350 rpm or more. If a spark jumps the 4.2 mm (0.166 in.) tester gap, the system is functioning properly.

To remove the armature and Magnetron module, remove the flywheel shroud. Disconnect the stop switch wire from the module. Remove the armature retaining screws and remove the Magnetron unit.

Position the armature so the air gap between armature legs and flywheel surface is 0.20-0.30 mm (0.008-0.012 in.).

VALVE ADJUSTMENT

Adjust valve clearance with the engine cold. Remove the rocker arm covers. Remove the spark plugs. Rotate the crankshaft so the No. 1 piston is at top dead center on the compression stroke. Using a suitable measuring device inserted through the spark plug hole, continue to rotate the crankshaft clockwise as viewed at the flywheel end so the piston is 6.35 mm (0.250 in.) past TDC.

Measure the clearance between the rocker arm and valve stem with a feeler gauge. Specified clearance is 0.10-0.16 mm (0.004-0.006 in.) for intake and exhaust. To adjust, loosen the lock nut (Fig. B213) and turn the adjusting screw to obtain desired clearance. Tighten the lock screw to 7 N·m (62 in.-lbs.).

Rotate the crankshaft one complete revolution and repeat the adjustment procedure for the No. 2 cylinder.

Install the valve covers and tighten the mounting screws to 3 N·m (27 in.-lbs.).

LUBRICATION

A rotor oil pump attached to the crankcase cover provides lubricating oil to the engine.

Periodically check the oil level; do not overfill. The oil dipstick should be screwed in until bottomed for a correct oil level reading.

Change the oil after first eight hours of operation and every 50 hours thereafter under normal operating conditions. Recommended oil change interval is 25 hours if severe service is encountered.

The engine may be equipped with a spin-on oil filter. If so equipped, the manufacturer recommends changing the oil filter after every 100 hours of operation. The filter should be changed more frequently if engine is operated in a severe environment.

Use engine oil that meets the latest API service classification. SAE 30 oil may be used when temperatures are above 40°F (4°C); SAE 10W-30 oil may be used for temperatures between 0°F (-18°C) and 100°F (38°C); below 0°F (-18°C) use petroleum based SAE 5W-20 or a suitable synthetic oil.

Crankcase capacity is 1.65 liters (3.5 pints) if equipped with an oil filter, 1.42 liters (3 pints) if not equipped with a filter.

A low oil pressure switch may be located on the oil filter housing. If so equipped, the switch should be closed at zero pressure and open at 31 kPa (4.5 psi).

CRANKCASE BREATHER

The engine is equipped with a crankcase breather that provides a vacuum for the crankcase. Vapor from the crankcase is evacuated to the air cleaner. A fiber disk acts as a one-way valve to maintain crankcase vacuum. The breather system must operate properly or excessive oil consumption may result.

The breather assembly is located in the valley between the cylinders. It should be possible to insert a 1 mm (0.045 in.) diameter wire between the fiber disc and breather body. Do not use excessive force when measuring the gap.

The disc should not stick or bind during operation. Replace the breather if the disc is distorted or damaged. Inspect the breather tube for leakage.

CYLINDER HEAD

Manufacturer recommends that after every 500 hours of operation the cylinder heads should be removed and cleaned of deposits.

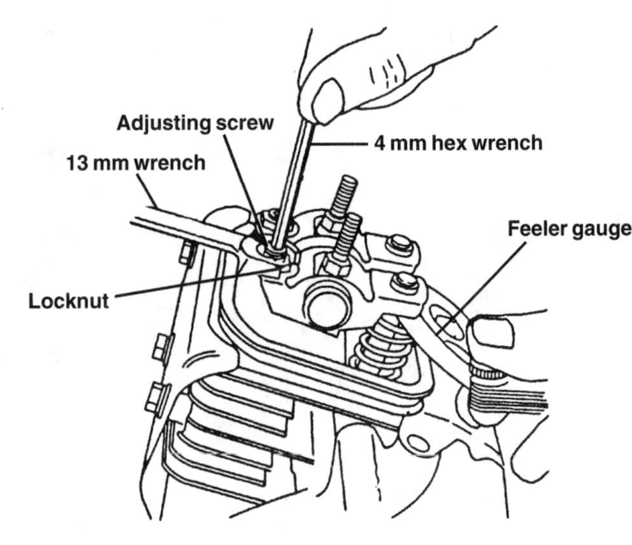

Fig. B213—After loosening lock nut, turn rocker arm adjusting screw so valve clearance is 0.10-0.16 mm (0.004-0.006 in.).

1/32 in. (.8 mm) fit for use

Margin

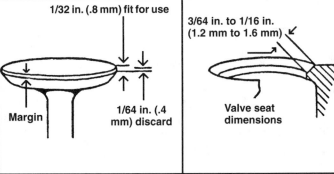

1/64 in. (.4 mm) discard

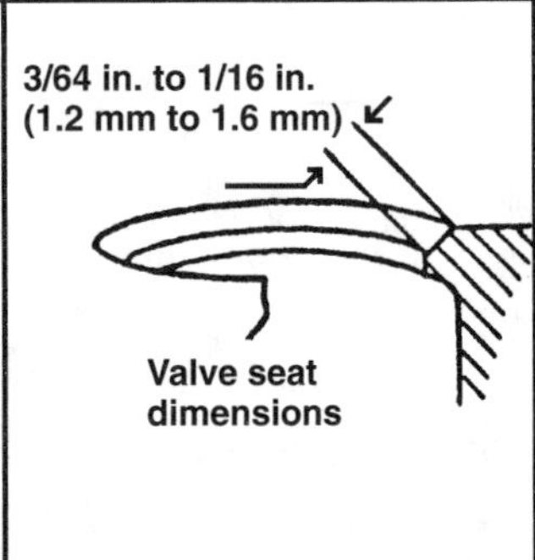

Fig. B214—Valve and valve seat dimensions.

REPAIRS

TIGHTENING TORQUES

Recommended tightening torque specifications are as follows:

Carburetor mounting screws	7 N·m (62 in.-lbs.)
Connecting rod	13 N·m (115 in.-lbs.)
Crankcase cover	17 N·m (150 in.-lbs.)
Cylinder head	19 N·m (165 in.-lbs.)
Flywheel nut	175 N·m (129 ft.-lbs.)
Oil pump	7 N·m (62 in.-lbs.)
Rewind starter	7 N·m (62 in.-lbs.)
Rocker arm cover	3.0 N·m (27 in.-lbs.)
Rocker arm lock screw	7 N·m (62 in.-lbs.)
Rocker shaft stud	16 N·m (142 in.-lbs.)
Spark plug	22.5 N·m (200 in.-lbs.)

CYLINDER HEAD

Cylinder heads are not interchangeable. Cylinder number is cast in area adjacent to the valve springs.

To remove the cylinder head, first remove the carburetor, intake manifold, muffler, exhaust manifold, air baffles and shields. Remove the rocker arm cover, rocker arms and push rods. Unscrew the cylinder head bolts and remove the cylinder head.

Valve face and seat angles are 45° for intake and exhaust. Specified seat width is 1.2-1.6 mm (0.047-0.063 in.). Minimum allowable valve margin is 0.4 mm (0.016 in.). See Fig. B214

The cylinder head is equipped with replaceable valve guides for both valves. Reject the guide if the inside diameter is 6.057 mm (0.2385 in.) or more. Use B&S tool 19274 to remove and install the guides. Guides may be installed either way. Top of the guide should protrude 7 mm (0.276 in.) as shown in Fig. B215. Use B&S tools 19345 and 19346 to ream the new valve guide to the correct size.

Note the following when installing the cylinder head: Do not apply sealer to the cylinder head gasket. Sealing washers are used under the heads of the two cylinder head bolts adjacent to the rocker shaft. Tighten the cylinder head bolts using the sequence shown in Fig. B216. Tighten the bolts in three

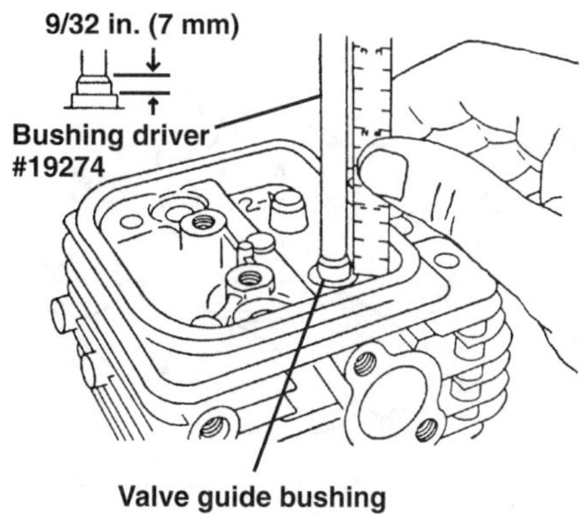

Fig. B215—Install valve guide so standout is 7 mm (0.276 in.) as shown above.

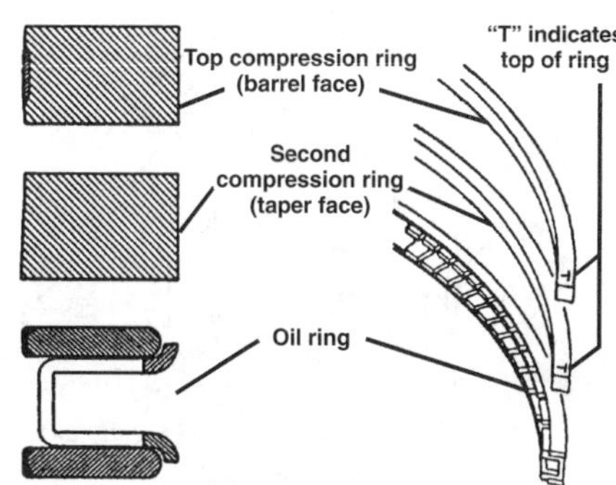

Fig. B218—Drawing showing correct installation of piston rings.

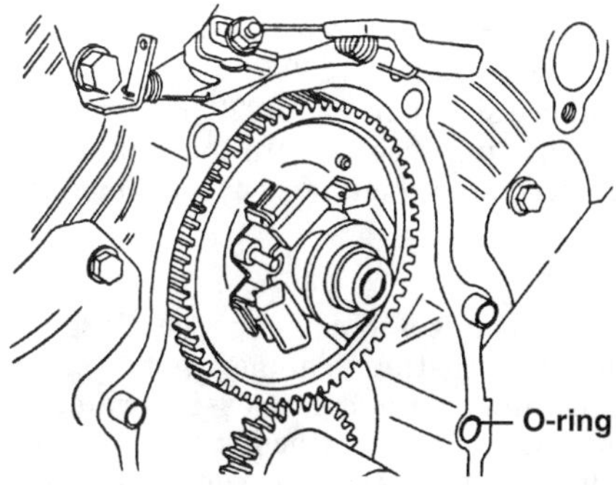

Fig. B221—Be sure O-ring (R) is in place before installing crankcase cover.

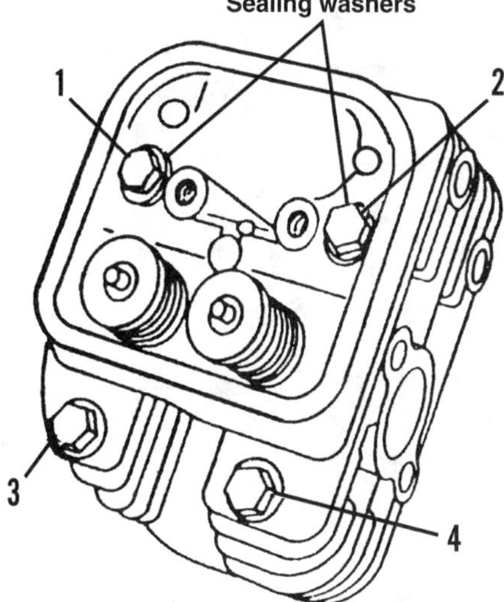

Fig. B216—Follow sequence shown above when tightening cylinder head bolts.

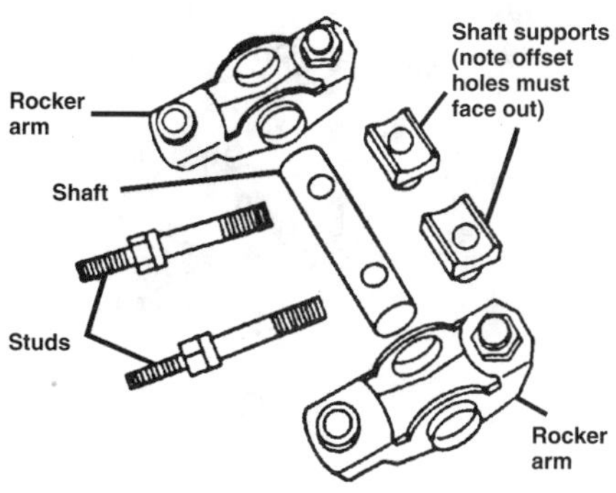

Fig. B217—Offset hole in rocker shaft supports must be nearer end of rocker shaft.

steps until final torque reading of 19 N·m (165 in.-lbs.) is obtained.

Rocker shaft studs are threaded into the cylinder head. Note that the rocker shaft stands have offset holes. The hole must be nearer the end of the shaft as shown in Fig. B217. Tighten the studs to 16 N·m (142 in.-lbs.).

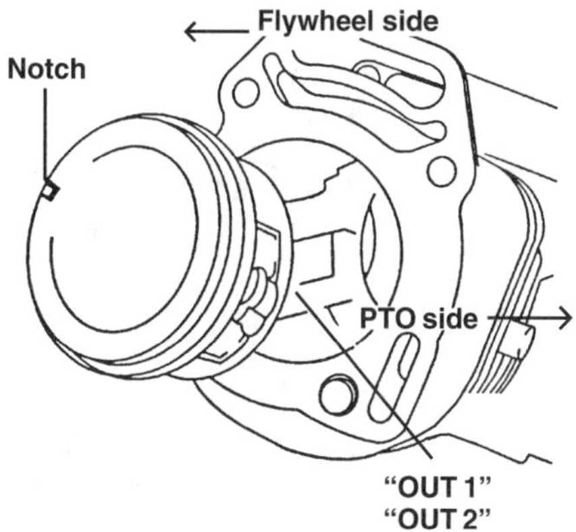

Fig. B219—Install piston and rod so notch in piston crown is toward flywheel and "OUT" mark on rod is toward PTO end of crankshaft.

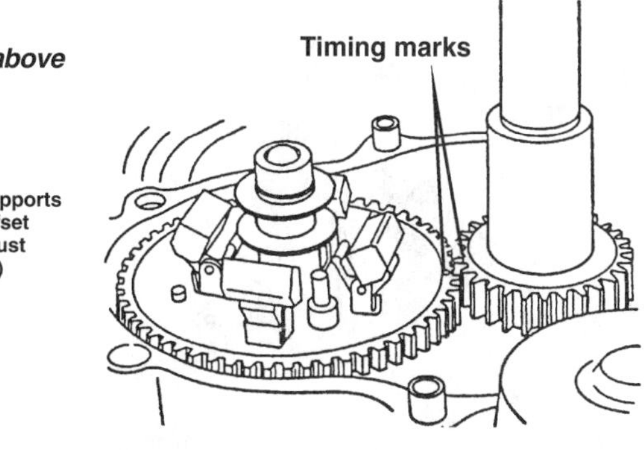

Fig. B220—Timing marks must align after installation of camshaft and crankshaft.

PISTON, PIN, RINGS AND CONNECTING ROD

To remove the piston and rod assemblies, drain the engine oil and remove the engine from the tractor. Remove the cylinder heads as previously outlined. Remove carbon or ring ridge (if present) from the top of the cylinder bore.

Clean the PTO end of the crankshaft and remove any burrs or rust. Unscrew the fasteners and remove the crankcase cover. Rotate the crankshaft so the timing marks on the crankshaft and camshaft gears are aligned. This will position the valve tappets out of way. Remove the camshaft.

Mark the connecting rods and caps so they can be installed in their original positions. Unscrew the connecting rod screws and remove piston and rod.

Inspect pistons for scoring, scuffing or excessive wear and replace when necessary. Check piston ring grooves for wear by inserting new rings in the grooves and measure the side clearance between the ring and ring land using a feeler gage. Replace the piston if ring side clearance exceeds 0.10 mm (0.004 in.) for compression rings and 0.20 mm (0.008 in.) for oil ring.

Piston pin is a slip fit in the piston and rod. Reject size for piston pin diameter is 17.056 mm (0.6715 in.). Reject size for pin bore in piston is 17.109 mm (0.6736 in.).

The connecting rod rides directly on the crankpin. The reject size for rod big end diameter is 37.109 mm (1.461 in.) and reject size for small end diameter is 17.081 mm (0.6725 in.). A connecting rod with 0.51 mm (0.020 in.) undersize big end diameter is available to accommodate a worn crankpin (machining instructions are included with the new rod).

Install the compression rings on the piston with the T-side towards the piston crown (Fig. B218). When assembling the piston and rod, be sure the notch in the piston crown is towards the flywheel and the OUT side of the rod is towards the PTO end of the engine (Fig. B219).

Install the rod cap so the marks on the rod and cap align and tighten rod screws to 13 N·m (115 in.-lbs.).

Install the camshaft while aligning the timing marks (Fig. B220) on the crankshaft and camshaft gears. Be sure the governor arm is in the proper position to contact the governor slider on the camshaft. Be sure the O-ring (R—Fig. B221) is in place. Install the crankcase cover and tighten the cover screws to 17 N·m (150 in.-lbs.) in the sequence shown in Fig. B222. Do not force the mating of cover with the crankcase. Reassemble remainder of components.

CAMSHAFT

Camshaft and camshaft gear are an integral casting. The governor weight assembly and compression release mechanism are attached to the camshaft. Camshaft, governor and compression release are available only as a unit assembly.

To remove the camshaft, proceed as follows: Remove the engine from the tractor and drain the crankcase oil. Clean the PTO end of the crankshaft and remove any burrs or rust. Remove the rocker arm push rods and mark them so they can be returned to their original position. Unscrew the fasteners and remove the crankcase cover.

Rotate the crankshaft so the timing marks on the crankshaft and camshaft gears are aligned. This will position valve tappets out of way. Remove the camshaft and tappets. Mark the tappets as they are removed so they can be returned to their original position.

The reject size for camshaft bearing journal at the flywheel end is 15.913 mm (0.6265 in.); the reject size for the bearing journal at the PTO end is 19.913 mm (0.7840 in.). The reject size for camshaft lobes is 30.25 mm (1.191 in.).

Be sure the compression release and governor components operate freely without binding. Check for loose and excessively worn parts.

Reverse the removal procedure to install components. Install the camshaft while aligning the timing marks (Fig. B220) on the crankshaft and camshaft gears. Be sure the governor arm is in the proper position to contact the governor slider on the camshaft. Be sure the O-ring (R—Fig. B221) is in place.

Install the crankcase cover and tighten the cover screws to 17 N·m (150 in.-lbs.) in the sequence shown in Fig. B222. Do not force the mating of the cover with the crankcase. Reassemble remainder of components.

CRANKSHAFT

The crankshaft is supported at the flywheel end by a bushing in the cylinder block and by a ball bearing at the PTO end. To remove the crankshaft, remove the engine from the tractor. Drain the engine oil. Remove the blower housing and flywheel. Remove the crankcase cover and camshaft as previously described. Remove the connecting rod caps and push the connecting rods and

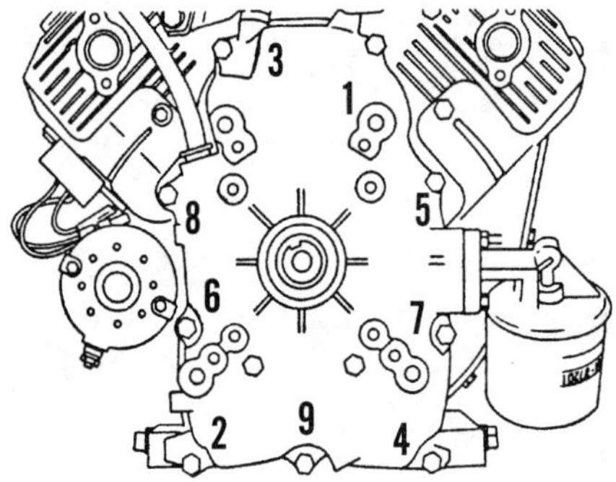

Fig. B222—Follow sequence shown above when tightening crankcase cover screws.

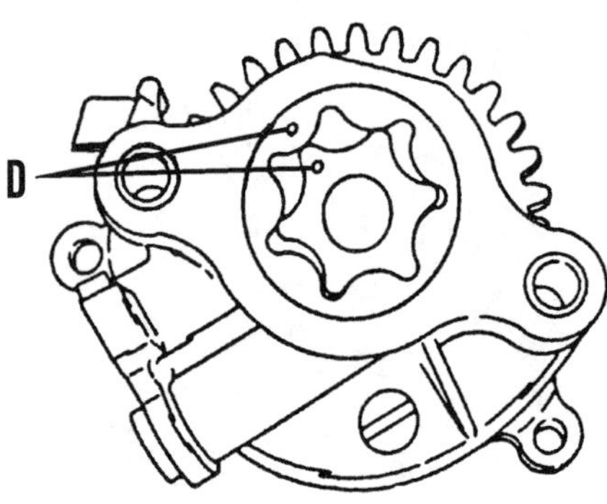

Fig. B223—Install oil pump rotors so dimples (D) are on same side.

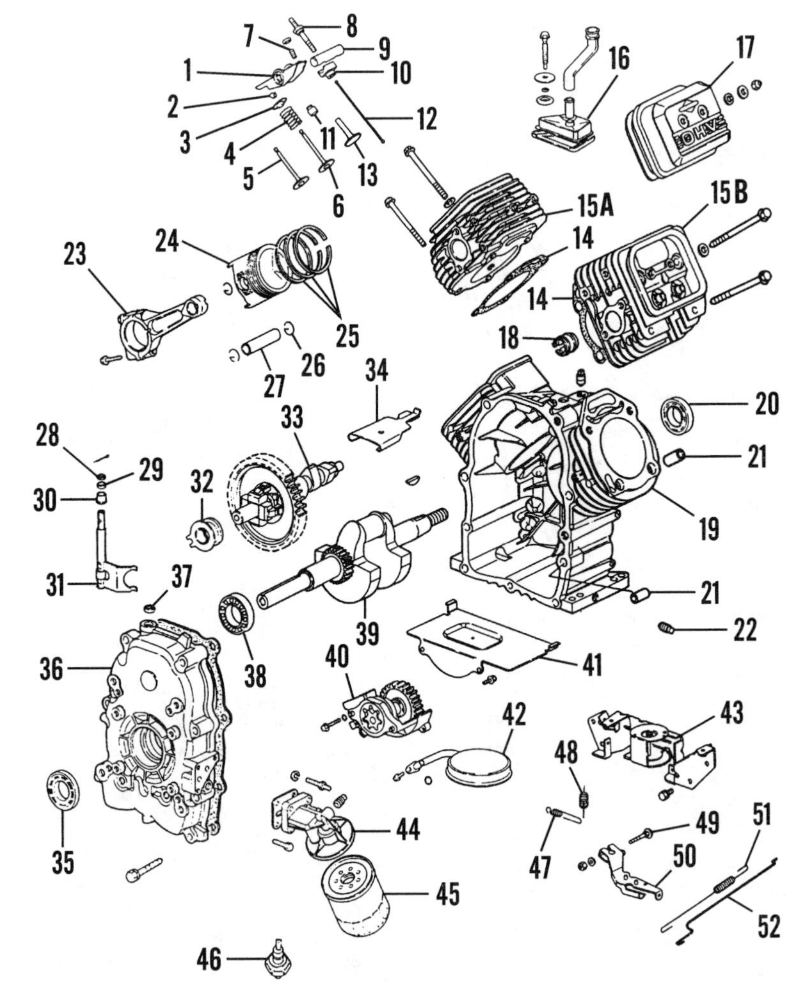

Fig. B224—Exploded view of horizontal crankshaft engine.

1. Rocker arm
2. Split retainer
3. Spring retainer
4. Spring
5. Intake valve
6. Exhaust valve
7. Adjusting screw
8. Rocker stud
9. Rocker shaft
10. Support
11. Seal
12. Push rod
13. Tappet
14. Head gasket
15A. Cylinder head, No. 1
15B. Cylinder head, No. 2
16. Crankcase breather
17. Valve cover
18. Exhaust port liner
19. Cylinder block
20. Oil seal
21. Dowels
22. Oil drain plug
23. Connecting rod
24. Piston
25. Piston rings
26. Retaining rings
27. Piston pin
28. Seal
29. Bushing
30. Bushing
31. Governor shaft
32. Governor slider
33. Camshaft & governor assy.
34. Baffle
35. Oil seal
36. Crankcase cover
37. Washer
38. Main bearing
39. Crankshaft
40. Oil pump
41. Windage plate
42. Oil pickup screen
43. Governor bracket
44. Oil filter adaptor
45. Oil filter
46. Oil pressure switch
47. Governor idle spring
48. Governor spring
49. Clamp bolt
50. Governor lever
51. Link spring
52. Governor link

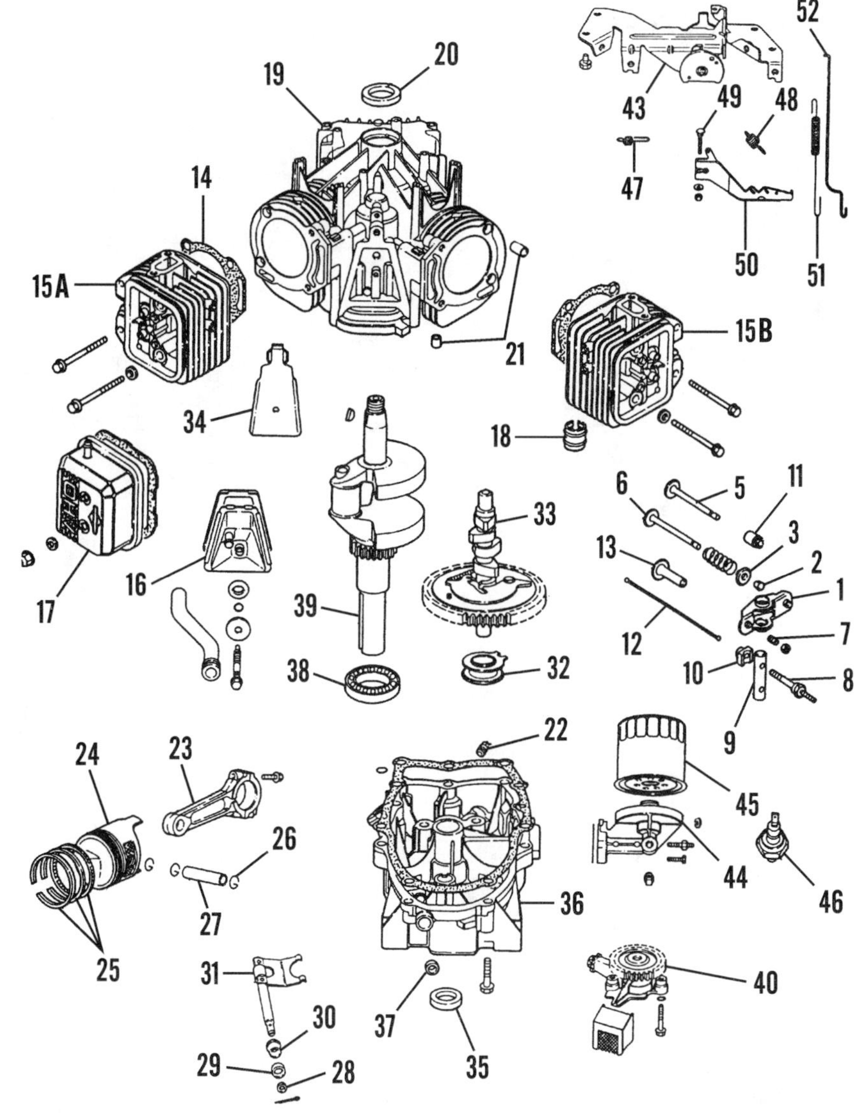

Fig. B225—Exploded view of vertical crankshaft engine. Refer to Fig. 224 for parts identification.

pistons away from the crankpin. Remove the crankshaft from the cylinder block.

Reject the crankshaft if worn to 34.943 mm (1.3757 in.) or less at the pto bearing journal or if worn to 29.95 mm (1.179 in.) or less at the flywheel bearing end.

Regrind the crankpin or replace the crankshaft if crankpin diameter is worn to 36.957 mm (1.4550 in.) or less. A 0.51 mm (0.020 in.) undersize connecting rod is available for use on a reground crankpin.

CYLINDER BLOCK

Standard cylinder bore diameter is 68.000-68.025 mm (2.6772-2.6781 inches). If cylinder bore wear exceeds 0.076 mm (0.003 in.) or if out-of-round of bore exceeds 0.038 mm (0.0015 in.), the cylinder should be bored to the next oversize or replaced.

Replace the main bearing at the flywheel side if the bore is 30.08 mm (1.184 in.) or less. Install a new bearing bushing so the notch is facing out and the locating pin hole and oil hole are aligned. Replace the crankcase cover if the bearing bore is 35.06 mm (1.380 in.) or less.

OIL PUMP

The rotor type oil pump is located in the crankcase cover and driven by the camshaft. Remove the crankcase cover for access to the pump.

Note that the pump rotors are installed so that the dimples (D—Fig. B223) are on the same side. Replace any components that are damaged or excessively worn. Tighten oil pump mounting screws to 7 N·m (62 in.-lbs.).

When installing the crankcase cover, be sure the governor arm is in the proper position to contact the governor slider on the camshaft. Be sure the O-ring (R—Fig. B221) is in place. Install the crankcase cover and tighten the cover screws to 17 N·m (150 in.-lbs.) in the sequence shown in Fig. B222. Do not force the mating of the cover with the crankcase. Reassemble the remainder of the components.

GOVERNOR SHAFT

The governor shaft, which is located in the crankcase cover, transmits motion from the governor assembly on the camshaft to the governor linkage. The shaft rides in two bushings in the cover.

Remove the crankcase cover for access to the shaft and bushings. Upper bushing is replaceable, but lower bushing is not. If the lower bushing is damaged, replace the crankcase cover.

When installing the crankcase cover, be sure the governor arm is in proper position to contact the governor slider on the camshaft. Be sure the O-ring (R—Fig. B221) is in place.

Install the crankcase cover and tighten the cover screws to 17 N·m (150 in.-lbs.) in sequence shown in Fig. B222. Do not force the mating of the cover with the crankcase. Reassemble the remainder of the components.

NOTES

HONDA

Model	No. Cyls.	Bore	Stroke	Displacement	Power Rating
GX360	2	58 mm (2.28 in.)	68 mm (2.68 in.)	359 cc (21.9 cu. in.)	9.7 kW (13 hp)

Model GX360 is a four-stroke, overhead cam, single cylinder, liquid cooled engine with a horizontal crankshaft.

MAINTENANCE

LUBRICATION

The engine oil level should be checked prior to operating the engine. Check the oil level with oil cap not screwed in, but just touching the first threads of the oil filler neck. Maintain the oil level between the upper and lower marks on the dipstick.

The oil should be changed after the first 20 hours of engine operation and every 100 hours thereafter. Change the oil filter after every 300 hours of operation or after two years, whichever occurs first.

Use SAE 10W-30 or 10W-40 oil. Crankcase capacity is 1.4 liters (1.5 qt.). After changing the oil filter, operate the engine for a few minutes and then recheck the oil level. Add oil if necessary.

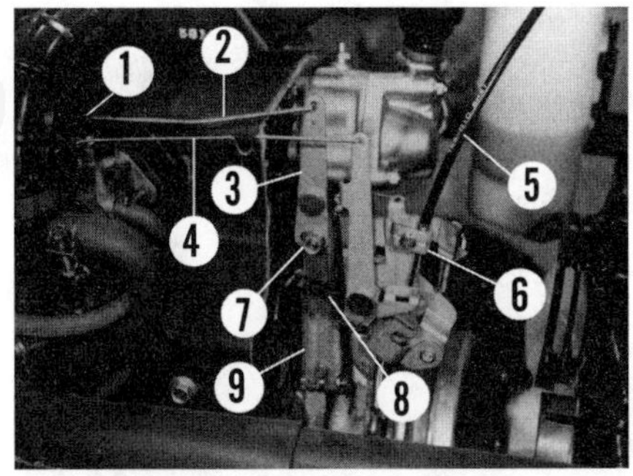

Fig. HE1-1—View of speed control linkage. Refer to text for adjustment procedure.

1. Carburetor throttle arm
2. Throttle link
3. Upper governor lever
4. Choke link
5. Throttle control cable
6. Cable clamp
7. Screw
8. Governor spring
9. Lower governor lever

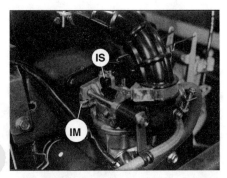

Fig. HE1-2—Adjust idle speed mixture screw (IS) and idle stop screw (IM) as outlined in text.

AIR CLEANER

Engine is equipped with a dry type air filter that should be cleaned and inspected after every 50 hours of operation. Replace the filter elements if holes, tears or other damage is evident.

Remove the foam and paper air filter elements from the air filter housing. Foam element should be washed in a mild detergent and water solution, rinsed in clean water and allowed to air dry. After drying, soak the foam element in clean engine oil. Squeeze out excess oil.

Gently tap the paper element to remove dust and other debris from the outside of the element. Low-pressure compressed air can be directed from the inside of the element toward the outside to remove dust and dirt from the element.

Reinstall the elements.

COOLANT SYSTEM

The engine is cooled by a 50:50 mixture of clean water and permanent antifreeze. Refer to the tractor section for maintenance requirements.

SPARK PLUG

The spark plug should be removed, cleaned and inspected after every 100 hours of use.

Recommended spark plug is a NGK BPR4HS. The spark plug electrode gap should be 0.6-0.7 mm (0.024-0.028 in.).

When installing the spark plug, install the spark plug finger tight. Then for a new plug, tighten an additional $\frac{1}{2}$ turn. For a used plug, tighten an additional $\frac{1}{4}$ turn.

CARBURETOR

The engine is equipped with a Keihin float carburetor with a fixed main fuel jet and an adjustable idle speed fuel mixture needle.

Proceed as follows to adjust the throttle control cable. Move the throttle control lever to the FAST position. Loosen the cable clamp (6—Fig. HE1-1) at the engine end of the throttle cable, then rotate the adjusting nuts at the upper end of the cable so the bottom end of the cable housing is flush with the bottom edge of the clamp (6).

To adjust the choke operation, move the throttle control lever to the START position. The choke plate in the carburetor should be closed. If necessary, bend the choke link (4) at the "U" to adjust the choke plate position.

Initial adjustment setting for the idle mixture screw (IS—Fig. HE1-2) is $1\frac{3}{4}$ turns out on Models HT3813 and HT4213. Initial idle mixture screw adjustment on Model H4514H is $1\frac{1}{4}$ turns out. Perform the final adjustment with the engine at normal operating temperature and running.

Operate the engine at idle speed and adjust the idle mixture screw (LS) to obtain a smooth idle and satisfactory acceleration. Adjust the idle speed by turning the idle speed screw (IM). Recommended idle speed is 1300-1500 rpm.

GOVERNOR

A mechanical flyweight governor is located inside a compartment on front of engine. Refer to the REPAIRS section for service information.

Before adjusting the external linkage, check the carburetor control adjustments described in previous section.

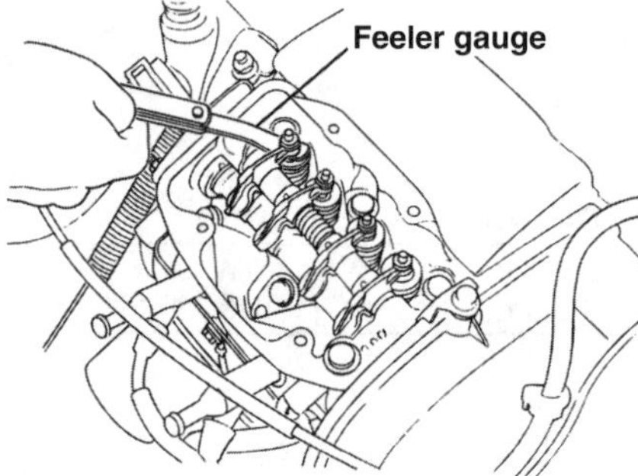

Fig. HE1-3—Check valve clearance with a feeler gauge.

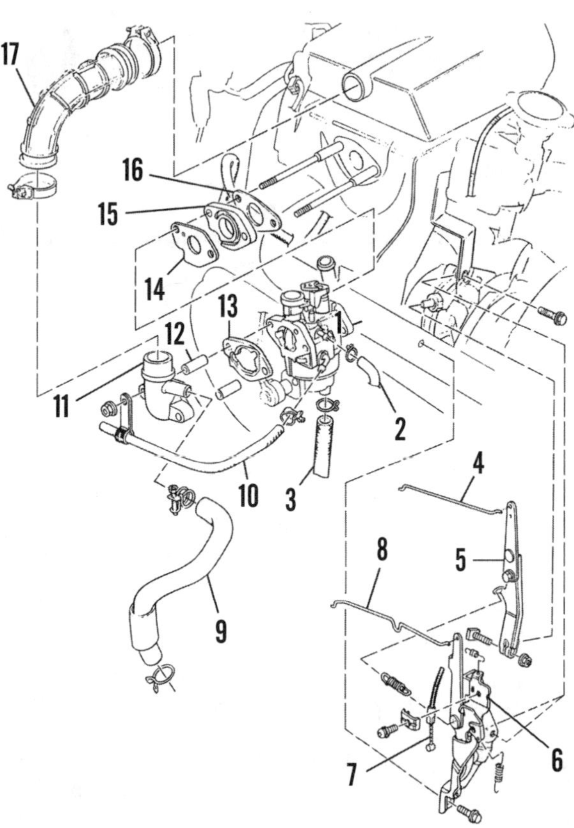

Fig. HE1-4—Carburetor and governor linkage components.

1. Carburetor
2. Air vent tube
3. Fuel drain tube
4. Governor link
5. Governor arm
6. Throttle control
7. Throttle cable
8. Choke link
9. Crankcase breather tube
10. Fuel line
11. Air cleaner elbow
12. Spacer
13. Gasket
14. Gasket
15. Insulator
16. Gasket
17. Air cleaner tube

To adjust the governor linkage, make certain all linkage is in good condition and governor spring (8—Fig. HE1-1) is not stretched or damaged. Loosen the governor lever screw (7). Push the lower governor lever (9) clockwise as far as possible and hold the governor lever in this position. Move the upper governor lever (3) so the throttle is completely open. Tighten the screw (7).

Start the engine and operate at an idle until its operating temperature has been reached. Attach a tachometer to the engine. Open the throttle so the engine is operating at maximum speed. Maximum unloaded engine speed should be 3300 rpm.

If engine speed is too slow, reposition the governor spring in the next farthest hole so spring length increases. If engine speed is too fast, reposition the governor spring in closer hole so the spring length decreases.

If the specified engine speed cannot be obtained by altering the governor spring length, change the throttle cable effective length. To change the throttle cable effective length, either loosen the cable clamp and reposition the cable or adjust the nuts at the upper end of the throttle cable.

IGNITION SYSTEM

The breakerless ignition system requires no regular maintenance. Ignition coil unit is mounted outside the flywheel. Air gap between flywheel and coil should be 0.2-0.6 mm (0.008-0.024 in.).

To check ignition coil primary side, connect one ohmmeter lead to the black primary coil lead and touch the iron coil laminations with the remaining lead. The ohmmeter should indicate 0.9-1.1 ohm.

To check the ignition coil secondary side, remove the spark plug caps and connect an ohmmeter lead to each spark plug lead wire. Ohmmeter should indicate 8.8k-13.3k ohms. If ohmmeter readings are not as specified, replace the ignition coil.

The specified spark plug cap resistance is 7.5k-12.5k ohms.

VALVE ADJUSTMENT

Valve-to-rocker arm clearance should be checked and adjusted after every 300 hours of operation.

To adjust valve clearance, remove the air filter housing and the rocker arm cover. Remove the spark plugs. Rotate the crankshaft so the piston in number one cylinder is at top dead center (TDC) on the compression stroke (both valves must be closed).

Insert a feeler gauge between the rocker arm and the end of the valve stem (Fig. HE1-3). Loosen the rocker arm jam nut and turn adjusting screw to obtain the desired clearance. Specified clearance is 0.10-0.14 mm (0.004-0.005 in.) for intake and 0.18-0.22 mm (0.007-0.008 in.) for exhaust. Tighten the jam nut and recheck the clearance.

Repeat the sequence to adjust the valves of the number two cylinder.

COMPRESSION PRESSURE

Compression pressure measured at cranking speed should be 980-1176 kPa (142-170 psi).

REPAIRS

TIGHTENING TORQUES

Recommended special tightening torque specifications are as follows:

Camshaft pulley nut (after serial No. 1142975) . . . . **35 N·m (26 ft.-lb.)**
Connecting rod . . . . **22 N·m (195 in.-lb.)**
Crankcase:
M6 . . . . **10 N·m (88 in.-lb.)**
M8 . . . . **23 N·m (17 ft.-lb.)**
Crankshaft pulley nut . . . . **25 N·m (18 ft.-lb.)**
Cylinder head . . . . **23 N·m (17 ft.-lb.)**
Exhaust manifold . . . . **22 N·m (195 in.-lb.)**
Flywheel nut . . . . **115 N·m (85 ft.-lb.)**
Intake manifold . . . . **10 N·m (88 in.-lb.)**
Water pump . . . . **10 N·m (88 in.-lb.)**

CARBURETOR

To remove the carburetor, disconnect the air vent tube (2—Fig. HE1-4), fuel drain tube (3) and fuel line (10) from the carburetor. If equipped with a fuel shutoff solenoid valve, disconnect the wire connector. Disconnect the air cleaner tube (17) and unscrew the two nuts retaining the air cleaner elbow and carburetor. Disconnect the governor link (4) and choke link (8) from the carburetor and remove the carburetor, gaskets and insulator from the engine.

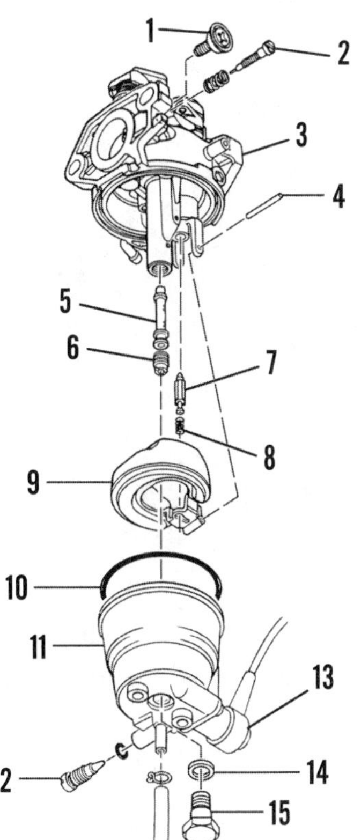

Fig. HE1-5—Exploded view of carburetor.

1. Idle speed screw
2. Pilot screw
3. Body
4. Float pin
5. Nozzle
6. Main jet
7. Fuel inlet valve
8. Spring
9. Float
10. O-ring
11. Fuel bowl
12. Drain screw
13. Fuel cutoff solenoid
14. Gasket
15. Screw

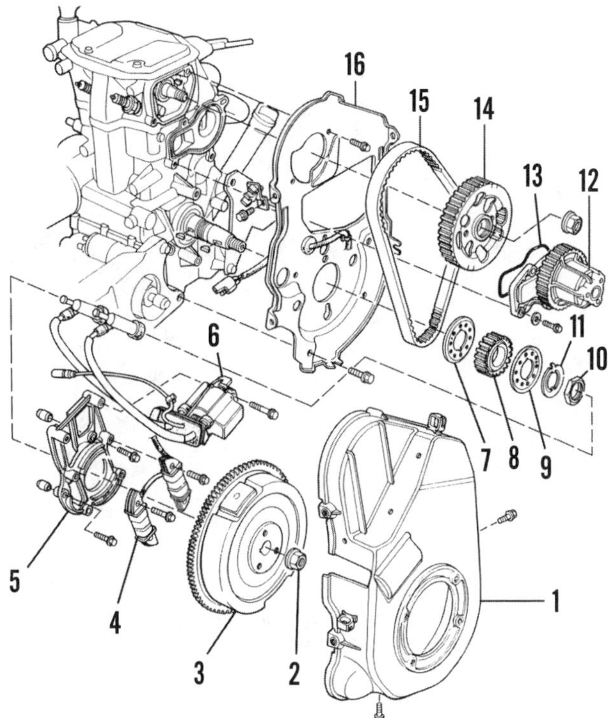

Fig. HE1-6—Engine timing belt is located on the rear of the engine beneath the rear cover.

1. Engine rear cover
2. Nut
3. Flywheel
4. Charge coil
5. Bracket
6. Ignition coil
7. Flange washer
8. Crankshaft pulley
9. Flange washer
10. Nut
11. Lockwasher
12. Water pump
13. Gasket
14. Camshaft pulley
15. Timing belt
16. Cover plate

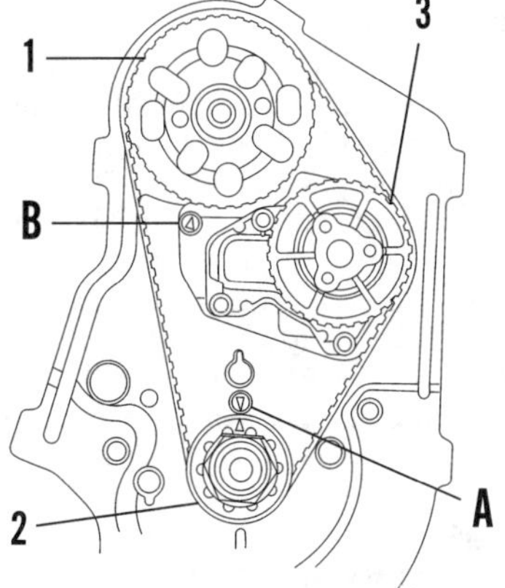

Fig. HE1-7—View of timing marks for crankshaft (A) and camshaft (B). Refer to text for timing procedure.

1. Camshaft pulley
2. Crankshaft pulley
3. Water pump

To disassemble the carburetor, unscrew the bolt (15—Fig. HE1-5) retaining the fuel bowl (11) to the carburetor body. Remove the fuel bowl and gasket (10). Withdraw the float pin (4) and remove the float 9), spring (8) and fuel valve (7). Unscrew the main jet (6), nozzle (5) and pilot screw (2).

Thoroughly clean all parts using a suitable carburetor cleaning solvent. Be sure the solvent will not damage plastic parts of the carburetor.

To check the float level, remove the fuel bowl and invert the carburetor. Measure from the top edge of the float to the fuel bowl mating edge of the carburetor body. The measurement should be 13.2 mm (0.52 in.). Float height is not adjustable. If the fuel inlet valve is in good condition, replace the float if float height is incorrect.

Standard main jet size is #88 on Models HT3813 and HT4213. Standard main jet size is #92 on Model H4514H. Install nozzle (5) so the fuel metering holes are toward the main jet.

When reinstalling the carburetor, install the outer gasket (14—Fig. HE1-4) so the vent hole is located on the left side. Install the insulator (15) so the vent passage is out.

CRANKCASE BREATHER

The engine is equipped with a crankcase breather located on the side of the cylinder block. The crankcase breather provides a vacuum for the crankcase. Vapor from the crankcase is evacuated to the air intake tube. A reed valve acts as a one-way valve to maintain crankcase vacuum. The breather system must operate properly or excessive oil consumption can result.

Check that reed valve is not damaged and seats properly. Replace if distorted or damaged. Inspect breather tube for leakage.

THERMOSTAT

A thermostat regulates the engine coolant temperature. The thermostat is contained in the thermostat housing located on the front of the cylinder head.

The thermostat should be fully open at 82° C (180° F). When installing the thermostat be sure the small hole in the mounting flange is up.

TIMING BELT

A cogged belt that engages a pulley on the crankshaft drives the water pump and camshaft. See Fig. HE1-6. No maintenance is required, however, a damaged or excessively worn belt or pulley should be replaced. Refer to camshaft and crankshaft service sections if pulley service is required.

Adjustment

Measure timing belt deflection at the midpoint between the camshaft pulley (1—Fig. HE1-7) and the crankshaft pulley (2). A force of 20 N (4.5 lb.) should deflect the belt 4-5 mm (0.16-0.20 in.).

To adjust timing belt tension, loosen the screws retaining the water pump (3) and relocate the water pump. Use care not to dislodge the O-ring behind the water pump. Retighten the water

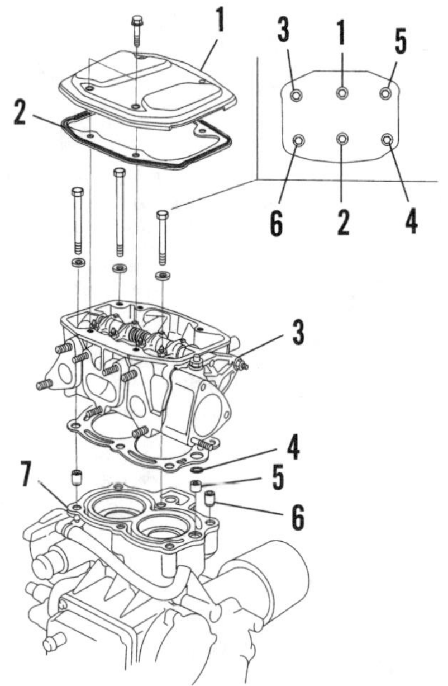

Fig. HE1-8—Tighten cylinder head screws in sequence shown. Note length of screws: short—1 & 5; medium—2, 4 & 6; long—3.

1. Cylinder head cover
2. Gasket
3. Cylinder head
4. O-ring
5. Oil metering orifice
6. Dowel pin (2)
7. Head gasket

Fig. HE1-9—Exploded view of cylinder head. Some engines are not equipped with seals on the exhaust valve.

1. Cylinder head
2. Intake valve
3. Exhaust valve
4. Valve stem seal
5. Spring seat
6. Valve spring
7. Valve spring retainer
8. Valve rotator
9. Split key
10. Valve spring retainer
11. Valve stem seal
12. Oil seal
13. Washer
14. Adjuster screw
15. Spacer
16. Spring
17. Rocker arm
18. Rocker arm shaft
19. Thrust washers
20. Camshaft
21. Thermostat housing
22. Gasket

pump retaining screws to 10 N·m (88 in.-lb.). Recheck timing belt tension.

Removal and Installation

Remove the engine rear cover (1—Fig. HE1-6). Remove the ignition coil (6). Use a suitable puller and remove the flywheel (3). Remove the charge coil assembly (4). Loosen the screws retaining the water pump (12) and move the pump to relieve the tension on the belt. Slide the belt off the pulleys.

Before installing the timing belt, align the timing marks as follows: Rotate the crankshaft so the triangle marks (A—Fig. HE1-7) on the crankshaft pulley and crankcase are aligned. Rotate camshaft so the T-mark on the camshaft for number one cylinder and triangle mark (B) on the cylinder block are aligned. Install the belt while keeping the marks aligned.

Move the water pump to the right until a 20 N (4.5 lb.) force will deflect the belt 4-5 mm (0.16-0.20 in.). Tighten the water pump retaining screws to 10 N·m (88 in.-lb.). Check the alignment of the timing marks.

Install the charge coil assembly. Install the flywheel and tighten the flywheel nut to 115 N·m (85 ft.-lb.). Install the ignition coil and adjust the air gap between the coil and flywheel magnet to 0.2-0.6 mm (0.008-0.0.24 in.). Install the rear cover.

WATER PUMP

The water pump (12—Fig. HE1-6) is located at the rear of the engine behind the engine rear cover. Remove the rear cover for access to the water pump.

If the engine is in the tractor, drain the coolant. Unscrew the water pump retaining screws. Remove the pump, but do not disturb the location of timing belt on camshaft and crankshaft pulleys so engine timing is not lost.

Water pump is available only as a unit assembly. Before installing the water pump be sure to install a new O-ring gasket (13—Fig. HE1-6) on the pump. Carefully install the water pump so the timing belt position is not changed on the camshaft and crankshaft pulleys. If camshaft or crankshaft pulleys move, check engine timing as described in the TIMING BELT section. Adjust the timing belt tension as described in the TIMING BELT section.

CYLINDER HEAD

To remove the cylinder head (3—Fig. HE1-8), proceed as follows. If the engine is in the tractor, drain the coolant and detach the coolant hoses. Remove the shrouds and spark plugs. Remove the air cleaner housing, carburetor, intake manifold, exhaust manifold, engine rear cover, flywheel and timing belt.

Remove the cylinder head cover (1—Fig. HE1-8). Remove the screws attaching the cylinder head (3) to the block. Lift the cylinder head and gasket off the cylinder block.

Inspect the cylinder head for cracks and other damage. Maximum allowable cylinder head surface warpage is 0.10 mm (0.004 in.).

Install the cylinder head with a new head gasket. Be sure to install the oil metering orifice (5—Fig. HE1-8) and O-ring (4) in the oil passage at the front end of the cylinder block and head. Note the different lengths of the head retaining screws and their respective location in the cylinder head (Fig. HE1-8). Tighten the cylinder head screws in the sequence shown in Fig. HE1-8 in three equal steps to final torque of 23 N·m (17 ft.-lb.).

CAMSHAFT AND VALVE SYSTEM

Remove the cylinder head as previously outlined. On engines using a nut to retain the drive pulley on the camshaft, the camshaft end is tapered. If equipped with a retaining nut, remove the camshaft drive pulley from the camshaft using Honda tool 89301-400-000.

Remove the thermostat housing (21—Fig. HE1-9). Extract the rocker arm shaft (18) while sliding components off the shaft as it is withdrawn.

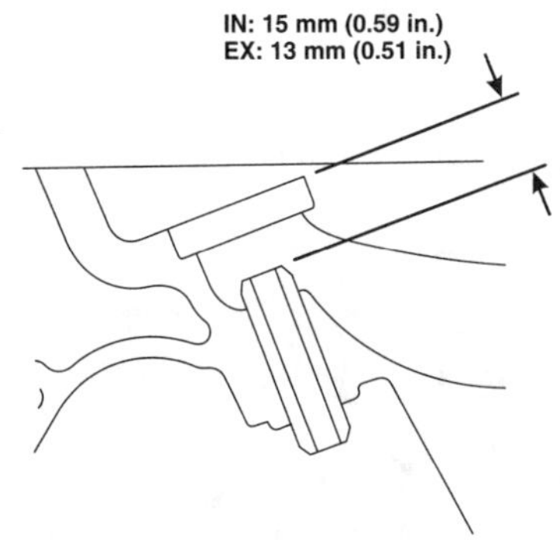

Fig. HE1-10—On Model HT3813 and HT4213 tractor engines that use clipless valve guides, drive in valve guides to dimension shown in the above drawing.

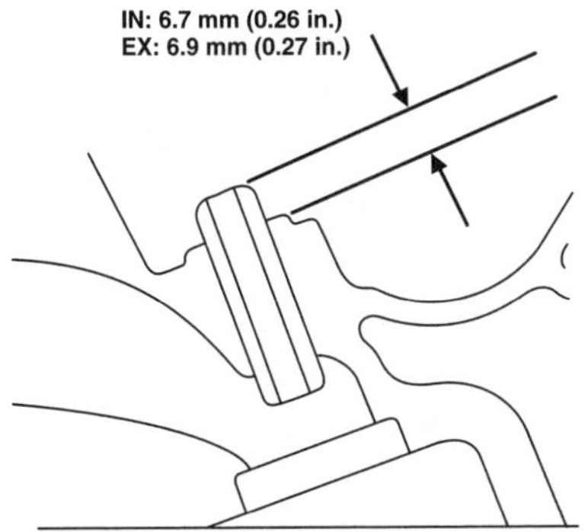

Fig. HE1-11—On Model H4514H tractor engines, drive in valve guides to dimension shown in the above drawing.

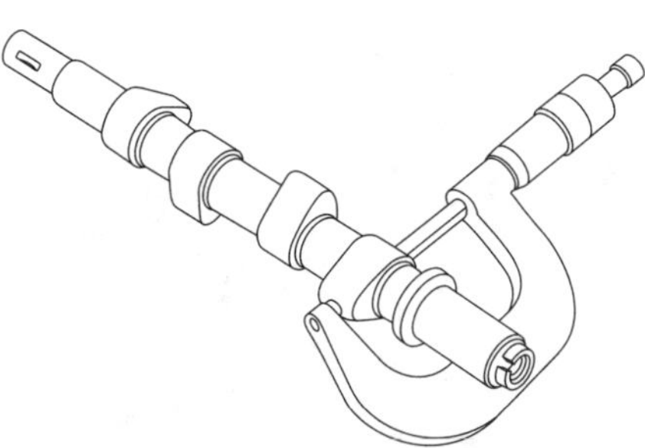

Fig. HE1-12—Measure camshaft lobe height as shown.

Identify the parts as they are removed so they can be returned to their original position on the cylinder head. Remove the camshaft (20).

Use a valve spring compressor tool to compress the valve springs. Remove the valve retainers. Note that split keys (9) are used to retain the intake valve in the valve retainer while a slotted retainer (7) is used on the exhaust valve. The exhaust valve is equipped with a valve rotator (8) on the valve stem.

Identify the valves and springs as they are removed so they can be returned to their original positions in the cylinder head. Some early models are not equipped with exhaust valve seals (4).

Valve face and seat angles are 45°. Standard valve seat width is 0.7 mm (0.028 in.). Narrow the seat if seat width is 2.0 mm (0.079) or more.

Standard valve spring free length is 29.0 mm (1.14 in.). Replace the valve spring if free length is 27.5 mm (1.08 in.) or less.

Standard valve guide inside diameter is 5.50 mm (0.216 in.). Replace the guide if inside diameter is 5.55 mm (0.218 in.) or more.

Intake valve stem diameter should be 5.48 mm (0.2157 in.). Discard the intake valve if the stem diameter is less than 5.32 mm (0.2094 in.). The exhaust valve stem diameter should be 5.45 mm (0.2146 in.). Discard the exhaust valve if the stem diameter is less than 5.29 mm (0.2083 in.).

To replace the valve guide, heat the entire cylinder head to 150°C (300°F). DO NOT heat the head above the recommended temperature as the valve seats may loosen. Use Honda valve guide driver 07942-8920000 to remove and install the guides. Drive out the valve guide toward the valve spring side of the head.

Chill the new valve guides in a freezer for approximately one hour prior to installation. On early models, a locating clip at the top of the guide determines the valve guide depth in the cylinder head. Drive in the valve guide toward the combustion side of the head so the clip is bottomed against the head.

On Model HT3813 and HT4213 tractor engines that use clipless valve guides, drive the new intake valve guide toward the combustion side of the head until the intake guide protrudes 15 mm (0.59 in.) below the valve seat surface (Fig. HE1-10). Drive in the new exhaust valve guide so the guide protrudes 13 mm (0.51 in.) below the valve seat surface. New valve guides must be reamed after installation.

On Model H4514H tractors, drive in the new intake valve guide toward the combustion side of the head so the guide protrudes 6.7 mm (0.26 in.) above the adjacent head surface. See Fig. HE1-11. Drive in the new exhaust valve guide toward the combustion side of the head so the guide protrudes 6.9 mm (0.27 in.) above the adjacent head surface. New valve guides must be reamed after installation.

Standard camshaft lobe height (Fig. HE1-12) is 24.96 mm (0.983 in.) for the intake lobe and 25.92 mm (1.020 in.) for the exhaust lobe. If the intake lobe measures less than 24.5 mm (0.964 in.), or the exhaust lobe measures less than 25.6 mm (1.008 in.), replace the camshaft.

Standard camshaft bearing journal diameter is 15.98 mm (0.629 in.). Replace the camshaft if the journal diameter is less than 15.9 mm (0.626 in.).

Standard rocker arm inside diameter is 13.00 mm (0.512 in.) with a wear limit of 13.04 mm (0.513 in.). Standard rocker shaft diameter is 12.957 mm (0.5101 in.) with a wear limit of 12.940 mm (0.5094 in.).

When reassembling the camshaft and valve system, install the threaded end of the camshaft away from the thermostat housing (21—Fig. HE1-9). On later engines that use a nut to secure the pulley to the camshaft, tighten the nut to 35 N·m (26 ft.-lb.).

Install the rocker shaft (18) so the threaded end is toward the thermostat housing.

GOVERNOR

The governor flyweight assembly is contained in a compartment on the front of the engine cylinder block (Fig. HE1-13). To remove the governor, loosen the clamp bolt (7) and slide the governor arm (2) off the governor shaft (5). Remove the screws attaching the governor cover (6) to the engine and withdraw the cover, fork (9), slider (12) and governor weight assembly (14).

Inspect the governor for damage and replace when necessary.

When reassembling the governor, position the flyweights (10) on the slider (12), place the slider on the governor weight shaft (14) and insert the pins (13). Insert the tapered end of the pin first. Be sure the flyweights and slider operate freely.

Adjust the governor linkage as previously outlined in the MAINTENANCE section.

OIL PUMP

The engine is equipped with a rotor oil pump located in the crankcase and driven by a gear on the crankshaft (Fig. HE1-14). To remove the pump, drain the oil from the crankcase. Remove the screws attaching the pump housing to the engine and remove the pump assembly (10) and drive gear (14).

To disassemble, remove the pump cover (1—Fig. HE1-15). Withdraw the pump rotors (2 and 3) from the pump housing.

NOTE: Note the orientation of the punch marks on the pump rotors for correct reassembly. When installing the rotors, make sure the punch marks face the

same direction as when removed.

Inspect the pump and make certain the oil passages are clear and the pump body is not damaged. Inner-to-outer rotor clearance should be 0.15 mm (0.006 in.). If clearance is 0.30 mm (0.012 in.) or more, replace the rotors. Oil pump body-to-outer rotor clearance should be 0.12-0.22 mm (0.005-0.008 in.). If clearance is 0.30 mm (0.012 in.) or more, replace the outer rotor and/or oil pump body (5). Side clearance between either rotor and pump cover should be 0.04-0.09 mm (0.002-0.0035 in.). Maximum allowable side clearance is 0.11 mm (0.004 in.).

When assembling the oil pump, install the rotors so the punch mark on each rotor is facing the same direction as when removed. Align the inner rotor with the cutout in the pump drive gear shaft (8). Be sure to install both O-rings (4 and 6).

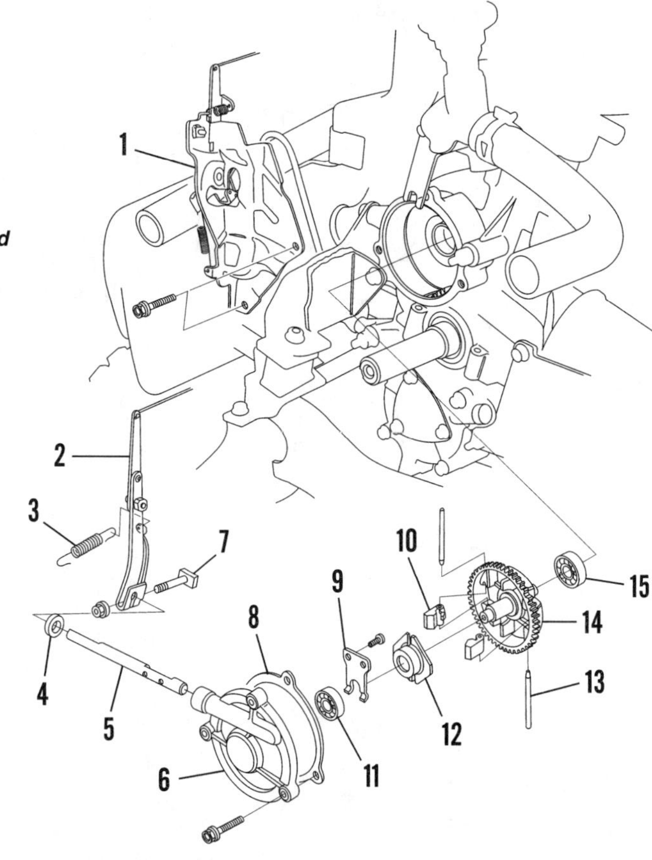

Fig. HE1-13—Exploded view of governor.

1. Governor control bracket
2. Governor arm
3. Return spring
4. Seal
5. Governor shaft
6. Cover
7. Clamp bolt
8. Gasket
9. Fork
10. Governor weight
11. Bearing
12. Slider
13. Pin
14. Gear
15. Bearing

PISTONS, PINS AND RINGS

The crankcase (15—Fig. HE1-14) must be separated from the cylinder block (3) for access to the crankshaft, piston and rod assemblies. Mark the connecting rods so they can be reinstalled in their original positions on the crankshaft. Detach the piston pin clip (5) and push out the piston pin (6) to separate the piston (4) from the rod.

Measure piston diameter 10 mm (0.4 in.) above the lower edge of the skirt and 90° from the piston pin. Specified standard diameter is 57.960-57.990 mm (2.2819-2.2831 in.). Wear limit is 57.9 mm (2.280 in.). Oversize pistons are available.

Standard piston pin bore diameter is 14.005 mm (0.5514 in.). Reject piston if the piston pin bore diameter is 14.055 mm (0.5533 in.) or more.

Standard piston pin diameter is 14.000 mm (0.5512 in.). Reject piston pin if the diameter is 13.954 mm (0.5494 in.) or less.

Side clearance for the compression rings in the piston ring grooves should be 0.03 mm (0.001 in.). Maximum allowable compression ring side clearance is 0.17 mm (0.007 in.). Replace the piston and rings if side clearance is excessive.

Ring end gap for compression rings should be 0.2 mm (0.008 in.). If the ring end gap for any ring is 0.6 mm (0.024 in.) or more, replace the ring and/or resize the cylinder for oversize piston and rings. Oversize piston rings are available.

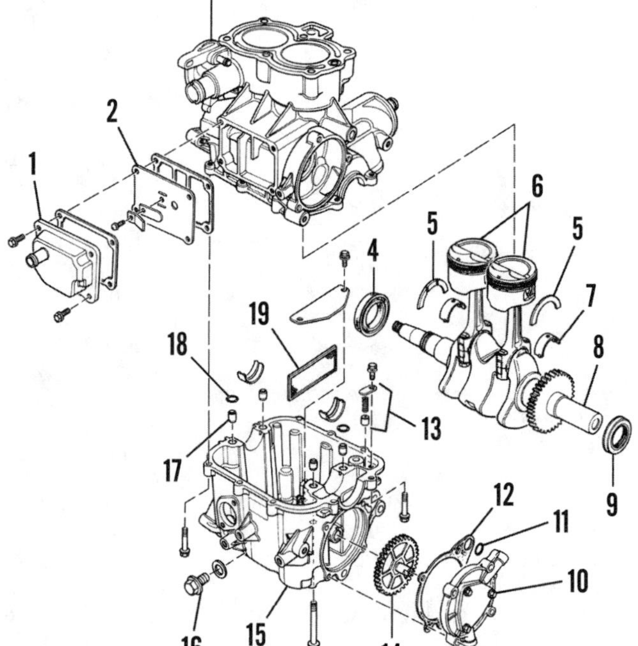

Fig. HE1-14—Separate the crankcase (15) from the cylinder block (3) to access crankshaft and pistons.

1. Breather cover
2. Breather plate
3. Cylinder block
4. Oil seal
5. Thrust bearings
6. Pistons
7. Main bearing insert
8. Crankshaft
9. Oil seal
10. Oil pump assy.
11. O-ring
12. Gasket
13. Oil check valve
14. Oil pump drive gear
15. Crankcase
16. Drain plug
17. Dowel
18. O-ring
19. Oil filter screen

Install the oil control ring (3—Fig. HE1-16) with the side rail end gaps at least 20 mm (0.8 in.) apart.

Install the compression rings (1 and 2—Fig. HE1-16) with the marked side toward piston crown. Do not interchange the rings. The chrome plated compression ring must be installed in the piston ring top groove. Stagger the ring end gaps equally around the piston.

When installing the piston on the rod, position the piston so the valve re-

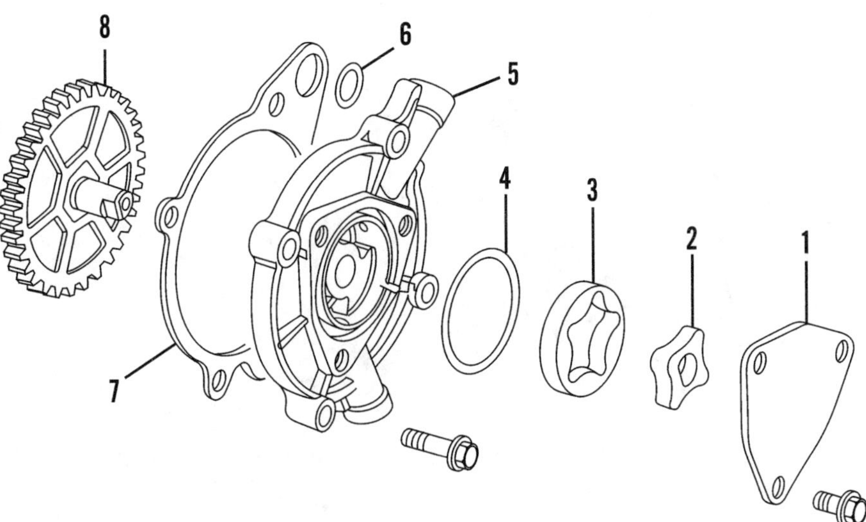

Fig. HE1-15—Exploded view of oil pump.

1. Cover
2. Inner rotor
3. Outer rotor
4. O-ring
5. Pump housing
6. O-ring
7. Gasket
8. Oil pump drive gear

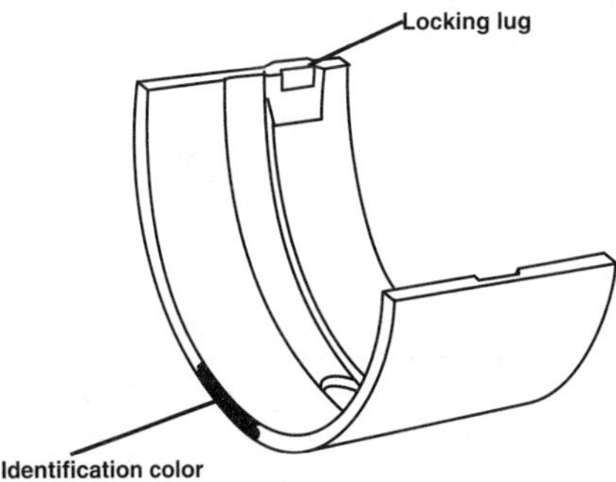

Fig. HE1-18—Bearing color code is located on side of both the rod and main bearing inserts.

Crankpin O.D. \ Connecting rod I.D.	Mark A	B	C
Mark A	Red	Yellow	Green
B	Yellow	Green	Brown
C	Green	Brown	Black

Fig. HE1-19—Select correct rod bearing according to chart using letters stamped on rod and crankshaft. See text.

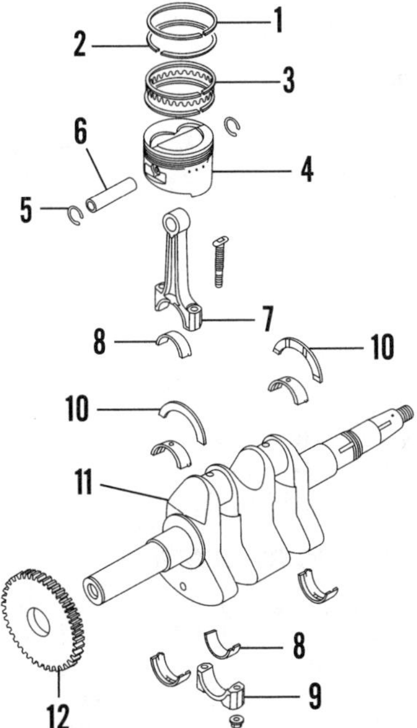

Fig. HE1-16—Exploded view of piston, connecting rod and crankshaft.

1. Top compression ring
2. Second compression ring
3. Oil control ring
4. Piston
5. Clip
6. Piston pin
7. Connecting rod
8. Rod bearing insert
9. Rod cap
10. Thrust bearings
11. Crankshaft
12. Oil pump drive gear

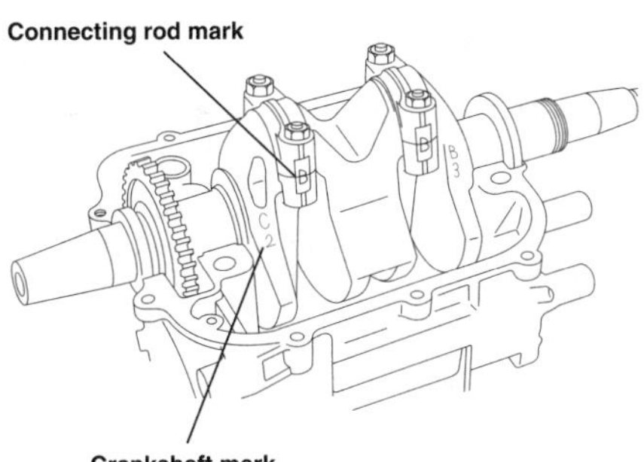

Fig. HE1-17—Connecting rods and crankshaft are stamped with bearing code letters and numbers. Refer to text for bearing selection procedure.

liefs in the piston crown are on the valve side of the engine. Install the piston pin retaining clip (5) so the end gap is opposite the notch in the piston pin bore. Tighten the connecting rod nuts to 22 N·m (195 in.-lb.).

Refer to CONNECTING ROD section for additional instructions for installing the piston and rod in the cylinder block.

CONNECTING RODS

Remove the cylinder head and separate the crankcase and cylinder block for access to the crankshaft, piston and rod assemblies (Fig. HE1-14). Mark the connecting rods so they can be reinstalled in their original positions on the crankshaft. Detach the piston pin clip (5—Fig. HE1-16) and push out the piston pin to separate the piston from the rod.

Standard piston pin bore diameter in the connecting rod is 14.016 mm (0.5518 in.). Replace the connecting rod if the diameter is 14.070 mm (0.5539 in.).

Connecting rod is equipped with replaceable insert bearings (8—Fig. HE1-16) in the big end. Standard connecting rod bearing bore-to-crankpin clearance is 0.025 mm (0.0010 in.). Renew the connecting rod bearing and/or crankshaft if clearance is 0.045 mm (0.0018 in.) or more.

Adjust rod clearance on the crankpin by installing one of five different thickness bearing inserts. To determine which bearing to install so correct bearing clearance is achieved, note the identifying letter on the side of the rod and adjacent to the crankpin (Fig. HE1-17). Bearing inserts are color-coded according to their thickness (Fig. HE1-18). The table in Fig. HE1-19 identifies the correct bearing for installation.

NOTE: When installing bearing inserts, be sure the tang on the bearing insert engages the notch in the rod or rod cap.

Connecting rod side play on crankpin should be 0.10 mm (0.004 in.). Replace connecting rod if side play is 0.30 mm (0.012 in.) or more.

When reinstalling the piston and connecting rod assembly in the cylinder, the arrowhead on the piston crown must be on the valve side of the engine. During assembly on the crankshaft, align the ribs on the rod and rod cap.

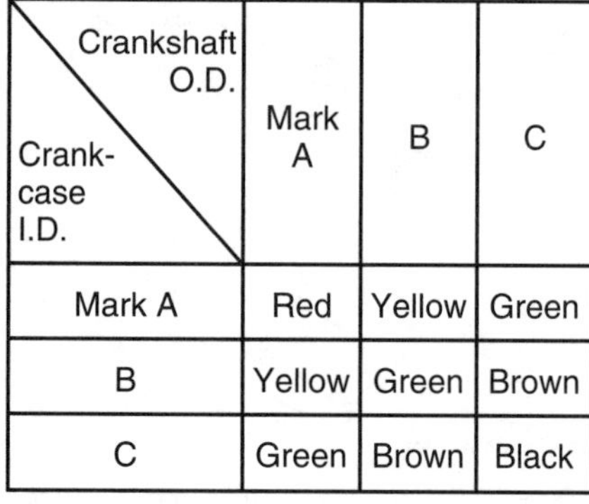

Crankcase I.D. \ Crankshaft O.D.	Mark A	B	C
Mark A	Red	Yellow	Green
B	Yellow	Green	Brown
C	Green	Brown	Black

Fig. HE1-20—Select correct main bearing according to chart using letters stamped on crankcase and crankshaft. See text.

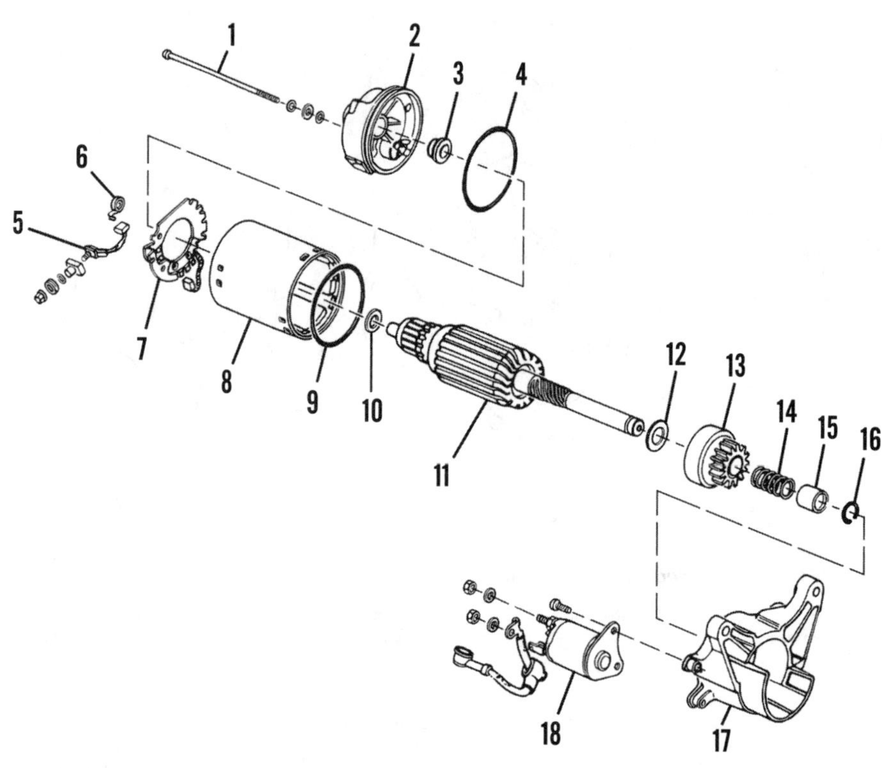

Fig. HE1-21—Exploded view of electric starter motor.

1. Bolt
2. End cap
3. Bushing
4. O-ring
5. Brush
6. Spring
7. Brush holder plate
8. Frame
9. O-ring
10. Thrust washer
11. Armature
12. Thrust washer
13. Drive gear
14. Spring
15. Collar
16. Snap ring
17. Drive housing
18. Solenoid

Tighten connecting rod nuts to 22 N·m (195 in.-lb.).

CRANKSHAFT, CRANKCASE AND CYLINDER BLOCK

Crankshaft rides in replaceable insert bearings (7—Fig. HE1-14) in the crankcase (15) and cylinder block (3). Crankshaft thrust is controlled by replaceable thrust bearings (5) located on the cylinder block.

Standard cylinder bore diameter should be 58.000-58.015 mm (2.2835-2.2840 in.). Maximum wear limit is 58.100 mm (2.2874 in.). Resize cylinder and install oversize piston if cylinder bore is excessively worn or damaged.

The crankcase contains an oil screen (19) and oil check valve (13). Clean oil passages, screen and check valve components. Be sure to install the screen and check valve assemblies during assembly.

Oil pump drive gear (12—Fig. HE1-16) is pressed on the crankshaft. Be sure to properly support the crankshaft when removing or installing the drive gear.

Crankshaft main journal diameter should be 33.009 mm (1.2996 in.). Renew crankshaft if main journal diameter is less than 32.96 mm (1.298 in.).

Adjust main bearing clearance by installing one of five different thickness bearing inserts. To determine which bearing to install so correct bearing clearance is achieved, note identifying letter on the side of the crankcase and adjacent to the crankshaft main journal (Fig. HE1-17). Bearing inserts are color-coded (see Fig. HE1-18) according to thickness. The table in Fig. HE1-20 identifies the correct bearing for installation.

NOTE: When installing bearing inserts, be sure the tang on the bearing insert engages the notch in the crankcase or cylinder block.

Inspect the thrust bearings (5—Fig. HE1-14) and replace if excessively worn. Install the thrust bearings in the cylinder block so the grooved side is toward the inside of the cylinder block.

When assembling the crankcase and cylinder block, be sure to install O-rings (18—Fig. HE1-14) on the dowels (17) at upper left and lower right of crankcase. Apply liquid-gasket sealer to the mating surfaces of the crankcase and cylinder block. Tighten the screws attaching the crankcase to the cylinder block to 10 N·m (88 in.-lb.) if M6 or to 23 N·m (17 ft.-lb.) if M8.

Install new oils seals (4 and 9) with oil seal lip facing inward. Install flange washers (7 and 9—Fig. HE1-6) on either side of the timing belt pulley (8) so the flanges are away from the pulley. Position the lockwasher (11) so the inner tab fits in the hole of the flange washer. Install the crankshaft nut, tighten the nut to 25 N·m (18 ft.-lb.) and bend the lockwasher against the flats of the nut.

Install and time the timing belt as previously outlined. Adjust the timing belt tension as previously outlined and tighten the water pump retaining screws to 10 N·m (88 in.-lb.). Install the flywheel and tighten the retaining nut to 115 N·m (83 ft.-lb.).

ELECTRIC STARTER

All models are equipped with an electric starter (Fig. HE1-21). Cranking voltage should be 8.5 volts DC under load and 11.5 volts DC under no load. Cranking current should be below 165 amps under load and below 20 amps under no load.

Push the collar (15—Fig. HE1-21) toward the starter for access to snap ring (16). Minimum brush length is 8.5 mm (0.34 in.). Align tabs and grooves when assembling brush plate, frame and drive end housing.

CHARGE COILS

Charge coils (4—Fig. HE1-6) located behind the flywheel provide electrical current for the battery charging circuit. To test the charge coils, disconnect the charge coil connector on the left side of the engine. Resistance between terminals should be 0.16-0.24 ohms.

HONDA

Model	No. Cyls.	Bore	Stroke	Displacement	Power Rating
GXV390	1	88 mm (3.46 in.)	64 mm (2.52 in.)	389 cc (23.7 cu. in.)	9.7 kW (13 hp)

Model GXV390 is a four-stroke, overhead valve, single-cylinder, air-cooled engine with a vertical crankshaft.

The engine model number is cast or stamped into the side of the crankcase (Fig. HE2-1). Engine model and serial number may be necessary when ordering parts.

MAINTENANCE

LUBRICATION

Engine oil level should be checked prior to operating the engine. Check the oil level with the oil cap not screwed in, but just touching the first threads.

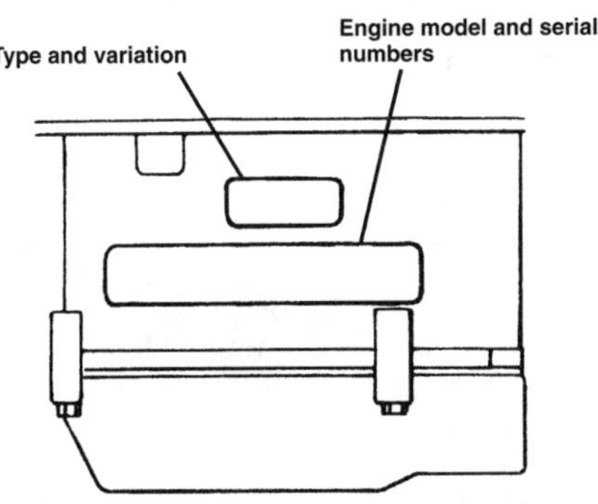

Fig. HE2-1—Engine model information is located on engine as shown.

Oil should be changed after the first 20 hours of engine operation and after every 100 hours thereafter.

Use oil that meets the latest API service classification. SAE 10W-30 or 10W-40 oil is recommended. Use SAE 10W-40 if temperature is above 90°F (32°C).

Crankcase capacity is 1.1 liters (1.16 qt.).

AIR CLEANER

The engine is equipped with a dry air filter that should be cleaned and inspected after every 50 hours of operation.

Remove the foam and paper air filter elements from the air filter housing. The foam element should be washed in a mild detergent and water solution, rinsed in clean water and allowed to air dry. When dry, soak the foam element in clean engine oil. Squeeze out excess oil.

Gently tap the paper element to dislodge dirt and other debris. The paper element may be cleaned by directing low-pressure compressed air stream from inside filter toward the outside.

Inspect the elements and replace them if any damage is evident. Reinstall the elements after cleaning.

SPARK PLUG

The spark plug should be removed, cleaned and inspected after every 100 hours of use.

Recommended spark plug is a NGK BPR5ES or ND W16EPR-U. Spark plug electrode gap should be 0.7-0.8 mm (0.028-0.031 in.).

When installing the spark plug, the manufacturer recommends installing the spark plug finger tight. Then for a new plug, tighten an additional ½ turn. For a used plug, tighten an additional ¼ turn.

CARBURETOR

The engine is equipped with a Keihin float type carburetor with a fixed main fuel jet and an adjustable idle speed fuel mixture needle.

To adjust the carburetor control cable and linkage, proceed as follows: Place the throttle control lever in full speed position. The gap (G—Fig. HE2-2) between the control lever (L) and choke lever (C) should be 3-5 mm (0.12-0.20 in.). To adjust the gap, loosen the cable housing clamp and relocate the cable.

If gap adjustment is not possible by relocating the cable housing, retighten the clamp screw. Adjust the throttle cable by rotating the adjusting nuts at the upper end of the throttle cable.

To adjust choke operation, move the throttle control lever to the start position. The choke plate in the carburetor should be closed. Bend the choke link at the (U—Fig. HE2-2) to adjust choke plate position. Rotate the choke screw (S) so the screw just touches the choke lever (C).

Initial setting for the idle mixture screw (LS—Fig. HE2-3) is 2½ turns out from a lightly seated position. Perform final adjustment with the engine at normal operating temperature and running.

Operate the engine at idle speed and adjust the idle mixture screw (LS) to obtain a smooth idle and satisfactory acceleration. Adjust the idle speed by turning the idle speed screw (TS). Recommended idle speed is 1750-1950 rpm.

Refer to Fig. HE2-4 for an exploded view of the carburetor. To disassemble for cleaning and inspection, remove the

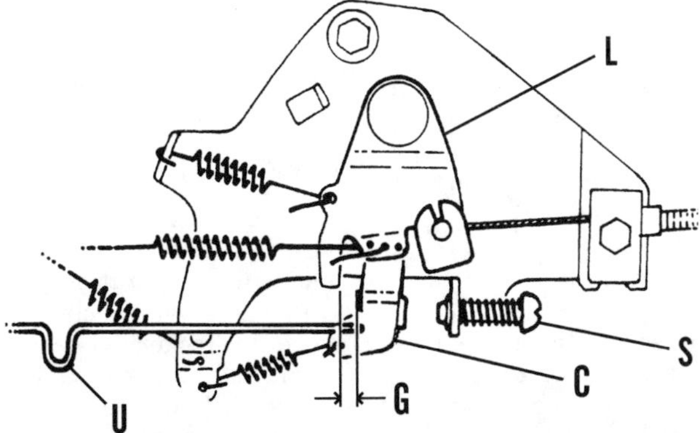

Fig. HE2-2—When throttle is in wide open position, gap (G) between control lever (L) and choke lever (C) must be 3-5 mm (0.12-0.20 in.). Refer to text for adjustment.

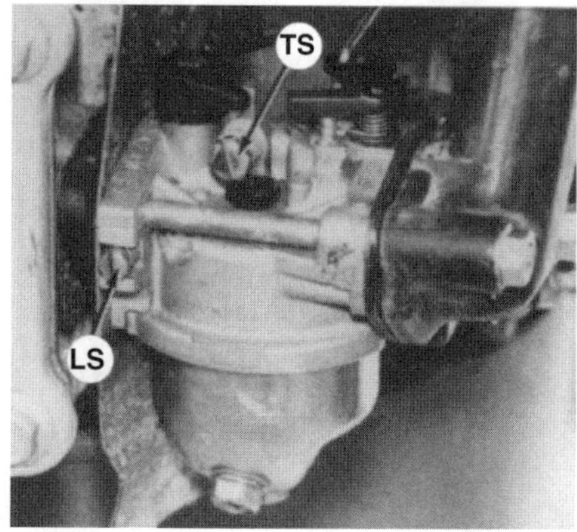

Fig. HE2-3—Adjust idle speed mixture screw (LS) and idle stop screw (TS) as outlined in text.

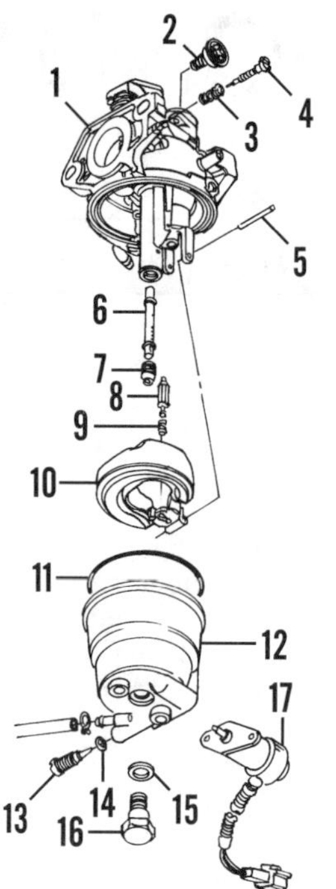

Fig. HE2-4—Exploded view of carburetor.

1. Body
2. Idle speed screw
3. Spring
4. Idle mixture screw
5. Float pin
6. Nozzle
7. Main jet
8. Fuel inlet valve
9. Spring
10. Float
11. O-ring
12. Fuel bowl
13. Drain screw
14. O-ring
15. Gasket
16. Screw
17. Fuel cutoff solenoid

Fig. HE2-5—View of typical external governor linkage.

1. Governor-to-carburetor rod
3. Governor lever
4. Choke rod
5. Tension spring
6. Governor shaft
7. Clamp bolt
8. Maximum speed screw

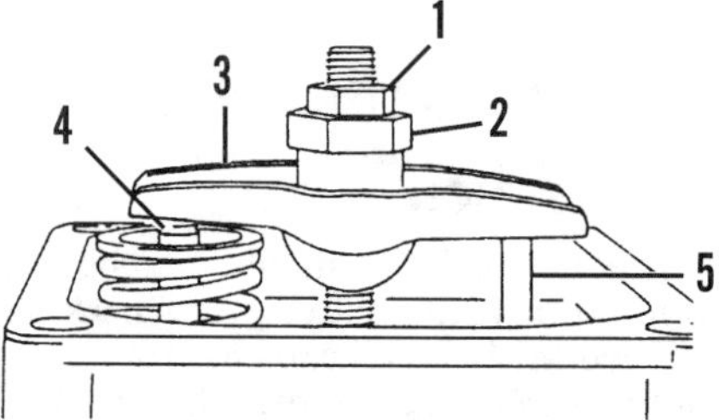

Fig. HE2-6—Valve clearance should be 0.13-0.17 mm (0.005-0.007 in.) for intake and 0.18-0.22 mm (0.007-0.009 in.) for exhaust. Loosen rocker arm jam nut (1) and turn adjusting nut (2) to obtain desired clearance.

1. Jam nut
2. Adjustment nut
3. Rocker arm
4. Valve stem clearance
5. Push rod

fuel shut-off solenoid (17). Remove the screw (16) and remove the fuel bowl (12). Push out the float pin (5) and remove the float (10) and fuel inlet valve (8) and spring (9). Unscrew the main jet (7) and nozzle (6) from the pump body. Remove the idle mixture screw (4).

If a cleaning solvent is used to clean the carburetor, be sure it will not damage the plastic parts of the carburetor.

To check float level, remove the fuel bowl and invert the carburetor. Measure from the top edge of the float to the fuel bowl mating edge of the carburetor body. Measurement should be 11.9-14.5 mm (0.47-0.57 in.). Float height is not adjustable. If the fuel inlet valve is in good condition, replace the float if float height is incorrect.

Standard main jet size is #95. Install the nozzle (6) so the fuel metering holes are toward the main jet.

When installing the carburetor, install the inner gasket so the vent hole is in the lower left corner. Install the insulator so the vent passage is out. Install the outer gasket so the vent hole is in the upper right corner.

GOVERNOR

A mechanical flyweight governor is located inside the engine crankcase. Before adjusting the external linkage, check the carburetor control adjustments described in previous section.

To adjust the governor linkage, make certain all linkage is in good condition and the governor spring (5—Fig. HE2-5) is not stretched or damaged. Governor spring should be attached to the center hole of the control lever (L—Fig. HE2-2).

Loosen the clamp bolt (7—Fig. HE2-5) and move the governor lever (3) so the throttle is completely open. Hold the governor lever in this position and rotate the governor shaft (6) in the same direction until it stops. Tighten the clamp bolt.

Start the engine and operate at an idle until operating temperature has been reached. Attach a tachometer to the engine. Open the throttle so the engine is operating at maximum speed. Maximum unloaded engine speed should be 3300 rpm.

If the engine speed is too slow, reposition the governor spring to the hole nearest to the throttle cable clamp. If the engine speed remains slow, loosen the cable clamp and reposition the cable.

If the engine speed is too fast, reposition the governor spring to the hole farthest from the throttle cable clamp. If the engine speed remains too fast, loosen the cable clamp and reposition the cable.

IGNITION SYSTEM

The breakerless ignition system requires no regular maintenance. An ignition coil unit is mounted outside the flywheel. Air gap between the flywheel and coil should be 0.2-0.6 mm (0.008-0.024 in.).

To check the ignition coil primary side, connect one ohmmeter lead to the black primary coil lead and touch the iron coil laminations with the remaining lead. Ohmmeter should indicate 0.7-0.9 ohm.

To check the ignition coil secondary side, remove the spark plug cap and connect one ohmmeter lead to the spark plug lead wire and the remaining lead to the iron core laminations. Ohmmeter should indicate 6.3k-7.7k ohms. If ohmmeter readings are not as specified, replace the ignition coil.

VALVE ADJUSTMENT

Valve-to-rocker arm clearance should be checked and adjusted after every 300 hours of operation.

To adjust valve clearance, first remove the rocker arm cover. Rotate the crankshaft so the piston is at top dead center (TDC) on the compression stroke. Insert a feeler gauge between the rocker arm (3—Fig. HE2-6) and the end of the valve stem. Loosen the rocker arm jam

Fig. HE2-7—Compression release spring (1) and weight (2) are installed on camshaft gear.

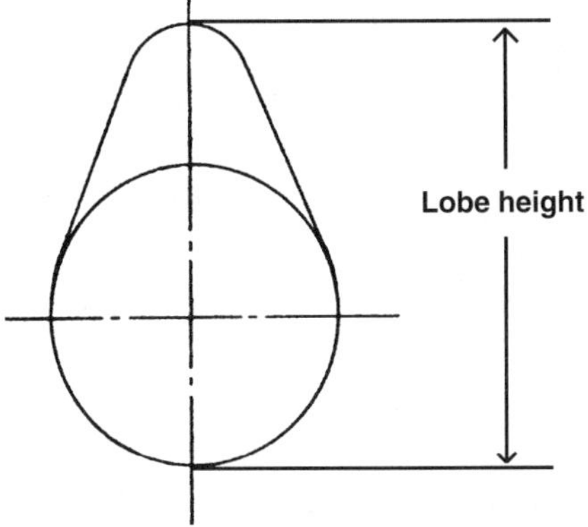

Fig. HE2-8—Measure camshaft lobe height as shown.

nut (1) and turn the adjusting nut (2) to obtain the desired clearance.

Specified clearance is 0.08-0.12 mm (0.003-0.005 in.) for intake and 0.13-0.17 mm (0.005-0.006 in.) for exhaust.

Tighten the jam nut and recheck clearance. Install the rocker arm cover gasket so the outer lip is toward the cylinder head. Install the rocker arm cover.

COMPRESSION PRESSURE

Compression pressure measured at cranking speed of 600 rpm should be 637-980 kPa (93-142 psi).

REPAIRS

TIGHTENING TORQUES

Recommended special tightening torque specifications are as follows:

Connecting rod . . . . **14 N·m (124 in.-lb.)**
Cylinder head . . . . **35 N·m (26 ft.-lb.)**
Flywheel nut . . . . **115 N·m (85 ft.-lb.)**
Oil pan . . . . **24 N·m (212 in.-lb.)**
Rocker arm jam nut . . . . **10 N·m (88 in.-lb.)**
Rocker arm pivot stud . . . . **24 N·m (212 in.-lb.)**

CYLINDER HEAD

To remove the cylinder head, remove the cooling shroud. Disconnect and remove the carburetor linkage and carburetor. Remove the muffler. Remove the rocker arm cover and the four cylinder head retaining screws. Remove the cylinder head and gasket.

Clean carbon deposits and any head gasket material from the cylinder head. Check the spark plug hole and valve seats for cracks. Check the cylinder head for warpage using a straightedge and feeler gauge. Maximum allowable warpage is 0.10 mm (0.004 in.).

Install the cylinder head using a new head gasket. Tighten the cylinder head retaining screws in a crossing pattern. Tighten the screws in three steps to a final torque of 35 N·m (26 ft.-lb.).

Adjust the valves as outlined in the VALVE ADJUSTMENT paragraph.

VALVE SYSTEM

Remove the cylinder head as previously outlined. Remove the rocker arms, compress the valve springs and remove the valve retainers. Note that the exhaust valve is equipped with a valve rotator on the valve stem, and the exhaust valve spring retainer has a recess to accept the valve rotator. Remove the valves and springs. Remove the push rod guide plate if necessary.

Valve face and seat angles are 45 degrees for intake and exhaust. Standard valve seat width is 1.1 mm (0.043 in.). Narrow the seat if seat width is 2.0 mm (0.079) or more.

Standard valve spring free length is 39.0 mm (1.54 in.). Replace the valve spring if free length is 37.5 mm (1.48 in.) or less.

Standard valve guide inside diameter is 6.60 mm (0.260 in.). Replace the guide if inside diameter is 6.66 mm (0.262 in.) or more.

Valve stem-to-guide clearance should be 0.010-0.037 mm (0.0004-0.0015 in.) for the intake valve and 0.050-0.077 mm (0.002-0.003 in.) for exhaust valve. Replace the valve guide and/or guide if clearance is 0.10 mm (0.004 in.) or more for the intake valve or 0.12 mm (0.005 in.) or more for the exhaust valve.

To replace the valve guide, heat the entire cylinder head to 150°C (300°F). DO NOT heat the head above the recommended temperature as the valve seats may loosen. Use valve guide driver 07942-6570100 to remove and install the guides. Drive out valve guide toward valve spring side of head.

A wire clip is attached to the upper end of each valve guide. Drive in the new valve guide toward the combustion side of the head so the clip is bottomed against the head. New valve guides must be reamed to the specified size after installation.

When assembling valve system components in the head, note that the exhaust valve spring retainer has a recess that fits the valve rotator.

OIL PUMP

The engine is equipped with a rotor oil pump that is located in the oil pan and driven by the camshaft. The oil pump is accessible by removing the pump cover from the outside of the oil pan.

Specified inner rotor-to-outer rotor clearance is 0.18 mm (0.007 in.) with a wear limit of 0.30 mm (0.012 in.). Specified outer rotor-to-bore clearance is 0.15-0.20 mm (0.006-0.008 in.) with a wear limit of 0.26 mm (0.010 in.). Minimum allowable outer rotor height is 7.45 mm (0.293 in.). Maximum allowable pump bore depth is 7.56 mm (0.298 in.). Specified rotor-to-body side clearance is 0.02-0.09 mm (0.0008-0.0040 in.) with a wear limit of 0.11 mm (0.004 in.). Pump bore wear limit is 29.21 mm (1.150 in.).

CAMSHAFT

Camshaft and camshaft gear are an integral casting equipped with a compression release mechanism (Fig. HE2-7). To remove the camshaft, drain the oil and remove the engine. Remove any parts attached to the engine crankshaft. Clean the crankshaft and remove any rust or burrs. Unscrew the oil pan retaining screws and remove the oil pan. Remove the camshaft. Identify the valve tappets if they are removed so they can be returned to their original locations.

Standard camshaft bearing journal diameter is 15.984 mm (0.6293 in.). Replace the camshaft if journal diameter is less than 15.916 mm (0.6266 in.).

Standard camshaft lobe height (Fig. HE2-8) is 32.60 mm (1.283 in.) for intake lobe and 32.09 mm (1.263 in.) for exhaust lobe. If the intake lobe measures less than 32.35 mm (1.274 in.), or the exhaust lobe measures less than 31.84 mm (1.254 in.), replace the camshaft.

Inspect the compression release mechanism for damage. The spring must pull the weight tightly against the camshaft so the decompressor lobe holds the exhaust valve slightly open.

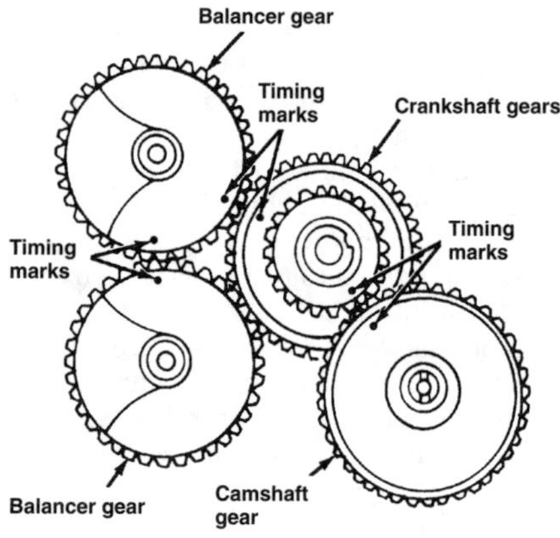

Fig. HE2-9—Drawing showing correct alignment of timing marks on crankshaft, camshaft and balancer shaft gears.

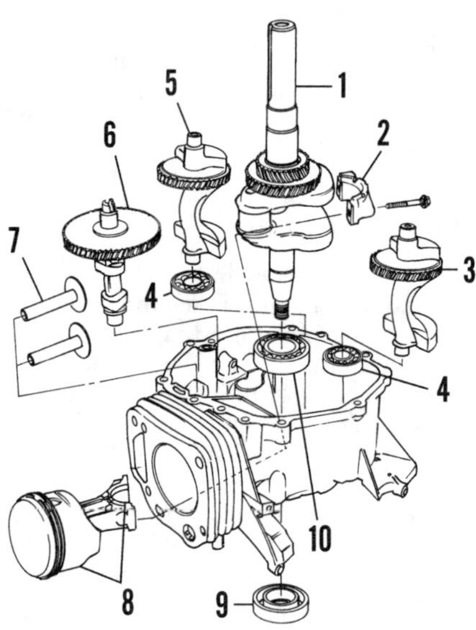

Fig. HE2-10—Exploded view of engine internal components.

1. Crankshaft
2. Rod cap
3. Balancer shaft
4. Bearings
5. Balancer shaft
6. Camshaft
7. Tappets
8. Piston & connecting rod assy.
9. Oil seal
10. Main bearing

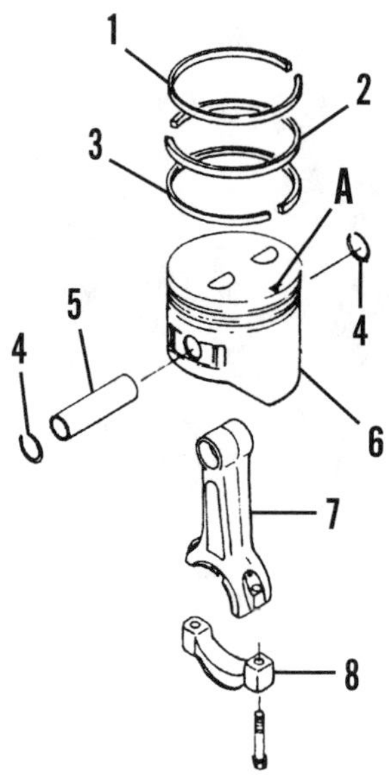

Fig. HE2-11—Long side of connecting rod and arrowhead (triangle) on top of piston must be on the same side and facing toward push rod side of engine after installation. Refer to text.

A. Arrowhead
1. Top ring
2. Second ring
3. Oil control ring
4. Retaining ring
5. Piston pin
6. Piston
7. Connecting rod
8. Rod cap

When installing the camshaft, make certain the camshaft and crankshaft gear timing marks are aligned as shown in Fig. HE2-9. Be sure the slot in the end of the camshaft aligns with the oil pump rotor when installing the oil pan. Tighten the oil pan screws to 24 N·m (212 in.-lb.).

BALANCER SHAFTS

The engine is equipped with two balancer shafts (3 and 5—Fig. HE2-10) that are accessible after removing the oil pan. See previous section for oil pan removal procedure. Each balancer shaft is supported by ball bearings (4) at both ends that are a press fit in the crankcase and oil pan. Crankcase or oil pan must be replaced if a ball bearing is loose in the bore.

Timing marks must be aligned as shown in Fig. HE2-9 during installation of the shafts.

PISTON, PIN AND RINGS

Piston and connecting rod are removed as an assembly. To remove the piston and connecting rod, remove the cylinder head and oil pan. Remove any carbon or ridge, if present, from the top of the cylinder prior to removing the piston. Remove the connecting rod cap screws and cap (2—Fig. HE2-10). Push the connecting rod and piston assembly (8) out of the cylinder.

The camshaft can also be removed if required. Remove the piston pin retaining rings (4—Fig. HE2-11) and separate the piston from the connecting rod.

Measure the piston diameter 10 mm (0.4 in.) above the lower edge of the skirt and 90 degrees from the piston pin. Specified standard diameter is 87.985 mm (3.4640 in.). Wear limit is 87.85 mm (3.459 in.). Oversize pistons are available.

Standard clearance between the piston pin and pin bore in the piston is 0.002-0.014 mm (0.0001-0.0006 in.) for all models. If the clearance is 0.08 mm (0.0031 in.) or greater, replace the piston and/or pin.

Standard piston pin bore diameter is 20.002 mm (0.7875 in.). Reject the piston if the piston pin bore diameter is 20.042 mm (0.7890 in.) or more.

Standard piston pin diameter is 20.000 mm (0.7874 in.). Reject the piston pin if diameter is 19.95 mm (0.785 in.) or less.

Clean any deposits from the piston ring grooves, being careful not to damage the ring lands. Insert a new compression ring into the ring groove and measure the side clearance between the ring and ring land with a feeler gauge. The specified compression ring side clearance is 0.030-0.060 mm (0.0012-0.0024 in.). Replace the piston if side clearance exceeds 0.15 mm (0.006 in.).

Ring end gap for the compression rings should be 0.2-0.4 mm (0.008-0.016 in.). If ring end gap for any ring is 1.0 mm (0.039 in.) or more, replace the ring and/or cylinder. Oversize piston rings are available.

Install the marked piston rings with the marked side toward the piston crown and stagger the ring end gaps equally around the piston. Install the chrome plated piston ring in the top piston ring groove.

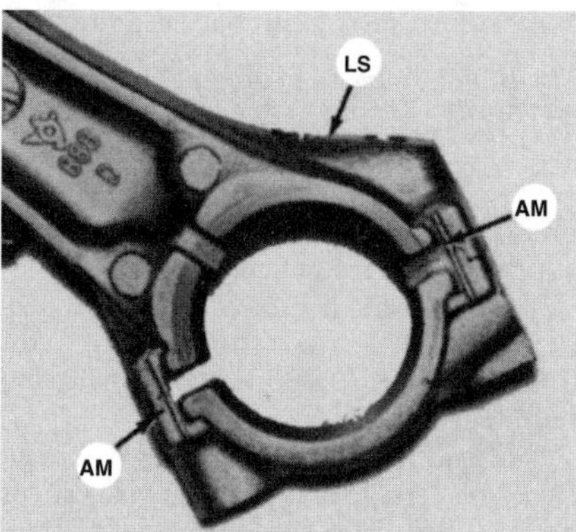

Fig. HE2-12—View of connecting rod. Match marks (AM) on rod and cap must be aligned.

When assembling the piston on the connecting rod, the long side of connecting rod (LS—Fig. HE2-12) and the arrowhead (A—Fig. HE2-11) on the piston crown must be on same side.

Lubricate the piston and cylinder with engine oil. Use a piston ring compressor tool to compress the rings and install the piston in the cylinder. Note that the arrowhead on the piston crown must be on the push rod side of the engine.

Align the connecting rod cap and connecting rod match marks (AM—Fig. HE2-12). Install connecting rod screws and tighten to 14 N·m (124 in.-lb.).

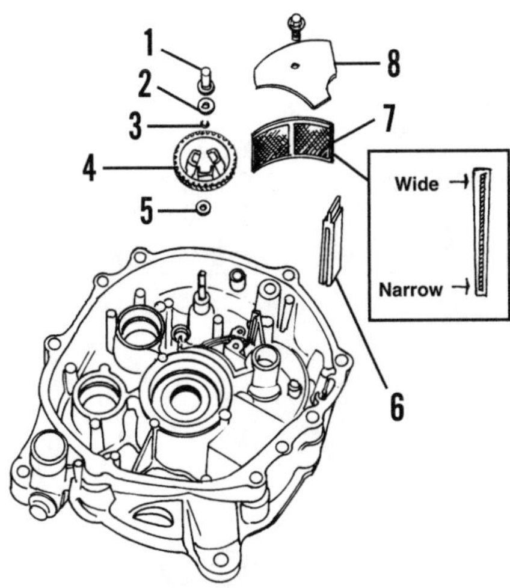

Fig. HE2-13—Exploded view of the governor assembly.

1. Governor slider
2. Washer
3. Retaining clip
4. Governor weight
5. Thrust washer
6. Oil return rubber
7. Oil strainer screen
8. Plate

Fig. HE2-14—Exploded view of electric starter motor.

1. Bolt
2. End cap
3. Bushing
4. O-ring
5. Brush
6. Spring
7. Brush holder plate
8. Frame
9. O-ring
10. Thrust washer
11. Armature
12. Thrust washer
13. Drive gear
14. Spring
15. Collar
16. Snap ring
17. Drive housing
18. Solenoid

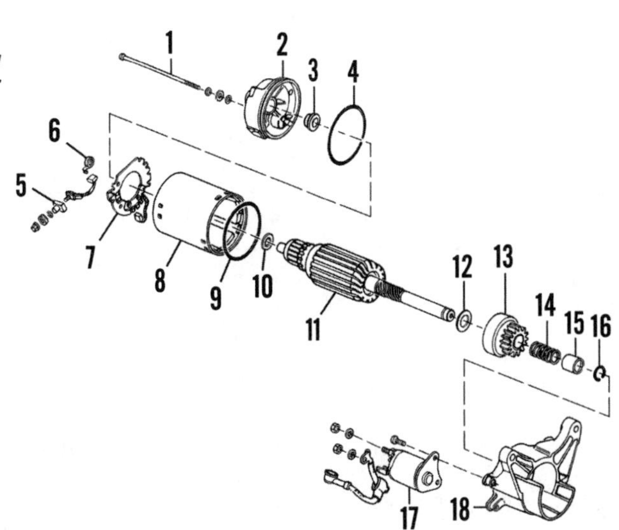

CONNECTING ROD

The aluminum alloy connecting rod rides directly on the crankpin journal. Refer to the previous PISTON, PIN AND RINGS paragraphs for removal and installation procedure.

Standard piston pin bore diameter in the connecting rod is 20.005 mm (0.7876 in.). Replace the connecting rod if the diameter is 20.07 mm (0.790 in.).

Standard connecting rod bearing bore-to-crankpin clearance is 0.040-0.066 mm (0.0016-0.0026 in.). Replace the connecting rod and/or crankshaft if clearance is 0.12 mm (0.005 in.) or more.

Standard big end diameter is 36.025-36.041 mm (1.4183-1.4189 in.). Maximum allowable standard big end diameter is 36.07 mm (1.420 in.). An undersize connecting rod is available.

Connecting rod side play on the crankpin should be 0.1-0.7 mm (0.004-0.028 in.). Replace the connecting rod if the side play is 1.0 mm (0.039 in.) or more.

When assembling the piston on the connecting rod, the long side (LS—Fig. HE2-12) of the connecting rod and the arrowhead on the piston crown (Fig. HE2-11) must be on the same side.

When installing the piston and connecting rod assembly in the cylinder, the arrowhead on the piston crown must be on the push rod side of engine. Align the connecting rod cap and connecting rod match marks (AM—Fig. HE2-12). Install the connecting rod screws and tighten to 14 N·m (124 in.-lb.).

CRANKSHAFT, MAIN BEARINGS AND SEALS

The crankshaft is supported at each end in the ball bearing main bearings (10—Fig. HE2-10). The crankshaft (1) may be removed after removing the piston as previously outlined.

The standard crankpin journal diameter is 35.975-35.985 mm (1.4163-1.4167 in) with a wear limit of 35.930 mm (1.4146 in.).

The timing gears are a press fit on the crankshaft. Prior to removal of the timing gears, mark the position of the gears on the crankshaft using the timing marks on the gears as a reference point. Transfer the marks to the new timing gears so they can be installed in the same position as the old gears.

Ball bearing main bearings are a press fit on the flywheel end of the crankshaft and in the bearing bore of the oil pan. Replace the bearings if damaged or rough. Replace the oil pan if the bearing bore is excessively worn.

Seals should be pressed into the seal bores until the outer edge of the seal is flush with the seal bore.

When installing the crankshaft, make certain the timing marks on the crankshaft gear, camshaft gear and balancer gears are aligned as shown in Fig. HE2-9.

CYLINDER AND CRANKCASE

Cylinder and crankcase are an integral casting. The specified standard cylinder bore size is 88.000 mm (3.4646 in.). Replace the cylinder if cylinder bore diameter exceeds 88.17 mm (3.471 in.).

GOVERNOR

The centrifugal flyweight governor located in the oil pan controls engine rpm via external linkage. Refer to the GOVERNOR paragraphs in the MAINTENANCE section for adjustment procedure.

To remove the governor, drain the oil and remove the engine. Remove any parts attached to the crankshaft. Clean the crankshaft and remove any rust or burrs. Unscrew the oil pan retaining screws and remove the oil pan. Remove the governor slider (1—Fig. HE2-13) and washer (2). Detach the retaining clip (3) and withdraw the governor weight (4) and thrust washer (5) from the stub shaft.

Install the governor assembly by reversing the removal procedure. Adjust the external linkage as outlined under GOVERNOR in the MAINTENANCE section.

OIL STRAINER SCREEN

An oil strainer screen (7—Fig. HE2-13) is located in the oil pan. The screen should be removed and cleaned whenever the oil pan is removed for service.

Install the screen with the narrow end toward the oil pan.

ELECTRIC STARTER

All models are equipped with an electric starter (Fig. HE2-14). Cranking voltage should be 8.5 volts dc under load and 11.5 volts dc under no load. Cranking current should be below 165 amps under load and below 20 amps under no load.

Push the collar (15—Fig. HE2-14) toward the starter for access to the snap ring (16). Remove the bolts (1) and separate the end housings, frame and armature.

Minimum brush length is 8.5 mm (0.34 in.). Align tabs and grooves when assembling the brush plate, frame and drive end housing.

HONDA

Model	No. Cyls.	Bore	Stroke	Displacement	Power Rating
GX640	2	76 mm (2.99 in.)	70 mm (2.76 in.)	635 cc (38.7 cu. in.)	9.7 kW (13 hp)

Model GX640 is a four-stroke, overhead cam, single-cylinder, liquid-cooled engine with a horizontal crankshaft. Flywheel is located at the front of the engine as it sits in the tractor.

MAINTENANCE

LUBRICATION

Engine oil level should be checked prior to operating the engine. Check the oil level with the oil cap just touching the first threads, but not screwed in.

The engine oil should be changed after the first 20 hours of engine operation and after every 100 hours thereafter. Change the oil filter after every 300 hours of operation or after two years, whichever occurs first.

Use engine oil that meets the latest API service classification. Use SAE 10W-30 or 10W-40 oil. SAE 10W-40 may be used if the temperature is above 90°F (32°C).

Crankcase capacity is 2.0 liters (2.2 qt.). After changing the oil filter, be sure to check the engine oil level after running the engine.

AIR CLEANER

The engine is equipped with a dry air filter that should be cleaned and inspected after every 50 hours of operation. Replace the filter element if any damage is evident.

Remove the foam and paper air filter elements from the air filter housing. The foam element should be washed in a mild detergent and water solution, rinsed in clean water and allowed to air dry. Soak the foam element in clean engine oil. Squeeze out excess oil.

The paper element may be cleaned by directing a low-pressure compressed air stream from inside the filter toward the outside. Reinstall the elements. Be sure elements fit properly.

COOLANT SYSTEM

The engine is cooled by a 50:50 mixture of clean water and permanent antifreeze. Refer to the tractor section for maintenance requirements.

SPARK PLUG

The spark plug should be removed, cleaned and inspected after every 100 hours of use.

Recommended spark plug is NGK BPR5ES-11 or ND W16PR-U11. Spark plug electrode gap should be 1.0-1.1 mm (0.039-0.043 in.).

When installing the spark plug, thread the spark plug in finger tight. Then for a new plug, tighten an additional ½ turn. For a used plug, tighten an additional ¼ turn.

CARBURETOR

Adjustment

The engine is equipped with a float carburetor with a fixed main fuel jet and an adjustable idle speed fuel mixture needle.

To adjust the carburetor control cable and linkage, proceed as follows: Place the speed control lever to the FAST position. The gap (G—Fig. HE3-1) between the throttle arm and choke arm should be 0-0.5 mm (0.0-0.02 in.). To adjust the gap, loosen the cable housing clamp and relocate the cable. If gap adjustment is not possible by relocating the cable housing, retighten the clamp screw. Adjust the throttle cable by rotating the adjusting nuts at the upper end of the throttle cable.

To adjust the choke control, move the speed control lever to the START position. The choke plate in the carburetor should be closed. Bend the choke link at the U to adjust the choke plate position.

Initial setting for the idle mixture screw (IM—Fig. HE3-2) is 1¼ turns out. Perform final adjustment with the engine at normal operating temperature and running.

Operate the engine at idle speed and adjust the idle mixture screw (IM) to obtain a smooth idle and satisfactory acceleration. Adjust the idle speed by turning idle speed screw (IS). Recommended idle speed is 1750 rpm.

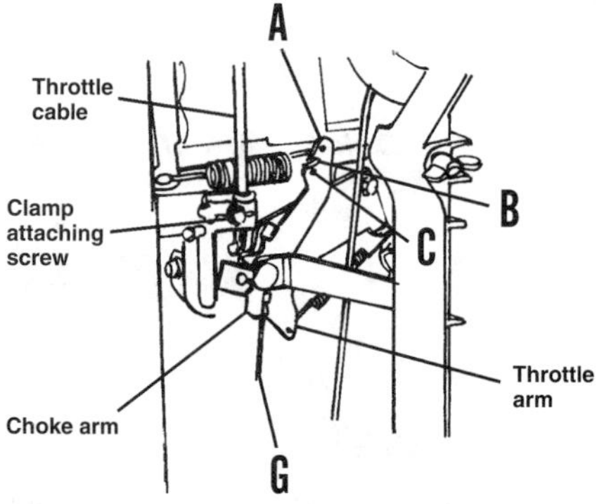

Fig. HE3-1—View of speed control linkage. Refer to text for adjustment procedure.

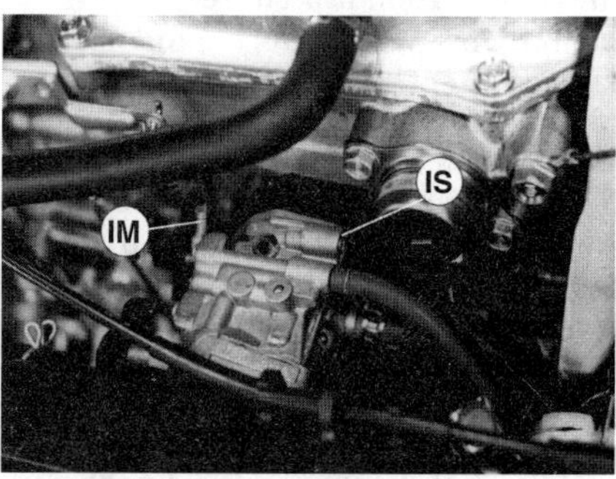

Fig. HE3-2—Adjust idle speed mixture screw (IM) and idle stop screw (IS) as outlined in text.

Removal and Installation

To remove the carburetor, open the hood and remove the air cleaner assembly. Detach the air vent tube from the frame clamp. Disconnect the fuel line from the carburetor. Disconnect the electrical connector from the fuel shut-off solenoid. Disconnect the throttle rod and choke rod and withdraw the carburetor (11—Fig. HE3-3).

To disassemble for cleaning and inspection, separate the solenoid valve (19—Fig. HE3-4) from the float chamber (15). Remove the screws attaching the float chamber to the carburetor body and remove the float chamber. Push out the float pin (6) and remove

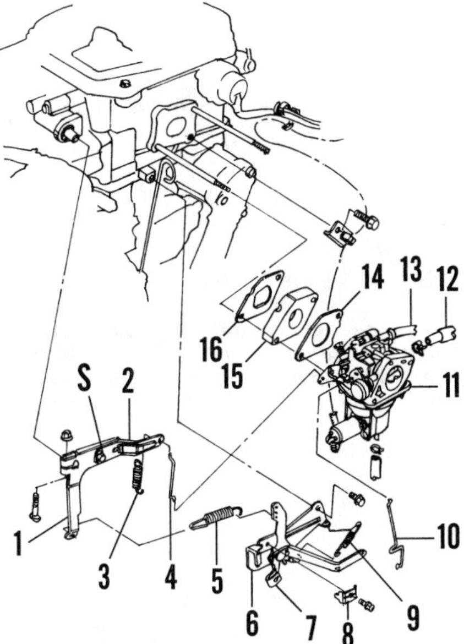

Fig. HE3-3—Exploded view of governor linkage. Note the position of notches in the carburetor gaskets and insulator when installing the carburetor.

1. Governor lower arm
2. Governor upper arm
3. Throttle return spring
4. Governor rod
5. Governor spring
6. Governor control plate
7. Choke arm
8. Cable clamp
9. Return spring
10. Choke rod
11. Carburetor
12. Fuel line
13. Air vent tube
14. Gasket
15. Insulator
16. Gasket

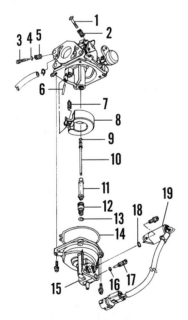

Fig. HE3-4—Exploded view of the carburetor.

1. Idle speed screw
2. Spring
3. Idle mixture screw
4. O-ring
5. Spring
6. Float pin
7. Fuel inlet valve
8. Float
9. O-ring
10. Jet needle
11. Nozzle
12. Main jet
13. O-ring
14. Gasket
15. Fuel bowl
16. O-ring
17. Drain screw
18. O-ring
19. Fuel cutoff solenoid

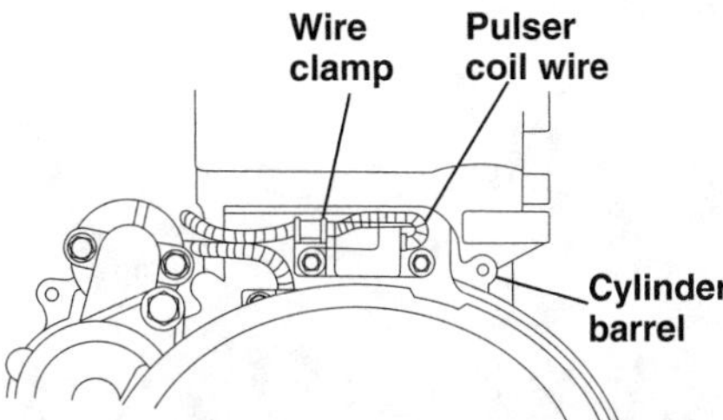

Fig. HE3-5—Ignition pulser coil is mounted on the cylinder barrel behind the flywheel.

the float (8) and fuel inlet valve (7). Remove the main jet (12), nozzle (11) and jet needle (10). Unscrew the idle mixture screw (3).

If a cleaning solvent is used to clean the carburetor, be sure it will not damage the plastic parts of carburetor.

Standard main jet size is #95. Install the nozzle (11) so the smaller diameter end is toward the carburetor body.

To check the fuel shut-off solenoid valve operation, connect a 12-volt battery to the solenoid connector. The valve needle should project out 3.5 mm (0.14 in.) if the solenoid is operating properly. Avoid applying voltage longer than 15 seconds when testing the solenoid.

To check the float level, position the carburetor so the float hangs down but just pushes against the fuel inlet valve. Measure from the top edge of the float to the float chamber mating edge of the carburetor body. Measurement should be 14 mm (0.55 in.). Float height is not adjustable. If the fuel inlet valve is in good condition, replace the float if float height is incorrect.

Assemble the carburetor using new O-rings. Assemble the float chamber to the body with the drain screw (17) facing to the rear.

When installing the carburetor, install inner gasket (16—Fig. HE3-3) and insulator (15) so the notch is on the upper left. Install the outer gasket (14) so the notched side is on the lower right.

The choke link (10) must be installed so the U points away from the carburetor.

GOVERNOR

A mechanical flyweight governor is located inside a compartment on the front of the engine. Refer to the REPAIRS section for service information.

Before adjusting the external linkage, check the carburetor control adjustments described in the previous section.

To adjust the governor linkage, make certain all linkage is in good condition and the governor spring (5—Fig. HE3-3) is not stretched or damaged.

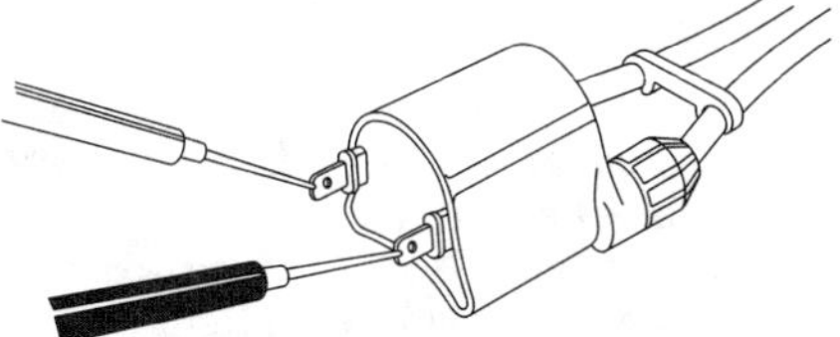

Fig. HE3-6—To check the ignition coil, use an ohmmeter to check the resistance of the primary winding (shown) and the secondary winding. Refer to text for specifications.

Loosen the governor lever screw (S). Push the inner governor lever (1) counterclockwise as far as possible and hold the governor lever in this position. Move the outer governor lever (2) so the throttle is completely open. Tighten the screw (S).

Start the engine and operate at an idle until operating temperature has been reached. Attach a tachometer to the engine. Open the throttle so the engine is operating at maximum speed. Maximum unloaded engine speed should be 2950 rpm. If engine speed is too slow, reposition the governor spring in the next farthest hole (C—Fig. HE1-1) so spring length increases. If engine speed is too fast, reposition the governor spring in the closer hole (A) so spring length decreases.

If the specified engine speed cannot be obtained by altering the governor spring length, change the throttle cable effective length. To change the throttle cable effective length, either loosen the cable clamp and reposition the cable or adjust the nuts at the upper end of the throttle cable.

IGNITION SYSTEM

The breakerless ignition system requires no regular maintenance. A pulsar coil mounted behind the flywheel triggers the ignition. Air gap adjustment is not required.

To check the pulsar coil (Fig. HE3-5), disconnect the pulsar coil wire connector located on the right side of the engine (black and blue wires). Resistance between the pulsar coil terminals should be 350-430 ohms.

To check the ignition coil primary side, connect ohmmeter leads to primary blade terminals (Fig. HE3-6). Ohmmeter should indicate 0.35-0.43 ohm.

To check ignition coil secondary side, remove the spark plug caps and connect the ohmmeter leads the spark plug lead wires. Ohmmeter should indicate 8.0k-9.8k ohms.

If ohmmeter readings are not as specified, replace the ignition coil.

VALVE ADJUSTMENT

Valve-to-rocker arm clearance should be checked and adjusted after every 300 hours of operation.

To adjust the valve clearance, first remove the rocker arm cover. Remove the spark plugs. Rotate the flywheel by turning the cooling fan so the T-mark on the flywheel is visible through the inspection hole (H—Fig. HE3-7) in the flywheel cover. Check the valve clearance on the cylinder with closed valves (rocker arms should be loose).

Insert a feeler gauge between the rocker arm and the end of the valve stem (Fig. HE3-8). Loosen the rocker arm jam nut and turn the adjusting screw to obtain desired clearance. Specified clearance is 0.10-0.14 mm (0.004-0.005 in.) for intake and 0.18-0.22 mm (0.007-0.008 in.) for exhaust. Tighten the jam nut and recheck the clearance.

Rotate the flywheel one revolution so the T-mark reappears and repeat the adjustment sequence to adjust the valves of the remaining cylinder.

COMPRESSION PRESSURE

Compression pressure measured at cranking speed should be 392-686 kPa (57-99 psi). Note that this pressure reading occurs when the decompressor operates. The decompressor holds open the intake valves when the electric starter rotates the engine.

REPAIRS

TIGHTENING TORQUES

The recommended special tightening torque specifications are as follows:

Camshaft pulley	**30 N·m (22 ft.-lb.)**
Connecting rod	**29 N·m (21 ft.-lb.)**
Crankcase:	
M8	**22 N·m (195 in.-lb.)**
M10	**44 N·m (32 ft.-lb.)**
Crankshaft nut	**67.5 N·m (50 ft.-lb.)**
Cylinder head	**55 N·m (40 ft.-lb.)**
Flywheel	**71 N·m (52 ft.-lb.)**
Muffler	**22 N·m (195 in.-lb.)**

CRANKCASE BREATHER

The engine is equipped with a crankcase breather located on the underside of the cylinder head cover. The crankcase breather provides a vacuum for the crankcase. Vapor from the crankcase is evacuated to the air cleaner. A reed valve acts as a one-way valve to maintain crankcase vacuum. The breather system must operate properly or excessive oil consumption can result.

Check that the reed valve is not damaged and seats properly. Replace if distorted or damaged. Inspect the breather tube for leakage.

Fig. HE3-7—Align "T" mark on flywheel with index mark in inspection hole (H) to set piston at top dead center.

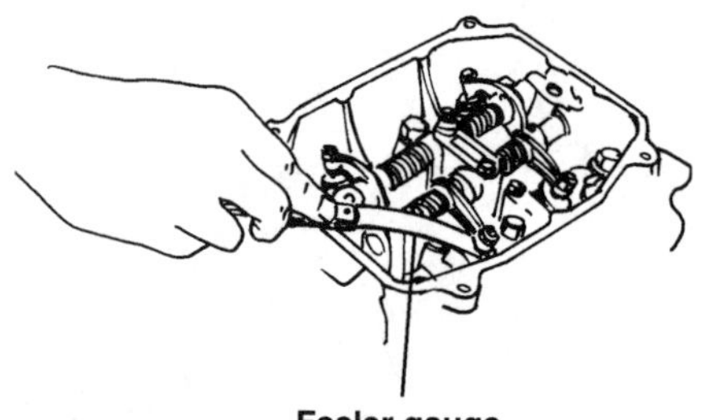

Fig. HE3-8—Check the intake and exhaust valve clearance for the cylinder that is at top dead center of its compression stroke. Use a feeler gauge to measure the clearance.

THERMOSTAT

A thermostat (19—Fig. HE3-9) regulates the engine coolant temperature. The thermostat is contained in the thermostat housing (21) on the side of the cylinder block. The thermostat should be fully open at 95° C (203° F).

When installing the thermostat be sure the small hole in the mounting flange is up.

TIMING BELT

A cogged belt, which engages a pulley on the crankshaft, drives the water pump and camshaft. See Fig. HE3-9. No maintenance is required, however, a damaged or excessively worn belt or pulley should be replaced. Refer to the camshaft or crankshaft service sections if pulley service is required.

Belt Tension

To check timing belt tension, remove the engine rear cover. Loosen the idler retaining screw (6—Fig. HE3-9) so the idler tension spring (8) pulls the idler against the belt. Rotate the crankshaft approximately ⅛ turn clockwise (viewed as shown in Fig. HE3-9), then rotate the crankshaft approximately 1/4 turn counterclockwise. Retighten the idler screw (5).

Measure timing belt deflection at the midpoint between the camshaft pulley (11) and crankshaft pulley (9). A force of 20 N (4.5 lb.) should deflect the belt 4-7 mm (0.16-0.27 in.). If belt tension is not correct, replace the idler spring (3). When installing the spring, attach the large end loop of the spring to the stud (18).

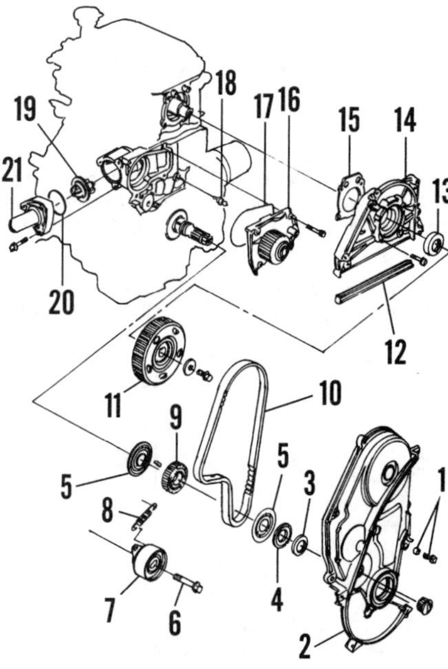

Fig. HE3-9—Exploded view of engine timing belt and pulleys.

1. Cap screw & spacer (7)
2. Timing belt cover
3. Nut
4. Lock washer
5. Flange washers
6. Idler bolt
7. Idler pulley
8. Spring
9. Crankshaft pulley
10. Timing belt
11. Camshaft pulley
12. Gasket
13. Oil seal
14. Rear cover
15. Gasket
16. Water pump assy.
17. Gasket
18. Spring anchor bolt
19. Thermostat
20. Gasket
21. Thermostat cover

Removal And Installation

Remove the engine rear cover (2—Fig. HE3-9). Detach the tension spring (8). Loosen the idler retaining screw (6). Move the idler away from the belt then retighten the screw to hold the pulley out of way. Remove the belt (10).

Before installing the belt, rotate the crankshaft so the mark on the drive pulley aligns with the mating surface of the crankcase and cylinder block (Fig.

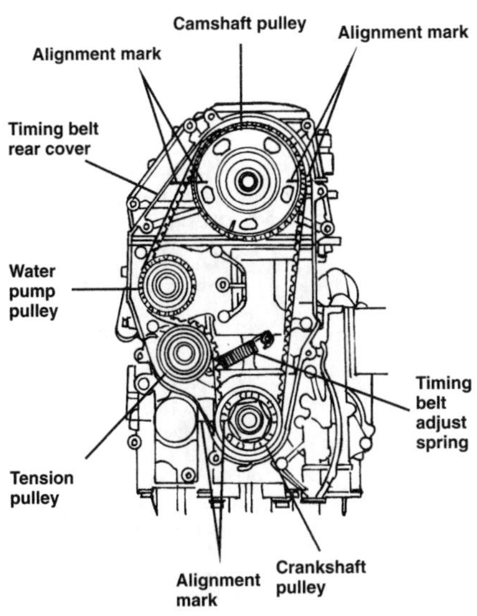

Fig. HE3-10—View of timing belt and drive pulleys. Refer to text for timing procedure.

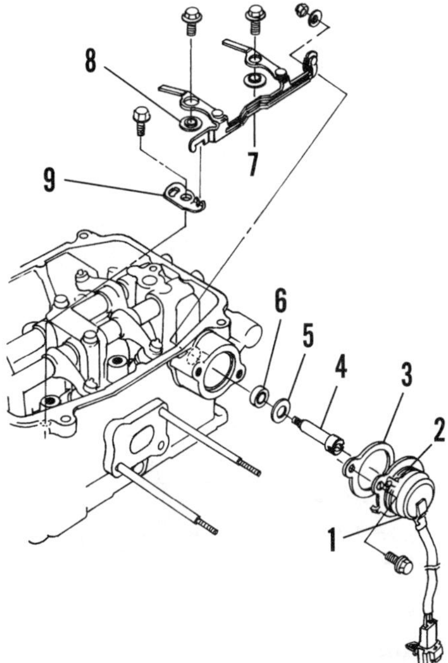

Fig. HE3-11—Exploded view of the decompressor assembly.

1. Decompressor solenoid
2. Spring pin
3. Gasket
4. Plunger
5. Washer
6. Oil seal
7. Decompressor lever assy.
8. Flange washer
9. Decompressor stop

HE3-10). Position the camshaft pulley so the UP mark is up and the two alignment lines on the pulley align with the marks on the upper timing cover (Fig. HE3-10).

Install the timing belt as shown in Fig. HE3-10. Loosen the idler screw (6—Fig. HE3-9) and attach the tension spring (8) to the pulley. Turn the crankshaft approximately ⅛ turn counterclockwise. Then turn the crankshaft clockwise ¼ turn and tighten the idler screw (6).

Rotate the crankshaft in the normal direction for two revolutions. Recheck the timing marks for alignment. Reinstall the belt if the marks do not align. Check the belt tension as previously described.

Install the timing belt cover (2), spacers (1) and cap screws. Tighten the cap screws to 8 N·m (70 in.-lb.).

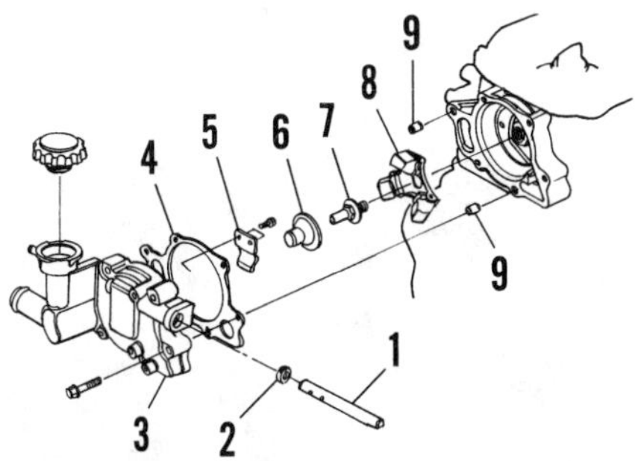

Fig. HE3-12—Exploded view of governor assembly.

1. Governor shaft
2. Oil seal
3. Governor housing
4. Gasket
5. Governor fork
6. Slider
7. Shaft stud
8. Flyweight assy.
9. Dowel pin

WATER PUMP

The water pump (16—Fig. HE3-9) is located at the rear of engine behind the engine rear cover. Remove the rear cover for access to the water pump.

Remove the timing belt as described in the previous section. Unscrew the water pump retaining screws and remove the pump.

The water pump is available only as a unit assembly. Before installing the water pump be sure to install the O-ring gasket (17—Fig. HE3-9) on the pump. Reinstall the timing belt and adjust the belt tension as previously described.

DECOMPRESSOR

The engine is equipped with a decompressor device that holds the intake valves open during starting. An electric solenoid (1—Fig. HE3-11) actuates the plunger (4). The plunger actuates the decompressor lever (7) causing the ends of the levers to be inserted under the intake rocker arms.

Adjustment

Remove the cylinder head cover. Rotate the flywheel by turning the cooling fan so the T-mark on the flywheel is visible through the window in the flywheel cover (Fig. HE3-7). Move the solenoid end of the decompressor lever (7—Fig. HE3-11) so the lever ends are pushed under the intake rocker arms.

The levers should not protrude from the side of the rocker arms more than 0.5 mm (0.02 in.). Loosen the retaining screw and move the stop (9) to adjust the position of the lever ends. Retighten the retaining screw.

Testing

The solenoid may be tested without removing the solenoid from the cylinder head. Disconnect the electrical connector. Connect an ohmmeter to the solenoid connector. Specified resistance reading between the connector terminals is 4.5-5.6 ohms at a temperature of 68° F (20° C).

Removal And Installation

To remove the decompressor, remove the screws attaching the solenoid (1—Fig. HE3-11) to the cylinder head. Disconnect the wiring connector and remove the solenoid. Remove the rocker cover. Unscrew the nut retaining the plunger (4) and withdraw the plunger from the cylinder head. Unscrew the two cap screws retaining the decompressor lever (7) and remove the lever and washers (8).

When assembling the decompressor, align the projections on the washers (8) engage the holes in the compressor levers (7). Align the notch in decompressor lever (7) end with the cutout on plunger (4). The notch in the outer end of the plunger (4) must engage the spring pin (2) on the solenoid (1).

GOVERNOR

The governor flyweight assembly is attached to the camshaft and contained in a compartment at the front of the cylinder head.

To disassemble the governor, remove the engine rear cover for access to the camshaft drive pulley. Remove the governor cover (3—Fig. HE3-12) from the front of the engine. Use a suitable spanner wrench to hold the camshaft drive pulley, then unscrew the slider shaft (7) from the camshaft.

To assemble the governor, place the flyweight assembly (8) on the camshaft and hold in place with the slider shaft (7). Be sure the flyweight base fits on camshaft properly. While holding the camshaft drive pulley, tighten the slider shaft (7) to 43 N·m (32 ft.-lb.).

Position the flyweights (8) over the slider (6) and install the slider onto the shaft (7). Be sure flyweights and slider move smoothly. If removed, install a new oil seal (2) with the lip facing inward. In-

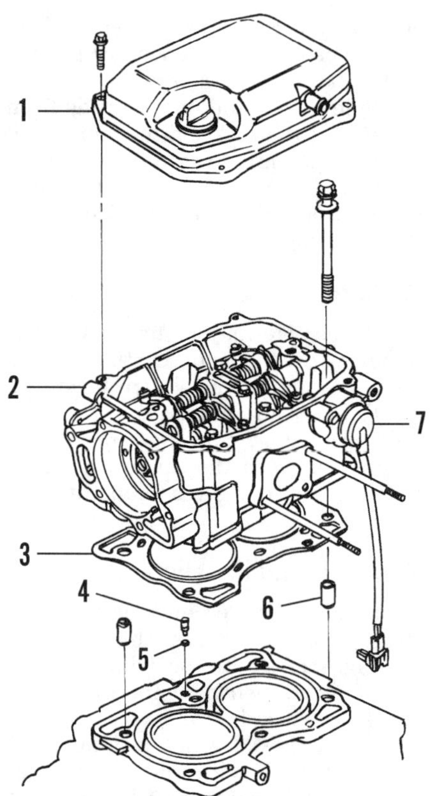

Fig. HE3-13—Drawing of the cylinder head.

1. Rocker cover
2. Cylinder head
3. Head gasket
4. Oil orifice
5. O-ring
6. Dowel pin (2)

Fig. HE3-14—Exploded view of cylinder head and valve components.

1. Long springs (3)
2. Short spring (1)
3. Rocker arm
4. Adjuster screw
5. Nut
6. Spacer
7. Bolt (2)
8. Keepers
9. Valve spring retainer
10. Valve spring
11. Spring seat
12. Valve seal
13. Intake valve
14. Exhaust valve
15. Camshaft
16. Intake rocker shaft
17. Exhaust rocker shaft

sert the governor shaft (1) and attach the fork (5) to the shaft. Install the governor cover (3) with a new gasket (4).

CYLINDER HEAD

To remove the cylinder head, proceed as follows. Drain the coolant and detach the coolant hoses. Remove the engine from the tractor.

Remove the shrouds and spark plugs. Remove the carburetor, intake manifold, exhaust manifold and timing belt. Disconnect the decompressor electrical connector. Remove the cylinder head bolts and lift the cylinder head from the engine.

Inspect the cylinder head for cracks and other damage. Maximum allowable cylinder head surface warpage is 0.10 mm (0.004 in.).

To install the cylinder head, reverse the removal procedure and note the following special instructions: Be sure to install the oil metering orifice (4—Fig. HE3-13) and the O-ring (5) in the oil passage located at the side of the cylinder block and head. Install a new cylinder head gasket with the UP mark on the gasket facing up and toward the intake side of the engine. Tighten the cylinder head screws in a crossing pattern starting with the inner screws. Tighten screws in three steps to final toque of 23 N·m (17 ft.-lb.).

CAMSHAFT AND VALVE SYSTEM

Remove the cylinder head as previously outlined. Remove the decompressor and governor as previously described. Use a suitable spanner wrench to hold the camshaft drive pulley (11—Fig. HE3-9), then remove the pulley retaining screw and pulley. Unscrew and remove the timing belt upper cover (14).

Unscrew the rocker shaft retaining screws (7—Fig. HE3-14) and extract the rocker arm shafts (16 and 17) while sliding components off the shafts. Identify the components as they are removed so they can be installed in their original locations. Remove the camshaft (15). Use a suitable valve spring compressor to compress the valve springs. Remove the valve keepers (8) and remove the valve assemblies from the head.

Valve face and seat angles are 45° for intake and exhaust. Standard valve seat width is 0.95-1.25 mm (0.037-0.049 in.). Narrow the seat if seat width is 2.0 mm (0.079) or more.

Standard valve spring free length is 38.64 mm (1.521 in.). Replace the valve spring if free length is 37.14 mm (1.462 in.) or less.

Standard valve guide inside diameter is 5.000-5.012 mm (0.1968-0.1973 in.). Replace the guide if inside diameter is 5.05 mm (0.199 in.) or more.

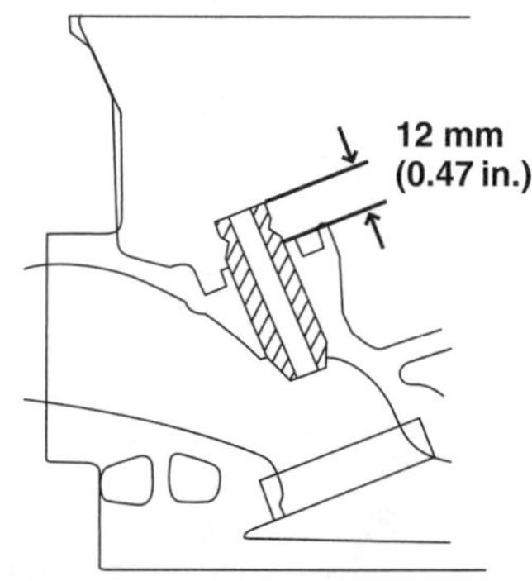

Fig. HE3-15—Drive in new valve guides so the guide protrudes 12 mm (0.47 in.).

Intake valve stem diameter should be 4.98-4.99 mm (0.1961-0.1964 in.). Discard the intake valve if stem diameter is less than 4.85 mm (0.191 in.).

Exhaust valve stem diameter should be 4.96-4.97 mm (0.1953-0.1957 in.). Discard the exhaust valve if stem diameter is less than 4.83 mm (0.190 in.).

Use valve guide driver 07942-MA60000 to remove and install guides. Drive out the valve guide toward the valve spring side of the head. Chill the new valve guides in a freezer for approximately one hour prior to installation. Drive the valve guide toward the combustion side of the head until the guide protrudes 12 mm (0.47 in.) above the adjacent head surface. See Fig. HE3-15. New valve guides must be reamed after installation.

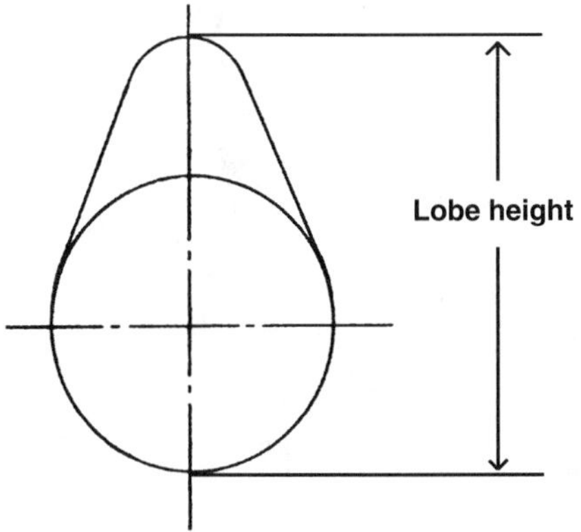

Fig. HE3-16—Measure camshaft lobe height as shown.

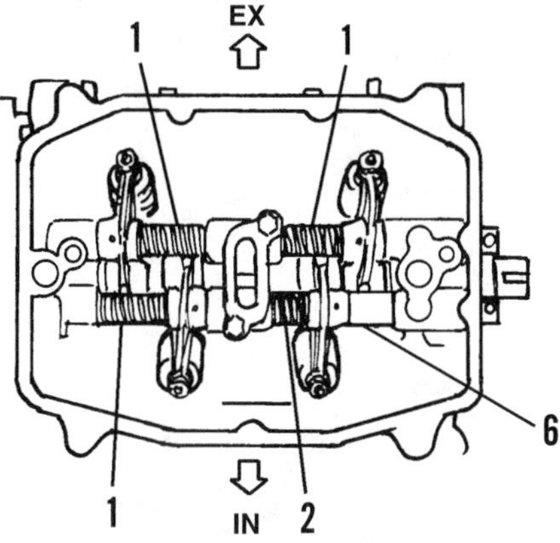

Fig. HE3-17—Assemble rocker shaft assemblies so the long springs (1), short spring (2) and spacer (6) are located as shown.

Standard camshaft lobe height (Fig. HE3-16) is 30.67-30.95 mm (1.207-1.218 in.) for the intake lobe and 30.71-30.99 mm (1.209-1.220 in.) for the exhaust lobe. If the intake or exhaust lobe measures less than 30.55 mm (1.203 in.), replace the camshaft.

The standard camshaft bearing journal diameter is 27.959-27.980 mm (1.1007-1.1016 in.). Replace the camshaft if journal diameter is less than 27.9 mm (1.098 in.).

The standard rocker arm inside diameter is 12.000-12.018 mm (0.4724-0.4731 in.) with a wear limit of 12.030 mm (0.4736 in.). Standard rocker shaft diameter is 11.976-11.994 mm (0.4715-0.4722 in.) with a wear limit of 11.970 mm (0.4713 in.).

When reassembling the camshaft and valve system, install the hollow rocker arm shaft (17—Fig. HE3-14) on the exhaust side. The notch on each rocker shaft must index with the retaining screw (7). Shaft end with a hole must be toward the timing belt end of the head. Refer to Fig. HE3-17 and note the arrangement of the three long springs (1), the short spring (2) and the spacer (6) on the rocker arm shafts.

Tighten the camshaft drive pulley retaining screw to 30 N·m (19 ft.-lb.). Install the cylinder head, governor and timing belt as previously described. Adjust the valve clearance, decompressor linkage and timing belt tension.

OIL PUMP

The oil pump is located on the front of the engine and includes a mounting pad for the oil filter (Fig. HE3-18). The left balancer shaft drives the oil pump.

An oil filter screen (10—Fig. HE3-19) is located in the crankcase/oil pan (11). Drain the engine oil prior to removing the screen.

To disassemble the oil pump, remove the oil pump housing (8—Fig. HE3-18) from the engine. Remove the oil pump cover (14) and separate the pump rotors (11 and 12) and shaft (10) from the housing.

Inspect the pump and make certain the oil passages are clear and the pump body is not damaged. Inner-to-outer rotor clearance should be 0.14 mm (0.0055 in.). If clearance is 0.28 mm (0.011 in.) or more, replace the rotors.

Oil pump body-to-outer rotor clearance should be 0.15-0.21 mm (0.006-0.008 in.). If clearance is 0.30 mm (0.012 in.) or more, replace the rotors and/or pump cover (14).

Side clearance between the face of the pump housing (14) and either rotor should be 0.04-0.09 mm (0.002-0.0035 in.). Maximum allowable side clearance is 0.11 mm (0.004 in.).

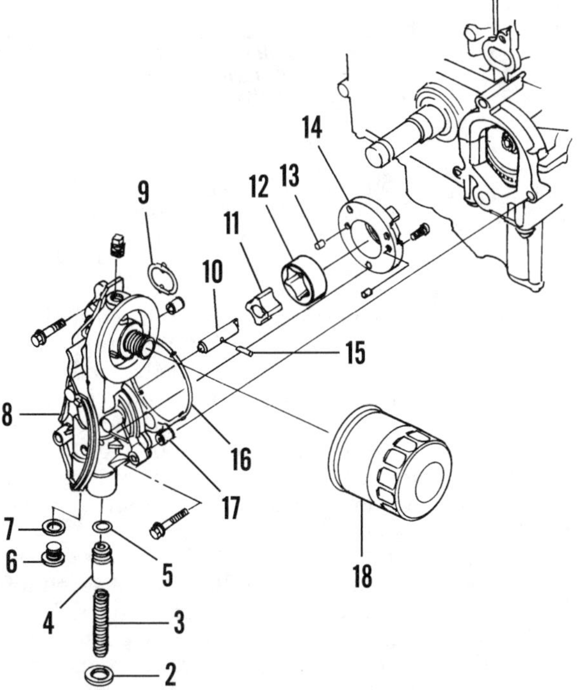

Fig. HE3-18—Exploded view of the oil pump.

1. Plug
2. Seal washer
3. Relief valve spring
4. Relief valve
5. O-ring
6. Plug
7. Seal washer
8. Oil pump housing
9. Gasket
10. Pump shaft
11. Inner rotor
12. Outer rotor
13. Dowel pin (2)
14. Pump body
15. Pin
16. Gasket
17. Dowel (2)
18. Oil filter

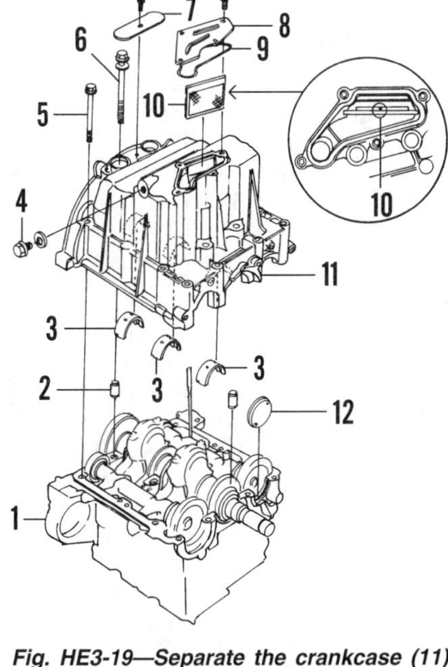

Fig. HE3-19—Separate the crankcase (11) from the cylinder block (1) for access to internal engine components. Two bolts (6) are located beneath the plate (7).

1. Cylinder block
2. Dowel pin
3. Main bearing inserts
4. Oil drain plug
5. Bolt (M8)
6. Bolt (M10)
7. Plate
8. Oil screen plate
9. O-ring
10. Oil filter screen
11. Crankcase/ oil pan
12. Seal plug

When assembling the oil pump, install the rotors so the punch mark on each rotor faces outward. Be sure the drive pin (15) engages the slot in the inner rotor (11). Apply Loctite to the threads of plugs (1 and 6). When installing the oil pump, the drive spline on the oil pump drive shaft must mesh with the notch on the balancer shaft.

Clean the oil filter screen (10—Fig. HE3-19) before installing. Install the screen so the arrow mark on the screen body is positioned as shown in Fig. HE3-19.

PISTONS, PINS AND RINGS

To remove the pistons, first remove the cylinder head as previously described. Separate the crankcase (11—Fig. HE3-19) and cylinder block (1) as outlined in the CRANKSHAFT, CRANKCASE AND CYLINDER BLOCK section. Remove the balance shafts (5 and 6—Fig. HE3-20). Mark the connecting rods and rod caps so they can be reinstalled in their original positions on the crankshaft. Remove the rod caps (1) and push the connecting rods and pistons (12) out of the cylinder block. Detach the piston pin clip (6—Fig. HE3-21) and push out the piston pin (5) to separate the piston from the rod.

Measure the piston diameter 10 mm (0.4 in.) above the lower edge of the skirt and 90 degrees from the piston pin. Specified standard diameter is 57.960-57.990 mm (2.2819-2.2831 in.). Wear limit is 57.9 mm (2.280 in.). Oversize pistons are available.

Standard piston pin bore diameter is 14.005 mm (0.5514 in.). Reject the piston if piston pin bore diameter is 14.055 mm (0.5533 in.) or more.

Standard piston pin diameter is 14.000 mm (0.5512 in.). Reject the piston pin if diameter is 13.954 mm (0.5494 in.) or less.

Clean the piston ring grooves being careful not to damage the ring lands. To check the piston ring grooves for wear, insert a new compression ring into the ring groove and measure the side clearance between the ring and ring land. Standard compression ring side clearance is 0.03 mm (0.001 in.). Replace the piston if side clearance is 0.17 mm (0.007 in.) or greater.

Insert each compression ring into the cylinder and measure the ring end gap. The ring end gap should be 0.2 mm (0.008 in.). If the ring end gap for any ring is 0.6 mm (0.024 in.) or more, replace the ring and/or the cylinder. Oversize piston rings are available.

Install the marked piston rings (Fig. HE3-21) with the marked side toward the piston crown. Note that the top ring

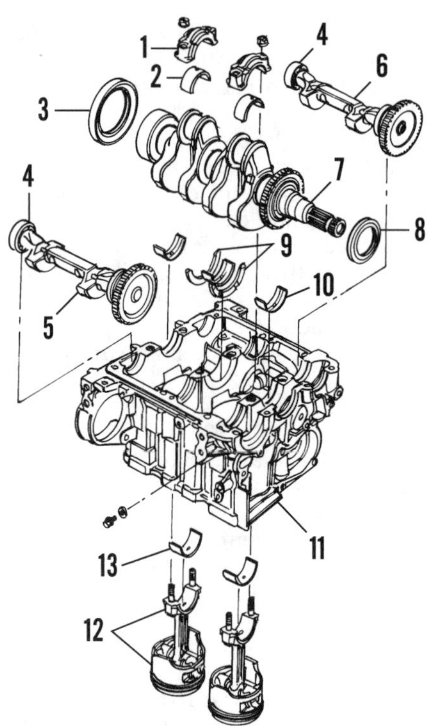

Fig. HE3-20—Exploded view of crankshaft, piston, connecting rod and balance shaft assemblies.

1. Rod cap
2. Rod bearing
3. Oil seal
4. Bearing
5. Balance shaft (left)
6. Balance shaft (right)
7. Crankshaft
8. Oil seal
9. Thrust bearing
10. Main bearing
12. Connecting rod & piston assy.
13. Rod bearing

(1) is chrome plated. Do not interchange it with the second ring.

Stagger the ring end gaps equally around the piston. Space the oil control ring (3) side rail end gaps at least 50 mm (2 in.) apart.

When assembling the piston on the connecting rod, be sure the oil hole (8—Fig. HE3-21) in the rod and the IN mark (9) on the piston crown are on the same side. Install the piston pin retaining ring (6) so the end gap is opposite the notch in the piston pin bore.

Refer to the CONNECTING ROD section when installing the piston and rod in the cylinder block.

CONNECTING RODS

Separate the crankcase and cylinder block for access to the connecting rod and piston assemblies. Remove the balance shafts. Mark the rods and rod caps so they can be reinstalled in original positions on crankshaft. Push the connecting rod and pistons out the top of the cylinders. Detach the piston pin clip and push out the piston pin to separate the piston from the rod.

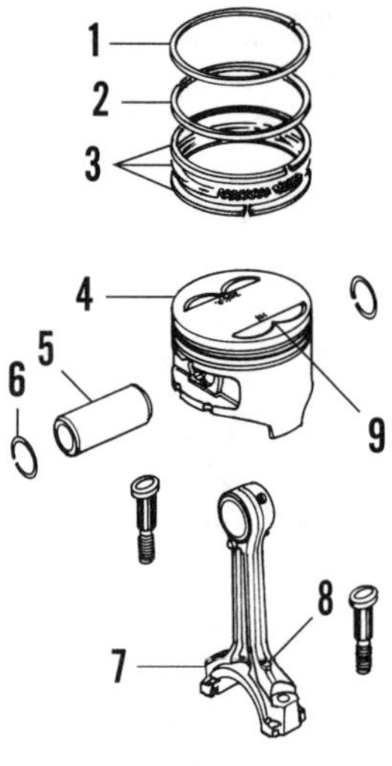

Fig. HE3-21—Exploded view of connecting rod, piston and rings. The "IN" mark on piston crown must be on same side as oil hole (8) in the rod.

1. Top compression ring
2. Second compression ring
3. Oil control ring
4. Piston
5. Piston pin
6. Retaining ring
7. Connecting rod
8. Oil hole
9. "IN" mark

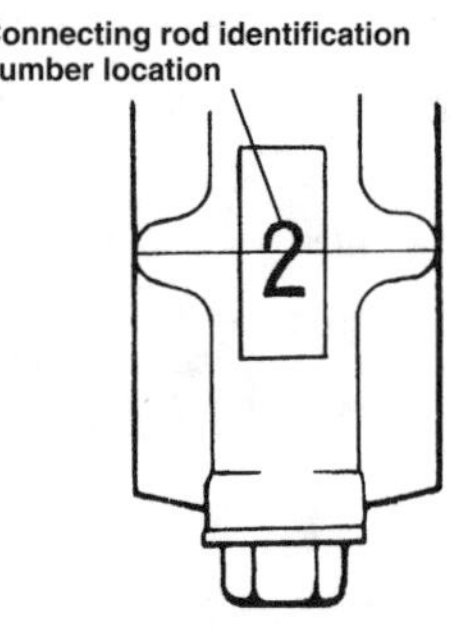

Fig. HE3-22—Code numbers on the connecting rod indicate the connecting rod inside diameter. Refer to text for bearing selection procedure.

Standard piston pin bore diameter in the connecting rod is 19.006-19.018 mm (0.7483-0.7487 in.). Replace the connecting rod if diameter is 19.066 mm (0.7506 in.).

Connecting rod is equipped with replaceable insert bearings (2 and 13—Fig. HE3-20) in the big end. Standard connecting rod bearing bore-to-crankpin clearance is 0.020-0.038 mm (0.0008-0.0015 in.). Replace the connecting rod bearing and/or crankshaft if clearance is 0.045 mm (0.0018 in.) or more.

Adjust the rod clearance on the crankpin by installing one of seven different thickness bearing inserts. To determine which bearing to install so the correct bearing clearance is achieved, note the identifying number on the side of the rod (Fig. HE3-22) and the identi-

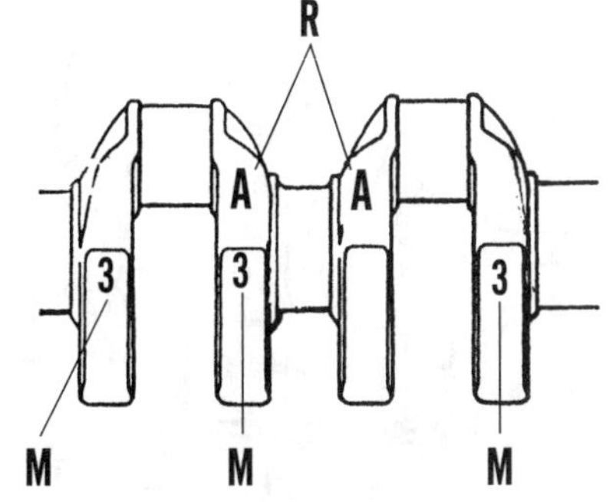

Fig. HE3-23—Bearing code letters for rod bearings (R) and numbers for main bearings (M) are stamped on the crankshaft.

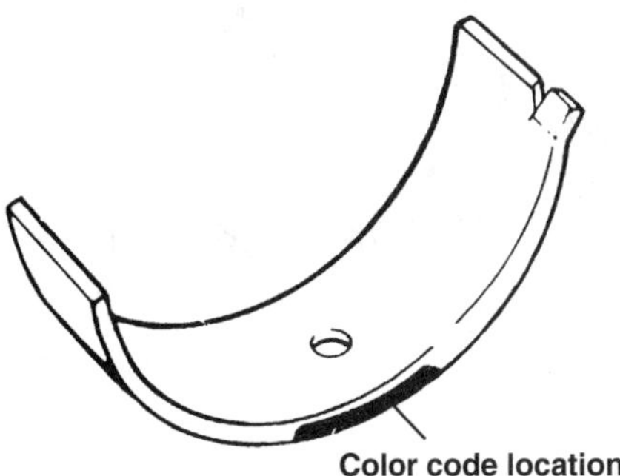

Fig. HE3-24—Bearing color code is located on the side of both the rod and main bearings.

	1	2	3	4
A	Red	Pink	Yellow	Green
B	Pink	Yellow	Green	Brown
C	Yellow	Green	Brown	Black
D	Green	Brown	Black	Blue

Fig. HE3-25—Select correct rod bearing according to chart using the numbers stamped on the rod and letters stamped on the crankshaft.

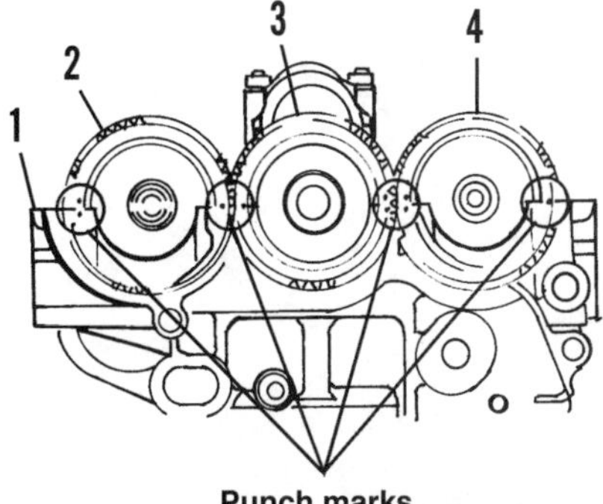

Fig. HE3-26—Refer to text when installing the crankshaft and balance shafts. Note the location of single timing punch marks and double timing marks.

fying letter (R—Fig. HE3-23) adjacent to the crankpin. Bearing inserts are color-coded (see Fig. HE3-24) according to thickness. The table in Fig. HE1-25 identifies the correct bearing for installation.

NOTE: When installing the bearing inserts, be sure the tang on the bearing insert fits the notch in the rod or rod cap.

Connecting rod side play on the crankpin should be 0.15-0.30 mm (0.006-0.012 in.). Replace the connecting rod if side play is 0.33 mm (0.013 in.) or more.

Assemble the piston on the connecting rod so the oil hole (8—Fig. HE3-21) and the IN mark (9) on the piston crown are on the same side. Lubricate the piston and cylinder with engine oil. Use a ring compressor to compress the piston rings. Install the piston and connecting rod assembly in the cylinder so the IN mark on the piston crown is on the carburetor intake valve side of the engine.

Install each rod cap on its respective connecting rod. Align the ribs on the rod and rod cap. Tighten the connecting rod nuts to 29 N·m (21 ft.-lb.).

BALANCE SHAFTS

The engine is equipped with two balance shafts located on both sides of the crankshaft. To gain access to the balance shafts, remove any components that interfere with crankcase removal. Position the engine so the cylinder block is down and the crankcase is on top. Remove the fasteners attaching the crankcase to the cylinder block. Note that two crankcase screws are located under the plate (7—Fig. HE3-19).

With the engine positioned as described, note that when viewed from the splined end of the crankshaft, the left balance shaft has an end slot that drives the oil pump. Lift out the balance shafts (5 and 6—Fig. HE3-20).

Inspect the balance shafts for damage and renew as necessary. The bearing (4) at the end of each shaft is replaceable.

The balance shafts must be timed with the crankshaft during installation. Rotate the crankshaft so the single punch mark on the balancer drive gear (3—Fig. HE3-26) aligns with the cylinder block surface on left side. The double punch marks on the gear (3) should be split by the block surface on the right side.

Install the left balance shaft (2) so the single punch mark on the balancer gear aligns with the single punch mark on the crankshaft gear (Fig. HE3-26). Install right balance shaft (4) so the two punch marks on gear align with the two punch marks on the crankshaft gear (Fig. HE3-26).

Rotate the crankshaft several revolutions and recheck the alignment of the punch marks. Assemble the crankcase to the cylinder block as described in the CRANKSHAFT, CRANKCASE AND CYLINDER BLOCK section.

CRANKSHAFT, CRANKCASE AND CYLINDER BLOCK

To remove the crankshaft, first remove the cylinder head as previously described. Remove any components that interfere with crankcase removal. Position the engine so the cylinder block is down and the crankcase is on top. Remove the fasteners retaining the crankcase (11—Fig. HE3-19) to the cylinder block. Note that two crankcase screws (6) are located under the plate [7]). Remove the balance shafts (5 and 6—Fig. HE3-20). Remove the connecting rod caps (1) and lift the crankshaft (7) from the cylinder block.

The crankshaft rides in renewable insert type bearings located in the crankcase and cylinder block. Crankshaft thrust is controlled by renewable thrust bearings (9—Fig. HE3-20) located on the cylinder block. The crankshaft gear is not replaceable.

Standard cylinder bore diameter should be 76.000-76.015 mm (2.9921-2.9927 in.). Maximum wear limit is 76.100 mm (2.9960 in.). Resize the cylinder and install an oversize piston if the cylinder bore is excessively worn or damaged.

The crankcase contains an oil screen (10—Fig. HE3-19). Clean the oil passages and the screen. Install the oil screen so the arrow on the screen points as shown in Fig. HE3-19.

The crankshaft main journal diameter should be 39.976-40.000 mm (1.5738-1.5748 in.). Replace the crankshaft if the main journal diameter is less than 39.93 mm (1.572 in.).

Adjust the main bearing clearance by installing one of seven different thickness bearing inserts. To determine which bearing to install so the correct bearing clearance is achieved, note the identifying letter (HE3-27) on the side of the crankcase and the identifying number (M—Fig. HE3-23) adjacent to the crankshaft main journal. Bearing inserts are color-coded (see Fig. HE3-24) according to their thickness. The table in Fig. HE3-28 identifies the correct bearing for installation.

NOTE: When installing the bearing inserts, be sure the tang on

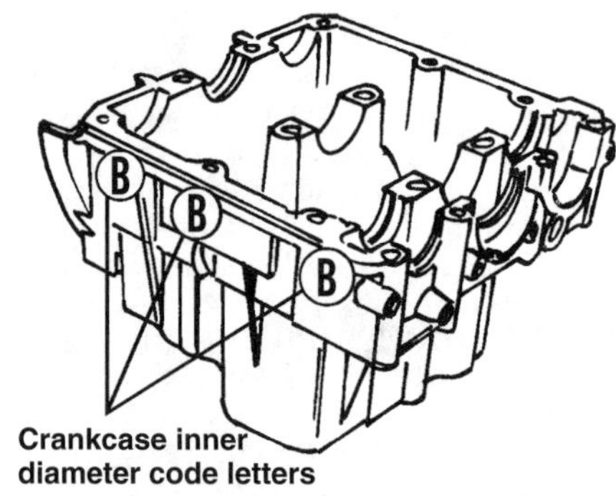

Fig. HE3-27—Bearing code letters for main bearings are stamped on the crankcase.

	A	B	C	D
1	Red	Pink	Yellow	Green
2	Pink	Yellow	Green	Brown
3	Yellow	Green	Brown	Black
4	Green	Brown	Black	Blue

Fig. HE3-28—Select correct main bearing according to the chart above and using the letters stamped on the crankcase and crankshaft.

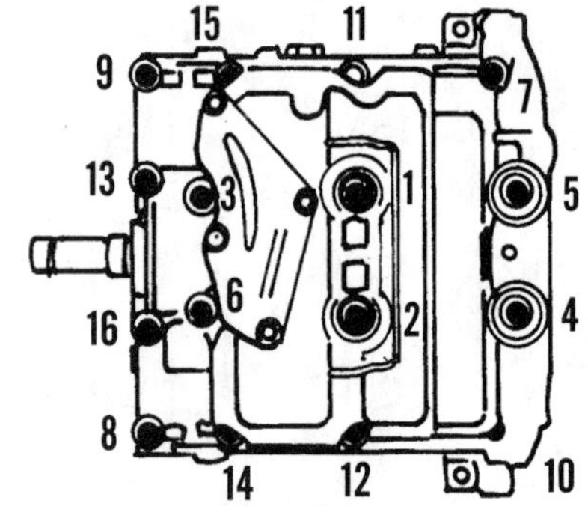

Fig. HE3-29—Tighten the crankcase screws in the sequence shown.

the bearing insert engages the notch in the crankcase or cylinder block.

Inspect the thrust bearings (9—Fig. HE3-20) and replace if excessively worn. Install the thrust bearings in the cylinder block so the grooved side is toward the inside of the cylinder block.

After installing the crankshaft and piston and rod assemblies, install the balance shafts as described in the BALANCE SHAFTS section.

Before assembling the crankcase and cylinder block, apply liquid-gasket sealer to mating surfaces of crankcase and cylinder block Do not allow sealer in the bolt holes or where sealer may contact the crankshaft journal. Tighten the crankcase screws in the sequence shown in Fig. HE3-29. Tighten the M8 screws to 22 N·m (195 in.-lb.) and M10 screws to 44 N·m (32 ft.-lb.).

Install the crankshaft timing belt pulley (9—Fig. HE3-30) so the OUT mark on the pulley faces outward. Install the flange washers (5) on either side of the timing belt pulley so the flanges are away from the pulley. Position the lockwasher (4) so its tab fits into the holes in the flange washer and pulley. Install the crankshaft nut, tighten the nut to 67.5 N·m (50 ft.-lb.) and bend the lockwasher against the nut flats.

Align the crankshaft and camshaft pulley timing marks (Fig. HE3-10) and install the timing belt as previously outlined in the TIMING BELT section.

ELECTRIC STARTER

All models are equipped with an electric starter. Cranking voltage should be 9 volts dc under load and 11.5 volts dc under no load. Cranking current should be below 150 amps under load and below 50 amps under no load.

CHARGE COILS

Charge coils mounted behind the flywheel provide electrical current for the battery charging circuit. To test the charge coils, disconnect the charge coil connector located on the right side of the engine. Measure the resistance between the terminals with an ohmmeter. Resistance should be 0.368-0.498 ohms.

When installing the charge coil, position the charge coil so the wire lead fits in the notch on the back side of the coil.

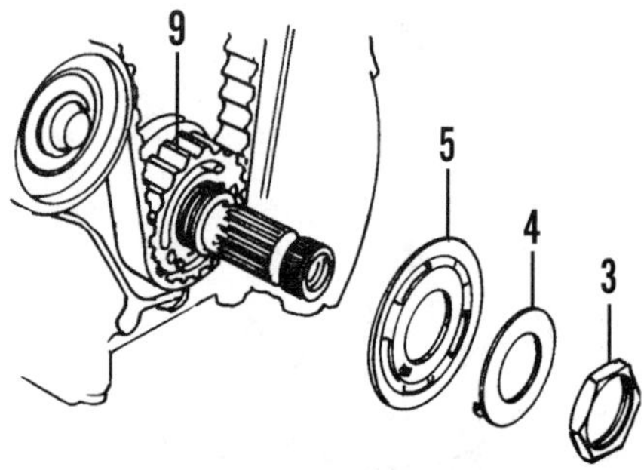

Fig. HE3-30—Install the crankcase pulley (9) with "OUT" mark facing out. Be sure the tab on the lock washer engages the hole in the flange washer (5) and pulley.

KAWASAKI

Model	No. Cyls.	Bore	Stroke	Displacement	Power Rating
FD440V	2	67 mm (2.64 in.)	62 mm (2.44 in.)	437 cc (26.7 cu. in.)	11 kW (15 hp)
FD501V	2	67 mm (2.64 in.)	62 mm (2.44 in.)	437 cc (26.7 cu. in.)	12.6 kW (17 hp)

All models are four-stroke, twin-cylinder, liquid-cooled engines with an overhead valve system. All Models are equipped with a vertical crankshaft and are lubricated by pressurized oil from an oil pump. The engine serial number decal is located on the cooling air duct on the right side.

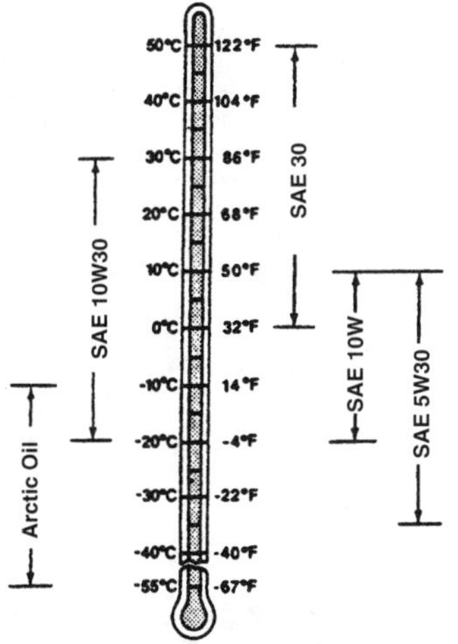

Fig. KW501–Use engine oil with viscosity based on expected air temperature as indicated in chart above.

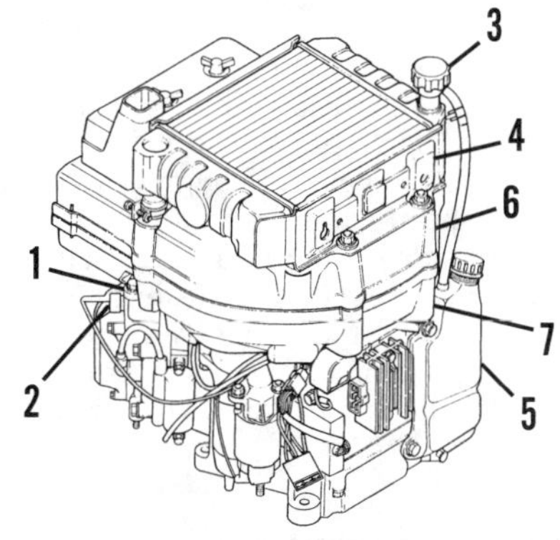

Fig. KW502–Drawing showing location of some cooling system components.

1. Thermostat cover
2. Coolant temperature switch
3. Radiator cap
4. Radiator
5. Overflow reservoir
6. Upper coolant duct
7. Lower cooling duct

MAINTENANCE

LUBRICATION

Engine oil level should be checked prior to each operating interval. Oil should be maintained between the reference marks on dipstick. The dipstick should just touch the first threads; do not screw the dipstick in to check the oil level.

Use oil of a suitable viscosity for the expected air temperature range during the period between oil changes. Refer to the temperature/viscosity chart shown in Fig. KW501.

Engine oil and oil filter should be changed after every 100 hours of operation or yearly, whichever comes first. Change the oil and oil filter after every 25 hours of operation if the engine is operated in severe conditions. Oil should be drained while the engine is warm. Crankcase oil capacity is approximately 1.5 L (3.2 pt.) without a new filter and 1.7 L (3.6 pt.) with a new filter.

The engine is equipped with an oil pressure switch located above the oil filter adapter on the side of the crankcase. The switch should be closed at zero pressure and open above 28 kPa (4.0 psi). The switch is connected to a warning device.

AIR FILTER

The air filter element should be removed and cleaned after every 25 hours of operation, or more often if operating in extremely dusty conditions. The paper element should be replaced if it is dirty or damaged in any way.

The engine may be used on equipment equipped with an air restriction indicator. Check the air filter elements when the air restriction indicator signals that service is necessary.

Clean the foam element in a solution of warm water and liquid detergent, then squeeze out the water and allow to air dry. DO NOT wash the paper element. Apply a light coat of engine oil to the foam element and squeeze out excess oil.

Clean the paper element by tapping gently to remove dust. DO NOT use compressed air to clean the element. Inspect the paper element and replace it if holes or other damage is evident.

COOLING SYSTEM

A radiator mounted above the engine transfers heat to air forced through the radiator by an engine-driven fan. A water pump driven by the engine camshaft circulates coolant through the cylinder block, cylinder heads and radiator. A thermostat regulates the coolant temperature.

Drain, flush and refill the cooling system annually. The manufacturer recommends using a low silicate antifreeze that does not contain stop leak additive. Cooling system capacity is 3.0 liters (3.2 qt.).

A thermostat is located under the cover (1—Fig. KW502). The thermostat should begin to open at 82°C (180°F) and open fully at 95°C (203°F).

A coolant temperature sensor (2) located on the engine controls the dash panel temperature gauge.

For water pump service, refer to the WATER PUMP section.

CRANKCASE BREATHER

Crankcase pressure is vented to an intake tube. A reed valve is located on top of the cylinder block as shown in Fig. KW503. Replace the reed valve if the tip of the reed stands up (S—Fig. KW504) more than 0.2 mm (0.008 in.) or if the reed is damaged or worn.

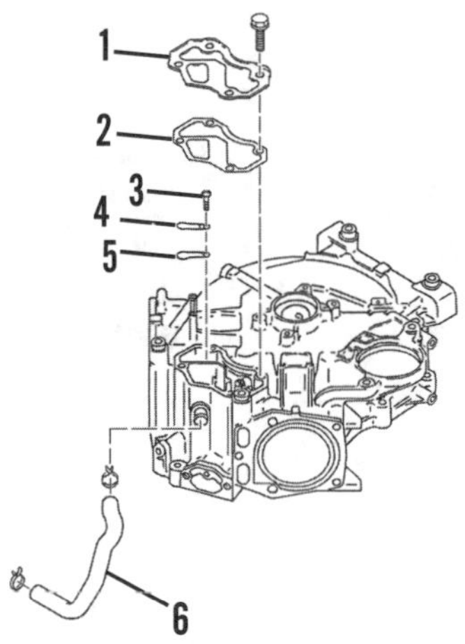

Fig. KW503–Exploded view of crankcase breather assembly. Breather hose routes crankcase gases to intake tube.

1. Cover
2. Gasket
3. Screw
4. Stop plate
5. Valve
6. Breather hose

SPARK PLUG

Recommended spark plug is NGK BMR6A.

The spark plug should be removed, cleaned and the electrode gap set after every 500 hours of operation. Specified spark plug gap is 0.76 mm (0.030 in.).

Tighten the spark plug to 17 N·m (150 in.-lb.) on Model FD440V or to 20 N·m (186 in.-lb.) on Model FD501V.

CARBURETOR

Both models are equipped with a float side draft carburetor.

Recommended engine idle speed is 1550 rpm. Turn the idle speed screw (IS—Fig. KW505) to adjust the idle speed.

Adjust the throttle control as follows: Place the engine throttle lever in fast position. Using a 15/64-inch drill bit, insert the bit (B—Fig. KW506) through the hole (H) in the speed control lever and bracket. Loosen the throttle cable housing clamp screw (S), pull the cable housing tight and retighten the cable clamp screw.

Rotate the choke lever screw (W) located on the rear of the bracket so there is a gap between the screw and the choke control lever (L), then turn the screw back in until it just touches the lever. Remove the drill bit.

With the throttle control lever in the choke position, the carburetor choke plate should be closed. If not, repeat the adjustment procedure. It may be necessary to bend the choke actuating rod slightly so the choke plate will close fully.

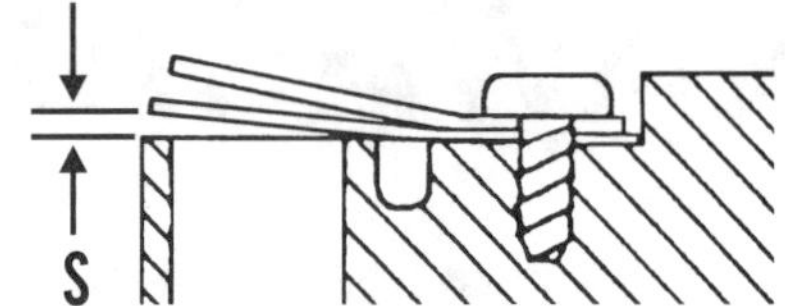

Fig. KW504–Replace reed valve if tip of reed stands up (S) more than 0.2 mm (0.008 in.)

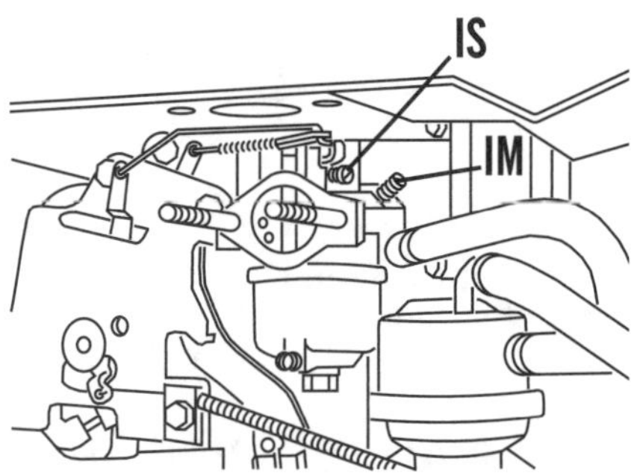

Fig. KW505–View showing location of idle mixture screw (IM) and idle speed screw (IS).

Initial adjustment of the idle mixture screw (IM—Fig. KW505) is 1⅛ turns open on Model FD440V and 1⅜ turns on Model FD501V. Make final adjustment with the engine at operating temperature and running.

Adjust the idle mixture screw to obtain maximum engine idle speed, then turn the idle mixture screw out counterclockwise an additional ¼ turn. Adjust the idle speed screw so the engine idles at 1550 rpm.

A fixed main jet controls the high-speed fuel mixture. Different size main jets are available for high altitude operation.

GOVERNOR

A gear-driven flyweight governor is located inside the engine crankcase. Before adjusting the governor linkage, make certain all linkage is in good condition.

To adjust external linkage, place the engine throttle control in the FAST position. Loosen the governor lever clamp nut (N—Fig. KW507). Push the governor lever (L) to the left and turn the governor shaft (S) counterclockwise as far as possible. Tighten the clamp nut.

Maximum no-load engine speed should be 3450 rpm on Model FD440V and 3550 rpm on Model FD501V. Adjust maximum no-load speed as follows: Run the engine until normal operating temperature is reached. Align the holes (H—Fig. KW506) in the speed control lever and bracket and insert a 15/64-inch drill bit.

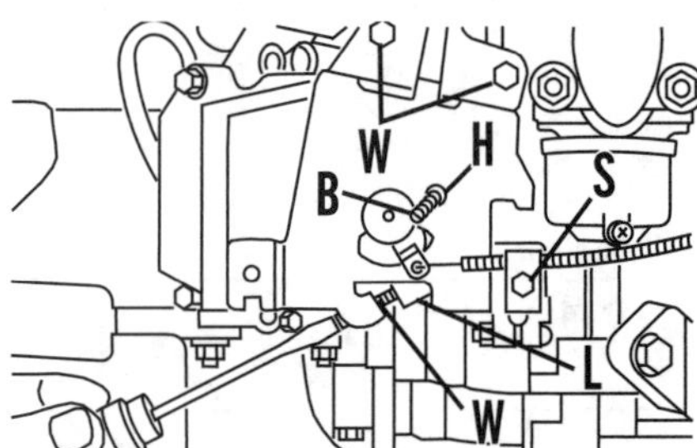

Fig. KW506–Refer to text for throttle cable adjustment.

Fig. KW507–To adjust governed speed, place throttle control lever in fast position. Loosen governor lever clamp nut (N), hold lever (L) and turn governor shaft (S) as far as possible counterclockwise.

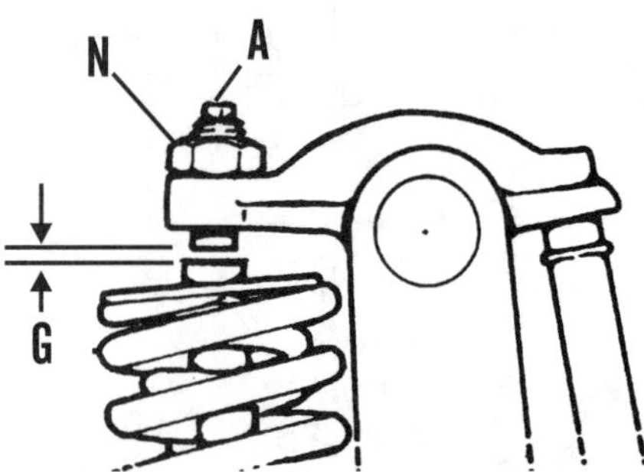

Fig. KW508–Loosen nut (N) and rotate adjusting screw (A) to adjust the clearance gap (G) between valve stem and rocker arm. Valve clearance should be 0.15 mm (0.006 in.).

Run the engine under no load and determine the engine speed using an accurate tachometer. If engine speed is not as specified, loosen the bracket retaining screws (W) and reposition the bracket to obtain the desired engine speed. Retighten the screws and recheck engine speed. Check choke operation as outlined in the CARBURETOR section.

IGNITION SYSTEM

All models are equipped with a solid-state ignition system and regular maintenance is not required. Ignition timing is not adjustable. The ignition coil is located outside the flywheel.

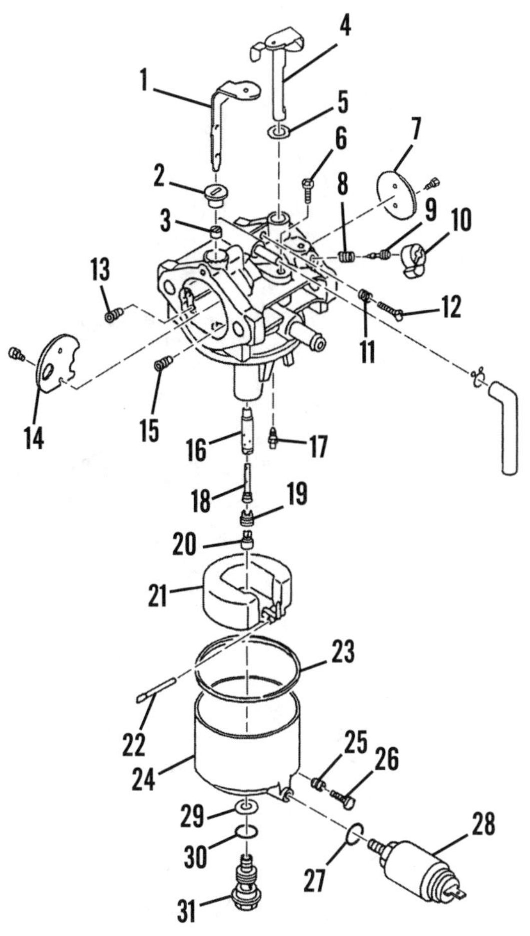

Fig. KW509–Exploded view of carburetor used on Model FD501V. Carburetor on Model FD440V is similar but components 16, 19, 27 and 28 are not used.

1. Choke shaft
2. Bushing
3. Ring
4. Throttle shaft
5. Seal
6. Pilot shaft
7. Throttle plate
8. Spring
9. Idle mixture screw
10. Restrictor cap
11. Spring
12. Idle speed screw
13. Main air jet
14. Choke plate
15. Pilot air jet
16. Main nozzle
17. Fuel inlet valve
18. Nozzle
19. Jet holder
20. Main jet
21. Float
22. Pin
23. Gasket
24. Fuel bowl
25. Spring
26. Drain screw
27. Gasket
28. Fuel shutoff solenoid
29. Washer
30. O-ring
31. Bolt

To test the ignition coil, disconnect the spark plug cable, positive wire (wide terminal) and negative wire (narrow terminal). To check primary coil resistance, connect ohmmeter test leads between the positive and negative wire terminals. Primary coil resistance should be 3.4-4.6 ohms.

To measure secondary coil resistance, remove the spark plug cap from the spark plug wire. Connect ohmmeter leads to the spark plug wire and positive terminal. Secondary coil resistance should be 10.4k-15.5k ohms.

Measure the resistance between the spark plug wire and coil core. The reading should be infinity. If readings vary significantly from the specifications, replace the ignition coil.

To check the pulsar coil, disconnect the pulsar coil connector. Measure the resistance between the terminals of the white/blue wire and pink wire. Resistance should be 85-270 ohms. Measure the resistance between the terminals of the green/white wire and yellow wire. Resistance should be 85-270 ohms.

VALVE ADJUSTMENT

Clearance between the valve stem ends and the rocker arms should be checked and adjusted after every 300 hours of operation. Engine must be cold for valve adjustment.

Rotate the crankshaft so the piston is at top dead center on the compression stroke. Remove the rocker arm cover. Valve clearance gap (G—Fig. KW508) for both valves should be 0.15 mm (0.006 in.).

To adjust the clearance, loosen the nut (N) and turn the adjusting screw (A) to obtain desired the clearance. Tighten the nut to 9 N·m (80 in.-lb.) and recheck the clearance.

COMPRESSION PRESSURE

Minimum compression reading is 1034 kPa (150 psi).

NOTE: When checking compression pressure, the spark plug leads must be grounded or the electronic ignition could be damaged.

REPAIRS

TIGHTENING TORQUES

The recommended special tightening torques are as follows:

Connecting rod . . . . 12 N·m (106 in.-lb.)
Cylinder head . . . . 21 N·m (186 in.-lb.)
Flywheel . . . . 90 N·m (66 ft.-lb.)
Intake manifold . . . . 6 N·m (53 in.-lb.)
Oil pan . . . . 21 N·m (186 in.-lb.)
Water pump
6 mm . . . . 8 N·m (71 in.-lb.)
8 mm . . . . 21 N·m (186 in.-lb.)

CARBURETOR

To disassemble, unscrew the fuel shut-off solenoid (28—Fig. KW509) and bolt (31) and remove the fuel bowl (24). Remove the float pin (22), float (21) and fuel inlet valve (17). Remove the main jet (20), jet holder (19) and nozzle. Remove the pilot jet (6) and idle mixture screw (9).

Clean the carburetor parts, except the plastic components, using suitable carburetor cleaner. Do not clean the jets or passages with drill bits or wire as enlargement of the passages could affect the carburetor calibration. Rinse parts in warm water to neutralize the corrosive action of the carburetor cleaner and dry with compressed air.

When assembling the carburetor note the following. Place a small drop of nonhardening sealant such as Permatex #2 or equivalent on the throttle and choke plate retaining screws. The float should be parallel with the carburetor body when the carburetor is inverted. Float height is not adjustable. If the float height is incorrect, replace any components that are damaged or worn and adversely affect the float position.

FUEL PUMP

The fuel pump is a mechanical pump driven by a lobe on the camshaft. The pump should maintain a minimum fuel pressure of 19.6 kPa (2.8 psi) at full throttle. Fuel flow at fuel throttle should be 160 ml (5.4 oz.) in 15 seconds. Fuel pump must be serviced as a unit assembly.

CYLINDER HEAD

To remove the cylinder head, remove the muffler, if not previously removed. Drain the engine coolant. Remove the radiator and components on top of engine to gain access to the carburetor. Remove the carburetor and intake manifold.

Rotate the crankshaft so the piston is at top dead center on the compression stroke. Remove the rocker arm cover. Detach the snap rings (8—Fig. KW510) from the rocker shaft, withdraw the rocker shaft and remove the rocker

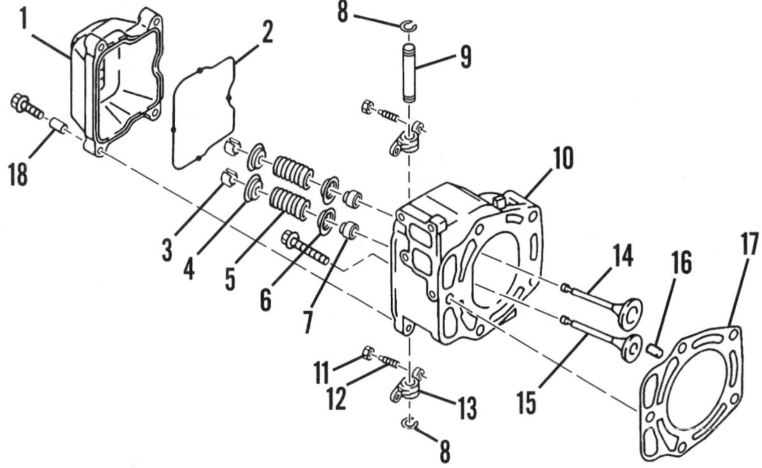

Fig. KW510–Exploded view of cylinder head and valve assembly.

1. Rocker cover
2. Gasket
3. Keepers
4. Valve spring retainer
5. Valve spring
6. Valve spring seat
7. Seal
8. Snap ring
9. Rocker shaft
10. Cylinder head
11. Nut
12. Screw
13. Rocker arm
14. Exhaust valve
15. Intake valve
16. Dowel pin
17. Head gasket

arms. Remove the push rods and mark them so they can be reinstalled in their original position. Unscrew the cylinder head screws in ¼-turn increments and remove the cylinder head.

Place the cylinder head on a flat surface and check for distortion. Replace the head if a 0.05 mm (0.002 in.) feeler gauge can be inserted under the head.

Follow the sequence shown in Fig. KW511 when tightening the cylinder head screws. Tighten the screws to an initial torque of 13 N·m (115 in.-lb.). Install the intake manifold and tighten the manifold screws to 6 N·m (53 in.-lb.). Tighten the cylinder head screws in steps until a final torque of 21 N·m (186 in.-lb.) is attained.

VALVE SYSTEM

The valves are located in the cylinder head. Valve seats and guides are not renewable.

Valve face and seat angles should be 45 degrees. Valve seat width should be 0.5-1.1 mm (0.02-0.043 in.). Minimum valve margin is 0.50 mm (0.020 in.). Maximum allowable valve guide inside diameter is 5.06 mm (0.199 in.). Minimum valve spring length is 27.30 mm (1.075 in.). Maximum valve stem run out measured with valve supported at ends is 0.05 mm (0.002 in.). Maximum push rod run out measured with push rod supported at ends is 0.8 mm (0.03 in.). Minimum rocker shaft diameter is 11.95 mm (0.470 in.). Maximum rocker arm inner diameter is 12.07 mm (0.475 in.).

PISTON, PIN, RINGS AND ROD

Remove the cylinder head as previously outlined. Remove any carbon or wear ridge at the top of the cylinder to prevent damage to the rings or piston during removal. Drain the engine oil and remove the oil pan (34—Fig. KW512).

Mark the rod cap so it can be reinstalled in its original position. Unscrew the rod cap screws, detach the rod cap and remove the piston and rod assembly through the cylinder bore.

Specified piston clearance in bore is 0.015-0.150 mm (0.0006-0.0060 in.). Standard piston diameter is 66.950-66.965 mm (2.6358-2.6364 in.). Measure the piston diameter 13.5 mm (0.53 in.) from the bottom of the piston and perpendicular to the piston pin.

Maximum allowable pin bore in the piston is 16.04 mm (0.631 in.). Minimum allowable piston pin diameter is 15.98 mm (0.629 in.). Maximum allowable piston ring end gap is 1.00 mm (0.039 in.). Maximum allowable piston ring side clearance is 0.10 mm (0.004 in.) for compression rings. Pistons and rings are available in standard and 0.50 mm oversizes. Refer to the CYLINDER BLOCK section if oversize pistons are required.

The connecting rod rides directly on the crankpin. Maximum allowable inside diameter at big end of rod is 31.06 mm (1.223 in.). The minimum allowable crankpin journal diameter is 30.93 mm (1.218 in.). Maximum allowable inside diameter at pin end of rod is 16.05 mm (0.632 in.).

Assemble the piston and rod so the arrow on the piston crown will be toward the flywheel as shown in Fig. KW513 and the chamfered side of the rod big end will be facing the crankshaft web. When properly installed, the arrow on the crown of both pistons will point towards the flywheel and the "MADE IN JAPAN" side of the rod will be towards

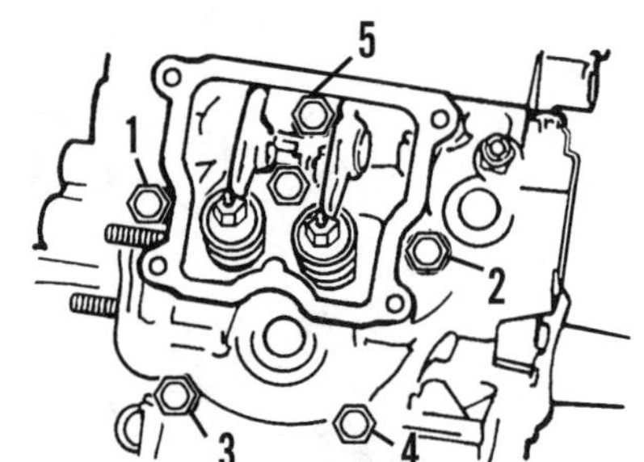

Fig. KW511–Tighten cylinder head screws in sequence shown above.

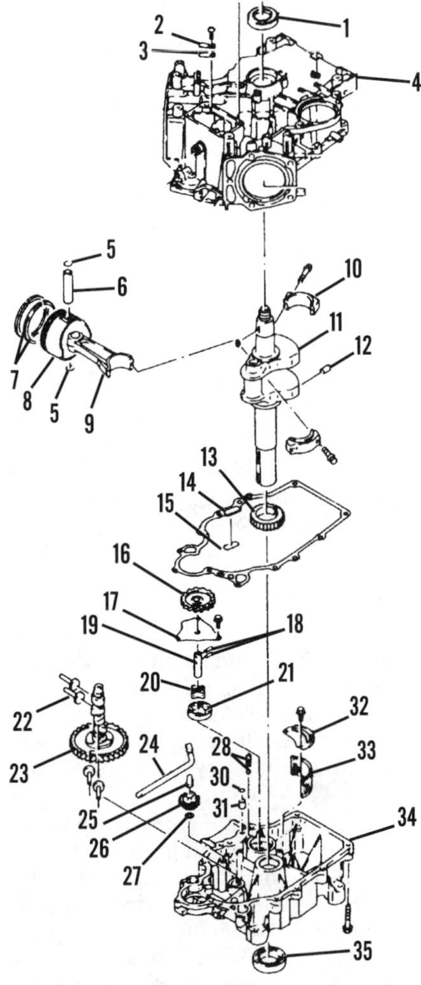

Fig. KW512–Exploded view of internal engine components.

1. Seal
2. Plate
3. Breather plate
4. Cylinder block
5. Retaining ring
6. Piston pin
7. Piston rings
8. Piston
9. Connecting rod
10. Rod cap
11. Crankshaft
12. Pin
13. Gear
14. Gasket
15. O-ring
16. Oil pump gear
17. Cover
18. Pins
19. Shaft
20. Inner rotor
21. Outer rotor
22. Tappets
23. Camshaft
24. Governor shaft
25. Sleeve
26. Governor
27. Washer
28. Relief valve spring
29. Relief valve
30. O-ring
32. Plate
33. Strainer
34. Oil pan
35. Seal

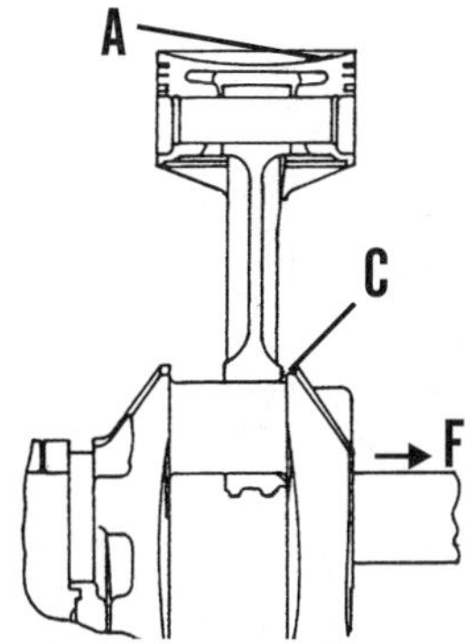

Fig. KW513–Assemble piston and rod so arrow (A) on piston crown is toward flywheel (F) and chamfer (C) is towards adjacent cranksahft web (W). Note that when both rods are installed on the crankshaft the non-chamfered sides will be together.

Fig. KW514–Tighten oil pan screws in sequence shown above.

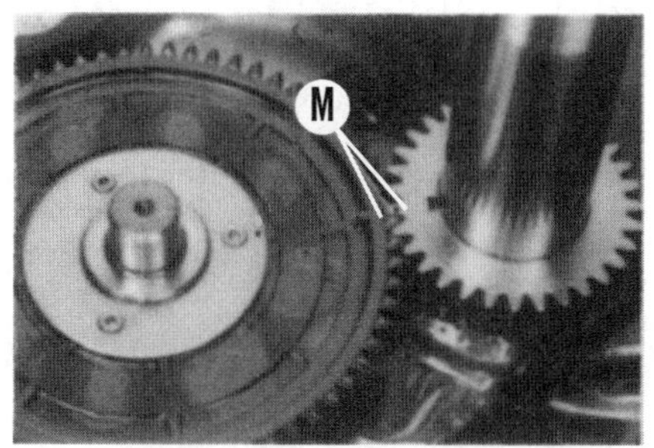

Fig. KW515–Align timing marks (M) on crankshaft and camshaft gears when installing camshaft.

the flywheel on the upper rod and towards the PTO on the lower rod.

Install the top compression piston ring with the lettered side toward the piston crown. Position the piston rings so the ring gaps are 180° apart.

Install the piston and rod assembly so the arrow on the piston crown points toward the flywheel end of the crankshaft. Make sure the rod cap matches the rod. Tighten the rod cap screws to 12 N·m (106 in.-lb.).

Tighten the oil pan screws to 21 N·m (186 in.-lb.) in the sequence shown in Fig. KW514. Install the cylinder head as previously outlined.

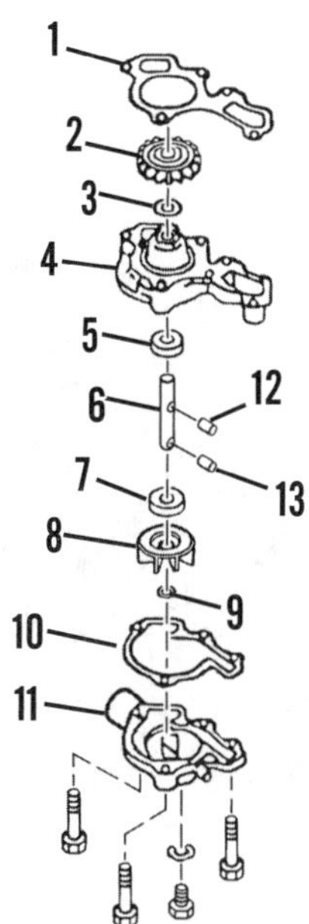

Fig. KW516–Exploded view of water pump.

1. Gasket
2. Gear
3. Washer
4. Housing
5. Seal
6. Shaft
7. Seal
8. Impeller
9. O-ring
10. Gasket
11. Cover
12. Pin
13. Pin

CAMSHAFT

The camshaft is accessible after removing the oil pan. The camshaft rides in nonreplaceable bushings in the cylinder block and oil pan. Replace the cylinder block or cover if the bushing diameter is greater than 14.07 mm (0.554 in.).

Minimum allowable camshaft bearing journal diameter is 13.91 mm (0.548 in.). Minimum allowable camshaft lobe height is 24.43 mm (0.962 in.). Minimum fuel pump lobe height is 19.50 mm (0.768 in.).

When installing the camshaft, be sure to align the timing marks (M—Fig. KW515). Tighten the oil pan screws evenly to 21 N·m (186 in.-lb.) in the sequence shown in Fig. KW514.

CRANKSHAFT AND MAIN BEARINGS

The crankshaft rides in nonreplaceable bushings in the cylinder block and oil pan.

Maximum allowable bushing diameter in the block and cover is 30.09 mm (1.185 in.). Minimum allowable crankshaft main bearing journal diameter is 29.92 mm (1.178 in.). Minimum allowable crankpin diameter is 30.93 mm (1.218 in.). Maximum allowable crankshaft run out is 0.05 mm (0.002 in.) measured at the main bearing journals with crankshaft supported at the ends.

Be sure the timing marks (M—Fig. KW515) on the crankshaft and camshaft gears are aligned. Tighten the oil pan screws to 21 N·m (186 in.-lb.) in the sequence shown in Fig. KW514.

CYLINDER BLOCK

The cylinders may be bored to accept oversize pistons. Standard bore diameter is 66.98-67.00 mm (2.637-2.638 in.) and maximum wear limit is 67.06 mm (2.640 in.).

GOVERNOR

A flyweight governor is located in the oil pan. The camshaft gear drives the governor gear. Remove the oil pan for access to the governor assembly. Governor components must move freely without binding.

NOTE: Removing the governor assembly from the shaft will damage the governor and require installation of a new governor assembly.

Remove the governor assembly by prying or pulling it off the shaft. The shaft must protrude above the boss 32.2-32.8 mm (1.27-1.29 in.).

Install the governor by pushing it down until it snaps onto the locating groove. Tighten the oil pan screws to 21 N·m (186 in.-lb.) in the sequence shown in Fig. KW514.

OIL PUMP

A gerotor oil pump is located in the oil pan. The pump provides pressurized oil directed to the crankshaft main bearing journals and crankpin. Drilled passages in the connecting rods squirt oil on the underside of the pistons.

To check the oil pressure, remove the oil pressure switch from the side of the cylinder block adjacent to the oil filter and connect an oil pressure gauge. With the engine at operating temperature and running at fast throttle setting, the oil pressure should be no less than 240 kPa (35 psi).

Remove the oil pan for access to the pump. Maximum inner rotor-to-outer rotor clearance is 0.3 mm (0.012 in.). Minimum allowable shaft diameter is 10.92 mm (0.430 in.). Maximum allowable bore diameter in the oil pan and pump cover is 11.07 mm (0.436 in.). Maximum rotor bore diameter in the oil pan is 40.80 mm (1.606 in.). Replace the relief valve spring (28—Fig. KW512) if its free length is less than 21.05 mm (0.829 in.).

WATER PUMP

Note the diameter and length of screws during removal for proper reinstallation. Refer to Fig. KW516 for an exploded view of the water pump.

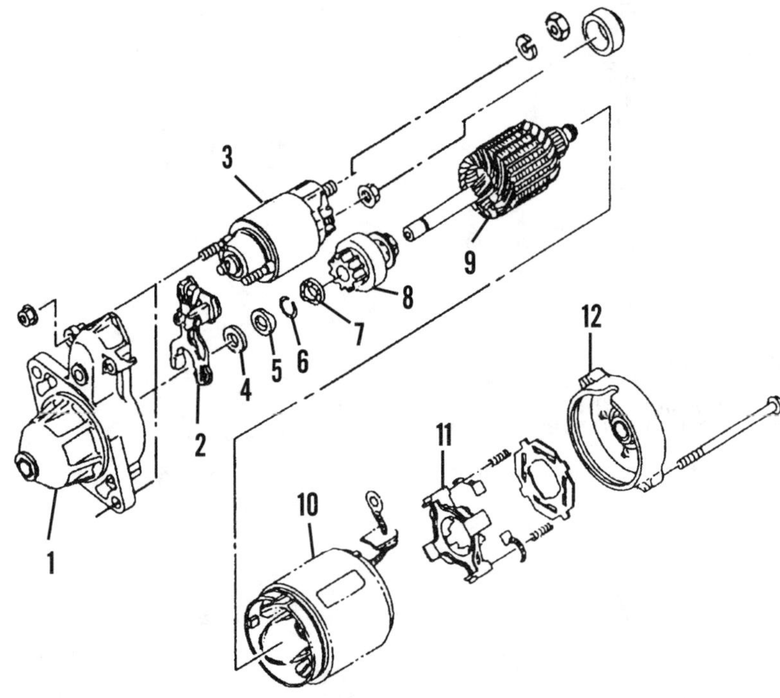

Fig. KW517–Exploded view of starter.

1. Drive housing
2. Fork
3. Solenoid
4. Washer
5. Pinion stop half
6. Snap ring
7. Pinion stop half
8. Clutch
9. Armature
10. Frame
11. Brush plate
12. End cap

The impeller (8), shaft (6) and pin (13) are available as a unit assembly only. Minimum allowable diameter of the shaft is 9.94 mm (0.391 in.). Maximum allowable diameter of the housing bore is 10.09 mm (0.397 in.).

Install the seal (10) using the driver provided in the seal kit. Tighten the 6 mm mounting screws to 8 N·m (71 in.-lb.) and 8 mm mounting screw to 21 N·m (186 in.-lb.).

ELECTRIC STARTER

Refer to Fig. KW517 for an exploded view of the electric starter. Place alignment marks on the pinion housing, frame and end cover before disassembly so they can be reinstalled in their original positions.

Replace the brushes if their length is less than 6 mm (0.24 in.). Starter no-load current draw should be 50 amps at starter speed of 6000 rpm.

ALTERNATOR

The alternator stator is located under the flywheel. To check the alternator, disconnect the black stator wires from the regulator/rectifier and check the voltage reading at the stator leads. With the engine running at full speed, the minimum voltage reading is 26 volts ac. Before renewing the stator, check the flywheel magnets.

REGULATOR/RECTIFIER

The regulator/rectifier should provide 15 amps direct current at 12.2-14.7 volts at full engine speed. If the regulator/rectifier output is below specification, check the alternator stator output. If stator output is satisfactory, replace the regulator/rectifier with a good unit.

ELECTRICAL WIRING DIAGRAM

Refer to Fig. WK518 for engine wiring diagram.

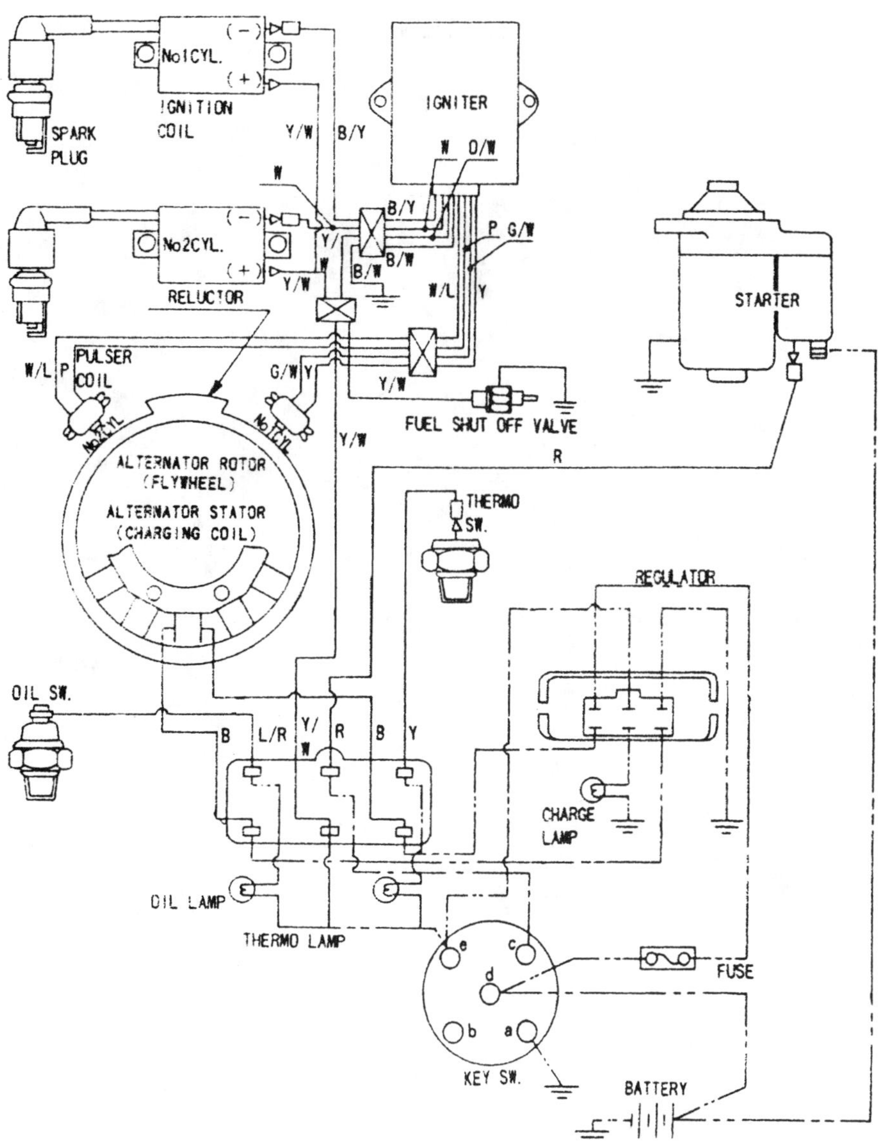

Fig. KW518–Engine wiring diagram.

B. Black
P. Pink
R. Red
W. White
Y. Yellow
L. Blue

NOTES

KOHLER

KOHLER COMPANY
Kohler, Wisconsin 53044

Model	No. Cyls.	Bore	Stroke	Displacement	Power Rating
CH11, CV11	1	87 mm (3.43 in.)	67 mm (2.64 in.)	398 cc (24.3 cu. in.)	10.5 kW (14 hp)
CH12.5, CV12.5	1	87 mm (3.43 in.)	67 mm (2.64 in.)	398 cc (24.3 cu. in.)	9.33 kW (12.5 hp)
CH14, CV14	1	87 mm (3.43 in.)	67 mm (2.64 in.)	398 cc (24.3 cu. in.)	10.5 kW (14 hp)
CV15	1	90 mm (3.60 in.)	67 mm (2.64 in.)	426 cc (26.0 cu. in.)	11.2 kW (15 hp)

NOTE: Metric fasteners are used throughout engine.

The Kohler engines covered in this section are four-stroke, air-cooled, single-cylinder engines using an overhead valve system. Engine identification numbers are located on a decal affixed to flywheel fan shroud. Refer to the preceding Kohler section for engine identification information.

MAINTENANCE

LUBRICATION

Periodically check the oil level. Do not overfill. The oil dipstick should be resting on the dipstick tube to check the oil level. Do not screw in the dipstick.

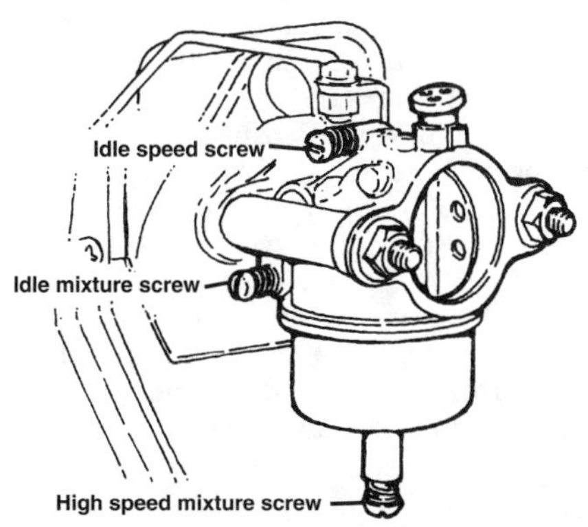

Fig. KO201–View of carburetor showing adjustment points. High speed mixture screw is not used on CV models. Some models may be equipped with a fuel shutoff solenoid valve on bottom of fuel bowl.

Change the oil after the first 5 hours of operation. Thereafter change the oil after every 100 hours of operation. Oil should be drained while the engine is warm. Oil capacity is approximately 1.9 liters (2.0 qt.). It is recommended that a new oil filter be installed at each oil change.

Use engine oil with the latest API service classification. Use 10W-30 or 10W-40 oil for temperatures above 0°F (-18°C). When operating in temperatures below 32°F (0°C), SAE 5W-20 or 5W-30 may be used.

SAE 10W-30 oil should be used for the first 5 hours of operation of an overhauled engine or a new short block. After the 5-hour break-in period, drain the oil and install new oil according to the ambient temperature requirements.

The engine may be equipped with a low-oil sensor. The sensor circuit may be designed to stop the engine or trigger a warning device if the oil level is low.

AIR FILTER

The engine is equipped with a foam precleaner element and paper type air filter. Service the precleaner after every 25 hours of operation and the paper air filter after every 100 hours of operation. Service more frequently if engine is operated in severe conditions.

Clean the precleaner element by washing in soapy water. Allow it to dry, then apply clean engine oil. Squeeze out excess oil.

The paper air filter should be replaced rather than cleaned. Do not wash or direct pressurized air at the filter.

FUEL FILTER

Periodically inspect the fuel filter, if so equipped. Replace the filter if it is dirty or damaged.

CRANKCASE BREATHER

A breather valve is attached to the top of the cylinder head under the rocker cover. A tube connects the breather to the air cleaner base to allow crankcase vapors to be burned by the engine. Inspect and clean the breather valve as needed to prevent or remove restrictions.

SPARK PLUG

The recommended spark plug is Champion RC12YC or equivalent. Specified electrode gap is 1.0 mm (0.040 in.). Tighten the spark plug to 38-43 N·m (28-32 ft.-lb.).

CARBURETOR

Initial setting of the idle mixture screw (Fig. KO201) is 1¼ turns out on Models CH11 and CH12.5, 1-3/4 turns out on Model CH14, and one turn out on all CV models. Initial setting of high-speed mixture screw is 1½ turns out on Models CH11 and CH12.5, and 1¼ turns out on Model CH14. There is no high-speed mixture screw on CV models.

Final adjustment of mixture screws should be made with the engine at normal operating temperature. Adjust the idle speed screw so the engine idles at 1500 rpm on CH models and at 1200 rpm on CV models, or at the speed specified by the equipment manufacturer.

Turn the idle mixture screw counterclockwise until engine rpm decreases and note the screw position. Turn the screw clockwise until engine rpm decreases again and note the screw position. Turn the screw to midpoint between the two noted positions. Reset the idle speed screw if necessary to obtain desired idle speed.

To adjust the high speed mixture screw (Fig. KO201) on CH models, run the engine at maximum speed with the engine under load. Slowly rotate the high-speed mixture screw in until engine speed decreases, then turn the screw out ¼ turn.

A fixed main jet controls the high-speed mixture on CV models. No optional jets are offered, although a high altitude kit is available.

To disassemble the carburetor, refer to Fig. KO202. Remove the retaining screw (16) and fuel bowl (14). Push out the float hinge pin (17) and remove the float (11) and fuel inlet valve (10). Unscrew the idle mixture screw (1).

Note that the edges of the throttle and choke plates (3 and 8) are beveled and must be reinstalled in their original positions. Mark choke and throttle plates before removal to ensure correct reassembly.

To remove the fuel inlet seat (9), thread a suitably sized screw into the seat and pull it out of the carburetor body. The seat must be replaced if removed. Do not reinstall a seat that has been removed.

Use a sharp punch to pierce the Welch plug and pry it from the carburetor body. Be careful to prevent the punch from contacting and damaging the carburetor body.

Clean all parts in suitable carburetor cleaner and blow out all passages with compressed air. Be careful not to enlarge any fuel passages or jets as calibration of carburetor may be altered.

If removed, press a new fuel inlet seat into the carburetor body so the seat is bottomed. Apply Loctite 609 to the throttle plate retaining screw. Be sure the throttle plate is properly seated against carburetor bore before tightening the screw. Be sure the choke shaft properly engages the detent spring (7). Locking tabs on the choke plate must straddle the choke shaft.

After installing the Welch plug, apply a fuel resistant sealant around the outer edge of the plug. Common fingernail polish is a suitable sealant.

IGNITION

The engine is equipped with a breakerless, electronic magneto ignition system. The electronic ignition module is mounted outside the flywheel. The ignition switch grounds the module to stop the engine. There is no periodic maintenance or adjustment required with this ignition system.

Air gap between the module and flywheel should be 0.20-0.30 mm (0.008-0.012 in.). Loosen the module retaining screws and position module to obtain the desired gap. Tighten the screws to 4 N·m (35 in.-lb.) for used engines or to 6.2 N·m (55 in.-lb.) on a new engine cylinder block.

If the ignition module fails to produce a spark, check for faulty kill switch or grounded wires. Measure resistance of the ignition module secondary circuit using a suitable ohmmeter. Connect one test lead to the spark plug terminal and the other test lead to the module core laminations. Resistance should be 7900-10850 ohms. If resistance is low or infinite, renew the module.

GOVERNOR

A flyweight governor is located in the crankcase. The camshaft gear drives the governor gear. Refer to REPAIRS section for overhaul information.

To adjust the governor linkage, proceed as follows: Loosen the governor lever clamp nut (N—Fig. KO203) and push the governor lever so the throttle is wide open. Rotate the governor cross shaft (S) counterclockwise as far as possible and tighten the clamp nut.

The engine should never run at speeds exceeding 3750 rpm. Maximum high-speed setting depends on engine application. Use a tachometer to check the engine speed.

To adjust the high idle speed setting on CV models, first loosen the throttle control cable clamp (Fig. KO204). Move the equipment speed control lever to the FAST position. Align the hole in the throttle lever with the hole in the speed control bracket by inserting a pencil or drill bit through the holes. Pull up on the throttle control cable shield to remove slack, and tighten cable clamp.

Start the engine and allow it to reach operating temperature. Align the hole in the throttle lever with the hole in the speed control bracket as previously outlined. Loosen the speed control bracket mounting screws and move the bracket up (toward flywheel) to increase high idle speed or down (toward PTO) to decrease high idle speed. When desired

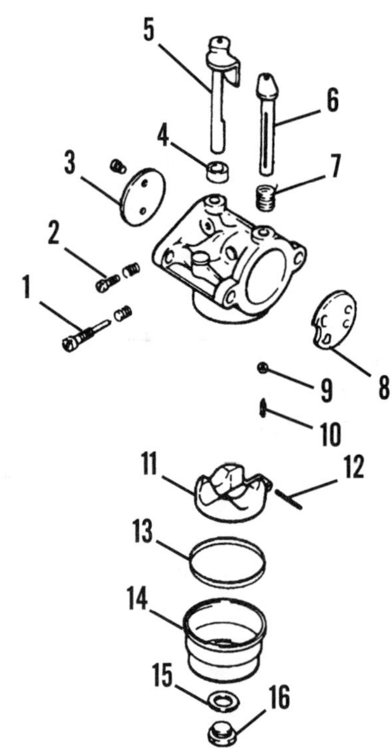

Fig. KO202–Exploded view of float-type carburetor used on all engines. A high speed screw is located in bottom of fuel bowl in place of retaining screw (16) on CH models. Some engines may be equipped with an electric fuel shut-off solenoid located in bottom of fuel bowl in place of retaining screw (16).

1. Idle mixture screw
2. Idle speed screw
3. Throttle plate
4. Throttle shaft dust seal
5. Throttle shaft
6. Choke shaft
7. Return spring
8. Choke plate
9. Fuel inlet valve seat
10. Fuel inlet valve
11. Float
12. Float shaft
13. Gasket
14. Fuel bowl
15. Gasket
16. Gasket

speed is obtained, tighten the control bracket screws to 10.7 N·m (95 in.-lb.) on a new short block or to 7.3 N·m (65 in.-lb.) on all other engines.

On CH models, the governor spring end should be located in the following specified hole from the end of the governor lever for specified high idle speed: (a) outer hole for 3800 rpm, (b) second hole for 3600 rpm, (c) third hole for 3400 rpm (d) fifth hole for 3200 (e) sixth hole for 3000 rpm. Note that the throttle end of the governor spring is attached to the third hole from the top of the throttle lever for 3800 rpm and the first hole for all other speeds.

Governor sensitivity is adjusted by positioning the governor spring in different holes in the governor lever arm. On CV models, it is recommended that the spring be installed in the hole closest to the governor shaft if high idle speed is 3600 rpm or less. If high idle

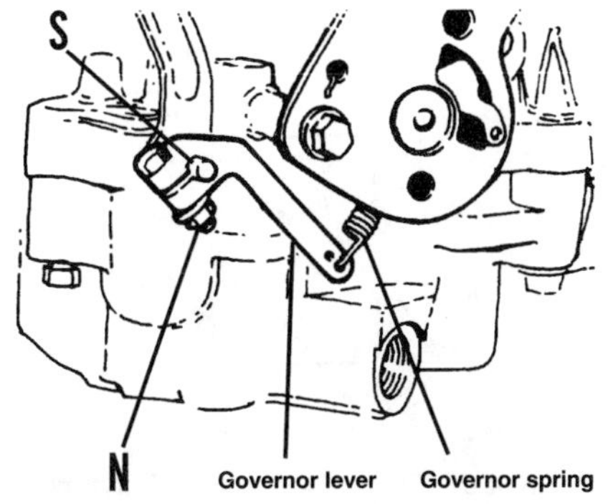

Fig. KO203–View of governor external linkage. Refer to text for adjustment procedure.

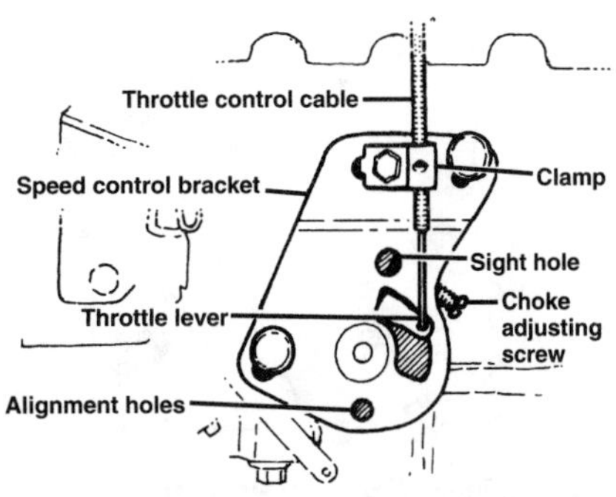

Fig. KO204–View of typical speed control linkage on CV models. Refer to text for adjustment procedure.

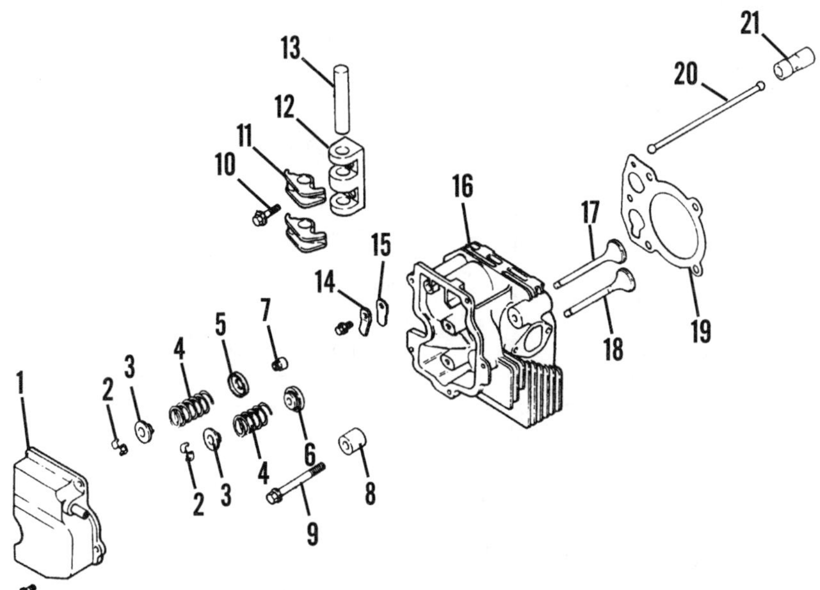

Fig. KO205–Exploded view of cylinder head and valve components. Exhaust valve rotator (7) is used on early production CV model engines before S.N. 1933593554.

1. Valve cover
2. Split retainer
3. Spring retainer
4. Valve spring
5. Spring seat
6. Valve seal (intake)
7. Valve rotator (exhaust)
8. Spacer
9. Head bolt
10. Screw
11. Rocker arm
12. Rocker bridge
13. Rocker shaft
14. Retainer plate
15. Breather reed
16. Cylinder head
17. Intake valve
18. Exhaust valve
19. Head gasket
20. Push rod
21. Valve fitter

speed is greater than 3600 rpm, use the second hole which is farthest from governor cross shaft.

On CH models, governor sensitivity is adjusted by reattaching the governor spring to another hole in the governor arm. Move the spring to an outer hole on the arm to decrease governor sensitivity.

VALVE CLEARANCE

All models are equipped with hydraulic valve lifters that automatically maintain proper valve clearance. No periodic adjustment is required.

REPAIRS

TIGHTENING TORQUE

The recommended special tightening torque values are as follows:

Connecting rod . . . . **22.6 N·m (200 in.-lb.)**
Crankcase cover/ Oil pan . . . . **24.4 N·m (216 in.-lb.)**
Cylinder head . . . . **41 N·m (30 ft.-lb.)**
Flywheel . . . . **66 N·m (49 ft.-lb.)**
Spark plug . . . . **38-43 N·m (28-32 ft.-lb.)**

FUEL PUMP

Some engines may be equipped with a mechanically operated diaphragm fuel pump. An eccentric on the engine camshaft actuates the fuel pump. Individual components are not available; the pump must be replaced as a unit assembly.

When installing the fuel pump assembly, make certain that the fuel pump lever is positioned to the right side of the camshaft. Damage to the fuel pump and engine may result if the lever is positioned on the left side of the camshaft. Tighten the fuel pump mounting screws to 9.0 N·m (80 in.-lb.) for first time installation on new short block. On all other engines, tighten mounting screws to 7.3 N·m (65 in.-lb.).

CYLINDER HEAD

To remove the cylinder head, remove the air cleaner assembly and base. Detach the speed control linkage and fuel line. Unbolt and remove the carburetor and muffler. Remove the blower housing and cylinder head air baffles and shields. Remove the rocker arm cover. Rotate the crankshaft so the piston is at top dead center on compression stroke. Mark the push rods and rocker arms so they can be reinstalled in their original position if reused. Unscrew the cylinder head bolts and remove the cylinder head and gasket.

To disassemble, remove the spark plug. Remove the breather retainer (14—Fig. KO205) and reed (15). Push the rocker shaft (13) out the breather side of the rocker arm bridge (12) and remove the rocker arms (11). Use a valve spring compressor tool to compress the valve springs. Remove the split retainers (2), release the spring tension and remove the valves from cylinder head.

Clean combustion deposits from the cylinder head and inspect for cracks or other damage. Maximum allowable warpage of the head surface is 0.076 mm (0.003 in.).

To reassemble the cylinder head components, reverse the disassembly procedure. Be sure the rocker pedestal (12) is installed with the small counterbored hole toward the exhaust port side of the cylinder head. Tighten the rocker pedestal mounting screws to 9.9 N·m (88 in.-lb.). Install a new stem seal (6) on the intake valve. Do not reuse the old seal.

Install the cylinder head with a new head gasket. Tighten the cylinder head screws in increments of 14 N·m (10 ft.-lb.) following the sequence shown in Fig. KO206 until the final torque of 41 N·m (30 ft.-lb.) is reached. Install the push rods in their original position, compress the valve springs and snap the push rods underneath the rocker arms.

Silicone sealant is used as a gasket between the valve cover and cylinder head. GE Silmate type RTV-1473 or RTV-108 sealant (or equivalent) is recommended. The use of a silicone removing solvent is recommended to remove old silicone gasket, as scrapping the mating surfaces may damage them and could cause leaks. Apply a 1.6 mm (1/16 in.) bead of sealant to the gasket surface of cylinder head. Install the valve cover and tighten the mounting screws in the sequence shown in Fig. KO207. Tighten the valve cover screws to 10.7 N·m (95 in.-lb.) if a new cylinder head is installed, or to 7.3 N·m (65 in.-lb.) if original head is installed.

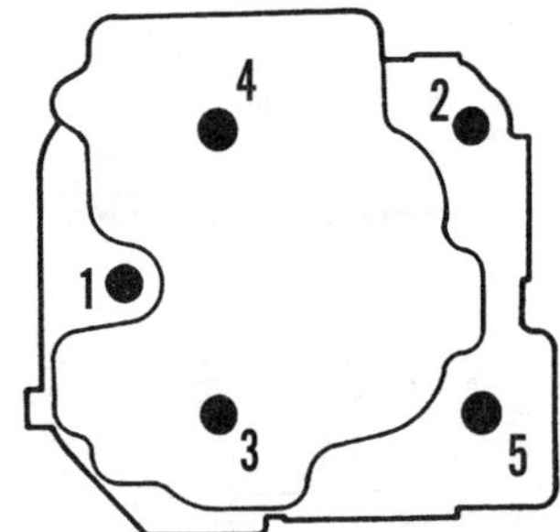

Fig. KO206–Follow sequence shown when tightening cylinder head bolts. Refer to text.

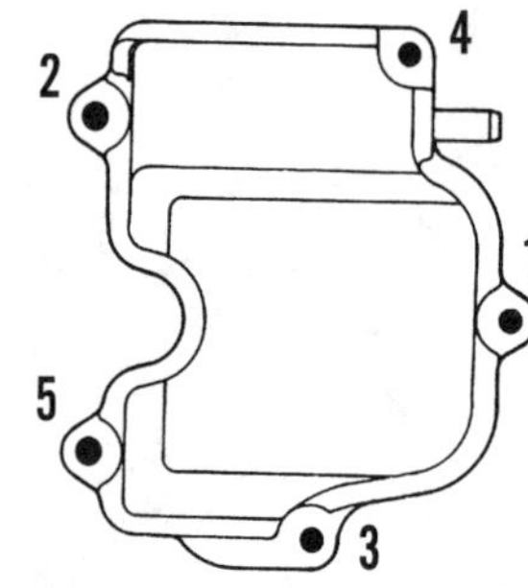

Fig. KO207–Follow sequence shown when tightening valve cover mounting screws. Refer to text.

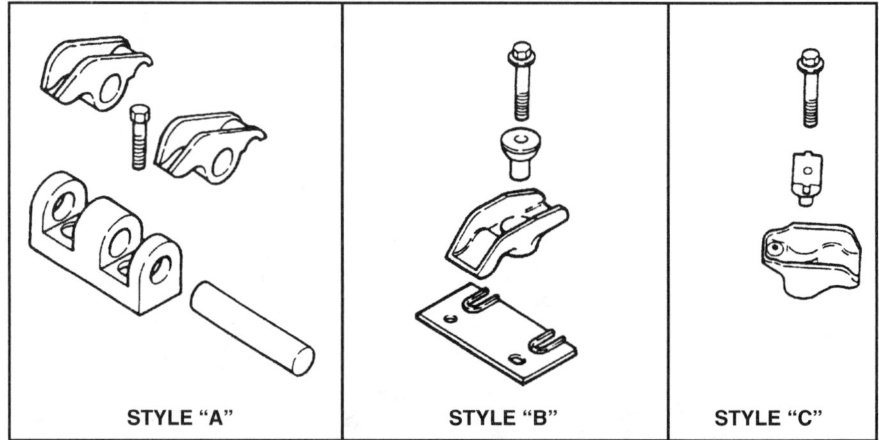

Fig. KO208–Different styles of rocker arms and pivots. Refer to text.

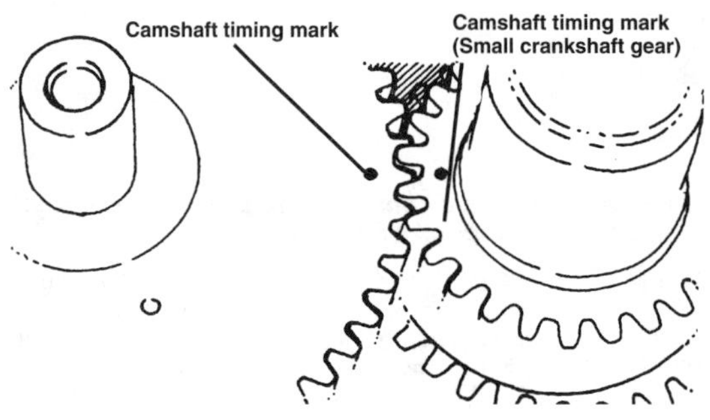

Fig. KO209–Align timing mark on the small crankshaft gear with timing mark on camshaft gear.

VALVE SYSTEM

Remove the valves from the cylinder head as previously outlined in the CYLINDER HEAD section. Clean valve heads and stems with a wire brush. Inspect each valve for warped or burned head, pitting or worn stem and replace as required.

Valve face and seat angles are 45° for intake and exhaust. Replace the valve if valve margin is less than 1.5 mm (0.060 in.) after grinding the valve face.

Specified valve stem-to-guide clearance is 0.038-0.076 mm (0.0015-0.0030 in.) for intake valve and 0.050-0.088 mm (0.0020-0.0035 in.) for exhaust valve. Specified new valve stem diameter is 6.982-7.000 mm (0.2749-0.2756 in.) for intake and 6.970-6.988 mm (0.2744-0.2751 in.) for exhaust. Specified new valve guide inside diameter for either valve is 7.033-7.058 mm (0.2769-0.2779 in.). Maximum allowable valve guide inside diameter is 7.134 mm (0.2809 in.) for intake guide and 7.159 mm (0.2819 in.) for exhaust guide. Valve guides are not renewable, however, guides can be reamed to accept valves with 0.25 mm oversize stem.

On late production CV engines, starting with serial number 1933503554, the exhaust valve rotator (7—Fig. KO205) has been eliminated and a new spring seat with different length valve spring is used in its place. Free length of the new valve spring is 55.8 mm (2.197 in.), and spring is color coded green for identification. Free length of early production exhaust valve spring is 48.69 mm (1.917 in.).

Note that three different styles of rocker arms and pivots (Fig. KO208) are used. Engines with serial No. 2617200734 and higher use the latest Style C rocker arm. If rocker arm replacement is required due to valve train wear, the Style B can be upgraded to Style C. Engines with Style A components can only be upgraded to Style C by installing a complete new cylinder head.

CAMSHAFT AND HYDRAULIC LIFTERS

To remove the camshaft, first rotate the crankshaft so the piston is at top dead center on compression stroke. Remove the rocker cover, compress the valve springs and disengage the push rods from the rocker arms. Remove the push rods while marking them so they can be returned to their original position.

Remove the crankcase cover or oil pan mounting screws, then pry the cover or oil pan from the crankcase at the prying lugs located on the cover or oil pan. Rotate the crankshaft so the timing marks on the crankshaft and camshaft gears are aligned. Remove the camshaft from the crankcase. Identify the valve lifters as either intake or exhaust so they can be returned to their original position, then remove the lifters from the crankcase.

NOTE: Do not use magnetic pick-up tools to remove the valve lifters. Using magnetic tools can magnetize the internal lifter components and lead to lifter malfunction.

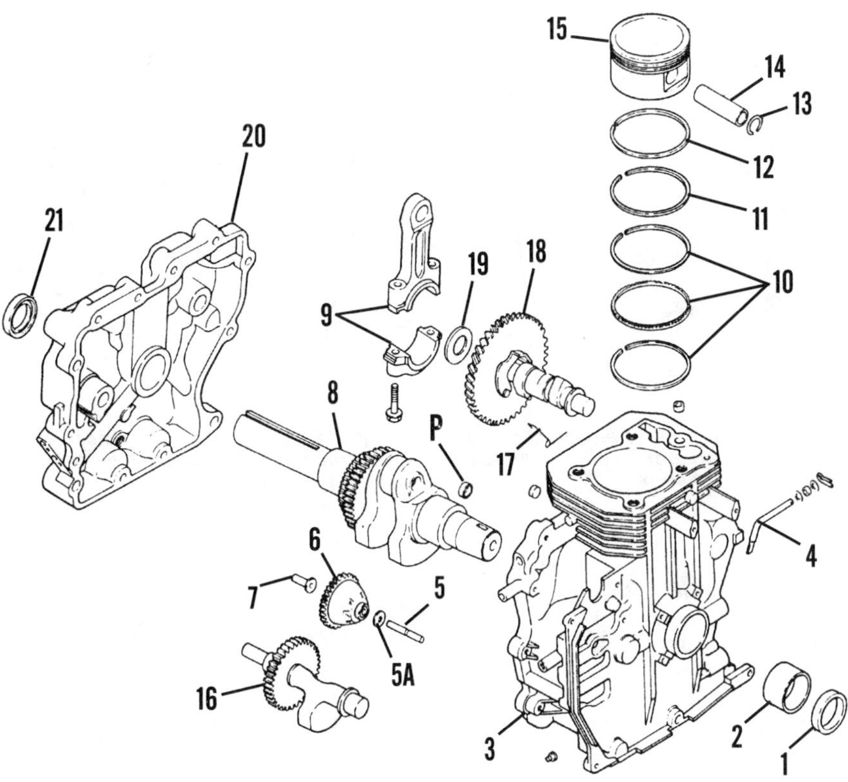

Fig. KO210–Exploded view of crankcase/cylinder block assembly of CH models.

1. Oil seal
2. Main bearing
3. Crankcase/cylinder block
4. Governor cross shaft
5. Governor gear shaft
5A. Thrust washer
6. Governor gear assy.
7. Governor pin
8. Crankshaft
9. Connecting rod
10. Oil control ring
11. Second compression ring
12. Top compression ring
13. Snap ring
14. Piston pin
15. Pisong
16. Balance shaft & gear assy.
17. Compression release spring
18. Camshaft & gear assy.
19. Shim
20. Crankcase cover
21. Oil seal

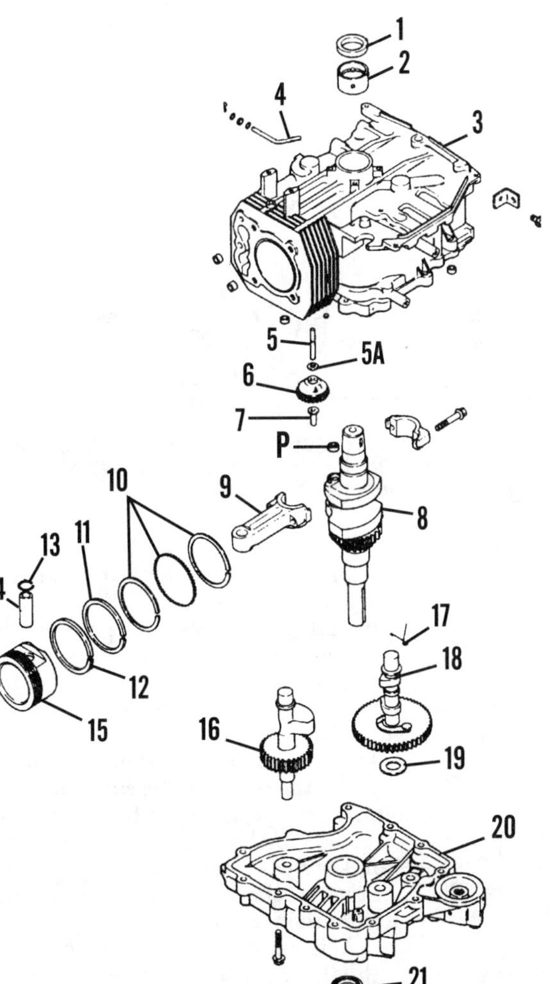

Fig KO211–Exploded view of crankcase/cylinder block assembly of CV models.

1. Oil seal
2. Main bearing
3. Crankcase/cylinder block
4. Governor cross shaft
5. Governor gear shaft
5A. Thrust washer
6. Governor gear assy.
7. Governor pin
8. Crankshaft
9. Connecting rod
10. Oil control ring
11. Second compression ring
12. Top compression ring
13. Snap ring
14. Piston pin
15. Piston
16. Balance shaft & gear assy.
17. Compression release spring
18. Camshaft & gear assy.
19. Shim
20. Oil pan
21. Oil seal

The camshaft is equipped with a compression reduction device to aid starting. The lever and weight mechanism on the camshaft gear moves a pin inside the exhaust cam lobe. During starting the pin protrudes above the cam lobe and forces the exhaust valve to stay open longer thereby reducing compression. At running speeds the pin remains below the surface of the cam lobe. Inspect the mechanism for proper operation.

Inspect the camshaft and lifters for scoring, pitting and excessive wear. Minimum cam lobe height is 8.96 mm (0.353 in.) for intake lobe and 9.14 mm (0.360 in.) for exhaust lobe. If the camshaft is replaced, the new valve lifters should also be installed.

If the hydraulic valve lifters are noisy after the engine has run for several minutes and reached operating temperature, it is probably an indication that contamination is preventing the lifter check ball from the seating or is there is internal wear in the lifter. Individual parts are not available for the hydraulic lifters. Lifters should be replaced if faulty.

Lubricate the lifter bores with oil and install hydraulic lifters in their original position. The exhaust lifter bore is closest to the crankcase gasket surface.

Install the camshaft, aligning the timing marks (Fig. KO209) on the crankshaft and camshaft gears as shown. Camshaft end play is adjusted with shims (19—Fig. KO210 or KO211), which are installed between the camshaft and oil pan. To determine camshaft end play, install the camshaft with the original thickness shim in the crankcase. Attach the end play checking tool KO-1031 to the crankcase and use a feeler gauge to measure the clearance between the shim and checking tool. Camshaft end play should be 0.076-0.127 mm (0.003-0.005 in.). Install different thickness shim as necessary to obtain the desired end play.

No gasket is used with the crankcase cover or oil pan. Apply a 1.6 mm (1/16 in.) bead of silicone gasket sealant (GE Silmate RTV-108, RTV-1473 or equivalent) around the crankcase cover or oil pan mating surface as shown in Fig. KO212. Tighten the crankcase cover or oil pan screws to 24.4 N·m (216 in.-lb.) using the sequence shown in Fig. KO213.

Rotate the crankshaft three full turns so the piston is at TDC between the exhaust and intake stroke. While rotating the crankshaft, observe the valve springs. If the valve spring coils compress completely, stop rotating the crankshaft and let the engine rest in this position for about 10 minutes. This will allow the valve spring pressure to collapse the hydraulic lifters.

Complete the assembly of the engine. Install the spark plug, then rotate the crankshaft by hand and check for compression on the compression stroke. If there is strong compression, the valves are seating and the engine can now be started.

PISTON, PIN AND RINGS

The piston and connecting rod are removed as an assembly. Remove the cylinder head and camshaft as previously outlined. Remove the balance shaft from the crankcase. Remove carbon deposits and ring ridge (if present) from the top of the cylinder before removing the piston and rod assembly. Remove the connecting rod cap and push the connecting rod and piston out of the cylinder. Remove the piston pin retaining rings and separate the piston and rod.

To determine piston clearance in the cylinder, measure the piston skirt diameter at a point 6 mm (0.24 in.) from the bottom of the skirt and perpendicular to the piston pin bore. Measure the cylinder bore inside diameter at the point of greatest wear, approximately 63 mm (2.5 in.) below the top of the cylinder and perpendicular to the piston pin. The difference between the two measurements is the piston clearance in the bore, which should be 0.031-0.043 mm (0.0012-0.0016 in.) for Model CV15 and 0.041-0.044 mm (0.0016-0.0017 in.) for all other models.

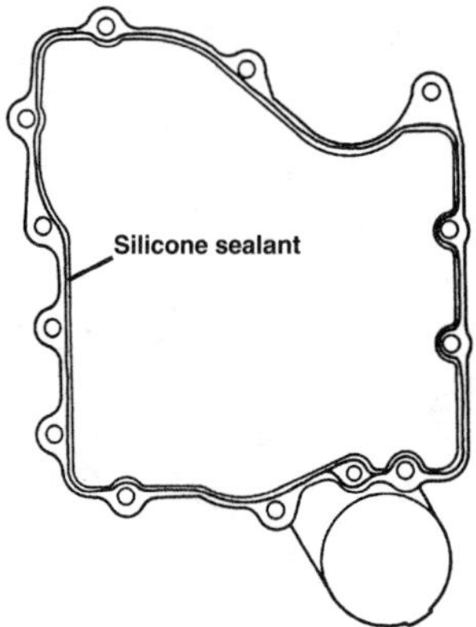

Fig. KO212–Apply silicone sealant in a 1.6 mm (1/16 in.) bead around crankcase cover mating surface as shown.

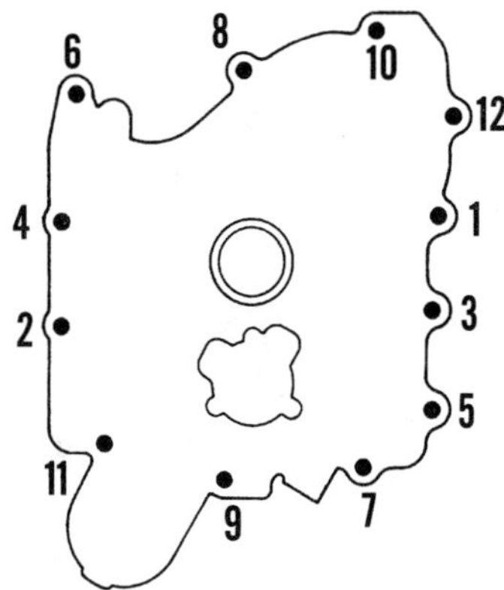

Fig. KO213–Follow the sequence shown when tightening crankcase cover or oil pan mounting screws.

Piston and rings are available in standard size and 0.25 and 0.50 mm (0.010 and 0.020 in.) oversize. Standard piston skirt diameter on Model CV15 is 89.951-89.969 mm (3.5413-3.5420 in.) with a wear limit of 89.824 mm (3.5363 in.). Standard piston skirt diameter on all other models is 86.941-86.959 mm (3.4229-3.4236 in.) with a wear limit of 86.814 mm (3.418 in.).

Specified piston pin bore is 19.006-19.012 mm (0.7483-0.7485 in.), and wear limit is 19.025 mm (0.749 in.). Specified piston pin diameter 18.995-19.000 mm (0.7478-0.7480 in.), and wear limit is 18.994 mm (0.7478 in.). Piston-to-piston pin clearance should be 0.006-0.017 mm (0.0002-0.0007 in.).

Insert new compression rings in the piston ring grooves and measure the clearance between the piston ring land and the piston ring using a feeler gauge. Replace the piston if the side clearance is excessive. Refer to the following specifications:

	Side Clearance
Top ring:	
CV15	0.060-0.105 mm (0.0023-0.0041 in.)
All other models	0.040-0.105 mm (0.0016-0.0041 in.)
Second ring:	
CV15	0.040-0.085 mm (0.0015-0.0033 in.)
All other models	0.040-0.072 mm (0.0016-0.0028 in.)

Specified piston ring end gap for compression rings is 0.27-0.50 mm (0.010-0.020 in.) for Model CV15 and 0.30-0.50 mm (0.012-0.020 in.) for all other models. Maximum allowable ring end gap in a used cylinder is 0.77 mm (0.030 in.).

When assembling piston rings on the piston, install the oil control ring expander (Fig. KO214) first and then the side rails.

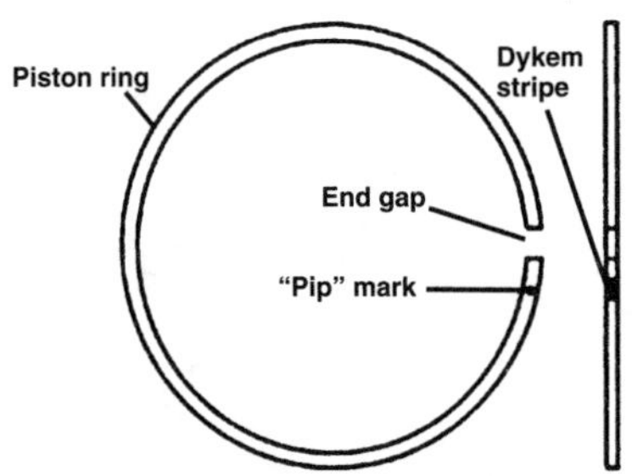

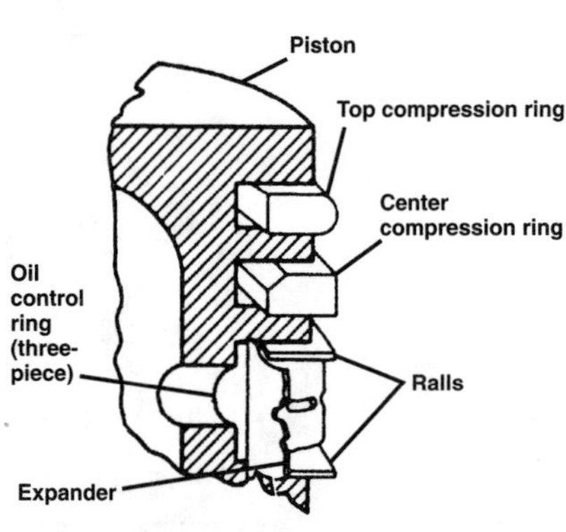

Fig. KO214–Cross-sectional view of piston showing correct installation of piston rings. Refer to text for details.

Install the compression rings so the side marked with "pip" mark is toward the piston crown and the stripe on the face of the ring is to the left of the end gap.

The second compression ring has a bevel on the inside of the ring and has a pink stripe on the ring face. Top compression ring has a barrel face and has a blue stripe on the ring face.

Stagger the ring end gaps evenly around the piston.

Lubricate the piston and cylinder with oil, then use a suitable ring compressor tool to the install piston and

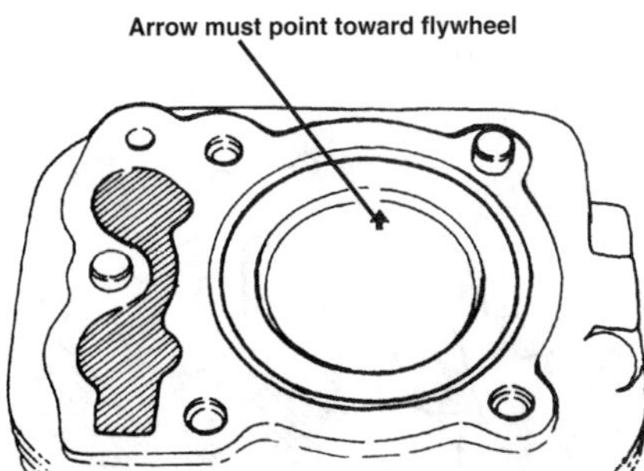

Fig. KO215–Piston must be installed with arrow pointing toward flywheel side of engine.

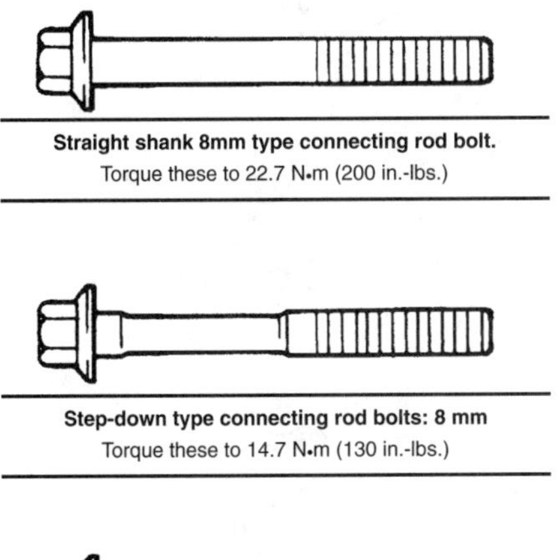

Straight shank 8mm type connecting rod bolt.
Torque these to 22.7 N•m (200 in.-lbs.)
Step-down type connecting rod bolts: 8 mm
Torque these to 14.7 N•m (130 in.-lbs.)
Straight shank 6 mm type connecting rod bolt.
Torque these to 11.3 N•m (100 in.-lbs.)

Fig. KO216–Different styles of connecting rod bolts. Refer to text.

rod. Be sure that the arrow on the piston crown is toward the flywheel side of the crankcase as shown in Fig. KO215.

Refer to the CONNECTING ROD section for connecting rod tightening torque. Install the balance shaft, camshaft, crankcase cover and cylinder head as outlined in the applicable sections.

CONNECTING ROD

Piston and connecting rod are removed as an assembly as outlined in the PISTON, PIN AND RINGS section. Remove the piston pin retaining rings and separate the piston and rod.

Replace the connecting rod if the bearing surfaces are scored or excessively worn. The specified connecting rod small end diameter is 19.015-19.023 mm (0.7486-0.7489 in.), and wear limit is 19.036 mm (0.7495 in.). Specified connecting rod-to-piston pin running clearance is 0.015-0.028 mm (0.0006-0.0011 in.).

Specified connecting rod-to-crankpin bearing clearance is 0.030-0.055 mm (0.0011-0.0022 in.), and maximum allowable clearance is 0.07 mm (0.0025 in.). A connecting rod with 0.25 mm (0.010 in.) undersize big end is available. The undersized rod can be identified by the drilled hole located in lower end of the rod.

Specified rod side clearance on the crankpin is 0.18-0.41 mm (0.007-0.016 in.).

To reinstall the connecting rod and piston assembly, reverse the removal procedure. Be sure the arrow mark on top of the piston is toward the flywheel side of the crankcase (Fig. KO215).

NOTE: Three different style connecting rod bolts are used (Fig. KO216). Each style bolt has a different tightening torque.

Lubricate the connecting rod and crankpin with engine oil. Install the rod cap and bolts. Tighten the rod bolts to the torque specified in Fig. KO216.

GOVERNOR

The engine is equipped with a flyweight mechanism mounted on the governor gear (6—Fig. KO210 or KO211). Remove the crankcase cover or oil pan (20) for access to the governor gear.

Inspect the gear assembly for excess wear and damage. The governor gear is held onto the governor shaft (5) by molded tabs on the gear. When the gear is removed, the tabs are damaged and replacement of the governor gear will be required. Gear and flyweight assembly are available only as a unit assembly.

If the governor gear shaft (5) requires replacement, tap a new shaft into the crankcase so it protrudes 32.64-32.84 mm (1.285-1.293 in.) above the crankcase boss.

Remove the cotter pin to remove the governor lever shaft (4). Inspect the shaft oil seal in the crankcase bore and replace if necessary.

No gasket is used with the crankcase cover or oil pan. Apply a 1.6 mm (1/16 in.) bead of silicone gasket sealant (GE Silmate RTV-108, RTV-1473 or equivalent) around the crankcase cover or oil pan mating surface as shown in Fig. KO212. Tighten the crankcase cover or oil pan screws to 24.4 N·m (216 in.-lb.) using the sequence shown in Fig. KO213. Adjust the governor as previously outlined in the MAINTENANCE section.

CRANKSHAFT

To remove the crankshaft, remove the starter and flywheel. Remove the crankcase cover or oil pan, piston, connecting rod and camshaft as previously outlined. Remove the balance shaft. Remove the crankshaft from the crankcase.

The crankshaft rides in a replaceable bushing (2—Fig. KO210 or KO211) in the crankcase and in an integral bearing in the crankcase cover or oil pan.

Specified main journal diameter at the flywheel end is 44.913-44.935 mm (1.7682-1.7691 in.), and the wear limit is 44.84 mm (1.765 in.). Bearing inside diameter at the flywheel end is 44.965-45.003 mm (1.7703-1.7718 in.), and wear limit is 45.016 mm (1.7723 in.). The crankshaft-to-bearing running clearance should be 0.03-0.09 mm (0.0012-0.0035 in.). When replacing the main bearing, make certain that the oil hole in the bearing aligns with the oil passage in the crankcase.

The specified main journal diameter at the PTO end is 41.915-41.935 mm (1.6502-1.6510 in.), and wear limit is 41.86 mm (1.648 in.). Crankshaft-to-oil pan bore running clearance should be 0.03-0.09 mm (0.0012-0.0035 in.).

The maximum allowable main journal taper is 0.020 mm (0.0008 in.) and the maximum allowable out-of-round is 0.025 mm (0.0010 in.). The main journals cannot be machined undersize.

Specified standard crankpin diameter is 38.958-38.970 mm (1.5338-1.5343 in.). Minimum allowable crankpin diameter is 38.94 mm (1.533 in.). Maximum allowable crankpin taper is 0.012 mm (0.0005 in.) and maximum allowable out-of-round is 0.025 mm (0.0010 in.). Crankpin can be ground to accept a connecting rod that is 0.25 mm (0.010 in.) undersize.

The plug (P—Fig. KO210 or KO211) should be removed after the machining operation so the oil passages can be cleaned thoroughly. Use a suitable screw puller to extract the plug. Be sure the new plug does not leak.

Maximum allowable crankshaft runout is 0.15 mm (0.006 in.) measured at the PTO end of the crankshaft with the crankshaft supported in the engine. The maximum allowable crankshaft runout is 0.10 mm (0.004 in.) measured at any point on the crankshaft with the crankshaft supported in V-blocks.

To install the crankshaft, reverse the removal procedure. Install the balance shaft, aligning the timing marks on the large crankshaft gear and balance shaft gear as shown in Fig. KO217. Install the camshaft, aligning the timing marks on the small crankshaft gear and the camshaft gear as shown in Fig. KO209.

No gasket is used with the crankcase cover or oil pan. Apply a 1.6 mm (1/16 in.) bead of silicone gasket sealant (GE Silmate RTV-108, RTV-1473 or equivalent) around the crankcase cover or oil pan mating surface as shown in Fig. KO212. Tighten the crankcase cover or oil pan screws to 24.4 N·m (216 in.-lb.) using the sequence shown in Fig. KO213.

Tighten the flywheel retaining nut to 66 N·m (90 ft.-lb.).

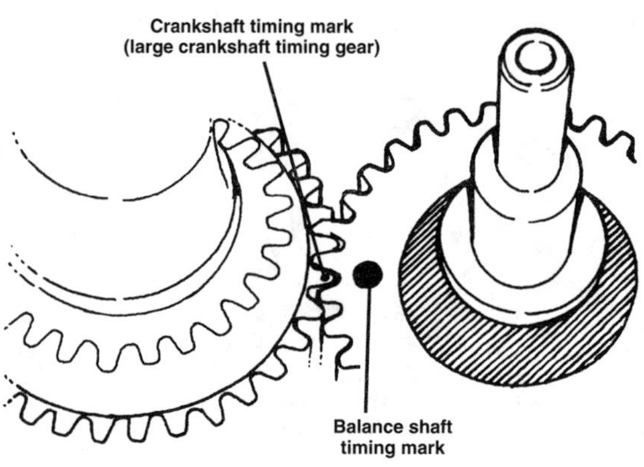

Fig. KO217–When assembling the engine, align the timing mark on large crankshaft gear with timing mark on balance shaft gear.

CYLINDER/CRANKCASE

Cylinder bore standard diameter is 90.000-90.025 mm (3.5433-3.5443 in.) on Model CV15 and 87.000-87.025 (3.4252-3.4262 in.) on all other models. Wear limit is 90.63 mm (3.5681 in.) for Model CV15 and 87.063 mm (3.4277 in.) for all other models. Maximum bore out-of-round is 0.12 mm (0.005 in.). Maximum bore taper is 0.05 mm (0.002 in.). Cylinder can be bored to accept an oversize piston.

Install new crankshaft oil seals in the crankcase and oil pan using seal driver KO-1036. Force the seal into the crankcase or oil pan until the tool bottoms.

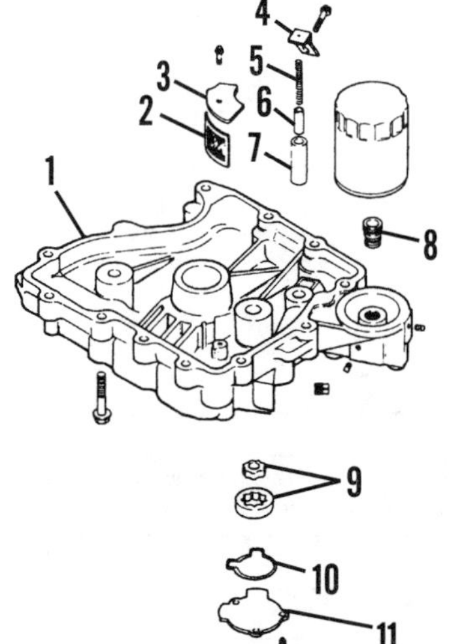

Fig. KO218–Gerotor type engine oil pump is mounted in crankcase cover on CH models or in oil pan on CV models. Oil pickup screen (2) and cover (3) are used on CV models. Not shown is oil pickup tube assembly used on CH models.

1. Crankcase cover/oil pan
2. Oil pick-up screen
3. Cover
4. Relief valve bracket
5. Relief valve spring
6. Relief valve piston
7. Relief valve body
8. Oil filter
9. Inner & outer rotors
10. O-ring
11. Pump cover

OIL PUMP

A gerotor oil pump is located in the crankcase cover of CH models or the oil pan of CV models. The engine balance shaft drives the oil pump.

The oil pump rotors (9—Fig. KO218) can be removed for inspection after removing the pump cover (11) from the bottom of the crankcase cover or oil pan. The crankcase cover or oil pan must be removed for access to oil pick-up or oil pressure regulator valve (5-7).

Check the oil pump rotors and oil pump cavity for scoring or excessive wear. The pressure relief valve body (7) and piston (6) must be free of scratches or burrs. The relief valve spring (5) free length should be approximately 25.20 mm (0.992 in.).

Lubricate the oil pump cavity and pump rotors with oil during reassembly. Install a new O-ring (10) in the groove in the crankcase cover or oil pan. Install the pump cover (11) and tighten the mounting screws to 6.2 N·m (55 in.-lb.) on a new crankcase cover or oil pan or 4.0 N·m (35 in.-lb.) on a used crankcase cover or oil pan.

No gasket is used with the crankcase cover or oil pan. Apply a 1.6 mm (1/16 in.) bead of silicone gasket sealant (GE Silmate RTV-108, RTV-1473 or equivalent) around crankcase cover or oil pan mating surface as shown in Fig. KO212. Tighten the crankcase cover or oil pan screws to 24.4 N·m (216 in.-lb.) using the sequence shown in Fig. KO213.

OIL SENSOR

Some engines are equipped with an Oil Sentry oil pressure monitor. The system uses a pressure switch installed in one of the main oil galleries of the crankcase cover or oil pan, or on the oil filter adapter. The pressure switch is designed to break contact as oil pressure increases to normal pressure, and to make contact when oil pressure decreases within the range of 20-35 kPa (3-5 psi). When the switch contacts close, either the engine will stop or a LOW OIL warning light will be activated, depending on the engine application.

To check the sensor pressure switch, a regulated supply of compressed air and a continuity tester are required. With zero pressure applied to the switch, the tester should indicate continuity across the switch terminal and ground. When pressure is increased through the range of 20-35 kPa (3-5 psi), the switch should open and the tester should indicate no continuity. If the switch fails the test, install a new switch.

SHIBAURA

Model	No. Cyls.	Bore	Stroke	Displ.	Power Rating
E643	3	64 mm (2.52 in.)	64 mm (2.52 in.)	617 cc (37.7 cu. in.)	10.4 kW (14 hp.)
E673	3	67 mm (2.64 in.)	64 mm (2.52 in.)	676 cc (41.2 cu. in.)	11.9 kW (16 hp.)

ENGINE IDENTIFICATION

The Shibaura E643 and E673 are four-stroke, three-cylinder, water-cooled, indirect injection diesel engines. The camshaft is located in the cylinder block. Valves in the cylinder head are operated through push rods and rocker arms. The number 1 cylinder is located at the fan end of the engine and the firing order is 1-2-3. The engine identification number is cast into the left side of the engine block.

MAINTENANCE

LUBRICATION

Use engine oil with API classification CD. Select oil viscosity depending on the expected ambient temperature range as shown on the temperature chart in Fig. SH101.

The recommended oil change interval is after every 100 hours of use. The recommended oil filter interval is after every 200 hours of use. The oil filter is a spin-on paper element cartridge. On new and reconditioned engines, lubricating oil and filter should be changed after first the 50 hours of operation. Change the oil and filter more frequently if severe operating conditions are encountered.

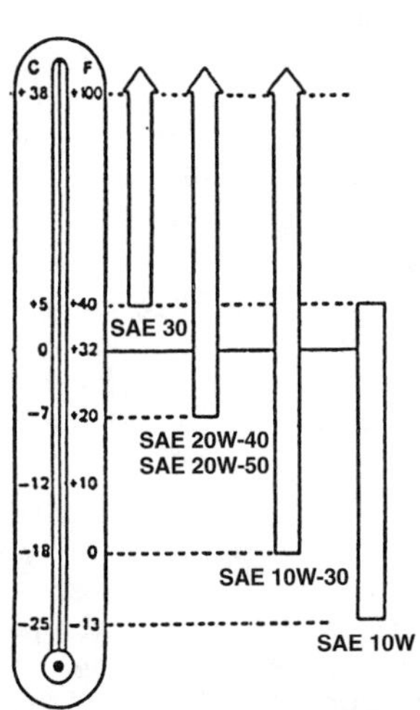

Fig. SH101–Select engine oil viscosity according to expected ambient air temperature.

AIR FILTER

The air filter should be cleaned after every 25 hours of operation or more frequently if operating in extremely dusty conditions. Remove dust from the filter element by tapping lightly with your hand, not on a hard surface. Compressed air at pressure under 30 psi (210 kPa) may also be directed inside the filter element, but be careful not to damage the element. Replace the filter once a year or as necessary.

FUEL FILTER

Refer to the applicable tractor section in this manual for fuel filter maintenance and fuel system bleeding instructions.

WATER PUMP BELT

Adjust belt tension so the belt will deflect approximately 13 mm (½ inch) when moderate thumb pressure is applied to the belt midway between the pump and alternator pulleys. Reposition the alternator to adjust belt tension.

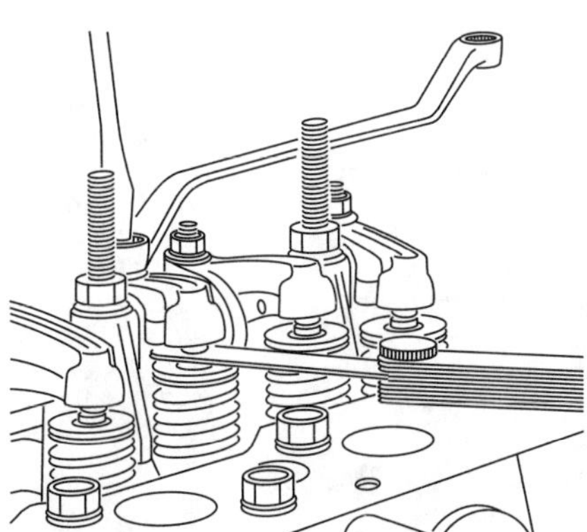

Fig. SH102–Use a feeler gauge to check and adjust valve clearance.

COOLING SYSTEM

Refer to the tractor section for cooling system maintenance information.

A thermostat regulates engine coolant temperature. Thermostat is contained in the thermostat housing located on the side of the cylinder head. Thermostat should be fully open at 90° C (194° F).

VALVE ADJUSTMENT

Adjust the valve clearance with the engine cold. The specified clearance is 0.2 mm (0.008 in.) for both intake and exhaust valves.

To adjust the clearance, remove the valve cover. Rotate the flywheel until the number 1 piston is at top dead center on the compression stroke. Both push rods for the number 1 cylinder should be loose. Loosen the rocker arm locknuts. Turn the adjusting screw at the push rod end of the rocker arm until a 0.2 mm (0.008 in.) thick feeler gauge is a slip fit between the end of the valve stem and the rocker arm pad (Fig. SH102). Hold the adjusting screw in this position and tighten the locknut.

Rotate the flywheel to position the next piston in the firing order at top dead center on the compression stroke. Repeat the valve adjustment procedure for each cylinder.

INJECTION PUMP TIMING

Timing of the fuel injection pump is accomplished by varying the thickness of shims installed between the injection pump and the mounting surface of the engine front cover.

To check the injection pump timing, thoroughly clean the injector, injector line and pump. Remove the fuel injection line to the number 1 cylinder (cylinder at fan end of the engine). Remove the number 1 delivery valve holder, delivery valve spring (2—Fig. SH103) and delivery valve (3) from the injection pump. Reinstall the holder without the spring and valve. Connect a suitable spill pipe to the delivery valve holder.

Remove the rocker arm cover and turn the crankshaft in normal direction until the number 1 piston is on the compression stroke and the notch in the crankshaft pulley is in line with the TOP mark (M—Fig. SH104) on the timing gear cover. Both rocker arms for the number 1 cylinder should be loose. If the number 1 cylinder rocker arms are not loose at this point, the piston is on the exhaust stroke and the crankshaft must be rotated one full turn.

Turn the crankshaft counterclockwise so the pulley notch is at the 30 degree mark on the timing gear cover. Turn the key switch to the ON position and move the throttle lever to the full speed position, but do not start the engine. Fuel should flow from the delivery valve holder.

Slowly turn the crankshaft in the normal direction of rotation (clockwise) so that number 1 piston is starting up on the compression stroke and observe fuel flow from the open fuel delivery valve. Fuel flow should change to drops and then stop. Just as the fuel stops, stop turning the crankshaft and check the injection timing marks (M—Fig. SH104). Notch (N) on the pulley should be aligned with the 17 degree timing mark. Note that if fuel does not stop flowing, the number 1 piston is on the exhaust stroke instead of compression stroke. Turn the crankshaft one complete revolution and repeat the test.

If the timing notch is not aligned with the specified timing mark, repeat the check several times to be sure you are observing fuel flow correctly. If the injection timing is not correct, remove the injection pump and adjust the timing as follows: If the notch has not reached the 17 degree timing mark when fuel stops flowing, retard the injection timing by increasing the thickness of the pump mounting shim gasket. If the notch has passed 17 degree timing mark, advance the timing by decreasing the thickness of the pump mounting shim. Changing the shim thickness 0.1 mm (0.004 in.) will change the timing mark about one degree.

Tighten the pump mounting bolts and recheck the timing. When the injection pump timing is within specifications, install the fuel delivery valve and spring. Tighten the delivery valve holder to 42 N·m (31 ft.-lb.). Install the fuel injection line and bleed air from the line before tightening the fitting at the injector.

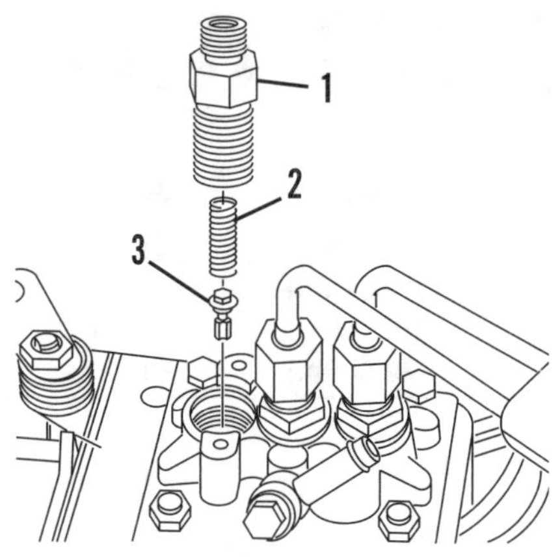

Fig. SH103–Exploded view of delivery valve holder (1), spring (2) and delivery valve (3).

GOVERNOR

The governor is located within the fuel injection pump camshaft housing on all models. Low idle speed should be 1450 rpm. Engine governed fast idle no-load speed should be 3350-3450 rpm. Fast idle adjusting screw (F—Fig. SH105) is located on the rear face of the timing gear housing and slow idle adjusting screw (S) is located on the side of the timing gear cover.

REPAIRS

TIGHTENING TORQUE

Refer to the following special tightening torque specifications:

Camshaft retainer	9-12 N·m (80-106 in.-lb.)
Connecting rod	21-25 N·m (186-221 in.-lb.)
Crankshaft pulley nut	88-98 N·m (65-72 ft.-lb.)
Cylinder head	35-39 N·m (26-28 ft.-lb.)
Flywheel	69-78 N·m (51-57 ft.-lb.)
Glow plug	15-19 N·m (133-168 in.-lb.)
Injector nozzle nut	40 N·m (30 ft.-lb.)
Injector	59-69 N·m (44-50 ft.-lb.)
Main bearing retaining screw	20-24 N·m (177-212 in.-lb.)
Main bearing holder	20-24 N·m (177-212 in.-lb.)
Rocker arm cover	10-11 N·m (89-97 in.-lb.)
Rocker shaft pedestal	20-24 N·m (177-212 in.-lb.)

ROCKER ARMS AND PUSH RODS

Rocker arm shaft assembly and push rods can be removed after removing the rocker arm cover. Rocker arms for all cylinders pivot on a one-piece shaft that is supported by pedestals attached to the cylinder head by cap screws. Loosen the rocker shaft support nuts one turn at a time to prevent bending the rocker shaft. All valve train components should be identified as they are removed so they can be reinstalled in their original locations if reused.

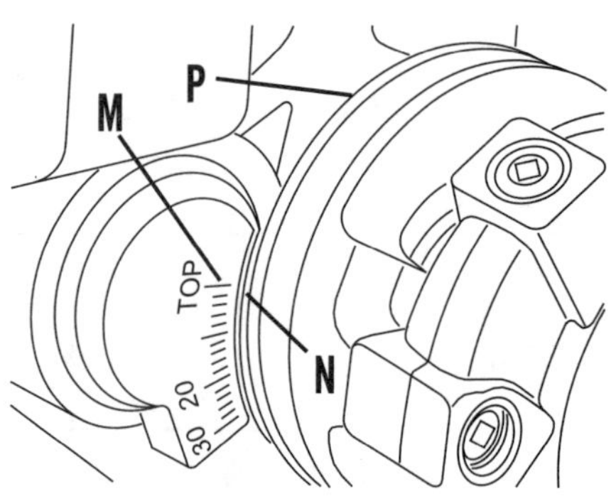

Fig. SH104–Timing marks (M) are located on timing gear cover. Refer to text for timing procedure.

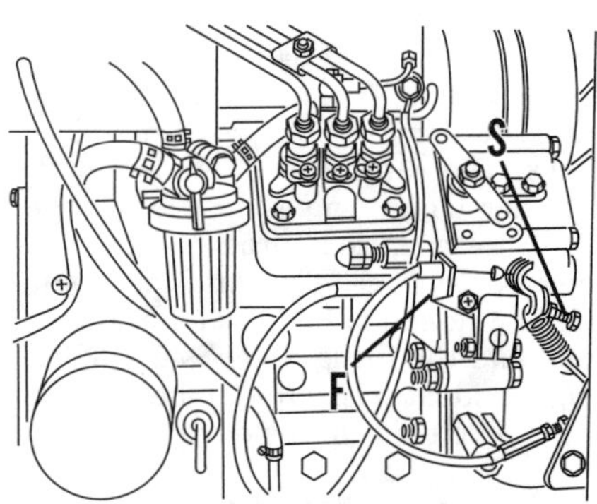

Fig. SH105–View showing location of fast idle adjustment screw F) and slow idle adjustment screw (S).

Rocker shaft diameter should be 11.65-11.67 mm (0.4587-0.4594 in.) with wear limit of 11.57 mm (0.4555 in.). The specified rocker arm-to-shaft clearance is 0.03-0.07 mm (0.001-0.003 in.). Clearance between rocker arm and shaft should not exceed 0.2 mm (0.008 in.).

Check push rods by rolling them on a flat plate and replace any that are bent or if the ends are galled, worn or chipped. Push rod length is 146 mm (5.738 in.).

Note the following when assembling the rocker arm shaft assembly. Lubricating oil passes through the roll pin securing the rocker shaft to the pedestal. Drive in the roll pin so the lower end just extends below the foot of the pedestal. Upper end of the pin must not bottom against the shaft wall or oil flow will be blocked.

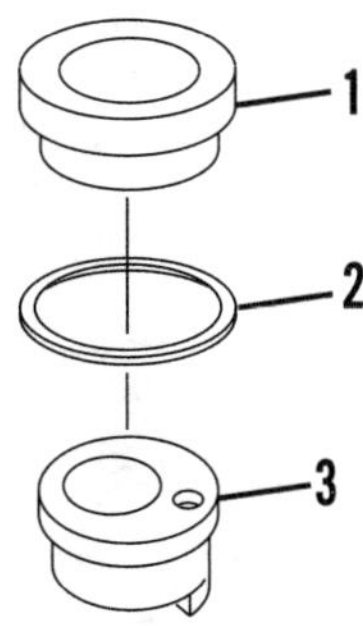

Fig. SH106–Exploded view of precombustion chamber assembly showing spacer (1), gasket ring (2) and chamber (3).

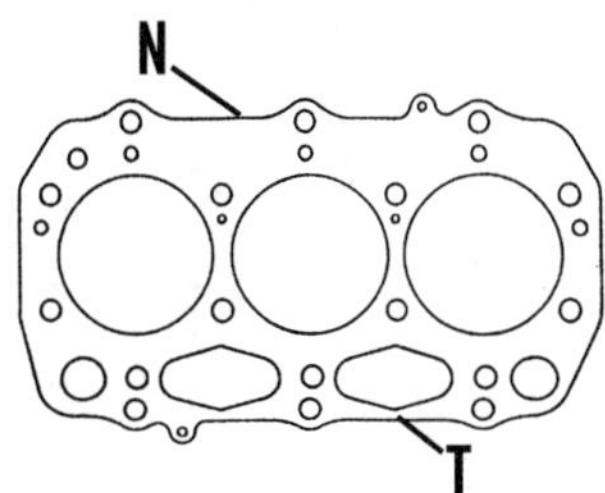

Fig. SH107–On Model 643, last four digits of cylinder head part number (N) are stamped on top side of head gasket in area indicated. Head gasket may also be identified by presence or absence of notches (T) on gasket edge. Refer to text.

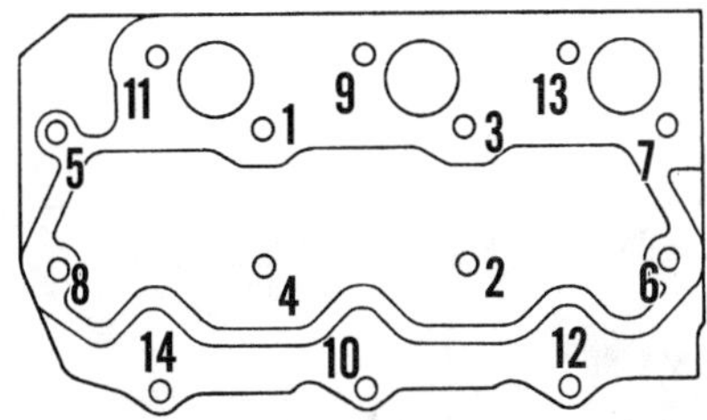

Fig. SH108–Tighten head bolts in sequnce shown to a final torque of 35-39 N•m (26-28 ft.-lb.).

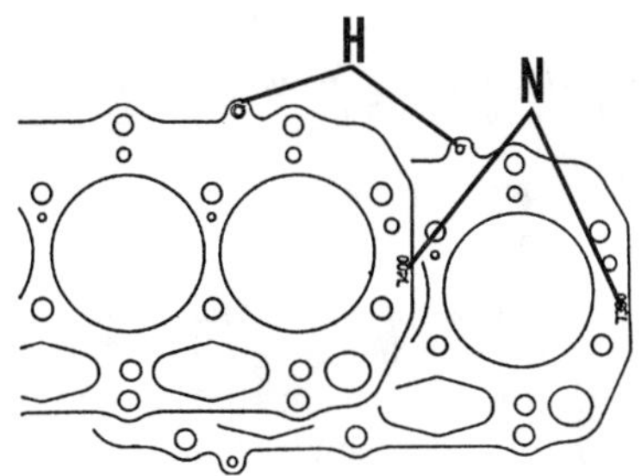

Fig. SH109–On Model 673, last four digits of cylinder head part number (N) are stamped on top side of head gasket in area indicated. Head gasket may also be identified by presence or absence of grommet in hole (H). Refer to text.

Tighten the rocker shaft pedestal nuts to 20-24 N·m (177-212 in.-lb.). Adjust the valves as previously outlined and install the rocker arm cover. Tighten the rocker arm cover nuts and screws to 10-11 N·m (89-97 in.-lb.).

CYLINDER HEAD

Model E643

To remove the cylinder head, drain the engine coolant and proceed as follows: Remove the exhaust manifold, water pump, fuel injectors, glow plugs, oil line, rocker arm cover, rocker arm assembly and push rods. Unscrew the cylinder head bolts in steps of one-half turn to prevent warping the head. Remove the cylinder head bolts and lift the cylinder head off the engine.

The cylinder head is equipped with a precombustion chamber (Fig. SH106) for each cylinder. The chamber is a press fit in the head. If the chamber is removed, a new chamber must be installed.

Before installing the cylinder head, thoroughly clean the head and block gasket surfaces and inspect the head for cracks, distortion or other defects. Check the cylinder head gasket surface with a straightedge and feeler gauge. The head must be reconditioned or replaced if distortion (warp or twist) exceeds 0.12 mm (0.005 in.).

To determine the correct cylinder head gasket thickness, measure the piston standout above the block surface for each piston at top dead center. Select a cylinder head gasket from the following table using the reading that indicates greatest standout.

Piston Standout	Gasket Number	Installed Thickness
0.55-0.65 mm (0.022-0.026 in.)	111147090	1.1 mm (0.043 in.)
0.65-0.75 mm (0.026-0.030 in.)	111147100	1.2 mm (0.047 in.)
0.75-0.85 mm (0.030-0.034 in.)	111147110	1.3 mm (0.051 in.)

Cylinder head gasket may be identified by the last four digits of the part number (N—Fig. SH107) stamped in the surface and by notches (T) in the outside edge. Gasket 111147090 has one notch, gasket 111147100 has two notches and gasket 111147110 has no notches.

Install the head gasket with the part number (N) up. Lubricate the cylinder head bolt threads with oil prior to installation. Tighten the head bolts in steps using sequence shown in Fig. SH108. Tighten the head bolts to a final torque of 35-39 N·m (26-28 ft.-lb.).

Complete the installation of the cylinder head by reversing the removal procedure.

MODEL E673

To remove the cylinder head, drain the engine coolant and proceed as follows: Remove the exhaust manifold, water pump, fuel injectors, glow plugs, oil line, rocker arm cover, rocker arm assembly and push rods. Unscrew the cylinder head bolts in steps of one-half turn to prevent warping the head. Remove the cylinder head bolts and lift the cylinder head off the engine.

Cylinder head is equipped with a precombustion chamber (Fig. SH106) for each cylinder. The chamber is a press fit in the head. If the chamber is removed, a new chamber must be installed.

Before installing the cylinder head, thoroughly clean the head and block gasket surfaces and inspect the head for cracks, distortion or other defects. Check the cylinder head gasket surface with a straightedge and feeler gauge. Head must be reconditioned or replaced if distortion (warp or twist) exceeds 0.12 mm (0.005 in.).

To determine the correct cylinder head gasket thickness, measure the depth of the piston below the block surface for each piston at top dead center. Select a cylinder head gasket from the following table using the reading indicating the greatest depth.

Piston Depth	Gasket Number	Installed Thickness
0.25-0.40 mm (0.010-0.016 in.)	111147390	0.4 mm (0.016 in.)
0.15-0.25 mm (0.006-0.010 in.)	111147400	0.5 mm (0.020 in.)

Cylinder head gasket may be identified by the last four digits of the part number (N—Fig. SH109) stamped in the surface and by the presence or absence of a grommet in the hole (H) in the outside edge. Gasket 111147390 does not have a grommet in hole (H) while gasket 111147400 has a grommet.

Install the head gasket with the part number (N) up. Lubricate the cylinder head bolt threads with oil prior to installation. Tighten the head bolts in steps using the sequence shown in Fig. SH108. Tighten the head bolts to a final torque of 35-39 N·m (26-28 ft.-lb.).

Complete the installation of the cylinder head by reversing the removal procedure.

VALVE SYSTEM

Valves seat directly in the cylinder head. Valve seat angle is 45° for intake and exhaust. Valve seat width should be 1.59-1.80 mm (0.062-0.070 in.).

Valve face angle is 45° for intake and exhaust. Specified valve margin is 0.93-1.08 mm (0.037-0.042 in.). Minimum valve margin is 0.51 mm (0.020 in.).

Valve guides are not replaceable. Refer to the following valve stem and guide specifications:

Intake valve stem OD . . . . . 5.960-5.980 mm (0.2346-0.2354 in.)
Wear limit . . . . . 5.90 mm (0.232 in.)
Exhaust valve stem OD . . . 5.940-5.960 mm (0.2338-0.2346 in.)
Wear limit . . . . . 5.90 mm (0.232 in.)
Intake valve clearance . . . . 0.025-0.052 mm (0.0010-0.0020 in.)
Wear limit . . . . . 0.2 mm (0.0078 in.)
Exhaust valve clearance . . 0.045-0.070 mm (0.0018-0.0028 in.)
Wear limit . . . . . 0.25 mm (0.0098 in.)

After reconditioning the seats and valves, check the distance (D—Fig. SH110) the valve head is below the cylinder head surface. Standard valve head recess distance is 0.65-0.95 mm (0.026-0.037 in.). If valve head recess is 1.8 mm (0.070 in.) or more, install new valves or cylinder head or both.

Minimum allowable valve spring pressure is 59 N (13.2 lb.) at a length of 28.3 mm (0.114 in.) for both intake and exhaust. Minimum valve spring length is 31.5 mm (1.240 in.). Replace the spring if out-of-square more than 1.2 mm (0.047 in.).

INJECTORS

Removal and Installation

Prior to removing the injectors, thoroughly clean the injectors, injector lines, fuel injection pump and surrounding area. Remove the fuel injection lines from the injection pump and injectors. Remove the fuel return line from the top of the injectors. Cap all openings to prevent entry of dirt. Unscrew the fuel injectors from the cylinder head. Remove the seal washer from the bottom of the injector bore in the cylinder head if it did not come out with the injector.

When installing the fuel injectors, first be sure the injector bores in the cylinder head are clean and all old seals are removed. Insert new seal washers in the injector bores and install the injectors. Tighten the injector to 59-69 N·m (44-50 ft.-lb.). Bleed air from the injector lines before tightening the high pressure fuel line fittings at the injector end.

Testing

A complete job of testing, cleaning and adjusting the fuel injector requires the use of special test equipment. Use

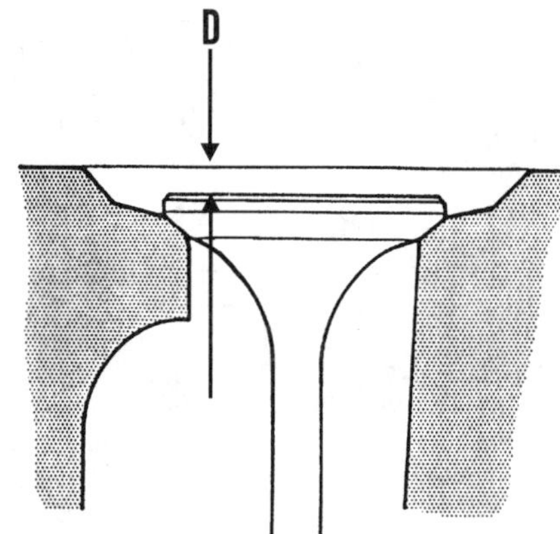

Fig. SH110–Top of valve should be below cylinder head surface. Refer to text for specifications.

only clean approved testing oil in the tester tank. Injector should be tested for opening pressure, seat leakage and spray pattern. Before connecting the injector to the test stand, operate the tester lever until oil flows, then attach the injector to the tester line.

WARNING: Fuel emerges from the injector with sufficient force to penetrate the skin. When testing injector, keep yourself clear of nozzle spray.

Close the valve to the tester gauge and operate the tester lever a few quick strokes to purge air from the injector and to be sure the nozzle valve is not stuck.

Opening Pressure

Open the valve to the tester gauge and operate the tester lever slowly while observing the gauge reading. Opening pressure should be 11730 kPa (1700 psi). Adjust the opening pressure by changing the thickness of the shim stack (2—Fig. SH111). Increasing the shim thickness will increase the opening pressure.

Spray Pattern

The spray pattern should be conical, well atomized, and emerging in a straight axis from the nozzle tip. If the spray is drippy, ragged or to one side, the nozzle must be cleaned or renewed.

Seat Leakage

Wipe the nozzle tip dry with clean blotting paper, then slowly actuate the tester lever to obtain a gauge pressure approximately 2070 kPa (300 psi) below the opening pressure and hold this tester pressure for 10 seconds. If a drop of oil appears at the nozzle tip, or oil

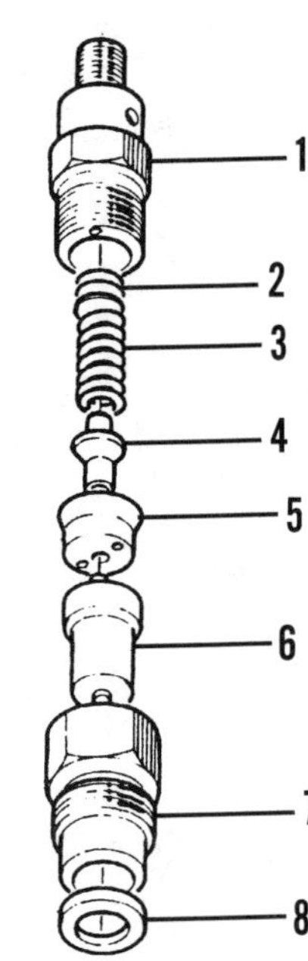

Fig. SH111–Exploded view of fuel injector.

1. Injector body
2. Shims
3. Spring
4. Spring seat
5. Spacer
6. Nozzle & needle
7. Nozzle nut
8. Sealing washer

drips from the nozzle, clean or replace the nozzle.

Overhaul

Hard or sharp tools, emery cloth, grinding compounds or other than approved tools, solvents and lapping compounds, must never be used. Wipe all dirt and loose carbon from the injector, then refer to Fig. SH111 and proceed as follows:

Secure the injector nozzle in a holding fixture or soft-jawed vise and loosen the nut (7). Unscrew the nut and remove the internal parts (2 to 6) from the injector. Be careful not to lose the shims (2). Place all parts in clean diesel fuel or calibrating oil as they are removed, and take care not to mix parts with those from other injector assemblies.

Clean exterior surfaces with a brass wire brush to loosen carbon deposits. Soak parts in approved carbon solvent if necessary. Rinse parts in clean diesel fuel or calibrating oil after cleaning to neutralize the carbon solvent.

Clean the nozzle spray hole from inside using a pointed hardwood stick. Scrape carbon from the nozzle pressure chamber using a hooked scraper. Clean the valve seat using a brass scraper.

Inspect the nozzle valve and body for scratches or wear. Be sure that nozzle valve slides smoothly in the nozzle body bore. The nozzle valve should slide down into the nozzle body by its own weight. If the valve sticks in the nozzle

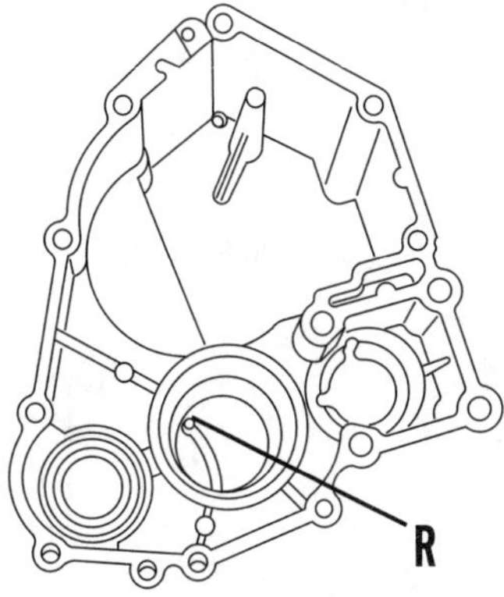

Fig. SH112A–When installing timing gear cover, roll pin (R) in timing gear cover must fit into hole (H–Fig. SH112B) in oil pump cover.

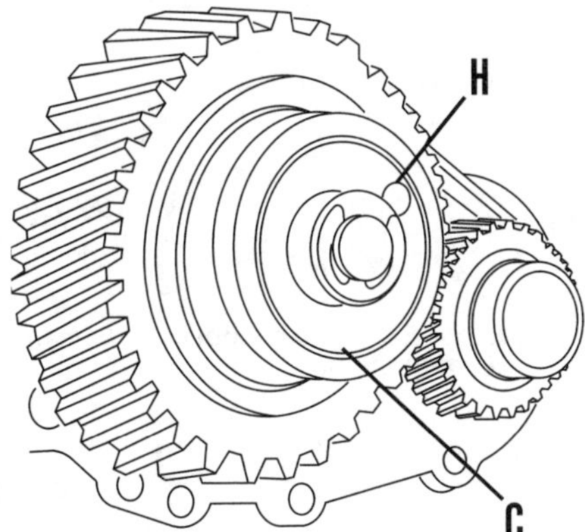

Fig. SH112B–View of oil pump and idler gear.

body, reclean or replace the nozzle assembly.

Reclean all parts by rinsing thoroughly in clean diesel fuel or calibrating oil and assemble the injector while immersed in fuel or oil. Be sure the shim stack is intact, then install the shims (2), spring (3), spring seat (4), spacer (5), nozzle valve assembly (6) and nozzle nut (7). Tighten the nozzle nut to 40 N·m (30 ft.-lb.). Do not overtighten the nozzle nut in an attempt to stop fuel leakage. Disassemble and clean the injector if a leak is noted. Retest the assembled injector.

INJECTION PUMP

The fuel injection pump is mounted on the engine block and is driven by lobes on the engine camshaft. To remove the injection pump, thoroughly clean the pump, fuel injectors, lines and surrounding area. Remove the high pressure fuel injection lines and disconnect the fuel supply line.

Plug all openings to prevent entry of dirt. Remove the fuel shut-off solenoid. Remove the nuts and screws retaining the pump. Lift the pump from the top of

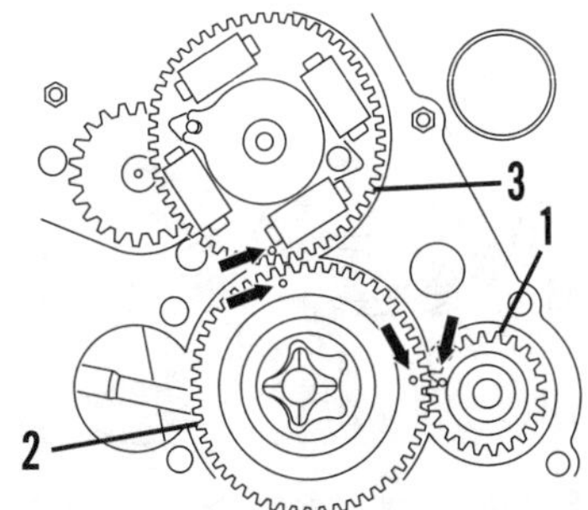

Fig. SH113–Timing marks on crankshaft gear (1), idler gear (2) and camshaft gear (3) must be aligned as shown.

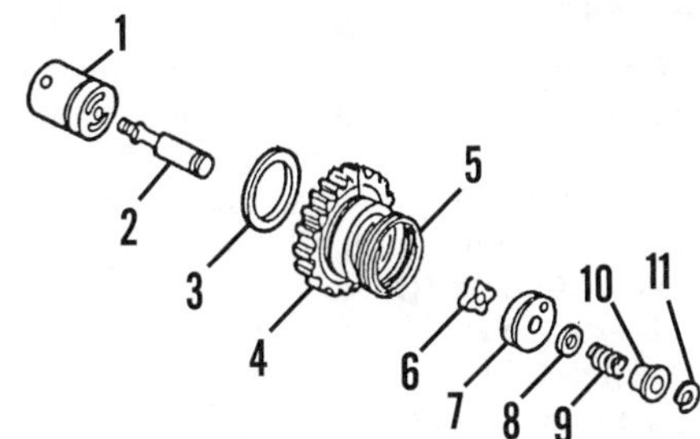

Fig. SH114–Exploded view of idler gear and oil pump assemblies.

1. Support
2. Shaft
3. Thrust washer
4. Idler gear & outer rotor
5. Spring
6. Inner rotor
7. Cover
8. Shim
9. Spring
10. Collar
11. E-ring

the timing gear housing so the governor link is accessible. Detach the governor link from the pump control rack, then remove the injection pump.

Only a qualified fuel injection repair shop should service the injection pump.

To install the injection pump, reverse the removal procedure using the same pump mounting shims as were removed. To bleed air from the fuel system, loosen the bleed screw located on the injection pump fuel inlet fitting. Turn the key switch ON, but do not start the engine. Tighten the bleed screw when air-free fuel flows from the fitting. Move the throttle to high-speed position. Loosen the injection line fittings at the injectors, then crank the engine until fuel flows from the lines. Tighten the fittings.

Check the injection pump timing as outlined in the MAINTENANCE section.

TIMING GEAR COVER

To remove timing gear cover, the engine must be removed from the tractor. Remove the alternator, fan, drive coupler and crankshaft pulley. Remove the fuel injection pump as previously described. Remove the cap screws attaching the timing gear cover to the engine and remove the timing gear cover.

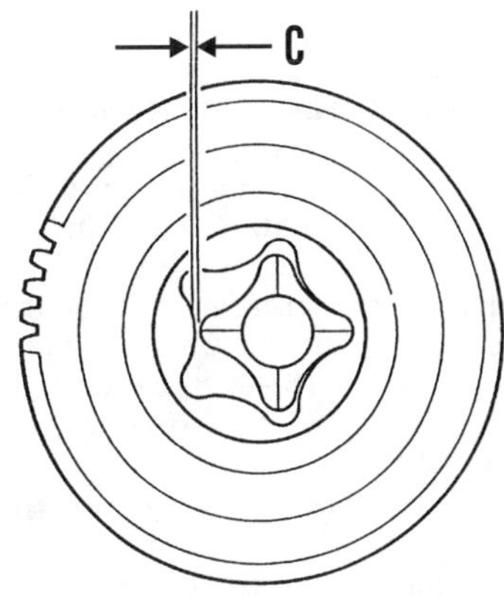

Fig. SH115–Clearance (C) between outer rotor and inner rotor should be 0.10-0.15 mm (0.004-0.006 in.)

The governor linkage is mounted on the timing gear cover. Refer to the GOVERNOR section.

Thoroughly clean the timing cover and mounting gasket surfaces. When installing the cover, the roll pin (R—Fig. SH112A) in the timing gear cover must fit into the hole (H—Fig. SH112B) in the oil pump cover. To complete reassembly, reverse the removal procedure.

TIMING GEARS

The timing gears can be inspected after removing the timing gear cover. Standard backlash between mating timing gears is 0.08 mm (0.003 in.); maximum allowable backlash is 0.25 mm (0.010 in.). Check the gear teeth for excessive wear or tooth damage and renew as necessary. If necessary to replace the gears, remove the valve cover, rocker arm assembly and the push rods to relieve valve spring pressure on the camshaft.

To remove the crankshaft gear or camshaft gear, it is recommended that the shafts be removed from the engine as the gears are a press fit on their respective shafts. Also refer to IDLER GEAR section.

When installing the timing gears, be sure all timing marks are aligned as shown in Fig. SH113.

OIL PUMP AND RELIEF VALVE

Oil pump (Fig. SH112B) is contained in the idler gear body and a portion of the gear body serves as the outer pump rotor. The timing gear cover must be removed for access to the oil pump. Detach the "E" ring (11—Fig. SH114), then disassemble pump.

Clearance (C—Fig. SH115) between the outer rotor and inner rotor should be 0.10-0.15 mm (0.004-0.006 in.). Maximum allowable rotor clearance is 0.25 mm (0.010 in.).

With the pump assembled, mount a dial indicator against the pump cover (C—Fig. SH112B) and measure the inner rotor end play against spring pressure. Cover movement should be 0.10-0.20 mm (0.004-0.008 in.). Less movement may cause internal pump damage, while greater movement may reduce pump pressure and volume. Adjust the shim (8—Fig. SH114) thickness to obtain the desired cover movement.

To reinstall the pump, reverse the removal procedure. When installing the timing gear cover, the roll pin (R—Fig. SH112A) in the timing gear cover must fit into the hole (H—Fig. SH112B) in the oil pump cover.

The system pressure relief valve is located on the side of the cylinder block below the fuel injection pump. The relief valve regulates oil pressure to 290-490 kPa (43-71 psi).

IDLER GEAR

The oil pump is mounted on the idler gear (4—Fig. SH114). The idler gear rides on a removable support (1) that routes oil to and from the oil pump. The support is a force fit in the front of the block.

The camshaft and adapter plate on the front of the block must be removed to remove the idler support (Fig. SH116). Remove the support using Ford tools 11097 and 11099. Engage the tools in the grooves of the support and pull the support out of the cylinder block.

To install the support, install guide pins of tool FTC-214080 in the holes adjacent to the support hole in block. Position the support and shaft in the driver, then place the driver on the guide pins as shown in Fig. SH117. Drive against the driver to force the support into the cylinder block. The driver must bottom against the block.

When installing the idler gear, be sure the timing marks are aligned as shown in Fig. SH113.

GOVERNOR

The governor flyweight assembly is mounted on the camshaft gear. Governor linkage is located inside the timing gear cover. If faulty governor operation is suspected, inspect components for binding, looseness, excessive wear or other damage. Flyweight assembly is available only as a unit assembly with the camshaft gear. The camshaft must be removed to remove the gear. Refer to the CAMSHAFT section.

Check and adjust the engine slow and fast idle speeds as outlined in the MAINTENANCE section.

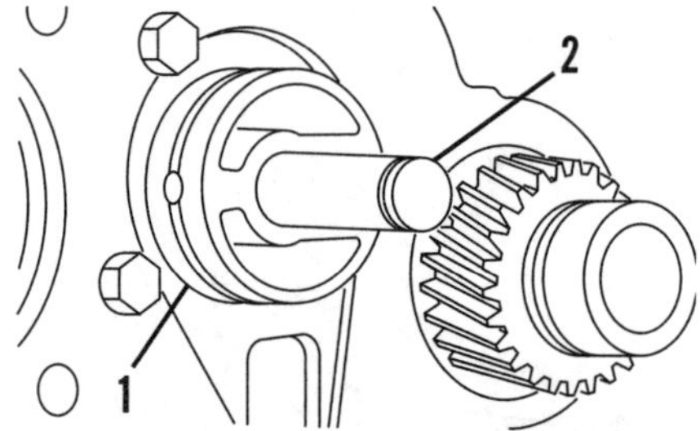

Fig. SH116–View of idler gear support (1). Support routes oil to and from oil pump in idler gear. Oil pump inner rotor rides on shaft (2).

CAMSHAFT

To remove the camshaft, remove the cylinder head and valve tappets. Mark the tappets so they can be returned to their original positions. Remove the fuel injection pump and timing gear cover. Remove the camshaft retainer (11—Fig. SH118) and withdraw the camshaft (1).

The governor flyweight assembly is mounted on the camshaft gear. Camshaft gear and flyweight assembly are available only as a unit assembly. Use a suitable press to separate the gear assembly from the camshaft.

Minimum allowable valve lobe height (H—Fig. SH119) is 26.10 mm (1.028 in.). Minimum allowable injection lobe height (H) is 34.30 mm (1.350 in.). Maximum allowable camshaft runout measured at the center of the camshaft is 0.1 mm (0.004 in.).

Inspect the camshaft bearings and replace if damaged.

Be sure the timing marks are aligned as shown in Fig. SH113 when installing the camshaft.

PISTON AND ROD UNITS

Engine must be removed from the tractor to remove the pistons and connecting rods. Piston and rod units may be removed from above after removing the oil pan, oil pump pickup tube and cylinder head. Be sure to remove the ridge (if present) from the top of the cylinders prior to removing the pistons. Mark the rod bearing cap and rod so they can be reassembled together.

When assembling the piston and rod, note the location of the arrow on the piston crown and the numbers on the rod and cap as shown in Fig. SH120. Position the piston rings so the gaps are approximately 90° apart. Lubricate the piston and cylinder with engine oil. Use a ring compressor to compress the rings, and install the piston and rod so the arrow on the piston crown is toward the timing gear end of the engine. Tighten the connecting rod nuts to 21-25 N·m (186-221 in.-lb.).

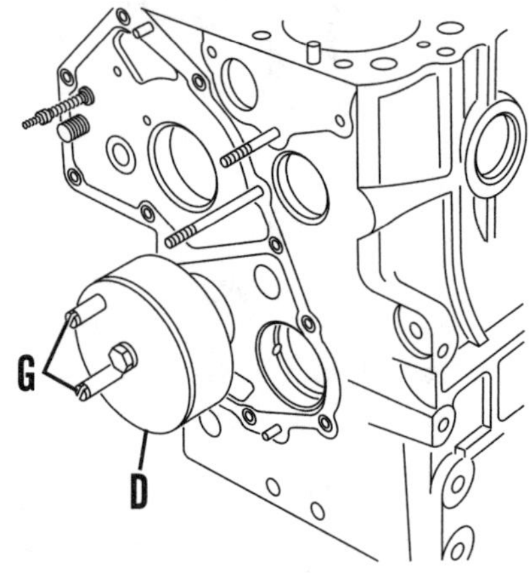

Fig. SH117–Guide pins (G) position the driver (D) so idler support is installed correctly.

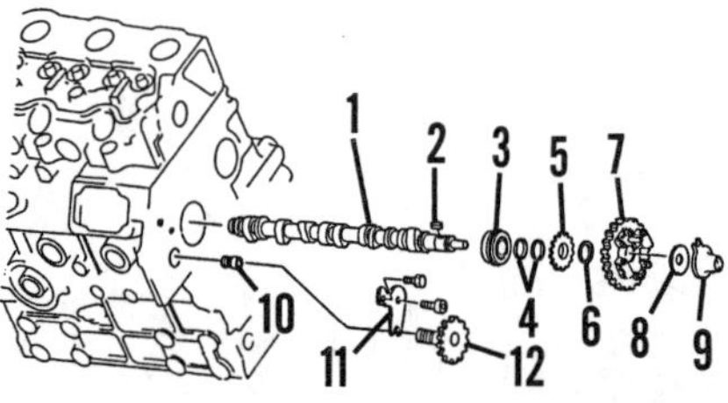

Fig. SH118–Exploded view of camshaft and related components.

1. Camshaft
2. Key
3. Bearing
4. Spacer
5. Tachometer drive gear
6. Spacer
7. Gear & governor flyweight assy.
8. Washer
9. Pusher
10. Bushing
11. Retainer
12. Tachometer drive

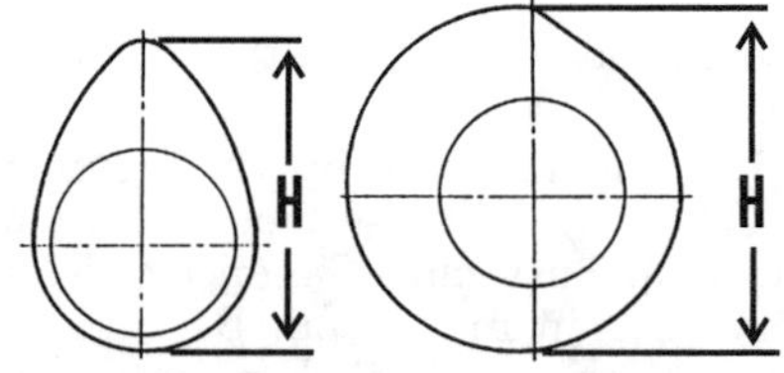

Valve lobe Injection pump lobe

Fig. SH119–Measure height (H) of camshaft valve lobes and injection pump lobes and refer to text.

PISTONS, PINS, AND RINGS

Pistons are fitted with two compression rings and one oil control ring with a coil expander under the oil ring. Piston pin is full floating and is retained by a snap ring at each end of the pin bore in the piston. If necessary to remove the piston from the connecting rod, remove the snap rings and push the pin from the piston and rod.

Inspect the piston skirt for scoring, cracks and excessive wear. Measure the piston skirt at right angle to the pin bore and at a distance of 10 mm (0.4 in.) from the bottom edge of the skirt.

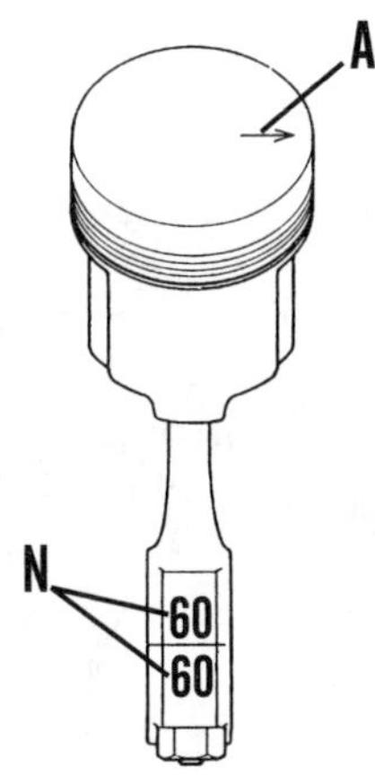

Fig. SH120–Assemble piston and rod so arrow (A) on piston crown and numbers on rod and cap (N) are positioned as shown. Install piston and rod unit so arrow on piston crown is toward timng gear end of engine.

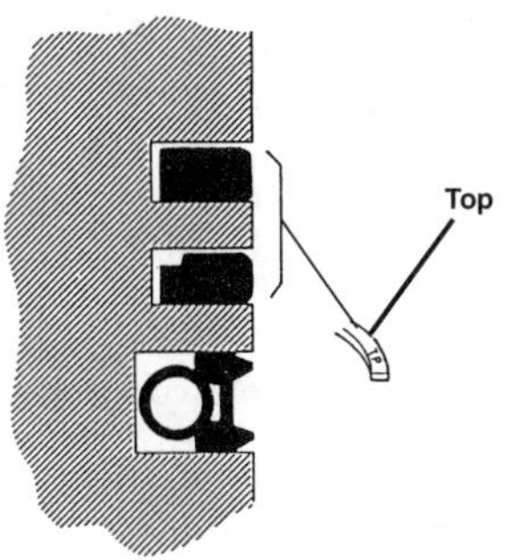

Fig. SH121–Install piston rings on piston as shown. TOP marking on compression rings must be toward piston crown.

Piston skirt standard diameter for Model E643 is 63.95-63.96 mm (2.5177-2.5181 in.) and wear limit is 63.70 mm (2.5079 in.). Piston skirt standard diameter for Model E673 is 66.94-66.95 mm (2.6354-2.6358 in.) and wear limit is 66.70 mm (2.6260 in.).

Specified piston clearance in the cylinder bore is 0.038-0.072 mm (0.0015-0.0028 in.) for Model E643 and 0.048-0.082 mm (0.0019-0.0032 in.). Maximum piston clearance for both models is 0.25 mm (0.010 in.).

Specified piston pin to piston pin bore clearance is 0.004 mm (0.0001 in.) interference to 0.004 mm (0.0001 in.) loose. Maximum allowable piston pin clearance in piston is 0.02 mm (0.0008 in.). Be sure the piston and connecting rod are positioned as shown in Fig. SH120 before installing the piston pin.

Install new rings in the piston ring grooves and use a feeler gauge to measure ring side clearance. Replace the piston if side clearance is excessive. Push each ring squarely into the cylinder bore and measure ring end gap using a feeler gauge. Refer to the following specifications:

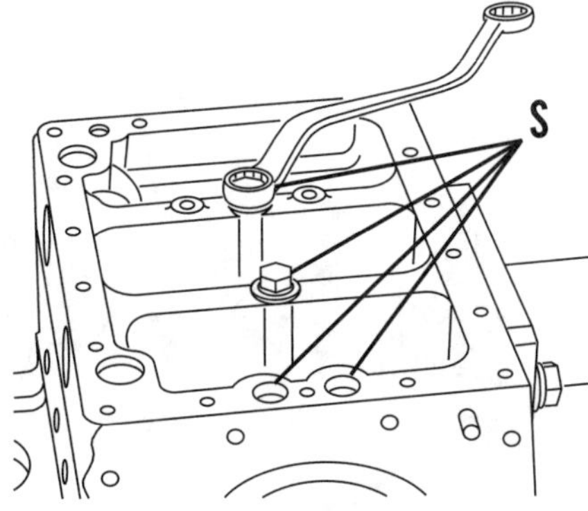

Fig. SH122–View showing location of bearing holder retaining screws (S).

Ring side clearance—

Top ring	0.06-0.10 mm (0.002-0.004 in.)
Second ring	0.06-0.10 mm (0.002-0.004 in.)
Oil ring	0.02-0.06 mm (0.0008-0.0024 in.)
Wear limit:	
Top & second ring	0.25 mm (0.010 in.)
Oil ring	0.15 mm (0.006 in.)

Ring end gap—

Top ring	0.13-0.28 mm (0.005-0.011 in.)
Second ring	0.10-0.25 mm (0.004-0.010 in.)
Oil ring	0.10-0.30 mm (0.004-0.012 in.)
Wear limit (all rings)	1.0 mm (0.039 in.)

Refer to Fig. SH121 when installing the piston rings. Place the oil ring expander in the groove first , then install the oil ring on top of the expander with the ring end gap at the opposite side of the piston from the expander ends. Install the compression rings with the side having the identification mark facing up and with end gaps approximately 90° from each other and the oil ring end gap.

CONNECTING RODS AND BEARINGS

The connecting rod is fitted with a replaceable bushing at the piston pin end and a slip-in precision fit bearing (9) at the crankpin end.

Rod twist should be less than 0.08 mm (0.003 in.) per 100 mm (4 in.). Maximum allowable rod twist is 0.20 mm (0.008 in.) per 100 mm (4 in.). The rod out-of-parallel condition should be less than 0.05 mm (0.002 in.) per 100 mm (4 in.). Maximum allowable rod out-of-parallel is 0.15 mm (0.006 in.) per 100 mm (4 in.).

Crankpin standard diameter is 34.96-34.98 mm (1.376-1.377 in.). The specified crankpin bearing oil clearance is 0.03-0.08 mm (0.0012-0.0032 in.). Maximum allowable rod bearing oil clearance is 0.2 mm (0.008 in.).

Rod side clearance on the crankpin journal should be 0.1-0.3 mm (0.004-0.012 in.). Maximum allowable side clearance is 0.7 mm (0.028 in.).

The crankshaft may be machined to accept undersize rod bearings. Manufacturer recommends fillet radius of 3 mm (0.118 in.). Oil hole chamfer should be 2 mm (0.079 in.) at widest point.

Specified piston pin outside diameter is 19.00 mm (0.748 in.). Minimum allowable piston pin diameter is 18.9 mm (0.744 in.). Pin-to-bushing clearance should be 0.013-0.028 mm (0.0005-0.0011 in.). Maximum allowable clearance is 0.08 mm (0.003 in.). If piston pin clearance is excessive, replace the piston pin or bushing or both. Ream the new bushing to obtain the specified oil clearance.

CRANKSHAFT AND BEARINGS

Crankshaft is supported by three main bearing holders equipped with bearing inserts and by a bushing in the cylinder block at the gear end.

To remove the crankshaft, remove the pistons and rods, timing gear cover and flywheel. Remove the adapter plate and seal carrier from the flywheel end of the engine. Free the bearing holders by unscrewing the locating screws (S—Fig. SH122). Carefully withdraw the crankshaft with the bearing holders out the flywheel end of the engine. Remove the screws securing the bearing holder halves and separate the halves from the crankshaft.

Specified standard diameter of the main journal at the flywheel end of the crankshaft is 45.96-45.98 mm (1.809-1.810 in.) with a minimum allowable diameter of 45.90 mm (1.807 in.). Specified standard diameter of all other crankshaft main journals is 42.96-42.98 mm (1.691-1.692 in.) with a minimum allowable diameter of 42.90 mm (1.689 in.).

Specified main bearing clearance for all journals is 0.04-0.09 mm (0.0016-0.0035 in.). Maximum allowable bearing clearance is 0.2 mm (0.008 in.) for all main bearing journals.

The crankshaft may be machined to accept undersize bearing inserts and bushing. Manufacturer recommends fillet radius of 3 mm (0.118 in.). Oil hole chamfer should be 2 mm (0.079 in.) at widest point.

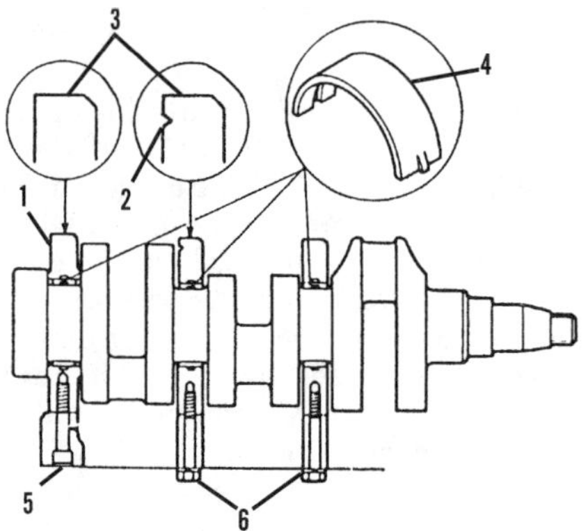

Fig. SH123–Drawing of crankshaft and bearing holder assemblies.

1. Bearing holder *(aluminum)
2. Groove
3. Chamfer
4. Upper bearing insert
5. Allen head screw
6. Cap screw

Fig. SH124–Exploded view of starter motor

1. Bushing
2. Drive end frame
3. Washer
4. Snap ring
5. Retainer
6. Drive pinion & clutch assy,
7. Shift lever
8. Cover
9. Shim
10. Solenoid assy.
11. Armature
12. Field coil assy.
13. Brush holder
14. Bushing
15. End cover

Crankshaft end play is controlled by the thrust surface on the aluminum bearing holder at the flywheel end of the crankshaft. Side clearance between the crankshaft and bearing holder should be 0.1-0.3 mm (0.004-0.012 in.). Maximum allowable side clearance is 0.5 mm (0.020 in.). The aluminum bearing holder must be renewed if side clearance is excessive.

Maximum allowable crankshaft runout measured at either of the center main bearing journals is 0.06 mm (0.0024 in.).

To reinstall the crankshaft, reverse the removal procedure. Install the grooved bearing inserts (4—Fig. SH123) in the upper (nearer camshaft) bearing holder halves. Install the bearing holders with chamfer (3) toward the gear end of the crankshaft. Note that the aluminum bearing holder (1) is located at the flywheel end of the crankshaft.

Allen head screws (5) secure the aluminum bearing holder in the cylinder block. Install the iron bearing holder with the grooved face (2) next to the aluminum bearing holder and the groove side toward the flywheel end of the crankshaft. Tighten the bearing holder retaining screws to 20-24 N·m (177-212 in.-lb.).

Before installing the crankshaft seal at the flywheel end, lubricate the crankshaft seal surface. Apply gasket sealant to the seal flange that mates with the cylinder block.

CRANKSHAFT REAR OIL SEAL

The crankshaft oil seal at the flywheel end can be renewed after removing the flywheel and adapter plate. Before installing the seal, lubricate the crankshaft seal surface. Apply gasket sealant to the seal flange that mates with the cylinder block.

FLYWHEEL

The flywheel ring gear is replaceable. To replace the ring gear, remove the old ring gear using a suitable chisel to cut and break through the ring gear. Heat the inside diameter of the new ring gear to 240-300° F (120-150° C) prior to installation on the flywheel. Do not overheat the gear teeth.

Note that the flywheel and crankshaft mounting holes are asymmetric. Tighten the flywheel mounting screws to 69-78 N·m (51-57 ft.-lb.).

ELECTRICAL SYSTEM

GLOW PLUGS

All engines utilize glow plugs as an aid in engine starting. The glow plugs are connected in parallel so that if one plug is burned out, the others will continue to operate. The glow plug indicator light will be on while the glow plugs are heating. A timer in the circuit will turn the indicator light off after about 10 seconds. At that time, turn the switch to the START position to start the engine.

The glow plugs can be checked with an ohmmeter. Renew the plug if there is no continuity. Glow plug resistance should be approximately 1 ohm.

ELECTRIC STARTER

To disassemble the starter, disconnect the solenoid wire. Remove the solenoid retaining screws and remove the solenoid and plunger assembly. Remove the starter through-bolts and retaining screws from the end cover (15—Fig. SH124).

Pry the springs away from the negative brushes, pull the brushes up and release the springs to hold the brushes in this position. Remove the field coil brushes from the brush holder, then remove the brush holder (13) from the field housing.

Separate the field coil housing from the armature. Withdraw the armature from the drive housing (2). Push the pinion stop (5) downward, remove the retaining ring (4) and remove the clutch assembly (6) from the armature shaft.

Inspect all components for wear or damage. Brush length wear limit is 11.5 mm (0.453 in.).

Use an ohmmeter or test light to test the armature for grounded or open windings. There should not be continuity between the commutator and armature shaft. There should be continuity between two different commutator bars. To test for short circuited winding, use an armature growler.

Use an ohmmeter or test light to check the field winding for grounded or open winding. There should not be continuity between the field coil brush and field frame. There should be continuity between the two field brushes.

To reassemble the starter, reverse the disassembly procedure. Install shims (9) as needed so clearance between the pinion stop (5) and drive gear (6) is 0.5-2.0 mm (0.02-0.08 in.) when the solenoid is engaged. Excessive clearance may be due to worn parts.

ALTERNATOR

To disassemble the alternator, clamp the alternator pulley in a vise and remove the nut (1—Fig. SH125). Tap the

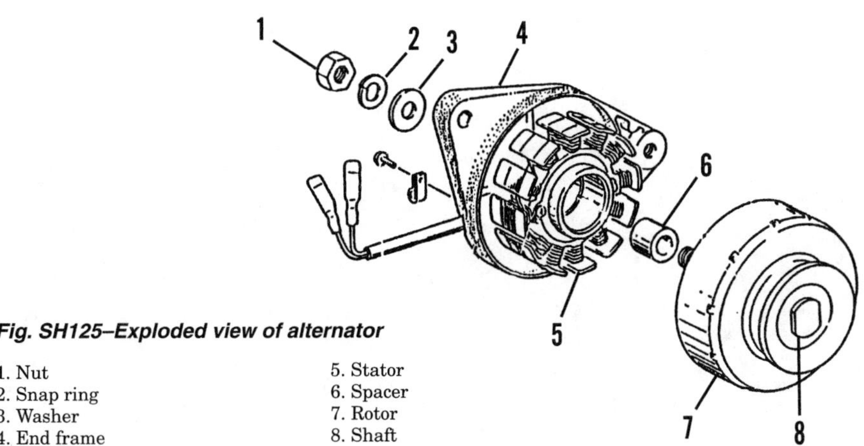

Fig. SH125–Exploded view of alternator

1. Nut
2. Snap ring
3. Washer
4. End frame
5. Stator
6. Spacer
7. Rotor
8. Shaft

end of the shaft (8) with a soft hammer to separate the rotor (7) from the stator assembly. Remove the harness clamp screw and remove the connector from the harness leads. Remove the stator mounting screws and remove the stator (5) from end frame (4).

Replace the flywheel if magnets are loose or damaged. Check the stator for indications of burned wiring or other damage and replace when necessary. Check the bearings for roughness or damage and replace when necessary.

To reassemble, reverse the disassembly procedure. Tighten the retaining nut (1) to 8-9 N·m (6-7 ft.-lb.).

NOTES

TECUMSEH

Model	No. Cyls.	Bore	Stroke	Displacement	Power Rating
OHV15	1	3.562 in. (92.8 mm)	3.00 in. (76.2 mm)	29.9 cu. in. (492 cc)	15 hp (11.2 kW)

All models are four-stroke, overhead-valve, single-cylinder gasoline engines. The engine is equipped with a horizontal crankshaft. The aluminum alloy cylinder and crankcase assembly is equipped with a cast iron cylinder sleeve that is an integral part of the cylinder. A rotor type oil pump located in the bottom of the oil pan provides pressurized lubrication.

Engine model number, serial number and specification number are stamped into the cooling shroud. Always furnish correct engine model, serial and specification numbers when ordering parts.

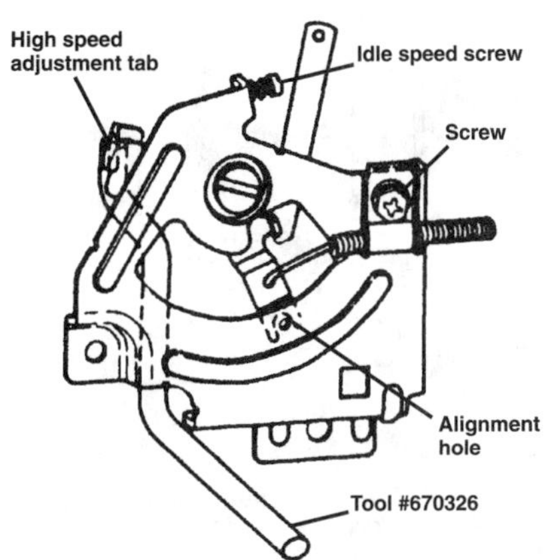

Fig. T901–Refer to text for idle and high speed adjustments.

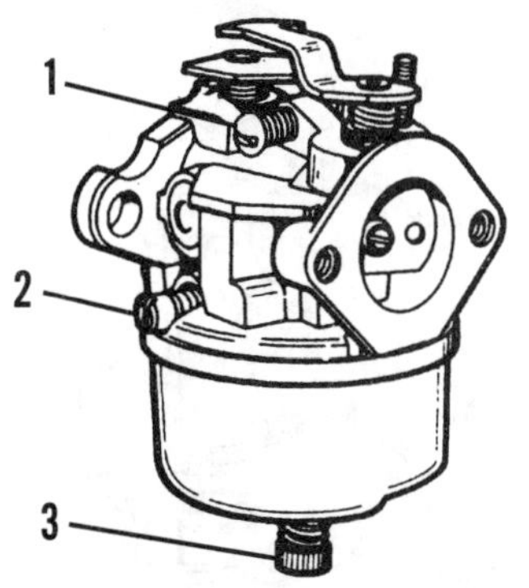

Fig. T902–View of carburetor showing idle speed screw (1), idle mixture adjusting screw (2) and high speed fuel mixture adjusting screw (3).

MAINTENANCE

LUBRICATION

The engine is equipped with a positive displacement oil pump that is located in the bottom of the oil pan. The oil pump is driven by a drive shaft that connects to the camshaft. A spin-on oil filter is mounted on the side of the oil pan.

Oil level should be checked before initial start-up and at five-hour intervals. Maintain oil level at the FULL mark on the dipstick.

Change oil after first two hours of operation if engine is new or overhauled. Recommended oil change interval is every 25 hours of normal operation. Oil should be drained when engine is warm. The oil filter should be changed whenever oil is changed.

Use oil meeting the latest API service classification. Use SAE 30 oil for temperatures above 32°F (0°C) and SAE 5W-30 or 10W-30 for temperatures below 32°F (0°C).

AIR CLEANER

Engine is equipped with a dry air filter that should be inspected after every 25 hours of operation or more frequently if operated in severe environment. Remove the foam and paper air filter elements from the air filter housing.

Clean the foam element after every 25 hours of operation. Wash the foam element in a mild detergent and water solution. Rinse the element in clean water, and then air-dry the element. Soak the foam element in clean engine oil. Squeeze out excess oil.

Manufacturer does not recommend cleaning the paper element. The paper element should be replaced annually or after every 100 hours of operation.

SPARK PLUG

The recommended spark plug is a Champion RN4C or equivalent. The recommended electrode gap is 0.030 in. (0.76 mm).

CARBURETOR

Adjust engine idle speed by turning the idle speed screw on the control cable bracket shown in Fig. T901.

Adjust the throttle control as follows: Place the engine throttle lever in fast position. Insert a drill bit through the alignment hole (Fig. T901) in the bracket and the notch in the speed control lever. Loosen the throttle cable housing clamp screw, pull the cable housing tight and retighten the cable clamp screw.

Adjust high speed by bending the adjustment tab (Fig. T901) using tool 670326 or a suitable equivalent. With the engine at normal operating temperature and equipment control lever in idle position, adjust the governed idle speed screw (Fig. T901) on the bracket so the engine idles at desired rpm.

Engine may be equipped with either a Tecumseh or Walbro float carburetor. Refer to appropriate following section.

Tecumseh Carburetor

Initial adjustment of the idle mixture screw (2—Fig. T902) is one turn open from a lightly seated position. Initial adjustment of the high-speed adjustment screw (3) is approximately 1¼ turns open from a lightly seated position.

Make final adjustments on all models with the engine at normal operating temperature. Set the engine speed at full throttle and turn the high-speed adjusting screw to find the lean drop-off point and the rich drop-off point. Then, set the adjusting screw midway between the two extremes. When correctly set, the engine should accelerate smoothly and run under load with steady governor operation. If the engine stumbles or hesitates when accelerating, turn the adjusting screw ⅛ turn counterclockwise and recheck operation.

Turn the idle speed adjustment screw (1) so the engine idles below the governed idle speed. Adjust the idle mixture adjustment screw (2) to obtain smoothest idle operation using the same procedure as outlined for the high-speed adjustment screw.

Because each adjustment affects the other, the adjustment procedure may have to be repeated.

To clean the carburetor, disassemble and clean all metallic parts with solvent or carburetor cleaner. Welch plugs should be removed from the carburetor body to expose drilled passages to thoroughly clean the carburetor. Use a small, sharp pointed chisel to pierce the Welch plug and pry plug out of carburetor body. When installing new plugs, use a flat punch equal, or greater in size than the plug and just flatten the plug. Do not drive the center of plug below the surface of the carburetor body.

NOTE: Do not remove the main nozzle tube in carburetor body. Tube is installed to a predetermined depth, and altering its position in the carburetor body will affect metering characteristics of the carburetor.

Fig. T903–Exploded view of Tecumseh carburetor.

1. Choke shaft
2. Choke return spring
3. Washer
4. Dust seal
5. Choke stop spring
6. Throttle shaft
7. Throttle return spring
8. Washer
9. Dust seal
10. Throttle plate
11. Idle speed screw
12. Spring
13. Welch plug
14. Idle mixture needle
15. Spring
16. Washer
17. O-ring
18. Carburetor body
19. Choke plate
20. Welch plug
21. Bowl gasket
22. Inlet valve seat
23. Fuel inlet valve
24. Clip
25. Float pin
26. Float
27. Drain stem
28. Gasket
29. Fuel bowl
30. Spring
31. Retainer
32. Washer
33. Bowl retainer
34. O-ring
35. Washer
36. Spring
37. High speed mixture screw

Use compressed air and solvent to clean drilled passages and jets. Do not use drill bits or wire to clean jets or passages because carburetor calibration may be affected if openings are enlarged.

There are two different types of bowl nuts (33—Fig. T903) that are used on carburetors equipped with an adjustable main jet. One type has one fuel inlet port at the bottom of the nut, and the other type has two fuel inlet ports at the bottom of the nut (Fig. T904). The difference between the nuts has to do with calibration changes of the carburetor, depending on engine application. DO NOT interchange bowl nuts. Fuel inlet port(s) and idle fuel transfer port, located in annular groove at top of nut, must be open and free of any debris to ensure proper fuel flow to high and low speed circuits.

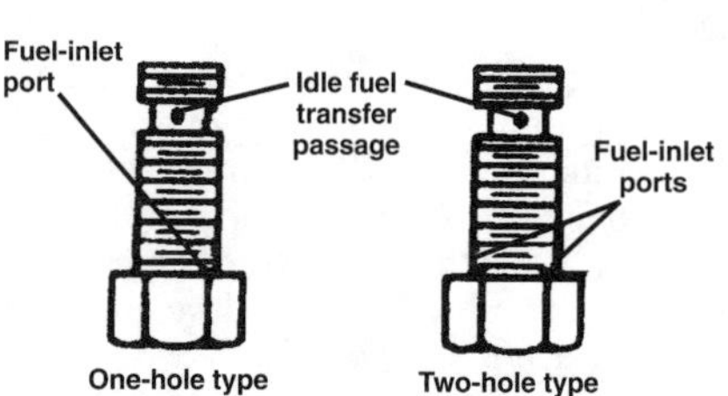

Fig. T904–Two different types of fuel bowl retaining nuts are used on adjustable mainjet type carburetors. Different type nuts must not be interchanged. Refer to text.

When reassembling the carburetor, it is important that the throttle plate (10—Fig. T903) is installed with the line on the plate facing outward and positioned at the 3 o'clock position. Choke plate (19) must be installed with the cut-out section facing downward. Be sure that the throttle and choke plates open and close without binding.

Fuel inlet needle (23—Fig. T903) and seat (22) are replaceable. If the needle tip or seat is worn or deformed, a new needle and seat should be installed. Make certain when installing the new seat that the grooved side of the seat is installed in the bore first so the inlet needle will seat against the smooth side of the seat (Fig. T905).

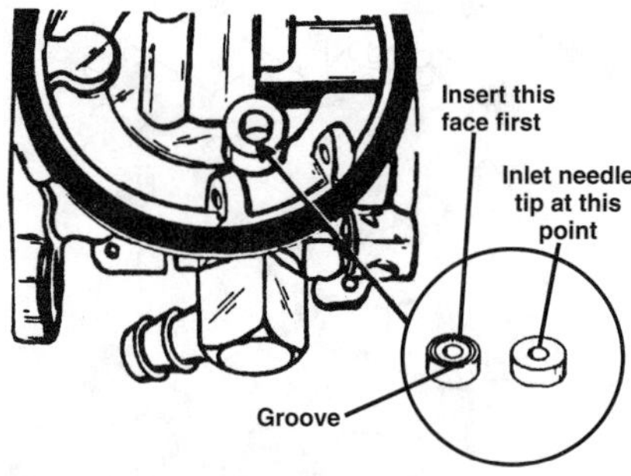

Fig. T905–Fuel inlet needle seat must be installed with grooved side against carburetor body. Refer to text.

Assemble the float, inlet needle and needle clip as shown in Fig. T906. To prevent binding, the long end of clip should face the choke end of the carburetor body.

To check float height, invert the carburetor body and use the float setting tool 670253A as shown in Fig. T907. Float height is correct if the float does not touch the step portion of tool (1) and contacts the step (2) as the tool is pulled toward the float hinge pin as shown.

If the tool is not available, measure the distance from the top of the main nozzle boss to the surface of the float. Distance should be 0.275-0.315 inch (7.0-8.0 mm). If adjustment is required, bend the float tab that contacts the fuel

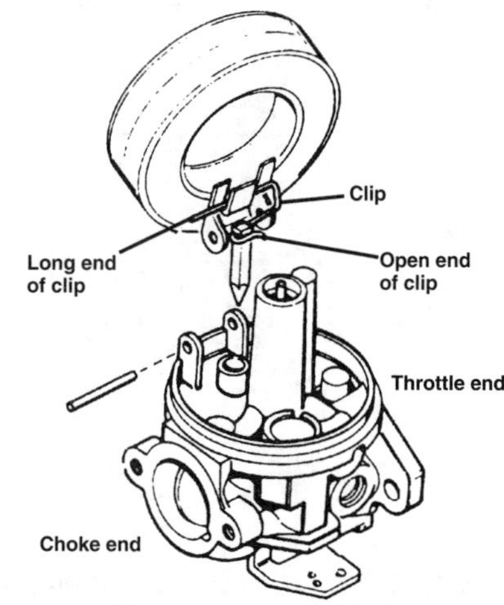

Fig. T906–Drawing showing correct installation of fuel inlet needle clip.

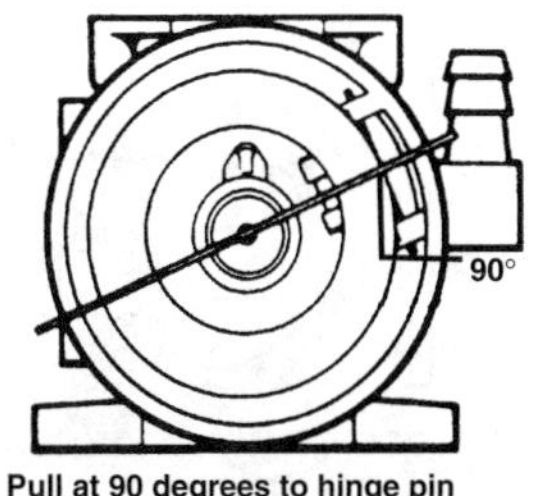

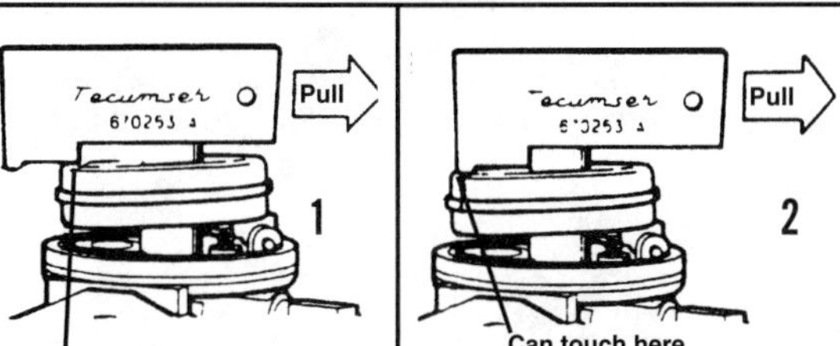

Fig. T907–Float height can be adjusted using float setting tool 670253A.

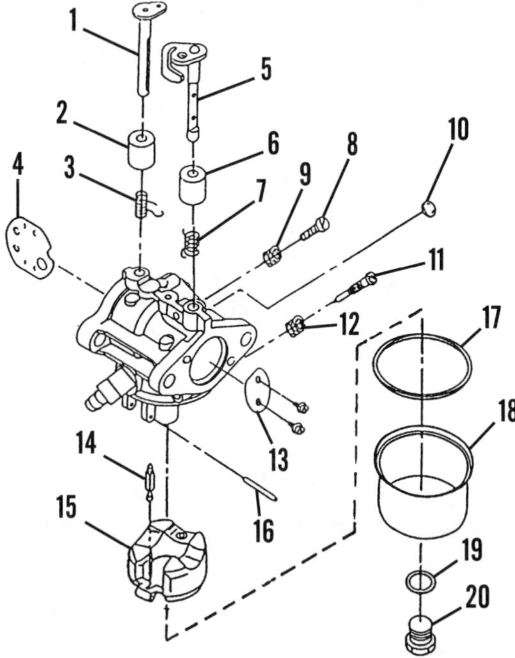

Fig. T908–Exploded view of Walbro LMK carburetor.

1. Choke shaft
2. Dust seal
3. Choke return spring
4. Choke plate
5. Throttle shaft
6. Dust seal
7. Throttle return spring
8. Idle speed screw
9. Spring
10. Welch plug
11. Idle mixture screw
12. Spring
13. Throttle plate
14. Fuel inlet valve
15. Float
16. Float pin
17. O-ring
18. Fuel bowl
19. Washer
20. Bowl nut

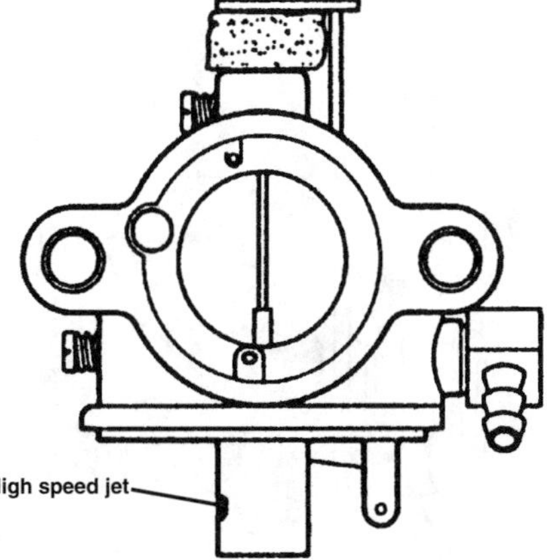

Fig. T909–High speed jet is located in side of body.

inlet needle being careful not to force the inlet needle onto its seat.

Walbro Carburetor

The Walbro carburetor is equipped with an adjustable idle mixture screw and a fixed main jet.

Initial setting of the idle mixture screw (11—Fig. T908) is 1⅛ turns out. With the engine at normal operating temperature, adjust the idle speed screw (8) so the engine idles below governed idle speed. With the engine running at idle speed, turn the idle mixture screw clockwise until the engine speed just starts to drop. Note the screw position. Turn the idle mixture screw counterclockwise until the engine speed just starts to drop again. Note the screw position, then turn the screw to midpoint between the noted screw positions. If the engine will not accelerate cleanly, slightly enrich the mixture by turning the idle mixture screw counterclockwise. If necessary, readjust the idle speed screw.

To clean the carburetor, remove the fuel bowl (18—Fig. T908), float (15) and fuel inlet valve (14). Unscrew the idle mixture screw (11). Mark the throttle and choke plates so they can be returned to their original positions. After removing the throttle or choke plate, remove any burrs on the shaft before withdrawing the shaft from the body. Do not remove the fixed high-speed jet (Fig. T909). Refer to Fig. T910 for drawing of a suitable tool for removing the Welch plug (10—Fig. T908). Clean and inspect components and discard any parts that are damaged or excessively worn.

When reassembling the carburetor, note the following: Do not deform the Welch plug during installation; it should be flat. Seal the outer edges of the plug with fuel resistant sealer. Note that the throttle return spring must force the throttle plate to the closed position. Choke return spring must force the choke plate to the open position. Float height is not adjustable. Tighten the fuel bowl retaining nut to 50 in.-lb. (5.6 N·m).

GOVERNOR

The engine is equipped with a mechanical flyweight governor located inside the crankcase.

To adjust the external governor linkage, stop the engine and loosen the screw (S—Fig. T911) securing the governor lever to the governor clamp. Push the governor lever to fully open the carburetor throttle. Turn the governor clamp counterclockwise as far as it will go. While holding the clamp and lever in this position, tighten the screw.

IGNITION SYSTEM

A solid-state ignition system is used on all models. Ignition system has no moving parts and is considered satisfactory if a spark will jump a ⅛ inch (3.2 mm) air gap when the engine is cranked at 125 rpm.

Ignition module is mounted on the outside of the flywheel. Air gap setting between the ignition module and flywheel magnets is 0.0125 inch (0.32 mm). To set the air gap, loosen the module mounting screws, move the module as necessary and retighten the screws.

VALVE ADJUSTMENT

Clearance between rocker arms and valve stem ends should be checked and adjusted with the engine cold. Specified clearance is 0.004 inch (0.10 mm) for both valves.

To adjust the valves, remove the rocker arm cover and rotate the crankshaft to position the piston at top dead center (TDC) on the compression stroke. Both valves should be closed and the push rods loose at this point. Use a feeler gauge to measure the clearance between the rocker arm and valve stem as shown in Fig. T912. Loosen the Allen screw (A), then rotate the pivot nut (N) to obtain the specified clearance. Retighten the Allen screw.

REPAIRS

TIGHTENING TORQUES

The recommended special tightening torque values are as follows:

Connecting rod	200-220 in.-lb. (22.6-24.8 N·m)
Cylinder head bolts	220-240 in.-lb. (24.8-27.1 N·m)
Flywheel nut	50-55 ft.-lb. (68-74 N·m)
Intake pipe	90-100 in.-lb. (10.2-11.3 N·m)
Oil pan	100-140 in.-lb. (11.3-15.8 N·m)
Rocker arm studs	170-210 in.-lb. (19.2-23.7 N·m)
Rocker cover	30-50 in.-lb. (3.4-5.6 N·m)
Spark plug	220-280 in.-lb. (24.9-31.6 N·m)

CRANKCASE BREATHER

The engine is equipped with a crankcase breather located on the side of the cylinder block. The crankcase breather provides a vacuum for the crankcase. Vapor from the crankcase is evacuated to the air intake tube. A reed valve acts as a one-way valve to maintain crankcase vacuum. The breather system must operate properly or excessive oil consumption can result.

Check that the reed valve is not damaged and seats properly. Replace if distorted or damaged. The reed and stop must be parallel to the upper side of the cover. After tightening the reed retaining screw, be sure the reed moves without binding. Inspect the breather tube for leakage.

CYLINDER HEAD

Always allow the engine to cool completely before loosening the cylinder head bolts. To remove the cylinder head, first locate the piston at top dead center of the compression stroke. Remove the air shrouds and intake and exhaust systems. Remove the rocker arm cover (1—Fig. T913). Loosen the rocker arm Allen screws (3), then remove the pivot nuts (4) and rocker arms (5). Remove the push rods, rocker arm studs (6) and push rod guide plate (7). Remove the cylinder head retaining screws and remove the cylinder head. Discard cylinder head gasket.

Thoroughly clean cylinder head and inspect for cracks or other damage. Position cylinder head on a flat plate and use a feeler gauge to check flatness of head gasket sealing surface. Replace cylinder head if necessary.

Use a new head gasket when installing the cylinder head. Install the Belleville washer (13) so the crown is toward the bolt head. Tighten the head bolts in 50 in.-lb. (5.6 N·m) increments following sequence shown in Fig. T914 until reaching final torque of 220-240 in.-lb. (24.8-27.1 N·m).

Install the push rod guide plate. Install the rocker arm studs and tighten to 170-210 in.-lb. (19.2-23.7 N·m). Push rods are aluminum with steel ends. Install the push rods so the long steel end is up (next to push rod guide plate). See Fig. T915. Install the rocker arm assemblies and adjust valve clearance as previously described. Install the remaining parts.

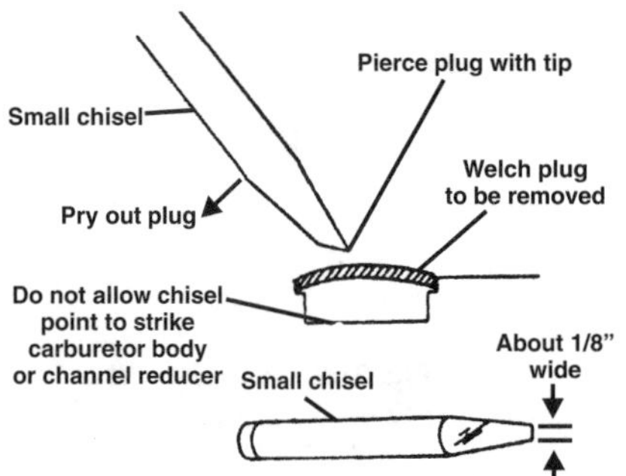

Fig. T910–Fabricate a tool as shown to remove Welch plug.

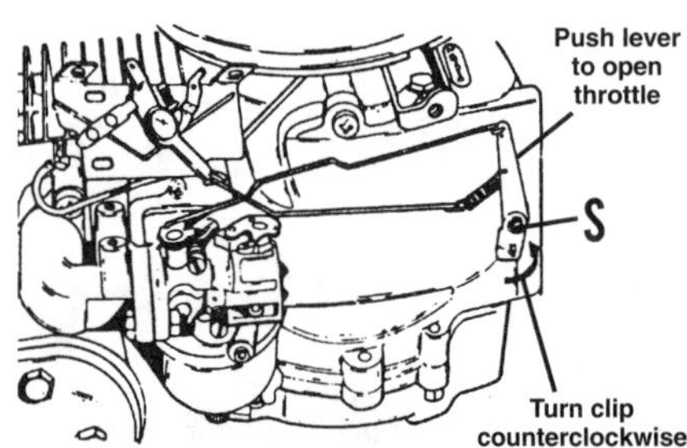

Fig. T911–Drawing of governor external linkage. Refer to text for adjustment.

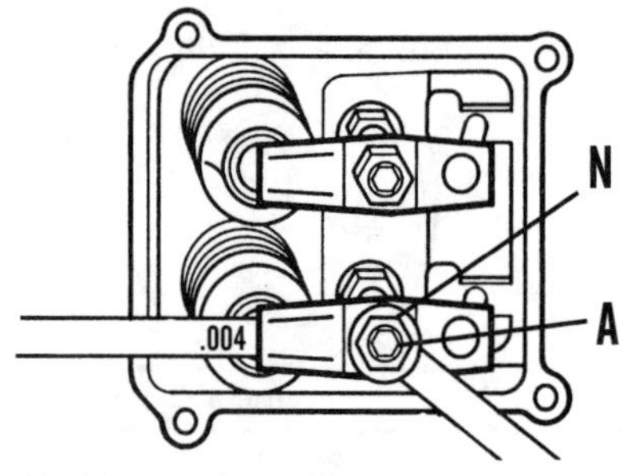

Fig. T912–Loosen Allen screw (A) then rotate pivot nut (N) to adjust valve clearance.

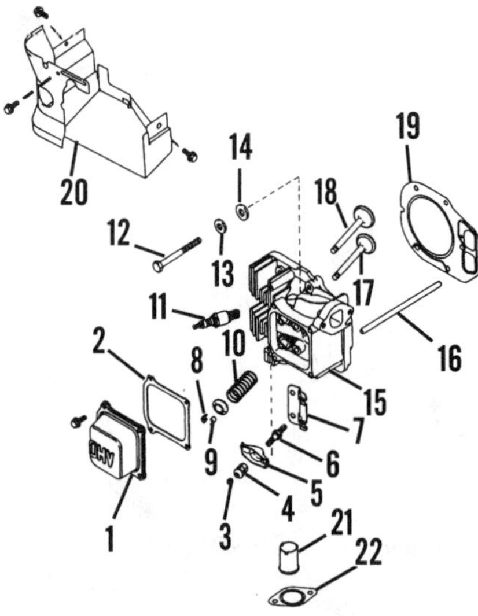

Fig. T913–Exploded view of cylinder head assembly.

1. Rocker arm cover
2. Gasket
3. Allen screw
4. Pivot nut
5. Rocker arm
6. Rocker arm stud
7. Push rod guide
8. Split retainer
9. Spring retainer
10. Valve spring
11. Spark plug
12. Head bolt
13. Belleville washer
14. Flat washer
15. Cylinder head
16. Push rod
17. Exhaust valve
18. Intake valve
19. Head gasket
20. Air shroud
21. Exhaust port liner
22. Gasket

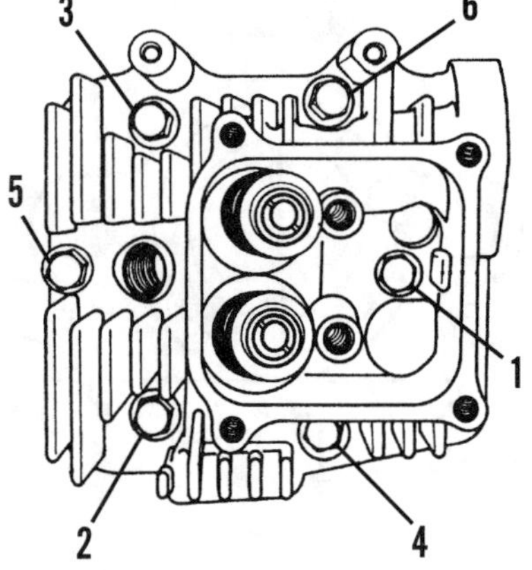

Fig. T914–Tighten cylinder head bolts in sequence shown.

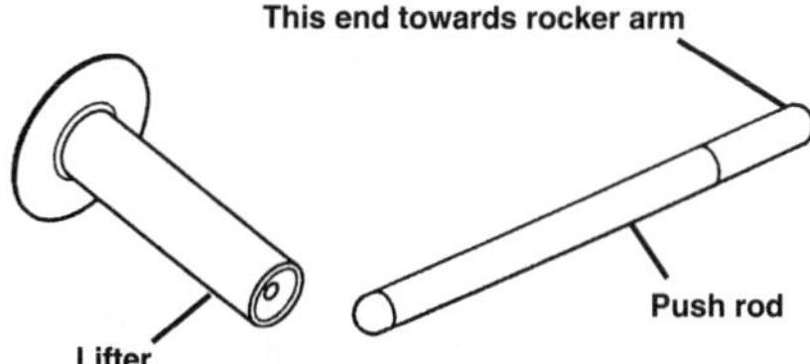

Fig. T915–Install push rods so long steel edn is up (next to push rod guide plate).

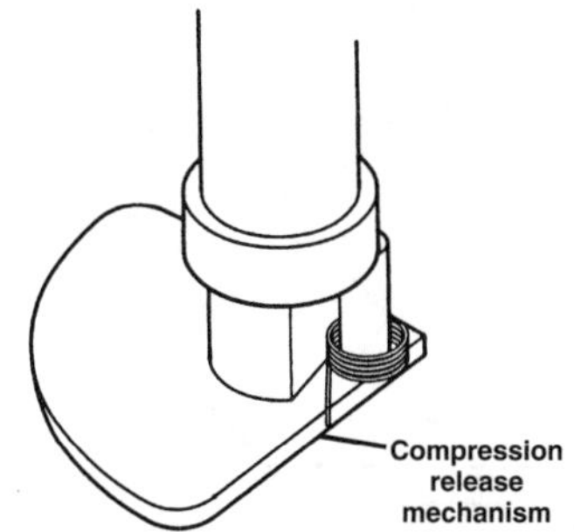

Fig. T916–Camshaft is equipped with a compression release mechanism.

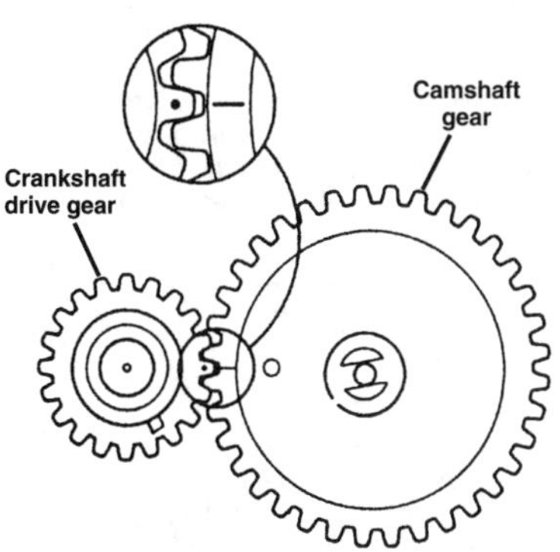

Fig. T917–Camshaft and crankshaft timing marks must be aligned after installation for proper valve timing.

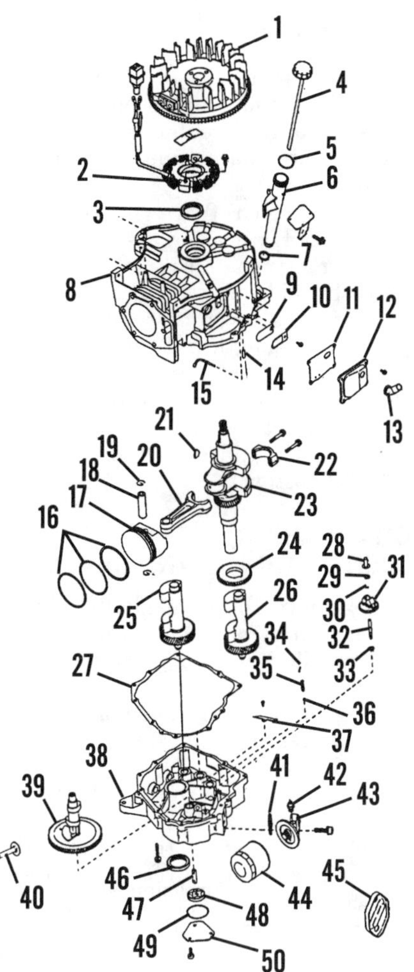

Fig. T918–Exploded view of engine. Also refer to T913.

1. Flywheel
2. Stator
3. Oil seal
4. Dipstick
5. O-ring
6. Tube
7. O-ring
8. Cylinder block
9. Breather reed plate
10. Reed stop
11. Gasket
12. Cover
13. Breather tube
14. Dowel pin
15. Governor shaft
16. Piston rings
17. Piston
18. Piston pin
19. Retaining ring
20. Connecting rod
21. Key
22. Rod cap
23. Crankshaft
24. Gear
25. Balancer shaft
26. Balancer shaft
27. Gasket
28. Thrust spool
29. Washer
30. Snap ring
31. Governor gear & weight assy.
32. Governor shaft
33. Washer
34. Pin
35. Oil pressure relief spring
36. Ball
37. Oil screen
38. Oil pan
39. Camshaft
40. Tappets
41. Cover
42. Oil pressure switch
43. Adapter
44. Oil filter
45. Cover
46. Oil seal
47. Drive saft
48. Oil pump rotor
49. O-ring
50. Cover

VALVE SYSTEM

Remove the cylinder head as previously described for access to the valves. To remove the valve springs, a lever type valve spring compressor tool (Tecumseh tool 670315A) may be used to compress the valve spring. Install a rocker arm stud to serve as a pivot point.

Valve seats are machined directly in the cylinder head. Seats should be cut at a 46° angle and valve faces cut or ground at a 45° angle. Valve seat width should be 3/64 inch (1.2 mm).

Intake and exhaust valves are not the same. Exhaust valve is non-magnetic. Clean all combustion deposits from the valves. Replace the valves that are burned, excessively pitted, warped or if valve head margin after grinding is less than 1/32 inch (0.8 mm).

Valve spring free length should be 1.980 inches (50.29 mm). It is recommended that valve springs be replaced when the engine is overhauled.

The valve spring dampening coils are coils wound closer together at one end than the other. The end with closer coils should be installed against the cylinder head.

Standard valve guide inside diameter is 0.312-0.313 inch (7.93-7.95 mm). Guides can be reamed to 0.3432-0.3442 inch (8.717-8.743 mm) for use with oversize valve stems.

CAMSHAFT

Camshaft and camshaft gear are an integral part that can be removed from the engine after removing the rocker arms, push rods and oil pan. Identify the position of the tappets as they are removed so they can be reinstalled in their original position if reused.

Camshaft bearings are an integral part of the crankcase and oil pan. Camshaft journal diameter should be 0.6235-0.6240 inch (15.84-15.85 mm). Camshaft bearing inside diameter should be 0.6245-0.6255 inch (15.86-15.89 mm). Clearance between the camshaft journal and camshaft bearing should not exceed 0.003 inch (0.08 mm). Inspect the camshaft lobes for pitting, scratches or excessive wear and replace when necessary. Tappets should be replaced whenever a new camshaft is installed.

Camshaft is equipped with a compression release mechanism (Fig. T916) to aid starting. Compression release mechanism parts should work freely with no binding or sticking. Parts are not serviced separately from camshaft.

When installing the camshaft, be sure that the timing marks on the camshaft gear and crankshaft gear are aligned as shown in Fig. T917. Before installing the oil pan, refer to the OIL PAN section.

PISTON, PIN AND RINGS

Refer to Fig. T918 for an exploded view of the engine. Piston and connecting rod are removed as an assembly. Refer to the CONNECTING ROD section for the removal procedure.

Standard piston skirt diameter, measured at the bottom of the skirt 90° from the piston pin bore, is 3.5595-3.5605 inches (84.05-84.09 mm) for all models. Specified clearance between the piston skirt and cylinder wall is 0.0015-0.0035 inch (0.038-0.089 mm). Oversize pistons are available. Oversize piston size should be stamped on top of the piston.

To check piston ring grooves for wear, clean carbon from ring grooves and install new rings in grooves. Use a feeler gauge to measure side clearance between the ring land and ring. Specified side clearance is 0.002-0.004 inch (0.05-0.10 mm) for compression rings and 0.001-0.003 inch (0.025-0.076 mm) for oil control ring. Replace the piston if ring side clearance is excessive.

Ring end gap should be 0.012-0.022 inch (0.30-0.56 mm) for all rings.

Assemble the piston and connecting rod so the arrow on the piston and the match marks on the rod are positioned as shown in Fig. T919. Rings must be installed on piston as shown in Fig. T920. Stagger ring end gaps around the piston. Install the piston and rod as described in the CONNECTING ROD section.

CONNECTING ROD

Remove the piston and connecting rod as an assembly as follows: Remove the cylinder head as previously outlined. Drain the oil and remove the oil pan. Remove the connecting rod cap. Remove any carbon or ring ridge (if present) from the top of cylinder before removing the piston. Push the connecting rod and piston out the top of the cylinder.

Connecting rod rides directly on the crankshaft crankpin. The inside diameter of the connecting rod bearing bore at the crankshaft end should be 1.6234-1.6240 inches (41.234-41.250 mm).

Assemble the piston and connecting rod so the arrow on the piston and the match marks on the rod are positioned as shown in Fig. T919. Lubricate the piston and cylinder with engine oil prior to installing the piston. Use a ring compressor tool to compress the piston rings. Install the piston and rod so the arrow on the side of the piston points toward the push rod side of the engine and the match marks on the connecting rod and cap are toward the open side of the crankcase. Tighten the connecting rod screws to 200-220 in.-lb. (22.6-24.8 N·m). Before installing the oil pan, refer to the OIL PAN section.

GOVERNOR

The camshaft gear drives the governor weight and gear assembly, which rides on a replaceable shaft that is pressed into the engine crankcase or crankcase cover.

Governor gear, flyweights and shaft are serviced only as an assembly. If the governor gear shaft is replaced, the new shaft should be pressed into the oil pan or crankcase cover boss until the exposed shaft length is 1$^{23}/_{64}$ inches (34.5 mm).

Before installing the oil pan, refer to the OIL PAN section. Adjust external linkage as outlined in the MAINTENANCE section.

CRANKSHAFT, MAIN BEARINGS AND SEALS

To remove the crankshaft, first remove all shrouds. Remove the flywheel. Remove the connecting rod and piston as previously outlined. Remove the balancer gear and shaft assembly. Remove the balancer drive gear from the crankshaft. Position the engine so the tappets fall away from the camshaft, then withdraw the camshaft from the cylinder block and remove the crankshaft.

Crankshaft rides directly in bores in the crankcase and oil pan. Specified main bearing inside diameter is 1.6265-1.6270 inches (41.313-41.326 mm).

Standard crankshaft main journal diameter is 1.6245-1.6250 inches (41.262-41.275 mm) for each end. The standard crankpin journal diameter is 1.6223-1.6228 inches (41.206-41.219 mm).

Crankshaft end play should be 0.0025-0.0035 inch (0.064-0.089 mm).

When replacing the crankshaft oil seals, note if the old seal is raised or flush with the outer surface of the crankcase and oil pan or the crankcase cover and install the new seal to the same dimension. Attempting to install the seal too far into the casting bore may damage the seal or engine. Use a suitable installing tool to install the new seal until it is lightly seated in the casting bore.

When installing the crankshaft, align the timing mark on the crankshaft gear with the timing mark on the camshaft gear to ensure correct valve timing. See Fig. T917. Refer to the BALANCER section and install the balancer gear(s). Before installing the oil pan, refer to OIL PAN section.

CYLINDER AND CRANKCASE

A cast iron liner is permanently cast into the aluminum alloy cylinder and

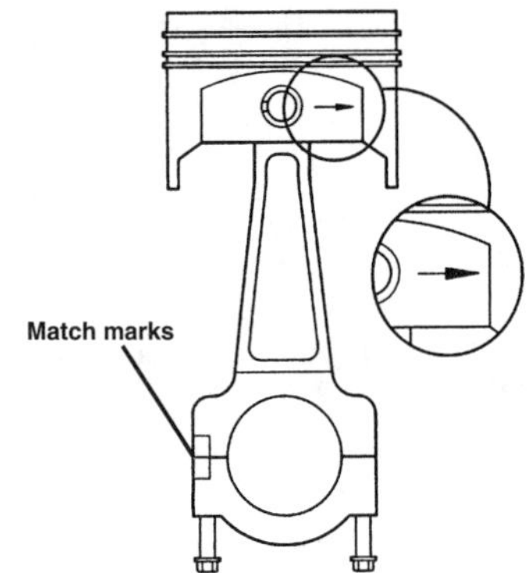

Fig. T919–Assemble piston and rod with arrow on piston and match marks on rod positioned as shown.

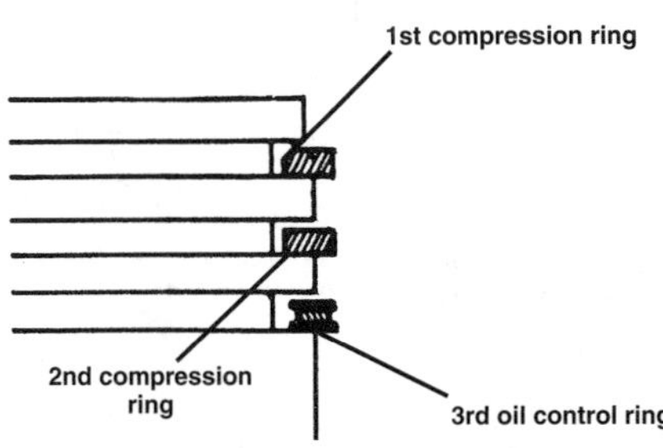

Fig. T920–Drawing showing piston ring locations. Note that chamfered edge of top ring is toward piston crown.

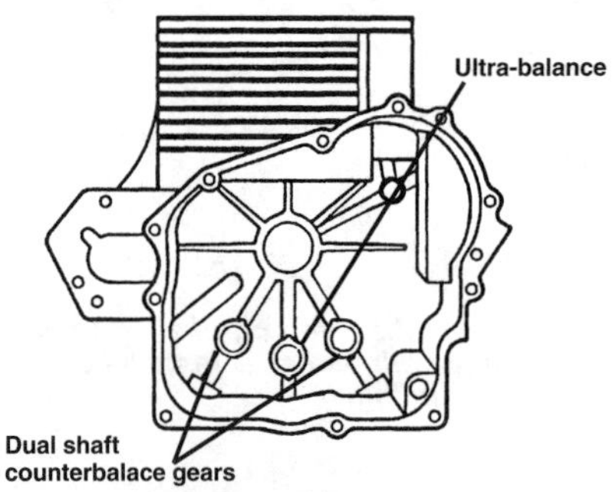

Fig. T921–Install balancer shaft(s) in correct crankcase bore.

crankcase assembly. Standard piston bore inside diameter is 3.562-3.563 inches (90.47-90.50 mm). If cylinder taper or out-of-round exceeds 0.004 inch (0.10 mm), cylinder should be bored to nearest oversize for which piston and rings are available.

BALANCER

The engine may be equipped with either one balance shaft (Ultra-Balance) or two balance shafts (dual-shaft).

Engines equipped with Ultra-Balance system have a single balance shaft that is driven by a gear on the crankshaft. The balance shaft rides

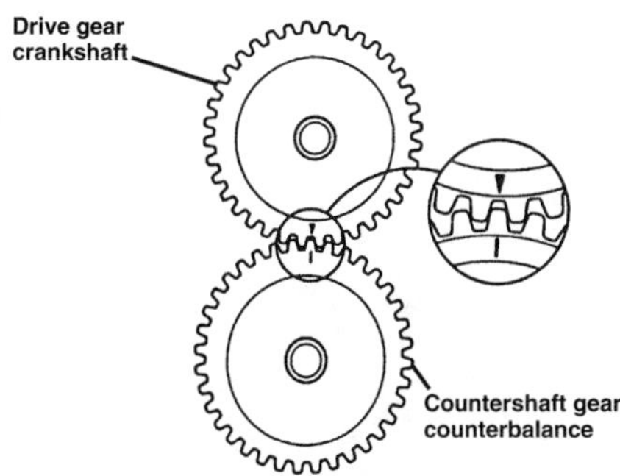

Fig. T922–Timing marks on crankshaft drive gear and Ultra-Balance gear must align when piston is at top dead center.

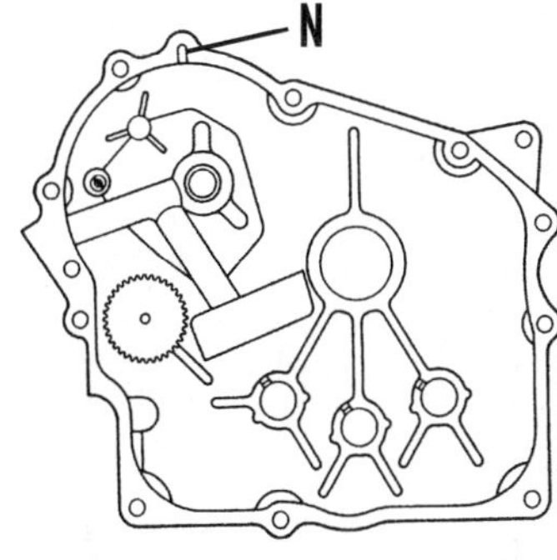

Fig. T924–Oil passage notch (N) in oil pan must not be obstructed.

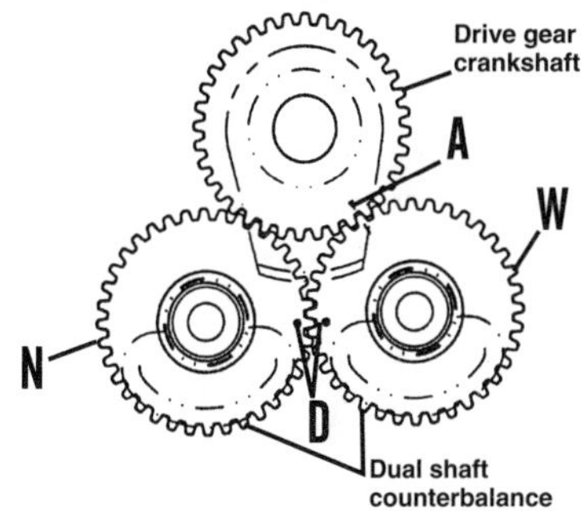

Fig. T923–View showing location of dual-balance shaft with narrow gear (N) and wide gear (W) as well as timing dots (D) and marks.

directly in bores in the crankcase and oil pan.

When installing the balance shaft, position the piston at top dead center and install the balance drive gear on the crankshaft so the arrow on the gear rim points toward the balance shaft. Insert the balance shaft into its boss in the crankcase (see Fig. T921) with the mark on the balance shaft gear aligning with the arrow on the drive gear as shown in Fig. T922.

Engines equipped with dual-shaft balance system have two balance shafts. A gear on the crankshaft drives the balance shaft with the wide gear. The balance shaft with the wide gear drives the balance shaft with the narrow gear. The balance shafts ride directly in bores in the crankcase and oil pan.

When installing the balance shafts, position the piston at top dead center and install the balance shaft with the wide gear in the right-hand bore in the crankcase (see Fig. T921). Install the balance shaft with the narrow gear in left-hand bore in the crankcase while rotating the gears so the timing dots (D—Fig. T923) on the gears are aligned. Slide the drive gear onto the crankshaft while aligning the arrow (A) on the drive gear with the mark on the balance shaft gear (Fig. T923). Be certain the drive gear properly engages the keyway on the crankshaft.

Before installing the oil pan, refer to the OIL PAN section.

OIL PAN

The oil pan may be removed after draining the oil and removing any burrs from the crankshaft.

CAUTION: To prevent damage to the camshaft, the oil pump must be removed before installing the oil pan.

When installing the oil pan, be sure the oil return passage notch (N—Fig. T924) is not restricted or blocked. Do not force the installation. Rotate the crankshaft as needed so the governor gear meshes with the camshaft gear. Apply Loctite 242 to the threads of the oil pan screws and tighten evenly to 100-140 in.-lb. (11.3-15.8 N·m). Install the oil pump.

OIL PUMP

A rotor oil pump is located in the oil pan. A drive shaft connected to the camshaft drives the oil pump. The oil pump rotors (47—Fig. T918) can be removed for inspection after removing the pump cover (49) from the bottom of the oil pan. A hooked tool may be used to extract the rotors. Use care to prevent damage to the rotor surfaces. The oil pan must be removed for access to the oil pressure regulator valve (34-36).

Check oil pump rotors and oil pump cavity for scoring or excessive wear.

CAUTION: If the oil pump was disassembled with the oil pan removed, install the oil pan before assembling the oil pump to prevent damage to the camshaft.

Lubricate the oil pump cavity and pump rotors with oil during reassembly.

Tighten the oil pump cover retaining screws to 50-70 in.-lb. (5.6-7.9 N·m).

NOTES

TORO

POWER PLUS P-SERIES

Model	Cyls.	Bore	Stroke	No. Displacement	Power Rating
P216	2	3.250 in. (82.55 mm)	2.625 in. (66.68 mm)	43.6 cu. in. (715 cc)	16 hp. (11.9 kW)
P220	2	3.250 in. (82.55 mm)	2.875 in. (73.03 mm)	47.7 cu. in. (782 cc)	20 hp. (14.9 kW)

Engines in this section are four-stroke, twin-opposed-cylinder engines. Engine is equipped with a horizontal crankshaft.

Refer to Fig. TO201 for explanation of engine model and specification identification numbers.

MAINTENANCE

LUBRICATION

Both models are equipped with a pressure lubrication system and an oil filter. Oil is routed from an oil pump located behind the gear cover and driven by the crankshaft gear.

Use SAE 30 oil for ambient temperatures above 32° F (0° C); use SAE 10W-30 oil for temperatures between 0° F (-18° C) and 80° F (27° C); below 20° F (-7° C) use SAE 5W-20.

Check oil at regular intervals and maintain at the FULL mark on the dipstick. DO NOT overfill.

Change engine oil and oil filter after first 25 hours of operation. Change engine oil after every 50 hours of operation and change oil filter after every 100 hours of operation. Change oil and filter more frequently if engine undergoes severe operation.

Crankcase capacity is 1.8 quarts (1.7 L) if oil filter is changed with oil refill, 1.5 quarts (1.4 L) if the oil filter is not changed.

Normal oil pressure should be 20 psi (138 kPa). If the engine oil pressure is less than 8 psi (55.2 kPa) at an engine speed of 1500 rpm, the cause for low oil pressure should be determined.

The engine may be equipped with a low oil pressure switch located on the oil filter adapter. The switch may be connected to a warning device or into the ignition circuit.

CRANKCASE BREATHER

The engine is equipped with a crankcase breather that provides a vacuum for the crankcase. The crankcase breather does not require periodic maintenance, but it should be replaced if it malfunctions.

Fig. TO201—Typical model and specification number showing digit interpretation.

1. Basic engine series
2. Number of cylinders
3. Power rating (BHP)
4. Crankshaft direction (G—horizontal, V—vertical)
5. Engine duty cycle
6. Designated optional equipment
7. Production specification letter

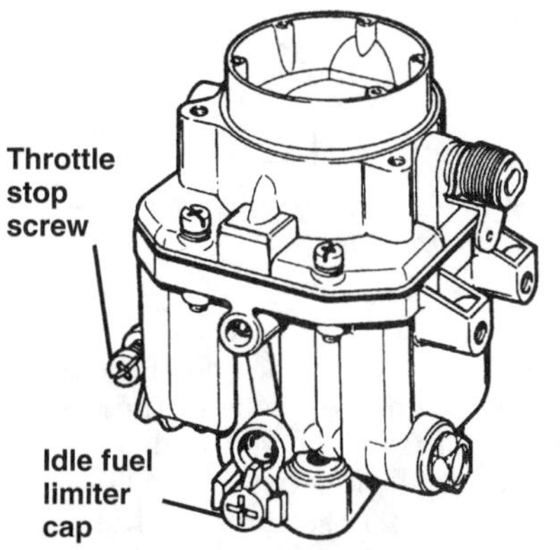

Fig. TO202—View showing location of throttle stop screw and idle mixture screw on carburetor. Limiter cap must be removed to perform initial adjustment of idle mixture screw.

SPARK PLUG

The recommended spark plug is Champion RS14YC or equivalent. The electrode gap should be 0.025 inch (0.64 mm).

CARBURETOR

Both models are equipped with a downdraft float carburetor. Note that idle mixture screw was originally equipped with a limiter cap (Fig. TO202). Remove cap for initial setting of idle mixture screw. Initial adjustment of idle mixture screw is 1¼ turns out. Run engine until normal operating temperature is reached.

Back out the governor idle screw or bend the governor idle tab (see GOVERNOR section) so the idle speed is determined by the throttle stop screw (Fig. TO202) on the carburetor. Rotate the throttle stop screw so the engine idle speed is 1000 rpm. Adjust the idle mixture screw so the engine idles at maximum speed and will accelerate cleanly, then readjust the throttle stop screw so the engine idles at 1000 rpm. Adjust the governed idle speed as outlined in the GOVERNOR section.

Install the limiter cap so it is at the midpoint of its travel. A fixed main jet controls the high speed mixture. An optional main jet may be installed for engine operation above 5000 feet.

To disassemble the carburetor for cleaning, remove the air horn (1—Fig. TO203). Slide out the float pin (3) and remove the float (2) and fuel inlet valve (4). Unscrew the idle mixture needle (8) and main jet (9).

Use care when cleaning the carburetor as caustic solvents may damage nonmetallic parts. To check the float level, position the carburetor as shown in Fig. TO204 so the float arm is just

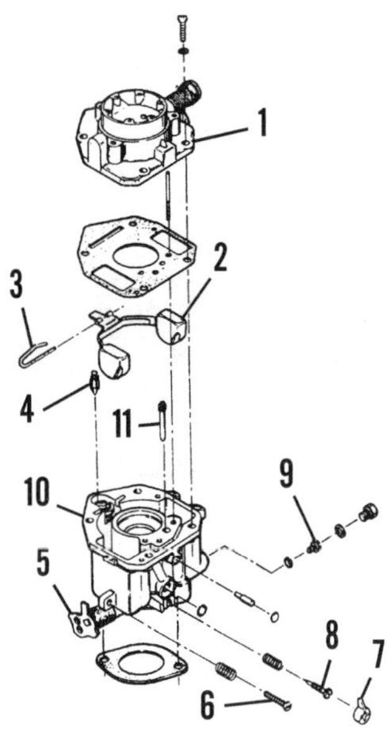

Fig. TO203—Exploded view of carburetor.

1. Air horn
2. Float
3. Pivot pin
4. Needle valve
5. Throttle shaft
6. Throttle stop screw
7. Cap
8. Idle adjustment needle
9. Main jet
10. Carburetor body
11. Main nozzle

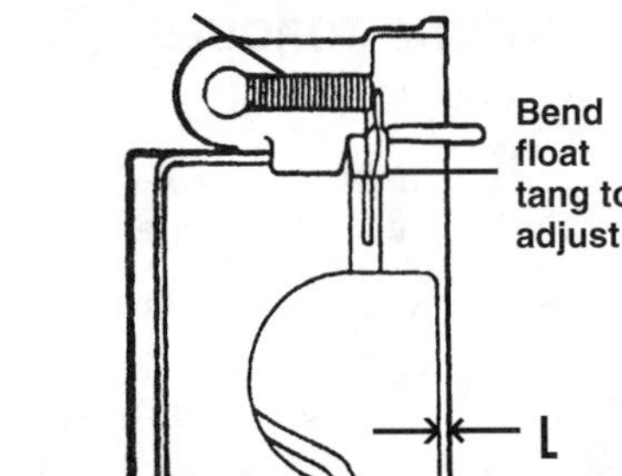

Fig. TO204—Position carburetor as shown when measuring float level (L). Float level should be 0.023-0.079 inch (0.58-2.00 mm).

touching the fuel inlet valve. Bend the float tang as required so the float level (L) is 0.023-0.079 inch (0.58-2.00 mm).

Float drop (D—Fig. TO205) should be 0.291 inch (7.40 mm). Bend the float arm to obtain the correct float drop.

GOVERNOR

Both models are equipped with a flyball weight governor located under the timing gear on the camshaft gear. The engine may be equipped with a front pull (Fig. TO206) or side pull (Fig. TO207) linkage arrangement. Service procedures are similar. Disconnect the link (L) from hole (H) and push the link and governor arm (A) toward the carburetor as far as possible. While held in this position, insert the end of the linkage into the nearest hole in the governor arm. Insert the rod end into the next outer hole if between two holes.

Normal factory setting is in the third hole from the pivot for side pull linkage and the second hole from the pivot for front pull linkage.

Sensitivity is increased by connecting the governor spring closer to the pivot and decreased by connecting the governor spring farther from the pivot.

Engine governed speed is adjusted by rotating the adjustment screw or bending the stop tab shown in Fig. TO208 or TO209. Governed idle speed should be set at 1100 rpm unless otherwise specified by the equipment manufacturer. Maximum governed speed should be set to the equipment manufacturer's specifications.

IGNITION SYSTEM

All engines are equipped with a battery ignition system that uses an electronic, breakerless triggering system. The trigger ring is attached to the

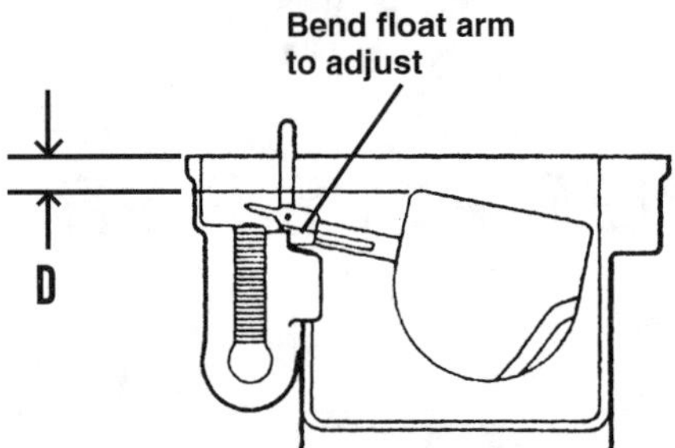

Fig. TO205—Float drop (D) should be 0.291 inch (7.40 mm).

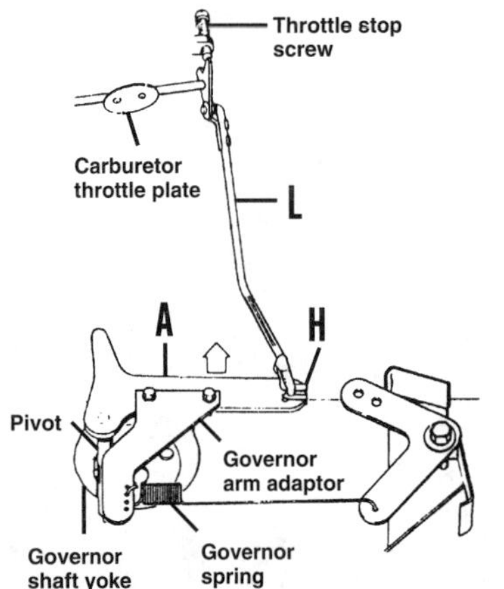

Fig. TO206—View of front pull variable speed governor linkage.

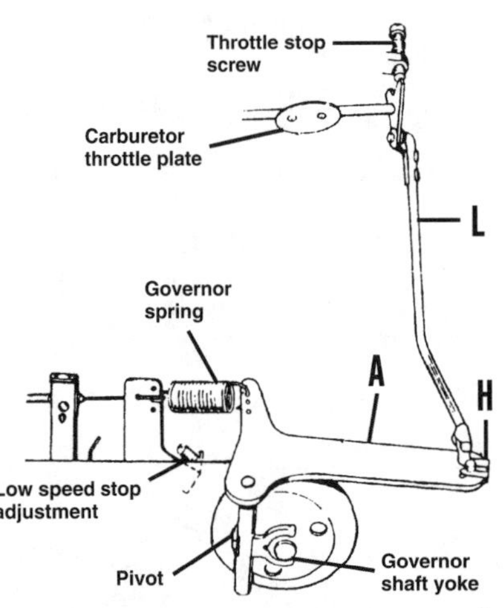

Fig. TO207—View of side pull variable speed governor linkage.

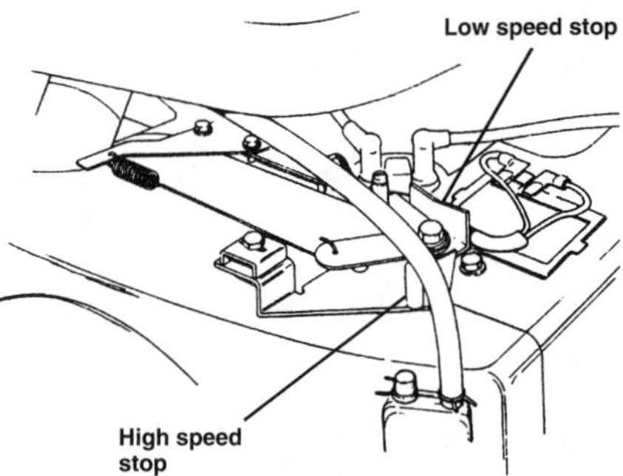

Fig. TO208—Low and high governed engine speeds are adjusted by bending stops on front pull governor linkage.

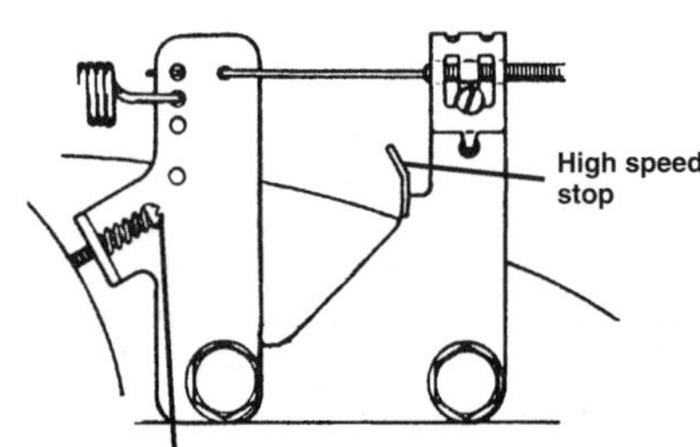

Fig. TO209—On side pull governor linkage, rotate adjustment screw to obtain desired low governed engine speed or bend high speed stop to adjust high governed engine speed.

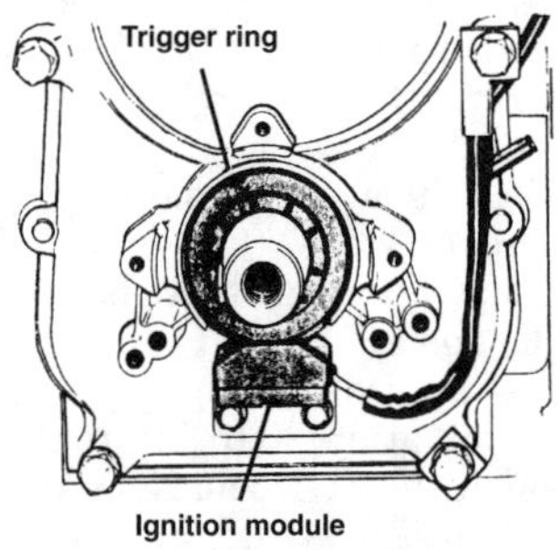

Fig. TO210—View of trigger ring and ignition module.

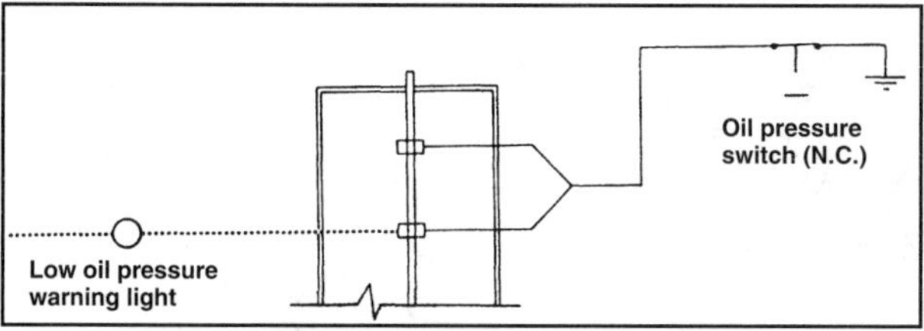

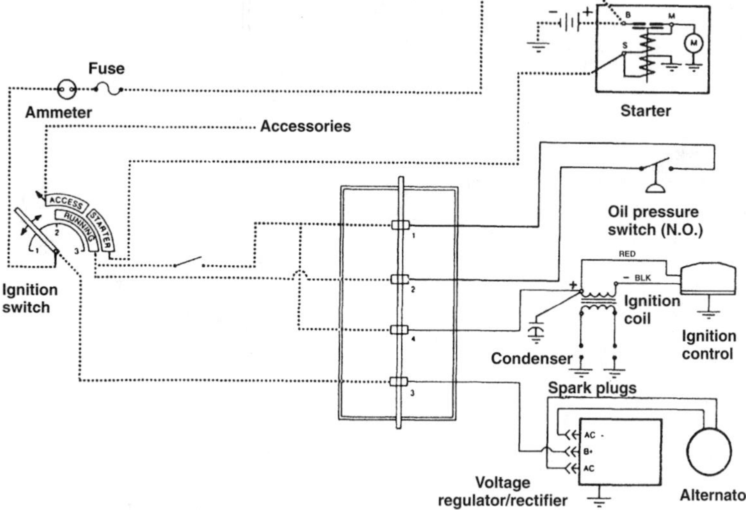

Fig. TO211—Typical wiring diagram. Circuit shown in inset is for an oil pressure switch connected to a warning device.

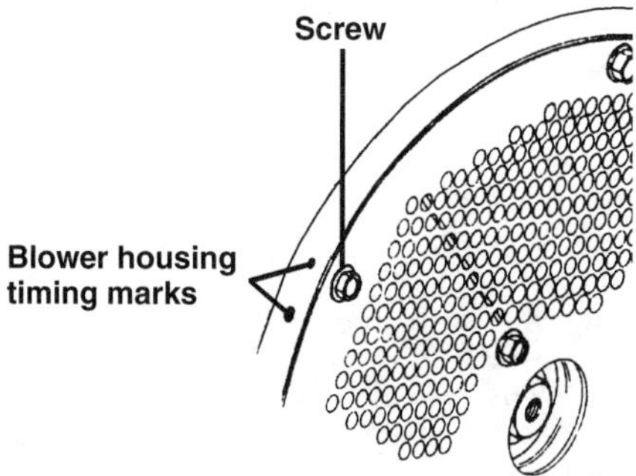

Fig. TO212—Ignition timing is correct if screen bolt aligns with timing marks when following ignition timing checking procedure in text.

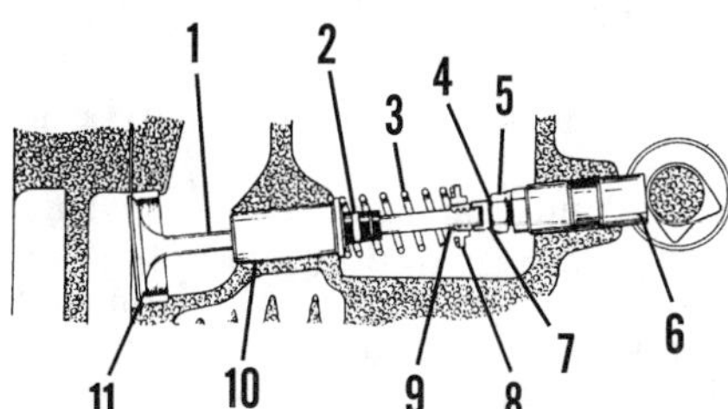

Fig. TO213—Cross-sectional view of intake valve assembly.

1. Valve
2. Valve stem seal
3. Valve spring
4. Tappet gap
5. Tappet adjusting screw
6. Tappet
7. Valve cap
8. Valve retainer
9. Valve keepers
10. Valve guide
11. Seat insert

crankshaft and the ignition module is located on the crankcase (see Fig. TO210). The spark plugs fire at the same time. Refer to Fig. TO211 for the wiring diagram. Regular maintenance is not required.

CAUTION: Due to the presence of the battery in circuit, improper test connections or incorrect wiring connections can damage the ignition module.

Ignition timing is 20° BTDC, but is not adjustable. To check ignition timing, remove the spark plugs. Using a voltmeter, connect the positive tester lead to the negative terminal (larger diameter) on the ignition coil and ground the negative tester lead to the engine.

Turn the ignition switch on and turn the flywheel clockwise slowly by hand. When voltmeter reading changes from 1-1.5 volts to battery voltage, a bolt on the rotating screen should be positioned between the timing marks on the blower housing shown in Fig. TO212. Note that the flywheel must be rotated in complete revolutions to obtain the required meter fluctuation; back-and-forth flywheel movement will not trigger the ignition.

To test the ignition module, follow the procedure in the previous paragraph to check ignition timing. If the voltmeter does not indicate fluctuation between 1-1.5 volts and battery voltage, the ignition module is faulty. Replace the module and recheck the ignition system.

To check the ignition coil primary windings, connect the ohmmeter leads to the negative and positive terminals on the coil. The ohmmeter should indicate 2.90-3.60 ohms. To check the ignition coil secondary windings, disconnect the spark plug wires from the ignition coil. Connect the ohmmeter leads to the two spark plug wire receptacles on the ignition coil. The ohmmeter should indicate 14.5k-19.8k ohms. If the ohmmeter readings are not as specified, replace the ignition coil.

VALVE ADJUSTMENT

The specified valve tappet clearance (cold) is 0.005 inch (0.13 mm) for the intake valve and 0.013 inch (0.33 mm) for the exhaust valve. The piston must be at top dead center for the cylinder requiring valve adjustment. Rotate the screw on the tappet shown in Fig. TO213 to adjust the valve stem-to-tappet clearance.

REPAIRS

TIGHTENING TORQUES

The recommended special tightening torque values are as follows:

Connecting rod	**144-168 in.-lb. (16.3-19 N·m)**
Exhaust manifold	**108-132 in.-lb. (12.2-14.9 N·m)**
Flywheel	**50-55 ft.-lb. (68-74 N·m)**
Gear case cover	**96-120 in.-lb. (10.8-13.6 N·m)**
Intake manifold	**96-120 in.-lb. (10.8-13.6 N·m)**
Oil base	**18-23 ft.-lb. (24.5-31.3 N·m)**
Oil pump	**84-108 in.-lb. (9.5-12.2 N·m)**
Rear bearing plate	**25-27 ft.-lb. (34-36.7 N·m)**

CYLINDER HEADS

The cylinder heads are accessible after removing the air shrouds.

CAUTION: Cylinder heads should not be detached from the block when hot due to possibility of head warpage.

Note the type of head gasket before installation. Use the following assembly procedure to prevent damage to the head gasket. Insert the cylinder head screws in the cylinder head, then place the gasket on the cylinder head around screws. Install the head with the gasket

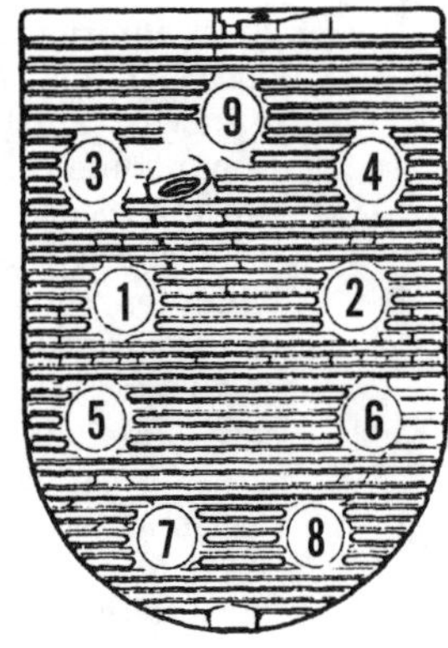

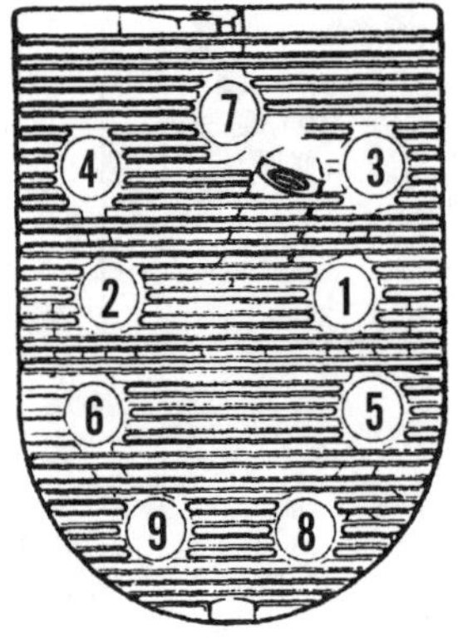

Fig. TO214—Tighten cylinder head screws in sequence shown.

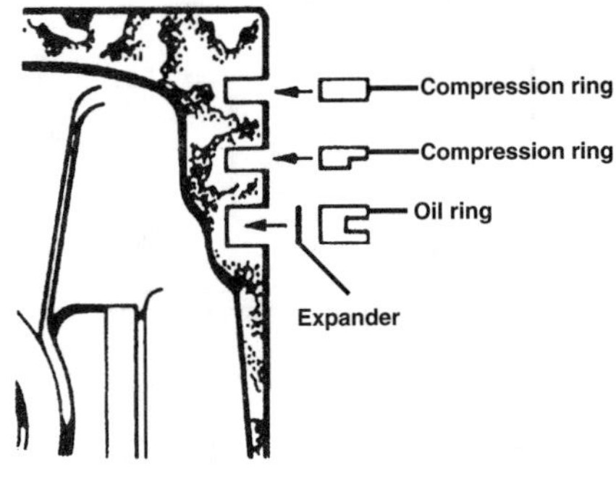

Fig. TO216—Install piston rings in piston grooves as shown.

on the block. Tighten the nuts in sequence shown in Fig. TO214. Initially tighten nuts in steps to 60 in.-lb. (6.8 N·m) and 120 in.-lb. (13.5 N·m), then tighten to a final torque of 192-216 in.-lb. (21.7-24.4 N·m) if head gasket is asbestos or 168-192 in.-lb. (19-21.7 N·m) if gasket is graphoil.

VALVE SYSTEM

Intake valve on all models is equipped with a stem seal that must be replaced whenever the valve is removed. All valves are equipped with valve caps (see Fig. TO213).

The valve seats are replaceable and are available in a variety of oversizes as well as standard. Seats are ground at a 45° angle. Seat width should be 0.031-0.047 inch (0.79-1.19 mm).

Valves should be ground at a 44° angle to provide an interference angle of one degree (Fig. TO215). Minimum valve margin is 0.030 inch (0.8 mm).

Valve stem clearance should be 0.0010-0.0025 inch (0.025-0.064 mm) for intake valve and 0.0020-0.0035 inch (0.051-0.089 mm) for the exhaust valve. The specified valve stem diameter is 0.2795-0.2800 inch (7.099-7.112 mm) for the intake valve and 0.2780-0.2785 inch (7.061-7.074 mm) for exhaust valve. The specified valve guide diameter is 0.2810-0.2820 inch (7.137-7.163 mm) for the intake valve guide and 0.2805-0.2815 inch (7.125-7.150 mm) for the exhaust valve guide.

Valve guides are replaceable. Intake valve guide is equipped with a gasket. Drive out the old guide towards the camshaft. The valve guide is tapered; the small end must be towards the valve seat. Use a suitable puller to install a new valve guide so the guide extends $^{11}/_{32}$ inch (8.7 mm) above surface at valve the spring end of the guide.

PISTON, PIN AND RINGS

The piston and connecting rod are removed from the cylinder head end of block as an assembly after removing the cylinder head and oil base.

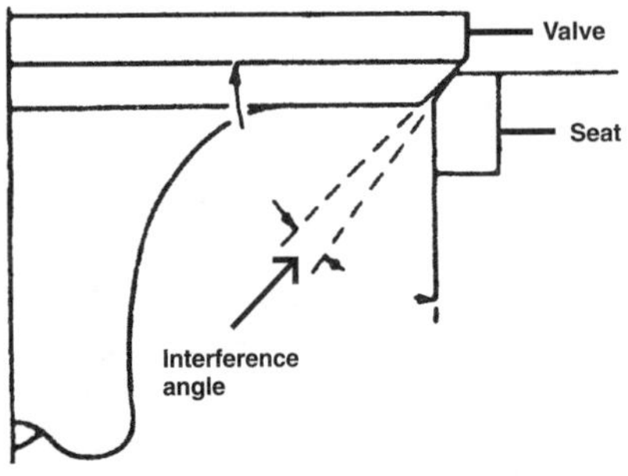

Fig. TO215—Valve seat and valve face are ground to obtain a one-degree interference angle. See text.

The specified piston ring end gap is 0.010-0.020 inch (0.25-0.51 mm). The piston should be replaced if the side clearance between the top compression ring and the ring land exceeds 0.008 inch (0.20 mm). The specified piston ring groove width is 0.0800-0.0810 inch (2.032-2.057 mm) for the compression rings and 0.1880-0.1890 inch (4.775-4.801 mm) for the oil control ring.

Piston pin-to-piston bore clearance should be 0.00004-0.00064 inch (0.0010-0.0163 mm). The specified pin bore in the piston is 0.6877-0.6882 inch (17.468-17.480 mm). The specified piston pin diameter is 0.6875-0.6877 inch (17.463-17.468 mm).

Piston clearance in bore should be 0.0033-0.0053 inch (0.084-0.135 mm). When determining piston clearance, measure the piston diameter at a point that is perpendicular to the piston pin bore and 1.187 inches (30.15 mm) from the piston crown.

Install piston rings as shown in Fig. TO216. When installing the piston and connecting rod, the oil hole (Fig. TO217) in the rod must be towards the camshaft. Tighten the connecting rod nuts to an initial torque of 60 in.-lb. (6.8 N·m) and then to a final torque of 144-168 in.-lb. (16.3-19 N·m).

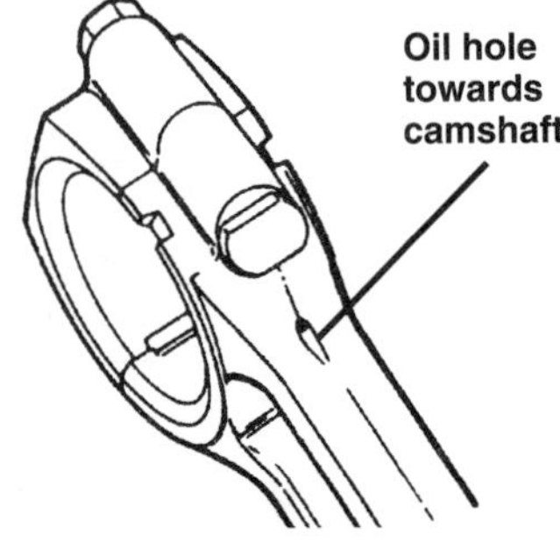

Fig. TO217—Install connecting rod so oil hole is towards camshaft.

CONNECTING ROD

The connecting rod and piston are removed from the cylinder head end of the block as an assembly after removing the cylinder head and oil base.

Connecting rods ride directly on the crankshaft journal. The specified connecting rod big end diameter is 1.6280-1.6285 inch (41.351-41.364 mm). The specified small end diameter is 0.6879-0.6882 inch (17.473-17.480 mm).

Connecting rod-to-crankpin clearance should be 0.0020-0.0033 inch (0.051-0.084 mm). The connecting rod side play should be 0.002-0.016 inch (0.05-0.41 mm). The undersize connecting rods are available to fit a reground crankshaft crankpin.

When installing the piston and connecting rod, the oil hole (Fig. TO217) in the rod must be towards the camshaft. Tighten the connecting rod nuts to an initial torque of 60 in.-lb. (6.8 N·m) and then to a final torque of 144-168 in.-lb. (16.3-19 N·m).

CRANKSHAFT, BEARINGS AND SEALS

The crankshaft (Fig. TO218) is supported at each end by precision sleeve bearings located in the cylinder block (Fig. TO219) and rear bearing plate.

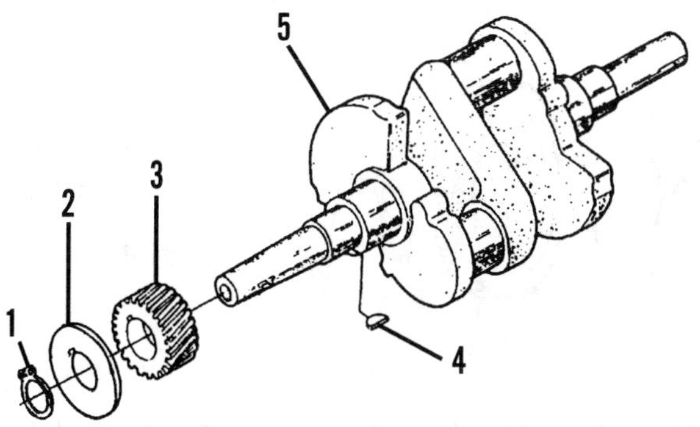

Fig. TO218—Exploded view of crankshaft used on all models.

1. Snap ring
2. Washer
3. Crankshaft gear
4. Key
5. Crankshaft

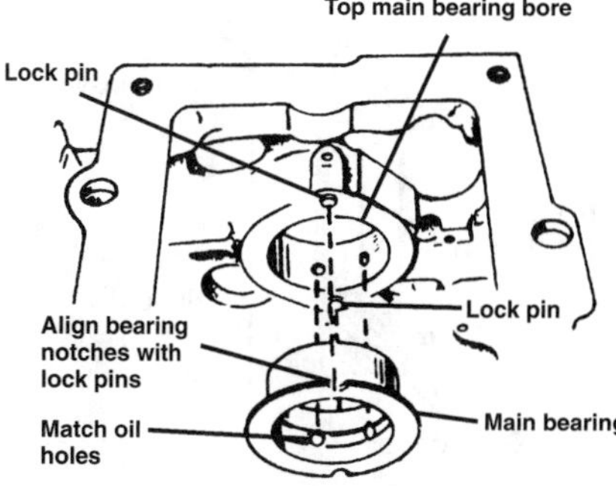

Fig. TO220—Align front main bearing as shown.

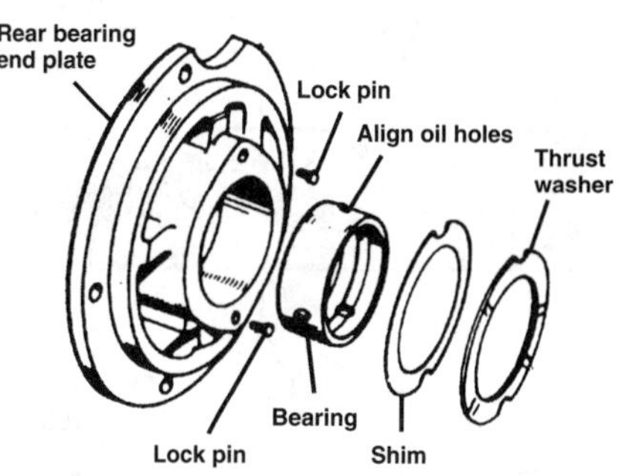

Fig. TO221—Align thrust washer and shim with lock pins on rear bearing plate. Oil grooves on thrust washer must be towards crankshaft.

Fig. TO219—Exploded view of crankcase assembly. Crankcase breather components (1 through 6) are used on early models while breather components (7 through 13) are used on later models.

1. Valve cap
2. Screen
3. O-ring
4. Clamp
5. Baffle
6. Breather tube
7. Breather cover
8. Gasket
9. Spring
10. Washer
11. Breather valve
12. Baffle
13. Gasket
14. Valve cover
15. Gasket
16. Tappet
17. Valve retainers
18. Valve cap
19. Valve spring retainer
20. Valve spring
21. Intake valve seal
22. Valve guide
23. Screw
24. Washer
25. Oil pressure relief valve spring
26. Oil pressure relief valve
27. Welch plug
28. Drive pin
29. Gasket
30. Shim
31. Main bearing
32. Rear bearing plate
33. Oil seal
35. Socket screw
36. Camshaft bearing
37. Oil pump gasket
38. Oil pump
39. Plug (early models)
40. Dowel
41. Drive pin
42. Main bearing
43. Oil tube
44. Plug
45. Rod cap
46. Connecting rod
47. Piston rings
48. Retainer ring
49. Piston pin
50. Piston
51. Exhaust valve seat
52. Intake valve seat
53. Exhaust valve
54. Intake valve
55. Head gasket
56. Cylinder head

The specified crankshaft main bearing journal diameter is 1.9992-2.0000 inches (50.780-50.800 mm) for both main bearings. The main bearing journals can be reqround to fit undersize main bearings.

The specified crankpin diameter is 1.6252-1.6260 inches (41.280-41.300 mm). The crankpin can be reground to accept an undersize connecting rod.

The new front main bearing is supplied with a cloth that is used to wipe the outside of the bearing and the bearing bore in the cylinder block. The main bearing should be chilled and the cylinder block should be heated to 200° F (93° C) to ease bearing installation. Apply Loctite to the outer bearing surface before installation. When installing the front main bearing in the cylinder block, make certain the bearing notches are aligned with the lock pins as shown in Fig. TO220.

Install the bearing in the rear bearing plate so the bearing is 0.000-0.015 in. (0.38 mm) from the surface and the oil holes are aligned. A thrust washer is located between the crankshaft and rear bearing plate (Fig. TO221). Install the thrust washer so the notches align with the lock pins and grooves on the thrust washer are towards the crankshaft.

Crankshaft end play should be 0.006-0.012 inch (0.15-0.30 mm) and is adjusted by installing shims between the thrust washer and oil base as shown in Fig. TO221. Be sure the shims and thrust washer are properly aligned with the lock pins during assembly.

To remove the crankshaft oil seals, the timing gear cover and rear bearing plate must be removed. Force out the oil seals from the inside. Install the oil seal in the

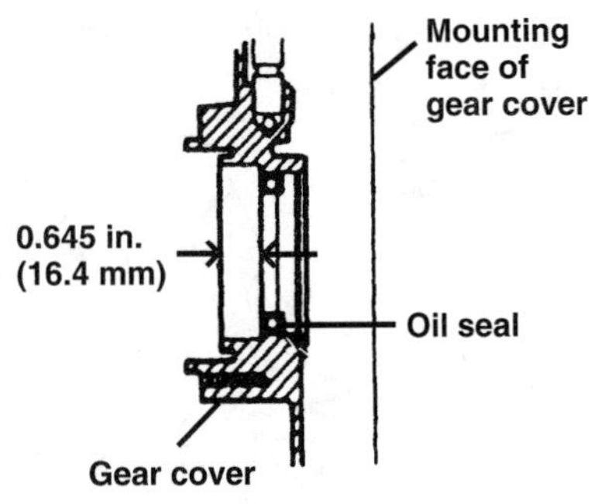

Fig. TO222—Install oil seal in timing gear cover as shown.

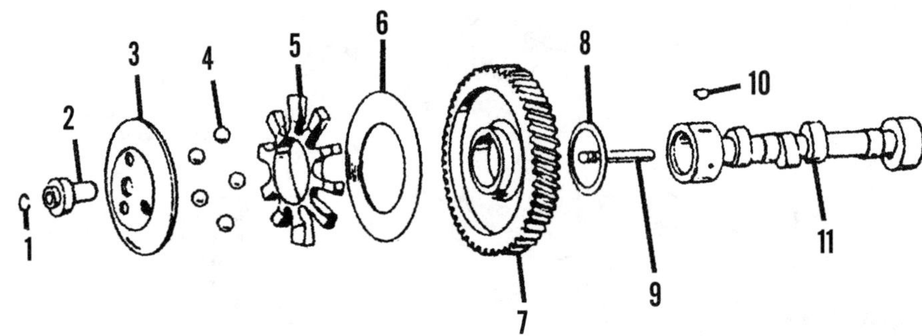

Fig. TO223—Exploded view of camshaft used on all models. Number of governor balls (4) may be five or ten depending on engine model and application.

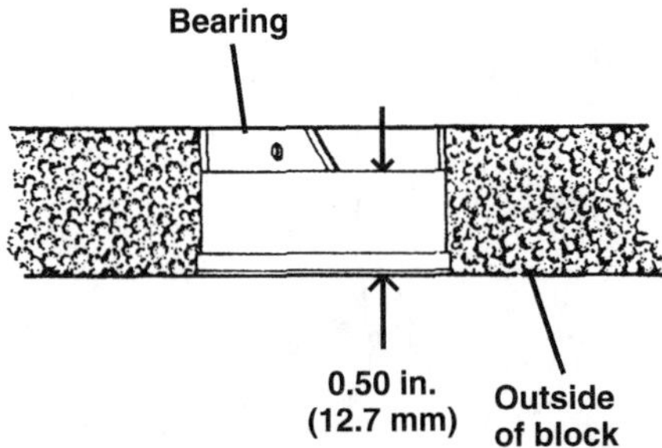

Fig. TO224—Press rear camshaft bearing in cylinder block as shown.

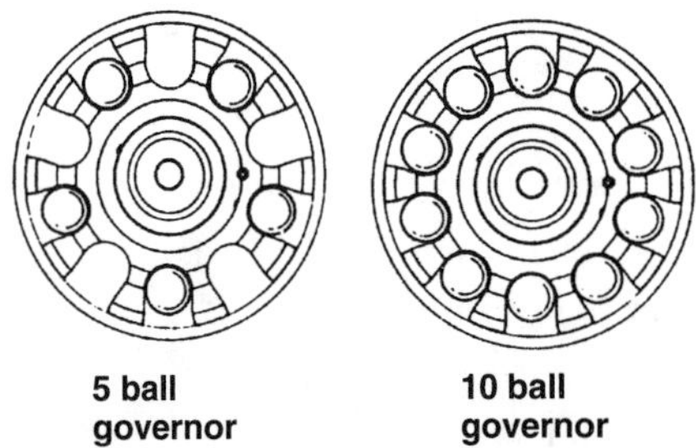

Fig. TO225—Flyballs must be arranged as shown, according to total number used to obtain desired governor sensitivity.

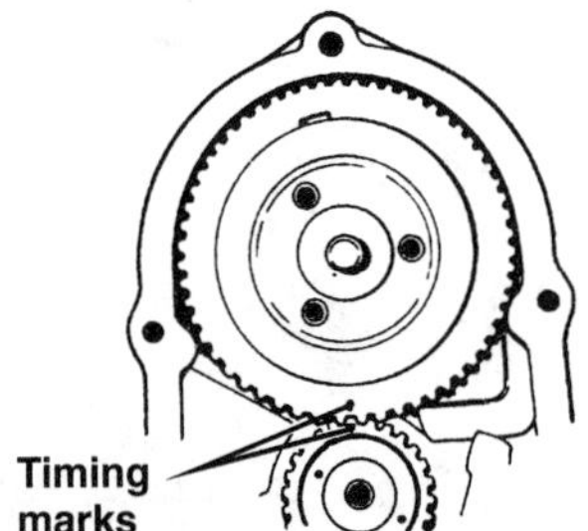

Fig. TO226—Timing marks on camshaft and crankshaft gears must be aligned during assembly.

timing gear cover so the seal is 0.645 inch (16.38 mm) below the face of the bore as shown in Fig. TO222. Drive the oil seal into the rear bearing plate until bottomed in the bearing plate.

CAMSHAFT, BEARINGS AND GOVERNOR

The camshaft (Fig. TO223) is supported at each end in the precision sleeve bearings. Apply Loctite Bearing Mount to the bearing before installation. Make certain the oil holes in the bearing and block are aligned.

Press the front bearing in flush with the outer surface of the block. Press the rear bearing in so it is 0.50 inch (12.7 mm) from the outer surface of the block as shown in Fig. TO224. Camshaft-to-bearing clearance should be 0.0015-0.0030 inch (0.038-0.076 mm).

Camshaft end play should be 0.011-0.048 inch (0.28-1.22 mm). Camshaft end play is adjusted by varying the thickness of the shim located between the camshaft timing gear and cylinder block.

Camshaft lobe height wear limit for the exhaust valve is 1.1570 inches (29.388 mm). The wear limit for the intake valve lobe is 1.1370 inches (28.880 mm) on Model P216 and 1.1670 inches (29.642 mm) on Model P220.

Camshaft timing gear is a press fit on the end of the camshaft and is designed to accommodate five or 10 flyballs arranged as shown in Fig. TO225. The number of flyballs is varied to alter governor sensitivity. Fewer flyballs are used on engines with variable speed applications and greater number of flyballs are used for continuous speed applications. Flyballs must be arranged in "pockets" as shown according to the total number used.

When installing the camshaft, align the timing marks on the camshaft gear and crankshaft gear as shown in Fig. TO226.

The center pin (Fig. TO227) should extend ¾ inch (19 mm) from the end of the camshaft to allow 7/32 inch (5.6 mm) in-and-out movement of the governor cup. If the distance is incorrect, remove the pin and press a new pin in to the correct depth.

Always make certain the governor shaft pivot ball is in the timing cover by measuring as shown in Fig. TO228 inset, and check the length of the roll pin that engages the bushed hole in the governor cup. This pin must extend ¾ inch (19.05 mm) from the timing cover mating surface.

OIL PUMP

The oil pump is a unit assembly; separate components are not available.

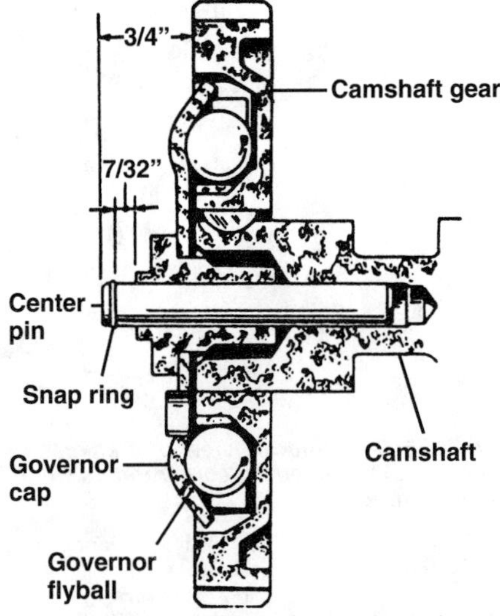

Fig. TO227—Cross-sectional view of camshaft gear and governor assembly showing correct dimensions for center pin extension from camshaft. Refer to text.

An oil pressure relief valve located in the cylinder block (Fig. TO229) regulates the engine oil pressure. Relief valve spring free length should be 1.00 inch (25.4 mm). Relief valve spring pressure should be 2.4-2.8 pounds (10.6-12.5 N) at spring length of 0.5 inch (12.7 mm). Relief valve diameter should be 0.3105-0.3125 inch (2.142-2.156 mm).

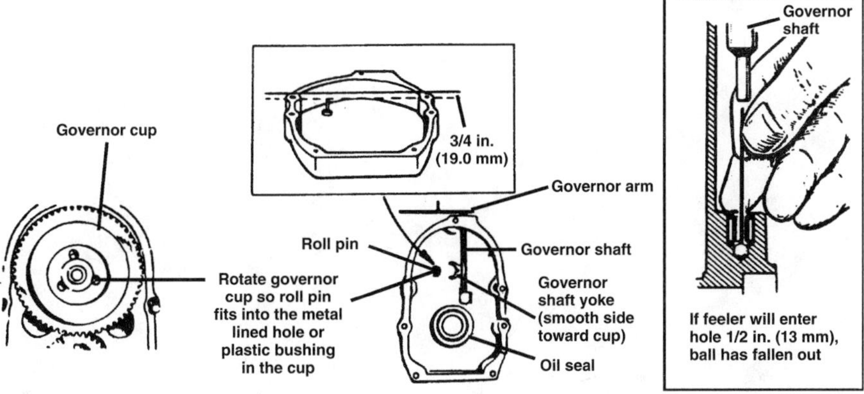

Fig. TO228—View of governor shaft, timing cover and governor cup showing assembly details. Refer to text.

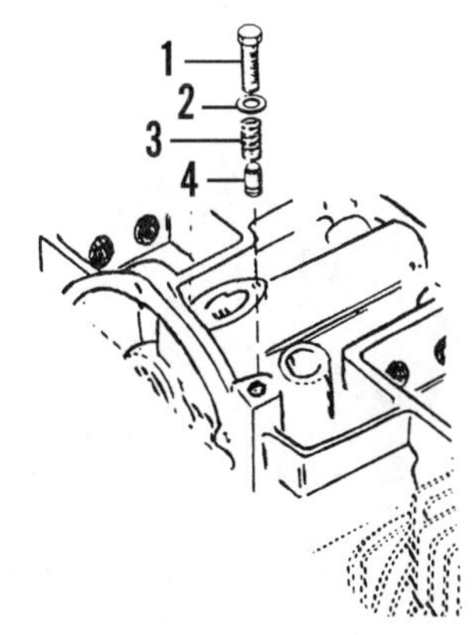

Fig. TO229—View showing location of oil pressure relief valve and spring.

1. Cap screw
2. Sealing washer
3. Spring
4. Valve

NOTES

YANMAR

Model	No. Cyls.	Bore	Stroke	Displacement	Power Rating
3TG66UJ	3	66 mm (2.6 in.)	64.2 mm (2.53 in.)	659 cc (40.2 cu. in.)	13.4 kW (18 hp.)

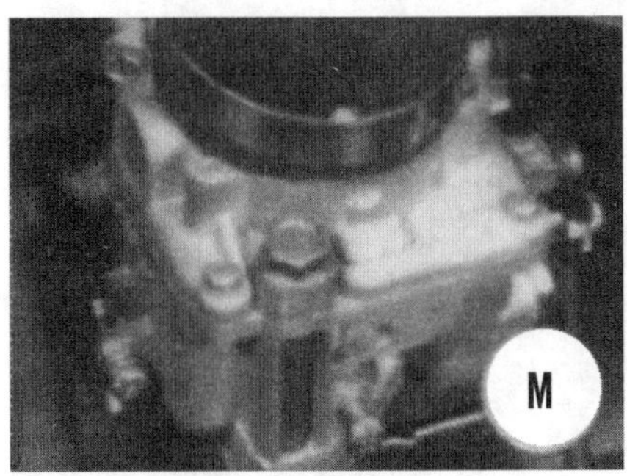

Fig. Y101—Initial adjustment of idle mixture screw (M) is 1½ turns out from a lightly seated position. Refer to text for adjustment procedure.

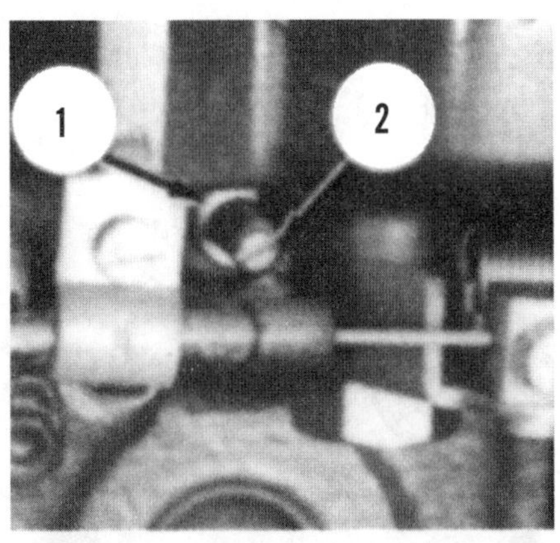

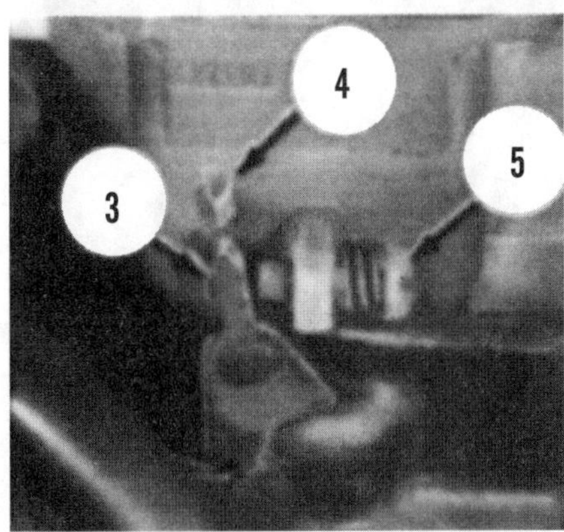

Fig. Y102—Loosen jam nut (1) and turn adjusting screw (2) so pointer on throttle shaft flange (3) is aligned with projection (4) on carburetor. Refer to text for adjustment of low idle stop screw (5).

ENGINE IDENTIFICATION

The Yanmar 3TG66UJ is a four-stroke, three-cylinder engine. The engine is liquid cooled and equipped with overhead valves. The engine identification plate is located on the rocker cover.

MAINTENANCE

LUBRICATION

The engine is equipped with an oil filter and an oil pump that provides pressurized oil to the engine.

Check the oil level before operation and after every 10 hours of operation. Oil level must be between the marks on the dipstick. Do not operate the engine if the oil level is at or below the lower mark.

The oil should meet the latest API service classification. Select the oil viscosity depending upon the ambient temperature. Use SAE 30 oil for temperatures above 0°C (32°F); use SAE 10W-30 oil for temperatures between -20°C (-4°F) and (86°F) 30°C; SAE 5W-30 may be used between 10°C (50°F) and -35°C (-31°F).

Change oil and filter after first 50 hours of operation and then after every 200 hours of operation, or more frequently if operation is severe. Crankcase capacity is 3 liters (3.1 qt.) with filter or 2.8 liters (2.9 qt.) without filter.

AIR FILTER

The air filter should be cleaned after every 200 hours of operation. The filter element is paper and should not be washed.

Tap the filter lightly to remove debris, or direct low-pressure air, approximately 210 kPa (30 psi), from the inside to the outside to blow away debris. Replace the filter if it cannot be satisfactorily cleaned or if it is damaged in any way.

FAN BELT

Adjust the fan belt tension so a 107 N (24 lb.) force applied midway between the fan and alternator pulleys will deflect the belt 13 mm (½ in.). Reposition the alternator to adjust the fan belt tension.

COOLING SYSTEM

Drain, flush and refill the cooling system annually. Manufacturer recommends low silicate antifreeze that does not contain stop leak additive. Cooling system capacity is 2.8 liters (2.9 qt.).

A thermostat is used to maintain the cooling system temperature. The thermostat should begin to open at 71°C (160°F) and open fully at 84°C (184°F).

SPARK PLUG

Recommended spark plug is NGK BPR4BS or Champion RN11YC. Spark plug electrode gap should be 0.8 mm (0.032 in.). Tighten the spark plug to 20 N·m (180 in.-lb.).

CARBURETOR

A fixed, nonadjustable main jet controls the high-speed mixture on standard equipment carburetors. A variable adjustable main jet kit is available for installation on tractors operating at high altitudes.

Initial adjustment of the idle mixture screw (M—Fig. Y101) is 1½ turns out from a lightly seated position. Final adjustment of the idle mixture screw must be performed with the engine at normal operating temperature. Run the engine at idle speed and the turn idle mixture screw (M) counterclockwise until the engine speed decreases. Turn the screw clockwise until the engine speed decreases again, then turn the screw to obtain fastest engine speed. Turn the screw out an extra ⅛ turn.

Shut off the engine, loosen the locknut (1—Fig. Y102) and turn the speed adjusting screw (2) so the pointer on the throttle shaft flange (3) aligns with the projection (4) on the side of the carburetor. Disconnect the throttle cable, start the engine and hold the throttle shaft flange against the stop screw (5). If necessary, adjust the idle speed by turning the stop screw (5) to obtain recommended speed of 1300 rpm.

Refer to the GOVERNOR paragraph for the high idle (no-load) speed adjustment.

GOVERNOR

The engine is equipped with a flyweight governor (4—Fig. Y103) located on the backside of the timing gear case. Refer to the REPAIRS section for service.

To adjust the governor linkage, proceed as follows: Run the engine until normal operating temperature is achieved. Disconnect the throttle cable. Move the governor lever against the high-speed stop screw (2—Fig. Y103) and check engine speed using an accurate tachometer. Specified engine speed is 3600-3800 rpm. If necessary, loosen the nut (1) and turn the high-speed stop screw (2) to obtain desired speed. Tighten the nut and recheck engine speed. Move the throttle control lever to the high speed position, loosen the throttle cable clamp, pull the cable to remove slack, reconnect the throttle cable and tighten the cable clamp.

IGNITION SYSTEM

The ignition system is an electronic type that uses three pulsars, an ignition module and three ignition coils. The pulsars are mounted equidistantly around the flywheel and trigger the ignition for each cylinder. Each cylinder is served by an ignition coil.

Ignition timing is not adjustable, but a viewing port is provided in the flywheel housing. The ignition module determines ignition timing, however, the timing should be the same for all cylinders.

If an ignition malfunction is suspected, refer to the REPAIRS section for service procedure.

VALVE ADJUSTMENT

To adjust the valve clearance, remove the plug from the flywheel viewing port located on the side of the flywheel housing. Rotate the flywheel so the mark (F—Fig. Y104) indicating the number 1 cylinder is aligned with the mark (M) on the flywheel housing and valves for the number one cylinder are both closed (rocker arms will be loose). Use a feeler gauge to measure the clearance between the rocker arm and valve stem end of both valves for the number one cylinder. The specified clearance (engine cold) for both the intake and exhaust valves is 0.2 mm (0.008 in.). If necessary, loosen the locknut and turn the rocker arm adjusting screw to obtain desired clearance.

Rotate the flywheel so the mark on the flywheel indicating number 2 cylinder is aligned with the mark (M) on the flywheel housing and the valves for number 2 cylinder are closed. Adjust the valve clearance for number 2 cylinder, then repeat the procedure for number 3 cylinder.

Fig. Y103—Adjust high idle speed by turning high-speed stop screw (2) as outlined in text.

1. Jam nut
2. High speed stop screw
3. Spring
4. Governor linkage & housing

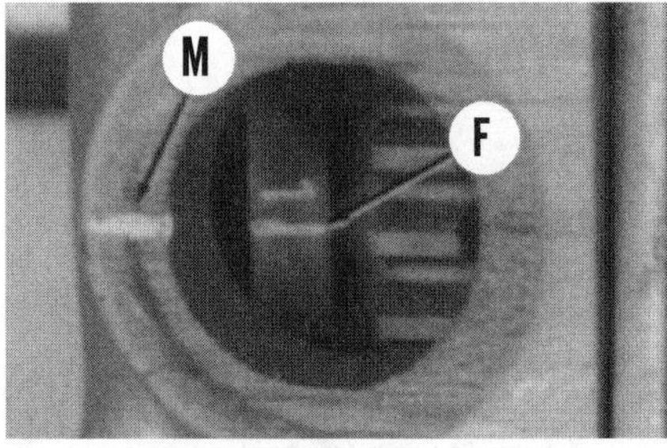

Fig. Y104—View showing index mark (M) on flywheel housing and TDC mark (F) for No. 1 cylinder on flywheel.

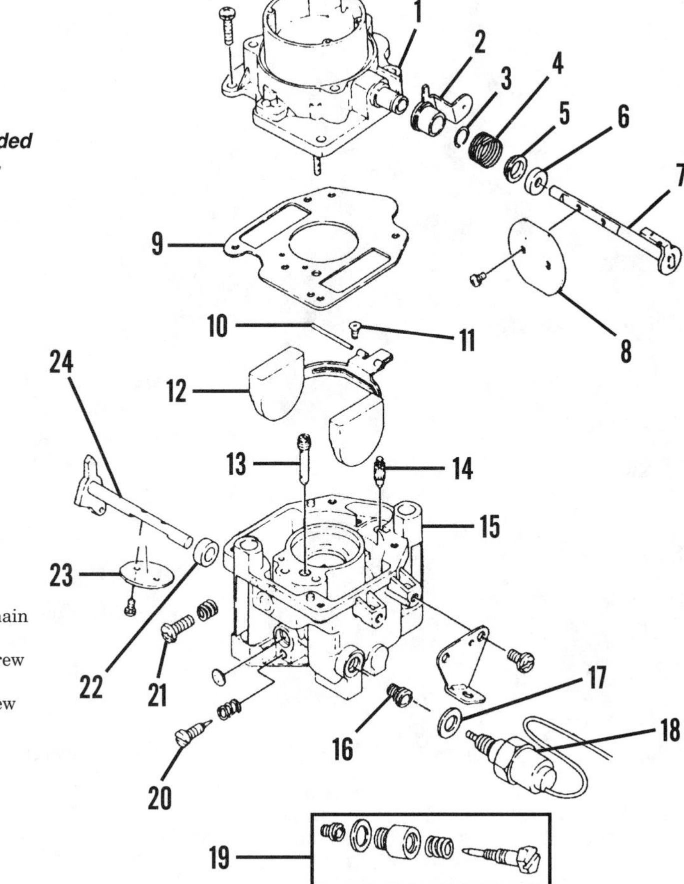

Fig. Y105—Exploded view of carburetor.

1. Cover
2. Lever
3. Snap ring
4. Spring
5. Bushing
6. Seal
7. Choke shaft
8. Choke plate
9. Gasket
10. Pin
11. Screw
12. Float
13. Nozzle
14. Fuel inlet valve
15. Body
16. Main jet
17. Gasket
18. Fuel shut-off solenoid
19. High altitude main jet kit
20. Idle mixture screw
21. Idle speed adjustment screw
22. Seal
23. Throttle plate
24. Throttle shaft

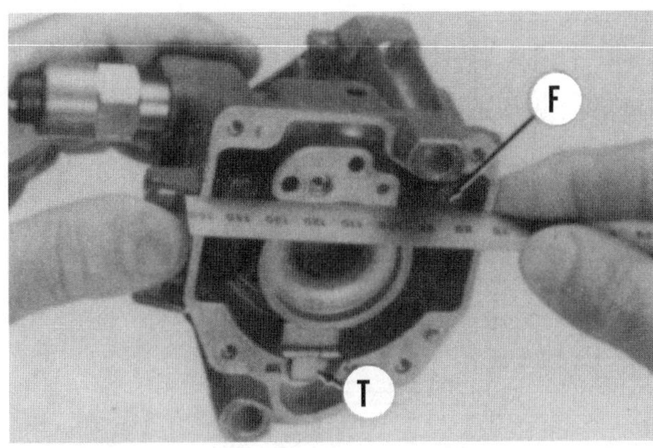

Fig. Y106—Refer to text and measure float level as shown. Bend float tab (T) to adjust float level.

Fig. Y107—Measure float drop from tip of float to body mating surface as shown. Bend float arm (A) to adjust.

COMPRESSION PRESSURE

At a cranking speed of 300 rpm, minimum compression pressure is 779 kPa (113 psi). Maximum variation between cylinders is 97 kPa (14 psi).

REPAIRS

TIGHTENING TORQUES

The recommended special tightening torque specifications are as follows:

Camshaft retainer . . . . 10-12 N·m (89-106 in.-lb.)
Connecting rod . . . . 23 N·m (17 ft.-lb.)
Cylinder head . . . . 34 N·m (25 ft.-lb.)
Exhaust manifold . . . . 11 N·m (97 in.-lb.)
Flywheel . . . . 83 N·m (61 ft.-lb.)
Flywheel housing
 8 mm . . . . 26 N·m (19 ft.-lb.)
 10 mm . . . . 49 N·m (36 ft.-lb.)
Intake manifold . . . . 11 N·m (97 in.-lb.)
Main bearing . . . . 54 N·m (40 ft.-lb.)
Oil pump. . . . . 11 N·m (97 in.-lb.)
Rear main seal . . . . 11 N·m (97 in.-lb.)
Rocker arm shaft . . . . 25 N·m (18 ft.-lb.)
Spark plug. . . . . 20 N·m (15 ft.-lb.)
Starter . . . . 49 N·m (36 ft.-lb.)
Stub shaft . . . . 59 N·m (43 ft.-lb.)
Timing cover. 9 N·m (80 in.-lb.)
Timing gear housing
 Aluminum . . . . 9 N·m (80 in.-lb.)
 Iron. . . . . 11 N·m (97 in.-lb.)
Water pump. 26 N·m (19 ft.-lb.)

CARBURETOR

To disassemble the carburetor for cleaning and inspection, separate the cover (1—Fig. Y105) from the carburetor body (15). Push out the float pin (10) and remove the float (12) and fuel inlet valve (14). Unscrew and remove the fuel shut-off solenoid (18), main jet (16), low speed jet (13) and idle mixture screw (20).

Thoroughly clean all parts with carburetor cleaner. Do not clean the passages in carburetor with drill bits or wire as any enlargement of the passages may change the calibration and performance of the carburetor. Do not polish or attempt to reshape the idle jet (13 and 20), main jet (16) or fuel inlet valve (14). Replace jets if they are worn or damaged. Use low-pressure air to dry out passages. Do not use cloth or paper towels to dry parts.

To check the float level, invert the carburetor. The end of the float (F—Fig. Y106 should be flush with the body surface. Bend the float tab (T) to adjust the float setting. With the carburetor upright, float drop should be at least 5 mm (0.20 in.) as measured from the highest point on the float to the carburetor body surface as shown in Fig. Y107. Bend the float arm (A) as needed, then recheck the float level.

Before tightening the throttle plate and choke plate screws, rotate the shaft so the plate is in the closed position, then tighten the screws. This will center the plate on the shaft.

IGNITION SYSTEM

Refer to Fig. Y108 for the engine wiring diagram. To test the ignition components, first turn the key switch ON and place the hydrostatic lever in the STOP position and the PTO switch in the OFF position. Check for voltage at the double pink/black wires at the engine harness connector.

If there is no voltage at the double pink/black wires, turn the key switch OFF. Connect a jumper wire across the seat safety switch terminals. Check for continuity between the black wire at the Time Delay Control Module (TDC) two-pin connector and ground. Turn the key switch ON and check for voltage at the pink wire at the TDC two-pin connector. Check for voltage at the pink wire, yellow/black wire, and purple/black wire at the TDC eight-pin connector.

If continuity and voltage checks are normal, the pink wire from TDC eight-pin connector to engine connector is open. If there is no continuity at the black wire, the ground wire is faulty. If there is no voltage at the pink wire at the two-pin connector, check for faulty wire or connections. If there is no voltage at the pink wire at the eight-pin connector, the TDC module is faulty. If there is no voltage at the yellow/black wire or purple/black wire at the eight-pin connector, check for faulty wires or connections.

If there is voltage at the double pink/black wires, perform an operational test of the ignition system as follows: Connect a test light to the negative terminal of each of the ignition coils in turn. Start the engine and run at low idle speed. The test light should blink rapidly.

If the test light fails to blink at all three coils, check the transistor module. If the test light does not blink at one coil, test the pulsar for that coil. If the test light does blink but there is no spark, test the coil.

To test the pulsars, disconnect the four-pin pulsar wiring connector. Use an ohmmeter to check resistance between the black ground wire and each of the remaining pulsar wires in the connector. Specified resistance is 15.5-23.3 ohms. If resistance is not as specified or there is no resistance, renew the pulsar or wiring as necessary.

To test the ignition coils, turn the key switch OFF and disconnect the wires from the coil. Measure the primary wind-

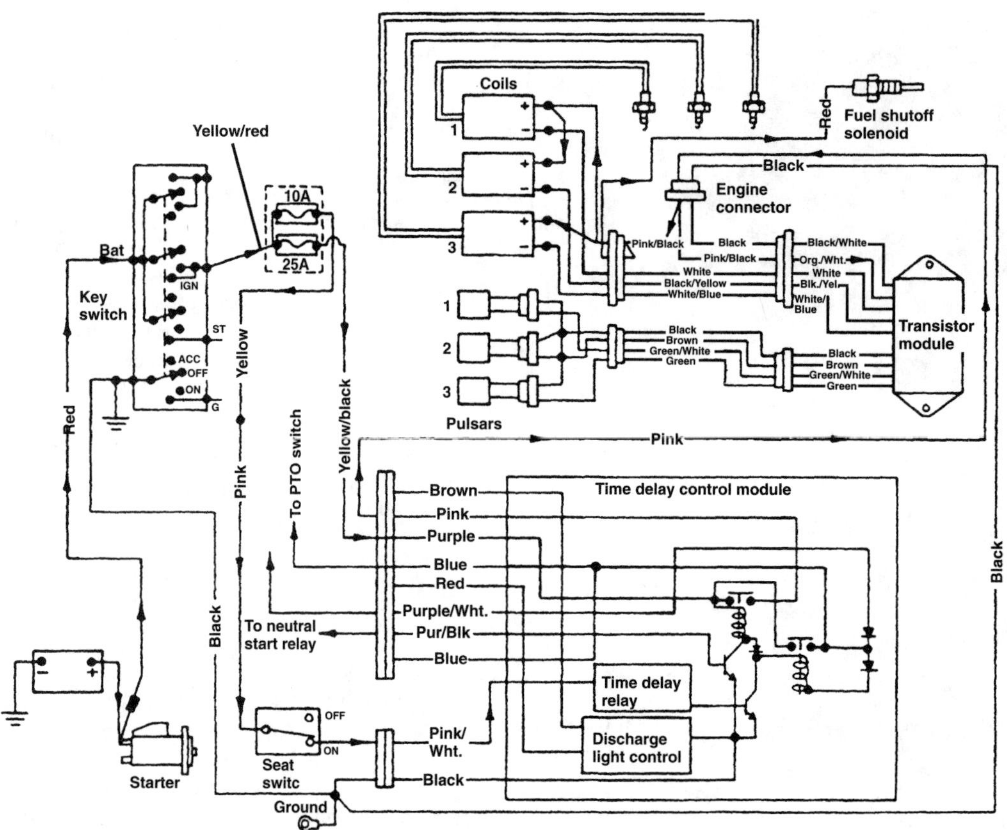

Fig. Y108—Wiring diagram of ignition circuit.

ing resistance across the coil terminals with an ohmmeter. Specified resistance is 3.8-5.2 ohms. Disconnect the spark plug wire and measure the resistance between the coil positive terminal and spark plug boot end of the high tension lead. Specified resistance is 10.8K-16.2K ohms. Check for continuity between the negative terminal of the coil and core. There should be infinite resistance. Replace the coil as necessary.

To check the transistor module, disconnect the transistor module wiring connectors and check resistance across the terminals as indicated in the chart shown in Fig. Y109. Note that the readings are approximate and may vary due to the condition and accuracy of the ohmmeter.

Ignition timing is not adjustable but may be checked at the flywheel inspection port using a timing light. The flywheel has three BTDC marks and a TDC mark for each cylinder. If ignition timing is correct, the center BTDC mark on the flywheel should align with the mark on the flywheel housing for all three cylinders.

If the BTDC mark is not in the same position for one cylinder, check the input voltage to the transistor module as follows: Run the engine at low idle speed and measure the voltage across

Black lead / Red lead	Black	Brown	Green White	Green	Black Yellow	White	White Blue	Orange White	Black White
Black		O (2.2 K)	O (2.2 K)	O (2.2 K)	O (2.4 K)	O (2.4 K)	O (2.4 K)	X	O (0Ω)
Brown	O (2.2 K)		O (4.4 K)	O (4.4 K)	O (5.1 K)	O (5.1 K)	O (5.1 K)	X	O (2.2 K)
Green White	O (2.2 K)	O (4.4 K)		O (4.4 K)	O (5.1 K)	O (5.1 K)	O (5.1 K)	X	O (2.2 K)
Green	O (2.2 K)	O (4.4 K)	O (4.4 K)		O (5.1 K)	O (5.1 K)	O (5.1 K)	X	O (2.2 K)
Black Yellow	X	X	X	X		X	X	X	X
White	X	X	X	X	X		X	X	X
White Blue	X	X	X	X	X	X		X	X
Orange White	O (15 K)	O (20 K)	O (20 K)	O (20 K)	O (50 K)	O (50 K)	O (50 K)		O (15 K)
Black White	O (0Ω)	O (2.2 K)	O (2.2 K)	O (2.2 K)	O (2.4 K)	O (2.4 K)	O (2.4 K)	X	

Fig. Y109—The chart shown above may be used to troubleshoot the ignition module. "O" denotes continuity and "X" denotes infinite resistance.

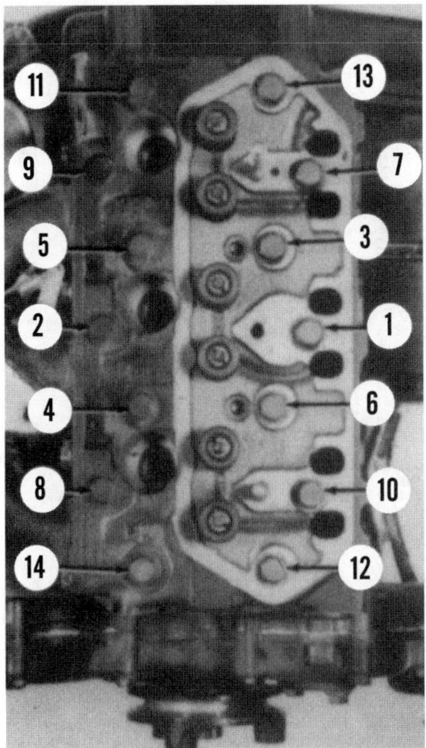

Fig. Y110—Tighten cylinder head screws in several steps following sequence shown above.

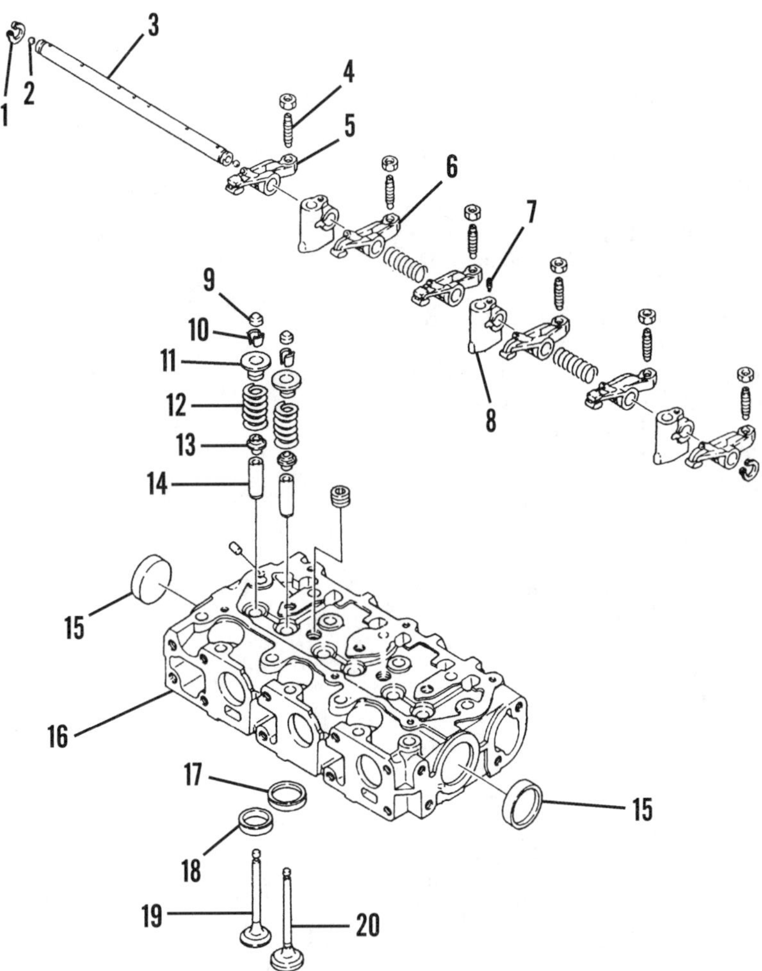

Fig. Y111—Exploded view of cylinder head and rocker arms. Center shaft support (8) is located in center of rocker shaft (3) by setscrew (7).

1. Snap ring
2. Ball
3. Rocker shaft
4. Adjusting screw
5. Rocker arm, exhaust
6. Rocker arm, intake
7. Setscrew
8. Shaft support
9. Valve stem cap
10. Split retainer
11. Spring retainer
12. Valve spring
13. Valve seal
14. Valve guide
15. Plugs
16. Cylinder head
17. Seat insert
18. Seat insert
19. Exhaust valve
20. Intake valve

the black wire in the module four-pin connector and each of the three remaining wires. Voltage at the three wires must be the same. If not, check for faulty wire or pulsar.

CYLINDER HEAD

The cylinder head is removable with the engine in the tractor. To remove the head, drain the engine coolant and disconnect the battery cables. Remove the exhaust manifold, water pump, carburetor, ignition coils and spark plugs. Remove the rocker arm cover, rocker arms and push rods. Mark the rocker arms and push rods so they can be returned to their original position. Remove the cylinder head screws and lift the head off the engine. Remove the intake manifold.

Inspect the cylinder head. The head gasket surface must be flat within 0.10 mm (0.004 in.), otherwise machine the surface. Maximum thickness that may be removed is 0.2 mm (0.008 in.). Check valve recession if the head is machined.

When installing the cylinder head refer to Fig. Y110 for screw tightening sequence. Tighten the cylinder head screws in several steps to final torque of 34 N·m (25 ft.-lb.).

VALVE SYSTEM

The valves are located in the cylinder head. When disassembling the valve components, mark the parts as they are removed so they can be installed in their original positions if reused. Valve seats (17 and 18—Fig. Y111) and guides (14) are replaceable.

Intake valve face and seat angles should be 30°. Exhaust valve face and seat angles should be 45°. Intake valve seat width should be 1.14 mm (0.045 in.). Exhaust valve seat width should be 1.37 mm (0.054 in.). Minimum valve margin is 0.51 mm (0.020 in.). Minimum valve stem diameter is 5.40 mm (0.213 in.).

Maximum allowable valve guide inside diameter is 5.57 mm (0.219 in.). Guide may be knurled if valve stem-to-guide clearance exceeds 0.15 mm (0.006 in.) but is less than 0.20 mm (0.008 in.). Replace the valve or guide if clearance is 0.20 mm (0.008 in.) or greater.

Use a suitable driver to remove and install guides. Install the guide so the grooved end is up. Valve guide standout above the valve spring seating surface is 7 mm (0.276 in.). Ream the new guide to obtain the desired clearance after installation.

Valve spring pressure should be 125 N (28 lb.) at a length of 17 mm (0.669 in.) for both intake and exhaust. Minimum valve spring length is 27.59 mm (1.083 in.). Install the spring so the end with paint mark (less distance between coils at end) is next to the head.

Maximum push rod runout measured with the push rod supported at the ends is 0.30 mm (0.012 in.). Minimum rocker shaft diameter is 9.9 mm (0.390 in.). Maximum rocker arm inner diameter is 10.1 mm (0.398 in.). Maximum rocker shaft support inner diameter is 10.1 mm (0.398 in.).

When reassembling, install the new valve stem seals (13). Note that the center rocker shaft support (8—Fig. Y111) is located on the rocker shaft by a setscrew (9).

FLYWHEEL AND STUB SHAFT

Remove the engine for access to the flywheel. Remove the PTO clutch assembly. Remove the flywheel housing (1—Fig. Y112). Unscrew the retaining cap screws and remove the stub shaft (3) and flywheel (4).

Stub shaft runout should not exceed 0.2 mm (0.008 in.). Mounting surfaces of the flywheel and stub shaft should be flat within 0.05 mm (0.002 in.).

The flywheel retaining cap screws should not be reused. Install new flywheel cap screws and tighten to 83 N·m (61 ft.-lb.). Tighten the stub shaft screws to 59 N·m (43 ft.-lb.). Tighten the flywheel housing 10 mm screws to 49 N·m (36 ft.-lb.) and 8 mm screws to 26 N·m (230 in.-lb.).

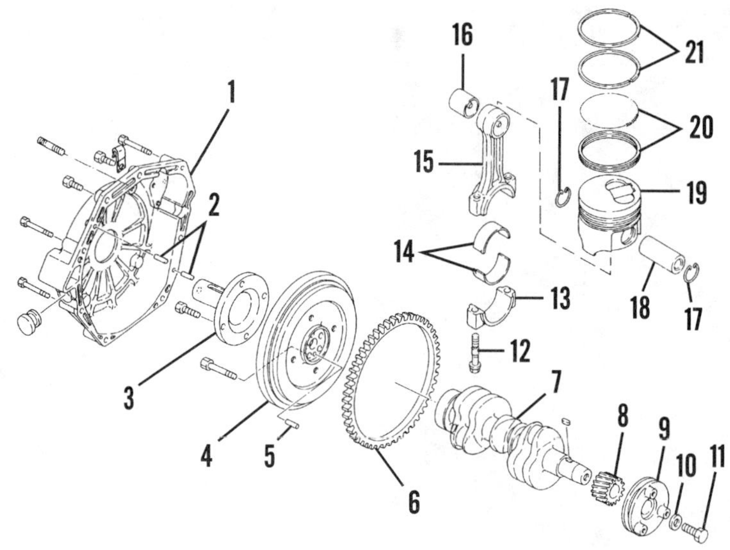

Fig. Y112—Exploded view of crankshaft, piston and rod assemblies.

1. Flywheel housing
2. Dowel pins
3. Stub shaft
4. Flywheel
5. Dowel pin
6. Ring gear
7. Crankshaft
8. Gear
9. Drive pulley
10. Washer
11. Screw
12. Rod bolt
13. Rod cap
14. Crankpin bearing insert
15. Connecting rod
16. Bushing
17. Snap rings
18. Piston pin
19. Piston
20. Oil ring
21. Compression rings

PISTON, PIN, RINGS AND CONNECTING ROD

To remove the piston and connecting rod units, remove the engine from the tractor. Remove the PTO clutch, flywheel, starter, pulsars, rear mounting plate, cylinder head and oil pan. Be sure to remove the ring ridge, if present, from the top of the cylinder before removing the piston. Mark the piston, connecting rod and rod cap so they can be returned to their original position. Remove the rod cap and push the piston and rod unit out of the cylinder block.

Inspect the pistons for cracks, scoring or scuffing and replace when necessary. To check the piston ring grooves for wear, first carefully clean any deposits from the ring grooves. Insert new rings in the piston grooves and use a feeler gauge to measure the side clearance between the ring and ring land. Replace the piston if the side clearance exceeds 0.25 mm (0.010 in.) for all rings.

Minimum allowable piston diameter, measured at the bottom of the skirt and perpendicular to the piston pin, is 65.85 mm (2.593 in.). The maximum allowable standard cylinder bore diameter is 66.12 mm (2.603 in.). The maximum allowable piston-to-bore clearance is 0.15 mm (0.006 in.). Pistons and rings are available in standard size and 0.25 mm oversize.

Maximum allowable ring end gap for the compression rings is 1.30 mm (0.051 in.). Maximum end gap for the oil ring is 1.80 mm (0.071 in.).

Maximum allowable pin bore in the piston is 20.1 mm (0.791 in.). Minimum allowable piston pin diameter is 19.9 mm (0.783 in.). Maximum allowable clearance between the pin and piston bore is 0.10 mm (0.004 in.).

Maximum allowable small end diameter of the connecting rod is 20.1 mm (0.791 in.). Maximum allowable clearance between the pin and connecting rod bushing is 0.15 mm (0.006 in.). The small end bushing is replaceable.

Maximum allowable big end bearing inside diameter is 36.07 mm (1.420 in.). Minimum allowable crankpin diameter is 35.93 mm (1.415 in.). Maximum allowable crankpin bearing clearance is 0.12 mm (0.005 in.). Crankpin may be reground to accept 0.25 mm undersize rod bearing. Maximum allowable rod side clearance on crankshaft is 0.8 mm (0.031 in.).

Manufacturer recommends discarding the used connecting rod screws. Assemble the connecting rod and piston so the depression (D—Fig. Y113) in the piston crown is on the side opposite of the bearing locating groove (G) in the rod.

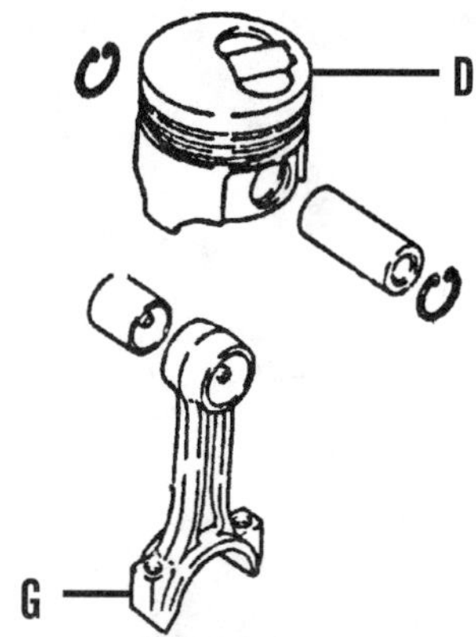

Fig. Y113—Assemble connecting rod and piston so depression (D) in piston crown is on side opposite of bearing locating groove (G) in rod.

Install the oil ring expander in the piston ring groove so the ends are located above either end of the piston pin. Install the oil ring so the ends are on the opposite side from the expander ends.

Install the second compression ring so the inside chamfer is towards the piston crown and the end gap is positioned 120° away from the oil ring end gap. Install the top piston ring so the marked side is towards the piston crown and the end gap is 120° away from the second ring end gap.

Lubricate the piston, rings, cylinder and crankpin bearing with engine oil. Use a suitable ring compressor tool to compress the piston rings and install the piston and rod assembly in the cylinder. Lubricate the crankpin bearing insert with engine oil, then install the rod cap with the tangs on the cap and connecting rod on the same side. Install new rod cap screws and tighten them to 23 N.m (203 in.-lb.).

TIMING GEARS, GEAR COVER AND HOUSING

Remove the engine from tractor for access to the gear housing. Remove the fan, alternator belt and alternator. Unscrew the crankshaft retaining screw, and using a suitable puller remove the crankshaft pulley. Detach the timing gear cover.

Fig. Y114—View showing location of timing gears. Note timing marks (M) on crankshaft, idler and camshaft gears that must align for correct valve timing.

C. Crankshaft gear
G. Governor gear
I. Idler gear
P. Oil pump gear
T. Camshaft gear

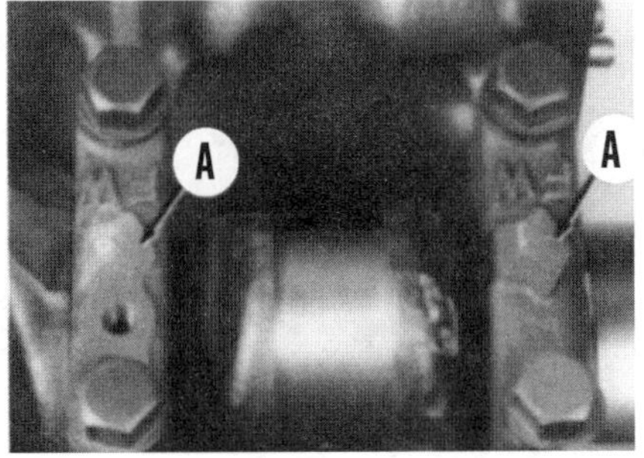

Fig. Y115—Arrow (A) on main bearing cap must point towards flywheel end of crankshaft.

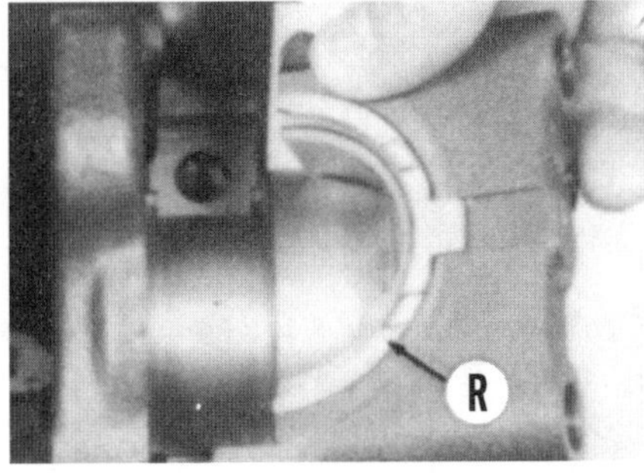

Fig. Y116—Install thrust ring (R) on main bearing cap so tab indexes in notch of cap and oil grooves face outward.

Refer to Fig. Y114 for timing gear identification. The camshaft and crankshaft gears are pressed onto their respective shafts. Note the timing marks (M) on the crankshaft, idler and camshaft gears that must align during installation.

Specified gear backlash is 0.2 mm (0.008 in.) for the camshaft, crankshaft and idler gears; 0.3 mm (0.012 in.) for oil pump gear; 0.38 mm (0.015 in.) for governor gear. Replace the gear if backlash is greater than specified.

The idler gear rides on a stub shaft attached to the cylinder block. Maximum allowable inside diameter of the idler gear bushing is 20.08 mm (0.790 in.). The bushing is replaceable. Minimum allowable idler shaft diameter is 19.9 mm (0.783 in.). Maximum allowable clearance is 0.1 mm (0.004 in.).

To remove the gear housing, remove all interfering geared components. Note that the camshaft must be removed as the gear is pressed on shaft. Remove the screws attaching the housing to the engine and remove the housing.

When installing the gear housing, tighten the mounting screws to 9 N·m (80 in.-lb.) if the housing is aluminum, or to 11 N·m (97 in.-lb.) if the housing is iron.

Install the timing cover crankshaft seal so the lip is towards the inside of the cover. Tighten the cover retaining screws to 9 N·m (80 in.-lb.).

CAMSHAFT AND LIFTERS

To remove the camshaft, remove the engine from the tractor. Remove the rocker arm cover. Remove the push rods and mark them so they can be returned to original position. Remove the cylinder head if the lifters (tappets) are to be removed. Remove the timing gear cover.

Prior to removing the camshaft, measure the camshaft end play. If end play is greater than 0.5 mm (0.020 in.), replace the thrust plate. Remove the screws securing the camshaft retainer. If the lifters were not removed, use suitable magnetic tools to hold the lifters away from the camshaft or tilt the engine so the lifters move away from the camshaft. Withdraw the camshaft from the engine.

Minimum allowable camshaft bearing journal diameter is 35.84 mm (1.411 in.) for end journals and 35.81 mm (1.410 in.) for the two inner journals. Minimum allowable lobe height is 29.7 mm (1.169 in.). Maximum bushing diameter in the block is 36.115 mm (1.4218 in.) for front bushing (nearest timing gears) and 36.075 mm (1.4203 in.) for inner and rear bushings. Maximum allowable camshaft bearing clearance is 0.18 mm (0.007 in.). Camshaft bushings are replaceable and must be installed so the oil hole aligns with the oil hole in the cylinder block.

Minimum allowable lifter diameter is 17.85 mm (0.703 in.). Maximum lifter bore diameter in the block is 18.1 mm (0.713 in.). Maximum allowable lifter clearance is 0.1 mm (0.004 in.). The lifters should be replaced if a new camshaft is installed.

If necessary to remove the camshaft gear, use a suitable press. Heat the gear to 150°C (300°F) before pressing the gear on the camshaft.

When installing the camshaft be sure to align the timing marks (M—Fig. Y114. Tighten the camshaft retainer plate screws to 10-12 N·m (89-106 in.-lb.).

CRANKSHAFT AND MAIN BEARINGS

To service the crankshaft, remove the engine from the tractor. Remove the cylinder head, oil pan and pistons and connecting rods. Remove the timing gears, timing gear housing, flywheel, starter, ignition pulsars and engine mounting plate. Remove the rear oil seal case.

Measure the crankshaft end play before disassembly. Maximum allowable end play is 0.30 mm (0.012 in.).

Mark the bearing caps prior to removal so they can be reinstalled in their original position. Notice that the arrow (A—Fig. Y115) on the cap points towards the flywheel end of the crankshaft.

Minimum allowable main bearing journal diameter is 39.93 mm (1.572 in.). Maximum bearing inside diameter is 40.93 mm (1.611 in.). Maximum allowable bearing clearance is 0.12 mm (0.005 in.). Main bearings are available in standard size and 0.25 mm (0.010 in.) undersize.

Crankshaft thrust is controlled by replaceable thrust rings located at the front main bearing web. If the crankshaft end play is excessive, install new thrust rings. Install thrust rings so the oil grooves face out and the tabs on the bottom rings index in notches on the bearing cap as shown in Fig. Y116.

If necessary to remove the crankshaft gear, use a suitable press. Heat the gear to 150°C (300°F) before pressing the gear on the crankshaft.

Lubricate the main bearing inserts with engine oil. Be sure that main bearing caps are installed in their original locations (caps and cylinder block are numbered). Lubricate the main bearing cap screws with engine oil, then tighten the screws to 54 N·m (40 ft.-lb.). Make certain the crankshaft turns freely as the main bearing cap screws are tightened.

Install a new oil seal in the seal retainer so the lip of the seal is towards the engine. The seal should be installed flush with the outer surface of the oil seal retainer. However, if the crankshaft flange is grooved at the original oil seal contact point, the new seal may be pressed 3 mm (1/8 in.) farther into the retainer so that the seal lip will contact an unworn portion of the crankshaft. Tighten the oil seal retainer cap screws to 11 N·m (97 in.-lb.).

When installing the timing gears be sure to align the timing marks (M—Fig. Y114).

GOVERNOR

The governor assembly is driven by the governor gear (G—Fig. Y114). The flyweight assembly is mounted on the back of the timing gear housing. To remove the governor unit, remove the engine from the tractor. Remove the timing gear cover and unscrew the special bolt (27—Fig. Y117) retaining the governor gear (25). Detach the governor linkage, unscrew the governor housing retaining screws and withdraw the governor housing (16) and linkage assembly.

Remove the screws retaining the bearing flange (23) and remove the governor weight assembly from the timing gear housing. Remove the two screws from the governor lever yoke (17), then remove the governor lever (9), spacer (13) and ball (14) from the governor housing. Drive the oil seal (12) from the housing if necessary.

Minimum allowable diameter of the governor shaft (19) is 7.90 mm (0.311 in.). Maximum allowable inside diameter of the flyweight carrier (22) is 8.15 mm (0.321 in.). Maximum allowable clearance between the shaft and bore is 0.18 mm (0.007 in.).

Inspect the governor weights (20) and pivot pins (21) for excessive wear and replace when necessary. The weights must pivot freely on the pins.

Bearings (24) are pressed on the carrier (22). Specified backlash for the governor gear is 0.38 mm (0.015 in.). Replace the gear if backlash is greater than specified.

To reassemble, reverse the disassembly procedure. Adjust the governor linkage as outlined in the MAINTENANCE section.

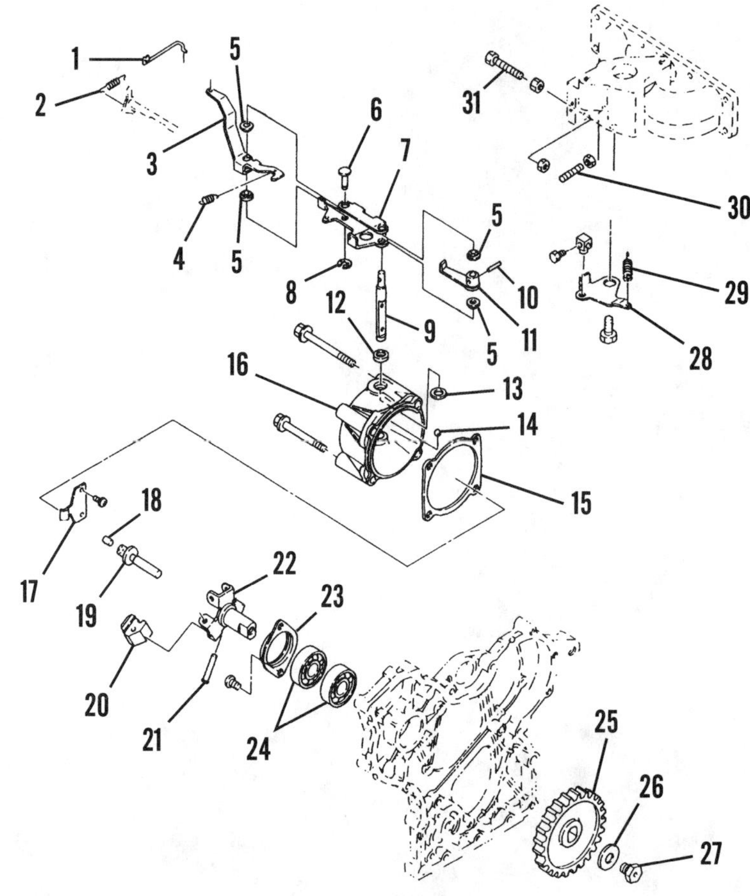

Fig. Y117—Exploded view of governor linkage and flyweights.

1. Carburetor link
2. Spring
3. Governor lever
4. Spring
5. Washers
6. Pin
7. Bracket
8. E-ring
9. Governor lever
10. Pin
11. Arm
12. Oil seal
13. Washer
14. Ball
15. Gasket
16. Governor housing
17. Yoke
18. Pin
19. Governor shaft
20. Flyweight
21. Pin
22. Flyweight carrier
23. Flange
24. Bearings
25. Governor gear
26. Washer
27. Special bolt

OIL PUMP

A gerotor oil pump is located on the front of the engine and driven by the crankshaft gear.

To check the oil pressure, remove the oil pressure switch from the side of the cylinder block and connect an oil pressure gauge. With the engine at operating temperature and running at half throttle setting, the oil pressure should be 294-440 kPa (43-64 psi).

The oil pressure relief valve is located in the oil filter nipple (1—Fig. Y118). To remove the nipple, remove the oil filter, loosen the nut (N) and unscrew the nipple from the cylinder block. Unscrew the plug (5) for access to the valve components.

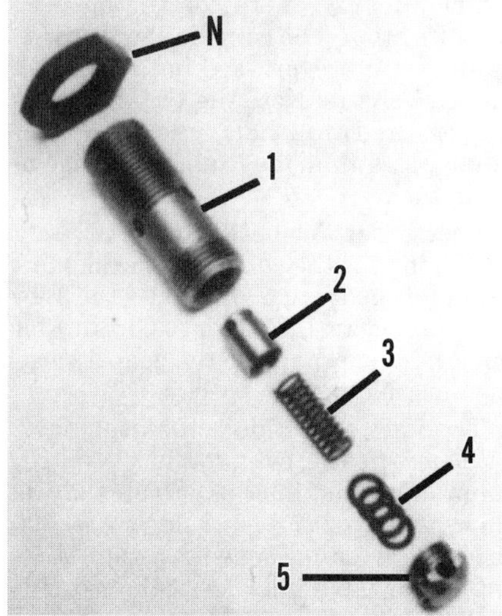

Fig. Y118—Exploded view of relief valve assembly contained in oil filter nipple.

N. Nut
1. Nipple
2. Relief valve
3. Spring
4. Shims
5. Plug

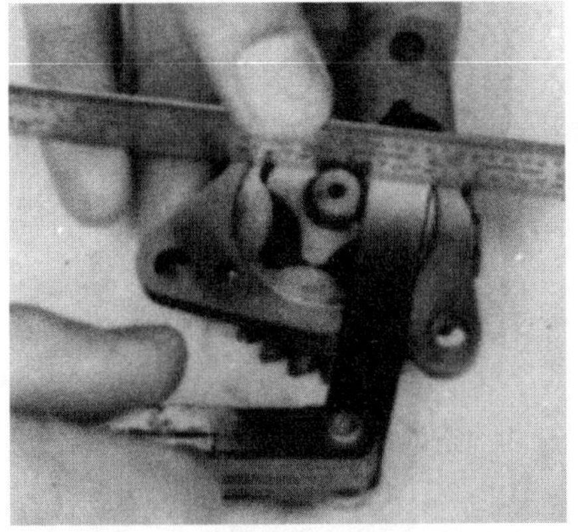

Fig. Y119—Pump rotors must be no more than 0.25 mm (0.010 in.) below face of pump body.

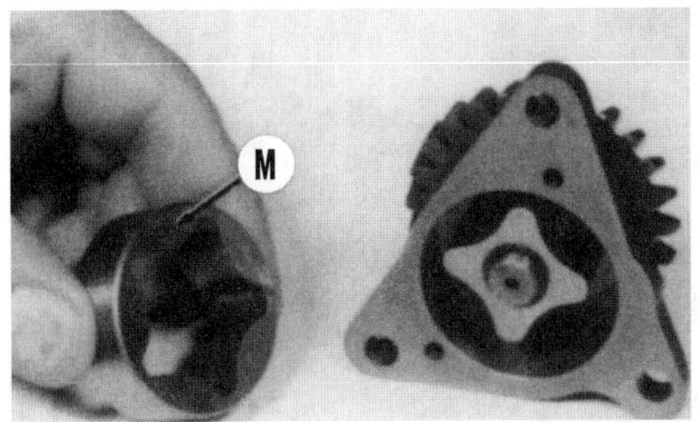

Fig. Y121—Install outer rotor so mark (M) is toward inside of pump.

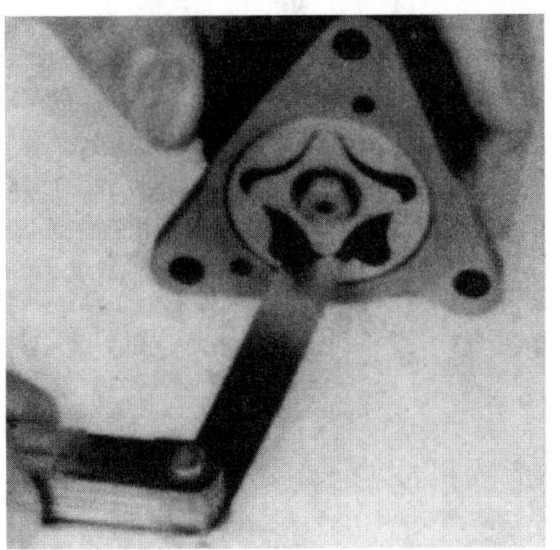

Fig. Y120—Maximum allowable clearance between inner rotor tip and outer rotor lobe is 0.25 mm (0.010 in.).

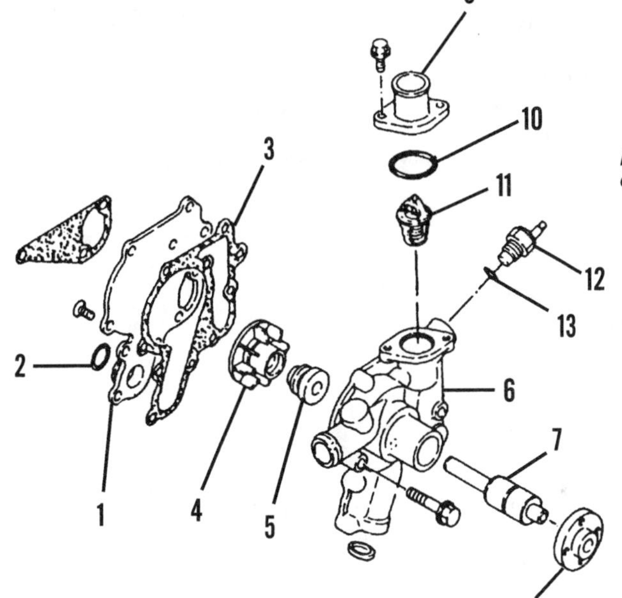

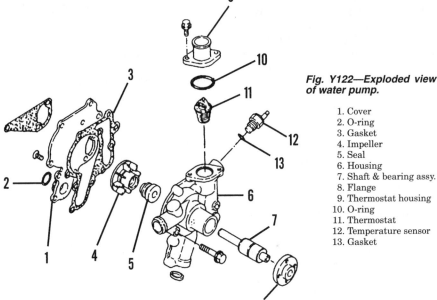

Fig. Y122—Exploded view of water pump.

1. Cover
2. O-ring
3. Gasket
4. Impeller
5. Seal
6. Housing
7. Shaft & bearing assy.
8. Flange
9. Thermostat housing
10. O-ring
11. Thermostat
12. Temperature sensor
13. Gasket

Relief valve pressure setting may be adjusted by adding or deleting shims (4). Spring free length should be 21.9-24.5 mm (0.862-0.965 in.). Compressed spring length should be 14.7 mm (0.579 in.) at 12 N (2.7 lb.).

Remove the timing gear cover for access to the oil pump. Specified oil pump drive gear backlash is 0.3 mm (0.012 in.). Replace the gear if the backlash is greater than specified.

Oil pump rotors must be no more than 0.25 mm (0.010 in.) below the face of the pump (see Fig. Y119). Maximum allowable clearance between the outer pump rotor and pump body is 0.25 mm (0.010 in.). Maximum allowable clearance between the inner rotor tip and outer rotor lobe is 0.25 mm (0.010 in.) as shown in Fig. Y120.

Pump drive gear is pressed onto the pump shaft. Install the outer rotor so the mark (M—Fig. Y121) is towards the inside of the pump. Tighten the oil pump retaining screws to 11 N·m (97 in.-lb.).

WATER PUMP AND THERMOSTAT

Thermostat (11—Fig. Y122) is located in the water pump coolant outlet. To remove the thermostat, drain the coolant and remove the thermostat cover (9).

The thermostat should start to open at 71°C (160°F) and be fully open at 85°C (184°F).

To remove the water pump, detach the drive belt and remove the fan. Unbolt and remove the water pump from the engine.

To disassemble pump, use a suitable puller and remove the pulley flange (8—Fig. Y122). Detach the rear cover (1). Support the housing (6) and press the shaft (7), seal (5) and impeller (4) as an assembly out the impeller end of the housing. Press the impeller off shaft.

When assembling the pump, press the shaft and bearing assembly (7) into the housing so the outer face of the bearing is flush with the front of the housing. To prevent possible damage to the bearing, be sure to use a suitable bearing driver tool that contacts only the outer race of the bearing.

Press the seal (5) into the housing until bottomed. Support the rear of the shaft and press the pulley flange (8) onto the front of the shaft until the outer face of the flange is flush with the end of the shaft. Install the ceramic seal into the impeller, making certain that the lapped sealing surface of the insert is clean and dry. Press the impeller onto the shaft so the outer face of the impeller and the end of the shaft are flush.

Tighten the cover screws to 9 N·m (80 in.-lb.). Tighten the thermostat housing screws to 9 N·m (80 in.-lb.). Tighten the water pump mounting screws to 26 N·m (230 in.-lb.). Tighten the fan screws to 11 N·m (97 in.-lb.).

ELECTRIC STARTER

Starter no-load current draw should be 60 amps or less at starter speed of 7000 rpm. Starter current draw under load should be 230 amps at starting rpm.

Refer to Fig. Y123 for an exploded view of the electric starter. Place alignment marks on the pinion housing, frame and end cover before disassembly so they can be reinstalled in their original position.

To disassemble the starter, disconnect the solenoid wire. Remove the through-bolts and retaining screws from the end cover. Pry the plastic cap (18) from the end cover (14). Remove the E-ring (17), shims (16) and end cover.

Pry the springs away from the negative brushes, pull the brushes up and release the springs to hold the brushes in this position. Remove the field coil brushes from the brush holder, then remove the brush holder (13) from the field housing. Separate the field coil housing from the armature.

Remove the screws retaining the solenoid and withdraw the solenoid assembly and armature from the housing. Push the pinion stop (4) downward, remove the retaining ring (3) and withdraw the clutch assembly (5) from the armature shaft.

Inspect all components for wear or damage. Brush length wear limit is 7.7 mm (0.030 in.).

Use an ohmmeter or test light to test the armature for grounded or open windings. There should not be continuity between the commutator and armature shaft. There should be continuity between two different commutator bars.

To test for short-circuited winding, use an armature growler.

Use an ohmmeter or test light to check the field winding for grounded or open winding. There should not be continuity between the field coil brush and field frame. There should be continuity between the two field brushes.

To reassemble the starter, reverse the disassembly procedure.

ALTERNATOR

To check alternator unregulated voltage output, disconnect the two-pin connector from the alternator. Use a voltmeter set at 100 volts ac to measure voltage across the alternator connector terminals. With the engine running at fast throttle, the alternator should produce a minimum voltage reading of 30 volts AC.

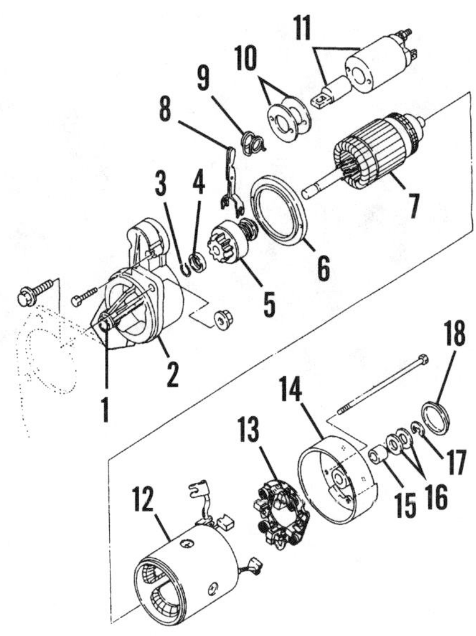

Fig. Y123—Exploded view of starter motor.

1. Sleeve
2. Drive end frame
3. Snap ring
4. Retainer
5. Drive pinion & clutch assembly
6. Cover
7. Armature
8. Shift lever
9. Spring
10. Shims
11. Solenoid assy.
12. Field coil assy.
13. Brush holder
14. End cover
15. Sleeve
16. Washers
17. E-ring
18. Cap

To disassemble the alternator, unscrew the nut (2) and tap the end of the shaft screw (13) to separate the rotor (11) from the housing (5). Press against the end of the shaft screw to force the shaft out of the bearing (8) and rotor. Remove the harness clamp screw and remove the connector from the wiring harness (1). Remove the stator mounting screws and remove the stator (6) from the housing.

Replace the rotor if the magnets are loose or damaged. Check the stator for indications of burned wiring or other damage and replace when necessary.

Fig. Y124—Exploded view of alternator.

1. Wiring harness
2. Nut
3. Washer
4. Bearing
5. Housing
6. Stator
7. Spacer
8. Bearing
9. Spacer
10. Washer
11. Rotor
12. Pulley half
13. Shaft

To reassemble, reverse the disassembly procedure. When installing the shaft screw, note that the pulley half (12) must bottom against the rotor (11) and the bearing (8) must bottom against the spacer (9). Bearing (4) must be discarded if removed. Install the new bearing (4) so it bottoms in the housing. Tighten the nut (2) to 27 N·m (20 ft.-lb.).

VOLTAGE REGULATOR/RECTIFIER

The voltage regulator/rectifier should provide 18 amps direct current at 13.5-15 volts at full engine speed. Rectifier/regulator is available only as a unit assembly.

YANMAR

Model	No. Cyls.	Bore	Stroke	Displ.	Power Rating
3TN66UJ	3	66 mm (2.60 in.)	64.2 mm (2.53 in.)	658 cc (40.15 cu. in.)	11.9 kW (16 hp.)
3TNA72UJ	3	72 mm (2.83 in.)	72 mm (2.83 in.)	879 cc (53.64 cu. in.)	15 kW (20 hp.)
3TNA72UJ3	3	72 mm (2.83 in.)	72 mm (2.83 in.)	879 cc (53.64 cu. in.)	16.4 kW (22 hp.)

NOTE: In the following text, 3TNA72UJ(3) applies to Models 3TNA72UJ and 3TNA72UJ3 unless otherwise indicated.

ENGINE IDENTIFICATION

The Yanmar 3TN66UJ, 3TNA72UJ and 3TNA72UJ3 are four-stroke, three-cylinder, water-cooled, indirect injection diesel engines. The camshaft is located in the cylinder block. Valves in the cylinder head are operated through push rods and rocker arms. Number 1 cylinder is at the flywheel end of the engine and the firing order is 1-3-2. The engine identification plate is located on the rocker cover.

MAINTENANCE

LUBRICATION

Use engine oil with an API classification CD. Select oil viscosity depending on the expected ambient temperature range as shown on temperature chart in Fig. Y150.

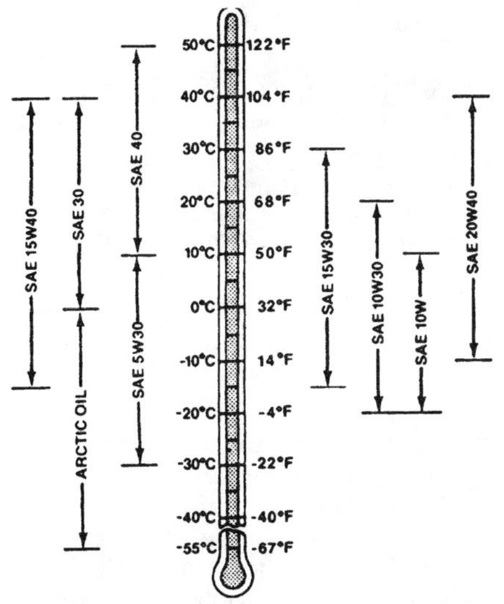

Fig. Y150—Select engine oil viscosity according to expected ambient air temperature range.

Recommended oil change interval is after every 200 hours of use. Oil filter is a spin-on paper element cartridge. On new and reconditioned engines, lubricating oil and filter should be changed after first 50 hours of operation.

AIR FILTER

The air filter should be cleaned after every 200 hours of operation or more frequently if operating in extremely dusty conditions.

Remove the dust from the filter element by tapping lightly with your hand, not on a hard surface. Compressed air at pressure under 30 psi (210 kPa) may also be directed inside the filter element, but be careful not to damage the element. Replace the filter once a year or when necessary.

WATER PUMP BELT

Adjust belt tension so the belt will deflect approximately 13 mm (½ inch) when moderate thumb pressure is applied to the belt midway between the pump and alternator pulleys. Reposition the alternator to adjust the belt tension.

COOLING SYSTEM

Drain, flush and refill the cooling system annually. The manufacturer recommends using low silicate antifreeze not containing stop leak additive. Refer to the tractor section for the cooling system capacity.

A thermostat is used to maintain the cooling system temperature. The manufacturer recommends replacing the thermostat annually.

THERMOSTAT

The thermostat is mounted in the water pump housing. To remove the thermostat, drain the cooling system and unbolt the water outlet from the top of the water pump housing.

The thermostat should start to open at 71°C (160°F) and be fully open at 85°C (185°F).

When installing the thermostat, be sure all gasket surfaces are clean and use a new gasket and sealing ring. Tighten the thermostat housing cap screws to 26 N·m (19 ft.-lb.).

FUEL FILTER

Models 3TN66UJ and 3TNA72UJ3

A replaceable paper element fuel filter (1—Fig. Y151) is located between the fuel feed pump and fuel injection pump. Water and sediment should be drained from the filter bowl (7) after every 50 hours of operation or as necessary.

To drain the water and sediment, unscrew the retaining ring (8) and remove the bowl and filter assembly. Clean the cover and reinstall the filter assembly. Loosen the vent screw (3) and turn the key switch to the ON position to activate the fuel feed pump. When fuel flows from the vent screw, tighten the screw and turn the key switch to the OFF position.

The filter element should be replaced annually, or sooner if loss of engine power is evident. Filter element may be removed and installed as outlined above. Be sure to bleed the air from the fuel system before attempting to start the engine.

Model 3TNA72UJ

A replaceable paper element fuel filter (1—Fig. Y152) is used between the fuel feed pump and fuel injection pump. Water and sediment should be drained from filter after 50 hours of operation or when necessary.

To drain water and sediment from the filter, raise the hood and remove the shield from the left side of the engine. Loosen the vent screw (3) and place the end of the filter drain hose in a container. Loosen the drain screw (7) and allow water and fuel to drain, then tighten the drain screw. With the vent screw still loose, turn the key switch to the ON position to activate the fuel feed pump, but do not start the engine. When fuel flows from the vent screw, tighten the vent screw and turn the key switch to the OFF position.

The filter element should be replaced annually, or sooner if the loss of power is evident. To replace the filter, loosen the vent screw (3) and drain screw (7) and allow all fuel to drain from the filter. Release the filter clamps (2) and remove the filter element (1). Install the new element and close the drain screw.

Air must be bled from the system after the new filter is installed. Turn the key switch to the ON position to activate the fuel feed pump. When air-free fuel begins to flow from the vent screw, tighten the vent screw and turn the key switch to the OFF position.

BLEED FUEL SYSTEM

Air must be bled from the fuel system after servicing any part of the fuel system. To bleed air from the fuel system, first loosen the bleed screw (3—Fig. Y151 or Fig. Y152) on the filter housing. Turn the key switch to the ON position to activate the fuel feed pump. When air-free fuel flows from the bleed screw, tighten the screw.

Loosen the bleed screw (9—Fig. Y151) on the fuel injection pump fuel inlet fitting. When air-free fuel flows from the bleed screw, tighten the screw and turn the key switch to the OFF position.

If the engine will not start, loosen the fuel injector line fittings at the injectors and crank the engine until fuel flows from all lines. Tighten the injector line fittings and start the engine.

VALVE ADJUSTMENT

Adjust the valve clearance with the engine cold. Specified clearance is 0.2 mm (0.008 in.) for both intake and exhaust valves.

Remove the rocker arm cover to access the rocker arms and valves. Adjust the valve clearance by loosening the locknut and turning the adjusting screw at the push rod end of the rocker arm until a 0.2 mm (0.008 in.) thick feeler gauge is a tight slip fit between the end of the valve stem and the rocker arm pad.

To adjust the valves, turn crankshaft in normal direction of rotation so that number 1 piston is at top dead center (Fig. Y153) on the compression stroke. Number 1 cylinder is at the flywheel end of the engine. Adjust the intake and exhaust valves on the number 1 cylinder. Continue to turn the crankshaft until the next piston in the firing order (1-3-2) is at top dead center on compression stroke and adjust the valves for that cylinder in the same manner. Repeat the procedure for each cylinder in the firing order.

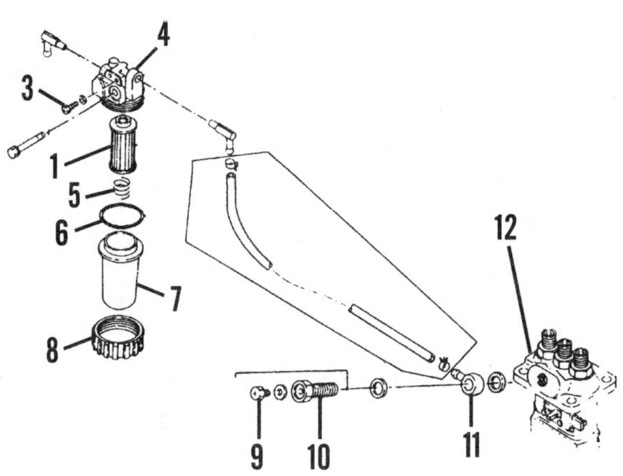

Fig. Y151—Exploded view of fuel filter assembly used on 3TN66UJ engine. Model 3TNA72UJ3 is similar, but the housing is also equipped with a fuel shutoff valve and bleed screw (3) is located above valve.

1. Filter element
3. Bleed screw
4. Filter housing
5. Spring
6. Gasket
7. Filter bowl
8. Retaining ring
9. Bleed screw
10. Fuel inlet fitting
11. Fuel inlet line
12. Injection pump

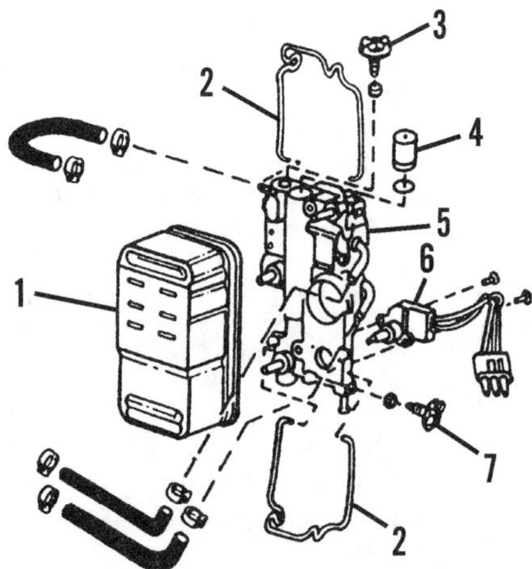

Fig. Y152—Exploded view of fuel filter assembly used on 3TNA72UJ engine.

1. Filter element
2. Clamps
3. Bleed screw
4. Heater core
5. Filter base
6. Water-in-fuel sensor
7. Drain screw

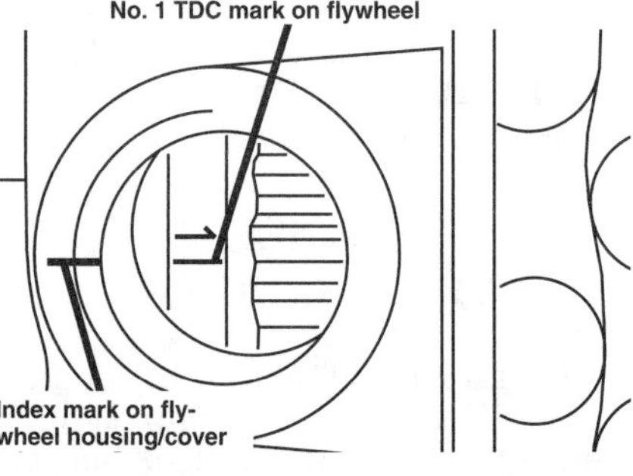

Fig. Y153—View of timing marks on flywheel. Number 1 cylinder top dead center mark is identified by "1" while injection timing mark is identified by "13." Refer to text to check injection timing.

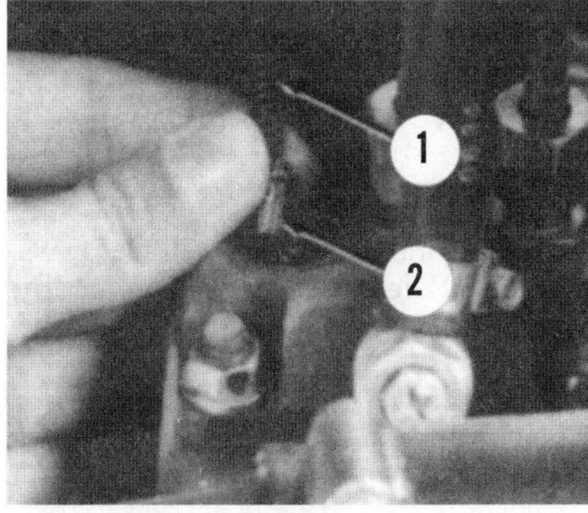

Fig. Y154—To check fuel injection pump timing, remove delivery valve spring (1) and valve (2) from number 1 cylinder fuel injection discharge fitting. Refer to text.

INJECTION PUMP TIMING

Timing of the fuel injection pump is accomplished by varying the thickness of shims installed between the injection pump and mounting surface of the engine front cover.

To check the injection pump timing, thoroughly clean the injector, injector line and pump and remove the fuel injection line to the number 1 cylinder, the cylinder at the flywheel end of the engine. Remove the number 1 delivery valve holder, delivery valve spring (1—Fig. Y154) and delivery valve (2), then reinstall the holder. Connect JDF-14 spill pipe adapter or other suit-

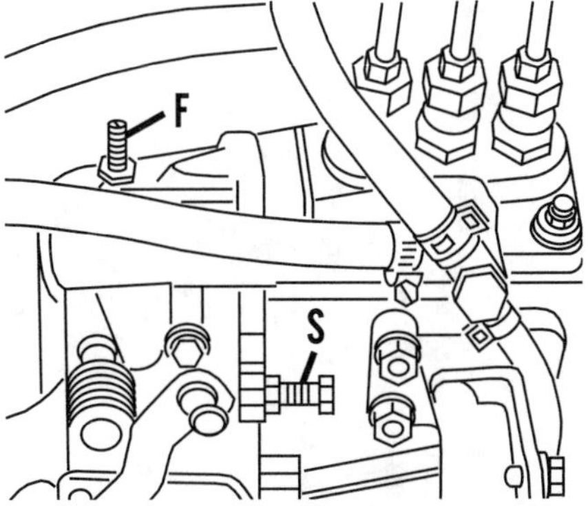

Fig. Y155—View showing location of fast idle speed screw (F) and slow idle speed screw (S).

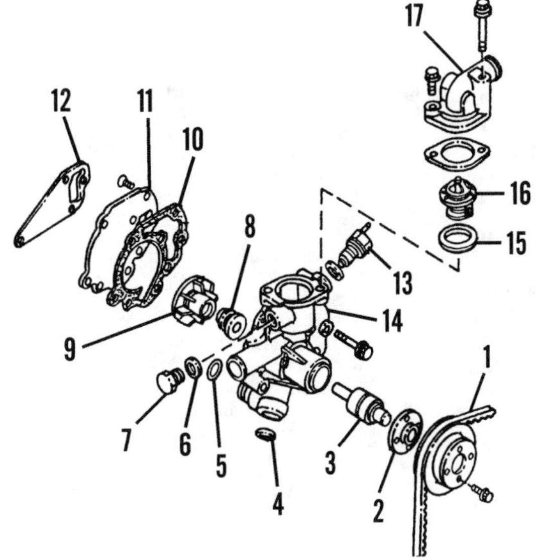

Fig. Y156—Exploded view of water pump assembly used on Model 3TNA72UJ. Water pump used on Model 3TN66UJ and 3TNA72UJ3 is similar. On Model 3TNA72UJ3, a temperature switch replaces plug (7).

1. Pulley
2. Hub
3. Shaft & bearing assy.
4. Plug
5. "O" ring
6. Gasket
7. Plug/switch
8. Seal
9. Impeller
10. Gasket
11. Plate
12. Gasket
13. Temperature sender
14. Pump housing
15. Gasket
16. Thermostat
17. Outlet elbow

able spill pipe to the delivery valve holder.

Turn the flywheel in normal direction until the number 1 piston TDC timing mark, the mark next to the number 1 as shown in Fig. Y153, on the flywheel aligns with the timing index mark. Turn the key switch to the RUN position, but do not start the engine.

Turn the flywheel clockwise approximately 90° and note that fuel should be flowing from the number 1 open delivery valve. Turn the flywheel slowly counterclockwise so that the number 1 piston is starting up on the compression stroke and observe the fuel flow from the open fuel delivery valve. The fuel flow should change to drops and then stop. Just as the fuel stops, stop turning the flywheel and check the injection timing mark, the mark next to number 13, on the flywheel.

Note that if fuel does not stop flowing, the number 1 piston is on the exhaust stroke instead of the compression stroke. Turn the flywheel one complete revolution and repeat the test.

If the timing mark is not aligned with the timing index mark, repeat the check several times to be sure you are observing the fuel flow correctly. If the injection timing is not correct, remove the injection pump and adjust the timing as follows:

If the timing mark has not reached the timing index mark when fuel stops flowing, retard the injection timing by increasing the total thickness of shims under the injection pump. If the timing mark has passed the timing index mark, advance the timing by decreasing the thickness of the pump mounting shims.

Changing the shim thickness 0.2 mm (0.008 in.) will change the position of the flywheel timing mark about 4.5 mm (0.180 in.).

Install the thickest shim against the injection pump and the thinnest shim against the timing gear housing. Tighten the pump mounting bolts and recheck the timing.

When the injection pump timing is within specifications, install the fuel delivery valve and spring using a new bronze gasket. Tighten the delivery valve holder to a torque of 42 N·m (31 ft.-lb.). Install fuel the injection line and bleed the air from the line before tightening the fitting at the injector.

GOVERNOR

The governor is located within the fuel injection pump camshaft housing on all models. The low idle speed should be 1650 rpm. Engine governed fast idle no-load speed should be 3600-3670 rpm for 3TN66UJ engines and 3400-3450 rpm for 3TNA72UJ(3) engines.

The fast idle adjusting screw (F—Fig. Y155) is located on top of the governor housing and the slow idle adjusting screw (S) is located on the side of the governor housing.

REPAIRS

TIGHTENING TORQUE

Refer to the following special tightening torque specifications:

Connecting rod bolts . . . . 23 N·m (203 in.-lb.)
Crankshaft pulley bolt . . . . 115 N·m (85 ft.-lb.)
Cylinder head bolts—
3TN66UJ . . . . 34 N·m (25 ft.-lb.)
3TNA72UJ(3) . . . . 61 N·m (45 ft.-lb.)
Exhaust manifold—
3TN66UJ . . . . 11 N·m (8 ft.-lb.)
3TNA72UJ(3) . . . . 26 N·m (19 ft.-lb.)
Flywheel bolts . . . . 83 N·m (61 ft.-lb.)
Injection pump . . . . 20 N·m (177 in.-lb.)
Injector nozzle nut . . . . 40 N·m (30 ft.-lb.)
Injector . . . . 50 N·m (37 ft.-lb.)
Intake manifold . . . . 11 N·m (97 in.-lb.)
Main bearing bolts—
3TN66UJ . . . . 54 N·m (40 ft.-lb.)
3TNA72UJ(3) . . . . 79 N·m (58 ft.-lb.)
Rocker arm cover nuts . . . . 18 N·m (160 in.-lb.)
Rocker arm shaft . . . . 26 N·m (19 ft.-lb.)
Timing gear housing bolts—
Aluminum housing . . . . 9 N·m (80 in.-lb.)
Cast iron housing . . . . 11 N·m (97 in.-lb.)
Water pump mounting bolts . . . . . . 26 N·m (19 ft.-lb.)

WATER PUMP AND COOLING SYSTEM

To remove the water pump, first drain the cooling system. Remove engine the side panels and grille. Loosen the alternator mounting and brace to remove the fan belt. Disconnect the coolant hoses from the pump. Disconnect the coolant temperature sender wire. Unbolt and remove water pump assembly.

To disassemble, unbolt and remove the thermostat housing (17—Fig. Y156) and thermostat (16). Remove temperature sender (13). Remove belt pulley (1), then use a suitable puller to remove pulley flange (2). Remove cover plate (11). Press the shaft and bearing assembly (3) back from the pump housing. Press the shaft out of the impeller (9).

To reassemble, press the new bearing and shaft, longer end of shaft first, into the pump housing from the front until bearing is flush with front surface of pump housing. Support impeller end of shaft, then press the pulley flange onto the shaft until the flange is flush with the end of the shaft. Press the new shaft seal (8) into the housing bore. Install a new ceramic insert in the impeller, being careful not to touch the lapped surface of the insert. Press the impeller onto the shaft until the top of the impeller is flush with the end of the shaft. Install the cover, pulley, thermostat and housing, and temperature sender.

Reinstall water pump and tighten mounting cap screws to 26 N·m (19 ft.-lb.). Adjust belt tension so the belt deflects about 13 mm (½ inch) when moderate thumb pressure is applied midway between the pump and alternator pulleys.

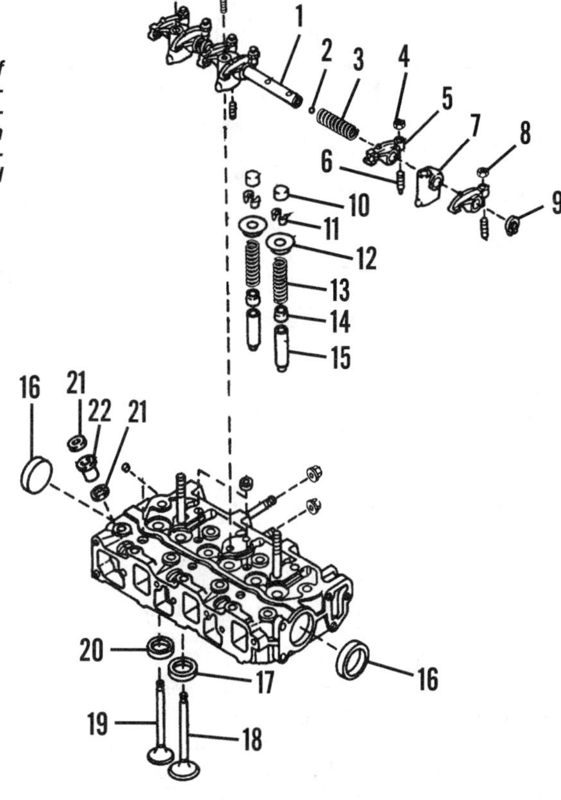

Fig. Y157—Exploded view of cylinder head and valve mechanism used on 3TNA72UJ(3) engine. Cylinder head used on 3TN66UJ engine is similar except valve seat inserts (17 and 20) are not used.

1. Rocker shaft
2. Ball
3. Spring
4. Locknut
5. Rocker arm, exhaust
6. Adjusting screw
7. Support
8. Rocker arm, intake
9. Snap ring
10. Valve caps
11. Split retainer
12. Spring seat
13. Valve spring
14. Seal
15. Valve guide
16. Plugs
17. Valve seat
18. Intake valve
19. Exhaust valve
20. Valve seat
21. Gaskets
22. Teflon seal

ROCKER ARMS AND PUSH RODS

Rocker arm shaft assembly (Fig. Y157) and push rods can be removed after removing the rocker arm cover. Rocker arms for all cylinders pivot on a full-length shaft that is held by support brackets attached to the cylinder head by cap screws. All valve train components should be identified as they are removed so they can be reinstalled in their original locations if reused.

The rocker shaft diameter should be 9.97-9.99 mm (0.3925-0.3933 in.) with a wear limit of 9.96 mm (0.392 in.) on Model 3TN66UJ. The specified rocker shaft diameter is 11.966-11.984 mm (0.471-0.472 in.) with a wear limit of 11.96 mm (0.471 in.) on Model 3TNA72UJ(3).

The rocker arm inside diameter should be 10.00-10.02 mm (0.3937-0.3945 in.) with a wear limit of 10.09 mm (0.397 inch) for Model 3TN66UJ, and 12.00-12.02 mm (0.4724-0.4732 in.) with a wear limit of 12.09 mm (0.476 in.) on Model 3TNA72UJ(3). Clearance between the rocker arm and shaft should not exceed 0.13 mm (0.005 in.) on any model engine.

Check the push rods for distortion by rolling them on a flat plate. Replace any that are bent or if the ends are galled, worn or chipped. The push rod length is 114-115 mm (4.488-4.528 in.) on Model 3TN66UJ and 141-142 mm (5.551-5.590 in.) on Model 3TNA72UJ(3).

On all models, loosen the rocker arm adjustment screw locknuts and back the screws (6) out before installing the push rods, rocker arm supports and rocker arms. Tighten the rocker arm support bolts to a torque of 26 N·m (19 ft.-lb.) on all models. Adjust the valves as previously outlined and install the rocker arm cover.

CYLINDER HEAD

To remove the cylinder head, drain the engine coolant and proceed as follows: Remove the intake and exhaust manifolds, water pump, fuel injectors, glow plugs, rocker arm cover, rocker arm assembly and push rods. Remove the cylinder head bolts and lift the cylinder head from the engine.

Before installing the cylinder head, thoroughly clean the head and block gasket surfaces and inspect the head for cracks, distortion or other defects. If alignment dowels (roll pins) were removed with the head, pull the pins from the head and install in the cylinder block.

Check the cylinder head gasket surface with a straightedge and feeler gauge. The head must be reconditioned or replaced if distortion (warp or twist) exceeds 0.15 mm (0.006 in.). A maximum of 0.20 mm (0.008 in.) of material may be removed from the cylinder head gasket surface.

Place a new head gasket on the block with the trademark or engine model number up and locate the gasket on the two roll pins. Place the cylinder head on the block so the two roll pins enter the matching holes in the head. Lubricate the bolt threads with engine oil. Tighten the head bolts in three steps in the sequence shown in Fig. Y158 until a final torque of 34 N·m (25 ft.-lb.) for Model 3TN66UJ or 61 N·m (45 ft.-lb.) for Model 3TNA72UJ(3) is reached.

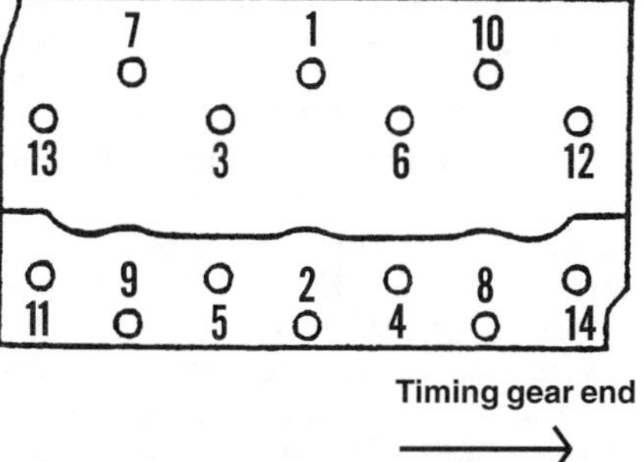

Fig. Y158—Cylinder head bolt tightening sequence for all engines.

Complete the installation of the cylinder head by reversing the removal procedure. Yanmar recommends retorqueing the cylinder head bolts after the first 50 hours of operation.

VALVE SYSTEM

Valves seat directly in the cylinder head on Model 3TN66UJ. The cylinder

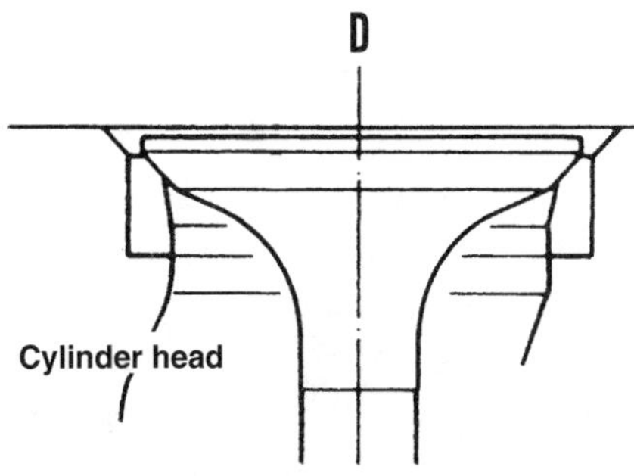

Fig. Y159—Top of valve head should be below cylinder head surface. Refer to text for specifications.

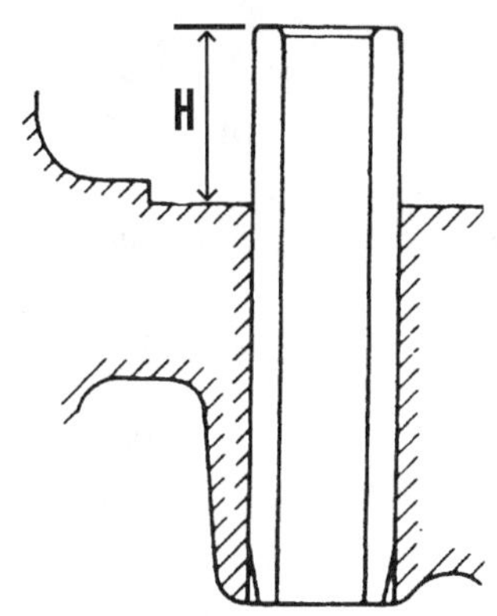

Fig. Y160—Valve guides must be installed to specified height (H) as outlined in text.

head on Model 3TNA72UJ(3) is equipped with replaceable valve seats. On all engines, valve seat and face angle is 30° for intake valves and 45° for exhaust valves. Recondition the exhaust seats using 45, 60 and 30° stones and recondition the intake seats using 30, 60 and 15° stones. Valve seat width specifications are as follows:

Model 3TN66UJ

Intake valve seat—

Desired width . . . . 1.15 mm (0.045 in.)

Maximum width . . . . 1.65 mm (0.065 in.)

Exhaust valve seat—

Desired width . . . . 1.41 mm (0.056 in.)

Maximum width . . . . 1.91 mm (0.075 in.)

Model 3TNA72UJ(3)

Intake valve seat—

Desired width . . . . 1.44 mm (0.057 in.)

Maximum width . . . . 1.98 mm (0.078 in.)

Exhaust valve seat—

Desired width. . . . . 1.77 mm (0.070 in.)

Maximum width . . . . 2.27 mm (0.089 in.)

After reconditioning the valve seats, check the distance (D—Fig. Y159) the valve head is below the cylinder head surface. The standard valve head recess distance for Model 3TN66UJ is 0.40 mm (0.016 in.) for the intake and 0.85 mm (0.033 in.) for the exhaust valve. Model 3TNA72UJ(3) intake valve recess should be 0.50 mm (0.020 in.) and the exhaust valve recess should be 0.85 mm (0.034 in.). If the valve head recess is 1.0 mm (0.039 in.) or more, install new valves, valve seats on Model 3TNA72UJ(3), and/or the cylinder head.

If new valve seats are installed, grind the new seats to the proper seat width and check to be sure the correct valve recess is maintained.

Refer to the following valve stem specifications:

Model 3TN66UJ

Intake valve stem OD. . . . . 5.460-5.475 mm (0.215-0.216 in.)

Wear limit . . . . 5.40 mm (0.213 in.)

Exhaust valve stem OD . . . 5.445-5.460 mm (0.214-0.215 in.)

Wear limit . . . . 5.40 mm (0.213 in.)

Model 3TNA72UJ(3)

Intake valve stem OD. . . . . 6.945-6.960 mm (0.273-0.274 in.)

Wear limit . . . . 6.90 mm (0.272 in.)

Exhaust valve stem OD . . . 6.945-6.960 mm (0.273-0.274 in.)

Wear limit . . . . 6.90 mm (0.272 in.)

Check the valve guides against the following specifications and replace any guides with excessive wear. When installing new guides, drive the old guide out toward the top of the head using a suitable piloted driver.

Install the new guide with a piloted driver so that the distance from the spring seat surface of the cylinder head to the top of the guide (H—Fig. Y160) is 7 mm (0.276 in.) for Model 3TN66UJ or 9 mm (0.354 in.) for Model 3TNA72UJ(3). Refer to the valve guide specifications in the following table:

Model 3TN66UJ

Guide ID . . . . 5.50-5.51 mm (0.2165-0.217 in.)

Wear limit . . . . 5.58 mm (0.220 in.)

Model 3TNA72UJ(3)

Guide ID . . . . 7.005-7.020 mm (0.2758-0.2764 in.)

Wear limit . . . . 7.08 mm (0.279 in.)

After installing new guides, measure the inside diameter of the guide and if necessary, use a suitable reamer to obtain the proper fit of the valve stem to the guide. The valve seats should be refaced so they are concentric with the new guides.

Intake and exhaust valve springs are alike on all models. Spring free length should be 28 mm (1.102 in.) for Model 3TN66UJ. Spring free length should be 37.4 mm (1.472 in.) for Model 3TNA72UJ(3). Be sure to install the springs with the closer spaced coils next to the cylinder head.

INJECTORS

Removal and Installation

Prior to removing the injectors, thoroughly clean the injectors, injector lines, fuel injection pump and surrounding area using suitable solvent and compressed air. Remove the fuel injection lines from the injection pump and injectors. Remove the fuel return line from the top of the injectors. Cap all openings to prevent entry of dirt. Unscrew the fuel injectors from the cylinder head. Remove the gaskets and Teflon seal from the bottom of the injector bores in the cylinder head if they did not come out with the injectors.

When installing the fuel injectors, first be sure the injector bores in the cylinder head are clean and all old seals are removed. Insert new bronze gaskets and the Teflon seals in the injector bores and install the injectors. Tighten the injector to a torque of 50 N·m (37 ft.-lb.).

Bleed air from the injector lines before tightening the high-pressure fuel line fittings at the injector end.

Testing

A complete job of testing, cleaning and adjusting the fuel injector requires use of special test equipment. Use only clean approved testing oil in the tester tank. Injector should be tested for opening pressure, seat leakage and spray pattern. Before connecting the injector to the test stand, operate the tester lever until oil flows, then attach the injector to the tester line.

WARNING: Fuel emerges from the injector with sufficient force to penetrate the skin. When testing the injector, keep clear of the nozzle spray.

Close the valve to the tester gauge and operate the tester lever a few quick strokes to purge air from the injector and to be sure the nozzle valve is not stuck.

Opening Pressure

Open the valve to the tester gauge and operate the tester lever slowly while observing gauge reading. Opening pressure should be 11242-12200 kPa (1630-1770 psi).

Opening pressure is adjusted by changing the thickness of the shim stack (4—Fig. Y161). Increasing shim thickness will increase the opening pressure.

Spray Pattern

The spray pattern should be conical, well atomized, and emerging in a straight axis from nozzle tip. If the spray is drippy, ragged or to one side, the nozzle must be cleaned or replaced.

Seat Leakage

Wipe the nozzle tip dry with clean blotting paper, then slowly actuate the tester lever to obtain a gauge pressure approximately 1960 kPa (285 psi) below the opening pressure and hold this tester pressure for 10 seconds. If a drop of oil appears at the nozzle tip, or oil drips from the nozzle, clean or replace the nozzle.

Overhaul

Hard or sharp tools, emery cloth, grinding compounds or other than approved tools, solvents and lapping compounds, must never be used. Wipe all dirt and loose carbon from the injector, then refer to Fig. Y161 and proceed as follows:

Secure the injector nozzle in the holding fixture or soft-jawed vise and loosen the nut (10). Unscrew the nut and remove the internal parts (4-9) from the injector. Be careful not to lose the shims (4). Place all parts in clean diesel fuel or calibrating oil as they are removed, and take care not to mix parts with those from other injector assemblies.

Clean exterior surfaces with a brass wire brush to loosen carbon deposits. Soak parts in approved carbon solvent if necessary. Rinse parts in clean diesel fuel or calibrating oil after cleaning to neutralize the carbon solvent.

Clean the nozzle spray hole from the inside using a pointed hardwood stick. Scrape carbon from the nozzle pressure chamber using a hooked scraper. Clean the valve seat using brass scraper.

Inspect the nozzle valve (8) and body (9) for scratches or wear. Be sure the nozzle valve slides smoothly in the nozzle body bore. The nozzle valve should slide down into the nozzle body by its own weight. If the valve sticks in the nozzle body, reclean or replace the nozzle assembly.

Reclean all parts by rinsing thoroughly in clean diesel fuel or calibrating oil and assemble the injector while immersed in fuel or oil. Be sure the shim stack is intact, then install the shims (4), spring (5), spring seat (6), stop plate (7), nozzle valve assembly (8 and 9) and the nozzle nut (10).

Tighten the nozzle nut to a torque of 40 N·m (30 ft.-lb.). Do not overtighten the nozzle nut in an attempt to stop any leakage. Disassemble and clean the injector if a leak is noted. Retest the assembled injector.

INJECTION PUMP

Thoroughly clean the pump, fuel injectors, lines and surrounding area using suitable solvent and compressed air. Disconnect the fuel return line from the injectors and remove the high pressure fuel injection lines.

Plug all openings to prevent entry of dirt. Remove the cover and fuel shut-off solenoid from the side of the fuel injection pump camshaft housing. Pull out the governor link snap pin and disconnect the governor link from the pump control rack. Remove the pump retaining screws and lift the pump from the top of the timing gear housing.

Only a qualified fuel injection repair shop should service the fuel injection pump.

To install the injection pump, reverse the removal procedure using the same pump mounting shims as were removed. Do not tighten the fuel injection line fittings at the injectors until air has been bled from the lines. Bleed air from the fuel system and check the injection pump timing as outlined in the MAINTENANCE section.

TIMING GEAR COVER

To remove the timing gear cover, the engine must be removed from the tractor. Remove the alternator, fan if equipped and the crankshaft pulley. Unbolt and remove the cover from the front of the engine.

Thoroughly clean the timing cover and mounting gasket surfaces. Install a new crankshaft oil seal with the lip to the inside and lubricate the seal with oil or grease. Apply a bead of silicone gasket material on the front cover mounting surface.

Install the timing cover on the engine, aligning the holes in the cover with the two hollow alignment dowel pins in the front of the engine. Tighten the retaining cap screws to 9 N·m (80 in.-lb.).

Clean the crankshaft pulley hub and apply lubricant on the seal contact surface. Install the crankshaft pulley and tighten the retaining bolt to 115 N·m (85 ft.-lb.).

To complete reassembly of the engine, reverse the removal procedure.

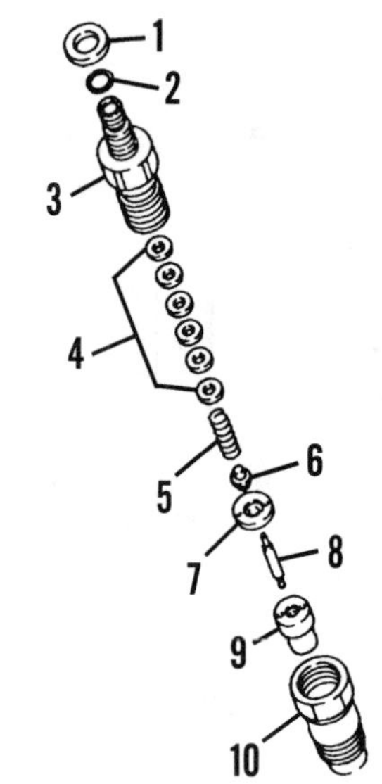

Fig. Y161—Exploded view of throttling pintle type fuel injector used on all engines.

1. Bronze gasket
2. O-ring
3. Nozzle holder
4. Shims
5. Spring
6. Spring seat
7. Stop plate
8. Nozzle needle
9. Nozzle body
10. Nozzle nut

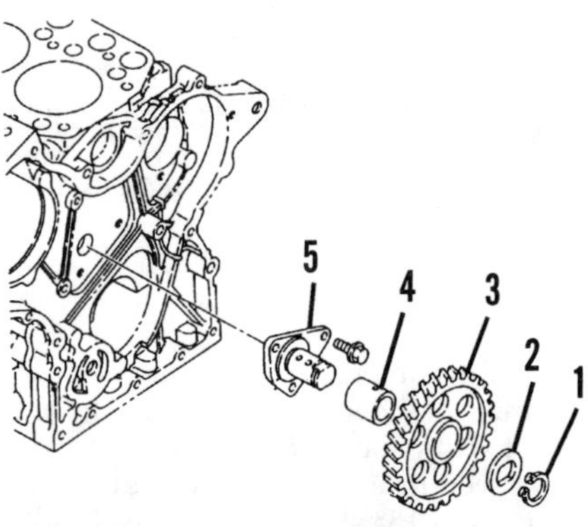

Fig. Y162—Idler gear (3) is mounted on stub shaft (5).

1. Snap ring
2. Washer
3. Idler gear
4. Idler gear bushing
5. Stub shaft

TIMING GEARS

The timing gears can be inspected after removing the timing gear cover. Standard backlash between mating timing gears is 0.04-0.12 mm (0.0016-0.0047 in.); maximum allowable backlash is 0.2 mm (0.008 in.). Check the gear teeth for excessive wear or tooth damage and replace when necessary. If necessary to replace the gears, remove the valve cover, rocker arm assembly and the push rods to relieve valve spring pressure on the camshaft.

To remove the idler gear and shaft, refer to Fig. Y162 and remove the snap ring (1), washer (2) and gear (3).

Fig. Y163—Engine is correctly "timed" when timing marks on idler gear are aligned with marks on injection pump camshaft gear (A), crankshaft gear (B) and engine camshaft gear (C). Timing gears shown are for 3TN66UJ engine; timing gears on 3TNA72UJ(3) engine have single marks instead of double marks.

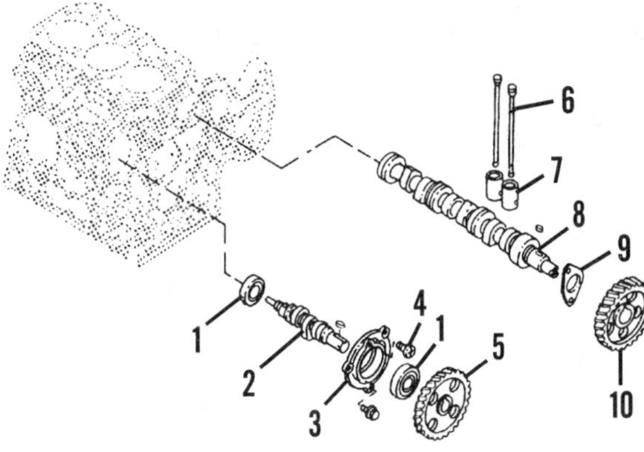

Fig. Y164—Exploded view of engine camshaft and fuel injection pump camshaft assemblies.

1. Bearing
2. Fuel injection pump camshaft
3. Bearing case
4. Bearing retaining screw
5. Gear
6. Push rods
7. Cam followers
8. Engine camshaft
9. Thrust plate
10. Gear

Stub shaft (5) is bolted to the cylinder block. Idler stub shaft diameter should be 19.959-19.980 mm (0.786-0.787 in.) and wear limit is 19.93 mm (0.785 in.). Specified bushing (4) to idler shaft oil clearance is 0.020-0.062 mm (0.001-0.002 in.) with maximum allowable clearance of 0.15 mm (0.006 in.). Replace the bushing (4) if worn and the idler gear (3) is otherwise serviceable.

To remove the crankshaft gear, engine camshaft gear or injection pump camshaft gear, it is recommended that the shafts be removed from the engine as the gears are a press fit on their respective shafts.

When installing the timing gears, be sure all timing marks are aligned as shown in Fig. Y163.

INJECTION PUMP CAMSHAFT

The engine must be removed from the tractor in order to remove the injection pump camshaft (2—Fig. Y164). Remove the fuel injection pump and timing gear cover. Remove the governor housing and governor flyweight assembly from the rear of the camshaft as outlined in the GOVERNOR section. Remove the idler gear. Remove the screw retaining the camshaft front bearing through the hole in the camshaft gear. Remove the camshaft and bearings from the engine.

Inspect the camshaft and bearings for wear or other damage and replace when necessary. Minimum allowable camshaft lobe height is 30.9 mm (1.217 in.) for all engines.

Install the camshaft in the timing gear housing, being careful not to damage the cam lobes or journals. Tighten the bearing retaining screw to 20 N·m (15 ft.-lb.). Install the governor flyweight assembly and governor housing. Install the idler gear, aligning the timing marks as shown in Fig. Y163.

Install the timing gear cover and tighten the retaining screws to 9 N·m (80 in.-lb.). Install the fuel injection pump, bleed air from the fuel system and check and adjust injection timing as outlined in MAINTENANCE section.

CAMSHAFT AND BEARINGS

The engine must be removed from the tractor in order to remove the engine camshaft. The camshaft (8—Fig. Y164), gear (10) and thrust plate (9) can be removed from the cylinder block after removing the timing cover, valve cover, rocker arm assembly and push rods.

Use magnetic tools to lift the cam followers away from the camshaft or invert the engine so the followers fall away from the cam. Remove the camshaft thrust plate retaining bolts through the web holes in the camshaft gear and pull the camshaft from the cylinder block.

If necessary to replace the camshaft, thrust plate or gear, carefully press the shaft from the plate and gear.

Camshaft end play in the block is controlled by the thrust plate. End play should be 0.05-0.15 mm (0.002-0.006 in.). Replace the thrust plate if end play exceeds 0.40 mm (0.016 in.); also check the thrust surface wear on the timing gear and camshaft.

The camshaft journal at the timing gear end of the engine rides in a replaceable bushing in the cylinder block, while the other journals ride directly in unbushed bores of block. Replace the camshaft bushing if oil clearance is 0.18 mm (0.007 in.) or more. Camshaft journal to unbushed block bore maximum oil clearance is also 0.18 mm (0.007 in.).

Refer to the following camshaft specifications:

Model 3TN66UJ

Journal OD (gear end)—
- Standard . . . . 35.94-35.96 mm (1.415-1.416 in.)
- Wear limit . . . . 35.85 mm (1.411 in.)

Journal OD (intermediate and flywheel end)—
- Standard . . . . 35.91-35.94 mm (1.414-1.415 in.)
- Wear limit . . . . 35.85 mm (1.411 in.)

Bushing ID—
- Standard . . . . 36.00-36.065 mm (1.417-1.420 in.)
- Wear limit . . . . 36.10 mm (1.421 in.)

Block bores ID—
- Standard . . . . 36.00-36.025 mm (1.417-1.418 in.)
- Wear limit . . . . 36.10 mm (1.421 in.)

Journal clearance (gear end)—
- Standard . . . . 0.040-0.125 mm (0.0016-0.0049 in.)
- Wear limit . . . . 0.18 mm (0.007 in.)

Journal clearance (intermediate and flywheel end)—
- Standard . . . . 0.065-0.115 mm (0.0026-0.0045 in.)
- Wear limit . . . . 0.18 mm (0.007 in.)

Cam lobe height—
- Standard . . . . 29.97-30.03 mm (1.180-1.182 in.)
- Wear limit . . . . 29.70 mm (1.169 in.)

Model 3TNA72UJ(3)

Journal OD (gear and flywheel ends)—
- Standard . . . . 39.94-39.96 mm (1.572-1.573 in.)
- Wear limit . . . . 39.85 mm (1.569 in.)

Journal OD (intermediate)—
- Standard . . . . 39.910-39.935 mm (1.571-1.572 in.)
- Wear limit . . . . 39.85 mm (1.569 in.)

Bushing ID—
- Standard . . . . 40.00-40.065 mm (1.575-1.577 in.)
- Wear limit . . . . 40.10 mm (1.579 in.)

Block bores ID—
Standard............. 40.00-40.065 mm (1.575-1.577 in.)
Wear limit.................. 40.10 mm (1.579 in.)
End journal clearance—
Standard............. 0.040-0.085 mm (0.0016-0.0033 in.)
Wear limit................... 0.18 mm (0.007 in.)
Intermediate journal clearance—
Standard.............. 0.065-0.115 mm (0.0026-0.0045 in.)
Wear limit................... 0.18 mm (0.007 in.)
Cam lobe height—
Standard............. 33.95-34.05 mm (1.337-1.341 in.)
Wear limit.................. 33.75 mm (1.329 in.)

To remove the cam followers (7—Fig. Y163), the cylinder head must first be removed. Be sure to identify each cam follower and its position in the cylinder block so they can be reinstalled in the same bore from which they were removed.

The cam follower standard diameter is 17.95-17.968 mm (0.7067-0.7074 in.) and the wear limit is 17.93 mm (0.706 in.) for Model 3TN66UJ. Cam follower standard diameter is 20.927-20.960 mm (0.824-0.825 in.) and the wear limit is 20.93 mm (0.824 in.) for Model 3TNA72UJ(3). The cam follower-to-bore clearance should not exceed 0.10 mm (0.004 in.) for Model 3TN66UJ and 0.15 mm (0.006 in.) for Model 3TNA72UJ(3).

Inspect the cam follower face for uneven wear, scuffing, pitting or other damage and replace when necessary. If the camshaft is replaced, the cam followers should also be replaced.

GOVERNOR

To remove the governor assembly, first remove the fuel shut-off solenoid and cover from the side of the timing gear cover. Remove the pin (9—Fig. Y165) and disconnect the governor link (10) from the injection pump rack. Unbolt and remove the governor linkage housing (8) from the rear of the timing gear housing. Remove the governor sleeve (15) and flyweight assembly (17, 18 and 19) from the rear of the injection pump camshaft. Remove the governor linkage from the housing as necessary.

Inspect all parts for wear or damage and replace when necessary.

To reassemble, reverse the removal procedure. Check and adjust engine slow and fast idle speeds as outlined in the MAINTENANCE section.

OIL PUMP AND RELIEF VALVE

The gerotor oil pump (Fig. Y166) is mounted on the front of the engine timing gear housing and the gear on the pump shaft is driven from the crankshaft gear.

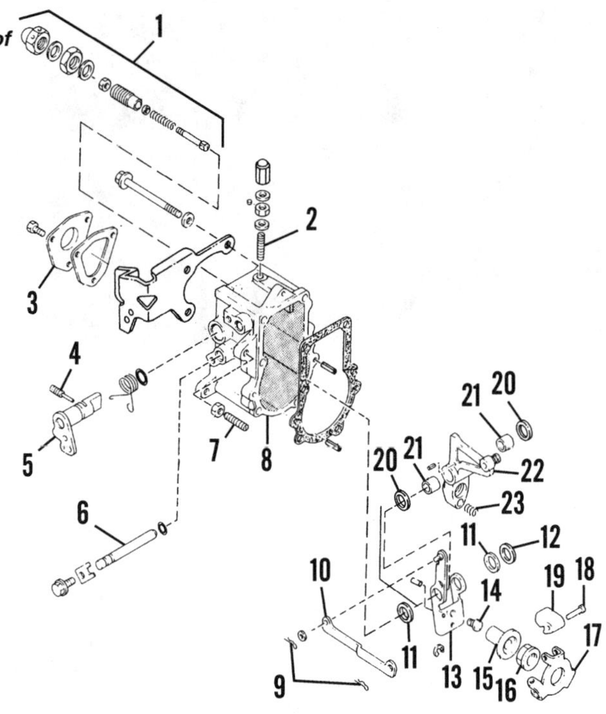

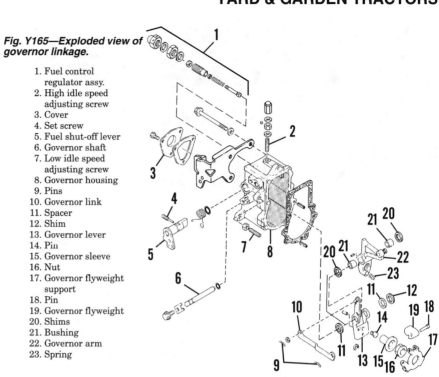

Fig. Y165—Exploded view of governor linkage.

1. Fuel control regulator assy.
2. High idle speed adjusting screw
3. Cover
4. Set screw
5. Fuel shut-off lever
6. Governor shaft
7. Low idle speed adjusting screw
8. Governor housing
9. Pins
10. Governor link
11. Spacer
12. Shim
13. Governor lever
14. Pin
15. Governor sleeve
16. Nut
17. Governor flyweight support
18. Pin
19. Governor flyweight
20. Shims
21. Bushing
22. Governor arm
23. Spring

To remove the pump, first remove the timing gear cover, then unbolt and remove the pump from the front of the engine. The pump rear plate (3) can then be removed from the pump body to inspect the pump.

Clearance between the outer rotor and pump body should be 0.10-0.17 mm (0.004-0.007 in.) with a wear limit of 0.25 mm (0.010 in.). Clearance between the lobes of the inner and outer rotors should be 0.05-0.1 mm (0.002-0.004 in.) with maximum allowable clearance being 0.25 mm (0.010 in.).

Rotor end clearance in the pump body should be 0.03-0.09 mm (0.0012-0.0035 in.) and maximum end clearance is 0.25 mm (0.010 in.).

Check for looseness of the drive shaft in the pump body and replace the pump if loose or wobbly.

When assembling the pump, lubricate all parts with clean engine oil. Be sure the outer rotor is installed with the punched marked side toward the inside of the pump housing (7).

To reinstall the pump, reverse the removal procedure. Tighten the mounting screws to 25 N·m (18 ft.-lb.).

The system pressure relief valve, located on the back side of oil filter mounting adapter (4—Fig. Y167), regulates oil pressure to 295-434 kPa (43-63 psi). Valve pressure setting may be adjusted by removing the cap (12) from the end of the valve and adding shims (11). Increasing shim thickness 1 mm (0.039 in.) will increase the oil pressure approximately 13.8 kPa (2.0 psi) on Model 3TN66UJ and 10.9 kPa (1.6 psi) on Model 3TNA72UJ(3).

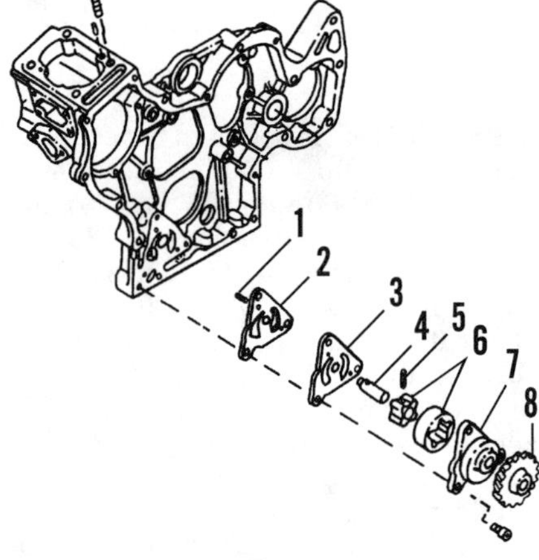

Fig. Y166—Exploded view of engine oil pump.

1. Dowel pin
2. Gasket
3. End cover
4. Pump shaft
5. Drive pin
6. Inner & outer rotors
7. Pump housing
8. Drive gear

PISTON AND ROD UNITS

The engine must be removed from the tractor to remove the pistons and connecting rods. Piston and rod units are removed from above after removing the PTO electric clutch, flywheel assembly, oil pan, oil pump pickup tube and the cylinder head. Be sure to remove the ridge (if present) from the top of the cylinders prior to removing the

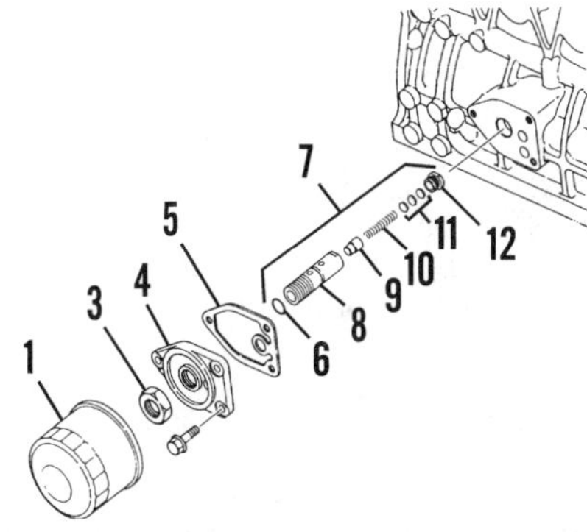

Fig. Y167—Oil pressure relief valve (7) is located on back side of oil filter base. If disassembled, be sure valve retainer (12) is securely staked to adapter body (8).

1. Oil filter
3. Hex nut
4. Filter base
5. Gasket
6. O-ring
7. Relief valve assy.
8. Adapter body
9. Relief valve poppet
10. Spring
11. Adjusting shims
12. Valve retainer

Fig. Y168—Identification mark on piston crown (1) must be on same side as identification marks on connecting rod (2) and face injection pump side of engine when installed in cylinder block.

pistons. Keep the rod bearing cap with its matching connecting rod.

To install the piston and rod units, be sure that recess in the top of the piston (1—Fig. Y168) is on the same side as the identification mark (2) on the connecting rod and that the marks face toward the fuel injection pump side of the engine.

Lubricate cylinder wall, crankpin, piston and rings and rod bearing with engine oil. Place ring end gaps at equal spacing at 120° around piston. Install the piston and rod unit using a suitable ring compressor.

Do not reuse the connecting rod bolts. Lubricate the connecting rod bolt threads with engine oil and tighten the bolts to 23 N·m (203 in.-lb.).

PISTONS, PINS, AND RINGS

Pistons are fitted with two compression rings and one oil control ring with a coil expander under the oil ring. The piston pin is full floating and is retained by a snap ring at the each end of the pin bore in the piston. If necessary to remove the piston from the connecting rod, remove the snap rings and push the pin from the piston and rod.

Inspect the piston skirt for scoring, cracks and excessive wear. Measure the piston skirt at a right angle to the pin bore and at a distance of 5 mm (0.2 in.) from the bottom edge of the skirt on Model 3TN66UJ, 8 mm (0.3 in.) on Model 3TNA72UJ(3). Piston skirt standard diameter for Model 3TN66UJ is 65.927-65.957 mm (2.596-2.597 in.) and wear limit is 65.85 mm (2.593 in.). Piston skirt standard diameter for Model 3TNA72UJ(3) is 71.922-71.952 mm (2.832-2.833 in.) and wear limit is 71.81 mm (2.827 in.). Pistons are available in standard size and 0.25 mm (0.010 in.) oversize.

Piston pin to piston pin bore clearance should be zero to 0.017 mm (0-0.0007 in.). Maximum allowable piston pin clearance in piston is 0.045 mm (0.0018 in.). Be sure the piston and connecting rod are positioned as shown in Fig. Y168 before installing the piston pin. Be sure the pin retaining snap rings are securely installed at each end of the pin bore in the piston.

Install new rings in the piston ring grooves and use a feeler gauge to measure ring side clearance. Replace the piston if the side clearance is excessive. Push each ring squarely into the cylinder bore and measure the ring end gap using a feeler gauge. Refer to the following specifications:

Model 3TN66UJ

Ring side clearance—
Top ring . . . . **0.065-0.100 mm (0.0026-0.0039 in.)**
Second ring . . . . **0.030-0.065 mm (0.0012-0.0026 in.)**
Oil ring . . . . **0.020-0.055 mm (0.0008-0.0022 in.)**
Wear limit (all rings) . . . . **0.20 mm (0.008 in.)**
Ring end gap—
Compression rings . . . . **0.15-0.30 mm (0.006-0.012 in.)**
Oil ring . . . . **0.15-0.35 mm (0.006-0.014 in.)**

Model 3TNA72UJ(3)

Ring side clearance—
Top ring . . . . **0.075-0.110 mm (0.0030-0.0043 in.)**
Second ring . . . . **0.030-0.065 mm (0.0012-0.0026 in.)**
Oil ring . . . . **0.020-0.055 mm (0.0008-0.0022 in.)**
Wear limit (all rings) . . . . **0.20 mm (0.008 in.)**
Ring end gap—
Compression rings . . . . **0.10-0.25 mm (0.004-0.010 in.)**
Oil ring . . . . **0.15-0.35 mm (0.006-0.014 in.)**

When installing the piston rings, place the oil ring expander in the groove first, then install the oil ring on top of the expander with the ring end gap located on opposite side of the piston from the expander ends. Install the compression rings with the side having the identification mark facing up and with the end gaps at 120° spacing from each other and the oil ring end gap.

CYLINDERS

The cylinder block for all engines is sleeveless and the pistons and rings ride directly in the cylinder block bores. Pistons and rings are available in standard size and 0.25 mm (0.010 in.) oversize. Cylinders may be bored and honed to this oversize if worn beyond limit for use of standard size pistons and rings.

Check cylinder bores in block for cracks, scoring or excessive wear. Measure the cylinder bore at six different places, taking two measurements 90° apart at the top, middle and bottom to determine the amount of cylinder wear and out-of-round. Cylinder bore specifications are as follows:

Model 3TN66UJ

Standard cylinder bore . . . **66.00-66.03 mm (2.599-2.600 in.)**
Wear limit . . . . **66.20 mm (2.606 in.)**

Model 3TNA72UJ(3)

Standard cylinder bore . . . **72.00-72.03 mm (2.835-2.836 in.)**
Wear limit . . . . **72.20 mm (2.843 in.)**

The cylinder out-of-round condition should be less than 0.01 mm (0.0004 in.). The maximum allowable out-of-round is 0.02 mm (0.001 in.). Bore and hone the cylinders or replace the block if the out-of-round condition or cylinder wear is excessive.

CONNECTING RODS AND BEARINGS

The connecting rod is fitted with a replaceable bushing at the piston pin end and a slip-in precision fit bearing (9) at the crankpin end.

Rod twist or out of parallel condition should be less than 0.05 mm (0.002 in.) per 100 mm (4 in.). Maximum allowable rod distortion is 0.08 mm (0.003 in.) per 100 mm (4 in.).

Crankpin standard diameter is 35.97-35.98 mm (1.416-1.417 in.) for Model 3TN66UJ and 39.97-39.98 mm (1.5736-1.574 in.) for Model 3TNA72UJ(3).

Specified crankpin bearing oil clearance is 0.02-0.07 mm (0.0008-0.0028 in.). Crankpin bearing oil clearance wear limit is 0.15 mm (0.006 in.) for all models.

Rod side clearance on the crankpin journal for all models should be 0.2-0.4 mm (0.008-0.016 in.). Maximum allowable side clearance is 0.55 mm (0.022 in.). Replace the connecting rod and/or crankshaft if clearance is excessive.

Refer to the following piston pin specifications:

Model 3TN66UJ

Pin OD................. 19.99-20.00 mm (0.7870-0.7874 in.)
Wear limit.................. 19.90 mm (0.786 in.)
Pin bushing ID........ 20.025-20.038 mm (0.788-0.789 in.)
Wear limit.................. 20.10 mm (0.791 in.)
Pin-to-bushing clearance—
Standard.............. 0.025-0.047 mm (0.001-0.002 in.)
Wear limit.................... 0.11 mm (0.004 in.)

Model 3TNA72UJ(3)

Pin OD................. 20.99-21.00 mm (0.826-0.827 in.)
Wear limit.................. 20.98 mm (0.826 in.)
Pin bushing ID........ 21.025-21.038 mm (0.826-0.827 in.)
Wear limit.................. 21.10 mm (0.831 in.)
Pin-to-bushing clearance—
Standard.............. 0.025-0.047 mm (0.001-0.002 in.)
Wear limit.................... 0.11 mm (0.004 in.)

When installing the connecting rod, make certain that the same rod cap is installed as was removed and that the tangs in the cap and rod are on the same side. Replace the connecting rod cap screws. Lubricate the threads of the rod cap screws with engine oil and tighten to 23 N·m (203 in.-lb.).

CRANKSHAFT AND MAIN BEARINGS

The crankshaft is supported in four main bearings. Split thrust washers, located at each side of the number 1 main bearing cap, control crankshaft end play.

To remove the crankshaft, first remove the engine from the tractor. Remove the water pump, timing gear cover, fuel injection pump, cylinder head and cam followers, idler gear, engine camshaft, fuel injection pump camshaft, oil pump gear and timing gear housing. Remove the piston and rod units, flywheel, flywheel housing and rear bearing seal retainer. Be sure that the position number is marked on each main bearing cap, then unbolt and remove the main bearing caps and lift the crankshaft from cylinder block.

Check all main bearing journals, thrust surfaces at rear journal, and the crankpin journals for scoring or excessive wear. Main bearings and rod bearings are available in standard size and 0.25 mm (0.010 in.) undersize. Refer to the CONNECTING RODS AND BEARINGS paragraph for information on crankpin journal specifications. Refer to the following table for main bearing specifications:

Model 3TN66UJ

Main journal OD—
Standard.............. 39.97-39.98 mm (1.5736-1.5740 in.)
Wear limit.................. 39.90 mm (1.572 in.)
Main bearing clearance—
Standard............. 0.020-0.072 mm (0.0008-0.0028 in.)
Wear limit.................... 0.15 mm (0.006 in.)

Model 3TNA72UJ(3)

Main journal OD—
Standard.............. 43.97-43.98 mm (1.731-1.732 in.)
Wear limit.................. 43.92 mm (1.729 in.)
Main bearing clearance—
Standard.............. 0.020-0.070 mm (0.0008-0.0028 in.)
Wear limit.................... 0.15 mm (0.006 in.)

Crankshaft end play should be 0.095-0.270 mm (0.004-0.011 inch). Maximum allowable end play is 0.33 mm (0.013 inch).

If the crankshaft gear was removed, heat the gear to approximately 150°C (300°F) before pressing it onto the crankshaft. Be sure that all bearing surfaces are clean and free of nicks or burrs.

Install the main bearing shells with the oil holes into cylinder block and the bearing shells without oil holes into the main bearing caps. Bearing sets for all journals are alike.

Lubricate the crankshaft and bearings with oil, then set the crankshaft in the bearings. Lubricate the upper thrust washer halves, those without locating projection, and insert the thrust washers between the block and crankshaft with the oil groove side of the thrust washers towards the crankshaft shoulders. Using light grease, stick the lower thrust washer halves in the number 1 main bearing cap with the tabs on the washers aligned with the notches in the cap and with the bearing side out.

Lubricate the bearings and install the caps, making certain that they are installed in the same positions as they were removed. Note that the side of the caps with the embossed letters FW and an arrow points toward the flywheel end of the engine.

Lubricate the threads of main bearing cap screws with engine oil. Tighten the main bearing cap screws to 54 N·m (40 ft.-lb.) on Model 3TN66UJ or 79 N·m (58 ft.-lb.) on Model 3TNA72UJ(3). Check to be sure that the crankshaft turns freely in bearings before completing reassembly of the engine.

CRANKSHAFT FRONT OIL SEAL

The crankshaft front oil seal is located in the timing gear cover and can be replaced after removing the crankshaft pulley. Pry the seal from the timing cover, taking care not to damage the cover.

The seal lip rides on the hub of the crankshaft pulley. Inspect the pulley hub for excessive wear at the point of seal contact. Install a new seal with the lip to the inside using a suitable driver.

Lubricate the seal lip and crankshaft pulley hub. Install the pulley on crankshaft with the hole in the pulley hub aligned with the dowel pin in the crankshaft gear. Tighten the pulley retaining bolt to 115 N·m (85 ft.-lb.).

CRANKSHAFT REAR OIL SEAL

The crankshaft rear oil seal can be replaced after removing the flywheel and the seal retainer. Install a new oil seal with the lip to the inside using a suitable driver. Press the seal into the retainer until flush with the outer surface of the retainer.

If the crankshaft is grooved at the original oil seal contact surface, the new seal can be installed 3 mm (1/8 in.) farther into the seal retainer.

Lubricate the seal lip and install the retainer with a new gasket. Tighten the retainer-to-cylinder block cap screws to 11 N·m (97 in.-lb.) and retainer-to-oil pan cap screws to 9 N·m (80 in.-lb.).

ELECTRICAL SYSTEM

GLOW PLUGS

All engines utilize glow plugs as an aid in engine starting. The glow plugs are connected in parallel so that if one plug is burned out, the others will continue to operate. The glow plug indicator light will be on while the glow plugs are heating. A timer in the circuit will turn the indicator light off after about 10 seconds; at that time, turn the switch to the START position to start engine.

The glow plugs can be checked with an ohmmeter; replace the plug if there

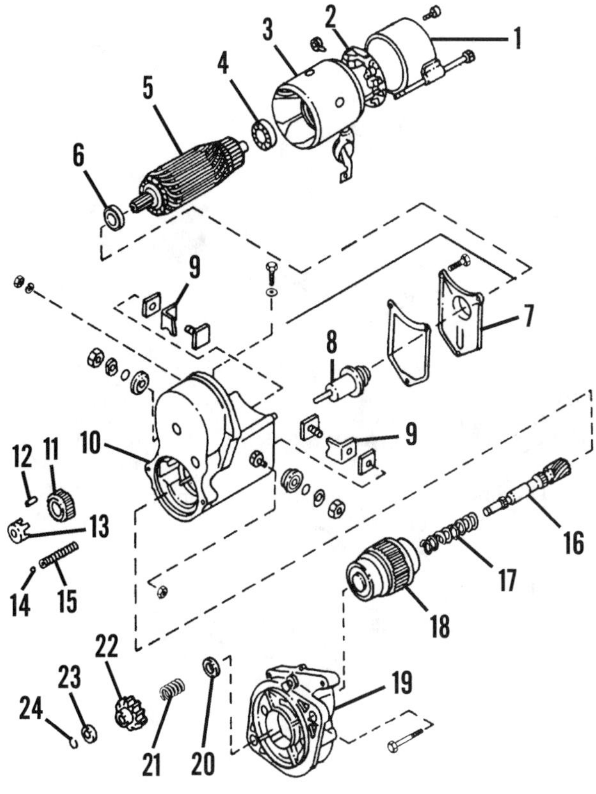

Fig. Y169—Exploded view of Nippon Denso starter motor used on some engines.

1. End frame
2. Brush holder
3. Field coil frame
4. Bearing
5. Armature
6. Bearing
7. Cover
8. Plunger
9. Contact plates
10. Solenoid housing
11. Pinion gear
12. Roller
13. Retainer
14. Ball
15. Spring
16. Clutch shaft
17. Spring
18. Clutch assy.
19. Clutch housing
20. Washer
21. Spring
22. Drive gear
23. Retainer
24. Snap ring

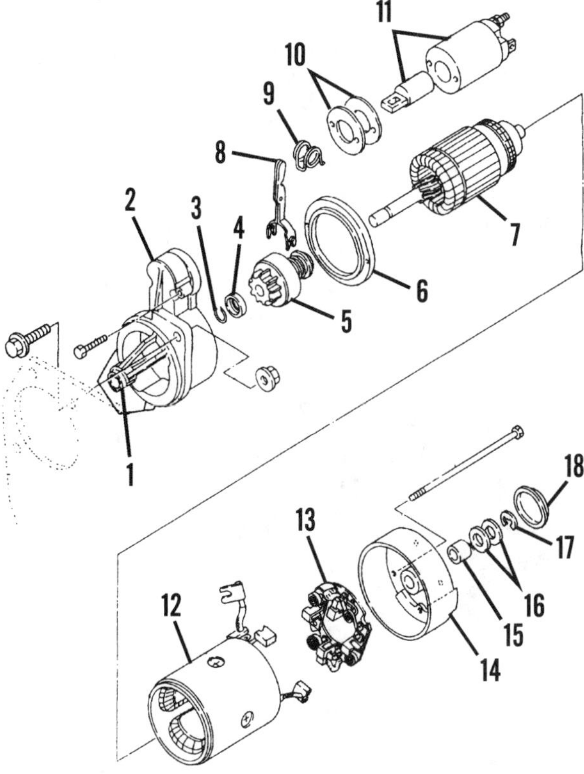

Fig. Y170—Exploded view of Hitachi starter motor used on some engines.

1. Sleeve
2. Drive end frame
3. Snap ring
4. Retainer
5. Drive pinion & clutch assy.
6. Cover
7. Armature
8. Shift lever
9. Spring
10. Shims
11. Solenoid assy.
12. Field coil assy.
13. Brush holder
14. End cover
15. Sleeve
16. Washers
17. E-ring
18. Cap

is no continuity. Glow plug resistance should be 1.35-1.65 ohms.

To check the glow plug controller circuit, check for voltage at the glow plug power lead when the key switch is turned to the ON position. If there is no voltage, remove the glow plug controller from the connector socket and turn the key switch ON. Check for voltage at the connector terminal red wire. If there is voltage, replace the controller unit.

ELECTRIC STARTER

Engines may be equipped with either a Nippon Denso or Hitachi starter. The Nippon Denso starter (Fig. Y169) uses a gear reduction drive system, while the Hitachi starter (Fig. Y170) drives directly from the armature shaft.

On all models, starter current draw under load should be 230 amps or less at 300 rpm (starting rpm). On a Nippon Denso starter, no-load current draw should be 90 amps or less at starter speed of about 3000 rpm. On a Hitachi starter, no-load current draw should be 60 amps or less at starter speed of about 7000 rpm.

Nippon Denso Starter

To disassemble, disconnect the field lead, remove the through-bolts and separate the starter motor from the solenoid housing. Remove the end frame (1—Fig. Y169).

Pry the brush springs away from the brushes and disengage the field coil brushes from the brush holder. Pull the negative brushes outward about 6.0 mm (1/4 in.), then release the springs to hold the brushes in this position. Separate the brush holder (2) from the field coil housing (3). Withdraw the armature (5) from the field housing.

To disassemble the reduction gears and clutch assembly, remove the retaining screws and separate the solenoid housing (10) from the clutch housing (19). Remove the clutch assembly and drive the pinion from the clutch housing. Push the retainer (23) back and remove the retaining ring (24), then withdraw the components from the clutch shaft (16).

Remove the cover (7) from the solenoid housing and withdraw the plunger (8). Remove the contact plates (9) if necessary. Note that the contact plate located on the left side of the housing is smaller than the contact plate on the right side.

Inspect all components for wear or damage. Brush length wear limit is 8.5 mm (0.035 in.).

Use an ohmmeter or test light to test the armature for grounded or open windings. There should not be continuity between the commutator and armature shaft. There should be continuity between two different commutator bars. To test for short-circuited winding, use an armature growler.

Use an ohmmeter or test light to check the field winding for grounded or open winding. There should not be continuity between the field coil brush and field frame. There should be continuity between the two field brushes.

To reassemble the starter, reverse the disassembly procedure while noting the following special instruction: Apply grease to the clutch shaft (16) and bearings and to the pinion (11), rollers (12) and retainer (13). Be sure that the steel ball (14) is installed in the end of the clutch shaft. When installing the end frame (1), be sure that field coil brush wires do not contact the end frame. Tighten the starter through-bolt nuts to 88 N·m (65 ft.-lb.).

Hitachi Starter

To disassemble the starter, disconnect the solenoid wire. Remove the through-bolts and retaining screws from the end cover. Pry the plastic cap (18—Fig. Y170) from the end cover (14), remove the E-ring (17) shims (16) and end cover.

Pry the springs away from the negative brushes, pull the brushes up and release the springs to hold the brushes in this position. Remove the field coil brushes from the brush holder, then remove the brush holder (13) from the field housing.

Separate the field coil housing from the armature. Remove screws retaining the solenoid and withdraw the solenoid assembly and armature from the drive housing. Push the pinion stop (4) downward, remove the retaining ring (3) and withdraw the clutch assembly (5) from the armature shaft.

Inspect all components for wear or damage. Brush length wear limit is 7.7 mm (0.30 in.).

Use an ohmmeter or test light to test the armature for grounded or open windings. There should not be continuity between the commutator and armature shaft. There should be continuity between two different commutator bars. To test for short-circuited winding, use an armature growler.

Use an ohmmeter or test light to check the field winding for grounded or open winding. There should not be continuity between the field coil brush and field frame. There should be continuity between the two field brushes.

To reassemble the starter, reverse the disassembly procedure.

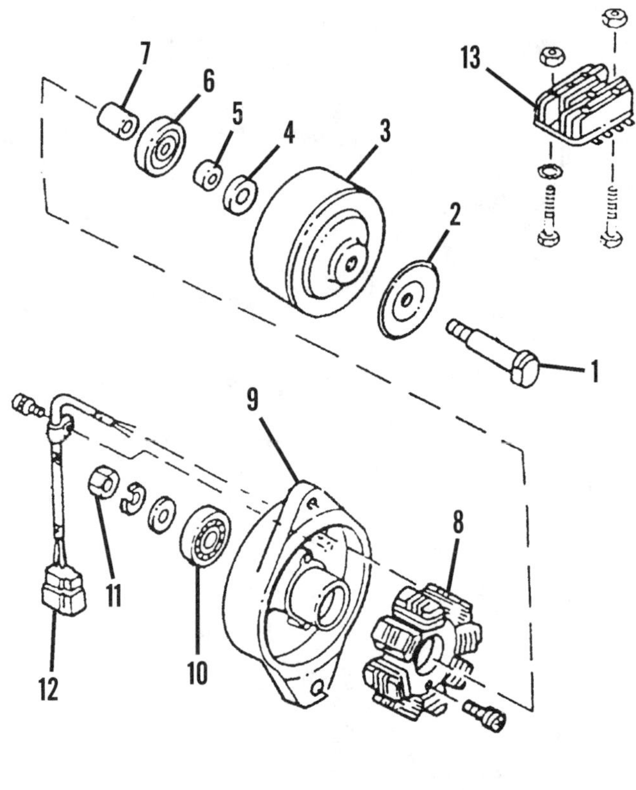

Fig. Y171—Exploded view of Kokosan alternator used on some engines.

1. Shaft
2. Plate
3. Flywheel
4. Washer
5. Spacer
6. Bearing
7. Locking collar
8. Stator
9. End frame
10. Bearing
11. Nut
12. Wiring harness
13. Voltage regulator

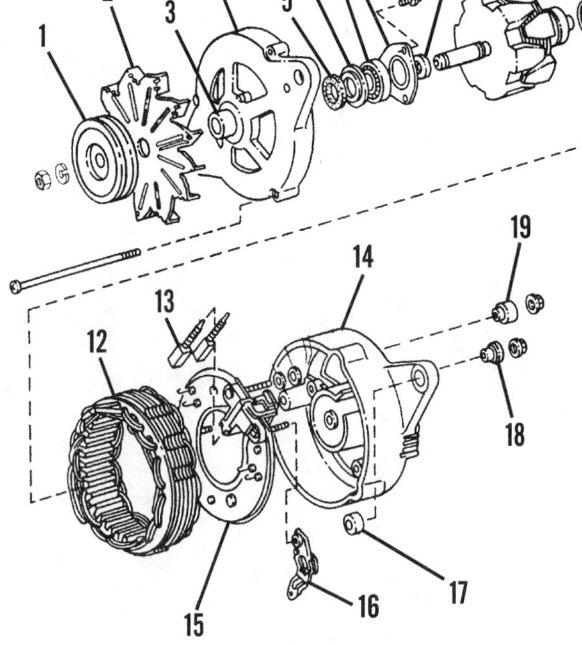

Fig. Y172—Exploded view of Nippon Denso alternator used on some engines.

1. Pulley
2. Fan
3. Locking collar
4. Drive end frame
5. Felt washer
6. Cover
7. Bearing
8. Retainer plate
9. Locking collar
10. Rotor
11. Bearing
12. Stator
13. Brushes
14. Stator housing
15. Rectifier assy.
16. Voltage regulator
17. Bushing
18. Insulator
19. Bushing

ALTERNATOR

Kokosan Alternator

To disassemble the alternator, clamp the alternator pulley in a vise and remove the retaining nut (11—Fig. Y171). Tap the end of the shaft (1) with a soft hammer to separate the flywheel (3) from the stator housing (9).

Remove the harness clamp screw and remove the connector from the harness leads (12). Remove the stator mounting screws and separate the stator (8) from the housing (9).

Replace the flywheel if magnets are loose or damaged. Check the stator for indications of burned wiring or other damage and replace when necessary. Check the bearings (6 and 10) for roughness or damage and replace when necessary.

To reassemble, reverse the disassembly procedure. Tighten the retaining nut (11) to 27 N·m (20 ft.-lb.).

Nippon Denso Alternator

To disassemble the alternator, remove the through-bolts and separate the drive end frame (4—Fig. Y172)

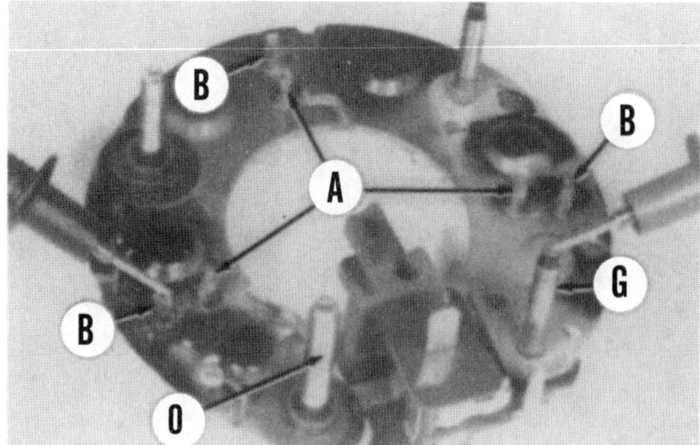

Fig. Y173—Use an ohmmeter or continuity test light to test rectifier diodes. Refer to text for procedure.

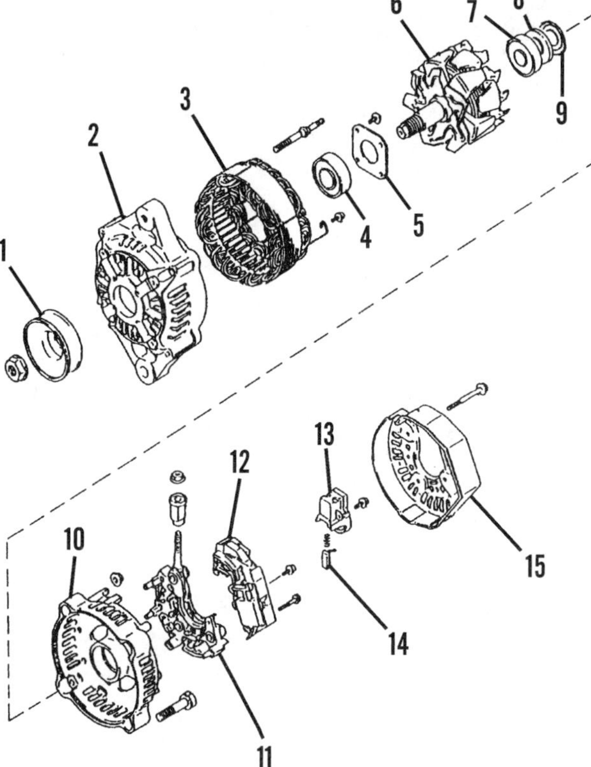

Fig. Y174—Exploded view of Hitachi alternator used on some models.

1. Pulley
2. End frame
3. Stator
4. Bearing
5. Retainer plate
6. Rotor
7. Bearing
8. Thrust washer
9. Cover
10. Housing
11. Rectifier assy.
12. Voltage regulator
13. Brush holder
14. Brush
15. End cover

from the stator housing (14). Remove the alternator pulley (2) and fan (3), then tap the rotor (10) from the end frame. Remove the bearing retainer (8), bearing (7), cover (6) and felt washer (5).

Remove the nuts and insulators from the rear of the stator housing, and pry the stator from the end frame. Unsolder the brush leads, voltage regulator leads and stator leads as necessary to remove the brushes, voltage regulator and rectifier assembly.

Use an ohmmeter or battery powered test light to check the rotor winding for short or open circuit. There should be continuity indicated when the tester leads are connected to the rotor slip rings. There should not be continuity when the tester leads are connected to the rotor frame and each of the slip rings.

Replace the brushes if the exposed length is less than 5.5 mm (0.220 in.). Check for continuity between each of the brushes and ground. Renew the rectifier-brush holder assembly if continuity is indicated.

Inspect the stator for discoloration or a burned odor that would indicate faulty wiring and renew as necessary. There should be equal resistance readings between each pair of stator lead wires. There should not be continuity indicated between any of the stator leads and the stator frame.

There should be continuity indicated between each of the three inner terminals (A—Fig. Y173) of the rectifier assembly. To check the rectifier diodes, touch the ohmmeter leads to the output post (O) and to each of the three outer terminals (B) in turn. Switch the ohmmeter test leads and check each terminal again. There should be continuity in only one direction.

Repeat the test, touching the ohmmeter test leads to the ground post (G) and to each of the three outer terminals (B). There should be continuity in only one direction. Renew the rectifier assembly if any of the six diodes tests defective.

To reassemble the alternator, reverse the disassembly procedure while noting the following special instruction: When soldering the lead wires, use only 60-40 rosin core solder. Do not heat the connections longer than necessary as excess heat will damage the rectifier assembly. Be sure that the stator lead wires do not contact the housing frame when assembled.

Depress the brushes into the brush holder and insert a wire through the hole in the rear of the stator housing to hold the brushes in place. Remove the wire after the drive end frame and stator housing are assembled. Tighten the rotor nut to 54 N·m (40 ft.-lb.).

Hitachi Alternator

To disassemble the alternator, remove the end cover (15—Fig. Y174). Remove the through-bolts and separate the drive end frame (2) from the stator housing (10). Remove the nut from the rotor shaft and tap the rotor (6) from the end frame. Remove the retainer plate (5) and bearing (4).

Unsolder the voltage regulator and brush holder wire leads and separate the voltage regulator (12) from the brush holder (13). Unsolder the stator wire leads and remove the rectifier assembly (11).

Use an ohmmeter or battery powered test light to check the rotor winding for short or open circuit. There should be continuity indicated when the tester leads are connected to the rotor slip rings. There should not be continuity when the tester leads are connected to the rotor frame and each of the slip rings.

Replace the brushes (14) if exposed length is less than 5.5 mm (0.220 in.). Check for continuity between each of the brushes and between each brush and ground. Renew the brush holder assembly if continuity is indicated.

Inspect the stator for discoloration or a burned odor that would indicate faulty wiring and replace when necessary. There should be equal resistance readings between each pair of stator lead wires. There should not be continuity indicated between any of the stator leads and the stator frame.

To test the rectifier diodes, connect the ohmmeter tester leads to the ground post (A—Fig. Y175) and each of the three outer terminals (C). Switch the ohmmeter test leads and check each terminal again. There should be continuity indicated in only one direction.

Connect the tester leads to the output terminal (B) and to each of the three outer terminals (C), then reverse the tester leads and repeat the test. There should be continuity indicated in only one direction. Replace the rectifier assembly if any of the diodes fails the test.

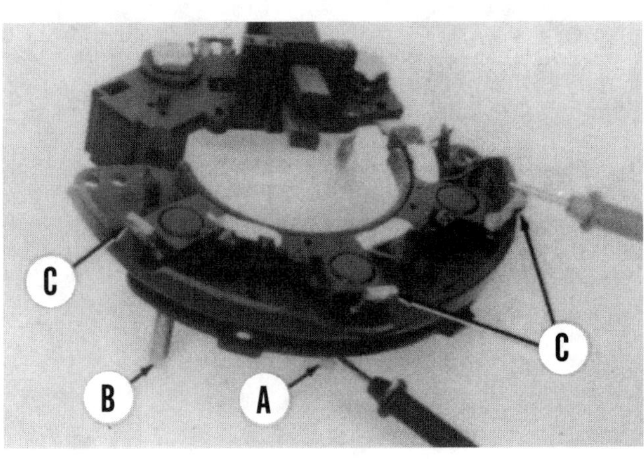

Fig. Y175—Use an ohmmeter or continuity test light to test rectifier diodes. Refer to text for procedure.

To reassemble the alternator, reverse the disassembly procedure. When soldering the lead wires, use only 60-40 rosin core solder. Do not heat the connections longer than necessary as excess heat will damage the rectifier assembly. Be sure that the stator lead wires do not contact the housing frame when assembled.

Depress the brushes into the brush holder and insert a wire through the hole in the rear cover to hold the brushes in place. Remove the wire after the alternator is assembled. Tighten the rotor nut to 54 N·m (40 ft.-lb.).

NOTES

NOTES

NOTES

NOTES

NOTES

Technical Information

Technical information is available from John Deere. Some of this information is available in electronic as well as printed form. Order from your John Deere dealer or call **1-800-522-7448**. Please have available the model number, serial number, and name of the product.

Available information includes:

- PARTS CATALOGS list service parts available for your machine with exploded view illustrations to help you identify the correct parts. It is also useful in assembling and disassembling.
- OPERATOR'S MANUALS providing safety, operating, maintenance, and service information. These manuals and safety signs on your machine may also be available in other languages.
- OPERATOR'S VIDEO TAPES showing highlights of safety, operating, maintenance, and service information. These tapes may be available in multiple languages and formats.
- TECHNICAL MANUALS outlining service information for your machine. Included are specifications, illustrated assembly and disassembly procedures, hydraulic oil flow diagrams, and wiring diagrams. Some products have separate manuals for repair and diagnostic information. Some components, such as engines, are available in separate component technical manuals
- FUNDAMENTAL MANUALS detailing basic information regardless of manufacturer:
  - Agricultural Primer series covers technology in farming and ranching, featuring subjects like computers, the Internet, and precision farming.
  - Farm Business Management series examines "real-world" problems and offers practical solutions in the areas of marketing, financing, equipment selection, and compliance.
  - Fundamentals of Services manuals show you how to repair and maintain off-road equipment.
  - Fundamentals of Machine Operation manuals explain machine capacities and adjustments, how to improve machine performance, and how to eliminate unnecessary field operations.

TS189 –UN–17JAN89

TS191 –UN–02DEC88

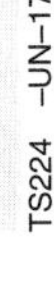

TS224 –UN–17JAN89

THE PRECISION-FARMING GUIDE FOR AGRICULTURISTS

TS1663 –UN–10OCT97